WILEY PLUS

WileyPLUS helps today's students succeed in the classroom using resources relevant to their everyday lives and to the workplace that will help make them globally competitive. With the complete e-book plus a variety of interactive tools, ***WileyPLUS*** makes teaching, learning, and retaining the material easier, more relevant, and more exciting than ever.

"I wish all my classes had WileyPLUS linked to their textbooks so I could study better in all my classes"

- Student David Delgado

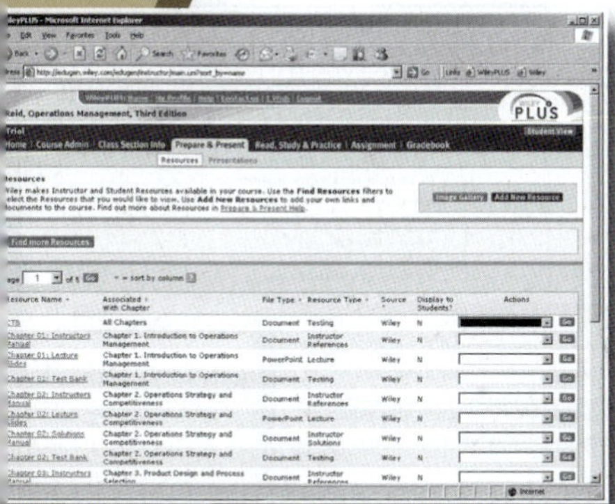

Instructors using ***WileyPLUS*** easily choose all of the resources they need to effectively design and deliver their courses with maximum impact and minimum preparation time. Conveniently organized and highly integrated resources include the Instructor's Manual, Test Bank, PowerPoint slides, Cases, Videos, and more.

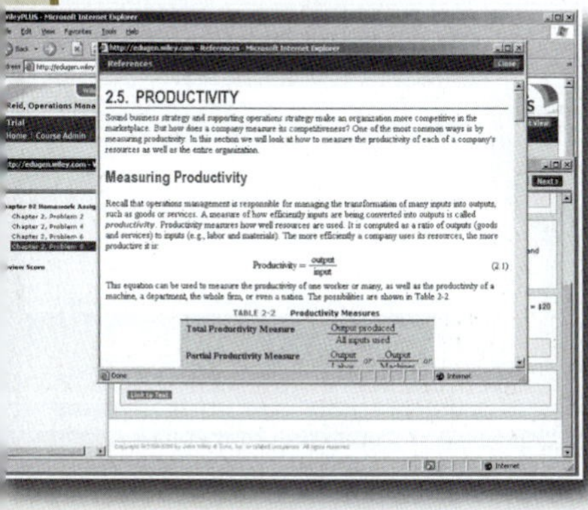

WileyPLUS links students directly from homework assignments to specific portions of the online text for the contextual help they need - when they need it.

See and try *WileyPLUS* in action!

• www.wileyplus.com •

CONTEMPORARY STRATEGY ANALYSIS

TEXT AND CASES

Seventh Edition

To Sue

CONTEMPORARY STRATEGY ANALYSIS

TEXT AND CASES

SEVENTH EDITION

ROBERT M. GRANT

A John Wiley & Sons, Ltd, Publication

Published by John Wiley & Sons Ltd

Registered office
John Wiley & Sons Ltd, The Atrium, Southern Gate, Chichester, West Sussex, PO19 8SQ, United Kingdom

For details of our global editorial offices, for customer services and for information about how to apply for permission to reuse the copyright material in this book please see our website at www.wiley.com.

Library of Congress Cataloging-in-Publication Data

Grant, Robert M., 1948-
Contemporary strategy analysis: text and cases/Robert M. Grant.—7th ed.
p. cm.
Includes bibliographical references.
ISBN 978-0-470-74709-4 (cloth)
1. Strategic planning. I. Title.
HD30.28.G7213 2010
658.4'012—dc22

2009052136

A catalogue record for this book is available from the British Library.

Set in 10/12pt Classical Garamond by Thomson Digital, India
Printed in Spain by Grafos Sa, Barcelona

I wrote *Contemporary Strategy Analysis* to equip managers and students of management with the concepts, frameworks and techniques needed to make better strategic decisions. I wanted a strategy text that would reflect the dynamism and intellectual rigor of this fast-developing field of management. At that time, the existing texts failed to incorporate either the enormous advances taking place in strategy research or the strategic management practices of leading-edge companies.

The result is a strategy text that endeavors to be both rigorous and relevant. While embodying the latest thinking in the strategy field, *Contemporary Strategy Analysis* aims to be accessible to students from different backgrounds and with varying levels of experience. I achieve this accessibility by combining clarity of exposition with concentration on the fundamentals of value creation and an emphasis on practicality.

These same objectives are unchanged in this seventh edition of *Contemporary Strategy Analysis*. My approach is simultaneously analytical and practical. If strategic management is all about managing to achieve outstanding success then the essential tasks of strategy are to identify the sources of superior business performance and to formulate and implement a strategy that exploits these sources of superior performance.

The seventh edition also reflects the developments that have occurred since 2007 both in the business environment and in strategy analysis. With regard to the former, the dominant feature is the global recession that followed the financial crisis of 2008–9. I view this financial crisis less as an isolated event than one in a series of shocks that have afflicted the twenty-first century business environment. Looking ahead, I anticipate that turbulence, unpredictability, and intense competition will continue to dominate the global business environment.

The principal implications I draw are, first, that strategy will become increasingly important to firms as they navigate a challenging and unpredictable business environment and, second, that a determined focus on the fundamentals of value creation will be critical to firm survival and prosperity. Despite the reaction against shareholder value maximization for its inducement to short-termism and crass materialism, strategy analysis must focus on the pursuit of long-run profitability. This requires a penetrating understanding of customer needs, competitive forces and the firm's strengths and weaknesses.

Achieving profitability in the face of intense competition means that competitive advantage must be the central focus of strategy. This new edition places a stronger emphasis on the primary sources of competitive advantage: the resources and capabilities of the enterprise.

This edition also places a greater emphasis on strategy implementation. Establishing competitive advantage in a complex and unpredictable business environment requires that firms reconcile scale economies with entrepreneurial flexibility, innovation with cost efficiency and globalization with local responsiveness. This creates new challenges for the design of organizational structures and management systems. At the same time I have maintained an integrated approach to strategy formulation and strategy implementation recognizing their codependence. A strategy that is formulated without regard to its implementation is likely to be fatally flawed. It is through the process of implementation that strategies adapt and emerge.

As well as emphasizing the fundamentals of strategy analysis, I draw upon promising new approaches to strategy analysis including the role of complementarity, the use of real options to analyze flexibility, the nature of complexity and the potential for self-organization, and the role of legitimacy and its relevance to corporate social responsibility.

There is very little in this book that is original—I have plundered mercilessly the ideas, theories and evidence of fellow scholars. My greatest debts are to my colleagues and students at the business schools where this book has been developed and tested—notably Georgetown University and Bocconi University. This edition has also benefitted from feedback and suggestions from professors and students in other schools where *Contemporary Strategy Analysis* is used. I am particularly grateful to Andrew Campbell for assisting with Chapters 16 and 17. With the enhanced Web-based support being provided by the publisher, I look forward to closer interaction with users.

The success of *Contemporary Strategy Analysis* owes much to the professionalism and enthusiasm of the editorial, production and sales and marketing teams at John Wiley & Sons, Ltd. I am especially grateful to Steve Hardman, Deborah Egleton, Catriona King and Rosemary Nixon.

Robert M. Grant
London

Guide to the Instructor and Student resources to accompany Contemporary Strategy Analysis

Visit **www.contemporarystrategyanalysis.com** to access all the teaching and learning materials that accompany this text.

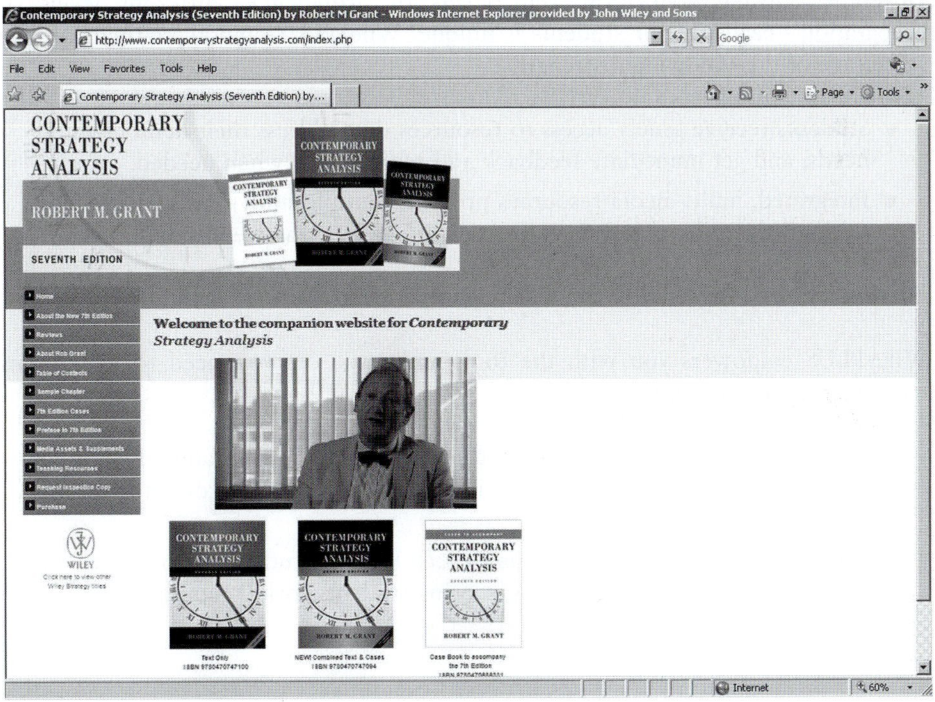

Students can see video clips of the author summarising and extending the learning in each chapter. There are also self-test quizzes and case study activities, including case-related video clips with questions.

Instructors can access the password-protected resources including the Instructor's Manual, case teaching notes, PowerPoint slides and a Test Bank with over 1500 questions.

Contemporary Strategy Analysis is also accompanied by a WileyPLUS course

WileyPLUS is an online teaching and learning environment that integrates the **entire digital textbook** with the most effective instructor and student resources to fit every learning style.

With WileyPLUS:

- Students achieve concept mastery in a rich, structured environment that is available 24/7.
- Instructors personalize and manage their course more effectively with assessment, assignments, grade tracking, and more.

***For Students* - Personalize the learning experience**

Different learning styles, different levels of proficiency, different levels of preparation—each of your students is unique. WileyPLUS empowers them to take advantage of their individual strengths:

- Students receive timely access to resources that address their demonstrated needs, and get immediate feedback and remediation when needed.
- Integrated, multi-media resources provide multiple study-paths to fit each student's learning preferences and encourage more active learning.

***For Instructors* - Personalize the teaching experience**

WileyPLUS empowers you with the tools and resources you need to make your teaching even more effective:

- With WileyPLUS you can identify those students who are falling behind and intervene accordingly, without having to wait for them to come to you in office hours.
- WileyPLUS simplifies and automates such tasks as student performance assessment, creating assignments, scoring student work, keeping grades, and more.

I

INTRODUCTION

1 The Concept of Strategy

Strategy is the great work of the organization. In situations of life or death, it is the Tao of survival or extinction. Its study cannot be neglected.

—SUN TZU, *THE ART OF WAR*

OUTLINE

Introduction and Objectives

Strategy is about winning. This chapter explains what strategy is and why it is important to success—both for organizations and individuals. We will distinguish strategy from planning. Strategy is not a detailed plan or program of instructions; it is a unifying theme that gives coherence and direction to the actions and decisions of an individual or an organization.

The principal task of this chapter will be to introduce the basic framework for strategy analysis that underlies this book. I will introduce the two basic components of strategy analysis: analysis of the external environment of the firm (mainly industry analysis) and the analysis of the internal environment (primarily analysis of the firm's resources and capabilities).

By the time you have completed this chapter, you will be able to:

- appreciate the contribution that strategy can make to successful performance, both for individuals and for organizations;
- recognize the key characteristics of an effective strategy;
- comprehend the basic framework of strategy analysis that underlies this book;
- become familiar with the major trends in the development of business strategy during recent decades;
- understand how strategy is made within organizations and the role played by strategic planning systems.

Since the purpose of strategy is to help us to win, we start by looking at the role of strategy in success.

The Role of Strategy in Success

Strategy Capsules 1.1, 1.2, and 1.3 outline examples of success in three very different arenas: Madonna in popular entertainment, General Giap and the North Vietnamese armed forces in warfare, and Lance Armstrong in cycling. Can the success of these diverse individuals and the organizations they led be attributed to any common factors?

STRATEGY CAPSULE 1.1
Madonna

The fifty-first birthday of Madonna Louise Veronica Ciccone on August 16, 2009 offered no respite from her hectic work schedule. The day before she had performed the 71st concert in her *Sweet and Sticky* world tour; a tour that would gross over $400 million. For yet another year it seemed unlikely that Madonna would be displaced in the *Guinness Book of Records* as the world's top-earning female entertainer and most successful female recording artist of all time.

In the summer of 1978, aged 19, Madonna arrived in New York with $35 to her name. After five years of struggle, she landed a recording contract. *Madonna* (1983) ultimately sold 10 million copies worldwide, while *Like a Virgin* (1984) topped 12 million copies. Between 1985 and 1990, six further albums, three world tours, and five movie roles had established Madonna with an image and persona that transcended any single field of entertainment: she was rock singer, actor, author, and pinup. Yet, she was more than this—as her website proclaims, she is "icon, artist, provocateur, diva, and mogul." She has also made a great deal of money.

What is the basis of Madonna's incredible and lasting success? Certainly not outstanding natural talent. As a vocalist, musician, dancer, songwriter, or actress, Madonna's talents seem modest. Few would regard her as an outstanding beauty.

She possesses relentless drive. Her wide range of activities—records, concerts, music videos, movies, books, and charity events—are unified by her dedication to a single goal: the quest for superstar status. "Even as a little girl, I knew I wanted the whole world to know who I was." She is widely regarded as a workaholic who survives on little sleep and rarely takes vacations: "I am a very disciplined person. I sleep a certain number of hours each night, then I like to get up and get on with it. All that means that I am in charge of everything that comes out."

She has drawn heavily on the talents of others: writers, musicians, choreographers, and designers. Many of her personal relationships have been stepping stones to career transitions. Her transition from dance to music was assisted by relationships, first, with musician Steve Bray, then with disc jockey John Benitex. Her entry into Hollywood was accompanied by marriage to Sean Penn and an affair with Warren Beatty. Most striking has been continuous reinvention of her image. From the street-kid look of the early 1980s, to the hard-core sexuality of the 90s, to the Madonna-with-children spirituality of the past decade, her fans have been treated to multiple reincarnations. As Jeff Katzenberg of Dreamworks observed: "She has always had a vision of exactly who she is, whether performer or businesswoman, and she has been strong enough to balance it all. Every time she comes up with a new look it is successful. When it happens once, OK, maybe it's luck, but twice is a coincidence, and three times it's got to be a remarkable talent. And Madonna's on her fifth or sixth time."

She was quick to learn the ropes both in Tin Pan Alley and in Hollywood. Like Evita Perón, whom Madonna portrayed in *Evita*, Madonna has combined determination, ambition, social acumen, and mastery of the strategic use of sex. As a self-publicist she is without equal, using nudity, pornography, bisexuality, spirituality and philanthropy as publicity tools. She is also astute at walking the fine line between the shocking and the unacceptable. Through Maverick Inc., a joint venture with Time Warner, she has been able to control her own creative output and also manage and develop younger entertainers and musicians. Her 2007, $120 million contract with Live Nation revealed her understanding of the shifting of economic power from recorded music to live performances.

STRATEGY CAPSULE 1.2

General Giap and the Vietnam Wars, 1948–75

As far as logistics and tactics were concerned, we succeeded in everything we set out to do. At the height of the war the army was able to move almost a million soldiers a year in and out of Vietnam, feed them, clothe them, house them, supply them with arms and ammunition and generally sustain them better than any army had ever been sustained in the field . . . On the battlefield itself, the army was unbeatable. In engagement after engagement the forces of the Vietcong and the North Vietnamese Army were thrown back with terrible losses. Yet, in the end, it was North Vietnam, not the United States that emerged victorious. How could we have succeeded so well yet failed so miserably?

Despite having the largest army in Southeast Asia, North Vietnam was no match for South Vietnam so long as the south was backed by the world's most powerful military and industrial nation. South Vietnam and its U.S. ally were defeated not by superior resources but by a superior strategy. North Vietnam achieved what Sun Tzu claimed was the highest form of victory: the enemy gave up.

The master of North Vietnam's military strategy was General Vo Nguyen Giap. In 1944, Giap became head of the Vietminh guerrilla forces. He was commander-in-chief of the North Vietnamese Army until 1974 and Minister of Defense until 1980. Giap's strategy was based on Mao Tse Tung's three-phase theory of revolutionary war: first, passive resistance to mobilize political support; second, guerrilla warfare aimed at weakening the enemy and building military strength; finally, general counteroffensive. In 1954, Giap's brilliant victory over the French at Dien Bien Phu fully vindicated the strategy. Against the U.S., the approach was similar.

> *Our strategy was . . . to wage a long-lasting battle . . . Only a long-term war could enable us to utilize to the maximum our political trump cards, to overcome our material handicap, and to transform our weakness into strength. To maintain and increase our forces was the principle to which we adhered, contenting ourselves with attacking when success was certain, refusing to give battle likely to incur losses.*

The strategy built on the one resource where the communists had overwhelming superiority: their will to fight. As Prime Minister Pham Van Dong explained: "The United States is the most powerful nation on earth. But Americans do not like long, inconclusive wars . . . We can outlast them and we can win in the end." Limited military engagement and the charade of the Paris peace talks helped the North Vietnamese prolong the conflict, while diplomatic efforts to isolate the U.S. from its Western allies and to sustain the U.S. peace movement accelerated the crumbling of American will.

The effectiveness of the U.S. military response was limited by two key uncertainties: what the objectives were and who the enemy was. Was the U.S. role one of supporting the South Vietnamese regime, fighting Vietcong terrorism, inflicting a military defeat on North Vietnam, conducting a proxy war against the Soviet Union, or combating world communism? The consistency and strength of North Vietnam's strategy allowed it to survive errors in implementation. Giap was premature in launching his general offensive. Both the 1968 Tet Offensive and 1972 Easter Offensive were beaten back with heavy losses. By 1974, U.S. resistance had been sapped by the Watergate scandal On April 29, 1975, Operation Frequent Wind began evacuating all remaining Americans from South Vietnam, and the next morning North Vietnamese troops entered the Presidential Palace in Saigon.

Sources: Col. Harry G. Summers Jr., *On Strategy* (Novato, CA: Presidio Press, 1982): 1; Vo Nguyen Giap, *Selected Writings* (Hanoi: Foreign Language Publishing House, 1977); J. Cameron, *Here Is Your Enemy* (New York: Holt, Rinehart, Winston, 1966).

STRATEGY CAPSULE 1.3

Lance Armstrong and the Tour de France

On July 24, 2005, Lance Armstrong became the first person to win the Tour de France seven times. His achievement was all the more remarkable for the fact that he had recovered from testicular cancer that had spread to his lungs and brain.

Even without cancer, Lance Armstrong was not an obvious candidate for title of the greatest cyclist ever. Despite certain natural advantages—notably a heart 30% larger than normal with an abnormally slow beat rate (32 times per minute while at rest)—Armstrong's aerobic rate was less than that of cycling greats such as Miguel Indurain and Greg LeMond. For most of his career, Armstrong was not the world's pre-eminent cyclist. He won the world championship just once (1993) and his Olympic best was a bronze medal in the 2000 Sydney games.

Armstrong's seven-year dominance of the Tour de France resulted from a combination of factors, not least of which was his single-minded focus, not just on cycling, but on a single race: between his seven Tour de France victories, Armstrong won only five other races.

Armstrong raised planning for the Tour to new levels of sophistication: with meticulous attention to training, diet and calorific intake and expenditure. His all-round abilities as a cyclist, mental resilience, and mastery of bluff and psychological warfare were well suited to the requirements of the Tour. His feigning exhaustion at critical junctures before devastating his rivals with a powerful breakaway has been deemed "worthy of a Hollywood Oscar." However, it was in team planning and coordination where the major differences between Armstrong and his competitors were most evident.

The principal prize in the Tour de France is for the individual who achieves the fastest overall time, but cyclists compete within teams. Team coordination and the willingness of the other team members (*domestiques*) to sacrifice themselves for the leader is critical to individual success. Armstrong's U.S. Postal Service team (which became the Discovery Channel team for the 2005 Tour) was remarkable not just for the quality of other team members but for the willingness of these world-class cyclists to serve their leader. Olympic gold medal winner Viatcheslav Ekimov—"The Russian Power House"—was critical to pulling Armstrong through the flatter stages of the Tour. Roberto Heras and Jose Asevedo defended Armstrong in the mountains—shielding him from the wind and supporting him during breakaways. George Hinkapie rode in all seven of Armstrong's Tour victories as a versatile all-rounder. Why did the team show a unique degree of loyalty to their team leader? Part was Armstrong's infectious commitment; part was his willingness to pay bonuses out of his own pocket to other riders, but also important was reciprocity—while team members gave total support to Armstrong on the Tour de France, in other competitions the roles were reversed and Armstrong served as a *domestique* to other team members.

The team's master planner was director, Johan Bruyneel, whose unrivaled knowledge of the Tour spanned sports physiology, game theory, psychology, and tactics. As well as team selection, role assignment, and discipline, Bruyneel managed a network of secret agreements with other teams. In return for financial support, other teams agreed to support Armstrong should he find himself split from his own team members. Bruyneel gave particular attention to team dynamics: fostering loyalty, camaraderie discussion, and shared emotions to overcome the notorious individualism of professional cyclists.

Armstrong's decision to come out of retirement electrified the 2009 Tour. In the Astana team, Armstrong rejoined Bruyneel and other former USPS/Discovery riders—but with one difference: Alberto Contador was team leader, not Armstrong. Contrador duly won the 2009 Tour de France; Lance Armstrong in third place.

For none of these three examples can success be attributed to overwhelmingly superior resources:

- Madonna possesses vitality, intelligence and magnetism, but lacks outstanding talents as a vocalist, musician or actress.

- The military, human, and economic resources of the Vietnamese communists were dwarfed by those of the U.S. and South Vietnam. Yet, with the U.S. evacuation from Saigon in 1975, the world's most powerful nation was humiliated by one of the world's poorest.
- Lance Armstrong possessed a powerful combination of physical and psychological attributes. Yet these endowments were not markedly superior to other top-class cyclists—especially after Armstrong's near-death encounter with cancer.

Nor can their success be attributed either exclusively or primarily to luck. For all three, lucky breaks provided opportunities at critical junctures. None, however, was the beneficiary of a consistent run of good fortune. More important than luck was the ability to recognize opportunities when they appeared and to have the clarity of direction and the flexibility necessary to exploit these chances.

My contention is that the key common ingredient in all three success stories was the presence of a soundly formulated and effectively implemented *strategy*. These strategies did not exist as a plan; in most the strategy was not even made explicit. Yet, in all three, we can observe a consistency of direction based on a clear understanding of the "game" being played and a keen awareness of how to maneuver into a position of advantage.

- Underpinning Madonna's many years as a superstar has been a strategy built on dedication, opportunism, reinvention of herself and a well-coordinated multimarket presence.
- The victory of the Vietnamese communist forces over the French and then the Americans is a classic example of how a sound strategy pursued with total commitment over a long period can succeed against vastly superior resources. The key was Giap's strategy of a protracted war of limited engagement. With the U.S. constrained by domestic and international opinion from unleashing its full military might, the strategy was unbeatable once it began to sap the willingness of the U.S. government to persevere with a costly, unpopular foreign war.
- Lance Armstrong's domination of the Tour de France from 1999 to 2005 was because he and his team did the most effective job of analyzing the requirements for success in the race, developing a strategy around those requirements and executing it almost faultlessly.

We can go further. What do these examples tell us about the characteristics of a strategy that are conducive to success? In all three stories, four common factors stand out (see Figure 1.1):

1 *Goals that are simple, consistent, and long term.* All three individuals displayed a single-minded commitment to a clearly recognized goal that was pursued steadfastly over a substantial part of their lifetime.
  - Madonna's career featured a relentless drive for stardom in which other dimensions of her life were absorbed within her career.
  - North Vietnamese efforts were unified and focused on the ultimate goal of reuniting Vietnam under communist rule and expelling a foreign army

FIGURE 1.1 Common elements in successful strategies

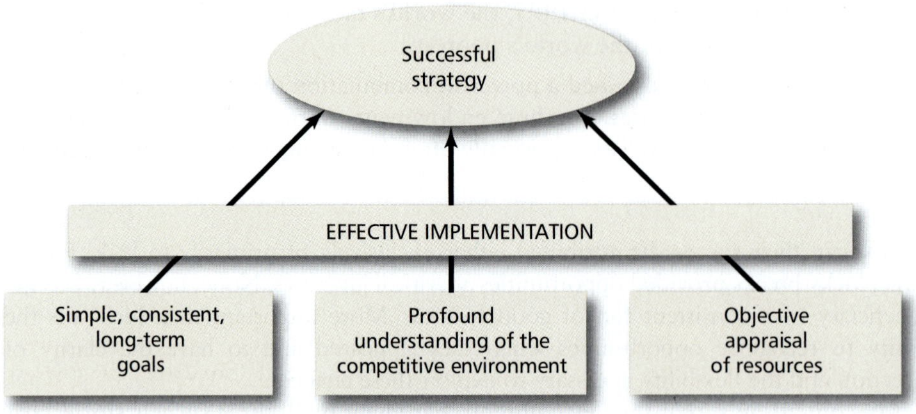

from Vietnamese soil. By contrast, U.S. efforts in Vietnam were bedeviled by confused objectives.

- On his return to professional cycling in 1998, Lance Armstrong committed to a single goal: winning the Tour de France.

2 *Profound understanding of the competitive environment*. All three individuals designed their strategies around a deep and insightful appreciation of the arena in which they were competing.

- Fundamental to Madonna's continuing success has been a shrewd understanding of the ingredients of stardom and the basis of popular appeal. This extends from the basic marketing principle that "sex sells" to recognition of the need to manage gatekeepers of the critical media distribution channels. Her periodic reincarnations reflect an acute awareness of changing attitudes, styles, and social norms.
- Giap understood his enemy and the battlefield conditions where he would engage them. Most important was appreciation of the political predicament of U.S. presidents in their need for popular support in waging a foreign war.
- Lance Armstrong and team director Johan Bruyneel took analysis of the requirements for success in the Tour de France to unprecedented levels of detail and sophistication.

3 *Objective appraisal of resources*. All three strategies were effective in exploiting internal strengths, while protecting areas of weakness.

- By positioning herself as a "star," Madonna exploited her abilities to develop and project her image, to self-promote and to exploit emerging trends while avoiding being judged simply as a rock singer or an actress. Her live performances rely heavily on a large team of highly qualified dancers, musicians, vocalists, choreographers and technicians, thus compensating for any weaknesses in her own performing capabilities.
- Giap's strategy was carefully designed to protect against his army's deficiencies in arms and equipment while exploiting the commitment and loyalty of his troops.

- Armstrong's campaign to win the Tour de France was based on two key strengths: unmatched determination to win and superior team-building capability.

4 *Effective implementation*. Without effective implementation, the best-laid strategies are of little use. Critical to the success of Madonna, Giap, and Armstong was their effectiveness as leaders in terms of their capacity to reach decisions, energy in implementing them, and ability to foster loyalty and commitment among subordinates. All three built organizations that allowed effective marshaling of resources and capabilities and quick responses to changes in the competitive environment.

These observations about the role of strategy in success can be made in relation to most fields of human endeavor. Whether we look at warfare, chess, politics, sport, or business, the success of individuals and organizations is seldom the outcome of a purely random process. Nor is superiority in initial endowments of skills and resources typically the determining factor. Strategies that build on the basic four elements almost always play an influential role.

Look at the "high achievers" in any competitive area. Whether we review the world's political leaders, the CEOs of the Fortune 500, or our own circles of friends and acquaintances, those who have achieved outstanding success in their careers are seldom those who possessed the greatest innate abilities. Success has gone to those who managed their careers most effectively—typically by combining the four strategic factors mentioned above. They are goal focused; their career goals have taken primacy over the multitude of life's other goals—friendship, love, leisure, knowledge, spiritual fulfillment—which the majority of us spend most of our lives juggling and reconciling. They know the environments within which they play and tend to be fast learners in terms of understanding the keys to advancement. They know themselves in terms of both strengths and weaknesses, and they implement their career strategies with commitment, consistency and determination. As the late Peter Drucker observed: "we must learn how to be the CEO of our own careers."[4]

There is a downside, however. Focus on a single goal may lead to outstanding success, but may be matched by dismal failure in other areas of life. Many people who have reached the pinnacles of their careers have led lives scarred by poor relationships with friends and families and stunted personal development. These include Howard Hughes and Jean Paul Getty in business, Richard Nixon and Joseph Stalin in politics, Marilyn Monroe and Elvis Presley in entertainment, Joe Louis and O. J. Simpson in sport, and Bobby Fischer in chess. Fulfillment in our personal lives is likely to require broad-based lifetime strategies.[5]

These same ingredients of successful strategies—clear goals, understanding the competitive environment, resource appraisal and effective implementation—form the key components of our analysis of business strategy.

The Basic Framework for Strategy Analysis

Figure 1.2 shows the basic framework for strategy analysis that we shall use throughout the book. The four elements of a successful strategy shown in Figure 1.1 are recast into two groups—the firm and the industry environment—with strategy forming a link between the two. The firm embodies three sets of these elements:

FIGURE 1.2 The basic framework: strategy as a link between the firm and its environment

goals and values ("simple, consistent, long-term goals"), resources and capabilities ("objective appraisal of resources"), and structure and systems ("effective implementation"). The industry environment ("profound understanding of the competitive environment") is defined by the firm's relationships with customers, competitors and suppliers.

This view of strategy as a link between the firm and its industry enviroment has close similarities with the widely used, but inferior, SWOT Framework (see strategy capsule 1.4).

The task of business strategy, then, is to determine how the firm will deploy its resources within its environment and so satisfy its long-term goals, and how to organize itself to implement that strategy.

STRATEGY CAPSULE 1.4

What's Wrong with SWOT?

Distinguishing between the external and the internal environment of the firm is common to most approaches to strategy analysis. The best known and most widely used of these approaches is the "SWOT" framework, which classifies the various influences on a firm's strategy into four categories: Strengths, Weaknesses, Opportunities, and Threats. The first two—strengths and weaknesses—relate to the internal environment; the last two—opportunities and threats—relate to the external environment.

Which is better, a two-way distinction between internal and external influences or the four-way SWOT taxonomy? The key issue is whether it is sensible and worthwhile to classify internal factors into strengths and weaknesses and external factors into opportunities and threats. In practice, such distinctions are difficult:

- Is Steve Jobs a strength or a weakness for Apple? As both founder and reincarnator of Apple, few major companies owe so much to a single person. Yet, having suffered pancreatic cancer and the subject of continuing health concerns, Jobs is also a critical source of vulnerability for Apple.
- Is global warming a threat or an opportunity to the world's automobile

producers? Global warming may encourage governments to raise taxes on motor fuels and support public transport, thereby threatening the demand for private motoring. At the same time, these circumstances create an opportunity for developing new, fuel-efficient cars that may encourage consumers to scrap their gas-guzzlers.

The lesson here is that an arbitrary classification of external factors into opportunities and threats, and internal factors into strengths and weaknesses, is less important than a careful identification of these external and internal factors followed by an appraisal of their implications. My approach to strategy analysis favors a simple two-way classification of *internal* and *external* factors. What will characterize our strategic appraisal will be the rigor and depth of our analysis of these factors, rather than a superficial categorization into strengths or weaknesses, and opportunities or threats.

Strategic Fit

Fundamental to this view of strategy as a link between the firm and its external environment is the notion of *strategic fit*. For a strategy to be successful, it must be consistent with the firm's external environment, and with its internal environment—its goals and values, resources and capabilities, and structure and systems. As we shall see, the failure of many companies is caused by lack of consistency with either the internal or external environment. General Motors' long-term decline is a consequence of a strategy that has failed to break away from its long-established ideas about multibrand market segmentation and adapt to the changing market for automobiles. In other cases, many companies have failed to align their strategies to their internal resources and capabilities. A critical issue for Nintendo in the coming years will be whether it possesses the financial and technological resources to continue to compete head-to-head with Sony and Microsoft in the market for video game consoles.

As you will discover, the notion of *strategic fit* extends beyond the simple notion that strategy must fit with the external and the internal environment of the firm. The principles of strategic fit extend to organizational design—what is called *contingency theory* (see Chapter 7) and the view of the firm as a system of interlinked activities (see the discussion of *contextuality* in Chapter 8 and *complementarity* in Chapter 11).

A Brief History of Business Strategy

Origins and Military Antecedents

Enterprises need business strategies for much the same reasons that armies need military strategies—to give direction and purpose, to deploy resources in the most effective manner and to coordinate the decisions made by different individuals. Many of the concepts and theories of business strategy have their antecedents in military strategy. The term *strategy* derives from the Greek word *strategia*, meaning "generalship." However, the concept of strategy did not originate with the Greeks. Sun Tzu's classic *The Art of War*, written circa 500 BC, is regarded as the first treatise on strategy.[6]

Military strategy and business strategy share a number of common concepts and principles, the most basic being the distinction between strategy and tactics. *Strategy* is the overall plan for deploying resources to establish a favorable position; a *tactic* is a scheme for a specific action. Whereas tactics are concerned with the maneuvers necessary to win battles, strategy is concerned with winning the war. Strategic decisions, whether in military or business spheres, share three common characteristics:

- they are important
- they involve a significant commitment of resources
- they are not easily reversible.

Many of the principles of military strategy have been applied to business situations. These include the relative strengths of offensive and defensive strategies; the merits of outflanking over frontal assault; the roles of graduated responses to aggressive initiatives; the benefits of surprise and the potential for deception, envelopment, escalation and attrition.[7] At the same time, the differences between business competition and military conflict must be recognized. The objective of war is (usually) to defeat the enemy. The purpose of business rivalry is seldom so aggressive: most business enterprises limit their competitive ambitions, seeking coexistence rather than the destruction of competitors.

The tendency for the principles of military and business strategy to develop along separate paths indicates the absence of a general theory of strategy. The publication of Von Neumann and Morgenstern's *Theory of Games* in 1944 gave rise to the hope that a general theory of competitive behavior would emerge. During the subsequent six decades, game theory has revolutionized the study of competitive interaction, not just in business but in politics, military conflict and international relations as well. Yet, as we shall see in Chapter 4, game theory has achieved only limited success as a practical and broadly applicable general theory of strategy.[8]

From Corporate Planning to Strategic Management

The evolution of business strategy has been driven more by the practical needs of business than by the development of theory. During the 1950s and 1960s, senior executives were experiencing increasing difficulty in coordinating decisions and maintaining control in companies that were growing in size and complexity. Financial budgeting, in the form of annual financial planning and investment appraisal provided short-term control and project selection but did little to guide the long-term development of the firm. Corporate planning (also known as *long-term planning*) was developed during the late 1950s to serve this purpose. Macroeconomic forecasts provided the foundation for the new corporate planning. The typical format was a five-year corporate planning document that set goals and objectives, forecasted key economic trends (including market demand, the company's market share, revenue, costs and margins), established priorities for different products and business areas of the firm, and allocated capital expenditures. The diffusion of corporate planning was accelerated by a flood of articles and books addressing this new science.[9] The new techniques of corporate planning proved particularly useful for developing and guiding the diversification strategies that many large companies were pursuing during the 1960s. By the mid-1960s , most large U.S. and European companies had set up corporate planning departments. Strategy Capsule 1.5 provides an example of such formalized corporate planning.

STRATEGY CAPSULE 1.5

Corporate Planning in a Large U.S. Steel Company, 1965

The first step in developing long-range plans was to forecast the product demand for future years. After calculating the tonnage needed in each sales district to provide the "target" fraction of the total forecast demand, the optimal production level for each area was determined. A computer program that incorporated the projected demand, existing production capacity, freight costs etc., was used for this purpose.

When the optimum production rate in each area was found, the additional facilities needed to produce the desired tonnage were specified. Then the capital costs for the necessary equipment, buildings, and layout were estimated by the Chief Engineer of the corporation and various district engineers. Alternative plans for achieving company goals were also developed for some areas, and investment proposals were formulated after considering the amount of available capital and the company debt policy. The Vice President who was responsible for long-range planning recommended certain plans to the President and, after the top executives and the Board of Directors reviewed alternative plans, they made the necessary decisions about future activities.

Source: Harold W. Henry, *Long Range Planning Processes in Forty-five Industrial Companies* (Englewood Cliffs, NJ: Prentice-Hall, 1967): 65.

During the 1970s and early 1980s, confidence in corporate planning and infatuation with scientific approaches to management were severely shaken. Not only did diversification fail to deliver the anticipated synergies but the oil shocks of 1974 and 1979 ushered in a new era of macroeconomic instability, combined with increased international competition from resurgent Japanese, European, and Southeast Asian firms. Faced with a more turbulent business environment, firms could no longer plan their investments, new product introductions and personnel requirements three to five years ahead, simply because they couldn't forecast that far into the future.

The result was a shift in emphasis from *planning* to *strategy making*, where the focus was less on the detailed management of companies' growth paths than on positioning the company in markets and in relation to competitors in order to maximize the potential for profit. This transition from *corporate planning* to what became termed *strategic management* was associated with increasing focus on competition as the central characteristic of the business environment and competitive advantage as the primary goal of strategy.

This emphasis on strategy as a quest for performance directed attention to the sources of profitability. During the late 1970s and into the 1980s, attention focused on sources of profit within the industry environment. Michael Porter of Harvard Business School pioneered the application of industrial organization economics to analyzing industry profitability.[10] Other studies focused on how profits were distributed between the different firms in an industry—in particular the impact of market share and experience upon costs and profits.[11] These two lines of inquiry—into interindustry and interfirm differences in profitability—were combined in the Strategic Planning Institute's PIMS (Profit Impact of Market Strategy) project.[12]

During the 1990s, the focus of strategy analysis shifted from the sources of profit in the external environment to the sources of profit within the firm. Increasingly the resources and capabilities of the firm became regarded as the main source of competitive advantage and the primary basis for formulating strategy.[13] This emphasis on what has been called the *resource-based view of the firm* represented a substantial shift in thinking about strategy. Rather than firms pursuing similar strategies, as in seeking attractive markets and favorable competitive positions, emphasis on internal resources and capabilities has encouraged firms to identify how they are different from their competitors and design strategies that exploit these differences. Michael Porter's answer to the question "What is strategy?" emphasized that: "Competitive strategy is about being different. It means deliberately choosing a different set of activities to deliver a unique mix of value."[14]

During the first decade of the twenty-first century, the principles and practice of strategy have been molded by the uniquely challenging circumstances of a new era. Technology has been a particularly potent force.[15] The beginning of the decade saw the bursting of the TMT (technology, media, telecommunications) bubble and the realization that the "new knowledge economy" and internet-based business models did not require a rewriting of the principles of strategy. Nevertheless, technology continues to reshape industries: digital technologies are associated with standards wars,[16] the emergence of "winner-take-all" markets, [17] and the potential for strategic innovation as firms seek the "blue oceans" of uncontested market space.[18]

In the face of continuous change and relentless competition, strategy becomes less about building positions of sustained competitive advantage and more about developing the responsiveness and flexibility to create successive temporary advantages. Reconfiguring resources and capabilities to achieve such responsiveness typically requires firms to collaborate within networks of strategic alliances.

The continuing traumas of the twenty-first century, including the recession of 2008–9, are encouraging new thinking about the purpose of business. Disillusion with "shareholder value capitalism" has been accompanied by renewed interest in corporate social responsibility, ethics, sustainability of the natural environment and the role of social legitimacy in long-term corporate success.

Figure 1.3 summarizes the main developments in strategic management over the past 60 years.

Strategic Management Today

What Is Strategy?

In its broadest sense, strategy is the means by which individuals or organizations achieve their objectives. Table 1.1 presents a number of definitions of the term strategy. Common to definitions of business strategy is the notion that strategy is focused on achieving certain *goals*; that the critical actions that make up a strategy involve *allocation of resources*; and that strategy implies some *consistency*, *integration*, or *cohesiveness* of decisions and actions.

FIGURE 1.3 Evolution of strategic management: dominant themes

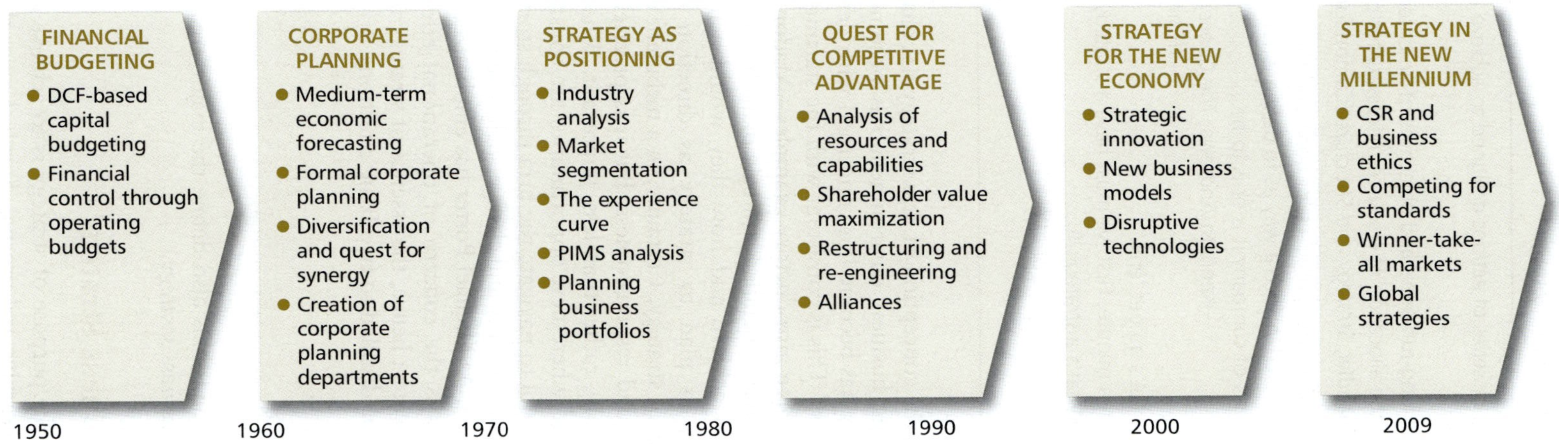

TABLE 1.1 Some definitions of strategy

- Strategy: a plan, method, or series of actions designed to achieve a specific goal or effect.
  —*Wordsmyth Dictionary*
- The determination of the long-run goals and objectives of an enterprise, and the adoption of courses of action and the allocation of resources necessary for carrying out these goals.
  —Alfred Chandler, *Strategy and Structure* (Cambridge, MA: MIT Press, 1962)
- Strategy is the pattern of objectives, purposes, or goals and the major policies and plans for achieving these goals, stated in such a way as to define what business the company is in or is to be in and the kind of company it is or is to be.
  —Kenneth Andrews, *The Concept of Corporate Strategy* (Homewood, IL: Irwin, 1971)
- Lost Boy: "Injuns! Let's go get 'em!"
  John Darling: "Hold on a minute. First we must have a strategy."
  Lost Boy: "Uhh? What's a *strategy*?"
  John Darling: "It's, er . . . it's a plan of attack."
  —Walt Disney's *Peter Pan*

Yet, as we have seen, the conception of firm strategy has changed greatly over the past half century. As the business environment has become more unstable and unpredictable, so strategy has become less concerned with detailed plans and more about the quest for success. This is consistent with the starting point to the chapter. If we think back to our three introductory examples—Madonna, General Giap and Lance Armstrong—none wrote detailed strategic plans but all possessed clear ideas of what they wanted to achieve and how they would achieve it. This shift in emphasis from strategy as plan to strategy as direction does not imply any downgrading of the role of strategy. Certainly, in a turbulent environment, strategy must embrace flexibility and responsiveness. But it is precisely in these conditions that strategy becomes more, rather than less, important. When the firm is buffeted by unforeseen threats and where new opportunities are constantly appearing, then strategy becomes a vital tool to navigate the firm through stormy seas.

In an environment of uncertainty and change, a clear sense of direction is essential to the pursuit of objectives. As Michael Porter has emphasized, strategy is not about doing things better—this is the concern of operational effectiveness—strategy is about doing things *differently*; hence, the essence of strategy is *making choices*.[19]

Strategic choices can be distilled to two basic questions:

- *Where* to compete?
- *How* to compete?

The answers to these questions also define the major areas of a firm's strategy: *corporate strategy* and *business strategy*.

Corporate and Business Strategy

If we start from basics, the purpose of strategy is to achieve certain goals. For the firm, the basic goal is to survive and prosper. Survival, over the long term, requires

FIGURE 1.4 The sources of superior profitability

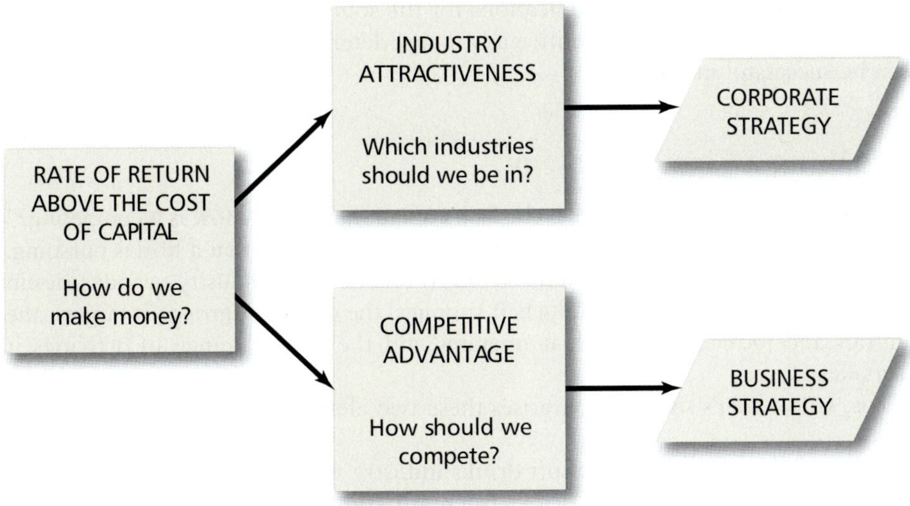

that the firm earns a rate of return on its capital that exceeds its cost of capital. There are two possible ways of achieving this. First, the firm may locate within an industry where overall rates of return are attractive. Second, the firm may attain a position of advantage vis-à-vis its competitors within an industry, allowing it to earn a return in excess of the industry average (see Figure 1.4).

These two sources of superior performance define the two basic levels of strategy within an enterprise:

- *Corporate strategy* defines the scope of the firm in terms of the industries and markets in which it competes. Corporate strategy decisions include choice over in diversification, vertical integration, acquisitions and new ventures; and the allocation of resources between the different businesses of the firm.
- *Business strategy* is concerned with how the firm competes within a particular industry or market. If the firm is to prosper within an industry, it must establish a competitive advantage over its rivals. Hence, this area of strategy is also referred to as *competitive strategy*.

This distinction may be expressed in even simpler terms. The basic question facing the firm is: "How do we make money?" The answer to this question corresponds to the two basic strategic choices we identified above: "Where to compete?" ("In which industries and markets should we be?") and "How should we compete?"

The distinction between corporate strategy and business strategy corresponds to the organization structure of most large companies. Corporate strategy is the responsibility of the top management team and the corporate strategy staff. Business strategy is primarily the responsibility of divisional management.

As an integrated approach to firm strategy, this book deals with both business and corporate strategy. However, my primary emphasis will be business strategy. This is because the critical requirement for a company's success is its ability to establish competitive advantage. Hence, issues of business strategy precede those of corporate strategy. At the same time, these two dimensions of strategy are intertwined: the scope of a firm's business has implications for the sources of competitive advantage, and the nature of a firm's competitive advantage determines the range of businesses it can be successful in.

Describing a Firm's Strategy

These same two questions "Where is the firm competing?" and "How is it competing?" also provide the basis upon which we can describe the strategy that a firm is pursuing. The *where* question has multiple dimensions. It relates to the industry or industries in which the firm is located, the products it supplies, the customer groups it targets, the countries and localities in which it operates and the vertical range of activities it undertakes.

Thus, Coca-Cola's strategy comprises these two elements. With regard to *where*:

- Coca-Cola competes in the soft drinks industry where it supplies concentrate for its branded carbonated drinks (such as Coca-Cola, Sprite, Fanta, Tab and Fresca) and supplies other drinks (such as Minute Maid, Hi-C and Five Alive fruit juices, and Dasani bottled water).
- Geographically, Coca-Cola competes worldwide. Its major markets are the U.S. (27% of sales) followed by Mexico, Brazil, Japan, and China.
- In terms of vertical scope, Coca-Cola's main activities are product development, brand management, and concentrate manufacture and distribution. The production and distribution of its soft drinks are undertaken by its sister company Coca-Cola Enterprises and franchised local bottlers.

With regard to *how*: Coca-Cola pursues a differentiation strategy where it relies on brand image developed through heavy advertising and promotion. It seeks market share leadership through its mass marketing and through close relationships with the leading bottlers in every country where it does business.

However, strategy is not simply about "competing for today"; it is also concerned with "competing for tomorrow." This dynamic concept of strategy involves establishing objectives for the future and determining how they will be achieved. Future objectives relate to the overall purpose of the firm (*mission*), what it seeks to become (*vision*) and specific performance targets.

In the case of Coca-Cola, this dynamic dimension of its strategy is outlined in broad terms in its statements of vision (to refresh the world) and mission which outlines goals in relation to its five Ps: people, products, planet, partners, and profit. More specific objectives are outlined in presentations to analysts: long-term volume growth of 3–4%, revenue growth of 5–6%, and operating profit growth of 6–8%. These objectives are to be achieved through growing sales of still drinks, exploiting growth opportunities in emerging markets, accelerating innovation and building core capabilities.[20]

These two dimensions of strategy—the static and the dynamic—are depicted in Figure 1.5. As we shall see, reconciling these two dimensions of strategy—what Derek Abell calls "competing with dual strategies" and Tushman and O'Reilly refer to as "the challenge of ambidexterity"—is one of the central dilemmas of strategic management.[21]

FIGURE 1.5 Describing firm strategy: competing in the present, preparing for the future

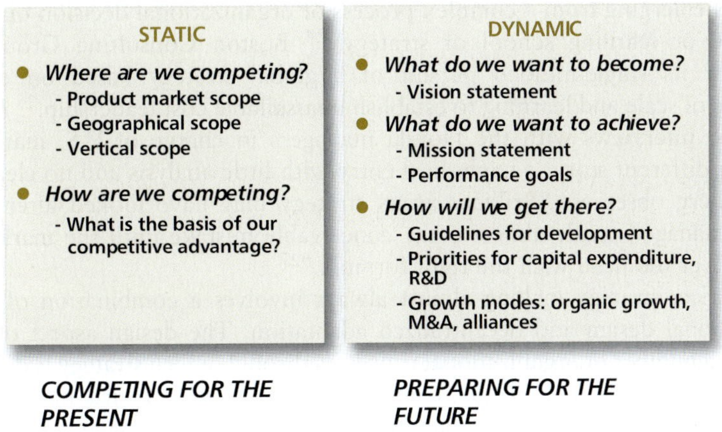

How Is Strategy Made? Design versus Emergence

How companies make strategy has been one of the most hotly debated issues in strategic management. Our emphasis on strategy analysis encourages the view that strategy is the result of managers engaging in deliberate, rational analysis. However, strategy may also emerge through adaptation to circumstances. In discussing Madonna's career, we discerned a consistency and pattern to her career decisions that we described as a strategy, yet there is no evidence that she engaged in any systematic strategic planning. Similarly many successful companies were not products of grand designs—for example Wal-Mart's winning strategy built on large-store formats, hub-and-spoke distribution, small-town locations and employee motivation emerged from Sam Walton's hunches and a series of historical accidents.

Henry Mintzberg is a leading critic of rational approaches to strategy design. He distinguishes *intended*, *realized* and *emergent* strategies. *Intended strategy* is strategy as conceived of by the top management team. Even here, intended strategy is less a product of rational deliberation and more an outcome of negotiation, bargaining and compromise among the many individuals and groups involved in the process. However, *realized strategy*—the actual strategy that is implemented—is only partly related to that which was intended (Mintzberg suggests only 10–30% of intended strategy is realized). The primary determinant of realized strategy is what Mintzberg terms *emergent strategy*—the decisions that emerge from the complex processes in which individual managers interpret the intended strategy and adapt to changing external circumstances.[22] According to Mintzberg, not only is rational design an inaccurate account of how strategies are actually formulated—it is a poor way of making strategy. "The notion that strategy is something that should happen way up there, far removed from the details of running an organization on a daily basis, is one of the great fallacies of conventional strategic management."[23] The emergent approaches to strategy making permit adaptation and learning though continuous interaction between strategy formulation and strategy implementation in which strategy is constantly being adjusted and revised in light of experience.

Honda's successful entry into the US motorcycle market has provided a central battleground between those who view strategy making as primarily a rational, analytical process of deliberate planning (the design school) and those that envisage strategy as emerging from a complex process of organizational decision making (the emergence or learning school of strategy).[24] Boston Consulting Group lauded Honda for its single-minded pursuit of a global strategy based on exploiting economies of scale and learning to establish unassailable cost leadership.[25] However, subsequent interviews with the Honda managers in charge of U.S. market entry revealed a different story: a haphazard entry with little analysis and no clear plan.[26] As Mintzberg observes: "Brilliant as its strategy may have looked after the fact, Honda's managers made almost every conceivable mistake until the market finally hit them over the head with the right formula."[27]

In practice, strategy making almost always involves a combination of centrally driven rational design and decentralized adaptation. The design aspect of strategy comprises a number of organizational processes through which strategy is deliberated, discussed, and decided. In larger companies these include board meetings and a formalized process of strategic planning process supplemented by more broadly participative events such as strategy workshops. I will discuss processes of strategic planning more fully in Chapter 6.

At the same time, strategy is being continually enacted through decisions that are made by every member of the organization—by middle management especially. The decentralized, bottom-up strategy emergence often precedes more formalized strategy formulation. Intel's historic decision to abandon memory chips and concentrate on microprocessors was initiated by incremental decisions taken by business unit and plant managers that were subsequently promulgated by top management into strategy.[28]

In all the companies I am familiar with, strategic planning combines design and emergence—a process that I have referred to as "planned emergence."[29] The balance between the two depends greatly upon the stability and predictability of a company's business environment. The Roman Catholic Church and the U.S. Postal Service inhabit relatively stable environments. For Google, Al Qaida and Zimbabwe Banking Corporation, strategic planning will inevitably be restricted to a few principles and guidelines; the rest must emerge as circumstances unfold.

As the business environment becomes more turbulent and less predictable, so strategy making becomes more concerned with guidelines and less with specific decisions. Bain & Company advocate the use of strategic principles— "pithy, memorable distillations of strategy that guide and empower employees"—to combine consistent focus with adaptability and responsiveness. [30] America's most successful airline, Southwest, encapsulates its strategy in a simple statement: "Meet customers' short-haul travel needs at fares competitive with the cost of automobile travel." Kathy Eisenhart and Don Sull make a similar argument when they advocate "simple rules" as the basis for successful strategies in fast-moving businesses. For example, Lego evaluates new product proposals by applying a checklist of rules: "Does the product have the Lego look?" "Will children learn while having fun?" "Does it stimulate creativity?"[31]

We shall return to the role of rules and principles to guide an organization's evolution and coordinate the decisions of its many members in our final chapter where we explore some of the implications of complexity theory for strategic management.

Identifying a Company's Strategy

Where do we look to find a company's strategy? Strategy is located in three places: in the heads of the chief executive and senior managers, in their articulations of strategy in speeches and written documents, and in the decisions through which strategy is enacted. Only the last two are observable.

While the most explicit statements of strategy—in board minutes and strategic planning documents—are almost invariably confidential, most companies—public companies in particular—see value in communicating their strategy to employees, customers, investors, and business partners—and, inevitably, to the public at large. Collis and Rukstad identify a hierarchy of strategy statements:

- The mission statement is the basic statement of organizational purpose, it addresses "Why we exist."
- A statement of principles or values states "What we believe in and how we will behave."
- The vision statement projects "What we want to be."
- The strategy statement articulates "What our competitive game plan will be." Collis and Rukstad argue that this should comprise three definitive components of strategy: *objectives*, *scope* (where we will compete) and *advantage* (how we will compete).[32]

A version of some or all of these statements is typically found on the corporate pages of companies' websites. More detailed statements of strategy—including qualitative and quantitative medium-term targets—are often found in top management presentations to analysts which are typically included in the "for investors" pages of company websites.

More detailed information on scope (*where?*) and advantage (*how?*) can be found in companies' annual reports. For U.S. corporations, the description of the business that forms Item 1 of the 10-K annual report to the SEC is particularly informative about strategy.

Strategy capsules 1.6 and 1.7 provide summary statements of strategy by Apple Inc. and Nokia Corp.

STRATEGY CAPSULE 1.6

Apple Computer, Inc.: Business Strategy

The Company is committed to bringing the best personal computing and music experience to students, educators, creative professionals, businesses, government agencies, and consumers through its innovative hardware, software, peripherals, services and internet offerings. The Company's business strategy leverages its unique ability, through the design and development of its own operating system, hardware, and many software applications and technologies, to bring to its customers new products and solutions with superior ease-of-use, seamless integration, and innovative industrial design. The Company believes continual investment in research and development is critical to facilitate innovation of new and improved products and technologies. Besides updates to its existing line of personal computers and related software, services, peripherals, and networking solutions, the Company continues to capitalize on the convergence of digital consumer electronics and the computer by creating innovations like the iPod and iTunes Music Store. The Company's strategy also includes expanding its distribution network to reach more of its targeted customers effectively and provide them a high-quality sales and after-sales support experience.

Source: Apple Computer, Inc., 10-K Report, 2005.

STRATEGY CAPSULE 1.7

Nokia's Strategy

VISION

Our vision is a world where everyone can be connected. Everyone has a need to communicate and share. Nokia helps people to fulfill this need and we help people feel close to what matters to them. We focus on providing consumers with very human technology—technology that is intuitive, a joy to use, and beautiful.

We are living in an era where connectivity is becoming truly ubiquitous. The communications industry continues to change and the internet is at the center of this transformation. Today, the internet is Nokia's quest.

Nokia's strategy relies on growing, transforming, and building the Nokia business to ensure its future success.

STRATEGY

We seek to grow, transform and build the Nokia business based on our business strategies and strategic capabilities.

Our business strategies reflect the primary focus of each of Nokia's business areas as follows:

- lead and win in mobile devices
- grow consumer internet services
- accelerate adoption of business solutions
- leverage scale and transform solutions in infrastructure.

Our strategic capabilities are the priority areas where we are investing with the aim of gaining a competitive advantage. The following capabilities can be shared among our several business areas:

- consumer understanding
- brand
- technology and architecture
- channels and supply chain.

Sources: www.nokia.com/A4126317 (accessed July 2, 2009); U.S. Securities and Exchange Commission, Nokia Form 20-F 2007 (March 20, 2008): 27–28.

However, the usefulness of public statements of strategy is limited by their role as public relations vehicles—this is particularly evident in vision and mission statements which are frequently grandiose and platitudinous. Hence, explicit statements of strategy need to be checked against decisions and actions:

- Where is the company investing its money? Notes to financial statements provide detailed breakdowns of capital expenditure by region and by business segment.
- What technologies are the company developing? Identifying the patents that a company has filed (using the online databases of the U.S. and E.U. patent offices) indicates the technological trajectory it is pursuing.
- What new products have been released, major investment projects initiated, and top management hired? A company's press releases usually announce these strategic decisions.

To identify a firm's strategy it is necessary to draw upon multiple sources of information in order to build an overall picture of what the company says it is doing and what it is actually doing. We will return to this topic when we discuss competitive intelligence in Chapter 4.

Multiple Roles of Strategy

The transition from corporate planning to strategic management has involved strategy moving from technocratic planning departments to the center of corporate leadership. As a result, strategy occupies multiple roles within an organization.

Strategy as Decision Support I have described strategy as a pattern or theme that gives coherence to the decisions of an individual or organization. But why can't individuals or organizations make optimal decisions in the absence of such a unifying theme? Consider the 1997 "man-versus-computer" chess epic in which Garry Kasparov was defeated by IBM's "Deep Blue." Deep Blue did not need strategy. Its phenomenal memory and computing power allowed it to identify its optimal moves based on a huge decision tree.[33] Kasparov—although the world's greatest chess player—was subject to *bounded rationality*: his decision analysis was subject to the cognitive limitations that constrain all human beings.[34] For chess players, a strategy offers guidelines and decision criteria that assist positioning and help create opportunities.

Strategy improves decision making in several ways. First, strategy simplifies decision making by *constraining* the range of decision alternatives considered and by acting as a *heuristic*—a rule of thumb that reduces the search required to find an acceptable solution to a decision problem. Second, a strategy-making process permits the knowledge of different individuals to be pooled and integrated. Third, a strategy-making process facilitates the use of analytic tools—the frameworks and techniques that we will encounter in the ensuing chapters of this book.

Strategy as a Coordinating Device The greatest challenge of managing an organization is coordinating the actions of different organizational members. Strategy can promote coordination in several ways. First, it is a communication device. Statements of strategy are a powerful means through which the CEO can communicate the identity, goals and positioning of the company to all organizational members. However, communication alone is not enough. For coordination to be effective, buy-in is essential from the different groups that make up the organization. The strategic planning process can provide a forum in which views are exchanged and consensus developed. Once formulated, the implementation of strategy through goals, commitments and performance targets that are monitored over the strategic planning period also provides a mechanism to ensure that the organization moves forward in a consistent direction.

Strategy as Target Strategy is forward looking. It is concerned not only with how the firm will compete now but also with what the firm will become in the future. A key purpose of a forward-looking strategy is not only to establish a direction of the firm's development but also to set aspirations that can motivate and inspire members of the organization. Gary Hamel and C. K. Prahalad use the term "strategic intent" to describe the articulation of a desired leadership position. They argue that: ". . . strategic intent creates an extreme misfit between resources and ambitions. Top management then challenges the organization to close the gap by building new competitive advantages."[35] The implication they draw is that strategy should be less about fit and resource allocation, and more about *stretch* and *resource leverage*.[36] The evidence from Toyota, Virgin, and Southwest Airlines is that resource scarcity may engender ambition, innovation, and a "success-against-the-odds" culture. Jim Collins and Jerry Porras make a similar point: U.S. companies that have been sector leaders for 50 years or more—Merck, Walt Disney, 3M, IBM, and Ford—have all generated commitment and drive through setting "Big, Hairy, Ambitious Goals."[37] Striving, inspirational goals are typical of most organizations' statements of vision and mission. One of the best known is the goal set by President Kennedy for NASA's space program: ". . . before this decade is out, of landing a man on the moon and returning him safely to Earth." British Airways aspires to be "The World's Favourite Airline," while Coca-Cola's drive for growth is driven by the quest to "have a Coca-Cola within arm's reach of everyone in the world."

The Role of Analysis in Strategy Formulation

Despite the criticism of rational, analytical approaches to strategy formulation by Henry Mintzberg and others, the approach of this book is to emphasize analytic approaches to strategy formulation. This is not because I wish to downplay the role of intuition, creativity and spontaneity—these qualities are essential ingredients of successful strategies. Nevertheless, whether strategy formulation is formal or informal, whether strategies are deliberate or emergent, systematic analysis is a vital input into the strategy process. Without analysis, strategic decisions are susceptible to power battles, individual whims, fads and wishful thinking. Concepts, theories, and analytic tools are complements not substitutes for experience, commitment and creativity. Their role is to provide frameworks for organizing discussion, processing information and opinions and assisting consensus.

This is not to endorse current approaches to strategy analysis. Strategic management is still a young field and the existing toolbox of concepts and techniques remains woefully inadequate. Our challenge is to do better. If existing analytical techniques do not adequately address the problems of strategy making and strategy implementation under conditions of uncertainty, technological change and complexity, we need to augment and extend our analytical toolkit. In the course of the book you will encounter concepts such as real options, tacit knowledge, hypercompetition, complementarity, and complexity that will help you address more effectively the challenges that firms are facing in today's turbulent business environment. We must also recognize the nature of strategy analysis. Unlike many of the analytical techniques in accounting, finance, market research, or production management, strategy analysis does not generate solutions to problems. It does not yield rules, algorithms, or formulae that tell us the optimal strategy to adopt. The strategic questions that companies face (like those that we face in our own careers and lives) are simply too complex to be programmed.

The purpose of strategy analysis is not to provide answers but to help us understand the issues. Most of the analytic techniques introduced in this book are frameworks that allow us to identify, classify and understand the principal factors relevant to strategic decisions. Such frameworks are invaluable in allowing us to come to terms with the complexities of strategy decisions. In some instances, the most useful contribution may be in assisting us to make a start on the problem. By guiding us to the questions we need to answer and by providing a framework for organizing the information gathered, strategy analysis places us in a superior position to a manager who relies exclusively on experience and intuition. Finally, analytic frameworks and techniques can improve our flexibility as managers. The analysis in this book is general in its applicability; it is not specific to particular industries, companies, or situations. Hence, it can help increase our confidence and effectiveness in understanding and responding to new situations and new circumstances. By encouraging depth of understanding in fundamental issues concerning competitive advantage, customer needs, organizational capabilities, and the basis of competition, the concepts, frameworks and techniques in this book will encourage rather than constrain innovation and flexibility.

Summary

This chapter has covered a great deal of ground—I hope that you are not suffering from indigestion. If you are feeling a little overwhelmed, not to worry: we shall be returning to most of the themes and issues raised in this chapter in the subsequent chapters of the book.

The next stage is to delve further into the basic strategy framework shown in Figure 1.2. The elements of this framework—goals and values, the industry environment, resources and capabilities, and structure and systems—comprise the basic components of strategy analysis. The next part of the book devotes separate chapters to each. We then deploy these tools in the analysis of competitive advantage (Part III), in the formulation and implementation of business strategies in different industry contexts (Part IV), and then in the development of corporate strategy (Part V). Figure 1.6 shows the framework for the book.

FIGURE 1.6 The structure of the book

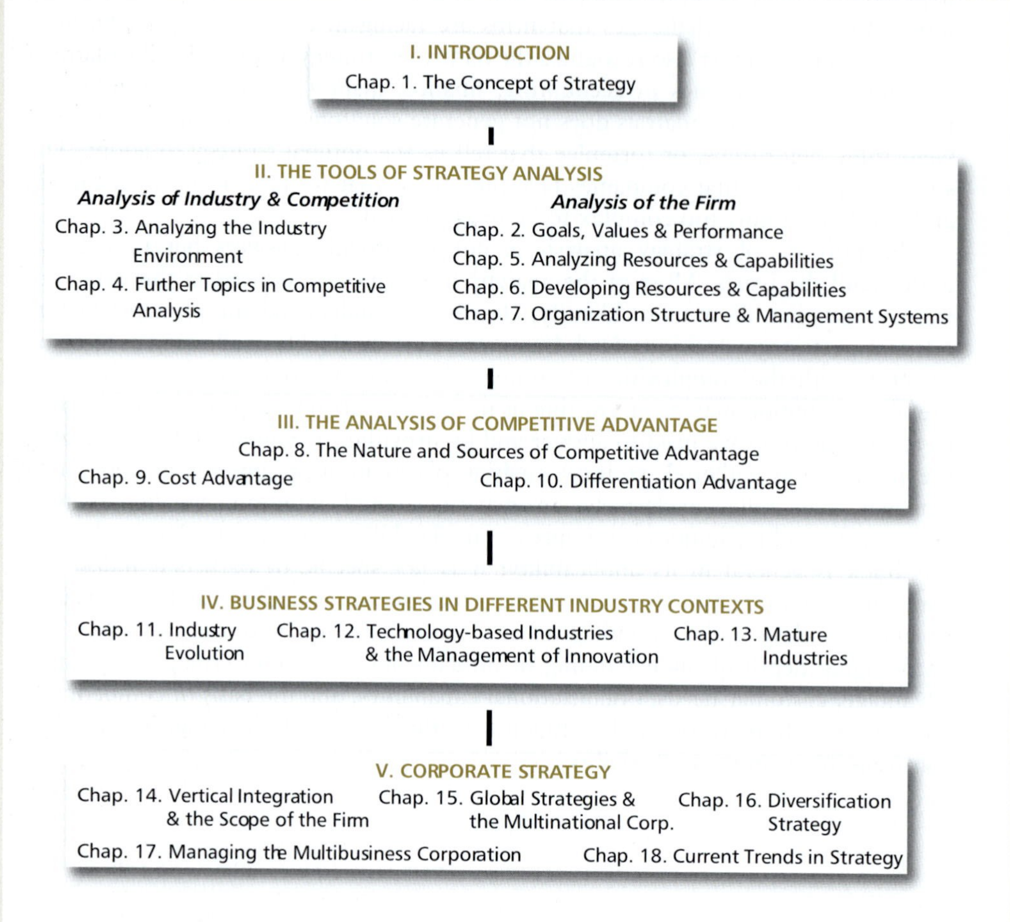

Self-Study Questions

1 In relation to the four characteristics of successful strategies (clear, consistent, long-term objectives; profound understanding of the environment; objective appraisal of resources and effective implementation), assess the U.S. strategy towards Iraq during 2003–9.

2 The discussion of the evolution of business strategy ("From Corporate Planning to Strategic Management") established that the characteristics of a firm's strategic plans and its strategic planning process are strongly influenced by the volatility and unpredictability of its external environment. On this basis, what differences would you expect in the strategic plans and strategic planning processes of Coca-Cola Company and Google Inc.?

3 I have noted that a firm's strategy can be described in terms of the answers to two questions: "Where are we competing?" and "How are we competing?" Applying these two questions, provide a concise description of Madonna's career strategy (see Strategy Capsule 1.1).

4 Using the structure outlined in Figure 1.5, describe the strategy of the business school you attend?

5 What is your career strategy for the next five years? To what extent does your strategy fit with your long-term goals, the characteristics of the external environment and your own strengths and weaknesses?

6 In relation to each of the "multiple roles of strategy" outlined above, what use (if any) is Nokia's statement of strategy as outlined in Strategy Capsule 1.7?

Notes

1 Col. Harry G. Summers Jr., *On Strategy* (Novato, CA: Presidio Press, 1982): 1.

2 Vo Nguyen Giap, *Selected Writings* (Hanoi: Foreign Language Publishing House, 1977).

3 J. Cameron, *Here Is Your Enemy* (New York: Holt, Rinehart & Winston, 1966).

4 P. F. Drucker, "Managing Oneself," *Harvard Business Review* (March–April 1999): 65–74.

5 Stephen Covey (*The Seven Habits of Highly Effective People*, Simon & Schuster, 1989) advises us to start at the end—to visualize our own funerals and imagine what we would like the funeral speakers to say about us and our lives. On this basis, he recommends that we develop lifetime mission statements based on the multiple roles that we occupy in life.

6 Sun Tzu, *The Art of Strategy: A New Translation of Sun Tzu's Classic "The Art of War,"* trans. R. L. Wing (New York: Doubleday, 1988).

7 See: R. Evered "So What is Strategy," *Long Range Planning* 16, no. 3 (June 1983): 57–72; E. Clemons and J. Santamaria, "Maneuver Warfare," *Harvard Business Review* (April 2002): 46–53.

8 On the contribution of game theory to business strategy analysis, see F. M. Fisher, "Games Economists Play: A Non-cooperative View," *RAND Journal of Economics* 20 (Spring 1989): 113–24; and C. F. Camerer, "Does Strategy Research Need Game Theory?" *Strategic Management Journal* 12, Special Issue (Winter 1991): 137–52.

9 During the late 1950s, *Harvard Business Review* featured a number of articles on corporate planning, for example D. W. Ewing, "Looking Around: Long-range Business Planning," *Harvard Business Review* (July–August 1956): 135–46; B. Payne, "Steps in Long-range Planning," *Harvard Business Review* (March–April 1957): 95–101.

10 M. E. Porter, *Competitive Strategy* (New York: Free Press, 1980).

11 Boston Consulting Group, *Perspectives on Experience* (Boston: Boston Consulting Group, 1978).

12 R. D. Buzzell and B. T. Gale, *The PIMS Principles* (New York: Free Press, 1987).

13 R. M. Grant, "The Resource-based Theory of Competitive Advantage: Implications for Strategy Formulation," *California Management Review* 33 (Spring 1991): 114–35; D. J. Collis and C. Montgomery, "Competing on Resources: Strategy in the 1990s," *Harvard Business Review* (July–August 1995): 119–28.

14 M. E. Porter, "What is Strategy?" *Harvard Business Review* (November–December 1996): 64.

15 C. Christensen, *The Innovator's Dilemma* (Boston: Harvard Business School Press, 1997).

16 C. Shapiro and H. R. Varian, *Information Rules* (Boston: Harvard Business School Press, 1998).

17 R. H. Frank and P. J. Cook, *The Winner-Take-All Society* (New York: Penguin, 1997).

18 W. C. Kim and R. Mauborgne, "Creating New Market Space," *Harvard Business Review* (January–February 1999): 83–93.

19 M. E. Porter, "What is Strategy?" op. cit.

20 Coca-Cola Company, Inc. Presentation to Lehman Brothers Conference, September 3, 2008 (http://media.corporate-ir.net/media_files/irol/94/94566/presentations/KO_Lehman_Conference_090308.pdf, accessed July 2, 2009).

21 D. F. Abell, *Managing with Dual Strategies* (New York: Free Press, 1993); M. L. Tushman and C. A. O'Reilly, "The Ambidextrous Organization," *Harvard Business Review* (April 2004): 74–81.

22 See H. Mintzberg, "Patterns of Strategy Formulation," *Management Science* 24 (1978): 934–48; "Of Strategies:

Deliberate and Emergent," *Strategic Management Journal* 6 (1985): 257–72; and *Mintzberg on Management: Inside Our Strange World of Organizations* (New York: Free Press, 1988).

23 H. Mintzberg, "The Fall and Rise of Strategic Planning," *Harvard Business Review* (January–February 1994): 107–14.

24 The two views of Honda are captured in two Harvard cases: *Honda [A]* (Boston: Harvard Business School, Case No. 384049, 1989) and *Honda [B]* (Boston: Harvard Business School, Case No. 384050, 1989).

25 Boston Consulting Group, *Strategy Alternatives for the British Motorcycle Industry* (London: Her Majesty's Stationery Office, 1975).

26 R. T. Pascale, "Perspective on Strategy: The Real Story Behind Honda's Success," *California Management Review* 26, no. 3 (Spring 1984): 47–72.

27 H. Mintzberg, "Crafting Strategy," *Harvard Business Review* 65 (July–August 1987): 70.

28 R. A. Burgelman and A. Grove, "Strategic Dissonance," *California Management Review* 38 (Winter 1996): 8–28.

29 R. M. Grant, "Strategic Planning in a Turbulent Environment: Evidence from the Oil and Gas Majors," *Strategic Management Journal* 14 (June 2003): 491–517.

30 O. Gadiesh and J. Gilbert, "Transforming Corner-office Strategy into Frontline Action," *Harvard Business Review* (May 2001): 73–80.

31 K. M. Eisenhardt and D. N. Sull, "Strategy as Simple Rules," *Harvard Business Review* (January 2001): 107–16.

32 D. J. Collis and M.G. Rukstad, "Can You Say What Your Strategy Is?" *Harvard Business Review* (April 2008): 63–73.

33 "Strategic Intensity: A Conversation with Garry Kasparov," *Harvard Business Review* (April 2005): 105–13.

34 The concept of bounded rationality was developed by Herbert Simon ("A Behavioral Model of Rational Choice," *Quarterly Journal of Economics* 69 (1955): 99–118).

35 G. Hamel and C. K. Prahalad, "Strategic Intent," *Harvard Business Review* (May–June 1989): 63–77.

36 G. Hamel and C. K. Prahalad, "Strategy as Stretch and Leverage," *Harvard Business Review* (March–April 1993): 75–84.

37 J. C. Collins and J. I. Porras, *Built to Last: Successful Habits of Visionary Companies* (New York: HarperCollins, 1995).

II

THE TOOLS OF STRATEGY ANALYSIS

2 Goals, Values, and Performance

The strategic aim of a business is to earn a return on capital, and if in any particular case the return in the long run is not satisfactory, then the deficiency should be corrected or the activity abandoned for a more favorable one.

—ALFRED P. SLOAN JR., *MY YEARS WITH GENERAL MOTORS*

OUTLINE

Introduction and Objectives

Our framework for strategy analysis (Figure 1.2) comprises four components: the firm's goals and values, its resources and capabilities, its structure and management systems and its industry environment. The chapters that form Part II of the book develop these four components of strategy analysis. We begin with goals and values and, by extension, the performance of the firm in attaining its goals.

Firms possess multiple goals. However, for the purpose of strategy analysis, we focus upon a single goal: the maximization of the value of the firm. The value of the firm is determined, primarily, by the profits it earns over its lifetime—hence, business strategy becomes a quest for profit. Most of the frameworks and techniques of strategy analysis that we will cover are concerned with identifying and exploiting the sources of profitability open to the firm.

This focus on profitability and value creation means that we will draw upon some of the tools of financial analysis for the purposes of performance appraisal, performance diagnosis, and target setting. At the same time we shall recognize that, while profit is the most useful measure of firm performance, firms are motivated by goals other than profit. Indeed, the companies that are most successful in generating profits over the long run are typically those driven by ambitions other than profit. Profit is the life-blood of the organization, but it is not a goal that inspires organizational members to outstanding achievement. Moreover, for a firm to survive and generate profit over the long run requires responsiveness to, and accommodation with, its social, political, and natural environment.

By the time you have completed this chapter you will be able to:

- appreciate the main arguments in the debate over shareholder versus stakeholder goals for the firm;
- understand the relationship between profit, cash flow and value;

- use financial and strategic information to diagnose the sources of a company's performance problems;
- translate the overall goals of long-term profit maximization into meaningful performance targets that can be measured and monitored;
- understand the linkages between financial analysis and strategic analysis, and how they can be used to complement one another;
- comprehend the role of values, mission and vision in formulating and implementing strategy.

Strategy as a Quest for Value

Business is about creating *value*. *Value* is the monetary worth of a product or asset. The purpose of business is, first, to create value for customers and, second, to extract some of that customer value in the form of profit, thereby creating value for the firm.

Value can be created in two ways: by production and by commerce. Production creates value by physically transforming products that are less valued by consumers into products that are more valued by consumers—turning clay into coffee mugs, for example. Commerce creates value not by physically transforming products but by repositioning them in space and time. Trade involves transferring products from individuals and places where they are less valued to individuals and locations where they are more valued. Similarly, speculation involves transferring products from a point in time where the product is valued less to a point in time where it is valued more. Thus, the essence of commerce is creating value through arbitrage across time and space.[1]

The difference between the value of a firm's output and the cost of its material inputs is its *value added*. Value added is equal to the sum of all the income paid to the suppliers of factors of production. Thus:

$$\begin{aligned}\text{value added} &= \text{sales revenue from output—cost of material inputs}\\ &= \text{wages/salaries} + \text{interest} + \text{rent} + \text{royalties/license fees}\\ &\quad + \text{taxes} + \text{dividends} + \text{retained profit}\end{aligned}$$

In Whose Interest? Shareholders versus Stakeholders

The value added created by firms is distributed among different parties: employees (wages and salaries), lenders (interest), landlords (rent), government (taxes) and owners (profit). In addition, firms also create value for their customers to the extent that the satisfaction customers gain exceeds the price they pay (they derive *consumer surplus*). It is tempting, therefore, to think of the firm as operating for the benefit of multiple constituencies. This view of the business enterprise as a coalition of interest groups where top management's role to balance these different—often conflicting—interests is referred to as the *stakeholder* approach to the firm.[2]

The notion of the corporation balancing the interests of multiple stakeholders has a long tradition, especially in Asia and continental Europe. By contrast, most English-speaking countries have endorsed *shareholder capitalism*, where companies' overriding duty is to produce profits for owners. These differences are reflected in international differences in companies' legal obligations. In the U.S., Canada, the U.K. and Australia, company boards are required to act in the interests of shareholders. In continental European countries, companies are legally required to take account of the interests of employees, the state and the enterprise as a whole. Whether companies should operate exclusively in the interests of their owners or should also pursue the goals of other stakeholders is an ongoing debate. During the 1990s, "Anglo-Saxon" shareholder capitalism was in the ascendant—many continental European and Japanese companies changed their strategies and corporate governance to increase their responsiveness to shareholder interests. However, during the twenty-first century, shareholder value maximization became associated with short-termism, financial manipulation (Enron, World.com), excessive CEO compensation, and the failures of risk management that precipitated the 2008–9 financial crisis. The responsibilities of business to employees, customers, society and the natural environment are central ethical and social issues. Nevertheless, in order to make progress in developing analytical tools for designing successful strategies I shall adopt the simplifying assumption that companies operate in the interests of their owners by seeking to maximize profits over the long term. Why do I make this assumption and how do I justify it? Let me point to four key considerations:

- *Competition*. Competition erodes profitability. As competition increases, the interests of different stakeholders converge around the goal of survival. Survival requires that, over the long term, the firm earns a rate of profit that covers its cost of capital otherwise it will not be able to replace its assets. Over half of America's publicly listed companies do not cover their cost of capital.[3] Across many sectors of industry, the heat of international competition is such that few companies have the luxury of pursuing goals that diverge from profit maximization.
- *The market for corporate control*. Management teams that fail to maximize the profits of their companies will be replaced by teams that do. In the "market for corporate control" companies that underperform financially suffer a declining share price that attracts acquirers—other public companies or private equity funds. In addition, activist investors, both individuals (Carl Icahn, Kirk Kerkorian) and funds (such as California Public Employees' Retirement System, The Children's Investment Fund) put pressure on boards of directors to improve shareholder returns. One result has been increased turnover of chief executives.[4]
- *Convergence of stakeholder interests*. Even beyond a common interest in the survival of the firm, there is likely to be more community of interests than conflict of interests among different stakeholders. Profitability over the long-term requires loyalty from employees, trusting relationships with suppliers and customers, and support from governments and communities. The

argument that firms require legitimacy in order to survive and prosper is reinforced by evidence that firms that pursue ethical principles and corporate social responsibility achieve superior financial performance.[5]

- *Simplicity*. A key problem of the stakeholder approach is that considering multiple goals and specifying tradeoffs between them vastly increases the complexity of decision making.[6] Virtually all the major tools of business decision making, from pricing rules to discounted cash flow analysis, are rooted in the assumption of profit maximization. Adopting stakeholder goals risks opening the door to political wrangling and management paralysis.

Assuming that firm strategy is directed primarily toward making profit doesn't mean that we have to accept that profit is the sole motivation driving business enterprises. As we noted in the previous chapter, the goals driving the architects of the world's great enterprises—Henry Ford at Ford Motor Company, Bill Gates at Microsoft, and Nicholas Hayek of Swatch—are seldom financial. The dominant drivers tend to be the fulfillment of a vision and the desire to make a difference in the world. Nevertheless, even when business goals transcend mere money making, their achievement requires enterprises that are commercially successful—this requires the adoption of strategies that generate profit.

What Is Profit?

Thus far, we have referred to firms' quest for profit in loose terms. It is time to look more carefully at what we mean by profit and how it relates to shareholder value.

Profit is the surplus of revenues over costs available for distribution to the owners of the firm. But, if profit maximization is to be a realistic goal, the firm must know what profit is and how to measure it. Otherwise, instructing managers to maximize profit offers little guidance. What is the firm to maximize: total profit or rate of profit? Over what time period? With what kind of adjustment for risk? And what is profit anyway—accounting profit, cash flow, or economic profit? The ambiguity is apparent once we consider the profit performance of companies. Table 2.1 shows that ranking companies by profitability depends critically on how profitability is measured.

From Accounting Profit to Economic Profit

A major problem of accounting profit is that it combines two types of returns: the *normal return to capital* that rewards investors for the use of their capital; and *economic profit*, which is the pure surplus available after all inputs (including capital) have been paid for. Economic profit represents a purer and more reliable measure of profit that is a better measure of performance. To distinguish economic profit from accounting profit, economic profit is often referred to as *rent* or *economic rent*.

A widely used measure of economic profit is *economic value added* (EVA), devised and popularized by the New York consulting firm Stern Stewart & Company.[7] Economic value added is measured as net operating profit after tax (NOPAT) less cost of capital, where cost of capital is calculated as capital employed *multiplied by* the weighted average cost of capital (WACC).

TABLE 2.1 Performance of the world's biggest companies using different profitability measures (2007)

Company	Market capitalization[a] ($ bn)	Net income[a] ($ bn)	Return on sales[b] (%)	Return on equity[c] (%)	Return on assets[d] (%)	Return to shareholders[e] (%)
ExxonMobil	453	40.61	17.42	33.35	29.69	24.30
PetroChina	424	20.75	24.48	19.99	18.85	28.90
General Electric	370	22.21	15.40	19.22	7.46	2.60
Gazprom	300	26.11	38.66	16.11	10.33	103.50
China Mobile	298	12.41	36.21	23.32	22.02	21.50
Microsoft	264	14.07	39.41	48.73	30.90	20.80
AT&T	231	11.95	15.31	10.36	7.40	20.50
Royal Dutch Shell	220	31.33	14.22	25.28	15.12	20.10
Procter & Gamble	216	10.34	19.25	17.38	11.86	16.60
Wal-Mart Stores	211	12.73	5.33	19.70	13.45	4.70
Berkshire Hathaway	207	13.21	17.05	10.94	8.08	28.70
Nestlé	197	10.72	12.57	20.99	13.10	31.60

Notes

[a] Source: *Financial Times*.

[b] Pretax profit as a percentage of sales revenues. Source: Hoovers

[c] Net income as a percentage of (year end) shareholders' equity. Source: Hoovers.

[d] Operating income as a percentage of (year end) total assets. Source: Hoovers.

[e] Dividend + share price appreciation during 2007. Source: *Fortune*.

Economic profit has two main advantages over accounting profit as a performance measure. First, it sets a more demanding performance discipline for managers. At many capital intensive companies seemingly healthy profits disappear once cost of capital is taken into account.

Second, using economic profit improves the allocation of capital between the different businesses of the firm by taking account of the real costs of more capital intensive businesses (see Strategy Capsule 2.1).

STRATEGY CAPSULE 2.1

Economic Value Added at Diageo plc.

At Guinness-to-Johnny-Walker drinks giant Diageo, EVA transformed the way in which Diageo measured its performance, allocated its capital and advertising expenditures, and evaluated its managers.

Taking account of the costs of the capital tied up in slow-maturing, vintage drinks such as Talisker and Lagavulin malt whisky, Hennessey cognac, and Dom Perignon champagne showed that these high-margin drinks were often not as profitable as the company had believed. The result was that Diageo's advertising expenditures were reallocated towards Smirnoff vodka, Gordon's gin, Bailey's and other drinks that could be sold within weeks of distillation.

Once managers had to report profits after deduction of the cost of the capital tied up in their businesses, they took measures to reduce their capital bases and make their assets work harder. At Diageo's Pillsbury food business, the economic profit of every product and every major customer was scrutinized. The result was the elimination of many products and efforts make marginal customers more profitable. Ultimately, EVA analysis resulted in Diageo selling Pillsbury to General Foods. This was followed by the sale of Diageo's Burger King chain to Texas Pacific, a private equity group.

Value-based management was extended throughout the organization by making EVA the primary determinant of the incentive pay earned by 1400 Diageo managers.

Sources: John McGrath, "Tracking Down Value," *Financial Times Mastering Management Review*, December 1998; www.diageo.com.

Linking Profit to Enterprise Value

There is also the problem of time. Once we consider multiple periods of time, then profit maximization means maximizing the net present value of profits over the lifetime of the firm.

Hence, profit maximization translates into maximizing the value of the firm. The value of the firm is calculated in the same way as any other asset: it is the net present value (NPV) of the returns that the asset generates. The relevant returns are the cash flows to the firm. Hence, firms are valued using the same discounted cash flow (DCF) methodology that we apply to the valuation of investment projects. Thus, the value of an enterprise (V) is the sum of its free cash flows (C) in each year t, discounted at the enterprise's cost of capital (r).[8] The relevant cost of capital is the weighted average cost of capital (r_{e+d}) that averages the cost of equity (r_e) and the cost of debt (r_d):

$$V = \sum_t \frac{C_t}{(1 + r_{e+d})^t}$$

where *free cash flow* (C) is measured as:

net operating profit + depreciation—taxes—investment in fixed and working capital

To maximize its value, a firm must maximize its future net cash flows (its *free cash flow*) while also managing its finances to minimize its cost of capital.

This value-maximizing approach implies that *cash flow* rather than *accounting profit* is the relevant performance measure. In practice, valuing companies by discounting economic profit gives the same result as by discounting net cash flows. The difference is in the treatment of the capital consumed by the business. The cash flow approach deducts capital at the time when the capital expenditure is made; the

EVA approach follows the accounting convention of charging capital as it is consumed (through charging depreciation). In principle, a full DCF approach is the most satisfactory approach to valuing companies. In practice, however, for DCF analysis to be meaningful requires forecasting cash flows several years ahead, since cash flow for a single year is a poor indicator of underlying profitability. Companies that are profitable and growing fast are likely to have negative cash flows. The preference of many financial analysts for cash-based accounting is also based on the fact that cash flows are less easily manipulated by company managers for cosmetic purposes than are accounting profits. For the same reason, operating earnings, EBIT (earnings before interest and tax) and EBITDA (earnings before interest, tax, depreciation, and amortization) are often preferred to net income as an indicator of profit.

If financial forecasts can only be made for a few years out, then economic profit is usually preferable to free cash flow as a performance indicator. Economic profit shows the surplus being generated by the firm in each year, whereas free cash flow depends on management choices over the level of capital expenditure. Thus, a firm can easily boost its free cash flow by slashing capital expenditures.

Enterprise Value and Shareholder Value How does maximizing enterprise value relate to the much-lauded goal of *maximizing shareholder value*? In the 1950s, Modigliani and Miller laid the foundations of modern financial theory by showing that the value of a company's assets must equal the value of the claims against those assets.[9] Hence, for public companies, the DCF value of the firm is equal to the market value of the firm's securities (plus any other financial claims such as debt and pension fund deficits). Thus, shareholder value is calculated by subtracting the debt (and other non-equity financial claims) from the DCF value of the firm.

Does enterprise value less debt really equal the stock market value of a firm's equity? So long as full information about a firm's prospects reaches the stock market and this information is efficiently reflected in stock prices—yes. But isn't the stock market subject to bubbles, fads, and crashes? Yes—but this instability is a reflection of volatile expectations of companies' future cash flows. Our emphasis in this book will be on maximization of enterprise value rather than maximization of shareholder value. This is principally for convenience: distinguishing debt from equity is not always straightforward due to the presence of preference stock and convertible debt, while junk bonds share the characteristics of both equity and debt. Also, focusing on the value of the enterprise as a whole assists us in identifying the fundamental drivers of firm value. In practice, however, maximization of enterprise value and maximization of shareholder value mean much the same in terms of our strategy analysis.

Applying DCF Analysis to Valuing Companies, Businesses and Strategies

Applying DCF to Uncertain Future Cash Flows The biggest difficulty in using DCF analysis to value companies and business units is forecasting cash flows sufficiently far into the future. Given the level of uncertainty affecting most businesses, even one-year forecasts of profits and cash flows may be difficult. To estimate future cash flows we may need to make assumptions. For example in a stable growth business (the sole dairy in an expanding village) it may be reasonable to assume that the current year's cash flow (C_0) will grow at a constant rate (g) to infinity. In this case, the above equation becomes:

$$V = \frac{C_0}{(r_{e+d} - g)^t}$$

A slightly more sophisticated approach is to forecast free cash flow over the medium term—say five years—then to calculate a horizon value (H) based either on the book value of the firm at that time or on some more arbitrary forecast of cash flows beyond the medium term:

$$V = C_0 + \frac{C_1}{(1+r)^1} + \frac{C_2}{(1+r)^2} + \frac{C_3}{(1+r)^3} + \frac{C_4}{(1+r)^4} + \frac{H_4}{(1+r)^4}$$

Valuing Strategies The same approach used to value companies and business units can be applied to evaluate alternative strategies. Thus, different strategy options can be appraised by forecasting the cash flows under each strategy and then selecting the strategy that produces the highest NPV.[10] Since the early 1990s, companies have increasingly integrated value analysis into their strategic planning processes. At PepsiCo, for example, value maximization provides the basis on which strategic plans are formulated, divisional and business unit targets are set and performance is monitored. A key merit of value maximization is its consistency. The same DCF methodology is used to value individual projects, individual business units, alternative business strategies and the company as a whole.

Applying enterprise value analysis to appraising business strategies involves several steps:

- Identify strategy alternatives (the simplest approach is to compare the current strategy with the preferred alternative strategy).
- Estimate the cash flows associated with each strategy.
- Estimate the implications of each strategy for the cost of capital—according to the risk characteristics of different strategies and their financing implications, each strategy will have a different cost of capital.
- Select the strategy that generates the highest NPV.

Although simple in principle, applying DCF analysis to strategy selection runs into major practical difficulties. The central problem is forecasting cash flows. A strategy that is implemented today will influence a company's cash flows long into the future. Given the unpredictability of future business conditions, forecasting the costs and revenues resulting from a particular strategy is exceedingly difficult. The problem of forecasting is compounded by the fact that choosing a strategy does not predetermine cash flows. As we discussed in the first chapter, a strategy is not a detailed plan, it is a direction and a set of guidelines. As such, a strategy will be consistent with a range of specific outcomes in terms of product introductions, output levels, prices and investments in new plans. Once we recognize that strategy is about reconciling flexibility with direction in an uncertain environment, there are two key implications for strategy analysis: first, it may be better to view strategy as a portfolio of options rather than a portfolio of investment projects; second, qualitative approaches to strategy analysis may be more useful than quantitative ones. Let me address each of these themes.

Strategy and Real Options

The simple idea that an *option*—the choice of whether to do something or not—has value has important implications for how we value firms. In recent years, the principles of option pricing have been extended from valuing financial securities to valuing investment projects and companies. The resulting field of *real option analysis* has emerged as one of the most important developments in financial theory over the past decade, with far-reaching implications for strategy analysis. The technical details of valuing real options are complex. However, the underlying principles are intuitive. Let me outline the basic ideas of real options theory and what they mean for strategy analysis.

In November 2005, BP announced the doubling of capital expenditure at its newly formed BP Alternative Energy division. Yet, it was highly unlikely that returns to this investment would match those of BP's oil and gas businesses. How could investing in renewable energy—wind and solar power—be consistent with shareholder interests?

The answer lies in the *option value* of alternative energy investments. BP's $600 million in alternative energy represented only 0.4% of overall 2006 capital expenditure. By developing a position in solar, wind and hydrogen energy technologies, BP was buying the option to become a leading player in these energy sources should hydrocarbon use be restricted by Middle East conflict, reserve exhaustion, or environmental concerns.

In a world of uncertainty, where investments, once made, are irreversible, flexibility is valuable. Instead of committing to an entire project, there is virtue in breaking the project into a number of phases, where the decision of whether and how to embark on the next phase can be made in the light of prevailing circumstances and the learning gained from the previous stage of the project. Most large companies have a *phases and gates* approach to product development in which the development process is split into distinct phases, at the end of which the project is reassessed before being allowed through the "gate." Such a phased approach creates the options to continue the project, to abandon it, to amend it, or to wait. The growth options that a company faces are valued by the stock market and by investors. The emphasis that venture capitalists place on "scalability"—the potential to scale up or replicate a business should the initial launch be successful similarly acknowledges the value of growth options. Strategy Capsule 2.2 addresses the calculation of real option values.

Strategy as Options Management

For strategy formulation, our primary interest is how we can use the principles of option valuation to create shareholder value. There are two types of real option: *growth options* and *flexibility options*. Growth options allow a firm to make small initial investments in a number of future business opportunities but without committing to them. Flexibility options relate to the design of projects and plants that permit adaptation to different circumstances—*flexible manufacturing systems*

STRATEGY CAPSULE 2.2

Calculating Real Option Value

Application of real option valuation to investment projects and strategies has been limited by the complexity of the valuation techniques. Yet, even without getting into the mathematics needed to quantify option values, we can use the basic principles involved to understand the factors that determine option values and to recognize how projects and strategies can be designed in order to maximize their option values.

The early work on real option valuation adapted the *Black–Scholes option-pricing formula* developed for valuing financial options to the valuation of real investment projects.[11] Black–Scholes comprises six determinants of option value, each of which has an analogy in the valuation of a real option:

1 Stock price = The NPV of the project: a higher NPV increases option value
2 Exercise price = Investment cost: the higher the cost, the lower the option value
3 Uncertainty: for both financial and real options, uncertainty *increases* option value
4 Time to expiry: for both financial and real options, the longer the option lasts, the greater its value
5 Dividends = Decrease in the value of the investment over the option period: lowers option value
6 Interest rate: a higher interest rate increases option value by making deferral more valuable.[12]

However, the dominant methodology used for real option valuation is the *binomial options pricing model*. By allowing the sources of uncertainty and key decision points in a project to be a modeled explicitly, the technique offers a more intuitive appreciation of the sources of option value. The analysis involves two main stages:

1 Create an event tree that shows the value of the project at each development period under two different scenarios.
2 Convert the event tree into a decision tree by identifying the key decision points on the event tree—typically the points where commitments of new funds to the project are required, or where there is the option to defer development. Incremental project values at each stage can then be calculated for each decision point by working back from the final nodes of the decision tree (using a discount factor based upon the *replicating portfolio* technique). If the incremental project value at the initial stage exceeds the initial investment, proceed with the first phase—and similarly for each subsequent phase.[13]

allow different product models to be manufactured on a single production line. Individual projects can be designed to introduce both growth options and flexibility options. This means avoiding commitment to the complete project and introducing decision points at multiple stages, where the main options are to delay, modify, scale up, or abandon the project. Merck, an early adopter of option pricing, noted, “When you make an initial investment in a research project, you are paying an entry fee for a right, but you are not obligated to continue that research at a later stage."[14]

In developing strategy, our main concern is with growth options. These might include:

- "Platform investments." These are investments in core products or technologies that create a stream of additional business opportunities.[15] 3M's investment in nanotechnology offers the opportunity to create new products across a wide range of its businesses, from dental restoratives and drug-delivery systems to adhesives and protective coatings. Google's search engine has provided the platform for a wide variety of initiatives that range from other search products (Google Maps, Google Scholar) to advertising management products, to downloadable software.[16]
- Strategic alliances and joint ventures, which are limited investments that offer options for the creation of whole new strategies.[17] Virgin Group has used joint ventures as the basis for creating a number of new businesses: with Stagecoach to create Virgin Rail, with AMP to create Virgin Money (financial services), with Deutsche Telecom to form Virgin Mobile. Shell has used joint ventures and alliances as a means of making initial investments in wind power, biodiesel fuel, solar power, and other forms of renewable energy.
- Organizational capabilities, which can also be viewed as options offering the potential to create competitive advantage across multiple products and businesses.[18] Sharp's miniaturization capability has provided a gateway to success in calculators, LCD screens, solar cells and PDAs.

Putting Performance Analysis into Practice

Our discussion so far has established the following:

- For the purposes of strategy formulation, profit maximization is a convenient and reasonable assumption. Once we look beyond a single period, maximizing profit translates into maximizing enterprise value.
- Discounted cash flow (DCF) valuation of enterprises and strategies encounters two problems. First, it is difficult to estimate cash flows more than a few years into the future. Second, it does not take account of option value.

Given these challenges, what practical guidance can I offer about using financial analysis to appraise and develop business strategies? Let me deal with four questions. First, how can we best appraise overall firm (or business unit) performance? Second, how can we diagnose the sources of poor performance? Third, how can we select strategies on the basis of their profit prospects? Lastly, how do we set performance targets?

Appraising Current and Past Performance

The first task of any strategy formulation exercise is to assess the current situation. This requires that we identify the current strategy of the firm and assess how well that strategy is doing in terms of the financial performance of the firm. The next stage is diagnosis—identifying the sources of unsatisfactory performance. Thus, good strategic practice emulates good medical practice: the first task is to determine the state of health of the patient, and then to determine the reasons for any sickness.

Forward-Looking Performance Measures: Stock Market Value If our goal is maximizing profit over the lifetime of the firm, then to evaluate the performance of a firm we need to look at its stream of profit (or cash flows) over the rest of its life. The problem, of course, is that we don't know what these will be. However, for public companies we do have a good indicator: stock market valuation, which represents the best available estimate of expected cash flows into the future. Thus, to evaluate the effectiveness of a firm's CEO, we can look at the change in the market value of the firm relative to that of competitors over the CEO's period of tenure. Of course, using stock market valuation as a performance indicator has its problems, the information upon which the stock market values companies is imperfect and expectations about a firm's future earnings tend to be volatile.

Backward-Looking Performance Measures: Accounting Ratios Given the volatility of performance measures based on stock market values, evaluation of firm performance for the purposes of assessing the current strategy or evaluating management effectiveness tends to concentrate on accounting-based performance. All of these are inevitably historical—financial reports appear, at minimum, three weeks after the period to which they relate.

In the light of our discussion over accounting profit versus economic profit versus cash flow, which are the best indicators to use? McKinsey & Company argue that, for practical purposes, the DCF value of the firm may be viewed as a function of three variables: the return on the firm's invested capital (ROIC), its weighted average cost of capital, and the rate at which it grows its operating profit.[19] Hence, return on invested capital, or its close relatives return on capital employed (ROCE), return on assets (ROA) and return on equity (ROE) are useful indicators of the effectiveness of the firm in generating profits from its assets. However, to evaluate a firm's return on capital, we must first compare it with cost of capital, and second take account of growth. The value of a firm is highly sensitive to the rate at which profit grows. Hence efforts to boost a firm's return on capital by cutting capital expenditure and disposing of less profitable businesses may fail to increase the value of the firm.

Different profitability measures are related. Indeed, in practice, the longer the time period under consideration, the greater their convergence.[20] Over shorter periods, the key issues are, first, to be aware of the limitations and biases inherent in any particular profitability measure and, second, to use multiple measures of profitability so that their consistency can be judged. Table 2.2 outlines some commonly used performance indicators.

Interpreting probability ratios requires benchmarks. Longitudinal comparisons examine whether a profitability ratio is improving or deteriorating. Interfirm comparisons tell us how a firm is performing relative to a competitor, relative to its industry average, or relative to firms in general (for example, the average for the Fortune 500 or FT 500). Another key benchmark is cost of capital. ROIC and ROCE should be compared with WACC, and ROE compared with the cost of equity capital.

TABLE 2.2 Profitability ratios

Ratio	Formula	Comments
Return on Invested Capital (ROIC)	$\frac{\text{operating profit before interest after tax}}{\text{fixed assets + net current assets}}$	ROIC measures the return on the capital invested in the business. ROIC is also referred to as return on capital employed (ROCE). It is sometimes calculated pre-tax and sometimes post-tax. The numerator can be operating profit or earnings (EBIT). Invested capital (capital employed) can also be measured as equity *plus* debt.
Return on Equity (ROE)	$\frac{\text{net income}}{\text{shareholders' equity}}$	ROE measures the firm's success in using shareholders' capital to generate profits that are available for remunerating investors. Net income should ideally be measured net of dividends on preferred stock. Net income is often measured net of income from discontinued operations and before any special items.
Return on Assets (ROA)	$\frac{\text{operating profit}}{\text{total assets}}$	Different measures of the numerator are common. Ideally the numerator should be a broad-based measure of profit: operating profit, EBITDA (earnings before interest, tax, depreciation, and amortization), or EBIT (earnings before interest and tax).
Gross margin	$\frac{\text{sales} - \text{cost of bought-in goods and services}}{\text{sales}}$	Gross margin measures the extent to which a firm adds value to the goods and services it buys in.
Operating margin	$\frac{\text{operating profit}}{\text{sales}}$	Operating margin and net margin measure a firm's ability to extract profit from its sales, but for comparing firms' performance, these ratios reveal little because margins vary so much between different sectors (see Table 2.1).
Net margin	$\frac{\text{net income}}{\text{sales}}$	

Notes

Few accounting ratios have agreed definitions. Hence, it is always advisable to be explicit about how you have calculated the ratio you are using.

A general guideline for rate of return ratios is that the numerator should be the profits that are available to remunerate the owners of the assets in the denominator. Profits are measured over a period of time (typically over a year).

Assets are valued at a point of time. Hence, in rate-of-return calculations, assets and capital employed need to be averaged between the end of the period and the end of the previous period.

Performance Diagnosis

If profit performance is unsatisfactory, we need to identify the sources of poor performance so that management can take corrective action. Diagnosis primarily involves disaggregation of return on capital in order to identify the fundamental "value drivers." A useful approach is to apply the *Du Pont Formula* to disaggregate return on invested capital into sales margin and capital turnover. We can go further: as Figure 2.1 shows, sales margin and capital productivity can be further disaggregated into their constituent items. This analysis allows us to identify the sources of poor performance in terms of specific activities.

Strategy Capsule 2.3 investigates the performance of Ford's automotive operations compared with those of the industry's top performer, Toyota. By disaggregating overall return on assets we can begin to pinpoint the sources of Ford's dismal profitability. We can also disaggregate performance by business and geographical segments. If we then combine the financial data with qualitative data on Ford's business strategy, its operations, its product strategy, the organizational issues it has faced, and the conditions in the world market for motor vehicles, we can begin to formulate hypotheses as to why Ford has performed so poorly. This can then provide the basis for identifying corrective measures.

FIGURE 2.1 Disaggregating return on capital employed

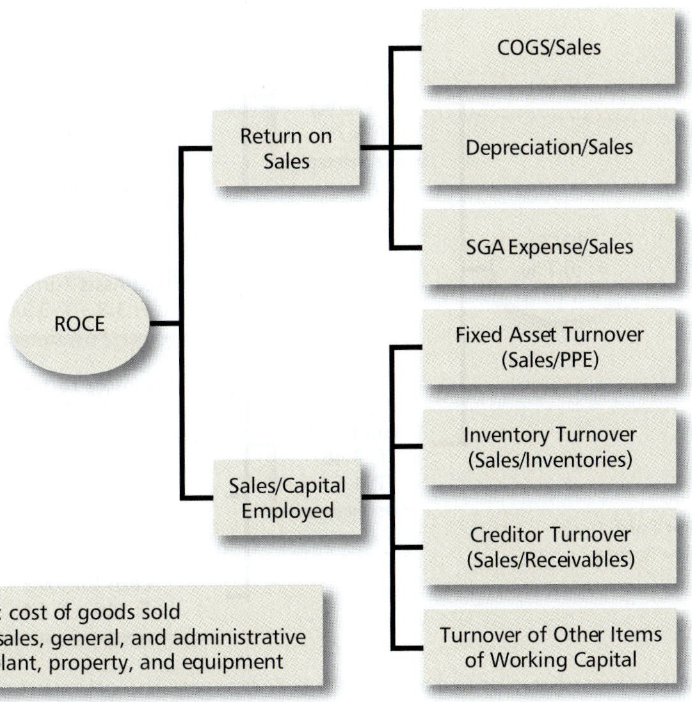

Note: For further discussion, see T. Koller, M. Goedhart, and D. Wessels, *Valuation*, 4th edn (New York: John Wiley & Sons, Inc., 2005): Chapter 7.

STRATEGY CAPSULE 2.3

Diagnosing Performance: What Ails Ford?

During the early years of the twenty-first century, Ford Motor Company continued the declining trend that had begun during the 1980s. During the five-year period 2003–7, return on equity averaged a negative 3.9% while operating losses in its automotive business totaled over $24 billion. Ford's share of the U.S. car and truck market declined from 21.8% to 16.8%. A new CEO, Alan Mulally, initiated vigorous cost cutting and asset sales, but without any significant upturn in profitability.

To understand the sources of Ford's poor financial performance, it is useful to compare Ford's automotive operations with those of the company that had displaced it as the world's second largest auto manufacturer (by volume)—Toyota. Combining data for 2006 and 2007, we can disaggregate Ford and Toyota's return on capital employed into sales margin and capital turnover, then disaggregate further into individual cost and asset productivity ratios:

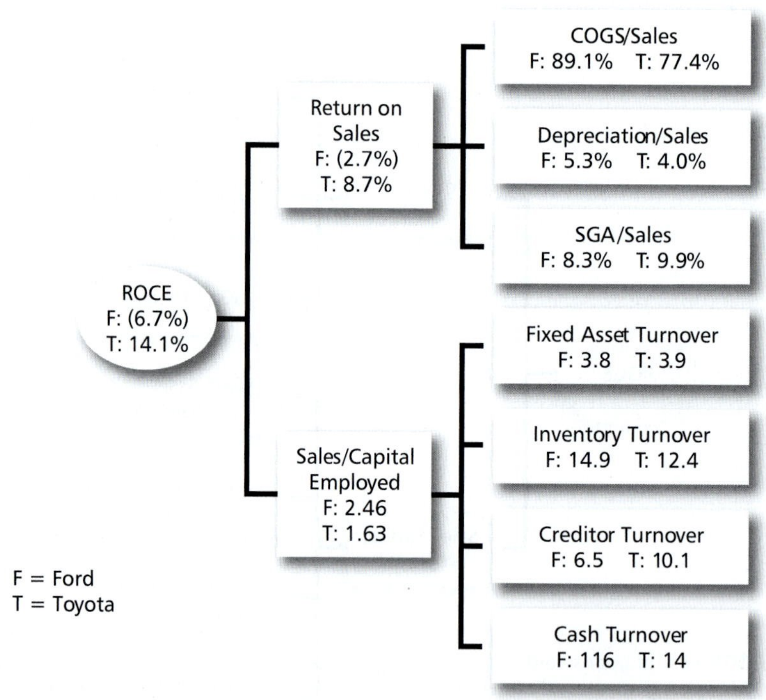

Note: These ratios relate to the automotive businesses only; financial services are excluded.

The analysis reveals the following:

- Ford's lower ROCE is wholly the result of a lower margin on sales than Toyota. This lower margin results from a substantially higher ratio of cost of goods sold to sales. This could be the result of higher costs (for example, of labor and parts), or lower unit prices for vehicles, or both. Additional analysis suggests that Ford's higher COGS/sales ratio is the result of lower productivity of labor—Ford produced 23.8 vehicles per employee compared with 31.9 for Toyota. Also, Toyota with just 17 manufacturing plants worldwide is likely to exploit scale economies more effectively than Ford with its 113 plants. Although Ford received more revenue per vehicle than Toyota ($22, 814 versus $21, 442), the difference seems to be accounted for by Toyota's greater emphasis on small cars. For comparable models, it appears that Toyota's prices are higher than Ford's—possibly the result of higher quality and better features.
- Ford's overall capital productivity is higher than Toyota's. Yet, when we review the disaggregated asset productivity ratios, it is difficult to find the source of this higher capital turnover. In turning fixed asset productivity, the two are the same. Ford's productivity advantages stem from two sources: first, higher inventory turnover; second, Ford's fewer current assets in the form of cash and receivables.

Can Past Performance Guide Strategies for the Future?

A probing diagnosis of a firm's recent performance—as outlined above—provides useful input into strategy formulation. If we can establish why a company has been performing badly then we have a basis for corrective actions. These corrective actions are likely to be both strategic (i.e. focused on the medium to long term) and operational (focused on the short term). The worse a company's performance, the more likely it is that management will concentrate on the short term. For companies teetering on the brink of bankruptcy, such as General Motors and American Airlines (AMR Corporation)—long-term strategy takes a back seat; survival is the dominant concern.

For companies that are performing well, financial analysis allows us to understand the sources of superior performance so that strategy can protect and enhance these determinants of success.

However, analyzing the past only takes us so far. The world of business is one of constant change and the role of strategy is to allow the firm to adapt to change. The challenge is to look into the future and identify factors that threaten performance or create new opportunities for profit. As we have already noted, financial analysis does not allow us to forecast cash flows or profits into the future. In making strategy recommendations to Toyota, our financial analysis can tell us some of the reasons why Toyota has been doing well up until now, but Toyota wants to know what its performance is likely to be in the future and what strategy will be most effective in maximizing that performance. Here, financial analysis is of little use. To look ahead into the future Toyota needs to understand the strategic factors that are the ultimate drivers of profitability. What will be happening in the industry in terms of competition and customer demand? Which companies will possess the resources and capabilities needed to establish a competitive advantage in tomorrow's markets? Applying the tools of strategy analysis will not enable us to forecast Toyota's profits and cash flows quantitatively but it will offer qualitative indications as to the implications of Toyota sticking to its present strategy and the likely consequences of adopting alternative strategies.

Setting Performance Targets

We noted in Chapter 1 that an important role for strategic planning systems is to drive corporate performance through setting performance goals then monitoring results against targets. To be effective, performance targets need to be consistent with long-term goals, linked to strategy, and relevant to the tasks and responsibilities of individual organizational members. The instruction to maximize long-run profits is meaningless outside the executive suite. Corporate targets need to be translated into specific goals that are meaningful for managers further down the organization. The key is to match performance targets to the variables over which different managers exert some control. Thus, for the CEO, it may make sense to set the overall goal of maximizing enterprise value. For the chief operating officer and divisional heads it makes sense to set more specific financial goals (such as maximizing ROCE on existing assets and investing in projects whose rate of return exceeds the cost of capital). More specific operating targets are preferable for functional, departmental and unit managers. Thus, in a retailing company, store managers might be given targets with regard to sales per square foot and gross margins. Warehouse managers might be required to achieve target levels of inventory turns. Purchasing managers might be required to reduce the cost of goods purchased as a percentage of sales revenue. The chief financial officer might be required to minimize average cost of capital and reduce cash balances.

The same procedure that we used to disaggregate return on capital for appraising past performance can be used to set performance targets appropriate to different levels and functions within the organization. Figure 2.2 uses the same breakout of the drivers of return on capital as Figure 2.1. The difference is that Figure 2.2 provides a basis for identifying the financial and operating ratios appropriate to managers at the different levels and in the different functions of the company.

Balanced Scorecards The problem with any system of performance management is that the performance goals are long term (for example, maximizing profits over the lifetime of the company) but to act as an effective control system performance targets need to be monitored over the short term. The problem with the above financially based approach of disaggregating profitability into its constituent ratios is that the short-term pursuit of financial targets is unlikely to result in long-term profit maximization. One solution to this dilemma is to link the overall corporate goal of value maximization to strategic and operational targets to ensure that the pursuit of financial goals is not at the expense of the longer term strategic position of the company. The most widely used method for doing this is the *balanced scorecard* developed by Robert Kaplan and David Norton.[21] The balanced scorecard methodology provides an integrated framework for balancing financial and strategic goals and cascading performance measures down the organization to individual

FIGURE 2.2 Linking value drivers to performance

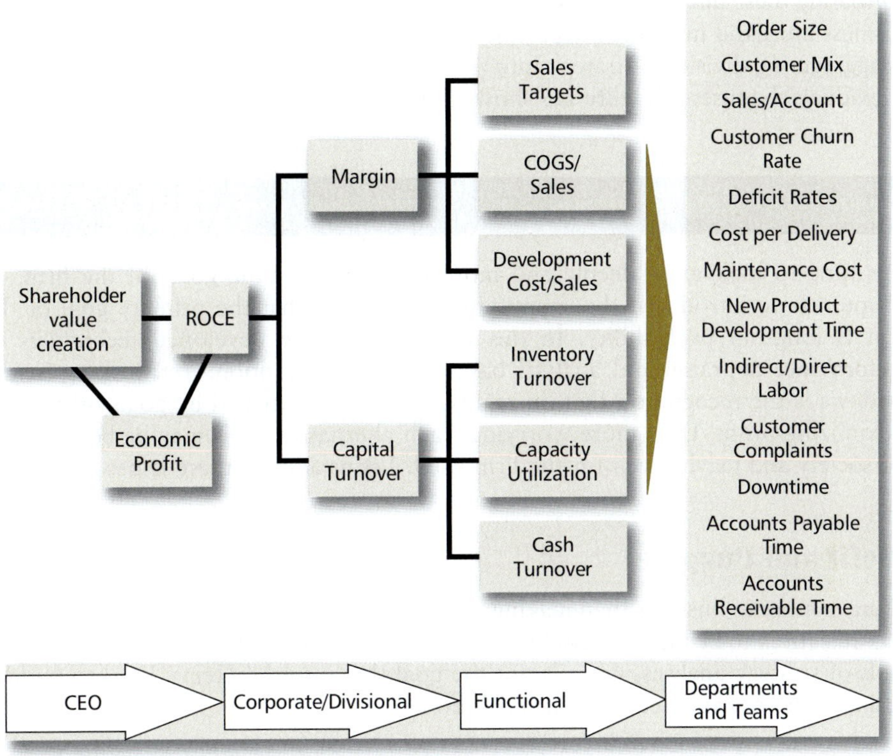

business units and departments. The performance measures combine the answers to four questions:

- *How do we look to shareholders?* The financial perspective is composed of measures such as cash flow, sales and income growth and return on equity.
- *How do customers see us?* The customer perspective comprises measures such as goals for new products, on-time delivery, and defect and failure levels.
- *What must we excel at?* The internal business perspective relates to internal business processes such as productivity, employee skills, cycle time, yield rates and quality and cost measures.
- *Can we continue to improve and create value?* The innovation and learning perspective includes measures related to new product development cycle times, technological leadership and rates of improvement.

By balancing a set of strategic and financial goals, the scorecard methodology allows the strategy of the business to be linked with the creation of shareholder value while providing a set of measurable targets to guide this process.

Mobil Corporation's North American Marketing and Refining business (NAM&R) was a pioneer of the balanced scorecard during the 1990s. Faced with pressures of unsatisfactory profit performance, the business adopted the scorecard methodology as a means of linking strategy with financial performance goals and translating these into operating objectives tailored to the circumstances of individual business units and functional departments. The scorecard provided a mechanism for disaggregating divisional strategy into specific operating goals which were linked to individuals' bonuses.[22] Figure 2.3 shows NAM&R's scorecard.

Beyond Profit: Values and Social Responsibility

It is time to look more deeply and more realistically at the goals of the firm. In Chapter 1 we introduced the simplifying assumption that the primary goal of the firm is long-run profitability. In this chapter we have developed techniques of performance appraisal and analysis based on this assumption. Yet, lurking in the shadows is the recognition that, in reality, firms are motivated by goals other than maximizing profit. Even more worrying, such alternative goals may be better, both for society and maybe even for the firm itself. Let us address these issues directly.

Profit and Purpose

There is more to business than making money. Profit maximization (enterprise value maximization, to be more precise) provides a convenient foundation for building our tools of strategy analysis, yet it is not the goal that inspired Henry Ford to build a business that precipitated a social revolution.

> I will build a motor car for the great multitude . . . It will be so low in price that no man making good wages will be unable to own one and to enjoy with his family the blessing of hours of pleasure in God's great open spaces . . . When I'm through, everyone will be able to afford one, and everyone will have one.[23]

Similar remarks can be made about entrepreneurs generally: they are driven less by the promise of riches as by the desire to create.

As we recognized in Chapter 1 (see *Strategy as Target*, pg 26), the world's most consistently successful companies in terms of profits and shareholder value tend to be those that are motivated by factors other than profit. A succession of studies point to the role of strategic intent, vision, and "big, hairy, ambitious goals" in driving sustained corporate success.[24] Indeed, the converse may also be true—the companies that are most focused on profitability and the creation of shareholder value are often remarkably unsuccessful at achieving those goals. The case of Boeing during the 1990s is instructive (see Strategy Capsule 2.4).

Why does the pursuit of profit so often fail to realize its goal? First, profit will only be an effective guide to management action if managers know what determines profit. Obsession with profitability can blinker managers' perception of the real drivers of superior performance. Conversely, a strategic goal "to build a motor car for the great multitude that everyone will be able to afford" (Ford), or to "build great planes" (Boeing), or to "become the company most known for changing the worldwide poor quality image associated with Japanese products" (Sony, 1950s)

FIGURE 2.3 Balanced scorecard for Mobil North American Marketing and Refining

		Strategic Objectives	Strategic Measures
Financially Strong	Financial	F1 Return on Capital Employed F2 Cash Flow F3 Profitability F4 Lowest Cost F5 Profitable Growth F6 Manage Risk	• ROCE • Cash Flow • Net Margin • Full cost per gallon delivered to customer • Volume growth rate vs. industry • Risk index
Delight the Consumer	Customer	C1 Continually delight the targeted consumer	• Share of segment in key markets • Mystery shopper rating
Win–Win Relationship	Customer	C2 Improve dealer/distributor profitability	• Dealer/distributor margin on gasoline • Dealer/distributor survey
Safe and Reliable	Internal	I1 Marketing 1. Innovative products and services 2. Dealer/distributor quality	• Non-gasoline revenue and margin per square foot • Dealer/distributor acceptance rate of new programs • Dealer/distributor quality ratings
	Internal	I2 Manufacturing 1. Lower manufacturing costs 2. Improve hardware and performance	• ROCE on refinery • Total expenses (per gallon) vs. competition • Profitability index • Yield index
Competitive Supplier	Internal	I3 Supply, Trading, Logistics 1. Reducing delivered cost 2. Trading organization 3. Inventory management	Delivered cost per gallon vs. competitors • Trading margin • Inventory level compared to plan and to output rate
Good Neighbor	Internal	I4 Improve health, safety, and environmental performance	• Number of incidents • Days away from work
On Spec On time	Internal	I5 Quality	• Quality index
Motivated and Prepared	Learning and growth	L1 Organization involvement L2 Core competencies and skills L3 Access to strategic information	• Employee survey • Strategic competitive availability • Strategic information availability

STRATEGY CAPSULE 2.4

The Pitfalls of Pursuing Shareholder Value: Boeing

Boeing was one of the most financially successful members of the Dow Jones Industrial Index between 1960 and 1990. Yet, financial management received little attention at Boeing over this period. CEO Bill Allen was interested in building great planes and leading the world market with them: "Boeing is always reaching out for tomorrow. This can only be accomplished by people who live, breathe, eat and sleep what they are doing." Allen bet the company on the 747, yet when asked by non-executive director Crawford Greenwalt for financial projections on the project, Allen was utterly vague. "My God," muttered Greenwalt, "these guys don't even know what the return on investment will be on this thing."

The change came in the mid-1990s when Boeing acquired McDonnell Douglas and a new management team of Harry Stonecipher and Phil Condit took over. Mr Condit proudly talked of taking the company into "a value-based environment where unit cost, return on investment, shareholder return are the measures by which you'll be judged."

The result was lack of investment in major new civil aviation projects and diversification into defense and satellites. Under Condit, Boeing relinquished market leadership in passenger aircraft to Airbus, while faltering as a defense contractor due partly to ethical lapses by key executives. When Condit resigned on December 1, 2003, Boeing's stock price was 20% lower than when he was appointed.

Source: Adapted from John Kay, "Forget how the Crow Flies," *Financial Times Magazine* (January 17, 2004): 17–27.

may lead a company to direct its efforts towards the sources of competitive advantage within its industry—ultimately leading to superior long-term profitability.

The second factor concerns motivation. Success is the result of coordinated effort. The goal of maximizing the return to stockholders is unlikely to inspire employees and other company stakeholders and it's unlikely to be especially effective in inducing cooperation and unity between them. Dennis Bakke, founder of the international power company AES, offers the following analogy:

> Profits are to business as breathing is to life. Breathing is essential to life, but is not the purpose for living. Similarly, profits are essential for the existence of the corporation, but they are not the reason for its existence.[25]

A sense of purpose is common to most new, entrepreneurial enterprises. Primary the impetus driving entrepreneurs to found new businesses is typically not the quest for riches—if that was the case, most would have pursued less uncertain avenues to wealth. According to Schumpeter, "The entrepreneur-innovator's motivation includes such aspects as the dream to found a private kingdom, the will to conquer and to succeed for the sake of success itself, and the joy of creating and getting things done."[26]

But what about established companies? What happened to the sense of purpose that was presumably present at their founding? Some companies have kept alive a keen sense of purpose—it is embedded in organizational culture and implicit in strategy and in the behavior of corporate leaders. However, sustaining a sense of purpose typically requires articulation in explicit statements of mission, vision, and purpose. For example:

- Google's mission is: ". . . to organize the world's information and make it universally accessible and useful."
- "The IKEA vision is to create a better everyday life for the many people. We make this possible by offering a wide range of well-designed, functional home furnishing products at prices so low that as many people as possible will be able to afford them."
- "SAP strives to define and establish undisputed leadership in the emerging market for business process platform offerings and accelerate business innovation powered by IT for companies and industries worldwide."
- Gaia House (a Buddhist retreat center in England) "exists for the liberation of all beings from greed, hatred and delusion."

Is organizational purpose instilled at birth, or can companies choose or adapt their *raison d'être* during the course of their lives? Certainly many of the companies that are most closely identified with clarity of purpose—HP, Johnson & Johnson, Walt Disney—have a sense of mission that is little changed from that articulated by their founders. Yet, Cynthia Montgomery argues that "forging a compelling organizational purpose" is the ongoing job of the CEO—indeed, it is the "crowning responsibility of the CEO."[27] The challenge is to link change with continuity. Some of the most successful corporate turnarounds have been engineered by corporate leaders—Gerstner at IBM, Eisner at Walt Disney—who have renewed and redirected organizational purpose while appealing to continuity of tradition and values.

Values and Principles

A sense of purpose—as articulated in statements of mission and vision—is often complemented by beliefs about how this purpose should be achieved. These company beliefs are likely to include a set of values that comprise commitments to different stakeholder groups and to ethical precepts. Company values may be articulated as a set of principles to guide the decisions and actions of organizational members. Strategy Capsule 2.5 summarizes Shell's values and business principles.

At one level, statements of values and principles may be regarded as instruments of companies' external image management. Yet, to the extent that companies are consistent and sincere in their adherence to values and principles, these ideals can be a critical component of organizational identity and an important influence on employees' commitment and propensity to collaborate. To the extent that values are shared among organizational members, they form a central component of organizational culture.

STRATEGY CAPSULE 2.5

Shell's Values and Principles

OUR VALUES

Shell employees share a set of core values—honesty, integrity and respect for people. We also firmly believe in the fundamental importance of trust, openness, teamwork and professionalism and pride in what we do.

PRINCIPLES

1 Economic. Long-term profitability is essential to achieving our business goals and to our continued growth . . .

2 Competition. Shell companies support free enterprise. We seek to compete fairly and ethically and within the framework of applicable competition laws . . .

3 Business integrity. Shell companies insist on honesty, integrity and fairness in all aspects of our business . . .

4 Political Activities . . . Shell companies act in a socially responsible manner within the laws of the countries in which we operate in pursuit of our legitimate commercial objectives . . .

5 Health, safety, security *and the environment.* Shell companies have a systematic approach to health, safety, security and environmental management in order to achieve continuous performance improvement.

6 Local communities. Shell companies aim to be good neighbors by continuously improving the ways in which we contribute directly or indirectly to the general wellbeing of the communities within which we work . . .

7 Communication and engagement. Shell companies recognize that regular dialogue and engagement with our stakeholders is essential. We are committed to reporting of our performance by providing full relevant information to legitimately interested parties . . .

8 Compliance. We comply with all applicable laws and regulations of the countries in which we operate.

Source: Extracted from Royal Dutch Shell plc *General Business Principles,* 2008(http://www.shell.com/home/content/aboutshell/who_we_are/our_values/sgbp/sgbp_30032008.html, accessed July 2, 2009).

The evidence that commitment to values and principles influences organizational performance is overwhelming. Peters and Waterman identified "shared values" as a key determinant of "excellence".[28] Jim Collins and Jerry Porras argue that "core values" and "core purpose"—the organization's most fundamental reason for being—unite to form an organization's "core ideology" which "defines an organization's timeless character" and is "the glue that holds the organization together."[29] When core ideology is put together with an "envisioned future" for the enterprise, the result is a powerful sense of strategic direction that provides the foundation for long-term success.

The Debate over Corporate Social Responsibility

Values and principles can enhance a sense of identity and motivate employees—but this still leaves the question of *what* values and principles should companies adopt? This issue is central to the recent debate over *corporate social responsibility* (CSR).What are a company's obligations to society as a whole? In a sharp rebuttal to calls for business to address the broader problems of society, free-market economist Milton Friedman declared CSR to be both unethical and undesirable. Unethical because it involved management spending owners' money on projects that owners had not approved; undesirable because it involved corporate executives determining the interests of society. Once business enterprises accept responsibility for society, does this justify support for political activities, for religious movements, for elitist universities? According to Friedman:

> There is one and only one social responsibility of business—to use its resources and engage in activities designed to increase its profits so long as it stays within the rules of the game, which is to say, engage in open and free competition without deception or fraud.[30]

Despite these arguments, companies are increasingly accepting responsibilities that extend well beyond the immediate interests of their owners. The case for CSR is based both on ethics and efficacy. Ethical arguments about management responsibility depend, ultimately, upon what we conceive the firm to be. William Allen contrasts two different notions of the public corporation: "the property conception", which views the firm as a set of assets owned by stockholders, and the "social entity conception", which views the firm as the community of individuals that is sustained and supported its relationships with its social, political, economic and natural environment. [31] The "firm as property" view implies that management's responsibility is to operate in the interests of shareholders. The "firm as social entity" implies a responsibility to maintaining the firm within its overall network of relationships and dependencies. Charles Handy dismisses the "firm as property" view as a hangover from the nineteenth century—in the twenty-first century shareholders invest in companies but are not "owners" in any meaningful sense. To regard profit as the purpose for which companies exist, he argues, is a tragic confusion.[32]

The efficacy argument for CSR also views the firm as embedded within the ecosystem of its social and natural environments implying congruence between the interests of the firm and those of the supporting ecosystem. Thus, according to former Shell executive, Arie De Geus, long-living companies are those that build strong communities, have a strong sense of identity, commit to learning and are sensitive to the world around them. In short, they recognize they are living organisms whose lifespans depend upon effective adaptation to a changing environment.[33] A narrower view of this dependency is the sociological concept of *legitimacy*: organizations that gain social legitimacy attract resources and customers.

Michael Porter and Mark Kramer outline a more focused and pragmatic approach to CSR.[34] Putting aside ethical arguments (what they call "the moral imperative"), they identify three reasons why CSR might also be in the interests of a company: the *sustainability argument*—CSR is in firms' interests due to a mutual interest in sustaining the ecosystem; the *reputation argument*—CSR enhances a firm's reputation with consumers and other third parties; and *license-to-operate* argument—to conduct their businesses firms the support of the constituencies upon which they depend. However, these fail to offer clear guidance as to what CSR initiatives firms should pursue. The critical task, according to Porter and Kramer, is to identify *specific intersections between the interests of the firm and those of society*: i.e. projects and activities that create competitive advantage for the firm while generating positive social outcomes—what they term *strategic CSR*. For example:

- Toyota's early efforts to address the problems of pollution and global warming resulted in its coming early to market with its Prius hybrid car—one of the most successful automobile launches of the past decade.
- To develop a dairy in the Moga, India, Nestlé established a refrigerated milk collection network and offered veterinary and nutrition services to farmers. The resulting fall in the mortality of newborn calves and rise in milk yield permitted a virtuous cycle of development of the local dairy industry that benefitted both farmers and Nestlé.

C. K. Prahalad also sees the potential for win-win relationships in the relationship between business and the world's poor: the four billion people at the "the bottom of the pyramid" living off less than $2 a day.[35] If multinationals can stop viewing the poor as victims or as a burden and recognize them as value-conscious consumers, resilient workers, and creative entrepreneurs then a whole world of opportunity opens up. At the bottom of the pyramid there are attractive growth markets. The shanty towns of Rio de Janeiro, Johannesburg and Mumbai house millions of people, vibrant economies and substantial collective purchasing power. Lack of disposable income does not necessarily mean lack of profit. Grameen Telecom's payphones sited in Bangladeshi villages generate strong profit margins. Moreover, engaging with the world's poor creates pathways to growth—and early mover advantage in the markets of the future. Finally, through meeting the challenges of serving this market, and forging relationships with local government, aid agencies and local businesses, multinational firms can generate innovations that they can apply more widely. The wind-up, batteryless radio was developed by British inventor Trevor Bayliss to allow Third World communities access to radio broadcasts—yet, wind-up radios and other mechanically powered electrical products have sold massively to sophisticated First World consumers. The use of mobile phones to make person-to-person financial transactions in the Third World has stimulated innovative thinking among telecom multinationals about the financial services potential of wireless telecommunications.

Summary

Chapter 1 introduced a framework for strategy analysis that provides the structure for Part II of this book. This chapter has explored the first component of that framework—the goals, values, and performance of the firm. My key assumption is that the firm operates in the interests of its owners through maximizing their returns (profits), which implies maximizing the value of the firm. Focusing upon profit and value maximization allows us to use the tools of financial analysis both in diagnosing the sources of superior or inferior performance and for setting performance targets.

At the same time, we must recognize that profit, while essential, is not the *raison d'être* for most business enterprises. Strategy is also about creating purpose and committing revenues and principles. The pursuit of wider social and environmental goals does not necessarily conflict with the interests of owners.

Financial analysis is primarily useful for analyzing past performance. Strategy's main concern is creating value in the future. This requires identifying and exploiting the fundamental drivers of firm value. That is the challenge we address in the next three chapters of the book. We begin with the industry environment of the firm.

Self-Study Questions

1 Table 2.1 compares companies according to different profitability measures.

(a) Which two of the six performance measures do you think are the most useful indicators of how well a company is being managed?
(b) Is return on sales or return on equity a better basis on which to compare the performance of the companies listed?
(c) Several companies are highly profitable yet have delivered very low returns to their shareholders. How is this possible?

2 Nike, supplier of sports footwear and apparel, is interested in the idea that it could increase its stock market value by creating options for itself. Advise Nike on some of the actions it might take in order to generate option value.

3 India's Tata Group is a diversified group. Some of its largest companies are: Tata Steel, Tata Motors, Tata Consultancy Services (IT), Tata Power (electricity generation), Tata Chemicals, Tata Tea, Indian Hotels, and Tata Communications. How do you think Tata Group's recent adoption of EVA as a performance management tool is likely to influence the way in which it allocates investment among the companies listed above?

4 With regard to Strategy Capsule 2.3, what additional data would you seek and what additional cost and productivity ratios would you calculate to shed further light on the reasons for Ford's inferior ROCE relative to Toyota?

5 The CEO of a chain of pizza restaurants is interested in initiating a program of corporate social responsibility to be funded by a 5% levy on the company's operating profit. The board of directors, fearing a negative shareholder reaction, is opposed to the plan. What arguments might the CEO use to persuade the board that CSR might be in the interests of shareholders, and what types of CSR initiatives might the program include to ensure that this is the case?

Notes

1 In this chapter, I use the term "value" in two distinct senses. Here I am referring to *economic value*, which is worth as measured in monetary units. We shall also be discussing *values* as moral principles or standards of behavior.

2 T. Donaldson and L. E. Preston, "The stakeholder theory of the corporation," *Academy of Management Review* 20 (1995): 65–91.

3 Stern Stewart & Co., "Russell 3000 Annual Ranking Data, 2003", (2004).

4 Weber Shandwick, "Global CEO Turnover Rises 10 Percent in Past 12 Months According To New Study," (March 3, 2008), www.webershandwick.com; M. Wiersema, "Holes at the Top: Why CEO Firings Backfire," *Harvard Business Review* (December 2002): 66–78; S. N. Kaplan and B. Minton, "How CEO Turnover Changed," NBER Working Paper No. 12465 (August, 2006).

5 S. L. Hart and M. B. Milstein, "Global Sustainability and the Creative Destruction of Industries," *Sloan Management Review* 41 (Fall, 1999): 23–33; M. Orlitzky, F. L. Schmidt and S. L. Rynes, "Corporate Social and Financial Performance: A Meta-Analysis," *Organization Studies* 24 (Summer, 2003): 403–41.

6 J. Figuero, S. Greco and M. Ehrgott, *Multiple Criteria Decision Analysis: State of the Art Surveys* (Berlin: Springer, 2005).

7 See www.sternstewart.com. See also: J. L. Grant, *Foundations of Economic Value Added,* 2nd edn (New York: Wiley, 2003).

8 The cost of equity capital is calculated using the capital asset pricing model: firm X's cost of equity = the risk-free rate of interest + a risk premium. The risk premium is the excess of the stock market rate of return over the risk-free rate multiplied by Firm X's beta coefficient (its measure of *systematic risk*). See T. Koller, M. Goedhart and D. Wessels, *Valuation: Measuring and Managing the Value of Companies*, 4th edn (New York: Wiley, 2005): Chapter 10.

9 F. Modigliani and M. H. Miller, "The Cost of Capital, Corporation Finance, and the Theory of Investments," *American Economic Review* 48 (1958): 261–97.

10 This "shareholder value" approach to strategy appraisal is outlined by A. Rappaport in *Creating Shareholder Value: The New Standard for Business Performance* (New York: Free Press, 1986); and "CFOs and Strategists: Forging a Common Framework," *Harvard Business Review* (May–June 1992): 84–91.

11 F. Black and M. Scholes, "The Pricing of Options and Corporate Liabilities," *Journal of Political Economy* 81 (1993): 637–54.

12 K. J. Leslie and M. P. Michaels, "The Real Power of Real Options", *McKinsey Quarterly Anthology: On Strategy* (Boston: McKinsey & Company, 2000). Also: A. Dixit and R. Pindyck, "The Options Approach to Capital Investment," *Harvard Business Review* (May–June 1995): 105–15.

13 This approach is developed in T. Copeland and P. Tufano, "A Real-world Way to Manage Real Options" *Harvard Business Review,* March, 2004. See also: T. Copeland, *Developing Strategy Using Real Options,* Monitor Company (October 2003).

14 N. Nichols, "Scientific Management at Merck: An Interview with CFO Judy Lewent," *Harvard Business Review* (January–February, 1994): 89–105.

15 B. Kogut and N. Kulatilaka, "Options Thinking and Platform Investments: Investing in Opportunity," *California Management Review* (Winter, 1994): 52–69.

16 A. Gower and M. A. Cusamano, "How Companies Become Platform Leaders," *Sloan School of Management Review* (Winter, 2008): 28–35.

17 T. Chi, "Option to Acquire or Divest a Joint Venture," *Strategic Management Journal* 21 (2000): 665–87.

18 B. Kogut and N. Kulatilaka, "Capabilities as Real Options," *Organization Science* 12 (2001): 744–58; R. G. McGrath, W. Furrier and A. Mendel, "Real Options as Engines of Choice and Heterogeneity," *Academy of Management Review* 29 (2004): 86–101.

19 Koller, Goedhart, and Wessels, *Valuation* op. cit.: Chapter 13.

20 J. A. Kay and C. Meyer, "On the Application of Accounting Rates of Return," *Economic Journal* 96 (1986): 199–207; J. A. Kay, *Foundations of Corporate Success: How Business Strategies Create Value* (Oxford: Oxford University Press, 1993): 207.

21 R. S. Kaplan and D. P. Norton. "The Balanced Scorecard: Measures that Drive Performance," *Harvard Business Review* (January–February, 1992) 71–79; R. S Kaplan and D. P. Norton: "Using the Balanced Scorecard as a Strategic Management System," *Harvard Business Review* (January-February, 1996): 75–85.

22 R. S. Kaplan and D. P. Norton, *The Strategy-focused Organization* (Boston: Harvard Business School Press, 2001): Chapter 2, "How Mobil Became a Strategy-focused Organization."

23 See www.abelard.org/ford.

24 J. Collins and J. Porras, "Building Your Company's Vision," *Harvard Business Review* (September–October, 1996): 65–77.

25 Author's interview.

26 Joseph Schumpeter, *The Theory of Economic Development* (Cambridge MA, Harvard University Press, 1934).

27 C. A. Montgomery, "Putting Leadership Back into Strategy" *Harvard Business Review* (January, 2008): 54–60.

28 T. Peters and R. Waterman *In Search of Excellence* (New York: HarperCollins, 1982).

29 Collins and Porras, "Building Your Company's Vision," op. cit.

30 M. Friedman, *Capitalism and Freedom* (Chicago: University of Chicago Press, 1963). See also: M. Friedman, "The Social Responsibility of Business is to Increase its Profits," *New York Times Magazine* (September 13, 1970).
31 W. T. Allen, "Our Schizophrenic Conception of the Business Corporation," *Cardozo Law Review* 14 (1992): 261–81.
32 C. Handy, "What's a Business For?" *Harvard Business Review* (December, 2002): 133–43.
33 A. De Geus, "The Living Company," *Harvard Business Review* (March–April, 1997): 51–9.
34 M. E. Porter and M. R. Kramer, "Strategy and Society: The Link Between Competitive Advantage and Corporate Social Responsibility," *Harvard Business Review* (December, 2006): 78–92.
35 C. K. Prahalad and A. Hammond, "Serving the World's Poor, Profitably," *Harvard Business Review* (September, 2002); C. K. Prahalad, *Fortune at the Bottom of the Pyramid, Eradicating Poverty Through Profits* (Philadelphia: Wharton Publishing, 2004).

3 Industry Analysis: The Fundamentals

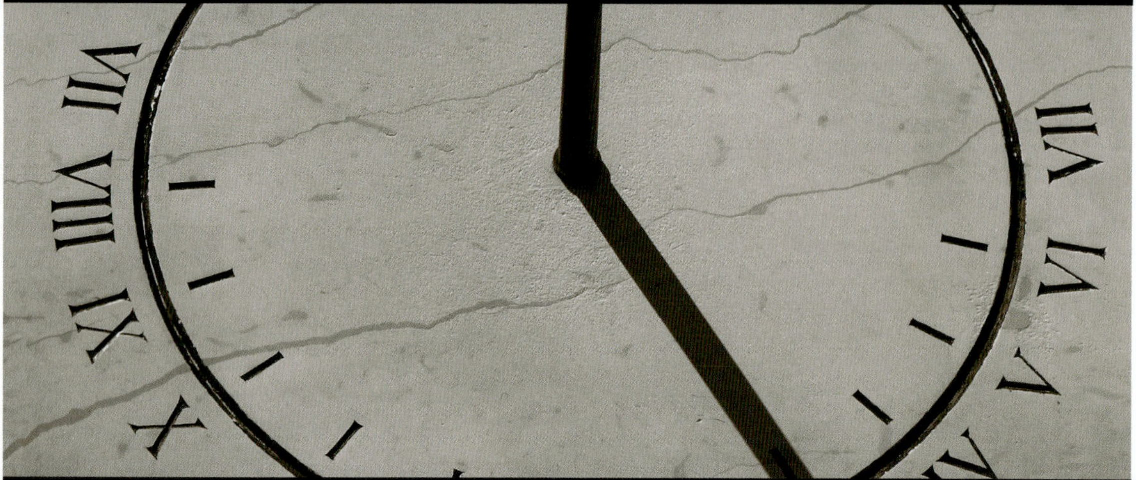

When a management with a reputation for brilliance tackles a business with a reputation for poor fundamental economics, it is the reputation of the business that remains intact.

—WARREN BUFFETT, CHAIRMAN, BERKSHIRE HATHAWAY

The reinsurance business has the defect of being too attractive-looking to new entrants for its own good and will therefore always tend to be the opposite of, say, the old business of gathering and rendering dead horses that always tended to contain few and prosperous participants.

—CHARLES T. MUNGER, CHAIRMAN, WESCO FINANCIAL CORP.

OUTLINE

Introduction and Objectives

In this chapter and the next we explore the external environment of the firm. In Chapter 1 we observed that profound understanding of the competitive environment is a critical ingredient of a successful strategy. We further noted that business strategy is essentially a quest for profit. The primary task for this chapter is to identify the sources of profit in the external environment. The firm's proximate environment is its industry environment; hence the focus of our environmental analysis will be industry analysis.

Industry analysis is relevant both to corporate-level and business-level strategy.

- Corporate strategy is concerned with deciding which industries the firm should be engaged in and how it should allocate its resources among them. Such decisions require assessment of the attractiveness of different industries in terms of their profit potential. The main objective of this chapter is to understand how the competitive structure of an industry determines its profitability.
- Business strategy is concerned with establishing competitive advantage. By analyzing customer needs and preferences and the ways in which firms compete to serve customers, we identify the general sources of competitive advantage in an industry—what we call *key success factors*.

By the time you have completed this chapter you will be able to:

- identify the main structural features of an industry that influence competition and profitability;
- use industry analysis to explain why in some industries competition is more intense and profitability lower than in other industries;
- use evidence on structural trends within industries to forecast changes in competition and profitability in the future;

- develop strategies that (a) position the firm most favorably in relation to competition and (b) influence industry structure in order to enhance industry attractiveness;
- analyze competition and customer requirements in order to identify opportunities for competitive advantage within an industry (*key success factors*).

From Environmental Analysis to Industry Analysis

The business environment of the firm consists of all the external influences that affect its decisions and performance. Given the vast number and range of external influences, how can managers hope to monitor, let alone analyze, environmental conditions? The starting point is some kind of system or framework for organizing information. For example, environmental influences can be classified by *source*—for example, into political, economic, social, and technological factors ("PEST analysis")—or by *proximity*—the "micro-environment" or "task environment" can be distinguished from the wider influences that form the "macro-environment".[1] Systematic, continuous scanning of the whole range of external influences might seem desirable but such extensive environmental analysis incurs high costs and creates information overload.

The prerequisite for effective environmental analysis is to distinguish the vital from the merely important. To do this let us return to first principles. For the firm to make profit it must create value for customers. Hence, it must understand its customers. Second, in creating value, the firm acquires goods and services from suppliers. Hence, it must understand its suppliers and manage relationships with them. Third, the ability to generate profitability depends on the intensity of competition among firms that vie for the same value-creating opportunities. Hence, the firm must understand competition. Thus, the core of the firm's business environment is formed by its relationships with three sets of players: customers, suppliers and competitors. This is its industry environment.

This is not to say that macro-level factors such as general economic trends, changes in demographic structure, or social and political trends are unimportant to strategy analysis. These factors may be critical determinants of the threats and opportunities a company will face in the future. The key issue is how these more general environmental factors affect the firm's industry environment (Figure 3.1). Consider the threat of global warming. For most companies this is not an important strategic issue (at least, not for the next hundred years). However, for the producers of automobiles, global warming is a vital issue. But, to analyze the strategic implications of global warming, the automobile manufacturers need to trace its implications for their industry environment. For example, what will be the impact on consumers and their preferences? Will there be a switch from private to public

FIGURE 3.1 From environmental analysis to industry analysis

transportation? With regard to competition, will there be new entry by manufacturers of electric vehicles into the car industry? Will increased R&D costs cause the industry to consolidate?

The Determinants of Industry Profit: Demand and Competition

The starting point for industry analysis is a simple question: what determines the level of profit in an industry?

The prerequisite for profit is the creation of value for the customer. Value is created when the price the customer is willing to pay for a product exceeds the costs incurred by the firm. But value creation does not translate directly into profit. The surplus of value over cost is distributed between customers and producers by the forces of competition. The stronger competition is among producers, the more of the surplus is received by customers in *consumer surplus* (the difference between the price they actually pay and the maximum price they would have been willing to pay) and the less is the surplus received by producers (as *producer surplus* or *economic rent*). A single supplier of bottled water at an all-night rave can charge a price that fully exploits the dancers' thirst. If there are many suppliers of bottled water, then, in the absence of collusion, competition causes the price of bottled water to fall toward the cost of supplying it.

The surplus earned by producers over and above the minimum costs of production is not entirely captured in profits. Where an industry has powerful suppliers—monopolistic suppliers of components or employees united by a strong labor union—a substantial part of the surplus may be appropriated by these suppliers (the profits of suppliers or premium wages of union members).

The profits earned by the firms in an industry are thus determined by three factors:

- the value of the product to customers
- the intensity of competition
- the bargaining power of producers relative to their suppliers and buyers.

Industry analysis brings all three factors into a single analytic framework.

Analyzing Industry Attractiveness

Table 3.1 shows the profitability of different U.S. industries. Some industries (such as tobacco and pharmaceuticals) consistently earn high rates of profit; others (airlines, paper, and food production) fail to cover their cost of capital. The basic premise that underlies industry analysis is that the level of industry profitability is neither random nor the result of entirely industry-specific influences—it is determined by the systematic influences of the industry's structure. The pharmaceutical industry and the personal computer industry not only supply very different products; they also have very different structures, which make one highly profitable and the other a nightmare of price competition and weak margins. The pharmaceutical industry produces highly differentiated products bought by price-insensitive consumers and new products receive monopoly privileges in the form of patents. The personal computer industry comprises many firms, produces commoditized products, and is squeezed by powerful suppliers (for example, Intel and Microsoft).

Small markets can often support much higher profitability that large markets for the simple reason that small markets can more easily be dominated by a single firm.

TABLE 3.1 The profitability of U.S. industries, 1999–2007

Industry	Median ROE 1999–2007 (%)	Leading companies
Household and personal products	26.0	Procter & Gamble, Kimberley-Clark, Colgate-Palmolive
Pharmaceuticals	21.0	Pfizer, Johnson & Johnson, Merck
Petroleum	20.1	ExxonMobil, Chevron, ConocoPhillips
Tobacco	19.7	Altria, Reynolds American, Universal
Food consumer products	19.5	PepsiCo, Sara Lee, Conagra
Securities and investment banking	18.4	Morgan Stanley, Merrill Lynch, Goldman Sachs
Mining, crude oil production	18.0	Occidental Petroleum, Devon Energy
Medical products and equipment	17.7	Medtronic, Baxter International
Beverages	17.2	Coca-Cola, Anheuser-Busch
Food services	16.6	McDonald's, Yum Brands
Scientific, photographic, and control equipment	15.6	Eastman Kodak, Danaher, Aligent
Diversified financials	15.5	General Electric, American Express
Commercial banks	14.8	Citigroup, Bank of America
Apparel	14.4	Nike, VF, Jones Apparel
Electronics, electrical equipment	14.3	Emerson Electric, Whirlpool
Oil and gas equipment and services	14.3	Halliburton, Baker Hughes
Computer software	14.0	Microsoft, Oracle, CA
Aerospace and defense	13.9	Boeing, United Technologies, Lockheed Martin
Specialty retailers	13.8	Home Depot, Costco, Lowe's
Chemicals	13.8	Dow Chemical, DuPont
Computers, office equipment	13.5	IBM, Hewlett-Packard, Dell Computer

TABLE 3.1 *(Continued)*

Industry	Median ROE 1999–2007 (%)	Leading companies
Healthcare	13.1	United Health Group, Wellpoint, HCA, Medco
Industrial and farm equipment	13.1	Caterpillar, Deere, Illinois Tool Works
Hotels, casinos, resorts	12.7	Marriott International, Harrah's Entertainment
Publishing, printing	12.5	R. R. Donnelley & Sons, Gannett
Engineering, construction	12.4	Flour, Jacobs Engineering
I.T. services	12.4	EDS, Computer Sciences, Science Applications Intl.
General merchandisers	12.3	Wal-Mart, Target, Sears Holdings
Trucking, truck leasing	12.2	YRC Worldwide, Ryder System
Metals	11.8	Alcoa, U.S. Steel, Nucor
Wholesalers: food and grocery	11.3	Sysco, Supervalu, CHS
Energy production	11.2	Constellation Energy, ONEOK
Pipelines	11.2	Plains All-American Pipeline, Enterprise Products
Packaging and containers	10.9	Smurfit-Stone Container, Owens-Illinois
Automotive retailing and services	10.7	AutoNation, United Auto Group
Utilities: gas and electric	10.6	DU.K.e Energy, Dominion Resources
Food and drug stores	10.6	Kroger, Walgreen, Albertson's
Furniture	10.4	Leggett & Platt, Steelcase
Real estate	9.9	Cendant, Host Marriott, Simon Property Group
Building materials, glass	9.9	Owens Corning, USG, Armstrong Holdings
Insurance: property and casualty	9.5	American Intl. Group, Berkshire Hathaway
Motor vehicles and parts	9.3	GM, Ford, Johnson Controls
Insurance: life and health	9.1	MetLife, New York Life
Forest and paper products	7.3	International Paper, Weyerhaeuser
Food production	6.5	Archer Daniels Midland, Tyson Foods
Semiconductors and electronic components	6.2	Intel, Texas Instruments, Sanmina-SCI
Network and communications equipment	5.9	Motorola, Cisco Systems, Lucent
Telecommunications	5.8	Verizon, AT&T, Sprint-Nextel
Entertainment	2.7	Time Warner, Walt Disney, News Corp.
Airlines	(12.6)	AMR, UAL, Delta Airlines

Note:

Median ROE for each industry averaged across the seven years 1999–2007. Industries with five or fewer firms were excluded. Also omitted were industries that were substantially redefined during 1999–2007.

Source:

Data from Fortune 1000 by industry.

Strategy Capsule 3.1 offers examples of niche markets that are havens from the rigors of fierce competition.

The underlying theory of how industry structure drives competitive behavior and determines industry profitability is provided by industrial organization (IO) economics. The two reference points are the *theory of monopoly* and the *theory of*

STRATEGY CAPSULE 3.1

Chewing Tobacco, Sausage Skins, and Slot Machines: The Joys of Niche Markets

UST Inc. was the most profitable company in the S&P500 over the period 2003–8 (in 2008 it was acquired by Altria, the owner of Philip Morris) with an average annual ROIC (operating profit as percentage of total assets less current liabilities) of 63%. What's the secret of UST's profitability? It controls 78% of the U.S. market for "smokeless tobacco" (chewing tobacco and snuff), with brands such as Skoal, Copenhagen and Red Seal. Despite its association with a bygone era of cowboys and farm workers, chewing tobacco has been a growth market in the U.S. UST's long-established brands, its distribution through tens of thousands of small retail outlets, and restrictions on advertising tobacco products have created formidable barriers to entry into this market.

Devro plc, based in the Scottish village of Moodiesburn, is the world's leading supplier of collagen sausage skins ("casings"). "From the British 'Banger' to the Chinese Lap Cheong, from the French Merguez to the South American Chourizo, Devro has a casing to suit all product types." Its overall world market share is around 60%, with about 80% of the U.K. and Australian markets. In recent years its ROIC has averaged 18% and its return on equity was 20%.

International Game Technology (IGT) based in Reno, Nevada, is the world's dominant manufacturer of slot machines for casinos. ITG maintains its 70% U.S. market share through close relations with casino operators and a continuous flow of new products. With heavy investment in R&D, new product saturation, tight control over distribution and servicing, and a policy of leasing rather than selling machines, IGT offers little opportunity to rivals. During 2004–7, IGT earned an average ROE of 31%.

Sources: www.ustinc.com, www.devro.com, www.igt.com.

perfect competition, which form end points of the spectrum of industry structures. *Monopoly* exists where an industry comprises a single firm protected by high barriers to entry. The monopolist can appropriate in profit the full amount of the value it creates. At the other extreme, *perfect competition* exists where there are many firms supplying an identical product with no restrictions on entry or exit. Here, the rate of profit falls to a level that just covers firms' cost of capital. In the real world, industries fall between these two extremes. The U.S. market for chewing tobacco is close to being a monopoly; the Chicago grain markets are close to being perfectly competitive. Most manufacturing industries and many service industries tend to be *oligopolies*: they are dominated by a small number of major companies. Table 3.2 identifies some key points on the spectrum. By examining the principal structural features and their interactions for any particular industry, it is possible to predict the type of competitive behavior likely to emerge and the resulting level of profitability.

TABLE 3.2 The spectrum of industry structures

	Perfect Competition	*Oligopoly*	*Duopoly*	*Monopoly*
Concentration	Many firms	A few firms	Two firms	One firm
Entry and exit barriers	No barriers	Significant barriers		High barriers
Product differentiation	Homogeneous product (Commodity)	Potential for product differentiation		
Information availability	No impediments to information flow	Imperfect availability of information		

Porter's Five Forces of Competition Framework

Table 3.2 identifies four structural variables influencing competition and profitability. In practice there are many features of an industry that determine the intensity of competition and the level of profitability. A helpful, widely used framework for classifying and analyzing these factors was developed by Michael Porter of Harvard Business School.[2] Porter's five forces of competition framework views the profitability of an industry (as indicated by its rate of return on capital relative to its cost of capital) as determined by five sources of competitive pressure. These five forces of competition include three sources of "horizontal" competition: competition from substitutes, competition from entrants, and competition from established rivals; and two sources of "vertical" competition: the power of suppliers and power of buyers (see Figure 3.2).

FIGURE 3.2 Porter's five forces of competition framework

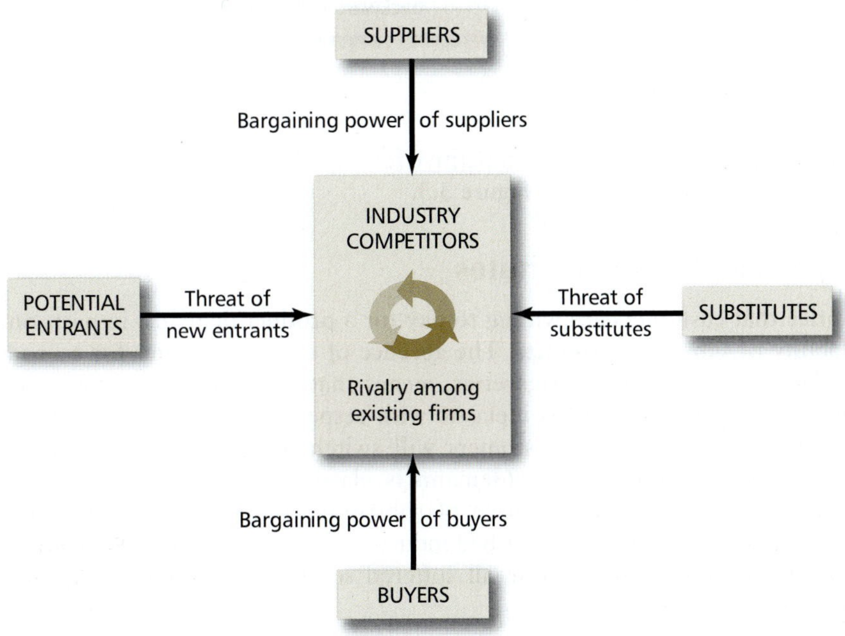

FIGURE 3.3 The structural determinants of the five forces of competition

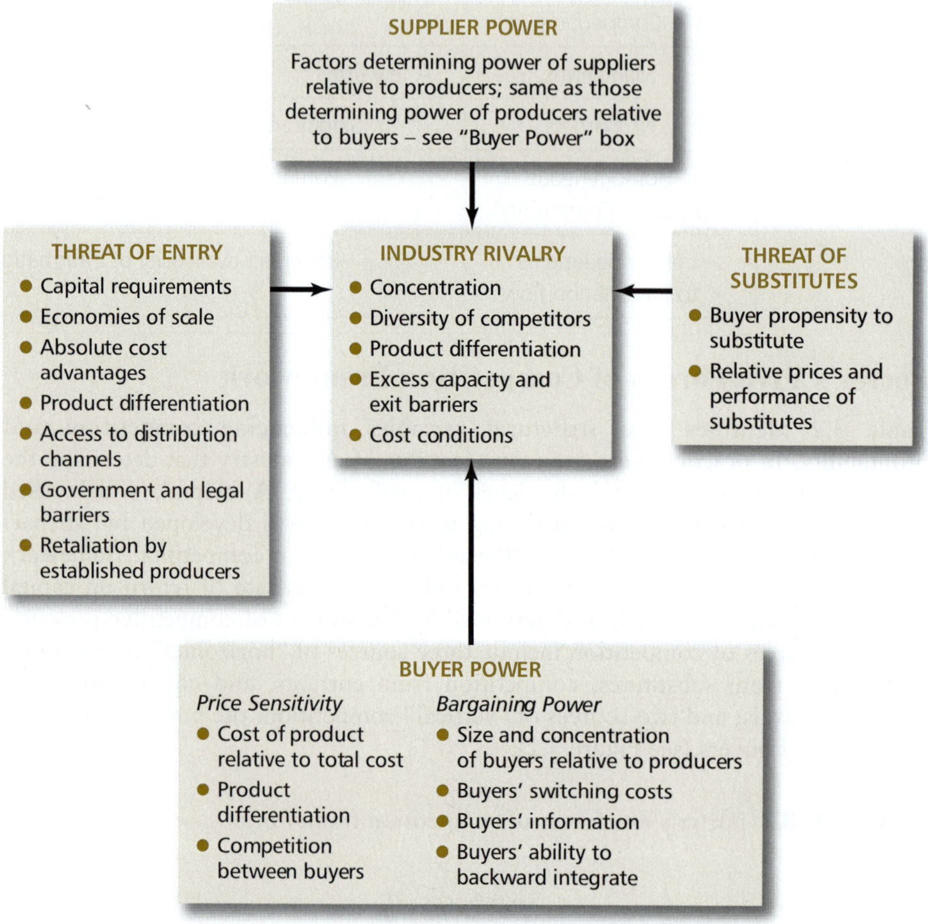

The strength of each of these competitive forces is determined by a number of key structural variables, as shown in Figure 3.3.

Competition from Substitutes

The price that customers are willing to pay for a product depends, in part, on the availability of substitute products. The absence of close substitutes for a product, as in the case of gasoline or cigarettes, means that consumers are comparatively insensitive to price (demand is inelastic with respect to price). The existence of close substitutes means that customers will switch to substitutes in response to price increases for the product (demand is elastic with respect to price). The internet has provided a new source of substitute competition that has proved devastating for a number of established industries. Travel agencies, newspapers and telecommunication providers have all suffered severe competition from internet-based substitutes.

The extent to which substitutes depress prices and profits depends on the propensity of buyers to substitute between alternatives. This, in turn, depends on their price-performance characteristics. If city-center to city-center travel between Washington and New York is 50 minutes quicker by air than by train and the average traveler values time at $30 an hour, the implication is that the train will be competitive at fares of $25 below those charged by the airlines. The more complex the product and the more difficult it is to discern performance differences, the lower the extent of substitution by customers on the basis of price differences. The failure of low-priced imitations of leading perfumes to establish significant market share reflects consumers' difficulty in recognizing the performance characteristics of different fragrances.

Threat of Entry

If an industry earns a return on capital in excess of its cost of capital, it will act as a magnet to firms outside the industry. If the entry of new firms is unrestricted, the rate of profit will fall toward its competitive level. The U.S. bagel industry faced a flood of new entrants in the late 1990s that caused a sharp decline in profitability.[3] Why is it that my wife, a psychotherapist, earns much less than our niece, a recently qualified medical doctor? Barriers to entry are one factor. In psychotherapy there are multiple accrediting bodies and limited state licensing, hence the entry barriers to psychotherapy are much lower than in medicine.

Threat of entry rather than actual entry may be sufficient to ensure that established firms constrain their prices to the competitive level. Only American Airlines offers a direct service between Dallas-Fort Worth and Santa Barbara, California, for example. Yet American may be unwilling to exploit its monopoly power to the full if Southwest or another airline can easily extend its routes to cover the same two cities. An industry where no barriers to entry or exit exist is *contestable*: prices and profits tend towards the competitive level, regardless of the number of firms within the industry.[4] Contestability depends on the absence of sunk costs—investments whose value cannot be recovered on exit. An absence of sunk costs makes an industry vulnerable to "hit-and-run" entry whenever established firms raise their prices above the competitive level.

In most industries, however, new entrants cannot enter on equal terms with those of established firms. A barrier to entry is any advantage that established firms have over entrants. The height of a barrier to entry is usually measured as the unit cost disadvantage faced by would-be entrants. The principal sources of barriers to entry are discussed below.

Capital Requirements The capital costs of becoming established in an industry can be so large as to discourage all but the largest companies. The duopoly of Boeing and Airbus in large passenger jets is protected by the huge capital costs of establishing R&D, production and service facilities for supplying these planes. Likewise with the business of launching commercial satellites: the costs of developing rockets and launch facilities make new entry highly unlikely. In other industries, entry costs can be modest. One reason why the e-commerce boom of the late 1990s ended in financial disaster for most participants is that the initial setup costs of new internet-based ventures were typically very low. Across the service sector more generally, startup costs tend to be low. For example, startup costs for a franchised pizza outlet begin at $120 000 for a Domino's and $638 000 for a Pizza Hut.[5]

Economies of Scale In industries that are capital or research or advertising intensive, efficiency requires large-scale operation. The problem for new entrants is that they are faced with the choice of either entering on a small scale and accepting high unit costs, or entering on a large scale and bearing the costs of underutilized capacity. In automobiles, cost efficiency means producing at least three million vehicles a year. As a result, the only recent entrants into volume car production have been state-supported companies (for example, Proton of Malaysia and Maruti of India). The main source of scale economies is new product development costs. Thus, developing and launching a new model of car typically costs over $1.5 billion. Airbus's A380 superjumbo cost about $18 billion to develop and must sell about 400 planes to break even. Once Airbus had committed to the project, then Boeing was effectively excluded from the superjumbo segment of the market.

Absolute Cost Advantages Established firms may have a unit cost advantage over entrants irrespective of scale. Absolute cost advantages often result from the acquisition of low-cost sources of raw materials. Saudi Aramco's access to the world's biggest and most accessible oil reserves give it an unassailable cost advantage over Shell, Exxon Mobil, and BP, whose costs per barrel are at least four times those of Saudi Aramco. Absolute cost advantages may also result from economies of learning. Sharp's cost advantage in LCD flat screen TVs results from its early entry into LCDs and its speed in moving down the learning curve.

Product Differentiation In an industry where products are differentiated, established firms possess the advantages of brand recognition and customer loyalty. The percentage of U.S. consumers loyal to a single brand varies from under 30% in batteries, canned vegetables and garbage bags, up to 61% in toothpaste, 65% in mayonnaise and 71% in cigarettes.[6] New entrants to such markets must spend disproportionately heavily on advertising and promotion to gain levels of brand awareness and brand goodwill similar to those of established companies. One study found that, compared to early entrants, late entrants into consumer goods markets incurred additional advertising and promotional costs amounting to 2.12% of sales revenue.[7]

Access to Channels of Distribution For many new suppliers of consumer goods, the principal barrier to entry is likely to be gaining distribution. Limited capacity within distribution channels (for example, shelf space), risk aversion by retailers and the fixed costs associated with carrying an additional product result in retailers being reluctant to carry a new manufacturer's product. The battle for supermarket shelf space between the major food processors (typically involving "slotting fees" to reserve shelf space) further disadvantages new entrants. One of the most important competitive impacts of the internet has been allowing new businesses to circumvent barriers to distribution.

Governmental and Legal Barriers Economists from the Chicago School claim that the only effective barriers to entry are those created by government. In taxi cabs, banking, telecommunications and broadcasting, entry usually requires a license from a public authority. From medieval times to the present day, companies and favored individuals have benefitted from governments granting them an exclusive right to ply a particular trade or offer a particular service. In knowledge-intensive industries, patents, copyrights and other legally protected forms of intellectual property are major barriers to entry. In the pharmaceutical industry, the major players seek to delay entry by generic drug makers by extending their original patents through changes in dosage and delivery modes. Regulatory requirements and environmental and safety standards often put new entrants at a disadvantage in comparison with established firms because compliance costs tend to weigh more heavily on newcomers.

Retaliation Barriers to entry also depend on the entrants' expectations as to possible retaliation by established firms. Retaliation against a new entrant may take the form of aggressive price cutting, increased advertising, sales promotion, or litigation. The major airlines have a long history of retaliation against low-cost entrants. Southwest and other budget airlines have alleged that selective price cuts by American and other major airlines amounted to predatory pricing designed to prevent its entry into new routes.[8] To avoid retaliation by incumbents, new entrants may seek initial small-scale entry into less visible market segments. When Toyota, Nissan and Honda first entered the U.S. auto market, they targeted the small car segments, partly because this was a segment that had been written off by the Detroit Big Three as inherently unprofitable.[9]

The Effectiveness of Barriers to Entry Industries protected by high entry barriers tend to earn above average rates of profit.[10] Capital requirements and advertising appear to be particularly effective impediments to entry.[11]

The effectiveness of barriers to entry depends on the resources and capabilities that potential entrants possess. Barriers that are effective against new companies may be ineffective against established firms that are diversifying from other industries.[12] Google has used its massive web presence as a platform for entering a number of other markets—including Microsoft's seemingly impregnable position in browsers.

Rivalry Between Established Competitors

For most industries, the major determinant of the overall state of competition and the general level of profitability is competition among the firms within the industry. In some industries, firms compete aggressively—sometimes to the extent that prices are pushed below the level of costs and industry-wide losses are incurred. In other industries, price competition is muted and rivalry focuses on advertising, innovation, and other nonprice dimensions. The intensity of competition between established firms is the result of interactions between six factors. Let us look at each of them.

Concentration Seller concentration refers to the number and size distribution of firms competing within a market. It is most commonly measured by the *concentration ratio*: the combined market share of the leading producers. For example, the four-firm concentration ratio (*CR4*) is the market share of the four largest producers. In markets dominated by a single firm (for example, Microsoft in PC operating systems, or UST in the U.S. smokeless tobacco market), the dominant firm can exercise considerable discretion over the prices it charges. Where a market is dominated by a small group of leading companies (an oligopoly), price competition may also be restrained, either by outright collusion, or more commonly through "parallelism" of pricing decisions.[13] Thus, in markets dominated by two companies, such as alkaline batteries (Duracell and Energizer), color film (Kodak and Fuji) and soft drinks (Coke and Pepsi), prices tend to be similar and competition focuses on advertising, promotion and product development. As the number of firms supplying a market increases, coordination of prices becomes more difficult and the likelihood that one firm will initiate price cutting increases. However, despite the frequent observation that the exit of a competitor reduces price competition, while the entry of a new competitor stimulates it, there is little systematic evidence that seller concentration increases profitability. Richard Schmalensee concluded that: "The relation, if any, between seller concentration and profitability is weak statistically and the estimated effect is usually small."[14]

Diversity of Competitors The extent to which a group of firms can avoid price competition in favor of collusive pricing practices depends on how similar they are in their origins, objectives, costs and strategies. The cozy atmosphere of the U.S. auto industry prior to the advent of import competition was greatly assisted by the similarities of the companies in terms of cost structures, strategies, and top management mindsets. The intense competition that affects the car markets of Europe and North America today is partly due to the different national origins, costs, strategies, and management styles of the competing firms. Similarly, the key challenge faced by OPEC is agreeing and enforcing output quotas among member countries that are sharply different in terms of objectives, production costs, politics and religion.

Product Differentiation The more similar the offerings among rival firms, the more willing are customers to switch between them and the greater is the inducement for firms to cut prices to boost sales. Where the products of rival firms are virtually indistinguishable, the product is a *commodity* and price is the sole basis for competition. Commodity industries such as agriculture, mining and petrochemicals tend to be plagued by price wars and low profits. By contrast, in industries where products are highly differentiated (perfumes, pharmaceuticals, restaurants, management consulting services), price competition tends to be weak, even though there may be many firms competing.

Excess Capacity and Exit Barriers Why does industry profitability tend to fall so drastically during periods of recession? The key is the balance between demand and capacity. Unused capacity encourages firms to offer price cuts to attract new business. Excess capacity may be cyclical (for example, the boom-bust cycle in the semiconductor industry); it may also be part of a structural problem resulting from overinvestment and declining demand. In these latter situations, the key issue is whether excess capacity will leave the industry. *Barriers to exit* are costs associated with capacity leaving an industry. Where resources are durable and specialized, and where employees are entitled to job protection, barriers to exit may be substantial.[15] In the European and North American auto industry, excess capacity together with high exit barriers have devastated industry profitability. Conversely, rapid demand growth creates capacity shortages that boost margins. Expanding world trade, fueled by the growth of China, pushed up charter rates of large bulk carriers ("Capesizes") from under \$18 000 a day at the beginning of 2003 to a peak of \$233 988 per day on June 5, 2008. With the onset of global recession and fleet expansion by ship owners, rates declined precipitously to a mere \$2773 a day by November 26, 2008.[16]

FIGURE 3.4 The impact of growth on profitability

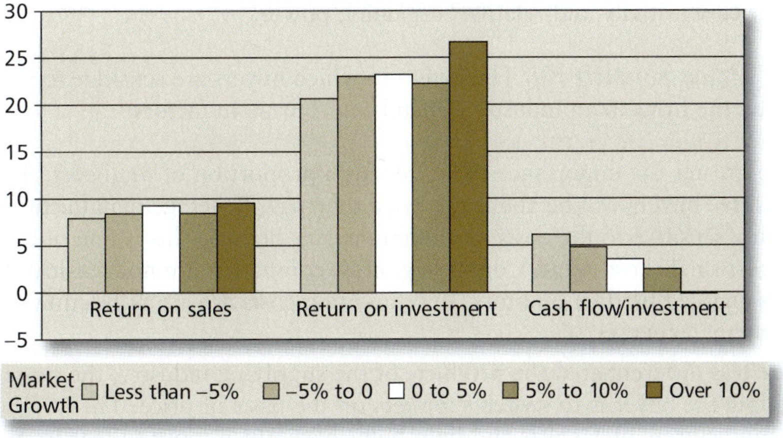

Source:

R. D. Buzzell and B. T. Gale, *The PIMS Principles* (New York: Free Press, 1987): 56–7. © 1987 The Free Press. Reproduced by permission of Simon & Schuster.

On average, companies in growing industries earn higher profits than companies in slow growing or declining industries (see Figure 3.4).

Cost Conditions: Scale Economies and the Ratio of Fixed to Variable Costs When excess capacity causes price competition, how low will prices go? The key factor is cost structure. Where fixed costs are high relative to variable costs, firms will take on marginal business at any price that covers variable costs. The consequences for profitability can be disastrous. In the airline industry, the emergence of excess capacity almost invariably leads to price wars and industry-wide losses. The willingness of airlines to offer heavily discounted tickets on flights with low bookings reflects the very low variable costs of filling empty seats. During the 2009 recession, the industries that have suffered the most drastic falls in profitability (autos, mining, hotels) tended to be those where fixed costs are high and firms are willing to accept additional business at any price that covers variable costs.

Scale economies may also encourage companies to compete aggressively on price in order to gain the cost benefits of greater volume. If scale efficiency in the auto industry means producing four million cars a year, a level that is currently achieved by only five companies, the outcome is a battle for market share as each firm tries to achieve critical mass.

Bargaining Power of Buyers

The firms in an industry compete in two types of markets: in the markets for inputs and the markets for outputs. In input markets firms purchase raw materials, components and financial and labor services. In the markets for outputs, firms sell their goods and services to customers (who may be distributors, consumers or other manufacturers). In both markets the transactions create value for both buyers and sellers. How this value is shared between them in terms of profitability depends on their relative economic power. Let us deal first with output markets. The strength of buying power that firms face from their customers depends on two sets of factors: buyers' price sensitivity and relative bargaining power.

Buyers' Price Sensitivity The extent to which buyers are sensitive to the prices charged by the firms in an industry depends on four main factors:

- The greater the importance of an item as a proportion of total cost, the more sensitive buyers will be about the price they pay. Beverage manufacturers are highly sensitive to the costs of aluminum cans because this is one of their largest single cost items. Conversely, most companies are not sensitive to the fees charged by their auditors, since auditing costs are a tiny fraction of total company expenses.
- The less differentiated the products of the supplying industry, the more willing the buyer is to switch suppliers on the basis of price. The manufacturers of T-shirts and light bulbs have much more to fear from Wal-Mart's buying power than have the suppliers of perfumes.
- The more intense the competition among buyers, the greater their eagerness for price reductions from their sellers. As competition in the world automobile industry has intensified, so component suppliers face greater pressures for lower prices.
- The more critical an industry's product to the quality of the buyer's product or service, the less sensitive are buyers to the prices they are charged. The buying power of personal computer manufacturers relative to the manufacturers of microprocessors (Intel and AMD) is limited by the vital importance of these components to the functionality of PCs.

Relative Bargaining Power Bargaining power rests, ultimately, on refusal to deal with the other party. The balance of power between the two parties to a transaction depends on the credibility and effectiveness with which each makes this threat. The key issue is the relative cost that each party sustains as a result of the transaction not being consummated. A second issue is each party's expertise in managing its position. Several factors influence the bargaining power of buyers relative to that of sellers:

- *Size and concentration of buyers relative to suppliers.* The smaller the number of buyers and the bigger their purchases, the greater the cost of losing one. Because of their size, health maintenance organizations (HMOs) can purchase healthcare from hospitals and doctors at much lower cost than can individual patients. Empirical studies show that buyer concentration lowers prices and profits in the supplying industry.[17]
- *Buyers' information.* The better informed buyers are about suppliers and their prices and costs, the better they are able to bargain. Doctors and lawyers do not normally display the prices they charge, nor do traders in the bazaars of Tangier and Istanbul. Keeping customers ignorant of relative prices is an effective constraint on their buying power. But knowing prices is of little value if the quality of the product is unknown. In the markets for haircuts, interior design, and management consulting, the ability of buyers

to bargain over price is limited by uncertainty over the precise attributes of the product they are buying.

- *Ability to integrate vertically*. In refusing to deal with the other party, the alternative to finding another supplier or buyer is to do it yourself. Large food-processing companies such as Heinz and Campbell Soup have reduced their dependence on the manufacturers of metal cans by manufacturing their own. The leading retail chains have increasingly displaced their suppliers' brands with their own-brand products. Backward integration need not necessarily occur—a credible threat may suffice.

Bargaining Power of Suppliers

Analysis of the determinants of relative power between the producers in an industry and their suppliers is precisely analogous to analysis of the relationship between producers and their buyers. The only difference is that it is now the firms in the industry that are the buyers and the producers of inputs that are the suppliers. The key issues are the ease with which the firms in the industry can switch between different input suppliers and the relative bargaining power of each party.

Because raw materials, semi-finished products and components are often commodities supplied by small companies to large manufacturing companies, their suppliers usually lack bargaining power. Hence, commodity suppliers often seek to boost their bargaining power through cartelization (for example, OPEC, the International Coffee Organization, and farmers' marketing cooperatives). A similar logic explains labor unions. Conversely, the suppliers of complex, technically sophisticated components may be able to exert considerable bargaining power. The dismal profitability of the personal computer industry may be attributed to the power exercised by the suppliers of key components (processors, disk drives, LCD screens) and the dominant supplier of operating systems (Microsoft).

Labor unions are important sources of supplier power. Where an industry has a high percentage of its employees unionized—as in steel, airlines, and automobiles—profitability is reduced (see Figure 3.5).

FIGURE 3.5 The impact of unionization on profitability

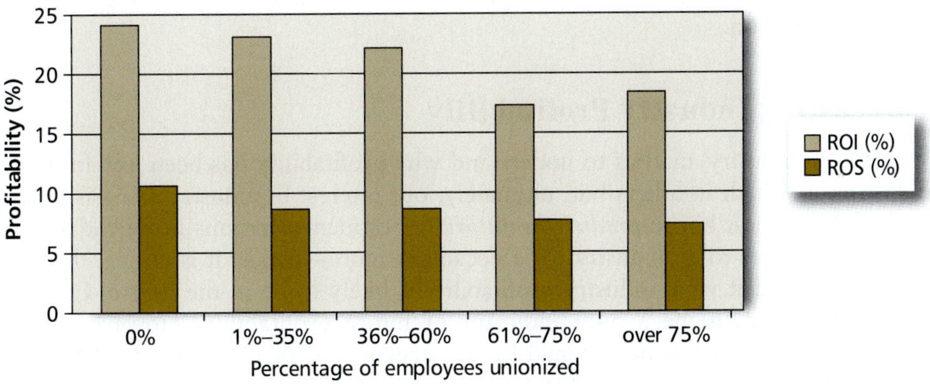

Source:

R. D. Buzzell and B. T. Gale, *The PIMS Principles* (New York: Free Press, 1987): 56–7. © 1987 The Free Press. Reproduced by permission of Simon & Schuster.

Applying Industry Analysis

Once we understand how industry structure drives competition, which, in turn, determines industry profitability, we can apply this analysis, first to forecast industry profitability in the future, second, to position the firm in relation it the competitive forces it faces and, third, to find ways of changing industry structure for the better.

Describing Industry Structure

The first stage of industry analysis is to identify the key elements of the industry's structure. In principle, this is a simple task. It requires identifying who are the main players—the producers, the customers, the input suppliers, and the producers of substitute goods—then examining some of the key structural characteristics of each of these groups that will determine competition and bargaining power.

In most manufacturing industries the identity of the different groups of players is usually straightforward, in other industries—particularly in service industries—building a picture of the industry may be more difficult. Consider the supply of television programming. There are a number of different types of player and establishing which are buyers, which are sellers, and where the industry boundaries lie is not simple. In terms of industry definition, do we consider all forms of TV distribution or identify separate industries for broadcast TV, cable TV and satellite TV? In terms of identifying buyers and sellers we see that there the industry has quite a complex value chain with the producers of the individual shows, networks that put together program schedules, and local broadcasting and cable companies that undertake final distribution. For the distribution companies there are two buyers—viewers and advertisers. Some companies are vertically integrated across several stages of the value chain—thus, networks such as Fox and NBC not only create and distribute program schedules, they are also backward integrated into producing some TV shows and they are forward integrated into local distribution through ownership of local TV stations.

Sorting out the different players and their relationships therefore involves some critical issues of industry definition. Which activities within the value chain do we include in the industry? What are the horizontal boundaries of the industry in terms of both products and geographical scope? We shall return to some of these issues of industry definition.

Forecasting Industry Profitability

We can use industry analysis to understand why profitability has been low in some industries and high in others but, ultimately, our interest in industry analysis is not to explain the past but to *predict the future*. Investment decisions made today will commit resources to an industry for a decade or more—hence, it is critical that we are able to predict what industry profitability is likely to be in the future. Current profitability tends to be a poor indicator of future profitability. However, if an industry's profitability is determined by the structure of that industry then we can use observations of the structural trends in an industry to forecast the likely changes in competition and profitability. Changes in industry structure tend to be the result of fundamental shifts in customer buying behavior, technology and firm strategies.

Hence we can use our current observations of the developments to identify emerging trends in industry structure.

To predict the future profitability of an industry, our analysis proceeds in three stages:

1 Examine how the industry's current and recent levels of competition and profitability are a consequence of its present structure.
2 Identify the trends that are changing the industry's structure. Is the industry consolidating? Are new players seeking to enter? Are the industry's products becoming more differentiated or more commoditized? Will additions to industry capacity will outstrip growth of demand?
3 Identify how these structural changes will affect the five forces of competition and resulting profitability of the industry. Will the changes in industry structure cause competition to intensify or to weaken? Rarely do all the structural changes move competition in a consistent direction—typically, some factors will cause competition to increase; others will cause competition to moderate. Hence, determining the overall impact on profitability is likely to be a matter of judgment.

Strategy Capsule 3.2 discusses the outlook for profitability in the wireless handset industry while Strategy Capsule 3.3 takes a retrospective look at the dotcom boom of 1998–2001. Could industry analysis have alerted us to the fact that that most e-commerce markets had limited scope for profitability?

STRATEGY CAPSULE 3.2

The Future of the Wireless Handset Industry

Wireless telephony has been one of the greatest growth industries of the past two decades—and almost as lucrative for the handset makers as for the service providers. During the 1990s, growth of handset sales in North America, Europe and Japan averaged close to 50% each year and generating massive profits and shareholder value for the early leaders, Motorola and Nokia.

The current decade has witnessed a profound change in competition and margins. Despite continued demand growth (especially in emerging markets), profitability has fallen. During 2000–5, the industry leaders—Nokia, Motorola, Sony-Ericsson, and Samsung—earned an average pretax margin of 20.2% on their sales of mobile devices; by 2006–8 this had fallen to 8.9% (with Motorola incurring substantial losses). Departures from the industry included Philips, Siemens, Mitsubishi and Sanyo.

The structural changes undermining industry profitability are not hard to find. Low entry barriers have resulted in a large number and a wide variety of companies competing. In addition to established telecom equipment manufacturers (Ericsson, Lucent, Alcatel) and consumer electronics companies (Sony, Sharp, LG, Samsung, Hitachi, Toshiba and Matsushita), a number of new players have emerged onto the international stage. These include a number of manufacturers from Taiwan (HTC, BenQ) and mainland China (Huawei, ZTE, Lenovo)—many of these recent entrants were former contract manufacturers now supplying under their own brands. During 2007/8, the world handset market was further shaken up with the entry of Apple's iPhone and Google's introduction of its Android mobile operating system.

The handset manufacturers also face strong vertical bargaining power on both sides. Not only are the service providers the biggest distributors of mobile handsets—they are in a continuous struggle with the handset manufacturers for preeminence in consumer brand loyalty. Thus, Vodafone, Orange and Verizon seek to strengthen their bargaining power by ordering specially-designed handsets manufactured under their own brands.

At the other end, the manufacturers deal with powerful suppliers including the suppliers of digital signaling chips and operating systems (Microsoft, Symbian, and Palm).

Over the period 2010–14, the structural trends that have eroded profitability over the past decade seem likely to continue. Market saturation will spread from the mature to the emerging markets. The global recession will further dampen demand growth. Yet despite the prospect of excess manufacturing capability, there is a continuous risk that new entry will continue to boost the already excessive number of mobile phone suppliers. Widespread outsourcing by the leading suppliers to contract manufacturers in Asia and elsewhere means that there are many firms with the manufacturing capability and know-how ready to enter the market with their own brands of handset.

Two major uncertainties are, first, the future of product differentiation and, second, the balance of bargaining power between handset manufacturers and service providers. In terms of product differentiation there are two conflicting forces: the growing demand for low-cost, technologically unsophisticated handsets in emerging markets, which suggests increasing commoditization, and the technological opportunities provided by 3G and 4G technologies, mobile internet, and convergence of handheld digital devices. While advancing technologies and multifunctionality (for example, mobile phone as a device for internet access, GPS, TV and music) increases the potential for product differentiation, it also appears that most forms of differentiation are easily imitated. The distinction between "smartphones", such as RIM's Blackberry and Apple's iPhone, and mainstream wireless handsets has been disappearing. During 2009, it seemed that, as a result of market power and control over distribution, the service producers would continue to hold the balance of vertical power. Much would depend upon which side had greater control over technology.

STRATEGY CAPSULE 3.3

The Internet: Value Creator or Value Destroyer?

The diffusion of the internet during the late 1990s and the wave of e-business startups that sought to exploit it contributed to one of the most spectacular stock market booms in history. Webvan, Pets.com, Kozmo, eToys.com, and Boo.com burned through hundreds of millions of dollars of venture capital and achieved stock market values that reached $1.2 billion (in the case of Webvan) before descending into oblivion.

Could the application of strategic analysis to e-business have revealed the dubious profit potential of dotcoms? Applying five forces analysis to the sectors offers some simple yet startling insights:

- *Substitutes.* Most new e-commerce startups were not fundamentally new businesses; they used a new distribution channel for existing goods and services: books (Amazon), airline tickets (Expedia), groceries (Peapod) and securities (E-trade). As such, they faced strong substitute competition from traditional retailers
- *Threat of entry.* Most e-commerce businesses are characterized by low costs of entry and ease of market access (setting up a web site costs little). Most markets suffered many more entrants than the level of demand could support.
- *Rivalry.* Ease of entry implied many competitors, the ubiquity of internet technology made differentiation difficult, while the internet's global span meant the absence of geographical niches.
- *Supplier power.* The suppliers of web software and owners of major portals possessed significant bargaining power.
- *Buyer power.* The transparency of prices and low switching costs resulted in high price sensitivity of customers.

The implication is that most "e-tailing" markets—whether for books, securities, household goods or hotel accommodation, will tend to be highly competitive and, on average, will generate low margins. Will any e-businesses offer high profitability? The key is the potential to reduce rivalry and raise barriers to entry through strategies that exploit network effects, economies of scale or product differentiation. For example, E-bay exploits network effects to dominate the person-to-person auction business. In books Amazon relies on scale economies and product differentiation through its range of customer services. Google exploits scale economies and differentiation based upon rapid innovation to dominate web search.

Sources: M. E. Porter, "Strategy and the Internet," *Harvard Business Review* (March 2001): 63–77; "The E-Commerce Winners," *Business Week* (August 3, 2001)

Positioning the Company

Recognizing and understanding the competitive forces that a firm faces within its industry allows managers to position the firm where competitive forces are weakest. The record industry, once reliance on sales of CDs, has been devastated by the substitute competition in the form of digital downloads, piracy and file sharing. Yet not all segments of the recorded music business have been equally affected. The old are less inclined to turn to digital downloading than younger listeners with the result that classical music, country and golden oldies have become comparatively more attractive than pop and hip-hop genres.

Porter describes the success of U.S. truck-maker, Paccar, in sheltering itself from the bargaining power of fleet buyers. By focusing on the preferences of independent owner-operators—for example by providing superior sleeping cabins, higher specification seats, a roadside assistance program—Paccar has consistently been able to earn the higher rate of return in the industry.[18]

Effective positioning requires the firm to anticipate changes in the competitive forces likely to affect the industry. Between 2006 and 2008, the pornographic video industry suffered a massive revenue decline as customers turned to free web sites that featured user-generated content. A leading survivor in the industry is Vivid Entertainment, which invested in its brand and in high-quality production in an effort to differentiate its DVDs from those available on free websites. Vivid has also initiated legal moves—suing AEBN, owner of PornTube—for copyright infringement.[19]

Strategies to Alter Industry Structure

Understanding how the structural characteristics of an industry determine the intensity of competition and the level of profitability provides a basis for identifying opportunities for changing industry structure to alleviate competitive pressures. The first issue is to identify the key structural features of an industry that are responsible for depressing profitability. The second is to consider which of these structural features are amenable to change through appropriate strategic initiatives. For example:

- The remarkable profit revival in the world steel industry between 2002 and 2008 was mainly the result of rising demand, however it was also supported by the rapid consolidation of the industry, led by Mittal Steel.[20]
- Excess capacity was a major problem in the European petrochemicals industry. Through a series of bilateral plant exchanges, each company built a leading position within a particular product area.[21]
- In the U.S. airline industry, the major airlines have struggled to change an unfavorable industry structure. In the absence of significant product differentiation, the airlines have used frequent-flier schemes to build customer loyalty. Through hub-and-spoke route systems, the companies have achieved dominance of particular airports: American at Dallas-Fort Worth, U.S. Airways at Charlotte NC, and Northwest at Detroit and Memphis. Mergers and alliances have reduced the numbers of competitors on many routes.[22]
- Building entry barriers is a vital strategy for preserving high profitability in the long run. A primary goal of the American Medical Association has been to maintain the incomes of its members by controlling the numbers of doctors trained in the U.S. and imposing barriers to the entry of doctors from overseas.

It is often assumed that dominant firms or firms acting in concert can change their industry structure. Michael Jacobides notion of *architectural advantage* begins with the premise that firms are in a continual state of evolution and all firms—even quite small ones—have the potential to influence the development of industry structure to suit their own interests.[23] Apple has profoundly influenced both the recorded music and audio hardware industries, positioning itself as an intermediary between the two. Google is seeking to influence the development of wireless communications through its Android operating system for mobile phones with a view to extending its dominance of web search to a wireless internet environment. Achieving "architectural advantage" is all about identifying and then controlling actual and potential "bottlenecks" within industries. Alleviating bottlenecks that are barriers to oneself (as IKEA did when it transferred furniture assembly from furniture manufacturers to furniture consumers) and creating new ones that protect one's own position (as Microsoft did when it became the supplier of the operating system for the IBM PC) can create massive profit for a firm. To identify opportunities for architectural advantage requires looking beyond the existing boundaries of an industry to consider interacting clusters of industries. Digital imaging comprises suppliers of cameras, printers, software, consumables, and memory. The key to making money in this fiercely competitive sector is to identify potential bottlenecks—activities and technologies where economic power can be established. These might include image editing software (such as Adobe's Photoshop) and sensors.

Defining Industries: Where to Draw the Boundaries

In our earlier discussion of the structure of the television broadcasting industry, I noted that a key challenge in industry analysis is defining the relevant industry. The Standard Industrial Classification (SIC) offers an official guide but this provides limited practical assistance. Suppose Jaguar, now part of the Tata Group, is assessing its future prospects. In forecasting the profitability of its industry, should Jaguar consider itself part of the "motor vehicles and equipment" industry (SIC 371), the automobile industry (SIC 3712), or the luxury car industry? Should it view its industry as national (U.K.), regional (Europe), or global?

Industries and Markets

The first issue is clarifying what we mean by the term "industry." Economists define an industry as a group of firms that supplies a market. Hence, a close correspondence exists between markets and industries. So, what's the difference between analyzing industry structure and analyzing market structure? The principal difference is that industry analysis—notably five forces analysis—looks at industry profitability being determined by competition in two markets: product markets and input markets.

Everyday usage makes a bigger distinction between industries and markets. Typically, industries are identified with relatively broad sectors, whereas markets refer to specific products. Thus, the firms within the packaging industry compete in many distinct product markets—glass containers, steel cans, aluminum cans, paper cartons, plastic containers and so on.

Similar issues arise in relation to geographical boundaries. From an economist's viewpoint, the U.S. automobile industry would denote all companies supplying the U.S. auto market—irrespective of their location. In everyday usage, the term "U.S. auto industry" typically refers to auto manufacturers located within the U.S., and is often restricted to U.S.-owned automakers (which now includes primarily Ford and General Motors).

For the purposes of industry analysis, I suggest we adopt the economist's approach to identifying and defining industries. Thus, our starting point is the market: which are the firms that compete to supply a particular product or service? This approach may lead us to discard conventional concepts of industry boundaries. For example, if we are examining competition within the banking industry, it is likely that we would want to regard banking as comprising a number of industries—banks supply a number of distinct services and competition in each product market comprises different sets of firms. Most basic is the distinction between retail banking, corporate (or "wholesale") banking and investment banking. Even retail banking we might want to disaggregate into several different product markets. Thus, deposit taking, transaction services, credit cards and mortgage lending are distinct product offerings with different groups of competing firms. We can disaggregate even further, Strategy Capsule 3.4 outlines a micro-level approach to competitive analysis that focuses on consumers' choices between rival offerings.

STRATEGY CAPSULE 3.4

Analyzing Competition in Markets for Offerings

Mathur and Kenyon argue that our conventional concept of industry is fundamentally flawed. To analyze competition, we must begin with customer choice. Customers do not choose a product or a company; their unit of choice is the single *offering*. To analyze competition, it makes no sense to talk about the "watch market" or the "watch industry"—the Patek Philippe 10-day Tourbillon (list price $335 000) does not compete with the $35 Timex Sport Watch. Similarly, a $1400 Swatch Lustrous Bliss Sapphire Watch is not a close competitor to Swatch's $39.95 Pampas Rider. Each model by each watch maker is a separate offering where competitors can be ranked according to their proximity to the focal offering in the mind of the customer.

This micro approach to analyzing competition focuses on customer choices and contrasts sharply with Porter's industry analysis, which examines competition at a much higher level of aggregation.

Should we abandon our more aggregated industry analysis in favor of the meticulously micro analysis advocated by Mathur and Kenyon? The critical consideration is the type of question that we want our competitive analysis to answer. For decisions relating to marketing strategy—including product design, pricing, advertising, distribution, and entry into specific market segments—analysis of competition between narrowly defined offerings in relation to specific customers and customer groups is likely to be particularly revealing.

For understanding and predicting medium-term profit trends, the conventional five forces analysis of broadly defined industries has two virtues. First, it allows us to consider competition in two markets simultaneously—the market for outputs and markets for inputs. Second, it takes account of supply-side substitution. Thus, the Swatch Group can easily switch production capacity between models. Given that it owns 16 brands—including Swatch, Omega, Longines, and Tissot—there is scope for reallocating resources between brands. Hence, for analyzing broad questions of profitability and competitive advantage, it can be useful to consider the watch industry in broad terms.

Source: Based on Shiv Mathur and Alfred Kenyon, *Winning Business Strategies* (Oxford: Butterworth-Heinemann, 2007).

Defining Markets: Substitution in Demand and Supply

I have argued that the key to defining industry boundaries is identifying the relevant market. By focusing on the relevant market, we do not lose sight of the critical relationship among firms within an industry: competition. But how do we define markets?

A market's boundaries are defined by *substitutability*. There are two dimensions to this—substitutability on the demand side and the supply side. Let us consider once more the market within which Jaguar competes. Starting with the demand side, if customers are unwilling to substitute trucks for cars on the basis of price differences, Jaguar's market should be viewed as automobiles rather than all motor vehicles. Again, if customers are only willing to substitute between Jaguars and other makes of luxury cars, then Jaguar's relevant market is luxury cars rather than the automobile market as a whole.

But this fails to take account of substitutability on the supply side. If manufacturers find it easy to switch their production from luxury cars to family sedans to sports cars and the like, such supply-side substitutability would suggest that Jaguar is competing within the broader automobile market. The ability of Toyota, Nissan and Honda to penetrate the luxury car market suggests that supply-side substitutability between mass-market autos and specialty autos is moderately high. Similarly, the automobile industry is frequently defined to include vans and light trucks, since these can be manufactured at the same plants as automobiles (often using the same platforms and engines). So too with "major appliance" manufacturers. They tend to be classified as a single industry, not because consumers are willing to substitute between refrigerators and dishwashers, but because the manufacturers can use the same manufacturing plants and distribution channels for different appliances.

The same considerations apply to the geographical boundaries of markets. Should Jaguar view itself as competing in a single global market or in a series of separate national or regional markets? The criterion here again is substitutability. If customers are willing and able to substitute cars available on different national markets, or if manufacturers are willing and able to divert their output among different countries to take account of differences in margins, then a market is global. The key test of the geographical boundaries of a market is price: if price differences for the same product between different locations tend to be eroded by demand-side and supply-side substitution, then these locations lie within a single market.

In practice, drawing the boundaries of markets and industries is a matter of judgment that depends on the purposes and context of the analysis. If Tata is considering the pricing and market positioning of its Jaguar cars, it must take a micro-level approach that defines markets around each model, in each country, and in relation to different categories of customer (for example, distinguishing between sales to car rental companies and sales to individual consumers). In considering decisions over investments in technology, component plants, and new products, Tata will view Jaguar as one part of its Tata Motor business and will define its market as global and extending across its full range of models. The longer term the decisions are that it is considering, the more broadly it will wish to consider its markets, since substitutability is higher in the long run than in the short term.

Second, the precise delineation of the boundaries of a market or industry is seldom critical to the outcome of our analysis so long as we remain wary of external influences. The market in which an offering competes is a continuum rather than a bounded space. Thus, we may view the competitive market of Disneyland, Anaheim as a set of concentric circles. Closest is Universal Studios Tour. Slightly more distant competitors are Sea World and Six Flags. Further still might be a trip to Las Vegas, or a skiing weekend. Beyond these would be the broader entertainment market that might include cinemas, the beach, or playing video games.

For the purposes of applying the five forces framework, industry definition is not critical. We define an industry "box" within which industry rivals compete, but because we include competitive forces outside the industry box—notably entrants and substitutes—the precise boundaries of the industry box are not greatly important. If we define Disneyland as competing within the broad entertainment industry, then beach and ski resorts are rivals; if we define Disneyland as competing in the theme park industry, then beach and ski resorts are substitutes.[24]

From Industry Attractiveness to Competitive Advantage: Identifying Key Success Factors

The five forces framework allows us to determine an industry's potential for profit. But how is industry profit shared between the different firms competing in that industry? Let us look explicitly at the sources of competitive advantage within an industry. In subsequent chapters we develop a more comprehensive analysis of competitive advantage. Our goal here is to identify those factors within the firm's market environment that determine the firm's ability to survive and prosper—its *key success factors*.[25] In Strategy Capsule 3.5, Kenichi Ohmae of McKinsey's Tokyo office discusses key success factors in forestry and their link with strategy.

STRATEGY CAPSULE 3.5

Probing for Key Success Factors

As a consultant faced with an unfamiliar business or industry, I make a point of first asking the specialists in the business, "What is the secret of success in this industry?" Needless to say, I seldom get an immediate answer and so I pursue the inquiry by asking other questions from a variety of angles in order to establish as quickly as possible some reasonable hypotheses as to key factors for success. In the course of these interviews it usually becomes quite obvious what analyses will be required in order to prove or disprove these hypotheses. By first identifying the probable key factors for success and then screening them by proof or disproof, it is often possible for the strategist to penetrate very quickly to the core of a problem.

Traveling in the U.S. last year, I found myself on one occasion sitting in a plane next to a director of one of the biggest lumber companies in the country. Thinking I might learn something useful in the course of the five-hour flight, I asked him, "What are the key factors for success in the lumber industry?" To my surprise, his reply was immediate: "Owning large forests and maximizing the yield from them." The first of these key factors is a relatively simple matter: purchase of forest land. But his second point required further explanation. Accordingly, my next question was: "What variable or variables do you control in order to maximize the yield from a given tract?"

He replied: "The rate of tree growth is the key variable. As a rule, two factors promote growth: the amount of sunshine and the amount of water. Our company doesn't have many forests with enough of both. In Arizona and Utah, for example, we get more than enough sunshine but too little water and so tree growth is very low. Now, if we could give the trees in those states enough water, they'd be ready in less than 15 years instead of the 30 it takes now. The most important project we have in hand at the moment is aimed at finding out how to do this."

Impressed that this director knew how to work out a key factor strategy for his business, I offered my own contribution: "Then under the opposite conditions, where there is plenty of water but too little sunshine—for example, around the lower reaches of the Columbia River—the key factors should be fertilizers to speed up the growth and the choice of tree varieties that don't need so much sunshine."

Having established in a few minutes the general framework of what we were going to talk about, I spent the rest of the long flight very profitably hearing from him in detail how each of these factors was being applied.

Source: Kenichi Ohmae, *The Mind of the Strategist* (New York: McGraw-Hill, 1982): 85. Reproduced by permission of McGraw-Hill.

Like Ohmae, our approach to identifying key success factors is straightforward and commonsense. To survive and prosper in an industry, a firm must meet two criteria: first, it must supply what customers want to buy; second, it must survive competition. Hence, we may start by asking two questions:

- What do our customers want?
- What does the firm need to do to survive competition?

To answer the first question we need to look more closely at customers of the industry and to view them, not as a threat to profitability because of their buying power but as *raison d'être* of the industry and its underlying source of profit. This requires that we inquire: Who are our customers? What are their needs? How do they choose between competing offerings? Once we recognize the basis of customers' preferences we can then identify the factors that confer success upon the individual firm. For example, if consumers choose supermarkets

FIGURE 3.6 Identifying key success factors

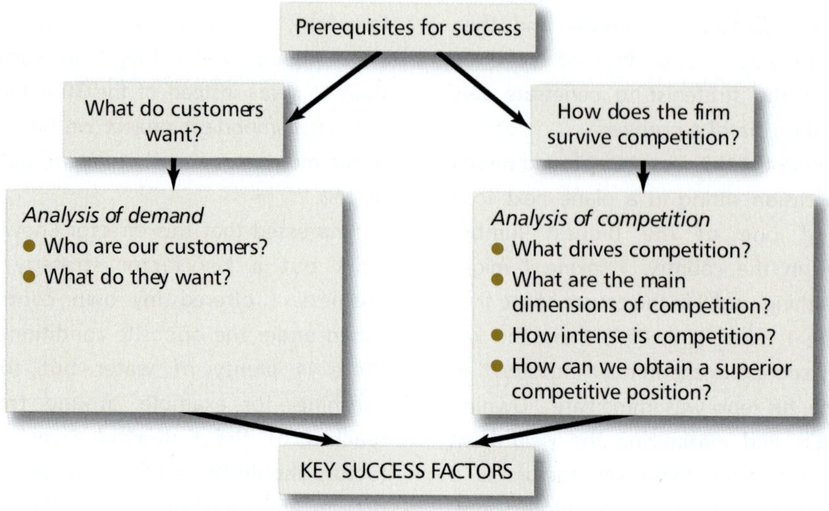

on the basis of price then cost efficiency is the primary basis for competitive advantage and the key success factors are the determinants of inter-firm cost differentials.

The second question requires that we examine the nature of competition in the industry. How intense is competition and what are its key dimensions? Thus, in airlines, it is not enough to offer low fares, convenience and safety. Survival requires sufficient financial strength to weather the intense price competition that accompanies cyclical downturns.

A basic framework for identifying key success factors is presented in Figure 3.6. Application of the framework to identify key success factors in three industries is outlined in Table 3.3.

Key success factors can also be identified through the direct modeling of profitability. In the same way that the five forces analysis models the determinants of industry-level profitability, we can also model firm-level profitability by identifying the drivers of a firm's relative profitability within an industry. Using the same approach as in Chapter 2 (see Figure 2.2), we can disaggregate return on capital employed into component ratios which then point to the main drivers of superior profitability. Figure 3.7 applies this analysis to identifying success factors in retailing.

In some industries, the key drivers of firm-level profitability are well known. Strategy Capsule 3.6 draws upon a well-known profitability formula used in the airline industry to identify key success factors.

The value of success factors in formulating strategy has been scorned by some strategy scholars. Pankaj Ghemawat observes that the "whole idea of identifying a success factor and then chasing it seems to have something in common with the ill-considered medieval hunt for the philosopher's stone, a substance that would

TABLE 3.3 Identifying key success factors: steel, fashion clothing, and supermarkets

	What do customers want? (Analysis of demand)	How do firms survive competition? (Analysis of competition)	Key success factors
Steel	Low price Product consistency Reliability of supply Specific technical specifications for special steels	Commodity products, excess capacity, high fixed costs, excess capacity, exit barriers, and substitute competition mean intense price competition and cyclical profitability Cost efficiency and financial strength essential	Cost efficiency requires: large-scale plants, low-cost location, rapid capacity adjustment Alternatively, high technology, small-scale plants can achieve low costs through flexibility and high productivity Differentiation through technical specifications and service quality
Fashion clothing	Diversity of customer preferences in terms of garment type, style, quality, color Customers willing to pay premium for brand, style, exclusivity, and quality Mass market highly price sensitive	Low barriers to entry and exit, low seller concentration, and buying power of retail chains imply intense competition Differentiation can yield substantial price premium, but imitation is rapid	Combining differentiation with low costs Differentiation requires speed of response to changing fashions, style, reputation, and quality Cost efficiency requires manufacture in low wage countries
Supermarkets	Low prices Convenient location Wide range of products adapted to local preferences Fresh/quality produce; good service; ease of parking; pleasant ambience	Intensity of price competition depends on number and proximity of competitors Bargaining power a critical determinant of cost of bought-in goods	Low costs require operational efficiency, scale-efficient stores, large aggregate purchases, low wage costs Differentiation requires large stores (to allow wide product range), convenient location, familiarity with local customer preferences

transmute everything it touched into gold."[26] Our goal is not to identify "generic strategies" that can guarantee success, simply to recognize commonalities in customer motivation and the nature of competition. In the fashion clothing business we identified key success factors (see Table 3.3). However, if we compare the strategies of Zara, H&M, Diesel, and Benetton, we can see that unique resources and capabilities applied to common success factors results in the adoption of very different strategies.

FIGURE 3.7 Identifying key success factors through analyzing profit drivers: the case of retailing

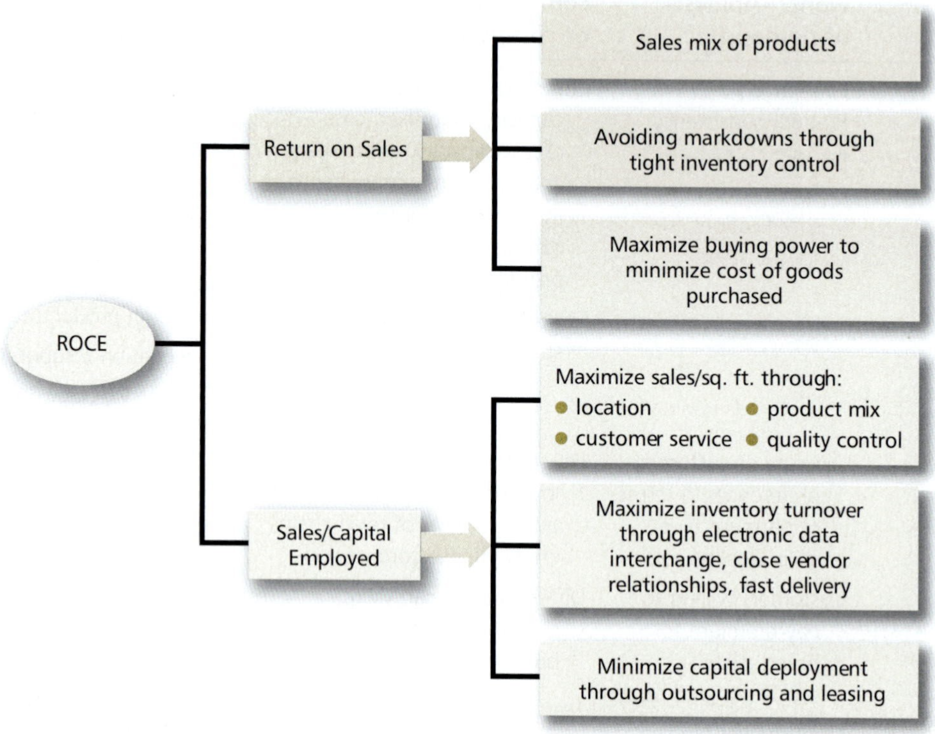

STRATEGY CAPSULE 3.6

Identifying Key Success Factors by Modeling Profitability: Airlines

Profitability, as measured by operating income per available seat-mile (ASM), is determined by three factors: yield, which is total operating revenues divided by the number of revenue passenger miles (RPMs); load factor, which is the ratio between RPMs and ASMs; and unit cost, which is total operating expenses divided by ASMs. Thus:

$$\frac{\text{income}}{\text{ASMs}} = \frac{\text{revenue}}{\text{RPMs}} \times \frac{\text{RPMs}}{\text{ASMs}} - \frac{\text{expenses}}{\text{ASMs}}$$

Some of the primary determinants of each of these measures are the following:

- Revenue/RPMs
  - intensity of competition on routes flown
  - effective yield management to permit quick price adjustment to changing market conditions
  - ability to attract business customers
  - superior customer service.

- Load factors
  - competitiveness of prices
  - efficiency of route planning (for example, through hub-and-spoke systems)
  - building customer loyalty through quality of service, frequent-flier programs
  - matching airplane size to demand for individual flights.
- Expenses/ASMs
  - wage rates and benefit levels
  - fuel efficiency of aircraft
  - productivity of employees (determined partly by their job flexibility)
  - load factors
  - level of administrative cost.

In their battle for survival, the airlines have sought to optimize as many of these factors as possible in order to improve their profitability. To enhance revenue, several airlines have withdrawn from their most intensely competitive routes; others have sought to achieve a fare premium over the cut-price airlines through superior punctuality, convenience, comfort, and services. To improve load factors, companies have become more flexible in their pricing and in allocating different planes to different routes. Most notably, companies have sought to cut costs by increasing employee productivity, reducing overhead, sharing services with other airlines and reducing salaries and benefits.

Summary

In Chapter 1 we established that profound understanding of the competitive environment is a critical ingredient of a successful strategy. In this chapter we have developed a systematic approach to analyzing a firm's industry environment in order to evaluate the industry's profit potential and to identify the sources of competitive advantage. The centerpiece of our approach is Porter's *five forces of competition* framework, which links the structure of an industry to the competitive intensity within it and to the profitability that it realizes. Although every industry is unique, competition and profitability are the result of the systematic influences of a common set of structural variables. The Porter framework provides a simple yet powerful organizing framework for identifying the relevant features of an industry's structure and predicting their implications for competitive behavior. The framework is particularly useful for predicting industry profitability, positioning the firm in relation to these forces, and identifying how the firm can improve industry attractiveness.

As with most of the tools for strategy analysis that we shall consider in this book, the Porter five forces framework is easy to comprehend. Its basis is a substantial body of microeconomic theory but the relationships it posits are straightforward and consistent with common sense. However, real learning about industry analysis and about the Porter framework in particular derives from its *application*. It is only when we apply the Porter framework to analyzing competition and diagnosing the causes of high or low profitability in an industry that we are forced to confront the complexities and subtleties of the model. What industry (or industries) does a company compete in? Where do the industry's boundaries lie? How wide a range of substitutes do we consider? How do the structural features of an industry interact with one another?

I urge you to put the tools of industry analysis to work—not just in your strategic management coursework, but also in your interpretation of everyday business events. What will be the impact of Google's *Android* software platform on the wireless handset industry? How will the financial crisis of 2008–9 affect the structure of U.S. and European banking and what will this mean for competition and profitability?

Through practical applications of the Porter framework, we shall also become aware of its limitations. In the next chapter we look to ways in which we can extend and augment our analysis with additional concepts, tools, and frameworks.

Self-Study Questions

1 The major forces shaping the business environment of the fixed-line telecom industry are technology and government policy. The industry has been influenced by fiber-optics (greatly increasing transmission capacity), new modes of telecommunication (wireless and internet telephony), deregulation, and privatization. Using the five forces of competition framework, show how each of these developments has influenced competition in the fixed-line telecom industry.

2 From Table 3.1, select a high-profit industry and a low-profit industry. From what you know of the structure of your selected industry, use the five forces framework to explain why profitability has been either high or low.

3 With reference to Strategy Capsule 3.1, use the five forces framework to explain why the U.S. smokeless tobacco industry is so profitable (as indicated by the profitability of its dominant firm).

4 The leading companies in the online travel agency industry are Expedia, Travelocity (which owns Lastminute.com), Orbitz, Priceline, Cheaptickets and a host of others. The online agents compete both with traditional travel agents (American Express, Thomas Cook, Carlson) and direct online sales by airlines, cruise lines and car rental companies. Their biggest business is selling airline tickets, where they employ the services of computerized airline reservation systems such as Sabre, Amadeus, Worldspan and Galileo. Use Porter's five forces framework to predict the likely profitability of the online travel agency industry over the next ten years.

5 Wal-Mart (like Carrefour, Ahold and Metro) competes in several countries of the world, yet most shoppers choose between retailers within a radius of a few miles. For the purposes of analyzing profitability and competitive strategy, should Wal-Mart consider the discount retailing industry to be global, national, or local?

6 What do you think are key success factors in:

(a) The pizza delivery industry?
(b) The investment banking industry?

Notes

1 "Pest Analysis," mindtools. www.mindtools.com/pages/article/newTMC_09.htm.

2 M. E. Porter, "The Five Competitive Forces that Shape Strategy," *Harvard Business Review* 57 (January 2008): 57–71.

3 "For Bagel Chains, Investment May Be Money in the Hole," *Wall Street Journal* (December 30, 1997): B8.

4 W. J. Baumol, J. C. Panzar and R. D. Willig, *Contestable Markets and the Theory of Industry Structure* (New York: Harcourt Brace Jovanovich, 1982). See also Michael Spence, "Contestable Markets and the Theory of Industry Structure: A Review Article," *Journal of Economic Literature* 21 (September 1983): 981–90.

5 "Annual Franchise 500," *Entrepreneur* (January 2009).

6 "Brand Loyalty is Rarely Blind Loyalty," *Wall Street Journal* (October 19, 1989): B1.

7 R. D. Buzzell and P. W. Farris, "Marketing Costs in Consumer Goods Industries," in H. Thorelli (ed.), *Strategy + Structure = Performance* (Bloomington, IN: Indiana University Press, 1977): 128–9.

8 In October 1999, the Department of Justice alleged that American Airlines was using unfair means in attempting to monopolize air traffic out of Dallas-Fort Worth (http://www.aeroworldnet.com/1tw05179.htm, accessed July 2, 2009).

9 M. Lieberman , "Excess Capacity as a Barrier to Entry," *Journal of Industrial Economics* 35, June 1987: 607–27 argues that, to be credible, the threat of retaliation needs to be supported by incumbents holding excess capacity giving them the potential to flood the market.

10 See for example: J. S. Bain, *Barriers to New Competition* (Cambridge, MA: Harvard University Press, 1956) and H. M. Mann, "Seller Concentration, Entry Barriers, and Rates of Return in Thirty Industries," *Review of Economics and Statistics* 48 (1966): 296–307.

11 W. S. Comanor and T. A. Wilson, *Advertising and Market Power* (Cambridge: Harvard University Press, 1974); J. L. Siegfried and L. B. Evans, "Empirical Studies of Entry and Exit: A Survey of the Evidence," *Review of Industrial Organization* 9 (1994): 121–55.

12 G. S. Yip, "Gateways to Entry," *Harvard Business Review* 60 (September-October 1982): 85–93.

13 F. M. Scherer and D. R. Ross, *Industrial Market Structure and Economic Performance*, 3rd edn (Boston: Houghton Mifflin, 1990); R. M. Grant, "Pricing Behavior in the U.K. Wholesale Market for Petrol. A 'Structure-Conduct Analysis'," *Journal of Industrial Economics* 30 (March 1982) 271–292.

14 R. Schmalensee, "Inter-Industry Studies of Structure and Performance," in R. Schmalensee and R. D. Willig, *Handbook of Industrial Organization*, 2nd edn (Amsterdam: North Holland, 1988): 976; M. A. Salinger, "The Concentration-Margins Relationship Reconsidered," *Brookings Papers: Microeconomics* (1990): 287–335.

15 The problems caused by excess capacity and exit barriers are discussed in C. Baden-Fuller (ed.), *Strategic Management of Excess Capacity* (Oxford: Basil Blackwell, 1990).

16 "Dry bulk shipping rates approach all-time low," *Financial Times* (November 27, 2008).

17 S. H. Lustgarten, "The Impact of Buyer Concentration in Manufacturing Industries," *Review of Economics and Statistics* 57 (1975): 125–32; T. Kelly and M. L. Gosman, "Increased Buyer Concentration and its Effects on Profitability in the Manufacturing Sector," *Review of Industrial Organization* 17 (2000): 41–59.

18 M. E. Porter, "The Five Competitive Forces that Shape Strategy" op. cit.

19 "Rude Awakening" *FT Weekend*, Financial Times (October 4/5, 2008): 16–23.

20 "Globalization or Concentration?" *Business Week* (November 8, 2004): 54; "Mittal: Blood, Steel and Empire Building," *Business Week* (February 13, 2006).

21 J. Bower, *When Markets Quake* (Boston: Harvard Business School Press, 1986).

22 M. Carnall, S. Berry and P. Spiller, "Airline Hubbing, Costs and Demand," in D. Lee (ed.), *Advances in Airline Economics,* vol. 1 (Amsterdam: Elsevier, 2006).

23 M. G. Jacobides, "Building Architectural Advantage: Don't just compete *in* your sector. Shape your sector and win!" AIM White Paper, London Business School (May 2008).

24 For a concise discussion of market definition see Office of Fair Trading, *Market Definition* (London: December 2004), especially pp. 7–17.

25 The term was coined by Chuck Hofer and Dan Schendel, *Strategy Formulation: Analytical Concepts* (St Paul: West Publishing, 1977): 77. They defined key success factors as "those variables that management can influence through its decisions and that can affect significantly the overall competitive positions of the firms in an industry."

26 P. Ghemawat, *Commitment: The Dynamic of Strategy* (New York: Free Press, 1991): 11.

4 Further Topics in Industry and Competitive Analysis

OUTLINE

Introduction and Objectives

The Porter five forces model offers a systematic approach to analyzing competition. At the same time, it offers a highly simplified view of industry and competition. Consider the following:

- The only relationships between products that we have considered are substitute relations. Many products—both goods and services—have *complementary* relationships with one another. What do complements imply for competition and the potential for profit?
- In many sectors industry structure may be much less stable than envisaged by the Porter model. Rather than structure determining competition in some predictable way, competition—particularly when it involves innovation—may reshape industry structure very rapidly. How do we analyze industries where structure is continually being recreated by firms' strategies?
- We have not explored the dynamic rivalry that characterizes business competition in the real world. Pepsi-Cola's competitive environment is determined more by the strategy and marketing tactics of Coca-Cola than by the structure of the world soft drinks industry—similarly with Reuters and Bloomberg and with Boeing and Airbus. To understand competition as a dynamic process we shall draw upon the tools of game theory and competitor analysis.
- In discussing the problems of drawing industry boundaries, we noted the advantages of analyzing competition at different levels. American Airlines competes in the world airline industry. However, each route comprises a different market with a different set of competitors. To take account of the internal heterogeneity of industries we shall disaggregate industries into segments and analyze each segment as a separate market.

This chapter will extend the analysis of industry and competition to address the above topics. In doing so, you will acquire the ability to:

- analyze relationships of *complementarity* between products and recognize the potential for the firm to make profit through managing these relationships;

- recognize the implications of *game theory* for competitive analysis—in particular, the potential gains from cooperative strategies and the use of threats, commitments, signaling, deterrence and preemption to gain and sustain competitive advantage;
- utilize *competitor analysis* to predict the competitive moves by rivals;
- *segment* an industry into its constituent markets, to appraise the relative attractiveness of different segments, and identify differences in key success factors among them;
- classify the firms within an industry into *strategic groups* based on similarities in their strategies.

Extending the Five Forces Framework

Does Industry Matter?

Porter's five forces of competition framework has been subject to two main attacks. Some have criticized its theoretical foundations, arguing that the structure-conduct-performance approach to industrial organization that underlies it lacks rigor (especially when compared with the logical robustness of game theory).

Others have noted its empirical weaknesses. It appears that industry environment is a relatively minor determinant of a firm's profitability. Studies of the sources of interfirm differences in profitability have produced very different results (see Table 4.1)—but all acknowledge that industry factors account for a minor part (less than 20%) of variation in return on assets among firms.

My defense of industry analysis in general, and the Porter framework in particular, is that it is very useful for understanding competition, for predicting profitability changes and for guiding strategy formulation. Nevertheless, these criticisms also point to the need to go further in our industry analysis. First, we must understand more deeply the determinants of competitive behavior between companies and how competition influences industry-level profitability. We need to reconsider the relationship between industry structure and competition and explore more rigorous and sophisticated approaches to analyzing competition—game theory in particular. Second, we need to disaggregate broad industry groupings and examine competition at the level of particular segments and strategic groupings of firms. Let us begin by considering the possibilities of extending the Porter framework.

Complements: A Missing Force in the Porter Model?

The Porter framework identifies the suppliers of substitute goods and services as one of the forces of competition that reduces the profit available to the firms within an industry. However, economic theory identifies two types of relationship between different products: *substitutes* and *complements*. While the presence of substitutes

TABLE 4.1 What determines interfirm differences in profitability? The role of industry

	Percentage of variance in firms' return on assets explained by:		
	Industry effects (%)	Firm effects (%)	Unexplained variance (%)
Schmalensee (1985)	19.6	0.6	79.9
Rumelt (1991)	4.0	44.2	44.8
McGahan & Porter (1997)	18.7	31.7	48.4
Hawawini et al. (2003)	8.1	35.8	52.0
Roquebert et al. (1996)	10.2	55.0	32.0
Misangyi et al. (2006)	7.6	43.8	n.a.

Notes:
"Firm effects" combine business unit and corporate effects. The rows do not sum to 100% because other sources of variance are not reported.

***Sources*:**
R. Schmalensee, "Do markets differ much?" *American Economic Review* 75 (1985): 341–51;
R. P. Rumelt, "How much does industry matter?" *Strategic Management Journal* 12 (1991): 167–85;
A. M. McGahan and M. E. Porter, "How much does industry matter, really?" *Strategic Management Journal* 18 (1997): 15–30; G. Hawawini, V. Subramanian, and P. Verdin, "Is Performance Driven by Industry or Firm-Specific Factors? A New Look at the Evidence," *Strategic Management Journal* 24 (2003): 1–16; J. A. Roquebert, R. L. Phillips, and P. A. Westfall, "Markets vs. Management: What 'Drives' Profitability?" *Strategic Management Journal* 17 (1996): 653–64; V. F. Misangyi, H. Elms, T. Greckhamer and J. A. Lepine, "A New Perspective on a Fundamental Debate: A Multilevel Approach to Industry, Corporate and Business Unit Effects," *Strategic Management Journal* 27 (2006): 571–90.

reduces the value of a product, complements increase value. The availability of ink cartridges for my printer transforms its value to me.

Given the importance of complements to most products—the value of my car depends on the availability of gasoline, insurance, and repair services—our analysis of the competitive environment needs to take them into account. The simplest way is to add a sixth force to Porter's framework (see Figure 4.1).[1]

Complements have the opposite effect to substitutes. While substitutes reduce the value of an industry's product, complements increase it. Indeed, where products are close complements, they have little value to customers individually—customers value the whole system. But how is the value shared between the producers of the different complementary products? Bargaining power and its deployment are the key. During the early 1990s, Nintendo earned huge profits from its video game consoles. Although most of the revenue and consumer value was in the software—mostly supplied by independent developers—Nintendo was able to appropriate most of the profit potential of the entire system through establishing dominance over the games developers. Nintendo used its leadership in the console market and ownership of the console operating system to enforce restrictive developer licenses to software producers of games, and maintain tight control over the manufacture and distribution of games cartridges (from which Nintendo earned a hefty royalty).[2]

FIGURE 4.1 Five forces, or six?

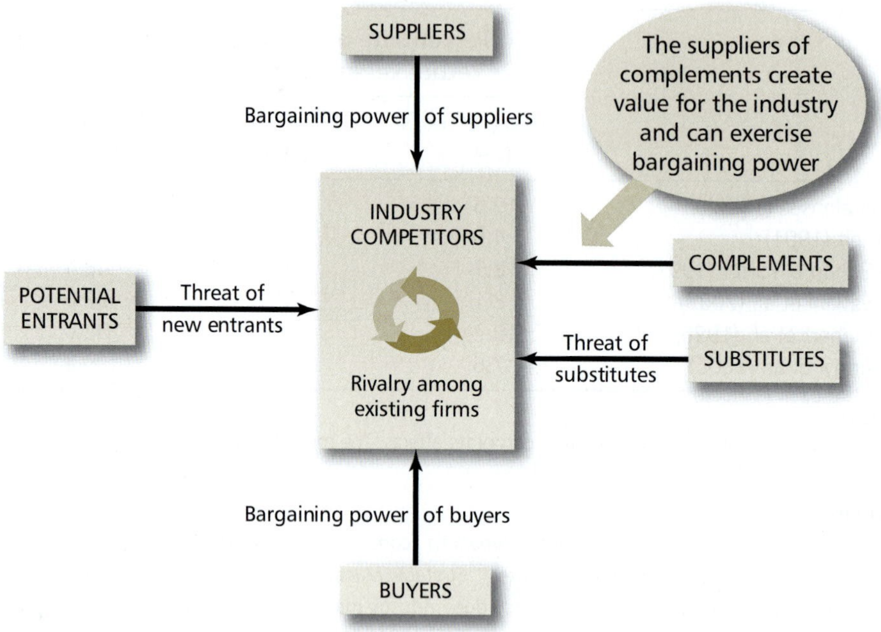

In PCs, by contrast, power has been on the side of the software suppliers—Microsoft in particular. IBM's adoption of open architecture meant that Microsoft Windows became a proprietary standard, while PCs were gradually reduced to commodity status. This is a very different situation from video games, where hardware suppliers keep proprietary control over their operating systems.

Where two products are complements to one another, profit will accrue to the supplier that builds the stronger market position and reduces the value contributed by the other. How is this done? The key is to achieve monopolization, differentiation and shortage of supply in one's own product, while encouraging competition, commoditization and excess capacity in the production of the complementary product. IBM is attempting to shift the balance of power between hardware and software producers through its promotion of Linux and other open-source software programs. By pressing to differentiate its hardware products while commoditizing software, it can reduce the power of Microsoft and garner a bigger share of the profit returns from systems of hardware and software.[3]

Dynamic Competition: Creative Destruction and Hypercompetition

The notion that industry structure is relatively stable and determines competitive behavior in a predictable way ignores the dynamic forces of innovation and entrepreneurship that transform industry structure. Joseph Schumpeter viewed competition as a "perennial gale of creative destruction" through which favorable industry structures—monopoly in particular—contain the seeds of their own destruction by attracting incursions from new and established firms deploying innovatory strategies and innovatory products to unseat incumbents.[4]

This view of Schumpeter (and the "Austrian school" of economics) that competition is a dynamic process that continually reformulates industry structure suggests that it may be more appropriate to view structure as the outcome of competitive behavior rather than vice versa.[5] The key consideration is the speed of structural change in the industry—if structural transformation is rapid, the five forces model has limited predictive value.

In practice, Schumpeter's process of "creative destruction" tends to be more of a breeze than a gale. In established industries entry occurs so slowly that profits are undermined only gradually,[6] while changes in industrial concentration tend to be slow.[7] One survey observed: "the picture of the competitive process . . . is, to say the least, sluggish in the extreme."[8] As a result, both at the firm and the industry level, profits tend to be highly persistent in the long run.[9]

What about recent decades? Has accelerating technological change and intensifying international competition reinforced the processes of "creative destruction"? Rich D'Aveni argues that a general feature of industries today is *hypercompetition*: "intense and rapid competitive moves, in which competitors must move quickly to build [new] advantages and erode the advantages of their rivals."[10] If industries are hypercompetitive, their structures are likely to be less stable than in the past, superior profitability will tend to be transitory and the only route to sustained superior performance is through continually recreating and renewing competitive advantage.

Despite the plausibility of this thesis and everyday observations that markets are becoming more volatile and market leadership more tenuous, systematic evidence of this trend is ambiguous. One large-scale statistical study concluded: "The heterogeneity and volatility of competitive advantage in U.S. manufacturing industries has steadily and astonishingly increased since 1950. Industry structures are destabilizing. These results suggest that a shift towards hypercompetition has indeed occurred."[11] This volatility is observed not just in technology-intensive industries and not just in manufacturing industries.[12] However, another study found a "lack of widespread evidence . . . that markets are more unstable now than in the recent past."[13]

The Contribution of Game Theory

Central to the criticisms of Porter's five forces as a static framework is its failure to take full account of competitive interactions among firms. In Chapter 1, we noted that the essence of strategic competition is the interaction among players, such that the decisions made by any one player are dependent on the actual and anticipated decisions of the other players. By relegating competition to a mediating variable that links industry structure with profitability, the five forces analysis offers little insight into competition as a process of interactive decision making by rival firms. Game theory allows us to model this competitive interaction. In particular, it offers two especially valuable contributions to strategic management:

- *It permits the framing of strategic decisions.* Apart from any theoretical value of the theory of games, game theory provides a structure, a set of concepts, and a terminology that allows us to describe a competitive situation in terms of:

- identity of the players;
- specification of each player's options;
- specification of the payoffs from every combination of options;
- the sequencing of decisions using game trees.

This permits us to understand the structure of the competitive situation and facilitates a systematic, rational approach to decision making.

- *It can predict the outcome of competitive situations and identify optimal strategic choices.* Through the insight that it offers into situations of competition and bargaining, game theory can predict the equilibrium outcomes of competitive situations and the consequences of strategic moves by any one player. Game theory provides penetrating insights into central issues of strategy that go well beyond pure intuition. Simple game models (for example, "prisoners' dilemma") predict cooperative versus competitive outcomes, whereas more complex games permit analysis of the effects of reputation,[14] deterrence,[15] information[16] and commitment[17]—especially within the context of multiperiod games. Particularly important for practicing managers, game theory can indicate strategies for improving the structure and outcome of the game through manipulating the payoffs to the different players.[18]

During the past two decades, game theory has provided illuminating insights into a wide variety of competitive situations, including the Cuban missile crisis of 1962,[19] rivalry between Boeing and Airbus,[20] NASCAR race tactics,[21] auctions of airwave spectrum,[22] and the reasons why evolution has conferred such magnificent tails upon male peacocks.[23]

Cooperation

One of the key merits of game theory is its ability to encompass both competition and cooperation. A key deficiency of the five forces framework is in viewing interfirm relations as exclusively competitive in nature. The central message of Adam Brandenburger and Barry Nalebuff's book *Co-opetition* is recognizing the competitive/cooperative duality of business relationships.[24] While some relationships are predominantly competitive (Coca-Cola and Pepsi-Cola) and others are predominantly cooperative (Intel and Microsoft), there is no simple dichotomy between competition and cooperation: all business relationships combine elements of both. For all their intense rivalry, Coca-Cola and PepsiCo cooperate on multiple fronts, including common policies on sales of soda drinks within schools, environmental issues and health concerns. There is also some evidence of coordination in pricing and product introductions.[25] Exxon and Shell have battled for over a century for leadership of the world petroleum industry. At the same time, Exxon and Shell cooperate in a number of joint ventures. The desire of competitors to cluster together—antique dealers in London's Bermondsey

Market and movie studios in Hollywood—points to the common interests of competing firms in growing the size of their market and developing its infrastructure.

In many business relationships, competition results in an inferior outcome for the players compared with cooperation. The prisoners' dilemma game analyzes this predicament (see Strategy Capsule 4.1).

STRATEGY CAPSULE 4.1

The Prisoners' Dilemma

The classic prisoners' dilemma game involves a pair of crime suspects who are arrested and interrogated separately. The dilemma is that each will "rat" on the other with the result that both end up in jail despite the fact that, if both had remained silent, both would have been released for lack of evidence.

The dilemma arises in almost all competitive situations—everyone could be better off with collusion. Consider competition between Coca-Cola and Pepsi-Cola in Ukraine where each has the choice of spending big or small on advertising. The matrix below shows the payoffs to each firm.

COCA-COLA (Payoffs in $ millions)

PEPSI		Small Advertising Budget	Big Advertising Budget
	Small Advertising Budget	10 (Pepsi) / 10 (Coke)	−2 (Pepsi) / 15 (Coke)
	Big Advertising Budget	15 (Pepsi) / −2 (Coke)	4 (Pepsi) / 4 (Coke)

In each cell, the lower-left number is the payoff to Pepsi; the upper-right the payoff to Coke.

Clearly, the best solution for both firms is for them to each restrain their advertising expenditure (the upper left cell). However, in the absence of cooperation, the outcome for both firms is to adopt big budgets (the lower right cell)—the reason being that each will fear that any restraint will be countered by the rival seeking advantage by shifting to a big advertising budget. The resulting maxi-min choice of strategies (each company chooses the strategy that maximizes the minimum payoff) is a Nash equilibrium: no player can increase his/her payoff by a unilateral change in strategy. Even if collusion can be achieved, it will be unstable because of the incentives for cheating—a constant problem for OPEC, where the member countries agree quotas but then cheat on them.

How can a firm escape from such prisoners' dilemmas? One answer is to change a one-period game (single transaction) into a repeated game.

In the case of the supplier–buyer relationship, moving from a spot transaction to a long-term vendor relationship gives the supplier the incentive to offer a better quality product and the buyer to offer a price that offers the seller a satisfactory return. In the case of price competition, markets dominated by two or three suppliers tend to converge toward patterns of price leadership where price competition is avoided.

A second solution is to change the payoffs through deterrence. In the classic prisoners' dilemma, the Mafia shifts the equilibrium from the suspects confessing to their not talking by using draconian reprisals to enforce its "code of silence". Similarly, if both Coca-Cola and Pepsi were to threaten one another with an aggressive price cuts should the other seek advantage through a big advertising budget, this could shift the equilibrium to the top left cell.

Sources: A. Dixit and B. Nalebuff, "Prisoners' Dilemma," *The Concise Encyclopedia of Economics* (www.econlib.org/library/Enc/PrisonersDilemma.html); "Prisoners' Dilemma," *Stanford Encyclopedia of Philosophy* (http://plato.stanford.edu/entries/prisoner-dilemma/).

Deterrence

As we saw in Strategy Capsule 4.1, one way of changing a game's equilibrium is through *deterrence*. The principle behind deterrence is to impose costs on the other players for actions deemed to be undesirable. By establishing the certainty that deserters would be shot, the British army provided a strong incentive to its troops to participate in advances on heavily fortified German trenches during the First World War.

The key to the effectiveness of any deterrent is that it must be credible. The problem here is that if administering the deterrent is costly or unpleasant for the threatening party, the deterrent is not credible. When King of Shaves (owned by KMI Ltd; annual sales $90 million) entered the U.K. razor market, Gillette might have threatened it with a price cut. But would such a threat have been credible? Once King of Shaves had entered, Gillette's dominant market share meant that a price cut would inflict more damage on itself than on rivals.[26] Investing in excess capacity can be an effective means of discouraging entry. Prior to the expiration of its NutraSweet patents, Monsanto invested heavily in unneeded plant capacity to deter manufacturers of generic aspartame.[27] Conversely, in compact disks, the reluctance of the dominant firm (Philips) to invest heavily in new capacity to meet growing demand encouraged a wave of new entrants.[28]

Deterrence has provided a central theme in international relations. The nuclear arms race between the U.S. and the then Soviet Union was based on the logic of "mutual assured destruction." However, the ability for deterrence to produce a stable, peaceful equilibrium depends on the willingness of the adversaries to be deterred. A central weakness of George W. Bush's "war on terror" was that ideologically motivated terrorists are not susceptible to deterrence.[29]

Commitment

For deterrence to be effective it must be credible, which means being backed by commitment. Commitment involves the elimination of strategic options: "binding an organization to a future course of action."[30] When Hernan Cortes destroyed his ships on arrival in Mexico in 1519, he communicated, both to Montezuma and his men, that there was no alternative to conquest of the Aztec empire. Once Airbus had decided to build its A380 superjumbo, it was critical to signal its commitment to the project. During 2000–2 Airbus spent heavily on advertising the plane, even before completing the design phase, in order encourage airlines to place orders and discourage Boeing from developing a rival plane.

These commitments to aggressive competition have been described as "hard commitments." A company may also make commitments that moderate competition; these are called "soft commitments."[31] The airlines' frequent-flier programs commit the airlines to redeem miles flown with free tickets. They also signal to other airlines a willingness to avoid price competition and indicate less vulnerability to a rival's price cuts. How these different types of commitment affect the profitability of the firm making the commitment depends on the type of game being played. Where companies compete on price, game theory shows that they tend to match one another's price changes.[32] Hence, under price adjustments, hard commitments (such as a commitment to cut price) tend to have a negative profit impact and soft commitments (such as a commitment to raise prices) have a positive impact. Conversely, where companies compete on output, game theory shows that increases in output by one firm results in output reductions by the other.[33] Hence, under quantity adjustments, a hard commitment (for example, a commitment to build new plants) will tend to have a positive effect on the committing firm's profitability because it will tend to be met by other firms reducing their output.[34]

Changing the Structure of the Game

Creative strategies can change the structure of the competitive game. A company may seek to change the structure of the industry within which it is competing in order to increase the profit potential of the industry or to appropriate a greater share of the available profit. Thus, establishing alliances and agreements with competitors can increase the value of the game by increasing the size of the market and building joint strength against possible entrants. There may be many opportunities for converting win-lose (or even lose-lose) games into win-win games. A cooperative solution was found to the 1997 bidding war between Norfolk Southern and CSX for control of Conrail, for example. The bidding war was terminated when the two firms agreed to cooperate in acquiring and dismembering Conrail. [35]

In some cases, it may be advantageous for a firm to create competition for itself. By offering second-sourcing licenses to AMD, Intel gave up its potential monopoly over its x86 microprocessors. Although Intel was creating competition for itself, it was also encouraging the adoption of the x86 chip by computer manufacturers (including IBM) who were concerned about overdependence on Intel. As we shall see in Chapter 11, standards battles often involve the deliberate sacrificing of potential monopoly positions by the main contestants.

Signaling

Competitive reactions depend on how the competitor perceives its rival's initiative. The term *signaling* is used to describe the selective communication of information to competitors (or customers) designed to influence their perception and hence to provoke or avoid certain types of reaction.[36] The use of misinformation is well developed in military intelligence. In 1944, Allied deception was so good that even during the D-Day landings in Normandy, the Germans believed that the main invasion would occur near Calais. But, as noted in discussing deterrence, information on its own is not enough: signals need to be credible. Thus, Allied misinformation concerning the invasion of Europe included the marshaling of a phantom army designed to convince the German military that the Normandy invasion was merely a diversionary mission.

The credibility of threats is critically dependent on reputation.[37] Even though carrying out threats against rivals is costly and depresses short-term profitability, exercising such threats can build a reputation for aggressiveness that deters competitors in the future. The benefits of building a reputation for aggressiveness may be particularly great for diversified companies where reputation can be transferred from one market to another.[38] Hence, Procter & Gamble's protracted market share wars in disposable diapers and household detergents have established a reputation for toughness that protects it from competitive attacks in other markets.

Signaling may also be used to communicate a desire to cooperate. Price announcements can facilitate collusive pricing among firms.[39]

Is Game Theory Useful?

The value of game theory to strategic management has generated lively debate. For economists this seems paradoxical because to them game theory *is* the theory of strategy. The great virtue of game theory is its rigor. In microeconomics, the game theory revolution of the past quarter-century has established the analysis of markets and firm behavior on a much more secure theoretical foundation.

However, the price of mathematical rigor has been limited applicability to real world situations. Game theory provides clear prediction in highly stylized situations involving few external variables and highly restrictive assumptions. The result is a mathematically sophisticated body of theory that suffers from unrealistic assumptions, lack of generality, and an analysis of dynamic situations through a sequence of static equilibriums. When applied to more complex (and more realistic) situations, game theory frequently results in either no equilibrium or multiple equilibriums, and outcomes that are highly sensitive to small changes in initial assumptions. In general, game theory has not developed to the point where it permits us to model real business situations in a level of detail that can generate precise predictions.[40]

In its empirical applications, game theory has done a much better job of explaining the past than of predicting the future. In diagnosing Nintendo's domination of the video games industry in the 1980s, Monsanto's efforts to prolong NutraSweet's market leadership beyond the expiration of its patents, or Airbus's wresting of market leadership from Boeing, game theory provides penetrating insight into the competitive situation and deep understanding of the rationale behind the strategies deployed. However, in predicting outcomes and designing strategies, game theory has been much less impressive—the use of game theory by U.S. and European governments to auction wireless spectrum has produced mixed results.[41]

So, where can game theory assist us in designing successful strategies? As with all our theories and frameworks, game theory is useful not because it gives us answers but because it can help us understand business situations. Game theory provides a set of tools that allows us to structure our view of competitive interaction. By identifying the players in a game, the decision choices available to each, and the implications of each combination of decisions, we have a systematic framework for exploring the dynamics of competition. Most importantly, by describing the structure of the game we are playing, we have a basis for suggesting ways of changing the game and thinking through the likely outcomes of such changes.

Game theory continues its rapid development and, although it is still a long way from providing the central theoretical foundation for strategic management, we draw upon it in several places in this book—especially in exploring competitive dynamics in highly concentrated markets. However, our emphasis in strategy formulation will be less on achieving advantage through influencing the behavior of competitors and much more on transforming competitive games through building positions of unilateral competitive advantage. The competitive market situations with which we shall be dealing will, for the most part, be different from those considered by game theory. Game theory typically deals with competitive situations with closely matched players where each has a similar range of strategic options (typically relating to price changes, advertising budgets, capacity decisions, and new product introductions). The outcome of these games is highly dependent on order of moves, signals, bluffs, and threats. Our emphasis will be less on managing competitive interactions and more on establishing competitive advantage through exploiting uniqueness.

Competitor Analysis

In highly concentrated industries, the dominant feature of a company's competitive environment is likely to be the behavior of its closest rivals. In household detergents, Unilever's industry environment is dominated by the strategy of Procter & Gamble. The same is true in soft drinks (Coca-Cola and Pepsi), jet engines (GE, United Technologies, and Rolls-Royce), and business news periodicals (*Business Week*, *Fortune*, and *Forbes*). Similar circumstances exist in more local markets. The competitive environment of my local Costa coffee shop is dominated by the presence of Starbucks across the road. Game theory provides a theoretical apparatus for analyzing competitive interaction between small numbers of rivals but, for everyday business situations, a less formal and more empirically based approach to predicting competitors' behavior may be more useful. Let us examine how information about competitors can help us to predict their behavior.

Competitive Intelligence

Competitive intelligence involves the systematic collection and analysis of public information about rivals for informing decision making. It has three main purposes:

- to forecast competitors' future strategies and decisions;
- to predict competitors' likely reactions to a firm's strategic initiatives;
- to determine how competitors' behavior can be influenced to make it more favorable.

For all three purposes, the key requirement is to understand competitors in order to predict their responses to environmental changes and our own competitive moves. To understand competitors, it is important to be informed about them. Competitive intelligence is a growth field, with a flood of recent books,[42] a dedicated journal,[43] specialist consulting firms, and professional associations.[44] About one-quarter of large U.S. corporations have set up competitive intelligence units.

The boundary between legitimate competitive intelligence and illegal industrial espionage is not always clear. The distinction between public and private information can be uncertain. Trade secrets law does not offer clear guidance. Well publicized cases of information theft include Procter & Gamble's acquisition of documents concerning Unilever's hair care business that had been removed from Unilever dumpsters[45] and the $100 million fine levied on the McLaren-Mercedes Formula One team for possessing confidential technical information belonging to Ferrari.[46]

A Framework for Predicting Competitor Behavior

Competitive intelligence is not simply about collecting information. The problem is likely to be too much rather than too little information. The key is a systematic approach that makes it clear what information is required and for what purposes it will be used. The objective is to *understand* one's rival. A characteristic of great generals from Hannibal to Patton has been their ability to go beyond military intelligence and to "get inside the heads" of their opposing commanders. Michael Porter proposes a four-part framework for predicting competitor behavior (see Figure 4.2).

- *Competitor's current strategy*. To predict how a rival will behave in the future, we must understand how that rival is competing at present. As we noted in Chapter 1, identifying a firm's strategy requires looking at what the

FIGURE 4.2 A framework for competitor analysis

company says and what it does. (See "Identifying a Company's Strategy" in Chapter 1). The key is to link the content of top management communication (with investors, the media, and financial analysts) with the evidence of strategic actions—particularly those that involve commitment of resources. For both sources of information, company web sites are invaluable.

- *Competitor's objectives.* To forecast how a competitor might change its strategy, we must identify its goals. A key issue is whether a company is driven by financial goals or market goals. A company whose primary goal is attaining market share is likely to be much more aggressive a competitor than one that is mainly interested in profitability. The willingness of the U.S. automobile and consumer electronics producers to cede market share to Japanese competitors was partly a result of their preoccupation with short-term profitability. By comparison, companies like Procter & Gamble and Coca-Cola are obsessed with market share and tend to react aggressively when rivals step on their turf. The most difficult competitors can be those that are not subject to profit disciplines at all—state-owned enterprises in particular. The level of current performance in relation to the competitor's objectives determines the likelihood of strategy change. The more a company is satisfied with present performance, the more likely it is to continue with its present strategy. But if performance is falling well short of target, radical strategic change, possibly accompanied by a change in top management, is likely.
- *Competitor's assumptions about the industry.* A competitor's strategic decisions are conditioned by its perceptions of itself and its environment. These perceptions are guided by the beliefs that senior managers hold about their industry and the success factors within it. Evidence suggests that not only do these systems of belief tend to be stable over time, they also tend to converge among the firms within an industry: what J. C. Spender refers to as *industry recipes*."[47] Industry recipes may engender "blindspots" that limit the capacity of a firm—even an entire industry—to respond to an external threat. During the 1960s, the Big Three U.S. automobile manufacturers firmly believed that small cars were unprofitable. This belief was partly a product of their own overhead allocation procedures. The result was a willingness to yield the fastest-growing segment of the U.S. automobile market to imports. The complacency of British and U.S. motorcycle manufacturers in the face of Japanese competition reflected similar beliefs (see Strategy Capsule 4.2).
- *Competitor's resources and capabilities.* Evaluating the likelihood and seriousness of a competitor's potential challenge requires assessing the strength of that competitor's resources and capabilities. If our rival has a massive cash pile, it would be unwise for our company to unleash a price war by initiating price cuts. Conversely, if we direct our competitive initiative towards our rivals' weaknesses, it may be difficult for them to respond. Richard Branson's Virgin Group has launched a host of entrepreneurial new ventures, typically in markets dominated by a powerful incumbent—British Airways in airlines, EMI in music, Vodafone in wireless telecommunications. Branson's strategy has been to adopt innovative forms of differentiation that are difficult for established incumbents to respond to.

STRATEGY CAPSULE 4.2

Motorcycle Myopia

During the 1960s, BSA was the leading motorcycle manufacturer in Britain, while Harley-Davidson was the leader in the U.S. During the 1960s, both markets experienced increased import penetration from Japan, but given the emphasis by Honda, Suzuki, and Yamaha on smaller motorcycles, the Japanese challenge was largely discounted.

Eric Turner, chairman of BSA Ltd (manufacturer of Triumph and BSA motorcycles), commented in 1965:

> *The success of Honda, Suzuki, and Yamaha has been jolly good for us. People start out by buying one of the low-priced Japanese jobs. They get to enjoy the fun and exhilaration of the open road and they frequently end up buying one of our more powerful and expensive machines.*

Similar complacency was expressed by William Davidson, president of Harley-Davidson:

> *Basically, we do not believe in the lightweight market. We believe that motorcycles are sports vehicles, not transportation vehicles. Even if a man says he bought a motorcycle for transportation, it's generally for leisure time use. The lightweight motorcycle is only supplemental. Back around World War I, a number of companies came out with lightweight bikes. We came out with one ourselves. We came out with another in 1947 and it just didn't go anywhere. We have seen what happens to these small sizes.*

By the end of the 1970s, BSA and Triumph had ceased production and Harley-Davidson was barely surviving. The world motorcycle industry, including the large bike segments, was dominated by the Japanese.

Sources: *Advertising Age* (December 27, 1965); *Forbes* (September 15, 1966); Richard T. Pascale, *Honda A* (Harvard Business School Case No. 9-384-049, 1983).

Segmentation Analysis[48]

The Uses of Segmentation

In Chapter 3 we noted the difficulty of drawing industry boundaries and the need to define industries both broadly and narrowly according to the types of question we are seeking to answer. Initially it may be convenient to define industries broadly, but for a more detailed analysis of competition we need to focus on markets that are drawn more narrowly in terms of both products and geography. This process of disaggregating industries into specific markets we call *segmentation*.

Segmentation is particularly important if competition varies across the different submarkets within an industry such that some are more attractive than others. A company can avoid some of the problems of an unattractive industry by judicious segment selection. In the intensely competitive personal computer industry, Dell has used its highly flexible direct distribution system to target products, geographical areas, and customers that offer the best margins: "We cut the market and then cut it again, looking for the most profitable customers to serve," says CEO Kevin Rollins.[49] In the cut-throat tire industry, Pirelli has achieved superior margins by investing heavily in technology and focusing on high-performance tires for sports and luxury cars.[50]

Stages in Segmentation Analysis

The purpose of segmentation analysis is to identify attractive segments, to select strategies for different segments, and to determine how many segments to serve. The analysis proceeds in five stages (see Strategy Capsule 4.3 for a summary and application).

1 Identify Key Segmentation Variables The first stage of segmentation analysis is to determine the basis of segmentation. Segmentation decisions are essentially choices about which customers to serve and what to offer them: hence

STRATEGY CAPSULE 4.3

Segmenting the European Metal Can Industry

1. Identify key segmentation variables and categories.
   - Identify possible segmentation variables. Raw material, can design, can size, customer size, customer's industry, location.
   - Reduce the number of segmentation variables. Which are most significant? Which are closely correlated and can be combined? Type of can, customer industry, customer location.
   - Identify discrete categories for each segmentation variable. Type of can: steel three-piece, steel two-piece, aluminum two-piece, general cans, composite cans, aerosols. Type of customer: food processing, fruit juice, pet food, soft drink, toiletries, beer, oil. Location: France, Germany, Spain/Portugal, Italy, U.K., Benelux.
2. Construct a segmentation matrix.
3. Analyze segment attractiveness. Apply five forces analysis to individual segments.
4. Identify key success factors in each segment. Within each segment, how do customers choose, and what is needed to survive competition?
5. Analyze attractions of broad versus narrow segment scope.
   - What is the potential to share costs and transfer skills across segments?
   - How similar are key success factors between segments?
   - Are there benefits of segment specialization?

FIGURE 4.3 The basis for segmentation: the characteristics of buyers and products

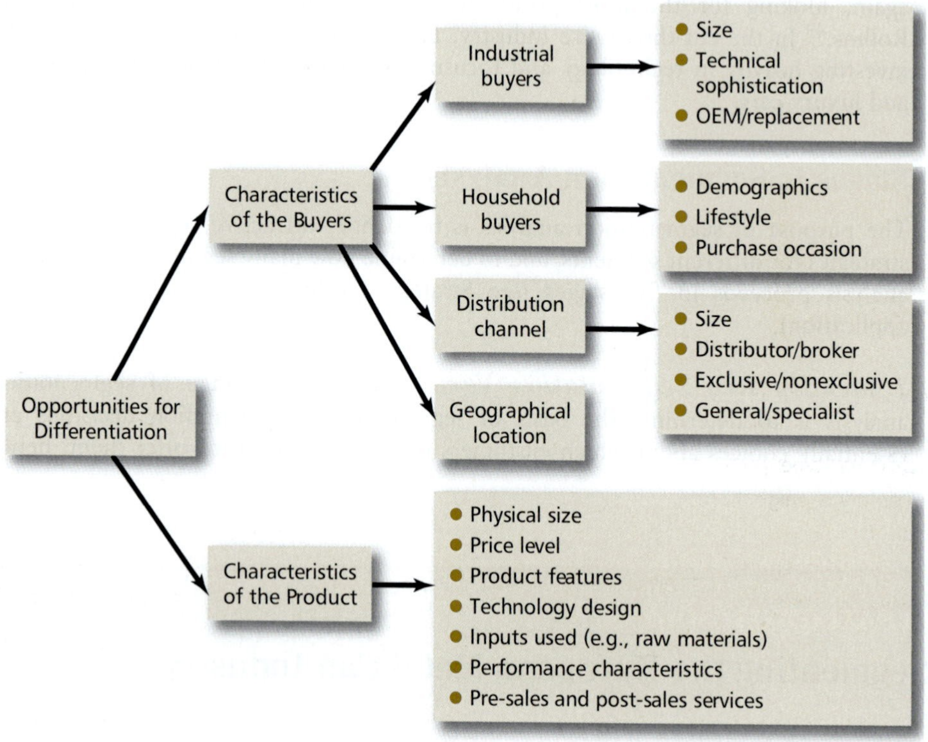

segmentation variables relate to the characteristics of customers and the product (see Figure 4.3). The most appropriate segmentation variables are those that partition the market most distinctly in terms of limits to substitution by customers (demand-side substitutability) and producers (supply-side substitutability). Price differentials are a good guide to market segments. Thus, in the auto industry, color is probably not a good segmentation variable (white and red Honda Civics sell at much the same price); size is a better segmentation variable (full-size cars sell at a price premium over subcompact cars). Typically, segmentation analysis generates far too many segmentation variables. For our analysis to be manageable, we need to reduce these to two or three. To do this we need to:

- Identify the most *strategically significant* segmentation variables. Which variables are most important in creating meaningful divisions in a market?
- Combine segmentation variables that are closely correlated. Thus, in the restaurant industry, price level, service level (waiter service/self-service), cuisine (fast-food/full meals), and alcohol license (wine served/soft drinks only) are likely to be closely related. We could use a single variable, restaurant type, with three categories—full-service restaurants, cafés, and fast-food outlets—as a proxy for all of these variables.

2 Construct a Segmentation Matrix Once the segmentation variables have been selected and discrete categories determined for each, the individual segments may be identified using a two- or three-dimensional matrix. Thus, the European metal container industry might be analyzed in a three-dimensional segmentation matrix (see Strategy Capsule 4.3), whereas the world automobile industry might be segmented simply by vehicle type and geographical region (see Strategy Capsule 4.4).

STRATEGY CAPSULE 4.4

Segmenting the World Automobile Market

A global automobile producer such as Ford or Toyota might segment the world auto market by product type and geography. A first-cut segmentation might be along the following lines:

To identify segments with the best profit prospects for the future, we need to understand why, in the past, some segments have been more profitable than others. For example, during the 1990s:

- The North American market for small cars was unprofitable due to many competitors (all the world's major auto producers were

REGIONS

PRODUCTS

	North America	Western Europe	Eastern Europe	Asia	Latin America	Australia & N.Z.	Africa
Luxury cars							
Full-size cars							
Mid-size cars							
Small cars							
Station wagons							
Minivans							
Sports cars							
Sport utility							
Pickup trucks							
Hybrids							

represented), lack of clear product differentiation, and customers' price sensitivity.

- Sport utility vehicles and passenger minivans were highly profitable segments due to strong demand relative to capacity, and comparatively few participants. However, the influx of companies into these segments has eroded margins.
- The luxury car segment is traditionally a high-margin segment due to few players, high product differentiation, and price insensitivity of buyers. However, new entry and excess capacity has increased competition.
- Hybrids have earned big margins due to few players and shortage of capacity relative to demand.

Once we understand the factors that determined segment profitability in the past, we can predict segment profitability in the future.

3 Analyze Segment Attractiveness Profitability within an industry segment is determined by the same structural forces that determine profitability within an industry as a whole. As a result, Porter's five forces of competition framework is equally effective in relation to a segment as to an entire industry. Strategy Capsule 4.4 points to some implications of a five forces analysis for certain segments of the world automobile industry.

There are, however, a few differences. First, when analyzing the pressure of competition from substitute products, we are concerned not only with substitutes from other industries but, more importantly, substitutes from other segments within the same industry. Second, when considering entry into the segment, the main source of entrants is likely to be producers established in other segments within the same industry. The barriers that protect a segment from firms located in other segments are called *barriers to mobility* to distinguish them from the *barriers to entry,* which protect the industry as a whole.[51] When barriers to mobility are low, then the superior returns of high-profit segments tend to be quickly eroded. Thus, the high margins earned on sport utility vehicles during the mid-1990s were competed away once most of the world's main auto producers had entered the segment.

Segmentation analysis can also be useful in identifying unexploited opportunities in an industry. For example, a segmentation matrix of the restaurant industry in a town or locality might reveal a number of empty segments. Companies that have built successful strategies by concentrating on unoccupied segments include Wal-Mart (discount stores in small towns), Enterprise Rent-A-Car (suburban locations), and Edward Jones (full-service brokerage for small investors in smaller cities). This can be an intermediate step in the quest for "blue oceans"—new markets untainted by competition.[52]

4 Identify the Segment's Key Success Factors (KSFs) Differences in competitive structure and in customer preferences between segments result in different key success factors. By analyzing buyers' purchase criteria and the basis of competition within individual segments, we can identify key success factors for individual segments. For example, we can segment the U.S. bicycle market into high-price enthusiasts' bikes sold through specialist bike stores. Key success factors in the enthusiast segment are technology, reputation and dealer relations. In the economy segment, KSFs are low-cost manufacture (most likely in China) and a supply contract with a leading retail chain.

5 Select Segment Scope Finally, a firm needs to decide whether it wishes to be a segment specialist, or compete across multiple segments. The advantages of a broad over a narrow segment focus depend on two main factors: similarity of key success factors and the presence of shared costs. If key success factors are different across segments, a firm will need to deploy distinct strategies and may have difficulties in drawing upon the same capabilities. Harley-Davidson's attempt to compete in sports motorcycles through its Buell brand has met limited success.

The ability to share costs across different segments has been a major factor in automobiles where very few specialist manufacturers survive and most of the world's main automakers offer a full range of vehicles allowing cost economies from common platforms and components.

Vertical Segmentation: Profit Pools

Segmentation is usually horizontal—markets are disaggregated according to products, geography and customer groups. An industry can also be segmented vertically by identifying different value chain activities. Bain & Company show that profitability varies greatly between different vertical activities and proposes *profit pool mapping* as a technique for analyzing the vertical structure of profitability.[53] For example, in the U.S. automobile industry, downstream activities such as finance, leasing, insurance, and service and repair are much more profitable than manufacturing (see Figure 4.4). During 2003-8, Ford and GM's sole source of profits were financial services to dealers and customers.

FIGURE 4.4 The U.S. auto industry profit pool

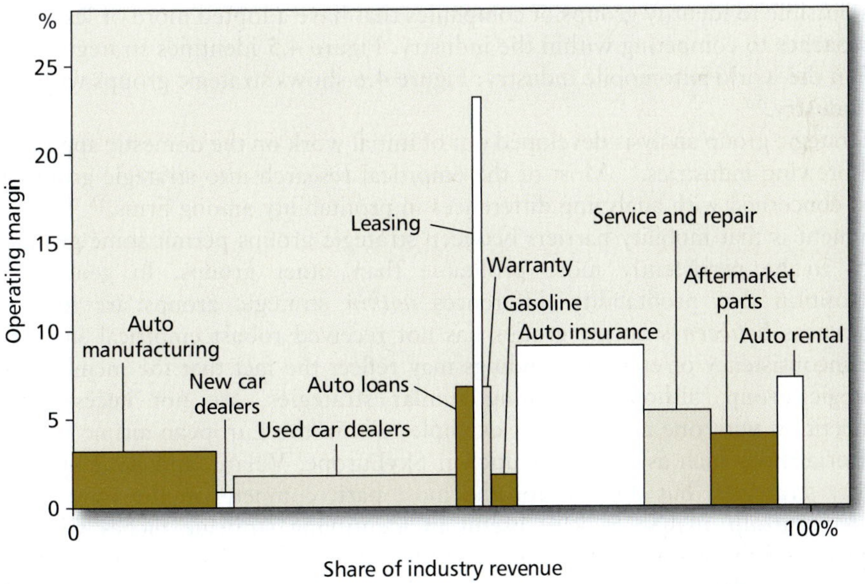

Source:
O. Gadiesh and J. L. Gilbert, "Profit Pools: A Fresh Look at Strategy," ***Harvard Business Review*** (May-June 1998): 142. © 1998 by the Harvard Business School Publishing Corporation, all rights reserved. Reproduced with permission.

To map an industry's profit pool, Bain & Company identifies four steps:

1 *Define the pool's boundaries.* What is the range of value-adding activities that your business sector encompasses? It may be useful to look upstream and downstream beyond conventional industry boundaries.

2 *Estimate the pool's overall size.* Total industry profit may be estimated by applying the average margin earned by a sample of companies to an estimate of industry total revenues.

3 *Estimate profit for each value chain activity in the pool.* Here is the key challenge. It requires gathering data from companies that are "pure players"—specialized in the single value chain activity—and disaggregating data for "mixed players"—those performing multiple activities.

4 *Check and reconcile the calculations.* Compare the aggregation of profits in each activity (stage 3) with the total for the industry (stage 2).

Strategic Groups

Whereas segmentation analysis concentrates on the characteristics of markets as the basis for disaggregating industries, strategic group analysis segments an industry on the basis of the strategies of the member firms. A strategic group is "the group of firms in an industry following the same or a similar strategy along the strategic dimensions."[54] These strategic dimensions might include product range, geographical breadth, choice of distribution channels, level of product quality, degree of vertical integration, choice of technology and so on. By selecting the most important strategic dimensions and locating each firm in the industry along them, it is possible to identify groups of companies that have adopted more or less similar approaches to competing within the industry. Figure 4.5 identifies strategic groups within the world automobile industry; Figure 4.6 shows strategic groups within the oil industry.[55]

Strategic group analysis developed out of initial work on the domestic appliance[56] and brewing industries.[57] Most of the empirical research into strategic groups has been concerned with analyzing differences in profitability among firms.[58] The basic argument is that mobility barriers between strategic groups permit some groups of firms to be persistently more profitable than other groups. In general, the proposition that profitability differences *within* strategic groups are less than differences *between* strategic groups has not received robust empirical support.[59] The inconsistency of empirical findings may reflect the fact that the members of a strategic group, although pursuing similar strategies, are not necessarily in competition with one another. For example, within the European airline industry, budget airlines such as EasyJet, BalticAir, SkyEurope, Volare, and Ryanair pursue similar strategies, but do not, for the most part, compete on the same routes. Strategic group analysis is very useful in identifying strategic niches within an industry and the strategic positioning of different firms; it is less useful as a tool for analyzing interfirm profitability differences.[60]

FIGURE 4.5 Strategic groups within the world automobile industry

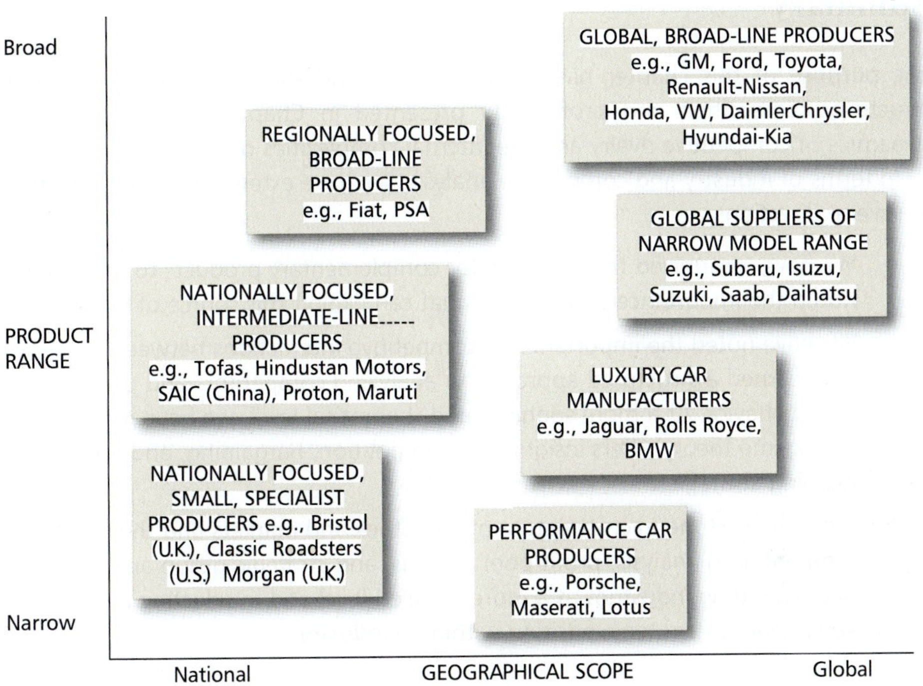

FIGURE 4.6 Strategic groups within the world petroleum industry

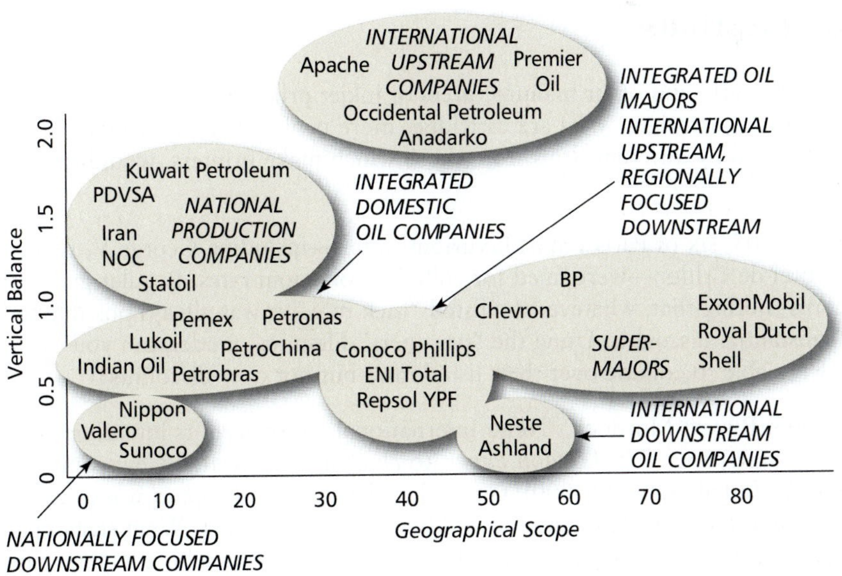

Summary

The purpose of this chapter has been to go beyond the basic analysis of industry structure, competition and profitability presented in Chapter 3, and consider the dynamics of competitive rivalry and the internal complexities of industries.

In terms of industry and competitive analysis, we have extended our strategy tool kit in several directions:

- We have recognized the potential for complementary products to add value and noted the importance of strategies that can exploit this source of value.
- We have noted the importance of competitive interactions between close rivals and learned a structured approach to analyzing competitors and predicting their behavior. At a more sophisticated theoretical level, we have recognized how game theory offers insight into competition, bargaining, and the design of winning strategies.
- We examined the microstructure of industries and markets and the value of segmentation analysis, profit pool analysis, and strategic group analysis in understanding industries at a more detailed level and in selecting an advantageous strategic position within an industry.

Self-Study Questions

1 HP, Canon, Lexmark, and other manufacturers of inkjet printers make most of their profits on the sales of ink cartridges. Why are cartridges more profitable than printers? If cartridges were manufactured by different firms from those which make printers, would the situation be different?

2 In November 2005, six of Paris's most luxurious hotels—including George V, Le Bristol, the Ritz, and Hotel de Crillon—were fined for colluding on room rates. Regular guests showed little concern—noting that, whatever the listed "rack rate," it was always possible to negotiate substantial discounts. Using the "prisoners' dilemma" model, can you explain why the hotels were able to collude over their listed rates but not over discounts?

3 In August 2006, Rupert Murdoch's News International announced its intention of launching a free evening newspaper, *The London Paper*, to challenge Associated Newspapers' London *Evening Standard* (daily sales 390 000). Given that the *Evening Standard* was already believed to be loss making, the new competition could be fatal for the paper. What steps might Associated Newspapers take to deter News International from launching its new paper, and if it goes ahead with the launch, what would Associated Newspapers' best response be?

4 During 2007–9, the Nintendo Wii established leadership over the Sony PS3 and Microsoft Xbox360 in the market for video game consoles. Unlike Sony and Microsoft, Nintendo is completely dependent upon the video games industry for its revenues. How might Nintendo use the competitor analysis framework outlined in Figure 4.2 to predict the likely reactions of Sony and Microsoft to its market success?

5 How would you segment the restaurant market in your home town? How would you advise someone thinking of starting a new restaurant which segments might be most attractive in terms of profit potential?

Notes

1 A. Brandenburger and B. Nalebuff, *Co-opetition* (New York: Doubleday, 1996) propose an alternative framework, the *value net*, for analyzing the impact of complements.

2 See A. Brandenburger and B. Nalebuff, "The Right Game: Use Game Theory to Shape Strategy," *Harvard Business Review* (July–August, 1995): 63-4 and A. Brandenburger, J. Kou and M. Burnett, *Power Play (A): Nintendo in 8-bit Video Games* (Harvard Business School Case No. 9-795-103, 1995).

3 C. Baldwin, S. O'Mahony and J. Quinn, *IBM and Linux (A)* (Harvard Business School Case No. 903-083, 2003).

4 J. A. Schumpeter, *The Theory of Economic Development* (Cambridge, MA: Harvard University Press, 1934).

5 See R. Jacobson, "The Austrian School of Strategy," *Academy of Management Review* 17 (1992): 782–807; and G. Young, K. Smith and C. Grimm, "Austrian and Industrial Organization Perspectives on Firm-Level Competitive Activity and Performance," *Organization Science* 7 (May-June 1996): 243–54.

6 R. T. Masson and J. Shaanan, "Stochastic Dynamic Limit Pricing: An Empirical Test," *Review of Economics and Statistics* 64 (1982): 413–22; R. T. Masson and J. Shaanan, "Optimal Pricing and Threat of Entry: Canadian Evidence," *International Journal of Industrial Organization* 5 (1987): 520–535.

7 R. Caves and M. E. Porter, "The Dynamics of Changing Seller Concentration," *Journal of Industrial Economics* 19 (1980): 1–15; P. Hart and R. Clarke, *Concentration in British Industry* (Cambridge: Cambridge University Press, 1980).

8 P. A. Geroski and R. T. Masson, "Dynamic Market Models in Industrial Organization," *International Journal of Industrial Organization* 5 (1987): 1–13.

9 D. C. Mueller, *Profits in the Long Run* (Cambridge: Cambridge University Press, 1986).

10 R. D'Aveni, *Hypercompetition: Managing the Dynamics of Strategic Maneuvering* (New York: Free Press, 1994): 217–18.

11 L. G. Thomas and R. D'Aveni, "The Rise of Hypercompetition in the U.S. Manufacturing Sector, 1950-2002." Tuck School of Business, Dartmouth College, Working Paper #2004-11 (2004).

12 R. R. Wiggins and T. W. Ruefli, "Schumpeter's Ghost: Is Hypercompetition Making the Best of Times Shorter?" *Strategic Management Journal* 26 (2005): 887–911.

13 G. McNamara, P. M. Vaaler, and C. Devers, "Same As It Ever Was: The Search for Evidence of Increasing Hypercompetition," *Strategic Management Journal* 24 (2003): 261–78.

14 K. Weigelt and C. F. Camerer, "Reputation and Corporate Strategy: A Review of Recent Theory and Applications," *Strategic Management Journal* 9 (1988): 137–42.

15 A. K. Dixit, "The Role of Investment in Entry Deterrence," *Economic Journal* 90 (1980): 95–106.

16 P. Milgrom and J. Roberts, "Informational Asymmetries, Strategic Behavior and Industrial Organization," *American Economic Review* 77, no. 2 (May 1987): 184–9; J. Tirole, *The Theory of Industrial Organization* (Cambridge, MA: MIT Press, 1988).

17 P. Ghemawat, *Commitment: The Dynamic of Strategy* (New York: Free Press, 1991).

18 See, for example: A. K. Dixit and B. J. Nalebuff, *Thinking Strategically: The Competitive Edge in Business, Politics, and Everyday Life* (New York: W. W. Norton, 1991) and J. McMillan, *Games, Strategies, and Managers* (New York: Oxford University Press, 1992).

19 G. T. Allison and P. Zelikow, *Essence of Decision: Explaining the Cuban Missile Crisis*, 2nd edn (Boston: Little Brown, 1999).

20 B. C. Esty and P. Ghemawat, "Airbus vs. Boeing in Superjumbos: A Case of Failed Preemption," Harvard Business School Working Paper No. 02-061 (2002).

21 D. Ronfelt, "Social Science at 190 mph on NASCAR's Biggest Superspeedways," *First Monday* 5 (February 7, 2000).

22 "Game Theory in Action: Designing the U.S. Airwaves Auction," *Financial Times* Mastering Strategy Supplement (October 11, 1999): 4.
23 J. Maynard Smith, "Sexual Selection and the Handicap Principle," *Journal of Theoretical Biology* 57 (1976): 239–42.
24 A. Brandenburger and B. Nalebuff (1996), op. cit.
25 T. Dhar, J.-P. Chatas, R. W. Collerill, and B. W. Gould, Strategic Pricing Between Coca-Cola Company and PepsiCo, *Journal of Economics and Management Strategy* 14 (2005): 905–31.
26 "A Sharp Act Gets an Edge" *Financial Times* (September 10, 2008).
27 *Bitter Competition: Holland Sweetener vs. NutraSweet (A)* (Harvard Business School Case No. 9-794-079, 1994).
28 A. M. McGahan, "The Incentive not to Invest: Capacity Commitments in the Compact Disk Introduction," in R. A. Burgelman and R. S. Rosenbloom (eds), *Research on Technological Innovation Management and Policy*, vol. 5 (Greenwich, CT: JAI Press, 1994).
29 D. K. Levine and R. A. Levine, "Deterrence in the Cold War and the War on Terror," working paper, UCLA Department of Economics (2006).
30 D. N. Sull, "Managing by Commitments," *Harvard Business Review* (June 2003): 82–91.
31 J. Chevalier, "When It Can Be Good to Burn Your Boats," *Financial Times* Mastering Strategy Supplement (October 25, 1999): 2–3.
32 Games where price is the primary decision variable are called Bertrand models after the 19th century French economist Joseph Bertrand.
33 Games where quantity is the primary decision variable are called Cournot models after the 19th century French economist Augustin Cournot.
34 F. Scott Morton, "Strategic Complements and Substitutes," *Financial Times* Mastering Strategy Supplement (November 8, 1999): 10–13.
35 R. Loving, *The Men who Loved Trains* (Bloomington, IA: Indiana University Press, 2006).
36 For a review of research on competitive signaling, see O. Heil and T. S. Robertson, "Toward a Theory of Competitive Market Signaling: A Research Agenda," *Strategic Management Journal* 12 (1991): 403–18.
37 For a survey of the strategic role of reputation, see K. Weigelt and C. Camerer, "Reputation and Corporate Strategy: A Review of Recent Theory and Applications," *Strategic Management Journal* 9 (1988): 443–54.
38 P. Milgrom and J. Roberts, "Predation, Reputation, and Entry Deterrence," *Journal of Economic Theory* 27 (1982): 280–312.
39 R. M. Grant, "Pricing Behavior in the U.K. Wholesale Market for Petrol," *Journal of Industrial Economics* 30 (1982): 271–92; L. Miller, "The Provocative Practice of Price Signaling: Collusion versus Cooperation," *Business Horizons* (July–August, 1993).
40 On the ability of game theory to predict almost any equilibrium solution (the "Pandora's Box Problem") see C. F. Camerer, "Does Strategy Research Need Game Theory?" *Strategic Management Journal*, Special Issue, 12 (Winter 1991): 137–52; and F. M. Fisher, "The Games Economists Play: A Noncooperative View," *Rand Journal of Economics* 20 (Spring 1989): 113–24. Steve Postrel illustrates the point with a game theory model to explain the rationality of bank presidents setting fire to their trousers. See S. Postrel, "Burning Your Britches Behind You: Can Policy Scholars Bank on Game Theory?" *Strategic Management Journal*, Special Issue, 12 (Winter 1991): 153–5.
41 P. Milgrom, *Putting Auction Theory to Work* (Cambridge: Cambridge University Press, 2004); J. McMillan, *Reinventing the Bazaar* (New York: Norton, 2002).
42 L. Field, *The Secret Language of Competitive Intelligence* (New York: Random House, 2006); J. E. Prescott and S. H. Miller, *Proven Strategies in Competitive Intelligence: Lessons from the Trenches* (Wiley: New York, 2001).
43 *Competitive Intelligence Review* (New York: John Wiley & Sons, Inc.).
44 The Society of Competitive Intelligence Professionals (www.scip.org).
45 "P&G's Covert Operation," *Fortune* (September 17, 2001).
46 "McLaren Docked F1 Points for Spying" *Financial Times* (September 14, 2007).
47 J.-C. Spender, *Industry Recipes: The Nature and Sources of Managerial Judgement* (Oxford: Basil Blackwell, 1989). How social interaction promotes convergence of perceptions and beliefs is discussed by Anne Huff in "Industry Influences on Strategy Reformulation," *Strategic Management Journal* 3 (1982): 119–31.
48 This section draws heavily on M. E. Porter, *Competitive Advantage* (New York: Free Press, 1985): Chapter 7.
49 O. Gadiesh and J. L. Gilbert, "Profit Pools: A Fresh Look at Strategy," *Harvard Business Review* (May–June 1998): 146.
50 "Pirelli's Bet on High-performance Tires," *International Herald Tribune* (April 2, 2005).
51 R. E. Caves and M. E. Porter, "From Entry Barriers to Mobility Barriers: Conjectural Decisions and Contrived Deterrence to New Competition," *Quarterly Journal of Economics* 91 (1977): 241–62.
52 W. C. Kim and R. Mauborgne, "Blue Ocean Strategy: From Theory to Practice," *California Management Review* 47 (Spring 2005): 105–21.
53 O. Gadiesh and J. L. Gilbert, "How to Map Your Industry's Profit Pools," *Harvard Business Review* (May-June 1998): 149–62.
54 M. E. Porter, *Competitive Strategy* (New York: Free Press, 1980): 129.
55 For more on strategic groups, see John McGee and Howard Thomas's "Strategic Groups: Theory, Research, and Taxonomy," *Strategic Management Journal* 7 (1986): 141–60.

56 M. Hunt, "Competition in the Major Home Appliance Industry," doctoral dissertation (Harvard University, 1973).
57 K. Hatten, D. Schendel and A. Cooper, "A Strategic Model of the U.S. Brewing Industry," *Academy of Management Journal* 21 (1978): 592–610.
58 K. Cool and D. Schendel, "Strategic Group Formation and Performance: The Case of the U.S. Pharmaceutical Industry," *Management Science* 33 (1987): 1102–24; A. Feigenbaum and H. Thomas, "Strategic Groups and Performance: The U.S. Insurance Industry," *Strategic Management Journal* 11 (1990): 197–215.
59 K. Cool and I. Dierickx, "Rivalry, Strategic Groups, and Firm Profitability," *Strategic Management Journal* 14 (1993): 47–59.
60 K. Smith, C. Grimm and S. Wally, "Strategic Groups and Rivalrous Firm Behavior: Toward a Reconciliation," *Strategic Management Journal* 18 (1997): 149–57.

5 Analyzing Resources and Capabilities

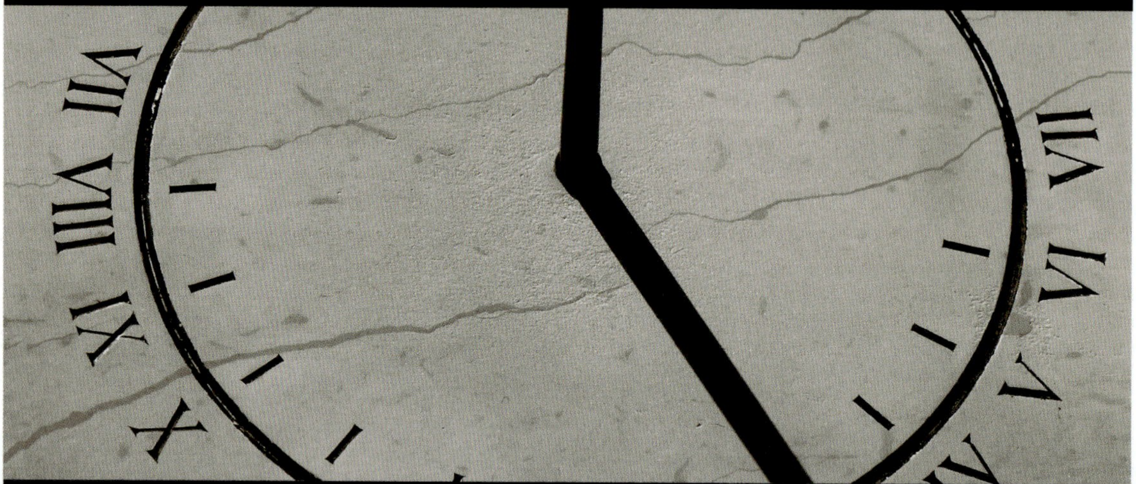

Analysts have tended to define assets too narrowly, identifying only those that can be measured, such as plant and equipment. Yet the intangible assets, such as a particular technology, accumulated consumer information, brand name, reputation, and corporate culture, are invaluable to the firm's competitive power. In fact, these invisible assets are often the only real source of competitive edge that can be sustained over time.

—HIROYUKI ITAMI, *MOBILIZING INVISIBLE ASSETS*

You've gotta do what you do well.

—LUCINO NOTO, FORMER VICE CHAIRMAN, EXXON MOBIL

OUTLINE

- **Introduction and Objectives**
- **The Role of Resources and Capabilities in Strategy Formulation**
  - Basing Strategy on Resources and Capabilities
  - Resources and Capabilities as Sources of Profit
- **The Resources of the Firm**
  - Tangible Resources
  - Intangible Resources
  - Human Resources
- **Organizational Capabilities**
  - Classifying Capabilities
  - The Nature of Capability
- **Appraising Resources and Capabilities**
  - Establishing Competitive Advantage
  - Sustaining Competitive Advantage
  - Appropriating the Returns to Competitive Advantage

Introduction and Objectives

In Chapter 1 I noted that the focus of strategy thinking has been shifted from the external environment towards its internal environment. In this chapter, we will make the same transition. Looking within the firm, we will concentrate our attention on the resources and capabilities that firms possess. In doing so, we shall build the foundations for our analysis of competitive advantage (which began in Chapter 3 with the discussion of key success factors).

By the time you have completed this chapter you will be able to:

- appreciate the role of a firm's resources and capabilities as a basis for formulating strategy;
- identify and appraise the resources and capabilities of a firm;
- evaluate the potential for a firm's resources and capabilities to confer sustainable competitive advantage;
- use the results of resource and capability analysis to formulate strategies that exploit internal strengths while defending against internal weaknesses.

We begin by explaining why a company's resources and capabilities are so important to its strategy.

The Role of Resources and Capabilities in Strategy Formulation

Strategy is concerned with matching a firm's resources and capabilities to the opportunities that arise in the external environment. So far, the emphasis of the book has been on the identification of profit opportunities in the external environment of the firm. In this chapter, our emphasis shifts from the interface between strategy and the external environment towards the interface between strategy and the internal environment of the firm—more specifically, with the resources and capabilities of the firm (see Figure 5.1).

Increasing emphasis on the role of resources and capabilities as the basis for strategy is the result of two factors. First, as firms' industry environments have become more unstable, so internal resources and capabilities rather than external market focus has been viewed as a more secure base for formulating strategy. Second, it has become increasingly apparent that competitive advantage rather than industry attractiveness is the primary source of superior profitability. Let us consider each of these factors.

Basing Strategy on Resources and Capabilities

During the 1990s, ideas concerning the role of resources and capabilities as the principal basis for firm strategy and the primary source of profitability coalesced into what has become known as the *resource-based view of the firm*.[1]

To understand why the resource-based view has had a major impact on strategy thinking, let us go back to the starting point for strategy formulation: typically some statement of the firm's identity and purpose (often expressed in a mission statement). Conventionally, firms have answered the question "what is our business?" in terms of the market they serve: "who are our customers?" and "which of their needs are we seeking to serve?" However, in a world where customer preferences are volatile and the identity of customers and the technologies for serving them are changing, a market-focused strategy may not provide the stability and constancy of direction needed to guide strategy over the long term.[2] When the external environment is in

FIGURE 5.1 Analyzing resources and capabilities: the interface between strategy and the firm

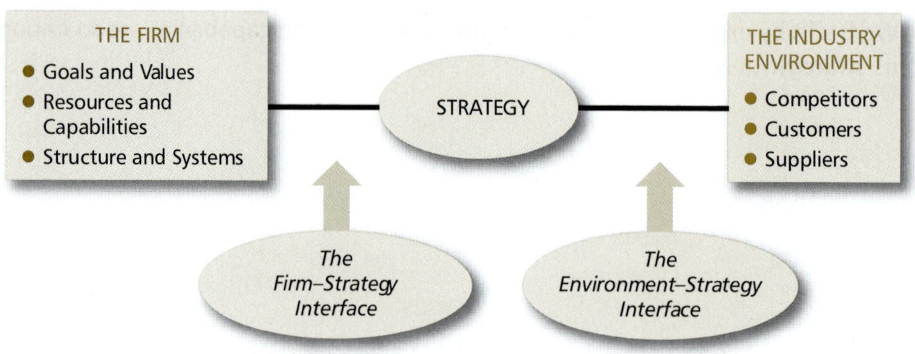

FIGURE 5.2 Honda Motor Company: product development milestones

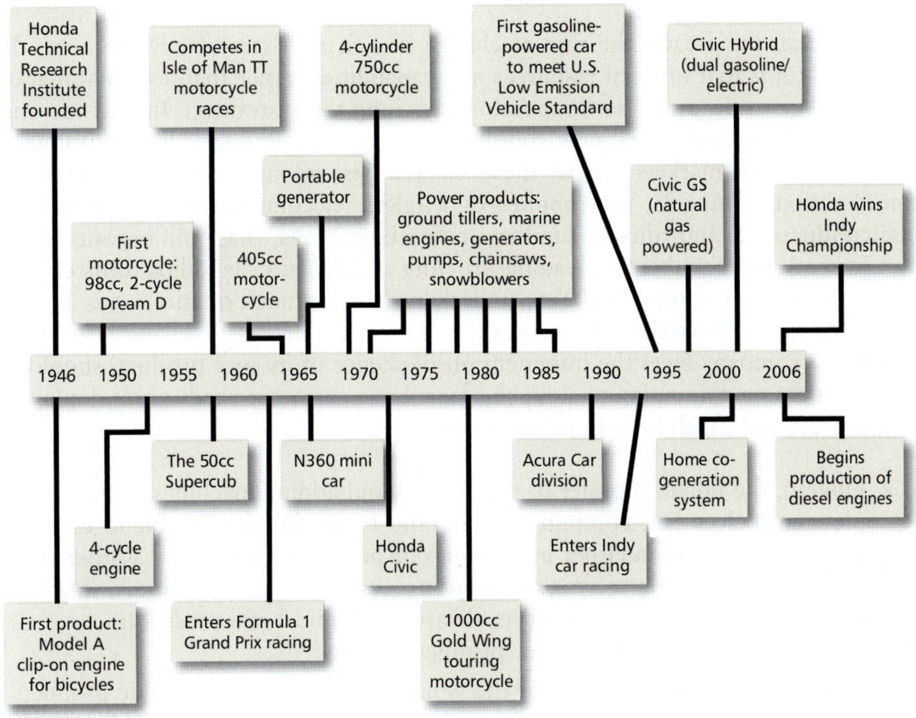

a state of flux, the firm itself, in terms of its bundle of resources and capabilities, may be a much more stable basis on which to define its identity.

In their 1990 landmark paper, "The Core Competence of the Corporation," C. K. Prahalad and Gary Hamel pointed to the potential for capabilities to be the "roots of competitiveness," source of new products and foundation for strategy.[3] For example:

- Honda Motor Company is the world's biggest motorcycle producer and a leading supplier of automobiles but it has never defined itself either as a motorcycle company or a motor vehicle company. Since its founding in 1948, its strategy has been built around its expertise in the development and manufacture of engines; this capability has successfully carried it from motorcycles to a wide range of gasoline-engined products (see Figure 5.2).
- Canon Inc. had its first success producing 35 mm cameras. Since then it has gone on to develop fax machines, calculators, copy machines, printers, video cameras, camcorders, semiconductor manufacturing equipment and many other products. Almost all of Canon's products involve the application of three areas of technological capability: precision mechanics, microelectronics and fine optics.
- 3M Corporation expanded from sandpaper into adhesive tapes, audio and videotapes, road signs, medical products and floppy disks. Its product list now comprises over 30 000 products. Is it a conglomerate? Certainly not, claims 3M. Its vast product range rests on a foundation of key technologies

relating to adhesives, thin-film coatings, and materials sciences supported by outstanding capability in the development and launching of new products.

In general, the greater the rate of change in a firm's external environment, the more likely it is that internal resources and capabilities rather than external market focus will provide a secure foundation for long-term strategy. In fast-moving, technology-based industries, new companies are built around specific technological capabilities. The markets where these capabilities are applied are a secondary consideration. Motorola, the supplier of wireless telecommunications equipment, semiconductors, and direct satellite communications, has undergone many transformations, from being a leading provider of TVs and car radios to its current focus on telecom equipment. Yet, underlying these transformations has been a consistent focus on wireless electronics.

When a company faces the imminent obsolescence of its core product, should its strategy focus on continuing to serve the same basic customer needs or on deploying its resources and capabilities in other markets?

- Olivetti, the Italian supplier of typewriters and adding machines, was a pioneer in electronic computers during the 1960s, but was unable to establish long-term viability in either mainframes or personal computers.[4] Rather than maintain its focus on serving the word processing needs of business, should Olivetti have sought to exploit its electro-mechanical and precision engineering capabilities in other product markets?
- Eastman Kodak's dominance of the world market for photographic products based on chemical imaging has been threatened by digital imaging. Since 1990, Kodak has invested billions of dollars developing digital technologies and digital imaging products. Yet profits and market leadership in digital imaging remain elusive for Kodak. Might Kodak have been better off sticking with its chemical know-how and developing its interests in specialty chemicals, pharmaceuticals and healthcare?[5]

The difficulties experienced by established firms in adjusting to technological change within their own markets are well documented—in typesetting and in disk-drive manufacturing, successive technological waves have caused market leaders to falter and have allowed new entrants to prosper.[6]

Resources and Capabilities as Sources of Profit

In Chapter 1, we identified two major sources of superior profitability: industry attractiveness and competitive advantage. Of these, competitive advantage is the more important. Internationalization and deregulation have increased competitive pressure within most sectors; as a result, few industries (or segments) offer cozy refuges from vigorous competition. As we observed in the previous chapter (see Table 4.1), industry factors account for only a small proportion of interfirm profit differentials. Hence, establishing competitive advantage through the development and deployment of resources and capabilities, rather than seeking shelter from the storm of competition, has become the primary goal for strategy.

The distinction between industry attractiveness and competitive advantage (based on superior resources) as sources of a firm's profitability corresponds to economists' distinction between different types of profit (or *rent*). The profits arising from market power are referred to as *monopoly rents*; those arising from superior resources are *Ricardian rents*, after the nineteenth-century British economist David Ricardo. Ricardo showed that, in a competitive wheat market, when land at the margin of cultivation earned a negligible return, fertile land would yield high returns. Ricardian rent is the return earned by a scarce resource over and above the cost of bringing it into production.[7]

Distinguishing between profit arising from market power and profit arising from resource superiority is less clear in practice than in principle. A closer look at Porter's five forces framework suggests that industry attractiveness derives ultimately from the ownership of resources. Barriers to entry, for example, are the result of patents, brands, distribution channels, learning, or some other resource possessed by incumbent firms. Monopoly is usually based on the ownership of a key resource such as a technical standard or government license.

The resource-based approach has profound implications for companies' strategy formulation. When the primary concern of strategy was industry selection and positioning, companies tended to adopt similar strategies. The resource-based view, by contrast, emphasizes the uniqueness of each company and suggests that the key to profitability is not through doing the *same* as other firms but rather through exploiting *differences*. Establishing competitive advantage involves formulating and implementing a strategy that exploit a firm's unique strengths.

The remainder of this chapter outlines a resource-based approach to strategy formulation. Fundamental to this approach is a thorough and profound understanding of the resources and capabilities of a firm. Such understanding provides a basis for selecting a strategy that exploits key resource and capability strengths of an organization—or an individual (see Strategy Capsule 5.1). Walt Disney's turnaround under Michael Eisner is a classic example of the benefits of exploiting underutilized resources (see Strategy Capsule 5.2).

Analyzing resources and capabilities is also concerned with filling resource gaps and building capability for the future. We shall consider the development of resources and capabilities in the next chapter.

Our starting point is to identify and assess the resources and capabilities available to the firm.

STRATEGY CAPSULE 5.1

Focusing Strategy around Core Capabilities: Lyor Cohen on Mariah Carey

2001 was a disastrous year for Mariah Carey. Her first movie, *Glitter*, was a flop, the soundtrack was Carey's most poorly received album in a decade, her $80 million recording contract was dropped by EMI, and she suffered a nervous breakdown.

Lyor Cohen, the aggressive, workaholic chief executive of Island Def Jam records was quick to spot an opportunity: *"I cold-called her on the day of her release from EMI and I said, I think you are an unbelievable artist and you should hold your head up high. What*

I said stuck on her and she ended up signing with us."

His strategic analysis of Carey's situation was concise: *"I said to her, what's your competitive advantage? A great voice, of course. And what else? You write every one of your songs—you're a great writer. So why did you stray from your competitive advantage? If you have this magnificent voice and you write such compelling songs, why are you dressing like that, why are you using all these collaborations [with other artists and other songwriters]? Why? It's like driving a Ferrari in first—you won't see what that Ferrari will do until you get into sixth gear."*

Cohen signed Carey in May 2002. Under Universal Music's Island Def Jam Records, Carey returned to her core strengths: her versatile voice, song-writing talents, and ballad style. Her next album, *The Emancipation of Mimi*, was the biggest-selling album of 2005, and in 2006 she won a Grammy award.

Source: "Rap's Unlikely Mogul," *Financial Times* (August 5, 2002).

STRATEGY CAPSULE 5.2

Resource Utilization: Revival at Walt Disney

In 1984, Michael Eisner became CEO of the Walt Disney Company. Between 1984 and 1988, Disney's sales revenue increased from $1.66 billion to $3.75 billion, net income from $98 million to $570 million, and the stock market's valuation of the company from $1.8 billion to $10.3 billion.

The key to the Disney turnaround was the mobilization of Disney's considerable resource base. Prominent among Disney's underutilized resources were 28000 acres of land in Florida. With the help of the Arvida Corporation, a land development company acquired in 1984, Disney began hotel, resort, and residential development of these land-holdings. New attractions were added to the Epcot Center, and a new theme park, the Disney-MGM Studio Tour, was built. Disney World expanded beyond theme parks into resort vacations, the convention business, and residential housing.

To exploit its huge film library, Disney introduced videocassette sales of Disney movies and licensed packages of movies to TV networks. The huge investments in the Disney theme parks were more effectively exploited through heavier marketing effort and increased admission charges. Encouraged by the success of Tokyo Disneyland, Disney embarked on further international duplication of its U.S. theme parks with Euro Disneyland just outside Paris, France. A chain of Disney Stores was established to push sales of Disney merchandise.

The most ambitious feature of the turnaround was Disney's regeneration as a movie studio. Eisner began a massive expansion of its Touchstone label, which had been established in 1983 with the objectives of putting Disney's film studios to fuller use and establishing the company in the teenage and adult markets. Disney Studios doubled the number of movies in production. In 1988, it became America's leading studio in terms of box office receipts. Studio production was further boosted by Disney's increasing TV presence, both through the Disney Channel and programs for network TV.

Above all, the new management team was exploiting Disney's most powerful and enduring asset: the affection of millions of people of different nations and different generations for the Disney name and the Disney characters.

The Resources of the Firm

It is important to distinguish between the resources and the capabilities of the firm: resources are the productive assets owned by the firm; capabilities are what the firm can do. Individual resources do not confer competitive advantage; they must work together to create *organizational capability*. It is capability that is the essence of superior performance. Figure 5.3 shows the relationships among resources, capabilities and competitive advantage.

Drawing up an inventory of a firm's resources can be surprisingly difficult. No such document exists within the accounting or management information systems of most corporations. The corporate balance sheet provides a limited view of a firm's resources—it comprises mainly financial and physical resources. To take a wider view of a firm's resources it is helpful to identify three principal types of resource: tangible, intangible, and human resources.

FIGURE 5.3 The links among resources, capabilities and competitive advantage

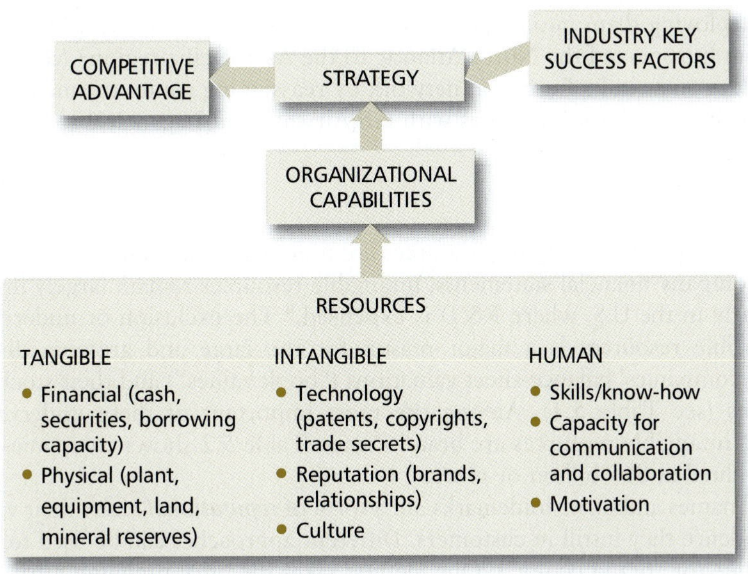

Tangible Resources

Tangible resources are the easiest to identify and evaluate: financial resources and physical assets are identified and valued in the firm's financial statements. Yet balance sheets are renowned for their propensity to obscure strategically relevant information and to distort asset values. Historic cost valuation can provide little indication of an asset's market value. Disney's movie library had a balance sheet value of only $5.4 billion in 2008, based on production cost less amortization. Its land assets (including its 28 000 acres in Florida) were valued at a paltry $1.2 billion.

However, the primary goal of resource analysis is not to value a company's assets but to understand their potential for creating competitive advantage. Information that British Airways possessed fixed assets valued at £8 billion in 2008 is of little use in assessing their strategic value. To assess British Airways' ability to compete effectively in the world airline industry we need to know about the composition of these assets: the location of land and buildings, the types of plane, the landing slots and gate facilities at airports, and so on.

Once we have fuller information on a company's tangible resources we explore how we can create additional value from them. This requires that we address two key questions:

- *What opportunities exist for economizing on their use?* It may be possible to use fewer resources to support the same level of business, or to use the existing resources to support a larger volume of business. In the case of British Airways there may be opportunities for consolidating administrative offices and engineering and service facilities. Improved inventory control may allow economies in inventories of parts and fuel. Better control of cash and receivables permits a business to operate with lower levels of cash and liquid financial resources.
- *What are the possibilities for employing existing assets more profitably?* Could British Airways generate better returns on some of its planes by redeploying them into cargo carrying? Should BA seek to redeploy its assets from Europe and the North Atlantic to the Asia-Pacific region? Might it reduce costs in its European network by reassigning routes to small franchised airlines (as it does with GB Airways and Loganair)?

Intangible Resources

For most companies, intangible resources are more valuable than tangible resources. Yet, in company financial statements, intangible resources remain largely invisible—particularly in the U.S. where R&D is expensed.[8] The exclusion or undervaluation of intangible resources is a major reason for the large and growing divergence between companies' balance-sheet valuations ("book values") and their stock-market valuations (see Table 5.1). Among the most important of these undervalued or unvalued intangible resources are brand names. Table 5.2 shows companies owning brands valued at $15 billion or more.

Brand names and other trademarks are a form of *reputational asset*: their value is in the confidence they instill in customers. Different approaches can be used to estimate brand value (or "brand equity"). One method takes the price premium attributable to a brand, multiplies it by the brand's annual sales volume, then calculates the present

TABLE 5.1 Major companies with the highest market-to-book ratios, December 2006

Company	Valuation Ratio	Country	Company	Valuation Ratio	Country
Yahoo! Japan	72.0	Japan	Coca-Cola	7.8	U.S.
Colgate-Palmolive	20.8	U.S.	Diageo	7.4	U.K.
GlaxoSmithKline	13.4	U.K.	3M	7.3	U.S.
Anheuser-Busch	12.6	U.S.	Nokia	6.7	Finland
eBay	11.2	U.S.	Sanofi-Aventis	6.3	France
SAP	10.8	Germany	AstraZeneca	5.9	U.K.
Yahoo!	10.7	U.S.	Johnson & Johnson	5.7	U.S.
Dell Computer	10.0	U.S.	Boeing	5.7	U.S.
Sumitomo Mitsui Financial	8.8	Japan	Eli Lily	5.6	U.S.
Procter & Gamble	8.4	U.S.	Cisco Systems	5.5	U.S.
Qualcomm	8.3	U.S.	Roche Holding	5.5	Switz.
Schlumberger	8.2	U.S.	L'Oréal	5.3	France
Unilever	8.1	Neth./U.K.	Altria	5.2	U.S.
PepsiCo	8.0	U.S.	Novartis	5.1	Switz.

Note: The table includes companies with the highest market capitalization as a proportion of balance-sheet net asset value among the top 200 companies of the world with the largest market capitalization at the end of 2006.

TABLE 5.2 The world's most valuable brands, 2008

Rank	Brand	Brand value in 2008, $ billion	Change from 2007	Country of origin
1	Coca-Cola	66.7	−1%	U.S.
2	IBM	59.0	+11%	U.S.
3	Microsoft	59.0	−2%	U.S.
4	GE	53.1	+14%	U.S.
5	Nokia	35.9	+35%	Finland
6	Toyota	34.1	+37%	Japan
7	Intel	31.3	6%	U.S.
8	McDonald's	31.0	0%	U.S.
9	Disney	29.3	+11%	U.S.
10	Google	25.6	+96%	U.S.
11	Mercedes Benz	25.6	+28%	Germany
12	Hewlett-Packard	23.9	+26%	U.S.
13	BMW	23.3	+36%	Germany
14	Gillette	22.1	+5%	U.S.
15	American Express	21.9	+18%	U.S.
16	Louis Vuitton	21.6	+34%	France
17	Cisco	21.3	+22%	U.S.
18	Marlboro	21.3	0%	U.S.
19	Citi	20.2	+1%	U.S.
20	Honda	19.1	+21%	Japan

Note: Brand values are calculated as the net present value of future earnings generated by the brand.
Source: Interbrand.

value of this revenue stream. The brand valuations in Table 5.2 are based upon the operating profits for each company (after taxation and a capital charge), estimating the proportion attributable to the brand, then capitalizing these returns.

The value of a company's brands can be increased by extending the range of products over which a company markets its brands. Johnson & Johnson, Samsung and General Electric derive considerable economies from applying a single brand to a wide range of products. As a result, companies that succeed in building strong consumer brands have a powerful incentive to diversify—for example, Nike's diversification from athletic shoes into apparel and sports equipment.[9]

Like reputation, technology is an intangible asset whose value is not evident from most companies' balance sheets. Intellectual property—patents, copyrights, trade secrets, and trademarks—comprise technological and artistic resources where ownership is defined in law. Since the 1980s, companies have become more attentive to the value of their intellectual property. For IBM (with the world's biggest patent portfolio) and Qualcomm (with its patents relating to CDMA digital wireless telephony), intellectual property is the most valuable resource that they own.

Human Resources

The firm's human resources comprise the expertise and effort offered by employees. Like intangible resources, human resources do not appear on the firm's balance sheet—for the simple reason that the firm does not own its employees; it purchases their services under employment contacts. The reason for including human resources as part of the resources of the firm is their stability—although employees are free to move from one firm to another (most employment contracts require no more than a month's notice on the part of the employee)—in practice most employment contracts are long term. In the U.S. the average length of time an employee stays with an employer is four years, in Europe it is longer—ranging from eight years in Britain to 13 in Greece.[10]

Most firms devote considerable effort to appraising their human resources. This appraisal occurs at the hiring stage when potential employees are evaluated in relation to the requirements of their job and as part of an ongoing appraisal process of which annual employee reviews form the centerpiece. The purposes of appraisal are to assess past performance for the purposes of compensation and promotion, set future performance goals and establish employee development plans. Trends in appraisal include greater emphasis on assessing results in relation to performance targets (for example, *management by objectives*) and broadening the basis of evaluation (for example, 360-degree appraisal).

Since the 1990s human resource appraisal has become far more systematic and sophisticated. Many organizations have established assessment centers specifically for the purpose of providing comprehensive, quantitative assessments of the skills and attributes of individual employees and appraisal criteria are increasingly based upon empirical research into the components and correlated of superior job performance. *Competency modeling* involves identifying the set of skills, content knowledge, attitudes, and values associated with superior performers within a particular job category, then assessing each employee against that profile.[11] An important finding of research into HR competencies is the critical role of psychological and social aptitudes in determining superior performance: typically these factors outweigh technical skills and educational and professional qualifications. Recent interest in *emotional intelligence* reflects growing recognition of these psychological and social attributes.[12] Overall, these finding explain the growing trend among companies to "hire for attitude; train for skills."

The ability of employees to harmonize their efforts and integrate their separate skills depends not only on their interpersonal skills but also the organizational context. This organizational context as it affects internal collaboration is determined by a key intangible resource: the *culture* of the organization. The term *organizational culture* is notoriously ill defined. It relates to an organization's values, traditions, and social norms. Building on the observations of Peters and Waterman that "firms with sustained superior financial performance typically are characterized by a strong set of core managerial values that define the ways they conduct business," Jay Barney identifies organizational culture as a firm resource of great strategic importance that is potentially very valuable.[13]

Organizational Capabilities

Resources are not productive on their own. A brain surgeon is close to useless without a radiologist, anesthetist, nurses, surgical instruments, imaging equipment and a host of other resources. To perform a task, a team of resources must work together. An *organizational capability* is a "firm's capacity to deploy resources for a desired end result."[14] Just as an individual may be capable of playing the violin, ice skating, and speaking Mandarin, so an organization may possess the capabilities needed to manufacture widgets, distribute them globally and hedge the resulting foreign exchange exposure. We use the terms *capability* and *competence* interchangeably.[15]

Our primary interest is in those capabilities that can provide a basis for competitive advantage. Selznick used *distinctive competence* to describe those things that an organization does particularly well relative to its competitors.[16] Prahalad and Hamel coined the term *core competences* to distinguish those capabilities fundamental to a firm's strategy and performance.[17] Core competences, according to Hamel and Prahalad, are those that:

- make a disproportionate contribution to ultimate customer value, or to the efficiency with which that value is delivered and
- provide a basis for entering new markets.[18]

Prahalad and Hamel criticize U.S. companies for emphasizing product management over competence management. They compare the strategic development of Sony and RCA in consumer electronics. Both companies were failures in the home video market. RCA introduced its videodisk system, Sony its Betamax videotape system. For RCA, the failure of its first product marked the end of its venture into home video systems and heralded a progressive retreat from the consumer electronics industry. RCA was acquired by GE and later sold to Thomson of France. Sony, on the other hand, acknowledged the failure of Betamax but continued to develop its capabilities in video technology and produced a string of successful video products including camcorders, digital cameras, and the PlayStation game console.

Classifying Capabilities

Before focusing upon "distinctive" or "core" capabilities, it is helpful to take a comprehensive look at the full range of an organization's capabilities. To identify a firm's capabilities, we need to have some basis for classifying and disaggregating its activities. Two approaches are commonly used:

- A *functional analysis* identifies organizational capabilities in relation to each of the principal functional areas of the firm. Table 5.3 classifies the principal functions of the firm and identifies organizational capabilities located within each function.
- A *value-chain analysis* separates the activities of the firm into a sequential chain. Michael Porter's representation of the value chain distinguishes between *primary activities* (those involved with the transformation of inputs and interface with the customer) and *support activities* (see Figure 5.4). Porter's generic value chain identifies a few broadly defined activities that can be disaggregated to provide a more detailed identification of the firm's activities (and the capabilities that correspond to each activity). Thus, marketing might include market research, test marketing, advertising, promotion, pricing and dealer relations.[19]

TABLE 5.3 A functional classification of organizational capabilities

Functional area	Capability	Exemplars
CORPORATE FUNCTIONS	Financial control	ExxonMobil, PepsiCo
	Management development	General Electric, Shell
	Strategic innovation	Google, Haier
	Multidivisional coordination	Unilever, Shell
	Acquisition management	Cisco Systems, Luxottica
	International management	Shell, Banco Santander
MANAGEMENT INFORMATION	Comprehensive, integrated MIS network linked to managerial decision making	Wal-Mart, Capital One, Dell Computer
RESEARCH AND DEVELOPMENT	Research	IBM, Merck
	Innovative new product development	3M, Apple
	Fast-cycle new product development	Canon, Inditex (Zara)
OPERATIONS	Efficiency in volume manufacturing	Briggs & Stratton, YKK
	Continuous improvements in operations	Toyota, Harley-Davidson
	Flexibility and speed of response	Four Seasons Hotels
PRODUCT DESIGN	Design capability	Nokia, Apple
MARKETING	Brand management	Procter & Gamble, Altria
	Building reputation for quality	Johnson & Johnson
	Responsiveness to market trends	MTV, L'Oréal
SALES AND DISTRIBUTION	Effective sales promotion and execution	PepsiCo, Pfizer
	Efficiency and speed of order processing	L. L. Bean, Dell Computer
	Speed of distribution	Amazon.com
	Customer service	Singapore Airlines, Caterpillar

FIGURE 5.4 Porter's value chain

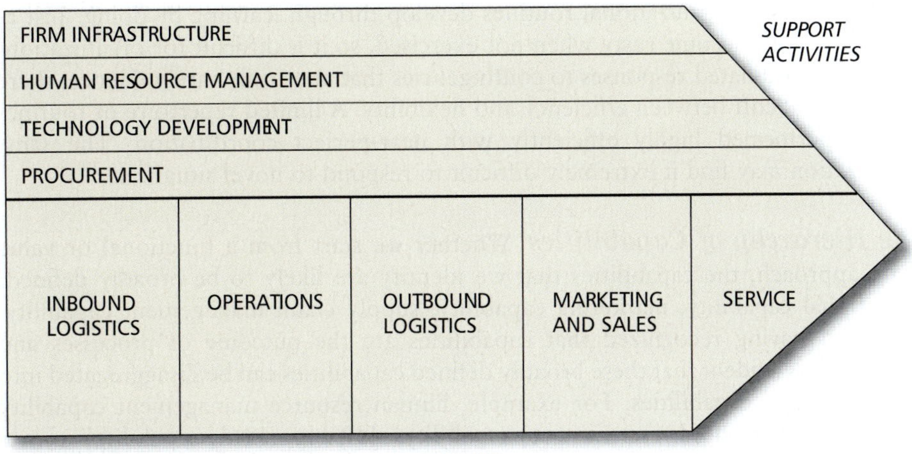

The Nature of Capability

Identifying and drawing up an inventory of a firm's resources is fairly straightforward. Organizational capabilities pose greater problems—they are much more elusive. Apple's distinctive capability in the design of consumer electronic products that combine pleasing aesthetics with a superior user interface is evident from its iMac, iPod, and iPhone products—but where within Apple is this capability located? To better understand organizational capabilities, let us take a look at their structure.

Capability as Process and Routine Organizational capability requires the efforts of various individuals to be integrated with one another and with capital equipment, technology and other resources. But how does this integration occur? Productive activity within an organization involves coordinated actions undertaken by teams of people engaged in a series of productive tasks. We refer to the sequence of actions through which a specific task is performed as an *organizational process.* The sequences that comprise organizational processes can be mapped using a flowchart.[20] For example, the process of fixing bugs in the operating system developed by a large computer company involved a sequence of 30 distinct activities that began with problem recognition and ended with changes in software documentation.[21]

A key feature of most processes performed by an organization is their routinized nature. Routinization is an essential step in translating directions and operating practices into capabilities—only by becoming routine do processes become efficient and reliable. In every McDonald's hamburger restaurant, operating manuals provide precise directions for a comprehensive range of tasks, from the placing of the pickle on the burger to the maintenance of the milkshake machine. In practice, the operating manuals are seldom consulted—tasks become routinized through continuous repetition.

These *organizational routines*—"regular and predictable behavioral patterns [comprising] repetitive patterns of activity"[22]—are viewed by evolutionary economists as the fundamental building blocks of what firms do and who they are. It is through the adaptation and replication of routines that firms develop. Like individual skills, organizational routines develop through learning by doing. Just as individual skills become rusty when not exercised, so it is difficult for organizations to retain coordinated responses to contingencies that arise only rarely. Hence, there may be a tradeoff between efficiency and flexibility. A limited repertoire of routines can be performed highly efficiently with near-perfect coordination. The same organization may find it extremely difficult to respond to novel situations.[23]

The Hierarchy of Capabilities Whether we start from a functional or value chain approach, the capabilities that we identify are likely to be broadly defined: operational capability, marketing capability, supply chain management capability. However, having recognized that capabilities are the outcome of processes and routines, it is evident that these broadly defined capabilities can be disaggregated into more specialist capabilities. For example, human resource management capability can be disaggregated recruitment capability, HR appraisal capability, career development capability,—and others too. We can also recognize that even broadly defined functional capabilities integrate to form wider cross-functional capabilities: new product development, business development, the provision of customer solutions. What we observe is a hierarchy of capabilities where more general,

FIGURE 5.5 The hierarchical nature of capabilities: a manufacturer of PBXs

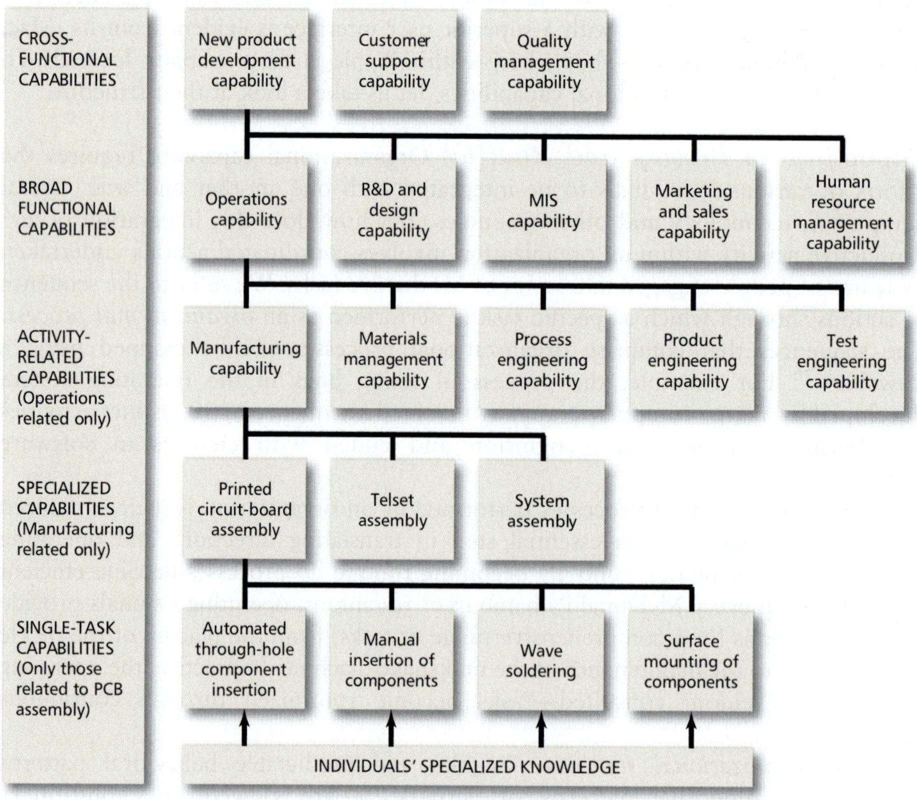

broadly defined capabilities are formed from the integration of more specialized capabilities. For example:

- A hospital's capability in treating heart disease depends on its integration of capabilities relating to patient diagnosis, physical medicine, cardiovascular surgery, preoperative and postoperative care, as well as capabilities relating to training, information technology and various administrative and support functions.
- Toyota's manufacturing capability—its system of "lean production"—integrates capabilities relating to the manufacture of components and subassemblies, supply-chain management, production scheduling, assembly, quality-control procedures, systems for managing innovation and continuous improvement, and inventory control.

Figure 5.5 offers a partial view of the hierarchy of capabilities of a telecom equipment maker. The capabilities at the highest level of integration—typically those that involve cross-functional and cross-divisional integration—are most difficult to develop, for the simple reason that they require integration across many individuals and across a broad spectrum of specialist knowledge. As a result, achieving excellence in new product development capabilities represents one of the greatest challenges that companies face in capability management—we will return to the topic of new product development in subsequent chapters.[24]

Appraising Resources and Capabilities

So far, we have established what resources and capabilities are, how they can provide a long-term focus for a company's strategy and how we can go about identifying them. However, given our emphasis on strategy as a quest for profit, the next stage of our analysis is to appraise the potential for resources and capabilities to earn profits for the company.

The profits that a firm obtains from its resources and capabilities depend on three factors: their abilities to *establish* a competitive advantage, to *sustain* that competitive advantage and to *appropriate* the returns to that competitive advantage. Each of these depends on a number of resource characteristics. Figure 5.6 shows the key relationships.

Establishing Competitive Advantage

For a resource or capability to establish a competitive advantage, two conditions must be present:

- *Scarcity*. If a resource or capability is widely available within the industry, then it may be essential to possess it in order to compete, but it will not be a sufficient basis for competitive advantage. In oil and gas exploration, new technologies such as directional drilling and 3-D seismic analysis are critical to reducing the costs of finding new reserves. However, these technologies are widely available from oilfield service and IT companies. As a result, such technologies are "needed to play," but they are not sufficient to win.

FIGURE 5.6 Appraising the strategic importance of resources and capabilities

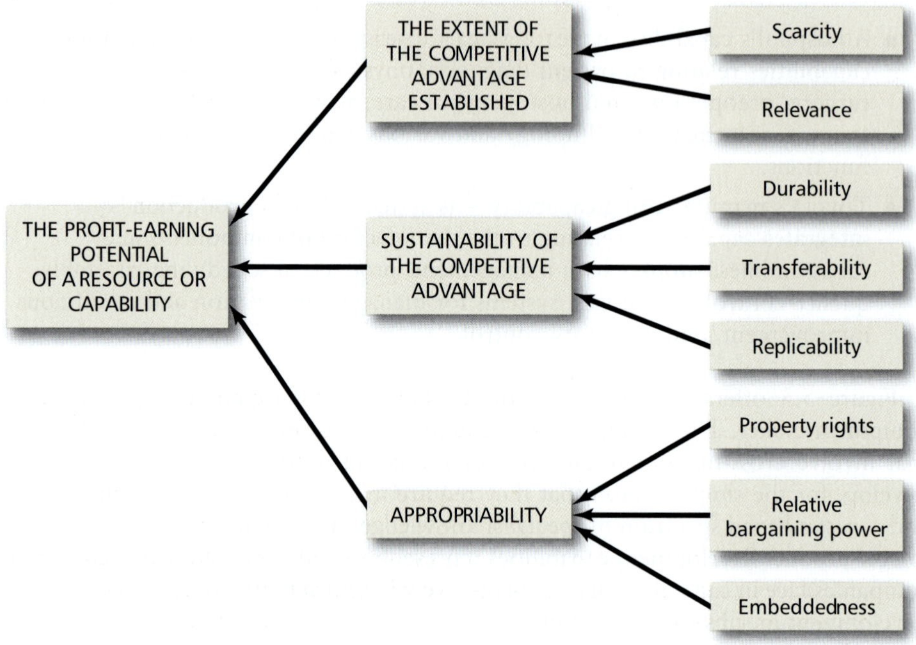

- *Relevance.* A resource or capability must be relevant to the key success factors in the market. British coal mines produced some wonderful brass bands. Unfortunately, musical capabilities did little to assist the mines in meeting competition from cheap imported coal and North Sea gas. As retail banking shifts toward automated teller machines and online transactions, so the retail branch networks of the banks have become less relevant for customer service.

Sustaining Competitive Advantage

The profits earned from resources and capabilities depend not just on their ability to *establish* competitive advantage but also on how long that advantage can be *sustained*. This depends on whether resources and capabilities are *durable* and whether rivals can *imitate* the competitive advantage they offer. Resources and capabilities are imitable if they are *transferable* or *replicable*.

Durability Some resources are more durable than others and, hence, are a more secure basis for competitive advantage. The increasing pace of technological change is shortening the useful life span of most resources including capital equipment and proprietary technologies. Brands, on the other hand, can show remarkable resilience to time. Heinz sauces, Kellogg's cereals, Guinness stout, Burberry raincoats and Coca-Cola have been market leaders for over a century.

Transferability The simplest means of acquiring the resources and capabilities necessary for imitating another firm's strategy is to buy them. The ability to buy a resource or capability depends on its *transferability*—the extent to which it is mobile between companies. Some resources, such as finance, raw materials, components, machines produced by equipment suppliers and employees with standardized skills (such as short-order cooks and auditors) are transferable and can be bought and sold with little difficulty. Some resources are not easily transferred—either they are entirely firm specific or their value depreciates on transfer.[25]

Sources of immobility include:

- Geographical immobility of natural resources, large items of capital equipment and some types of employees may make it difficult for firms to acquire these resources without relocating themselves. The competitive advantage of the Laphroaig distillery and its 10-year-old, single-malt whiskey is its water spring on the Isle of Islay, which supplies water flavored by peat and sea spray.
- Imperfect information regarding the quality and productivity of resources creates risks for buyers. Such imperfections are especially important in relation to human resources—hiring decisions are typically based on very little knowledge of how the new employee will perform. Sellers of resources have better information about the characteristics of the resources on offer than potential buyers—this creates a "lemons problem" for firms seeking to acquire resources.[26] Jay Barney has shown that different valuations of resources by firms can result in their being either underpriced or overpriced, giving rise to differences in profitability between firms.[27]
- Complementarity between resources means that the detachment of a resource from its "home team" causes it to lose productivity and value. Thus, if brand reputation is associated with the company that created it, a change in ownership of the brand erodes its value. The sale of Jaguar Cars, first to Ford and then to Tata Motors of India has almost certainly eroded its brand value.[28]
- Organizational capabilities, because they are based on teams of resources, are less mobile than individual resources. Even if the whole team can be transferred (in investment banking it has been commonplace for whole teams of analysts or mergers and acquisitions specialists to defect from one bank to another), the dependence of the team on a wider network of relationships and corporate culture may pose difficulties for recreating the capability in the new company.

Replicability If a firm cannot buy a resource or capability, it must build it. In financial services, most innovations in new derivative products can be imitated easily by competitors. In retailing, too, competitive advantages that derive from store layout, point-of-sale technology, charge cards and extended opening hours can be copied easily by competitors.

Capabilities based on complex organizational routines are less easily replicable. Federal Express's national, next-day delivery service and Nucor's system for steel manufacturing, which combines efficiency with flexibility, are complex capabilities based on unique corporate cultures. Some capabilities appear simple but prove difficult to replicate. Throughout the 1980s and 1990s, General Motors struggled to understand and replicate the Toyota lean production system. The NUMMI joint venture between the two companies gave GM a birds-eye view of Toyota's system in operation. Yet, after two decades of benchmarking, capital investment and employee training, GM was still lagging in efficiency, quality, and flexibility.[29]

Even where replication is possible, incumbent firms benefit from the fact that resources and capabilities that have been accumulated over a long period can only be replicated at disproportionate cost by would-be imitators. Dierickx and Cool identify two major sources of incumbency advantage:

- *Asset mass efficiencies* occur where a strong initial position in technology, distribution channels, or reputation facilitates the subsequent accumulation of these resources.
- *Time compression diseconomies* are the additional costs incurred by imitators when attempting to accumulate rapidly a resource or capability. Thus, "crash programs" of R&D and "blitz" advertising campaigns tend to be less productive than similar expenditures made over a longer period.[30]

Appropriating the Returns to Competitive Advantage

Who gains the returns generated by superior capabilities? We should normally expect that such returns accrue to the owner of that capability. However, ownership is not always clear-cut: capabilities depend heavily on the skills and efforts of employees—who are not owned by the firm. For companies dependent on human ingenuity and know-how, the mobility of key employees represents a constant threat to their competitive advantage (see Strategy Capsule 5.3). In investment banks and other human capital-intensive firms, the struggle between employees and shareholders to appropriate rents is reminiscent of the war for surplus value between labor and capital that Marx analyzed. It is notable that in 2006, average employee pay among Goldman Sachs' 27 000 staff (including secretaries and janitors) was $622 000.[31] The prevalence of partnerships (rather than joint-stock companies) in professional service industries (lawyers, accountants, and management consultants) reflects the desire to avoid conflict between its owners and its human resources.

STRATEGY CAPSULE 5.3

When Your Competitive Advantage Walks Out the Door: Gucci

On September 10, 2001, French retailer Pinault Printemps Redoute (PPR) agreed to acquire Gucci Group—the Italian-based fashion house and luxury goods maker. On November 4, 2003, the managers and shareholders of the two companies were stunned to learn that Chairman Domenico De Sole and Vice Chairman Tom Ford would be leaving Gucci in April, 2004.

The duo had masterminded Gucci's transformation from a near-bankrupt family firm with an over-extended brand into one of the world's hottest fashion houses. As creative director, Tom

Ford had established Gucci as a style leader and hired young designers such as Stella McCartney and Alexander McQueen. De Sole's astute leadership had instituted careful planning and financial discipline, and built Gucci's global presence—especially in Asia.

How great a blow was De Sole and Ford's departure to the parent PPR? In principle, a new CEO and new head of design could be hired. In practice, talent of the ilk of De Sole and Ford was rare—especially a combination of designer and CEO who could collaborate around a shared vision.

The stock market's reaction was ominous. On November 3, 2003, Gucci's share price was $86.10; on November 6 it had fallen to $84.60. However, in the absence of PPR's guarantee to acquire Gucci's shares at $85.52, analysts estimated that Gucci would be trading at around $74. The implication was that Gucci was worth $1.2 billion less without De Sole and Ford than with them.

Source: Adapted from articles in the *Financial Times* during November 5–8, 2003.

The less clearly defined are property rights in resources and capabilities, the greater the importance of relative bargaining power in determining the division of returns between the firm and its individual members. In the case of team-based organizational capabilities, this balance of power between the firm and an individual employee depends crucially on the relationship between individuals' skills and organizational routines. The more deeply embedded are individual skills and knowledge within organizational routines, and the more they depend on corporate systems and reputation, the weaker the employee is relative to the firm.

Conversely, the closer an organizational capability is identified with the expertise of individual employees, and the more effective those employees are at deploying their bargaining power, the better able employees are to appropriate rents. If the individual employee's contribution to productivity is clearly identifiable, if the employee is mobile, and if the employee's skills offer similar productivity to other firms, the employee is in a strong position to appropriate most of his or her contribution to the firm's value added. Does the $29 million annual salary paid to Alex Rodriguez fully exploit his value to the New York Yankees? In most professional sports, it appears that strategies based exclusively on signing superstar players result in the players appropriating most of the rents, with little surplus available for the clubs—this was certainly the fate of Real Madrid, Chelsea, and Manchester City soccer clubs in recent years. The emphasis by investment banks and consulting companies upon the capabilities of their teams, rather than upon the role of star employees, is a strategy for improving the bargaining power of the firm relative to that of its key employees.

Putting Resource and Capability Analysis to Work: A Practical Guide

We have covered the principal concepts and frameworks for analyzing resources and capabilities. How do we put this analysis into practice? Let me offer a simple, step-by-step approach to how a company can appraise its resources and capabilities and then use the appraisal to guide strategy formulation.

Step 1 Identify the Key Resources and Capabilities

To draw up a list of the firm's resources and capabilities we can begin from outside or inside the firm. From an external focus, we begin with key success factors (see Chapter 3). Which factors determine why some firms in an industry are more successful than others and on what resources and capabilities these success factors are based? Suppose we are evaluating the resources and capabilities of Volkswagen AG, the German-based automobile manufacturer. We can start with key success factors in the world automobile industry: low-cost production, attractively designed new models embodying the latest technologies, the financial strength to weather the heavy investment requirements and cyclical nature of the industry. What capabilities and resources do these key success factors imply? They would include manufacturing capabilities, new product development capability, effective supply-chain management, global distribution, brand strength, scale-efficient plants with up-to-date capital equipment, a strong balance sheet, and so on.

To organize these various resources and capabilities, it is useful to take an inside view of VW and examine the company's value chain, identifying the sequence of activities from new product development to purchasing, to supply chain management, to component manufacture, assembly, and right the way through to dealership support and after-sales service. We can then look at the resources that underpin the capabilities at each stage of the value chain. Table 5.4 lists VW's principal resources and capabilities.

Step 2 Appraising Resources and Capabilities

Resources and capabilities need to be appraised against two key criteria. First, their *importance*: which resources and capabilities are most important in conferring sustainable competitive advantage? Second, where are strengths and weaknesses as compared with competitors?

Assessing Importance The temptation in assessing which resources and capabilities are most important is to concentrate on customer choice criteria. What we must bear in mind, however, is that our ultimate objective is not to attract customers but to make superior profit through establishing a sustainable competitive advantage. For this purpose we need to look beyond customer choice to the underlying strategic characteristics of resources and capabilities. To do this we need to apply the set of appraisal criteria outlined in the previous section on "Appraising Resources and Capabilities." In the case of VW, many resources and capabilities are essential to compete in the business but several of them are not scarce (for example, total quality management capability and technologically advanced assembly plants have become widely diffused within the industry), while others (such as IT capability and design capability) are outsourced to external providers—either way, they are "needed to play" but not "needed to win." On the other hand, resources such as brand strength and a global distribution network and capabilities such as fast-cycle new product development and global logistics capability, cannot be easily acquired or internally developed—they are critical to establishing and sustaining advantage.

Assessing Relative Strengths It is difficult to appraise objectively the comparative strengths and weaknesses of a company's resources and capabilities relative to competitors. In assessing their own competencies, organizations

TABLE 5.4 Appraising VW's resources and capabilities

	Importance[a]	VW's relative strength[b]	Comments
RESOURCES			
R1. Finance	6	6	Credit rating is above average for the industry but free cash flow remains negative
R2. Technology	7	5	Despite technical strengths, VW is not a leader in automotive technology
R3. Plant and equipment	8	8	Has invested heavily in upgrading plants
R4. Location	4	4	Plants in key low-cost, growth markets (China, Mexico, Brazil) but German manufacturing base is very expensive
R5. Distribution (dealership network)	8	5	Geographically extensive distribution with special strength in emerging markets. Historically weak position within the U.S.
R6. Brands	6	5	VW, Audi, Bentley and Bugatti are strong brands but, together with Skoda and Seat, VW's brand portfolio lacks coherence and clear market positioning
CAPABILITIES			
C1. Product development	9	4	Traditionally weak at VW. Despite a few big hits: Beetle (introduced 1938), Golf (1974), Passat (1974), Vanagon (1979), VW still not an industry leader in new product development
C2. Purchasing	7	5	Traditionally weak—strengthened by senior hires from Opel and elsewhere
C3. Engineering	7	9	The core technical strength of VW
C4. Manufacturing	8	4	VW is a high-cost producer, but struggles to attain above average quality
C5. Financial management	6	4	Has traditionally lacked a strong financial orientation
C6. R&D	5	4	Despite several technical strengths, VW is not a leader in automotive innovation
C7. Marketing and sales	9	4	Despite traditional weakness in recognizing and meeting customer needs in different national markets, VW has increased its sensitivity to the market, improved brand management, and managed its advertising and promotion with increasing dexterity
C8. Government relations	4	8	Important in emerging markets
C9. Strategic management	7	4	Effective restructuring and cost cutting, but lack of consistency and consensus at top management level

[a]Both scales range from 1 to 10 (1 = very low, 10 = very high).

[b]Volkswagen's resources and capabilities are compared with those of GM, Ford, Toyota, DaimlerChrysler, Nissan, Honda, Fiat, and PSA, where 5 represents parity. The ratings are based on the author's subjective judgment.

frequently fall victim to past glories, hopes for the future and their own wishful thinking. The tendency toward hubris among companies—and their senior managers—means that business success often sows the seeds of its own destruction.[32] Among the failed industrial companies in America and Europe are many whose former success blinded them to their stagnating capabilities and declining competitiveness: examples include the cutlery producers of Sheffield, England, and the integrated steel giants of the U.S.

To identify and appraise a company's capabilities, managers must look both inside and outside. Internal discussion can be valuable in sharing insights and evidence and building consensus regarding the organization's resource and capability profile. The evidence of history can be particularly revealing in reviewing instances where the company has performed well and those where it has performed poorly: do any patterns appear?

Finally, to move the analysis from the subjective to the objective level, *benchmarking* is a powerful tool for quantitative assessment of performance relative to that of competitors. Benchmarking is "the process of identifying, understanding, and adapting outstanding practices from organizations anywhere in the world to help your organization improve its performance."[33] Benchmarking offers a systematic framework and methodology for identifying particular functions and processes and then for comparing their performance with other companies. Strategy Capsule 5.4 offers some examples. As McKinsey & Co. has shown, performance differentials between top-performing and average-performing companies in most activities tends to be wide.[34]

STRATEGY CAPSULE 5.4

Using Benchmarking to Assess Capabilities

By systematically comparing processes and activities with those of other firms, benchmarking allows a company to make an objective appraisal of its capabilities. The key stages in the benchmarking process are

1 Deciding what to benchmark.
2 Identifying partners.
3 Establishing benchmarking metrics.
4 Gathering data.
5 Analysis.

This then forms the foundation for programs to imitate the superior capabilities of other firms.

Xerox Corporation was the pioneer of benchmarking. Losing market share during the 1980s, logistics engineer Robert Camp performed detailed comparisons that showed the massive superiority of Japanese competitors in cost efficiency, quality and new product development. Every department at Xerox was encouraged to look beyond competitors to identify best-in-class companies against which to benchmark. For inventory control and customer responsiveness, Xerox benchmarked against L. L. Bean, the direct-mail clothing company.

During the early 1990s, Chrysler benchmarked its new product development against Honda. The result was a total reorganization of Chrysler's product development organization, which resulted in greatly reduced cycle time for new models and enhanced launch quality.

Bank of America (B of A) engaged in a series of benchmarking studies with Royal Bank of Canada which was similar in size and philosophy but was not a direct competitor. These allowed B of A first to highlight anomalies and then carry out more detailed comparisons of processes.

However, benchmarking carries risks. Jeff Pfeffer laments the propensity for benchmarking to encourage uniformity: "Take an airplane flight. With very few exceptions, can you tell them apart?" Dan Levinthal points to the danger of looking at specific practices without taking account of interdependencies with other processes and the organizational context more broadly: "Companies should be cautious about benchmarking or imitating certain policies and practices of other firms . . . the implicit assumption in this thinking is that the policy that is benchmarked and adopted is independent of what my firm is already doing. The best human resource management practice for Nordstrom may not be the best for McDonald's. It may actually be dysfunctional."

Sources: Robert C. Camp, *Benchmarking: The Search for Industry Best Practices that Lead to Superior Performance* (Florence, KY: Productivity Press, 2006). J. Pfeffer, *What Were They Thinking?* (Boston: Harvard Business School Press, 2007, Chapter 23 "Dare to be Different"). "A New Tool for Resurrecting an Old Theory of the Firm," Knowledge@Wharton, May 17, 2006 (http://knowledge.wharton.upenn.edu/article/1480.cfm, accessed 16 June, 2009).

Ultimately, appraising resources and capabilities is not about data—it is about insight and understanding. Every organization has some activity where it excels or has the potential to excel. For Federal Express, it is a system that guarantees next-day delivery anywhere within the U.S. For BMW it is the ability to integrate world-class engineering with design excellence and highly effective marketing. For McDonald's, it is the ability to supply millions of hamburgers from thousands of outlets throughout the world, with remarkable uniformity of quality, customer service and hygiene. For General Electric, it is a system of corporate management that reconciles coordination, innovation, flexibility and financial discipline in one of the world's largest and most diversified corporations. All these companies are examples of highly successful enterprises. One reason why they are successful is that they have recognized what they can do well and have based their strategies on their strengths. For poor-performing companies the problem is not necessarily an absence of distinctive capabilities but a failure to recognize what they are and to deploy them effectively.

Bringing Together Importance and Relative Strength Putting the two criteria—importance and relative strength—together allows us to highlight a company's key strengths and key weaknesses. Consider, for example, Volkswagen AG. Table 5.4 provides a partial (and hypothetical) identification and appraisal of VW's resources and capabilities at the beginning of the 21st century in relation to the two criteria of importance and relative strength outlined above. Figure 5.7 then brings the two criteria together into a single display. Dividing this display into four quadrants allows us to identify those resources and capabilities that we may regard

FIGURE 5.7 Appraising VW's resources and capabilities (hypothetical)

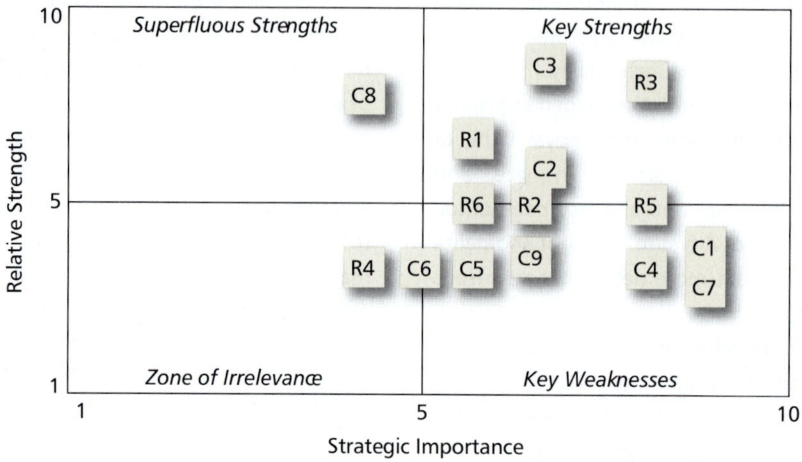

Note: Figure 5.7 is based on the ratings of resources and capabilities in Table 5.4.

as key strengths and those that we may identify as key weaknesses. For example, our assessment suggests that plant and equipment, engineering capability and supply chain management are key strengths of VW, whereas distribution (a relatively weak presence in the U.S. and Japan), new product development (no consistent record of fast-cycle development of market-winning new models) and financial management are key weaknesses.

Step 3 Developing Strategy Implications

Our key focus is on the two right-hand quadrants of Figure 5.7. How do we exploit our key strengths most effectively? How can we address our key weaknesses in terms of both reducing our vulnerability to them and correcting them? Finally, what about our "inconsequential" strengths? Are these really superfluous or are there ways in which we can deploy them to greater effect?

Exploiting Key Strengths Having identified resources and capabilities that are important and where our company is strong relative to competitors, the key task is to formulate our strategy to ensure that these resources are deployed to the greatest effect. If engineering is a key strength of VW, then it may wish to seek differentiation advantage through technical sophistication and safety features. If VW is effective in managing government relations and is well positioned in the potential growth markets of China, Eastern Europe, and Latin America, exploiting this strength may require developing models that will appeal to these markets.

To the extent that different companies within an industry have different capability profiles, this implies differentiation of strategies within the industry. Thus, Toyota's outstanding manufacturing capabilities and fast-cycle new product development, Hyundai's low-cost manufacturing capability that derives from its South Korean location, and Peugeot's design flair suggest that each company should be pursuing a distinctively different strategy.

Managing Key Weaknesses What does a company do about its key weaknesses? It is tempting to think of how companies can upgrade existing resources and capabilities to correct such weaknesses. However, converting weakness into strength is likely to be a long-term task for most companies. In the short to medium term, a company is likely to be stuck with the resources and capabilities that it inherits from the previous period.

The most decisive—and often most successful—solution to weaknesses in key functions is to outsource. Thus, in the automobile industry, companies have become increasingly selective in the activities they perform internally. During the 1930s, Ford was almost completely vertically integrated. At its massive River Rouge plant, which once employed over 100 000 people, coal and iron ore entered at one end, completed cars exited at the other. In 2004, Ford opened its Dearborn Truck Plant on the old River Rouge site. The new plant employed 3 200 Ford workers and an equal number of suppliers' employees. Almost all component production was outsourced along with a major part of design, engineering, assembly, IT and security. In athletic shoes and clothing, Nike undertakes product design, marketing, and overall "systems integration," but manufacturing, logistics, and many other functions are contracted out. We shall consider the vertical scope of the firm at greater depth in Chapter 14.

Through clever strategy formulation a firm may be able to negate the impact of its key weaknesses. Consider Harley-Davidson: in competition with Honda, Yamaha, and BMW and with sales of 300 000 bikes a year (compared with 10 million at Honda), Harley is unable to compete on technology. How has it dealt with this problem? It has made a virtue out of its outmoded technology and traditional designs. Harley-Davidson's obsolete push-rod engines and recycled designs have become central to the retro-look appeal of the "hog."

What about Superfluous Strengths? What about those resources and capabilities where a company has particular strengths, but these don't appear to be important sources of sustainable competitive advantage? One response may be to lower the level of investment from these resources and capabilities. If a retail bank has a strong but increasingly underutilized branch network, this may be an opportunity to prune its real estate assets and invest in web-based customer services.

However, in the same way that companies can turn apparent weaknesses into competitive strengths, so it is possible to develop innovative strategies that turn apparently inconsequential strengths into key strategy differentiators. Edward Jones' network of brokerage offices and 8 000-strong sales force looked increasingly irrelevant in an era when brokerage transactions were going online. However, by emphasizing personal service, trustworthiness, and its traditional, conservative investment virtues, Edward Jones has built a successful contrarian strategy based on its network of local offices.[35]

In the fiercely competitive MBA market, business schools should also seek to differentiate on the basis of idiosyncratic resources and capabilities. Georgetown's Jesuit heritage is not an obvious source of competitive advantage for its MBA programs. Yet, the Jesuit approach to education is about developing the whole person; this fits well with an emphasis on developing the values, integrity and emotional intelligence necessary to be a successful business leader. Similarly, Dartmouth College's location in woods of New Hampshire far from any major business center is not an obvious benefit to its business programs. However, Dartmouth's Tuck Business School has used the isolation and natural beauty of its locale to create an MBA program that features unparalleled community and social involvement that fosters personal development and close network ties.

Summary

We have shifted the focus of our attention from the external environment of the firm to its internal environment. This internal environment comprises many features of the firm but, for the purposes of strategy analysis, the key issue is what the firm *can do*. This means looking at the resources of the firm and the way resources combine to create organizational capabilities. Our interest is the potential for resources and capabilities to establish sustainable competitive advantage. Systematic appraisal of a company's resources and capabilities provides the basis for formulating (or reformulating) strategy. How can the firm deploy its strengths to maximum advantage? How can it minimize its vulnerability to its weaknesses? Figure 5.8 provides a simplified view of the approach to resource analysis developed in this chapter.

FIGURE 5.8 Summary: a framework for analyzing resources and capabilities

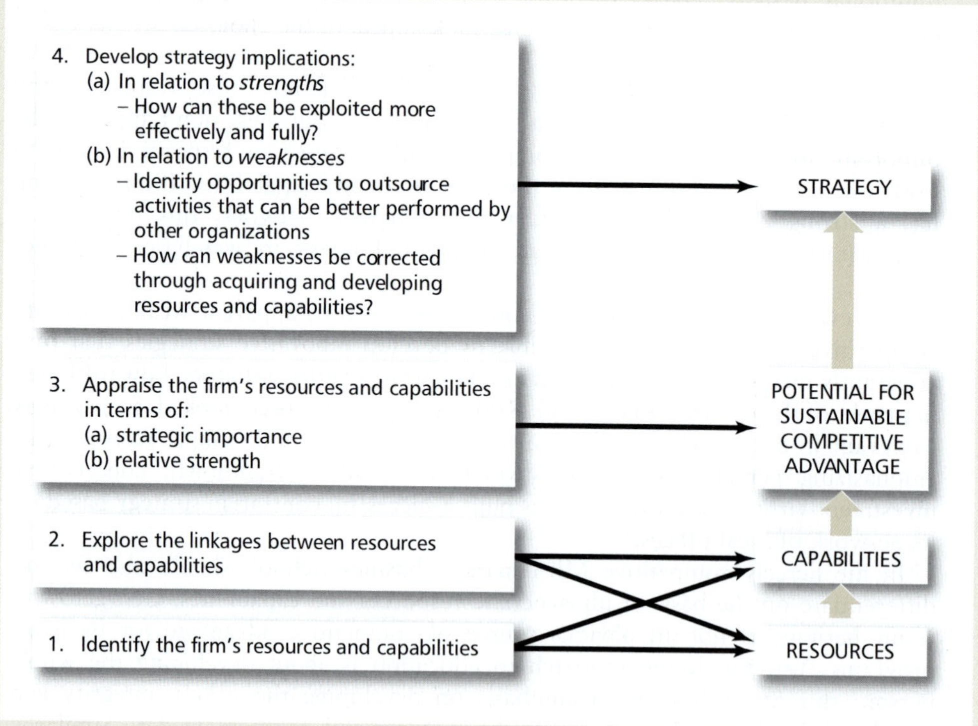

Although much of the discussion has been heavy on concepts and theory, the issues are practical. The management systems of most firms devote meticulous attention to the physical and financial assets that are valued on their balance sheets; much less attention has been paid to the critical intangible and human resources of the firm, and even less to the identification and appraisal of organizational capability. Most senior managers are now aware of the importance of their resources and capabilities but the techniques of identifying, assessing and developing them are woefully underdeveloped.

Because the resources and capabilities of the firm form the foundation for building competitive advantage, we shall return again and again to the concepts of this chapter. At the same time, I have deliberately limited the scope of this chapter. My emphasis has been on identifying, appraising and deploying firms' existing resources and capabilities. What about developing resources and capabilities for the future? In particular, can firms develop entirely new capabilities or are they restricted to playing the hand that the past has dealt them? This is our next port of call.

Self-Study Questions

1 In recent years Google has expanded from internet search across a broad range of internet services, including email, photo management, satellite maps, digital book libraries, blogger services, and telephony. To what extent has Google's strategy been built upon a common set of resources and capabilities rather than specific customer needs? What are Google's principal resources and capabilities?

2 Microsoft's main capabilities relate to the development and marketing of complex computer software and its greatest resource is its huge installed base of its Windows operating system. Does Microsoft's entry into video game consoles indicate that its strategy is becoming divorced from its principal resources and capabilities?

3 During 1984–8, Michael Eisner, the newly installed CEO of Walt Disney Company, successfully exploited Disney's existing resources to boost profitability (see Strategy Capsule 5.2). During the last eight years of Eisner's tenure (1998–2005), however, profitability stagnated and share price declined. To what extent did Eisner focus too much on exploiting existing resources and not enough on developing Disney's capabilities to meet the entertainment needs of a changing world?

4 Many companies announce in their corporate communications: "Our people are our most important resource." In terms of the criteria listed in Figure 5.6, can employees be considered to be of the utmost strategic importance?

5 Given the profile of VW's resources and capabilities outlined in Table 5.4 and Figure 5.7, what strategy recommendations would you offer VW?

6 Apply the approach outlined in the section "Putting Resource and Capability Analysis to Work" to your own business school. Begin by identifying the resources and capabilities relevant to success in the market for business education, appraise the resources and capabilities of your school, then make strategy recommendations regarding such matters as the programs to be offered and the overall positioning and differentiation of the school and its offerings.

Notes

1 The "resource-based view" is described in J. B. Barney, "Firm Resources and Sustained Competitive Advantage," *Journal of Management* 17 (1991): 99–120; J. Mahoney and J. R. Pandian, "The Resource-Based View within the Conversation of Strategic Management," *Strategic Management Journal* 13 (1992): 363–80; M. A. Peterlaf, "The Cornerstones of Competitive Advantage: A Resource-Based View," *Strategic Management Journal* 14 (1993): 179–92; and R. M. Grant, "The Resource-based Theory of Competitive Advantage," *California Management Review* 33 (1991): 114–35.

2 Ted Levitt, "Marketing Myopia," *Harvard Business Review* (July–August 1960): 24–47 proposed that firms should define their strategies on the basis of customer needs rather than products, for example, railroad companies should view themselves as in the transportation business. However, this fails to address the resource implications of serving these broad customer needs.

3 C. K. Prahalad and G. Hamel, "The Core Competence of the Corporation," *Harvard Business Review* (May–June 1990): 79–91.

4 E. Danneels, B. Provera and G. Verona, "Legitimizing Exploration: Olivetti's Transition from Mechanical to Electronic Technology" Management Department, Bocconi University, 2008; also "Olivetti Reinvents Itself Once More," *Wall Street Journal* (February 22, 1999): A.1.

5 "Eastman Kodak: Meeting the Digital Challenge," in R. M. Grant, *Cases to Accompany Contemporary Strategy Analysis* 6th edn (Oxford: Blackwell, 2008).

6 M. Tripsas, "Unraveling the Process of Creative Destruction: Complementary Assets and Incumbent Survival in the Typesetter Industry," *Strategic Management Journal* 18, Summer Special Issue (1997): 119–42; J. Bower and C. M. Christensen, "Disruptive Technologies: Catching the Wave," *Harvard Business Review* (January-February 1995): 43–53.

7 A. Madhok and S. Li, "Ricardo Revisited: The Resource Based View, Comparative Advantage and Competitive Heterogeneity" (September 28, 2004). Available at SSRN: http://ssrn.com/abstract=611182, accessed 16 June, 2009.

8 "Why It Is So Hard to Value a Mystery," *Financial Times* Special Report (January 7, 2008): 2.

9 Economies of scope in brands can also be exploited by licensing. Harley-Davidson licenses its brands to the manufacturers of apparel, toys, autos, and toiletries.

10 *Economic Survey of the European Union, 2007* (Paris: OECD, 2007).

11 E. Lawler, "From Job-Based to Competency-Based Organizations," *Journal of Organizational Behavior* 15 (1994): 3–15; L. Spencer, D. McClelland, and S. Spencer, *Competency Assessment Methods: History and State of the Art* (Hay/McBer Research Group, 1994); L. Spencer and S. Spencer, *Competence At Work: Models for Superior Performance* (New York: John Wiley & Sons, Inc., 1993).

12 D. Goleman, *Emotional Intelligence* (New York: Bantam, 1995).

13 J. Barney, "Organizational Culture: Can It Be a Source of Sustained Competitive Advantage?" *Academy of Management Review* 11 (1986): 656–65.

14 C. E. Helfat and M. Lieberman, "The Birth of Capabilities: Market Entry and the Importance of Prehistory," *Industrial and Corporate Change* 12 (2002): 725–60.

15 G. Hamel and C. K. Prahalad argue (*Harvard Business Review*, May-June 1992: 164–5) that "the distinction between competencies and capabilities is purely semantic."

16 P. Selznick, *Leadership in Administration: A Sociological Interpretation* (New York: Harper & Row, 1957).

17 C. K. Prahalad and G. Hamel, "The Core Competence of the Corporation," op. cit.

18 G. Hamel and C. K. Prahalad, letter, *Harvard Business Review* (May-June 1992): 164–5.

19 Porter's value chain is the main framework of his *Competitive Advantage* (New York: Free Press, 1984). McKinsey & Company refers to the firm's value chain as its "business system." See: C. F. Bates, P. Chatterjee, F. W. Gluck, D. Gogel, A. Puri, "The Business System: A New Tool for Strategy Formulation and Cost Analysis," in *McKinsey on Strategy* (Boston: McKinsey & Company, 2000).

20 T. W. Malone, K. Crowston, J. Lee and B. Pentland, "Tools for Inventing Organizations: Toward a Handbook of Organizational Processes" *Management Science* 45 (1999): 425–43.
21 K. Crowston, "A Coordination Theory Approach to Organization Design" *Organization Science* 8 (1997): 157–75.
22 R. R. Nelson and S. G. Winter, *An Evolutionary Theory of Economic Change* (Cambridge, MA: Belknap, 1982).
23 As a result, specialists perform well in stable environments while generalists do well in variable conditions. See J. Freeman and M. Hannan, "Niche Width and the Dynamics of Organizational Populations," *American Journal of Sociology* 88 (1984): 1116–45.
24 K. B. Clark and T. Fujimoto, *Product Development Performance* (New York: Free Press, 1991).
25 See Richard Caves' discussion of "specific assets" in "International Corporations: The Industrial Economics of Foreign Investment," *Economica* 38 (1971): 1–27.
26 G. Akerlof, "The Market for Lemons: Qualitative Uncertainty and the Market Mechanism," *Quarterly Journal of Economics* 84 (1970): 488–500.
27 J. B. Barney, "Strategic Factor Markets: Expectations, Luck and Business Strategy," *Management Science* 32 (October 1986): 1231–41.
28 "Is India Bad for Jaguar," *Time* (December 14, 2007).
29 K. Ichijo and I. Nonaka, *Knowledge Creation and Management* (New York: Oxford University Press, 2006): 127–8; "The Open Secret of Success," *The New Yorker* (May 12, 2008).
30 I. Dierickx and K. Cool, "Asset Stock Accumulation and Sustainability of Competitive Advantage," *Management Science* 35 (1989): 1504–13.
31 "Good deal," *Boston Globe* (December 12, 2006).
32 D. Miller, *The Icarus Paradox: How Exceptional Companies Bring About Their Own Downfall* (New York: Harper-Business, 1990).
33 Benchnet: The Benchmarking Exchange (www.benchnet.com, accessed 16 June, 2009).
34 S. Walleck, D. O'Halloran, and C. Leader, "Benchmarking World-Class Performance," *McKinsey Quarterly* (1991): 3–24; "The Link Between Management and Productivity," *McKinsey Quarterly* (February, 2006). http://www.mckinseyquarterly.com/The_link_between_management_and_productivity_1725
35 C. Markides, *All the Right Moves* (Boston: Harvard Business School Press, 1999).

6 Developing Resources and Capabilities

An organization's ability to learn, and translate that learning into action rapidly is the ultimate competitive advantage.

— JACK WELCH, CHAIRMAN AND CEO, GENERAL ELECTRIC 1980–2001

OUTLINE

Introduction and Objectives

Our analysis of resources and capabilities has focused upon appraising and then deploying the firm's existing stock of resources and capabilities. Ultimately, however, sustaining and renewing competitive advantage in a changing world requires the continuous development and extension of existing resources and capabilities, and the nurturing of new ones. So what's the big deal? How difficult can this be? The short answer is "very difficult". In this chapter we shall address the challenge of developing and creating resources and capabilities. Our emphasis will be on organizational capabilities as this is where the critical challenges lie.

By the time you have completed this chapter, it is my intention that you will have achieved the following:

- recognition of the difficulties that managers face in developing the resources and capabilities of the organization—capabilities in particular;
- familiarity with the different approaches that firms have taken in developing organizational capabilities—and the merits and pitfalls of each;
- appreciation of the role of knowledge as the most important resource of the firm and the contribution knowledge management can play in developing organizational capability.

Developing Resources

Resources are comparatively simple—we know what they are and we have a formidable arsenal of concepts and techniques that we can deploy in developing them. In the case of brands, marketing has developed sophisticated approaches to understanding the nature of brand loyalty and the dynamics through which it can be built. In the case of technology, a substantial body of research and practical knowledge informs us about the sources of invention, the nurturing of innovation and the management of intellectual capital (which we shall encounter in Chapter 12). Human resource management has been one of the most active and rich areas of management where the principles of job design, motivation, training, and appraisal have developed enormously since the early days of scientific management 100 years ago.

There is still scope for improvement. As the 2007–8 credit crisis revealed, many financial institutions lacked good understanding of the risk characteristics of some of their financial assets—mortgage-backed securities in particular. Indeed, a major outcome of the credit crisis was recognition of the strategic importance of the liquidity characteristics of financial resources once financial markets had become frozen by risk aversion.[1] Nevertheless, for most categories of resource—whether tangible or intangible, human or nonhuman—we are aware both of the problems of limited information that is the primary risk of acquiring resources from the market and of the challenges involved in developing resources internally. Organizational capabilities are a different matter altogether.

The Challenge of Capability Development

Possibly the most difficult problem in developing capabilities is that we know little about the linkage between resources and capabilities. One observation that is confirmed repeatedly across very different fields of competitive endeavor is that capabilities are not simply an outcome of the resources upon which they are based.

In sport it is common to see resource-rich teams failing to match the achievements of teams that create strong capabilities from modest resources. In European soccer, teams built with modest finances and without the acquisition of top-class players (Arsenal, Bayern Munich, PSV Eindhoven and Valencia) frequently outplay star-studded teams built from massive finance outlays (Chelsea, Real Madrid, Manchester City and Inter Milan). In my former home town, Washington DC, the Redskins (NFL), Wizards (NBA), and Capitols (NHL) were among the most financially well-endowed teams in their leagues but succeeded in consistently disappointing their long-suffering fans. International competition tells a similar story; it is small, resource-poor countries that regularly outperform the pre-eminent national teams. Despite dominating the ranks of the world's best basketball players, the U.S. has won the World Basketball Championship just once since 1986. At the Beijing Olympics, the U.S. sprint relay teams—despite having some of the world's fastest runners—failed to win a single medal.

It is the same in business: the firms that demonstrate the most outstanding capabilities are not necessarily those with the greatest resource endowments:

- In automobiles, GM has four times the output of Honda and four times the R&D expenditure, yet, since 1980, it is Honda, not GM, that has been the world leader in power train technology.
- In animated movies, the most successful productions in recent years were by newcomers Pixar (Toy Story, The Incredibles) and Aardman Animations (Wallace and Gromit) rather than by industry giant, Walt Disney.
- In telecom equipment it was the upstart Cisco rather than established incumbents Alcatel-Lucent, Ericsson and Siemens that led the new era of package switching.

That said, there is one resource that does seem to be critical to the development of capabilities: the managers with the requisite knowledge for capability building. There is a great deal that we do not know about why some companies have developed certain capabilities to higher levels than other firms but one thing is clear—managers play a critical role in nurturing and shaping those capabilities. Among the founders of new companies, a substantial number have prior managerial experience within the same sector.[2] In new industries, the best-performing firms are often those whose founders had prior experience in closely related sector.[3] It is reasonable to suppose that the key knowledge that these entrepreneurs carry with them is an understanding of what it takes to build key organizational capabilities.

Path Dependency and the Role of Early Experiences

If organizational capability is not simply the result of the application of resources, what determines the capabilities in which a firm achieves distinctiveness? If we examine the types of capability that make different firms distinctive in their particular industries (the companies listed in Table 5.3 for example), one obvious feature is that these capabilities have developed over significant periods of time. In many cases we can trace the origins of a distinctive capability (or "core competence") to the circumstances which prevailed during the founding and early development of the company. In other words, organizational capability is *path dependent*—a company's capabilities today are the result of its history.[4]

Consider Wal-Mart Inc., the world's biggest retailer. How did it develop its outstanding capability in supply chain logistics? This superefficient system of warehousing, distribution and vendor relationships was not the result of careful planning and design; it evolved from the circumstances that Wal-Mart faced during its early years of existence. Its small-town locations in Arkansas and Oklahoma resulted in unreliable delivery from its suppliers, consequently Wal-Mart established its own distribution system. Similarly with its remarkable commitment to cost efficiency. Its management systems are undoubtedly important but ultimately it is Wal-Mart's origins in the rural South and the values and personality of its founder, Sam Walton, that sustain its obsession with cutting cost and eliminating waste.

Consider too the world's largest oil and gas majors (see Table 6.1). Despite long histories of competing together in the same markets, with near-identical products and similar strategies, the majors display very different capability profiles. Industry

TABLE 6.1 Distinctive capabilities as a consequence of childhood experiences: the oil majors

Company	Distinctive capability	Early history
Exxon	Financial management	Exxon's predecessor, Standard Oil (NJ), was the holding company for Rockefeller's Standard Oil Trust
Royal Dutch Shell	Coordinating a decentralized global network of 200 operating companies	Shell Transport & Trading headquartered in London and founded to sell Russian oil in China and the Far East Royal Dutch Petroleum headquartered in The Hague; founded to exploit Indonesian reserves
BP	"Elephant hunting"	Discovered huge Persian reserves, went on to find Forties field (North Sea) and Prudhoe Bay (Alaska)
ENI	Deal making in politicized environments	The Enrico Mattei legacy; the challenge of managing government relations in postwar Italy
Mobil	Lubricants	Vacuum Oil Co. founded in 1866 to supply patented petroleum lubricants

leaders Exxon and Royal Dutch Shell exemplify these differences. Exxon (now ExxonMobil) is known for its outstanding financial management capabilities exercised through rigorous investment controls and unrelenting cost efficiency. Shell is known for its decentralized, international management capability, which allows it to adapt to different national environments and to become an "insider" wherever it does business. These differences can be traced back to the companies' nineteenth-century origins. Exxon (then Standard Oil New Jersey) acted as holding company for Rockefeller's Standard Oil Trust, exercising responsibility for overall financial management. Shell was established to sell Russian oil in China and the Far East, while Royal Dutch was established to exploit Indonesian oil reserves. With head offices thousands of miles away in Europe, both parts of the group developed a decentralized, adaptable management style.

The Linkage between Resources and Capabilities

These observations are troubling for ambitious executives anxious to adapt and regenerate their companies: if a firm's capabilities are determined during the early stages of its life, is it really possible to develop the new capabilities needed to meet the challenges of tomorrow?

To explore this question let us look more closely at the structure of organizational capability—a topic we addressed briefly in Chapter 5. Capabilities, we observed, involve coordination between organizational members such that they integrate their skills with one another and with a variety of other resources. We will explore coordination more fully in the next chapter. Here let us focus on the primary means through which multiple resources become integrated and organizational members coordinate their activities. Figure 6.1 provides the framework for the discussion that follows.

As we shall explore further in the next chapter, coordination is the essence of what organizations do. We can distinguish formal and informal dimensions of this coordination. The literature on organizational routines emphasizes the informal

FIGURE 6.1 Integrating resources to create organizational capabilities

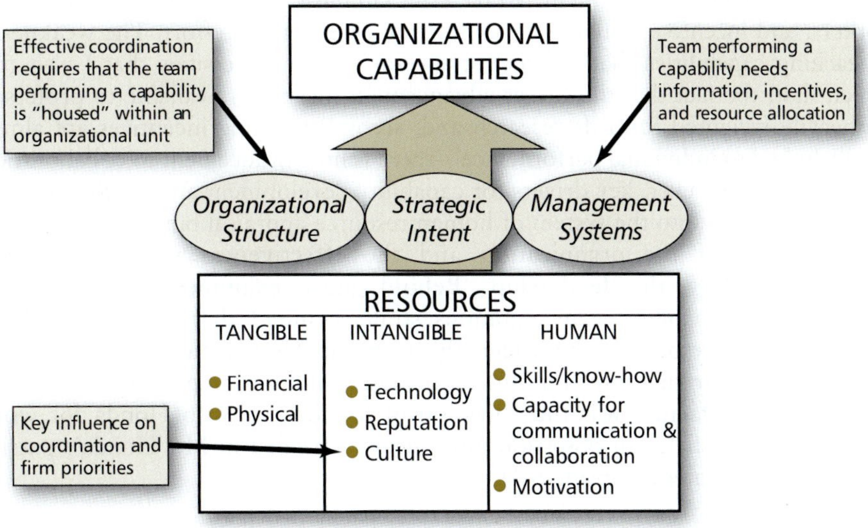

dimension. Routinization involves "repetitive patterns of activity," which are "ordinarily accomplished without conscious awareness."[5] Two factors contribute to the efficiency and effectiveness with which teams of individuals perform these repetitive patterns of activity. The first is *organizational learning*. Coordination is perfected through repetition. The more complex the task, the greater the gains from learning-by-doing.

The second is *culture*. Recall that in Chapter 5, I included culture as one of the intangible resources of the firm. In relation to capabilities, culture plays a pivotal role. The capacity for organizational members to comprehend one another and collaborate together without continual managerial direction depends upon shared perceptions, common values, and behavioral norms—all elements of the complex phenomenon that we refer to as *organizational culture*.

There is also an important formal dimension to the organizational aspects of capability. At the most basic level, coordination requires that the individuals required to perform a particular capabilities need to be located within a defined organizational unit. This seems obvious—yet organizations often disregard it. The major reason for the superior product development performance of Japanese car companies relative to their U.S. and European competitors was their creation of crossfunctional product development teams. Until the end of the 1980s, most U.S. auto companies operated a sequential "over-the-wall" product development system where new product development involved first marketing, then design, then engineering, then manufacturing, and finally finance.[6]

At several of the business schools I have worked, a common complaint among students has been lack of integration across courses while a common aspiration of several MBA course directors has been to introduce multidisciplinary courses that involve students in cross-functional problem solving. However, little can be achieved if faculty members are located within specialist, discipline-defined departments and coordination across courses is limited to a single "teachers' meeting" held each semester.

The coordination needed for organizational capability also requires appropriate management systems. These include information systems to allow each organizational member to identify changing circumstances and the actions of co-workers, and incentive systems to promote cooperation and effort. The weaknesses in teaching capabilities that I detect at several of the universities that I visit may reflect, first, the fact that the career-advancement incentives available to professors are heavily weighted towards research and, second, teaching incentives are almost wholly linked to individual performance—there is little inducement to collaboration.

Ultimately, however, key drivers for capability development are not the penalties and rewards built into the system of human resource appraisal but the overall drive and direction of the organization and the effectiveness with which it is communicated by the leadership. Behind most examples of outstanding organizational capability is an ambitious strategic intent that is instilled among organizational members by the leadership. Consider Honda's leadership in engine technology. The driving force for innovation and continuous improvement in engine design and manufacture was the obsession of founder Soichiro Honda for world leadership in this field, an obsession most clearly revealed in Mr. Honda's passion for racing (see Strategy Capsule 6.1).

STRATEGY CAPSULE 6.1

Siochiro Honda and the Isle of Man TT

The Isle of Man TT, which takes place on a rocky, rainswept island between England and Ireland, is one of the world's oldest—and most dangerous—motorcycle races. On March 20, 1954, when Honda Motor Company was still a tiny company less than six years old, company president, Soichiro Honda, made the following declaration to employees:

> *. . . Since I was a small child, one of my dreams has been to compete in motor vehicle races all over the world . . . I have reached the firm decision to enter the TT Races next year.*
>
> *I will fabricate a 250 cc (medium class) racer for this race, and as the representative of our Honda Motor Co., I will send it out into the spotlight of the world. I am confident that this vehicle can reach speeds exceeding 180 km/h . . . I address all employees!*
>
> *Let us bring together the full strength of Honda Motor Co. to win through to this glorious achievement. The future of Honda Motor Co. depends on this, and the burden rests on your shoulders. I want you to turn your surging enthusiasm to this task, endure every trial, and press through with all the minute demands of work and research, making this your own chosen path. The advances made by Honda Motor Co. are the growth you achieve as human beings, and your growth is what assures our Honda Motor Co. its future.*
>
> *With this, I announce my determination, and pledge with you that I will put my entire heart and soul, and turn all my creativity and skills to the task of entering*

the TT Races and winning them.
This I affirm.

A series of impediments (including opposition by the Japanese government and difficulties in conforming to the TT rules and regulations) delayed Honda's entry until 1958. In that year Honda won the manufacturer's prize.

Source: Honda Motor Company

We have examined the role of strategic intent and "big, hairy, ambitious goals" in discussing the drivers of firm success and in observing how such ambition is articulated in statements of corporate vision and mission. However, closer examination reveals that it is through its impact on the development of organizational capabilities that strategic intent impacts performance. In case after case, a similar story emerges: a business leader (very often the company founder) communicates a sincere and passionate commitment to a vision of the company. This communication typically takes the form of words and example, and inspires organizational members not only to substitute organizational goals for their own personal goals, but—equally importantly—to subordinate their personal preferences, principles and prejudices to team collaboration. This spirit of community and achievement is apparent at Samsung Electronics under the leadership of Jong-Yong Yun, at Swatch under Nicolas Hayek, and Southwest Airlines under Herb Kelleher. One of the roles of these leaders was to motivate capability upgrading by raising performance aspirations above levels of actual and expected performance levels.[7]

Are Organizational Capabilities Rigid or Dynamic?

If capabilities develop over long time periods, are embodied within organizational structure and are embedded within organizational culture, they act as barriers to a firm's ability to change. The more highly developed a firm's organizational capabilities are, the narrower its repertoire, and the more difficult it is for the firm to adapt them to new circumstances. Because Dell Computer's direct sales model was so highly developed, Dell found it difficult to adapt to selling though retail outlets as well. Thus, Dorothy Leonard-Barton argues that core capabilities are simultaneously *core rigidities*—they inhibit firms' ability to access and develop new capabilities.[8]

The idea that capabilities impose rigidities on firms has been challenged from two directions:

- *Flexibility in organizational routines*. The notion that routines are fixed patterns of interaction that function through automatic stimulus-response mechanisms has been undermined by studies that demonstrate that even basic operations display variation and the capacity to adapt.[9]
- *Dynamic capability*. Many companies are able to adapt to changing circumstances. The capacity to change may itself be regarded as an

organizational capability. David Teece and his colleagues introduced the term *dynamic capabilities* to refer to a "firm's ability to integrate, build, and reconfigure internal and external competences to address rapidly changing environments."[10] The precise definition of a dynamic capability has proven contentious. Eisenhardt and Martin consider dynamic capabilities to be any capabilities that allow an organization to reconfigure its resources in order to adapt and change.[11] Winter and Zollo are more precise: a dynamic capability is a "higher level" process through which the firm modifies its operating routines.[12]

What is agreed is that dynamic capabilities are far from common. For most companies, highly developed capabilities in existing products and technologies create barriers to developing capabilities in new products and new technologies. When adapting to radical change within an industry, or in exploiting entirely new business opportunities, are new firms at an advantage or disadvantage compared with established firms? It depends on whether the change or the innovation is competence enhancing or competence destroying. In TV manufacturing, the most successful new entrants were existing producers of radios—the new technology was compatible with their capabilities. However, in most new industries, the most successful firms tend to be startups rather than established firms. In personal computers, it was newcomers such as Dell, Acer, Compaq and Gateway that emerged as most successful during the 1990s. Among established firms, relatively few (IBM, Hewlett-Packard, and Toshiba) went on to significant success. Many others (such as, Xerox, GE, Texas Instruments, AT&T and Olivetti) exited. In wireless telephony, too, startups—Vodafone, McCaw Cellular, Orange—were more successful than established telephone companies.[13]

Approaches to Capability Development

So, how do companies go about developing new capabilities? Our focus here is on the internal development of capabilities. However, we need to acknowledge that firms can also import capabilities from outside—either by acquisition or alliance. Let us begin with a brief review of the issues involved in acquiring and accessing other firms' capabilities (we shall deal with mergers and, acquisitions more fully in Chapter 17), before considering different approaches to the internal development of organizational capability.

Acquiring Capabilities: Mergers, Acquisitions and Alliances

Acquiring a company that has already developed the desired capability can short-circuit the tortuous process of capability development. Among the many motives for corporate acquisition, obtaining another company's capabilities is common—especially in technologically fast-moving environments where established firms target specific technical capabilities. Microsoft's adaptation to the internet and its entry into video games was facilitated by multiple acquisitions. Each year, Microsoft hosts its VC Summit, where venture capitalists from all over the world are invited to market their companies. In building digital imaging capabilities, Eastman Kodak has made a host of acquisitions since 1994. Acquisitions are also used for obtaining other types of capability: Procter & Gamble's takeover of Gillette was motivated by P&G's desire to acquire Gillette's new product development capability.

However, using acquisitions to extend a company's capability base involves major risks. To begin with, acquisitions are expensive. In addition to the acquisition premium that must be paid, the targeted capability comes with a mass of additional resources and capabilities that are most likely surplus to requirements for the acquiring firm. Most important, once the acquisition has been made, the acquiring company must find a way to integrate the acquiree's capabilities with its own. All too often, culture clashes, personality clashes between senior managers, or incompatibility of management systems can result in the degradation or destruction of the very capabilities that the acquiring company was seeking. Selecting and integrating company acquisitions is itself an organizational capability. Cisco Systems' 136 acquisitions between 1996 and 2004 were critical to its expanding its base of technological and product development capabilities.[14]

These costs and risks add to the attractions of strategic alliances as a targeted and cost-effective means to access another company's capabilities. A *strategic alliance* is a cooperative relationship between firms involving the sharing of resources in pursuit of common goals. Long-running technical collaboration between HP and Canon has allowed both firms to enhance their printer technology. Prior to acquisition in 2005, Pixar's alliance with Disney allowed it to access Disney's marketing and distribution capabilities.

A key issue that arises in the formation and management of strategic alliances is whether their purpose is to gain *access* to the capabilities of the partner firm or to *acquire* those capabilities through one partner learning from the other.[15] The strategic alliance between Intel and DreamWorks Animation allows each company to access the other's capabilities in order to jointly develop next-generation stereoscopic 3D films.[16] Conversely, General Motors' NUMMI joint venture with Toyota to make cars at the former GM Fremont, California plant was primarily motivated by GM's desire to learn about the Toyota Production System.[17] Where both alliance partners are trying to acquire one another's capabilities, the result may well be a "competition for competence" that ultimately destabilizes the relationship.[18]

It is tempting to view strategic alliances as a quick and low-cost means of extending the capabilities available to a firm. However, managing alliance relationships is itself a critically important organizational capability. "Relational capability" comprises building trust, developing interfirm knowledge sharing routines, and establishing mechanisms for coordination.[19] The more a company outsources its value chain activities to a network of alliance partners, the more it needs to develop the "systems integration capability" to coordinate and integrate the dispersed activities.[20]

Internal Development: Focus and Sequencing

We have observed that, to build organizational capability, obtaining the necessary resources is the easy part. The challenge is in integrating these resources in order to do something. Indeed, achieving excellence in resources may militate against achieving high levels of integration. At London's Arsenal Football Club, manager Arsene Wenger sold his star players, Patrick Viera and Thierry Henry, on the basis that their presence inhibited coordinated effort from his young team.

Integrating resources into capabilities, we have seen, requires *organization* and *management systems* and is facilitated by culture and strategic intent. The implication is that capability development needs to be *systematic*. It needs to bring together the requisite human and nonhuman resources, locate these resources within a suitable organizational unit, establish the processes that perform the capability, allow these processes to develop through routinization, design management systems that support the capability and lead the entire effort through appropriate strategic intent.[21]

Achieving this complex task is likely to mean that an organization must limit the number and scope of the capabilities that it is attempting to create at any point in time. Hamel and Prahalad argue that the key to developing superior capabilities is "resource leveraging." Two key components of this leveraging are, first, "concentrating resources" by *focusing* the efforts of each group, department, and business unit on specific priorities and, second, "accumulating resources" through "mining experience" in order to accelerate learning.[22]

Focusing implies developing capabilities *sequentially*. Thus, complex capabilities can be developed incrementally through several stages and, in order to develop multiple capabilities, it is advisable to target no more than a few capabilities in each time period.

Given our limited knowledge about how capabilities are created and developed, companies often find it helpful to focus their capability development efforts not on the organizational capabilities themselves but on developing and supplying the products that use those capabilities. A trajectory through time of related, increasingly sophisticated products allows a firm to develop the "integrative knowledge" that is at the heart of organizational capability.[23] Matsushita utilizes this approach in developing operational capabilities in countries where it is establishing plants for the first time:

> In every country batteries are a necessity, so they sell well. As long as we bring a few advanced automated pieces of equipment for the processes vital to final product quality, even unskilled labor can produce good products. As they work on this rather simple product, the workers get trained, and this increased skill level then permits us to gradually expand production to items with increasingly higher technology levels, first radios, then televisions.[24]

Where a company is developing an entirely new area of business, such an approach can allow the sequential upgrading of products to be linked to targeting specific capabilities. Strategy Capsule 6.2 considers the development of Hyundai Motor.

Where a new capability requires structure, systems and culture that are different from those that support the firm's existing capabilities it may be helpful to develop the new capability within a new unit that is organizationally—and, preferably, geographically—separated from the main organization. Strategy Capsule 6.3 discusses examples of this approach.

STRATEGY CAPSULE 6.2

Hyundai Motor: Developing Capabilities through Product Sequencing

Hyundai's emergence as a world-class automobile producer is a remarkable example of capability development over a sequence of compressed phases. Each phase of the development process was characterized by a clear objective in terms of product outcome, a tight time deadline, an empowered development team, a clear recognition of the capabilities that needed to be developed in each phase, and an atmosphere of impending crisis should the project not succeed. The first phase was the construction of an assembly plant in the unprecedented time of 18 months in order to build Hyundai's first car—a Ford Cortina imported in semi-knocked down (SKD) form. Subsequent phases involved products of increasing sophistication and the development of more advanced capabilities.

Source: L. Kim, "Crisis construction and organizational learning: Capability building and catching up at Hyundai Motor," *Organizational Science* 9 (1998): 506–21.

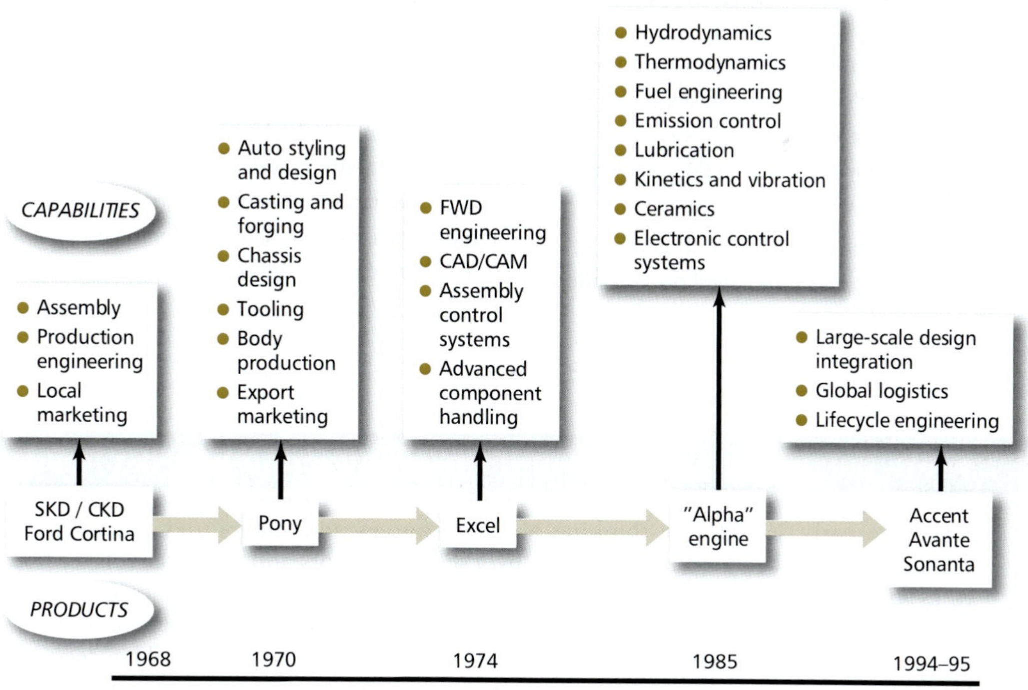

STRATEGY CAPSULE 6.3

Incubating Capabilities in Separate Organizational Units

The model for organizationally separate development units was Lockheed's "skunk works"—a product development team established in Burbank, California during the Second World War to develop innovative new military aircraft. Since then, a number of companies have used satellite units to develop new organizational capabilities:

- IBM developed its PC at a new unit led by veteran executive Bill Lowe and located in Florida—a thousand miles from IBM's corporate headquarters in New York. Lowe claimed that isolation from IBM's main organization was critical to the team's creation of a product design and business system that were radically different from those of IBM's mainframe business. In particular, the PC unit relied heavily on outsourcing in contrast to IBM's traditional emphasis on vertical integration.[25]
- The pioneering online financial services company Egg was established by its London-based parent, Prudential Insurance, in the Midlands towns of Dudley and Derby—well away from the London headquarters.

These separate incubator units combine the flexibility and autonomy of a startup, while drawing on the resources and capabilities of the parent. However, the critical challenge is in reintegrating the new capabilities back into the parent company. Xerox's Palo Alto Research Center (PARC) pioneered many of the technologies that formed the basis of the microcomputer revolution of the 1980s. However, it was much easier for these technologies to flow to nearby competitors—Hewlett-Packard, Apple, Microsoft, and Sun Microsystems—than it was for them to be absorbed by Xerox's east coast establishment.[26] GM's Saturn has had a similar experience. The Tennessee-based subsidiary achieved its objective of developing new manufacturing and marketing capabilities, but the Saturn experiment did little to revitalize the parent organization.[27]

Knowledge Management and the Knowledge-based View

Since the early 1990s, our thinking about resources and capabilities and their management has been extended greatly by a set of concepts and practices referred to as *knowledge management*. Knowledge management is an umbrella term that comprises a range of organizational processes and practices whose common feature is their concern with generating value from knowledge. The term "knowledge management" is of recent vintage but much of its content is not: it includes many long-established organizational functions such as R&D, management information systems, employee training, and managing intellectual property—even strategic planning could be regarded as a knowledge management activity. Initially, knowledge management was primarily concerned with information technology—especially the use of databases, intranets, expert systems and groupware for storing, analyzing and disseminating information. Subsequent developments in knowledge management have been concerned less with data and more with organizational learning—especially the transfer of best practices and the derivation of "lessons learned" from ongoing activities. Knowledge management has attracted its share of skepticism and ridicule. Lucy Kellaway of the *Financial Times* observes that it has "attracted more needless obfuscation and wooly thinking by academics and consultants than any other [area]."[28] *The Wall Street Journal* reports Saatchi & Saatchi's director of knowledge management as "absorbing everything under the sun" including an interest in Japanese pantyhose "embedded with millions of microcapsules of vitamin C and seaweed extract that burst when worn to provide extra nourishment for the limbs."[29]

The real value of knowledge management is, first, in providing a single overall view of the multiplicity of knowledge development, knowledge transfer and knowledge utilization activities that occur within the firm and, second, in explicitly recognizing their commonalities and differences. In terms of resources, almost all the resources of the firm can be viewed as a form of knowledge. While information and technology may be the only "pure" knowledge resources, the value of people derives almost entirely from the knowledge they can deploy. Similarly capital equipment may be viewed as the physical embodiment of knowledge. Capabilities represent knowledge at the organizational level resulting from the integration of the knowledge of multiple individuals.[30]

At the foundation of knowledge management is recognition of knowledge as the most important resource of the firm and the essence of organizational capability. What has become known as the *knowledge-based view of the firm* is a conception of the firm as an assemblage of knowledge assets where value is created by deploying this knowledge. The knowledge-based view offers a revealing perspective on the existence of the firm, the determination of its boundaries and its design and management.[31]

To appreciate how the knowledge-based view and knowledge management can further our understanding of how resources and capabilities can be developed within the firm, let us consider, first, the characteristics of knowledge and, second, the processes through which knowledge is created and applied.

Types of Knowledge

The single most important insight that knowledge management offers to the strategic management of resources and capabilities is recognizing that different types of knowledge have different characteristics. A key distinction is between *knowing how* and *knowing about*:

- *Know-how* is primarily *tacit* in nature—it involves skills that are expressed through their performance (riding a bicycle, playing the piano).
- *Knowing about* is primarily *explicit*—it comprises facts, theories, and sets of instructions.

The principal implication of this distinction between tacit and explicit knowledge relates to transferability:

- Explicit knowledge can be communicated at negligible marginal cost between individuals and across space and time. This ability to disseminate knowledge such that any one person's use does not limit any one else's access to the same knowledge means that explicit knowledge has the characteristic of a *public good*: once created, it can be replicated among innumerable users at low cost. The digital revolution and the internet have further reduced the costs of disseminating explicit knowledge.
- Tacit knowledge, on the other hand, cannot be directly articulated or codified. It can only be observed through its application and acquired through practice. Hence, its transfer between people is slow, costly, and uncertain.

This distinction has major implications for strategy. If explicit knowledge can be transferred so easily, it is seldom the foundation of sustainable competitive advantage. It is only secure from rivals when it is protected, either by intellectual property rights (patents, copyrights, trade secrets) or by secrecy ("The formula for Coca-Cola will be kept in a safe in the vault of our Atlanta headquarters guarded by heavily-armed Coca-Cola personnel."). The challenge of tacit knowledge is the opposite. If the culinary skills of award-winning chef Daniel Boulud have been acquired through intuition and learning-by-doing, how does he transfer this knowhow to the chefs and managers of his six restaurants in New York, Las Vegas, and Palm Beach, Florida? For consulting companies, the distinction between tacit ("personalized") and explicit ("systematized") knowledge defines their business model and is a central determinant of their strategy.[32]

The result is a "paradox of replication". In order to utilize knowledge—whether it is in the form of technology, human capital, or organizational capability— we need to replicate it; and replication is much easier if the knowledge is in explicit form. Yet, in doing so, we also make it easier for rivals to imitate our knowledge. Facilitating internal replication, while limiting external replication, is a key challenge for firms.[33]

Knowledge Processes that Promote Capability Development

A key distinction is between those knowledge processes that focus on the acquisition of new knowledge and those which exploit existing knowledge—James March refers to this as the tradeoff between *exploration* and *exploitation*.[34] Figure 6.2 categorizes the main knowledge processes that are relevant to developing organizational capabilities.

In the context of our previous discussion of types of capability, exploration activities are associated most closely with *dynamic capabilities*—they are processes through which the firm changes itself. Exploration activities that build the organization's stock of knowledge include both the internal creation of knowledge (*knowledge creation*) and the identification and absorption of existing knowledge from outside the organization (*knowledge acquisition*). The mechanisms for acquiring outside knowledge include: hiring skilled employees, acquiring companies or their knowledge resources, benchmarking "best-in-class" companies, and learning through alliances. We shall return to the themes creativity and innovation in Chapter 12.

FIGURE 6.2 Types of knowledge process within an organization

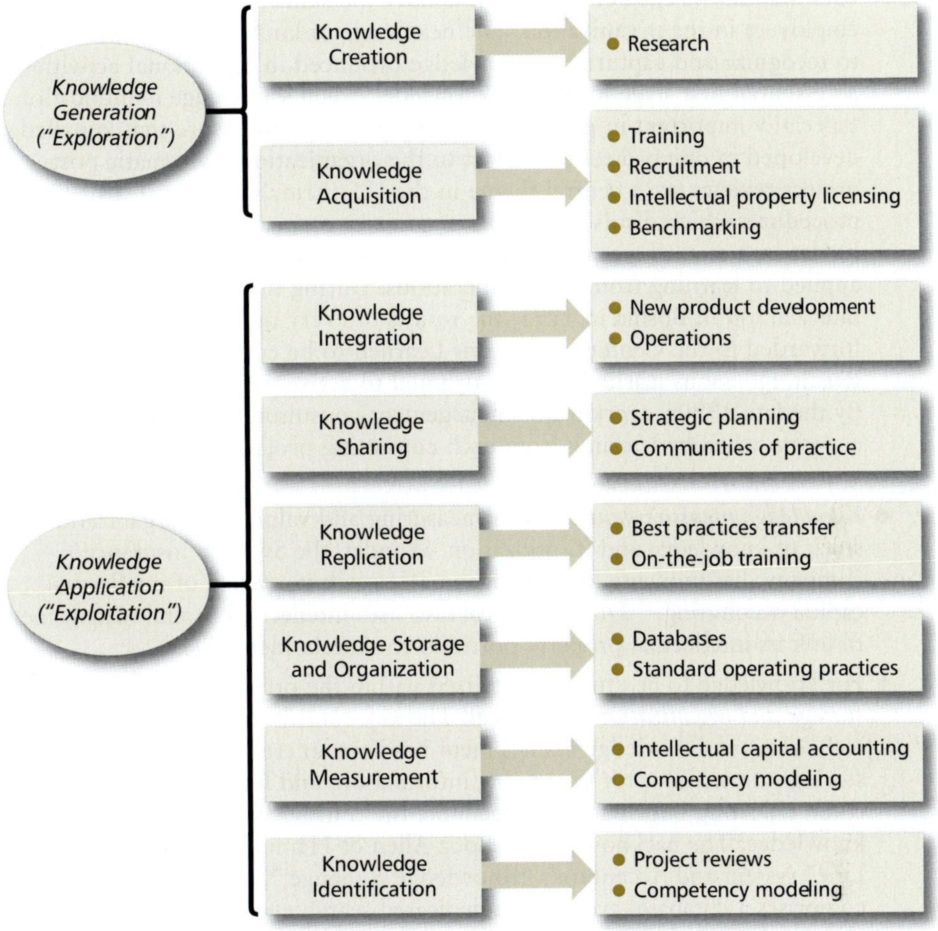

The exploration-exploitation distinction is less clear in practice than in principle—exploitation involves not only the use of existing knowledge but also its development.[35] These development processes are critical to the ungrading and improvement of existing operational and functional capabilities. Some of the most important contributions of knowledge management to capability building are in improving the utilization of existing knowledge and capturing knowledge generated by the firm's ongoing operations.

The best-developed and most widely applied techniques of knowledge management have focused on some of the most basic aspects of knowledge application and exploitation. For example:

- In the area of *knowledge identification*, the basic challenge is to recognize the knowledge assets that are available within the firm. This includes identifying and assessing the intellectual property of the firm (the patent portfolio in particular) and identifying the skills and know-how of employees. BP's *Connect* is a corporate yellow pages comprising personnel data that allows each employee to identify the skills and experience of other employees in the organization. The next stage of knowledge identification is to recognize and capture the knowledge produced in operational activities—an essential first stage in reusing knowledge. Such knowledge identification is especially important in project-based organizations to ensure that knowledge developed in one project is not lost to the organization. Systematic post-project reviews are a central theme in the U.S. Army's "lessons learned" procedure, which distils the results of practice maneuvers and simulated battles into tactical guidelines and recommended procedures. A process is applied to learning from actual operations. During the NATO military intervention in Bosnia in 1995, the results of every operation were forwarded to the Center for Lessons Learned to be collected and codified. Resulting lessons learned were distributed to active units every 72 hours.[36] By the late 1990s, every major management consulting firm had introduced a system whereby learning from each consulting project was identified, written up, and submitted to the firm's database.

- *Knowledge measurement* involves measuring and valuing the organization's stock of knowledge and its utilization. Skandia, the Swedish insurance company, has pioneered knowledge metrics with its system of intellectual capital accounting.[37] Dow Chemical also uses intellectual capital management to link its intellectual property portfolio to shareholder value.
- For knowledge to be efficiently utilized within the organization, *knowledge storage and organization* are critical. The key contribution of information technology to knowledge management has been in creating databases for storing information, for organizing information, and for accessing and communicating information, to facilitate the transfer of and access to knowledge. The backbone of the Booz-Allen & Hamilton's "Knowledge-On-Line" system and Accenture's "Knowledge Xchange," is an IT system that comprises a database, groupware, dedicated search engine, and an intranet that permits employees to input and access information.[38]
- *Knowledge sharing and replication* involves the transfer of knowledge from one part of the organization (or from one person) to be replicated in another part (or by another individual). A central function of IT-based knowledge management systems is to facilitate such transfer. However, tacit knowledge is not amenable to codification within an IT system. The traditional answer to the problem of replicating tacit knowledge is to use apprenticeships and other forms of on-the-job training. Recently, organizations have discovered the important role played by informal networks in transferring experiential knowledge. These self-organizing *communities of practice* are increasingly being deliberately established and managed as a means of facilitating knowledge sharing and group learning.[39] Replicating capabilities poses an even greater challenge. Transferring best practices within companies is not simply about creating appropriate incentives; complexity and credibility of the knowledge involved are key impediments.[40]
- *Knowledge integration* represents one of the greatest challenges to any company. Ultimately, organizational capability is about integrating knowledge

across a broad range of expertise for the purposes of supplying goods and services. While knowledge management provides few specific tools or techniques for integrating knowledge, appreciating the conditions under which knowledge is transferred and combined can offer profound insight into the role of rules, structure, information systems, leadership, and interpersonal relations on the ability to integrate knowledge effectively and efficiently.[41] For certain corporate functions knowledge integration plays a critical role. A strategic planning system is a vehicle for integrating the different knowledge bases of managers at different levels of the organization and from different functions in order to design the possible strategy for a company. New product development teams are systems for integrating the knowledge of many experts and across a range of functions and technical areas.[42]

Knowledge Conversion and the Challenge of Replication

The close linkage between the use of knowledge and its generation is evident from the key role of learning-by-doing in upgrading the firm's capability. Nonaka goes further: his theory of knowledge creation distinguishes types of knowledge (tacit and explicit) and levels of knowledge (individual and organizational). He argues that knowledge *conversion* between tacit and explicit forms and between individual and organizational levels produce a "knowledge spiral" in which the organization's stock of knowledge broadens and deepens (see Figure 6.3). For example, explicit knowledge is *internalized* into tacit knowledge in the form of intuition, know-how, and routines, while tacit knowledge is *externalized* into explicit knowledge through articulation and codification.[43]

In business schools, education is concerned primarily with the acquisition of explicit knowledge; however, it is often argued that the real learning takes place

FIGURE 6.3 Knowledge conversion

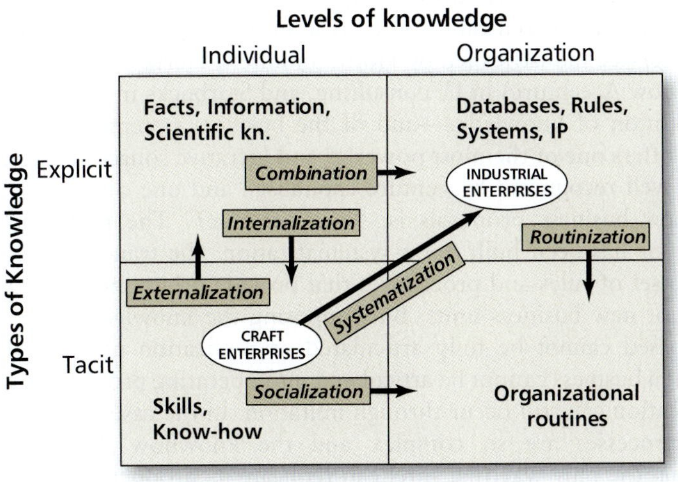

Source:

Based upon I. Nonaka, "A Dynamic Theory of Organizational Knowledge Creation," *Organization Science* 5 (1994): 14–37.

when the concepts, frameworks and theories of business become internalized through repeated application. The result is the development of tacit managerial knowledge in the form of judgment, intuition, and the ability to assess business situations.

Knowledge conversion is also critical to the development of companies—and societies as well. The transition from the *craft enterprise*, based upon individual tacit knowledge, to the industrial enterprise based upon explicit knowledge owned by the organization is a stage in firm development and marks the emergence of the industrial society. This transition is depicted in Figure 6.3 and is illustrated by the following examples:

- Henry Ford's Model T was initially produced on a small scale by skilled metal workers one car at a time. Ford's assembly line mass-production technology systematized that tacit knowledge and built it into machines and processes. The Ford industrial system was no longer dependent upon skilled craftsmen—the assembly lines could be operated by former farm workers and immigrants straight off the boat.
- When Ray Kroc discovered the McDonald brothers' hamburger stand in Riversdale, California, he quickly recognized the potential for systematizing and replicating their process. The result was a global fast-food empire in which the McDonald's business model was replicated through operating manuals and training programs and now serves 47 million customers using some 400 000 employees—few of whom possess significant culinary skills.

This systematization of knowledge offers massive potential for value creation. The craft enterprise is typically small scale and skilled employees appropriate a major share of the value that is created. Systematization allows replication and deskilling. Ford built his assembly-line plants not only in Detroit but also in Canada, the U.K., France, Denmark, Germany, Austria, Argentina, South Africa, Australia, and the Soviet Union. The industrialization of craft industries has been a key feature of the evolution of service industries led by Hilton in hotels, Hertz in car rental, Andersen Consulting (now Accenture) in IT consulting, and Starbucks in coffee shops.[44]

The replication of knowledge—and of the business systems within which it is embedded—offers one of the most powerful and lucrative sources of scale economy. Its power is well recognized by venture capitalists, and one of the key criteria for evaluating new business proposals is: "Is it scalable?" The replication we have discussed so far has been built upon systematization: the translation of a business system into a set of rules and procedures that provide programmed instructions for the creation of new business units. But supposing the knowledge upon which the business is based cannot be fully articulated, is replication possible? Even if the knowledge of a business cannot be articulated into operating procedures and training videos, replication can still occur through imitation. In the case of microprocessors, fabrication processes are so complex and the knowhow involved so deeply embedded that the only way that Intel can replicate its production capabilities is by replicating its lead plant in every detail—a process called "Copy Exactly."[45] However, firms may also seek a middle way between full systematization and pure imitation by basing their replication on a set of fundamental principles that act as guidelines in setting up new business units.[46]

Designing Knowledge Management Systems

Knowledge management covers a wide range of practices—indeed, there are few management activities that do not involve managing knowledge in one form or another. A focus on capability development can provide focus and direction for an organization's knowledge management practices. The starting point is to identify the capabilities needed to ensure continuing success in the face of a changing external environment. This allows identification of the knowledge required to develop the required capabilities and the knowledge processes through which that knowledge can be acquired and deployed. The implication is that knowledge management systems are likely to vary greatly between companies. Consider the following examples:

- For Dow Chemical, the core of its value creation is in developing new chemical products and exploiting globally the intellectual property that is created. Enhancing Dow's capabilities in research, product development, and intellectual property protection are the core goals of Dow's knowledge management practices. Dow's "Intellectual Capital Management" places its central emphasis on the company's patent portfolio and links its intellectual property to a broad range of intellectual capital variables and processes and ultimately to the company's total value.[47]
- For McKinsey & Co., creating value for clients requires continually building on the knowledge it generates from client assignments, and conceptualizing and sharing that knowledge base. This is achieved through a system that ensures the knowledge generated from each project is captured and made available for subsequent client projects; a matrix structure of industry and functional practices that permits specialized knowledge to be created and stored; and an R&D function in the form of the McKinsey Global Institute.[48]
- For McDonald's Corporation, knowledge management has traditionally involved the global replication of the McDonald's system. This has required the development of a standardized set of operating practices that are disseminated through meticulously managed training practices, which include formal training programs at Hamburger University, and on-the-job training at individual establishments. However, competition and changing consumer preferences have required adaptation and innovation from McDonald's. Developing decentralized capabilities in market research, new product development, restaurant design and the internal transfer of product and process innovations has required major changes in the processes through which McDonald's collects information, stimulated creativity among middle managers and disseminated knowledge internally. The result has been the introduction of new products into national markets (see Chapter 15, Strategy Capsule 15.3, McDonalds Goes Glocal), new restaurant designs and new concepts (McCafes, Ronald Gym Clubs).[49]

The design of every knowledge process must take account of the characteristics of the knowledge being deployed. The fundamental distinction here is between explicit and tacit knowledge. Take a simple example of the transfer of best practice between the different fabrication plants of a multinational semiconductor plant. If the knowledge is explicit, then such knowledge can be disseminated in the form of reports, or directives requiring every plant to adopt a new standard operating procedure. If the knowledge is tacit—it is the result of the experience or intuition of a single plant manager—the task is more difficult. Transferring the best practice is likely to require either visits by other plant managers to the innovating plant, or for the innovating plant manager to adopt a consulting role and visit other plants in the group for the purpose of teaching employees there.

It is in the area of managing tacit knowledge (which includes, typically, the major part of the knowledge relevant to organizational capability) where the major challenges and opportunities in knowledge management lie. Information technology has made huge strides in the storage, analysis and systematization of explicit knowledge. However, the greater part of organizational learning is experience based and intuitive. Identifying this knowledge, and transferring it to other parts of the organization in order to utilize it more effectively, remains a fundamental management challenge.

Summary

For a company to be successful—even to survive—over the long-term requires that it upgrades it resource and capability base. The critical management challenges are in developing existing capabilities and acquiring or creating new ones.

Some of the most important developments in strategic management research in recent years are in deepening our understanding of what organizational capabilities are and how they develop. A number of key themes, principles and tools are emerging. These include: the role of top management leadership through establishing strategic intent, the role of organizational structure and corporate culture in facilitating coordination and critical contributions that knowledge management can offer. At the same time we have much to learn. The reasons why some companies are able to reinvent themselves through the development of new capabilities (and whole new areas of business) such as Nokia and SMH/Swatch, while others, such as Eastman Kodak and General Motors struggle to develop the new capabilities needed to thrive under changed market circumstances remain poorly understood. In the subsequent chapters we shall return repeatedly to the challenge of adaptation to a changing business environment. In the next chapter we will focus attention upon the structures and systems through which companies deploy their resources and build and exercise organizational capability.

Self-Study Questions

1 Identify two sports teams: one that is rich in resources (such as talented players) but whose capabilities (as indicated by performance) have been poor; one that is resource-poor but has displayed strong team capabilities. What clues can you offer as to the determinants of capabilities among sports teams?

2 In 2006, Disney completed its acquisition of the film animation company Pixar for $7.4 billion. The high purchase price reflected Disney's eagerness to gain Pixar's animation capabilities, its talent (animators, technologists and storytellers) and its culture of creativity. What risks does Disney face in achieving the goals of this acquisition?

3 The dean of your business school wishes to upgrade the effectiveness with which the school designs and delivers its educational programs and increase the effectiveness of its graduates in their subsequent careers. Advise your dean on what tools and systems of knowledge management might be deployed in order to support these goals.

Notes

1 "Modern Management: All You Need is Cash," *Economist* (November 20, 2008): 78–80.

2 C. B. Schoonhoven and E. Romanelli, "The Local Origins of New Firms" in C. B. Schoonhoven and E. Romanelli (eds), *The Entrepreneurship Dynamic* (Stanford: Stanford University Press, 2001): 40–67.

3 S. Klepper, "The Capabilities of New Firms and the Evolution of the U.S. Automobile Industry" *Industrial and Corporate Change* 11, 4 (2001): 645–6.

4 B. Wernerfelt, "Why do Firms Tend to Become Different?" in Constance Helfat (ed.) *Handbook of Organizational Capabilities* (Oxford: Blackwell, 2006): 121–33.

5 R. R. Nelson and S. G. Winter, *An Evolutionary Theory of Economic Change* (Cambridge, MA: Belknap, 1982): 15, 97.

6 K. B. Clark and T. Fujimoto, *Product Development Performance* (New York: Free Press, 1991).

7 S. G. Winter, "The Satisficing Principle in Capability Learning," *Strategic Management Journal* 21 (2000): 981–96; G. Gavetti and D. Levinthal, "Looking Forward and Looking Backward: Cognitive and Experiential Search," *Administrative Science Quarterly* 45 (2000): 113–37.

8 D. Leonard-Barton, "Core Capabilities and Core Rigidities," *Strategic Management Journal*, Summer Special Issue (1992): 111–26.

9 M. S. Feldman and B. T. Pentland, "Reconceptualizing Organizational Routines as a Source of Flexibility and Change," *Administrative Science Quarterly*, 48 (2003): 94–118.

10 D. J. Teece, G. Pisano, and A. Shuen, "Dynamic Capabilities and Strategic Management," *Strategic Management Journal* 18 (1997): 509–33.

11 K. M. Eisenhardt and J. A. Martin, "Dynamic Capabilities: What Are They?" *Strategic Management Journal* 21 (2000): 1105–21 and H. Volberda, *Building the Flexible Firm* (Oxford: Oxford University Press, 1998).

12 M. Zollo and S. G. Winter, "Deliberate Learning and the Evolution of Dynamic Capabilities," *Organization Science* 13 (2002): 339–51; S. G. Winter, "Understanding Dynamic Capabilities" *Strategic Management Journal* 24 (2003): 991–5.

13 Established firms typically fail to survive radical innovation. See, for example, R. M. Henderson and K. B. Clark, "Architectural Innovation: The Reconfiguration of Existing Product Technologies and Failure of Established Firms," *Administrative Science Quarterly* 35 (1990): 9–30; C. Christensen, "The Rigid Disk Drive Industry: A History of Commercial and Technological Turbulence," *Business History Review* 67 (1993): 531–88; M. Tripsas, "Unravelling the Process of Creative Destruction: Complementary Assets and Incumbent Survival in the Typesetter Industry," *Strategic Management Journal* 18 (Summer Special Issue, 1997): 119–42; A. Henderson, "Firm Strategy and Age Dependence: A Contingent View of the Liabilities of Newness, Adolescence and Obsolescence," *Administrative Science Quarterly* 44 (1999): 281–314.

14 C. E. Helfat, S. Finkelstein, W. Mitchell, M. A. Peteraf, H. Singh, D. J. Teece, S. G. Winter, *Dynamic Capabilities: Understanding Strategic Change in Organizations* (Malden, MA: Blackwell Publishing, 2007): Chapter 6.

15 See, for example, A. Mody, "Learning Through Alliances," *Journal of Economic Behavior and Organization* 20 (1993): 151–70; D. C. Mowery, J. E. Oxley and B. S. Silverman, "Strategic Alliances and Interfirm Knowledge Transfer," *Strategic Management Journal* 17, Winter Special Issue (1996): 77–93; A. C. Inkpen and M. M. Crossan, "Believing Is Seeing: Joint Ventures and Organizational Learning," *Journal of Management Studies* 32 (1995): 595–618.

16 Intel News Release, "*Intel, Dreamworks Animation Form Strategic Alliance to Revolutionize 3-D Filmmaking Technology*" (July 8, 2008), http://www.intel.com/pressroom/archive/releases/20080708corp.htm, accessed July 3, 2009.

17 J. A. Badaracco, *The Knowledge Link: How Firms Compete Through Strategic Alliances* (Boston: Harvard Business School Press, 1991).

18 G. Hamel, "Competition for Competence and Inter-partner Learning within International Strategic Alliances," *Strategic Management Journal* 12, Summer Special Issue (1991): 83–103.

19 P. Kale, J. H. Dyer and H. Singh. "Alliance Capability, Stock Market Response and Long Term Alliance Success" *Strategic Management Journal* 23 (2002): 747–67; C. E. Helfat et al. *Dynamic Capabilities* op. cit.: Chapter 5.

20 A. Prencipe, "Corporate Strategy and Systems Integration Capabilities" in A. Prencipe, A. Davies and M. Hobday, *The Business of Systems Integration* (Oxford University Press, 2003): 114–32.

21 A. Bakhru and R. M. Grant, "A Managerial Process Model of Organizational Capability Development: Evidence from New E-commerce Businesses", CROMA Discussion Paper, Bocconi University, Milan, 2008.

22 G. Hamel and C. K. Prahalad, *Competing for the Future* (Boston: Harvard Business School Press, 1994).

23 C. E. Helfat and Ruth S. Raubitschek, "Product Sequencing: Co-evolution of Knowledge, Capabilities and Products," *Strategic Management Journal* 21 (2000): 961–79. The parallel development of capabilities and products has also been referred to as "dynamic resource fit". See: H. Itami, *Mobilizing Invisible Assets* (Boston: Harvard University Press, 1987): 125.

24 A. Takahashi, *What I Learned from Konosuke Matsushita* (Tokyo: Jitsugyo no Nihonsha, 1980); in Japanese, quoted by Itami, op. cit.: 25.

25 T. Elder, "Lessons from Xerox and IBM," *Harvard Business Review* (July–August 1989): 66–71.

26 *Xerox PARC: Innovation without Profit*? ICMR Case Study, 2004.

27 J. O'Toole, *Forming the Future: Lessons from the Saturn Corporation* (New York: Harper, 1996).

28 Lucy Kellaway column, *Financial Times* (June 23, 1999): 13.

29 "Saatchi's 'Manager of Knowledge' Keeps Track of What's Trendy," *Wall Street Journal* (February 28, 1997): B.16.

30 R. M. Grant, "Prospering in Dynamically-competitive Environments: Organizational Capability as Knowledge Integration", *Organization Science* 7 (1996): 375–87.

31 "The knowledge-based view" offers a rationale for the firm that is based on its effectiveness as an institution for creating, assembling, and transforming knowledge into goods and services. See: B. Kogut and U. Zander, "Knowledge of the Firm, Combinative Capabilities and the Replication of Technology", *Organization Science* 3 (1992): 387–99; R. M. Grant, "Toward a Knowledge-based Theory of the Firm," *Strategic Management Journal* 17, Winter Special Issue (1996): 109–22.

32 M. Hansen, N. Nohria and T. Tierney, "What's Your Strategy for Managing Knowledge?" *Harvard Business Review* (March 1999): 106–16.

33 See: B. Kogut and U. Zander, "Knowledge of the Firm, Combinative Capabilities, and the Replication of Knowledge" *Organization Science* 3 (1992): 383–97. However, at moderate levels of complexity, internal replication can be achieved while avoiding imitation by rivals: J. Rivkin, "Reproducing Knowledge: Replication without Imitation at Moderate Complexity" *Organization Science* 12 (2001): 274–93.

34 J. G. March, "Exploration and Exploitation in Organizational Learning," *Organization Science* 2 (1991): 71–87. J.-C. Spender makes a similar distinction between *knowledge generation* and *knowledge application* ("Limits to Learning from the West," *The International Executive* 34 (September/October 1992): 389–410.

35 This distinction between use and development within knowledge exploitation is made by P. McNamara and C. Baden-Fuller, "Shareholder returns and the exploration–exploitation dilemma: R&D announcements by biotechnology firms" *Research Policy* 36 (2007): 548–65.

36 "Lessons Learned: Army Devises System to Decide What Does and What Does Not Work," *Wall Street Journal* (May 23, 1997): A1 and A10.

37 L. Edvinsson and S. Malone, *Intellectual Capital: Realizing Your Company's True Value by Finding its Hidden Brainpower* (New York: Harper Business, 1997); D. Marchand and J. Roos, *Skandia AFS: Measuring and Visualizing Intellectual Capital*, Case No. GM 624 (Lausanne: IMD, 1996).

38 *Cultivating Capabilities to Innovate: Booz-Allen & Hamilton*, Case No. 9-698-027 (Boston: Harvard Business School, 1997); "Recycling Internal Know-How: Knowledge Management at Accenture", *Corporate Universities International* 8, No. 2 (March 2002).

39 E. C. Wenger and W. M. Snyder, "Communities of Practice: The Organizational Frontier," *Harvard Business Review* (January–February 2000).

40 G. Szulanski, "Exploring Internal Stickiness: Impediments to the Transfer of Best Practices within the Firm," *Strategic Management Journal* 17, Winter Special Issue (1996): 27–44.

41 S. Brusoni and L. Cassi, "Re-Inventing the Wheel: Knowledge Integration in Fact-Changing Environments" CESPRI WP no. 209, Bocconi University (Milan: December 2007); C. Schmickl and A. Kieser "How much do specialists have to learn from each other when they jointly develop radical product innovations?" *Research Policy* 37 (2008): 473–91.

42 See, for example, M. C. Becker and F. Zirpoli, "Organizing New Product Development: Knowledge Hollowing-out and Knowledge Integration: The Fiat Auto Case." DRUID Working Paper No 03-05 (2003).

43 I. Nonaka and H. Takeuchi, *The Knowledge-Creating Company* (Oxford: Oxford University Press, 1995).

44 S. Segal-Horn, "Strategy in Service Organizations," in D. O. Faulkner and A. Campbell (eds) *The Oxford Handbook of Strategy* (Oxford University Press, 2006): 472–508.

45 "Copy Exactly Factory Strategy" (www.intel.com/design/quality/mq_ce.htm). See also: G. Szulanski and S. Winter, "Getting it Right the Second Time," *Harvard Business Review* (January 2002): 62–9.

46 C. Baden-Fuller and S. G. Winter, "Replicating Organizational Knowledge: Principles or Templates?" Papers on Economics and Evolution, Max Planck Institute, 2005.

47 D. Near, "Intellectual Capital Management," Dow Chemical Company (April 15, 2002), http://www.km-iptask.org/ICM_Overview_4_15.ppt#371,1.

48 *McKinsey & Company: Managing Knowledge and Learning*, Case No. 9-396-357 (Boston: Harvard Business School, 1996).

49 "A Golden Recipe for McDonald's Europe," *Business Week* (July 17, 2008).

7 Organization Structure and Management Systems: The Fundamentals of Strategy Implementation

Ultimately, there may be no long-term sustainable advantage other than the ability to organize and manage.

—JAY GALBRAITH AND ED LAWLER

I'd rather have first-rate execution and second-rate strategy anytime than brilliant ideas and mediocre management.

—JAMIE DIMON, CEO, JP MORGAN CHASE & CO.

OUTLINE

Introduction and Objectives

"Great strategy; lousy implementation," is an epithet that has been applied to organizational failures from Philip II of Spain's attempted invasion of England with the Spanish Armada in 1588[1] to the dismal outcome of the 2006 merger between Alcatel and Lucent that created "a new global leader in telecommunication equipment".[2] The idea that the formulation of strategy can be separated from its implementation has become institutionalized by the numerous strategic management texts that devote separate sections to strategy formulation and strategy implementation.

This supposed division between formulation and implementation is fiction. At the most obvious level, formulating a strategy without taking into account the conditions under which it will be implemented will result in a poorly designed strategy. A fundamental flaw in the corporate planning systems of 25 years ago was separating strategy formulation—the task of corporate executives and strategic planners—from its implementation by divisional heads and middle managers.

The design of organization structure and management form key components of strategy implementation. Hence, the view of strategy formulation and strategy implementation as a sequential process is summed up in the adage "structure follows strategy." Yet, management guru Tom Peters argues the reverse: if capabilities are the primary basis of strategy, and if capabilities are a product of organizational structure, then *strategy follows structure*.[3] The key point, however, is not whether strategy or structure takes precedence but the recognition that the two are closely interdependent.[4] For Domino's Pizza with its global network of 8000 franchised outlets, or Amway, with its pyramid of commission-based, independent distributors, the structure is the strategy.

Having established that the way in which a company organizes itself is fundamental to its strategy and performance, the goal of this chapter is to introduce the key concepts and ideas necessary to understand and design companies' structures and systems. The approach is concise and selective. I do not intend to offer a potted overview of organizational theory. My aim is to introduce some basic principles of organizational design and to apply these to key aspects of firm structure. The principles outlined here will be further developed in later chapters when we consider strategies within particular business contexts. For example, Chapter 12 considers the organizational conditions conducive to innovation; Chapter 13 considers organization and organizational change within mature industries; Chapter 14 discusses vertical structures and outsourcing; Chapter 15 examines the structure and systems of the multinational corporation; and Chapter 16 deals with organizing the multibusiness company.

By the time you have completed this chapter you will be able to:

- recognize the key organizational innovations that have shaped the evolution of the modern corporation;
- understand the basic principles that determine the structural characteristics of complex human organizations;
- apply the principles of organizational design to recommend the types of organizational structure suited to particular tasks and particular business environments;
- understand the role of information systems, strategic planning, financial control, and human resource management in the coordination and control of corporations;
- appreciate the forces that are causing companies to seek new organizational structures and management systems.

The Evolution of the Corporation

Firms and Markets

This book is concerned with the strategy of business organizations—entities that I have referred to, more or less synonymously, as *firms*, *companies* or *enterprises*. Firms are the dominant feature of the capitalist economy—it is through them that we obtain our food, clothing and shelter and they provide us with the income to enjoy this consumption. Yet despite their central role, economists have paid them limited attention. Their focus has been upon the role of markets. In practice, firms and markets are twin institutions that organize the capitalist economy. Markets are organized by the "invisible hand" of the price mechanism; firms are organized by the "visible hand" of management.[5]

One reason for economists' neglect of firms is that they are of recent origin. At the beginning of the nineteenth century, most production—even in Britain, the most industrially advanced economy of the time—was undertaken by individuals and by families. Woolen textile production—upon which much British prosperity was based—involved networks of self-employed workers producing in their own homes. Mechanization and the rise of the factory system changed all this; however, most of the new factories were owner-proprietorships employing small numbers of workers. In the United States, the biggest business organizations in the mid-nineteenth century, in terms of numbers of employees, were family-owned farms—especially some of the large plantations of the South.[6]

The modern firm—the business corporation—is one of the greatest innovations of modern society. Its emergence is the result of two developments: legal and organizational.

Legal Development

A *corporation* is an organization that has a legal identity—it can own property, enter contacts, sue and be sued. Such a legal identity is essential to the operation of a business enterprise that involves more than a few people. Corporations were originally created by royal decree of acts of legislation. Some of the first business corporations were the colonial trading companies—the British East India Company (1600), the Dutch East India Company (1602), the Virginia Company of London (1606) and Hudson's Bay Company (1670) which were given monopoly rights over development and trade with specific colonies. Because corporations were legally distinct from their owners, this means that they could have large numbers of owners (shareholders) and ownership could be transferred.

Britain's Joint Stock Companies Act of 1844 allowed corporations to be established without the need for a royal decree or act of parliament. The Limited Liability Act of 1844 established that shareholders of corporations were not liable for the debts of a corporation beyond the share capital they owned—this opened up the potential for large-scale financing of industry.[7]

Organizational Development

Until the late nineteenth century, the world's only large-scale organizations—apart from colonial trading companies the aforementioned were the Roman

Catholic Church and national armies. Most ideas about organizing large companies derived from the organizational structure of armies. Indeed, prior to the development of business education, the role of the military as the training ground for most business leaders meant that a large proportion of management principles derived from the military. General Von Moltke's reorganization of the Prussian army into divisions and a functionally specialized general staff during the 1860s provided the basic model for large industrial corporations until well into the twentieth century.[8]

The emergence of the modern corporation occurred in the U.S. in what has been termed "the Second Industrial Revolution." Business historian, Alfred Chandler, identifies the modern corporation as a result of two "critical organizational transformations."[9]

Line-and-Staff Structure Until the mid-nineteenth century, companies were located in just one place—lack of transportation placed limits on firms' market reach; lack of communication prevented firms from operating in multiple locations. The railroad and the telegraph changed all that. In the U.S., the railroad companies were the first to create geographically separate operating units managed by an administrative headquarters. This *line-and-staff* structure divided employees into those allocated to operational tasks within operating units (*line*) and administrators and functional specialists located at head office (*staff*).

By the end of the late nineteenth century, simple line-and-staff structures had developed into more complex *functional structures*—companies such as DuPont, Sears Roebuck & Co. and Shell Transport and Trading managed a number of separate operating units with large functional departments that conducted sales, finance, R&D, legal affairs and other specialist activities.

The other organizational form for large business enterprises was the *holding company*. Standard Oil (of the U.S.), Mitsui (of Japan), and the British South Africa Company were financial enterprises created by a series of acquisitions in which the parent bought controlling equity stakes in a number of subsidiary companies. The management structure of these holding companies was primitive: the parent appointed the board of directors of the subsidiaries and received dividends, but otherwise there was little integration or overall managerial control.

The Multidivisional Corporation The second critical transformation was the emergence during the 1920s of the divisionalized corporation, which, over time, replaced both the centralized, functional structures that characterized most industrial corporations and the loose-knit holding companies created in the merger wave of the early twentieth century. The pioneers were DuPont and General Motors.

At DuPont, increasing size and a widening product range strained the functional structure and overloaded top management:

> . . . the operations of the enterprise became too complex and the problems of coordination, appraisal and policy formulation too intricate for a small number of top officers to handle both long-run, entrepreneurial and short-run, operational administrative activities.[10]

The solution devised by Pierre Du Pont was to decentralize: ten product divisions were created, each with their own sales, R&D, and support activities. The corporate

FIGURE 7.1 General Motors Corporation: organizational structure, 1921

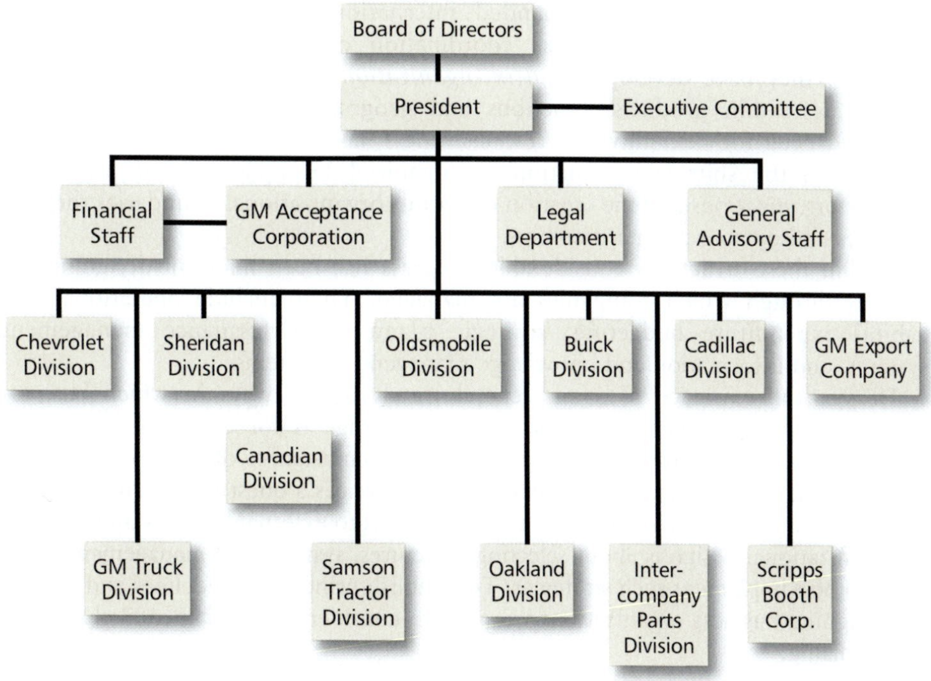

Source:
A. P. Sloan, *My Years with General Motors* (Orbit Publishing, 1972): 57. © 1963 by Alfred P. Sloan. © renewed 1991, Alfred P. Sloan Foundation. Reproduced with permission.

head office headed by an Executive Committee took responsibility for coordination, strategy, and resource allocation.[11]

General Motors, which had grown by acquisition into a loose holding company, adopted a similar structure as a solution to the problems of weak financial control and a confused product line. The new structure (shown in Figure 7.1) divided decision making responsibility between the chief executives of the divisions who were responsible for their divisions' operation and performance and the president who headed the general office and was responsible for the development and control of the corporation as a whole.[12]

Organizational Change since the 1950s

The rise of the public (i.e. stock market listed), divisionalized corporation as the dominant organizational form in large-scale American business was followed by its diffusion internationally. This diffusion was accelerated, first, by the success of American multinationals overseas and, second, by international political developments—including the U.S. occupation of Japan after the Second World War, the collapse of the Soviet Union and China's transition to capitalism.

At the same time, the organizational forms of business enterprise have continued to evolve. If the divisionalized corporation represented a fundamental breakthough in the problem of how to reconcile overall coordination with flexibility and responsiveness, subsequent developments have addressed the same problem. As companies have diversified, expanded internationally and developed greater functional sophistication, so their coordination challenges have increased. In response, they have developed *matrix organizations*—where separate hierarchies coordinate within products, functions and geographical areas. Simultaneously, increased need for flexibility and responsiveness has resulted in the *delayering* of hierarchies, the shift from functionally organized headquarters staff to *shared services organizations* and the creation of porous organizational boundaries through alliances and outsourcing partnerships.

Within these structures considerable progress has been made in designing the systems through which companies are managed. These include operational and capital expenditure budgeting, strategic planning, performance management systems, and information and knowledge management systems.

Despite the existence of some general trends in the ways in which business enterprises organize themselves, the critical challenge is for companies to design structures and systems that match the particular circumstances of their own business situations. In the same way that strategic management is a quest for unique solutions to the matching of internal resources and capabilities to external business opportunity, so organizational design is about selecting structures, systems and management styles that can best implement such strategies. To establish principles, guidelines and criteria for designing business organizations we need to consider the fundamental challenges of organizing.

The Organizational Problem: Reconciling Specialization with Coordination and Cooperation

To design a firm we must first recognize what it is supposed to do. According to Henry Mintzberg:

> Every organized human activity—from making pots to placing a man on the moon—gives rise to two fundamental and opposing requirements: the division of labor into various tasks, and the coordination of these tasks to accomplish the activity. The structure of the organization can be defined simply as the ways in which labor is divided into distinct tasks and coordination is achieved among these tasks.[13]

Specialization and Division of Labor

Firms exist because they are efficient institutions for the organization of economic activities, particularly the production of goods and services. The fundamental source of efficiency in production is *specialization* through the *division of labor* into separate tasks. The classic statement on the gains due to specialization is Adam Smith's description of pin manufacture:

> One man draws out the wire, another straightens it, a third cuts it, a fourth points it, a fifth grinds it at the top for receiving the head; to make the head

> requires two or three distinct operations; to put it on is a peculiar business, to whiten the pins is another; it is even a trade by itself to put them into the papers.[14]

Smith's pin makers produced about 4 800 pins per person each day. "But if they had all wrought separately and independently, and without any of them having been educated to this peculiar business, they certainly could not each have made 20, perhaps not one pin, in a day." Similarly, Henry Ford achieved huge productivity gains by his assembly-line system, which assigned individuals to highly specific tasks. Between the end of 1912 and early 1914 the time taken to assemble a Model T fell from 106 hours to six hours.

But specialization comes at a cost. The more a production process is divided between different specialists, the more complex is the challenge of integrating the efforts of individual specialists. The more volatile and unstable the external environment, the greater the number of decisions that need to be made and the greater are these coordination costs. Hence, the more stable is the environment, the greater is the optimal division of labor. This is true both for firms and for entire societies. Civilizations are built on increased division of labor, which is only possible through stability. As the strife-torn parts of Somalia, Haiti, and the Congo have demonstrated so tragically, once chaos reigns, societies regress toward subsistence mode where each family unit must be self-sufficient.

The Cooperation Problem

Integrating the efforts of specialist individuals involves two organizational problems: there is the *cooperation problem*—that of aligning the interests of individuals who have divergent goals—and *coordination problem*—even in the absence of goal conflict, how do individuals harmonize their different activities?

The economics literature analyzes cooperation problems arising from goal misalignment as the *problem of agency*.[15] An *agency relationship* exists when one party (the principal) contracts with another party (the agent) to act on behalf of the principal. The problem is ensuring that the agent acts in the principal's interest. Within the firm, the major agency problem is between owners (shareholders) and managers. The problem of ensuring that managers operate companies to maximize shareholder wealth is at the center of the corporate governance debate. During the 1990s, changes in top management remuneration—in particular the increasing emphasis given to stock options—were intended to align the interests of managers with those of shareholders.[16] However, at Enron, WorldCom, and other companies, these incentives induced managers to manipulate reported earnings rather than to work for long-term profitability.

Agency problems exist throughout the hierarchy. For individual employees, systems of incentives, monitoring and appraisal are designed to encourage pursuit of organizational objectives and overcome employees' tendency to do their own thing or simply shirk. The organization structure may create its own problems. Organizational departments create their own subgoals that do not align with one another. The classic conflicts are between different functions: sales wishes to please customers, production wishes to maximize output, R&D wants to introduce mind-blowing new products, while finance worries about profit and loss.

Several mechanisms are available to management for achieving goal alignment within organizations:

- *Control mechanisms* typically operate through hierarchical supervision. Managers supervise the behavior and performance of subordinates who must seek approval for actions that lie outside their defined area of discretion. Control is enforced through positive and negative incentives: the primary positive incentive is the opportunity for promotion up the hierarchy; negative incentives are dismissal and demotion.
- *Performance incentives* link rewards to output: they include piece-rates for production workers and profit bonuses for executives. Such performance-related incentives have two main benefits: first, they are *high powered*—they relate rewards directly to output—and second, they economize on the need for costly monitoring and supervision of employees. Pay-for-performance becomes more difficult where employees work in teams or on activities where output is difficult to measure.
- *Shared values.* Some organizations are able to achieve high levels of cooperation and low levels of goal conflict without extensive control mechanisms or performance-related incentives. Churches, charities, clubs and voluntary organizations typically display a commonality of purpose and values among members. Similarly with firms: the presence of shared core values appears to be a key influence on sustained success.[17] The role of culture as a control mechanism that is an alternative to bureaucratic control or the price mechanism is central to Bill Ouchi's concept of *clan control.*[18] The role of shared values and behavioral norms among organizational members is a powerful force aligning individual actions with company strategy. The key advantages of culture as a control device are, first, it is cheap: it saves on costs of monitoring and providing financial incentives; second, it permits flexibility: when individuals internalize the goals and principles of the organization, they can be allowed to use their initiative and creativity in their work. However, to view corporate culture as a tool of management control fails to recognize that culture is a property of the organization as a whole, which is not amenable to top management manipulation. At the British bank NatWest during the 1990s, John Weeks identified a "culture of complaining", which was resistant to top-down cultural change initiatives.[19]

The Coordination Problem

The desire to cooperate is not enough to ensure that organizational members integrate their efforts—it is not lack of a common goal that causes Olympic relay teams to drop the baton. Unless individuals can find ways of coordinate their efforts, production doesn't happen. As we have already seen in our discussion of organizational capabilities, the exceptional performance of Wal-Mart, the Cirque du Soleil, and the U.S. Marine Corp Band derives less from the skills of the individual members as from superb coordination between them. Among the mechanism for coordination, the following can be found in all firms:

- *Rules and directives.* A basic feature of the firm is the existence of general employment contracts under which individual agree to perform a range of duties as required by their employer. This allows managers to exercise authority by means of *general rules* ("Secret agents on overseas missions will have essential expenses reimbursed only on production of original receipts") and *specific directives* ("Miss Moneypenny, show Mr. Bond his new cigarette case with 4G communication and a concealed death ray").

- *Routines*. Where activities are performed recurrently, coordination based on mutual adjustment and rules becomes institutionalized within organizational routines. As we noted in the previous chapter, these "regular and predictable sequences of coordinated actions by individuals" are the foundation of organizational capability. If organizations are to perform complex activities at extreme levels of efficiency and reliability, coordination by rules, directives, or mutual adjustment is not enough—coordination must become embedded in routines.
- *Mutual adjustment*. The simplest form of coordination involves the mutual adjustment of individuals engaged in related tasks. In soccer or doubles tennis, each player coordinates with fellow team members without any authority relationship among them. Such mutual adjustment occurs in leaderless teams and is especially suited to novel tasks where routinization is not feasible.

The relative roles of these different coordination devices depend on the types of activity being performed and the intensity of collaboration required. Rules tend to work well for activities where standardized outcomes are required and the decision-making abilities of the operatives involved may be limited—most quality control procedures involve the application of simple rules. Routines form the basis for coordination in most activities where close interdependence exists between individuals, whether a basic production task (supplying customers at Starbucks) or a more complex activity (performing a heart bypass operation or implementing a systems integration project for a multinational corporation). Mutual adjustment works best where the individuals involved are well-informed of the actions of their co-workers, either because they are in close visual contact (a chef de cuisine and her sous-chefs), or through information exchange (designers using interactive CAD software).

Hierarchy in Organizational Design

Hierarchy is the fundamental feature of organizational structure. It is the primary means by which companies achieve specialization, coordination, and cooperation. Despite the negative images that hierarchy often stimulates, I shall argue that hierarchical structures are essential for efficiency and flexibility in firms. The critical issue is not whether or not to organize by hierarchy—there is little alternative—but how the hierarchy should be structured and how the various parts should be linked.

Hierarchy as Coordination: Modularity

Hierarchy is a feature, not only of human organizations but of almost all complex systems:[20]

- The human body which is hierarchy of cells, organs and subsystems such as the respiratory system, nervous system, digestive system and so on.

FIGURE 7.2 How hierarchy economizes on coordination

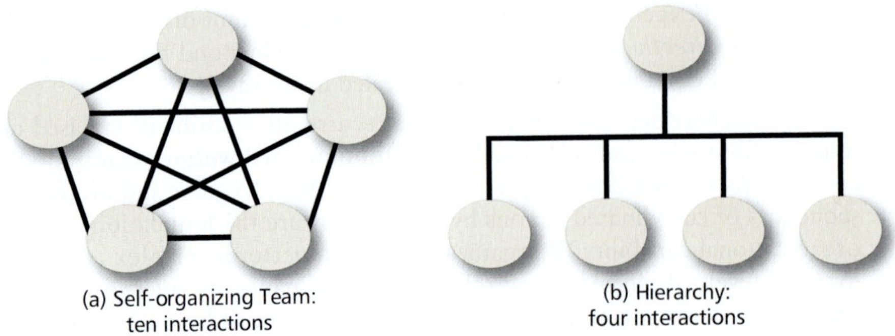

- Physical systems are composed at the macro level of planets, stars, and galaxies and at the micro level of subatomic particles, atoms and molecules.
- Social systems comprises of individuals, families, communities, and nations.
- A book consists of letters, words, sentences, paragraphs, and chapters.

This systems view of hierarchy (in contrast to the concept of an *administrative hierarchy*) points to two key advantages of hierarchical structures:

- *Economizing on coordination*. As we have noted, the gains from specialization come at the cost of coordination. Suppose there are five programmers designing a piece of customized computer software. If they are structured as a "self-organized team," where coordination is by mutual adjustment (see Figure 7.2a), ten bilateral interactions must be managed. Alternatively, suppose the programmer with the biggest feet is selected to be supervisor. In this simple hierarchy (Figure 7.2b), there are only four relationships to be managed. Of course, this says nothing about the *quality* of the coordination: if the programmers' work is highly interdependent, hierarchical relationships may not allow for rich collaboration among team members.

  However, even if individual units are organized as self-managed teams, hierarchy can still be an effective structure for linking the teams in a modular structure. By breaking up a complex system into discrete pieces—which can then communicate with one another through standard interfaces within a standardized architecture—one can eliminate what would otherwise be an unmanageable spaghetti tangle of interconnections.[21]

- *Adaptability*. Hierarchical, modular systems are able to evolve more rapidly than unitary systems that are not partitioned into subsystems. Such adaptability requires some degree of *decomposability*: the ability of each component subsystem to operate with some measure of independence from the other subsystems. Modular systems that allow significant independence for each module are referred to as *loosely coupled*.[22] The modular structure of an automobile allows the gearbox to be replaced without the need to scrap the whole car. Organizing the development of a new car is similar: if separate teams work on different subassemblies (power train, brakes, steering, electricals and so forth), so long as there is agreement on how the different subassemblies fit together, each team can get on with its design without the need for constant communication and coordination with every other team.[23] The multidivisional firm is a modular structure. At Procter & Gamble, decisions about developing new shampoos can be made by the Global Hair Care division without involving the Global Fabric Care, Global Health Care or the Duracell divisions. A divisional structure also makes it easier for P&G to add new businesses (Gillette; Wella) and to divest them (Folgers Coffee; paper products).[24]

The merits of hierarchical structures in economizing on efficiency in communication and permitting decentralized flexibility are evident in Nelson Mandela's restructuring of the ANC (see Strategy Capsule 7.1). But what about the role of hierarchies as a vehicle for top-down control through *bureaucracy*?

STRATEGY CAPSULE 7.1

Hierarchical Structures: The 1952 Mandela Plan for the ANC

Along with many others, I had become convinced that the government intended to declare the ANC (African National Congress) and the SAIC (South African Indian Congress) illegal organizations, just as it had done with the Communist Party. It seemed inevitable that the state would attempt to put us out of business as a legal organization. With this in mind, I approached the National Executive with the idea that we must come up with a contingency plan . . . They instructed me to draw up a plan that would enable the organization to operate from underground. This strategy came to be known as the Mandela-Plan, or simply, M-Plan.

The idea was to set up organizational machinery that would allow the ANC to take decisions at the highest level, which could then be swiftly transmitted to the organization as a whole without calling a meeting. In other words, it would allow the organization to continue to function and enable leaders who were banned to continue to lead. The M-Plan was designed to allow the organization to recruit new members, respond to local and national problems and maintain regular contact between the membership and the underground leadership.

I worked on it for a number of months and came up with a system that was broad enough to adapt itself to local conditions and not fetter individual initiative, but detailed enough to facilitate order. The smallest unit was the cell, which in urban townships consisted of roughly ten houses on a street. A cell steward would be in charge of each of these units. If a street had more than ten houses, a street steward would take charge and the cell stewards would report to him. A group of streets formed a zone directed by a chief steward, who was in turn responsible to the secretariat of the local branch of the ANC. The secretariat was a subcommittee of the branch executive, which reported to the provincial secretary. My notion was that every cell and street steward would know every person and family in his area, so that he would be trusted by his people and know whom to trust. The cell steward arranged meetings, organized political classes, and collected dues. He was the linchpin of the plan.

The plan was accepted and was implemented immediately. Word went out to the branches to begin to prepare for this covert restructuring . . . As part of the M-Plan, the ANC introduced an elementary course of political lectures for its members throughout the country. These lectures were meant not only to educate but to hold the organization together. They were given in secret by branch leaders. Those members in attendance would in turn give the same lectures to others in their homes and communities.

Source: Nelson Mandela, *Long Walk to Freedom* (London: Little Brown, 1994): 134-5. © 1994, 1995 by Nelson Rolihlahla Mandela. Reproduced by permission of Little Brown.

Hierarchy as Control: Bureaucracy

Hierarchy, I have argued, is an efficient solution to the problem of *coordination* in organizing complex tasks. However, what hierarchies are best known for is their ability to resolve the problem of *cooperation* in organizations through the imposition of top-down control.

The notion of the hierarchy as an administrative mechanism through which centralized power can be exercised can be traced back to the government system of the Ch'in dynasty of China around 220 BC. For Max Weber, "the father of organizational theory," hierarchy was the central feature of his system of *bureaucracy* which involved: "each lower office under the control and supervision of a higher one"; a "systematic division of labor"; formalization in writing of "administrative acts, decisions, and rules", and work governed by standardized rules and operating procedures, where authority is based on "belief in the legality of enacted rules and the right of those elevated to authority under such rules to issue commands."[25]

Weber's obsession with rationality, efficiency, and controlling against the personal use of hierarchical authority resulted in organizational designs that sought safeguards against human traits such as emotion, creativity, fellowship, and idiosyncrasies of personality. As a result bureaucratic organizations have been described as *mechanistic*[26] or as *machine bureaucracies*.[27]

Contingency Approaches to Organization Design

Led by the military and the civil service, the bureaucratic model dominated thinking about organizational structure during the first half of the twentieth century. However, it soon became clear that bureaucratic systems also nurtured inertia, alienation and a lack of initiative and innovation.

During the 1950s and 1960s, the *human relations school* recognized that cooperation and coordination within organizations was about social relationships, which bureaucracy stifled. Studying Scottish engineering companies, Burns and

TABLE 7.1 Mechanistic versus organic organizational forms

Feature	Mechanistic forms	Organic forms
Task definition	Rigid and highly specialized	Flexible and broadly defined
Coordination and control	Rules and directives vertically imposed	Mutual adjustment, common culture
Communication	Vertical	Vertical and horizontal
Knowledge	Centralized	Dispersed
Commitment and loyalty	To immediate superior	To the organization and its goals
Environmental context	Stable with low technological uncertainty	Dynamic with significant technological uncertainty and ambiguity

Source:
Adapted from Richard Butler, *Designing Organizations: A Decision-Making Perspective* (London: Routledge, 1991): 76.

Stalker found that firms in stable environment had *mechanistic* forms, characterized by bureaucracy; those in less stable market had *organic* forms that were less formal and more flexible. Table 7.1 contrasts key characteristics of the two forms.

These findings fueled *contingency approaches* to organizational design—the idea that a firm's optimal structure and systems depended upon the strategy it pursued, the technology it employed and the environment it inhabited. [28] Although Google and McDonald's are of similar sizes in terms of revenue, their structures and systems are very different. McDonald's is highly bureaucratized: high levels of job specialization, formal systems, a strong emphasis on rules and procedures. Google's freewheeling informality with low job specialization, emphasis on horizontal communication and emphasis of principles over rules reflects its emphasis on innovation, rapid growth, and its fast changing business environment. The more standardized goods or services are (beverage cans, blood tests, or haircuts for army inductees) and the more stable the environment is, the greater the efficiency advantages of the bureaucratic model with its standard operating procedures and high levels of specialization. But as soon as market turbulence arrives, innovation becomes a priority, or heterogeneous outputs are required from heterogeneous inputs—then the bureaucratic model breaks down.

These contingency factors also cause functions within companies to be organized differently. Stable, standardized activities such as payroll, treasury, taxation, customer support and purchasing activities tend to operate well when organized along bureaucratic principles; research, new product development, marketing, and strategic planning require more organic modes of organization.

Rethinking Hierarchy

Increasing turbulence of the business environment over time has created difficulties for large companies run on bureaucratic lines. Since the mid-1980s almost all large companies have made strenuous efforts to restructure and reorganize in order to achieve greater flexibility and responsiveness. Giant corporations such as BP and General Electric have retained their basic multidivisional structures, but have decentralized decision making, reduced their number of hierarchical layers, shrunk headquarters staffs, emphasized horizontal rather than vertical communication, and shifted the emphasis of control from *supervision* to *accountability*.[29]

The trend towards decentralization has not been one way. The need to build capabilities that integrate across products, across countries and across technologies has encouraged many large companies—including GE and BP—to recentralize many aspects of their strategy and operation. These cycles of centralization and decentralization may be a means by which companies are able to balance the tradeoff between integration and flexible responsiveness.[30]

Achieving effective integration while avoiding the cost and rigidities associated with centralized coordination has encouraged organizations to explore informal approaches to coordination—including many of the features of coordination associated with "organic" organizational forms. Here, companies have been assisted by developments in information and communication technology (ICT), the huge leaps in the availability of information available to organizational members and the ease with which they can communicate with one another has increased vastly the capacity for mutual adjustment without the need for intensive hierarchical guidance and leadership.

Applying the Principles of Organizational Design

We have established that the fundamental problem of organization is reconciling specialization with coordination and cooperation. The basic design for complex organizations—whether they are business enterprises, religious orders, political associations, or criminal organizations—is hierarchy. The essence of hierarchy is creating specialized units coordinated and controlled by a superior unit. But this does not take us very far. On what basis should specialized units be defined? How should decision-making authority be allocated? And what kind of relationships should there be between different organizational units?

In this section we will tackle the first two of these questions: the basis of grouping and the allocation of decision-making power. In the next section, we identify some typical organizational structures found in business enterprises. Then, in the following section we shall look at structuring relations between units—the operation and design of management systems.

Defining Organizational Units

In creating a hierarchical structure, on what basis are individuals assigned to organizational units within the firm? This issue is fundamental and complex. Multinational, multiproduct companies are continually grappling with the issue of whether they should be structured around product divisions, country subsidiaries, or functional departments, and periodically they undergo the disruption of changing from one to another. Some of the principal bases for grouping employees are common tasks, products, geography, and process:

- *Tasks*. Organizational units can be created around common tasks. This usually means grouping together employees who do the same job—thus, a firm might create a machine shop, a maintenance department, a secretarial pool, and a sales office.

- *Products*. Where a company offers multiple products, these can provide a basis for structure. In a department store, departments are defined by products: kitchen goods, bedding, lingerie, and so on. PepsiCo comprises three main product groups: PepsiCo Beverages, Frito-Lay (snack foods), and Quaker Foods (cereals and processed foods).
- *Geography*. Where a company serves multiple local markets, organizational units can be defined around these localities. Wal-Mart is organized by individual stores, groups of stores within an area, and groups of areas within a region. The Roman Catholic church is organized into parishes, dioceses, and archdioceses.
- *Process*. A process is a sequence of interlinked activities. An organization may be viewed as a set of processes: the product development process, the manufacturing process, the sales and distribution process, and so on. A process may correspond closely with an individual product, or a process may be dominated by a single task. Functional organizations tend to combine task-based and process-based grouping.

Organizing on the Basis of Coordination Intensity

How do we decide whether to use task, product, geography, or process to define organizational units? The fundamental issue is achieving the coordination necessary to integrate the efforts of different individuals. This implies grouping individuals according to the intensity of their coordination needs. Those individuals whose tasks require the most intensive coordination should work within the same organizational unit.

- In a geographically dispersed organization where coordination across distance is difficult, the organization must be built on local units. The ANC is an example (see Strategy Capsule 7.1), as are most large service companies.
- Where an organization has a narrow product range and does not need to be differentiated by location, but possesses strong functional specializations, then a grouping around functional tasks is appropriate. For example, British Airways is organized primarily around functions: flight operations, engineering, marketing, sales, customer service, human resources, information, and finance.
- Where a company is diversified over many products and these products are substantially different in terms of technology and markets, it is vital that individuals who work on the same product should interact closely—a product-based organization is the appropriate structure. Virtually all diversified companies—General Electric, 3M, Sony, Siemens, and Unilever—are organized by product divisions.

Having created organizational units that bring together individuals whose coordination needs are most intense, the next challenge is to create hierarchical control that permits effective coordination while giving as much operational autonomy as possible to the subordinate units. Oliver Williamson refers to this as the *principle of hierarchical decomposition*. At the operating level (where decision making is high frequency), organization units are created where the interactions are strong. At the strategic level (where decision making is low frequency), a separate organization unit is created to exercise coordination and direction. Hence:

> The hierarchical decomposition principle can be stated as follows: Internal organization should be designated in such a way as to effect quasi-independence between the parts, the high frequency dynamics (operating activities) and low frequency dynamics (strategic planning) should be clearly distinguished, and incentives should be aligned within and between components so as to promote both local and global effectiveness.[31]

To organize according to intensity of coordination needs requires understanding the nature of interdependence within an organization. James Thompson distinguished three levels of interdependence: *pooled interdependence* (the loosest), where individuals operate independently but depend on one another's performance; *sequential interdependence*, where the output of one individual is the input of the other; and *reciprocal interdependence* (the most intense), where individuals are mutually dependent. Thompson argued that organizational design needed to begin with creating organizational units where interdependence was the most intense.[32]

Over time, the relative importance of these different dependencies changes. Hence, companies need to change the basis on which they define their structure. For example, as trade and communication between countries has become easier and consumer preferences between countries have become more homogeneous, multinational corporations have shifted from geographically based structures to worldwide product divisions.

Other Factors Influencing the Definition of Organizational Units

Coordination requirements are not the only consideration in deciding how to group together employees and activities within the firm. Additional factors that influence the efficiency of different organizational arrangements include:

- *Economies of scale*. There may be advantages in grouping together activities where scale economies are present. Thus, it may be desirable to group together research activities even if there is little coordination among different research projects, simply to exploit scale economies in specialized facilities and technical personnel.
- *Economies of utilization*. It may also be possible to exploit efficiencies from grouping together similar activities that result from fuller utilization of employees. Even though there may be little need for individual maintenance engineers to coordinate with one another, establishing a single maintenance department permits maintenance personnel to be utilized more fully than assigning a maintenance engineer to each manufacturing cell.
- *Learning*. If establishing competitive advantage requires building distinctive capabilities, firms must be structured to maximize learning. Typically, it was

assumed that learning was best achieved by grouping together individuals doing similar jobs—creating a manufacturing engineering department, a quality control department, and a finance function. More recently, it has been observed that the specialized functional and discipline-based knowledge may be less important than *architectural knowledge*—knowing how to link together specialized knowledge from different fields. This implies the creation of multifunctional work groups comprising experts from different knowledge bases.

- *Standardization of control systems*. Tasks may be grouped together to achieve economies in standardized control mechanisms. An advantage of the typing pool and the sales department was that employees doing near-identical jobs could be subject to the same system of monitoring, performance measurement, training, and behavioral norms. Creative activities such as research and new product development need to be managed in a different way from routine activities such as manufacturing and accounting—hence they should be located in different organizational units.[33]

Alternative Structural Forms

On the basis of these alternative approaches to grouping tasks and activities we can identify three basic organizational forms: the functional structure, the multidivisional structure and the matrix structure.

The Functional Structure

Single-business firms tend to be organized along functional lines. Grouping together functionally similar tasks is conducive to exploiting scale economies, promoting learning and capability building, and deploying standardized control systems. Since cross-functional integration occurs at the top of the organization, functional structures are conducive to a high degree of centralized control by the CEO and top management team.

However, even for single-product firms, functional structures are subject to the problems of cooperation and coordination. Different functional departments develop their own goals, values, vocabularies and behavioral norms that make cross-functional integration difficult. As the size of the firm increases, the pressure on top management to achieve effective integration increases. Because the different functions of the firm tend to be *tightly coupled* rather than *loosely coupled*, there is limited scope for decentralization. In particular, it is very difficult to operate individual functions as semi-autonomous profit centers.

The real problems arise when the firm grows its range of products and businesses. As we noted with DuPont during the early twentieth century, once a functionally organized company expands its product range, coordination within each product area becomes difficult.

Although the long-term trend among very large companies has been for product-based, divisionalized companies to replace functionally organized companies, the trend is not entirely one way. As companies mature, the need for strong centralized control and well-developed functional capabilities has caused some companies to revert to functional structures. For example:

- When John Scully became CEO of Apple in 1984, the company was organized by product: Apple II, Apple III, Lisa, and Macintosh. Despite strong cross-functional coordination within each product group, there was little integration across products. Each product was completely incompatible with the others, and the structure failed to exploit scale economies within functions. Scully's response was to reorganize Apple along functional lines to gain control, reduce costs, and achieve a more coherent product strategy.
- General Motors, pioneer of the multidivisional structure, has adopted a more functional structure. As its strategic priorities have shifted from differentiation and segmentation toward cost efficiency, it has maintained its brand names (Cadillac, Chevrolet, Buick) but merged the separate divisions into a more functionally based structure to exploit scale economies and faster technical transfer (see Figure 7.3 and compare it with Figure 7.1).

The Multidivisional Structure

We have seen how the product-based, multidivisional structure emerged during the twentieth century in response to the coordination problems caused by diversification. The key advantage of divisionalized structures (whether product based or geographically based) is the potential for decentralized decision making. The

FIGURE 7.3 General Motors Corporation: organizational structure, 1997

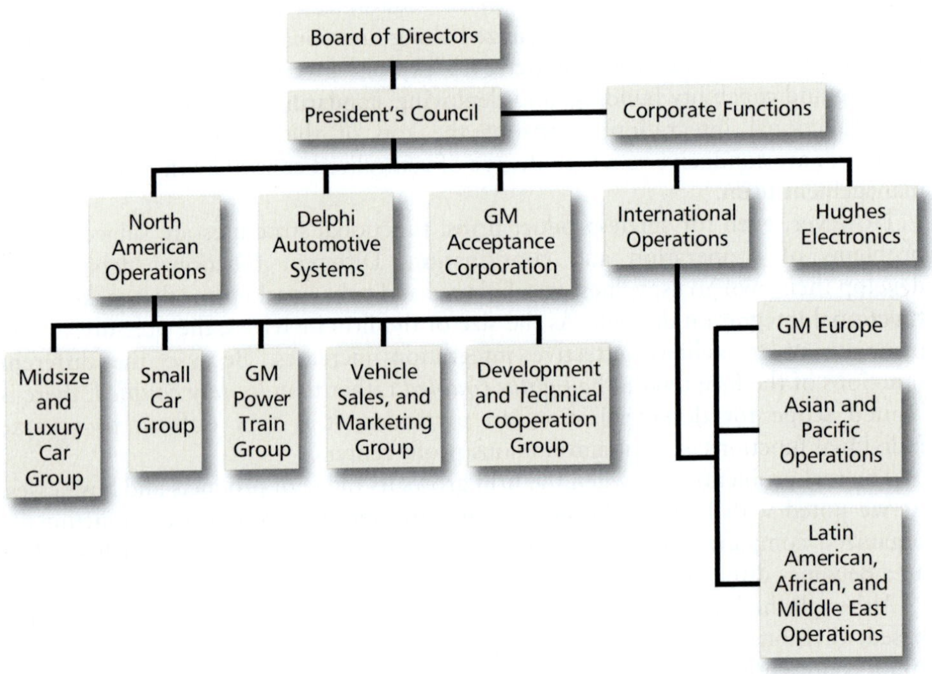

multidivisional structure is the classic example of a loose-coupled, modular organization where business-level strategies and operating decisions can be made at the divisional level, while the corporate headquarters concentrates on corporate planning, budgeting, and providing common services.

Central to the efficiency advantages of the multidivisional corporation is the ability to apply a common set of corporate management tools to a range of different businesses. At ITT, Harold Geneen's system of "managing by the numbers" allowed him to cope with over 50 divisional heads reporting directly to him. At British Petroleum, John Browne's system of "performance contracts" allowed direct reporting by over 20 "strategic performance units." Divisional autonomy also fosters the development of top management leadership capability among divisional heads—an important factor in CEO succession.

The large, divisionalized corporation is typically organized into three levels: the corporate center, the divisions, and individual business units, each representing a distinct business for which financial accounts can be drawn up and strategies formulated. Figure 7.4 shows General Electric's organizational structure at the corporate and divisional levels.

In Chapter 17, we shall look in greater detail at the organization of the multibusiness corporation.

Matrix Structures

Whatever the primary basis for grouping, all companies that embrace multiple products, multiple functions, and multiple locations must coordinate across all three dimensions. Organizational structures that formalize coordination and control across multiple dimensions are called *matrix structures*.

FIGURE 7.4 General Electric: organizational structure, 2009

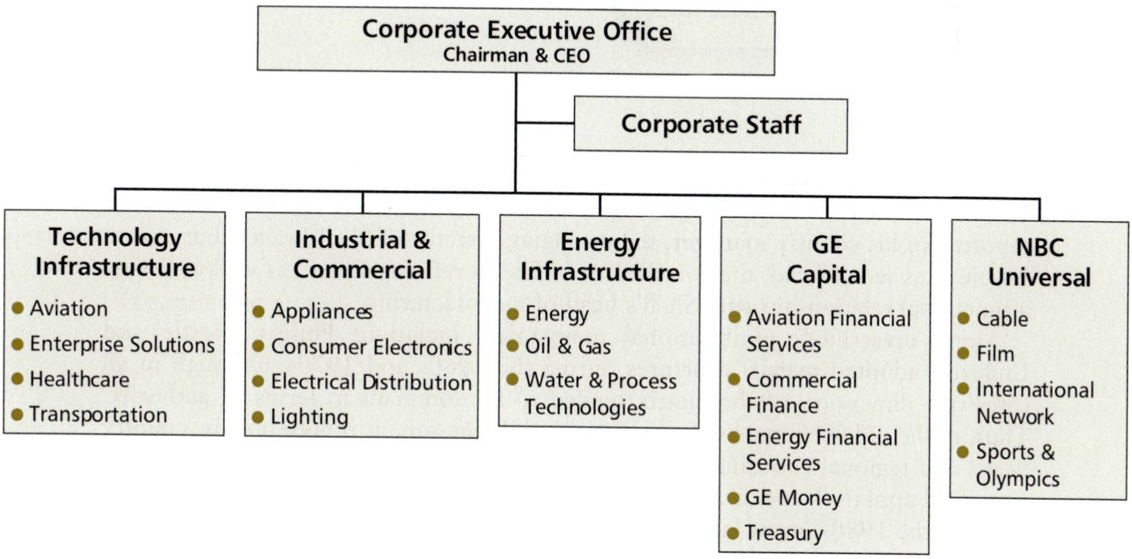

Source:
Based on information in General Electric Annual Report, 2008.

FIGURE 7.5 Royal Dutch Shell Group: pre-1996 matrix structure

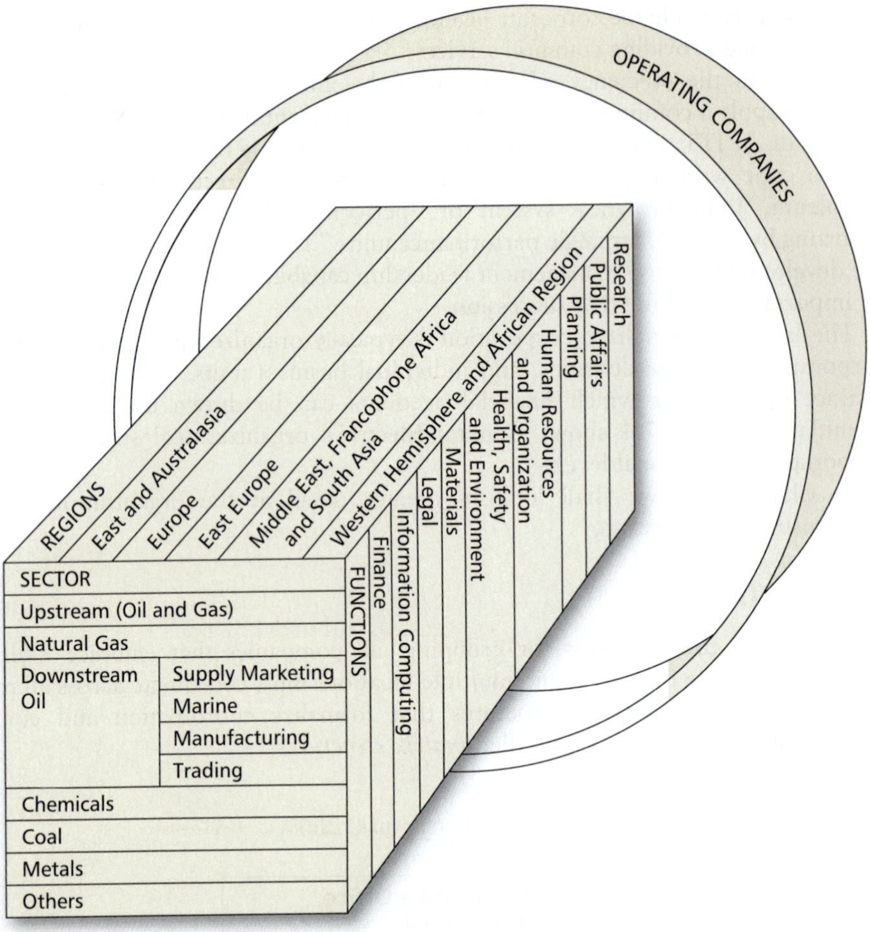

Figure 7.5 shows the Shell management matrix (prior to reorganization in 1996). Within this structure, the general manager of Shell's Berre refinery in France reported to his country manager, the managing director of Shell France, but also to his business sector head, the coordinator of Shell's refining sector, as well as having a functional relationship with Shell's head of manufacturing.

Many diversified, multinational companies, including Philips, Nestlé and Unilever, adopted matrix structures during the 1960s and 1970s, although in all cases one dimension of the matrix tended to be dominant in terms of authority. Thus, in the old Shell matrix the geographical dimension, as represented by country heads and regional coordinators, had primary responsibility for budgetary control, personnel appraisal, and strategy formulation.

Since the 1980s, most large corporations have dismantled or reorganized their matrix structures. Shell abandoned its matrix during 1995–6 in favor of a structure based on four business sectors: upstream, downstream, chemicals, and gas and power. During 2001–2, the Swiss-Swedish engineering giant ABB abandoned its much-lauded matrix structure in the face of plunging profitability and mounting debt. In fast-moving business environments companies have found that the benefits from formally coordinating across multiple dimensions have been outweighed by excessive complexity, larger head-office staffs, slower decision making, and diffused authority. Bartlett and Ghoshal observed that matrix structures "led to conflict and confusion; the proliferation of channels created informational logjams as a proliferation of committees and reports bogged down the organization; and overlapping responsibilities produced turf battles and a loss of accountability."[34]

Yet, all complex organizations that comprise multiple products, multiple functions, and multiple geographical markets need to coordinate within each of these dimensions. The problem of the matrix organization is not that it attempts to coordinate across multiple dimensions—in complex organizations such coordination is essential—but that this multiple coordination is overformalized, resulting in excessive corporate staffs and overcomplex systems that slow decision making and dull entrepreneurial initiative. The trend has been for companies to focus formal systems of coordination and control on one dimension, then allowing the other dimensions of coordination to be mainly informal.[35] Thus, while Shell is organized primarily around four business sectors and these sectors exercise financial and strategic control over the individual operating companies, Shell still has country heads, responsible for coordinating all Shell activities in relation to legal, taxation and government relations within each country, and functional heads, responsible for technical matters and best-practice transfer within their particular function, whether it is manufacturing, marketing, or HR.

Beyond Hierarchy?

For several decades consultants and management scholars have proclaimed the death of hierarchical structures in business firms. In 1993, two of America's most prominent scholars of organization announced: ". . . the new organizational revolution is sweeping one industry after another . . . quantum changes in manufacturing and computer-mediated communication technologies have given managers radical new options for designing organizations." The new organizations featured ". . . flatter hierarchies, decentralized decision making, greater tolerance for ambiguity, permeable internal and external boundaries, empowerment of employees, capacity for renewal, self-organizing units, self-integrating coordination mechanisms."[36]

As I noted in the earlier section on "Rethinking Hierarchy," there have been substantial changes in the way in which corporate hierarchies have been organized. Layers have been removed; mechanistic formality has been replaced by organic informality. Yet, hierarchy remains as the basic structural form of almost all companies. Are there alternative modes of organization?

Several organizational forms have been identified which, although they comprise some hierarchical elements, are sufficiently distinctive to be regarded as alternative organizational forms:

- *Adhocracies.* In some organizations, the presence of shared values, motivation and willingness to participate, mutual respect and communication effectiveness may allow a high level of coordination with little need for hierarchy, authority, or tools of control. These organizations, which Henry

Mintzberg calls *adhocracies*,[37] feature flexible, spontaneous coordination and collaboration around problem solving and other nonroutine activities. Adhocracies tend to exist among organizations where expertise is prized. In research organizations, new product development groups, jazz bands, and consulting firms, each specialist is valued for his or her expertise and there is little exercise of authority.

- *Team-based and project-based organizations.* Adhocracies are one example of an organizational form based on informal structure with flexible patterns of coordination. Flexibility and adaptability can also be achieved in project-based organizations—common in sectors such as construction, consulting, oil exploration, and engineering services—where business takes the form of projects of limited duration. Because every project is different, and every project goes through a changing sequence of activities, each project needs to be undertaken by a closely interacting team that relies on problem solving and mutual adjustment as well as rules and routines. Increasingly, companies are introducing elements of team- and project-based organizations into their conventional divisional and functional structures. For example, in most divisionalized corporations, new product development, change management, knowledge management, and research is organized in projects and undertaken by teams.
- *Networks.* Localized networks of small, closely interdependent firms have been a feature of manufacturing for many hundreds of years. In Italy such networks are prominent in the clothing industry of Prato, near Florence, and in packaging equipment.[38] Hollywood movie making[39] and microelectronics in Silicon Valley have similar structures—highly specialized firms that coordinate to design and produce complex products. Often these networks feature a central firm that acts as a "systems integrator,"[40] as in the case of Benetton and Toyota.[41] In fast-moving industries, the ability of highly specialized, knowhow-intensive firms to reconfigure their relationships can be conducive to innovation, product differentiation, and rapid new product development. In the developing world, such networks can be a viable alternative to industrial development where large enterprises are lacking.[42]

These different organizational forms share several common characteristics:

- *A focus on coordination rather than control.* In contrast to the "command-and-control" hierarchy, these structures focus almost wholly upon achieving coordination. Financial incentives, culture, and social controls take the place of hierarchical control.
- *Reliance on coordination by mutual adjustment.* Central to all nonhierarchical structures is their dependence on voluntaristic coordination through bilateral and multilateral adjustment. The capacity for coordination through mutual adjustment has been greatly enhanced by information technology.
- *Individuals in multiple organizational roles.* Reconciling complex patterns of coordination with high levels of flexibility and responsiveness is difficult if job designs and organizational structures are rigidly defined. Adhocracies and team-based organizations feature individuals switching their organizational

roles and occupying multiple roles simultaneously. For example, for most of the 1990s AES had no finance function, no HR function, no safety or environmental affairs functions, and no public relations department. These functions were performed by teams of operatives and line managers.

Management Systems for Coordination and Control

The relationship between management systems and organizational structure is similar to that between the skeleton and bodily systems in the human body. The skeleton provides the framework; the respiratory system, digestive system, and nervous system are the means by which the body operates. Computer networks offer another analogy: the hardware provides the structure and the software provides the systems that make the network operational.

Management systems provide the mechanisms of communication, decision making, and control that allow companies to solve the problems of achieving both coordination and cooperation. Four management systems are of primary importance: the information systems, the strategic planning systems, the financial systems, and the human resource management systems.

Information Systems

Information is fundamental to the operation of all management systems. Communication technology—the telephone and telegraphy—were essential for the companies to span multiple locations. The computer has had an equally dramatic impact during the past half century. Accounting systems are key components of firms' information systems. They collect, organize, and communicate financial information to top management facilitating hierarchical control.

Administrative hierarchies are founded on vertical information flows: the upward flow of information to the manager and the downward flow of instructions. The trend towards decentralization and informality in organizations rests on two key aspects of increased information availability: *information feedback* to the individual on job performance, which has made self-monitoring possible, and *information networking*, which has allowed individuals to coordinate their activities voluntarily without hierarchical supervision. For example, a central element of total quality management has been recognition that regular, real-time, performance feedback to employees permits them to take responsibility for quality control, reducing or eliminating the need for supervisors and quality controllers. During the past decade, corporate intranets, web-based information systems, and groupware have transformed organizations' capacity for decentralized coordination.

Strategic Planning Systems

Small enterprises can operate successfully without an explicit strategy. The firm's strategy may exist only in the head of the founder and, unless the founder needs to write a business plan in order to attract outside financing, the strategy may never be articulated. Most large companies have a regular (normally annual) strategic planning process. For a multibusiness company, the strategic planning process creates business plans for the individual divisions that are then integrated into a corporate plan.

Whether formal or informal, systematic or *ad hoc,* documented or not, the strategy formulation process is an important vehicle for achieving coordination within a company. As discussed in Chapter 1, the strategy process brings together knowledge from different parts of the company, ensures consistency between the decisions being made at different levels and in different parts of the company, and commits managers to ambitious performance targets.

The system through which strategy is formulated varies considerably from company to company. Even after the entrepreneurial startup has grown into a large company, strategy making may remain the preserve of the chief executive. Functional managers may provide key inputs such as financial projections and market analysis, but the key elements of strategy—goals, new business developments, capital investment, and key competitive initiatives—are often decided by the chief executive.[43] At MCI Communications former CEO Orville Wright observed: "We do it strictly top-down at MCI."[44] The first director of strategic planning was warned: "If you ever write a strategic plan, you will be fired!"

As companies mature, their strategic planning processes become more systematized and typically follow an annual cycle. Strategic plans tend to be for three to five years and combine top-down initiatives (indications of performance expectations and identification of key strategic initiatives) and bottom-up business plans (proposed strategies and financial forecasts for individual divisions and business units). After discussion between the corporate level and the individual businesses, the business plans are amended and agreed and integrated into an overall corporate plan that is presented to and agreed by the board of directors. Figure 7.6 shows a typical strategic planning cycle.

The resulting strategic plan typically comprises the following elements:

- *A statement of the goals* the company seeks to achieve over the planning period with regard to both financial targets (for example, targets for revenue growth, cost reduction, operating profit, return on capital employed, return to shareholders) and strategic goals (such as market share, new products,

FIGURE 7.6 The generic strategic planning cycle

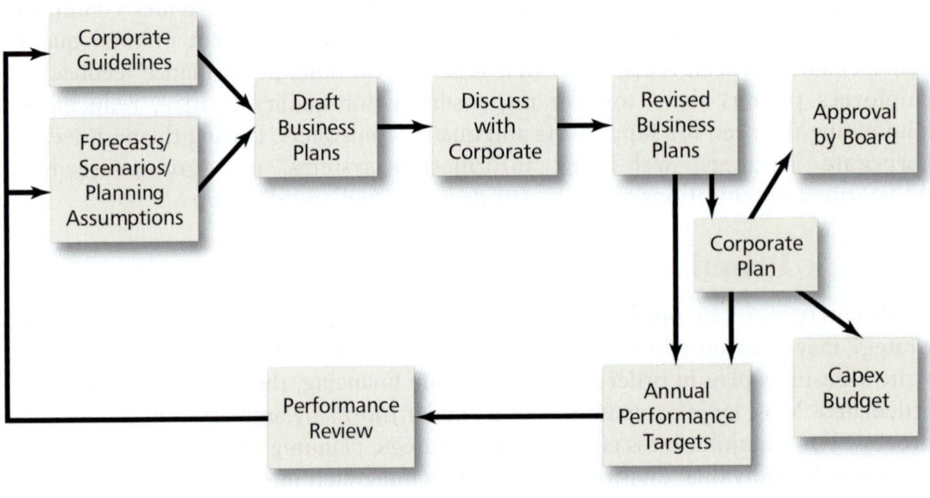

overseas market penetration and new business development). For example, in BP's February 2006 strategy statement, the company established that its "primary objective is to deliver sustainable growth in free cash flow," which it would achieve through "growing production by about 4% a year to 2010" and "delivering further improvements in return on average capital employed relative to our peer group."[45]

- *A set of assumptions or forecasts* about key developments in the external environment to which the company must respond. For example, BP's 2006–10 strategic plan assumed an oil price of $40 a barrel.
- *A qualitative statement* of how the shape of the business will be changing in relation to geographical and segment emphasis, and the basis on which the company will be establishing and extending its competitive advantage. For example, BP's 2006–10 strategy emphasized capital discipline (capex to increase by $0.5 billion per year) and upgrading BP's asset portfolio by selective divestments of about $3 billion per year.
- *Specific action steps* with regard to decisions and projects, supported by a set of mileposts stating what is to be achieved by specific dates. For example, BP's strategic commitments included 24 start-ups of upstream projects during 2006-8, $6 billion capital expenditure on its Russian joint venture, and growth in wind power to 450 MW.
- *A set of financial projections*, including a capital expenditure budget and outline operating budgets. For example, BP's 2006 strategy statement set a capital expenditure budget of $15–16 billion per year, shareholder distribution of $50 billion during 2006–8, and operating costs to increase at less than the rate of inflation.

Although strategic planning tends to emphasize the specific commitments and decisions that are documented in written strategic plans, the most important aspect of strategic planning is the *strategy process*: the dialog through which knowledge is shared and ideas communicated, the consensus that is established, and the commitment to action and results that is built.

Increasing turbulence in the business environment has caused strategic planning processes to become less formalized and more flexible. For example, among the world's largest petroleum majors, the key changes have been as follows:

- Strategic plans have become less concerned with specific actions and became more heavily focused on performance targets, especially on financial goals such as profitability and shareholder return. Planning horizons have also shortened (two to five years is the typical planning period).
- Companies recognized the impossibility of forecasting the future and based their strategies less on medium- and long-term economic and market forecasts of the future and more on more general issues of strategic direction (in the form of vision, mission, and strategic intent) and alternative views of the future (for example, using scenario analysis).
- Strategic planning shifted from a *control perspective*, in which senior management used the strategic planning mechanisms as a means of controlling decisions and resource deployments by divisions and business

units and departments, toward more of a *coordination perspective*, in which the strategy process emphasized dialog involving knowledge sharing and consensus building. As a result, the process became increasingly informal and put less emphasis on written documents.

- A diminishing role for strategic planning staff as responsibility for strategic decisions and the strategy-making process become located among senior managers.[46]

Financial Planning and Control Systems

Financial flows form the life blood of the enterprise. Revenues from customers provide the funds to pay suppliers and employees and any surplus remunerates owners. If inflows are insufficient to cover outflows, the firm becomes insolvent. Hence, financial systems are inevitably the primary mechanism through which top management seeks to control the enterprise. At the center of financial planning is the *budgetary process*. This involves setting and monitoring financial estimates with regard to income and expenditure over a specified time period, both for the firm as a whole and for divisions and departments. Budgets are in part an estimate of incomes and expenditures for the future, in part a target of required financial performance in terms of revenues and profits, and in part a set of authorizations for expenditure up to specified budgetary limits. Two types of budget are set: the capital expenditure budget and the operating budget.

The Capital Expenditure Budget *Capital expenditure budgets* are established through both top-down and bottom-up processes. From the top down, strategic plans establish annual capital expenditure budgets for the planning period both for the company as a whole and for individual divisions. From the bottom up, capital expenditures are determined by the approval of individual capital expenditure projects. Companies have standardized processes for evaluating and approving projects. Requests for funding are prepared according to a standardized methodology, typically based on a forecast of cash flows discounted at the relevant cost of capital (adjusted for project risk). The extent to which the project's returns are sensitive to key environmental uncertainties is also estimated. Capital expenditure approvals take place at different levels of a company according to their size. Projects up to \$5 million might be approved by a business unit head; projects up to \$25 million might be approved by divisional top management; larger projects might need to be approved by the top management committee, while the biggest projects require approval by the board of directors.

The Operating Budget The *operating budget* is a pro forma profit and loss statement for the company as a whole and for individual divisions and business units for the upcoming year. It is usually divided into quarters and months to permit continual monitoring and the early identification of variances. The operating budget is part forecast and part target. It is set within the context of the performance targets established by the strategic plan. Each business typically prepares an operating budget for the following year that is then discussed with the top management committee and, if acceptable, approved. At the end of the financial year, business-level divisional managers are called upon to account for the performance over the past year.

Human Resource Management Systems

Strategies may arise from principles, formulae, or divine inspiration, but their implementation depends on people. Ultimately, strategic and financial plans come to nothing unless they influence the ways in which people within the organization behave. To support strategic and financial plans, companies need systems for setting goals, creating incentives and monitoring performance at the level of the individual employee. Human resource management has the task of establishing an incentive system that supports the implementation of strategic plans and performance targets through aligning employee and company goals, and ensuring that each employee has the skills necessary to perform his or her job. The general problem, we have noted, is one of agency: how can a company induce employees to do what it wants?

The problem is exacerbated by the imprecision of employment contracts. Unlike most contracts, employment contracts are vague about employee performance expectations. The employer has the right to assign the employee to a particular category of tasks for a certain number of hours per week but the amount of work to be performed and the quality of that work are unspecified. Employment contracts give the right to the employer to terminate the contract for unsatisfactory performance by the employee, but the threat of termination is an inadequate incentive: it imposes costs on the employer and only requires the employee to perform better than a new hire would. Moreover, the employer has imperfect information as to employees' work performance—in team production individual output is not separately observable.[47]

The firm can ensure the employee's compliance with organizational goals using direct supervision of the type that administrative hierarchies are designed to do. The weaknesses of such administrative supervision are, first, there is little incentive for performance in excess of minimum requirements, second, supervision imposes costs, and third, the system presupposes that the supervisor has the knowledge required to direct the employee effectively.

The key to promoting more effective cooperation is for more sophisticated incentives than the threat of dismissal. The principal incentives available to the firm for promoting cooperation are compensation and promotion. The key to designing compensation systems is to link pay either to the inputs required for effective job performance (hours of work, punctuality, effort, numbers of customers visited) or to outputs. The simplest form of output-linked pay is piecework (paying for each unit of output produced) or commission (paying a percentage of the revenue generated).

Relating pay to individual performance is suitable for tasks performed individually. However, firms exist primarily to permit complex coordination among individuals; encouraging such collaboration requires linking pay to team or departmental performance. Where broad-based, enterprise-wide collaboration is required, there may be little alternative to linking pay to company performance through some form of profit sharing.

Corporate Culture as a Control Mechanism

We have already noted how shared values can align the goals of different stakeholders within the organization. More generally, we can view the culture of the organization as a mechanism for achieving coordination and control. *Corporate culture* comprises the beliefs, values and behavioral norms of the company, which influence how employees think and behave.[48] It is manifest in symbols, ceremonies, social practices, rites, vocabulary, and dress. It is embedded within national cultures, and incorporates elements of social and professional cultures. As a result, a corporate culture may be far from homogeneous: very different cultures may be evident in the research lab, on the factory floor, and within the accounting department. To this extent, culture is not necessarily an integrating device—it can contribute to divisiveness.

Culture can play an important role in facilitating both cooperation and coordination. In companies such as Starbucks, Shell, Nintendo, and Google, strong corporate cultures create a sense of identity among employees that facilitates communication and the building of organizational routines, even across national boundaries. The unifying influence of corporate culture is likely to be especially helpful in assisting coordination through mutual adjustment in large cross-functional teams of the type required for new product development. One of the advantages of culture as a coordinating device is that it permits substantial flexibility in the types of interactions it can support.

The extent to which corporate culture assists coordination depends on the characteristics of the culture. Salomon Brothers (now part of Citigroup) was renowned for its individualistic, internally competitive culture; this was effective in motivating drive and individual effort, but did little to facilitate cooperation. The British Broadcasting Corporation has a strong culture that reflects internal politicization, professional values, internal suspicion and a dedication to the public good, but without a strong sense of customer focus.[49] However, culture is far from being a flexible management tool. Cultures take a long time to develop and cannot easily be changed. As the external environment changes, a highly effective culture may become dysfunctional. The Los Angeles Police Department's culture of professionalism and militarism, which made it one of the most admired and effective police forces in America, later contributed to problems of isolation and unresponsiveness to community needs.[50]

While recognizing the importance of corporate culture—according to Merck's CEO, "Culture eats strategy for lunch!"—chief executives have limited power to change the culture that they inherit. The key issue is to recognize the culture of the organization and to ensure that structure and systems work with the culture and not against it.[51]

Integrating Different Control Mechanisms

The past ten years have seen substantial progress in integrating different control systems. As strategy has become more and more focused on creating shareholder value, so financial planning has become more closely integrated with strategic planning. Performance management systems have also done much to link strategic and financial planning with human resource management—especially in terms of goal setting and performance appraisal. The central aspect of the "metrics" movement within management is the ability not just to establish quantitative goals for individual employees and groups, but to create mechanisms for measuring and reporting the attainment of these targets. The balanced scorecard system outlined in Chapter 2 is but one approach to this linking of employee goals to company-wide goals.

Summary

The internal structure and systems of the firm are not simply a matter of "strategy implementation," which can be separated from the hard analytics of strategy formulation. Not only is strategy implementation inseparable from strategy formulation, but issues of structure and systems are central to the fundamental issues of competitive advantage and strategy choice—the existence of organizational capability in particular.

Despite the importance of these issues, this chapter provides only a brief introduction to some of the key issues in organization design. Subsequent chapters develop many of the themes more fully in relation to particular areas of strategy and particular business contexts. Nevertheless, our progress is limited by the weakness of theory in this area. Organization theory is an exceptionally rich field that still lacks adequate integration of its component disciplines: sociology, psychology, organizational economics, systems theory, population ecology, and organizational evolution. While business enterprises continue to experiment with new organizational forms, we business school academics are still struggling to articulate general principles of organizational design.

The chapters that follow will have more to say on the organizational structures and management systems appropriate to different strategies and different business contexts. In the final chapter (Chapter 18) we shall explore some of the new trends and new ideas that are reshaping our thinking about organizational design.

Self-Study Questions

1 As DuPont expanded its product range (from explosives into paints, dyes, plastics, and synthetic fibers) why do you think that the functional structure (organized around manufacturing plants and other functions such as sales, finance and R&D) became unwieldy? Why did the multidivisional structure based on product groups improve management effectiveness?

2 Within your own organization (whether a university, company, or not-for-profit organization), which departments or activities are organized mechanistically and which organically? To what extent does the mode of organization fit the different environmental contexts and technologies of the different departments or activities?

3 In 2008, Citigroup announced that its Consumer business would be split into Consumer Banking, which would continue to operate through individual national banks, and Global Cards, which would form a single global business (similar to Citi's Global Wealth Management division). On the basis of the arguments relating to *Organizing on the Basis of Coordination Intensity*, why should credit cards be organized as a global unit and all other consumer banking services as national units?

4 The examples of Apple Computer and General Motors (see section on "Functional Structure") point to the evolution of organizational structures over the industry life cycle. During the growth phase many companies adopt multidivisional structures, during maturity and decline many companies revert to functional structures. Why might this be? (*Note*: you may wish to refer to Chapter 11, which outlines the main features of the life-cycle model.)

5 Draw an organizational chart for a business school that you are familiar with. Does the school operate with a matrix structure (for instance, are there functional/discipline-based departments together with units managing individual programs)? Which dimension of the matrix is more powerful, and how effectively do the two dimensions coordinate? How would you reorganize the structure to make the school more efficient and effective?

Notes

1 G. Parker, *The Grand Strategy of Philip II* (New Haven: Yale University Press, 1998).
2 "Alcatel-Lucent: Goodbye and Adieu," *Economist* (July 13, 2008).
3 T. Peters, "Strategy Follows Structure," *California Management Review*, 26 (Spring, 1984): 114–28.
4 R. Whittington, A. Pettigrew, S. Peck, E. Fenton, and M. Conyon, "Change and Complementarities in the New Competitive Landscape," *Organization Science* 10 (1999): 583–96.
5 A. D. Chandler, *The Visible Hand: The Managerial Revolution in American Business* (Cambridge, MA: MIT Press, 1977): Chapter 2.
6 Ibid.
7 J. Micklethwait and A. Wooldridge, *The Company: a Short History of a Revolutionary Idea* (New York: Modern Library, 2005).
8 R. Stark, *Sociology*, 10th edn (Belmont, CA: Wadsworth, 2006).
9 A. D. Chandler, *Strategy and Structure* (Cambridge: MIT Press, 1962); Chandler, *The Visible Hand*, op. cit.
10 Chandler, *Strategy and Structure*, op. cit.: 382–3.
11 See http://heritage.dupont.com/floater/fl_management/floater.shtml.
12 A. P. Sloan, *My Years at General Motors* (London: Sidgwick & Jackson, 1963): 42–56.
13 H. Mintzberg, *Structure in Fives: Designing Effective Organizations* (Englewood Cliffs: Prentice Hall, 1993): 2.
14 A. Smith, *The Wealth of Nations* (London: Dent, 1910): 5.
15 S. Ross, "The Economic Theory of Agency," *American Economic Review*, 63 (1973): 134–9; K. Eisenhardt, "Agency Theory: An Assessment and Reviews," *Academy of Management Review*, 14 (1989): 57–74.
16 I. T. Kay and S. Van Ritten, *Myths and Realities of Executive Pay* (Cambridge University Press, 2007): Chapter 6.
17 T. Peters and R. Waterman, *In Search of Excellence* (New York: Harper & Row, 1982).
18 W. G. Ouchi, *Theory Z* (Reading, MA: Addison-Wesley, 1981).
19 J. Weeks, *Unpopular Culture: The Ritual of Complaint in a British Bank* (Chicago: University of Chicago Press, 2004).
20 H. A. Simon, "The Architecture of Complexity," *Proceedings of the American Philosophical Society* 106 (1962): 467–82.
21 R. N. Langlois, "Modularity in Technology and Organization," *Journal of Economic Behavior and Organization* 49 (September 2002): 19–37.
22 J. D. Orton and K. E. Weick, "Loosely Coupled Systems: A Reconceptualization," *Academy of Management Review* 15 (1990): 203–23.
23 M. Sako and F. Murray, "Modular Strategies in Car and Computers," *Financial Times*, Mastering Strategy Part 11 (December 6, 1999): 4–7.
24 Modularity in organizations is explored in: R. Sanchez and J. T. Mahoney, "Modularity, Flexibility, and Knowledge Management in Product and Organizational Design," *Strategic Management Journal* 17, Winter Special Issue (1996): 63–76; M. A. Schilling, "Toward a General Modular Systems Theory and its Application to Interfirm Product Modularity," *Academy of Management Review* 25 (2000): 312–34; and C. Baldwin and K. Clark, "Managing in an Age of Modularity," *Harvard Business Review* (September-October 1997): 84–93.
25 M. Weber, *Economy and Society: An Outline of Interpretive Sociology* (Berkeley: University of California Press, 1968).

26 T. Burns and G. M. Stalker, *The Management of Innovation* (London: Tavistock Institute, 1961).
27 H. Mintzberg, op. cit.: Chapter 9.
28 "The Contingency Theory of Organizational Design: Challenges and Opportunities" in R. M. Burton, B. Eriksen, D. D. Hakenssen and C. C. Snow, *Organization Design: The Evolving State of the Art* (New York: Springer-Verlag, 2006): 19–42.
29 H. J. Leavitt, "Why Hierarchies Thrive," *Harvard Business Review* (March 2003): 97–102.
30 J. Nickerson and T. Zenger refer to this as "structural modulation": "Being Efficiently Fickle: A Dynamic Theory of Organizational Choice," *Organization Science* 13 (September–October 2002): 547–67.
31 O. E. Williamson, "The Modern Corporation: Origins, Evolution, Attributes," *Journal of Economic Literature* 19 (1981): 1537–68.
32 J. D. Thompson, *Organizations in Action* (New York: McGraw-Hill, 1967). The nature of interdependence in organizational processes is revisited in T. W. Malone, K. Crowston, J. Lee, and B. Pentland, "Tools for Inventing Organizations: Toward a Handbook of Organizational Processes," *Management Science* 45 (March 1999): 489–504.
33 The need for organizations to differentiate management and organization between different functional departments and product units is discussed in P. R. Lawrence and J. W. Lorsch, *Organization and Environment* (Boston: Harvard Business School Press, 1986).
34 C. A. Bartlett and S. Ghoshal, "Matrix Management: Not a Structure, a Frame of Mind," *Harvard Business Review* (July–August 1990): 138–45.
35 "A Survey of the Company: The New Organization," *Economist* (January 21, 2006).
36 R. Daft and A. Lewin, "Where are the theories for the new organizational forms?" *Organization Science* 3 (1993): 1–6.
37 H. Mintzberg, op. cit.: Chapter 12.
38 M. H. Lazerson and G. Lorenzoni, "The Firms that Feed Industrial Districts: A Return to the Italian Source," *Industrial and Corporate Change* 8 (1999): 235–66; G. Lorenzoni and A. Lipparini, "The leveraging of interfirm relationships as a distinctive organizational capability: a longitudinal study," *Strategic Management Journal* 20 (1999): 317–38; A. Grandori, *Interfirm Networks* (London: Routledge, 1999).
39 R. J. DeFilippi and M. B. Arthur, "Paradox in Project-based Enterprise: The Case of Film Making," *California Management Review* 42 (1998): 186–91.
40 G. Lorenzoni and C. Baden-Fuller, "Creating a Strategic Center to Manage a web of Partners," *California Management Review* 37, no. 3 (1995): 146–63.
41 J. H. Dyer and K. Nobeoka, "Creating and managing a high-performance knowledge-sharing network: the Toyota case," *Strategic Management Journal* 21 (2000): 345–67; A. Camuffo, P. Romano, and A. Vinelli, "Back to the Future: Benetton Transforms Its Global Network," *Sloan Management Review* 43 (Fall 2001): 46–52.
42 D. Wheeler, K. McKague, J. Thomson, R. Davies, J. Medalye, and M. Prada, "Sustainable Local Enterprise Networks," *Sloan Management Review* (Fall 2005): 33–40.
43 W. C. Finnie, *Hands-On Strategy: The Guide to Crafting Your Company's Strategy* (New York: John Wiley & Sons, Inc., 1994).
44 *MCI Communications: Planning for the 1990s*, Case No. 9-190-136 (Boston: Harvard Business School, 1990): 1.
45 BP Strategy and Fourth Quarter 2005 Results Presentation, February 7, 2006 (www.bp.com).
46 R. M. Grant, "Strategic Planning in a Turbulent Environment: Evidence from the Oil Majors," *Strategic Management Journal* 24 (2003): 491–518. Similar findings have been reported by the American Productivity and Quality Center among "best practice companies" (*Strategic Planning: Final Report*, Houston: APQC, 1996).
47 A. Alchian and H. Demsetz, "Production, Information Costs, and Economic Organization," *American Economic Review* 62 (1972): 777–97.
48 E. H. Schein, "Organizational Culture," *American Psychologist* 45 (1990): 109–19.
49 T. Burns, *The BBC: Public Institution and Private World* (London: Macmillan, 1977).
50 "LAPD: Storming the Rampart," *Economist* (December 2, 2000): 72.
51 J. Weeks, "On Management: Culture Eats Strategy" *Management Today* (June 2006).

III

THE ANALYSIS OF COMPETITIVE ADVANTAGE

8 The Nature and Sources of Competitive Advantage

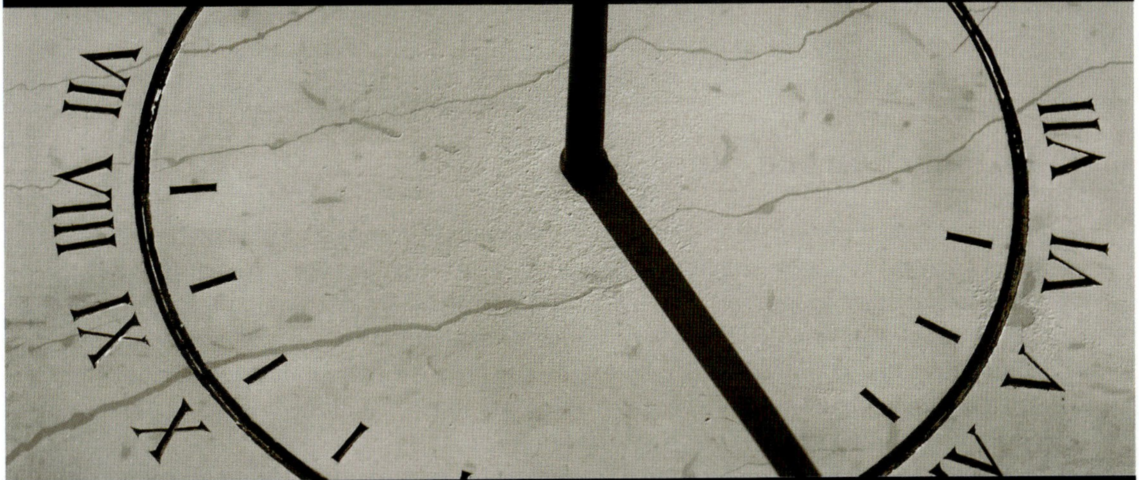

One Saturday afternoon in downtown Chicago, Milton Friedman, the famous free-market economist, was shopping with his wife.

"Look, Milton!" exclaimed Mrs. Friedman. "There's a $20 bill on the sidewalk!"
"Don't be foolish, my dear," replied the Nobel laureate. "If that was a $20 bill, someone would have picked it up by now."

—ECONOMIST'S ANECDOTE OF DOUBTFUL AUTHENTICITY

OUTLINE

Introduction and Objectives

In this chapter, we integrate and develop the elements of competitive advantage that we have analyzed in prior chapters. Chapter 1 noted that a firm can earn superior profitability either by locating in an attractive industry or by establishing a competitive advantage over its rivals. Of these two, competitive advantage is the more important. As competition has intensified across almost all industries, very few industry environments can guarantee secure returns; hence, the primary goal of a strategy is to establish a position of competitive advantage for the firm.

Chapters 3 and 5 provided the two primary components of our analysis of competitive advantage. The last part of Chapter 3 analyzed the external sources of competitive advantage: customer requirements and the nature of competition determine the *key success factors* within a market. Chapter 5 analyzed the internal sources of competitive advantage: the potential for the firm's resources and capabilities to establish and sustain competitive advantage.

This chapter looks more deeply at competitive advantage. We focus on the dynamic relationship between competitive advantage and the competitive process. Competition provides the incentive for establishing advantage and is the means by which advantage is eroded. By understanding the characteristics of competition in a market we can identify the opportunities for competitive advantage.

By the time you have completed this chapter you will be able to:

- identify the circumstances in which a firm can create a competitive advantage over a rival;
- predict the potential for competition to erode competitive advantage through imitation;
- recognize how resource conditions create imperfections in the competitive process which offer opportunities for competitive advantage;
- distinguish the two primary types of competitive advantage: cost advantage and differentiation advantage;
- apply this analysis to assess the potential for a business strategy to establish and sustain competitive advantage given the characteristics of the industry setting.

The Emergence of Competitive Advantage

To understand how competitive advantage emerges, we must first understand what competitive advantage is. Most of us can recognize competitive advantage when we see it: Wal-Mart has a competitive advantage in discount retailing within the U.S.; Toyota has a competitive advantage in making mass-produced cars; SAP has a competitive advantage in enterprise resource planning (ERP) software. Yet, defining competitive advantage is troublesome. At a basic level we can define it as follows: "When two or more firms compete within the same market, one firm possesses a competitive advantage over its rivals when it earns (or has the potential to earn) a persistently higher rate of profit."

The problem here is that if we identify competitive advantage with superior profitability, why do we need the concept of competitive advantage at all? The key difference is that competitive advantage may not be revealed in higher profitability—a firm may forgo current profit in favor of investment in market share, technology, customer loyalty, or executive perks.[1]

External Sources of Change

In the long run, competition eliminates differences in profitability between competing firms—hence, competitive advantage is a disequilibrium phenomenon that is a consequence of change. The source of the change may be external or internal to the industry (see Figure 8.1). For an external change to create competitive advantage, the change must have differential effects on companies because of their different resources and capabilities or strategic positioning. For example, during 2000–4, General Motors' return on assets (ROA) was 14.0%; Toyota's was 8.1%. During 2004–7, General Motors' ROA was −5.2%; Toyota's was 7.6%. Over the period oil prices had tripled and demand had shifted away from the advanced industrialized countries. Toyota, with its fuel-efficient product range and superior distribution in emerging market countries, was the advantaged competitor.

FIGURE 8.1 The emergence of competitive advantage

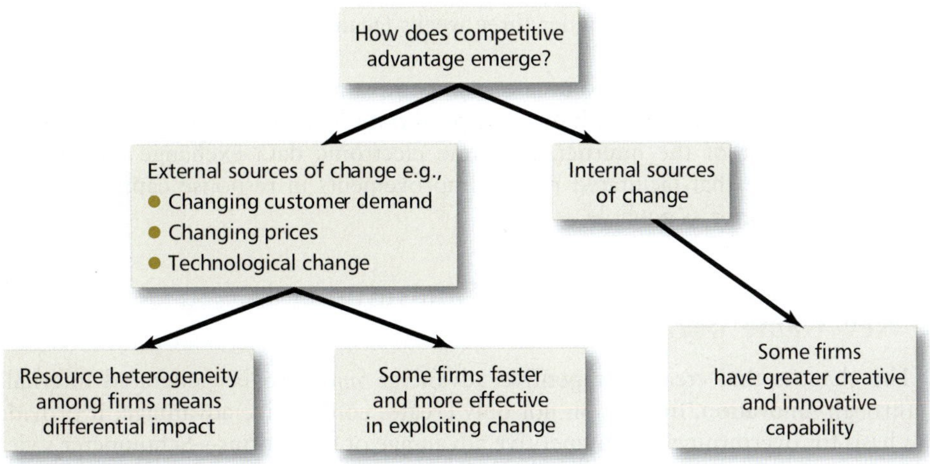

The extent to which external change creates competitive advantage and disadvantage depends on the magnitude of the change and the extent of firms' strategic differences. The more turbulent an industry's environment, the greater the number of sources of change and the greater the differences in firms' resources and capabilities, the greater the dispersion of profitability within the industry. In the world tobacco industry, the external environment is fairly stable and the leading firms pursue similar strategies with similar resources and capabilities. Hence, competitive advantages, as reflected in interfirm profit differentials, tend to be small. The toy industry, on the other hand, comprises a heterogeneous group of firms that experience unpredictable shifts in consumer preferences and technology. As a result, profitability differences are wide and variable.

Competitive Advantage from Responsiveness to Change

The competitive advantage that arises from external change also depends on firms' ability to respond to change. Any external change creates opportunities for profit, including opportunities for new business initiatives (what is known as *entrepreneurship*).

Responsiveness involves one of two key capabilities. The first is the ability to anticipate changes in the external environment. Thus, Nokia's ability to maintain market leadership in wireless handsets owes much to its anticipation of the shift in demand from advanced to emerging economies. The second is speed. An unexpected rain shower creates an upsurge in the demand for umbrellas. Those street vendors who are quickest to position themselves outside a busy railroad station will benefit most.

As markets become more turbulent and unpredictable, so speed of response through greater flexibility has become increasingly important as a source of competitive advantage. The first requirement for quick response capability is information. As conventional economic and market forecasting has become less effective, so companies rely increasingly on "early warning systems" through direct relationships with customers, suppliers and even competitors. The second requirement is short cycle times that allow information on emerging market developments to be acted upon speedily. In fashion retailing, fast response to emerging fashion trends is critical to success. Zara, the chain of retail clothing stores owned by the Spanish company Inditex, has pioneered leading-edge fashion clothes for budget-minded young adults through a tightly-integrated vertical structure that cuts the time between a garment's design and retail delivery to under three weeks (against an industry norm of three to six months.[2]

The notion of speed as a source of competitive advantage was pioneered by the Boston Consulting Group with its concept of *time-based competition*.[3] However, it was the advent of the internet, real-time electronic data exchange and wireless communication that facilitated radical improvements in response capability across the business sector as a whole.

Competitive Advantage from Innovation: "New Game" Strategies

The changes that create competitive advantage may also be generated internally through innovation. Innovation not only creates competitive advantage; it provides a basis for overturning the competitive advantage of other firms—Schumpeter's view of competition as "a gale of creative destruction." Although innovation is typically thought of as new products or processes that embody new technology, a key source of competitive advantage is *strategic innovation*— new approaches to doing business including new business models.

Strategic innovation typically involves creating value for customers from novel products, experiences, or modes of product delivery. Thus, in the retail sector competition is driven by a constant quest for new retail concepts and formats. This may take the form of: big-box stores with greater variety (Toys-R-Us, Home Depot); augmented customer service (Nordstrom) and novel approaches to display and store layout (Sephora in cosmetics).

Strategic innovation may also be based on redesigned processes and novel organizational designs:

- In the U.S. steel industry, Nucor achieved unrivaled productivity and flexibility by combining new process technologies, flat and flexible organizational structures and innovative management systems. Since 1997, it has been the biggest steel producer in the U.S.
- Southwest Airlines' point-to-point, no-frills airline service using a single type of plane and flexible, nonunion employees has made it the only consistently profitable airline in North America and the model for budget airlines throughout the world.
- Nike built its large and successful businesses on a business system that totally reconfigured the shoe industry's traditional value chain—notably by outsourcing manufacturing and concentrating upon design and marketing, and orchestrating a vast global network of producers, logistics providers and retailers.
- Apple Computer's resurgence during 2003-6 was the result of its reinvention of the recorded music business by combining an iconic MP3 player with its iTunes music download service.

How do we go about formulating innovative strategies? Strategic innovations tend to involve pioneering along one or more dimensions of strategy:

- New industries. Some companies launch products which create a whole new market. Xerox created the plain-paper copier industry; Freddie Laker pioneered budget air travel; Craig McCaw and McCaw Communications launched the mass market for wireless telephony. For Kim and Mauborgne, creating new markets is the purest form of blue ocean strategy—the creation of "uncontested market space."[4]
- New customer segments. Creating new customer segments for existing product concepts can also open up vast new market spaces. Apple did not invent the personal computer, but it launched the market for computers in the home. The video cassette recorder was developed by Ampex for use in television studios; Sony and Matsushita's innovation was in designing VCRs for domestic use. The success of the Nintendo Wii video games console has been based upon extending video gaming into new customer segments.
- New sources of competitive advantage. As Kim and Mauborgne acknowledge, most successful blue-ocean strategies do not launch whole new industries but introduce novel approaches to creating customer value. Thus, Dell's strategic

innovation was an integrated system for ordering, assembling and distributing PCs, which permitted unprecedented customer choice and speedy fulfillment of orders. Cirque de Soleil has reinvented the circus business as a multimedia entertainment spectacle that meshes technology with highly developed acrobatic and choreographic capabilities.[5] McKinsey & Company show that a key element of strategic innovation—what they call new game strategy—involves reconfiguring the industry value chain in order to change the "rules of the game" within a market.[6] For example, Canon's successful penetration of the plain-paper copier market during 1973–6, was based upon a strategy that was radically different from that of the incumbent, Xerox. While Xerox's dominance was based upon large machines, which used dry toner and were leased to customers, Canon introduced small machines that used liquid toner and were sold outright to customers.[7] In their study of rejuvenation among mature firms, Charles Baden-Fuller and John Stopford observe that strategic innovation often involves combining performance dimensions that were previously viewed as conflicting. For example, Richardson, a U.K. kitchen knife producer, used an innovative design, process innovation, and a lean, entrepreneurial management to supply kitchen knives that combined price competitiveness, durability, sharpness, and responsive customer service.[8] However, according to Gary Hamel, even innovative strategies are subject to imitation. He argues that the most durable forms of competitive advantage are those that derive from management innovation such as Procter & Gamble's invention of modern brand management and Toyota's lean production system.[9]

Sustaining Competitive Advantage

Once established, competitive advantage is subject to erosion by competition. The speed with which competitive advantage is undermined depends on the ability of competitors to challenge either by imitation or innovation. Imitation is the most direct form of competition; thus, for competitive advantage to be sustained over time, barriers to imitation must exist. Rumelt uses the term *isolating mechanisms* to describe "barriers that limit the *ex post* equilibration of rents among individual firms."[10] The more effective these isolating mechanisms are, the longer competitive advantage can be sustained against the onslaught of rivals. In most industries the erosion of the competitive advantage of industry leaders is a slow process: interfirm profit differentials often persist for period of a decade or more.[11] However, as we discussed in Chapter 4 (see the section on "Dynamic Competition"), the advent of hypercompetition has accelerated the erosion of profit differentials.

To identify the sources of isolating mechanisms, we need to examine the process of competitive imitation. For one firm successfully to imitate the strategy of another, it must meet four conditions:

- *Identification*. The firm must be able to identify that a rival possesses a competitive advantage.
- *Incentive*. Having identified that a rival possesses a competitive advantage (as shown by above-average profitability), the firm must believe that by investing in imitation, it too can earn superior returns.

FIGURE 8.2 Sustaining competitive advantage: types of isolating mechanism

REQUIREMENT FOR IMITATION	*ISOLATING MECHANISM*
Identification	—*Obscure* superior performance
Incentives for imitation	—*Deterrence*: signal aggressive intentions to imitators —*Preemption*: exploit all available investment opportunities
Diagnosis	—Rely on multiple sources of competitive advantage to create *"causal ambiguity"*
Resource acquisition	—Base competitive advantage on resources and capabilities that are *immobile* and *difficult to replicate*

- *Diagnosis*. The firm must be able to diagnose the features of its rival's strategy that give rise to the competitive advantage.
- *Resource acquisition*. The firm must be able to acquire through transfer or replication the resources and capabilities necessary for imitating the strategy of the advantaged firm.

Figure 8.2 illustrates these stages and the types of isolating mechanism that exist at each stage.

Identification: Obscuring Superior Performance

A simple barrier to imitation is to obscure the firm's superior profitability. According to George Stalk of the Boston Consulting Group: "One way to throw competitors off balance is to mask high performance so rivals fail to see your success until it's too late."[12] In the 1948 movie classic *The Treasure of the Sierra Madre*, Humphrey Bogart and his partners went to great lengths to obscure their find from other gold prospectors.[13] The Mongolian gold rush of 2002–3 also featured secretive behavior as miners with positive test results sought to acquire exploration rights on nearby properties.[14]

For firms that dominate a niche market, one of the attractions of remaining a private company is to avoid disclosing financial performance. Few food processors realized just how profitable cat and dog food could be until the U.K. Monopolies Commission revealed that the leading firm, Pedigree Petfoods (a subsidiary of Mars Inc.) earned a return on capital employed of 47%.[15]

Avoiding competition through avoiding disclosure of a firm's profits is much easier for a private than a public company. For Mars Inc., the nondisclosure of financial results assited the firm in protecting the profitably of its pet food and confectionery businesses.

The desire to avoid competition may be so strong as to cause companies to forgo short-run profits. The *theory of limit pricing*, in its simplest form, postulates that a firm in a strong market position sets prices at a level that just fails to attract entrants.[16]

Deterrence and Preemption

A firm may avoid competition by undermining the incentives for imitation. If a firm can persuade rivals that imitation will be unprofitable, it may be able to avoid competitive challenges. In Chapter 4 we discussed strategies of deterrence and the role of signaling and commitment in supporting them.[17]

As we have seen, reputation is critically important in making threats credible. Brandenburger and Nalebuff argue that in the aspartame market, NutraSweet's aggressive price war against the Holland Sweetener Company deterred other would-be entrants.[18]

A firm can also deter imitation by preemption—occupying existing and potential strategic niches to reduce the range of investment opportunities open to the challenger. Preemption can take many forms:

- Proliferation of product varieties by a market leader can leave new entrants and smaller rivals with few opportunities for establishing a market niche. Between 1950 and 1972, for example, the six leading suppliers of breakfast cereals introduced 80 new brands into the U.S. market.[19]
- Large investments in production capacity ahead of the growth of market demand also preempt market opportunities for rivals. Monsanto's heavy investment in plants for producing NutraSweet ahead of its patent expiration was a clear threat to would-be producers of generic aspartame.
- Patent proliferation can protect technology-based advantage by limiting competitors' technical opportunities. In 1974, Xerox's dominant market position was protected by a wall of over 2000 patents, most of which were not used. When IBM introduced its first copier in 1970, Xerox sued it for infringing 22 of these patents.[20]

The ability to sustain competitive advantage through preemption depends on the presence of two imperfections of the competitive process. First, the market must be small relative to the minimum efficient scale of production, such that only a very small number of competitors is viable. Second, there must be first-mover advantage that gives an incumbent preferential access to information and other resources, putting rivals at a disadvantage.

Diagnosing Competitive Advantage: "Causal Ambiguity" and "Uncertain Imitability"

If a firm is to imitate the competitive advantage of another, it must understand the basis of its rival's success. In most industries there is a serious identification problem in linking superior performance to the strategic decisions that generate that performance. Consider the remarkable success of Wal-Mart in discount retailing.

For Wal-Mart's struggling competitor, Sears Holdings (owner of the Kmart chain of discount stores), it is easy to point to the differences between Wal-Mart and itself. As one Wal-Mart executive commented: "Retailing is an open book. There are no secrets. Our competitors can walk into our stores and see what we sell, how we sell it, and for how much." The difficult task is to identify which differences are the critical determinants of superior profitability. Is it Wal-Mart's store locations (typically in small towns with little direct competition)? Its tightly integrated supply chain? Its unique management system? The information system that supports Wal-Mart's logistics and decision-making practices? Or is it a culture built on traditional rural American values of thrift and hard work?

The problem for Kmart/Sears and other wannabe Wal-Marts is what Lippman and Rumelt refer to as *causal ambiguity*.[21] The more multidimensional a firm's competitive advantage and the more it is based on complex bundles of organizational capabilities, the more difficult it is for a competitor to diagnose the determinants of success. The outcome of causal ambiguity is *uncertain imitability*: where there is ambiguity associated with the causes of a competitor's success, any attempt to imitate that strategy is subject to uncertain success.

Recent research suggests that the problems of strategy imitation may run even deeper. We observed in Chapter 5 that capabilities are the outcome of complex combinations of resources and that different capabilities interact to confer competitive advantage. However, work in complementarity among firms' activities suggests that these interactions extend across the whole range of management practices.[22] Where these linkages are tight, complexity theory—NK modeling in particular—predicts that within a particular competitive environment a number of "fitness peaks" will appear, each associated with a unique combination of strategic variables.[23] Michael Porter and Nicolaj Siggelkow quote Urban Outfitters as an example of a unique "activity system" (see Strategy Capsule 8.1).[24] If company success is the outcome of a complex configuration of strategy, structure, management systems, personal leadership, and host of business processes, the implication is that imitation may well be impossible.

STRATEGY CAPSULE 8.1

Urban Outfitters

During the three years to January 2009, Urban Outfitters Inc., which comprises 130 Urban Outfitters stores (together with Anthropologie and Free People chains), has grown at an average of 20% annually and earned a return on equity of 21%. The company describes itself as

> *targeting well-educated, urban-minded, young adults aged 18 to 30 through its unique merchandise mix and compelling store environment . . . We create a unified environment in our stores that establishes an emotional bond with the customer. Every element of the environment is tailored to the aesthetic preferences of our target customers. Through creative design, much of the existing retail space is modified to incorporate a mosaic of fixtures, finishes*

and revealed architectural details. In our stores, merchandise is integrated into a variety of creative vignettes and displays designed to offer our customers an entire look at a distinct lifestyle.

According to Michael Porter and Nicolaj Siggelkow, Urban Outfitters offers a set of management practices that is both distinctive and highly interdependent. The urban-bohemian-styled product mix, which includes clothing, furnishings and gift items are displayed within bazaar-like stores each of which have a unique design. To encourage frequent customer visits, the layout of each store is changed every two weeks, creating a new shopping experience whenever customers return. Emphasizing community with its customers, it foregoes traditional forms of advertising in favor of blogs and word-of-mouth transmission. Each practice makes little sense on its own, but together they represent a distinctive, integrated strategy. Attempts to imitate Urban Outfitters' competitive advantage would most likely fail because of the difficulty of replicating every aspect of the strategy then integrating them in the right manner.

Sources: Urban Outfitters Inc. 10-K Report to January 31, 2009 (Washington: SEC, 2008); M.E. Porter and N. Siggelkow, "Contextuality Within Activity Systems and Sustainable Competitive Advantage," *Academy of Management Perspectives* 22 (May 2008): 34–56.

One of the challenges for the would-be imitator is deciding which management practices are generic best practices and which are "contextual"—complementary with other management practices. For example, if we consider Sears Holdings' deliberation of which of Wal-Mart's management practices to imitate in its Kmart stores, some practices (for example, employees required to smile at customers, point-of-sale data transferred direct into the corporate database) are likely to be generically beneficial. Others, such as Wal-Mart's "everyday low prices" pricing policy, low advertising sales ratio, and hub-and-spoke distribution are likely to be beneficial only when combined with other practices.[25]

Acquiring Resources and Capabilities

Having diagnosed the sources of an incumbent's competitive advantage, the imitator can mount a competitive challenge only by assembling the resources and capabilities necessary for imitation. As we saw in Chapter 5, a firm can acquire resources and capabilities in two ways: it can buy them or it can build them. The period over which a competitive advantage can be sustained depends critically on the time it takes to acquire and mobilize the resources and capabilities needed to mount a competitive challenge.

There is little to add here to the discussion of transferability and replicability in Chapter 5. The ability to buy resources and capabilities from outside factor markets depends on their transferability between firms. Even if resources are mobile, the market for a resource may be subject to *transaction costs* including search costs, negotiation costs, and contract enforcement costs. Transaction costs are greater for highly differentiated (or "idiosyncratic") resources.[26]

The alternative to buying a resource or capability is to create it through internal investment. As we noted in Chapter 5, where capabilities are based on organizational routines, accumulating the coordination and learning required for their efficient operation can take considerable time.

Businesses that require the integration of a number of complex, team-based routines may take years to reach the standards set by industry leaders. General Motors' attempt to transfer team-based, lean production from its NUMMI joint venture with Toyota at Fremont, California, to the GM Van Nuys plant 400 miles to the south involved complex management problems that remained unsolved two years later.[27]

Conversely, where a competitive advantage does not require the application of complex, firm-specific resources, imitation is often fast. In financial services, most new products are copied quickly by competitors. *Collateralized debt obligations*, the derivative securities that played a central role in the financial crisis of 2008 were developed first by Drexel Burnham Lambert. During the late 1990s, several leading investment banks began issuing CDOs and by 2005 the annual volume of new CDOs exceeded $500 billion.[28]

A key issue for would-be imitators is the extent to which first-mover advantage exists within the market. The idea of first-mover advantage is that the initial occupant of a strategic position or niche gains access to resources and capabilities that a follower cannot match. This is either because the first-mover is able to preempt the best resources, or can use early entry to build superior resources and capabilities.[29] We shall return to the issue of first-mover advantage when we consider competitive advantage in emerging and technology-based industries (Chapter 12).

Competitive Advantage in Different Market Settings

To identify opportunities for establishing and sustaining competitive advantage requires that we understand the competitive process in the specific market. For competitive advantage to exist, there must be some imperfection of competition. To understand these imperfections in the competitive process, we need to identify the types of resources and capabilities necessary to compete and the circumstances of their availability.

Our initial discussion of the nature of business in Chapter 1 identified two types of value-creating activity: trading and production. Trading involves arbitrage across space (trade) and time (speculation). Production involves the physical transformation of inputs into outputs. These different types of business activity correspond to different market types: trading markets and production markets (see Figure 8.3). We begin with a discussion of a special type of trading market: an efficient market.

Efficient Markets: The Absence of Competitive Advantage

In Chapter 3, we introduced the concept of perfect competition. Perfect competition exists where there are many buyers and sellers, no product differentiation, no barriers to entry or exit, and free flow of information. In equilibrium, all firms earn the competitive rate of profit, which equals the cost of capital. The closest real-world examples of perfect competition are financial and commodity markets (for example, the markets for securities, foreign exchange and

FIGURE 8.3 Competitive advantage in different industry settings: trading and production

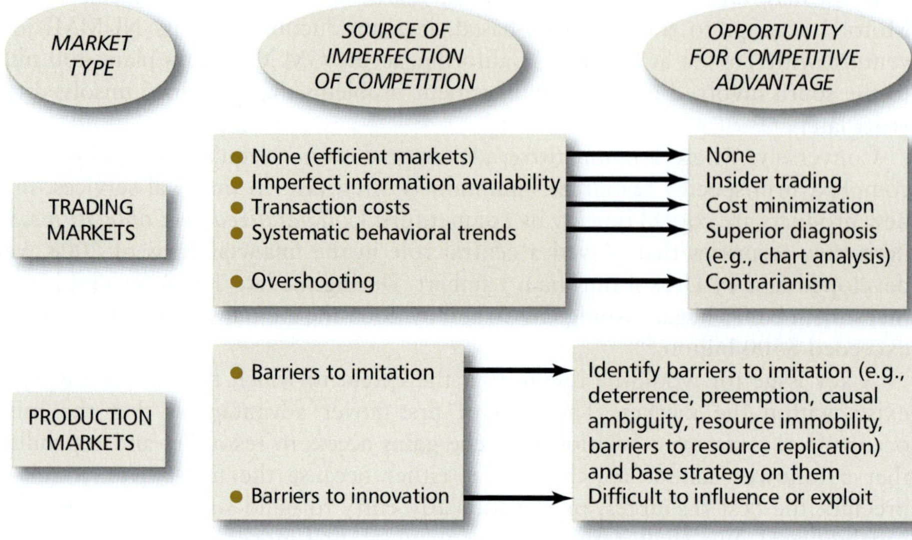

grain futures). These markets are sometimes described as *efficient*. An *efficient market* is one in which prices reflect all available information. Because prices adjust instantaneously to newly available information, no market trader can expect to earn more than any other. Any differences in *ex post* returns reflect either different levels of risk selected by different traders or purely random factors (luck). Because all available information is reflected in current prices, no trading rules based on historical price data or any other available information can offer excess returns: it is not possible to "beat the market" on any consistent basis. In other words, competitive advantage is absent.

The absence of competitive advantage in efficient markets can be linked to resource availability. If financial markets are efficient, it is because only two types of resource are required to participate—finance and information. If both are equally available to all traders, there is no basis for one to gain competitive advantage over another.

Competitive Advantage in Trading Markets

For competitive advantage to exist, imperfections (or "inefficiencies") must be introduced into the competitive process. In trading markets, several types of imperfection to the competitive process create opportunities for competitive advantage.

Imperfect Availability of Information Financial markets (and most other trading markets) are subject to imperfect availability of information. This provides opportunities for competitive advantage through superior access to information. Trading on the basis of privileged private information is a key source of advantage in markets for traded goods and securities—although such trading is affected by legal restrictions on "insider trading." Insider information creates advantage but the advantage is often short lived: once detected insider trading tends to be imitated by other market participants.

Transaction Costs If markets are efficient except for the presence of transaction costs, then competitive advantage accrues to the traders with the lowest transaction costs. In stock markets, low transaction costs are attained by traders who economize on research and market analysis and achieve efficient portfolio diversification. John Bogle estimated that actively managed U.S. mutual funds underperformed the market index by about 2.5% annually—roughly equal to the funds' costs of transactions and administration.[30] Bogle's Vanguard S&P 500 Index fund with transaction and operating costs of 0.5% annually has outperformed 90% of U.S. equity mutual funds.

Systematic Behavioral Trends If the current prices in a market fully reflect all available information, then price movements are caused by the arrival of new information and follow a random walk.[31] If, however, other factors influence price movements, there is scope for a strategy that uses insight into how prices really do move. Some stock market anomalies are well documented, notably the "small firm effect," the "January effect," and "weekend effects." More generally, there is evidence that prices in financial markets follow systematic patterns that result from "market psychology", allowing trends and turning points to be deduced from past data. Chart analysis uses patterns of price movements—such as "support and resistance levels," "head and shoulders," "double tops," "flags," and "candlesticks"—as prediction tools. Despite mixed evidence on the success of chart analysis in financial markets,[32] systematic behavior among market participants offers opportunity for competitive advantage by traders with superior skill in diagnosing such behavior.

Overshooting One well-documented behavioral aberration is the propensity towards "herd behavior" where imitative trading and converging expectations cause prices to overshoot.[33] The implication is that competitive advantage can be gained, in the short term, by following the herd—"momentum trading." In the long run, overshooting is corrected by an opposite corrective movement, offering opportunity for a *contrarian* strategy. The world's richest man, Warren Buffett, is a prominent contrarian who is "fearful when others are greedy, and greedy when others are fearful."

Competitive Advantage in Production Markets

The transitory nature of competitive advantage in trading markets is a result of the characteristics of the resources required to compete: finance and information. Finance is a relatively homogeneous resource that is widely available. Information, although highly differentiated, is transferable easily and at very low cost; hence, the competitive advantage it offers tends to be fleeting.

Production markets are quite different. Production activities require complex combinations of resources and capabilities and these resources and capabilities are highly differentiated. The result, as we have noted, is that each producer possesses a unique combination of resources and capabilities. The greater the heterogeneity of firms' endowments of resources and capabilities, the greater the potential for competitive advantage. In the European electricity generating industry, the growing diversity of players—utilities (GdF, ENEL, Iberdrola), oil and gas majors (Shell, Eni), independent power producers (AES, Powergen), and wind power generators—has expanded opportunities for competitive advantage and widened the profit differentials between them.

Differences in resource endowments among firms also influence the erosion of competitive advantage. Where firms possess very similar bundles of resources and capabilities, imitation of the competitive advantage of the incumbent firm is most likely. Where resource bundles are highly differentiated, competition is more likely to be through distinctive strategies that substitute the incumbent's competitive advantage.[34] For example:

- In video game consoles, Nintendo, with a very different resource base from Sony and Microsoft, gained market leadership with a distinctive strategy for its *Wii* console.
- In the U.S. airline industry, newcomer Virgin America has drawn upon its distinctive resources and capabilities to position itself differently from either the "legacy airlines" (American, United) and the low-cost carriers (Southwest, AirTran).

Since substitute competition can come from many directions its deterrence requires building defenses on multiple fronts—including commitments to key stakeholders.[35]

Types of Competitive Advantage: Cost and Differentiation

A firm can achieve a higher rate of profit (or potential profit) over a rival in one of two ways: either it can supply an identical product or service at a lower cost, or it can supply a product or service that is differentiated in such a way that the customer is willing to pay a price premium that exceeds the additional cost of the differentiation. In the former case, the firm possesses a cost advantage; in the latter, a differentiation advantage. In pursuing cost advantage, the goal of the firm is to become the cost leader in its industry or industry segment. Cost leadership requires that the firm "must find and exploit all sources of cost advantage . . . [and] . . . sell a standard, no-frills product."[36] Differentiation by a firm from its competitors is achieved "when it provides something unique that is valuable to buyers beyond simply offering a low price."[37] Figure 8.4 illustrates these two types of advantage.

The two sources of competitive advantage define two fundamentally different approaches to business strategy. A firm that is competing on low cost is distinguishable from a firm that competes through differentiation in terms of market positioning, resources and capabilities, and organizational characteristics. Table 8.1 outlines some of the principal features of cost and differentiation strategies.

FIGURE 8.4 Sources of competitive advantage

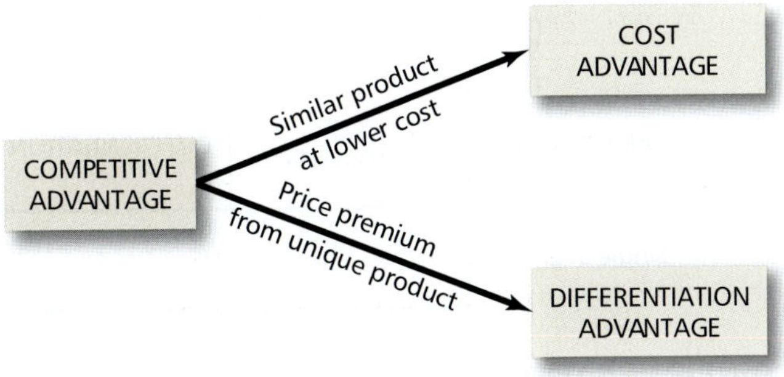

TABLE 8.1 Features of cost leadership and differentiation strategies

Generic strategy	Key strategy elements	Resource and organizational requirements
Cost leadership	Scale-efficient plants Design for manufacture Control of overheads and R&D Process innovation Outsourcing (especially overseas) Avoidance of marginal customer accounts	Access to capital Process engineering skills Frequent reports Tight cost control Specialization of jobs and functions Incentives linked to quantitative targets
Differentiation	Emphasis on branding advertising, design, service, quality, and new product development	Marketing abilities Product engineering skills Cross-functional coordination Creativity Research capability Incentives linked to qualitative performance targets

By combining the two types of competitive advantage with the firm's choice of scope—broad market versus narrow segment—Michael Porter has defined three generic strategies: cost leadership, differentiation, and focus (see Figure 8.5). Porter views cost leadership and differentiation as mutually exclusive strategies. A firm that attempts to pursue both is "stuck in the middle":

> The firm stuck in the middle is almost guaranteed low profitability. It either loses the high-volume customers who demand low prices or must bid away its profits to get this business from the low-cost firms. Yet it also loses high-margin business—the cream—to the firms who are focused on high-margin targets or have achieved differentiation overall. The firm that is stuck in the middle also probably suffers from a blurred corporate culture and a conflicting set of organizational arrangements and motivation system.[38]

FIGURE 8.5 Porter's generic strategies

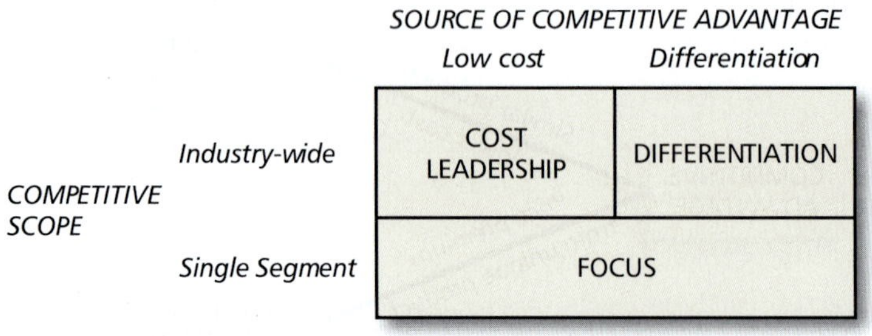

In practice, few firms are faced with such stark alternatives. Differentiation is not simply an issue of "to differentiate or not to differentiate." All firms must make decisions as to which customer requirements to focus on and where to position their product or service in the market. A cost leadership strategy typically implies a narrow-line, limited-feature, standardized offering. However, such a positioning does not necessarily imply that the product or service is an undifferentiated commodity. In the case of IKEA furniture and Southwest Airlines, a low-price, no-frills offering is also associated with clear market positioning and a unique brand image. The VW Beetle shows that a low-cost, utilitarian, mass-market product can achieve cult status. At the same time, firms that pursue differentiation strategies cannot be oblivious to cost.

In most industries, market leadership is held by a firm that maximizes customer appeal by reconciling effective differentiation with low cost—Toyota in cars, McDonald's in fast food, Nike in athletic shoes. In many industries, the cost leader is not the market leader but is a smaller competitor with minimal overheads, nonunion labor and cheaply acquired assets. In oil refining, the cost leaders tend to be independent refining companies rather than integrated giants such as ExxonMobil or Shell. In car rental, the cost leader is more likely to be Rent-A-Wreck (a division of Bundy American Corporation) rather than Hertz or Avis. Simultaneously pursuing differentiation, cost efficiency and innovation was a key element in the global success of Japanese companies in cars, motorcycles, consumer electronics and musical instruments. Reconciling different performance dimensions has been facilitated by new management techniques. For example, total quality management has refuted the perceived tradeoff between quality and cost.

Summary

Making money in business requires establishing and sustaining competitive advantage. Both these conditions for profitability demand profound insight into the nature and process of competition within a market. Competitive advantage depends critically on the presence of some imperfection in the competitive process—under perfect competition, profits are transitory. Our analysis of the imperfections of the competitive process has drawn us back to the resources and capabilities that are required to compete in different markets and to pursue different strategies. Sustaining competitive advantage depends on the existence of *isolating mechanisms*: barriers to rivals' imitation of successful strategies. The greater the difficulty that rivals face in accessing the resources and capabilities needed to imitate or substitute the competitive advantage of the incumbent firm, the greater the sustainability of that firm's competitive advantage. Hence, one outcome of our analysis is to reinforce the argument made in Chapter 5: the characteristics of a firm's resources and capability are fundamental to its strategy and its performance in decision making and long-term success.

In the next two chapters, we analyze the two primary dimensions of competitive advantage: cost advantage and differentiation advantage. In both of these areas we emphasize the importance of a deep understanding of both the firm and its industry environment. To this end, it is useful to disaggregate the firm into a series of separate but interlinked activities. A useful and versatile framework for this purpose is the value chain, which is an insightful tool for understanding the sources of competitive advantage in an industry, for assessing the competitive position of a particular firm, and for suggesting opportunities to enhance a firm's competitiveness.

Self-Study Questions

1 Figure 8.1 implies that stable industries, where firms have similar resources and capabilities, offer less opportunity for competitive advantage than industries where change is rapid and firms are heterogeneous. Think of an example of each of these two types of industry. Is there any evidence that interfirm profit differences are wider in the more dynamic, heterogeneous industry than in the more stable, homogeneous industry?

2 Apple has been successful in dominating the market for both MP3 players with its iPod and for music downloads with its iTunes service. Can Apple sustain its leadership in these markets? How?

3 Illy, the Italian-based supplier of quality coffee and coffee-making equipment, is launching an international chain of gourmet coffee shops. What advice would you offer Illy for how it can best build competitive advantage in the face of Starbucks' market leadership?

4 Do you believe that some mutual funds ("unit trusts" in British parlance) can deliver consistently superior returns (once adjusted for risk)? If so, what is the basis for such superior performance and what can fund managers do to achieve superior performance?

5 Target (the U.S. discount retailer), H&M (the Swedish fashion clothing chain) and Primark (the U.K. discount clothing chain) have pioneered "cheap chic"—combining discount store prices with fashion appeal. What are the principal challenges of designing and implementing a "cheap chic" strategy? Design a "cheap chic" strategy for a company entering another market, e.g. restaurants, sports shoes, cosmetics, or office furniture.

Notes

1 Richard Rumelt argues that competitive advantage lacks a clear and consistent definition ("What in the World is Competitive Advantage," Policy Working Paper 2003-105, Anderson School, UCLA, August, 2003).

2 K. Ferdows, M. A. Lewis, and J. Machuca, "Rapid-Fire Fulfillment," *Harvard Business Review* (November 2004): 104–10.

3 G. Stalk Jr., "Time—The Next Source of Competitive Advantage," *Harvard Business Review* (July–August, 1988): 41–51.

4 C. Kim and R. Mauborgne, "Blue Ocean Strategy," *Harvard Business Review* (October 2004).

5 Ibid.

6 R. Buaron, "New Game Strategies," *McKinsey Quarterly Anthology* (2000): 34–6.

7 "Canon Inc.: Worldwide Copier Strategy," Harvard Business School Case 9-384-151 (1988).

8 C. Baden-Fuller and J. M. Stopford, *Rejuvenating the Mature Business* (London and New York: Routledge, 1992).

9 G. Hamel, "The Why, What, and How of Management Innovation," *Harvard Business Review* (February 2006).

10 R. P. Rumelt, "Toward a Strategic Theory of the Firm," in R. Lamb (ed.), *Competitive Strategic Management* (Englewood Cliffs, NJ: Prentice Hall, 1984): 556–70.

11 See J. Cubbin and P. Geroski, "The Convergence of Profits in the Long Run: Interfirm and Interindustry Comparisons," *Journal of Industrial Economics* 35 (1987): 427–42; R. Jacobsen, "The Persistence of Abnormal Returns," *Strategic Management Journal* 9 (1988): 415–30; and R. R. Wiggins and T. W. Ruefli, "Schumpeter's Ghost: Is Hypercompetition Making the Best of Times Shorter?" *Strategic Management Journal* 26 (2005): 887–911.

12 G. Stalk, "Curveball: Strategies to Fool the Competition," *Harvard Business Review* (September 2006): 114–22.

13 The film was based on the book, by B. Traven, *The Treasure of the Sierra Madre* (New York: Knopf, 1947).

14 "The Great Mongolian Gold Rush," *Fortune Investors Guide 2004* (December, 2003).

15 Monopolies and Mergers Commission, *Cat and Dog Foods* (London: Her Majesty's Stationery Office, 1977).

16 S. Martin, *Advanced Industrial Economics*, 2nd edn. (Oxford: Blackwell Publishers, 2001): Chapter 8.

17 T. C. Schelling, *The Strategy of Conflict*, 2nd edn. (Cambridge: Harvard University Press, 1980): 35–41.

18 A. Brandenburger and B. Nalebuff, *Co-opetition* (New York: Doubleday, 1996): 72–80.

19 R. Schmalensee, "Entry Deterrence in the Ready-to-Eat Breakfast Cereal Industry," *Bell Journal of Economics* 9 (1978): 305–27.

20 Monopolies and Mergers Commission, *Indirect Electrostatic Reprographic Equipment* (London: Her Majesty's Stationery Office, 1976): 37, 56.

21 S. A. Lippman and R. P. Rumelt, "Uncertain Imitability: An Analysis of Interfirm Differences in Efficiency under Competition," *Bell Journal of Economics* 13 (1982): 418–38. See also: R. Reed and R. DeFillippi, "Causal Ambiguity, Barriers to Imitation, and Sustainable Competitive Advantage," *Academy of Management Review* 15 (1990): 88–102.

22 P. R. Milgrom and J. Roberts, "Complementarities and Fit: Strategy, Structure and Organizational Change in Manufacturing," *Journal of Accounting and Economics* 19 (1995): 179–208.

23 J. W. Rivkin, "Imitation of Complex Strategies," *Management Science* 46 (2000): 824–44.

24 M. E. Porter and N. Siggelkow, "Contextuality Within Activity Systems and Sustainable Competitive Advantage," *Academy of Management Perspectives* 22 (May 2008): 34–56.

25 Ibid.

26 See O. E. Williamson, "Transaction Cost Economics: The Governance of Contractual Relations," *Journal of Law and Economics* 19 (1979): 153–6.

27 C. Brown and M. Reich, "When Does Union-Management Cooperation Work? A Look at NUMMI and GM-Van Nuys," *California Management Review* 31 (Summer 1989): 26–44.

28 "CDOs May Bring Subprime-like Bust for LBOs, Junk Debt," www.bloomberg.com (March 13, 2007).

29 For an analysis of first-mover advantage, see M. Lieberman and D. Montgomery, "First-Mover Advantages," *Strategic Management Journal* 9 (1988): 41–58; M. Lieberman and D. Montgomery, "First-Mover (Dis)Advantages: Retrospective and Link with the Resource-based View," *Strategic Management Journal* 19 (1998): 1111–25.

30 J. C. Bogle, *Common Sense on Mutual Funds* (Chichester: John Wiley & Sons, Ltd, 2000).

31 E. F. Fama, "Efficient Capital Markets: A Review of Theory and Empirical Work," *Journal of Business* 35 (1970): 383–417.

32 A. W. Lo, H. Mamaysty and J. Wang, "Foundations of Technical Analysis," *Journal of Finance* 55 (2000): 1705–70.

33 W. De Bondt and R. Thaler, "Does the Stock Market Overreact?" *Journal of Finance* 42 (1985): 793–805.

34 J. B. Barney, "Firm Resources and Sustained Competitive Advantage," *Journal of Management* 17 (1991): 99–120.

35 S. K. McEvily, S. Das and K. McCabe, "Avoiding Competence Substitution through Knowledge Sharing," *Academy of Management Review* 25 (2000): 294–311.

36 M. E. Porter, *Competitive Advantage* (New York: Free Press, 1985): 13.

37 Ibid.: 120.

38 M. E. Porter, *Competitive Strategy* (New York: Free Press, 1980): 42.

9 Cost Advantage

SEARS MOTOR BUGGY: $395

For car complete with rubber tires, Timken roller bearing axles, top, storm front, three oil-burning lamps, horn, and one gallon of lubricating oil. Nothing to buy but gasoline.

. . . We found there was a maker of automobile frames that was making 75 percent of all the frames used in automobile construction in the United States. We found on account of the volume of business that this concern could make frames cheaper for automobile manufacturers than the manufacturers could make them themselves. We went to this frame maker and asked him to make frames for the Sears Motor Buggy and then to name us prices for those frames in large quantities. And so on throughout the whole construction of the Sears Motor Buggy. You will find every piece and every part has been given the most careful study; you will find that the Sears Motor Buggy is made of the best possible material; it is constructed to take the place of the top buggy; it is built in our own factory, under the direct supervision of our own expert, a man who has had fifteen years of automobile experience, a man who has for the past three years worked with us to develop exactly the right car for the people at a price within the reach of all.

—EXTRACT FROM AN ADVERTISEMENT IN THE SEARS ROEBUCK & CO. CATALOG, 1909: 1150

OUTLINE

Introduction and Objectives

In the last chapter, we identified cost and differentiation as the two principal forms of competitive advantage. Here we consider cost advantage. For some industries, particularly those that supply commodity products, cost advantage is the predominant basis for competitive advantage. But even where competition focuses on product differentiation, intensifying competition means that cost efficiency is a prerequisite for profitability. During recessionary periods the pressure for cost efficiency becomes intense. During 2008-9, lack of cost effectiveness led to the demise of many thousands of firms.

By the time you have completed this chapter, you will be able to:

- Identify the determinants of relative cost within the industry or activity ("cost drivers").
- Assess a firm's cost position relative to its competitors and identify the factors responsible for cost differentials.
- Recommend cost-reduction measures.

The analysis in this chapter is oriented around these objectives. In pursuing these objectives, we shall examine techniques for:

- Identifying the primary sources of cost advantage in an industry.
- Appraising the cost position of a firm within its industry by disaggregating the firm into its separate activities.
- Using the analysis of costs and relative cost position as a basis for recommending strategies for enhancing cost competitiveness.

Strategy and Cost Advantage

Historically, strategic management has emphasized cost advantage as the primary basis for competitive advantage in an industry. This focus on cost reflected the traditional emphasis by economists on price as the principal medium of competition—price competitiveness requires cost efficiency. It also reflected the strategy preoccupations of large industrial corporations. For much of the twentieth century, the development of large corporations was dominated by the quest for economies of scale and scope through investments in mass production and mass distribution. During the 1970s and 1980s, the analysis of cost advantage became focused around the *experience curve*—the relationship between unit cost and cumulative output identified by the Boston Consulting Group (see Strategy Capsule 9.1).

STRATEGY CAPSULE 9.1

BCG and the Experience Curve

The experience curve has its basis in the systematic reduction in the time taken to build airplanes and Liberty ships during the Second World War.[1] In a series of studies, ranging from bottle caps and refrigerators to long-distance calls and insurance policies, the Boston Consulting Group (BCG) observed a remarkable regularity in the reductions in unit costs with increased cumulative output, which it called the "Law of Experience": *the unit cost of value added to a standard product declines by a constant percentage (typically between 20 and 30%) each time cumulative output doubles.* ("Unit cost of value added" is total cost per unit of production less the cost per unit of production of bought-in components and materials.) The figure below shows examples of experience curves.

The relationship between unit cost and production volume may be expressed as follows:

$$C_n = C_1 \cdot n^{-a}$$

where C_1 is the cost of the first unit of production
C_n is the cost of the nth unit of production
n is the cumulative volume of production
a is the elasticity of cost with regard to output.

The experience curve has important implications for strategy. If a firm can expand its output faster than its competitors, it can move down the experience curve more rapidly and open up a widening cost differential. The inference drawn by BCG was that a firm's primary strategic goal should be maximizing market share.[2]

To achieve this, firms should price not on the basis of current costs, but on the basis of anticipated costs—using *penetration pricing* rather than *full-cost pricing*. In the British motorcycle market, BCG observed that local manufacturers adopted cost-plus pricing, whereas Honda priced to meet market share objectives.[3] The quest for experience-based economies also points to the advantages of increasing volume by broadening product range and expanding internationally.[4]

The quest for market share was supported by numerous studies confirming a positive relationship between profitability and market share.[5] However, *association* does not imply *causation*—it seems likely that market share and profitability are both outcomes of some other source of competitive advantage—product innovation or superior marketing.[6]

The experience curve lost favor as a strategy tool, first, because it combines several sources of cost reduction (learning, scale, process innovation) that can be better understood individually; second, because of the realization that cost reductions from experience are not automatic—they must be managed.

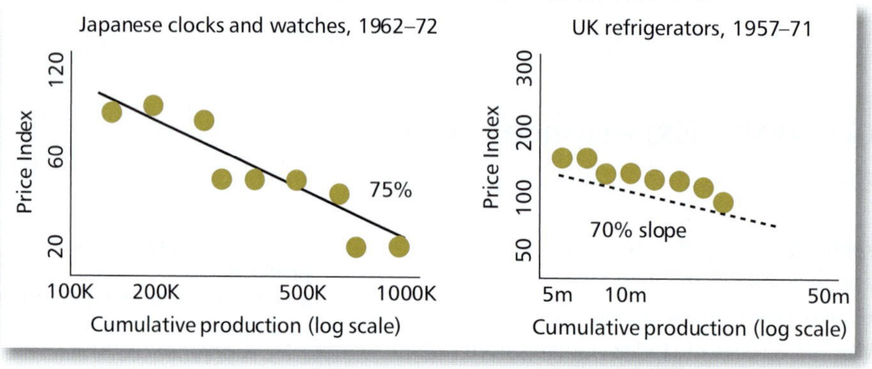

In recent decades, companies have been forced to think more broadly and radically about cost efficiency. The most dramatic shifts in cost advantage have been the result of international differences in labor costs (e.g. the declining competitiveness of Western manufactures to Chinese firms manufacturing), exchange rate shifts (e.g. the rising costs of Euro zone and Japanese firms during 2007–9) and new technologies (e.g. internet telephony). The response has been novel approaches to cost reduction involving outsourcing, process re-engineering and organizational delayering.

Cost analysis requires taking account of multiple factors, the importance of each depending on industry context. In the clothing industry, wage rates are the critical factor; in petrochemicals, it is feedstock costs; in semiconductors, it is yield rates. Some industries offer alternative routes to low cost—in the steel industry, Severstal of Russia with its low input costs and Nucor of the U.S. with its advanced ninimill technologies are both low-cost producers. Our approach to analyzing cost advantage will be to identify the basic determinants of a firm's cost position within its particular industry.

The Sources of Cost Advantage

There are seven principal determinants of a firm's unit costs (cost per unit of output) relative to its competitors; we refer to these as *cost drivers* (see Figure 9.1).

The relative importance of these different cost drivers varies across industries, across firms within an industry and across the different activities within a firm. By examining each of these different cost drivers in relation to a particular firm we can do the following:

- Analyze a firm's cost position relative to its competitors and diagnose the sources of inefficiency.
- Make recommendations as to how a firm can improve its cost efficiency.

Let's examine the nature and the role of each of these cost drivers.

FIGURE 9.1 The drivers of cost advantage

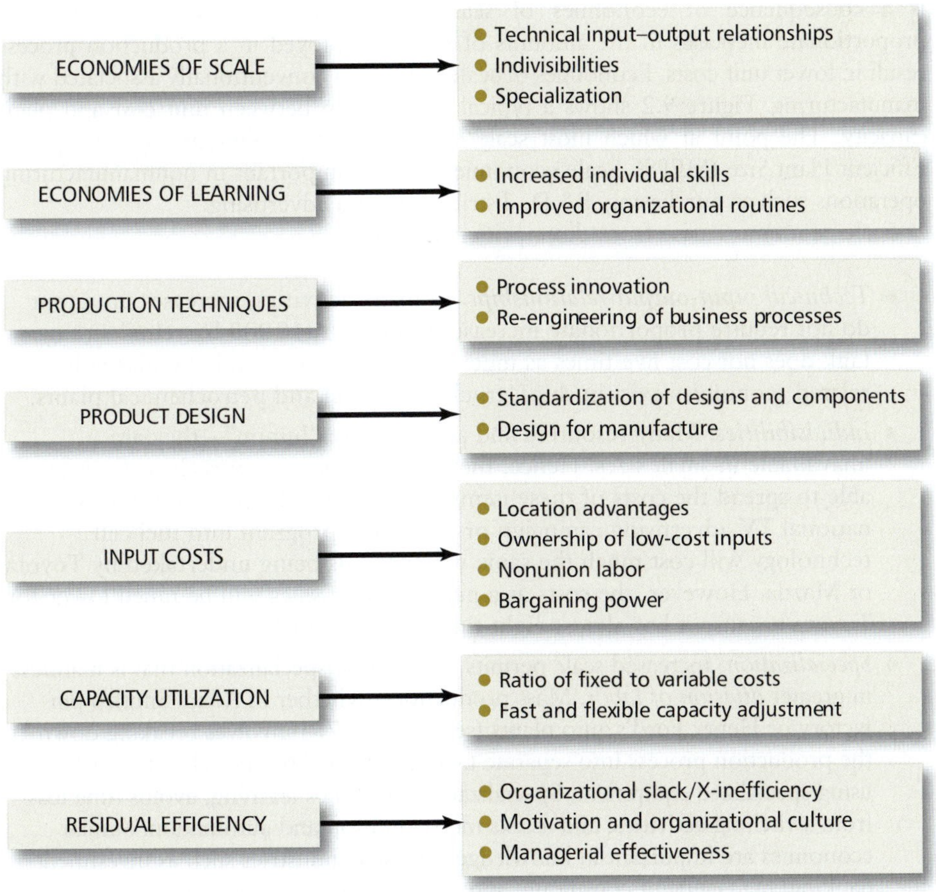

FIGURE 9.2 The long-run average cost curve for a plant

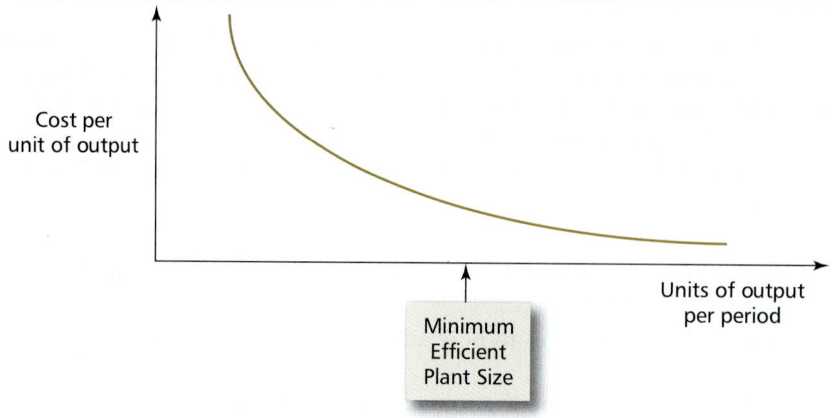

Economies of Scale

The predominance of large corporations in most manufacturing and service industries is a consequence of economies of scale. Economies of scale exist wherever proportionate increases in the amounts of inputs employed in a production process result in lower unit costs. Economies of scale have been conventionally associated with manufacturing. Figure 9.2 shows a typical relationship between unit cost and plant capacity. The point at which most scale economies are exploited is the Minimum Efficient Plant Size (MEPS). Scale economies are also important in nonmanufacturing operations such as purchasing, R&D, distribution, and advertising.

Scale economies arise from three principal sources:

- *Technical input-output relationships.* In many activities, increases in output do not require proportionate increases in input. A 10 000-barrel oil storage tank does not cost five times as much as a 2000-barrel tank. Similar volume-related economies exist in ships, trucks, and steel and petrochemical plants.
- *Indivisibilities.* Many resources and activities are "lumpy"—they are unavailable in small sizes. Hence, they offer economies of scale as firms are able to spread the costs of these items over larger volumes of output. A national TV advertising campaign or a research program into fuel cell technology will cost much the same whether it is being undertaken by Toyota or Mazda. However, the costs as a percentage of sales will be much lower for Toyota because it has almost eight times the sales of Mazda.
- *Specialization.* Increased scale permits greater task specialization that is manifest in greater *division of labor*. Mass production—whether in Adam Smith's pin factory or Henry Ford's auto plants (see Chapter 7)—involves breaking down the production process into separate tasks performed by specialized workers using specialized equipment. Specialization promotes learning, avoids time loss from switching activities, and assists mechanization and automation. Similar economies are important in knowledge-intensive industries such as investment banking, management consulting, and design engineering, where large firms are able to offer specialized expertise across a broad range of knowhow.

FIGURE 9.3 Economies of scale in advertising: U.S. soft drinks

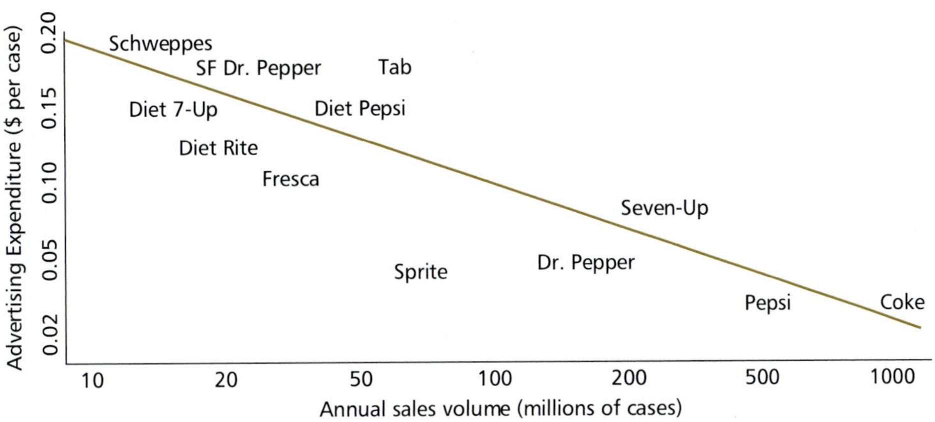

Scale Economies and Industry Concentration Scale economies are a key determinant of an industry's level of concentration (the proportion of industry output accounted for by the largest firms). However, the critical scale advantages of large companies are seldom in production. In packaged consumer goods—cigarettes, household detergents, beer, and soft drinks—economies of scale in marketing are the key factor causing world markets to be dominated by a few giant companies. Advertising is a key indivisibility: a 60-second TV commercial can cost over $5 million to produce but the real cost is in showing it—Sony's launch of its PlayStation 3 incurred advertising costs of over half a billion dollars. Figure 9.3 shows the relationship between sales volume and average advertising costs for different brands of soft drinks.

Consolidation in the world car industry has been driven by the escalating huge costs associated with new model development. Most small and medium-sized auto companies have been acquired by larger rivals because they lacked the volume necessary to amortize new model development costs. Volkswagen acquired Skoda, Seat and Rolls-Royce; Ford acquired Jaguar, Mazda, Land Rover, Aston Martin and Volvo (before subsequently divesting many of them).[7] Table 9.1 gives examples of some of the world's most costly new product development programs.

The huge development costs of new aircraft models mean that global market leadership within a product segment is critical to profitability. The Boeing 747 was a hugely profitable project because 1415 were built. Concorde, with only 20 planes built, was a financial disaster.

Limits to Scale Economies Despite the prevalence of scale economies, small and medium-sized companies continue to survive and prosper in competition with much bigger rivals. In the automobile industry, the most profitable companies in recent years have been medium-sized producers such as Peugeot, Renault, and BMW. In U.S. and European banking, there is no evidence that big players outperform smaller banks either on profitability or costs.[8] How do small and medium-sized firms offset the disadvantages of small scale? First, by exploiting the

TABLE 9.1 Some of the world's most expensive new product development projects

Product	Lead company	Estimated development cost	Launch date
F-35 Lightening II joint strike fighter	Lockheed Martin	$40 billion[a]	2012[b]
B-2 Spirit "stealth bomber"	Northrup Grumman	$23 billion	December 1993[b]
A380 "super-jumbo"	Airbus Industrie	$19 billion	October 2007[b]
787 Dreamliner	Boeing	$16–18 billion	3rd Quarter 2010[b]
Windows Vista	Microsoft	$7 billion	January 2007
Playstation 3	Sony	$7 billion[c]	November 2006
Iridium wireless satellite communication system	Motorola/Iridium Satellite LLC	$6 billion	July 1999
Ford Contour/Modeo	Ford Motor Company	$6 billion[d]	October 1992

Notes:

[a] Total program cost estimated at $300 billion; [b] Date of entering service; [c] Including development of Blu-ray DVD; [d] Including costs of tooling.

flexibility advantages of smaller size; second, by avoiding the difficulties of motivation and coordination that accompanies large scale.[9]

Economies of Learning

The experience curve is based primarily on learning-by-doing on the part of individuals and organizations. Repetition develops both individual skills and organizational routines. In 1943 it took 40 000 labor-hours to build a B-24 Liberator bomber. By 1945 it took only 8000 hours.[10] The more complex a process or product, the greater the potential for learning. Learning curves are exceptionally steep in semiconductor fabrication. When IBM introduced 0.18 micron, copper-interconnector chips, yields increased from zero to over 50% within the first two months. LCD flat screens are notoriously difficult to manufacture—a single defective chip may render an entire screen useless. The dominant position of Sharp and Samsung in flat screens is primarily a result of volume-based learning resulting in exceptionally high yields.[11] Learning occurs both at the individual level through improvements in dexterity and problem solving, and at the group level through the development and refinement of organizational routines.[12]

Process Technology and Process Design

For most goods and services, alternative process technologies exist. A process is technically superior to another when, for each unit of output, it uses less of one input without using more of any other input. Where a production method uses more of some inputs but less of others, then cost efficiency depends on the relative prices of the inputs. Hence, in the assembly of desktop PCs, Dell's Palmer North 2 plant in Austin, Texas is highly automated, while its two plants in Xiamen, China (where wages are about 90% lower) are much more labor intensive.

New process technology may radically reduce costs. Pilkington's float glass process gave it (and its licensees) an unassailable cost advantage in producing flat glass. Ford's moving assembly line reduced the time taken to assemble a Model T from 106 hours to six hours between 1912 and 1914.

When process innovation is embodied in new capital equipment, diffusion is likely to be rapid. However, the full benefits of new processes typically require system-wide changes in job design, employee incentives, product design, organizational structure and management controls.[13] Between 1979 and 1986, General Motors spent $40 billion on new process technology with the goal of becoming the world's most efficient manufacturer of automobiles. Yet, in the absence of fundamental changes in organization and management, the productivity gains were meager. After a tour of Cadillac's state-of-the-art Hamtramck plant in Detroit, Toyota chairman Eiji Toyoda told a colleague, "It would have been embarrassing to comment on it."[14] By contrast, the cost leadership established by Toyota, Nucor, Dell Computer, McDonald's, and Wal-Mart is the result of matching their structures, decision processes and human resource management to the requirements of their process technologies.

Indeed, the greatest productivity gains from process innovation are typically the result of organizational improvements rather than technological innovation and new hardware. The central components of Toyota's system of lean production are just-in-time scheduling, total quality management, continuous improvement (*kaisan*), teamworking, job flexibility, and supplier partnerships rather than robotics or IT.[15] Harley-Davidson's gains in productivity during the 1984-94 resulted from reorganizing around team-based production and commitment to continuous improvement, but with limited investment in advanced automation.[16]

Business Process Re-engineering During the 1990s, recognition that the redesign of operational processes could achieve substantial efficiency gains stimulated a surge of interest in a new management tool called *business process re-engineering* (BPR). "Re-engineering gurus" Michael Hammer and James Champy defined BPR as: "the fundamental rethinking and radical redesign of business processes to achieve dramatic improvements in critical contemporary measures of performance, such as cost, quality, service, and speed."[17]

Business process re-engineering recognizes that operational and commercial processes involve evolve over time without consistent direction or systematic appraisal of their efficiency or effectiveness. With information technology, the temptation is to automate existing processes—"paving over cowpaths," as Michael Hammer calls it.[18] The key is to detach from the way in which a process is currently organized and to begin with the question: "If we were starting afresh, how would we design this process?" Hammer and Champy point to the existence of a set of "commonalities, recurring themes, or characteristics" that can guide BPR. These include:

- Combining several jobs into one.
- Allowing workers to make decisions.
- Performing the steps of a process in a natural order.
- Recognizing that processes have multiple versions and designing processes to take account of different situations.

- Performing processes where it makes the most sense, for example, if the accounting department needs pencils, it is probably cheaper for such a small order to be purchased directly from the office equipment store along the block than to be ordered via the firm's purchasing department.
- Reducing checks and controls to the point where they make economic sense.
- Minimizing reconciliation.
- Appointing a case manager to provide a single point of contact at the interface between processes.
- Reconciling centralization with decentralization in process design—for example, via a shared database, decentralized decisions can be made while permitting overall coordination simply through information sharing.

Despite major gains in efficiency, quality and speed from BPR projects (see Strategy Capsule 9.2), there are also many disappointing outcomes. One of the major realizations to emerge from BPR is that most business processes are complex. To redesign a process one must first understand it. Process mapping exercises reveal that even seemingly simple business processes, such as the procurement of office supplies, involve complex and sophisticated systems of interactions among multiple organizational members. In Chapter 5 we saw that a process is often embodied within an organizational routine that is not fully comprehended by any single person. To this extent, Hammer and Champy's recommendation to "obliterate" existing processes and start with a "clean sheet of paper" runs the risk of destroying organizational capabilities that have been nurtured over a long period of time.

While BPR may be a "faded fad," it is still true that businesses processes are the fundamental productive activities of the firm and their design and development is critical to cost efficiency. Over the past decade, BPR has evolved into ***business process management***, where the emphasis has shifted form workflow management to the broader application of information technology (web-based applications in particular) to the redesign and enhancement of organizational processes.[19]

STRATEGY CAPSULE 9.2

Process Re-engineering at IBM Credit

IBM Credit offers credit to IBM customers purchasing IBM hardware and software. Under the old system, five stages were involved: first, an IBM salesperson telephoned a request for financing, which was logged on a piece of paper; second, the request was sent to the Credit Department where it was logged onto a computer and the customer's creditworthiness was checked; third, the request and credit check were sent to the Business Practices Department where a loan covenant was drawn up; fourth, the paperwork was passed to a pricer who determined the interest rate; finally, the clerical group prepared a quote letter that was sent to the salesperson.

The process took an average of six days, resulting in many lost sales. After many efforts to improve the process, two managers undertook an experiment. They took a financing request and walked it around through all five steps. The process took 90 minutes!

On this basis, the credit approval process was redesigned by replacing the specialists (credit checkers, pricers, and so on) with generalists who undertook all five processes. Only where the request was nonstandard or unusually complex were specialists called in. The basic problem was that the system had been designed for the most complex credit requests that IBM received, whereas in the vast majority of cases no specialist judgment was called for—simply looking up credit ratings, plugging numbers into standard formulae, and so on.

The result was that credit requests were processed in four hours compared to six days, total employees were reduced, while the total number of deals increased one hundred times.

Source: Adapted from M. Hammer and J. Champy, *Re-engineering the Corporation: A Manifesto for Business Revolution* (New York: HarperBusiness, 1993): 36–9.

Product Design

Design-for-manufacture—designing products for ease of production rather than simply for functionality and esthetics—can offer substantial cost savings, especially when linked to the introduction of new process technology.

- Volkswagen cut product development and component costs by redesigning its 30 different models around just four separate platforms. The VW Beetle, Audi TT, Golf, and Audi A3, together with several Seat and Skoda models, all share a single platform.
- The IBM "Proprinter," one of the most successful computer printers of the 1980s, owed its low costs (and reliability) to an innovative design that:
  - reduced the number of parts from 150, found in the typical PC printer, to 60;
  - designed the printer in layers so that robots could build it from the bottom up;
  - eliminated all screws, springs, and other fasteners that required human insertion and adjustment and replaced them with molded plastic components that clipped together.[20]
- Service offerings too can be designed for ease and efficiency of production. Motel 6, cost leader in U.S. budget motels, carefully designs its product to keep operating costs low. Its motels occupy low-cost, out-of-town locations, it uses standard motel designs, it avoids facilities such as pools and restaurants and it designs rooms to facilitate easy cleaning and low maintenance. However, efficiency in service design is compromised by the tendency for customers to "interfere" in service delivery. This requires a clear strategy to manage variability either through accommodation or restriction.[21]

Capacity Utilization

Over the short and medium term, plant capacity is more-or-less fixed and variations in output cause capacity utilization to rise or fall. Underutilization raises unit costs because fixed costs must be spread over fewer units of production. In businesses where virtually all costs are fixed (for example, airlines, theme parks), profitability is highly sensitive to shortfalls in demand. Conversely, pushing output beyond normal full-capacity operation also creates inefficiencies. As Boeing discovered in 1997 and then in 2006, operating above normal capacity increased unit costs due to overtime pay, premiums for night and weekend shifts, increased defects and higher maintenance.

In cyclical industries, the ability to speedily adjust capacity to downturns in demand can be a major source of cost advantage. During the 2008–9 recession, survival in hard-hit sectors such as housebuilding, construction equipment and retailing required moving early to cut capacity through shedding jobs and closing units. The key is to make adjustments in advance of downturns in demand: Caterpillar announced it was cutting 20 000 jobs on January 28, 2008, the same day it revealed that its sales in the previous quarter had increased from the previous year.[22] A critical challenge to effective capacity adjustment is distinguishing *cyclical* overcapacity which is short-term from *structural* overcapacity that is long-term.[23]

Input Costs

The firms in an industry do not necessarily pay the same price for identical inputs. There are several sources of lower input costs:

- *Locational differences in input prices.* The prices of inputs may vary between locations, the most important being differences in wage rates from one country to another. In the U.S., software engineers earned an average of \$89 000 in 2007. In India the average was \$29 000. In less-skilled occupations, differentials are much wider: in auto assembly the hourly rate in Chinese plants was about \$2 an hour in 2008 compared with \$60–\$70 in the U.S. (inclusive of benefits).[24]
- *Ownership of low-cost sources of supply.* In raw material-intensive industries, ownership or access to low-cost sources can offer crucial cost advantage. In oil and gas, lifting costs for the three "supermajors" (ExxonMobil, Royal Dutch Shell, and BP) were over \$11 per barrel in 2007; for Saudi Aramco they were about \$4.
- *Nonunion labor.* Labor unions result in higher levels of pay and benefits and work restrictions that lower productivity. In the U.S. airline industry, nonunion AirTran had average salary and benefit cost per employee of \$60 863 in 2007 compared with \$87 245 for United (80% unionized).
- *Bargaining power.* Where bought-in products are a major cost item, differences in buying power among the firms in an industry can be an

important source of cost advantage.[25] Wal-Mart's U.K. entry (with its acquisition of Asda) was greeted with dismay by other British supermarket chains—they recognized that Wal-Mart would be able to use its massive bargaining power to extract additional discounts from Asda's suppliers, which it could use to fuel aggressive price competition.

Residual Efficiency

In many industries, the basic cost drivers—scale, technology, product and process design, input costs, and capacity utilization—fail to provide a complete explanation for why one firm in an industry has lower unit costs than a competitor. Even after taking all these cost drivers into account, unit cost differences between firms remain. These residual efficiencies relate to the extent to which the firm approaches its efficiency frontier of optimal operation. Residual efficiency depends on the firm's ability to eliminate "organizational slack"[26] or "X-inefficiency"[27]—surplus costs that keep the firm from maximum-efficiency operation. These costs are often referred to as "organizational fat" and build up unconsciously as a result of employees—both in management and on the shop floor—maintaining some margin of slack in preference to the rigors of operating at maximum efficiency.

Eliminating excess costs is difficult. It may take a shock to a company's very survival to provide the impetus for rooting out institutionalized inefficiencies. When faced with bankruptcy or a precipitous fall in profitability, companies can demonstrate a remarkable capacity for paring costs. In his first year as CEO of Nissan Motor, Carlos Ghosn cut operating costs by 20%.[28]

In the absence of a threat to survival, high levels of residual efficiency are typically the result of management system and company values that are intolerant toward unnecessary costs and glorify frugality.[29] At companies such as Wal-Mart, Ryanair, IKEA, and Air Asia, relentless cost efficiency is embodied in management systems and embedded in the corporate culture.

Using the Value Chain to Analyze Costs

To analyze costs and make recommendations for building cost advantage, the company or even the business unit is too big a level for us to work at. As we saw in Chapter 5, every business may be viewed as a chain of activities. In most value chains each activity has a distinct cost structure determined by different cost drivers. Analyzing costs requires disaggregating the firm's value chain to identify:

- the relative importance of each activity with respect to total cost;
- the cost drivers for each activity and the comparative efficiency with which the firm performs each activity;
- how costs in one activity influence costs in another;
- which activities should be undertaken within the firm and which activities should be outsourced.

The Principal Stages of Value Chain Analysis

A value chain analysis of a firm's cost position comprises the following stages:

1 *Disaggregate the firm into separate activities.* Determining the appropriate value chain activities is a matter of judgment. It requires understanding the chain of processes involved in the transformation of inputs into output and its delivery to the customer. Very often, the firm's own divisional and departmental structure is a useful guide. Key considerations are:
- the separateness of one activity from another;
- the importance of an activity;
- the dissimilarity of activities in terms of cost drivers;
- the extent to which there are differences in the way competitors perform the particular activity.

2 *Establish the relative importance of different activities in the total cost of the product.* Our analysis needs to focus on the activities that are the major sources of cost. In disaggregating costs, Michael Porter suggests the detailed assignment of operating costs and assets to each value activity. Though the adoption of activity-based costing has made such cost data more available, detailed cost allocation can be a major exercise.[30] Even without such detailed cost breakdown it is usually possible to identify which activities are the principal sources of total cost and establish which activities are performed relatively efficiently or inefficiently.

3 *Identify cost drivers.* For each activity, what factors determine the level of cost relative to other firms? For some activities, cost drivers can be deduced simply from the nature of the activity and the types of cost incurred. For capital-intensive activities such as the operation of a body press in an auto plant, the principal factors are likely to be capital equipment costs, weekly production volume, and downtime between changes of dies. For labor-intensive assembly activities, critical issues are wage rates, speed of work, and defect rates.

4 *Identify linkages.* The costs of one activity may be determined, in part, by the way in which other activities are performed. Xerox discovered that its high service costs relative to competitors reflected the complexity of design of its copiers, which required 30 different interrelated adjustments.

5 *Identify opportunities for reducing costs.* By identifying areas of comparative inefficiency and the cost drivers for each, opportunities for cost reduction become evident. For example:
- If scale economies are a key cost driver, can volume be increased? One feature of Caterpillar's cost-reduction strategy was to broaden its model range and begin selling diesel engines to other vehicle manufacturers in order to expand its sales base.
- Where wage costs are the issue, can wages be reduced either directly or by relocating production?
- If a certain activity cannot be performed efficiently within the firm, can it be outsourced?

Figure 9.4 shows how the application of the value chain to automobile manufacture can yield suggestions for possible cost reductions.

FIGURE 9.4 Using the value chain in cost analysis: an automobile manufacturer

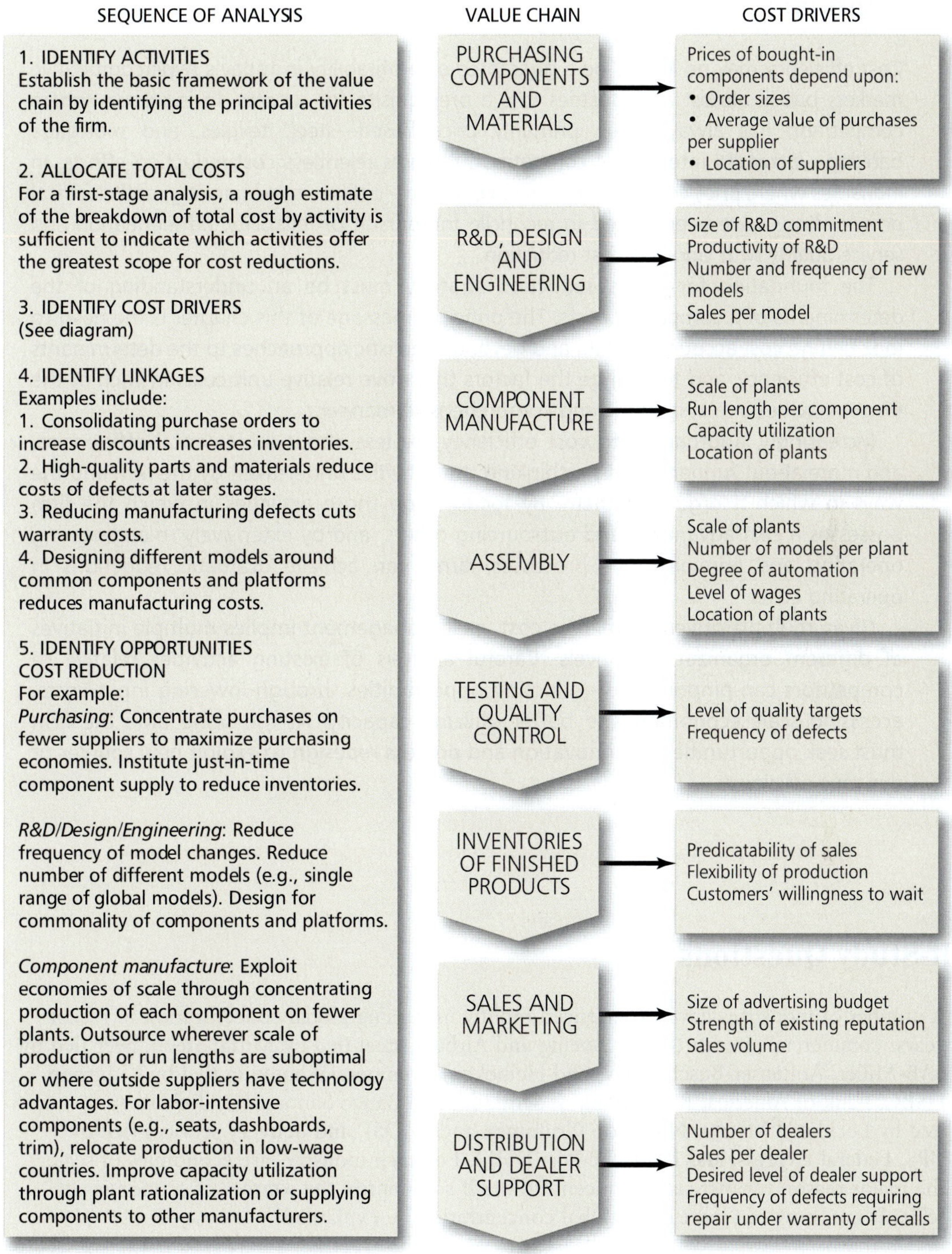

Summary

Cost efficiency may no longer be a guarantee of profitability in today's hypercompetitive markets but in almost all industries it is a prerequisite for success. In industries where competition has always been primarily price based—steel, textiles, and mortgage banking—increased intensity of competition requires relentless cost-reduction efforts. In industries where price competition was once muted—airlines, retail banking, and electrical power—firms have been forced to reconcile the pursuit of reliability, differentiation and service quality with vigorous cost reduction.

The foundation for a cost-reduction strategy must be an understanding of the determinants of a company's costs. The principal message of this chapter is the need to look behind cost accounting data and beyond simplistic approaches to the determinants of cost efficiency, and to analyze the factors that drive relative unit costs in each of the firm's activities in a systematic and comprehensive manner.

Increasingly, approaches to cost efficiency are less about incremental efficiencies, and more about fundamentally rethinking the activities undertaken by the firm and the ways in which it organizes them. By focusing on those activities in which the firm possesses a cost advantage and outsourcing others, and by extensively re-engineering operating and administrative processes, firms can achieve dramatic reductions in operating costs.

Given multiple drivers of relative cost, cost management implies multiple initiatives at different organizational levels. Careful analysis of existing activities relative to competitors can pinpoint cost-reduction opportunities through lowering input costs, accessing scale economies and better utilizing capacity. At the same time the firm must seek opportunities for innovation and process redesign to exploit new sources of dynamic efficiency.

Self-Study Questions

1 A number of industries have experienced rapidly increasing global concentration in recent years: commercial aircraft (led by Boeing and Airbus), steel (led by Mittal Steel), beer (led by SAB-Miller, Anheuser-Busch-Inbev, and Heineken), commercial banking (led by Citigroup, HSBC, Bank of America, Royal Bank of Scotland, and Banco Santander), defense equipment (led by Lockheed Martin, Northrop Grumman and EADS), and delivery services (led by UPS, Federal Express, and Deutsche Post/DHL). For each industry, are economies of scale the major reason for increasing concentration? If so, identify the sources of economies of scale. If not, how can increasing global concentration be explained?

2 In Strategy Capsule 2.3 (Chapter 2), we observed that Ford's profitability was low primarily because its costs were high. Using the value chain shown in Figure 9.4 and what you know

about Ford (including the information in Strategy Capsule 2.3), what suggestions would you offer as to how Ford might lower its costs of producing cars?

3 To what extent are the seven cost drivers shown in Figure 9.1 relevant in analyzing the costs per student at your business school? What recommendations would you make to your dean for improving the cost efficiency of the school?

Notes

1 Louis E. Yelle, "The Learning Curve: Historical Review and Comprehensive Survey," *Decision Sciences* 10 (1979): 302–28.

2 See D. Ross, "Learning to Dominate," *Journal of Industrial Economics* 34 (1986): 337–53.

3 Boston Consulting Group, *Strategy Alternatives for the British Motorcycle Industry* (London: Her Majesty's Stationery Office, 1975).

4 C. Baden-Fuller, "The Implications of the Learning Curve for Firm Strategy and Public Policy," *Applied Economics* 15 (1983): 541–51.

5 R. Jacobsen and D. Aaker, "Is Market Share All That It's Cracked up to Be?" *Journal of Marketing* 49 (Fall 1985): 11–22.

6 R. Wensley, "PIMS and BCG: New Horizons or False Dawn?" *Strategic Management Journal* 3 (1982): 147–58.

7 To be more precise, the economies of amortizing product development costs are *economies of volume* rather than *economies of scale*. The product development cost per unit depends on the total volume of production over the life of the model.

8 M. Venzin, *Building an International Financial Services Firm: How Successful Firms Design and Execute Cross-border Strategies* (Oxford: Oxford University Press, 2009)

9 R. P. McAfee and J. McMillan, "Organizational Diseconomies of Scale," *Journal of Economics and Management Strategy* 4 (1996): 399–426.

10 L. Rapping, "Learning and World War II Production Functions," *Review of Economics and Statistics* (February 1965): 81–6.

11 G. Linden, J. Hart, S. A. Lenway, and T. P. Murtha, "Flying Geese as Moving Targets," *Industry and Innovation* 5 (June 1998): 11–34.

12 L. Argote, S. L. Beckman, and D. Epple, "The Persistence and Transfer of Learning in Industrial Settings," *Management Science* 36 (1990): 140–54; M. Zollo and S. G. Winter, "Deliberate Learning and the Evolution of Dynamic Capabilities," *Organization Science* 13 (2002): 339–51.

13 R. H. Hayes and R. Jaikumar, "Manufacturing's Crisis: New Technologies, Obsolete Organizations," *Harvard Business Review* (September-October 1988): 85; and R. M. Grant, A. B. Shani, R. Krishnan, and R. Baer, "Appropriate Manufacturing Technology: A Strategic Approach," *Sloan Management Review* 33, no. 1 (Fall 1991): 43–54.

14 M. Keller, *Collision* (New York: Doubleday, 1993): 169–71.

15 J. Womack and D. T. Jones, "From Lean Production to Lean Enterprise," *Harvard Business Review* (March-April 1994); J. Womack and D. T. Jones, "Beyond Toyota: How to Root Out Waste and Pursue Perfection," *Harvard Business Review* (September–October, 1996).

16 R. Teerlink and L. Ozley, *More than a Motorcycle* (Cambridge, MA: Harvard Business School Press, 2000).

17 M. Hammer and J. Champy, *Re-engineering the Corporation: A Manifesto for Business Revolution* (New York: HarperBusiness, 1993): 32.

18 M. Hammer, "Re-engineering Work: Don't Automate, Obliterate," *Harvard Business Review* (July–August, 1990).

19 V. Glover and M. L. Marcus, "Business Process Transformation," *Advances in Management Information Systems* 9 (M.E. Sharpe, March 2008); R. Merrifield, J. Calhoun, and D. Stevens, "The Next Revolution in Productivity," *Harvard Business Review* (November 2006): 72–9.

20 R. E. Gomory, "From the Ladder of Science to the Product Development Cycle," *Harvard Business Review* (November–December 1989): 103.

21 F. X. Frei, "Breaking the Tradeoff between Efficiency and Service," *Harvard Business Review* (November 2006): 92–103.

22 "Caterpillar to Cut 20 000 Jobs as Downturn Worsens," *Wall Street Journal* (January 28, 2009).

23 J. Billington, "Listening to Overcapacity—Lessons from the Auto and Health Care Industries," *Harvard Management Update* (Boston: Harvard Business School, 1998, Reprint # U98068).

24 *Plunkett's Automotive Almanac 2008.*

25 "Buying Power of Multiproduct Retailers," *OECD Journal of Competition Law and Policy* 2 (March, 2000).

26 R. Cyert and J. March, *A Behavioral Theory of the Firm* (Englewood Cliffs, NJ: Prentice Hall, 1963).
27 H. Leibenstein, "Allocative Efficiency Versus X-Efficiency," *American Economic Review* 54 (June, 1966): 392-415.
28 K. Kase, F. J. Saez and H. Riquelme, *The New Samurais of Japanese Industry* (Cheltenham: Edward Elgar, 2006).
29 At the head office of Amazon.com, employees' desks built from doors became symbols of frugality. See "Jeff Bezos," in J. Middleton, *Gurus on E-business* (Abingdon: Thorogood Publishing, 2006): 37–9.
30 On activity-based costing, see R. S. Kaplan and S. R. Anderson, "Time-Driven Activity-based Costing," *Harvard Business Review* (November 2004): 131–8; J. Billington, "The ABCs of ABC: Activity-based Costing and Management," *Harvard Management Update* (Boston: Harvard Business School Publishing, May 1999).

10 Differentiation Advantage

If the three keys to selling real estate are location, location, location, then the three keys of selling consumer products are differentiation, differentiation, differentiation.

—ROBERT GOIZUETA, FORMER CHAIRMAN, COCA-COLA COMPANY

If you gave me $100 billion and said, "Take away the soft drink leadership of Coca-Cola in the world," I'd give it back to you and say, "It can't be done."

—WARREN BUFFETT, CHAIRMAN, BERKSHIRE HATHAWAY, AND COCA-COLA'S BIGGEST SHAREHOLDER

OUTLINE

- **Introduction and Objectives**
- **The Nature of Differentiation and Differentiation Advantage**
  - Differentiation Variables
  - Differentiation and Segmentation
  - The Sustainability of Differentiation Advantage
- **Analyzing Differentiation: The Demand Side**
  - Product Attributes and Positioning
  - The Role of Social and Psychological Factors
- **Analyzing Differentiation: The Supply Side**
  - The Drivers of Uniqueness
  - Product Integrity
  - Signaling and Reputation

Introduction and Objectives

A firm differentiates itself from its competitors "when it provides something unique that is valuable to buyers beyond simply offering a low price."[1] Differentiation advantage occurs when a firm is able to obtain from its differentiation a price premium in the market that exceeds the cost of providing the differentiation.

Every firm has opportunities for differentiating its offering to customers, although the range of differentiation opportunities depends on the characteristics of the product. An automobile or a restaurant offers greater potential for differentiation than cement, wheat or memory chips. These latter products are called "commodities" precisely because they lack physical differentiation. Yet, even commodity products can be differentiated in ways that create customer value: "Anything can be turned into a value-added product or service for a well-defined or newly created market," claims Tom Peters.[2] Consider the following:

- Cement is the ultimate commodity product, yet Cemex, the Mexican-based supplier of cement and ready-mix concrete, has established itself as the world's biggest supplier using a strategy that emphasizes "building solutions." One component of this strategy is ensuring that 98% of its deliveries are on time (compared to 34% for the industry as a whole).[3]
- Online bookselling is inherently a commodity business—any online bookseller has access to the same titles and same modes of distribution. Yet Amazon has exploited the information generated by the business to offer a range of value-adding services: best-seller lists, reviews and customized recommendations.

The lesson is this: differentiation is not simply about offering different product features; it is about identifying and understanding every possible interaction between the firm and its customers and asking how these interactions can be enhanced or changed in order to deliver additional value to the customer.

Analyzing differentiation requires looking at both the firm (the supply side) and its customers (the demand side). While supply-side analysis identifies the firm's potential to create uniqueness, the critical issue is whether such differentiation creates value for customers and whether the value created exceeds the cost of the differentiation. Hence, in this chapter we shall be concerned especially with the demand side of the market. By understanding what customers want, how they choose, and what motivates them, we can identify opportunities for profitable differentiation.

Differentiation strategies are not about pursuing uniqueness for the sake of being different. Differentiation is about understanding customers and how our product can meet their needs. To this extent, the quest for differentiation advantage takes us to the heart of business strategy. The fundamental issues of differentiation are also the fundamental issues of business strategy: Who are our customers? How do we create value for them? And how do we do it more effectively and efficiently than anyone else?

Because differentiation is about uniqueness, establishing differentiation advantage requires creativity—it cannot be achieved simply through applying standardized frameworks and techniques. This is not to say that differentiation advantage is not amenable to systematic analysis. As we have observed, there are two requirements for creating profitable differentiation. On the supply side, the firm must be aware of the resources and capabilities through which it can create uniqueness (and do it better than competitors). On the demand side, the key is insight into customers and their needs and preferences. These two sides form the major components of our analysis of differentiation.

By the time you have completed this chapter you will be able to:

- understand what differentiation is, recognize its different forms and appreciate its potential for creating competitive advantage;
- analyze the sources of differentiation in terms of customers' preferences and characteristics, and of the firm's capacity for supplying differentiation;
- formulate strategies that create differentiation advantage by linking the firm's differentiation capability to customers' demand for differentiation.

The Nature of Differentiation and Differentiation Advantage

Let us begin by exploring what differentiation is and why it is such an important basis for competitive advantage.

Differentiation Variables

The potential for differentiating a product or service is partly determined by its physical characteristics. For products that are technically simple (a pair of socks, a brick), that satisfy uncomplicated needs (a corkscrew, a nail) or must meet rigorous technical standards (a spark plug, a thermometer), differentiation opportunities are constrained by technical and market factors. Products that are technically complex (an airplane), that satisfy complex needs (an automobile, a vacation) or that do not need to conform to particular technical standards (wine, toys) offer much greater scope for differentiation.

Beyond these constraints, the potential in any product or service for differentiation is limited only by the boundaries of the human imagination. For seemingly simple products such as shampoo, toilet paper, and bottled water, the proliferation of brands on any supermarket's shelves is testimony both to the ingenuity of firms and the complexity of customer preferences. Differentiation extends beyond the physical characteristics of the product or service to encompass everything about the product or service that influences the value that customers derive from it. This means that differentiation includes every aspect of the way in which a company relates to its customers. Starbucks' ability to charge up to $4 for a cup of coffee rests not just on the characteristics of the coffee but also on the overall "Starbucks Experience," which encompasses the retail environment, the values the company projects and a sense of community in which customers participate. Differentiation is not an activity specific to particular functions such as design and marketing; it infuses all activities through which an organization relates to its customers and is built into the identity and culture of a company.

In analyzing differentiation opportunities, we can distinguish *tangible* and *intangible* dimensions of differentiation. Tangible differentiation is concerned with the observable characteristics of a product or service that are relevant to customers' preferences and choice processes. These include size, shape, color, weight, design, material and technology. Tangible differentiation also includes the performance of the product or service in terms of reliability, consistency, taste, speed, durability, and safety.

Tangible differentiation extends to products and services that complement the product in question. There is little that is distinctive about Dell's computers. The differentiation lies in the speed with which they are delivered, the flexibility with which customers can configure their own systems, and after-sales services including technical support, online training courses, repair service, upgrading service, and customer discussion forum—to mention but a few.

Opportunities for intangible differentiation arise because the value that customers perceive in a product or service does not depend exclusively on the tangible aspects of the offering. There are few products where customer choice is determined solely by observable product features or objective performance criteria. Social, emotional, psychological and esthetic considerations are present in choices over all products and services. The desires for status, exclusivity, individuality, and security are powerful motivational forces in choices relating to most consumer goods. Where a product or service is meeting complex customer needs, differentiation choices involve the overall image of the firm and its offering. Image differentiation is especially important for those products and services whose qualities and performance are difficult to ascertain at the time of purchase ("experience goods"). These include cosmetics, medical services, and education.

Differentiation and Segmentation

Differentiation is different from segmentation. Differentiation is concerned with *how* a firm competes—the ways in which it can offer uniqueness to customers. Such uniqueness might relate to consistency (McDonald's), reliability (Federal Express), status (American Express), quality (BMW), and innovation (Apple). Segmentation is concerned with *where* a firm competes in terms of customer groups, localities and product types.

Whereas segmentation is a feature of market structure, differentiation is a strategic choice by a firm. A segmented market is one that can be partitioned according to the characteristics of customers and their demand. Differentiation is concerned with a firm's positioning within a market (or market segment) in relation to the product, service and image characteristics that influence customer choice.[4] By locating within a segment, a firm does not necessarily differentiate itself from its competitors within the same segment. Ameritrade, E-Trade, and Scottrade are all located within the online segment of the brokerage industry, yet are not significantly differentiated from one another. Conversely, IKEA, Honda, Amazon and Starbucks pursue differentiation, but position themselves within the mass market and span multiple demographic and socioeconomic segments.

Nevertheless, differentiation decisions tend to be closely linked to choices over the segments in which a firm competes. By offering uniqueness in its offerings, a firm may inevitably target certain market niches. By selecting performance, engineering and style as the basis on which BMW competes in the automobile industry, it inevitably appeals to different market segments than does VW. To the extent that differentiation is imitated by other companies, the result can be the creation of new market segments. In the beer industry innovative differentiation to offer light beer, high-alcohol beer, microbrews, and brewpubs has resulted in the emergence of new market segments.[5]

The Sustainability of Differentiation Advantage

Differentiation offers a more secure basis for competitive advantage than low cost. The growth of international competition has revealed the fragility of seemingly well-established positions of domestic cost leadership. The cost advantages of Ford in autos, Honda in motorcycles, Indesit in domestic appliances, and Matsushita in consumer electronics have all been overturned by the emergence of new competitors from countries with low labor costs.

In addition, cost advantage is highly vulnerable to unpredictable external forces. During 2008, the Japanese yen appreciated by 19% against the U.S. dollar and 68% against the Korean won. During 2009, Japanese manufacturers were facing reduced demand and massive losses in export markets.

Cost advantage is also vulnerable to new technology and strategic innovation. United States' integrated iron and steel producers lost ground to the minimill producers—Nucor, Chaparral Steel, and Steel Dynamics. Discount brokers such as Quick & Reilly, Brown & Company, Olde, and Siebert were undercut by online brokers such as Ameritrade and E-Trade. Internet telephony (VoIP) offered by Skype, Vonage, and other upstarts has devastated the profitability of fixed-line, long-distance telecom providers.

Hence, sustained high profitability is associated more with differentiation than cost leadership. Large companies that consistently earn above average return on equity—such as Colgate-Palmolive, Diageo, Nokia, Johnson & Johnson, Kellogg's, Procter & Gamble, 3M, and Wyeth—tend to be those that have pursued differentiation through quality, branding and innovation.

Analyzing Differentiation: The Demand Side

Successful differentiation involves matching customers' demand for differentiation with the firm's capacity to supply differentiation. Let's begin with the demand side. Analyzing customer demand enables us to determine which product characteristics have the potential to create value for customers, customers' willingness to pay for differentiation, and a company's optimal competitive positioning in terms of differentiation variables.

Analyzing demand begins with understanding why customers buy a product or service. What are the needs and requirements of a person who is purchasing a personal computer? What is motivating a company when it hires management consultants? Market research systematically explores customer preferences and customer perceptions of existing products. However, the key to successful differentiation is to *understand* customers. To gain insight into customer requirements and preferences, simple, direct inquiry into the purpose of a product and the needs of its customers can often be far more illuminating than statistically validated market research (see Strategy Capsule 10.1).

STRATEGY CAPSULE 10.1

Understanding What a Product is About

Getting back to strategy means getting back to a deep understanding of what a product is about. Some time ago, for example, a Japanese home appliance company was trying to develop a coffee percolator. Should it be a General Electric-type percolator, executives wondered? Should it be the same drip type that Philips makes? Larger? Smaller? I urged them to ask a different kind of question: Why do people drink coffee? What are they looking for when they do? If your objective is to serve the customer better, then shouldn't you understand why that customer drinks coffee in the first place? Then you would know what kind of percolator to make.

The answer came back: good taste. Then I asked the company's engineers what they were doing to help the consumer enjoy good taste in a cup of coffee. They said they were trying to design a good percolator. I asked them what influences the taste in a cup of coffee. No one knew. That became the next question we had to answer. It turns out that lots of things can affect taste—the beans, the temperature, the water. We did our homework and discovered all the things that affect taste . . .

Of all the factors, water quality, we learned, made the greatest difference. The percolator in design at the time, however, didn't take water quality into account at all . . . We discovered next the grain distribution and the time between grinding the beans and pouring in the water were crucial. As a result we began to think about the product and its necessary features in a new way. It had to have a built-in dechlorinating function. It had to have a built-in grinder. All the customer should have to do is pour in water and beans . . .

To start you have to ask the right questions and set the right kinds of strategic goals. If your only concern is that General Electric has just brought out a percolator that brews coffee in ten minutes, you will get your engineers to design one that brews it in seven minutes. And if you stick to that logic, market research will tell you that instant coffee is the way to go . . . Conventional marketing approaches won't solve the problem. If you ask people whether they want their coffee in ten minutes or seven, they will say seven, of course. But it's still the wrong question. And you end up back where you started, trying to beat the competition at its own game. If your primary focus is on the competition, you will never step back and ask what the customers' inherent needs are, and what the product really is about.

Source: Kenichi Ohmae, "Getting Back to Strategy," *Harvard Business Review* (November–December 1988): 154.

Product Attributes and Positioning

Virtually all products and services serve multiple customer needs. As a result, understanding customer needs requires the analysis of multiple attributes. Market research has developed several techniques for analyzing customer preferences in relation to product attributes. These can guide decisions concerning the positioning of new products, repositioning of existing products, and pricing.

Multidimensional Scaling Multidimensional scaling (MDS) permits customers' perceptions of competing products' similarities and dissimilarities to be represented graphically and for the dimensions to be interpreted in terms of key product attributes.[6] For example, a survey of consumer ratings of competing pain relievers resulted in the mapping shown in Figure 10.1. Multidimensional scaling has also been

FIGURE 10.1 Consumer perceptions of competing pain relievers: a multidimensional scaling mapping

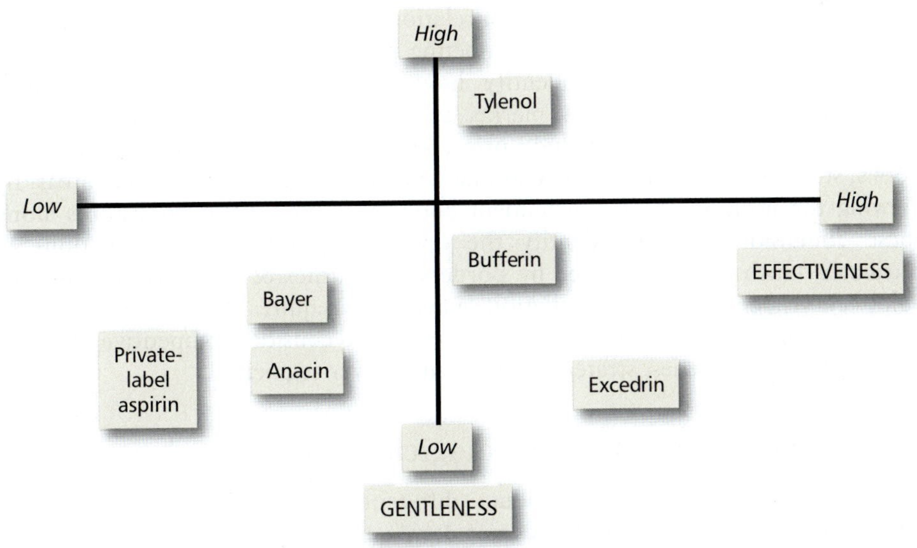

used to classify 109 single-malt Scotch whiskies according to the characteristics of their color, nose, palate, body and finish.[7]

Conjoint Analysis Conjoint analysis measures the strength of customer preferences for different product attributes. The technique requires, first, an identification of the underlying attributes of a product and, second, market research to rank hypothetical products that contain alternative bundles of attributes. The results can then be used to estimate the proportion of customers who would prefer a hypothetical new product to competing products already available in the market.[8] Conjoint analysis has been used to predict market shares of forthcoming new models of personal computer, to analyze windsurfer preferences, and to design new products, including Marriott's Courtyard hotel chain and nature tourism in the Amazon basin.

Hedonic Price Analysis The demand for a product may be viewed as the demand for the underlying attributes that the product provides.[9] The price at which a product can sell in the market is the aggregate of the values derived from each of these individual attributes. Hedonic price analysis uses regression to relate price differences for competing products to the levels of different attributes offered by each, thereby allowing the implicit market price for each attribute to be calculated. For example:

- For European automatic washing machines, price differences were related to differences in capacity, spin speed, energy consumption, number of programs, and reliability. For example, a machine that spins at 1000 rpm sold at about a $200 price premium to one that spins at 800 r.p.m.[10]
- Price differences between models of personal computer reflected differences in processor speed, memory and hard drive capacity.[11]

Value Curve Analysis Selecting the optimal combination of attributes depends not only on which attributes are valued by customers but also on where competitors' offerings are positioned in relation to different attributes. By mapping the performance characteristics of competing products on to a *value curve*, Chan Kim and Renee Mauborgne identify how superior combinations of product characteristics or a whole new market space can be created.[12] Thus, in book retailing, key value metrics include price, knowledge levels of staff, selection of books, store ambiance, store hours and facilities such as cafés and reading areas. By viewing the positioning of independent book stores and chain bookstores along these dimensions we can identify the opportunity for new combinations of attributes—such as those offered by Borders and Barnes & Noble. Deploying the value curve to create differentiation advantage requires looking beyond the conventionally defined boundaries of competition to consider competitive offerings from different industries, strategic groups, and buyer segments.

The Role of Social and Psychological Factors

The problem with analyzing product differentiation in terms of measurable performance attributes is that it does not delve very far into customers' underlying motivations. Very few goods or services are acquired to satisfy basic physical needs: most buying is motivated by social and psychological needs such as the desire to find community with others and to reinforce one's own identity. Psychologist Abraham Maslow proposed a hierarchy of human needs. Once basic needs for survival are established, there is a progression from security needs, to belonging needs, to esteem needs, to self-actualization needs.[13] For most goods, brand equity has more to do with status and identity than with tangible product performance. The disastrous introduction of "New Coke" in 1985 was the result of Coca-Cola giving precedence to tangible differentiation (taste preferences) over intangible differentiation (authenticity).[14] Harley-Davidson harbors no such illusions: it recognizes quite clearly that it is in the business of selling lifestyle, not transportation.

If the key customer needs that a product satisfies are identity and social affiliation, the implications for differentiation are far reaching. In particular, to understand customer demand and identify profitable differentiation opportunities requires that we analyze the product and its characteristics, but also customers, their lifestyles and aspirations, and the relationship of the product to these lifestyles and aspirations. Market research that explores the demographic (age, sex, race, location), socioeconomic (income, education), and psychographic (lifestyle, personality type) characteristics of potential customers may be less useful than deep understanding of consumers' relationship with a product. According to Tom Peters, the answer is simple: business people need to "get out from behind their desks to where the customers are . . . [and] construct settings so as to maximize 'naive' listening."[15]

In practice, understanding customer needs and preferences is likely to require more than listening. Typically, consumers cannot clearly articulate the motives that drive them and the emotions that different products trigger. Companies must observe carefully their customers to understand how a product relates to their lifestyles. Before opening its *Fresh and Easy* chain of foodstores in the western U.S., British supermarket giant, Tesco, sent a team of executives to live with local families.[16] Going beyond functionality to explore the emotional and esthetic aspects of consumers' relationships with products is central to Japanese approaches to marketing.[17]

Figure 10.2 summarizes the key points of this discussion by posing some basic questions that explore the potential for demand-side differentiation.

Analyzing Differentiation: The Supply Side

Demand analysis identifies customers' demands for differentiation and their willingness to pay for it, but creating differentiation advantage also depends on a firm's ability to offer differentiation. To identify the firm's potential to supply differentiation, we need to examine the activities that the firm performs and the resources it has access to.

The Drivers of Uniqueness

Differentiation is concerned with the provision of uniqueness. A firm's opportunities for creating uniqueness in its offerings to customers are not located within a particular function or activity, but can arise in virtually everything that it does.

FIGURE 10.2 Identifying differentiation potential: the demand side

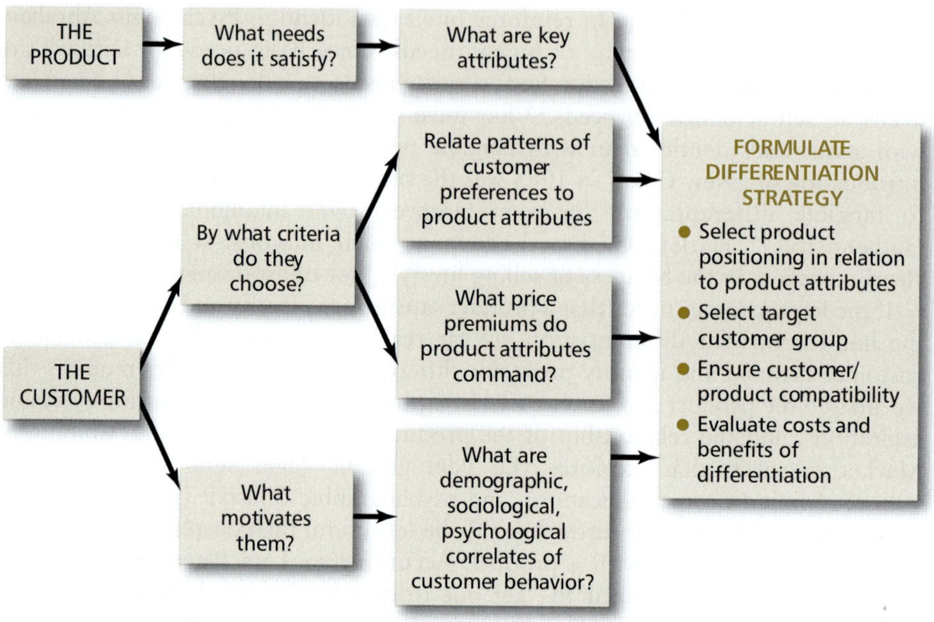

Michael Porter identifies a number of drivers of uniqueness that are decision variables for the firm:

- product features and product performance;
- complementary services (such as credit, delivery, repair);
- intensity of marketing activities (such as rate of advertising spending);
- technology embodied in design and manufacture;
- the quality of purchased inputs;
- procedures influencing the conduct of each of the activities (for example, rigor of quality control, service procedures, frequency of sales visits to a customer);
- the skill and experience of employees;
- location (for example, with retail stores);
- The degree of vertical integration (which influences a firm's ability to control inputs and intermediate processes).[18]

Most offerings do not involve a single product or a single service, but are a combination of products and services. In analyzing the potential for differentiation, we can distinguish between differentiation of the product ("hardware") and ancillary services ("software"). On this basis, four transaction categories can be identified (see Figure 10.3).[19]

As markets mature, so systems comprising both hardware and software tend to "unbundle." Products become commoditized while complementary services become provided by specialized suppliers. However, as customer preferences become

FIGURE 10.3 Differentiation of merchandise (hardware) and support (software)

		SUPPORT (SOFTWARE) Differentiated	SUPPORT (SOFTWARE) Undifferentiated
MERCHANDISE (HARDWARE)	Differentiated	SYSTEM	PRODUCT
	Undifferentiated	SERVICE	COMMODITY

Source: Shiv Mathur and Alfred Kenyon, *Creating Value* (Oxford: Butterworth-Heinemann, 1997). Reproduced by permission of Elsevier.

increasingly sophisticated and companies seek new opportunities for differentiation advantage, so hardware and software is repackaged into new systems. Service stations once offered a comprehensive array of services to motorists—gasoline, oil changes, car repair, tires, car washing and so on. As more and more of these services have become commodities provided by specialist suppliers, so the oil companies have sought differentiation through creating new bundles of retail services at their service stations.

A critical issue is whether such bundling really creates customer value. Thus, "one-stop shopping" by financial service companies diversified across retail banking, brokerage, fund management and insurance has had limited appeal to customers. Electronic commerce allows customers to assemble their own bundles of goods and services at low cost with little inconvenience. This trend explains the declining fortunes of European tour operators: most vacationers enjoy the flexibility of online information and reservations systems to create their own customized vacations.[20] The result, according to McKinsey consultants Hagel and Singer, is not just unbundling of products, but the unbundling of the corporation itself.[21]

Product Integrity

All companies face a range of differentiation opportunities. The primary issue is likely to be determining which forms of differentiation may be most successful in distinguishing the firm in the market and which are most valued by customers. Such choices cannot be made on a piecemeal basis. Establishing a coherent and effective differentiation position requires that the firm assembles a complementary package of differentiation attributes. If Beck's beer wishes to differentiate itself on the basis of the quality of its ingredients then it must adopt production methods that are consistent with quality ingredients, and packaging, advertising, and distribution appropriate to a quality, premium-priced product.

Product integrity refers to the consistency of a firm's differentiation; it is the extent to which a product achieves:

> . . . total balance of numerous product characteristics, including basic functions, esthetics, semantics, reliability, and economy . . . Product integrity has both internal and external dimensions. Internal integrity refers to consistency between the function and structure of the product—e.g., the parts

> fit well, components match and work well together, layout achieves maximum space efficiency. External integrity is a measure of how well a product's function, structure, and semantics fit the customer's objectives, values, production system, lifestyle, use pattern, and self-identity.[22]

In their study of product development in the auto industry, Clark and Fujimoto argue that simultaneously achieving internal and external integrity is the most complex organizational challenge facing automakers because it requires linking close cross-functional collaboration with intimate customer contact. The organizational changes among U.S. and European automakers, including the growing role of product managers, have attempted to imitate the success of Toyota and Honda in achieving internal-external integration.[23]

Combining internal and external product integrity is especially important to those supplying "lifestyle" products whose differentiation is based on customers' social and psychological needs. Here, the credibility of the image depends critically on the consistency of the image presented. A critical factor in such differentiation is the ability of employees and customers to identify with one another. Thus:

- Harley-Davidson's ability to develop its image of ruggedness, independence, and individuality is supported by a top management team that dons biking leathers and rides its "hogs" to owners' group rallies, and a management system that empowers shop-floor workers and fosters quality, initiative, and responsibility.
- MTV's capacity to stay at the leading edge of popular culture and embody "coolness" for new generations of young people owes much to its internal culture and human resource management, which rely heavily on the ideas and enthusiasm of its youngest employees.[24]

Maintaining integrity of differentiation is ultimately dependent on a company's ability to live the values embodied in the images with which its products are associated.

Signaling and Reputation

Differentiation is only effective if it is communicated to customers. But information about the qualities and characteristics of products is not always readily available to potential customers. The economics literature distinguishes between *search goods*, whose qualities and characteristics can be ascertained by inspection, and *experience goods*, whose qualities and characteristics are only recognized after consumption. This latter class of goods includes medical services, baldness treatments, frozen TV dinners, and wine. Even after purchase, performance attributes may be slow in revealing themselves. Bernie Madoff established Bernard L. Madoff Investment Securities LLC in 1960—it took almost half a century before the renowned investment house was revealed as a "giant Ponzi scheme."[25]

In the terminology of game theory (see Chapter 4), the market for experience goods corresponds to a classic "prisoners' dilemma." A firm can offer a high-quality or a low-quality product. The customer can pay either a high or a low price. If quality cannot be detected, then equilibrium is established, with the customer offering a low price and the supplier offering a low-quality product, even though both would be better off with a high-quality product sold at a high price (see Figure 10.4).

FIGURE 10.4 The problem of quality in experience goods: a "prisoners' dilemma"

Consumer's strategies		Producer's strategies: *High quality*	Producer's strategies: *Low quality*
	High price	7 (consumer) / 7 (producer)	−5 (consumer) / 10 (producer)
	Low price	10 (consumer) / −5 (producer)	3 (consumer) / 3 (producer)

Note: In each cell, the lower-left number is the payoff to the consumer and the upper-right number the payoff to the producer.

The resolution of this dilemma is for producers to find some credible means of signaling quality to the customer. The most effective signals are those that change the payoffs in the prisoners' dilemma. Thus, an extended warranty is effective because providing such a warranty would be more expensive for a low-quality producer than a high-quality producer. Brand names, warranties, expensive packaging, money-back guarantees, sponsorship of sports and cultural events and a carefully designed retail environment in which the product is sold are all signals of quality. Their effectiveness stems from the fact that they represent significant investments by the manufacturer that will be devalued if the product proves unsatisfactory to customers.

The need for signaling variables to complement performance variables in differentiation depends on the ease with which performance can be assessed by the potential buyer. The more difficult it is to ascertain performance prior to purchase, the more important signaling is.

- A perfume can be sampled prior to purchase and its fragrance assessed, but its ability to augment the identity of the wearer and attract attention remains uncertain. Hence, the key role of branding, packaging, advertising, and lavish promotional events in establishing an identity for the perfume in terms of the implied personality, lifestyle and aspirations of the user.
- In financial services, the customer cannot easily assess the honesty, financial security, or competence of the supplier. Hence, financial service companies emphasize symbols of security and stability: imposing head offices, conservative office decor, smartly dressed employees, and trademarks such as Prudential's rock and Travelers' red umbrella. Bernie Madoff's multi-billion investment swindle was sustained by his close association with leading figures among New York's Jewish community, his prominent role in cultural and charitable organizations, and the aura of exclusivity around his investment club.[26]

Strategies for reputation building have been subjected to extensive theoretical analysis.[27] Some of the propositions that arise from this research include the following:

- Quality signaling is primarily important for products whose quality can only be ascertained after purchase ("experience goods").

- Expenditure on advertising is an effective means of signaling superior quality, since suppliers of low-quality products will not expect repeat buying and hence it is not profitable for them to spend money on advertising.
- A combination of premium pricing and advertising is likely to be superior in signaling quality than either price or advertising alone.
- The higher the sunk costs required for entry into a market and the greater the total investment of the firm, the greater the incentives for the firm not to cheat customers through providing low quality at high prices.

Brands

Brand names and the advertising that supports them are especially important as signals of quality and consistency—because a brand is a valuable asset, it acts as a disincentive to provide poor quality. For many consumer goods (and some producer goods) companies, their brand is their most important asset.

Brands fulfill multiple roles. Most importantly, a brand provides a guarantee by the producer to the consumer of the quality of the product. It does so in several ways. At its most basic, a brand identifies the producer of a product. This ensures that the producer is legally and morally accountable for the products supplied to market. Further, the brand represents an investment that provides an incentive to maintain quality and customer satisfaction. Hence, the brand represents a guarantee to the customer that reduces uncertainty and search costs. The more difficult it is to discern quality on inspection, and the greater the cost to the customer of purchasing a defective product, the greater the value of a brand. Thus, a well-known brand name is likely to be more important to us when we purchase mountaineering equipment than when we buy a pair of socks.

The traditional role of the brand as a guarantor of reliability is particularly significant in e-commerce. Internet transactions are characterized by the anonymity of buyers and sellers and lack of government regulation. As a result, well-established players in e-commerce—Amazon, Microsoft, eBay, and Yahoo!—can use their brand to reduce consumers' perceived risk.

By contrast, the value conferred by consumer brands such as Red Bull, Harley-Davidson, Mercedes-Benz, Gucci, Virgin, and American Express is less a guarantee of reliability and more an embodiment of identity and lifestyle. Traditionally, advertising has been the primary means of influencing and reinforcing customer perceptions. Increasingly, however, consumer goods companies are seeking new approaches to brand development that focus less on product characteristics and more on "brand experience," "tribal identity," "shared values," and "emotional dialogue." Traditional mass-market advertising is less effective for promoting this type of brand identity as word-of-mouth promotion deploying web-based social networks—what has been referred to as *viral marketing* or *stealth marketing*.[28]

The Costs of Differentiation

Differentiation adds cost. The direct costs of differentiation include higher quality inputs, better trained employees, higher advertising costs and better after-sales service. The indirect costs of differentiation arise through the interaction of differentiation variables with cost variables. If differentiation narrows a firm's segment scope, it also limits the potential for exploiting scale economies. If differentiation requires continual product redesign, it hampers the exploitation of learning economies.

One means of reconciling differentiation with cost efficiency is to postpone differentiation to later stages of the firm's value chain. Economies of scale and the cost advantages of standardization are frequently greatest in the manufacturing of basic components. Modular design with common components permits scale economies while maintaining considerable product variety. All the major automakers have reduced the number of platforms and engine types and increased the commonality of components across their model ranges, while offering customers a greater variety of colors, trim and accessory options.

New manufacturing technology and the internet have redefined traditional tradeoffs between efficiency and variety. Flexible manufacturing systems and just-in-time scheduling have increased the versatility of many plants, made model changeovers less costly and made the goal of an "economic order quantity of one" increasingly realistic. Automobile and domestic appliance plants increasingly produce multiple models on a single assembly line.[29] Internet communication allows consumers to design their own products and quickly communicate their requirements to manufacturers. Pioneers of mass-customization include Capital One, which offers a unique package of credit facilities and interest rate charges to its credit card customers,[30] and Adidas, whose *mi adidas* program offers individually customized sports shoes through foot scanners installed in its retail stores.[31]

Bringing It All Together: The Value Chain in Differentiation Analysis

There is little point in identifying the product attributes that customers value most if the firm is incapable of supplying those attributes. Similarly, there is little purpose in identifying a firm's ability to supply certain elements of uniqueness if these are not valued by customers. The key to successful differentiation is matching the firm's capacity for creating differentiation to the attributes that customers value most. For this purpose, the value chain provides a particularly useful framework. Let's begin with the case of a producer good, i.e., one that is supplied by one firm to another.

Value Chain Analysis of Producer Goods

Using the value chain to identify opportunities for differentiation advantage involves four principal stages:

1. *Construct a value chain for the firm and the customer.* It may be useful to consider not just the immediate customer but also firms further downstream in the value chain. If the firm supplies different types of customers—for example, a steel company may supply steel strip to automobile manufacturers and white goods producers—draw separate value chains for each major category of customer.
2. *Identify the drivers of uniqueness in each activity.* Assess the firm's potential for differentiating its product by examining each activity in the firm's value chain and identifying the variables and actions through which the firm can

FIGURE 10.5 Using the value chain to identify differentiation potential on the supply side

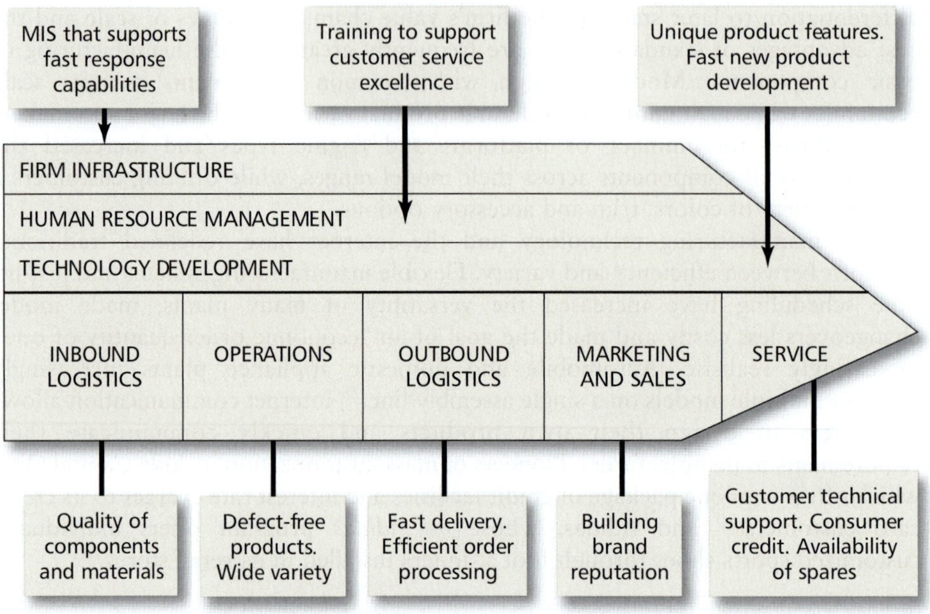

achieve uniqueness in relation to competitors' offerings. Figure 10.5 identifies sources of differentiation within Porter's generic value chain.

3 *Select the most promising differentiation variables for the firm.* Among the numerous drivers of uniqueness that we can identify within the firm, which one should be selected as the primary basis for the firm's differentiation strategy? On the supply side, there are three important considerations.
   - First, we must establish where the firm has greater potential for differentiating from, or can differentiate at lower cost than, rivals. This requires some analysis of the firm's internal strengths in terms of resources and capabilities.
   - Second, to identify the most promising aspects of differentiation, we also need to identify linkages among activities, since some differentiation variables may involve interaction among several activities. Thus, product reliability is likely to be the outcome of several linked activities: monitoring purchases of inputs from suppliers, the skill and motivation of production workers, and quality control and product testing.
   - Third, the ease with which different types of uniqueness can be sustained must be considered. The more differentiation is based on resources specific to the firm or skills that involve the complex coordination of a large number of individuals, the more difficult it will be for a competitor to imitate the particular source of differentiation. Thus, offering business-class passengers wider seats and more leg room is an easily imitated source of differentiation. Achieving high levels of punctuality represents a more sustainable source of differentiation.

4 *Locate linkages between the value chain of the firm and that of the buyer.* The objective of differentiation is to yield a price premium for the firm. This requires that the firm's differentiation creates value for the customer. Creating value for customers requires either that the firm lowers customers' costs, or that customers' own product differentiation is facilitated. Thus, by reorganizing its product distribution around quick-response technologies, Procter & Gamble has radically reduced distribution time and increased delivery reliability. This permits retailers to reduce costs of inventory while simultaneously increasing their reliability to shoppers through lowering the risk of stockouts. To identify the means by which a firm can create value for its customers it must locate the linkages between differentiation of its own activities and cost reduction and differentiation within the customer's activities. Analysis of these linkages can also evaluate the potential profitability of differentiation. The value differentiation created for the customer represents the maximum price premium the customer will pay. If the provision of just-in-time delivery by a component supplier costs an additional $1000 a month but saves an automobile company $6000 a month in reduced inventory, warehousing, and handling costs, then it should be possible for the component manufacturer to obtain a price premium that easily exceeds the costs of the differentiation.

Strategy Capsule 10.2 demonstrates the use of value chain analysis in identifying differentiation opportunities available to a manufacturer of metal containers.

STRATEGY CAPSULE 10.2

Analyzing Differentiation Opportunities for a Manufacturer of Metal Containers

The metal container industry is a highly competitive, low-growth, low-profit industry. Cans lack much potential for differentiation and buyers (especially beverage and food canning companies) are very powerful. Clearly, cost efficiency is essential but are there also opportunities for differentiation advantage? A value chain analysis can help a metal can manufacturer identify profitable opportunities for differentiation.

STAGE 1. Construct a value chain for firm and customers. The principal activities of the can manufacturer and its customers are shown in the diagram below.

STAGE 2. Identify the drivers of uniqueness. For each of the canmaking activities it is possible to suggest several possible differentiation variables. Examples are shown in the diagram.

STAGE 3. Select key variables. To select the most promising differentiation variables, the company's internal strengths must be considered. If the firm has strong technical capabilities, then it might design and manufacture products to meet difficult technical and design specifications, and provide sophisticated technical services to customers. If its logistics capabilities are strong it might offer fast and reliable delivery, possibly extended to electronic data interchange with customers.

STAGE 4. Identify linkages. To determine differentiation likely to create value for the customer, identify linkages between the canmaker's potential for differentiation and the potential for reducing cost or enhancing differentiation within the customer's value chain. The diagram identifies five such linkages.

Identifying differentiation opportunities through linking the value chains of the firm and its customers: can manufacture

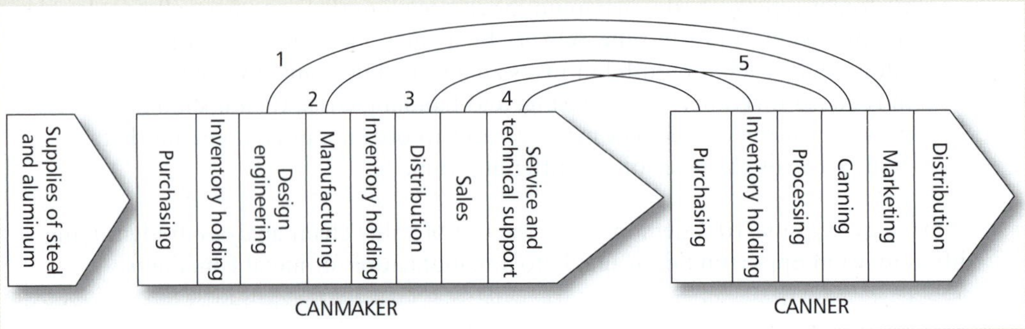

1. Distinctive can designs support canners' own marketing activities.
2. High manufacturing tolerances minimize breakdowns on customers' canning lines.
3. Frequent, punctual deliveries enable canners to minimize inventories.
4. Efficient order processing system reduces canners' ordering costs.
5. Speedy, competent technical support increases capacity utilization of canning lines.

Value Chain Analysis of Consumer Goods

Value chain analysis of differentiation opportunities can also be applied to consumer goods. Few consumer goods are consumed directly; in most cases consumers are involved in a chain of activities involving the acquisition and purchase of the product. Hence, even when the customer is a consumer, it is still feasible to draw a value chain showing the activities that the consumer engages in when purchasing and consuming a product.

In the case of consumer durables, customers are involved in a long chain of activities from search, purchase, financing, acquiring accessories, operation, service and repair to eventual disposal. Complex consumer value chains offer many potential linkages with the manufacturer's value chain, with considerable opportunity for innovative differentiation. Japanese producers of automobiles, consumer electronics and domestic appliances have a long tradition of observing their customers' behavior in selecting and utilizing products, then using the information of customer usage and selection processes in planning product design and marketing. Harley-Davidson has been particularly effective at achieving differentiation advantage through careful examination of the activities that customers undertake in selecting, purchasing, using, and maintaining their motorcycles. Harley creates value for its customers through providing test ride facilities at its dealerships, financing, driving instruction, insurance, service and repair facilities, owners' club activities, and various sponsored events for Harley riders. Even nondurables involve the consumer in a chain of activities. Consider a frozen TV dinner: it must be purchased, taken home, removed from the package, heated and served before it is consumed. After eating, the consumer must clean any used dishes, cutlery, or other utensils. A value chain analysis by a frozen foods producer would identify ways in which the product could be formulated, packaged, and distributed to assist the consumer in performing this chain of activities.

Summary

The attraction of differentiation over low cost as a basis for competitive advantage is its potential for sustainability. It is less vulnerable to being overturned by changes in the external environment, and it is more difficult to replicate.

The potential for differentiation in any business is vast. It may involve physical differentiation of the product, it may be through complementary services, it may be intangible. Differentiation extends beyond technology, design, and marketing to include all aspects of a firm's interactions with its customers.

The essence of differentiation advantage is to increase the perceived value of the offering to the customer either more effectively or at lower cost than do competitors. This requires that the firm matches the requirements and preferences of customers with its own capacity for creating uniqueness.

The value chain provides a useful framework for analyzing differentiation advantage. By analyzing how value is created for customers and by systematically appraising the scope of each of the firm's activities for achieving differentiation, the value chain permits matching demand-side and supply-side sources of differentiation.

Successful differentiation requires a combination of astute analysis and creative imagination. The two are not antithetical. A systematic framework for the analysis of differentiation can act as a stimulus to creative ideas.

Self-Study Questions

1 Bottled water sells at least 200 times the price of tap water, with substantial price differentials between different brands. What are the key differentiation variables that determine the price premium that can be obtained for bottled water?

2 The section on "Differentiation and Segmentation" notes that IKEA furnishings, Honda cars, Amazon, and Starbucks have achieved differentiation while maintaining a broad market appeal. How do companies achieve differentiate their products without limiting their appeal to certain market segments? If The Gap wishes to develop differentiation advantage while still appealing to customers across a broad demographic and socioeconomic range, what advice would you offer it?

3 Sony, which once dominated the market for portable music players with its Walkman products, has been the big loser to Apple in the market for MP3 music players. Using the framework shown in Figure 10.2, suggest opportunities for how Sony might differentiate its MP3 Walkman to increase its customer appeal.

4 Advise a chain of movie theaters on a differentiation strategy to restore its flagging profitability. Use the value chain framework outlined in Strategy Capsule 10.2 to identify potential linkages between the company's value chain and that of its customers in order to identify differentiation opportunities.

Notes

1 M. E. Porter, *Competitive Advantage* (New York: Free Press, 1985): 120.
2 T. Peters, *Thriving on Chaos* (New York: Knopf, 1987): 56.
3 "Cemex: Cementing a Global Strategy," Insead Case No. 307-233-1 (2007).
4 These distinctions are developed in more detail by P. R. Dickson and J. L. Ginter, "Market Segmentation, Product Differentiation and Marketing Strategy," *Journal of Marketing* 51 (April 1987): 1–10.
5 G. R. Carroll and A. Swaminathan, "Why the Microbrewery Movement?" *American Journal of Sociology* 106 (2000): 715–62.
6 S. Schiffman, M. Reynolds and F. Young, *Introduction to Multidimensional Scaling: Theory, Methods, and Applications* (Cambridge, MA: Academic Press, 1981).
7 F.-J. Lapointe and P. Legendre, "A Classification of Pure Malt Scotch Whiskies," *Applied Statistics* 43 (1994): 237–57. On principles of MDS, see I. Borg and P. Groenen, *Modern Multidimensional Scaling: Theory and Application* (Springer Verlag, 1997).
8 See P. Cattin and D. R. Wittink, "Commercial Use of Conjoint Analysis: A Survey," *Journal of Marketing* (Summer 1982): 44–53.
9 K. Lancaster, *Consumer Demand: A New Approach* (New York: Columbia University Press, 1971).
10 P. Nicolaides and C. Baden-Fuller, "Price Discrimination and Product Differentiation in the European Domestic Appliance Market," discussion paper (London: Center for Business Strategy, London Business School, 1987).
11 A. Pates, "A Reconsideration of Hedonic Price Indexes with an Application to PCs," *American Economic Review* 93 (2003): 1578–96.
12 C. Kim and R. Mauborgne, "Creating New Market Space," *Harvard Business Review* (January–February 1999): 83–93.
13 A. Maslow, "A Theory of Human Motivation," *Psychological Review* 50 (1943): 370–96.
14 M. Bastedo and A. Davis, "God, What a Blunder: The New Coke Story," December 17, 1993 (http://www.reference.com/browser/wiki.New_Coke).
15 T. Peters, op. cit.: 149.
16 "Fresh, but far from Easy," *Economist* (June 21, 2007).
17 J. K. Johansson and I. Nonaka, *Relentless: The Japanese Way of Marketing* (New York: HarperBusiness, 1996).
18 M. E. Porter, op. cit.: 124–5.
19 S. Mathur, "Competitive Industrial Marketing Strategies," *Long Range Planning* 17, no. 4 (1984): 102–9.
20 "Turbulent times for air charters," *Financial Times* (October 21, 2003): 21.
21 J. Hagel and M. Singer, "Unbundling the Corporation," *McKinsey Quarterly* no. 3 (2000).
22 K. Clark and T. Fujimoto, *Product Development Performance* (Boston: Harvard Business School Press, 1991): 29–30.
23 Ibid.: 247–85; K. B. Clark and T. Fujimoto, "The Power of Product Integrity," *Harvard Business Review* (November–December, 1990): 107–18.
24 J. Seabrook, "Rocking in Shangri-La," *The New Yorker* (October 10, 1994): 64–78.

25 "The Madoff Affair: Going Down Quietly," *Economist* (March 14, 2009).
26 "The Madoff Affair: Con of the Century," *Economist* (December 20, 2008): 119–20.
27 For a survey, see K. Weigelt and C. Camerer, "Reputation and Corporate Strategy: A Review of Recent Theory and Applications," *Strategic Management Journal* 9 (1988): 443–54.
28 D. J. Watts and J. Peretti, "Viral Marketing for the Real World," *Harvard Business Review* (May 2007): 22–3.
29 J. Pine, B. Victor, A. Boynton, "Making Mass-customization Work," *Harvard Business Review* (September–October 1993): 108–16; "Flexible Manufacturing Strategy lets Chrysler add New Model to Plant," *Industry Week* (June 6, 2007).
30 *Capital One Financial Corporation*, Harvard Business School Case No. 7-900-124 (2000).
31 "Adidas' High Tech Footwear," *Business Week* (November 3, 2006).

IV

BUSINESS STRATEGIES IN DIFFERENT INDUSTRY CONTEXTS

11 Industry Evolution and Strategic Change

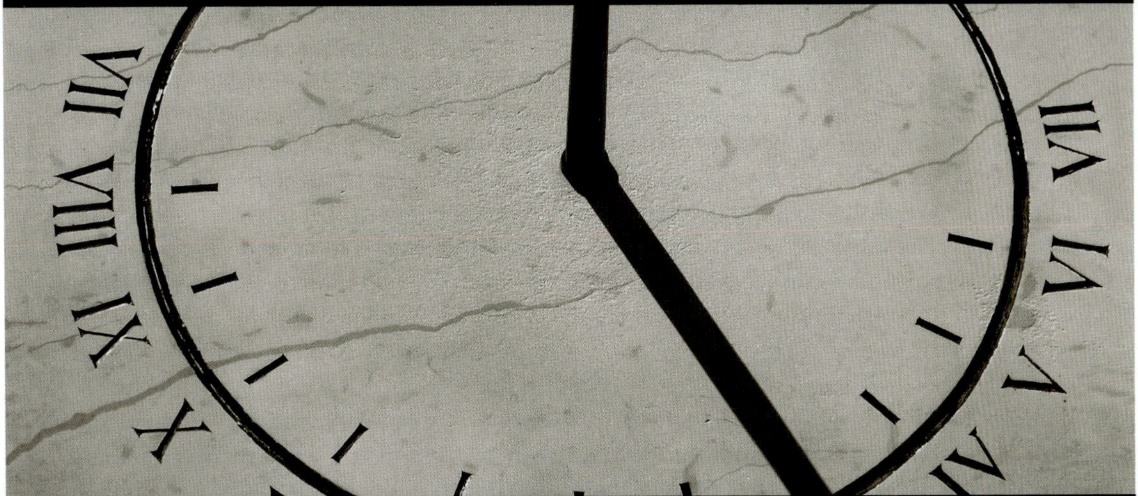

No company ever stops changing . . . Each new generation must meet changes—in the automotive market, in the general administration of the enterprise, and in the involvement of the corporation in a changing world. The work of creating goes on.

—ALFRED P. SLOAN JR., PRESIDENT OF GENERAL MOTORS 1923–37, CHAIRMAN 1937–56

OUTLINE

Introduction and Objectives

Everything is in a state of constant change—the business environment especially. Management's greatest challenge is to ensure that the enterprise adapts to the changes occurring within its environment.

Change in the industry environment is driven by the forces of technology, consumer need, politics, economic growth and a host of other influences. In some industries, these forces for change combine to create massive, unpredictable changes. For example, in telecommunications new digital and wireless technologies combined with regulatory changes have resulted in the telecom industry of 2009 being almost unrecognizable from that which existed 20 years previously. In other industries—food processing, aircraft production, and funeral services—change is more gradual and more predictable. Change is the result both of external forces and the competitive strategies of the firms within the industry. As we have seen, competition is a dynamic process in which firms vie for competitive advantage, only to see it eroded through imitation and innovation by rivals. The outcome is an industry environment that is being continually recreated by competition.

The purpose of this chapter is to help us to understand, predict, and manage change. To do this we shall explore the forces that drive change and look for patterns of change that can help us to predict how industries are likely to evolve over time. While recognizing that every industry follows a unique development path, we shall look for common drivers of change that produce similar patterns. Recognizing such patterns can help us to identify and exploit opportunities for competitive advantage.

However, understanding and predicting changes in the industry environment is only one aspect of the management challenge. By far the greater challenge is ensuring the adaptation of the firm to these changes. Change is disruptive, costly, and uncomfortable for individuals; for organizations the forces of inertia are even stronger. As a result, the life cycles of firms tend to be much shorter than the life cycles of industries: changes at the industry level tend to occur through the death of existing firms and birth of new firms rather than through continuous adaptation by a constant population of firms.

Our starting point is the *industry life cycle*. We shall consider the extent to which industries follow a common development pattern, examine the changes in industry structure over the cycle, and explore the implications for business strategy. We will then study the challenges of managing organizational change, including threats posed by technological change. While our main emphasis will be on the problems of adaptation to changing external circumstances, we shall also investigate the potential for firms to become agents of change—using strategy as a means of transforming their business environments.

By the time you have completed this chapter, you will be able to:

- recognize the different stages of industry development and understand the factors that drive the process of industry evolution;

- identify the key success factors associated with industries at different stages of their development;
- identify the strategies, organizational structures, and management systems appropriate to different stages of industry development;
- use scenarios to explore industry futures;
- appreciate the challenges of managing organizational change and be familiar with alternative approaches to strategic change.

The Industry Life Cycle

One of the best known and most enduring marketing concepts is the *product life cycle*.[1] Products are born, their sales grow, they reach maturity, they go into decline, and they ultimately die. If products have life cycles, so too do the industries that produce them. The *industry life cycle* is the supply-side equivalent of the product life cycle. To the extent that an industry produces multiple generations of a product, the industry life cycle is likely to be of longer duration than that of a single product.

The life cycle comprises four phases: *introduction* (or *emergence*), *growth*, *maturity*, and *decline* (see Figure 11.1). Before we examine the features of each of these stages, let us examine the forces that are driving industry evolution. Two factors are fundamental: demand growth and the production and diffusion of knowledge.

FIGURE 11.1 The industry life cycle

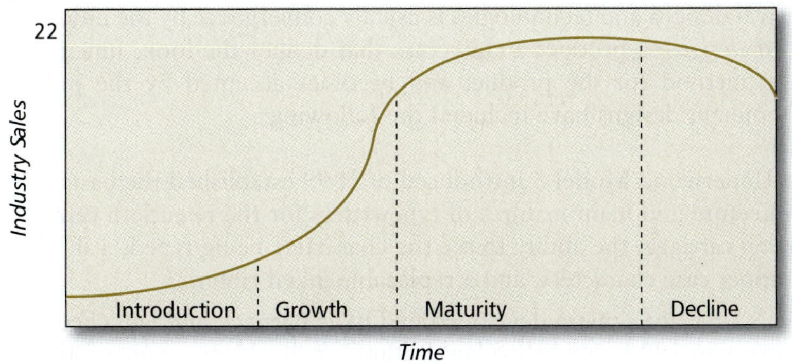

Demand Growth

The life cycle and the stages within it are defined primarily by changes in an industry's growth rate over time. The characteristic profile is an S-shaped growth curve.

1. In the *introduction stage*, sales are small and the rate of market penetration is low because the industry's products are little known and customers are few. The novelty of the technology, small scale of production, and lack of experience means high costs and low quality. Customers for new products tend to be affluent, innovation-oriented, and risk-tolerant.
2. The *growth stage* is characterized by accelerating market penetration as technical improvements and increased efficiency open up the mass market.
3. Increasing market saturation causes the onset of the *maturity stage*. Once saturation is reached, demand is wholly for replacement.
4. Finally, as the industry becomes challenged by new industries that produce technologically superior substitute products, the industry enters its *decline stage*.

Creation and Diffusion of Knowledge

The second driver of the industry life cycle is knowledge. New knowledge in the form of product innovation is responsible for an industry's birth, and the dual processes of knowledge creation and knowledge diffusion exert a major influence on industry evolution.

In the introduction stage, product technology advances rapidly. There is no dominant product technology, and rival technologies compete for attention. Competition is primarily between alternative technologies and design configurations:

- The first 30 years of steam ships featured competition between paddles and propellers, wooden hulls and iron hulls and, eventually, between coal and oil.
- The beginnings of the home computer industry during 1978–82 saw competition between different data storage systems (audio tapes versus floppy disks), visual displays (TV receivers versus dedicated monitors), operating systems (CPM versus DOS versus Apple II) and microprocessors.

Dominant Designs and Technical Standards The outcome of competition between rival designs and technologies is usually convergence by the industry around a *dominant design*—a product architecture that defines the look, functionality and production method for the product and becomes accepted by the industry as a whole. Dominant designs have included the following:

- The Underwood Model 5 introduced in 1899 established the basic architecture and main features of typewriters for the twentieth century: a moving carriage, the ability to see the characters being typed, a shift function for upper case characters, and a replacable inked ribbon.[2]
- Leica's Ur-Leica camera developed by Oskar Barnack and launched in Germany in 1924 established key features of the 35 mm camera, though it

was not until Canon began mass-producing cameras based on the Leica original that this design of 35 mm camera came to dominate still photography.

- When Ray Kroc opened his first McDonald's hamburger restaurant in Illinois in 1955, he established what would soon become a dominant design for the fast-food restaurant industry: a limited menu, no waiter service, eat-in and take-out options, roadside locations for motorized customers and a franchising model of business system licensing.

The concepts of *dominant design* and *technical standard* are closely related. Dominant design refers to the overall configuration of a product or system. A technical standard is a technology or specification that is important for compatibility. A dominant design may or may not embody a technical standard. IBM's PC established the MS-DOS operating system and Intel x86 series of microprocessor as technical standards for personal computing. Conversely, the Boeing 707 was a dominant design for large passenger jets but did not set industry standards in aerospace technology that would dominate subsequent generations of airplanes. Technical standards emerge where there are *network effects*—the need for users to connect in some way with one another. Network effects cause each customer to choose the same technology as everyone else to avoid being stranded. Unlike a proprietary technical standard, which is typically embodied in patents or copyrights, a firm that sets a dominant design does not normally own intellectual property in that design. Hence, except for some early mover advantage, there is not necessarily any profit advantage from setting a dominant design.

Dominant designs also exist in processes. In the flat glass industry there has been a succession of dominant process designs from glass cylinder blowing to continuous ribbon drawing to float glass.[3] Dominant designs are present, too, in business models. In many new markets, competition is between rival *business models*. In home grocery delivery, dotcom startups such as Webvan and Peapod soon succumbed to competition from "bricks 'n' clicks" retailers such as Giant, Safeway, and Wal-Mart.

From Product to Process Innovation The emergence of a dominant design marks a critical juncture in an industry's evolution. Once the industry coalesces around a leading design, there's a shift from radical to incremental product innovation. This transition may be necessary to inaugurate the industry's growth phase: greater standardization reduces risks to customers and encourages firms to invest in production capacity. The shift in emphasis from design to manufacture typically involves increased attention to process innovation as firms seek to reduce costs and increase product reliability through large-scale production methods (see Figure 11.2). The combination of process improvements, design modifications, and scale economies results in falling costs and greater availability that drives rapidly increasing market penetration. Strategy Capsule 11.1 uses the history of the automobile industry to illustrate these patterns of development.

Knowledge diffusion is also important on the customer side. Over the course of the life cycle, customers become increasingly informed. As they become more knowledgeable about the performance attributes of rival manufacturers' products, so they are better able to judge value for money and become more price sensitive.

FIGURE 11.2 Product and process innovation over time

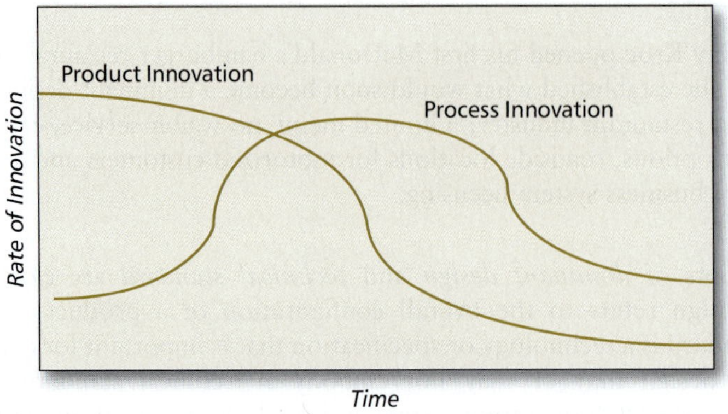

STRATEGY CAPSULE 11.1

Evolution of the Automobile Industry

The period 1890–1912 was one of rapid product innovation in the auto industry. After 1886, when Karl Benz received a patent on his three-wheel motor carriage, a flurry of technical advances occurred in Germany, France, the U.S. and Britain. Developments included:

- the first four-cylinder four-stroke engine (by Karl Benz in 1890);
- the honeycomb radiator (by Daimler in 1890);
- the speedometer (by Oldsmobile in 1901);
- automatic transmission (by Packard in 1904);
- electric headlamps (by General Motors in 1908);
- the all-steel body (adopted by General Motors in 1912).

Ford's Model T, introduced in 1908, with its front-mounted, water-cooled engine and transmission with a gearbox, wet clutch, and rear-wheel drive, acted as a dominant design for the industry. During the remainder of the twentieth century, automotive technology and design converged. A key indicator of this was the gradual elimination of alternative technologies and designs. Volkswagen's Beetle was the last mass-produced car with a rear-mounted, air-cooled engine. Citroën abandoned its distinctive suspension and braking systems. Four-stroke engines with four or six inline cylinders became dominant. Distinctive national differences eroded as American cars became smaller and Japanese and Italian cars became bigger. The fall of the Iron Curtain extinguished the last outposts of nonconformity: by the mid-1990s, East German two-stroke Wartburgs and Trabants were collectors' items.

As product innovation slowed, so process innovation took off. In October 1913, Ford opened its Highland Park Assembly Plant, with its revolutionary production methods based on interchangeable parts and a moving assembly line. In the space of one year, chassis assembly time was cut from 12 hours and 8 minutes to 1 hour and 33 minutes. The price of the Model T fell from $628 in 1908 to $260 in 1924.

Between 1908 and 1927 over 15 million Model Ts had been produced.

The second revolutionary process innovation in automobile manufacturing was Toyota's system of "lean production," involving a tightly integrated "pull" system of production embodying just-in-time scheduling, team-based production, flexible manufacturing and total quality management. During the 1970s and 1980s, lean production diffused throughout the world vehicle industry in the same way that Ford's mass-production system had transformed the industry half a century before.

Sources: www.ford.com; http://en.wikipedia.org/wiki/History_of_the_automobile

How General is the Life-Cycle Pattern?

To what extent do industries conform to this life-cycle pattern? To begin with, the duration of the life cycle varies greatly from industry to industry:

- The introduction phase of the U.S. railroad industry extended from the building of the first railroad, the Baltimore and Ohio in 1827, to the growth phase of the 1870s. With the growth of road transport, the industry entered its decline phase during the late 1950s.
- The introduction stage of the U.S. automobile industry lasted about 25 years, from the 1890s until growth took off in 1913–15. Maturity set in during the mid-1950s followed by decline during the past decade.
- In personal computers, the introduction phase lasted only about four years before growth took off in 1978. Between 1978 and 1983 a flood of new and established firms entered the industry. Toward the end of 1984, the first signs of maturity appeared: growth stalled, excess capacity emerged, and the industry began to consolidate around fewer companies; however, growth remained strong until the end of the 1990s.
- Digital audio players (MP3 players) were first introduced by Seehan Information Systems and Diamond Multimedia during 1997–8. With the launch of Apple's iPod in 2001 the industry entered its growth phase. By 2008–9, slackening growth indicated entry into the mature phase.

The tendency over time has been for life cycles to become compressed. This is especially evident in e-commerce. Businesses such as online gambling, business-to-business online auctions, and online travel services have gone from initial introduction to apparent maturity within a few years. "Competing on internet time" requires a radical rethink of strategies and management processes.[4]

Patterns of evolution also differ. Industries supplying basic necessities such as residential construction, food processing and clothing may never enter a decline phase because obsolescence is unlikely for such needs. Some industries may experience a rejuvenation of their life cycle. In the 1960s, the world motorcycle industry, in decline in the U.S. and Europe, re-entered its growth phase as Japanese manufacturers pioneered the recreational use of motorcycles. The market for TV

FIGURE 11.3 Innovation and renewal in the industry life cycle: retailing

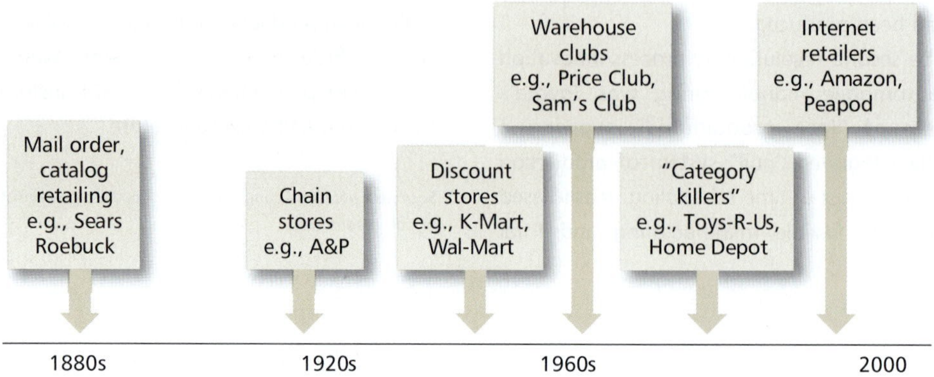

receivers has experienced multiple revivals: color TVs, computer monitors, flat-screen TVs and, most recently, HDTVs. Similar waves of innovation have revitalized retailing (see Figure 11.3). These rejuvenations of the product life cycle are not natural phenomena—they are typically the result of companies resisting the forces of maturity through breakthrough product innovations or developing new markets.

An industry is likely to be at different stages of its life cycle in different countries. Although the automobile markets of the E.U., Japanese, and U.S. have entered their decline phase, those of China, India, and Russia are in their growth phases. Multinational companies can exploit such differences: developing new products and introducing them into the advanced industrial countries, then shifting attention to other growth markets once maturity sets in.

A more fundamental critique of the life-cycle model is posed by recent work on industrial dynamics by Michael Jacobides. A key feature industrial evolution, he argues, is the shifting boundaries of industries. As a result industrial evolution needs to explore changes in "industry architecture" at the sectoral level—focusing in particular on the shifting vertical structure of clusters of related industries. In the computer sector and mortgage banking sector the major trend has been towards vertical deintegration.[5]

Structure, Competition and Success Factors over the Life Cycle

Changes in demand growth and technology over the cycle have implications for industry structure, competition, and the sources of competitive advantage (key success factors). Table 11.1 summarizes the principal features of each stage of the industry life cycle.

Product Differentiation

The introduction stage typically features a wide variety of product types that reflect the diversity of technologies and designs—and the lack of consensus over customer

TABLE 11.1 The evolution of industry structure and competition over the life cycle

	Introduction	Growth	Maturity	Decline
Demand	Limited to early adopters: high-income, avant-garde	Rapidly increasing market penetration	Mass market, replacement/repeat buying. Customers knowledgeable and price sensitive	Obsolescence
Technology	Competing technologies, rapid product innovation	Standardization around dominant technology, rapid process innovation	Well-diffused technical knowhow: quest for technological improvements.	Little product or process innovation
Products	Poor quality, wide variety of features and technologies, frequent design changes.	Design and quality improve, emergence of dominant design	Trend to commoditization. Attempts to differentiate by branding, quality, bundling	Commodities the norm: differentiation difficult and unprofitable
Manufacturing and distribution	Short production runs, high-skilled labor content, specialized distribution channels	Capacity shortages, mass production, competition for distribution.	Emergence of overcapacity, deskilling of production, long production runs, distributors carry fewer lines	Chronic overcapacity, reemergence of specialty channels
Trade	Producers and consumers in advanced countries	Exports from advanced countries to rest of world	Production shifts to newly industrializing then developing countries.	Exports from countries with lowest labor costs
Competition	Few companies	Entry, mergers and exits	Shakeout, price competition increases	Price wars, exits
Key success factors	Product innovation, establishing credible image of firm and product	Design for manufacture, access to distribution, brand building, fast product development, process innovation	Cost efficiency through capital intensity, scale efficiency, and low input costs	Low overheads, buyer selection, signaling commitment, rationalizing capacity

requirements. Convergence around a dominant design is often followed by commoditization during the mature phase unless producers develop new dimensions for differentiation. Personal computers, credit cards, online financial services, wireless communication services, and internet access have all become commodity items which buyers select primarily on price.

Organizational Demographics and Industry Structure

The number of firms in an industry changes substantially over the life cycle. The field of *organizational ecology*, founded by Michael Hannan, John Freeman and Glen Carroll, analyzes the population of industries and the processes of founding and selection that determine entry and exit.[6] Some of the main findings of the organizational ecologists in relation to industry evolution are:

- The number of firms in an industry increases rapidly during the early stages of an industry's life. Initially an industry may be pioneered by a few firms. However, as the industry gains legitimacy, failure rates decline and the rate of new firm foundings increases. New entrants have very different origins. Some are startup companies (*de novo* entrants); others are established firms diversifying from related industries (*de alio* entrants). The U.S. automobile industry comprised 272 manufacturers in 1909,[7] while in TV receivers there were 92 companies in 1951.[8]
- With the onset of maturity, the number of firms begins to fall. Very often, industries go through one or more "shakeout" phases during which the rate of firm failure increases sharply. After this point, rates of entry and exit decline and the survival rate for incumbents increases substantially.[9] The shakeout phase of intensive acquisition, merger, and exit occurs, on average, 29 years into the life cycle and results in the number of producers being halved.[10] In the U.S. tire industry, the number of firms grew from one (Goodrich) in 1896 to 274 in 1922 before shakeout reduced the industry to 49 firms in 1936.[11]
- As industries become increasingly concentrated and the leading firms focus on the mass market, so a new phase of entry may take place as new firms create niche positions in the market. An example of this "resource partitioning" is the U.S. brewing industry: as the mass market became dominated by a handful of national brewers, so opportunities arose for new types of brewing companies—microbreweries and brew pubs—to establish themselves in specialist niches.[12]

However, in different industries structural change follows very different evolutionary paths. In most industries maturity is associated with increasing concentration but in industries where scale economies are unimportant and entry barriers are low, maturity and commoditization may cause concentration to decline (as in credit cards, television broadcasting, and frozen foods). Some industries, especially where the first mover achieves substantial patent protection, may start out as near-monopolies, then become increasingly competitive. Plain-paper copiers were initially monopolized by the Xerox Corporation and it was not until the early 1980s that the industry was transformed by a wave of new entry. Seemingly stable mature industries can be transformed within a few years by a wave of mergers. The world petroleum industry consolidated considerably during 1998–2001, as did the world steel industry during 2001–7.

Location and International Trade

Industries move internationally during their life cycles as a result of shifts in demand decreasing dependence on advanced knowledge. New industries begin in the advanced industrial countries because of the presence of affluent consumers and the availability of technical and scientific resources. As demand grows in other countries, they are serviced initially by exports, but reduced need for sophisticated labor skills makes production attractive in newly industrialized countries. The advanced industrialized countries begin to import. With maturity, commoditization, and deskilling of production processes, production eventually shifts to developing countries where labor costs are lowest.

At the beginning of the 1990s, the production of wireless handsets was concentrated in the U.S., Japan, Finland and Germany. By the end of the 1990s, South Korea had joined this leading group. During 2009, production in North America, western Europe and Japan was in rapid decline as manufacturers shifted output to China, India, Brazil, Vietnam, Hungary and Romania.

The Nature and Intensity of Competition

The changes in industry structure that we have identified over the life cycle—commoditization, new entry, and international diffusion of production—have implications for competition. First, there is a shift from nonprice competition to price competition. Second, the intensity of competition grows, causing margins to narrow. During the introduction stage, competitors battle for technological leadership and competition focuses on technology and design. Gross margins can be high, but heavy investments in innovation and market development tend to depress return on capital. The growth phase is more conducive to profitability as market demand outstrips industry capacity—especially if incumbents are protected by barriers to entry. With the onset of maturity, increased product standardization and excess capacity stimulates price competition—especially during shakeout. How intense this is depends a great deal on the capacity/demand balance and the extent of international competition. In food retailing, airlines, motor vehicles, metals and insurance, maturity was associated with strong price competition and slender profitability. In household detergents, breakfast cereals, cosmetics and cigarettes, high seller concentration and successful maintenance of product differentiation has limited price rivalry and supported high margins. The decline phase is almost always associated with strong price competition (often degenerating into destructive price wars) and dismal profit performance.

Key Success Factors and Industry Evolution

These same changes in structure together with changes in demand and technology over the industry life cycle also have important implications for the sources of competitive advantage at each stage of industry evolution:

1 During the introductory stage, product innovation is the basis for initial entry and for subsequent success. Soon, however, other requirements for success emerge. In moving from the first generation of products to subsequent generations, investment requirements grow and financial resources become increasingly important. Capabilities in product development also need to be supported by capabilities in manufacturing, marketing, and distribution.

2 Once the growth stage is reached, the key challenge is scaling up. As the market expands, the firm needs to adapt its product design and its manufacturing capability to large-scale production. As Figure 11.4 shows,

investment in R&D, plant and equipment and sales tends to be high during the growth phase. To utilize increased manufacturing capability, access to distribution becomes critical. At the same time, the tensions that organizational growth impose create the need for internal administrative and strategic skills. We consider these issues in Chapter 12.

3 With the maturity stage, competitive advantage is increasingly a quest for efficiency—particularly in industries that tend toward commoditization. Cost efficiency through scale economies, low wages and low overheads become the key success factors. Figure 11.4 shows that R&D, capital investment, and marketing are lower in maturity than during the growth phase.

4 The transition to decline intensifies pressures for cost cutting. It also requires maintaining stability by encouraging the orderly exit of industry capacity and capturing residual market demand. We consider the strategic issues presented by mature and declining industries more fully in Chapter 13.

FIGURE 11.4 Differences in strategy and performance between businesses at different stages of the industry life cycle

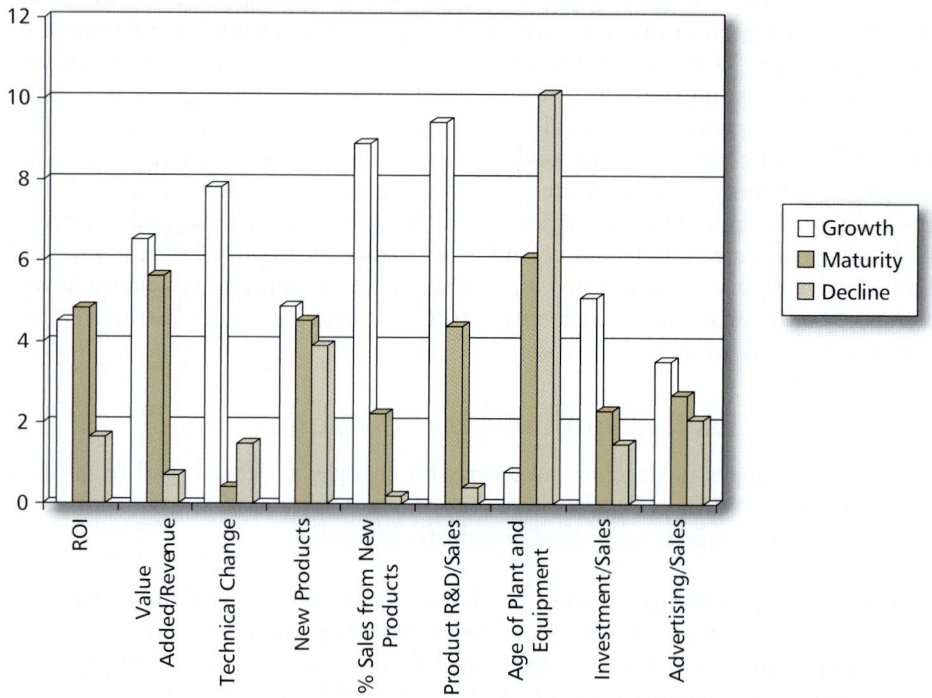

Note: The figure shows standardized means for each variable for businesses at each stage of the life cycle.

Source: C. Anderson and C. Zeithaml, "Stage of the Product Life Cycle, Business Strategy and Business Performance," *Academy of Management Journal* 27 (1984): 5–24. Reproduced with permission.

Organizational Adaptation and Change

The problem of change is that it is difficult. It is stressful and painful for individuals; it is even more difficult for companies—they comprise multiple individuals who must change in a coordinated way. Hence, our starting point for the analysis of organizational change is to understand why change is so problematic for companies.

The Sources of Organizational Inertia

Different theories of organizational and industrial change emphasize different barriers to change:

- *Organizational routines*. Evolutionary economists emphasize the fact that capabilities are based on organizational routines—patterns of coordinated interaction among organizational members that develop through continual repetition. The more highly developed are an organization's routines, the more difficult it is to develop new routines. Hence, organizations get caught in *competency traps*[13] where "core capabilities become core rigidities."[14]
- *Social and political structures*. Organizations develop social patterns of interaction that make organizational change stressful and disruptive.[15] Similarly, organizations create stable systems of political power. To the extent that change disrupts social patterns and threatens the power of those in positions of authority, organizations tend to resist change.
- *Conformity*. Institutional sociologists emphasize the propensity of firms to imitate one another to gain legitimacy.[16] The process of *institutional isomorphism* locks organizations into common structures and strategies that make it difficult for them to adapt to change. External pressures for conformity arise from governments, investment analysts, banks and other sources of resources and legitimacy but also through voluntary imitation—risk aversion encourages companies to adopt similar strategies and structures to their peers.[17]
- *Limited search*. The Carnegie School of organizational theory (associated with Herbert Simon, Jim March and Richard Cyert) views organizations' capacity for major changes as limited by a combination of cognitive and behavioral factors. Organizations tend to limit search to areas close to their existing activities—they prefer *exploitation* of existing knowledge over *exploration* for new opportunities. This is reinforced, first, by *bounded rationality*—human beings limited information processing capacity which constrains the set of choices that managers are capable of considering and, second, *satisficing*—the propensity for individuals (and organizations) to terminate the search for better solutions when they reach a satisfactory level of performance rather than to pursue optimal performance. The implication is that organizational change is triggered by declining performance.[18]
- *Complementarities between strategy, structure, and systems*. Organizational economics,[19] sociotechnical systems[20] and complexity theory[21] have all emphasized the importance of *fit* between an organization's strategy, structure, management systems, culture, employee skills—indeed, all the characteristics

of an organization. Organizations struggle to establish complex, idiosyncratic combinations of multiple characteristics during their early phases of development in order to match the conditions of their business environment. However, once established, this complex configuration becomes a barrier to change. To respond to a change in its external environment, it is not enough to make incremental changes in few dimensions of strategy—it is likely that the firm will need to find a new configuration that involves a comprehensive set of changes.[22] The implication is that organizations tend to evolve through a process of *punctuated equilibrium*, involving long periods of stability during which the widening misalignment between the organization and its environment ultimately forces radical and comprehensive change on the company.[23] Systematic changes that involve establishing a new configuration of activities that better matches the requirements of the external environment may require the appointment of a CEO from outside who is not wedded to the previous configuration.

Evolutionary Theory and Organizational Change

Different theories of organizational change are distinguished, not only by their focus on different sources of inertia, but also by their emphasis on different processes of change. The two major approaches to industry evolution—the organizational ecology school and the evolutionary economics school—both draw upon biological theories of evolution which view organizations adapting to external change through *variation*, *selection*, and *retention*.[24] However, they differ according to the level at which these evolutionary processes occur:

- *Organizational ecology*—at least in its initial formulation, views organizational change as restricted by powerful forces of inertia, hence, evolutionary processes work at the level of the industry through changes in the population of firms. Industries develop and grow through new entry which is spurred by the imitation of initial successful entrants. The competitive process is a *selection mechanism*, in which organizations whose characteristics match the requirements of their environment can attract resources, those that do not are eliminated. Thus, industry evolution occurs through changes in the *population of firms* rather than through changes in the firms themselves.[25]
- *Evolutionary economics* focuses upon individual organizations as the primary agents of evolution. The process of variation, selection, and retention takes place at the level of the *organizational routine*—unsuccessful routines are abandoned; successful routines are replicated within the organization.[26] As we discussed in Chapter 5, these patterns of coordinated activity are the basis for organizational capability. While evolutionary theorists view firms as adapting to external change through the search for new routines, replication of successful routines, and abandonment of unsuccessful routines, such adaptation is neither fast nor costless.

Empirical Evidence on Organizational Adaptation

The ability of some companies to adapt is indicated by the fact that many have been leaders in their industries for a century or more—BASF, the world's largest

TABLE 11.2 World's biggest companies in terms of market capitalization, 1912 and 2009

1912	$ bn	2009	$ bn
U.S. Steel	0.74	ExxonMobil	395
Exxon	0.39	PetroChina	241
J&P Coates	0.29	Wal-Mart Stores	202
Pullman	0.20	ChinaMobile	197
Royal Dutch Shell	0.19	Procter & Gamble	179
Anaconda	0.18	Microsoft	174
General Electric	0.17	BP	233
Singer	0.17	General Electric	168
American Brands	0.17	AT&T	157
Navistar	0.16	Chevron	148
BAT	0.16	BP	148
De Beers	0.16	Nestlé	139

Sources: *Financial Times, Economist.*

chemical company, has been a leader in chemicals since it was founded in 1865 as a producer of synthetic dyes. ExxonMobil and Royal Dutch Shell have led the world's petroleum industry for over a century.[27] Budweiser Budvar, the Czech beer company that has been involved in a trademark dispute with Anheuser Busch for several decades, traces its origins to 1785. Mitsui Group, the Japanese conglomerate is even older—its first business, a retail store, was established in 1673. Yet these companies are exceptions. Among the companies forming the original Dow Jones Industrial Average in 1896, only General Electric remains in the index today. Of the world's 12 biggest companies in 1912, just three were in the top 12 in 2009 (see Table 11.2).

A firm's ability to adapt to external change depends on the nature of that change. Generally, evolutionary change is less threatening than radical change—major technological shifts in particular. Let us look at some of the evidence.

Adapting to Changes over the Life Cycle Even though the industry life cycle involves changes that are largely predictable, the changes in key success factors that we have already identified imply that the different stages of the life cycle require different resources and capabilities. Markides and Geroski show that the "innovators" that pioneer the creation of a new industry are typically different companies from the "consolidators" that develop it:

> The fact that the firms that create new product and service markets are rarely the ones that scale them into mass markets has serious implications for the modern corporation. Our research points to a simple reason for this phenomenon: the skills, mind-sets, and competences needed for discovery and invention are not only different from those needed for commercialization; they conflict with the needed characteristics. This means that the firms good at invention are unlikely to be good at commercialization and vice versa.[28]

In plant biotechnology, the pioneers were research-based start-ups such as Calgene, Cetus Corporation, DNA Plant Technologies and Mycogen. By 2008, the leading suppliers of genetically modified seeds were DuPont, Monsanto, Syngenta, and Dow Chemical. In U.S. wireless telephony the pioneer was McCaw Communications; the current market leaders are AT&T and Verizon.

Adapting to Technological Change: Architectural Innovation The ability of firms to adapt to technological change depends to a great extent on the implications of the new technology. Some new technologies may enhance a company's existing capabilities, others may be "competence destroying."[29] This depends, in part, on whether the technology's impact is at the "component" or the "architectural" level—whether it involves a single process or product feature or whether it necessitates a new configuration of the product.[30] In many sectors of e-commerce—online grocery purchases and online banking—the internet involved innovation at the component level (it provided a new channel of distribution for existing products). Hence, existing supermarket chains and established retail banks with their "clicks-and-bricks" business models have dominated online groceries and online financial services. Conversely, the transistor radio involved an architectural innovation that required established radio producers to radically change their approaches to product design, manufacturing and marketing:

> In the mid-1950s engineers at RCA's corporate R&D center developed a prototype of a portable, transistorized radio receiver. The new product used technology in which RCA was accomplished (transistors, radio circuits, speakers, tuning devices), but RCA saw little reason to pursue such an apparently inferior technology. In contrast, Sony, a small, relatively new company, used the small transistorized radio to gain entry into the U.S. market. Even after Sony's success was apparent, RCA remained a follower in the market as Sony introduced successive models with improved sound quality and FM capability. The irony of the situation was not lost on the R&D engineers: for many years Sony's radios were produced with technology licensed from RCA, yet RCA had great difficulty matching Sony's product in the marketplace.[31]

Disruptive Technologies Clay Christiansen argues that the ability of established firms to successfully adopt new technology depends upon whether the new technology is *sustaining*, i.e., it augments existing performance attributes, or whether it is *disruptive,* incorporating different performance attributes than the existing technology.[32] In the disk drive industry, some technological innovations—such as thin-film heads and more finely-dispersed ferrous oxide disk coatings—have enhanced the dominant performance criterion: recording density. Such innovation has typically been led by established industry leaders.

Other disk-drive technologies—notably new product generations with smaller diameters—were disruptive in their impact: established companies were, on average, two years behind newcomers in launching the new disk sizes and typically lost their industry leadership.[33] Incumbents' resistance to the new disk sizes reflected inferior initial performance and customer resistance. In 1987 Connor Peripherals began shipping a 3.5 inch disk drive. Industry leader Seagate had developed a 3.5 inch drive but recognized that in terms of capacity and cost per megabyte of memory, it was inferior to the existing 5.25 inch disk. However, the key reason that Seagate abandoned development of the 3.5 inch disks was lack of interest among its major customers—the manufacturers of desktop PCs. The 3.5 inch disks were adopted initially by Compaq for its compact PCs and makers of laptop computers who appreciated its small size and robustness. However, within a year the rapid development of 3.5 inch disks resulted in their closing the gap with 5.25 inch disks in terms of cost and capacity. By 1990 even desktop computers were being fitted with 3.5 inch drives.[34]

Similarly with other technologies. Steam-powered ships were initially slower, more expensive and less reliable than sailing ships. However, they were useful on inland waters, which lacked constant winds. The leading shipbuilders failed to make the transition to steam power because their leading customers—the transocean shipping companies—remained loyal to sail until after the turn of the twentieth century.

However, the evidence is not wholly one way—in some industries, established firms have successfully adjusted to technological changes that were both architectural and disruptive. Since the late 19th century, the typesetting industry has undergone three waves of wrenching technological change. Yet, although new entrants had advantages in technology and new product development, incumbent firms have been able to use their strengths in certain key resources that newcomers were unable to replicate—notably customer relationships, sales and service networks, and font libraries—to survive and prosper.[35]

Established Firms in New Industries If established companies have difficulties adapting to evolutionary and technological changes within their own industries, it seems reasonable to expect that they would experience difficulties entering into entirely new industries. In most new industries we find both new startup companies ("*de novo* entrants") competing with established companies that have diversified from other sectors ("*de alio* entrants"). The issue is the same as within an existing industry that is undergoing change: do the flexibility advantages of new firms outweigh the superior resources and capabilities of established firms? It depends upon the extent to which the resources and capabilities required in the new industry are similar to those present in an existing industry. Where linkages are close, then diversifying entrants are likely to have an advantage over new startups. Thus:

- In the U.S. automobile industry, former bicycle, carriage, and engine manufacturers tended to be the best performers.[36]
- The U.S. television manufacturing industry was dominated by former producers of radios.[37]

However, some of the best performing firms in a new industry are often spinoffs from existing companies within that industry—i.e. new ventures established by former employees of existing companies. This was evident in the Akron tire industry[38] and the Silicon Valley semiconductor industry—where most of the leading players, including Intel, trace their origins to Shockley Semiconductor Laboratories, the pioneering producer of integrated circuits.[39]

Managing Organizational Change

Given the many barriers to organizational change, how can companies adapt to changes in their environment? Traditionally the management of organizational change has been viewed as a distinct area of management: *organizational development* (OD) comprises a set of methodologies through which an internal or external consultant acts as a catalyst for systemic change within a team or organizational unit.[40] In recent years the management of organizational change has been viewed as a continuous activity that forms the central component of a manager's responsibilities. The starting point for managing ongoing change is to recognize the sources of inertia: by identifying the barriers to change it becomes possible to identify opportunities for alleviating and circumventing them.

Dual Strategies and Separate Organizational Units Given the tendency for strategies and structures to be founded upon routinized behavior patterns and locked into complex patterns of interdependency, it may be easier to effect change by creating new organizational units rather than trying to change the existing organization. For example, faced with the challenge of disruptive technologies, Christensen and Overdorf suggest that established companies develop products and businesses that embody the new technologies in organizationally separate units.[41]

The broader issue is the challenge of *dual strategies*: how a company manages its existing activities while also nurturing new initiatives will form the basis for its business in the future. Most of the evidence points to the difficulties of reconciling strategies that require different capabilities and management systems within the same company: attempts by Continental, United and British Airways to establish budget airline subsidiaries were costly failures; attempts by the oil and gas majors to set up business development units that would create new businesses out of their technological innovations made little progress. Nevertheless, some companies have been able to reconcile the launch of new businesses with the effective management of established businesses (e.g. 3M, Google). Other companies have achieved coexistence of cost leadership and differentiation strategies (HSBC in full-service and internet banking; Merck in patented and generic drugs). Costas Markides argues that the successful pursuit of dual strategies requires either organizational separation (e.g. the allocation of new strategic initiatives to a separate organizational unit) or the development of "ambidexterity" such that the different strategy can access and deploy the same resources and capabilities.[42]

Given the general challenge of competing for today and developing the resources, capabilities and business initiatives needed to compete for tomorrow (see the discussion on strategic and dynamic notions of strategy in Chapter 1), all companies must—to some extent—pursue dual strategies. According to Derek Abell, such dual strategies require dual planning systems: short-term planning that focuses on strategic fit and performance over a one- or two-year period; and longer term planning to develop vision, reshape the corporate portfolio, redefine and reposition individual businesses, develop new capabilities and redesign organizational structures over periods of five years or more.[43] Given companies' bias towards the exploitation of current resources and capabilities in relation to known opportunities, the challenge for top management is to shift the emphasis towards building opportunities and new capabilities for the future.

Bottom-up Processes of Decentralized Organizational Change In Chapter 6, we noted that the appeal of modular, loosely coupled organizational structures was the potential for decentralized adaptation that avoided disrupting the whole organization. Yet, typically, simply decentralizing decision making is not enough to speed the processes of organizational adaptation. The strategy literature points to the need for top management to manage the conditions that foster and extend the processes of change. For example:

- If search for new strategies and new opportunities is limited by satisficing behavior, then top management needs to stimulate performance by raising performance expectations—establishing "stretch targets" for example.
- Corporate top management can challenge divisional and business unit managers to seek new opportunities by issuing specific company-wide initiatives. General Electric's former CEO, Jack Welch, would issue a new corporate challenge every two or three years: "Be number 1 or number 2 in your industry," "six-sigma quality," "destroy-your-business.com."
- Andy Grove of Intel has pointed to the necessity for top management to be alert to the emergence of "strategic dissonance" created by divergent strategic directions within the company. Such dissonance is likely to signal a "strategic inflection point"—a fundamental change in industry dynamics—at which point the company must be willing to make a radical strategic shift. For Intel, such an inflection point occurred when it recognized that its future lay in microprocessors rather than its initial business of DRAM chips.[44]
- By periodically changing organizational structure, a company can stimulate decentralized search and local initiatives while encouraging more effective exploitation of the outcomes of such search.[45] A typical pattern is to oscillate from periods of decentralization to periods of centralization.[46]

Imposing Top-down Organizational Change If organizational change occurs periodically through a punctuated equilibrium process, the implication is that these instances of concentrated organizational change must be orchestrated from the top. Most large companies exhibit periodic restructuring involving simultaneous changes in strategy, structure, management systems, and top management personnel. Such restructuring typically follows declining performance. For example, the oil and gas majors all experienced far-reaching restructuring during 1986–92 following depressed profitability that accompanied the oil price decline of 1986.[47] The challenge for top management is to undertake large-scale change before the company is pressured by declining performance. This may require that the CEO manufactures a perception of impending crisis within the company.

Using Scenarios to Prepare for the Future A company's ability to adapt to changes in its environment depends on its capacity to anticipate such changes. Yet predicting the future is hazardous, if not impossible. "Only a fool would make predictions—especially about the future," remarked movie mogul Samuel Goldwyn. But the inability to predict does not mean that it is not useful to think about what might happen in the future. *Scenario analysis* is a systematic way of thinking about how the future might unfold that builds on what we know about current trends and signals. Scenario analysis is not a forecasting technique, but a process for thinking and communicating about the future.

Herman Kahn, who pioneered their use first at the Rand Corporation and subsequently at the Hudson Institute, defined scenarios as "hypothetical sequences of events constructed for the purpose of focusing attention on causal process and decision points."[48] The multiple scenario approach constructs several distinct, internally consistent views of how the future may look five to 25 years ahead (shorter in the case of fast-moving sectors). Its key value is in combining the interrelated impacts of a wide range of economic, technological, demographic and political factors into a few distinct alternative stories of how the future might unfold. Scenario analysis can be either qualitative or quantitative or involve some combination of the two. Quantitative scenario analysis models events and runs simulations to identify likely outcomes. Qualitative scenarios typically take the form of narratives and can be particularly useful in engaging the insight and imagination of decision makers.

For the purposes of strategy making, scenario analysis is used to explore likely paths of industry evolution, to examine developments in particular country markets, to think about the impact of new technologies, and to analyze prospects for specific investment projects. Applied to industry evolution, scenarios can clarify and develop alternative views of how changing customer requirements, emerging technologies, government policies and competitor strategies might have an impact on industry structure and what the implications for competition and competitive advantage might be.

However, as with most strategy techniques, the value of scenario analysis is not in the results but in the process. Scenario analysis is a powerful tool for bringing together different ideas and insights, for surfacing deeply held beliefs and assumptions, for identifying possible threats and opportunities, for generating and evaluating alternative strategies, for encouraging more flexible thinking by managers and for building consensus. Evaluating the likely performance of different strategies under different scenarios can help identify which strategies are most robust and can assist in contingency planning by forcing managers to address "what if?" questions. Strategy Capsule 11.2 outlines the use of scenarios at Shell.

STRATEGY CAPSULE 11.2

Multiple Scenario Development at Shell

Royal Dutch Shell has pioneered the use of scenarios as a basis for long-term strategic planning in an industry where the life of investment projects (up to 50 years) far exceeds the time horizon for forecasting (two or three years). In 1967, a "Year 2000" study was inaugurated and scenario development soon became fundamental to Shell's planning process. Mike Pocock, Shell's former chairman, observed: "We believe in basing planning not on single forecasts, but on deep thought that identifies a coherent pattern of economic, political, and social development."

Shell views its scenarios as critical to its transition from planning toward strategic management, in which the role of the planning function is not so much to produce a plan, but to manage a process, the outcome of which is improved decision making by managers. This involves continually challenging current thinking within the group, encouraging a wider look at external influences on the business, promoting learning, and forging coordination among Shell's 200-odd subsidiaries.

Shell's global scenarios are prepared about every four years by a team comprising corporate planning staff, executives, and outside experts. Economic, political, technological, and demographic trends are analyzed 20 years into the future. Shell's 2005–25 scenarios were based on three sets of forces—market incentives, community, and coercion and regulation; and three objectives—efficiency, social cohesion, and security. Their interactions produced three scenarios each embodying different social, political, and economic conditions:

- *Low Trust Globalization*. A legalistic world where emphasis is on security and efficiency at the expense of social cohesion.
- *Open Doors*. A pragmatic world emphasizing social cohesion and efficiency with the market providing built-in solutions to crises of security and trust.
- *Flags*. A dogmatic world where community and security values are emphasized at the expense of efficiency.

Once approved by top management, the scenarios are disseminated by reports, presentations, and workshops, where they form the basis for long-term strategy discussion by business sectors and operating companies.

Shell is adamant that its scenarios are not forecasts. They represent carefully thought-out stories of how the various forces shaping the global energy environment of the future might play out. Their value is in stimulating the social and cognitive processes through which managers envisage the future. CEO Van Der Veer commented: ". . . the imperative is to use this tool to gain deeper in sights into our global business environment and to achieve the cultural change that is at the heart of our group strategy . . . I know that they broaden one's mindset and stimulate discussions."

Sources: Pierre Wack, "Scenarios: Uncharted Waters Ahead," *Harvard Business Review* (September–October, 1985): 72 and "Scenarios: Shooting the Rapids," *Harvard Business Review* (November-December 1985): 139; Arie De Geus, "Planning as Learning," *Harvard Business Review* (March–April 1988): 70–4; Paul Schoemacher, "Multiple Scenario Development: Its Conceptual and Behavioral Foundation," *Strategic Management Journal* 14 (1993): 193–214; *Shell Global Scenarios to 2025* (Shell International, 2005).

Shaping the Future

A succession of management gurus from Tom Peters to Gary Hamel have argued that the key to organizational change is not to adapt to external change but to create the future. Companies that adapt to change are doomed to playing catch-up; competitive advantages accrue to those companies that act as leaders and initiate change. Hamel and Prahalad's "new strategy paradigm" emphasizes the role of strategy as a systematic and concerted approach to redefining both the company and its industry environment in the future.[49]

According to Gary Hamel, in an age of revolution, "the company that is evolving slowly is already on its way to extinction."[50] The only option is to give up incremental improvement and adapt to a nonlinear world—revolution must be met by revolution. Achieving internal revolution requires changing the psychological and sociological norms of an organization that restrict innovation (see Figure 11.5).

Hamel's challenge for managers to cast off their bureaucratic chains and become revolutionaries is invigorating and inspiring. But is revolution among established

FIGURE 11.5 Shaking the foundations

OLD BRICK	NEW BRICK
Top management is responsible for setting strategy	Everyone is responsible for setting strategy
Getting better, getting faster is the way to win	Rule-busting innovation is the way to win
IT creates competitive advantage	Unconventional business concepts create competitive advantage
Being revolutionary is high risk	More of the same is high risk
We can merge our way to competitiveness	There's no correlation between size and competitiveness
Innovation equals new products and new technology	Innovation equals entirely new business concepts
Strategy is the easy part; implementation the hard part	Strategy is the easy part only if you're content to be an imitator
Change starts at the top	Change starts with activists
Our real problem is execution	Our real problem is incrementalism
Big companies can't innovate	Big companies can become gray-haired revolutionaries

Source: adapted from G. Hamel, *Leading the Revolution* (Boston: Harvard Business School Press, 2000): 280–1. Reproduced with permission.

companies either feasible or desirable? Some established companies have achieved radical change:

- Nokia underwent a metamorphosis from a manufacturer of paper and rubber goods into the world's leading supplier of mobile phones;
- BP transformed itself from a bureaucratic state-owned oil company to one of the most flexible and innovative of the supermajors;
- Microsoft has successfully ridden a series of disruptive changes in the world's computer industry, including the transition to object-oriented computing and the networking revolution of the late 1990s, and is currently positioning itself for the conversion of computing, telecommunications, and home entertainment.

However, for most established companies, efforts at radical change have resulted in disaster:

- Enron's transformation from a utility and pipeline company to a trader and market-maker in energy futures and derivatives ended in its demise in 2001;
- Vivendi's multimedia empire built on the base of French water and waste utility fell apart in 2002;
- GEC's reincarnation as Marconi, a telecom equipment supplier, was swiftly followed by bankruptcy in 2002;

- ICI, the former British chemical giant, has yet to recover from its attempt to reinvent itself as a specialty chemical company;
- Skandia's quest to become one of the world's most innovative insurance companies ended in top management scandal and the sale of most of the company's businesses outside of Sweden.

The perils of radical strategic change are not difficult to understand. We have noted that competitive advantage depends on the deployment of superior organizational capabilities and these capabilities develop slowly. Strategic changes that take a company beyond its competence domain involve massive risks.

Summary

Strategy is about establishing an identity and a direction for the development of a business into the future. How can we formulate a strategy for the future if the future is unknown and difficult to predict?

In this chapter we have learned that some regularities are evident in the evolutionary paths that industries follow. The life cycle model is a useful approach to exploring the impact of temporal processes of market saturation and technology development and dissemination, and their impact on industry structure and the basis of competitive advantage. Classifying industries according to their stage of development can in itself be an insightful exercise:

- It acts as a shortcut in strategy analysis. Categorizing an industry according to its stage of development can alert us to the type of competition likely to emerge and the kinds of strategy likely to be effective.
- Classifying an industry encourages comparison with other industries. By highlighting similarities and differences with other industries, such comparisons can help us gain a deeper understanding of the strategic characteristics of an industry.
- It directs attention to the forces of change and direction of industry evolution, thereby helping us to anticipate and manage change.

Even if we can identify certain regularities in the pattern of industry evolution, adapting to change presents a huge challenge to companies. Organizational theories that emphasize inertia and conformity among organizations suggest that industry adjustment may occur more through the birth of new firms and death of old ones than through adaptation by established firms. This analysis is supported by empirical evidence that points to the limited success of established firms in dealing with industry evolution and disruptive technologies.

While various management consultants and commentators advocate radical and continuous change among established companies, there is little evidence that most companies have the capacity to manage such change. Certain tools and techniques—scenario analysis in particular—may help managers understand and cope with change in the external environment; nevertheless, the fundamental truth is that, so long as developing new capabilities is slow and risky, a firm's capacity to undergo radical change successfully is inherently uncertain.

In the next two chapters, we discuss strategy formulation and strategy implementation in industries at different stages of their development: emerging industries, those characterized by technology-based competition, and mature industries.

Self-Study Questions

1 Consider the changes that have occurred in a comparatively new industry (for example, wireless communication services, wireless handsets, video game consoles, online auctions, bottled water, online book retailing). To what extent has the evolution of the industry followed the pattern predicted by the industry life-cycle model? What particular features does the industry have that have influenced its pattern of evolution? At what stage of development is the industry today? How is the industry likely to evolve in the future?

2 Select a product that has become a *dominant design* for its industry (for example, the IBM PC in personal computers, McDonald's in fast food, Harvard in MBA education, Southwest in budget airlines). What factors caused one firm's product architecture to become dominant? Why did other firms imitate this dominant design? To what extent has the dominant design evolved or been displaced?

3 The "resource partitioning" model argues that as industries become dominated by a few major companies whose strategies and products converge, so opportunities open for new entrants to build specialist niches. Identify an opportunity for establishing a specialist new business in an industry dominated by mass market giants.

4 Consider an industry facing fundamental technology change (e.g. the recorded music Industry and digital technology, computer software and open-source, newspapers and the internet, automobiles and alternative fuels, corporate IT services and cloud computing). Develop two alternative scenarios for the future evolution of your chosen industry. In relation to one leading player in the industry, identify the problems posed by the new technology and develop a strategy for how the company might adapt to and exploit the changes you envisage.

Notes

1 T. Levitt, "Exploit the Product Life Cycle," *Harvard Business Review* (November–December 1965): 81–94; G. Day, "The Product Life Cycle: Analysis and Applications," *Journal of Marketing* 45 (Autumn 1981): 60–7.

2 J. M. Utterback and F. F. Suarez, "Patterns of Industrial Evolution, Dominant designs, and Firms' Survival," Sloan working paper #3600-93 (MIT, 1993).

3 P. Anderson and M. L. Tushman, "Technological Discontinuities and Dominant Designs," *Administrative Science Quarterly* 35 (1990): 604–33.

4 M. A. Cusumano and D. B. Yoffie, *Competing on Internet Time: Lessons From Netscape and Its Battle with Microsoft* (New York: Free Press, 1998).

5 In Shiv Mathur and Alfred Kenyon's "transaction cycle," differentiation re-emerges as products and service are bundled into new systems. See "Competitive System Dynamics," in *Creating Wealth: Shaping Tomorrow's Business* (Oxford: Butterworth-Heinemann, 1997): Chapter 9.

6 M. G. Jacobides, "Industry Change through Vertical Disintegration: How and why Markets Emerged in Mortgage Banking," *Academy of Management Journal* 48, no. 3: 465–98; M. G. Jacobides, C. Y. Baldwin and R. Dizaji, "From the Structure of the Value Chain to the Strategic Dynamics of Industry Sectors," Academy of Management Presentation (Philadelphia, August 7, 2007).

7 G. Carroll and M. Hannan, *The Demography of Corporations and Industries* (Princeton: Princeton University Press, 2000). For a survey see: J. Baum, "Organizational Ecology," in S. R. Clegg, C. Hardy and W. R. Nord, *Handbook of Organizational Studies* (Thousand Oaks: Sage, 1996); D. Barron, "Evolutionary Theory," in D. O. Faulkner and A. Campbell (eds), *The Oxford Handbook of Strategy* (Oxford: Oxford University Press, 2003), vol. 1: 74–97.

8 G. R. Carroll, L. S. Bigelow, M.-D. Seidel and B. Tsai, "The Fates of *de novo* and *de alio* Producers in the American Automobile Industry, 1885–1981," *Strategic Management Journal* 17, Summer Special Issue (1996): 117–37.

9 S. Klepper and K. L. Simons, "Dominance by Birthright: Entry of Prior Radio Producers and Competitive Ramifications in the U.S. Television Receiver Industry," *Strategic Management Journal* 17 (2000): 997–1016.

10 High rates of entry and exit may continue well into maturity. In U.S. manufacturing industries in any given year, it was found that 39% of larger companies were not industry participants five years earlier and 40% would not be participants five years later. See T. Dunne, M. J. Roberts, and L. Samuelson, "Patterns of Firm Entry and Exit in U.S. Manufacturing Industries," *Rand Journal of Economics* 19 (1988): 495–515.

11 S. Klepper and E. Grady, "The Evolution of New Industries and the Determinants of Industry Structure," *Rand Journal of Economics* (1990): 27–44.

12 S. Klepper and K. Simons, "The Making of an Oligopoly: Firm Survival and Technological Change in the Evolution of the U.S. Tire Industry," *Journal of Political Economy* 108 (2000): 728-760.

13 G. Carroll and A. Swaminathan, "Why the Microbrewery Movement? Organizational Dynamics of Resource Partitioning in the American Brewing Industry," *American Journal of Sociology* 106 (2000): 715–62.

14 J. G. March, "Exploration and Exploitation in Organizational Learning," *Organizational Science* 2 (1991): 71–87.

15 D. Leonard-Barton, "Core Capabilities and Core Rigidities: A Paradox in Managing New Product Development," *Strategic Management Journal*, Summer Special Issue (1992): 111–25.

16 M. T. Hannan, L. Polos, and G. R. Carroll, "Structural Inertia and Organizational Change Revisited III: The Evolution of Organizational Inertia," Stanford GSB Research Paper 1734 (April 2002).

17 P. J. DiMaggio and W. Powell, "'The Iron Cage Revisited': Institutional Isomorphism and Collective Rationality in Organizational Fields," *American Sociological Review* 48 (1983): 147–60.

18 J.-C. Spender, *Industry Recipes* (Oxford: Blackwell, 1989).

19 J. G. March and H. A. Simon, *Organizations* (New York: John Wiley & Sons, Inc., 1958); J. G. March, "Exploration and Exploitation . . ." op. cit.

20 P. R. Milgrom and J. Roberts, "Complementarities and Fit: Strategy, Structure, and Organizational Change in Manufacturing," *Journal of Accounting and Economics* 19 (1995): 179–208; M. E. Porter and N. Siggelkow, "Contextual Interactions within Activity Systems and Sustainable Competitive Advantage," Working Paper, Harvard Business School, Boston, 2002.

21 E. Trist, "The Sociotechnical Perspective." In Van de Ven and Joyce (eds) *Perspectives on Organization Design and Behavior* (New York: John Wiley & Sons, Inc., 1984).

22 J. W. Rivkin, "Imitation of Complex Strategies," *Management Science* 46 (2000): 824–44.

23 M. E. Porter and N. Siggelkow, "Contextual Interactions within Activity Systems," *Academy of Management Perspectives* 22 (May 2008): 34–56.

24 M. L. Tushman and E. Romanelli, "Organizational Evolution: A Metamorphosis Model of Convergence and Reorientation," in L. L. Cummins and B. M. Staw (eds), *Research in Organizational Behavior* 7 (1985): 171–26; E. Romanelli and M. L. Tushman, "Organizational Transformation as Punctuated Equilibrium: An Empirical Test," *Academy of Management Journal* 37 (1994): 1141–66.

25 H. E. Aldrich, *Organizations and Environments* (Stanford University Press, 2007).

26 For an introduction to organizational ecology, see: M. T. Hannan and G. R. Carroll, "An introduction to organizational ecology," in *Organizations in Industry* (Oxford: Oxford University Press, 1995): 17–31.

27 For a survey of evolutionary approaches, see R. R. Nelson, "Recent Evolutionary Theorizing About Economic Change," *Journal of Economic Literature* 33 (March 1995): 48–90.

28 ExxonMobil Corporation is a descendent of Standard Oil; Royal Dutch Shell was created in 1907 by Royal Dutch Petroleum Co. and Shell Transport and Trading Co.

29 C. Markides and P. Geroski, "Colonizers and Consolidators: The Two Cultures of Corporate Strategy," *Strategy and Business* 32 (Fall, 2003). http://www.strategy-business.com/press/16635507/03306.

30 M. L. Tushman and P. Anderson, "Technological Discontinuities and Organizational Environments," *Administrative Science Quarterly* 31 (1986): 439–65.

31 R. M. Henderson and K. B. Clark, "Architectural Innovation: The Reconfiguration of Existing Systems and the Failure of Established Firms," *Administrative Science Quarterly* (1990): 9–30.

32 Ibid.

33 J. Bower and C. M. Christensen, "Disruptive Technologies: Catching the Wave," *Harvard Business Review* (January–February 1995): 43–53.

34 C. M. Christensen, *The Innovator's Dilemma* (Harvard Business School Press, 1997).

35 M. Tripsas, "Unravelling the Process of Creative Destruction: Complementary Assets and Incumbent Survival in the Typesetter Industry," *Strategic Management Journal* 18, Summer Special Issue (July 1997): 119–42.

36 S. Klepper, "The Capabilities of New Firms and the Evolution of the U.S. Automobile Industry," *Industrial and Corporate Change* 11 (2002): 645–66.

37 S. Klepper and K. L. Simons, "Dominance by Birthright: Entry of Prior Radio Producers and Competitive Ramifications in the U.S. Television Receiver Industry," *Strategic Management Journal* 21 (2000): 997–1016.

38 G. Buenstorf and S. Klepper, "Heritage and Agglomeration: The Akron Tire Cluster Revisited," Department of Social and Decision Sciences Working Paper, Carnegie Mellon University, March 2005.

39 D. A. Kaplan, *The Silicon Boys and Their Valley of Dreams* (New York: Morrow, 1999).

40 T. G. Cummins and C. G. Worley, *Organization Development and Change,* 8th edn. (Cincinatti, Ohio: Southwestern College Publishing: 2005).

41 C. M. Christensen and M. Overdorf, "Meeting the Challenge of Disruptive Change," *Harvard Business Review* (March–April 2000): 66–76.

42 C. Markides and C. D. Charitou, "Competing with Dual Strategies," *Academy of Management Executive* 18 (2004): 22–36.

43 D. F. Abell, *Managing with Dual Strategies* (New York: Free Press, 1993).

44 A. Grove, *Only the Paranoid Survive* (New York: Doubleday, 1996).

45 N. Siggelkow and D. A. Levinthal, "Escaping Real (Non-benign) Competency Traps: Linking the Dynamics of Organizational Structure to the Dynamics of Search," *Strategic Organization* 3 (2005): 85–115.

46 J. Nickerson and T. Zenger, "Being Efficiently Fickle: A Dynamic Theory of Organizational Choice," *Organization Science* 13 (September–October 2002): 547–67.

47 R. Cibin and R. M. Grant, "Restructuring among the World's Leading Oil Companies," *British Journal of Management* 7 (1996): 283–308.

48 H. Kahn, *The Next 200 Years: A Scenario for America and the World* (New York: William Morrow, 1976). For a guide to the use of scenarios in strategy making, see K. van der Heijden, *Scenarios: The Art of Strategic Conversation* (Chichester: John Wiley & Sons, Ltd, 2005).

49 G. Hamel and C. K. Prahalad, *Competing for the Future* (Boston: Harvard Business School Press, 1995).

50 G. Hamel, *Leading the Revolution* (Boston: Harvard Business School Press, 2000): 5.

12 Technology-based Industries and the Management of Innovation

Whereas a calculator on the ENIAC is equipped with 18 000 vacuum tubes and weighs 30 tons, computers in the future may have only 1000 vacuum tubes and perhaps weigh only 1.5 tons.

—POPULAR MECHANICS, *MARCH 1949*

I can think of no conceivable reason why an individual should wish to have a computer in his own home.

—KENNETH OLSEN, CHAIRMAN, DIGITAL EQUIPMENT CORPORATION, 1977

OUTLINE

Introduction and Objectives

In the previous chapter we saw that technology is the primary force that creates new industries and transforms existing ones. In the past quarter century, new technology-based industries include wireless telephony, biotechnology, photovoltaic power, fiber optics, online financial services, nanotechnology and laser printing. Industries transformed by technology include the telecom sector, which has been turned upside-down by wireless technology and the internet. The new global leaders are companies that pioneered the new technologies: on the service side Vodafone, China Mobile, and Skype (owned by eBay); on the hardware side Cisco Systems, Nokia, and Qualcomm.

The impact of technology has not been limited to science-based industries such as chemicals, healthcare, and electronics. A key feature of the past decade has been the pervasive influence of digital technologies—including communication technologies and the internet.

Our focus in this chapter is on business environments where technology is a key driver of change and an important source of competitive advantage. These technology-intensive industries include both emerging industries (those in the introductory and growth phases of their life cycle) and established industries where technology continues to be the major driver of competition (such as pharmaceuticals, chemicals, telecommunications and electronics). The issues we examine, however, are also relevant to a much broader range of industries where technology has the potential to create competitive advantage.

In the last chapter, we viewed technology as an external force that drove industrial change. In this chapter our primary concern will be the use of technology as a tool of competitive strategy. How does the firm use technology to establish competitive advantage?

By the time you have completed this chapter, you will be able to:

- analyze how technology affects industry structure and competition;
- identify the factors that determine the returns to innovation, and evaluate the potential for an innovation to establish competitive advantage;
- formulate strategies for exploiting innovation and managing technology, focusing in particular on:
  - the relative advantages of being a leader or a follower in innovation;
  - identifying and evaluating strategic options for exploiting innovation;
  - how to win standards battles;
  - how to manage risk;
- design the organizational conditions needed to implement such strategies successfully.

This chapter is organized as follows. First, we examine the links between technology and competition in technology-intensive industries. Second, we explore the potential for innovation to establish sustainable competitive advantage. Third, we deal with key issues in designing technology strategies, including timing (to lead or to follow), alternative strategies for exploiting an innovation, setting industry standards, and managing risk. Finally, we examine the organizational conditions for the successful implementation of technology-based strategies.

Competitive Advantage in Technology-intensive Industries

The principal link between technology and competitive advantage is *innovation*. It is the quest for competitive advantage that causes firms to invest in innovation; it is innovation that is responsible for new industries coning into being; and it is innovation that allows some firms to dominate their industries. Let us begin by exploring the conditions under which innovation generates profit.

The Innovation Process

Invention is the creation of new products and processes through the development of new knowledge or from new combinations of existing knowledge. Most inventions are the result of novel applications of existing knowledge. Samuel Morse's telegraph, patented in 1840, was based on several decades of research into electromagnetism from Ben Franklin to Orsted, Ampere and Sturgion. The compact disk embodies knowledge about lasers developed several decades previously.

Innovation is the initial commercialization of invention by producing and marketing a new good or service or by using a new method of production. Once introduced, innovation diffuses: on the demand side, through customers purchasing the good or service; on the supply side, through imitation by competitors. An innovation may be the result of a single invention (most product innovations in chemicals and pharmaceuticals involve discoveries of new chemical compounds) or it may combine many inventions. The first automobile, introduced by Benz in 1885, embodied a multitude of inventions, from the wheel, invented some 5000 years previously, to the internal combustion engine, invented nine years earlier. Not all invention progresses into innovation: among the patent portfolios of most technology-intensive firms are inventions that have yet to find a viable commercial application. Many innovations may involve little or no new technology: the personal computer brought together existing components and technologies; most new types of packaging—including the vast array of tamper-proof packages—involve novel design but no new technology.

Figure 12.1 shows the pattern of development from knowledge creation to invention and innovation. Historically, the lags between knowledge creation and innovation have been long:

- Chester F. Carlson invented xerography in 1938 by combining established knowledge about electrostatics and printing. The first patents were awarded in 1940. Xerox purchased the patent rights and launched its first office copier in 1958. By 1974, the first competitive machines were introduced by IBM, Kodak, Ricoh, and Canon.

FIGURE 12.1 The development of technology: from knowledge creation to diffusion

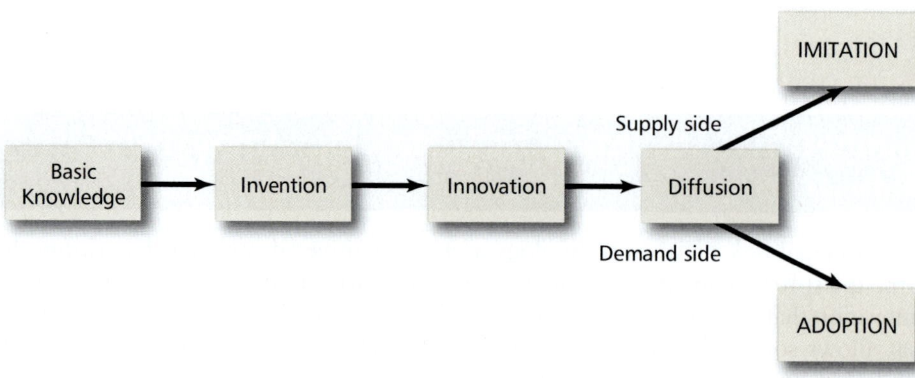

- The jet engine, employing Newtonian principles, was patented by Frank Whittle in 1930. The first commercial jet airliner, the DeHavilland Comet, flew in 1957. Two years later, the Boeing 707 was introduced.

Recently, the innovation cycle has speeded up:

- The mathematics of *fuzzy logic* were developed by Lofti Zadeh at Berkeley during the 1960s. By the early 1980s, Dr. Takeshi Yamakawa of the Kyushu Institute of Technology had registered patents for integrated circuits embodying fuzzy logic and in 1987 a series of fuzzy logic controllers for industrial machines was launched by Omron of Kyoto. By 1991, the world market for fuzzy logic controllers was estimated at $2 billion.[1]
- MP3, the audio file compression software, was developed at the Fraunhofer Institute in Germany in 1987; by the mid-1990s, the swapping of MP3 music files had taken off in U.S. college campuses and in 1998 the first MP3 player, Diamond Multimedia's *Rio*, was launched. Apple's iPod was introduced in 2001.

The Profitability of Innovation

"If a man can . . . make a better mousetrap than his neighbor, though he build his house in the woods, the world will make a beaten path to his door," claimed Emerson. Yet the inventors of new mousetraps, and other gadgets too, are more likely to be found at the bankruptcy courts than in the millionaires' playgrounds of the Caribbean. Certainly, innovation is no guarantor of fame and fortune, either for individuals or for companies. There is no consistent evidence that either R&D intensity or frequency of new product introductions are positively associated with profitability.[2]

The profitability of an innovation to the innovator depends on the value created by the innovation and the share of that value that the innovator is able to appropriate. The value created by an innovation is distributed among a number of different parties (see Figure 12.2). In the case of the personal computer, the innovators—MITS, Tandy, Apple, and Xerox—earned modest profits from their innovation. The imitators—IBM, Dell, Compaq, Acer, Toshiba and a host of other

FIGURE 12.2 Appropriation of value: who gets the benefits from innovation?

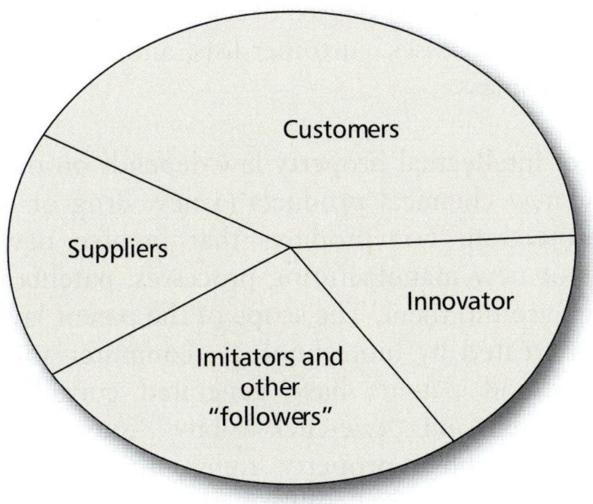

later entrants did somewhat better but their returns were overshadowed by the huge profits earned by the suppliers to the industry: Intel in microprocessors, Seagate in disk drives, Sharp in flat-panel displays and Microsoft in operating systems. However, because of strong competition in the industry, the greatest part of the value created by the personal computer was appropriated by customers, who typically paid prices for their PCs that were far below the value that they derived.[3]

The term *regime of appropriability* is used to describe the conditions that influence the distribution of returns to innovation. In a strong regime of appropriability, the innovator is able to capture a substantial share of the value created: NutraSweet artificial sweetener (developed by Searle, subsequently acquired by Monsanto), Pfizer's Viagra, and Pilkington's float glass process generated huge profits for their owners. In a weak regime of appropriability, other parties derive most of the value. In internet telephony (VoIP), ownership of technologies is diffused and standards are public, with the result that no players are likely to earn massive profits. Four factors are critical in determining the extent to which innovators are able to appropriate the value of their innovation: property rights, the tacitness and complexity of the technology, lead time and complementary resources.

Property Rights in Innovation Appropriating the returns on innovation depends, to a great extent, on the ability to establish property rights in the innovation. It was the desire to protect the returns to inventors that prompted the English Parliament to pass the 1623 Statute of Monopolies, which established the basis of patent law. Since then, the law has been extended to several areas of *intellectual property*, including:

- *Patents*—exclusive rights to a new and useful product, process, substance, or design. Obtaining a patent requires that the invention is novel, useful, and not excessively obvious. Patent law varies from country to country. In the U.S., a patent is valid for 17 years (14 for a design).
- *Copyrights*—exclusive production, publication, or sales rights to the creators of artistic, literary, dramatic, or musical works. Examples include articles, books, drawings, maps, photographs, and musical compositions.
- *Trademarks*—words, symbols, or other marks used to distinguish the goods or services supplied by a firm. In the U.S. and U.K., they are registered with the Patent Office. Trademarks provide the basis for brand identification.
- *Trade secrets*—offer a modest degree of legal protection for recipes, formulae, industrial processes, customer lists, and other knowledge acquired in the course of business.

The effectiveness of intellectual property law depends on the type of innovation being protected. For new chemical products (a new drug or plastic), patents can provide effective protection. For products that involve new configurations of existing components or new manufacturing processes, patents may fail to prevent rivals from innovating around them. The scope of the patent law has been extended to include life forms created by biotechnology, computer software, and business methods. Business method patents have generated considerable controversy—especially Amazon's patent on "one-click-to-buy" internet purchasing.[4] While patents and copyright establish property rights, their disadvantage (from the inventor's viewpoint) is that they make information public. Hence, companies may prefer secrecy to patenting as a means of protecting innovations.

In recent decades, companies have devoted increased attention to protecting and exploiting the economic value of their intellectual property. When Texas Instruments began exploiting its patent portfolio as a revenue source during the 1980s, the technology sector as a whole woke up to the value of its knowledge assets. During the 1990s, TI's royalty income exceeded its operating income from other sources. One outcome has been an upsurge in patenting. An average of 180 000 patents were granted by the U.S. Patent Office in each year between 2000 and 2008—well over double the annual rate during the 1980s.

Tacitness and Complexity of the Technology In the absence of effective legal protection the extent to which an innovation can be imitated by a competitor depends on the ease with which the technology can be comprehended and replicated. This depends, first, on the extent to which the technical knowledge is codifiable. *Codifiable knowledge*, by definition, is that which can be written down. Hence, if it is not effectively protected by patents or copyright, diffusion is likely to be rapid and the competitive advantage not sustainable. Financial innovations such as mortgage-backed securities and credit default swaps embody readily codifiable knowledge that can be copied very quickly. Similarly, Coca-Cola's recipe is codifiable and, in the absence of trade secret protection, is easily copied. Intel's designs for advanced microprocessors are codified and copyable; however, the processes for manufacturing these integrated circuits are based on deeply tacit knowledge.

The second key factor is *complexity*. Every new fashion, from the Mary Quant miniskirt of 1962 to Frida Giannini's "folkboho" look of 2009, involves simple, easy-to-copy ideas. Airbus's A380 and Nvidia's GT212 graphics chip represent entirely different challenges for the would-be imitator.

Lead Time Tacitness and complexity do not provide lasting barriers to imitation, but they do offer the innovator *time*. Innovation creates a *temporary* competitive advantage that offers a window of opportunity for the innovator to build on the initial advantage.

The innovator's *lead time* is the time it will take followers to catch up. The challenge for the innovator is to use initial lead time advantages to build the capabilities and market position to entrench industry leadership. Microsoft, Intel, and Cisco Systems were brilliant at exploiting lead time to build advantages in efficient manufacture, quality, and market presence. Conversely, British companies are notorious for having squandered their lead-time advantage in jet planes, radars, CT scanners, and genomics.

Lead time allows a firm to move down its learning curve ahead of followers. In new generations of microprocessors, Intel has traditionally been first to market, allowing it to move quickly down its experience curve, cut prices and so pressure the profit margins of its rival, AMD.

Complementary Resources Bringing new products and processes to market requires not just invention—it also requires the diverse resources and capabilities needed to finance, produce, and market the innovation. These are referred to as *complementary resources* (see Figure 12.3). Chester Carlson invented xerography but was unable for many years to bring his product to market because he lacked the complementary resources needed to develop, manufacture, market, distribute and service his invention. Conversely, Searle (and its later parent, Monsanto) was able to provide almost all the development, manufacturing, marketing and distribution resources needed to exploit its NutraSweet innovation. As a result, Carlson was able to appropriate only a tiny part of the value created by his invention of the plain-paper

FIGURE 12.3 Complementary resources

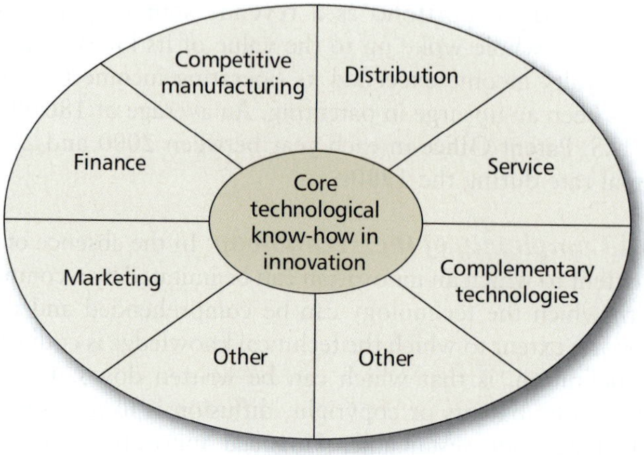

Xerox copier, whereas Searle/Monsanto was successful in appropriating a major part of the value created by its new artificial sweetener.

Complementary resources may be accessed through alliances with other firms—for example, biotech firms ally with large pharmaceutical companies for clinical trials, manufacture and marketing.[5] When an innovation and the complementary resources that support it are supplied by different firms, the division of value between them depends on their relative power. A key determinant of this is whether the complementary resources are *specialized* or *unspecialized*. Fuel cells may eventually displace internal combustion engines in many of the world's automobiles. However, the problem for the developers of fuel cells is that their success depends on automobile manufacturers making specialized investments in designing a whole new range of cars, service station owners providing specialized refueling facilities, and repair firms investing in training and new equipment. For fuel cells to be widely adopted will require that the benefits of the innovation are shared widely with the different providers of these complementary resources. Where complementary resources are generic, the innovator is in a much stronger position to capture value. Because Adobe Systems' Acrobat Portable Document Format (pdf) works with files created in almost any software application, Adobe is well positioned to capture most of the value created by its innovatory software product. However, one advantage of co-specialized complementary resources is that they raise barriers to imitation. Consider the threat that Linux presents to Microsoft Window's dominance of PC operating systems. Intel has adapted its microprocessors to the needs of Windows and most applications software is written to run on Windows, so the challenge for the Linux community is not just to develop a workable operating system but also to encourage the development of applications software and hardware that are compatible with the Linux operating system.

Which Mechanisms are Effective at Protecting Innovation?

How effective are these different mechanisms in protecting innovations? Table 12.1 shows that, despite considerable variation across industries, patent protection is of limited effectiveness as compared with lead-time, secrecy, and complementary

TABLE 12.1 The effectiveness of mechanisms for protecting innovation: percentage of innovations for which different mechanisms were considered effective

	Product innovations					Process innovations				
	Secrecy (%)	Patents (%)	Lead-time (%)	Sales/ service[1] (%)	Manufacturing (%)	Secrecy (%)	Patents (%)	Lead-time (%)	Sales/ service[1] (%)	Manufacturing[1] (%)
Food	59	18	53	40	51	56	16	42	30	47
Chemicals	53	37	49	45	41	54	20	27	28	42
Drugs	54	50	50	33	49	68	36	36	25	44
Computers	44	41	61	35	42	43	30	40	24	36
Electronic components	34	21	46	50	51	47	15	43	42	56
Telecom equipment	47	26	66	42	41	35	15	43	34	41
Medical equipment	51	55	58	52	49	49	34	45	32	50
All industries	51	35	53	43	46	51	23	38	31	43

[1]Shows the percentage of companies that reported that complementary capabilities in sales and service, and in manufacturing, were effective in protecting their innovations.

Source:

W. M. Cohen, R. R. Nelson, And J. P. Walsh, "Protecting their Intellectual Assets: Appropriability Conditions and Why us Manufacturing Firms Patent (or not)," NBER Working Paper No. W7552 (February 2000). © 2000. Reprinted by Permission of the Authors.

TABLE 12.2 Why do companies patent? (Responses by 674 US manufacturers)

	Product Innovations (%)	Process Innovations (%)
To prevent copying	95	77
For licensing revenue	28	23
To prevent law suits	59	47
To block others	82	64
For use in negotiations	47	43
To enhance reputation	48	34
To measure performance	6	5

Source: W. M. Cohen, R. R. Nelson, and J. P. Walsh, "Protecting their Intellectual Assets: Appropriability Conditions and Why us Manufacturing Firms Patent (Or Not)," NBER Working Paper No. W7552 (February 2000). Reproduced with permission.

manufacturing and sales/service resources. Indeed, since the late 1980s, the effectiveness of patents appeared to have declined despite the strengthening of patent law. Although patents are effective in increasing the lead time before competitors are able to bring imitative products to market, these gains tend to be small. The great majority of patented products and processes are duplicated within three years.[6]

Given the limited effectiveness of patents, why do firms continue to engage in patenting? As shown in Table 12.2, although protection from imitation is the principal motive, several others are also very important. In particular, much patenting activity appears to be strategic—it is directed towards blocking the innovation efforts of other companies and establishing property rights in technologies that can then be used in bargaining with other companies for access to their proprietary technologies. In semiconductors and electronics, cross-licensing arrangements—where one company gives access to its patents across a field of technology in exchange for access to another company's patents—are critical in permitting "freedom to design": the ability to design products that draw on technologies owned by different companies.[7]

Strategies to Exploit Innovation: How and When to Enter

Having established some of the key factors that determine the returns to innovation, let us consider some of the main questions concerning the formulation of strategies to manage technology and exploit innovation.

Alternative Strategies to Exploit Innovation

How should a firm maximize the returns to its innovation? A number of alternative strategies are available. Figure 12.4 orders them according to the size of the commitment of resources and capabilities that each requires. Thus, licensing requires little involvement by the innovator in subsequent commercialization; hence a limited

FIGURE 12.4 Alternative strategies for exploiting innovation

	Licensing	Outsourcing certain functions	Strategic alliance	Joint venture	Internal commercialization
Risk and return	Little investment risk but returns also limited. Risk that the licensee either lacks motivation or steals the innovation	Limits capital investment, but may create dependence on suppliers/partners	Benefits of flexibility. Risks of informal structure	Shares investment and risk. Risk of partner disagreement and culture clash	Biggest investment requirement and corresponding risks. Benefits of control
Resource requirements	Few	Permits external resources and capabilities to be accessed	Permits pooling of the resources and capabilities of more than one firm		Substantial requirements in terms of finance, production capability, marketing capability, distribution, etc.
Examples	Ericsson with its Bluetooth wireless technology; Dolby Labs with its sound reduction technology; Qualcomm and CDMA	Microsoft's XBox was largely designed by other companies and Flextronics does the manufacturing	Ballard's strategic alliance with DaimlerChrysler to develop fuel cells	Psion created Symbian as a joint venture with Ericsson, Nokia, and Motorola to develop the Symbian mobile phone operating system	Larry Page and Sergey Brin established Google Inc. to develop and market their Internet search technology

investment. Internal commercialization—possibly through creating a new enterprise or business unit—involves a much greater investment of resources and capabilities. In between there are various opportunities for collaboration with other companies. Joint ventures and strategic alliances typically involve substantial resource sharing between companies. On a more limited scale, specific activities may be outsourced to other companies.

The choice of strategy mode depends on two main sets of factors: the characteristics of the innovation, and the resources and capabilities of the firm.

Characteristics of the Innovation The extent to which a firm can establish clear property rights in an innovation critically determines the choice of strategy options. Licensing is only viable where ownership in an innovation is clearly defined by patent or copyrights. Thus, in pharmaceuticals, licensing is widespread because patents are clear and defensible. Many biotech companies engage only in R&D and license their drug discoveries to large pharmaceutical companies that possess the necessary complementary resources. Royalties from licensing its sound-reduction technologies accounted for 76% of Dolby Laboratories' 2006 revenues. Conversely, Steve Jobs and Steve Wozniak, developers of the Apple I and Apple II computers, had little option other than to go into business themselves—the absence of proprietary technology ruled out licensing as an option.

The advantages of licensing are, first, that it relieves the company of the need to develop the full range of complementary resources and capabilities needed for commercialization and, second, that it can allow the innovation to be commercialized quickly. If the lead time offered by the innovation is short, multiple licensing can allow for a fast global rollout. The problem, however, is that the success of the innovation in the market is totally dependent on the commitment and effectiveness of the licensees. James Dyson, the British inventor of the bagless vacuum cleaner, created his own company to manufacture and market his "dual cyclone" vacuum cleaners after failing to interest any major appliance company in a licensing deal for his technology.

Resources and Capabilities of the Firm As Figure 12.4 shows, different strategies require very different resources and capabilities. Hence, the choice of how to exploit an innovation depends critically upon the resources and capabilities that the innovator brings to the party. Startup firms possess few of the complementary resources and capabilities needed to commercialize their innovations. Inevitably they will be attracted to licensing or to accessing the resources of larger firms through outsourcing, alliances, or joint ventures. In several industries we observe a sequential process of innovation where different stages are conducted by different types of firm. In biotechnology and electronics, technology is typically developed initially by a small, technology-intensive startup, which then licenses to, or is acquired by, a larger established firm.

Conversely, large, established corporations, which can draw on their wealth of resources and capabilities, are better placed for internal commercialization. Companies such as Sony, DuPont, Siemens, Hitachi, and IBM have traditionally developed innovations internally—yet, as technologies evolve, converge and splinter, even these companies have increasingly resorted to joint ventures, strategic alliances, and outsourcing arrangements to access technical capabilities outside their corporate boundaries.

Ron Adner observes that innovation increasingly requires coordinated responses by multiple companies. Innovating firms need to identify and map their *innovation ecosystem,* then manage the interdependencies within it. The failed introduction of HDTV can be attributed to inadequate coordination among TV manufacturers, production studios and broadcasters.[8]

Timing Innovation: To Lead or to Follow?

To gain competitive advantage in emerging and technologically intensive industries, is it best to be a leader or a follower in innovation? As Table 12.3 shows, the evidence is mixed: in some products the leader has been the first to grab the prize, in others the leader has succumbed to the risks and costs of pioneering. Optimal timing of entry into an emerging industry and the introduction of new technology are complex issues. The advantage of being an early mover depends on the following factors:

- *The extent to which innovation can be protected by property rights or lead-time advantages.* If an innovation is appropriable through a patent, copyright, or lead-time advantage, there is advantage in being an early mover. This is especially the case where patent protection is important, as in pharmaceuticals. Notable patent races include that between Alexander Bell and Elisha Gray to patent the telephone (Bell got to the Patent Office a few hours before Gray),[9] and between Celera Inc. and the National Institutes of Health to patent the sequence of the human genome.[10]

TABLE 12.3 Leaders, followers, and success in emerging industries

Product	Innovator	Follower	The winner
Jet airliner	De Havilland (Comet)	Boeing (707)	Follower
Float glass	Pilkington	Corning	Leader
X-ray scanner	EMI	General Electric	Follower
Office PC	Xerox	IBM	Follower
VCRs	Ampex/Sony	Matsushita	Follower
Instant camera	Polaroid	Kodak	Leader
Pocket calculator	Bowmar	Texas Instruments	Follower
Microwave oven	Raytheon	Samsung	Follower
Fiber-optic cable	Corning	Many companies	Leader
Video games player	Atari	Nintendo/Sony	Followers
Disposable diaper	Procter & Gamble	Kimberley-Clark	Leader
Ink jet printer	IBM and Siemens	Hewlett Packard	Follower
Web browser	Netscape	Microsoft	Follower
MP3 music players	Diamond Multimedia	Apple (iPod)	Follower
Operating systems for mobile phones	Symbian	Microsoft	Leader
Laser printer	Xerox, IBM	Canon	Follower
Flash memory	Toshiba	Samsung, Intel	Followers
E-book reader	Sony (Digital Reader)	Amazon (Kindle)	Follower

Source: Based in Part on D. Teece, *the Competitive Challenge: Strategies for Industrial Innovation and Renewal* (Cambridge: Ballinger, 1987): 186–8.

- *The importance of complementary resources.* The more important complementary resources are in exploiting an innovation, the greater the costs and risks of pioneering. Several firms—from Clive Sinclair with a battery-driven car to General Motors with a fuel-cell car—have already failed in their attempts to develop and market an electric automobile. The problem for the pioneer is that the development costs are huge because of the need to orchestrate multiple technologies and establish self-sufficiency across a range of business functions. Followers are also favored by the fact that, as an industry develops, specialist firms emerge as suppliers of complementary resources. Thus, in pioneering the development of the British frozen foods industry, Unilever's Bird's Eye subsidiary had to set up an entire chain of cold stores and frozen distribution facilities. Later entrants were able to rely on the services of public cold stores and refrigerated trucking companies.
- *The potential to establish a standard.* As we shall see later in this chapter, some markets converge toward a technical standard. The greater the importance of technical standards, the greater the advantages of being an early mover in order to influence those standards and gain the market momentum needed to establish leadership. Once a standard has been set, displacing it becomes exceptionally difficult. IBM had little success with its OS/2 operating system against the entrenched position of Microsoft Windows. Linux has succeeded in taking market share from Windows. However, the main reason is that Linux is free!

Optimal timing depends also on the resources and capabilities that the individual firm has at its disposal. Different companies have different *strategic windows*—periods in time when their resources and capabilities are aligned with the opportunities available in the market. A small, technology-based firm may have no choice but to pioneer innovation: its opportunity is to grab first-mover advantage and then develop the necessary complementary resources before more powerful rivals appear. For the large, established firm with financial resources and strong production, marketing, and distribution capabilities, the strategic window is likely to be both longer and later. The risks of pioneering are greater for an established firm with a reputation and brands to protect, while to exploit its complementary resources effectively typically requires a more developed market. Consider the following examples:

- In personal computers, Apple was a pioneer, IBM a follower. The timing of entry was probably optimal for each. Apple's resources were its vision and its technology: only by pioneering could it hope to become a leading player. IBM had enormous strengths in manufacturing, distribution, and reputation. It could build competitive advantage even without a clear technological advantage. The key for IBM was to delay its entry until the time when the market had developed to the point where IBM's strengths could have their maximum impact.
- In the browser war between Netscape and Microsoft, Microsoft had the luxury of being able to follow the pioneer, Netscape. Microsoft's huge product development, marketing, and distribution capabilities, and—most important—its vast installed base of the Windows operating system allowed it to overhaul Netscape's initial lead.
- Although General Electric entered the market for CT scanners some four years after EMI, GE was able to overtake EMI within a few years because of its ability to apply vast technological, manufacturing, sales, and customer service capabilities within the field of medical electronics.

The most effective follower strategies are those that initiate a new product's transition from niche market to mass market. According to Markides and Geroski, successful first movers pioneer new products that embody new technologies and new functionality.[11] The opportunity for the fast-second entrant is to grow the niche market into a mass market by lowering cost and increasing quality. Timing is critical. Don Sull argues that a successful follower strategy requires "active waiting": a company needs to monitor market developments and assemble resources and capabilities while it prepares for large scale market entry.[12]

Managing Risks

Emerging industries are risky. There are two main sources of uncertainty:

- *Technological uncertainty* arises from the unpredictability of technological evolution and the complex dynamics through which technical standards and dominant designs are selected. Hindsight is always 20/20, but *ex ante* it is difficult to predict how technologies and the industries that deploy them will evolve.

- *Market uncertainty* relates to the size and growth rates of the markets for new products. When Xerox introduced its first plain-paper copier in 1959, Apple its first personal computer in 1977, or Sony its Walkman in 1979, none had any idea of the size of the potential market. Forecasting demand for new products is hazardous since all forecasting is based on some form of extrapolation or modeling based on past data. One approach is to use analogies.[13] Another is to draw on the combined insight and experience of experts through the *Delphi technique*.[14]

If reliable forecasting is impossible, the keys to managing risk are alertness and responsiveness to emerging trends together with limiting vulnerability to mistakes through avoiding large-scale commitments. Useful strategies for limiting risk include:

- *Cooperating with lead users.* During the early phases of industry development, careful monitoring of and response to market trends and customer requirements is essential to avoid major errors in technology and design. Von Hippel argues that lead users provide a source of leading market indicators, they can assist in developing new products and processes, and offer an early cash flow to fund development expenditures.[15] In computer software, "beta versions" are released to computer enthusiasts for testing. Nike has two sets of lead users: professional athletes who are trendsetters for athletic footwear and gang members and hip-hop artists who are at the leading edge of urban fashion trends. In communications and aerospace, government defense contracts play a crucial role in developing new technologies.[16]
- *Limiting risk exposure.* The financial risks of emerging industries can be mitigated by financial and operational practices that minimize a firm's exposure to adversity. By avoiding debt and keeping fixed costs low, a firm can lower its financial and operational gearing. Outsourcing and strategic alliance can also hold down capital investment and fixed costs.
- *Flexibility.* Uncertainty necessitates rapid responses to unpredicted events. Achieving such flexibility means keeping options open and delaying commitment to a specific technology until its potential becomes clear. Large, well-resourced companies have the luxury of pursuing multiple strategic options (see Strategy Capsule 12.1).

STRATEGY CAPSULE 12.1

Keeping your Options Open: Microsoft in Operating Systems

In 1988, as I wandered about the floor of Comdex, the computer industry's vast annual trade show, I could feel the anxiety among the participants. Since the birth of the IBM PC, six years earlier, Microsoft's Disk Operating System (DOS) had been the de facto standard for PCs. But DOS was now starting to age. Everyone wanted to know what would replace it.

Apple Computer, at the peak of its powers, had one of the largest booths showcasing the brilliantly graphical Macintosh operating system . . . Two different alliances of major companies, including AT&T, HP, and Sun Microsystems, offered graphical versions of Unix . . . And IBM was touting its new OS/2.

Amid the uncertainty, there was something very curious about the Microsoft booth . . . [which] resembled a Middle Eastern bazaar. In one corner, the company was previewing its highly criticized Windows system . . . In another, Microsoft touted its latest release of DOS. Elsewhere it was displaying OS/2, which it had developed with IBM. In addition, Microsoft was demonstrating new releases of Word and Excel that ran on Apple's Mac. Finally, in a distant corner, Microsoft displayed SCO Unix . . .

"What am I supposed to make of this?" grumbled a corporate buyer standing next to me. Columnists wrote that Microsoft was adrift, that its chairman and COO, Bill Gates, had no strategy.

Although the outcome of this story is now well known, to anyone standing on the Comdex floor in 1988 it wasn't obvious which operating system would win. In the face of this uncertainty, Microsoft followed the only robust strategy: betting on every horse.

Source: E. D. Beinhocker, "Robust Adaptive Strategies," *Sloan Management Review* (Spring 1999): 95–106. © 1999 Massachusetts Institute of Technology.

Competing for Standards

In the previous chapter, I noted that the establishment of standards is a key event in industry evolution. The emergence of the digital, networked economy has made standards increasingly important, and companies that own and influence industry standards are capable of earning returns that are unmatched by any other type of competitive advantage. The shareholder value generated by Microsoft and Intel from the "Wintel" PC standard, by Qualcomm from its CDMA digital wireless communications technology, and Cisco from its leadership role in setting internet protocol standards are examples of this potential. Table 12.4 lists several companies whose success is closely associated with their control of standards within a particular product category.

Types of Standard

A standard is a format, an interface, or a system that allows interoperability. It is adherence to standards that allows us to browse millions of different web pages, that ensures the light bulbs made by any manufacturer will fit any manufacturer's lamps, and that keeps the traffic moving in Los Angeles (most of the time). Standards can be *public* or *private*.

- Public (or *open*) standards are those that are available to all either free or for a nominal charge. Typically they do not involve any privately owned intellectual property, or the IP owners make access free (such as Linux). Public standards are set by public bodies and industry associations. Thus, the GSM mobile phone standard was set by the European Telecom Standards Institute. Internet protocols—standards governing internet addressing and

TABLE 12.4 Examples of companies that own de facto industry standards

Company	Product category	Standard
Microsoft	PC operating systems	Windows
Intel	PC microprocessors	x86 series
Matsushita	Videocassette recorders	VHS system
Sony/Philips	Compact disks	CD-ROM format
ARM (Holdings)	Microprocessors for mobile devices	ARM architecture
Sun Microsystems	Programming language for web apps	Java
Rockwell and 3Com	56K modems	V90
Qualcomm	Digital cellular wireless communication	CDMA
Adobe Systems	Common file format for creating and viewing documents	Acrobat Portable Document Format
Bosch	Antilock braking systems	ABS and TCS (Traction Control System)
Symbian	Operating systems for mobile phones	Symbian OS
Sony	High definition DVD	Blu-ray

routing—are mostly public. They are governed by several international bodies, including the internet Engineering Task Force.

- Private (*proprietary*) standards are those where the technologies and designs are owned by companies or individuals. If I own the technology that becomes a standard, I can embody the technology in a product that others buy (Microsoft Windows) or license the technology to others who wish to use it (Qualcomm's CDMA).

Standards can also be classified according to who sets them. *Mandatory standards* are set by government and have the force of law behind them. They include standards relating to automobile safety and construction specifications and to TV broadcasting. *De facto standards* emerge through voluntary adoption by producers and users. Table 12.4 gives examples.

A problem with *de facto* standards is that they may take a long time to emerge, resulting in duplication of investments and delayed development of the market. It was 40 years before a standard railroad gauge was agreed in the U.S.[17] One reason for the slow transition of wireless telecoms in the U.S. from analog to digital technology was continuing competition between TDMA and CDMA standards. By contrast, Europe officially adopted GSM (a close relative of TDMA) in 1992.[18] Delayed emergence of a standard may kill the technology altogether. The failure of quadraphonic sound to displace stereophonic sound during the 1970s resulted from incompatible technical standards, which inhibited audio manufacturers, record companies and consumers from investing in the technology.[19]

Why Standards Appear: Network Externalities

Standards emerge in markets that are subject to *network externalities*. A network externality exists whenever the value of a product to an individual customer depends on the number of other users of that product. The classic example of network externality is the telephone. Since there is little satisfaction to be gained from talking to oneself on the telephone, the value of a telephone to each user depends on the number of other users connected to the same telephone system. This is different from most products. When I pour myself a glass of Glenlivet after a couple of exhausting MBA classes, my enjoyment is independent of how many other people in the world are also drinking Glenlivet. Indeed, some products may have *negative* network externalities—the value of the product is less if many other people purchase the same product. If I spend $3000 on an Armani silver lamé tuxedo and find that half my colleagues at the faculty Christmas party are wearing the same jacket, my satisfaction is lessened.

Network externalities do not require everyone to use the same product or even the same technology, but rather that the different products are *compatible* with one another through some form of common interface. In the case of wireless telephone service, it doesn't matter (as far as network access is concerned) whether I purchase service from AT&T, Nextel, or T-Mobile because compatibility between each network allows connectivity. Similarly with railroads; if I am transporting coal from Wyoming to Boston, my choice of railroad company is not critical. Unlike in the 1870s, every railroad company now uses a standard gauge and is required to give "common carrier" access to other companies' rolling stock.

Network externalities arise from several sources:

- *Products where users are linked to a network.* Telephones, railroad systems, and email instant messaging groups are networks where users are linked together. Applications software, whether spreadsheet programs or video games, also link users—they can share files and play games interactively. User-level externalities may also arise through social identification. I watch *American Idol* and the Hollywood Oscar presentations on TV not because I enjoy them, but so that I have something to talk to my colleagues about in the faculty common room.[20]
- *Availability of complementary products and services.* Where products are consumed as systems, the availability of complementary products and services depends on the number of customers for that system. Apple's key problem in the computer market is that, because the Macintosh accounts for only 9% of the installed base of personal computers, few leading software firms are writing Mac-based applications. I choose to drive a Ford Focus rather than a Ferrari Testarossa because I know that, should I break down 200 miles from Bismarck, North Dakota, spare parts and a repair service will be more readily available.
- *Economizing on switching costs.* By purchasing the product or system that is most widely used, there is less chance that I shall have to bear the costs of switching. By using Microsoft Office rather than Lotus SmartSuite, it is more likely that I will avoid the costs of retraining and file conversion when I become a visiting professor at another university.

The implication of network externalities is that they create *positive feedback.* Once a technology or system gains market leadership, it attracts a growing proportion of new buyers. Conversely, once market leadership is lost, a downward spiral is likely. This process is called *tipping*: once a certain threshold is reached, cumulative forces become unstoppable.[21] The result is a tendency toward a *winner-takes-all* market. The markets subject to significant network externalities tend to be dominated by a single supplier (Microsoft in PC operating systems and office applications, eBay in internet auctions).

Once established, technical and design standards tend to be highly resilient. Standards are difficult to displace due to learning effects and collective lock-in. Learning effects cause the dominant technology and design to be continually improved and refined. Even where the existing standard is inherently inferior, switching to a superior technology may not occur because of collective lock in. The classic case is the QWERTY typewriter layout. Its 1873 design was based on the need to *slow* the speed of typing to prevent typewriter keys from jamming. Although the jamming problem was soon solved, the QWERTY layout has persisted, despite the patenting in 1932 of the more ergonomic Dvorak Simplified Keyboard (DSK).[22]

Winning Standards Wars

In markets subject to network externalities, control over standards is the primary basis for competitive advantage. Sony and Apple are unusual in that they lost their standards wars (in VCRs and personal computers, respectively) but returned as winners in other markets. Most of losers in standards wars—Lotus in spreadsheet software, Netscape in browsers, WordPerfect in word processing software—become mere footnotes in the history of technology. What can we learn from these and other standards wars about designing a winning strategy in markets subject to network externalities?

The first key issue is to determine whether we are competing in a market that will converge around a single technical standard. This requires a careful analysis of the presence and sources of network externalities.

The second strategic issue in standards setting is recognizing the role of positive feedback: the technology that can establish early leadership will rapidly gain momentum. Building a "bigger bandwagon," according to Shapiro and Varian,[23] requires the following:

- *Before you go to war, assemble allies.* You'll need the support of consumers, suppliers of complements, even your competitors. Not even the strongest companies can afford to go it alone in a standards war.
- *Preempt the market*—enter early, achieve fast-cycle product development, make early deals with key customers and adopt penetration pricing.
- *Manage expectations.* The key to managing positive feedback is to convince customers, suppliers and the producers of complementary goods that you will emerge as the victor. These expectations become a self-fulfilling prophecy. The massive pre-launch promotion and publicity built up by Sony prior to the American and European launch of PlayStation 2 in October 2000 was an effort to convince consumers, retailers and game developers that the product would be the blockbuster consumer electronics product of

the new decade, thereby stymieing Sega and Nintendo's efforts to establish their rival systems.

The lesson that has emerged from the classic standards battles of the past is that in order to create initial leadership and maximize positive feedback effects, a company must share the value created by the technology with other parties (customers, competitors, complementors, and suppliers). If a company attempts to appropriate too great a share of the value created, it may well fail to build a big enough bandwagon to gain market leadership (see Strategy Capsule 12.2). Thus, recent standards battles involve broad alliances, where the owner enlists the support of complementors and would-be competitors. In the 2006–8 struggle between Sony (Blu-ray) and Toshiba (HD-DVD) each camp recruited movie studios, software firms and producers of computers and consumer electronics using various inducements—including direct cash payments. The defection of Warner Brothers to the Sony camp was critical to the market tipping suddenly in Sony's favor. However, it appears that all the financial gains from owning the winning DVD standard were dissipated by the costs of the war.[24]

Achieving compatibility with existing products is a critical issue in standards battles. Advantage typically goes to the competitor that adopts an *evolutionary strategy* (i.e., offers backward compatibility) rather than one that adopts a *revolutionary strategy*.[25] Microsoft Windows won the PC war against the Apple Macintosh for many reasons. Both companies offered an operating system with a graphical user interface. However, while Windows was designed for compatibility with the DOS operating system, the Apple Mac was incompatible both with DOS and the Apple II. Similarly, a key advantage of the Sony PlayStation 2 over the Sega Dreamcast and Nintendo Cube was its compatibility with the PlayStation 1.

What are the key resources needed to win a standards war? Shapiro and Varian emphasize the following:

- control over an installed base of customers;
- owning intellectual property rights in the new technology;
- the ability to innovate in order to extend and adapt the initial technological advance;
- first-mover advantage;
- strength in complements (e.g., Intel has preserved its standard in microprocessors by promoting standards in buses, chipsets, graphics controllers, and interfaces between motherboards and CPUs);
- reputation and brand name.[26]

As companies become more familiar with the dynamics of standards competition, they are launching their strategic initiatives earlier—long before product release dates. As a result, standards wars are increasingly about the management of expectations. Companies are also more alert to the emergence of tipping points. As a result, standards wars are being resolved quicker: in high definition DVDs a mere 19 months elapsed between Toshiba's launch of its HD-DVD and its withdrawal announcement.

STRATEGY CAPSULE 12.2

Building a Bandwagon by Sharing Value: Lessons from VCRs and PCs

Profiting from standards requires, first, setting the standard; second, retaining a proprietary interest in the standard in order to appropriate part of its value. There is a tradeoff between the two—the more value a company tries to appropriate, the greater the difficulty in building early support for its technology. Consider the standards wars in VCRs and PCs:

- In VCRs, Matsushita's VHS format won against Sony's Betamax format not because of the technical superiority of VHS, but—in contrast to Sony's tight proprietary control of Betamax—Masushita licensed its VHS system to Sharp, Philips, GE, RCA, and others, allowing it to gain market leadership.
- In personal computers, IBM was highly successful in setting the standard, partly because it did not restrict access to its technology. Its product specifications were openly available to "clone makers," and its suppliers (including Microsoft and Intel) were free to supply them with microprocessors and the MS-DOS operating system. IBM was remarkably successful at setting the standard, but failed to appropriate much value because it retained no significant proprietary interest in the standard—it was Intel and Microsoft that owned the key intellectual property. For Apple, the situation was the reverse. It kept tight control over its Macintosh operating system and product architecture, it earned high margins, but it forfeited the opportunity to set the industry standard.

The tradeoff between market acceptance of a technology and appropriating the returns to a technology is shown above. Realizing the lessons of these two epic contests, the owners of technical standards have forfeited more and more value to complementors, competitors, and customers in order to establish market leadership. In the browser war of 1995–8, both Netscape (Navigator) and Microsoft (Explorer) ended up giving away their products.

Companies are now seeking ways to reconcile market acceptance with value appropriation. Adobe gives away its Acrobat Reader to broaden the user base, but charges for the software needed to create pdf documents.

Sources: *The World VCR Industry,* Case No. 9-387-098 (Boston: Harvard Business School, 1990); *Apple Computer—1992,* Case No. 9-792-081 (Boston: Harvard Business School, 1994); *The Browser Wars, 1994-1998,* Case No. 9-798-094 (Boston: Harvard Business School, 1998).

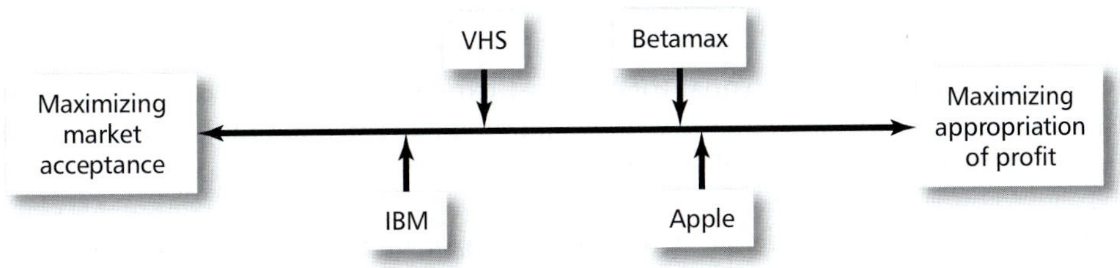

Implementing Technology Strategies: Creating the Conditions for Innovation

As we have noted previously, strategy formulation cannot be separated from its implementation. Nowhere is this more evident than in technology-intensive businesses.

Our analysis so far has taught us about the potential for generating competitive advantage from innovation and about the design of technology-based strategies but has said little about the conditions under which innovation is achieved. The danger is that strategic analysis can tell us a great deal about making money out of innovation, but this isn't much use if we cannot generate innovation in the first place. While innovation requires certain resources—people, facilities, information, and time—there is no predetermined relationship between R&D input and innovation output.[27] Clearly the productivity of R&D depends heavily on the organizational conditions that foster innovation. Hence, the crucial challenge facing firms in emerging and technology-based industries is to create the conditions conducive to innovation.

To address this issue, we must return to the critical distinction between invention and innovation. While these activities are complementary, they require different resources and different organizational conditions. While invention depends on creativity, innovation requires collaboration and cross-functional integration.

Managing Creativity

The Conditions for Creativity Invention is an act of creativity requiring knowledge and imagination. The creativity that drives invention is typically an individual act that establishes a meaningful relationship between concepts or objects that had not previously been related. This reconceptualizing can be triggered by accidents: an apple falling on Isaac Newton's head or James Watt observing a kettle boiling. Creativity is associated with particular personality traits. Creative people tend to be curious, imaginative, adventurous, assertive, playful, self-confident, risk taking, reflective, and uninhibited.[28]

Individual creativity also depends on the organizational environment in which they work—this is as true for the researchers and engineers at Amgen and Google as it was for the painters and sculptors of the Florentine and Venetian schools. Few great works of art or outstanding inventions are the products of solitary geniuses. Creativity is stimulated by human interaction: the productivity of R&D laboratories depends critically on the communication networks that the engineers and scientists establish.[29] An important catalyst of interaction is *play*, which creates an environment of inquiry, liberates thought from conventional constraints, and provides the opportunity to establish new relationships by rearranging ideas and structures at a safe distance from reality. The essence of play is that it permits unconstrained forms of experimentation.[30] The potential for low-cost experimentation has expanded vastly thanks to advances in computer modeling and simulation that permit prototyping and market research to be undertaken speedily and virtually.[31]

Organizing for Creativity Creativity requires management systems that are quite different from those appropriate for efficiency. In particular, creatively oriented people tend to be responsive to distinctive types of incentive. They desire to work in an egalitarian culture with enough space and resources to provide the opportunity to be spontaneous, experience freedom, and have fun in the performance of a task that, they feel, makes a difference to the strategic performance of the firm. Praise, recognition and opportunities for education and professional growth are also more important than assuming managerial responsibilities.[32] Nurturing the drive to create may require a degree of freedom and flexibility that conflicts with conventional HR practices. At Google engineers have considerable discretion as to which project they join.

Organizational environments conducive to creativity tend to be both nurturing and competitive. Creativity requires a work context that is secure but not cozy. Dorothy Leonard points to the merits of *creative abrasion* within innovative teams—fostering innovation through the interaction of different personalities and perspectives. Managers must resist the temptation to clone in favor of embracing diversity of cognitive and behavioral characteristics within work groups—creating "*whole brain teams*."[33] Exploiting diversity may require constructive conflict. Microsoft's development team meetings are renowned for open criticism and intense disagreement. Such conflict can spur progress towards better solutions.

Table 12.5 contrasts some characteristics of innovative organizations compared with those designed for operational efficiency.

From Invention to Innovation: The Challenge of Integration

Balancing Creativity and Commercial Direction For creativity to create value—both for the company and for society—it must be directed and harnessed. Balancing creative freedom with discipline and integration is a key issue to companies such as Apple and Google which position themselves on the leading edge of

TABLE 12.5 The characteristics of "operating" and "innovating" organizations

	Operating organization	Innovating organization
Structure	Bureaucratic. Specialization and division of labor. Hierarchical control. Defined organizational boundaries.	Flat organization without hierarchical control. Task-oriented project teams. Fuzzy organizational boundaries.
Processes	Emphasis on eliminating variation (e.g. six-sigma). Top-down control. Tight financial controls.	Emphasis on enhancing variation. Loose controls to foster idea generation. Flexible strategic planning and financial control.
Reward systems	Financial compensation, promotion up the hierarchy, power, and status symbols.	Autonomy, recognition, equity participation in new ventures
People	Recruitment and selection based on the needs of the organization structure for specific skills: functional and staff specialists, general managers, and operatives.	Key need is for idea generators that combine required technical knowledge with creative personality traits. Managers must act as sponsors and orchestrators.

Source: Based on J. K. Galbraith and R. K. Kazanjian, *Strategy Implementation: Structure, Systems and Processes,* 2nd Edn (St. Paul, Mn: West, 1986).

innovation. The problem is especially acute in media companies: "The two cultures—of the ponytail and the suit—are a world apart, and combustible together."[34] Many creative companies have been formed by frustrated innovators leaving established companies. Disney's 2006 acquisition of Pixar was motivated by its desire to reinvigorate its animated movies. Yet Pixar's John Lasseter, who was appointed creative head of Disney's animation studio had been fired from Disney 20 years earlier for his advocacy of computer animation![35] Conversely, HBO's remarkable run of successful TV series between 1999 and 2007 (*The Sopranos*, *Sex in the City*, *The Wire* and *Six Feet Under*) reveals a remarkable ability to mesh creativity with commercial acuity.

The critical linkage between creative flair and commercial success is *market need.* Few important inventions have been the result of spontaneous creation by technologists; almost all have resulted from grappling with practical problems. The invention of the Xerox copying process (xerography) by Chester Carlson, a patent attorney, was inspired by his frustration with the tedious task of making multiple copies of patent applications for submission to the U.S. Patent Office. The old adage that "necessity is the mother of invention" explains why customers are such fertile sources of innovation—they are most acutely involved with matching existing products and services to their needs.[36] Involving customers in the innovation process is an initial stage in the move towards *open innovation* (which I will say more about below).

Organizational Approaches to the Management of Innovation The key organizational challenge is the one that we explored back in Chapter 7—that of reconciling *differentiation* and *integration.* As we have already noted, creative activities require different organizational structures and management systems than operational activities. Yet, the commercialization of new technology—developing and introducing new products and implementing new processes—requires the integration of creativity and technological expertise with capabilities in production, marketing, finance, distribution, and customer support. Achieving such integration is difficult. Tension between the operating and the innovating parts of organizations is inevitable. Innovation upsets established routines and threatens the status quo. The more stable the operating and administrative side of the organization, the greater the resistance to innovation. A classic example was the opposition by the U.S. naval establishment to continuous-aim firing, a process that offered huge improvements in gunnery accuracy.[37]

As innovation has become an increasing priority for established corporations, so chief executives have sought to emulate the flexibility, creativity, and entrepreneurial spirit of technology-based startups. Organizational initiatives aimed at stimulating new product development and the exploitation of new technologies include the following:

- *Cross-functional product development teams.* Cross-functional product development teams have proven to be highly effective mechanisms for integrating creativity with functional effectiveness. Conventional approaches to new product development involved a sequential process that began in the corporate research lab then went "over the wall" to engineering, manufacturing, finance, and so on. Japanese companies pioneered autonomous product development teams staffed by specialists seconded from different departments with leadership from a "heavyweight" team manager who was able to protect the team from undue corporate influence.[38] Such teams have proven effective in deploying a broad range of specialist knowledge and, most importantly, integrating that knowledge flexibility and quickly—for example, through rapid prototyping and concurrent engineering.[39]

- *Product champions* provide a means, first, for incorporating individual creativity within organizational processes and, second, for linking invention to subsequent commercialization. The key is to permit the individuals who are sources of creative ideas to lead the teams which develop those ideas—but also to allow this leadership to continue through into the commercialization phases. Companies that are consistently successful in innovation have the ability to design organizational processes that capture, direct and exploit individuals' drive for achievement and success and their commitment to their innovations. The rationale for creating product champions is that these committed individuals can overcome resistance to change within the organization and generate the enthusiasm that attracts the involvement of others and forges cross-functional integration. Schön's study of 15 major innovations concluded that: "the new idea either finds a champion or dies."[40] A British study of 43 matched pairs of successful and unsuccessful innovations similarly concluded that a key factor distinguishing successful innovation was the presence of a "business innovator" to exert entrepreneurial leadership.[41] 3M Corporation has a long tradition of using product champions to develop new product ideas and grow them into new businesses (see Strategy Capsule 12.3).

STRATEGY CAPSULE 12.3

Innovation at 3M: The Role of the Product Champion

START LITTLE AND BUILD

We don't look to the president or the vice-president for R&D to say, all right, on Monday morning 3M is going to get into such-and-such a business. Rather, we prefer to see someone in one of our laboratories, or marketing, or manufacturing units bring forward a new idea that he's been thinking about. Then, when he can convince people around him, including his supervisor, that he's got something interesting, we'll make him what we call a "project manager" with a small budget of money and talent, and let him run with it. Throughout all our 60 years of history here, that has been the mark of success. Did you develop a new business? The incentive? Money, of course. But that's not the key. The key . . . is becoming the general manager of a new business . . . having such a hot project that management just has to become involved whether it wants to or not. (Bob Adams, Vice-President for R&D, 3M Corporation)

SCOTCHLITE

Someone asked the question, "Why didn't 3M make glass beads, because glass beads were going to find increasing use on the highways?"

. . . I had done a little working in the mineral department on trying to color glass beads and had learned a little about their reflecting properties. And, as a little extra-curricular activity, I'd been trying to make luminous house numbers.

Well, this question and my free-time lab project combined to stimulate me to search out where glass beads were being used on the highway. We found a place where beads had been sprinkled on the highway and we saw that they did provide a more visible line at night . . . From there, it was only natural for us to conclude that, since we were a coating company, and probably knew more than anyone else about putting particles onto a web, we ought to be able to coat glass beads very accurately on a piece of paper.

So, that's what we did. The first reflective tape we made was simply a double-coated tape—glass beads sprinkled on one side and an adhesive on the other. We took some out here in St. Paul and, with the cooperation of the highway department, put some down. After the first frost came, and then a thaw, we found we didn't know as much about adhesives under all weather conditions as we thought . . .

We looked around inside the company for skills in related areas. We tapped knowledge that existed in our sandpaper business on how to make waterproof sandpaper. We drew on the expertise of our roofing people who knew something about exposure. We reached into our adhesive and tape division to see how we could make the tape stick to the highway better.

The resulting product became known as "Scotchlite." Its principal application was in reflective signs; only later did 3M develop the market for highway marking. The originator of the product, Harry Heltzer, interested the head of the New Products Division in the product, and he encouraged Heltzer to go out and sell it. Scotchlite was a success and Heltzer became the general manager of the division set up to produce and market it.

Source: "The Technical Strategy of 3M: Start More Little Businesses and More Little Businesses," *Innovation* 5 (1969).

- *Buying innovation.* Recognition that small, technology-intensive startups have advantages in the early stages of the innovation process, while large corporations have superior capabilities, has encouraged large companies to enhance their technological performance by acquiring innovation from other firms. Such acquisition may involve licensing, outright purchase of patents, or acquiring the whole company. In biotechnology, pharmaceutical companies have pioneered this outsourcing of innovation. In addition to licensing drug patents, signing marketing agreements, and acquiring specialist biotech firms (these include Genentech by Roche in 2009, ICOS by Eli Lily in 2007, Chiron by Novartis in 2006, Scious by Johnson & Johnson in 2003), pharmaceutical companies have formed research alliances with biotech specialists.[42] In telecom equipment, Cisco Systems built its leading position in internet protocol switching technologies through acquiring small technology intensive firms—55 of them between 1993 and 2000 alone.[43]
- *Open innovation.* The shift from vertically integrated systems of innovation, where companies develop their own technologies in house then exploit them internally, to more market-based systems, where companies buy in technology while also licensing out their own technologies, has given way to ideas of *open innovation.* As innovation increasingly requires the integration

of multiple technologies often from traditionally separate scientific areas, so firms have been forced to look wider in their sourcing technology and in sharing knowhow and ideas. Evidence that external linkages promote innovation has reinforced firms' desire to seek technological knowledge from beyond their own borders.[44] Open innovation requires creating a network of collaborative relationships that comprises licensing deals, component outsourcing, joint research, collaborative product development, and informal problem solving and exchanges of ideas. Strategy Capsule 12.4 outlines Procter & Gamble's approach to open innovation.

STRATEGY CAPSULE 12.4

Procter & Gamble's Open Innovation Initiative

In 2000 it became clear that P&G's internally focused approach to innovation and new product development was incapable of delivering the growth targets that the company had set itself. Despite a research staff numbering 7500, P&G estimated that for every one of its on research scientists there were probably 200 outside the company with the potential to contribute to P&G's development efforts. When CEO A. G. Laffey challenged the company to obtain 50% of its innovations from outside the company, the quest for a new innovation model began.

P&G's *Connect and Develop* innovation model seeks to "identify promising ideas throughout the world and apply our own R&D, manufacturing, marketing and purchasing capabilities to them to create better and cheaper products, faster."

The starting point is to identify what P&G is looking for. The approach was to avoid "blue sky" innovation and seek ideas that had already been successfully embodied in a product, a prototype or a technology. To focus the search each business was asked to identify its top ten customer needs. These included: "reduce wrinkles, improve skin texture and tone . . . softer paper products with higher wet strength." These needs were then translated into specific technical requirements: for example, biotechnology solutions that permit detergents to perform well at low temperatures. Priorities are then reordered by identifying initiatives which fit with existing areas of brand strength ("adjacencies") and those which have permit strengthening of P&G's strategically important areas of technology ("technology game boards").

P&G's innovation network comprises a number of organizations:

- Within P&G, 70 *technology entrepreneurs* are responsible for developing external contacts and exploring for innovation in particular localities and with a focus around particular product or technology area.
- *Suppliers.* P&G has an IT platform that allows it to share technology briefs with its suppliers. This is complemented by regular meetings between senior P&G executives and senior executives at individual suppliers which explore mutual development opportunities.
- *Technology brokers.* P&G is a member (in some cases a founder member) of several prominent technology brokering networks. These include *NineSigma* which links companies with universities, private

labs, government bodies, consultants and other potential solutions providers; *Innocentive,* which brokers solutions to science-based problems; *YourEncore,* a network of retired scientists and engineers; and *Yet2.com,* an online marketplace for intellectual capital.

These networks generate an enormous flow of suggestions and proposals that are initially screened and disseminated through P&G's *Eureka* online catalog. It is then up to executives within the business groups to identify interesting proposals, to pursue these with the external provider through P&G's External Business Development group, and to then to take move the initiative into their own product development process.

By 2005, 35% of P&G's new product launches had their origins outside the company. Some of P&G's most successful new products—including Swiffer cleaning cloths, Olay Regeneration, and Crest Spinbrush—had been initiated by outsiders.

Source: L. Huston and N. Sakkab, "Connect and Develop: Inside Procter & Gamble's New Model for Innovation" *Harvard Business Review* (March 2006): 58–66. Reproduced with permission.

- *Corporate incubators* are business developments established to fund and nurture new businesses based upon technologies that have been developed internally but have limited applications within a company's established businesses. Corporate incubators became very popular during the IT boom at the end of the 1990s when companies saw the potential to generate substantial value from establishing then spinning off new tech-based ventures.[45] Despite a sound strategic and organizational logic, few major companies have achieved sustained success from the incubator units that they established and among the successful ones, many have been sold to venture capital firms. A key problem, according to Gary Hamel, is that: "Many corporate incubators became orphanages for unloved ideas that had no internal support or in-house sponsorship."[46] Despite their uneven track record, several leading companies have experienced considerable success in introducing company-wide processes for developing new businesses based upon internally generated innovations. Strategy Capsule 12.5 outlines the approaches of IBM and Cisco Systems.

STRATEGY CAPSULE 12.5

Incubating innovation at IBM and Cisco Systems

IBM uses *Innovation Jam*—a massive online brainstorming process—to generate, select, and develop new business ideas. The 2006 Jam was based upon an initial identification of 25 technology clusters grouped into six broad categories. Web sites were built for each technology cluster and, for a 72-hour period, IBM employees, their families and friends, suppliers and customers from all around the world were invited to contribute ideas for innovations based on these technologies. The 150 000 participants generated vast and diverse sets of suggestions that were subject to text mining software and review by 50 senior executives and technical specialists who worked in nine separate teams to identify promising ideas. The next phase of the Jam subjected the selected innovation ideas to comments and review by the online community. This was followed by a further review process in which the 10 best proposals were selected and a budget of $100 million was allocated to their development. The selected business ideas included a real-time foreign language translation service, smart healthcare payment systems, IT applications to environmental projects, and 3-D internet. The new businesses were begun as incubator projects and were then transferred to one or other of IBM's business groups. As well as divisional links, the new ventures were also subject to monthly review by IBM's corporate top management.

Cisco Systems created its *Emerging Technology Business Group* with the goal of creating 20 new ventures by 2012. Within 18 months, 400 ideas for new businesses had been posted on the Cisco wiki and the Emerging Technology Business Group had begun developing several of these suggestions including *TelePresence*, a video surveillance security system and an IP interoperability and collaboration systems server for emergency services. By 2008 *TelePresence* was established as a regular business group. Like IBM's *Innovation Jam* a key feature of Cisco's incubator model is its close linkage with the rest of the company: the Emerging Technology Group is part of Cisco's R&D organization and is subject to close involvement by Cisco's senior management—including CEO John Chambers.

Sources: O. M. Bjelland and R. C. Wood, "An Inside View of IBM's Innovation Jam" MIT Sloan Management Review (Fall 2008): 32–43. Tom Sanders "Cisco Reinvents the Corporate Incubator" (July 27, 2007): http://www.vnunet.com/vnunet/news/2194961/ cisco-reinvents-corporate, accessed 6 July, 2009.

Summary

In emerging and technology-based industries, nurturing and exploiting innovation is the fundamental source of competitive advantage and the focus of strategy formulation. Yet the basic tools of strategy analysis are the same as those that we have already encountered in this book. The fundamental strategic issues we are concerned with include the drivers of competition in these markets, the resources and capabilities through which a firm can establish competitive advantage, and the design of structures and systems to implement strategy.

Yet, the unpredictability and instability of these industries mean that strategic decisions in technology-driven industries have a very special character. The remarkable dynamics of these industries mean that difference between massive value creation and ignominious failure may be the result of small errors of timing or technological choices.

In technology-based industries, traditional approaches to strategy based upon forecasting and detailed planning are inadequate. The combination of speed and unpredictability of change means that effective strategies are those which combine clarity of vision with flexibility and responsiveness. The companies that have succeeded in emerging and technology based industries are those that recognized most clearly the strategic characteristics of their industries and adapted most effectively to them. In industries that have been turned upside-down by technological change—whether telecommunications equipment, medical imaging, information storage, or sports equipment—it is companies that have understood the sources of competitive advantage and assembled the resources and capabilities needed to exploit them that have emerged as winners.

I hope to have persuaded you that, despite the turbulence and uncertainty of these industries, there are analytic principles that can guide us towards strategies which do not guarantee success but certainly improve the odds. For example, our learning has included:

- evaluating an innovation's potential to generate profit;
- assessing the relative merits of licensing, alliances, joint ventures and internal development as alternative strategies for exploiting an innovation;
- identifying the factors that determine the comparative advantages of being a leader or a follower in innovation.

This chapter also pointed to the central importance of strategy implementation in determining success. The key to successful innovation is not resource allocation decisions, but creating the structure, integration mechanisms, and organizational climate conducive to innovation. No other type of industry environment reveals so clearly the inseparability of strategy formulation and strategy implementation. Strategies aimed at the exploitation of innovation, choices of whether to be a leader or a follower, and the management of risk must take careful account of organizational characteristics.

Technology-based industries also reveal some of the dilemmas that are a critical feature of strategic management in complex organizations and complex business environments. For example, technology-based industries are unpredictable, yet some investments in technology have time horizons of a decade or more. Successful strategies must be responsive to changing market conditions, but successful strategies also require long-term commitment. The fundamental dilemma is that innovation is an unpredictable process that requires creating a nurturing organizational context, whereas strategy is about resource-allocation decisions. How can a company create the conditions for nurturing innovation while planning the course of its development? John Scully, a former CEO of Apple, observed: "*Management and creativity might even be considered antithetical states. While management demands consensus, control, certainty, and the status quo, creativity thrives on the opposite: instinct, uncertainty, freedom, and iconoclasm.*"[47]

Fortunately, the experiences of companies such as 3M, Cisco Systems, Amgen and Nintendo point to solutions to these dilemmas. The need for innovation to reconcile individual creativity with coordination points toward the advantages of cross-functional team-based approaches over the isolation of R&D in a separate "creative" environment. Moreover, the need to reconcile innovation with efficiency indicates the advantage of parallel organizational structures where, in addition to the "formal" structure geared to the needs of existing businesses and products, an informal structure exists, which is the source of new products and businesses. The role of top management in balancing creativity with order and innovation with efficiency becomes critical—such reconciliation requires senior executives who are not necessarily experts in technology but who, at minimum appreciate its strategic implications.

The increasing pace of technological change and intensifying international competition suggests that the advanced, industrialized countries will be forced to rely increasingly on their technological capabilities as the basis for international competitiveness. Strategies for promoting innovation and managing technology will become more important in the future.

Self-Study Questions

1 Trevor Bayliss, a British inventor, submitted a patent application in November 1992 for a wind-up radio for use in Africa in areas where there was no electricity supply and people were too poor to afford batteries. He was excited by the prospects for radio broadcasts as a means of disseminating health education in areas of Africa devastated by AIDS. After appearances on British and South African TV, Bayliss attracted a number of entrepreneurs and companies interested in manufacturing and marketing his clockwork radio. However, Bayliss was concerned by the fact that his patent provided only limited protection for his invention: most of the main components—a clockwork generator and transistor radio—were long-established technologies. What advice would you offer Baylis as to how he can best protect and exploit his invention?

2 Table 12.1 shows that:

(a) Patents have been more effective in protecting product innovations in drugs and medical equipment than in food or electronic components;

(b) Patents are more effective in protecting product innovations than process innovations.

Can you suggest reasons why?

3 Page 306 refers to James Dyson's difficulties in licensing his innovative vacuum cleaner (see http://www.cdf.org/issue_journal/dyson_fills_a_vacuum.html for further information). What lessons would you draw from Dyson's experience concerning the use of licensing by small firms to exploit innovation?

4 From the evidence presented in Table 12.3, what conclusions can you draw regarding the factors that determine whether leaders or followers win out in the markets for new products?

5 In the battle for dominance of the ebook reader market, Amazon with Kindle 2 was ahead of Sony with its Reader Digital Book. Kindle 2 had the biggest number of recent titles available, but thanks to a deal with Google, Sony had a huge number of out-of-copyright titles. What are the sources of network externalities in this market? Will ebook readers become a winner-take-all market? Why has Amazon been able to gain a lead over Sony (and Samsung)? What can Sony do to fight back?

Notes

1 "The Logic that Dares Not Speak its Name," *Economist* (April 16, 1994): 89–91.

2 In the U.S., the return to R&D spending was estimated at between 3.7% and 5.5%. See M. Warusawitharana, "Research and Development, Profits and Firm Value: A Structural Estimation," Discussion Paper (Washington, DC: Federal Reserve Board, September, 2008).

3 The excess of the benefit received by the consumer over the price they paid is called *consumer surplus*. See: D. Besanko, D. Dranove and M. Shanley, *Economics of Strategy* (New York: John Wiley & Sons, Inc., 1996): 442–3.

4 "Knowledge Monopolies: Patent Wars," *Economist* (April 8, 2000): 95–9.

5 F. T. Rothermael, "Incumbent Advantage Through Exploiting Complementary Assets via Interfirm Cooperation," *Strategic Management Journal* 22 (2001): 687–99.

6 R. C. Levin, A. K. Klevorick, R. R. Nelson and S. G. Winter, "Appropriating the Returns from Industrial Research and Development," *Brookings Papers on Economic Activity* 18, no. 3(1987):783–832.

7 P. Grindley and D. J. Teece, "Managing Intellectual Capital: Licensing and Cross-Licensing in Semiconductors and Electronics," *California Management Review* 39 (Winter 1997): 8-41.

8 R. Adner, "Match your Innovation Strategy to your Innovation Ecosystem," *Harvard Business Review* (April 2006): 17–37.

9 S. Shulman, *The Telephone Gambit* (New York: Norton, 2008).

10 "The Human Genome Race," *Scientific American* (April 24, 2000).

11 C. Markides and P. A. Geroski, *Fast Second* (San Francisco: Jossey-Bass, 2005).

12 D. Sull, "Strategy as Active Waiting," *Harvard Business Review* (September 2005): 120–9.

13 For example, data on penetration rates for electric toothbrushes and CD players were used to forecast the market demand for HD TVs in the United States (B. L. Bayus, "High-Definition Television: Assessing Demand Forecasts for the Next Generation Consumer Durable," *Management Science* 39 (1993): 1319–33).

14 See B. C. Twiss, *Managing Technological Innovation*, 2nd edn (New York: Longman, 1980).

15 E. Von Hippel, "Lead Users: A Source of Novel Product Concepts," *Management Science* 32 (July, 1986).

16 In electronic instruments, customers' ideas initiated most of the successful new products introduced by manufacturers. See E. Von Hippel, "Users as Innovators," *Technology Review* 5 (1976): 212–39.

17 A. Friedlander, *The Growth of Railroads* (Arlington, VA: CNRI, 1995).

18 C. Shapiro and H. R. Varian, *Information Rules: A Strategic Guide to the Network Economy* (Boston: Harvard Business School Press, 1999): 264–7.

19 S. Postrel, "Competing Networks and Proprietary Standards: The Case of Quadraphonic Sound," *Journal of Industrial Economics* 24 (December 1990): 169–86.

20 S. J. Liebowitz and S. E. Margolis ("Network Externality: An Uncommon Tragedy," *Journal of Economic Perspectives* 8, Spring 1994: 133–50) refer to these user-to-user externalities as *direct externalities*.

21 M. Gladwell, *The Tipping Point* (Boston: Little Brown, 2000).

22 P. David, "Clio and the Economics of QWERTY," *American Economic Review* 75 (May 1985): 332–7; S. J. Gould, "The Panda's Thumb of Technology," *Natural History* 96, no. 1 (1986): 14-23. For an alternative view see S. J. Leibowitz and S. Margolis, "The Fable of the Keys," *Journal of Law and Economics* 33 (1990): 1–26.

23 C. Shapiro and H. R. Varian, "The Art of Standards Wars," *California Management Review* 41 (Winter 1999): 8–32.

24 R. M. Grant "The DVD War of 2006-8: Blu-Ray vs. HD-DVD" (2010) John Wiley & Sons, Chichester Cases to Accompany Contemporary Strategy Analysis, 7th edn.

25 C. Shapiro and H. R. Varian, "The Art of Standards Wars," op cit: 15–16.
26 Ibid.: 16–18.
27 S. Ahn, "Firm Dynamics and Productivity Growth: A Review of Micro Evidence from OECD Countries," Economics Department Working Paper 297 (OECD, 2001).
28 J. M. George, "Creativity in Organizations," *Academy of Management Annals* 1 (2007): 439–77.
29 M. L. Tushman, "Managing Communication Networks in R&D Laboratories," *Sloan Management Review* (Winter 1979): 37–49.
30 D. Dougherty and C. H. Takacs, "Team Play: Heedful Interrelating as the Boundary for Innovation," *Long Range Planning* 37 (December 2004): 569–90.
31 S. Thomke, "Enlightened Experimentation: The New Imperative for Innovation," *Harvard Business Review* (February, 2001): 66–75.
31 L. Grundy, J. Kickel and C. Prather, "Building the Creative Organization," *Organizational Dynamics* (Spring 1994): 22–37.
32 R. Florida and J. Goodnight, "Managing for Creativity," *Harvard Business Review* (July–August 2005): 124–131.
33 D. Leonard and S. Straus, "Putting Your Company's Whole Brain to Work," *Harvard Business Review* (July–August 1997): 111–21; D. Leonard and P. Swap, *When Sparks Fly: Igniting Creativity in Groups* (Boston: Harvard Business School Press, 1999).
34 "How to Manage a Dream Factory," *Economist* (January 16, 2003).
35 "Lunch with the FT: John Lasseter," *Financial Times* (January 17, 2009).
36 E. Von Hippel, *The Sources of Innovation* (New York: Oxford University Press, 1988), provides strong evidence of the dominant role of users in the innovation process.
37 E. Morrison, "Gunfire at Sea: A Case Study of Innovation," in M. Tushman and W. L. Moore (eds), *Readings in the Management of Innovation* (Cambridge, MA: Ballinger, 1988): 165–78.
38 K. Clark and T. Fujimoto, *Product Development Performance: Strategy, Organization, and Management in the World Auto Industry* (Boston: Harvard Business School Press, 1991).
39 K. Imai, I. Nonaka and H. Takeuchi, "Managing the New Product Development Process: How Japanese Companies Learn and Unlearn," in K. Clark, R. Hayes and C. Lorenz (eds), *The Uneasy Alliance* (Boston: Harvard Business School Press, 1985).
40 D. A. Schön, "Champions for Radical New Inventions," *Harvard Business Review* (March–April, 1963): 84.
41 R. Rothwell, C. Freeman, A. Horlsey, V. T. Jervis, A. B. Robertson and J. Townsend, "SAPPHO Updated—Project SAPPHO Phase II," *Research Policy* 3 (1974): 258–91.
42 G. P. Pisano, *Science Business: The Promise, the Reality, and the Future of Biotech* (Boston: Harvard Business School Press, 2006).
43 "Cisco's Chambers: The Route Ahead," ICFASI Case Study No. 306-172-1 (Chennai, 2006),
44 A. Arora, A, Fosfur and A. Gambardella, *Markets for Technology* (Cambridge: MIT Press, 2001); S. Breschi and F. Malerba, *Clusters, Networks and Innovation* (Oxford: Oxford University Press, 2005).
45 M. T. Hansen, H. W. Chesborough, N. Nohria and D. N. Sull, "Networked Incubators: Hothouse of the New Economy," *Harvard Business Review* (September–October, 2000): 74–88; "How to Make the Most of a Brilliant Idea," *Financial Times* (December 6, 2000): 21.
46 "Nurturing Creativity: Putting Passions to Work" *Shell World* (Royal Dutch Shell, 14 September, 2007): 1–12.
47 J. Scully, *Odyssey* (Toronto: Fitzhenry and Whiteside, 1987): 18.

13 Competitive Advantages in Mature Industries

We are a true "penny profit" business. That means that it takes hard work and attention to detail to be financially successful—it is far from being a sure thing. Our store managers must do two things well: control costs and increase sales. Cost control cannot be done by compromising product quality, customer service, or restaurant cleanliness, but rather by consistent monitoring of the "vital signs" of the business through observation, reports, and analysis. Portion control is a critical part of our business. For example, each Filet-O-Fish sandwich receives 1 fluid ounce of tartar sauce and 0.5 ounces of cheese. Our raw materials are fabricated to exacting tolerances, and our managers check them on an ongoing basis. Our written specification for lettuce is over two typewritten pages long. Our French fries must meet standards for potato type, solid and moisture content, and distribution of strand lengths.

—EDWARD H. RENSI, PRESIDENT AND CHIEF OPERATING OFFICER, MCDONALD'S U.S.A.[1]

OUTLINE

Introduction and Objectives

Although technology-based industries grab the attention of both business journalists and strategy researchers, if importance is measured by share of GDP rather than share of media output, mature industries—food, energy, construction, vehicles, financial services, and restaurants—retain their preeminence, even in the advanced industrialized nations.

Despite their heterogeneity—they range from massage parlors to steel—mature industries present several similarities from a strategic perspective. The purpose of this chapter is to explore these characteristics of mature industries, identify strategies through which competitive advantage can be established within them, and recognize the implications of these strategies for structure, systems, and leadership style. As we shall see, maturity does not imply lack of opportunity. Companies such as Hennes & Mauritz (fashion clothing), Ryanair (airlines), Starbucks (coffee shops) and Nucor (steel) have successfully deployed novel strategies in mature sectors. Mature sectors are typically inhabited by mature companies—Coca-Cola, ExxonMobil, and HSBC Holdings were founded in the nineteenth century, yet, over the past two decades, have achieved combinations of profitability and growth that would make most high-tech companies envious. Nor does maturity mean lack of innovation: as we shall see, many mature industries have been transformed by new technologies and new strategies.

By the time you have completed this chapter, you will be able to:

- recognize the principal strategic characteristics of mature industries;
- identify key success factors within mature industries and formulate strategies directed toward their exploitation;

- locate and analyze opportunities for strategic innovation in mature industries to establish competitive advantage;
- design organizational structures and management systems that can effectively implement such strategies.

Competitive Advantage in Mature Industries

Our analysis of the industry life cycle (Chapter 11) suggests that maturity has two principal implications for competitive advantage: first, it tends to reduce the number of opportunities for establishing competitive advantage; second, it shifts these opportunities from differentiation-based factors to cost-based factors.

Diminishing opportunities for sustainable competitive advantage in mature industries stem from:

- Less scope for differentiation advantage resulting from increased buyer knowledge, product standardization, and less product innovation.
- Diffusion of process technology means that cost advantages based on superior processes or more advanced capital equipment methods are difficult to obtain and sustain. Once a cost advantage is established, it is vulnerable to exchange rate movements and the emergence of low-cost overseas competitors.
- A highly developed industry infrastructure together with the presence of powerful distributors makes it easier to attack established firms that occupy particular strategic niches.

Using different terminology, Warren Buffett—"The Sage of Omaha"—views the process of maturity as one of value destruction during which enterprises make the transition from "franchises" into "businesses":

> An economic franchise arises from a product or service that (1) is needed or desired; (2) is thought by customers to have no close substitute; and (3) is not subject to price regulation. Franchises earn high rates of return on capital . . . [and] can tolerate mismanagement . . . In contrast, "a business" earns exceptional profits only if it is a low-cost operator or if supply of its product or service is tight. And a business, unlike a franchise, can be killed by poor management.[2]

This trend toward deteriorating industry profitability is a constant threat in mature industries. The propensity towards overinvestment in capacity, internationalization and commoditization exacerbate price competition and make competitive advantage difficult to attain and even harder to sustain.

Cost Advantage

If cost is the overwhelmingly important key success factor in most mature industries, what are the primary sources of low cost? Three cost drivers tend to be especially important:

- *Economies of scale.* In capital-intensive industries, or where advertising, distribution, or new product development is an important element of total cost, economies of scale are important sources of interfirm cost differences. The increased standardization that accompanies maturity greatly assists the exploitation of such scale economies. The significance of scale economies in mature industries is indicated by the fact that the association between return on investment and market share is stronger in mature industries than in emerging industries.[3]
- *Low-cost inputs.* Where small competitors are successful in undercutting the prices of market leaders in mature industries, it is frequently through their access to low-cost inputs. Established firms can become locked into high salaries and benefits, inefficient working practices and bloated overheads inherited from more prosperous times. New entrants into mature industries may gain cost advantages by acquiring plant and equipment at bargain-basement levels and by cutting labor costs. Valero Energy Corporation is the largest oil refiner in the U.S.: it acquired loss-making refineries from the majors at below book prices then operated them with rigorous cost efficiency. A lower cost of capital can also be a key source of cost advantage. Prior to the 2008 credit crunch, the acquisition of retailers, hotels, hospital groups, and chemical firms by private equity funds was motivated by the attractions of substituting low-cost debt for high-cost equity.[4]
- *Low overheads.* During the early 1990s, some of the most profitable companies in mature industries tended to be those that had achieved the most substantial reductions in overhead costs. In discount retailing, Wal-Mart is famous for its parsimonious approach to costs. Among the oil majors, Exxon is known for its rigorous control of overhead costs. Exxon's headquarters cost (relative to net worth) was estimated at less than one-quarter that of Mobil's.[5] When Exxon merged with Mobil, it was able to extract huge cost savings from Mobil. In newspaper and magazine publishing, newcomers such as EMAP in the U.K. and Media News Group in the U.S. (run by "Lean" Dean Singleton) have acquired multiple titles then slashed overhead costs.

As cost inefficiencies tend to become institutionalized within mature enterprises, cost reduction may require drastic interventions. *Corporate restructuring*—intensive periods of structural and strategic change—typically involves cost reduction through outsourcing, headcount reduction and downsizing—especially at corporate headquarters.[6] Successful turnaround strategies typically involve aggressive cost cutting. Empirical research among mature U.S. businesses has identified three successful approaches:

- *Asset and cost surgery*—aggressive cost reduction through reduction of excess capacity; halting of new investment in plant and equipment; and cutbacks in R&D, marketing expenditures, receivables, and inventories.

- *Selective product and market pruning*—refocusing on segments that were most profitable or where the firm possessed distinctive strength.
- *Piecemeal productivity moves*—adjustments to current market position rather than comprehensive refocusing or reorganizing, including reductions in marketing and R&D expenditures, higher capacity utilization, and increased employee productivity.[7]

Segment and Customer Selection

Sluggish demand growth, lack of product differentiation, and international competition tend to depress the profitability of mature industries. Yet, even unattractive industries may offer attractive niche markets with strong growth of demand, few competitors, and abundant potential for differentiation. As a result, segment selection can be a key determinant of differences in the performance of companies within the same industry. Wal-Mart's profitability was boosted by locating its stores in small and medium-sized towns where it faced little competition. In the auto industry, there is a constant quest to escape competition by creating new market segments with "crossover" vehicles that span existing segments. Opportunities for establishing new segments can arise from the strategies of market leaders. The more that incumbents focus on the mass market, the more likely it is that new entrants can carve out new market niches by supplying underserved customer needs.[8]

The logic of segment focus implies further disaggregation of markets—down to the level of the individual customer. Information technology permits new approaches to *customer relationship management* (CRM), making it possible to analyze individual characteristics and preferences, identify individual customers' profit contribution to the firm, and organize marketing around individualized, integrated approaches to customers. In the same way that Las Vegas casinos have long recognized that the major part of their profits derives from a tiny minority of customers—the "high rollers"—so banks, supermarkets, credit card companies, and hotels increasingly use transactions data to identify their most attractive customers, and those that are a drag on profitability.

The next stage in this process is to go beyond customer selection to actively target more attractive customers and transform less valuable customers into more valuable customers. Alan Grant and Leonard Schlesinger point to the need for companies to optimize their *value exchange*—the relationship between the investment a company makes in a customer relationship and the return that investment generates.[9] For example:

- Credit card issuer Capital One has long been a leader in using data warehousing, experimentation, simulation, and sophisticated statistical modeling to adjust the terms and features of its credit card offers to the preferences and characteristics of individual customers. Capital One estimates the lifetime profitability of each customer and analyzes the four key events in the credit card life cycle: acquiring the customer, stimulating the customer's card use, retaining the customer, and managing default.[10]
- Amazon.com uses information on customers' prior transactions and comparisons with other customers making similar purchases to generate individualized purchase suggestions.

The Quest for Differentiation

Cost leadership, we noted in Chapter 10, is difficult to sustain, particularly in the face of international competition. Hence, differentiating to attain some insulation from the rigors of price competition is particularly attractive in mature industries. The problem is that the trend toward commoditization narrows the scope for differentiation and reduces customer willingness to pay a premium for differentiation:

- In tires and domestic appliances, companies' investments in differentiation through product innovation, quality and brand advertising reputation have generated disappointing returns. Vigorous competition, price-sensitive customers and strong, aggressive retailers have limited the price premium that differentiation will support.
- Attempts by airlines to gain competitive advantage through offering more legroom, providing superior in-flight entertainment, and achieving superior punctuality have met little market response from consumers. The only effective differentiators appear to be frequent flier programs and services offered to first- and business-class travelers.

Standardization of the physical attributes of a product and convergence of consumer preferences constrains, but does not eliminate, opportunities for meaningful and profitable differentiation. Product standardization is frequently accompanied by increased differentiation of complementary services—financing terms, leasing arrangements, warranties, after-sales services and the like. In consumer goods, maturity often means a shift from physical differentiation to image differentiation. Entrenched consumer loyalties to specific brands of cola or cigarettes are a tribute to the capacity of brand promotion over long periods of time to create distinct images among near-identical products.

The intensely competitive retail sector produces particularly interesting examples of differentiation strategies. The dismal profitability earned by many retail chains (Toys-R-Us, J. C. Penney, and Circuit City in the U.S.; J. Sainsbury, Mothercare, and Kingfisher in the U.K.; Royal Ahold in the Netherlands) contrasts sharply with the sales growth and profitability of stores that have established clear differentiation through variety, style, and ambiance (Target, Lowe's, TJX, Bed, Bath and Beyond, and Wholefoods in the U.S.; Zara-Inditex from Spain; Hennes & Mauritz and IKEA from Sweden). A further lesson from highly competitive mature sectors such as retailing is that competitive advantage is difficult to sustain. Most of the outstandingly successful retailers of the previous decade—Toys-R-Us, Body Shop, and Marks & Spencer—have been displaced in the affections of consumers and investors by the rising stars of retail.

Innovation

We have characterized mature industries as industries where the pace of technical change is low. In many mature industries—steel, textiles, food processing, insurance, and hotels—R&D expenditure is below 1% of sales revenue, while in U.S. manufacturing as a whole just three sectors—computers and electronics, pharmaceuticals, and aerospace—account for 65% of R&D spending.[11] Nevertheless, measured by patenting activity, there is evidence that many mature industries are as innovative as emerging industries.[12] Even in mature low-tech products such as tires, brassieres and fishing rods, continuing inventiveness is indicated by a steady flow of new patents (see Strategy Capsule 13.1).

Despite an increased pace of technological change in many mature industries, the most opportunities for establishing competitive advantage are likely to arise from *strategic innovation*—including "new game strategies" and "blue ocean strategies" that we discussed in Chapter 8. Indeed, as identified in Chapter 11, it may be that strategic innovation constitutes a third phase of innovation that becomes prominent once product and process innovation slacken. In addition to the "value chain reconfiguration" approach discussed in Chapter 8, firms can seek strategic innovation by redefining markets and market segments. This may involve:

- *Embracing new customer groups*. Harley-Davidson has created a market for expensive motorcycles among the middle-aged, while in the maturing market

STRATEGY CAPSULE 13.1

Innovation in Mature Industries: Brassiere Technology

The first patent for a "breast-supporting device" was issued in the U.S. in 1864. However, the first patent relating to an undergarment named "brassiere" was issued to Mary Phelps Jacob in 1913. By 1940 over 550 U.S. patents for brassieres and related breast supporters had been issued.

The technological quest for a better bra continued into the twenty-first century—the U.S. Patent Office has issued over 200 patents relating to brassieres since January 2000. The design innovations of recent years include:

- Wonderbra (owned by Sara Lee) introduced a "variable cleavage" bra equipped with a system of pulleys;
- the Airotic bra designed by Gossard (also owned by Sara Lee) features "twin air bags as standard"—these are inflatable by a "unique G-pump system";
- Charnos's Bioform bra replaces underwiring with soft molded polypropylene around a rigid ring—a design inspired by the Frisbee and engineered by Ove Arup, who also engineered London's Millennium Bridge (which had to be closed because of excessive wobbling);
- The Ultimo bra, designed by Scottish model Michelle Mone assisted by a team of German scientists, is equipped with silicone gel pads;
- A number of new brassieres use "spacer fabric" which comprises "two outer textile layers separated by a ventilated inner layer of spacer yarns, to allow heat and moisture to escape. Various properties can be added to the fabrics, including anti-microbial, anti-mildew, anti-static, flame-retardant, absorptive, water-repellent, and abrasion-resistant attributes . . ."

Sources: "Bra Wars," *Economist* (December 2, 2000): 112; salon.com (August 28, 2000); U.S. Patent Database.

for video game consoles, Nintendo achieved remarkable success with its *Wii* by appealing to consumers outside the core market of teenage and preteenage boys. The most rapidly growing churches—for example Jehovah's Witnesses in Russia and Amway Christian Fellowship in America—tend to be those that recruit among non-church going social and demographic groups.

- *Augmenting products and services*. Some of the most successful approaches to differentiation in mature industries involve bundling additional products or services with the core offering. In book retailing, Barnes & Noble offer, not only a wide range of titles, but also include Starbucks coffee shops within its stores. Neighborhood bookstores that have survived competition from the megastores and Amazon.com are often those that have added poetry readings, live music and other recreational services. The adoption of themes by retail stores and restaurants—Virgin Megastores, Hard Rock Café and Planet Hollywood—reflect the desire to involve customers in an experience that goes beyond the product being sold. In the *experience economy*, companies go beyond providing a product or service that meets a clearly defined customer need and involve their customers in a process that engages them at the emotional, intellectual, even spiritual level.[13]
- The ability to create competitive advantage requires that managers free themselves from the cognitive limits associated with notions of maturity. Baden-Fuller and Stopford argue that maturity is a state of mind, not a state of the business—every enterprise has the potential for rejuvenation. The key to strategic innovation is for managers to prevent industry conventions from imprisoning their companies into conventional thinking about strategy. This is likely to cultivate an entrepreneurial organization where middle managers are encouraged to experiment and learn.[14]

Costas Markides identifies several firms that have successfully broken away from conventional wisdom to establish a unique positioning within mature industries:

- Edward Jones, with 2000 offices, mostly in the U.S. but also in Canada and the U.K., has rejected the conventional wisdom that successful brokerage firms require scale economies, product diversification, e-commerce and integration with investment banks. Edward Jones' office has just one investment adviser who is motivated to grow local business through face-to-face relationships; there are no proprietary investment products and no online investing.
- Enterprise Rent-A-Car has adopted a location strategy that is quite different from its major competitors, Hertz and Avis. Rather than concentrate on serving the business traveler through locating at airports and downtown, Enterprise concentrates on suburban locations, where it caters primarily to the consumer market.[15]

How do companies break away from the pack and achieve strategic innovation? The problem is that breaking with industry conventions requires confronting industry-wide systems of belief—what J.-C. Spender refers to as "industry recipes."[16] This is likely to require that managers find ways of altering their *cognitive maps*—the mental frameworks through which they perceive and understand their industry environments.[17] This may explain why strategic innovation in mature industries is so often associated with firms that are either outsiders or peripheral players.

According to Gary Hamel, the role of strategy should be to foster revolution through reorganizing the strategy-making process. This means breaking top management's monopoly over strategy formulation, bringing in younger people from further down the organization, and gaining involvement from those on the periphery of the organization.[18] Ultimately, strategic innovation is likely to require a process of organization-wide change—a "journey of strategic renewal."[19]

Strategy Implementation in Mature Industries: Structure, Systems and Style

Across most mature industries, the primary basis for competitive advantage is operational efficiency, however, as we have seen, cost efficiency must be reconciled with innovation and customer responsiveness. What kinds of organizational structures, management systems, and leadership styles do mature businesses need to adopt in order to achieve these multiple performance goals?

Efficiency through Bureaucracy

As we observed in Chapter 6, the conventional prescription for stable environments was "mechanistic" organizations characterized by centralization, precisely-defined roles, and predominantly vertical communication.[20] Henry Mintzberg describes this formalized type of organization dedicated to the pursuit of efficiency as the *machine bureaucracy*.[21] Efficiency is achieved through standardized routines, division of labor and close management control based on bureaucratic principles. Division of labor extends to management as well as operatives—high levels of vertical and horizontal specialization are typical among managers. Vertical specialization is evident in the concentration of strategy formulation at the apex of the hierarchy, while middle and junior management supervise and administer through the application of standardized rules and procedures. Horizontal specialization takes the form of functional structures.

The machine bureaucracy as described by Mintzberg is a caricature of actual organizations—probably the closest approximations are found in government departments performing highly routine administrative duties (for example, the Internal Revenue Service or departments of motor vehicle licensing). However, in most mature industries, the features of mechanistic organizations are evident in highly routinized operations controlled by detailed rules and procedures. McDonald's is far from being a typical bureaucracy—in particular, the majority of outlets are franchises operated by independent companies—however, the cost efficiency and consistency that characterizes its performance is the highly standardized and detailed operating procedures that govern virtually every aspect of how it does business (see the quotation that introduces this chapter). Similarly, in Marriott Hotels, HSBC, Toyota Motor Company, and Wal-Mart—the ability of these huge organizations to achieve efficiency and consistent high quality is the result of management systems that draw heavily upon the principles of bureaucracy. The key features of these mature organizations are summarized in Table 13.1.

Table 13.1 Strategy implementation in mature industries: the conventional model

STRATEGY	Primary goal is cost advantage through economies of scale and capital-intensive production of standardized products/services. Strategy formulation primarily the realm of top managers; middle managers responsible for strategy implementation.
STRUCTURE	Functional departments (e.g., production, marketing, customer service, distribution). Distinction between line and staff. Clearly defined job roles with strong vertical reporting/delegation relationships.
CONTROLS	Performance targets are primarily quantitative and short term and are specified for all members of the organization. Performance is closely monitored by well-established, centralized management information systems and formalized reporting requirements. Financial controls through budgets and profit targets particularly important.
INCENTIVES	Incentives are based on achievement of individual targets and take the form of financial rewards and promotion up the hierarchy. Penalties exist for failure to attain quantitative targets, for failure to adhere to the rules, and for lack of conformity to company norms.
COMMUNICATION	Primarily vertical for the purposes of delegation and reporting. Lateral communication limited, often achieved through interdepartmental committees.
LEADERSHIP	Primary functions of top management: control and strategic direction. Typical CEO profiles include: the *administrator* who guides the organization through establishing and operating organizational systems and principles and building consensus (e.g., Alfred Sloan Jr. of General Motors); the *autocrat*, who uses top-down decision making and leads through centralization of power and force of personality (Lee Iacocca of Chrysler and Al Dunlap of Sunbeam); and the *strategic leader* who combines clear strategic direction with considerable decentralization of decision making (John Brown at BP, Carlos Ghosn at Nissan, Jack Welch at GE).

Trends in Strategy Implementation among Mature Businesses

When competitive advantage in mature industries was all about cost advantage through scale and division of labor, management practices based upon standardized processes, elaborately defined rules, hierarchical control, quantitative performance targets and incentives closely linked to individual performance work well. However, as we have discussed, the requirements for success in mature industries and the strategies needed to achieve success given these requirements have become much more complex. In terms of cost efficiency, scale advantages have become less important than the flexibility to exploit low cost inputs and to outsource to low-cost specialists, and an organizational environment that constantly strives to eliminate waste and discover new sources of efficiency.

The efficiency leaders in mature industries are not necessarily the biggest firms that are able to exploit scale benefits to the maximum: they are more likely to be companies that have dedicated themselves to efficiency through implementing performance-oriented management systems. Top performing companies in mature businesses—UPS in delivery services, Wal-Mart in discount retailing, Nucor in steel, ExxonMobil in petroleum—are characterized by management systems that comprise integrated systems where performance goals are the centerpiece of strategy and these goals are implemented through financial controls, human resource policies, and operating practices which are closely integrated with these goals.

Unifying an organization around the pursuit of efficiency requires management systems that allow disaggregation of company-wide goals into specific performance targets for departments and individuals—the *balanced scorecard* is one of the most widely used techniques for achieving this (see Chapter 2). Most important, however, is embedding performance goals within the company's organizational culture:

- Central to UPS's performance driven management style is a corporate culture that simultaneously embraces high levels of employee autonomy and the company's "obsessive-compulsive personality".[22]
- Wal-Mart's culture of frugality reflects the values of founder Sam Walton. According to Wal-Mart executive Ron Loveless: "Sam valued every penny. People say that Wal-Mart is making $10 billion a year, or whatever. But that's not how people within the company think of it. If you spent a dollar, the question was: 'How many dollars of merchandise would you need to sell to make that dollar?'"[23]
- Ryanair is master of the art of managing for cost efficiency. From a simple strategic goal of being Europe's lowest cost airline, Ryanair's route structure, choice of airports, fleet, ticketing system and human resource practices are meticulously aligned to cost minimization. Ryanair's obsession with cost cutting is reflected in the large proportion of employees that are on temporary contracts, the requirement that crews pay for their own uniforms and training, and a heavy emphasis on incentive pay (cabin crew receive a commission on all inflight sales).[24]

Reconciling differentiation and innovation with a relentless drive for cost efficiency creates difficult challenges for designing management systems that promote these goals without blunting the imperatives for cost minimization. The conventional model for reconciling efficiency with innovation in mature companies is internal differentiation: innovation and entrepreneurship are the responsibility of specialist R&D, new product development and business development units. However, some established companies in mature industries have embraced *open innovation*. In the intensely competitive world market for domestic appliances, Whirlpool committed itself to innovation as the primary basis on which it would seek competitive advantage. Its decade-long program for opening up the company to innovation has involved creating a company-wide system for generating new ideas, establishing criteria for assessing proposals and funding them, and training people in the different phases of innovation—including some 600 I-mentors to facilitate the process and some 240 consultants to develop innovation projects.[25]

Strategies for Declining Industries

The transition from maturity to decline can be a result of technological substitution (typewriters, photographic film), changes in consumer preferences (canned food, men's suits), demographic shifts (children's toys in Europe), or foreign competition (textiles in the advanced industrialized countries). Shrinking market demand gives rise to acute strategic issues. Among the key features of declining industries are:

- excess capacity;
- lack of technical change (reflected in a lack of new product introduction and stability of process technology);
- a declining number of competitors, but some entry as new firms acquire the assets of exiting firms cheaply;
- high average age of both physical and human resources;
- aggressive price competition.

Despite the inhospitable environment offered by declining industries, research by Kathryn Harrigan has uncovered declining industries where at least some participants earned surprisingly high profits. These included electronic vacuum tubes, cigars, and leather tanning. However, elsewhere—notably in prepared baby foods, rayon, and meat processing—decline was accompanied by aggressive price competition, company failures, and instability.[26]

What determines whether or not a declining industry becomes a competitive blood-bath? Two factors are critical: the balance between capacity and output, and the nature of the demand for the product.

Adjusting Capacity to Declining Demand

The smooth adjustment of industry capacity to declining demand is the key to stability and profitability during the decline phase. In industries where capacity exits from the industry in an orderly fashion, decline can occur without trauma. Where substantial excess capacity persists, as has occurred in the steel industries of America and Europe, in the bakery industry, in gold mining, and in long-haul bus transportation, the potential exists for destructive competition. The ease with which capacity adjusts to declining demand depends on the following factors:

- *The predictability of decline*. If decline can be forecast, it is more likely that firms can plan for it. The decline of traditional photography with the advent of digital imaging was anticipated and planned for. Conversely, the long-term decline of the U.S. and Western European steel industries has been obscured by periodic cyclical upswings—most notably that of 2004–7. The more cyclical and volatile the demand, the more difficult it is for firms to perceive the trend of demand even after the onset of decline.
- *Barriers to exit*. Barriers to exit impede the exit of capacity from an industry. The major barriers are:
  - Durable and specialized assets. Just as capital requirements impose a barrier to entry into an industry, those same investments also discourage exit. The longer they last and the fewer the opportunities for using those assets in another industry, the more companies are tied to that particular industry.
  - Costs incurred in plant closure. Apart from the accounting costs of writing off assets, substantial cash costs may be incurred in redundancy payments to employees, compensation for broken contacts with customers and suppliers, dismantling the plant, and environmental clean up.

- Managerial commitment. In addition to financial considerations, firms may be reluctant to close plants for a variety of emotional and moral reasons. Resistance to plant closure and divestment arises from pride in company traditions and reputation, managers' unwillingness to accept failure, and loyalties to employees and the local community.
- *The strategies of the surviving firms*. Smooth exit of capacity ultimately depends on the willingness of the industry players to close plants and divest assets. The sooner companies recognize and address the problem, the more likely it is that independent and collective action can achieve capacity reduction. In European gasoline retailing, for example, the problem of excess capacity was partially solved by bilateral exchanges of service stations among the major oil companies. Stronger firms in the industry can facilitate the exit of weaker firms by offering to acquire their plants and take over their after-sales service commitments. A key strategy among private equity firms has been initiating "roll-ups" in declining industries—consolidating multiple acquisitions.

The Nature of Demand

Where a market is segmented, the general pattern of decline can obscure the existence of pockets of demand that are not only comparatively resilient, but also price inelastic. For example, despite the obsolescence of vacuum tubes after the adoption of transistors, GTE Sylvania and General Electric earned excellent profits supplying vacuum tubes to the replacement, high-end audio, and military markets.[27] In fountain pens, survivors in the quality pen segment such as Cross and Mont Blanc have achieved steady sales and high margins through appealing to high-income professionals and executives. Despite overall decline of the cigar market, quality cigars have benefitted from strong demand and attractive margins.

Strategies for Declining Industries

Conventional strategy recommendations for declining industries are either to divest or to harvest, i.e., to generate the maximum cash flow from existing investments without reinvesting. However, these strategies assume that declining industries are inherently unprofitable. If profit potential exists, then other strategies may be attractive. Harrigan and Porter identify four strategies that can profitably be pursued either individually or sequentially in declining industries:[28]

- *Leadership*. By gaining leadership, a firm is well placed to outstay competitors and play a dominant role in the final stages of the industry's life cycle. Once leadership is attained, the firm is in a good position to switch to a harvest strategy and enjoy a strong profit stream from its market position. Establishing leadership can be done by acquiring competitors, but a cheaper way is to encourage competitors to exit (and then acquire their plants). Inducements to competitors to exit may include showing commitment to the industry, helping to lower their exit costs, releasing pessimistic forecasts of the industry's future, and raising the stakes—for example, by supporting more stringent environmental controls that make it costly for them to stay in business.

- *Niche.* Identify a segment that is likely to maintain a stable demand and that other firms are unlikely to invade, then pursue a leadership strategy to establish dominance within the segment. The most attractive niches are those that offer the greatest prospects for stability and where demand is most inelastic.
- *Harvest.* By harvesting, a firm maximizes its cash flow from existing assets, while avoiding further investment. A harvesting strategy seeks to boost margins wherever possible through raising prices and cutting costs by rationalizing the number of models, number of channels, and number of customers. Note, however, that a harvest strategy can be difficult to implement. In the face of strong competition, harvesting may accelerate decline, particularly if employee morale is adversely affected by a strategy that offers no long-term future for the business.
- *Divest.* If the future looks bleak, the best strategy may be to divest the business in the early stages of decline before a consensus has developed as to the inevitability of decline. Once industry decline is well established it may be extremely difficult to find buyers.

Choosing the most appropriate strategy requires a careful assessment both of the profit potential of the industry and the competitive position of the firm. Harrigan and Porter pose four key questions:

- Can the structure of the industry support a hospitable, potentially profitable decline phase?
- What are the exit barriers that each significant competitor faces?
- Do your company strengths fit the remaining pockets of demand?
- What are your competitors' strengths in these pockets? How can their exit barriers be overcome?

Selecting an appropriate strategy requires matching the opportunities remaining in the industries to the company's competitive position. Figure 13.1 shows a simple framework for strategy choice.

FIGURE 13.1 Strategic alternatives for declining industries

		COMPANY'S COMPETITIVE POSITION	
		Strengths in remaining demand pockets	Lacks strength in remaining demand pockets
INDUSTRY STRUCTURE	Favorable to decline	LEADERSHIP or NICHE	HARVEST or DIVEST
	Unfavorable to decline	NICHE or HARVEST	DIVEST QUICKLY

Summary

Mature industries present challenging environments for the formulation and implementation of business strategies. Competition—price competition in particular—is usually strong and competitive advantage is often difficult to build and sustain: cost advantages are vulnerable to imitation, differentiation opportunities are limited by the trend to standardization. Stable positions of competitive advantage in mature industries are traditionally associated with cost advantage from economies of scale or experience, and differentiation advantage through brand loyalty. Such strategies are typically implemented through hierarchical organizations, with high levels of specialization and formalization, and centralized decision making directed toward maximizing static efficiency.

Increased dynamism of mature industries resulting from international competition, economic turbulence, and greater pressure for innovation has had two consequences. First, the conditions for cost efficiency have changed. In a dynamic environment, cost efficiency is less dependent on scale, specialization, and rigid control, and more on rapid adjustment to change. Second, as competition has become more intense, companies (especially those in the advanced industrialized countries) have been forced to seek new sources of competitive advantage through innovation and differentiation. Reconciling the pursuit of scale economies with the need for responsiveness and flexibility, and the requirements of cost efficiency with the growing need for innovation and differentiation, poses complex strategic and organizational challenges. Some of the most successful companies in mature industries—Wal-Mart in retailing, BP in oil and gas, Nike in shoes and sportswear, and Coca-Cola in beverages—are companies that have achieved flexibility through dismantling bureaucratic structures and procedures, exploiting new technology to combine variety and flexibility with efficiency, encouraging high levels of employee commitment, and relentlessly pursuing financial targets. We return to some of these challenges in Chapter 18.

Self-Study Questions

1 The clothing manufacturers of northern Italy are facing rapid decline as retail chains and fashion houses increasingly outsource to China and other low-cost countries. What strategies would you recommend to small and medium-sized Italian garment manufacturers to assist them in surviving the onslaught of low-cost foreign competition?

2 Under Jacques Nasser, Ford's response to intensifying competition in the auto industry was to acquire a stable of luxury brands and forward integrate into car rental (Hertz), car repair (Kwik Fit), and financial services. The present CEO, Alan Mulally, has moved in the opposite

direction: divesting car rental, car repair and the luxury brands (including Aston Martin, Land Rover and Jaguar), while aggressively cutting costs and capacity. Given the characteristics of the industry and the company, which CEO has the better strategy?

3 In both Europe and North America, established airlines are desperately cutting costs to compete with the increasing number of budget airlines. However, it is highly unlikely that these airlines will ever match the cost efficiency of Southwest, Jet Blue, or Ryanair. What opportunities are there for established airlines to improve their competitive position through differentiation strategies? Make specific proposals for how established airlines can differentiate their customer offerings more effectively.

4 Department stores (for example, Federated Department Stores and Mays in the U.S., Selfridges and House of Fraser in the U.K.) face increasing competition from specialized chain retailers and discount stores. What innovative strategies might department stores adopt to revitalize their competitiveness?

5 In an era of budget airlines, online booking for travel, hotels, and car hire, the elimination of commissions paid by airlines, and declining demand for "package vacations" (air travel + hotel reservations + other services), is there a future for retail travel agents? What survival strategies can you recommend?

Notes

1 E. H. Rensi, "Computers at McDonald's," in J. F. McLimore and L. Larwood (eds), *Strategies, Successes: Senior Executives Speak Out* (New York: Harper & Row, 1988): 159–60.

2 Letter to Shareholders, Annual Report of Berkshire Hathaway Inc., 1991.

3 R. D. Buzzell and B. T. Gale, *The PIMS Principles* (New York: Free Press, 1987): 279.

4 "European Leveraged Buy-outs," *Economist* (August 10, 2006).

5 T. Copeland, T. Koller and J. Murrin, *Valuation: Measuring and Managing the Value of Companies*, 3rd edn (New York: John Wiley & Sons, Inc. 2000): 305.

6 R. Cibin and R. M. Grant, "Restructuring among the World's Leading Oil Companies," *British Journal of Management* 7 (December 1996): 283–308.

7 D. C. Hambrick and S. M. Schecter, "Turnaround Strategies for Mature Industrial-Product Business Units," *Academy of Management Journal* 26, no. 2 (1983): 231–48.

8 G. R. Carroll and A. Swaminathan, "Why the Microbrewery Movement? Organizational Dynamics of Resource Partitioning in the American Brewing Industry," *American Journal of Sociology* 106 (2000): 715–62; C. Boone, G. R. Carroll and A. van Witteloostuijn, "Resource Distributions and Market Partitioning: Dutch Daily Newspapers 1964–94," *American Sociological Review* 67 (2002): 408–31.

9 A. W. H. Grant and L. A. Schlesinger, "Realize Your Customer's Full Profit Potential," *Harvard Business Review* (September–October 1995): 59–72.

10 *Capital One Financial Corporation*, Harvard Business School Case No. 9-700-124 (2000).

11 National Science Foundation, *Research and Development in Industry: 2002* (www.nsf.gov/statistics/industry).

12 A. M. McGahan and B. S. Silverman, "How Does Innovative Activity Change as Industries Mature?" *International Journal of Industrial Organization* 19, no. 7 (2001): 1141–60.

13 B. J. Pine and J. Gilmore, "Welcome to the Experience Economy," *Harvard Business Review* (July–August 1998): 97–105.

14 C. Baden-Fuller and J. Stopford, *Rejuvenating the Mature Business* (Boston: HBS Press, 1994): especially Chapters 3 and 4.

15 C. C. Markides, *All the Right Moves* (Boston: Harvard Business School Press, 1999).

16 J.-C. Spender, *Industry Recipes: The Nature and Sources of Managerial Judgment* (Oxford: Blackwell,

1989). On a similar theme, see also A. S. Huff, "Industry Influences on Strategy Reformulation," *Strategic Management Journal* 3 (1982): 119–31.

17 P. S. Barr, J. L. Stimpert, and A. S. Huff, "Cognitive Change, Strategic Action, and Organizational Renewal," *Strategic Management Journal* 13, Summer Special Issue (1992): 15–36.

18 G. Hamel, "Strategy as Revolution," *Harvard Business Review* 96 (July–August 1996): 69–82.

19 H. Volberda, C. Baden-Fuller, and F. van den Bosch, "Mastering Strategic Renewal," *Long Range Planning* 34 (April, 2001): 159–78.

20 T. Burns and G. M. Stalker, *The Management of Innovation* (London: Tavistock Institute, 1961).

21 H. Mintzberg, *Structure in Fives: Designing Effective Organizations* (Englewood Cliffs, NJ: Prentice Hall, 1983): Chapter 9.

22 G. Nieman, *Big Brown: The Untold Story of UPS* (Chichester: John Wiley & Sons, Ltd, 2007): 70.

23 C. Fishman, *The Wal-Mart Effect: The High Cost of Everyday Low Prices* (Harmondsworth: Penguin, 2006).

24 "Ryanair: Defying Gravity," IMD Case No. 3-1633 (2007). Available from www.ecch.com.

25 "How Whirlpool Defines Innovation," *Business Week* (March 6, 2006).

26 K. R. Harrigan, *Strategies for Declining Businesses* (Lexington, MA: D. C. Heath, 1980).

27 K. R. Harrigan, "Strategic Planning for Endgame," *Long Range Planning* 15 (1982): 45–8.

28 K. R. Harrigan and M. E. Porter, "End-Game Strategies for Declining Industries," *Harvard Business Review* (July–August 1983): 111–20.

V

CORPORATE STRATEGY

14 Vertical Integration and the Scope of the Firm

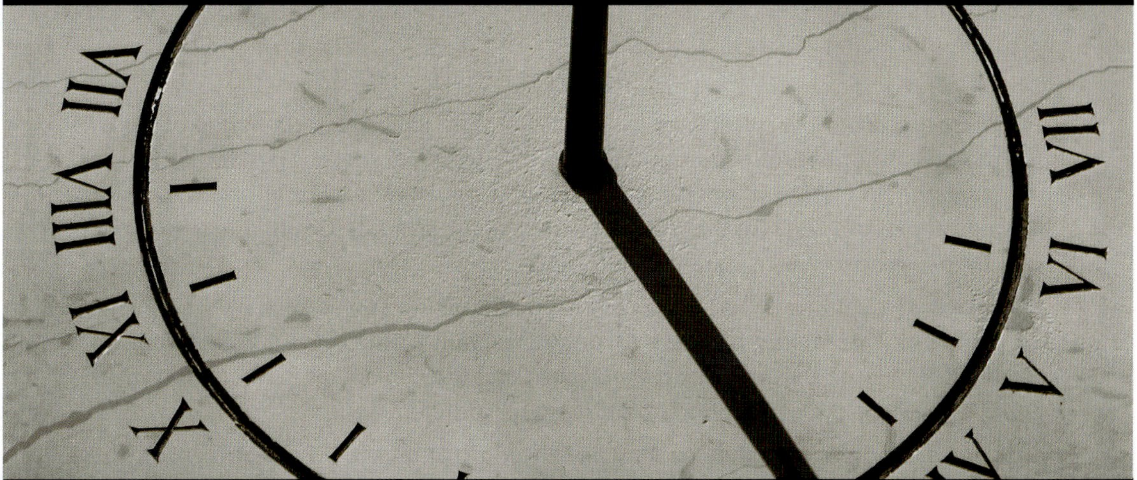

The idea of vertical integration is anathema to an increasing number of companies. Most of yesterday's highly integrated giants are working overtime at splitting into more manageable, more energetic units—i.e., de-integrating. Then they are turning around and re-integrating—not by acquisitions but via alliances with all sorts of partners of all shapes and sizes.

—TOM PETERS, LIBERATION MANAGEMENT

OUTLINE

Introduction and Objectives

Chapter 2 introduced the distinction between *corporate strategy* and *business strategy*. Corporate strategy is concerned primarily with the decisions over the *scope* of the firm's activities, including:

- *Product scope*. How specialized should the firm be in terms of the range of products it supplies? Coca-Cola (soft drinks), SAB-Miller (beer), Gap (fashion retailing), and SAP (software) are specialized companies: each is engaged in a single industry sector. Sony Corporation, General Electric and Tata Group are diversified companies: each spans multiple industries.
- *Geographical scope*. What is the optimal geographical spread of activities for the firm? In the restaurant business, Clyde's Restaurant Group owns 13 restaurants in the Washington DC area, Popeye's Chicken and Biscuits operates throughout the U.S., McDonald's Corporation operates in 121 different countries.
- *Vertical scope.* What range of vertically linked activities should the firm encompass? Walt Disney is a vertically integrated company: it produces its own movies, distributes them to cinemas and through its own TV networks (ABC and Disney Channel) and uses the movies' characters in its retail stores and theme parks. Nike is much more vertically specialized: it design and markets footwear and apparel, but outsources most activities in its value chain, including manufacturing, distribution, and retailing.

The distinction between business and corporate strategy may be summarized as follows: *corporate strategy* is concerned with *where* a firm competes; *business strategy* is concerned with *how* a firm competes with a particular area of business.[1] The major part of this book has been concerned with issues of business strategy. For the next four chapters, the emphasis is on corporate strategy: decisions that define the *scope of the firm.* I devote separate chapters to the different dimensions of scope—vertical scope (*vertical integration*), geographical scope (*multinationality*) and product scope (*diversification*). However, as we shall discover, the key underlying concepts for analyzing these different dimensions—economies of scope in resources and capabilities, transaction costs, and costs of corporate complexity—are common to all three.

In this chapter we begin by considering the overall scope of the firm. We then focus specifically on vertical integration. This takes us to the heart of the determinants of firm boundaries—in particular, the role of *transaction costs*. As we shall discover, vertical integration has been a hot topic in corporate strategy during the past decade. Opportunities for outsourcing, alliances, and electronic commerce have caused companies to rethink which of their activities should remain within their organizational boundaries.

By the time you have completed this chapter, you will be able to:

- identify the relative efficiencies of firms and markets in organizing economic activity and apply the principles of *transaction cost economics* to explain why boundaries between firms and markets shift over time;
- assess the relative advantages of vertical integration and outsourcing in organizing vertically-related activities, understand the circumstances that influence these relative advantages, and advise a firm whether a particular activity should be undertaken internally or outsourced;
- identify alternative ways of organizing vertical transactions—including spot market transactions, long-term contracts, franchise agreements, and alliances—and advise a firm on the most advantageous transaction mode given the characteristics and circumstances of the transaction.

Transaction Costs and the Scope of the Firm

In Chapter 7, we noted that firms came into existence because they were more efficient in organizing production than were market contracts between self-employed workers. Let us explore this issue and consider the determinants of firm boundaries.

Firms, Markets, and Transaction Costs

Although the capitalist economy is frequently referred to as a "market economy," in fact, it comprises two forms of economic organization. One is the *market mechanism*, where individuals and firms, guided by market prices, make independent decisions to buy and sell goods and services. The other is the *administrative mechanism* of firms, where decisions concerning production and resource allocation are made by managers and imposed through hierarchies. The market mechanism was characterized by Adam Smith, the eighteenth-century Scottish economist, as the "invisible hand" because its coordinating role does not require conscious planning. Alfred Chandler has referred to the administrative mechanism of firms as the "visible hand" because coordination involves active planning.[2]

Firms and markets may be viewed as alternative institutions for organizing production. Firms are distinguished by the fact that they comprise a number of individuals bound by employment contracts with a central contracting authority. But firms are not essential for organizing production. When I remodeled my basement, I contracted with a self-employed builder to undertake the work. He in turn subcontracted parts of the work to a plumber, an electrician, a joiner, a drywall installer and a painter. Although the job involved the coordinated activity of several individuals, these self-employed specialists were not linked by employment relations but by market contracts ("$4000 to install wiring, lights and sockets").

Firms and markets coexist, but their relative roles vary. If we compare the mainframe computer industry with the personal computer industry, the administrative mechanisms of firms predominate in the former, markets are more important in the latter. Thus, in mainframes, the dominant supplier, IBM, remains highly vertically integrated. It produces many of its own components (such as microprocessors), develops its own operating and applications software, and undertakes distribution, marketing, and customer support. Personal computers, by contrast, involve a network of firms linked by market contracts: design and marketing is undertaken by firms such as HP, Acer and Lenovo. Components are produced by firms such as Intel, Seagate, and Samsung. Assembly is outsourced to contract manufactures such as Asustek and Quanta Computer. Customer support is also outsourced to specialist suppliers—often located in India or Eastern Europe.

What determines which particular activity is undertaken within a firm and which through the market? Ronald Coase's answer was *relative cost*.[3] Markets are not costless: making a purchase or sale involves search costs, the costs of negotiating and drawing up a contract, the costs of monitoring to ensure that the other party's side of the contract is being fulfilled and the enforcement costs of arbitration or litigation should a dispute arise. All these costs are types of *transaction costs*.[4] If the transaction costs associated with organizing across markets are greater than the *administrative costs* of organizing within firms, we can expect the coordination of productive activity will be internalized within firms.

This situation is illustrated in Figure 14.1. With regard to vertical scope, which is more efficient: three independent companies—one producing steel, the next rolling the steel into sheet, and the third producing steel cans—or having all three stages of production within a single company? In the case of geographical scope, which is

FIGURE 14.1 The scope of the firm: specialization versus integration

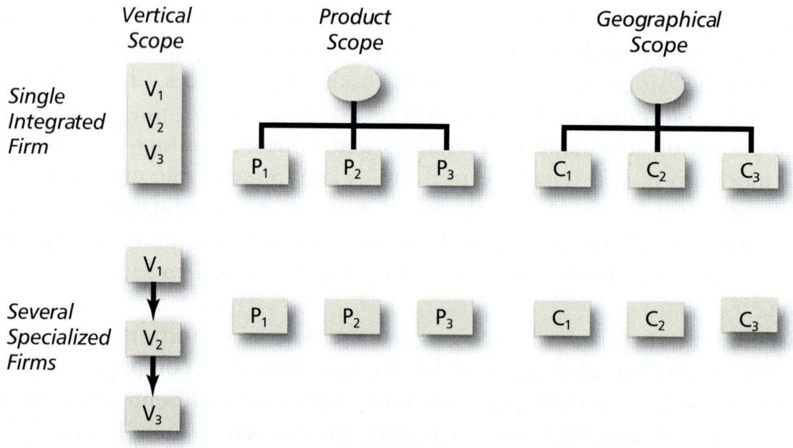

In the integrated firm there is an administrative interface between the different vertical units (V), product units (P), and country units (C). Where there is specialization, each unit is a separate firm linked by market interfaces.

more efficient: three independent companies producing cans in the U.S., U.K. and Italy, or a single multinational company owning and operating the can making plants in all three countries? In the case of product scope, should metal cans, plastic packaging, and domestic appliances be produced by three separate companies, or are there efficiencies to be gained by merging all three into a single company?

The Shifting Boundary between Firms and Markets

The answers to these questions have changed over time. During the nineteenth and for most of the twentieth century, companies grew in size and scope, absorbing transactions that had previously taken place across markets. This was part of the evolutionary process we observed in Chapter 7: companies that were once small, specialized and localized became large, integrated, diversified and multinational. Using the Coase principle, can we attribute this trend to a fall in the administrative costs firms relative to the transaction costs of markets? Certainly there are two factors that have greatly increased the efficiency of firms in organizing economic activity:

- *Technology*. The telegraph, telephone, and computer have played an important role in facilitating communications within firms and expanding the decision-making capacity of managers.
- *Management techniques*. Developments in the principles and techniques of management have greatly expanded the organizational and decision-making effectiveness of managers. Beginning with the dissemination of double-entry bookkeeping in the nineteenth century,[5] and the introduction of scientific management in the early twentieth century,[6] the past six decades have seen rapid advances in all areas of management theory and methods.

By the late 1960s, the growth in large corporations and the impressive achievements of the new tools of management science and corporate planning encouraged a widespread view that the *market economy* had been replaced by a *corporate economy*. J. K. Galbraith predicted that the inherent advantages of firms over markets in planning and resource allocation would result in increasing dominance of capitalist economies by a small number of giant corporations.[7]

Yet, by the end of the 1990s, these predictions had been refuted by a sharp reversal of the trend toward increased corporate scope. Although large companies continued to expand internationally, the dominant trends of the past three decades have been "downsizing" and "refocusing," as large industrial companies reduced both their product scope through focusing on their core businesses, and their vertical scope through outsourcing. As a result, the Forbes 500's share of total U.S. private sector employment fell from 21.2% in 1980 to 14.9% in 1995.[8]

The contraction of corporate boundaries points to markets increasing their efficiency relative to firms' administrative processes. A key factor is greater turbulence of the business environment in recent decades. During periods of instability, the costs of administration within large, complex firms tend to rise as the need for flexibility and speed of response overwhelms traditional management systems. A second factor is the developments of information and communications technology (ICT). The advent of computers reinforced the advantages of the giant corporation—only large organizations could afford them. But with the PC, internet, and mobile communication revolution, the benefits of leading-edge ICT have diffused to small firms and individuals, and the creation of virtual digital markets and electronic data interchange have revolutionized market transactions.

Let us focus now on just one dimension of corporate scope: vertical integration. The question we will consider is this: is it better to be vertically integrated or vertically specialized? With regard to a specific activity, the simple question for the firm is: *to make, or to buy?* To answer this question, we shall draw in particular on Oliver Williamson's analysis of transaction costs, which forms the basis for a theory of economic organization that is particularly useful in designing vertical relationships.[9]

The Costs and Benefits of Vertical Integration

Strategies towards vertical integration have been subject to shifting fashions. For most of the twentieth century the prevailing wisdom was that vertical integration was generally beneficial because it allowed superior coordination and reduced risk. During the past 25 years there has been a profound change of opinion: outsourcing, it is claimed, enhances flexibility and allows firms to concentrate on those activities where they possess superior capabilities. Moreover, many of the coordination benefits associated with vertical integration can be achieved through collaboration between vertically-related companies.

However, as in other areas of management, fashion is fickle. In the media sector, vertical integration between content and distribution has become viewed as a critical advantage in the face of rapid technological change. The resulting wave of mergers between content producers and distributors (TV broadcasters, cable companies, and internet portals) has transformed the industry (see Strategy Capsule 14.1).

Our task is to go beyond fads and fashions to uncover the factors that determine whether vertical integration enhances or weakens performance.

STRATEGY CAPSULE 14.1

Vertical Integration in the Media Sector: Value Creating or Value Destroying?

Considerable vertical integration has occurred between content companies (film studios, music publishing, newspapers) and distribution companies (TV broadcasting, cable, satellite TV, telecom providers). News Corp. has expanded from newspapers into movie production (Twentieth Century Fox), broadcast TV (Fox), satellite TV and other sectors of the media business; Disney acquired TV broadcaster ABC; Viacom, formerly a cable company, acquired Paramount and Dreamworks; GE's NBC Universal combines studio production with cable and broadcast TV distribution; and AOL merged with Time Warner, a leading magazine, film, and music company. In 2004, Comcast, America's biggest cable operator, made a $54 billion hostile bid for Walt Disney Company.

Does vertical integration between media content and media distribution create or destroy value? Here are two contrasting views:

STEVE ROSENBUSH, BUSINESS WEEK, FEBRUARY 11, 2004

The economics of the TV-distribution business have been under siege for some time. That's why many of the business' smartest operators, like Liberty Media's John Malone and Viacom's Sumner Redstone, started shifting their investments into media years ago. Under Redstone, Viacom has been transformed from a cable operator into a media hothouse that includes everything from MTV to CBS. Buying Disney "shouldn't be a surprise. It's the logical next step," Comcast CEO Brian Roberts said at his February 11 press conference announcing his bid for the Mouse House.

It isn't enough to be just a media company, either. Most content providers benefit from having a certain amount of distribution, which helps lower their costs. That's why, in the future, media and communications will be dominated by hybrids such as News Corp. which recently acquired satellite-TV operator DirecTV.

Comcast's Roberts has embraced this future. The question now is whether Disney CEO Michael Eisner—who spurned an offer for a friendly deal—can accept the same future. For decades, Disney and other programmers have held the balance of power in distribution deals. That's changing. The cable-TV business isn't just a collection of small family companies running regional outfits anymore. Comcast, which began life in Tupelo, Mississippi, in 1963, now has national reach. It has a greater market cap than Disney.

And it's competing with satellite-distribution companies like DirecTV that are also national in scope. Now that DirecTV is under Rupert Murdoch's control, it would be folly for Disney to pretend that it can still compete without a distribution partner of comparable stature. Comcast fits the bill.

JOHN KAY, FINANCIAL TIMES, MARCH 3, 2004

Media content needs delivery, and vice versa. And the same channels can often be used to disseminate text, images and music. This discovery was made at least 1000 years ago by people who developed religious services, still among the most moving and spectacular multimedia displays.

But this old idea is frequently rediscovered by visionary chief executives, excitable consultants, and greedy investment bankers: the people who proclaimed the AOL-Time Warner deal a marriage made in heaven. And it was revealed with Damascene force to Jean-Marie Messier, a humble French water carrier.

But activities can converge without requiring that the companies that undertake them converge. The erstwhile *maître du monde* might have drawn a useful lesson from his experience at Compagnie Générale des Eaux before his apotheosis as chief executive of Vivendi Universal: sewers and the stuff that goes down them do not need common ownership.

Defining Vertical Integration

Vertical integration refers to a firm's ownership of vertically related activities. The greater a firm's ownership extends over successive stages of the value chain for its product, the greater its degree of vertical integration. The extent of vertical integration is indicated by the *ratio of a firm's value added to its sales revenue*: the more a firm makes rather than buys, the lower are its bought-in goods and services relative to its sales revenue.

Vertical integration can be either *backward*, where the firm takes over ownership and control of producing its own components or other inputs, or *forward*, where the firm takes over ownership and control of activities previously undertaken by its customers.

Vertical integration may also be *full* or *partial*. Some California wineries are fully integrated: they produce wine only from the grapes they grow, and sell it all through direct distribution. Most are partially integrated: their home-grown grapes are supplemented with purchased grapes; they sell some wine through their own tasting rooms, but most through independent distributors.

Technical Economies from the Physical Integration of Processes

Analysis of the benefits of vertical integration has traditionally emphasized the *technical economies* of vertical integration: cost savings that arise from the physical integration of processes. Thus, most steel sheet is produced by integrated producers in plants that first produce steel, then roll hot steel into sheet. Linking the two stages of production at a single location reduces transportation and energy costs. Similar technical economies arise in pulp and paper production and from linking oil refining with petrochemical production.

However, although these considerations explain the need for the co-location of plants, they do not explain why vertical integration in terms of *common ownership* is necessary. Why can't steel and steel strip production or pulp and paper production be undertaken by separate firms that own facilities which are physically integrated with one another? To answer this question, we must look beyond technical economies and consider the implications of linked processes for *transaction costs*.

The Sources of Transaction Costs in Vertical Exchanges

Consider the value chain for steel cans, which extends from mining iron ore to delivering cans to food processing companies (see Figure 14.2). Between the production of steel and steel strip, most production is vertically integrated. Between the production of steel strip and steel cans, there is very little vertical integration: can producers such as Crown Holdings and Ball Corporation are specialist packaging companies that purchase steel strip from steel companies on contracts.[10]

The predominance of market contracts between steel strip production and can production is the result of low transaction costs in the market for steel strip: there are many buyers and sellers, information is readily available and the switching costs for buyers and suppliers are low. The same is true for many other commodity products: few jewelry companies own gold mines; few flour-milling companies own wheat farms.

FIGURE 14.2 The value chain for steel cans

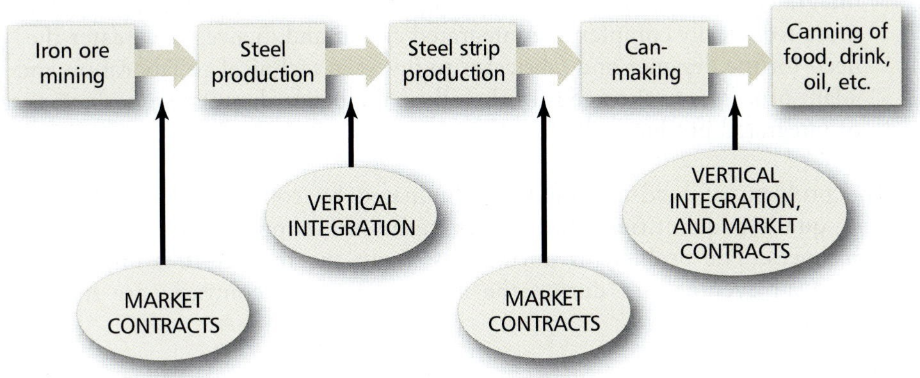

To understand why vertical integration predominates across steel production and steel strip production, let us see what would happen if the two stages were owned by separate companies. Because there are technical economies from hot-rolling steel as soon as it is poured from the furnace, steel makers and strip producers must invest in integrated facilities. A competitive market between the two stages is impossible; each steel strip producer is tied to its adjacent steel producer. In other words, the market becomes a series of *bilateral monopolies*.

Why are these relationships between steel producers and strip producers problematic? To begin with, where a single supplier negotiates with a single buyer, there is no market price: it all depends on relative bargaining power. Such bargaining is likely to be costly: the mutual dependency of the two parties is likely to give rise to *opportunism* and *strategic misrepresentation* as each company seeks to both enhance and exploit its bargaining power at the expense of the other. Hence, once we move from a competitive market situation to one where individual buyers and sellers are locked together in close bilateral relationships, the efficiencies of the market system are lost.

The culprits in this situation are *transaction-specific investments*. When a can maker buys steel strip, neither the steel strip producer nor the can maker needs to invest in equipment or technology that is specific to the needs of the other party. In the case of the steel producer and the steel roller, each company's plant is built to match the other party's plant. Once built, the plant's value depends upon the availability of the other party's complementary facilities—each seller is tied to a single buyer, which gives each the potential to *hold up* the other.

Thus, transaction-specific investments result in transaction costs arising from the difficulties of framing a comprehensive contract and the risks of disputes and opportunism that arise from contracts that do not cover every possible eventuality. Empirical research confirms the likelihood of vertical integration where transaction specific investments are required:[11]

- Among automakers, specialized components are more likely to be manufactured in-house than commodity items such as tires and spark plugs.[12] Similarly, in aerospace, company-specific components are more likely to be produced in house rather than purchased externally.[13]

- In the semiconductor industry, some companies specialize either in semiconductor design or in fabrication, while other companies are vertically integrated across both stages (for example, Intel, ST Microelectronics). The more technically complex the integrated circuit and, hence, the greater the need for the designer and fabricator to invest in technical collaboration and adapt processes to the needs of the other, the better the relative performance of integrated producers.[14]

The problem of hold-up could be eliminated by contracts that fully specify prices, quality, quantities, and other terms of supply under all possible circumstances. The problem is uncertainty about the future—it is impossible to anticipate all eventualities during the contract period—contracts are inevitably incomplete.

Administrative Costs of Internalization

Just because there are transaction costs in intermediate markets does not mean that vertical integration is necessarily an efficient solution. Vertical integration avoids the costs of using the market, but internalizing a transaction imposes administrative cost. The size of this cost depends on several factors.

Differences in Optimal Scale between Different Stages of Production Suppose that Federal Express requires delivery vans that are designed and manufactured to meet its particular needs. To the extent that the van manufacturer must make transaction-specific investments, there is an incentive for Federal Express to avoid the ensuing transaction costs by building its own vehicles. Would this be an efficient solution? Almost certainly not: the transaction costs avoided by Federal Express are likely to be trivial compared with the inefficiencies incurred in manufacturing its own vans. Federal Express purchases over 40 000 trucks and vans each year, well below the 200 000 minimum efficient scale of an assembly plant. (Ford produced two million commercial vehicles in 2005.)

The same logic explains why specialist brewers such as Anchor Brewing of San Francisco or Adnams of Suffolk, England are not backward integrated into cans and bottles like Anheuser-Busch-InterBev or SAB-Miller. Dedicated can making plants involve specific investments, creating problems of opportunism that vertical integration can avoid. However, small brewers simply do not possess the scale needed for scale efficiency in can manufacture.

Developing Distinctive Capabilities A key advantage of a company that is specialized in a few activities is its ability to develop distinctive capabilities in those activities. Even large, technology-based companies such as Xerox, Kodak and Philips cannot maintain IT capabilities that match those of IT services specialists such as EDS, IBM, and Accenture. The ability of these IT specialists to work with many different customers stimulates learning and innovation. If General Motors' IT department only serves the in-house needs of GM, this does not encourage the rapid development of its IT capabilities.

However, this assumes that capabilities in different vertical activities are independent of one another. Where one capability builds on capabilities in adjacent activities, vertical integration may help develop distinctive capabilities. Thus, IBM's half-century of success in mainframe computers owes much to its technological leadership in semiconductors and software. The efficiency of Wal-Mart's retailing operations depends critically on specialized IT and logistics from its in-house departments.

Managing Strategically Different Businesses These problems of differences in optimal scale and developing distinctive capabilities may be viewed as part of a wider set of problems—that of managing vertically related businesses that are strategically very different. A major disadvantage to FedEx of owning a truck-manufacturing company is that the management systems and organizational capabilities required for truck manufacturing are very different from those required for express delivery. These considerations may explain the lack of vertical integration between manufacturing and retailing. Firms that are integrated across design, manufacturing, and retailing, such as Zara and Gucci are rare. Most of the world's leading retailers—Wal-Mart, Gap, Carrefour—do not manufacture. Similarly, few manufacturing companies retail their own products. Not only do manufacturing and retailing require very different organizational capabilities, they also require different strategic planning systems, different approaches to control and human resource management, and different top management styles and skills.

These strategic dissimilarities are a key factor in the trend to vertical deintegration. Marriott's split into two separate companies, Marriott International and Host Marriott, was influenced by the belief that *owning* hotels is a strategically different business from *operating* hotels. Similarly, the Coca-Cola Company spun off its bottling activities as Coca-Cola Enterprises Inc. partly because managing local bottling and distribution operations is very different from managing the global Coca-Cola brand and the production and distribution of concentrates.

The Incentive Problem Vertical integration changes the incentives between vertically related businesses. Where a market interface exists between a buyer and a seller, profit incentives ensure that the buyer is motivated to secure the best possible deal and the seller is motivated to pursue efficiency and service in order to attract and retain the buyer—these are termed *high-powered incentives.* With vertical integration, internal supplier-customer relationships are subject to *low-powered incentives*—if Shell's tanker fleet is inefficient, employees will lose their bonuses and the head of shipping may be fired. However, these consequences tend to be slow and undramatic. Most of us who have worked in large organizations have found that external contractors are often more responsive to our requests than internal service providers.

One approach to creating stronger performance incentives within vertically integrated companies is to open internal divisions to external competition. As we shall examine more fully in Chapter 17, many large corporations have created *shared service organizations* where internal suppliers of corporate services such as IT, training, and engineering compete with external suppliers of the same services to serve internal operating divisions.

Competitive Effects of Vertical Integration Vertical integration can be used to extend a monopoly position at one stage of an industry's value chain to adjacent stages. The classic cases are Standard Oil, which used its dominance of transportation and refining to foreclose markets to independent oil producers; and Alcoa, which used its monopoly position in aluminum production to squeeze independent fabricators of aluminum products and favor its own fabrication subsidiaries. Such cases are rare. Economists have shown, once a company monopolizes one stage of the industry's value chain, there is no additional monopoly profit to be extracted by extending that monopoly to other stages.[15]

A more common situation is that a company which is strong at one vertical stage may disadvantage its market position by vertical integration. The firm's suppliers and customers are less willing to do business with the company if, through vertical integration, it becomes a competitor. Disney's acquisition of the ABC TV network adversely affected Disney's relationships with other TV networks and made other studios (for example, Dreamworks) more reluctant to collaborate with ABC in developing new TV productions.

Flexibility Both vertical integration and market transactions can claim advantage with regard to different types of flexibility. Where the required flexibility is rapid responsiveness to uncertain demand, there may be advantages in market transactions. The lack of vertical integration in the construction industry reflects, in part, the need for flexibility in adjusting both to cyclical patterns of demand and to the different requirements of each project. Vertical integration may also be disadvantageous in responding quickly to new product development opportunities that require new combinations of technical capabilities. Some of the most successful new electronic products of recent years—Apple's iPod, Microsoft's Xbox, Dell's range of notebook computers—have been produced by contract manufacturers. Extensive outsourcing has been a key feature of fast-cycle product development throughout the electronics sector.

Yet, where system-wide flexibility is required, vertical integration may allow for speed and coordination in achieving simultaneous adjustment throughout the vertical chain. American Apparel is a rare example of a successful U.S. *manufacturer* of apparel. Its tightly coordinated vertical integration from its Los Angeles design and manufacturing base to its 160 retail stores across 10 countries allows a super-fast design-to-distribution cycle. Vertical integration is also a central theme of brand identity. Figure 14.3 shows one of its advertisements.

Zara is another fashion clothing business that has cut cycle times and maximized market responsiveness through a vertically integrated strategy that challenges the industry's dominant model of contract manufacture (see Strategy Capsule 14.2).

Compounding Risk To the extent that vertical integration ties a company to its internal suppliers, vertical integration represents a compounding of risk insofar as problems at any one stage of production threaten production and profitability at all other stages. When union workers at a General Motors brake plant went on strike in 1998, GM's 24 U.S. assembly plants were quickly brought to a halt. If Disney animation studios fail to produce blockbuster animation movies with new characters, then the knock-on effects are felt through DVD sales, merchandise sales in Disney Stores, and lack of new attractions at Disney theme parks.

FIGURE 14.3 An American Apparel advertisement

Source:
American Apparel Inc.

STRATEGY CAPSULE 14.2

Making Vertical Integration Work: Zara

Zara is the main division and brand of the Spanish clothing company, Inditex (Industria de Diseño Textil, S.A). Zara contributes 68% of Inditex's sales. Between 2000 and 2006, Inditex achieved sales growth of 30% a year, a net margin of 11%, and a return on average equity of 29%—well ahead of Gap, H&M, or Mango. By the end of 2006, Zara operated over 1400 stores in 40 countries.

Zara's success is based on a business system that achieves a speed of response to market demand that is without precedent in the fast-moving fashion clothing sector. Zara's cycles of design, production, and distribution are substantially faster than any of its main competitors. For most fashion retailers there is a six-month lag between completing a new design and deliveries arriving at retail stores. Zara can take a new design from drawing board to retail store in as little as three weeks.

Products are designed at the Inditex headquarters in La Coruna on the northwest tip of Spain. Over 40 000 garments are designed annually with about one-quarter entering production. Designs are sketched, committed to the CAD system, then a sample is handmade by skilled workers located within the design facility. Working alongside the designers are "market specialists" who monitor sales and market trends in a particular country or region, and "buyers" who handle procurement and production planning. The three groups coordinate closely and jointly select which products go into production.

Close to half of Zara's products are manufactured within Zara's local network, which comprises Zara's own factories and subcontractors who undertake all sewing operations. The rest is outsourced to third-party manufacturers.

For its own production, 40% of fabric requirements are supplied by Comidex—a wholly owned subsidiary of Inditex. Most fabric is supplied undyed. Postponing dying until later in the production process allows colors to be changed at short notice.

Finished products are ironed, labeled (including tags with prices in local currencies), bagged in boxes or on hangers ready for retail display, then transferred by monorail to the La Coruna distribution center. Each retail store submits its orders twice a week and receives shipments twice a week. Orders are dispatched within eight hours of receipt and are delivered within 24 hours in Europe, 48 hours in the U.S., and 72 hours in Japan.

Zara owns and manages almost all its retail stores. This allows standardized layout and window displays and close communication and collaboration between store managers and headquarters.

Zara's tightly coordinated system allows quick response to market demand. At the beginning of each season only small numbers of each new item are produced and are placed in a few lead stores. According to market response, Zara then adjusts production. Typically, Zara's products spend no more than two weeks in a retail store. Product market specialists provide critical feedback that is used both to adjust production levels and to make design or color modifications to existing items.

The close, informal information networks within Zara are critical to product design. Although designers begin working on new designs some nine months before each new season, continuous adjustments to designs are made in response to new information on fashion trends and customer preferences. Designers and market specialists are encouraged to be alert to the new ranges released by the fashion houses of Milan, Paris, London, and New York; to the styles worn by trendsetters on TV, in popular music, and in the leading-edge clubs; and to feedback from store managers and other employees.

Zara's compressed product cycles have induced changes in customers' retail buying behavior. Zara customers make more frequent visits to their local stores than is typical for other fashion retailers. They also make faster purchase decisions in the knowledge that garments move quickly and are unlikely to be restocked.

Sources: Kasra Ferdows, Jose Machuca and Michael Lewis, *Zara*, ECCH Case Number 602-002-01, 2002; www.inditex.com.

TABLE 14.1 Vertical integration (VI) versus outsourcing: some key considerations

Characteristics of the vertical relationship	Implication
How many firms are there in the vertically adjacent activity?	The fewer the number of firms, the greater are the transaction costs and bigger the advantages of VI
Do transaction-specific investments need to be made by either party?	Transaction-specific investments increase the advantages of VI
How evenly distributed is information between the vertical stages?	The greater are information asymmetries, the more likely is opportunistic behavior and the greater the advantages of VI
Are market transactions in intermediate products subject to taxes or regulations?	Taxes and regulations are a cost of market contracts that can be avoided by VI
How uncertain are the circumstances of the transactions over the period of the relationship?	The greater are uncertainties concerning costs, technologies, and demand, the greater the difficulty of writing contracts, and the greater the advantages of VI
Are two stages similar in terms of the optimal scale of operation?	The greater the dissimilarity, the greater the advantages of market contracts as compared with VI
Are the two stages strategically similar (e.g., similar key success factors, common resources/capabilities)?	The greater the strategic similarity, the greater the advantages of VI over outsourcing
How great is the need for continual investment in upgrading and extending capabilities within individual activities?	The greater the need to invest in capability development, the greater the advantages of outsourcing over VI
How great is the need for entrepreneurial flexibility and drive in the separate vertical activities?	The greater the need for entrepreneurship and flexibility, the greater the advantages of high-powered incentives provided by market contracts, and the greater the administrative disadvantages of VI
How uncertain is market demand?	The greater the unpredictability of demand, the greater the flexibility advantages of outsourcing
Does vertical integration compound risk, exposing the entire value chain risks affecting individual stages?	The heavier the investment requirements and the greater the independent risks at each stage, the more risky is VI

Assessing the Pros and Cons of Vertical Integration

We have seen that vertical integration is neither good nor bad. As with most questions of strategy: it all depends. The value of our analysis is that we are now able to identify the factors that determine the relative advantages of the market transactions *versus* internalization within the firm. Table 14.1 summarizes some of the key criteria. However, our analysis is not yet complete, we must consider some additional factors that influence the choice of vertical strategy—in particular, the fact that vertical relationships are not limited to the simple choice of make or buy.

Designing Vertical Relationships

Our discussion so far has compared vertical integration with arm's-length market contracts. In practice buyers and sellers can interact and coordinate their interests through a variety of relationships. Figure 14.4 shows a number of different types of relationship between buyers and sellers. These relationships may be classified in relation to two characteristics. First, the extent to which the buyer and seller commit resources to the relationship: arm's-length, spot contracts involve no resource commitment beyond the single deal; vertical integration typically involves a substantial investment. Second, the formality of the relationship: long-term contracts and franchises are formalized by the complex written agreements they entail; spot contracts may involve little or no documentation, but are bound by the formalities of common law; collaborative agreements between buyers and sellers are usually informal, while the formality of vertical integration is at the discretion of the firm's management.

Different Types of Vertical Relationship

These different types of vertical relationship offer different combinations of advantages and disadvantages. For example:

- *Long-term contracts*. Market transactions can be either *spot contracts*—buying a cargo of crude oil on the Rotterdam petroleum market—or *long-term contracts* that involve a series of transactions over a period of time and specify the terms of sales and the responsibilities of each party. Spot transactions work well under competitive conditions (many buyers and sellers and a standard product) where there is no need for transaction-specific investments by either party. Where closer supplier-customer ties are needed—particularly when one or both parties need to make transaction-specific

FIGURE 14.4 Different types of vertical relationship

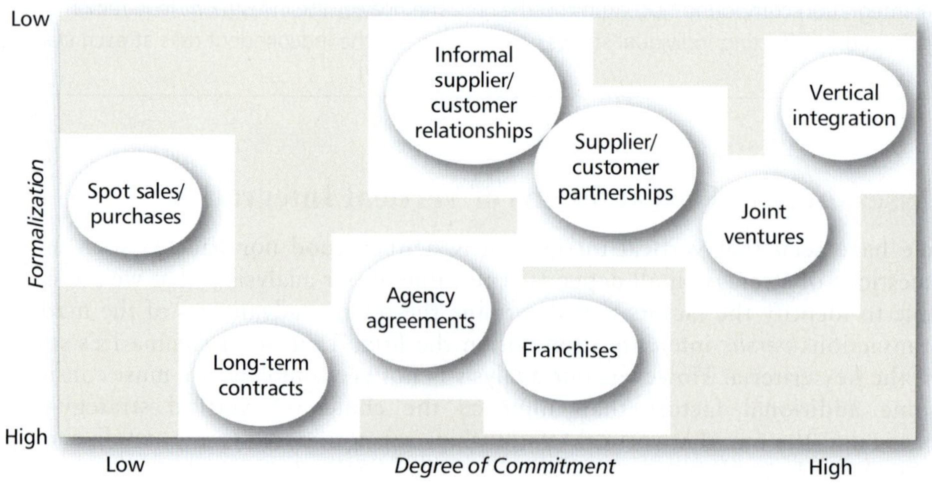

investments—then a longer term contract can help avoid opportunism and provide the security needed to make the necessary investment. However, long-term contracts face the problem of anticipating the circumstances that may arise during the life of the contract: either they are too restrictive, or so loose that they give rise to opportunism and conflicting interpretation. Long-term contracts often include provisions for the arbitration of contract disputes.

- *Vendor partnerships*. The greater the difficulties of specifying complete contracts for long-term supplier-customer deals, the greater the advantage of vertical relationships based on trust and mutual understanding will be. Such relationships can provide the security needed for transaction-specific investments, the flexibility to meet changing circumstances, and the incentives to avoid opportunism. Such arrangements may be entirely *relational contracts* with no written contract at all. The model for vendor partnerships has been the close collaborative relationships that many Japanese companies have with their suppliers. Japanese automakers have been much less backward integrated than their U.S. or European counterparts but have also achieved close collaboration with component makers in technology, design, quality, and production scheduling.[16]
- *Franchising*. A franchise is a contractual agreement between the owner of a business system and trademark (the franchiser) that permits the franchisee to produce and market the franchiser's product or service in a specified area. Franchising brings together the brand, marketing capabilities, and business systems of the large corporation with the entrepreneurship and local knowledge of small firms. The franchising systems of companies such as McDonald's, Century 21 Real Estate, Hilton Hotels and Seven-Eleven convenience stores facilitate the close coordination and investment in transaction-specific assets that vertical integration permits with the high-powered incentives, flexibility and cooperation between strategically dissimilar businesses that market contracts make possible.

Choosing between Alternative Vertical Relationships

The criteria listed in Table 14.1 establish the basic features of the vertical relation that favor either market transactions or vertical integration. However, the availability of other types of vertical relationships, such as vendor partnerships and franchises mean that vertical integration is not the sole solution to problems of transaction costs. Moreover, many of these relational contracts and hybrid arrangements have the capacity to combine the advantages of both vertical integration and market contracts.

Choosing the optimal vertical relationships needs to take account of additional factors than those listed in Table 14.1. In particular:

- *Resources, capabilities, and strategy*. Within the same industry, different companies will choose different vertical arrangements according to their reactive resource and capability strengths and the strategies they pursue. Thus in fashion clothing, Zara's high level of vertical integration compared to Hennes & Mauritz or Gap reflects strategy based upon fast-cycle new product development and tight integration between its retail stores, designers, and manufacturers. While most fast food chains have expanded through franchising, California-based In-N-Out Burger seeks to maintain its unique culture and distinctive business practices by directly owning and managing its restaurants. While most banks have been outsourcing IT to companies such as IBM and EDS, U.S. credit card group Capital One sees IT as a key source of competitive advantage: "IT is our central nervous system . . . if we outsourced tomorrow we might save a dollar or two on each account, but we would lose flexibility and value and service levels."[17]

- *Allocation of risk.* Any arrangement beyond a spot contract must cope with uncertainties over the course of the contract. A key feature of any contract is that its terms involve, often implicitly, an allocation of risks between the parties. How risk is shared is dependent partly on bargaining power and partly on efficiency considerations. In franchise agreements, the franchisee (as the weaker partner) bears most of the risk—it is the franchisee's capital that is at risk and the franchisee pays the franchiser a flat royalty based on sales revenues. In oil exploration, outsourcing agreements between the oil majors (such as Chevron, ExxonMobil, and Eni) and drilling companies (such as Schlumberger and Halliburton) have moved from fixed-price contracts to risk-sharing agreements where the driller often takes an equity stake in the project.
- *Incentive structures.* Incentives are central to the design of vertical relationships: incentives for opportunistic behavior are the bugbear of market contacts, while weak ("low-powered") incentives for performance are the central problem of vertical integration. It seems possible that hybrid and intermediate governance modes offer some of the best solutions to the problems of appropriate incentives. Toyota, Benetton, Boeing, and Marks & Spencer have relationships with their vendors that may involve formal contracts, but their essence is that they are long-term and trust based. The key to these relationships is that the promise of a long-term, mutually beneficial relationship trumps short term opportunism.

Recent Trends

The main feature of recent years has been a growing diversity of hybrid vertical relationships that have attempted to reconcile the flexibility and incentives of market transactions with the close collaboration provided by vertical integration. Although collaborative vertical relationships are viewed as a recent phenomenon—associated with microelectronics, biotechnology, and other hi-tech sectors—local clusters of vertically collaborating firms are a long-time feature of the craft industries of Europe. This is especially true of northern Italy—both in traditional sectors such as textiles[18] and newer sectors such as packaging equipment[19] and motorcycles.[20]

The supplier networks of Japanese manufacturers with their knowledge sharing and collaborative new product development have become models for many large American and European companies.[21] There has been a massive shift from arm's-length supplier relationships to long-term collaboration with fewer suppliers. In many instances, competitive tendering and multiple sourcing have been replaced by single-supplier arrangements. Vendor relationships frequently involve supplier certification and quality management programs and technical collaboration.

Enthusiasm for exploiting lower labor costs in emerging countries has intensified outsourcing among companies in North America, Europe, and Japan.[22] In the electronics sector, companies such as Nokia, Hewlett Packard, and Sony have outsourced manufacturing to China and services (including call centers and software development) to India. We shall return to these international dimensions of outsourcing in Chapter 15.

The mutual dependence that results from close, long-term supplier-buyer relationships creates vulnerability for both parties. While trust may alleviate some of the risks of opportunism, companies can also reinforce their vertical relationships and discourage opportunism through equity stakes and profit sharing arrangements. For example: Commonwealth Bank of Australia took an equity stake in its IT supplier, EDS Australia; pharmaceutical companies often acquire equity stakes in the biotech companies that undertake much of their R&D; and, as already noted, oilfield services companies are increasingly equity partners in upstream projects.

However, in this world of closer vertical relationships, some trends have been in the opposite direction. The internet has radically reduced the transaction costs of markets—particularly in pruning search costs and facilitating electronic payments. The result has been a revival in arm's-length competitive contracting through business-to-business e-commerce hubs such as Covisint (auto parts), Elemica (chemicals), and Rock and Dirt (construction equipment).[23]

The scope of outsourcing has extended from basic components to a wide range of business services including payroll, IT, training, and customer service and support. Increasingly, outsourcing involves not just individual components and services but whole chunks of the value chain. In electronics, the design and manufacture of entire products are often outsourced to contract manufacturers such as Hon Hai Precision Industry Co., which makes Apple iPods, Nokia phones, and Sony's PlayStation.

Extreme levels of outsourcing have given rise to the concept of the *virtual corporation*: a firm whose primary function is to coordinate the activities of a network of suppliers and downstream partners.[24] In this organizational form the hub company has the role of *systems integrator*. The critical issue is whether a company that outsources most functions can retain *architectural capabilities* needed to manage the *component capabilities* of the various partners and contractors. The risk is that the virtual corporation may degenerate into a "hollow corporation," where it loses the capability to evolve and adapt to changing circumstances.[25] If, as Prahalad and Hamel argue, core competences are embodied in "core products" then the more these core products are outsourced, the greater is the potential for the erosion of core competence.[26] Andrea Prencipe's research into aero engines points to the complementarity between architectural capabilities and component capabilities. Thus, even when the aero engine manufacturers outsource key components, they typically maintain R&D into those component technologies.[27] The problems experienced by Boeing in managing the outsourced network model it adopted for its 787 Dreamliner point to the complexity of the system integrator role.[28]

Summary

Deciding which parts of the value chain to engage in presents companies with one of their most difficult strategic decisions. The conventional analysis of vertical integration has looked simply at the efficiency of markets as compared with the efficiency of firms: if the cost of transacting through the market is greater than the cost of administering within the firm, then the company should vertically integrate across the stages. Transaction cost analysis does not, however, provide the complete answer. In the first place, vertical strategies are not simply make-or-buy choices—there is a wide variety of ways in which a company can structure vertical relationships. Secondly, the most critical long-run consideration is the development of organizational capability. If a company is to sustain competitive advantage, it must restrict itself to those activities where it possesses the capabilities that are superior to those of the other companies that perform those activities. If my company's data-processing capabilities are inferior to those of IBM and its logistics capabilities are inferior to those of Federal Express, I should consider outsourcing these activities. The most difficult issues arise where there are linkages between value chain activities. Even though a contract manufacturer may be able to manufacture my remote-controlled lawnmower more efficiently than I can internally, what would be the implications for my new product development capability if I no longer have in-house manufacturing?

Ultimately, vertical integration decisions revolve around two key questions. First, which activities will we undertake internally and which will we outsource? Second, how do we design our vertical arrangements with both external and internal suppliers and buyers? In the case of external relations, these may be conducted through spot contracts, long-term contracts, or some form of strategic alliance. Similar ranges of alternatives face the vertically integrated firm—including the option of arm's-length negotiated contracts. Both types of decision are critically dependent on the firm's competitive strategy and the capabilities it possesses. As we have already noted, the critical issue for the individual business is not to follow conventional wisdom but to carefully evaluate its strategic needs, its resources and capabilities at different stages in the value chain, the characteristics of the transactions involved and the relative attractiveness of different stages of the value chain.

Self-Study Questions

1 The discussion of "The Shifting Boundary between Firms and Markets" argues that the developments in information and communication technology (for example, telephone and computer) during most of the twentieth century tended to lower the costs of administration within the firm relative to the costs of market transactions, thereby increasing the size and scope of firms. What about the internet? How has this influenced the efficiency of large integrated firms relative to small, specialized firms coordinated by markets?

2 The discussion of "The Shifting Barrier between Firms and Markets" notes that the large U.S. companies account for a smaller percentage of total employment—a development that is attributed to a more turbulent business environment. Explain why external turbulence encourages outsourcing and increased focus on core business.

3 A large proportion of major corporations outsource their IT function to specialist suppliers of UIT services such as IBM, EDS (now owned by Hewlett Packard), Accenture, and Cap Gemini. What transaction costs are incurred by these outsourcing arrangements and why do they arise? What are the offsetting benefits from IT outsourcing?

4 In Strategy Capsule 14.1, Steve Rosenbush argues that integration between media content and media distribution companies (and, specifically, between Disney and Comcast) is strategically advantageous. John Kay suggests that there is little need for common ownerships between distribution channels and the content they carry. Explain the arguments of each. Who do you agree with? As more content is being viewed via the internet and on mobile devices, how does this affect the arguments?

5 For its Zara brand, Inditex manufactures the majority of the garments sells and undertakes all of its own distribution from manufacturing plants to its directly managed retail outlets. Benetton outsources most of its production, and most of its retail outlets are owned and operated by franchisees. Which is a superior system?

Notes

1 M. J. Piskorski ("A Note on Corporate Strategy," Harvard Business School 9-705-449, 2005) defines corporate strategy as: "a set of choices that a corporation makes to create value through configuration and coordination of its multimarket activities." In practice, determining the boundary between business strategy and corporate strategy depends on where we draw the boundaries of industries and markets.

2 A. Chandler Jr., *The Visible Hand: The Managerial Revolution in American Business* (Cambridge: MIT Press, 1977).

3 R. H. Coase, "The Nature of the Firm," *Economica* 4 (1937): 386–405.

4 The term *interaction costs* has also been used to describe "the time and money expended whenever people and companies exchange goods, services or ideas." See J. Hagel and M. Singer, "Unbundling the Corporation," *Harvard Business Review* (March–April 1999): 133–44.

5 Double-entry bookkeeping has its origins in fourteenth-century Italy and developed in Venice in the sixteenth century. See: L. Zan, "Accounting and Management Discourse in Preindustrial Settings: The Venice Arsenal at the Turn of the Sixteenth Century," *Accounting and Business Research* 32 (2004): 145–75.

6 F. W. Taylor, *The Principles of Scientific Management* (New York: Bulletin of the Taylor Society, 1916).

7 J. K. Galbraith, *The New Industrial State* (Harmondsworth: Penguin, 1969).

8 L. J. White, "Trends in Aggregate Concentration in the United States," *Journal of Economic Perspectives* 16 (Fall 2002): 137–60.

9 O. E. Williamson, *Markets and Hierarchies: Analysis and Antitrust Implications* (New York: Free Press, 1975); O. E. Williamson, *The Economic Institutions of Capitalism: Firms, Markets and Relational Contracting* (New York: Free Press, 1985).

10 The situation is different in aluminum cans, where aluminum producers such as Alcoa and Pechiney and users such as Coca-Cola and Anheuser-Busch are major producers of beverage cans.

11 For a review of empirical evidence on transaction costs and vertical integration see: J. T. Macher and B. D. Richman "Transaction Cost Economics: An Assessment of Empirical Research in the Social Sciences." *Business and Politics* 10 (2008): Article 1; M.D, Whinston, "On the Transaction Cost Determinants of Vertical Integration," *Journal of Law Economics and Organization* 19 (2003): 1–23.

12 K. Monteverde and J. J. Teece, "Supplier Switching Costs and Vertical Integration in the Automobile Industry," *Bell Journal of Economics* 13 (Spring 1982): 206–13.
13 S. Masten, "The Organization of Production: Evidence from the Aerospace Industry," *Journal of Law and Economics* 27 (October 1984): 403–17.
14 J. T. Macher, "Technological Development and the Boundaries of the Firm: A Knowledge-based Examination in Semiconductor Manufacturing," *Management Science* 52 (2006): 826–43; K. Monteverde, "Technical Dialogue as an Incentive for Vertical Integration in the Semiconductor Industry," *Management Science* 41 (1995): 1624–38.
15 R. Rey and J. Tirole, "A Primer on Foreclosure," Chapter 33 in R. Schmalensee, M. Armstrong, R. D. Willig and R.H. Porter, *Handbook of Industrial Organization* (Elsevier, 2007).
16 J. H. Dyer, "Effective Interfirm Collaboration: How Firms Minimize Transaction Costs and Maximize Transaction Value," *Strategic Management Journal* 18 (1997): 535–56; J. H. Dyer, "Specialized Supplier Networks as a Source of Competitive Advantage: Evidence from the Auto Industry," *Strategic Management Journal* 17 (1996): 271–92.
17 L. Willcocks and C. Sauer, "High Risks and Hidden Costs in IT Outsourcing," *Financial Times*, Mastering Risk (May 23, 2000): 3.
18 N. Owen and A. C. Jones, "A Comparative Study of the British and Italian Textile and Clothing Industries," Department of Trade and Industry (London: HMSO, 2003).
19 G. Lorenzoni and A. Lipparini, "The Leveraging of Interfirm Relationships as Distinctive Organizational Capabilities: A Longitudinal Study," *Strategic Management Journal* 20 (1999): 317–38.
20 G. Lorenzoni and A. Lipparini, "Organizing Around Strategic Relationships: Networks of Suppliers in the Italian Motorcycle Industry," in K. O. Cool, J. E. Henderson and R. Abate (eds), *Restructuring Strategy* (Oxford: Blackwell, 2005): 44–67.
21 J. H. Dyer and K. Nobeoka, "Creating and Managing a High-performance Knowledge-sharing Network: The Toyota Case," *Strategic Management Journal* 21 (2000): 345–68.
22 D. Farrell, "Smarter Offshoring," *Harvard Business Review* (June 2006): 85–92.
23 See www.covisint.com; www.elemica.com; www.rockanddirt.com.
24 "The Virtual Corporation," *Business Week* (February 8, 1993): 98–104; W. H. Davidow and M. S. Malone, *The Virtual Corporation* (New York: HarperCollins, 1992).
25 H. W. Chesborough and D. J. Teece, "When is Virtual Virtuous? Organizing for Innovation," *Harvard Business Review* (May–June 1996): 68–79.
26 C. K. Prahalad and G. Hamel, "The Core Competences of the Corporation," *Harvard Business Review* (May–June 1990): 79–91.
27 S. Brusoni, A. Prencipe, and K. Pavitt, "Knowledge Specialization, Organizational Coupling and the Boundaries of the Firm: Why Do Firms Know More Than They Make?" *Administrative Science Quarterly* 46 (2001): 597–621.
28 "Boeing's Dreamliner Delays Are a Nightmare" *SeekingAlpha*, http://seekingalpha.com/article/110735-boeing-s-dreamliner-delays-are-a-nightmare, accessed July 7, 2009.

15 Global Strategies and the Multinational Corporation

The speed of light does not merely transform the world. It becomes the world. Globalization is the speed of light.

—PAUL VIRILIO, PHILOSOPHER OF CULTURE AND SCIENCE

Globalization has changed us into a company that searches the world, not just to sell or to source, but to find intellectual capital—the world's best talent and greatest ideas.

—JACK WELCH, FORMER CHAIRMAN, GENERAL ELECTRIC

OUTLINE

Introduction and Objectives

In September 2007, Britain experienced its first bank run in 140 years as depositors queued to withdraw money from Northern Rock, a Newcastle-based mortgage bank. Despite having no direct exposure to the U.S. real estate market (only 0.24% of its assets were in U.S. collateralized debt obligations or U.S. home equity mortgage-backed securities), Northern Rock became the first non-U.S. casualty of the of the subprime mortgage crisis that began to unfold during spring 2007.

A year later the wave of bankruptcies precipitated by U.S. subprime mortgages claimed its first victim among sovereign nations: on October 9, 2008 Iceland's financial system collapsed and the government was forced to seek emergency support from the IMF. As with Northern Rock, the Icelandic banks that failed had almost no direct exposure to the U.S. real estate market or to securities based upon U.S. real estate loans.

The massive global fallout from the bursting of real estate bubbles in Miami, Las Vegas, Los Angeles, and other U.S. cities is a tribute to the power of internationalization to transmit and amplify local economic factors. Internationalization is the most important and pervasive force that has reshaped the competitive environment of business during the past half-century. While recent events have identified internationalization with global contagion, for most the past 60 years, internationalization has been a source of expanding opportunity for both firms and individuals. The opening of national markets has resulted in widening consumer choice, huge increases in efficiency, and growth options for both large and small firms.

Internationalization occurs through two mechanisms: trade and direct investment. The growth of world trade has consistently outstripped the growth of world output, increasing export/sales and import penetration ratios for all countries and all industries. For the OECD countries, total trade (imports and exports) rose from 11% of GDP in 1960 to 52% in 2007. The total stock of direct investment by OECD firms amounted to $13 trillion at the beginning of 2009—equivalent to 34% of OECD GDP.[1]

The forces driving both trade and direct investment are, first, the quest to exploit market opportunities in other countries, and, second, the desire to exploit resources and capabilities located in other countries. The resulting "globalization of business" has created vast flows of international transactions comprising payments for trade and services, flows of factor payments (interest, profits, and licensing fees) and flows of capital.

What does the internationalization of the world economy mean for our strategy analysis? As we shall see, internationalization is both a threat and an opportunity. Internationalization opens domestic markets to competitors from different countries—often with tragic consequences not just for individual firms but often for entire domestic industries. Internationalization also offers vast opportunity allowing firms with small domestic markets to become global leaders: Nokia (from Finland) in wireless handsets, Swatch (from Switzerland) in watches, A. P. Moller-Maersk (from Denmark) in shipping, Anheuser-Busch-InBev (from Belgium) in beer, BHP (from Australia) in metals mining, Research in Motion (from Canada) in smart phones. Most of all, the international dimension adds considerable complexity to our strategy analysis—not just in broadening the scope of markets (and competition) but also in complicating the analysis of competitive advantage.

By the time you have completed this chapter, you will be able to:

- use the tools of industry analysis to examine the impact of internationalization on industry structure and competition;
- analyze the implications of a firm's national environment for its competitive advantage;
- formulate strategies for exploiting overseas business opportunities, including overseas market entry strategies and overseas production strategies;
- shape international strategies that achieve an optimal balance between global integration and national differentiation;
- design organizational structures and management systems appropriate to the pursuit of international strategies.

We begin by exploring the implications of international competition, first for industry analysis, and then for the analysis of competitive advantage.

Implications of International Competition for Industry Analysis

Patterns of Internationalization

Internationalization occurs through *trade*—the sale and shipment of goods and services from one country to another—and *direct investment*—building or acquiring productive assets in another country. On this basis we can identify different types of industry according to the extent and mode of their internationalization (see Figure 15.1):

- *Sheltered industries* are served exclusively by indigenous firms. They are sheltered from both imports and inward direct investment by regulation, trade barriers, or because of the localized nature of the goods and services they offer. The forces of internationalization have made this category progressively smaller over time. Sheltered industries are primarily fragmented service industries (dry cleaning, hairdressing, auto repair, funeral services), some small-scale manufacturing (handicrafts, residential construction) and industries producing products that are nontradable because they are perishable (fresh milk, bread) or difficult to move (four-poster beds, garden sheds).
- *Trading industries* are those where internationalization occurs primarily through imports and exports. If a product is transportable, if it is not nationally differentiated and if it is subject to substantial scale economies, exporting from a single location is the most efficient means to exploit overseas markets. This is the case with commercial aircraft, shipbuilding, and defense

FIGURE 15.1 Patterns of industry internationalization

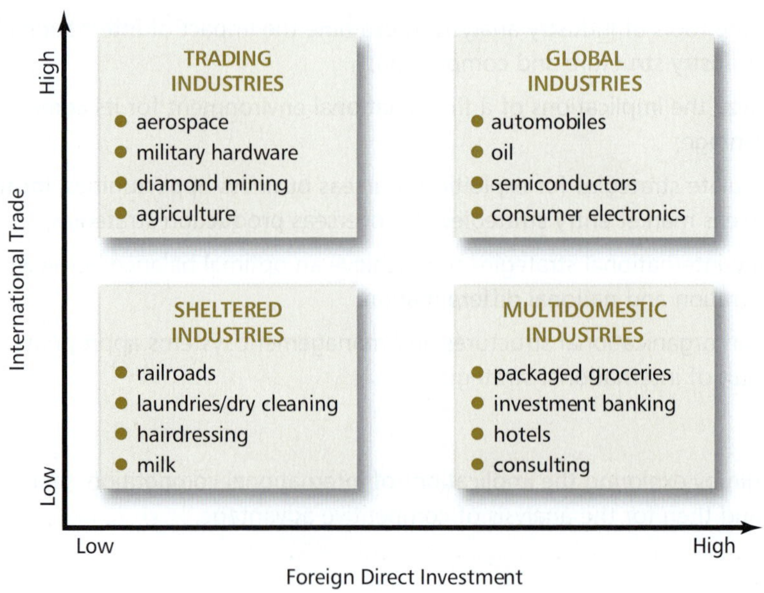

equipment. Trading industries also include products whose inputs are available only in a few locations: diamonds from South Africa; caviar from Iran and Azerbaijan.

- *Multidomestic industries* are those that internationalize through direct investment—either because trade is not feasible (as in the case of service industries such as banking, consulting, or hotels) or because products are nationally differentiated (for example, frozen dinners, recorded music).
- *Global industries* are those in which both trade and direct investment are important. Most large-scale manufacturing industries tend to evolve towards global structures: in automobiles, consumer electronics, semiconductors, pharmaceuticals, and beer, levels of both trade and direct investment are high.

By which route does internationalization typically occur? In the case of manufacturing companies, internationalization normally begins with exports—typically to countries with the least "psychic distance" from the home country. Later a sales and distribution subsidiary is established in the overseas country. Eventually the company develops a more integrated overseas subsidiary that undertakes manufacturing and product development as well.[2] In service industries, internationalization may involve replication (McKinsey & Company), acquisition (HSBC), or franchising (McDonald's).[3]

Implications for Competition

Internationalization usually means more competition and lower industry profitability. In 1976, the U.S. automobile market was dominated by GM, Ford, and Chrysler with 84% of the market. By 2009 there were 14 companies with auto plants within the U.S.; with the former "Big Three" accounting for just 43% of auto sales.

We can use Porter's five forces of competition framework to analyze the impact of internationalization on competition and industry profitability. If we define the industry in terms of the national market, internationalization directly influences three of the five forces of competition.

Competition from Potential Entrants Barriers to entry into most national markets have fallen substantially. Tariff reductions, falling real costs of transportation, the removal of exchange controls, internationalization of standards, and convergence between customer preferences have made it much easier for producers in one country to supply customers in another. Many of the entry barriers that were effective against potential domestic entrants may be ineffective against potential entrants that are established producers in overseas countries.

Rivalry Among Existing Firms Internationalization increases internal rivalry primarily because it increases the number of firms competing within each national market—it *lowers seller concentration*. In my youth, the European market for motor scooters was dominated by Piaggio (Vespa) and Innocenti (Lambretta). Apart from Piaggio, there are now over 25 manufacturers supplying scooters to the European market which include Japanese firms (Honda, Yamaha, Suzuki), Taiwanese (Kymco, Kwang Yang), Chinese (BenZhou/Yiying, Baotian, ZheJiang XingYue), Indian (Bajaj) and American (Baron, Vectrix).

Increasing global concentration is often accompanied by falling concentration in national markets. There has been massive consolidation of the global beer industry. Yet, in most countries I visit, I am struck by the widening range of beer available from more countries and more brewers. Moreover, even where global consolidation has been rapid (for example, paper, telecoms, oil, airlines, and aluminum), Ghemawat and Ghadar show that global concentration has declined as a result of national producers entering the global market.[4]

In addition, internationalization intensifies rivalry, first, by increasing the diversity of competitors in terms of goals, strategies and cost structures and, second, when internationalization occurs through direct investment in new plants, excess capacity increases. In the automobile industry, the massive overcapacity in the U.S. and China is primarily the result of direct investment by foreign auto producers.

Increasing the Bargaining Power of Buyers A further implication of the internationalization of business is that large customers can exercise their buying power far more effectively. Global sourcing provides a key tool for cost reduction by manufacturers. The growth of internet-based markets for components and materials enhances the power of industrial buyers.

Analyzing Competitive Advantage in an International Context

The growth of international competition over the past 20 years has been associated with some stunning reversals in the competitive positions of different companies. In 1989, U.S. Steel was the world's biggest steel company; in 2009 ArcelorMittal based in Luxemburg and India was the new global giant. In 1989, IBM, Compaq and Apple were world market leaders in PCs. By 2009, Hewlett-Packard and Acer were the new brand leaders, however, Asustek was the biggest manufacturer of PCs.

To understand how internationalization has shifted the basis of competition, we need to extend our framework for analyzing competitive advantage to include the influence of firms' national environments. Competitive advantage, we have noted, is achieved when a firm matches its internal strengths in resources and capabilities to the key success factors of the industry. In international industries, competitive advantage depends not just upon a firm's internal resources and capabilities, but also their national environments—in particular, the availability of resources within the countries where they do business. Figure 15.2 summarizes the implications of internationalization for our basic strategy model in terms of the impact both on industry conditions and firms' access to resources and capabilities.

National Influences on Competitiveness: Comparative Advantage

The effect of national resource availability on international competitiveness is the subject of the *theory of comparative advantage*. The theory states that a country has a comparative advantage in those products that make intensive use of those resources available in abundance within that country. Thus, Bangladesh has an abundant supply of unskilled labor. The U.S. has an abundant supply of technological

FIGURE 15.2 Competitive advantage in an international context

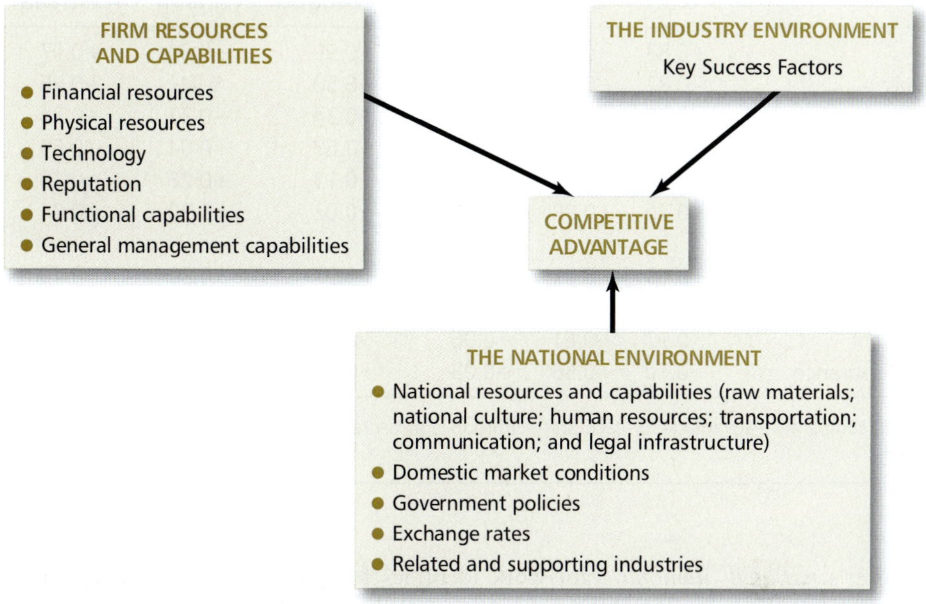

resources: trained scientists and engineers, research facilities, and universities. Bangladesh has a comparative advantage in products that make intensive use of unskilled labor, such as clothing, handicrafts, leather goods and assembly of consumer electronic products. The U.S. has a comparative advantage in technology-intensive products such as microprocessors, computer software, pharmaceuticals, medical diagnostic equipment and management consulting services.

The term "comparative advantage" refers to the *relative* efficiencies of producing different products. So long as exchange rates are well behaved (do not deviate far from their purchasing power parity levels), then comparative advantage translates into competitive advantage. Hence, comparative advantages are revealed in trade performance. Table 15.1 shows revealed comparative advantages for several product categories and several countries. Positive values show comparative advantage; negative values show comparative disadvantage.

Trade theory initially emphasized the role of natural resource endowments, labor supply and capital stock in determining comparative advantage. More recently emphasis has shifted to the central role of knowledge (including technology, human skills, and management capability) and the resources needed to commercialize knowledge (capital markets, communications facilities, and a legal system).[5] For industries where scale economies are important, a large home market is an additional source of comparative advantage (for example the U.S. in aerospace).[6]

Porter's National Diamond

Michael Porter has extended our understanding of comparative advantage by examining the dynamics through which particular industries within a country develop the resources and capabilities that confer international competitive advantage.[7]

TABLE 15.1 Indexes of revealed comparative advantage for certain broad product categories

	U.S.	U.K.	Japan	Switzerland	Canada	Australia	Taiwan
Cereals	+0.83	−0.24	−0.99	−0.99	+0.80	+0.97	−0.78
Mineral fuels	−0.82	−0.11	−0.93	−0.50	0.41	+0.26	−0.54
Pharmaceuticals	−0.25	+0.19	−0.51	+0.34	−0.32	−0.34	−0.78
Vehicles	−0.41	−0.25	+0.81	−0.68	+0.04	−0.69	+0.31
Aerospace	+0.58	−0.14	−0.44	−0.13	+0.26	−0.70	−0.50
Electrical and electronic equipment	−0.26	+0.08	+0.41	−0.02	−0.30	−0.74	+0.25
Optical, photo, medical and scientific equipment	+0.09	−0.02	+0.21	+0.37	−0.36	−0.46	+0.20
Apparel (woven)	−0.92	−0.61	−0.96	−0.40	−0.59	−0.92	−0.29
Finance and insurance	−0.10	+0.56	+0.08	+0.69	−0.08	+0.05	−0.85

Note: Revealed comparative advantage for each product group is measured as: (exports less imports)/(exports + imports).
Source: OECD.

Porter's *national diamond* framework identifies four key factors that determine a country's competitive advantage within a particular sector (see Figure 15.3):[8]

Factor Conditions Whereas the conventional analysis of comparative advantage focuses on endowments of broad categories of resource, Porter emphasizes the role of highly specialized resources many of which are "home-grown" rather than "endowed." For example, in analyzing Hollywood's preeminence in film production, Porter points to the local concentration of highly skilled labor, including the roles of UCLA and USC schools of film. Also, resource constraints may encourage the development of substitute capabilities: in post-war Japan, raw material shortages spurred miniaturization and low-defect manufacturing; in Italy, restrictive labor laws have stimulated automation.

FIGURE 15.3 Porter's national diamond framework

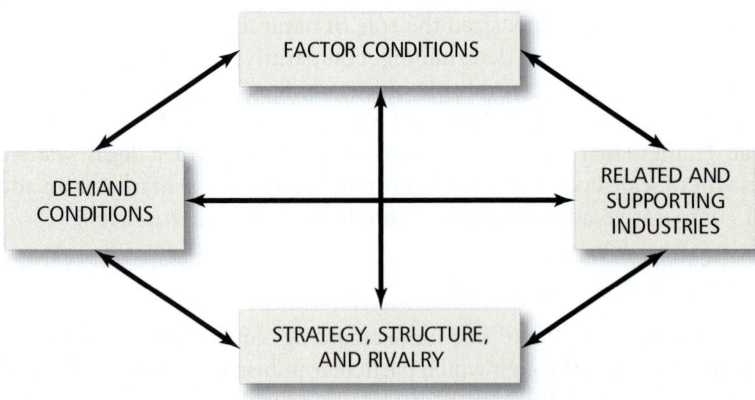

Related and Supporting Industries

One of Porter's most striking empirical findings is that national competitive strengths tend to be associated with "clusters" of industries. Silicon Valley's cluster comprises semiconductor, computer, software and venture capital firms. For each industry, closely related industries are sources of critical resources and capabilities. Denmark's global leadership in wind power is based upon a cluster comprising wind turbine manufacturers, offshore wind farm developers and operators, and utilities.

Demand Conditions Demand conditions in the domestic market provide the primary driver of innovation and quality improvement. For example:

- Switzerland's preeminence in watches is supported by the obsessive punctuality of the Swiss.
- Japanese dominant share of the world market for cameras by companies owes much to Japanese enthusiasm for amateur photography and their eager adoption of innovation in cameras.
- German dominance of the high-performance segment of the world automobile industry through Daimler, BMW, Porsche and VW-Audi reflects German motorists' love of quality engineering and their irrepressible urge to drive on autobahns at terrifying speeds.

Strategy, Structure and Rivalry National competitive performance in particular sectors is inevitably related to the strategies and structures of firms in those industries. Porter puts particular emphasis on the role of intense domestic competition in driving innovation, efficiency, and the upgrading of competitive advantage. The international success of the Japanese in autos, cameras, consumer electronic and office equipment is based upon domestic industries that feature at least six major producers, all strongly competitive with one another. Conversely, European failure in many hi-tech industries may be a result of European governments' propensity to kill domestic competition by creating "national champions."

Consistency Between Strategy and National Conditions

Establishing competitive advantage in global industries requires congruence between business strategy and the pattern of the country's comparative advantage. In audio equipment, it is sensible for Chinese producers, such as Skyworth and Desay, to concentrate on the low end of the market and to supply western mass retailers under their own brands. For Bose, international competitiveness requires exploiting U.S. strengths in basic research. For Danish consumer electronics maker Bang & Olufsen, international competitiveness requires exploiting European strengths in design and high-end marketing. Japanese producers such as Sony and Matsushita compete most effectively in the broad mid-market, exploiting national strengths in consumer electronic technology.

Achieving congruence between firm strategy and national conditions also extends to the embodiment of national culture within strategy and management systems. The success of U.S. companies in many areas of high technology, including computer software and biotechnology, owes much to a business system of entrepreneurial capitalism which exploits a national culture that emphasizes individuality, opportunity, and wealth acquisition. The global success of Korean corporate giants such as Samsung and LG reflects organizational structures and management systems that embody Korean cultural characteristics such as loyalty, respect for authority, conformity to group norms, commitment to organizational goals, and work ethic—what Professor Young-Ryeol Park refers to as "dynamic collectivism."[9]

Applying the Framework: International Location of Production

To examine how national resource conditions influence international strategies, we look at two types of strategic decision in international business: first, where to locate production activities and, second, how to enter a foreign market. Let us begin with the first of these.

Firms move beyond their national borders not only to seek foreign markets, but also to access the resources and capabilities available in other countries. Traditionally, multinationals established plants to serve local markets. Increasingly, decisions concerning where to produce are being separated from decisions over where to sell. For example, ST Microelectronics, the world leader in application-specific integrated circuits (ASICs), is headquartered in Switzerland; production is mainly in France, Italy, and Singapore; R&D is conducted mainly in France, Italy, and the U.S.; and the biggest markets are Singapore, the Netherlands, the U.S., and Japan.

Determinants of Geographical Location

The decision of where to manufacture requires consideration of three sets of factors:

- *National resource availability.* Where key resources differ between countries in their availability or cost, then firms should manufacture in countries where resource supplies are favorable. For the oil industry this means exploring in Kazakhstan, offshore Angola, and the Gulf of Mexico. In most areas of manufacturing, offshoring by companies from the advanced industrial nations has been driven primarily by the quest for lower wage costs. Table 15.2 shows differences in employment costs between countries. For many industries, gaining access to specialized knowhow is a critical consideration.
- *Firm-specific competitive advantages.* For firms whose competitive advantage is based on internal resources and capabilities, optimal location depends on where those resources and capabilities are situated and how mobile they are. Wal-Mart has experienced difficulty recreating its capabilities outside of the U.S. Conversely, Toyota and Goldman Sachs have successfully transferred their operational capabilities to their overseas subsidiaries.
- *Tradability.* The more difficult it is to transport a product and the more it is subject to trade barriers (such as tariffs and quotas), the more production will need to take place within the local market. Services—hairdressing, restaurant meals, and banking—typically need to be produced in close proximity to where they are consumed.

TABLE 15.2 Hourly compensation costs in U.S. dollars for production workers in manufacturing

	1975	2000	2006
U.S.	6.36	19.76	24.18
Mexico	1.47	2.08	2.75
Australia	5.62	14.47	26.00
Japan	3.00	22.27	19.99
Korea	0.32	8.19	14.72
Taiwan	0.40	5.85	6.56
Sri Lanka	0.28	0.48	0.56
France	4.52	15.70	24.90
Germany	6.31	24.42	34.21
Italy	4.67	14.01	25.07
Spain	2.53	10.78	18.83
Switzerland	6.09	21.24	30.67
U.K.	3.37	16.45	26.37

Source: U.S. Department of Labor, Bureau of Labor Statistics.

Location and the Value Chain

The production of most goods and services comprises a vertical chain of activities where the input requirements of each stage vary considerably. Hence, different countries offer advantage at different stages of the value chain. Table 15.3 shows the pattern of international specialization within textiles and apparel. Similarly with consumer electronics: component production is research and capital intensive and is concentrated in the U.S., Japan, Korea, and Taiwan; assembly is labor intensive and is concentrated in China, Thailand, and Latin America.

A key feature of recent internationalization has been the international fragmentation of value chains as firms seek to locate countries whose resource availability and cost best matches each stage of the value chain.[10] Strategy Capsule 15.1 describes ECCO's globally dispersed value chain.

TABLE 15.3 Comparative advantage in textiles and clothing by vertical stage

	Fiber production	Spun yarn	Textiles	Apparel
Hong Kong	−0.96	−0.81	−0.41	+0.75
Italy	−0.54	+0.18	+0.14	+0.72
Japan	−0.36	+0.48	+0.78	−0.48
U.S.	+0.96	+0.64	+0.22	−0.73

Note: Fiber production includes both natural and synthetic fibers. Revealed comparative advantage is measured as (exports − imports)/(exports + imports).

Source: United Nations.

STRATEGY CAPSULE 15.1

The Globally-dispersed Value Chain: ECCO A/S

ECCO is the world's second biggest supplier of "leisure casual branded footwear" behind Clarks and ahead of Rockport and Geoxx. ECCO was founded in Denmark in 1963 by Karl Toosbuy and is now owned and managed by his daughter Hanni and her husband. Its shoe making operations are characterized by their vertical integration ("from cow to consumer") and a proprietary process technology in which the shoe's sole and heel are molded directly on to the upper. Production was initially based in its home country, but its activities now span the globe:

- *Design* is based primarily at the company's headquarters in Bredebro, Denmark.
- *R&D* is centered in Portugal.
- *Leather production* takes place at three tanneries in the Netherlands, Indonesia and Thailand.
- *Production of shoe uppers* is a relatively labor-intensive activity and was concentrated in specialized factories in Thailand, Indonesia and China.
- *Shoe production* uses ECCO's direct injection technology and is fairly capital intensive. The main plants are in Thailand, China, Slovakia, Portugal and Indonesia. The Portuguese plant is the most technically advanced, deploying robotic production and laser technology.
- *Primary distribution centers* are in the Netherlands and Hong Kong.
- *Regional sales organizations* are based in the Netherlands (Western Europe), Denmark (Central Europe), Poland (Eastern Europe and Middle East), the U.S. (the Americas), and Hong Kong (Asia Pacific).
- *Retail distribution* is undertaken both by exclusive franchised retailers and independent retailers serviced by wholesalers.

Sources: www.ecco.com; B. B. Nielsen, T. Pedersen and J. Pyndt, *ECCO A/S—Global Value Chain Management* Ivey School of Business Case 908M14 (2008).

However, cost is just one factor in offshoring decisions. Cost advantages are vulnerable to exchange rate changes, so it is important to consider underlying issues concerning the availability and quality of resources and capabilities. For most Western and Japanese companies it is the potential for overall operational efficiency rather than local wage rates that is the key criterion influencing choice of location:

> [W]estern companies are finding that offshoring locations such as China and India offer access to world-class skills. For example, Jim Breyer, managing partner of Accel Partners, a Silicon Valley venture capitalist, observed: "Taiwan and China have some of the world's best designers of wireless chips and wireless software." In certain types of precision manufacturing, including the processes that produce magnesium alloy casing for notebook computers, companies such as Waffer in Taiwan offer some of the most sophisticated technology in the world.

> Most of the leading Indian IT outsourcing companies operate at level 5—the highest level of expertise—of the Capability Maturity Model (CMM), an international measure of technical skill, while most internal IT departments in western companies operate at level 2 or 3. Call centers, such as those operated by eTelecare—a Manila-based outsourcing provider—offer better average handling times and customer satisfaction relative to leading companies in the U.S.[11]

The modern laptop computer is the epitome of a globally dispersed value chain where every component and every process is located according the best combination of cost and technical knowhow (see Table 15.4).

The benefits from fragmenting the value chain must be traded off against the added costs of coordinating globally dispersed activities. Apart from costs of transportation costs and higher inventories, a key cost of dispersed activities is time. Just-in-time scheduling often necessitates that production activities are carried out in close proximity to one another. Companies that compete on speed and reliability of delivery (for example, Zara and Dell Computer) typically forsake the cost advantages of a globally dispersed value chain in favor of integrated operations with fast access to the final market. The financial crisis of 2008 created an additional cost of highly fragmented value chains—the need to ensure that distant suppliers have adequate access to credit.[12]

Figure 15.4 summarizes the relevant criteria in location decisions.

TABLE 15.4 Global production: the Hewlett Packard Pavilion 8000 laptop computer

Component/Process	Provider and Location
Design	HP, California; also, HP design studios in Taiwan and China collaborate with third-party manufacturers
Assembly	Contracted to Quanta (Taiwan); assembled in China by Quanta and by third-party contractors
Microprocessor	Designed by Intel in California; manufactured at Intel plants in Oregon, New Mexico, and Israel
Graphics card	Designed by ATI Technologies in Canada; manufactured in Taiwan
Screen	Manufactured by LG Philips LCD Co. (a joint venture between LG of Korea and Philips of the Netherlands). Manufactured in South Korea
Hard disk drive	By Seagate. Designed in California; manufactured in Malaysia
Lithium ion battery	Manufactured by Sony in Japan
Logistics	Contracted to 40 third-party providers (some global, such as Federal Express, DHL, and TNT; others local)
Telephone sales and customer support	Contracted to third-party providers in Canada, U.K., Ireland and India

Sources:
www.hp.com; "The Laptop Trail" *Wall Street Journal* (June 9, 2005).

FIGURE 15.4 Determining the optimal location of value chain activities

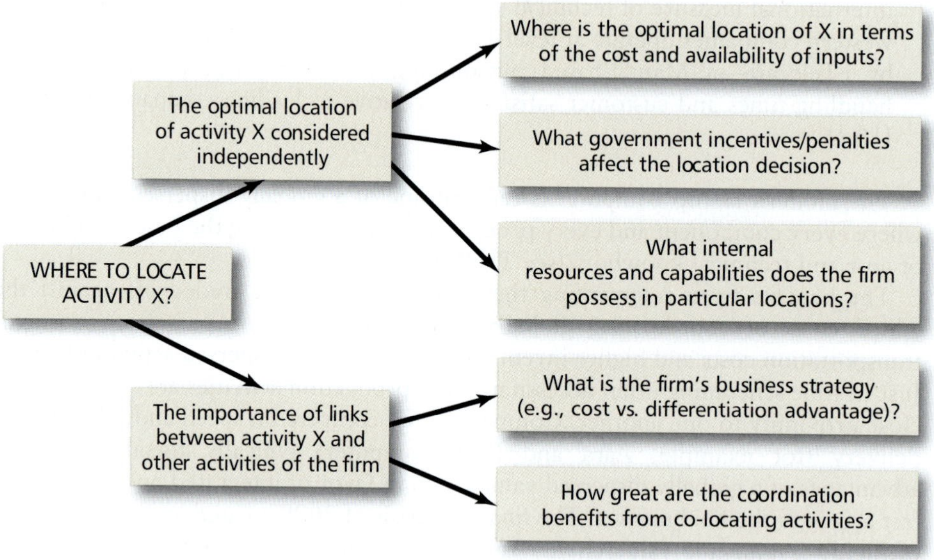

Applying the Framework: Foreign Entry Strategies

Firms enter foreign markets in pursuit of profitability. The profitability of entering a foreign market depends upon the attractiveness of that market and whether the firm can establish a competitive advantage within it. While market attractiveness can be a magnet for foreign multinationals—the size and growth of the Chinese economy has been irresistible to many Western companies—over the longer term, the key determinant of profitability is likely to be ability to establish competitive advantage *vis-à-vis* local firms and other multinationals.

A firm's potential for establishing competitive advantage has important implications for the means by which it enters a foreign market. The basic distinction is between market entry by means of *transactions* and market entry by means of *direct investment*. Figure 15.5 shows a spectrum of market entry options arranged according to the degree of resource commitment by the firm. Thus, at one extreme there is exporting through individual spot-market transactions; at the other, there is the establishment of a wholly owned, fully integrated subsidiary.

How does a firm weigh the merits of different market entry modes? Five key factors are relevant:

1 *Is the firm's competitive advantage based on firm-specific or country-specific resources?* If the firm's competitive advantage is country based, the firm must exploit an overseas market by exporting. Thus, to the extent that Tata Motor's competitive advantage in Western car markets is its low domestic cost base, it must produce in India and export to foreign markets. If Toyota's competitive advantage is its production and management capabilities, then as

FIGURE 15.5 Alternative modes of overseas market entry

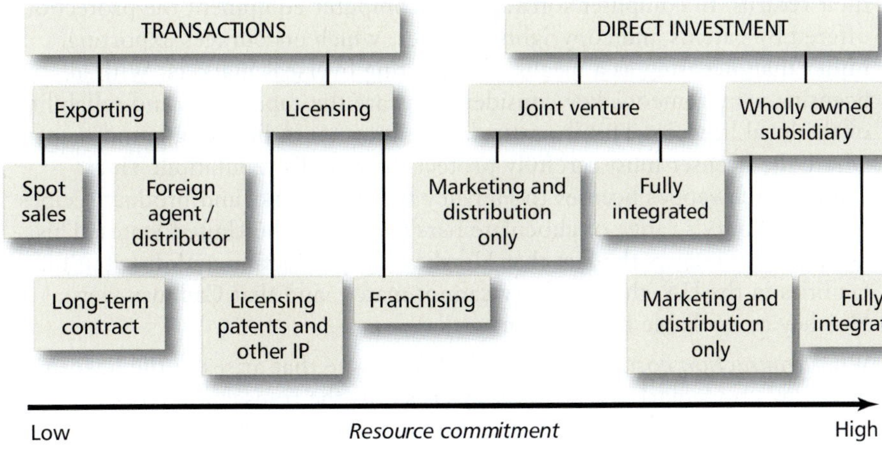

long as it can transfer and replicate these capabilities, Toyota can exploit foreign markets either by exports or by direct investment.[13]

2 *Is the product tradable and what are the barriers to trade?* If the product is not tradable because of transportation constraints or import restrictions, then accessing that market requires entry either by investing in overseas production facilities or by licensing the use of key resources to local companies within the overseas market.

3 *Does the firm possess the full range of resources and capabilities for establishing a competitive advantage in the overseas market?* Competing in an overseas market is likely to require that the firm acquires additional resources and capabilities, particularly those related to marketing and distributing in an unfamiliar market. Accessing such country-specific resources is most easily achieved by collaborating with a firm in the overseas market. The form of the collaboration depends, in part, on the resources and capabilities required. If a firm needs marketing and distribution, it might appoint a distributor or agent with exclusive territorial rights. If a wide range of manufacturing and marketing capabilities is needed, the firm might license its product and/or its technology to a local manufacturer. In technology-based industries, licensing technology to local companies is common. In marketing-intensive industries, firms with strong brands can license their trademarks to local companies. Alternatively, a joint venture might be sought with a local manufacturing company. United States' companies entered the Japanese market by joint ventures with local companies (for example, Fuji-Xerox, Caterpillar-Mitsubishi). These combined the technology and brand names of the U.S. partner with the market knowledge and manufacturing and distribution facilities of the Japanese firm.

4 *Can the firm directly appropriate the returns to its resources?* Whether a firm licenses the use of its resources or chooses to exploit them directly (either through exporting or direct investment) depends partly on appropriability considerations. In chemicals and pharmaceuticals, the patents protecting product innovations tend to offer strong legal protection, in which case patent licenses to local producers can be an effective means of appropriating their returns. In computer software and computer equipment the protection offered by patents and copyrights is looser, which encourages exporting rather than licensing as a means of exploiting overseas markets. With all licensing arrangements, key considerations are the capabilities and reliability of the local licensee. This is particularly important in licensing brand names, where the licenser must carefully protect the brand's reputation. Thus, Cadbury-Schweppes licenses to Hershey the trademarks and product recipes for its Cadbury's range of chocolate bars for sale in the United States. This arrangement reflects the fact that Hershey has production and distribution facilities in the U.S. that Cadbury cannot match, and that Cadbury views Hershey as a reliable business partner.

5 *What transaction costs are involved?* A key issue that arises in the licensing of a firm's trademarks or technology concerns the transaction costs of negotiating, monitoring and enforcing the terms of such agreements as compared with internationalization through a fully owned subsidiary. In expanding overseas, Starbucks owns and operates most of its coffee shops while McDonald's franchises its burger restaurants. McDonald's competitive advantage depends primarily upon the franchisee faithfully replicating the McDonald's system. This can be enforced effectively by means of franchise contracts. Starbucks believes that its success is achieved through creating the "Starbucks experience" which is as much about ambiance as it is about coffee. It is difficult to articulate the ingredients of this experience, let alone write it into a contract.

Issues of transaction costs are fundamental to the choices between alternative market entry modes. Barriers to exporting in the form of transport costs and tariffs are types of transaction costs; other costs include exchange rate risk and information costs. Transaction cost analysis has been central to theories of the existence of multinational corporations. In the absence of transaction costs in the markets either for goods or for resources, companies exploit overseas markets either by exporting their goods and services or by selling the use of their resources to local firms in the overseas markets.[14] Thus, multinationals tend to predominate in industries where:

- firm-specific intangible resources such as brands and technology are important (transaction costs in licensing the use of these resources favor direct investment);
- exporting is subject to transaction costs (for example, through tariffs or import restrictions);
- customer preferences are reasonably similar between countries.

International Alliances and Joint Ventures

Strategic alliances—collaborative arrangements between firms—have become increasingly popular means of accessing foreign markets. International strategic alliances take many forms—some are informal collaborative arrangements, some involve one partner taking an equity stake in the other, others may involve equity cross-holdings. An international venture is where partners from different countries form a new company which they jointly own.

The traditional reason for cross-border alliances and joint ventures was the desire by multinational companies to access the market knowledge and distribution capabilities of a local company, together with the desire by local companies to access the technology, brands and product development of the multinationals. Western banks entering China's booming credit card market have usually formed marketing alliances with local banks, often reinforced with an equity stake.[15] Governments in emerging market countries often oblige foreign companies to take a local partner in order to encourage the flow of technology and management capabilities to the host country.

By sharing resources and capabilities between the partners, alliances not only economize on investment, they also allow access to more highly developed resources and capabilities than a firm could create for itself. Thus, the Freemove alliance formed by Telefonica Moviles (Spain), TIM (Italy), T-Mobile (Germany) and Orange (France) created a seamless third-generation, wireless communication network across Europe at a fraction of the cost incurred by Vodafone; it also allowed each firm access to the mobile network of the leading operator in at least five major European markets.[16] Fiat's joint venture with Tata motors gives Fiat access to the Indian market while allowing Tata to augment its product range by building and marketing Fiat-designed small cars.[17]

Some companies have based their international strategies almost entirely on alliances with foreign partners. For Gazprom, the Russian gas giant, alliances relate to shared pipeline projects with Eni (Italy), CNPC (China), EON (Germany), PDVSA (Venezuela) and MOL (Hungary); liquefied natural gas projects with PetroCanada and Sonotrach (Algeria) and long-term supply arrangements with Gaz de France.

While the strategic rationale is strong, the success of cross-border alliance (including joint ventures) has been mixed. The Fuji-Xerox copier joint venture, the Sony-Ericsson mobile phone joint venture, the Renault-Nissan alliance, and the collaboration between Hewlett Packard and Canon in printers have been very successful. Conversely, BT and AT&T's Concert alliance, the GM-Fiat alliance, and Swissair's network of airline alliances were all disasters. Disagreements over the sharing of the contributions to and returns from an alliance are a frequent source of friction, particularly in alliances between firms that are also competitors. When each partner seeks to access the other's capabilities, "competition for competence" results.[18] In several of the alliances between Japanese and Western firms, the Japanese partner was better at appropriating the benefits of the alliance.[19] We shall return to some of these issues of interfirm collaboration in the next chapter when we consider diversification.

Multinational Strategies: Global Integration versus National Differentiation

So far, we have viewed international expansion, whether by export or by direct investment, as a means by which a company can exploit its competitive advantages not just in its home market but also in foreign markets. However, international scope may itself be a source of competitive advantage over geographically focused competitors. In this section, we explore whether, and under what conditions, firms that operate on an international basis are able to gain a competitive advantage over nationally focused firms. What is the potential for such "global strategies" to create competitive advantage? In what types of industry are they likely to be most effective? And how should they be designed and deployed in order to maximize their potential?

The Benefits of a Global Strategy

A global strategy is one that views the world as a single, if segmented, market. The late Ted Levitt argued that companies that compete on a national basis are highly vulnerable to companies that compete on a global basis.[20] Global players win out over their national competitors for two reasons. First, supplying the world market allows access to scale economies in product development, manufacturing, and marketing. (Ghemawat refers to these as benefits from cross-border *aggregation*.[21]) Second, the key barriers to exploiting these scale economies, locally differentiated customer preferences, are fast disappearing in the face of the uniformity imposed by technology, communication and travel. "Everywhere everything gets more and more like everything else as the world's preference structure is relentlessly homogenized," observed Levitt. Subsequent contributions to the analysis of global strategy have elaborated Levitt's analysis of the potential for global strategies to create value.[22] Five major benefits have been proposed:

Cost Benefits of Scale and Replication As we noted in Chapter 9, the primary source of scale economy is product development—Boeing and Airbus in commercial aircraft and Microsoft and SAP in computer software have to operate on a global scale to amortize their huge investments in developing new products. In industries where internationalization occurs through direct investment rather than exporting, the major cost efficiencies from international operation derives from economies in the replication of knowledge-based assets—including organizational capabilities.[23] When a company has created a knowledge-based asset or product—whether a recipe, a piece of software, or an organizational system—subsequent replication costs a fraction of the original. With Disneyland theme parks in Tokyo, Paris, Hong Kong, and soon Shanghai, as well as Anaheim and Orlando, Disney can achieve significant economies in developing new rides. Similarly with McDonald's: it developed its business system within the U.S. and has subsequently replicated it across some 200 countries throughout the world.

Serving Global Customers In several industries—investment banking, audit services, advertising—the primary driver of globalization has been the need to service global customers.[24] Thus, the internationalization of auto parts manufacturers has tended to follow the internationalization patterns of the auto assemblers.

Exploiting National Resources—Arbitrage Benefits As we have already seen, global strategy does not necessarily involve production in one location and then distributing globally. Global strategies also involve exploiting the efficiencies from locating different activities in different places. As we have seen, companies internationalize not just in search of market opportunities but also in search of resource opportunities. Traditionally this has meant a quest for raw materials and low-cost labor. Increasingly it means a quest for knowledge. For example, among semiconductor firms, a critical factor determining the location of overseas subsidiaries is the desire to access knowledge within the host country.[25] Ghemawat refers to this exploitation of differences between countries as *arbitrage*.[26] While such arbitrage strategies are conventionally associated with exploiting wage differentials by offshoring production to low wage locations, increasingly arbitrage is about exploiting the distinctive knowledge available in different locations.

Learning Benefits The learning benefits of multinational operations refer not only to MNCs ability to access and transfer localized knowledge (*knowledge arbitrage*) but also integration of knowledge from different locations and the creation of new knowledge through interacting with different national environments. IKEA's expansion has required it to adjust to the Japanese style and design preferences, Japanese modes of living, and Japanese fanatical quality-consciousness. As a result, IKEA has developed its capabilities with regard to both quality and design that it believes will enhance its competitiveness worldwide. According to the CEO of IKEA Japan, "One reason for us to enter the Japanese market, apart from hopefully doing very good business, is to expose ourselves to the toughest competition in the world. By doing so, we feel that we are expanding the quality issues for IKEA all over the world." [27]

Recent contributions to the international business literature suggest that this ability of MNCs to develop knowledge in multiple locations, to synthesize that knowledge and transfer it across national borders may be their greatest advantage over nationally focused companies.[28] The critical requirement for exploiting these learning benefits is that the company possesses some form of global infrastructure for managing knowledge that permits new experiences, new ideas, and new practices to be diffused and integrated.

Competing Strategically A major advantage of the Romans over the Gauls, Goths, and other barbarian tribes, was the Romans' ability to draw upon the military and economic resources of the Roman Empire to fight local wars. Similarly, multinational companies possess a key strategic advantage over their nationally focused competitors: multinationals can fight aggressive competitive battles in individual national markets using their resources (cash flows in particular) from other national markets. At its most simple, this *cross-subsidization* of competitive initiatives in one market using profits from other markets involves *predatory pricing*—cutting prices to a level that drives competitors out of business. Such pricing practices are likely to contravene both the World Trade Organization's antidumping rules and national antitrust laws. More usually, cross-subsidization involves using cash flows from other markets to finance aggressive sales and marketing campaigns.[29] There is some evidence that Asian electronics firms use the profits from higher prices at home to subsidize expansion in Western markets.[30]

Strategic competition between MNCs presents more complex opportunities for attack, retaliation and containment.[31] The most effective response to competition in one's home market may be to retaliate in the foreign MNC's own home market. Fuji Film's incursion into Kodak's backyard was symbolized by Fuji's sponsorship of the 1984 Olympic Games in Los Angeles. Kodak responded by expanding its marketing efforts in Japan.[32] To effectively exploit such opportunities for national leveraging, some overall global coordination of competitive strategies in individual national markets is required.

Kenichi Ohmae has argued that to become effective global competitors, multinationals must become true insiders in all of the world's leading economic centers. This used to mean positioning within the "triad": North America, Europe, and Japan.[33] This doctrine has been weakened, first, by the rise of new industrial powers (notably China and India) and, second, the disappointing outcomes of several attempts to build "triad power"—for example, Daimler-Benz's acquisitions of Chrysler in the U.S. and Mitsubishi in Japan.

The Need for National Differentiation

For all the advantages of global strategy, the evidence of the past decade is that national differences in customer preferences continue to exert a powerful influence in most markets: products designed to meet the needs of the "global customer" tend to be unappealing to most consumers. Moreover, costs of national differentiation can be surprisingly low if common basic designs and common major components are used. Most auto firms have abandoned attempts to create global car models in favor of common platforms.[34] Flexible manufacturing systems have reduced the costs of customizing products to meet the preferences of particular customer groups.

Domestic appliances provide an interesting refutation of the globalization hypothesis. In washing machines, national preferences have shown remarkable resilience: French and U.S. washing machines are primarily top loading, elsewhere in Europe they are mainly front loading; the Germans prefer higher spin speeds than the Italians; U.S. machines feature agitators rather than revolving drums; and Japanese machines are small. The pioneers of globalization in domestic appliances, such as Electrolux and Whirlpool, still struggle to outperform national and regional specialists.[35] Similarly in retail banking, despite some examples of successful internationalization (Banco Santander, HSBC), most of the evidence points to few economies from cross-border integration and the critical need to adapt to local market conditions.[36]

Every nation represents a unique combination of distinctive characteristics. How can we recognize and assess the extent of similarities and differences between countries? Pankaj Ghemawat proposes four key components: cultural distance, administrative and political distance, geographical distance, and economic distance—his "CAGE" framework (see Table 15.5).

Ghemawat's broad categories are only a starting point for exploring the national idiosyncrasies that make international expansion such a minefield. For consumer products firms, the structure of distribution channels are likely to be a critical barrier to global marketing and distribution. Procter & Gamble must adapt its marketing, promotion, and distribution of toiletries and household products to take account of the fact that, in the U.S., a few chains account for a major share of its U.S. sales; in southern Europe, most sales are through small, independent retailers; while in Japan, P&G must sell through a multitiered hierarchy of distributors. The closer an industry to the final consumer, the more important cultural factors are likely to be. Strategy Capsule 15.2 considers some dimensions of national culture. It is notable that so few retailers have become successful abroad. With the exception of IKEA, Hennes & Mauritz, and a handful of others, there are few international retailers that are truly global and few that have been as successful overseas as at home. For many, franchising has provided a lower risk internationalization strategy.

TABLE 15.5 Ghemawat's CAGE framework for assessing country differences

	Cultural distance	Administrative and political distance	Geographical distance	Economic differences
Distance between two countries increases with	• Different languages, ethnicities, religions, social norms • Lack of connective ethnic or social networks	• Absence of shared political or monetary association • Political hostility • Weak legal and financial institutions	• Lack of common border, water way access, adequate transportation or communication links • Physical remoteness	• Different consumer incomes • Different costs and quality of natural, financial, and human resources • Different information or knowledge
Industries most affected by source of distance	Industries with high linguistic content (TV, publishing) and cultural content (food, wine, music)	Industries viewed by government as strategically important (for example, energy, defense, telecommunications)	Products with low value-to-weight (cement), that are fragile or perishable (glass, milk) or dependent upon communi-cations (financial services)	Products whose demand is sensitive to consumer income levels (luxury goods). Labor intensive products (clothing)

Source:
Adapted from P. Ghemawat, "Distance Still Matters: The Hard Reality of Global Expansion," *Harvard Business Review* (September, 2001): 137–147. Used with permission.

STRATEGY CAPSULE 15.2

How do National Cultures Differ?

Do people differ between countries with regard to beliefs, norms, and value systems? The answer from a series of research studies is "yes."

The best known study of national cultural differences is by Geert Hofstede. The principal dimensions of national values he identified were:

- *Power distance*—the extent to which inequality, decision-making power in particular, is accepted within organizations and within society. Power distance was high in Malaysia, and most Latin American and Arab countries; low in Austria and Scandinavia.
- *Uncertainty avoidance*. Preference for certainty and established norms was high in most southern European and Latin American countries; tolerance for uncertainty and ambiguity was high in Singapore, Sweden, the U.K., the U.S., and India.

- *Individualism*. Concern for individual over group interests was highest in the U.S., the U.K., Canada, and Australia. Identification with groups and the collective interest was strongest in Latin America and Asia (especially Indonesia, Pakistan, Taiwan and South Korea).
- *Masculinity/femininity*. Hofstede identifies emphasis on work and material goals and demarcation of gender roles as "masculine"; emphasis on personal relationships rather than efficiency and belief in gender equality was viewed as "feminine." Japan, Austria, Venezuela, and Italy scored high on masculinity; Scandinavia and the Netherlands scored very low.

Other studies have used different measures for characterizing national cultures. Fons Trompenaars (another Dutchman) emphasizes "universalism" versus "particularism" in outlook (the U.S. and Australia score highest on universalism); "neutral" versus "affective" relationships (Japan and the U.K. are highest in terms of neutrality; Mexico and the Netherlands the most affective); and achievement orientation (Australia and the U.S. very high; Venezuela, Indonesia, and China very low).

Sources: G. Hofstede, *Culture's Consequences: International Differences in Work-related Values* (Thousand Oaks, CA: Sage, 1984); F. Trompenaars, *Riding the Waves of Culture* (London: Economist Books, 1993).

Reconciling Global Integration with National Differentiation

Choices about internationalization strategy have been viewed as a tradeoff between the benefits of global integration and those of national adaptation (see Figure 15.6).[37] Industries where scale economies are huge and customer preferences homogeneous call for a global strategy (for example, jet engines). Industries where national preferences are pronounced and where customization is not prohibitively expensive favor a "multidomestic" strategy (for example, retail banking). Indeed, if there are no significant benefits from global integration, then we may see these industries supplied almost entirely by locally specialized firms (as in funeral services and hairdressing). However, some industries may be low on most dimensions—cement and car repair services are fairly homogeneous worldwide, but also lack significant scale economies or other major benefits from global presence. Conversely, other industries offer substantial benefits from operating at global scale (telecommunications equipment, military hardware), but national preferences and standards may also necessitate considerable adaptation to the needs of specific national markets.

Reconciling conflicting forces for global efficiency and national differentiation represents one of the greatest strategic challenges facing MNCs. Achieving "global localization" involves standardizing product features and company activities where scale economies are substantial, and differentiating where national preferences are strongest and where achieving them is not over-costly. Thus, a global car such as the Honda Civic (introduced in 1972 and sold in 110 countries of the world) now embodies considerable local adaptations—not just to meet national safety and environmental standards, but also to meet local preferences for leg room, seat specifications, accessories, color, and trim. McDonald's too meshes global standardization with local adaptation (see Strategy Capsule 15.3).

FIGURE 15.6 Benefits of global integration versus national differentiation

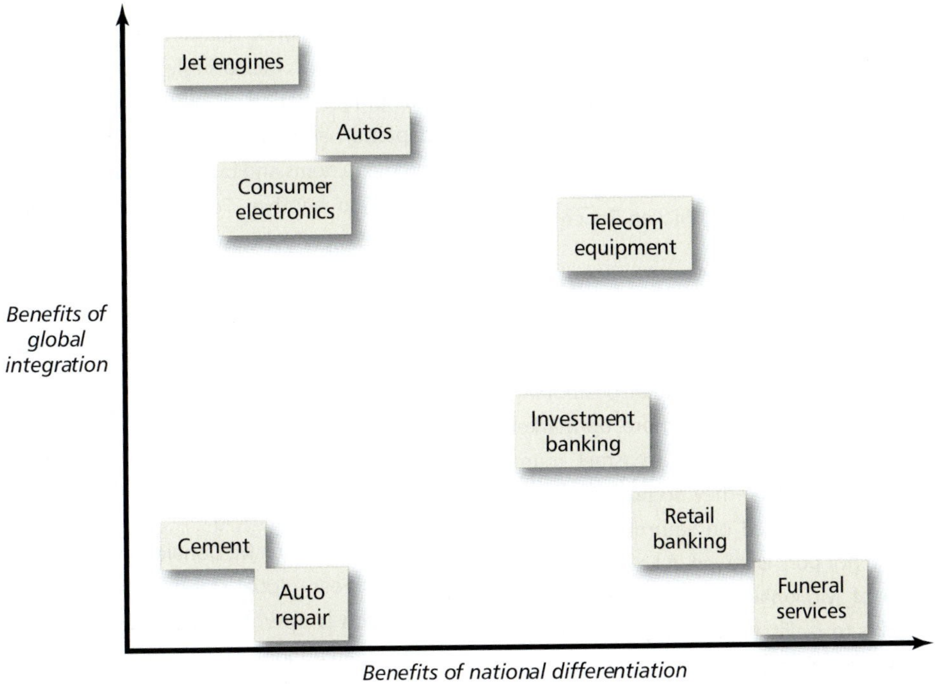

STRATEGY CAPSULE 15.3

McDonald's Goes "Glocal"

For antiglobalization activists, McDonald's is a demon of globalization: it crushes national cuisines and small, traditional family businesses with the juggernaut of U.S. fast-food corporate imperialism. In reality, its global strategy is a careful blend of global standardization and local adaptation.

McDonald's menus include a number of globally standardized items—the Big Mac and potato fries are international features—however, in most countries McDonald's menus feature an increasing number of locally developed items. These include:

- Australia—a range of wraps including Seared Chicken, Tandoori Chicken and Crispy Sweet Chili Chicken;
- France—Croque McDo (a toasted ham and cheese sandwich);
- Hong Kong—Grilled Pork Twisty Pasta and Fresh Corn Cup;
- India—Shahi Paneer McCurry Pan, McAloo Tikki, Veg Pizza McPuff;
- Saudi Arabia—McArabia Kofta, McArabia Chicken;

- Switzerland—Shrimp Cocktail, Chickenburger Curry;
- U.K.—A range of deli sandwiches including "Spicy Veggie Deli" (chickpea patty with coriander and cumin) , and "Sweet Chili Chicken Deli";
- U.S.A.—Premium Grilled Chicken Ranch BLT Sandwich.

There are differences too in restaurant decor, service offerings (internet access in the U.K.; home delivery in India), and market positioning (McDonald's tends to have a more up-market positioning outside the U.S.). In Israel many McDonald's are kosher—they do not offer dairy products and are closed on Saturdays. In India neither beef nor pork is served. A key reason that almost all of McDonald's non-U.S. outlets are franchised is to facilitate adaptation to national environments and access to local knowhow.

Yet, the principal features of the McDonald's business system are identical throughout the world. McDonald's values and business principles are seen as universal and invariant. Its emphasis on families and children is intended to identify McDonald's with fun and family life wherever it does business. Community involvement and the Ronald McDonald children's charity are also worldwide. Corporate trademarks and brands are mostly globally uniform—including the golden arches logo and "I'm lovin' it" tag line. The business system itself—the franchising, the training of managers and franchisees through Hamburger University, restaurant operations, and supplier relations—is also highly standardized.

Traditionally, McDonald's international strategy was about adapting its U.S. model to local conditions. Increasingly McDonald's is using local differentiation as a basis for worldwide adaptation and innovation through transferring new menu items and business concepts from one country to another. For example, the McCafe gourmet coffeehouses within McDonald's restaurants were first developed in Australia. By 2003, McCafes had become established in 30 countries, including the U.S. In responding to the growing tide of concern over nutrition and obesity in the developed world, McDonald's has drawn upon country initiatives with regard to sandwiches, salads, and information labeling as a basis for global learning.

Whether or not McDonald's has the balance right between global standardization and local adaptation is open to debate. Simon Anholt, a British marketing expert, argues: "By putting local food on the menu, all you are doing is removing the logic of the brand, because this is an American brand. If McDonald's serves what you think is a poor imitation of your local cuisine, it's going to be an insult." But according to McDonald's C.E.O. Jim Skinner: "We don't run our business from Oak Brook. We are a local business with a local face in each country we operate in." His chief marketing manager, Mary Dillon, adds: "McDonald's is much more about local relevance than a global archetype. Globally we think of ourselves as the custodian of the brand, but it's all about local relevance."

Sources: www.mcdonalds.com; *McDonald's Localization Strategy: Brand Unification, Menu Diversification?* ICFAI Case Study 306-316-1 (2006).

Reconciling global efficiency with appealing to customer preferences in each country also means looking at the globalization/national differentiation tradeoff for individual products and individual functions. In retail banking, different products and services have different potential for globalization. Credit cards and basic savings products such as certificates of deposit tend to be globally standardized; checking accounts and mortgage lending are much more nationally differentiated. Similarly with business functions: R&D, purchasing, IT, and manufacturing have strong globalization potential; sales, marketing, customer service, and human resource management need to be much more nationally differentiated. These differences have important implications for how the MNC is organized.

Strategy and Organization within the Multinational Corporation

These same factors—the benefits from global integration and need for national differentiation—that influence the design of international strategies also have critical implications for the design of organizational structures and management systems to implement these strategies. As we shall see, one of the greatest challenges facing the senior managers of MNCs is aligning organizational structures and management systems and their fit with the strategies being pursued.

The Evolution of Multinational Strategies and Structures

Over the past hundred years, the forces driving the internationalization of companies have changed considerably; the tradeoff between the benefits of global integration and those of national differentiation has also shifted markedly. Hence, during different periods international firms have adopted different strategies and different structural configurations. Yet, these structural configurations have tended to persist. Although all companies are subject to organizational inertia, MNCs because of their complexity face particular difficulties in structural change. Hence, MNCs are captives of their history: their strategy-structure configurations today reflect choices they made at the time of their international expansion. Radical changes in strategy and structure are difficult: once an international distribution of functions, operations, and decision-making authority has been determined, reorganization is slow, difficult and costly—particularly when host governments become involved. Bartlett and Ghoshal argue that the "administrative heritage" of an MNC—its configuration of assets and capabilities, its distribution of managerial responsibilities, and its network of relationships—is a critical determinant of its current capabilities and a key constraint upon its ability to build new strategic capabilities.[38]

Bartlett and Ghoshal identify three eras in the development of the MNC (see Figure 15.7):

- *Early twentieth century: era of the European multinational.* European companies such as Unilever, Shell, ICI, and Philips were pioneers of multinational expansion. Because of the conditions at the time of internationalization—poor transportation and communications, highly differentiated national markets—the companies created "multinational federations": each national subsidiary was operationally autonomous and undertook the full range of functions, including product development, manufacturing, and marketing.

FIGURE 15.7 The development of the multinational corporation: alternative parent-subsidiaries relations

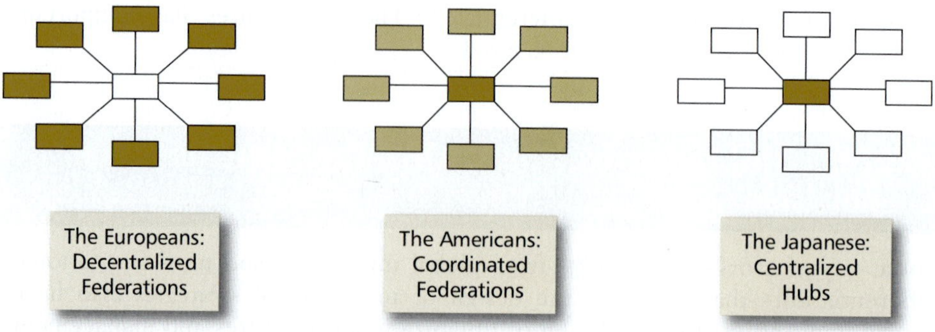

Note: The density of shading indicates the concentration of decision making.

Source: C. A. Bartlett and S. Ghoshal, *Managing Across Borders: The Transnational Solution* (Boston: Harvard Business School Press, 1998). Copyright © 1989 by the Harvard Business School Publishing Corporation, all rights reserved. Reprinted by permission of Harvard Business School Publishing.

- *Post-Second World War: era of the American multinational.* United States economic dominance was the basis for the pre-eminence of U.S. multinationals such as GM, Ford, IBM, Coca-Cola, Caterpillar, and Procter & Gamble. While their overseas subsidiaries were allowed considerable autonomy, this was within the context of the dominant position of their U.S. parent in terms of capital, new product and process technology, management capabilities, and management systems. United States-based resources and capabilities were their primary competitive advantages in world markets.
- *The 1970s and 1980s: the Japanese challenge.* Japanese MNCs—Honda, Toyota, Matsushita, NEC, and YKK—pursued global strategies from centralized domestic bases. R&D and manufacturing were concentrated in Japan; overseas subsidiaries were responsible for sales and distribution. Globally standardized products manufactured in large-scale plants provided the basis for unrivalled cost and quality advantages. Over time, manufacturing and R&D were dispersed—initially because of trade protection by consumer countries and the rising value of the yen against other currencies.

The different administrative heritage of these different groups of MNCs continues to shape their organizational capabilities today. The strength of European multinationals is adaptation to the conditions and requirements of individual national markets. The strength of the U.S. multinationals is their ability to transfer technology and proven new products from their domestic strongholds to their national subsidiaries. That of the Japanese MNCs is the efficiency of global production and new product development. Yet, these core capabilities are also core rigidities. The challenge for European MNCs has been to achieve greater integration of their sprawling international empires—for Shell and Philips this has involved reorganizations over a period of more than two decades. For U.S. MNCs such as Ford and Procter & Gamble it has involved nurturing the ability to tap their foreign subsidiaries for technology, design, and new product ideas. For Japanese MNCs such as Nomura, Hitachi, and NEC the challenge is to become true insiders in the overseas countries where they do business.

Reconfiguring the MNC: The Transnational Corporation

Changing Organization Structure For North American and European-based MNCs, the principal structural changes of recent decades have been a shift from organization around national subsidiaries and regional groupings to the creation of worldwide product divisions. For most MNCs, country and regional organizations are retained, but primarily for the purposes of national compliance and customer relationships. Thus, Hewlett-Packard conducts its business through global product groups: Technology Solutions Group (comprising Enterprise Storage and Servers, Services, and Software), Personal Systems Group (its personal computer and entertainment business), and Imaging and Printing Group (printers and cameras). At the same time, it maintains three regional headquarters: for the Americas (located in Houston), for Europe, Middle East and Africa (located in Geneva), and for Asia Pacific (located in Singapore).

New Approaches to Reconciling Localization and Global Integration However, the formal changes in structure are less important than the changes in responsibilities, decision powers, and modes of coordination within these structures. The fundamental challenge for MNCs has been reconciling the advantages of global integration with those of national differentiation. Escalating costs of research and new product development have made global strategies with global product platforms essential. At the same time, meeting consumer needs in each national market and responding swiftly to changing local circumstances requires greater decentralization. Accelerating technological change further exacerbates these contradictory forces: despite the cost and "critical mass" benefits of centralizing research and new product development, innovation occurs at multiple locations within the MNC and requires nurturing of creativity and initiative throughout the organization. "It's the corporate equivalent of being able to walk, chew gum, and whistle at the same time," notes Chris Bartlett.

According to Bartlett, the simultaneous pursuit of responsiveness to national markets and global coordination requires, "a very different kind of internal management process than existed in the relatively simple multinational or global organizations. This is the *transnational organization*."[39] The distinguishing characteristic of the transnational is that it becomes an integrated network of distributed and interdependent resources and capabilities (see Figure 15.8). This necessitates that:

- Each national unit is a source of ideas, skills and capabilities that can be harnessed for the benefit of the total organization.
- National units access global scale economies by designating them the company's world source for a particular product, component, or activity.
- The center must establish a new, highly complex managing role that coordinates relationships among units but in a highly flexible way. The key is to focus less on managing activities directly and more on creating an organizational context that is conducive to the coordination and resolution of differences. Creating the right organizational context involves "establishing clear corporate objectives, developing managers with broadly based perspectives and relationships, and fostering supportive organizational norms and values."[40]

FIGURE 15.8 The transnational corporation

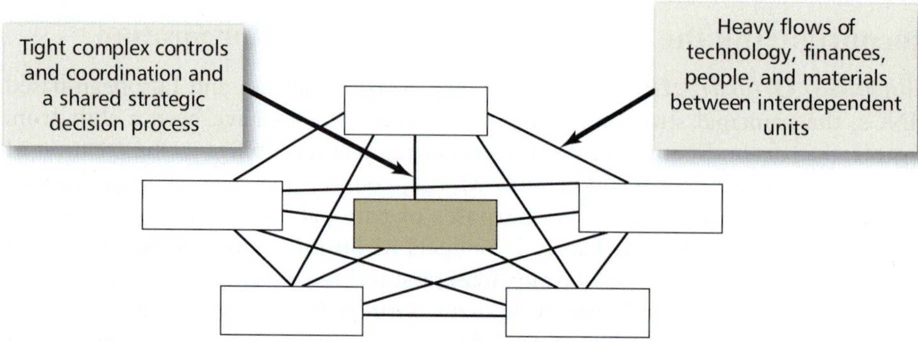

Balancing global integration and national differentiation requires that a company adapts to the differential requirements of different products, different functions, and different countries. Procter & Gamble adopts global standardization for some of its products (Pringles potato chips and high-end perfumes, for example); for others (hair care products and laundry detergent, for example) it allows significant national differentiation. Across countries, P&G organizes global product divisions to serve most of the industrialized world because of the similarities between their markets, while for emerging market countries (such as China and India) it operates through country subsidiaries in order to adapt to the distinctive features of these markets. Among functions, R&D is globally integrated while sales are organized by national units that are differentiated to meet local market characteristics.

The transnational firm is a concept and direction of development rather than a distinct organizational archetype. It involves convergence of the different strategy configurations of MNCs. Thus, companies such as Philips, Unilever, and Siemens have reassigned roles and responsibilities to achieve greater integration within their traditional "decentralized federations" of national subsidiaries. Japanese global corporations such as Toyota and Matsushita have drastically reduced the roles of their Japanese headquarters. American multinationals such as Citigroup and IBM are moving in two directions: reducing the role of their U.S. bases while increasing integration among their different national subsidiaries.

Multinational corporations are increasingly locating management control of their global product divisions outside their home countries. When Philips adopted a product division structure, it located responsibility for medical electronics in its U.S. subsidiary and leadership in consumer electronics in Japan. Nexans, the world's biggest manufacturer of electric cables, has moved the head office of five of its 20 product divisions outside of France. For example, the head of ships' cables is based in South Korea—the world leader in shipbuilding.[41] Aligning structure, strategy, and national resources may even require shifting the corporate headquarters—HSBC moved from Hong Kong to London, Tetra Pak from Lund, Sweden to Lausanne, Switzerland.[42]

Organizing R&D and New Product Development Probably the greatest challenges facing the top managers of MNCs are organizing, fostering and exploiting innovation and new product development. Innovation is stimulated by diversity and autonomy, while its exploitation and diffusion require critical mass and coordination. The traditional European decentralized model is conducive to local initiatives—but not to their global exploitation. Philips has an outstanding record of innovation in consumer electronics. In its TV business, its Canadian subsidiary developed its first color TV; its Australian subsidiary developed its first stereo sound TV and its British subsidiary developed teletext TVs. However, lack of global integration constrained its success on a worldwide scale. Building a globally integrated approach to new product development has been a major priority of the past two decades.

Assigning national subsidiaries global mandates allows them to take advantage of local resources and develop distinctive capabilities while exploiting globally the results of their initiatives.[43] For example, P&G, recognizing Japanese obsessiveness over cleanliness, assigned increasing responsibility to its Japanese subsidiary for developing household cleaning products. Its "Swiffer" dust-collecting products were developed in Japan (using technology developed by other firms) then introduced into other markets. Where a local unit possesses unique capabilities, it can be designated a *center of excellence*.[44]

Summary

Moving from a national to an international business environment represents a quantum leap in complexity. In an international environment, a firm's potential for competitive advantage is determined not just by its own resources and capabilities but also by the conditions of the national environment in which it operates, including input prices, exchange rates and a host of other factors. The extent to which a firm is positioned across multiple national markets also influences its economic power.

Our approach in this chapter has been to simplify the complexities of international strategy by applying the same basic tools of strategy analysis that we developed in earlier chapters. For example, to determine whether a firm should enter an overseas market, our focus has been the profit implications of such an entry. This requires an analysis of (a) the attractiveness of the overseas market using the familiar tools of industry analysis, and (b) the potential of the firm to establish competitive advantage in that overseas market, which depends on the firm's ability to transfer its resources and capabilities to the new location and their effectiveness in conferring competitive advantage.

However, establishing the potential for a firm to create value from internationalization is only a beginning. Subsequent analysis needs to design an international strategy: do we enter an overseas market by exporting, licensing, or direct investment? If the latter, should we set up a wholly owned subsidiary or a joint venture? Once the strategy has been established, then a suitable organizational structure needs to be designed.

The fact that so many companies that have been outstandingly successful in their home market have failed so miserably in their overseas expansion demonstrates the complexity of international management. In some cases, the companies have failed to recognize that the resources and capabilities that underpinned their competitive advantages in their home market could not be readily transferred or replicated in overseas markets. In others, the problems were in designing the structures and systems that could effectively implement the international strategy.

As the lessons of success and failure from international business become recognized and distilled into better theories and analytical frameworks, so we advance our understanding of how to design and implement strategies for competing globally. We are at the stage where we recognize the issues and the key determinants of competitive advantage in an international environment. However, there is much that we do not fully understand. Designing strategies and organizational structures that can reconcile critical tradeoffs between global scale economies versus local differentiation, decentralized learning and innovation versus worldwide diffusion and replication, and localized flexibilities versus international standardization remain key challenges for senior managers.

Self-Study Questions

1 With reference to Figure 15.1, identify a "sheltered industry" (one that has been subject to little penetration either by imports or foreign direct investment). Explain why the industry has escaped internationalization. Explore whether there are opportunities for profitable internationalization within the industry and, if so, the strategy that would offer the best chance of success.

2 With reference to Table 15.1, what characteristics of national resources explain the different patterns of comparative advantage for the U.S. and Japan?

3 According to Michael Porter's *Competitive Advantage of Nations*, some of the industries where British companies have an international advantage are: advertising, auctioneering of antiques and artwork, distilled alcoholic beverages, hand tools, and chemical preparations for gardening and horticulture. Some of the industries where U.S. companies have an international competitive advantage are: photo film, aircraft and helicopters, computer hardware and software, oilfield services, management consulting, cinema films and TV programs, healthcare products and services, and financial services. For either the U.K. or the U.S., use Porter's national diamond framework (Figure 15.3) to explain the observed pattern of international competitive advantage.

4 When Porsche decided to enter the SUV market with its luxury Cayenne model, it surprised the auto industry by locating its new assembly plant in Leipzig in Eastern Germany. Many observers believed that Porsche should have located the plant either in Central or Eastern Europe where labor costs were very low, or (like Mercedes and BMW) in the U.S. where it would be close to its major market. Using the criteria outlined in Figure 15.4, can you explain Porsche's decision?

5 British expatriates living in the U.S. frequently ask friends and relatives visiting from the U.K. to bring with them bars of Cadbury's chocolate on the basis that the Cadbury's chocolate available in the U.S. (manufactured under license by Hershey's) is inferior to "the real thing." Should Cadbury-Schweppes plc maintain its licensing agreement with Hershey or should it seek to supply the U.S. market itself, either by export from the U.K. or by establishing manufacturing facilities in the U.S.?

6 Has McDonald's got the balance right between global standardization and national differentiation (see Strategy Capsule 15.3)? Should it offer its franchisees in overseas countries greater initiative in introducing products that meet national preferences? Should it also allow greater flexibility for its overseas franchisees to adapt store layout, operating practices, and marketing? What aspects of the McDonald's system should McDonald's top management insist on keeping globally standardized?

Notes

1 *OECD in Figures 2008* (Organization for Economic Cooperation and Development, 2008). Note that the OECD members comprise the world's advanced industrialized countries.

2 This process was proposed by J. Johanson and J.-E. Vahlne, "The Internationalization Process of the Firm," *Journal of International Business Studies* 8 (1977): 23–32. See also L. Melin, "Internationalization as a Strategy Process," *Strategic Management Journal* 13 (1992 Special Issue): 99–118.

3 S. L. Segal-Horn, "Globalization of service industries," in J. McGee (ed.) *The Blackwell Encyclopedia of Management: Strategic Management* (Oxford: Blackwell Publishing, 2005): 147–54.

4 P. Ghemawat and F. Ghadar, "Global Integration—Global Concentration," *Industrial and Corporate Change* 15 (2006): 595–624.

5 A key finding was that *human capital* (knowledge and skills) was more important than *physical capital* in explaining U.S. comparative advantage. See W. W. Leontief, "Domestic Production and Foreign Trade," in R. Caves and H. Johnson (eds), *Readings in International Economics* (Homewood, IL: Irwin, 1968).

6 P. Krugman, "Increasing Returns, Monopolistic Competition, and International Trade," *Journal of International Economics* 9 (November, 1979): 469–79.

7 M. E. Porter, *The Competitive Advantage of Nations* (New York: Free Press, 1990).

8 For a review of the Porter analysis, see R. M. Grant, "Porter's *Competitive Advantage of Nations*: An Assessment," *Strategic Management Journal* 12 (1991): 535–48.

9 Y.-R. Park, "Korean Business Culture," Presentation, December 15, 2005, http://gc.sfc.keio.ac.jp/class/2005_14969/slides/10/, accessed July 7, 2009.

10 The linking of value-added chains to national comparative advantages is explained in B. Kogut, "Designing Global Strategies and Competitive Value-Added Chains," *Sloan Management Review* (Summer, 1985): 15–38.

11 J. Hagel and J. S. Brown, "Thinking Global, Acting Local," *Financial Times* (August 9, 2005).

12 "Sum of the Parts," *Financial Times* (November 17, 2008).

13 The role of firm-specific assets in explaining the multinational expansion is analyzed in R. Caves, "International Corporations: The Industrial Economics of Foreign Investment," *Economica* 38 (1971): 1–27.

14 D. J. Teece, "Transactions Cost Economics and Multinational Enterprise," *Journal of Economic Behavior and Organization* 7 (1986): 21–45. See also "Creatures of Imperfection," in "Multinationals: A Survey," *Economist* (March 27, 1993): 8–10.

15 D. von Emloh and Y. Wang, "Competing for China's Credit Card Market," *McKinsey Quarterly* (November, 2005): www.mckinseyquarterly.com.

16 "Freemove: Creating Value through Strategic Alliance in the Mobile Telecommunications Industry," IESE Case 0-305-013 (2004).

17 "Tata motors, Fiat to Halt competitive Launches," *Hindustan Times* (June 13, 2009).

18 G. Hamel, "Competition for Competence and Inter-partner Learning within International Strategic Alliances," *Strategic Management Journal* 12 (1991): 83–103.

19 See R. Reich and E. Mankin, "Joint Ventures with Japan Give Away our Future," *Harvard Business Review* (March–April 1986).

20 T. Levitt, "The Globalization of Markets," *Harvard Business Review* (May–June 1983): 92–102.

21 P. Ghemawat, *Redefining Global Strategy: Crossing Borders in a World Where Differences Still Matter* (Boston: Harvard Business School, 2007).

22 G. S. Yip, *Total Global Strategy II* (Upper Saddle River, NJ: Prentice Hall, 2003); C. Baden-Fuller and J. Stopford, "Globalization Frustrated," *Strategic Management Journal* 12 (1991): 493–507; "Rough and Tumble Industry," *Financial Times* (July 2, 1997): 13.
23 S. G. Winter and G. Szulanski, "Replication as Strategy," *Organization Science* 12 (2001): 730–43.
24 D. B. Montgomery, G. S. Yip, and B. Villalonga, "Explaining Supplier Behavior on Global Account Management," Stanford Research Paper No. 1767 (November, 2002). Abstract available at SSRN: http://ssrn.com/abstract=355240, accessed July 7, 2009.
25 P. Almeida, "Knowledge Sourcing by Foreign Multinationals: Patent Citation Analysis in the U.S. Semiconductor Industry," *Strategic Management Journal* 17, Winter Special Issue (1996): 155–65. See the McDonald's individual country web sites, such as www.mcdonalds.com (U.S.), www.mcdonalds.co.uk (U.K.), www.mcdonalds.fr (France).
26 P. Ghemawat, "The Forgotten Strategy," *Harvard Business Review* (November 2003): 76–84.
27 Comments by Tommy Kullberg (IKEA Japan) in "The Japan Paradox," Conference organized by the European Commission, Director General for External Affairs (December 2003): 62–3, available at http://www.deljpn.ec.europa.eu/data/current/japan-paradox.pdf, accessed July 7, 2009.
28 A. K. Gupta and P. Govindarajan, "Knowledge Flows within Multinational Corporations," *Strategic Management Journal* 21 (April 2000): 473–96; P. Almeida, J. Song and R. M. Grant, "Are Firms Superior to Alliances and Markets? An Empirical Test of Cross-Border Knowledge Building," *Organization Science* 13 (March–April 2002): 147–61.
29 G. Hamel and C. K. Prahalad, "Do You Really Have a Global Strategy?" *Harvard Business Review* (July–August 1985): 139–48.
30 H. Simon and Y. Eriguchi, "Pricing Challenges for Japanese Companies in the Twenty-first Century," *Journal of Professional Pricing* 14, no. 4 (2005), www.pricingsociety.com. B. Y. Aw, G. Batra, and M. J. Roberts, "Firm Heterogeneity and Export—Domestic Price Differentials: A Study of Taiwanese Electrical Products," *Journal of International Economics* 54 (2001): 149–69.
31 I. C. Macmillan, A. van Ritten and R. G. McGrath, "Global Gamesmanship," *Harvard Business Review* (May, 2003): 62–71.
32 R. C. Christopher, *Second to None: American Companies in Japan* (New York: Crown, 1986).
33 K. Ohmae, *Triad Power: The Coming Shape of Global Competition* (New York: Free Press, 1985).
34 The Ford Mondeo/Contour is a classic example of a global product that failed to appeal strongly to any national market. See M. J. Moi, "Ford Mondeo: A Model T World Car?" Working Paper, Rotterdam School of Management, Erasmus University (2001). C. Chandler, "Globalization: The Automotive Industry's Quest for a World Car": GlobalEdge working paper, Michigan State University (1997).
35 C. Baden-Fuller and J. Stopford, "Globalization Frustrated," *Strategic Management Journal* 12 (1991): 493–507.
36 M. Venzin, *Building an International Financial Services Firm: How Successful Firms Design and Execute Cross-border Strategies* (Oxford: Oxford University Press, 2009).
37 P. Ghemawat (*Redefining Global Strategy* op. cit.) proposes a three-way rather than a two-way analysis. In his Adaptation-Aggregation-Arbitrage ("AAA") framework he divides integration into aggregation and arbitrage.
38 C. A. Bartlett and S. Ghoshal, *Managing Across Borders: The Transnational Solution*, 2nd edn (Boston: Harvard Business School Press, 1998).
39 C. Bartlett, "Building and Managing the Transnational: The New Organizational Challenge," in Michael E. Porter (ed.) *Competition in Global Industries* (Boston: Harvard Business School Press, 1986): 377.
40 Ibid.: 388.
41 "The Country Prince Comes of Age," *Financial Times* (August 9, 2005).
42 J. Birkinshaw, P. Braunerhjelm, U. Holm and S. Terjesen, "Why do some Multinational Corporations Relocate their Headquarters Overseas?" *Strategic Management Journal* 27 (2006): 681–700.
43 J. Birkinshaw, N. Hood and S. Jonsson, "Building Firm-specific Advantages in Multinational Corporations: The Role of Subsidiary Initiative," *Strategic Management Journal* 19 (1998): 221–42.
44 T. S. Frost, J. M. Birkinshaw and P. C. Ensign, "Centers of Excellence in Multinational Corporations," *Strategic Management Journal* 23 (2002): 997–1018.

16 Diversification Strategy

Telephones, hotels, insurance—it's all the same. If you know the numbers inside out, you know the company inside out.

—HAROLD SYDNEY GENEEN, CHAIRMAN OF ITT, 1959–78, AND INSTIGATOR OF 275 COMPANY TAKEOVERS

For a company that has taken its original or main business as far as it can go, diversification as a means of channeling surplus resources should certainly be considered. For the company that has not yet developed its main business to the full potential, however, diversification is probably one of the riskiest strategic choices that can be made.

—KENICHI OHMAE, FORMER HEAD OF MCKINSEY & CO.'S TOKYO OFFICE

OUTLINE

Introduction and Objectives

Deciding "What business are we in?" is the starting point of strategy and the basis for defining the firm's identity. In their statements of vision and mission, some companies define their businesses broadly. Shell's objective is "to engage efficiently, responsibly, and profitably in oil, oil products, gas, chemicals, and other selected businesses." Other companies define their businesses more narrowly: McDonald's vision is "to be the world's best quick-service restaurant chain"; Caterpillar will "be the leader in providing the best value in machines, engines, and support services for companies dedicated to building the world's infrastructure and developing and transporting its resources."

The business scope of firms changes over time. The dominant trend of the past two decades has been "refocusing on core businesses." Philip Morris Companies, Inc. (now renamed Altria Group, Inc.) sold off 7-Up, Miller Brewing and Kraft Foods and became a specialist tobacco company. Most diversified industrial groups—U.S. and European conglomerates such as ITT, Hanson, Gulf & Western, Cendant, Vivendi Universal, and Tyco—have broken up altogether.

Some companies have moved in the opposite direction. Microsoft, once a supplier of operating systems, expanded into application and networking software, information services, entertainment systems and video games consoles. Google is no longer simply a search engine company—it supplies a wide array of information products, advertising management services, an internet browser (Chrome), an operating system for mobile phones (Android), and a wide array of applications software.

Diversification is a conundrum. The quest to enter new fields of business has probably caused more value destruction than any other type of strategic decision. Yet, diversification also offers growth options and the potential for a firm to free itself of the restrictions of a single industry.

Our goal in this chapter is to establish the basis on which companies can make corporate strategy decisions that create rather than destroy value. Is it better to be specialized or diversified? Is there an optimal degree of diversification? What types of diversification are most likely to create value?

In practice, we make these types of decision every day in our personal lives. If my car doesn't start in the morning, should I try to fix it myself or have it towed directly to the garage? There are two considerations. First, is repairing a car an attractive activity to undertake? If the garage charges $85 an hour but I can earn $600 an hour consulting, then car repair is not attractive to me. Second, am I any good at car repair? If I am likely to take twice as long as a skilled mechanic then I possess no competitive advantage in car repair.

Diversification decisions by firms involve the same two issues:

- How attractive is the industry to be entered?
- Can the firm establish a competitive advantage within the new industry?

These are the very same factors we identified in Chapter 1 (see Figure 1.4) as determining a firm's profit potential. Hence, no new analytic framework is needed for appraising diversification decisions: diversification may be justified either by the superior profit potential of the industry to be entered, or by the ability of the firm to create competitive advantage in the new industry. The first issue draws on the industry analysis developed in Chapter 3; the second draws on the analysis of competitive advantage developed in Chapters 5 and 8.

Our primary focus will be the latter question: under what conditions does operating multiple businesses assist a firm in gaining a competitive advantage in each? This leads into exploring linkages between different businesses within the diversified firm—a phenomenon often referred to as "synergy." By the time you have completed this chapter, you will be able to:

- understand the factors that caused both the earlier trend of diversification and the recent trend toward refocusing;
- identify the conditions under which diversification creates value for shareholders and, in particular, to evaluate the potential for sharing and transferring resources and capabilities within the diversified firm;
- determine the relative merits of diversification and strategic alliances in exploiting the linkages between different businesses;
- recognize the organizational and managerial issues to which diversification gives rise and why diversification so often fails to realize its anticipated benefits.

Trends in Diversification over Time

As a background to our analysis of diversification decisions, let's begin by examining the factors that have influenced diversification strategies in the past.

The Era of Diversification, 1950–80

In Chapter 14, we identified diversification as a major component of the widening scope of the modern corporation during the twentieth century. Between 1950 and 1980, the expansion of companies into different product markets was a major source of corporate growth in all the advanced industrial nations.[1] The 1970s saw the peak of the diversification boom, with the emergence of a new corporate form—the *conglomerate*—represented in the U.S. by ITT, Textron, and Allied-Signal, and in the U.K. by Hanson, Slater-Walker, and BTR. These highly diversified enterprises were created from multiple, unrelated acquisitions. Their existence reflected the view that senior management no longer needed industry-specific experience; corporate management simply needed to deploy the new techniques of financial and strategic management.[2] Figure 16.1 shows changing patterns of diversification strategy during the latter part of the twentieth century.

Refocusing, 1980–2009

After 1980, the diversification trend went into sharp reverse. Between 1980 and 1990, the average index of diversification for the Fortune 500 declined from 1.00 to

FIGURE 16.1 Diversification strategies of large U.S. and U.K. companies during the late twentieth century

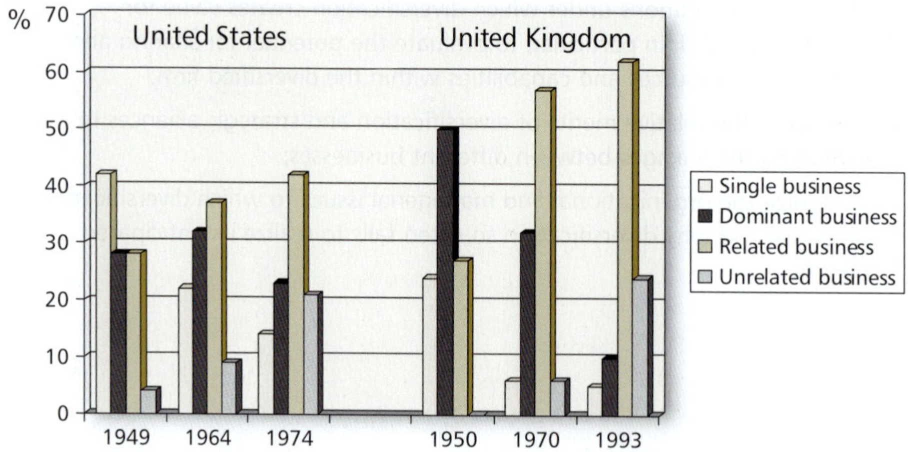

Sources: R. P. Rumelt, "Diversification Strategy and Profitability," *Strategic Management Journal* 3 (1982): 359–70; R. Whittington, M. Mayer, and F. Curto, "Chandlerism in Post-war Europe: Strategic and Structural Change in France, Germany and the UK, 1950–1993," *Industrial and Corporate Change* 8 (1999): 519–50; D. Channon, *The Strategy and Structure of British Enterprise* (Cambridge: Harvard University Press, 1973).

0.67.[3] Unprofitable "noncore" businesses were divested and many diversified companies fell prey to acquirers who promptly restructured them.[4] Acquisition activity was extremely heavy during the 1980s—some $1.3 trillion in assets were acquired, including 113 members of the Fortune 500—but, unlike the previous decade, only 4.5% of acquisitions represented unrelated diversification.[5] Moreover, acquisitions by the Fortune 500 were outnumbered by dispositions. The refocusing trend was strongest in the U.S., but was also evident in Canada and Europe and, to a lesser extent, in Japan.[6]

This trend towards specialization was the result of three principal factors.

Emphasis on Shareholder Value The primary driver of refocusing was the reordering of corporate goals from growth to profitability. Sluggish growth and high interest rates during the early 1980s and 1989–90 exposed the inadequate profitability of many large, diversified corporations. Institutional shareholders, including pension funds such as California's Public Employees Retirement system, became more active in pressuring top management for better shareholder returns—this led to increased CEO turnover.[7]

The surge in leveraged buyouts put further pressure on executives to boost shareholder returns. Kohlberg Kravis Roberts' $31 billion takeover of the tobacco and food giant RJR Nabisco in 1989 demonstrated that even the largest U.S. companies were vulnerable to attack from corporate raiders.[8] The result was a rush by diversified giants to restructure before leveraged buyout specialists did it for them. Evidence of "conglomerate discounts"—that the stock market was valuing diversified companies at less than the sum of their parts—provided a further incentive for breakups.[9]

Turbulence and Transaction Costs In Chapter 14, we observed that the relative costs of organizing transactions within firms and across markets depend on the conditions in the external environment. Administrative hierarchies are very efficient in processing routine transactions, but in turbulent conditions the pressure of decision making on top management results in stress, inefficiency and delay. As the business environment has become more volatile, specialized companies are more agile than large diversified corporations where strategic decisions require approval at divisional and corporate levels. At the same time, external markets for resources—capital markets especially—have become increasingly efficient. Many diversified companies have spun off their growth businesses because of the greater potential of external capital markets to fund their development.

Outside the mature industrialized countries, the situation is very different. Highly diversified business groups dominate the industrial sectors of many emerging countries: Tata Group and Reliance in India, Charoen Pokphand (CP) in Thailand, Astra in Indonesia, Sime Darby in Malaysia, Grupo Alfa and Grupo Carso in Mexico. One reason for the continued dominance of large conglomerates in emerging market countries may be higher transaction costs associated with their less sophisticated markets for finance, information, and labor that offer diversified companies advantages over their specialized competitors.[10]

Trends in Management Thinking Optimism that new tools and systems of financial and strategic management would enable companies to span many different businesses has been replaced by recognition that competitive advantage requires focusing on key strengths in resources and capabilities. Where core resources and

FIGURE 16.2 Diversification: the evolution of strategy and management thinking

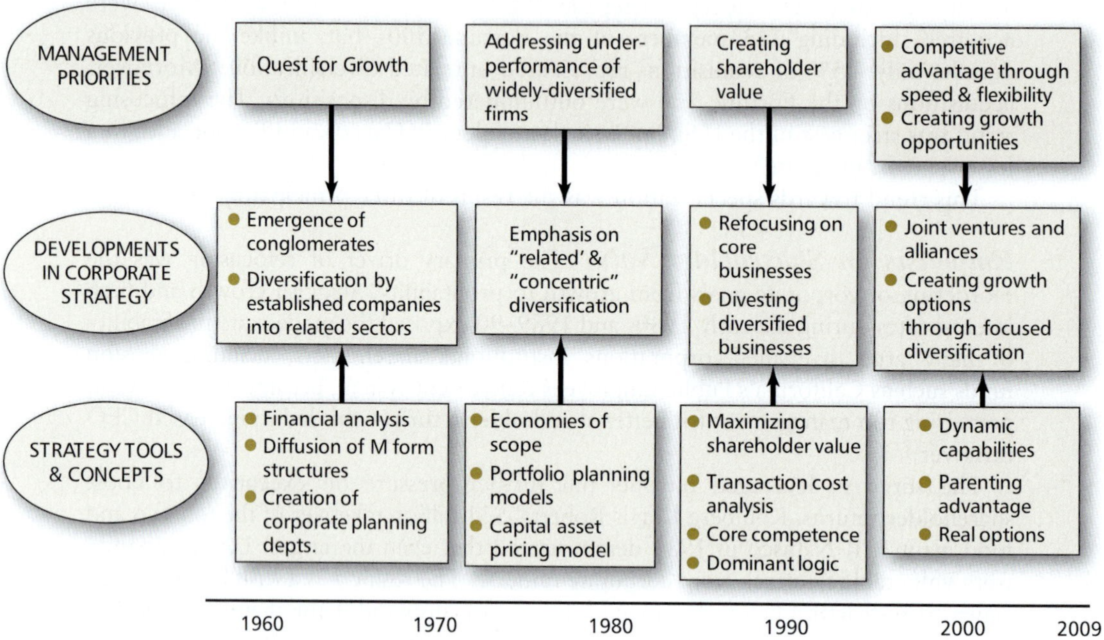

capabilities can be deployed across different product markets, this can support profitable diversification. Hence, the focus of diversification analysis has been to identify the circumstances in which multibusiness activity can create value. Analysis of economies of scope, the transferability of resources and capabilities across industry boundaries, and the role of transaction costs has allowed us to be more precise about these circumstances. Mere linkages between businesses are not enough: the key to creating value is the ability of the diversified firm to share resources and transfer capabilities more efficiently than alternative institutional arrangements. Moreover, it is essential that the benefits of these linkages are not outweighed by the additional management costs of exploiting them. Figure 16.2 summarizes some of the key developments in diversification strategy over the past 50 years.

Motives for Diversification

A critical development in the transition from diversification to refocusing has been the reordering of corporate objectives. The era of corporate diversification was influenced by two key objectives—growth and risk reduction—neither of which are consistent with the creation of shareholder value.

Growth

In the absence of diversification firms are prisoners of their industry. For firms in stagnant or declining industries this is a daunting prospect—especially for top management. The urge to achieve corporate growth that outstrips that of a firm's primary industry is an appealing prospect for managers. Companies in low-growth, cash flow-rich industries such as tobacco and oil have been especially susceptible to the temptations of diversification. During the 1980s, Exxon diversified into copper and coal mining, electric motors, and computers and office equipment; RJR Nabisco transformed itself from a tobacco company into a diversified consumer products company. In both cases diversification was highly destructive of shareholder value. Shareholders are quite happy to invest in companies in low growth, even declining industries, so long as these companies throw off plenty of cash flow which shareholders can invest in promising growth companies.

Risk Reduction

If the cash flows of different businesses are imperfectly correlated, then bringing them together under common ownership reduces the variance of the combined cash flow. However, such risk reduction appeals to managers more than to owners. Shareholders can diversify risk by holding diversified portfolios. Hence, what advantage can there be in companies diversifying for them? The only possible advantage could be if firms can diversify at lower cost than individual investors. In fact the reverse is true: the transaction costs to shareholders of diversifying their portfolios are far less than the transaction costs to firms diversifying through acquisition. Not only do acquiring firms incur the heavy costs of using investment banks and legal advisers, they must also pay an acquisition premium to gain control of an independent company.

The *capital asset pricing model* (CAPM) formalizes this argument. The theory states that the risk that is relevant to determining the price of a security is not the overall risk (variance) of the security's return, but *systematic risk*: that part of the variance of the return that is correlated with overall market returns. This is measured by the security's *beta coefficient*. Corporate diversification does not reduce systematic risk: if three separate companies are brought under common ownership, in the absence of any other changes, the beta coefficient of the combined company is simply the weighted average of the beta coefficients of the constituent companies. Hence, the simple act of bringing different businesses under common ownership does not create shareholder value through risk reduction.[11]

Empirical studies are generally supportive of the absence of shareholder benefit from diversification that simply combines independent businesses under a single corporate umbrella.[12] Unrelated diversification may even fail to lower unsystematic risk.[13]

Special issues arise once we consider the risk of bankruptcy. For a marginally profitable firm, diversification can help avoid cyclical fluctuations of profits that can push it into insolvency. However, diversification that reduces the risk of bankruptcy is beneficial to bondholders (and other creditors) rather than shareholders.[14]

Are there circumstances where reductions in unsystematic risk can create shareholder value? If there are economies to the firm from financing investments internally rather than resorting to external capital markets, the stability in the firm's cash flow that results from diversification may reinforce independence from external capital markets. For ExxonMobil, BP, and the other major oil companies, one of the benefits of extending across upstream (exploration and production), downstream (refining and marketing), and chemicals is that the negative correlation of the returns from these businesses increases the overall stability of their cash flows. This in turn increases their capacity to undertake huge, risky investments in offshore oil production, transcontinental pipelines, and natural gas liquefaction. These benefits also explain why firms pursue hedging activities that only reduce unsystematic risk.[15]

The financial turmoil of 2008–9 has created a new appreciation of the risk spreading benefits of diversification. The seizing up of credit markets towards the end of 2008 was less serious for large firms with diversified cash flows that were less dependent on banks providing working capital.

Value Creation: Porter's "Essential Tests"

If we return to the assumption that corporate strategy should be directed toward the interests of shareholders, what are the implications for diversification strategy? We have already revisited our two sources of superior profitability: industry attractiveness and competitive advantage. For firms contemplating diversification, Michael Porter expands on these. He proposes three "essential tests" to be applied in deciding whether diversification will truly create shareholder value:

- *The attractiveness test.* The industries chosen for diversification must be structurally attractive or capable of being made attractive.
- *The cost-of-entry test.* The cost of entry must not capitalize all the future profits.
- *The better-off test.* Either the new unit must gain competitive advantage from its link with the corporation, or vice versa.[16]

The Attractiveness and Cost-of-entry Tests A critical realization in Porter's "essential tests" is that industry attractiveness is insufficient on its own. Although diversification allows a firm to access more attractive investment opportunities than are available in its own industry, it faces the challenge of entering a new industry. The second test, *cost of entry*, recognizes that for outsiders, the cost of entry may counteract the attractiveness of the industry. Pharmaceuticals, corporate legal services, and defense contracting offer above-average profitability precisely because they are protected by barriers to entry. Firms seeking to enter these industries have a choice. They may acquire an established player, in which case the acquisition price will almost certainly fully capitalize the target firm's profit prospects (especially given the need to pay an acquisition premium over the market price of the target).[17] Alternatively, entry may occur through establishing a new corporate venture. In this case, the diversifying firm must directly confront the barriers to entry protecting that industry.[18]

The Better-off Test Porter's third criterion for successful diversification—*the better-off test*—addresses the basic issue of competitive advantage: if two businesses producing different products are brought together under the ownership and control of a single enterprise, is there any reason why they should become any more profitable? Combining different, but related, businesses can enhance the competitive advantages of the original business, the new business, or both. For example:

- Procter & Gamble's 2005 acquisition of Gillette was intended to boost the competitive position of both companies through combining the two companies' global marketing and distribution networks, transferring

Gillette's new product development capabilities to P&G, and increasing both companies' bargaining power relative to retail giants such as Wal-Mart.

- Bank of America's $50 billion takeover of Merrill Lynch in October 2008 to create the world's largest diversified financial services companies was justified by the strengthening of the core businesses of both firms. The combination of Merrill's investment banking business and Bank of America's corporate banking businesses created a massive presence in corporate financial services. The augmenting of Bank of America's retail banking presence with Merrill's huge network of stockbrokers created a broad U.S. platform for wealth management services.[19]

Primacy of the Better-Off Test In most normal circumstances it is only the better-off test that matters. In the first place, industry attractiveness is rarely a source of value from diversification—in most cases, the attractiveness test and the cost-of-entry test cancel each other out.

The second reason why the better-off test normally dominates is that it can make sense for a company to enter an unattractive industry so long as the cost of entry is sufficiently discounted and the better-off test is met. When private equity firm Golden Gate Capital bought Eddie Bauer Inc. in August 2009, the deal was motivated, not by the attractiveness of the retail clothing sector, but by Golden Gate's ability to by the 400-store chain for a mere $286 million, then apply its financial and strategic management capabilities to revitalizing the sportswear chain. Similarly, Disney's acquisition of marvel entertainment, also in August 2009, reflected Disney's desire to exploit the marvel characters in its movie and theme park businessed rather than Disney's desire to invest in the comic industry.

So, let us now explore further into the ways in which diversification can make businesses "better off" through analyzing the relationship between diversification and competitive advantage.

Competitive Advantage from Diversification

If the primary source of value creation from diversification is exploiting linkages between different businesses, what are these linkages and how are they exploited? The critical linkages are those that arise through the sharing of resources and capabilities across different businesses. In addition, there is the potential for diversification to enhance or exploit a firm's market power—this issue is addressed in the appendix to this chapter.

Economies of Scope

The most general argument concerning the benefits of diversification focuses on the presence of *economies of scope* in common resources: "Economies of scope exist when using a resource across multiple activities uses less of that resource than when the activities are carried out independently."[20]

Economies of scope exist for similar reasons as *economies of scale*. The key difference is that the economies of scale relate to cost economies from increasing output of a *single product*; economies of scope are cost economies from increasing the output of *multiple products*.[21] The nature of economies of scope varies between different types of resources and capabilities.

Tangible Resources Tangible resources—such as distribution networks, information technology systems, sales forces and research laboratories—offer economies of scope by eliminating duplication between businesses through creating a single shared facility. The greater the fixed costs of these items, the greater the associated economies of scope are likely to be. Entry by cable TV companies into telephone services and telephone companies into cable TV are motivated by the desire to spread the costs of networks and billing systems over as great a volume of business as possible. Common resources such as customer data bases, customer service centers, and billing systems have encouraged British Gas, a former publicly owned gas utility, to diversify into supplying electricity, fixed-line and mobile telephone services, broadband internet connections, home security systems, home insurance and home appliance repair.

Economies of scope also arise from the centralized provision of administrative and support services to the different businesses of the corporation. Within diversified companies, accounting, legal services, government relations and information technology tend to be centralized—often through *shared service organizations* that supply common administrative and technical services to the operating businesses. Similar economies arise from centralizing research activities in a corporate R&D lab.

Intangible Resources Intangible resources such as brands, corporate reputation and technology offer economies of scope from the ability to extend them to additional businesses at low marginal cost.[22] Exploiting a strong brand across additional products is called *brand extension*. Starbucks has extended its brand to ice cream, packaged cold drinks, home espresso machines, audio CDs and books.

Organizational Capabilities Organizational capabilities can also be transferred within the diversified company. For example:

- LVMH is the world's biggest and most diversified supplier of branded luxury goods. Its distinctive capability is the management of luxury brands. This capability comprises market analysis, advertising, promotion, retail management, and quality assurance. These capabilities are deployed across Louis Vuitton (accessories and leather goods); Hennessey (cognac); Moet et Chandon, Dom Perignon, Veuve Clicquot, and Krug (champagne); Celine, Givenchy, Kenzo, Dior, Guerlain, and Donna Karan (fashion clothing and perfumes); TAG Heuer and Chaumet (watches); Sephora and La Samaritaine (retailing); and some 25 other branded businesses.
- Sharp Corporation—originally established to manufacture metal products and the Ever Sharp Pencil—developed capabilities in the miniaturization of electronic products. It has developed and introduced a stream of innovative products, beginning with the world's first transistor calculator (1964), the first LCD pocket calculator (1973), LCD color TVs, PDAs, internet viewcams, ultraportable notebook computers, and 3G mobile telephones.

Some of the most important capabilities in influencing the performance of diversified corporations are *general management capabilities*. General Electric possesses strong technological and operational capabilities at business level and it is good at sharing these capabilities between businesses (for example, turbine knowhow between jet engines and electrical generating equipment). However, its core capabilities are in general management and these reside primarily at the corporate level. They include its ability to motivate and develop its managers, its outstanding strategic and financial management that reconciles decentralized decision making with strong centralized control, and its international management capability. Similar observations could be made about 3M. While 3M's capabilities in technical know-how, new product development, and international marketing reside within the individual businesses, it is the corporate management capabilities and the systems through which they are exercised that maintain, nourish, coordinate, and upgrade these competitive advantages.[23]

Economies from Internalizing Transactions

Although economies of scope provide cost savings from sharing and transferring resources and capabilities, does a firm have to diversify across these different businesses to exploit those economies? The answer is no. Economies of scope in resources and capabilities can be exploited simply by selling or licensing the use of the resource or capability to another company. In Chapter 12, we observed that a firm can exploit proprietary technology by licensing it to other firms. In Chapter 15, we noted how technology and trademarks are licensed across national frontiers as an alternative to direct investment. Similarly across industries: Starbucks' extension of its brand to other products has been achieved primarily through licensing: Pepsi produces and distributes Starbucks Frappaccino; Unilever produces Tazo Tea beverages, Dreyer's produces Starbucks ice cream. Walt Disney exploits the enormous value of its trademarks, copyrights, and characters partly through diversification into theme parks, live theater, cruise ships, and hotels; but it also licenses the use of these assets to producers of clothing, toys, music, comics, food, and drinks, as well as to the franchisees of Disney's retail stores. Disney's income from licensing fees and royalties was over $2 billion in 2005.

Even tangible resources can be shared across different businesses through market transactions. Airport and railroad station operators exploit economies of scope in their facilities not by diversifying into catering and retailing but by leasing out space to specialist retailers and restaurants.

Are economies of scope better exploited internally within the firm through diversification, or externally through market contracts with independent companies? The key issue is relative efficiency: what are the transaction costs of market contracts, as compared with the administrative costs of diversified activities? Transaction costs include the costs involved in drafting, negotiating, monitoring, and enforcing a contract, plus the costs of protecting against exploitation by the partner. The costs of internalization consist of the management costs of establishing and coordinating the diversified business.[24]

Consider the following:

- In the case of Walt Disney Company, it licenses Donald Duck trademarks to Florida's Natural Growers rather than setting up its own orange-juice company; it owns and operates Disneyland and Disney World theme parks but licenses its trademarks and technology to Oriental Land Company, the owner and operator of Tokyo Disneyland.

- Both Mars and Cadbury used their confectionary brands to enter the European ice cream market. Cadbury decided to license its brands to Nestlé; Mars entered the business itself by setting up production and distribution facilities, competing with Unilever and Nestlé. The result was that Cadbury made significant profits from its licenses whereas Mars experienced years of losses or low returns on its investment.

Finding the right answer is complex. It depends on the nature of the resource or capability that is generating the "better off" benefits. If the resource can be traded or licensed out for anything close to its real value—as in the case of the Donald Duck trademark or the confectionery brands, then it is not necessary to enter another business in order to capture the extra profitability. Cadbury captured more profitability by not entering the ice cream-business. If, on the other hand, the resource is one that cannot easily be traded, such as general management capabilities, then it will be necessary to enter the new business in order to create the extra profitability. There is little scope for 3M to deploy its new product development capabilities other than within its own business. Similarly, for Apple Computer, the only way for it to exploit its capabilities in user-friendly design was to diversify outside of its core computer business. Virgin has a separate licensing company but only licenses its brand to companies within the Virgin group. So why doesn't Virgin license its brand to companies it does not own? The answer presumably is that the brand is part of a package of benefits that Virgin offers, some of which could not be traded or licensed. For example, Virgin has developed special marketing skills around its brand, often using the brand and Richard Branson to gain press comment in place of expensive advertising.

Parenting Advantage

The recognition that it is only certain kinds of economies of scope that justify diversification led Goold, Campbell and Alexander to propose the concept "parenting value added" (an alternative to Porter's better-off test).[25] Parenting value comes from the resources and general management skills possessed by the parent company, holding company or corporate centre that is thinking of diversifying into a new business. In Virgin's case they include the brand, Richard Branson's skill at getting press coverage and Virgin's attractiveness to partners. If these skills add value to a new business, then Virgin should think of entering that business. If the "better-off" value comes from combining manufacturing or sales forces, then Goold and his colleagues argue that it is the skills of the managers in the parent company that make these combinations happen. Hence, they argue that parenting value added explains nearly all successful diversification because parenting is the main resource that is hard to trade and it is the activities of parent-level managers that lower internal transaction costs.

The Diversified Firm as an Internal Market

We see that economies of scope on their own do not provide an adequate rationale for diversification—they must be supported by potential to economize on transaction costs. In fact, the lower costs of managing transactions internally can offer "better off" efficiencies, even when no economies of scope are present.

Internal Capital Markets Consider the case of financial capital. The diversified firm represents an internal capital market: the corporate allocating capital between the different businesses through the capital expenditure budget. Which is more efficient, the internal capital markets of diversified companies or the external capital market? Diversified companies have two key advantages:

- By maintaining a balanced portfolio of cash-generating and cash-using businesses, diversified firms can avoid the costs of using the external capital market, including the margin between borrowing and lending rates and the heavy costs of issuing new debt and equity.
- Diversified companies have better access to information on the financial prospects of their different businesses than that typically available to external financiers.[26]

Against these advantages is the critical disadvantage that investment allocation within the diversified company is a politicized process in which strategic and financial considerations are subordinated by turf battles and ego building. Evidence suggests that diversified firms' internal capital markets tend to cross-subsidize poorly performing divisions and are reluctant to transfer cash flows to the divisions with the best prospects.[27] However, the efficiency of capital allocation varies greatly across companies. Makron Associates identified several conglomerates with exceptional performance in terms of ten-year shareholder returns. They included GE and Berkshire Hathaway of the U.S., Hutchison Wampoa of Hong Kong, Bouygues and Lagardere of France, Wesfarmers of Australia, ITC of India, and Carso of Mexico. These companies were characterized by: "Strict financial discipline, rigorous analysis and valuation, a refusal to overpay for acquisitions, and a willingness to close or sell existing businesses."[28]

Another form of organization that reduces the transaction costs of external capital markets is the *private equity firm*. These firms raise money into a fund that is then used to buy businesses. Instead of raising money each time they want to buy a business, they do the money raising once. Moreover, they have developed ways of avoiding the agency problems of self-seeking managers. Each fund has to be closed and returned to investors within a set number of years, often 10–14 years. This encourages the managers in the private equity firm to take particular care when allocating money from the fund. They want to make sure that each allocation will produce a good return before the fund is closed. They also give equity stakes to the managers in charge of each business that will pay out when the business is sold. This reduces the motivation for playing politics. Finally, the managers leading the individual businesses do not participate in the management decisions of the private equity firm. Many corporations, in contrast, have the heads of the biggest divisions sitting on the corporate-level management committee (more on this in the next chapter).

Internal Labor Markets Efficiencies also arise from the ability of diversified companies to transfer employees—especially managers and technical specialists—between their divisions, and to rely less on hiring and firing. As companies develop and encounter new circumstances, so different management skills are required. The costs associated with hiring include advertising, time spent in interviewing and selection and the costs of "head-hunting" agencies. The costs of dismissing employees can be very high where severance payments must be offered. A diversified corporation has a pool of employees and can respond to the specific needs of any one business through transfer from elsewhere within the corporation.

The broader set of opportunities available in the diversified corporation as a result of internal transfer may also result in attracting a higher caliber of employee. Graduating students compete intensely for entry-level positions with diversified corporations such as Canon, General Electric, Unilever and Nestlé in the belief that these companies can offer richer career development than more specialized companies.

The informational advantages of diversified firms are especially important in relation to internal labor markets. A key problem of hiring from the external labor market is limited information. A résumé, references, and a day of interviews are poor indicators of how a new hire will perform in a particular job. The diversified firm that is engaged in transferring employees between different positions and different internal units can build detailed information on the competencies and characteristics of its employees. This informational advantage exists not only for individual employees but also for groups of individuals working together as teams. Hence, in exploiting a new business opportunity an established firm is at an advantage over the new firm which must assemble its team from scratch.

Diversification and Performance

Where diversification exploits economies of scope in resources and capabilities in the presence of transaction costs, it has the potential to create value for shareholders. Diversification that seeks only growth or risk reduction is likely to destroy value. How do these predictions work in practice?

The Findings of Empirical Research

Empirical research into diversification has concentrated on two major issues: first, how do diversified firms perform relative to specialized firms and, second, does related diversification outperform unrelated diversification?

The Performance of Diversified and Specialized Firms Despite many empirical studies since the 1960s, consistent, systematic relationships between diversification and performance are lacking. Beyond a certain threshold, high levels of diversification appear to be associated with lower profitability—probably because of the organizational complexity that diversification creates. Among British companies, diversification was associated with increased profitability up to a point, after which further diversification was accompanied by declining profitability.[29] Several other studies have detected a similar curvilinear relationship between diversification and profitability.[30] McKinsey & Company also point to the benefits of moderate diversification—"a strategic sweet spot between focus and broader diversification." Diversification, they argue, makes most sense when a company has exhausted growth opportunities in its existing markets and can match its existing capabilities to emerging external opportunities.[31]

A key problem is distinguishing *association* from *causation*. If moderately diversified companies are generally more profitable than specialized firms, is it because diversification increases profitability or because profitable firms channel their cash flows into diversifying investments?

The performance effects of diversification depend on the mode of diversification. Mergers and acquisitions involving companies in different industries appear to perform especially poorly.[32]

More consistent evidence concerns the performance results of refocusing initiatives by North American and European companies: when companies divest diversified businesses and concentrate more on their core businesses, the result is typically increased profitability and higher stock market valuation.[33] These findings may reflect a changing relationship between diversification and profitability over time: growing turbulence of the business environment may have increased the costs of managing widely diversified corporations.

Related and Unrelated Diversification Given the importance of economies of scope in shared resources and capabilities, it seems likely that diversification into *related* industries should be more profitable than diversification into *unrelated* industries. Empirical research initially supported this prediction. Rumelt discovered that companies that diversified into businesses closely related to their core activities were significantly more profitable than those that pursued unrelated diversification.[34] By 1982, Tom Peters and Robert Waterman were able to conclude: "virtually every academic study has concluded that unchanneled diversification is a losing proposition."[35] This observation supported one of their "golden rules of excellence":

> *Stick to the Knitting*
>
> Our principal finding is clear and simple. Organizations that do branch out but stick very close to their knitting outperform the others. The most successful are those diversified around a single skill, the coating and bonding technology at 3M for example. The second group in descending order, comprise those companies that branch out into related fields, the leap from electric power generation turbines to jet engines from GE for example. Least successful are those companies that diversify into a wide variety of fields. Acquisitions especially among this group tend to wither on the vine.[36]

Subsequent studies have clouded the picture: the superiority of related diversifiers may be the result of risk factors and industry influences;[37] unrelated diversification may even outperform related.[38] Several factors may be confusing the relationship. First, related diversification offers greater potential benefits than unrelated but the linkages it involves also create more difficult management problems. (I shall address this issue in the next chapter.) Second, the apparently poor results from unrelated diversification might be the result of poorly performing companies seeking to get far away from their existing businesses.[39] Finally, the distinction between "related" and "unrelated" diversification is not always clear—it may depend upon the strategy and characteristics of individual firms. Champagne and luggage are not obviously related products, but LVMH applies similar brand management capabilities to them both. Let us consider this issue further.

The Meaning of Relatedness in Diversification

If relatedness refers to the potential for sharing and transferring resources and capabilities between businesses, there are no unambiguous criteria to determine whether two industries are related—it all depends on the company undertaking the diversification. Empirical studies have defined relatedness in terms of similarities between industries in technologies and markets. These similarities emphasize relatedness at the *operational* level—in manufacturing, marketing, and distribution—typically activities where economies from resource sharing are small and achieving them is costly in management terms. Conversely, some of the most important sources of value creation within the diversified firm are the ability to apply common general management capabilities, strategic management systems, and resource allocation processes to different businesses. Such economies depend on the existence of *strategic* rather than *operational* commonalities among the different businesses within the diversified corporation.[40]

- Berkshire Hathaway is involved in insurance, candy stores, furniture, kitchen knives, jewelry and footwear. Despite this diversity, all these businesses have been selected on the basis of their ability to benefit from the unique style of corporate management established by chairman Warren Buffett and CEO Charles Munger.
- Richard Branson's Virgin Group covers a huge array of businesses from airlines to bridal stores. Yet, they share certain strategic similarities: almost all are startup companies that benefit from Branson's entrepreneurial zeal and expertise; almost all sell to final consumers and are in sectors that offer opportunities for innovative approaches to differentiation.

The essence of such strategic-level linkages is the ability to apply similar strategies, resource allocation procedures, and control systems across the different businesses within the corporate portfolio.[41] Table 16.1 lists some of the strategic factors that determine similarities among businesses in relation to corporate management activities.

TABLE 16.1 The determinants of strategic relatedness between businesses

Corporate Management Tasks	Determinants of Strategic Similarity
Resource allocation	Similar sizes of capital investment projects Similar time spans of investment projects Similar sources of risk Similar general management skills required for business unit managers
Strategy formulation	Similar key success factors Similar stages of the industry life cycle Similar competitive positions occupied by each business within its industry
Performance management and control	Targets defined in terms of similar performance variables Similar time horizons for performance targets

Source: R. M. Grant, "On Dominant Logic, Relatedness, and the Link Between Diversity and Performance," *Strategic Management Journal* 9 (1988): 641. Reproduced by permission of John Wiley & Sons, Inc.

Unlike operational relatedness, where the opportunities for exploiting economies of scope in joint inputs are comparatively easy to identify—even to quantify—strategic relatedness is more elusive. It necessitates an understanding of the overall strategic approach of the company and recognition of its corporate-level management capabilities.

Ultimately, the linkage between the different businesses within a company may depend upon the strategic rationale of the company. Prahalad and Bettis use the term *dominant logic* to refer to managers' cognition of the rationale that unifies the different parts of the company.[42] Such a common view of a company's identity and *raison d'être* is a critical precondition for effective integration across its different businesses. However, dominant logic needs to be underpinned by economic synergies. Otherwise an appealing dominant logic—such as Allegis Corporation's desire to meet travelers' needs by combining airlines and hotels or General Mills meeting "the needs and wants of the homemaker" by diversifying into toys, fashion clothing, specialty retailing, and restaurants—will fail to translate into real value creation.

Summary

Diversification is like sex: its attractions are obvious, often irresistible. Yet, the experience is often disappointing. For top management it is a minefield. The diversification experiences of large corporations are littered with expensive mistakes: Exxon's attempt to build Exxon Office Systems as a rival to Xerox and IBM; Vivendi's diversification from water and environmental services into media, entertainment, and telecoms; Royal Bank of Scotland's quest to transform itself from a retail bank into a financial services giant. Despite so many costly failures, the urge to diversify continues to captivate senior managers. Part of the problem is the divergence between managerial and shareholder goals. While diversification has offered meager rewards to shareholders, it is the fastest route to building vast corporate empires. A further problem is hubris. A company's success in one line of business tends to result in the top management team becoming overconfident of its ability to achieve similar success in other businesses.

Nevertheless, for companies to survive and prosper over the long term they must change; inevitably this involves redefining the businesses in which they operate. The world's two largest IT companies—IBM and Hewlett-Packard—are both over six decades old. Their longevity is based on their ability to adapt their product lines to changing market opportunities. Essentially they have applied existing capabilities to developing new products which have provided new growth trajectories. Similarly with most other long established companies: for 3M, Canon, Samsung, and DuPont diversification has been central to the process of evolution. In most cases, this diversification was not a major discontinuity, but an initial incremental step in which existing resources and capabilities were deployed to exploit a perceived opportunity.

If companies are to use diversification as part of their long-term adaptation and avoid the many errors that corporate executives have made in the past, then better strategic analysis of diversification decisions is essential. The objectives of diversification need to be clear and explicit. Shareholder value creation has provided a demanding and illuminating criterion with which to appraise investment in new business opportunities. Rigorous analysis also counters the tendency for diversification to be a diversion—corporate escapism resulting from the unwillingness of top management to come to terms with difficult conditions within the core business.

The analytic tools at our disposal for evaluating diversification decisions have developed greatly in recent years. In the late 1980s, diversification decisions were based on vague concepts of synergy that involved identifying linkages between different industries. We are now able to be much more precise about the need for economies of scope in resources and capabilities *and* the economies of internalization that are prerequisites for diversification to create shareholder value. Recognizing the role of these economies of internalization has directed attention to the role of top management capabilities and effective corporate management systems in determining the success of diversification.

Self-Study Questions

1 An ice cream manufacturer is proposing to acquire a soup manufacturer on the basis that, first, its sales and profits will be more seasonally balanced and, second, from year to year, sales and profits will be less affected by variations in weather. Will this risk spreading create value for shareholders? Under what circumstances could this acquisition create value for shareholders?

2 Tata Group is one of India's largest companies, employing 203 000 people in many different industries, including steel, motor vehicles, watches and jewelry, telecommunications, financial services, management consulting, food products, tea, chemicals and fertilizers, satellite TV, hotels, motor vehicles, energy, IT, and construction. Such diversity far exceeds that of any North American or Western European company. What are the conditions in India that might make such broad-based diversification both feasible and profitable?

3 Giorgio Armani SpA is an Italian private company owned mainly by the Armani family. Most of its clothing and accessories are produced and marketed by the company (some are manufactured by outside contractors). For other products, notably fragrances, cosmetics, and eyewear, Armani licenses its brand names to other companies. Armani is considering expanding into athletic clothing, hotels, and bridal shops. Advise Armani on whether these new businesses should be developed in-house, by joint ventures, or by licensing the Armani brands to specialist companies already within these fields.

4 General Electric, Berkshire Hathaway and Richard Branson's Virgin Group each comprise a wide range of different businesses that appear to have few close technical or customer linkages. Are these examples of unrelated diversification and do the corporate and ownership links within each of the groups result in the creation of any value? If so, what are the sources of this value creation?

Appendix: Does Diversification Confer Market Power?

The potential for diversification to enhance profitability by increasing a firm's market power and suppressing competition has been a continuing interest for antitrust authorities in the U.S. and Europe—and more recently in Japan and South Korea. It has been claimed that large diversified companies can exercise market power through four mechanisms:

- *Predatory pricing*. Just as global corporations derive strength from their ability to finance competitive battles in individual markets through cross-subsidization, so multibusiness companies can use their size and diversity to discipline or even drive out specialized competitors in particular product markets through predatory pricing—cutting prices to below the level of rivals' costs. In 2003, following up complaints from AOL, the European Commission fined France Telecom 10 million euros for the predatory pricing of ISP services by its subsidiary, Wanadoo.[43]
- *Bundling*. A diversified firm can extend its monopoly in one market into a related market by bundling the two products together. The U.S. Justice Department claimed Microsoft abused its monopoly power in PC operating systems by bundling its Explorer web browser with Windows, thereby squeezing Netscape from the browser market. The E.U. made a similar case against Microsoft regarding its bundling of its media player with Windows.[44]
- *Reciprocal dealing*. A diversified company can leverage its market share across its businesses by reciprocal buying arrangements. These involve offers of the type: "I'll buy from you if you buy from me." A recent case involved Intel, which refused to supply microprocessors to Intergraph Corporation unless Intergraph licensed certain technology to Intel free of charge.[45] The potential for reciprocal dealing is greatest in those emerging market economies where a few large companies span many sectors.
- *Mutual forbearance*. Corwin Edwards argued that:

> When one large conglomerate enterprise competes with another, the two are likely to encounter each other in a considerable number of markets. The multiplicity of their contacts may blunt the edge of their competition. A prospect of advantage in one market from vigorous competition may be weighed against the danger of retaliatory forays by the competitor in other markets. Each conglomerate may adopt a live-and-let-live policy designed to stabilize the whole structure of the competitive relationship.[46]

Game theory shows that such *multimarket competition* is likely to inhibit aggressive action in any one market for fear of triggering more generalized warfare.[47] Empirical evidence suggests that such behavior is most likely among companies that meet in multiple geographical markets for the same product or service—the airline industry, for example.[48] Such tendencies may also exist where diversified companies meet in multiple product markets.[49]

Notes

1 A. D. Chandler Jr., *Strategy and Structure: Chapters in the History of the Industrial Enterprise* (Cambridge, MA: MIT Press, 1962); R. P. Rumelt, *Strategy, Structure and Economic Performance* (Cambridge, MA: Harvard University Press, 1974); H. Itami, T. Kagono, H. Yoshihara and S. Sakuma, "Diversification Strategies and Economic Performance," *Japanese Economic Studies* 11, no. 1 (1982): 78–110.

2 M. Goold and K. Luchs, "Why Diversify? Four Decades of Management Thinking," *Academy of Management Executive* 7, no. 3 (August, 1993): 7–25.

3 G. F. Davis, K. A. Diekman and C. F. Tinsley, "The Decline and Fall of the Conglomerate Firm in the 1980s: A Study in the De-Institutionalization of an Organizational Form," *American Sociological Review* 49 (1994): 547–70.

4 R. E. Hoskisson and M. A. Hitt, *Downscoping: How to Tame the Diversified Firm* (New York: Oxford University Press, 1994).

5 A. Shleifer and R. W. Vishny, "The Takeover Wave of the 1980s," *Science* 248 (July–September 1990): 747–9.

6 L. G. Franko, "The Death of Diversification: The Focusing of the World's Industrial Firms, 1980–2000," *Business Horizons* (July–August, 2004): 41–50.

7 During 2004-6 CEO turnover reached an all-time high. See Booz Allen Hamilton, "CEO Succession 2006: The Era of the Inclusive Leader," *strategy+business* (Summer 2007): www.strategy-business.com.

8 B. Burrough, *Barbarians at the Gate: The Fall of RJR Nabisco* (New York: Harper & Row, 1990).

9 L. Laeven and R. Levine, "Is there a Diversification Discount in Financial Conglomerates?" *Journal of Financial Economics* 82 (2006): 331–367.

10 T. Khanna and K. Palepu, "Why Focused Strategies May Be Wrong for Emerging Markets," *Harvard Business Review* (July–August, 1997): 41–51; D. Kim, D. Kandemir and S. T. Cavusgil, "The Role of Family Conglomerates in Emerging Markets," *Thunderbird International Business Review* 46 (January, 2004): 7–20.

11 See any standard corporate finance text, for example R. A. Brealey, S. Myers and F. Allen, *Principles of Corporate Finance*, 8th edn (McGraw-Hill, 2006): Chapter 8.

12 See, for example, H. Levy and M. Sarnat, "Diversification, Portfolio Analysis and the Uneasy Case for Conglomerate Mergers," *Journal of Finance* 25 (1970): 795–802; R. H. Mason and M. B. Goudzwaard, "Performance of Conglomerate Firms: A Portfolio Approach," *Journal of Finance* 31 (1976): 39–48; J. F. Weston, K. V. Smith and R. E. Shrieves, "Conglomerate Performance Using the Capital Asset Pricing Model," *Review of Economics and Statistics* 54 (1972): 357–63.

13 M. Lubatkin and S. Chetterjee, "Extending Modern Portfolio Theory into the Domain of Corporate Strategy: Does It Apply?" *Academy of Management Journal* 37 (1994): 109–36.

14 The reduction in risk that bondholders derive from diversification is termed the *coinsurance effect.* See: L. W. Lee, "Coinsurance and the Conglomerate Merger," *Journal of Finance* 32 (1977): 1527–37.

15 S. M. Bartram, "Corporate Risk Management as a Lever for Shareholder Value Creation," *Financial Markets, Institutions and Instruments* 9 (2000): 279–324.

16 M. E. Porter, "From Competitive Advantage to Corporate Strategy," *Harvard Business Review* (May–June 1987): 46.

17 M. Hayward and D. C. Hambrick, "Explaining the Premiums Paid for Large Acquisitions," *Administrative Science Quarterly* 42 (1997): 103–27.

18 A study of 68 diversifying ventures by established companies found that, on average, breakeven was not attained until the seventh and eighth years of operation: R. Biggadike, "The Risky Business of Diversification," *Harvard Business Review* (May–June, 1979):103–111.

19 Ken Lewis and John Thain, "Creating the Premier Financial Services Company in the World," A joint Bank of America and Merrill Lynch Presentation, September 15, 2008.

20 The formal definition of economies of scope is in terms of "subadditivity." Economies of scope exist in the production of goods $x_1, x_2, \ldots, xn$, if $C(X) < \Re iCi(xi)$ where: $X = \Re i(xi)$

C(X) is the cost of producing all n goods within a single firm

$\Re iCi(xi)$ is the cost of producing the goods in n specialized firms.

See W. J. Baumol, J. C. Panzar and R. D. Willig, *Contestable Markets and the Theory of Industry Structure* (New York: Harcourt Brace Jovanovich, 1982): 71–2.

21 Economies of scope can arise in consumption as well as in production: customers may prefer to buy different products from the same supplier. See T. Cottrell and B. R. Nault, "Product Variety and Firm Survival in Microcomputer Software," *Strategic Management Journal* 25 (2004): 1005–26.

22 There is some evidence to the contrary. See H. Park, T. A. Kruse, K. Suzuki and K. Park, "Long-term Performance Following Mergers of Japanese Companies: The Effect of Diversification and Affiliation," *Pacific Basin Finance Journal* 14 (2006); and P. R. Nayyar, "Performance Effects of Information Asymmetry and Economies of Scope in Diversified Service Firms," *Academy of Management Journal* 36 (1993): 28–57.

23 The role of capabilities in diversification is discussed in C. C. Markides and P. J. Williamson, "Related Diversification, Core Competencies and Corporate

Performance," *Strategic Management Journal* 15 (Special Issue, 1994): 149–65.
24 This issue is examined more fully in D. J. Teece, "Towards an Economic Theory of the Multiproduct Firm," *Journal of Economic Behavior and Organization* 3 (1982): 39–63.
25 M. Goold, A. Campbell and M. Alexander, *Corporate-Level Strategy: Creating Value in the Multibusiness Company* (New York: John Wiley & Sons, Inc., 1994).
26 J. P. Liebeskind, "Internal Capital Markets: Benefits, Costs and Organizational Arrangements," *Organization Science* 11 (2000): 58–76.
27 D. Scharfstein and J. Stein, "The Dark Side of Internal Capital Markets: Divisional Rent Seeking and Inefficient Investment," *Journal of Finance* 55 (2000): 2537–64; V. Maksimovic and G. Phillips, "Do Conglomerate Firms Allocate Resources Inefficiently Across Industries?" *Journal of Finance* 57 (2002): 721–67; R. Rajan, H. Servaes and L. Zingales, "The Cost of Diversity: The Diversification Discount and Inefficient Investment," *Journal of Finance* 55 (2000): 35–84.
28 C. Kaye and J. Yuwono, "Conglomerate Discount or Premium? How Some Diversified Companies Create Exceptional Value," Marakon Associates (2003). www.marakon.com/.
29 R. M. Grant, A. P. Jammine and H. Thomas, "Diversity, Diversification and Performance in British Manufacturing Industry," *Academy of Management Journal* 31 (1988): 771–801.
30 L. E. Palich, L. B. Cardinal and C. C. Miller, "Curvi-linearity in the Diversification-Performance Linkage: An Examination of over Three Decades of Research," *Strategic Management Journal* 22 (2000): 155–74.
31 N. Harper and S. P. Viguerie, "Are You Too Focused?" *McKinsey Quarterly* (2002 Special Edition): 29–37.
32 J. D. Martin and A. Sayrak, "Corporate Diversification and Shareholder Value: A Survey of Recent Literature," *Journal of Corporate Finance* 9 (2003): 37–57.
33 C. C. Markides, "Consequences of Corporate Refocusing: Ex Ante Evidence," *Academy of Management Journal* 35 (1992): 398-412; C. C. Markides, "Diversification, Restructuring and Economic Performance," *Strategic Management Journal* 16 (1995): 101–18.
34 R. P. Rumelt, *Strategy, Structure and Economic Performance* (Cambridge, MA: Harvard University Press, 1974).
35 T. Peters and R. Waterman, *In Search of Excellence* (New York: Harper & Row, 1982): 294.
36 Ibid.
37 H. K. Christensen and C. A. Montgomery, "Corporate Economic Performance: Diversification Strategy versus Market Structure," *Strategic Management Journal* 2 (1981): 327-43; R. A. Bettis, "Performance Differences in Related and Unrelated Diversified Firms," *Strategic Management Journal* 2 (1981): 379–83.
38 See, for example, A. Michel and I. Shaked, "Does Business Diversification Affect Performance?" *Financial Management* 13, no. 4 (1984): 18–24; G. A. Luffman and R. Reed, *The Strategy and Performance of British Industry, 1970-80* (London: Macmillan, 1984).
39 C. Park, "The Effects of Prior Performance on the Choice between Related and Unrelated Acquisitions," *Journal of Management Studies* 39 (2002): 1003–19.
40 For a discussion of relatedness in diversification, see J. Robins and M. F. Wiersema, "A Resource-Based Approach to the Multibusiness Firm: Empirical Analysis of Portfolio Interrelationships and Corporate Financial Performance," *Strategic Management Journal* 16 (1995): 277–300; J. Robins and M. F. Wiersema, "The Measurement of Corporate Portfolio Strategy: Analysis of the Content Validity of Related Diversification Indexes," *Strategic Management Journal* 24 (2002): 39–59.
41 R. M. Grant, "On Dominant Logic, Relatedness, and the Link Between Diversity and Performance," *Strategic Management Journal* 9 (1988): 639–42.
42 C. K. Prahalad and R. A. Bettis, "The Dominant Logic: A New Linkage Between Diversity and Performance," *Strategic Management Journal* 7 (1986): 485–502.
43 "Wanadoo Fined £10m for Predatory Pricing," *Financial Times* (July 17, 2003).
44 "Microsoft on Trial," *Economist* (April 28, 2006) (www.economist.com).
45 E. D. Cavanagh, "Reciprocal Dealing: A Rebirth?" *St. Johns Law Review* 75 (2001): 633–47.
46 US Senate, Subcommittee on Antitrust and Monopoly Hearings, *Economic Concentration*, Part 1, Congress, 1st session (1965): 45.
47 B. D. Bernheim and M. D. Whinston, "Multimarket Contact and Collusive Behavior," *Rand Journal of Economics* 2 (1990): 1–26.
48 In the U.S. airline industry, extensive multimarket contact resulted in a reluctance to compete on routes dominated by one or other of the airlines. See J. A. C. Baum and H. J. Korn, "Competitive Dynamics of Interfirm Rivalry," *Academy of Management Review* 39 (1996): 255–91.
49 S. Jayachandran, J. Gimeno, and P. R. Varadarajan, "The Theory of Multimarket Competition: A Synthesis and Implications for Marketing Strategy," *Journal of Marketing* 63 (July 1999): 49–66.

17 Implementing Corporate Strategy: Managing the Multibusiness Firm

Some have argued that single-product businesses have a focus that gives them an advantage over multibusiness companies like our own—and perhaps they would have, but only if we neglect our own overriding advantage: the ability to share the ideas that are the result of wide and rich input from a multitude of global sources.

GE businesses share technology, design, compensation and personnel evaluation systems, manufacturing practices, and customer and country knowledge. Gas Turbines shares manufacturing technology with Aircraft Engines; Motors and Transportation Systems work together on new propulsion systems; Lighting and Medical Systems collaborate to improve x-ray tube processes; and GE Capital provides innovative financing packages that help all our businesses around the globe. Supporting all this is a management system that fosters and rewards this sharing and teamwork, and, increasingly, a culture that makes it reflexive and natural at every level and corner of our Company.

—JACK WELCH, CHAIRMAN, GENERAL ELECTRIC COMPANY, 1981–2001

OUTLINE

Introduction and Objectives

In the last chapter, I concluded that the case for diversification depends on whether the diversified company can create value by operating across multiple businesses. Chapters 14 and 15 arrived at the same conclusion in relation to vertical integration and multinational operations. Having determined the potential for vertical integration, international expansion, or diversification to create value, the challenge is managing the company to exploit these sources of value. Implementing corporate strategy requires answering the following questions: How should the multibusiness corporation be structured? Through what systems and tools should management exercise control and coordination? What roles do the chief executive and top management team need to fulfill and what styles of leadership are likely to be most effective? Answering these questions requires that we look closely at the activities of the corporate head office and its relationships with the various businesses.

In this chapter we begin by addressing the problem of corporate governance in the large, multibusiness corporation and then go on to examine the main activities through which corporate management creates value, namely: managing the business portfolio, managing individual businesses, managing linkages between businesses, and leading change. We then assess the role of external strategies—mergers, acquisitions and alliances—in developing the corporation.

By the time you have completed this chapter you will be able to:

- appreciate the governance issues that impact the work of managers within the large corporation;
- recognize the principal organizational features of the multibusiness corporation;
- apply the techniques of portfolio analysis to corporate strategy decisions;
- understand how corporate headquarters manages its individual businesses through strategic planning and financial control and by managing linkages across businesses;
- analyze the fit between a firm's corporate strategy, organization structure, management systems, and leadership style;
- analyze the potential for value creation through restructuring a multibusiness corporation;
- identify the circumstances in which mergers and acquisitions can create value for a company—and be aware of their pitfalls.

Governance and the Structure of the Multibusiness Corporation

Chapter 1 introduced the distinction between business strategy and corporate strategy and observed that, within the multibusiness company,[1] corporate management takes primary responsibility for corporate strategy, and business-level management takes primary responsibility for business strategy. This distinction is the key management feature of the multibusiness corporation irrespective of whether the individual businesses are defined vertically (ExxonMobil), geographically (SAB-Miller), or by product (3M). In these *multidivisional* companies business decisions are located at the business level and the corporate center exercises overall coordination and control. While the multidivisional structure is the dominant organizational form for multibusiness companies, many multibusiness private companies are organized as holding companies (see Strategy Capsule 17.1).

STRATEGY CAPSULE 17.1

Alternatives to the Divisional Structure: the Holding Company

Despite the success of the multidivisional structure—especially in the U.S.—it is important to recognize that there are many multibusiness companies that have organizational and governance structures quite different from that of the divisionalized firm. By far the most common is the *holding company*. A holding company is a company that owns a controlling interest in a number of subsidiary companies. The term "holding company" is used to refer both to the parent company and to the group as a whole.

A holding company exercises control over the subsidiary through appointing its board of directors. The individual subsidiaries typically retain high levels of strategic and operational autonomy. A distinctive difference between a holding company and a divisionalized company is in financial integration. A divisionalized company almost always has a centralized treasury that manages cash holdings and hedges foreign exchange for the group as a whole; profits accrue to the corporate head office and operating funds and capital budgets are allocated by head quarters to the divisions. In the holding company each subsidiary manages is a separate financial entity. The parent company provides equity and debt capital to the subsidiary and receives dividends from the subsidiary.

Although the potential for exploiting synergies between businesses is more limited in the holding company than the divisionalized corporation, the holding company structure has important advantages for large family-owned companies. The attractiveness of holding companies is that they allow family dynasties to retain ownership and control of business empires that diversify family wealth across multiple sectors. At the same time their decentralization allows effective management of the group without the need for the parent company to develop tremendous depth of management capability.

Thus, Tata Group—India's biggest business concern with over $60 billion in revenue and over 330 000 employees—is controlled by the Tata family through Tata Sons Ltd., parent company of the group. Among the several hundred subsidiaries, several are leading companies within their industries—including Tata Steel, Tata Motors (owner of Jaguar and Land Rover), Tata Tea (owner of the Tetley brand), and Tata Consulting Services. Twenty-seven Tata companies are publicly listed.

Holding companies are common elsewhere in Asia—including the traditional Japanese *zaibatsu* (Mitsubishi and Mitsui), the Korean *chaebols* (Samsung and Hyundai), and the Hong Kong trading houses (Swire Group, Jardine Matteson and Hutchison Wampoa). In the U.S., bank holding companies are companies that own several banks. Because each bank must be separately regulated and have its own financial reserves, the holding company provides common ownership and control, but not the level of integration that exists within the typical divisionalized corporation.

By allowing the corporate headquarters to specialize in managing corporate issues and divisional units to specialize in managing the individual businesses, the multidivisional structure uses the principles of *modularity* to reconcile integration with decentralized responsiveness (see Chapter 7). However, separating corporate managers from divisional managers and managers from owners gives rise to problems of goal alignment—what referred to as the *agency problem* (see Chapter 7). The stream of corporate scandals of the past nine years—from Enron, WorldCom and Parmalat through to Lehman Brothers, AIG, and the Royal Bank of Scotland—involving acquisitive CEOs presiding over massive destruction of shareholder value raise critical issues over the efficacy of *corporate governance*—the system through which companies are directed and controlled.

The Theory of the M-form

While Alfred Chandler identified the invention and diffusion of the multidivisional form as critical to the development of the modern corporation (see Chapter 14), Oliver Williamson provided its theoretical rationale.[2] Williamson identified four key efficiency advantages of the divisionalized firm (or, in his terminology, the *M-form*):

- *Adaptation to "bounded rationality."* If managers are limited in their cognitive, information-processing, and decision-making capabilities, the top management team cannot be responsible for all coordination and decision making within a complex organization. The M-form permits decision making to be dispersed.
- *Allocation of decision making.* Decision-making responsibilities should be separated according to the frequency with which different types of decisions are made. The M-form allows high frequency decisions (such as operating decisions) to be made at divisional level and decisions that are made infrequently (such as strategic decisions) to be made at corporate level.
- *Minimizing coordination costs.* In the functional organization, decisions concerning a particular product or business area must pass up to the top of the company where all the relevant information and expertise can be brought to bear. In the divisionalized firm, so long as close coordination between different business areas is not necessary, most decisions concerning a particular business can be made at the divisional level. This eases the information and decision-making burden on top management.
- *Avoiding goal conflict.* In functional organizations, department heads emphasize functional goals over those of the organization as a whole. In multidivisional companies, divisional heads, as general managers, are more likely to pursue profit goals that are consistent with the goals of the company as a whole.

As a result, Williamson believed that the multidivisional form provided a solution to two central problems of corporate governance:

- *Allocation of resources.* Resource allocation within any administrative structure is a political process in which power, status, and influence can triumph over purely commercial considerations.[3] To the extent that the multidivisional company can create a competitive internal capital market in which capital is allocated according to financial and strategic criteria, it can avoid much of the politicization inherent in purely hierarchical systems. The multidivisional company does this through operating an internal capital market where budgets are linked to past and projected divisional profitability, and individual projects are subject to a standardized appraisal process.

- *Resolution of agency problems*. The basic agency problem is that owners (shareholders) desire maximization of the value of the firm, while their agents (managers) are more interested in salaries, security and power. Given the limited power of shareholders to discipline and replace managers and the weakness of boards to control management, the corporate head office of multidivisional firm can act as an interface between shareholders and the divisional managers and enforce adherence to profit goals. With divisions designated as profit centers, financial performance can readily be monitored by the head office and divisional managers can be held responsible for performance failures. According to Williamson, multibusiness companies can be more effective profit maximizers than specialist companies because of two critical advantages of the corporate head office over the board of directors of a single business company: first, the corporate head office has better access to information about the business, second, it is easier for a corporate head office to replace business managers than it is for a board of directors.[4] At General Electric, ExxonMobil, and PepsiCo, this capacity for corporate headquarters to create strongly profit-oriented systems is particularly evident.

The Challenge of Corporate Governance

Is Williamson right that the corporate head office can be relied upon to act as an "agent of the stockholders whose purpose is to monitor the operations of the constituent parts"? Among diversified firms, it seems that multidivisional structures are more conducive to profitability than alternative structural forms,[5] yet it is also clear that multidivisional structures are no safeguard against agency problems. The most notorious examples of chief executives operating their companies as personal fiefdoms are found among divisionalized, multibusiness corporations—Howard Hughes at Hughes Corporation, Ken Lay at Enron, Dennis Kozlowski at Tyco, Jean-Marie Messier at Vivendi Universal and Fred Goodwin at Royal Bank of Scotland. While the CEOs of diversified companies may avoid emotional commitment to particular businesses, this does not mean that they are more predisposed to share-holder return over the quest for Napoleonic personal grandeur.

Top management's pursuit of personal goals related to the aggrandizement of wealth, power, influence, and status in preference to owners' goals of value maximization are primarily a problem for public companies.[6] The critical problem is that the ability of shareholders to exercise effective control over management is limited by their large number. This creates, first, a coordination problem and, second, an incentive problem—if each shareholder owns only a small fraction of a company and if that company's shares only account for a small fraction of the shareholder's total wealth, then the costs of active engagement are high relative to the likely returns. Disgruntled shareholders typically sell their shares rather than oppose the incumbent management team.

Yet, even in the face of widespread shareholder apathy, the mechanisms and rules through which public companies are governed—in particular the rights accorded to shareholders and the responsibilities applied to companies' boards of directors—reinforce the power of owners relative to that of managers.

Rights of Shareholders Company law relating to the rights of shareholders typically covers shareholders' rights to sell their shares, their rights to company information (including access to audited financial statements), their rights to elect and remove members of the board of directors, and their right to share in the profits of the company.

Although seemingly straightforward, these rights are often abrogated by companies. For example, managers are more likely than shareholders to oppose takeover by another company—while shareholders benefit financially, senior executives often lose their jobs. Hence, companies frequently create impediments to hostile takeover either in the form of special voting rights for certain classes of share or "poison pill" defenses. Yahoo! defended against a 2008 takeover bid from Microsoft through a provision that any hostile bid would trigger the creation of a rights issue to existing shareholders. To resist takeover by Mittal Steel, Arcelor attempted to make itself indigestible by arranging a merger with Russian steel giant Severstal.

Managers desire to manipulate their companies' share prices has resulted in misreporting their financial results. Financial misreporting was at the center of the scandals that engulfed Enron and WorldCom in the U.S. and Parmalat and Royal Ahold in Europe.[7] New standards of financial reporting include America's Sarbanes Oxley Act.

The Board of Directors, according to *OECD Principles of Corporate Governance*, has the responsibility to: "...ensure the strategic guidance of the company, the effective monitoring of management by the board, and the board's accountability to the company and the shareholders."[8] This requires that:

- Board members act in good faith, with due diligence and care, in the best interest of the company and its shareholders.
- Board members review and guide corporate strategy, major plans of action, risk policy, annual budgets and business plans; set and monitor performance objectives; and oversee major capital expenditures; select, monitor, and compensate key executives; ensure the integrity of the corporation's accounting and financial reporting systems; and oversee the process of disclosure and communication.

The ability of the board to achieve these goals has been compromised by key impediments:

- The dominance of the board by executive directors—in both the U.S. and U.K. and some other countries, the top management team (the CEO, CFO and other senior executives) are likely to be board members.
- Combining the roles of board chair and CEO—this is common in the U.S., less so in most European companies. United States opinion suggests that splitting board chair and CEO roles is neither an advantage nor disadvantage—it depends entirely upon the attributes of the person doing

the job.[9] However, interlocking boards—where CEOs serve as independent members on one another's boards—does appear to be an unambiguous constraint on board independence.

The harshest criticisms of board oversight have been in relation to management compensation. The escalation of CEO compensation among large public companies since the early 1990s has been little short of staggering. The paradox is that the massive payouts to CEOs have been the result of compensation systems designed to align management goals with those of shareholders—especially through the grant of stock options and emphasis on performance-related bonuses. Yet, some of the biggest executive payouts have been by companies that have experienced shareholder returns that have ranged from indifferent to disastrous (see Table 17.1). Performance bonuses and options packages have been extended down corporate hierarchies to include middle managers as well as the top management team. In the U.K., salary comprised 54% of overall executive compensation as compared with bonuses 24%, and options and long-term incentive plans 22%.[10] Aspects of the poor alignment between executive compensation and shareholder value creation include linking bonuses to short term performance, a failure to correct for overall stockmarket movements, and incentives for creating shareholder value not being matched by penalties for its destruction.[11]

In short, there is little evidence to support Williamson's claim that the large multidivisional firm is a successful solution to the agency problem. While corporate CEOs may be able to avoid the distortions of judgment that result from emotional commitment to a particular business, the evidence suggest that they are far more prone to the delusions associated with hubris and the quest for power, influence and status.

Other Problems of Divisionalized Firms

Multidivisional structures may also suffer from other problems. In principle, the divisionalized corporation reconciles decentralization with coordination through

TABLE 17.1 Highest earning CEOs of U.S. companies 2003–7

CEO	Company	Total 5-year compensation (million $)
Steve Jobs	Apple	662
Ray Irani	Occidental Petroleum	550
Barry Diller	IAC/InterActive Corp.	462
Larry Ellison	Oracle	429
Angelo Mozilo	Countrywide Financial	392
Richard Fairbank	Capital One Financial	380
Richard Fuld	Lehman Brothers Holdings	354
Lew Frankfort	Coach	254
John Chambers	Cisco Systems	229
Bob Simpson	XTO Energy	215

Source:
"Special Report: CEO Compensation," *Fortune* (April 30, 2008).

embracing the principles of modularity (see Chapter 7). Yet, according to Henry Mintzberg, the multidivisional structure suffers from two key rigidities:[12]

- *Constraints on decentralization*. Although operational authority in the M-form firm is dispersed to the divisional level, the individual divisions often feature highly centralized power that arises from divisional presidents' personal accountability to the head office. In addition, the operational freedom of the divisional management exists only so long as the corporate head office is satisfied with divisional performance. As we have seen in the recent financial crisis, divisional underperformance typically results in a speedy end to divisional autonomy as the corporate head office intervenes.
- *Standardization of divisional management*. In principle, each division can adapt itself to the requirements of its business sector. In practice, there are powerful forces for standardizing control systems and management styles across the multidivisional corporation. The imposition by Exxon of its standard financial control systems and hierarchical management style on its IT subsidiary, Exxon Office Systems, was a key factor in the venture's eventual failure. The difficulties that many large, mature corporations experience with new business development often result from applying to new businesses the same management systems designed for existing businesses.[13]

The Role of Corporate Management

For the multibusiness corporation to be viable, the benefits from bringing businesses under common ownership and control must exceed the costs of the corporate overlay. Indeed, Goold, Campbell and Alexander go further. They propose a tougher hurdle for multibusiness companies: for each and every business within the corporate portfolio, not only must the additional profit from inclusion within the corporate fold exceed the cost of headquarters management, but the net gain should be bigger than that which any other potential corporate parent can offer.[14] (Otherwise it would be profitable to sell the business.) This notion of "parenting advantage"—that a company must be able to add more value to a business than rivals could—raises important issues concerning how multibusiness corporations create value and the tools needed to do so.

We shall focus on four activities through which corporate management adds value within the multibusiness company:

- managing the overall corporate portfolio, including acquisitions, divestments, and resource allocation;
- managing each individual business;
- managing linkages among businesses;
- managing change.

Let us consider each of these activities and establish the conditions under which they create value.

Managing the Corporate Portfolio

The basic questions of corporate strategy are "what businesses should we be in?" and "how should we manage these business in order to generate as much value from them as possible?" *Portfolio planning models* can assist help managers with both of these questions.

General Electric and the Development of Strategic Planning

Portfolio planning techniques were one outcome of the pioneering work in corporate strategy initiated by General Electric at the end of the 1960s.[15] GE comprised 46 divisions and over 190 businesses. To manage this sprawling industrial empire more effectively, GE launched a series of initiatives together with Boston Consulting Group, McKinsey & Company, Arthur D. Little, and Harvard Business School. The result was three key developments in strategic management at the corporate level. The first was the identification of *strategic business units (SBUs)*–businesses that were sufficiently self-contained to formulate a separate competitive strategy.[16] The other two were *portfolio planning models* and the *PIMS database,* which we discuss below.

Portfolio Planning: The GE/McKinsey Matrix

The basic idea of a portfolio planning model is to represent graphically the individual businesses of a multibusiness company in terms of key strategic variables that determine their potential for profit. These strategic variables typically relate to the attractiveness of their market and their competitive advantage within that market. This analysis can guide:

- allocating resources between the businesses on the basis of each business's market attractiveness and competitive position;
- formulating business unit strategy—by comparing the strategic positioning of different businesses opportunities for repositioning (including divestment) can be identified.
- analyzing portfolio balance—a single display of all the company's businesses permits assessment of the overall balance of the portfolio in terms of *cash flow generation* and *growth prospects*;
- setting performance targets on the basis of each business's market attractiveness and its competitive position.

In the GE/McKinsey matrix (see Figure 17.1) the industry attractiveness axis combines market size, market growth rate, market profitability (return on sales over three years), cyclicality, "inflation recovery" (potential to increase productivity and product prices), and international potential (ratio of foreign to domestic sales). Business unit competitive advantage combines: market share, return on sales relative to competitors, and relative position with regard to quality, technology, manufacturing, distribution, marketing, and cost.[17] The strategy implications are shown by three regions of Figure 17.1.

FIGURE 17.1 The GE/McKinsey portfolio planning matrix

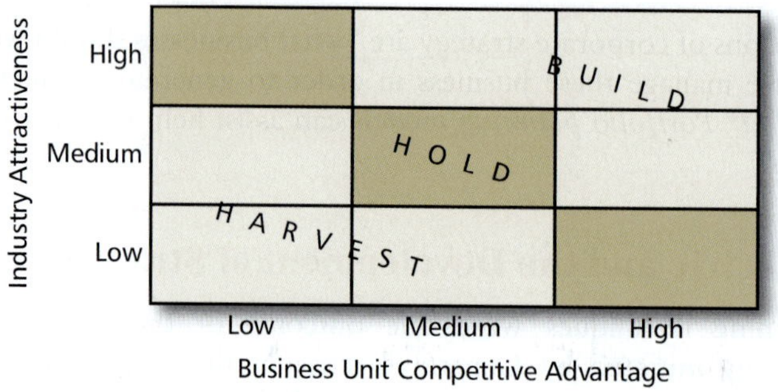

Portfolio Planning: BCG's Growth-Share Matrix

The Boston Consulting Group's *growth-share matrix* also uses industry attractiveness and competitive position to compare the strategic positions of different businesses. However, it uses a single indicator as a proxy for each of these dimensions: industry attractiveness is measured by *rate of market growth*, competitive advantage by *relative market share* (the business unit's market share relative to that of its largest competitor). The four quadrants of the BCG matrix predict patterns of profits and cash flow and indicate strategies to be adopted (see Figure 17.2).[18]

The simplicity of BCG matrix is both its limitation and its usefulness. It can be prepared very easily and offers a clear picture of a firm's business portfolio in relation to some important strategic characteristics. Moreover, the analysis is versatile—it can be applied to business units and to the positioning of different

FIGURE 17.2 The BCG growth-share matrix

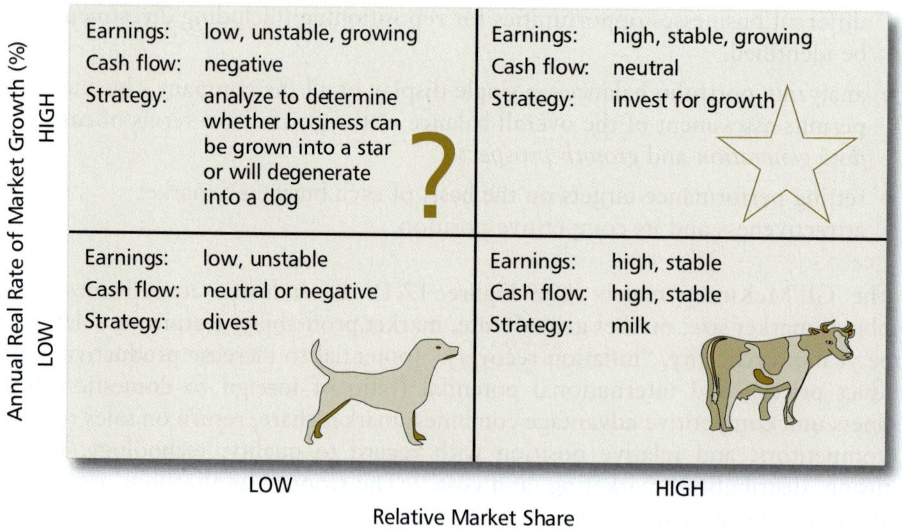

products, brands, distribution channels and customers. Though simplistic, it can be useful as a preliminary view before embarking upon a more detailed and rigorous analysis.

However, the simplistic approach of both the BCG and McKinsey business portfolio matrices has resulted in both losing their popularity as analytic tools. Apart from their simplistic approaches to the determinants of industry attractiveness and competitive advantage, there are problems relating to market definition. For example, in the BCG matrix, is BMW's auto business a "dog" because it holds less than 2% of the world auto market, or a cash cow because it is market leader in the luxury car segment? An even greater problem is the implicit assumption that every business in the portfolio is independent—a direct denial of the basic rational for the multibusiness corporation: the synergistic linkages between businesses.[19]

Portfolio Planning: The Ashridge Portfolio Display

The Ashridge Portfolio Display is based upon Goold, Campbell and Alexander's *parenting advantage* framework.[20] It takes account of the fact that the value creating potential of a business within a company's business portfolio depends not just upon the characteristics of the business (as assumed by the McKinsey and BCG matrices) but also on the characteristics of the parent. The focus, therefore, is on the *fit* between a business and its parent company. The horizontal axis of Figure 17.3 shows the parent's potential for creating additional profit within the business, for example, from applying corporate-level management capabilities to the business, from sharing resources and capabilities with other businesses, from economizing on transaction costs, and so on. The vertical axis measures the potential for value destruction by the

FIGURE 17.3 Ashridge portfolio display: the potential for patenting advantage

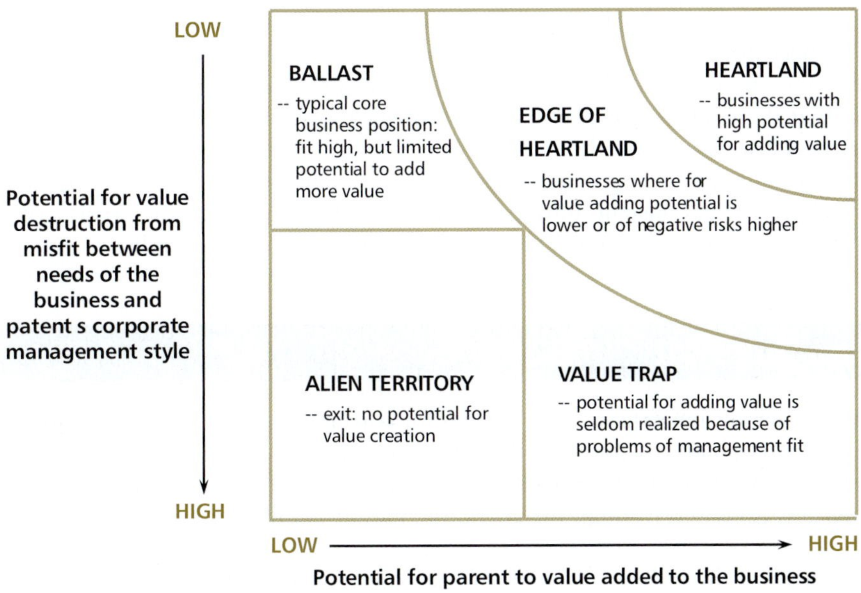

Source: Ashridge Strategic Management Centre.

FIGURE 17.4 Ashridge portfolio display applied to a diversified leisure company

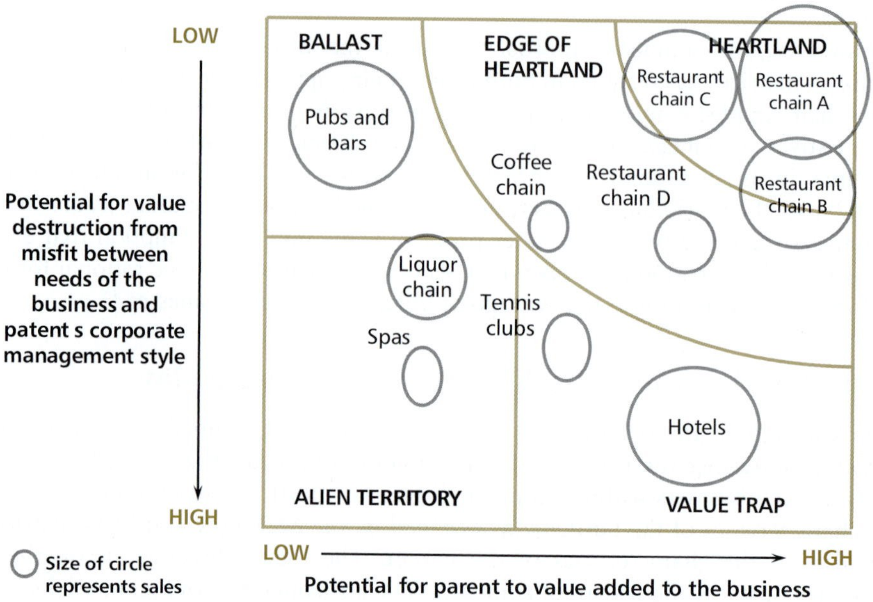

Source: Ashridge Strategic Management Centre.

parent—these result both from the costs of corporate overhead and mismatch between the management needs of the business and the management systems and style of the parent. These might include bureaucratic rigidity, incompatibility with top management mindset, politicization of decision making and risks of inappropriate strategic guidance. Figure 17.4 applies the framework to position the businesses of a diversified hospitality company.

The need for assessment of complex issues of fit between the business and the parent and the fact that these assessments inevitably require subjective judgments mean that the Ashridge Display is more difficult to use than GE/McKinsey or BCG matrices. However, this is the reality of the subject matter: creating value from the configuration and reconfiguration of a portfolio of business involves complex issues of fit that requires insight into the fundamental strategic characteristics of the businesses and the nature of corporate management systems and style.

Managing Individual Businesses

Some of the most important opportunities for corporate headquarters to create value arise from its ability to improve the strategic and operational management of its businesses—what Goold, Campbell, and Alexander call "standalone influence." This influence is exercised through the corporate parent's ability to:

> . . . appoint the general manager of each business and influence management development and succession planning within the businesses. It can approve or reject budgets, strategic plans, and capital expenditure proposals and it can

> influence the shape and implementation of these plans and proposals. It can provide advice and policy guidance to the businesses. The parent also influences the businesses by the hints and pressures passed on through both formal and informal line management meetings and contacts, and, more indirectly, through the corporate culture.[21]

The mechanisms through which the corporate headquarters exercises control over individual businesses can be divided into two types. Corporate management can control decisions, through requiring that certain decisions—typically those involving significant resource commitments— are referred upward for corporate approval. For example, the corporate HQ might require that capital expenditure requests that exceed $5 million are approved by the executive committee. Alternatively, corporate management can control businesses through setting and monitoring performance targets, backed by incentives and penalties to motivate their attainment. The distinction is between *input* and *output* control: the company can control the inputs into strategy (the decisions) or the output from strategy (the performance). Although most companies use a combination of input and output controls, there is an unavoidable tradeoff between the two: more of one implies less of the other. If the corporate HQ micromanages divisional decisions, it must accept the performance outcomes that result. If the corporate HQ imposes rigorous performance targets, it must give divisional managers the freedom to make the decisions necessary to achieve those targets.

The Strategic Planning System

In Chapter 1, I identified corporate strategy as being set at the corporate level and business strategy as set at the business level. In reality, business strategies are formulated jointly by corporate and divisional managers. In most diversified, divisionalized companies, business strategies are initiated by divisional managers and the role of corporate managers is to probe, appraise, amend and approve divisional strategy proposals. The challenge for corporate management is to create a strategy-making process that reconciles the decentralized decision making essential to fostering flexibility, responsiveness, and a sense of ownership at the business level, with the ability of the corporate level to bring to bear its knowledge, perspective, and responsibility for the shareholder interest. Achieving an optimal blend of business-level initiative and corporate-level guidance and discipline is a difficult challenge for the multibusiness corporation. Common to the success of General Electric, ExxonMobil, Samsung, and Unilever is a system of strategic management that has managed this difficult tradeoff between business initiative and corporate control. Strategy Capsule 17.2 describes key elements of the strategic planning process at Exxon.

Rethinking the Strategic Planning System Since the early 1980s, the strategic planning systems of large firms have been bombarded by criticism from academics and consultants. Two features of corporate strategic planning systems have attracted particular scorn:

- *Strategic planning systems don't make strategy*. Ever since Henry Mintzberg attacked the "rational design" school of strategy (see Chapter 1), strategic planning systems have been castigated as ineffective for formulating strategy.

STRATEGY CAPSULE 17.2

Strategic Planning at Exxon

Exxon (now ExxonMobil) is the world's biggest company (in terms of revenue and market value) and is the most financially successful oil and gas major. Exxon's strategic planning system has successfully reconciled long-term strategic planning with rigorous, short-term financial control; and strong centralized direction with flexible, responsive, business-level decision making. Exxon's strate-gic planning process follows an annual cycle that is similar to the "generic" strategic planning process outlined in Chapter 6 (see Figure 6.6).

The principal stages of the planning cycle are as follows:

1 *Economic review and energy review* are forecasts of the economy and energy markets prepared in spring by the corporate planning department to provide a basis for strategic planning.

2 *Business plans* are developed during the spring and summer by individual businesses and are aggregated and refined at the divisional level. Their time horizon is ten years for upstream, five years for downstream and chemicals. Prior to discussion, negotiation, and approval by the management committee, the plans are discussed with each division's contact director and evaluated by the corporate planning department (during October).

3 *The corporate plan* results from the aggregation of individual business plans. The approved business and corporate plans then provide the basis for the financial and performance plans (formulated during November).

4 *The financial forecast* comprises forecasts of revenues, operating costs, capital expenditures, interest and other expenses, income, and cash flow for divisions and for the company as a whole over a two-year period.

5 *The operating and capital budgets* are set for the upcoming year (the first year of the plans).

6 *The stewardship basis* comprises annual targets against which the next year's performance by each division will be judged. They include financial objectives, operating targets, safety and environmental objectives and strategy mileposts.

7 *Stewardship reviews*. In February of each year, each division's performance for the previous year is evaluated against its stewardship objectives. These reviews involve presentations by the divisional top management to the management committee.

8 *Investment reappraisals* occur in August and September and involve the divisions reporting back on the outcomes of specific investment projects.

In addition to this annual strategic planning cycle, *Strategic Studies* are *ad hoc* projects by the corporate planning department that address specific issues such as country and product studies and responses to major market, techn-ological, and political changes.

Exxon's strategic management system features clearly defined corporate, divisional, and business unit responsibilities (with matching accountability). At the same time there is close communication and coordination between these levels. This takes place formally through the strategic planning and financial control system and informally through ongoing communication between the management committee (composed of Exxon's executive board members) and the divisional presidents and their management teams. Each member of the management committee is "contact director" for two or three divisions. The dialog between the divisional presidents and the contact directors is a mechanism for knowledge sharing and initiating strategic changes that adds flexibility to the formal strategic planning process. The result is a system of strategy formulation and performance management that is simultaneously top-down and bottom-up.

Fundamental to Exxon's close integration of financial management with strategic planning is Exxon's emphasis on *stewardship*—a doctrine of managerial responsibility and accountability that makes each executive personally responsible to the corporation and its shareholders.

In particular, formalized strategic planning has been viewed as the enemy of flexibility, creativity and entrepreneurship. Marakon consultants Mankins and Steele have observed that "strategic planning doesn't really influence most companies' strategy."[22] The principal reasons are its rigid annual cycle and its preoccupation with business unit plans—as a result "senior executives . . . make the decisions that really shape their companies' strategies . . . outside the planning process typically in an ad hoc fashion without rigorous analysis or productive debate." The approach they identify at companies such as Microsoft, Boeing and Textron is what they call "continuous, decision-oriented planning" where the emphasis is, first, on analyzing the critical issues that face the company and, second, on decision making. The central feature of the process is that the top management team—the executive committee—drives the strategy-making process.

- *Weak strategy execution*. A major theme of recent years has been the need for more effective strategy execution by large companies. This means a more effective linkage between strategic planning and operational management. Larry Bossidy and Ram Charan point to the key role of *milestones* that can ". . . bring reality to a strategic plan."[23] Thus, to keep Honeywell's strategy for cost cutting in its automotive business on track, managers developed short- and medium-term milestones for shifting production overseas. As was noted in Chapter 2, the *balanced scorecard* is another technique for translating strategy into specific functional and operational targets. Building on their balanced scorecard approach, Kaplan and Norton propose that *strategy maps* are used to plot the relationships between strategic actions and overall goals.[24] To ensure a close linkage between strategic planning and strategy implementation they recommend that companies establish an *office of strategy management*, responsible not just for managing the annual strategic planning cycle but also for overseeing the execution of strategic plans.[25] The risk is that such a unit is the potential for it to conflict with the roles and responsibilities of divisional and business unit managers.

Performance Control and the Budgeting Process

Most multidivisional companies have a dual planning process: strategic planning concentrates on the medium and long term, financial planning controls short-term performance. Typically, the first year of the strategic plan includes the performance plan for the upcoming year in terms of an operating budget, a capital expenditure budget, and strategy targets relating to market share, output and employment levels, and specific strategic milestones. Annual performance plans are agreed between senior business-level managers and corporate-level managers. They are monitored on a monthly and quarterly basis. At the end of each financial year, they are probed and evaluated in performance review meetings between business and corporate management.

Performance targets emphasize financial indicators (return on invested capital, gross margin, growth of sales revenue) and also include strategic goals (market share, new product introductions, market penetration, quality) and operational performance (output, productivity). Performance targets are usually specified in detail for the next year, with less detailed performance targets set for up to five years ahead. Monthly and quarterly monitoring focuses on early detection of deviations from targets.

Performance targets are supported by management incentives and sanctions. Companies whose management systems are heavily orientated towards demanding profit targets typically use powerful individual incentives to create an intensely motivating environment for divisional managers. At ITT, Geneen's obsession with highly detailed performance monitoring, ruthless interrogation of divisional executives, and generous rewards for success developed an intensely competitive cadre of executives. They worked relentless long hours and applied the same performance demands on their subordinates as Geneen did of them.[26] Creating a performance-driven culture requires unremitting focus on a few quantitative performance targets that can be monitored on a short-term basis. PepsiCo's obsession with monthly market share nourishes an intense, marketing-oriented culture. Chief executive Indra Nooyi observed: "We are a very objective-driven company. We spend a lot of time up front setting objectives and our guys rise to the challenge of meeting those objectives. When they don't meet the objectives, we don't have to flog them because they do it themselves."[27] One executive put it more bluntly: "The place is full of guys with sparks coming out of their asses."[28] Even in businesses where interdependence is high and investment gestation periods are long, as in petroleum, short- and medium-term performance targets can be highly effective. The performance-oriented culture built by former CEO John Browne at BP was based upon a system of performance contracts in which each business unit general manager agrees a set of financial, strategic and operational targets with the CEO.[29] However, as we have observed, performance-based compensation can lead to unanticipated and dysfunctional consequences—especially with regard to prioritizing short-term over long-term performance.

Balancing Strategic Planning and Financial Control

One implication of the tradeoff between *input control* (controlling decisions) and *output control* (controlling performance) is that companies must choose a balance between strategic planning and financial control. Michael Goold and Andrew Campbell found that the corporate management systems of British multibusiness

TABLE 17.2 Characteristics of different strategic management styles

	Strategic planning	Financial control
Business Strategy Formulation	Businesses and corporate HQ jointly formulate strategy. The HQ coordinates strategies of businesses.	Strategy formulated at business unit level. Corporate HQ largely reactive, offering little coordination.
Controlling Performance	Primarily strategic goals with medium- to long-term horizon.	Financial budgets set annual targets for ROI and other financial variables with monthly and quarterly monitoring.
Advantages	Effective in managing (a) linkages among businesses, (b) innovation, (c) long-term competitive positioning.	Business unit autonomy encourages initiative, responsiveness, and the development of business leaders.
Disadvantages	Loss of divisional autonomy and initiative. Conducive to unitary strategic view. Resistance to abandoning failed strategy.	Short-term focus discourages innovation and long-term development. Limited sharing of resources and skills among businesses.
Style suited to:	Companies with a small number of closely related businesses. In sectors where technology and competition are important and projects are large and long term.	Companies with many businesses across a wide range of industries, and with limited linkages between them. Approach works best in mature, technologically stable sectors where investment projects are relatively small and short term.
U.K. Examples	BP, BOC, Cadbury-Schweppes, Lex Group, STC, United Biscuits.	Hanson, BTR, General Electric Company, Ferranti, Tarmac.

Source:
Based on M. Goold and A. Campbell, *Strategies and Styles* (Oxford: Blackwell, 1987).

companies emphasized one or the other.[30] The *strategic planning companies* emphasized the longer term development of their businesses and had corporate HQs that were was heavily involved in business-level planning. The *financial control companies* had corporate HQs that emphasized short-term budgetary control and rigorously monitored financial performance against ambitious targets, but had limited involvement in business strategy formulation—this was left to divisional and business unit managers. Table 17.2 summarizes key features of the two styles.

The trend over time has been a growing influence of financial control—even among oil and gas majors (BP in particular), strategic planning has become less concerned with strategic decision making and more focused on managing financial performance.[31]

Using PIMS in Strategy Formulation and Performance Appraisal

The PIMS (Profit Impact of Market Strategies) project offers corporate managers a set of techniques for appraising the performance of businesses and developing strategies towards them. PIMS grew out of General Electric's internal database and is now maintained by the Strategic Planning Institute.[32] Using information on about 4000 business units, it deploys multiple regression analysis to estimate the impact on profitability of a large number of strategy and market structure variables. PIMS is used by multibusiness companies to assist in two main areas of corporate management:

- *Setting performance targets for business units.* Using the regression coefficients in the PIMS profitability equations allows a business to calculate its "Par ROI"—the return on investment that would be expected for a specific business given its profile of strategic and industry characteristics if its performance were typical of the sample as a whole. "Par ROI" can be used as a benchmark to evaluate profitability and set profitability targets.
- *Formulating business unit strategy.* Using the PIMS regression equations, the effects of changes in business strategy on profitability can be simulated.

The PIMS analysis assumes that the various strategy and market structure variables have independent influences on profitability. The more complex are the interactions between different strategy and market structure variables, the less valid is the guidance based upon the results of large database regression estimates.

Managing Linkages between Businesses

As we saw in the previous chapter, the main opportunities for creating value in the multibusiness company arise from sharing resources and transferring capabilities among the different businesses within the company. This sharing occurs both through the centralization of common services at the corporate level and through direct linkages between the businesses.

Common Corporate Services

The simplest form of resource sharing in the multidivisional company is the centralized provision of common services and functions. These include corporate management functions such as strategic planning, financial control, treasury, risk management, internal audit, taxation, government relations and shareholder relations. They also include business services that are more efficiently provided on a centralized basis, such as research, engineering, human resources management, legal services, management development, purchasing and any other administrative services subject to economies of scale or learning. By 2000, shared corporate services accounted for 43% of headquarters staff among large U.K. corporations.[33]

In practice, the benefits of centralized provision of common services tend to be smaller than many corporate managers anticipate. Centralized provision can avoid costs of duplication but there can be little incentive among headquarters staff and specialized corporate units to meet the needs of their business-level customers. The experience of many companies is that corporate staffs tend to grow under their own momentum with few obvious economies from central provision and few benefits of superior services.

As a result, many companies separated their corporate headquarters into two groups: a *corporate management unit* responsible for supporting the corporate management team in core support activities such as strategic planning, finance and legal, and a *shared services organization* responsible for supplying common services such as research, engineering, training, and information technology to the businesses. Market incentives have been created for these shared service organizations by requiring them to supply services on an arm's-length basis to internal operating units, sometimes in competition with independent suppliers.

For example, Alcoa's Global Business Services was created in 2003. It offers financial accounting services; procurement; environment, health and safety services; people services; global credit; and information services. Its 1900 employees are based in Pittsburgh, Monterrey (Mexico), Quebec (Canada), Szekesfehervar (Hungary), Booragoon (Australia), Sao Paulo (Brazil) and Bangalore (India). Its vision is to "deliver valuable services to Alcoa's business and resource units at a cost and quality better than competitive alternatives."[34]

Business Linkages and Porter's Corporate Strategy Types

Exploiting economies of scope doesn't necessarily mean centralizing resources at the corporate level. Resources and capabilities can also be shared between the businesses. Michael Porter has argued that the way in which a company manages these linkages determines its potential to create value for shareholders.[35] He identifies four corporate strategy types:

- *Portfolio management*. The most limited form of resource sharing is where the parent company simply acquires a portfolio of attractive, soundly managed companies, allows them to operate autonomously, and links them through an efficient internal capital market. The typical organizational structure for portfolio management is the *holding company*—a parent company that owns controlling stakes in a number of (typically unrelated) subsidiaries but, beyond appointing the boards of the subsidiary companies, does not exert significant management control. Investor AB of Sweden (controlled by the Wallenberg family), Koor Industries of Israel and Berkshire Hathaway of the U.S. (headed by legendary investor Warren Buffett) are leading examples. Value is created by acquiring companies at favorable prices, closely monitoring their financial performance and operating an effective internal capital market.
- *Restructuring*. Conglomerates, such as Tyco International and Textron in the U.S., and Tomkins plc and Invensys plc in the U.K., create value primarily by restructuring: acquiring poorly managed companies, then intervening to appoint new management, dispose of underperforming businesses, restructure balance sheets and cut costs. As conglomerates have increasingly restructured themselves into oblivion (either transforming themselves into more focused industrial companies or breaking up entirely) private equity groups—such as Carlyle, KKR, Blackstone, and Texas Pacific in the U.S., and Alchemy and Candover in the U.K.—have increasingly taken on the same restructuring role.[36]
- *Transferring skills*. Organizational capabilities can be transferred between business units. LVMH transfers brand management and distribution capabilities among its different luxury-brand businesses. Sharp transfers its

optoelectronics and miniaturization capabilities across a number of consumer, electronic, and office equipment products. Creating value by sharing skills requires that the same capabilities are applicable to the different businesses and also that mechanisms are established to transfer these skills through personnel exchange and best practice transfer.

- *Sharing activities*. Porter argues that the most important source of value arises from exploiting economies of scope in common resources and activities. For these economies to be realized, corporate management must play a key coordinating role, including involvement in formulating business unit strategies and intervention in operational matters to ensure that opportunities for sharing R&D, advertising, distribution systems and service networks are fully exploited. In many countries, Unilever has a single marketing and distribution organization that handles a wide range of different consumer products.[37] The emergence of Samsung Electronics as a global leader in digital consumer products during 2000-4 owed much to its development of advanced design capabilities. These were located in four design centers in London, Tokyo, San Francisco and Seoul and are shared across Samsung's different business units.[38]

The Corporate Role in Managing Linkages

The closer the linkages among businesses, the greater the opportunities for creating value from sharing resources and transferring capabilities, and the greater the need for corporate headquarters to coordinate across businesses. We noted earlier that the "financial control" style of management occurs mainly in conglomerates where the independence of each business limits the coordinating role of the head office to manage the budgetary process and establish "framework conditions" for divisional planning.

In more closely related companies, such as the vertically integrated oil companies, or companies with close market or technological links (such as IBM, Procter & Gamble, American Express, and Alcoa), corporate management uses a "strategic planning" style, which is likely to involve not only coordination of strategies but also operational coordination to exploit the economies of scope and transferable skills discussed in Chapter 16. Corporate involvement in interdivisional affairs has implications for the size of the corporate headquarters. Berkshire Hathaway, which has almost no linkages among its businesses, has a corporate staff of about 50. Hewlett-Packard, with about the same sales but much closer linkages between its divisions, has close to 3000 employees at its Palo Alto head office. Where business units are linked through their sharing of a common resource or capability then the corporate headquarters is likely to be closely involved in the development and deployment of that resource or capability. For example, Pfizer and Corning have strong corporate R&D groups; Dow has a strong corporate manufacturing function; and Virgin's corporate team plays a key role in managing the Virgin brand.[39]

Developing and sharing resources and capabilities may require *ad hoc* organizational arrangements such as *cross-divisional task forces*. Such task forces might be formed for the introduction and dissemination of total quality management, to reengineer financial management practices, to promote fast-cycle new product development, or to coordinate business development in China.

The CEO can play an important role in initiating and pushing these kinds of cross-business initiatives. Corporate initiatives sponsored by the CEO are a key mechanism for disseminating strategic changes, best practices and management innovations.[40] At General Electric, Jack Welch was an especially effective exponent of period corporate initiatives as drivers of organizational change. These were built around communicable and compelling slogans such as "GE's growth engine," "boundarylessness," "six-sigma quality" and "destroy-your-business-dot-com."

Exploiting linkages between businesses imposes costs. Though Porter may be right that the *potential* for value creation increases as a company moves from a loose, "portfolio management" strategy toward the more integrated, "shared activity" strategy, this potential is not always realized. For example, most attempts at exploiting the potential for cross-selling across different businesses have yielded disappointing results, especially in financial services.[41] Lorsch and Allen point to some of management costs incurred in exploiting linkages between businesses. They compared three conglomerates with three vertically integrated paper companies.[42] The coordination requirements of the paper companies resulted in greater involvement of head office staff in divisional operations, larger head office staffs, more complex planning and control devices, and lower responsiveness to change in the external environment. By contrast, the conglomerates made little attempt to exploit linkages even if they were present:

> The conglomerate firms we had studied seemed to be achieving appreciable degrees of financial and managerial synergy but little or no operating synergy. Some of the firms saw little immediate payoff in this operating synergy; others met with little success in attempting to achieve it.[43]

The success with which the corporate headquarters manages linkages between businesses depends on top management's understanding of the commonalities among its different businesses. Ultimately, these commonalities have their basis in the underlying rationale for the corporation—what C. K. Prahalad and Rich Bettis have called *dominant logic*: "the way in which managers conceptualize the business and make critical resource allocation decisions."[44] The success of the multibusiness corporation depends upon strategic similarity among the different businesses that is consistent with an overall dominant logic.

Managing Change in the Multibusiness Corporation

Conceptions of the role of corporate management in the multibusiness company have shifted greatly over time. These shifting roles have been associated with different priorities with regard to value creation within the multibusiness corporation. During the 1970s and early 1980s, corporate management was concerned with the creation of large business empires. The motivation was partly growth but also the belief in the power of new tools of strategic and financial management to transcend industry boundaries. During the late 1980s a profound shift in top management priorities occurred and throughout the 1990s the dominant theme was applying the logic and principles of shareholder value maximization to restructure diversified corporate empires. The principal sources of value were pruning business portfolios and exercising "stand-alone" influence to boost the performance of individual businesses. During the present decade the primary challenges have been, first, creating value through exploiting linkages between businesses and improving integration within the corporation; second, increasing responsiveness to external change and accelerating the pace of organizational evolution. These shifts in strategic priorities have been associated with different leadership styles. Let me address each of these two major transitions.

Value Creation through Corporate Restructuring

During the late 1980s and 1990s, a large proportion of the largest corporations of North America and Europe underwent intense phases of corporate change typically triggered by declining financial performance or some external threat. Given the tendency for most multibusiness corporations to develop through a series of incremental strategy initiatives, periodic corporate restructuring based upon a comprehensive corporate review that appraises individual businesses and review of the overall business portfolio can be critical to revitalization.

McKinsey & Company's *pentagon framework* offers a systematic approach to analyzing the potential for increasing the market value of a multibusiness company through corporate restructuring.[45] The analysis comprises five stages—these correspond to the five nodes of Figure 17.5:

1 *The current market value of the company*. The starting point of the analysis is current enterprise value, which comprises the value of equity plus the value of debt. (As we know from Chapter 2, if securities markets are efficient, this equals the net present value of anticipated cash flow over the life of the company.)

2 *The value of the company as is*. Even without any changes to strategy or operations, it may be possible to value simply by managing external

FIGURE 17.5 The McKinsey restructuring pentagon

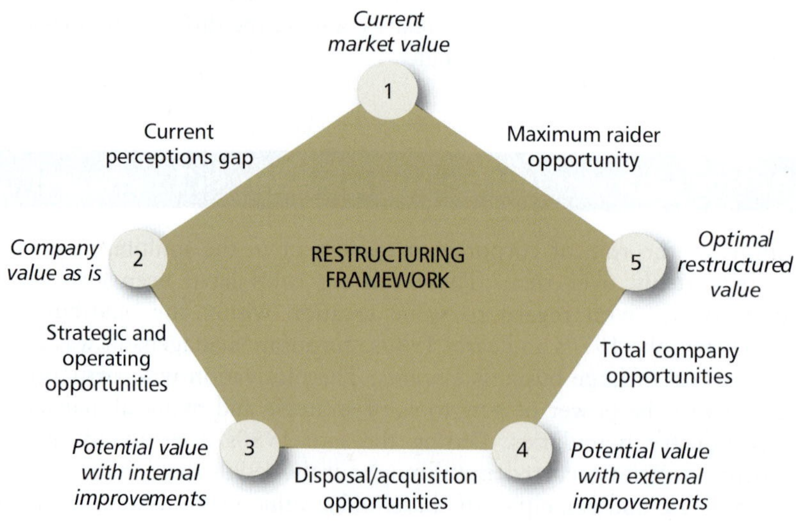

Source: T. E. Copeland, T. Koller, and J. Murrin, *Valuation* (New York: John Wiley & sons, Inc., 1990).

perceptions of a company's future prospects. Over the past two decades, companies have devoted increasing attention to managing investor expectations by increasing the quantity and quality of information flow to shareholders and investment analysts and establishing departments of investor relations for this purpose.

3. *The potential value of the company with internal improvements.* As we have seen, corporate management has opportunities for increasing the overall value of the company by making strategic and operational improvements to individual businesses that increase their cash flows. These might include exploiting global expansion opportunities, outsourcing certain activities and cost-cutting opportunities.
4. *The potential value of the company with external improvements.* Having determined the potential value of its constituent businesses, corporate management needs to determine whether changes in the business portfolio can increase overall company value. The key is to apply the principle of parenting advantage: even after strategic and operating improvements have been made, can a business be sold for price greater than its value to the company?
5. *The optimum restructured value of the company.* The previous four steps establish maximum value potential of a company. Assuming that these changes could also be undertaken by an alternative owner of the company, the difference between the maximum restructured value and the current market value represents the profit potential available to a corporate raider.

This type of analysis has been traditionally associated with leveraged buyout specialists and other corporate raiders. Faced with this threat, comprehensive corporate restructuring became widespread among large multibusiness companies (for example, the restructuring wave by the oil majors during 1986–92.)[46]

Leadership style associated with corporate restructuring is indicated by the nicknames given to some of the prominent exponents—"Chainsaw" Al Dunlap (at Scott Paper and Sunbeam), "Neutron" Jack Welch (at General Electric), "Fred-the Shred" Goodwin (at Royal Bank of Scotland). This points to an emphasis on cost cutting and asset divestment. The leadership mode associated with this approach is characterized by obsessive commitment to the shareholder value maximization and the bottom-line results needed to achieve it, managing through performance targets and an emphasis on performance incentives—both compensation incentives and the threat of termination threats for underperformance.

Beyond Restructuring: Value Creation from Business Linkages and Innovation

Disillusion with the shareholder value maximization model, diminishing returns to cost cutting, and the need to create new sources of corporate value have resulted in profound shifts in the corporate strategies of multibusiness companies. Increasingly, large multibusiness companies have sought to identify opportunities for innovation, for new product development and for creating value from exploiting new and more sophisticated linkages between companies. Corporate headquarters are concerned less with the problem of control and more with the problem of identifying and implementing the means for creating value within and between their individual businesses. The use of the term "parenting" to describe the corporate role, as opposed to the notion of "systems of corporate control," reflects this shift in thinking.

Changes in the management of multibusiness corporations have included decentralization of decision making from corporate to divisional levels, a shift from formal to informal coordination and a more multidimensional role for the corporate headquarters. From being simply a control center, the corporate HQ acts as a service center, a guide to the future, and a knowledge hub.

Managing transition has been a key role for chief executives. The most celebrated of these "change masters" was Jack Welch, Chairman and CEO of General Electric from 1981 to 2001. Welch's style and the system he created has become a model for other large, multibusiness corporations—not just in North America, but in Europe and Asia too. Strategy Capsule 17.3 outlines Welch's style and methods.

STRATEGY CAPSULE 17.3

General Electric: Welch's Reinvention of Corporate Management

Jack Welch's 20 years as Chairman and CEO of General Electric began with an intensive period of restructuring, which transformed the composition of GE's business portfolio through acquisitions and disposals and extended the conglomerate's global reach. Toward the mid-1980s, Welch's attention shifted from the business portfolio to the structure, systems and style of GE. Among the changes he initiated were the following.

- *Delayering*. Welch's fundamental criticism of GE's management was that it was slow and unresponsive. Welch eliminated GE's sector level of organization so that business heads reported directly to him. He pressured them to flatten their management pyramids. Overall, GE's layers of hierarchy were cut from nine or ten to four or five.
- *Changing the strategic planning system*. During the 1970s, GE had developed a systematic and formalized approach to strategy formulation and appraisal. Welch believed that not only was the system slow and inefficient, it also stifled innovation and opportunism. Welch replaced the staff-led, document-driven process with more personal, less formal but very intensive face-to-face discussions. Instead of data-heavy documents, each business head was asked to produce a slim "play-book" that summarized key strategic issues and actions. Concise answers were required to questions about market dynamics, competitive activity, risks, and proposed GE business responses. These documents became the basis for a half-day review session where business heads and key executives met with the Office of the CEO in an open dialog on strategy and performance.[47]
- *Redefining the role of headquarters*. The changes in the strategic planning system reflected broader changes in the role of the corporate headquarters. Welch viewed headquarters as interfering too much, generating too much paper, and failing to add value. His objective was to "turn their role 180 degrees from checker, inquisitor,

and authority figure to facilitator, helper, and supporter" so that decisions could move more quickly: "What we do here at headquarters . . . is to multiply the resources we have, the human resources, the financial resources, and the best practices . . . Our job is to help, it's to assist, it's to make these businesses stronger, to help them grow and be more powerful."[48]

- *The coordinating role of corporate*. A key role of corporate was facilitating coordination across GE's businesses. The Corporate Executive Council was reconstituted to include the leaders of GE's 13 businesses and several key corporate executives. It met two days each quarter to discuss common problems and issues. The Council became an important vehicle for identifying and exploiting synergies. In 1990, Welch launched his concept of the "boundaryless company." This involved blurring internal divisions so that people could work together across functional and business boundaries. Welch aimed at "integrated diversity"—the ability to transfer the best ideas, most developed knowledge and most valuable people freely and easily between businesses:

Boundaryless behavior is the soul of today's GE . . . Simply put, people seem compelled to build layers and walls between themselves and others, and that human tendency tends to be magnified in large, old institutions like ours. These walls cramp people, inhibit creativity, waste time, restrict vision, smother dreams and, above all, slow things down . . . Boundaryless behavior shows up in the actions of a woman from our Appliances business in Hong Kong helping NBC with contacts needed to develop satellite television service in Asia . . . And finally, boundaryless behavior means exploiting one of the unmatchable advantages a multibusiness GE has over almost any other company in the world. Boundaryless behavior combines 12 huge global businesses—each number one or number two in its markets—into a vast laboratory whose principal product is new ideas, coupled with a common commitment to spread them throughout the company.[49]

As Welch has shown, managing large-scale organizational change is not simply about top-down decision making. A key component is fostering change processes at lower levels of the organization—GE's "Work-Out" is a prime example. A critical feature of organizational design is building structures and systems that permit adaptation. While CEOs cannot be the primary initiators of change, they need to be alert and responsive to signals. Intel's former CEO, Andy Grove, emphasizes the importance of CEOs identifying *strategic inflection points*—instances where seismic shifts in a firm's competitive environment require a fundamental redirection of strategy.[50] At Intel, such inflection points included the transition from DRAM chips to microprocessors, the decision to focus on its x86 series of microprocessors in favor of RISC architecture, and the decision to replace its faulty Pentium chips.[51]

Above all, CEOs need to be adept at managing contradiction and dilemma. For example:

- companies must strive for efficiency, which requires rigorous financial controls; they must also be innovative and entrepreneurial, which requires autonomy and loose, flexible controls;

- maximizing current performance requires strategies that exploit existing resources and capabilities across different markets; success for the future is dependent on the creation of new resources and capabilities and their deployment in new markets;
- innovation, efficiency, and responsiveness require autonomy for business-level managers; yet the competitive advantage of the multibusiness corporation ultimately depends on integrating resources and capabilities across businesses. Is it possible for companies like Microsoft, Siemens, or Samsung to mesh the resource advantages of the giant corporation with the responsiveness and creativity of small enterprises?

Resolving these dilemmas requires that organizations operate in multiple modes simultaneously. In particular, they need to combine both decentralized flexibility and initiative *and* centralized purpose and integration. The transformation of IBM under Lou Gerstner offers some guidance as to how this can be achieved. Resisting Wall Street pressure to break up IBM, Gerstner was able to combine aggressive cuts in costs and jobs, entrepreneurship, and flexibility through decentralized decision making, and integration of technology and know-how by breaking down barriers both within IBM and between IBM and other companies.[52]

Flexible integration—whether it is sharing capabilities, harmonizing market initiatives in different countries, or collaborating to develop the new products and technologies required—cannot be hierarchically decreed: headquarters does not possess the necessary knowledge to be in the driver's seat. It must happen through horizontal collaboration among the businesses units. This requires that business-level general managers identify not only with their particular businesses, but also with the corporation as a whole. Fostering the necessary identity and direction within the multibusiness corporation is probably the most important task that the CEO must perform.

Creating this sense of identity is much more challenging for a company that spans several businesses than for one whose identity is determined by the products it offers (McDonald's or De Beers). It goes beyond "strategic relatedness" and "dominant logic" and embraces notions of vision and mission—concepts which were identified in Chapter 1 as lying at the foundations of companies' strategy formulation.[53] In the previous chapter, I observed that the luxury goods giant LVMH deploys its core brand management capabilities across many different businesses. Its success in doing so depends critically upon establishing a corporate identity that forms a "cultural glue" between these disparate businesses: "The common cultural trunk is based on the permanent search for quality of the products and the management, human relations based on responsibility and initiative, and rewarding competences and services."[54]

External Strategy: Mergers and Acquisitions

If the central concern of corporate strategy is managing the scope of the firm, then mergers and acquisitions are key instruments of corporate strategy as they are the principal means by which firms achieve major extensions in the scope of their activities. Mergers and acquisitions also represent one of the greatest paradoxes in strategic management. Given the absence of evidence that acquisitions create shareholder value for the acquiring firm, why is acquisition the preferred means of corporate growth for so many companies?

In Chapter 6 we examined the role of mergers and acquisitions in building the resources and capabilities of the firm (see "Acquiring Capabilities: Mergers, Acquisitions and Alliances"). In the previous chapter we looked at the role of acquisition in diversification strategy. In this chapter our goal is to look more generally at the efficacy of mergers, acquisitions and alliances as instruments of corporate strategy, the circumstances where they can be successful, and how they should be managed.

Acquisitions involve one company purchasing another. This involves the acquiring company making an offer for the common stock of another for a fixed price per share. Acquisitions can be "friendly," that is when they are supported by the board of the target company, or unfriendly, when they are opposed by the target company's board—in the latter case they are known as a *hostile takeover*.

Mergers are where two companies amalgamate to form a new company.[55] This requires agreement by the shareholders of the two companies who then exchange their shares for shares in the new company. Mergers occur when the companies involved are of roughly similar size and strength. Where the companies involved are in different countries, a merger may be preferred to an acquisition for political reasons. Thus, the amalgamations between Daimler Benz and Chrysler, Alcatel and Lucent, and Mittal Steel and Alcelor all took the form of mergers.

Table 17.3 shows the biggest acquisitions of the past decade.

TABLE 17.3 Deals of the decade: mergers and acquisitions with bid value exceeding $50 billion, 1999–2009

Year	Purchaser	Purchased	Transaction value (U.S. $ bn.)
1999	Vodafone Airtouch Plc.	Mannesmann	183
2000	America Online Inc.	Time Warner	165
1999	Pfizer	Warner-Lambert	90
2007	ABN-AMBRO	Royal Bank of Scotland, Banco Santander, Fortis	79
2000	Glaxo Wellcome Plc.	SmithKline Beecham Plc.	76
2004	Royal Dutch Petroleum Co.	Shell Transport & Trading Co	75
1999	Citicorp	Travelers Group	73
2006	AT&T Inc.	BellSouth Corporation	73
2001	Comcast Corporation	AT&T Broadband & Internet Services	72
2009	Pfizer	Wyeth	68
1999	SBC Communications	Ameritech Corporation	63
2004	Sanofi-Synthelabo SA	Aventis SA	60
1999	Vodafone Group	AirTouch Communications	60
2002	Pfizer Inc.	Pharmacia Corporation	60
2007	Endesa SA	Enel SpA, Acciona SA	60
2004	JP Morgan Chase & Co	Bank One Corp	59
2007	Procter & Gamble	Gillette	57
2008	InBev	Anheuser-Busch	52
2008	Bank of America	Merrill Lynch	50

Empirical Evidence on Mergers and Acquisitions

The performance effects of mergers and acquisitions have been measured using both shareholder returns (typically the stock market reaction to takeover announcements) and using accounting data on profitability. The only unambiguous evidence is that acquisitions benefit the shareholders of the acquired firms. For acquiring firms, studies show that the returns are either negative or insignificant from zero. Combining the effects on both acquirers and acquirees, the overall picture is one of small gains to mergers—typically around 2% of the combined market value of the companies involved.[56]

Studies that use accounting data measure the actual outcomes of mergers and acquisitions rather than stock market expectations of their results. However, attempts to compare post-merger performance with pre-merger performance are fraught with difficulties— "results from these accounting-based studies are all over the map."[57]

This outcome of several decades of research into the performance effects of mergers and acquisitions—that, overall, the only clear-cut effect is the shareholders of acquired firms gain—is disappointing. Yet it is not altogether unsurprising. Mergers and acquisitions are motivated by multiple factors; they each involve a unique combination of circumstances; and distinguishing their effects from the multiplicity of other influences on company performance is exceptionally difficult.

When do Mergers and Acquisitions Make Sense?

Inevitably, any lessons about when and how companies should use mergers and acquisitions as instruments of corporate strategy requires analysis of the specific circumstances of the merger or acquisition. Again, empirical research gives us limited insight into these circumstances. Even highly plausible propositions—for example, that horizontal mergers which increase market share result in gains in efficiency and profitability, or that acquisitions of firms in related businesses outperform unrelated acquisitions—fail to gain systematic empirical support.

Beginning with strategic analysis, it seems obvious that a merger or acquisition should be based upon a sound strategic rationale. Yet, it is not always apparent that this is the case. Michael Jensen suggests that CEOs of companies with overvalued equity will make equity financed acquisitions to help support their share price.[58] AOL's merger with Time Warner may reflect this motive. More typical is the propensity of CEOs to vastly overestimate the gains from mergers. Many diversifying mergers within financial services have been motivated by wildly optimistic forecasts of the potential for cross-selling and customers' desire for "one-stop-shopping."

The most common reason that mergers and acquisitions lack a strong strategic rationale is the propensity for imitation. Acquisitions go in waves: the petroleum mergers of the 1998-2002; the 1990s rush for banks and insurance companies to combine; the telecoms urge-to-merge of 1998-2005; and the global consolidation of the beer, pharmaceuticals, and metals sectors during the past decade. In these situations, the propensity of firms to "follow the leader" is reinforced by the fear of being alone at the fringes of the dance floor with only unattractive dancing partners left.

A realistic assessment of the potential gains from a merger or acquisition requires intimate knowledge of the target company. This is a bigger problem for hostile takeovers than for agreed acquisitions. However, even friendly takeovers are still prone to the *lemons problem:* the seller knows much more about the acquisition target than the buyer, so the acquirer can be hoodwinked into overpaying. One year after its acquisition of Jaguar, a Ford executive commented: "If we had known what a terrible shape Jaguar was in, we would never had paid the price we did."

Acquirers can also fall victims of believing their own propaganda—in seeking to persuade the stock market about the benefits of an acquisition, they risk believing their own inflated estimates of potential synergies.

Postmerger Integration

Case-study evidence shows that some of the most carefully planned mergers and acquisitions can end up as failures because of the problems of managing postmerger integration. The combination of Daimler Benz and Chrysler was exemplary in its premerger planning; the outcome was disastrous. Not only did Chrysler's problems appear to be intractable but Chrysler's demands on the group's top management negatively impacted the core Mercedes-Benz business.[59]

Frequently, it appears that where the potential benefits of mergers and acquisitions are large, the costs and risks of integrations are also large. Thus, Capron and Anand argue that cross-border acquisitions typically have the strongest strategic logic.[60] Yet, the evidence of Daimler-Chrysler, BMW-Rover, and Alcatel-Lucent suggests that when differences in corporate culture are accentuated by differences in national culture, the challenge of post-merger integration becomes immense.

A growing body of literature views acquisition as an organizational capability and points to the need for acquisition capability to be developed through explicit and experiential learning. Acquisition performance tends to increase with experience—although not at first. A learning threshold appears, after which subsequent acquisitions add value.[61] Explicit learning through the codification of acquisition processes also appears to be conducive to acquisition success.[62]

In common with my approach throughout this book, I consider that it is important to separate issues of preacquisition planning and postacquisition management. In the long and rich history of acquisition disasters, poor postacquisition management has been identified as the source of the problem. Yet, in many of these cases the integration problems could have been anticipated: the critical problem was going ahead with the acquisition without adequate assessment of post-merger management problems. Thus, in the case of Quaker Oats acquisition of Snapple ("the billion dollar blunder"), the critical problem—the impediments to integrating Snapple's distribution system with that of Quaker's Gatorade—were evident to the marketing managers and the franchised distributors of the two companies prior to the takeover.[63]

Summary

Formulating and implementing corporate strategy in the multibusiness company presents complex issues. We must extend our tools of strategy analysis to address challenging issues of organizational design, management control, and coordination between businesses. Developing generic recommendations as to how a multibusiness company should implement its corporate strategy is impossible: each firm is unique in terms of its portfolio of products and markets; its resources and capabilities; its corporate culture, and its administrative heritage. Given these factors, it is hardly surprising that empirical research offers limited guidance as to the correlates of superior performance—close relationships between businesses may or may not lead to higher profitability; sharing resources and capabilities offers economies but also imposes management costs; some mergers create value, others don't.

Managing the multibusiness firm inevitably requires abstracting from the complexities of the large, multifunctional, multiproduct, multinational firm. Tools such as portfolio planning matrices are simplistic but they offer a starting point for addressing the complexity of dealing with the firm as a whole.

The key to this complexity is *strategic fit*. Corporate strategy, business strategy, the external environment, together with the firm's resource, capabilities, structure, systems, leadership style, and culture need to be consistent and closely linked. To get to grips with these issues we need to characterize the firm in terms of its few fundamental features. For example, its strategic rationale can be described by its *dominant logic*,[64] its "personality" and "self-image" can be described by its *organizational identity*,[65] the consistency of its overall configuration by its *corporate coherence*.[66]

Internal fit is not enough: the critical requirement is fit with the external environment. As the business environment changes, so large, multibusiness companies need to adapt. Very often, the scale of this adaptation makes the task impossible. Conglomerates had strategies and structures that fitted well with the business environment of the 1970s. By the mid-1990s almost all of them had been dismantled. As we shall explore in the next chapter, the business environment has entered a new phase of discontinuous change. Large, multibusiness companies face critical challenges of adaption.

Self-Study Questions

1 Williamson's "M-form" concept argues that the efficiency of the multidivisional firm is the result of (a) the separation of responsibilities between divisional and corporate management and (b) overcoming the "agency problem" of managers pursuing their own interests rather than those of shareholders. How effective are most multibusiness companies in achieving these advantages? Are there other performance advantages associated with multibusiness companies?

2 If you were VP of strategic planning for a large multibusiness company, would you use portfolio planning techniques in your work? If so, for what purposes? If not, why not? Would your preference be to use the GE/McKinsey matrix or the BCG matrix?

3 Identify a poorly performing multibusiness company (examples might include Sony, Time Warner, Bombardier, Pearson, Matsushita, Dubai World, or Tyco). Using the McKinsey

pentagon framework, in which stage do you perceive the greatest opportunities for value creation through restructuring? (Use the company's web site or Hoovers.com to access information on the company.)

4 For technology-based companies, building linkages across different businesses is critical to sustaining competitive advantage. Select a technology-based company that you are familiar with (possibilities might include Microsoft, HP, Apple Computer, Canon, Sony, or Finmeccanica), then identify how linkages between businesses are currently being exploited and identify opportunities for additional exploitation of cross-business linkages.

Notes

1 A *multibusiness company* is a company that comprises multiple business units. These business units may comprise different vertical activities, different geographical units, or different product sectors.
2 O. E. Williamson, *Markets and Hierarchies: Analysis and Antitrust Implications* (New York: Free Press, 1975) and O. E. Williamson, "The Modern Corporation: Origins, Evolution, Attributes," *Journal of Economic Literature* 19 (1981): 1537–68.
3 J. L. Bower, *Managing the Resource Allocation Process* (Boston: Harvard Business School Press, 1986).
4 Williamson, "The Modern Corporation," op. cit.
5 See, for example, P. Steer and J. Cable, "Internal Organization and Profit: An Empirical Analysis of Large U.K. Companies," *Journal of Industrial Economics* 21 (September 1978): 13–30; H. Armour and D. Teece, "Organizational Structure and Economic Performance: A Test of the Multidivisional Hypothesis," *Bell Journal of Economics* 9 (1978): 106–22; D. Teece, "Internal Organization and Economic Performance," *Journal of Industrial Economics* 30 (1981): 173–99.
6 Among private companies, the key governance problem is typically one set of owners (for example, the founding family) enriching themselves at the expense of the other owners. See J. C. Coffee, "A Theory of Corporate Scandals: Why the U.S. and Europe Differ" *Columbia Law School Working Paper* No. 274 (March, 2005).
7 R. M. Grant and M. Visconti, "The Strategic Background to Corporate Accounting Scandals," *Long Range Planning* 39 (August 2006): 361–83.
8 *OECD Principles of Corporate Governance* (Paris: OECD, 2004).
9 "Splitting the Chairman and CEO Roles," *Business Week* (January 10, 2008): http://www.businessweek.com/managing/content/jan2008/ca2008018_642807.htm, accessed July 8, 2009.
10 M. J. Conyon, S. I. Peck, L. E. Read and G. V. Sadler, "The Structure of Executive Compensation Contracts: The U.K. Evidence," *Long Range Planning* 33 (August 2000): 478–503.
11 See for example: P. Bolton, J. Scheinkman and W. Xiong, "Pay for Short-term Performance: Executive Compensation in Speculative Markets," NBER Working Paper 12107 (March 2006); M. C. Jensen and K. J. Murphy, "Remuneration: Where We've Been, How We Got Here, What are the Problems," ECGI-Finance Working Paper 44 (2004).
12 H. Mintzberg, *Structure in Fives: Designing Effective Organizations* (Englewood Cliffs, NJ: Prentice Hall, 1983): Chapter 11.
13 J. Birkinshaw and A. Campbell, "Know the Limits of Corporate Venturing," FT Summer School, *Financial Times* (August 10, 2004).
14 M. Goold, A. Campbell, and M. Alexander, *Corporate-Level Strategy: Creating Value in the Multibusiness Company* (New York: John Wiley & Sons Inc., 1994).
15 *General Electric: Strategic Position—1981*, Case No. 381-174 (Boston: Harvard Business School, 1981): 1.
16 McKinsey & Company has recently reconceptualized SBUs as *value cells*. See M. Giordano and F. Wenger, "Organizing for Value" *Perspectives on Finance and Strategy* No. 18 (McKinsey & Company, Summer, 2008).
17 For a fuller discussion of the GE/McKinsey matrix see: "Enduring Ideas: The GE-McKinsey Nine-box Matrix," *McKinsey Quarterly* (September 2008).
18 For a fuller discussion of the BCG matrix see: B. Henderson, "The Experience Curve Reviewed: IV. The Growth Share Matrix or Product Portfolio," Boston Consulting Group (1973). www.bcg.com/publications/files/Experience_Curve_IV_Growth_Share_Matrix_1973.pdf
19 Booz Allen Hamilton claim that "dog" businesses can offer promising potential (H. Quarls, T. Pernsteiner and K. Rangan, "Love Your Dogs," Booz Allen Hamilton, March 15, 2005).
20 Goold, Campbell, and Alexander, *Corporate-Level Strategy* op. cit.
21 Ibid.: 90.
22 M. C. Mankins and R. Steele, "Stop Making Plans; Start Making Decisions," *Harvard Business Review* (January 2006): 76–84.

23 L. Bossidy and R. Charan, *Execution: The Discipline of Getting Things Done* (New York: Crown Business, 2002): 197–201.
24 R. S. Kaplan and D. P. Norton, "Having Trouble With Your Strategy? Then Map It," *Harvard Business Review* (September–October 2000): 67–76.
25 R. S. Kaplan and D. P. Norton, "The Office of Strategy Management," *Harvard Business Review* (October 2005): 72–80.
26 Geneen's style of management is discussed in Chapter 3 of R. T. Pascale and A. G. Athos, *The Art of Japanese Management* (New York: Warner Books, 1982).
27 Tuck School of Business, CEO Speaker Series, September 23, 2002.
28 "Those Highflying PepsiCo Managers," *Fortune* (April 10, 1989): 79.
29 BP, "Performance Contracts" (www.bp.com/genericarticle?Id=25&contentId=2000476).
30 M. Goold and A. Campbell, *Strategies and Styles* (Oxford: Blackwell, 1987).
31 R. M. Grant, "Strategic Planning in a Turbulent Environment: Evidence from the Oil and Gas Majors," *Strategic Management Journal* 24 (2003): 491–518.
32 Information on PIMS analysis and the PIMS database is available from: http://pimsonline.com/index.htm.
33 M. Goold, D. Pettifer and D. Young, "Redesigning the Corporate Center," *European Mangement Review* 19, no. 1 (2001): 83–91.
34 IQPC, "Most Admired Shared Service Organizations, 2005" (www.iqpc.com).
35 M. E. Porter, "From Competitive Advantage to Corporate Strategy," *Harvard Business Review* (May–June 1987): 46.
36 "Going Private," *Business Week* (February 27, 2006).
37 F. A. Maljers, "Corporate Strategy from a Unilever Perspective," in F. A. J. van den Bosch and A. P. de Man (eds.) *Perspectives on Strategy: Contributions of Michael E. Porter* (Boston: Kluwer, 1997): 35–45.
38 "How Samsung became a Global Champion," *Financial Times* (September 5, 2004).
39 M. Goold, D. Pettifer and D. Young, op. cit.
40 J. Darragh and A. Campbell, "Why Corporate Initiatives Get Stuck," *Long Range Planning* 34 (January 2001): 33–52.
41 "Cross-selling's Elusive Charms," *Financial Times* (November 16, 1998): 21.
42 J. W. Lorsch and S. A. Allen III, *Managing Diversity and Interdependence: An Organizational Study of Multi-divisional Firms* (Boston: Harvard Business School Press, 1973).
43 Ibid.: 168.
44 C. K. Prahalad and R. Bettis, "The Dominant Logic: A New Linkage Between Diversity and Performance," *Strategic Management Journal* 7 (1986): 485–502.
45 T. Copeland, T. Koller and J. Murrin, *Valuation: Measuring and Managing the Value of Companies*, 3rd edn (New York: John Wiley & Sons, Inc., 2000).
46 R. Cibin and R. M. Grant, "Restructuring Among the World's Largest Oil Companies," *British Journal of Management* 7 (December 1996): 411–28.
47 *General Electric: Jack Welch's Second Wave (A)*, Case No. 9-391-248 (Boston: Harvard Business School, 1991).
48 Jack Welch, "GE Growth Engine," speech to employees (1988).
49 "Letter to Share Owners," General Electric Company 1993 Annual Report (Fairfield, CT, 1994): 2.
50 A. S. Grove, *Only the Paranoid Survive: How to Exploit the Crisis Points that Challenge Every Company* (New York: Bantam, 1999).
51 R. A. Burgelman and A. Grove, "Strategic Dissonance," *California Management Review* 38 (Winter, 1996): 8–28.
52 L. V. Gerstner, *Who Says Elephants Can't Dance?* (New York: Harper Business, 2002).
53 Albert, S. and Whetten, D. A. (1985) "Organizational identity". In Cummings, L. L. and M. M. Staw (eds.) *Research in Organizational Behavior*, 7, 263–95.
54 *LVMH: Building Star Brands*, ICFAI Case MKTA016 (2004); R. Calori, "How Successful Companies Manage Diverse Businesses," *Long Range Planning* 21 (June, 1988): 85.
55 In everyday usage, the term "merger" is often used to refer to both mergers and acquisitions.
56 S. N. Kaplan, "Mergers and Acquisitions: A Financial Economics Perspective," University of Chicago, Graduate School of Business Working Paper (February, 2006). Also, Paul A. Pautler, "Evidence on Mergers and Acquisitions," Bureau of Economics, Federal Trade Commission (September 25, 2001).
57 S. N. Kaplan, "Mergers and Acquisitions," op. cit.: 8.
58 M. Jensen, "Agency costs of overvalued equity." Working paper, Harvard Business School (2004).
59 "DaimlerChrysler: Stalled," *Business Week* (September 10, 2003).
60 L. Capron and J. Anand, "Acquisition-based Dynamic Capabilities," in C. E. Helfat, S. Finkelstein, W. Mitchell, M. A. Peteraf, H. Singh, D. J. Teece and S. G. Winter, *Dynamic Capabilities* (Malden, MA: Blackwell, 2007): 80–99.
61 S. Finkelstein and J. Haleblian, "Understanding Acquisition Performance: The Role of Transfer Effects" *Organization Science* 13 (2002): 36–47.
62 M. Zollo and H. Singh, "Deliberate Learning in Corporate Acquisitions: Post-acquisition Strategies and Integration Capabilities in U.S. Bank Mergers," *Strategic Management Journal* 24 (2004): 1233–56.
63 C. E. Helfat *et al., Dynamic Capabilities,* op. cit.: 57–62.
64 C. K. Prahalad and R. Bettis, "The Dominant Logic" op cit.
65 B. Kogut and U. Zander, "What Firms Do? Coordination, Identity and Learning", *Organization Science* 7 (1996): 502–18.
66 D. J. Teece, R. Rumelt, G. Dosi and S. G. Winter, "Understanding Corporate Coherence: Theory and Evidence," *Journal of Economic Behavior and Organization,* 23 (1994): 1–30.

18 Current Trends in Strategic Management

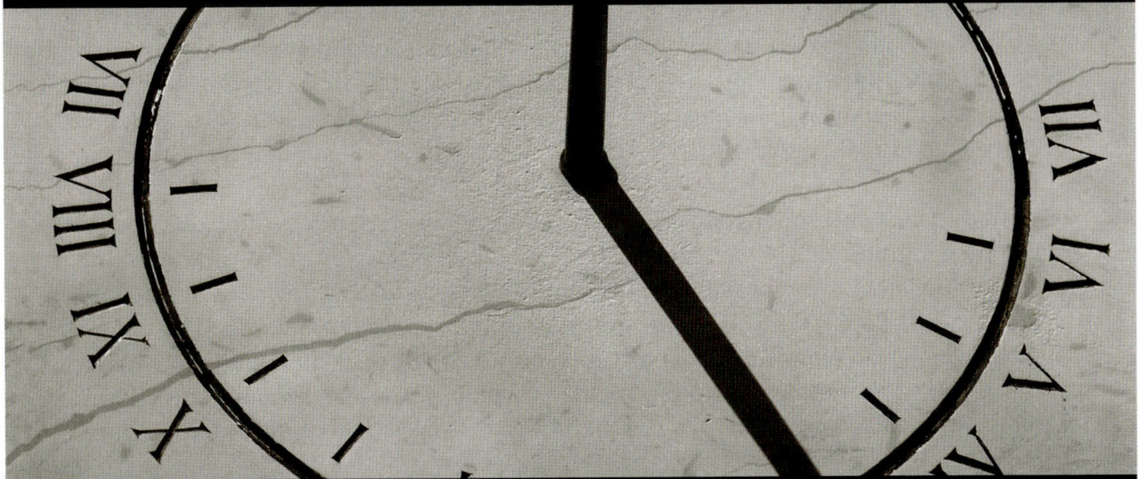

There are things we know we know. We also know there are known unknowns—We know there are some things we do not know. But there are also unknown unknowns: the ones we don't know we don't know.

—DONALD RUMSFELD, U.S. SECRETARY OF DEFENSE, 2000–6

In theory there is no difference between theory and practice. In practice there is.

—YOGI BERRA, PLAYER AND COACH, NEW YORK YANKEES, 1946–64, 1976–85

OUTLINE

Introduction

With the world mired in the worst economic downturn since the 1930s, it has become increasingly clear that the first decade of the twenty-first century has marked a fundamental break point both in global economic history and in the development of the business enterprise. Our challenge in this chapter is to assess what has changed in the business environment, what the implications for strategic management are, and what concepts and tools can help managers guide their businesses through these turbulent times.

We are in uncharted waters and, unlike the other chapters of this book, this chapter will not equip you with proven tools and frameworks that you can deploy directly in your own companies or in case analysis. The approach is exploratory. My goal is to identify the forces that are reshaping the environment of business, to introduce you to some of the concepts and approaches that are influencing current thinking about strategy, and to draw lessons from leading-edge companies about strategies, organizational forms, and management styles that may prove effective during this era of rapid, unpredictable change.

The New External Environment of Business

Since the financial crisis claimed its first major corporate casualty, Lehman Brothers, in September 2008, followed by the world's first sovereign state, Iceland, four weeks later, business leaders and politicians alike have surveyed the precarious world economy with shocked disbelief. Yet, for all the drama and tragedy of the banking crisis of 2008–9, it would appear that breakup of the world economic order began at the beginning of the decade rather than the end.

The NASDAQ stock market index hit its all time high on March 10, 2000. The ensuing meltdown of internet, technology, media and telecom stocks was the first evidence that U.S. credit expansion would not be enough to sustain the investment bubbles that had built up during the roaring 1990s.

The first major external shock of the decade was the terrorist attacks of September 11. The train of events that followed—the invasions of Afghanistan and Iraq, and further bombings in Bali, Madrid, London and Mumbai—had a major impact on world trade, financial flows, political tensions and risk perceptions.

Two months later, Enron, one of America's most successful and admired companies of the 1990s, entered bankruptcy. This was the first of a series of financial scandals that was to engulf companies on both sides of the Atlantic and revealed the downside of the aggressive pursuit of shareholder value through leverage, financial engineering and high-powered management incentives.

Unprecedented market turbulence was particularly evident in commodities and foreign exchange. In the two years up to July 2008, NYMEX crude oil rose from $49 to $147 a barrel before dropping to $37 before year end. Ship charter rates showed even more extreme gyrations: driven by booming Chinese demand for raw materials, bulk carrier daily rates reached a peak of $233 988 on June 5, 2008, before collapsing to $3670 five months later. In the foreign exchange markets, daily fluctuations of 5% between major currencies became quite normal during 2006–9.

The natural world has also emerged as a source of instability. A slew of scientific evidence suggests that climate change has reached "tipping point," triggering rapidly accelerating global warming accompanied by greatly increased risks of natural disasters.

At present we still have little idea as to the likely outcome of the present economic downturn—efforts to draw parallels with the Great Depression of the 1930s, the oil-shock of the early 1970s, or Japan's "lost decade" of the 1990s only emphasize the unique features of each of these major economic downturns. But whatever the length and depth of the current recession, a few general features of the prevailing business environment can be identified.

The Economy: Volatility and Low Growth

While the response of the world economy to the massive monetary and fiscal initiatives introduced by governments and international organizations remains unknown, one certainty does exist: even if successful, these policies will saddle all the world's leading economies with levels of public debt that are unprecedented in peacetime. Thus, even if the current expenditures on refinancing banks, acquiring "toxic securities," and supporting failing industrial enterprises are successful, the costs of servicing public debt will inevitably be major drag on future economic growth.

Meanwhile, it seems highly likely that the levels of volatility and unpredictability that we have experienced in recent years will continue into the future. A key feature of the global economy is the high level of interconnectedness that results from high levels of trade, internationalization of financial markets, flexibility of exchange and interest rates, and speed of communication. As predicted by systems theory, high levels of interconnectedness increase the tendency for the system to amplify small initial movements in unpredictable ways.

Shifts in the global balance of economic power will continue to undermine the ability of the leading industrial nations to control these disruptive forces. The rise of the BRIC countries is creating a multipolar world where the Old Order—the U.S., the E.U. and Japan and the institutions they created (the World Bank, IMF and OECD) are less able to offer global leadership. Looking ahead to 2025, the U.S. National Intelligence Council predicts:

> The international system—as constructed following the Second World War—will be almost unrecognizable . . . owing to the rise of emerging powers, a globalizing economy, an historic transfer of relative wealth and economic power from west to east, and the growing influence of non-state actors.[1]

Technology

Despite overblown expectations concerning the ability of new digital and communications technologies to create a "New Economy," we have witnessed a transition from an industrial economy to a knowledge economy, where software rather than hardware is the primary source of value. The digitally driven knowledge revolution also creates what Brian Arthur calls the "casino of technology," where markets are transformed and established market leaders deposed.[2] The ability of two maverick entrepreneurs operating out of Estonia, Niklas Zennstrom and Janus Friis, to initiate revolutions in two industries—recorded music through their Kazaa file sharing system and telephony through their Skype VoIP telephony service—exemplifies the disruptive potential of new internet-based business models.[3]

Digital technologies are also causing competition to intensify the dissolution of industry barriers. In hand-held devices, Nokia cell phones, Apple iPods, Nintendo Gameboys, Palm PDAs, and RIM's BlackBerry smartphones are increasingly sharing functions and increasingly competing in a shared marketplace.

Societal Pressures

For organizations to survive and prosper requires that they adapt to the values and expectations of society—what organizational sociologists refer to as *legitimacy*.[4] One of the profoundest impacts of the recent financial crisis on business may be implications for the legitimacy of particular types of business—which influences acceptability among consumers, motivation of employees, willingness of investors and financiers to provide funding, and government support. Loss of social legitimacy may be as great a threat to the survival of commercial and investment banks as their weak balance sheets.[5]

The notion that the business enterprise is a social institution which must identify with the goals and aspirations of society has been endorsed by several leading management thinkers—including Peter Drucker, Charles Handy and Sumantra Ghoshal.[6] The implication is that when the values and attitudes of society are changing, so must the strategies and behaviors of companies.

While anti-business sentiment has for the most part been restricted to the fringes of the political spectrum—neo-Marxists, environmentalist and anti-globalization activists—the corporate scandals of the early part of the decade (Enron, Worldcom, Parmalat) and the financial crisis of 2008–9 have moved disdain for business corporation and their leaders into the mainstream of public opinion. Three issues have been paramount: equity, ethics and environmental sustainability.

Equity issues have been fueled by the growing income disparity within organizational hierarchy. In 1980 the multiple of CEO compensation to that of first-tier employees within U.S. companies was around 40. By 2000, that ratio had risen to 400 in many U.S. companies. Increasingly, claims that bloated CEO bonuses and option packages were justified by the dictates of "the market" or the need to align top management incentives with shareholder value creation were no longer credible. However, it was the payoffs earned by top executives and star traders at failing financial institutions such as Merrill Lynch and Royal Bank of Scotland that turned disquiet into popular outrage.

Similarly with ethical issues. While the offences that put Michael Milken (the "junk-bond king") and Martha Stewart ("America's favorite housewife") behind bars seem modest transgressions, recent examples of rogue executive behavior are far more shocking, whether grossly extravagant (John Thain's $1200 trash bin for his office at Merrill Lynch), criminal (Bernard Madoff), or both (Allen Stanford).

Finally, as public concern over the degradation of the natural environment grows, so businesses are increasingly pressured to adopt strategies and actions that are conducive to environmental sustainability.[7]

Adapting to society's growing demands for fairness, ethics and sustainability presents challenges for business leaders that extend beyond the problems of reconciling societal demands with shareholder interests. Should a company determine unilaterally the values that will govern its behavior, or does it seek to reflect those of the society in which it operates? Companies that embrace the values espoused by their founders are secure in their own sense of mission and can ensure a long-term consistency in their strategy and corporate identity (for example, Walt Disney Company and Wal-Mart with respect to founders Walt Disney and Sam Walton). However, there is a risk that these values become out of step with those of the society as a whole or with the requirements for business effectiveness. Thus, Marks & Spencer's paternalism towards employees and suppliers became a source of rigidity rather than competitive advantage. Conversely, seeking to embrace the concerns and values of society presents the challenge of identifying what these are in a society characterized by diversity and rapid change. These increasing societal pressures have reinforced the attractions of private status: between 1998 and 2008, the number of companies listed on the NYSE fell from 2722 to 1978.

Managing in an Economic Crisis

When demand falls as quickly as it has between the fourth quarter of 2008 and third quarter of 2009, and credit markets seize up, business as normal gives way to crisis management. The problem, for most companies, is managing under conditions which are unlike anything in living memory, where the outlook is uncertain, and even the current situation is difficult to recognize, let alone comprehend. The evidence available so far points to several key themes and areas of management action which can help companies navigate their way through these troubled times.

New Top Management Requirements When events are moving at unprecedented speed, the time intervals between obtaining information, analyzing information, taking decisions and implementing those decisions need to be tightly compressed. Management consultant Ram Charan identifies the need for "management intensity": plans and progress must be revisited on a daily basis and every top executive must be involved, visible, and in continuous conversation with employees, customers and suppliers. Management intensity requires:

> . . . immersion in the business's operational details and the day-to-day competitive climate the business is facing, along with hands-on involvement and follow-through . . . Surviving a volatile environment requires frequent operational adjustments . . . your guiding principle should be: Head in, hands on. Only in this way will you be able to anticipate what's coming next and respond quickly and appropriately.[8]

The implication is that normal management processes must be bypassed—this can be facilitated by creating an alternative top management structure dedicated to crisis management. In December 2008, LG Electronics established a crisis war room comprising senior executives from LG's five business units, its eight regional headquarters and key functional areas. The team developed 11 key action items and every business unit was required to set up task-force teams to implement them.[9]

Other companies have adapted existing crisis management structures (see Strategy Capsule 18.1).

Dual Strategies: Surviving Today, Competing for Tomorrow We discussed *dual strategies* in Chapter 1. Strategic management involves making the most of the firm's existing resources and capabilities to maximize performance in the present while also developing to meet the requirements of the future. In times of crisis this conflict becomes more much more acute. The economic crisis has foreshortened management time horizons for most companies. The greater the impact of the downturn, the more firms are likely to be focusing their energies on surviving the present. The danger, however, is that in retrenching to secure survival,

STRATEGY CAPSULE 18.1

Crisis Management at DuPont

DuPont's CEO Chad Holliday was alerted to the spread of the subprime crisis when, on a visit to Japan, a major customer there announced cash flow concerns. A meeting with senior managers on his return to Wilmington, Delaware, resulted in a fragmentary but consistent picture of an accelerating downturn: sharp falls in orders by automakers for paint, falling occupancy rates for local hotels, etc. Holliday activated DuPont's Corporate Crisis Management Plan, which had last been initiated on the September 11, 2001. The next day the 17 standing committees met at DuPont HQ for four days of meetings. The committees assigned to security and safety issues were stood down, while the remaining teams worked on initial financial, operational and HR responses. To alert all employees, DuPont's chief economist and the head of its pension fund prepared a communication to employees on the business outlook, which also addressed pension fund issues. Within 10 days of initiating the crisis plan all DuPont employees had had a face-to-face meeting with a manager who outlined expectations with regard to cost cutting.

The initial measure involved heavy cutbacks of discretionary costs such as travel, consultants, overtime and outside contracts. But as the financial situation continued to deteriorate it became clear that additional measures would be needed. Together with his COO and CFO, Holliday had meetings with each of DuPont's 14 leaders to discuss their responses to the crisis. With evidence that cost cutting and cash conservation measures were not being implemented fast enough the top trio introduced sharply reduced targets for cost and working for the remainder of 2008 and first quarter of 2009.

Revised sales projections allowed a reassessment of capacity and labor requirements. On December 4, 2008 DuPont announced a series of plant closures, the elimination of 4000 contractors, and 2500 job losses.

Within six weeks Du Pont had achieved a major financial and operational repositioning of its entire company.

Source: Based on Ram Charan, *Leadership in the Era of Economic Uncertainty* (New York: McGraw-Hill, 2009)

for example by cutting back investments in technology, facilities, brands and people, companies will undermine their future competitiveness. One of the great challenges of managing in a downturn is to safeguard core capabilities and to make shrewd investments to prepare for the next upturn. Firms that perform best across economic cycles tend to be those which adjust activity levels early on in a downcycle, then invest in technology, human resources, and acquisitions at the depth of a recession.[10] However, timing is difficult. Recessions offer unique opportunities for acquiring resources on the cheap—however, as Bank of America discovered in its opportunistic acquisition of Merrill Lynch, moving too early may result in overpaying.

Adjusting Performance Criteria Emphasis on survival rather than long run profitability or growth has implications for the performance criteria a firm adopts to set targets and monitor performance. When battling for survival many of the conventional indicators—earnings per share for example—lose relevance. Standard indicators of solvency—debt/equity, excess of assets over liabilities, current ratio—take second place to indicators of liquidity such as cash reserves and free cash flow. When so many asset markets—for real estate, industrial equipment, or debt instruments—suffer from lack of trading volume, a liquidity problem can easily become a solvency problem. During recession cash is king, which means planning and monitoring of cash flows and cash balances. Tatum, the financial consulting firm recommends: "focus on managing the funds that are available . . . This requires the company to maintain a meaningful 13-week cash flow forecast, tracking and regularly updating the forecast to perpetually keep it running one quarter ahead, reflecting new information as it is gleaned."[11] Active cash management requires careful management of receivables, which must go beyond the numbers. What is the financial health of individual customers? Which ones are being unusually slow in settling their invoices? When cash flows are uncertain, contingency planning is essential—will suppliers extend lengthen payment periods what nonbank sources of credit are available, which assets can be sold?

Linking Environment Scanning to Financial Management A key feature of the 2008–9 downturn was a high level of uncertainty as managers sought to make sense of a mass of confusing economic and financial information—all of which pointed to rapid deterioration, but none of which was helpful in indicating the depth or length of the recession. Given human propensities to interpret new information in the light of individual emotional disposition, prior belief structures and outright denial, top management access to real time information from the periphery of the organization and group processes to interpret that information are critical. Cisco's corporate information systems allow senior executives to track orders from around the world on a real time basis and quickly identify potential deviations from budgets. Lego uses a monthly meeting of senior managers—the "operations board"—to pool knowledge of what is happening in its various markets and take a view about what is likely to happen in the 12 months to come.[12] Given the impossibility of forecasting, scenarios and simulations can be valuable ways of thinking about the future and exploring its implications. Early in the financial crisis, J. P. Morgan Chase examined the effect of a 50% fall in the stock market and 10% unemployment on its budgets. Lego generated a number of different scenarios as part of its 2009 budget and developed contingency plans for each scenario so that it can react swiftly to emerging events.

Innovative Approaches to Strategy Recessionary times offer opportunities for doing things differently—as well as opportunities for acquiring assets at fire-sale prices. Cash-strapped consumers offer a willing market for companies that can offer superior value propositions. According to Peter Williamson and Ming Zeng, companies that adapt low-cost technical solutions can quickly take market share from established market leaders. China's BYD now leads the world market for lithium ion batteries after developing a battery that uses lower cost materials and can be manufactured using a lower cost process. Another Chinese company, Zhongxing Medical, has developed a direct digital radiography scanner using a less sophisticated technology that allows it to undercut GE and Philips by about 75%. By developing products for emerging market countries, Western MNCs can find innovative low-cost customer solution. In India, HP has developed its *Shop Owner's Management Assistant*, a low-cost Linux-based device for inventory management and billing. Designed for India's mom-and-pop stores, HP is now discovering a global market for the product.[13]

The key to developing promising new strategies during a severe recession, according to Richard Rumelt, is to recognize that a serious economic downturn is not part of a normal business cycle but is a *structural break*: a point where trends become discontinuous and established cause-and-effect relationships break down.[14] Such periods are often associated with massive industrial change—some established industries go into terminal decline but others flourish. The Great Depression of the 1930s coincided with the golden years of Hollywood, the rise of air travel and the emergence of many branded consumer goods, including ready-to-eat breakfast cereals. Investment banking will never be the same and the auto industry may never bounce back, yet in the new networked, big-government economy struggling to save the ecosystem, massive opportunities are available in water supply systems, waste management, high-speed rail systems, alternative energy, next generation wireless services, healthcare, and crime prevention.

New Directions in Strategic Thinking

Reorienting Shareholder Value Maximization

As outlined in Chapter 1, the late twentieth century saw a broad acceptance of shareholder value maximization as the dominant goal of firms. The pursuit of shareholder value has resulted in major gains in cost efficiency and a wave of corporate restructuring involving divestment, outsourcing and delayering. During the present decade, the unremitting quest for shareholder value has also had unforeseen and undesired consequences. Rather than maximize the flow of profits on which stock market valuation depended, many companies had focused excessively on short-term earnings, while others had gone further and had attempted to directly manage their stock market valuations through smoothing fluctuations in reported earnings and, in some cases, artificially manipulating financial statements. The alleged alignment of management incentives with shareholder value through grants of stock options and bonuses to senior managers have, for many companies, become a mechanism for the enrichment of executives at the expense of shareholders.

However, none of these outcomes implies that the goal of maximizing the value of the firm is misguided. Maximizing shareholder value is essentially about maximizing the present value of economic profit over the lifetime of the firm. The key issue is how it is translated into strategy. The problem for many public companies is that shareholder value creation was interpreted by management to mean the management of a firm's stock market value. Management cannot create stock market value—only the stock market can do that. What management can do is to generate the stream of profits that the stock market capitalizes into market value. The danger is that CEO obsession with their companies' share price can divert them from the task of long-term profit maximization. Indeed, as I argued in Chapter 2, the critical focus of top management should be less on profits and more upon the factors that drive profits: operational efficiency, customer satisfaction, new product development and the like.

The implication is not that firms abandon shareholder value maximization in favor of some woolly notion of stakeholder satisfaction but that they should focus more determinedly on identifying the basic drivers of value creation and seek to manage them. Following this line of reasoning, the answer to the present crisis of confidence among business leaders lies not in some new model of capitalism but in refocusing upon the fundamentals of strategic management.

The corporate disasters of the present decade from Enron to Citigroup, Lehman Brothers and Royal Bank of Scotland have their roots in strategies that were a poor fit both with the key success factors of the industries within which the firms operated and with their resources and capabilities. The universal banking model pursued by Citigroup rested upon dubious assumptions about supply-side and demand-side economies of scope. RBS's acquisition-based growth strategy never adequately addressed the question of how cost savings from integrating the target firms would match the acquisition premiums that were paid.

The most powerful antidote to the triple threat of corporate empire building, CEO hubris, and unwarranted faith in new business models is fundamental strategic analysis: strate-gies which build value are those which are based upon choosing markets whose structural characteristics can support profitability over the long term, creating com-petitive advantage through matching internal strengths to emerging success factors and maintaining the flexibility to adapt to unexpected changes.

Managing Options

Deploying shareholder value maximization also means recognizing that shareholder value derives not only from the net present value of profits, but also from *real options*. During turbulent times, options are likely to become increasingly important as sources of value. A failure to take account of option value has been a critical flaw in the ways in which the shareholder value model has been applied. In the interests of reducing cost of capital and boosting after-tax profits, firms have substituted debt for equity. In doing so they have simultaneously reduced options: highly leveraged firms have fewer opportunities to take advantage of unexpected investment opportunities (including acquisition). In the event of an unexpected downturn, highly leveraged firms may experience a catastrophic lack of strategic options.

Analysis of strategy in terms of option-creation has focused on particular types of strategic decisions—for example, R&D decisions,[15] acquisitions,[16] and alliance formation.[17] However, application of real options thinking to strategic analysis at a broader level has been limited to broad generalizations, such as the value of flexibility. If we are to take on board options thinking more widely, then we need to reconsider many of our core strategy models and strategy techniques. For example:

- Industry analysis has taken the view that decisions about industry attractiveness depend on profit potential. However, if industry structure becomes so unstable that forecasting industry profitability is no longer viable, it is likely that industry attractiveness will depend much more on option value. From an options perspective, an attractive industry is one that is rich in options—for example, an industry that produces a number of different products is comprised of multiple segments, has many strategic groups, utilizes a diversity of alternative technologies and raw materials, and where internal mobility barriers tend to be low. Thus, consumer electronics, semiconductors, packaging, and investment banking would seem to be more attractive in terms of options than electricity or steel or car rental.
- An options approach also has major implications for the analysis of resources and capabilities. In terms of option value, an attractive resource is one that can be deployed in different businesses and support alternative strategies. Owning a patent on a breakthrough in nanotechnology is likely to offer greater option value than owning a blast furnace. Similarly with capabilities: highly specialized capabilities such as expertise in the design of petrochemical plants offers less option potential than expertise in the marketing of fast-moving consumer goods. Dynamic capabilities are important because they can create new options: "Dynamic capabilities are the organizational and strategic routines by which firms achieve new resource combinations as markets emerge, collide, split, evolve, and die."[18]

Seeking More Complex Sources of Competitive Advantage

Focus on strategy fundamentals does not necessarily lead to simple strategies. In many industries, increasing pressure of competition and the entry of firms with unassailable cost advantages requires that established players access new sources of profitability. As we observed in Chapter 7, there are few competitive advantages that are sustainable over a significant period of time in today's dynamic business environment. Ultimately, the only sustainable competitive advantage is the ability to create new sources of competitive advantage. A key fear of companies that have maintained both profitability and market share over periods of many years is their capacity to build layers of competitive advantage—for example, Toyota, Wal-Mart, 3M, Canon, Swatch and L'Oreal. These companies have meshed the diverse performance goals of cost efficiency, differentiation, innovation, responsiveness and global learning. As we shall see, reconciling the different requirements of different performance dimensions imposes highly complex organizational challenges that are pushing companies to fundamentally rethink their structures and management systems.

Thus the ability of some companies to combine multiple capabilities recalls Isaiah Berlin's classification of intellectuals into foxes and hedgehogs: "The fox knows many things; the hedgehog knows one big thing."[19] Despite Jim Collins' praise for companies that have a single penetrating insight into the complexities of their business environments, it appears that companies that have built their strategy on such insight often have difficulty in fending off new competitors: Toys-R-Us with its big-box retailing, Dell with its direct sales model, AOL with dial-up internet access.[20]

The Challenge of Strategic Fit: Complementarity and Complexity

Central to just about everything in this book is the notion of *strategic fit*. Strategy must *fit* with the business environment and with resources and capabilities; strategy must *fit* with structure; the individual components of strategy must *fit* one with another; organization structure must *fit* with management systems . . . We have examined these issues of fit intuitively using logic to explore individual relationships ("in a commodity market, the dominant strategy will be to be a cost leader"). However, two areas—the *economics of complementarity* and *complexity theory*—offer approaches to the analysis of strategic fit that not only offer vastly increased rigor but have troubling implications for strategy formulation and implementation.

Complementarity Complementarity research addresses the linkages among a firm's management practices such that adopting an apparently superior practice is likely to be ineffective or even counterproductive—the key is a system-wide shift to a new configuration of management practices. Much of the research has addressed the transition from mass manufacturing to lean manufacturing—reorganizing production processes achieves little without simultaneous adaptation of a wide range of human resource practices.[21] Similarly, a six-sigma quality management program is likely to be of little value unless it is accompanied by adjustments in incentives, recruitment policies, product strategy, and capital budgeting practices.

At one extreme, recognition of complementarities in management practices implies a retreat from rules and generalizations in formulating and implementing of strategy in favor of particularism: every firm is unique and must create a unique combination of strategic variables and management practices. In practice, the implications of complementarity are less stark. While every firm is unique, management choices tend to converge to a limited number of *configurations*. Thus, successful adaptation among large European companies was associated with a small number of configurations of organizational structure, processes and boundaries.[22]

Complexity Theory Organizations—like the weather, ant colonies, flocks of birds, human crowds, and seismic activity—are *complex systems* whose behavior results from the interactions of a large number of independent agents. This behavior has a number of interesting features:

- *Unpredictability*. The behavior of complex adaptive systems cannot be predicted in any precise sense. There is no tendency to stable equilibria; cascades of change are constantly interacting and reshaping competitive landscapes. Patterns of change tend to follow *power-law distributions*: small changes typically result in small consequences but may also trigger major movements—dropping grains of sand onto a sand pile results in small movements interspersed by occasional major landslides.[23]
- *Self-organization*. Complex systems—especially biological and social systems—have a capacity for self-organizing. A bee colony or shoal of fish shows coordinated responses to external threats and opportunities without anyone giving orders. Humans too can often do as well as bees and ants in organizing themselves, adapting to change and creating new structures and

systems without any formal authority. Quite sophisticated synchronized behavior can be achieved through adopting just a few simple rules. For human organizations there are three main requirements for self-organization: *identity* that permits a common sense-making process within the organization, *information* that provides the possibility of synchronized behavior, and *relationships* that are the pathways through which information is transformed into intelligent, coordinated action. The more access individuals have to one another, the greater the possibilities for organized activity.[24]

- *Inertia and chaos*. Evolutionary processes can produce orderly outcomes where change is so limited that the system falls into stasis, or disorder leading to chaotic outcomes. In between is an intermediate region where disturbances produce both small and large shifts (with a power-law distribution) that achieves the most rapid evolutionary adaptation. These results point to the advantages of systems that are positioned at the *edge of chaos*—they are capable of small, localized adaptations, but also have the potential to make larger leaps toward higher *fitness peaks*.[25] The implications of these ideas for strategic management are radical and far-reaching. Complexity implies that business is inherently unpredictable—not only is it impossible to forecast the business environment but managers cannot predict with any certainty what the outcomes of their actions will be. The concept of the CEO as the peak decision maker and strategy architect is not only unrealistic—it is undesirable. Managers must rely on the self-organizing properties of their companies. The critical issues are how can they select the structures, systems, and management styles that will allow these self-organizing properties to generate the best outcomes? Some of the recommendations arising from applications of complexity theory to strategic management include:[26]
- *Setting up conditions for both incremental and radical change*. Kaufman's *NK model* (and the *fitness landscapes* that it generates) is a widely used tool for exploring the implications among choices of strategy, organizational form, and management behavior.[27] Achieving the highest level of adaptive performance typically requires a combination of incremental changes with occasional radical leaps. Management systems can be designed to encourage these outcomes. For example the reorientation of companies' strategic planning systems from resource allocation decisions to agreeing performance targets is likely to encourage incentives for incremental measures—cost reduction and continuous improvement—while establishing conditions where serious performance shortfalls trigger corporate intervention involving major strategic changes. NK models also show that the optimal balance between incremental and radical management measures depend upon the degree of interdependency of the organizational environment: the stronger the linkages, the more rugged the landscape, and the greater the need for major strategic leaps to move to new performance peaks.
- *Establishing simple rules*. If the coordinated behaviors of complex systems (e.g. the flying formations of flocks of birds) can be simulated with a few simple rules, it seems feasible that companies can be managed by a few simple rules and very little managerial direction. For instance, rather than plan strategy in any formal sense, rules of thumb in screening opportunities

(*"boundary rules"*) can locate the company where the opportunities are richest. Thus, Cisco's acquisitions strategy is guided by the rule that it will acquire companies with fewer than 75 employees of which 75% are engineers. Second, rules can designate a common approach to how the company will exploit opportunities (*"how-to rules"*). Thus, Yahoo! has a few rules regarding the look and functionality of new web pages, but then gives freedom to developers to design new additions. Third, companies have rules to determine priorities in resource allocation (*"priority rules"*).[28] Jack Welch's corporate initiatives at GE—"Be number 1 or number 2 in your industry," "Six-sigma," "Destroy-your-business-dot-com"—fulfilled a similar role. They were not directives, but guidelines to stimulate and focus decentralized adaptation.[29]

- *Accelerating evolution through flexibility*. Organizational structures tend to ossify over time as power centers build and interactions become institutionalized. Periodic large-scale corporate reorganizations are not enough: to exploit innovation and entrepreneurial initiative, flexibility in organizational structure is essential. Eisenhardt and Brown use the term "patching" to describe a process in which new organizational units are continually being created, merged, and redefined to foster initiative.[30] Achieving flexibility may require leaving structures only partially defined. This may be especially effective in assisting collaboration between different business units within a company. Rather than attempt to manage business unit linkages from the corporate level, it may be better for corporate to create a context within which businesses can co-evolve. This requires allowing considerable autonomy to business units while keeping their boundaries porous to permit a multiplicity of voluntary collaborations between individuals across the businesses. Walt Disney Company exemplifies co-evolution between different internal divisions. Disney's *The Lion King* movie spawned videos, theme park attractions, a stage musical, and over 150 kinds of merchandise. These spinoffs were not planned by corporate strategists; they occurred through voluntary cooperation across Disney's different divisions.[31]
- *Using adaptive tension to position at the edge of chaos*. If too little tension produces inertia and too much creates chaos, the challenge for top management is to create a level of adaptive tension that optimizes the pace of organizational change and innovation. Bill McKelvey interprets Jack Welch's management style from a complexity viewpoint—by imposing initiatives ("be number 1 or number 2 in your industry") and powerful performance incentives—he turned up the level of pressure in the organization to the point where changes began occurring spontaneously.[32]

Applications of complexity theory to strategy management add analytic depth to Mintzberg's arguments in favor of *emergent* approaches to strategy making. Mintzberg's critique of the "rational design" school of strategy emphasized the superiority of decentralized strategy making that embraced intuition and responsiveness.[33] Complexity theory provides an intellectual basis for emergence in strategy making. Changes in large companies' strategic planning practices in recent years—reduced formality, emphasis on performance goals, focus on direction rather than content—are consistent with the tenets of complexity theory.[34]

Analyzing Linkages within the Firm Porter and Siggelkow observe that common to both complementarity and complexity approaches to linkages among a firm's activities is the concept of *contextuality*—the benefits from any particular activity depend upon what other activities are taking place.[35] In Chapter 8, I observed that one implication of this idea is that imitation of a firm's competitive advantage becomes more difficult: imitating a particular resource or process is unlikely to do the trick. However, Porter and Siggelkow's main contribution is the recognition of different types of linkage and their implications for management. Two dimensions are important:

- Generic activities *versus* strategy-specific activities. Some management activities have performance effects that are independent of other activities—for example using computers for managing accounting systems is optimal for virtually all firms. For other activities, how they are configured depends upon the other choices that the firm makes. Thus, the optimal employee incentive system depends upon a number of strategic choices.
- Generic interactions *versus* contextual interactions. The interactions between management activities can also be different across firms. Some activities may interact in the same way for all firms. For example, the benefits from flexibility in manufacturing will tend to increase with increased product differentiation for all firms. For other pairs of activities, interactions may be different across firms—depending either on the levels of the two activities, or on choices regarding other activities.

Redesigning the Organization

As business environments become more complex, more competitive and less predictable, survival requires that companies perform at a higher level with a broader repertoire of capabilities. Building multiple capabilities and achieving excellence across multiple performance dimensions requires managing dilemmas that cannot be resolved as simple tradeoffs. A company must produce at low cost, while also innovating; it must deploy the massed resources of a large corporation, while showing the entrepreneurial flair of a small startup; it must achieve high levels of reliability and consistency while also being flexible. All of these dilemmas are aspects of the underlying conflict between achieving operational efficiency today and adapting for tomorrow. Reconciling these conflicts within a single organization presents huge management challenges. We know how to devise structures and incentive systems that drive cost efficiency; we also know the organizational conditions conducive to innovation. But how on earth do we do both simultaneously?

Changes in organizational design are being driven by two major forces: first, the need for organizations to deploy more capabilities developed to a higher level; second, the need to respond quicker to external change.

Capability-based Structures

In Chapter 6, we noted that organizational design has been dominated by the requirements of cooperation rather than coordination. As a result, hierarchical structures have emphasized control and the need for unitary lines of command. Once we acknowledge that building outstanding capabilities is the primary goal of organizational design then the emphasis shifts to the need to achieve effective coordination. If we accept that most enterprises need to deploy multiple capabilities and the coordination needs of different capabilities vary, it follows that our organizational structure must encompass different patterns of interaction. Hence, most business enterprises are unlikely to be successful with a unitary structure and will need to encompass multiple structures.

Beyond Unitary Structures Developing multiple capabilities requires that organizational members coordinate in different ways for different purposes, which requires structures that simultaneously support multiple patterns of coordination.[36] Matrix structures—organizing to develop capabilities around businesses, geographical markets and functions—have been around for a long time. But these dimensions of the traditional matrix relate primarily to operational activities. The literature on organizational learning knowledge management distinguishes productive activities according to whether they are building the firm's stock of knowledge or deploying that knowledge: the former is referred to as *exploration*, the latter as *exploitation*.[37] When exploration activities were carried out by specialized functions—R&D, market research, strategic planning—organizations could simply differentiate these departments to meet the organizational requirements of exploration. Increasingly, however, these functions are not the preserve of specialized departments but are diffused across the organization.

Adding exploration activities—product development teams, innovation initiatives, communities of practice—on top of the standard dimensions of the organizational matrix requires additional structures to support coordination. Structures directed towards acquiring new knowledge and promoting change within the formal organization have been described as *parallel learning structures*.[38] They are designed to foster communication and interaction, but typically involve little specialization or rules. For example:

- 3M has a parallel structure for new product development whereby individuals are encouraged, to "bootleg" time, materials, and use of facilities to work on new product ideas. Promising new products that emerge from this informal structure are ultimately taken up by the formal structure.
- The "Work-Out" program implemented by Jack Welch at GE was a parallel structure designed to effect change within the formal structure. During Work-Out sessions the norms that governed the formal organization were suspended, and free interchange of ideas was encouraged.
- IBM's massive online "*Innovation Jam*" (more on this later) creates a temporary organization that administers a biannual, 72-hour online session involving tens of thousands of contributors from inside and outside the company, then harvesting the results.[39]

Team-based, Project-based and Process-based Structures The structures needed to support coordination are different from those required to ensure compliance and control. Increased reliance on teams reflects the recognition that routines require patterns of interaction that are spontaneous and poorly understood—hence, they cannot be "managed" in any directive sense. Flexible, team-based structures can achieve the kinds of adaptable integration that are the basis of dynamic capabilities, yet beyond some very basic requirements of team structure we know little about the dynamics of team interaction.[40]

More companies are organizing their activities less around functions and continuous operations and more around time-designated projects where a team is assigned to a specific project with a clearly defined outcome and a specified completion date. While construction companies and consulting firms have always been structured around projects, a wide range of companies are finding that project-based structures featuring temporary cross-functional teams charged with clear objectives are more able to achieve innovation, adaptability, and rapid learning than more traditional structures:

- About half of Google's employees—including almost all of its software engineers—are organized into teams comprising three or four people. Team leadership revolves, individuals work on multiple teams, and individuals can move between teams without HR approval. According to Shona Brown, Google's head of operations: "If at all possible, we want people to commit to things, rather than be assigned to things . . . If you see an opportunity, go for it."[41]
- W. L. Gore, the supplier of Gore-Tex and wide a range of hi-tech fabric products, also has a team-based structure with minimal top-down direction—there are no formal job titles and leaders are selected by peers. Employees ("associates") may apply to join particular teams and it is up to the team members to choose new members. The teams are self-managed and team goals are not assigned from above but are agreed through team commitments. Associates are encouraged to work on multiple teams.[42]

Non-hierarchical, team-based organizations can achieve high levels of innovation, flexibility and employee motivation. But absence of hierarchical control can also produce chaos. Oticon, the Danish manufacturer of hearing aids, initiated radical decentralization, abolished most formal controls, and reorganized around over 100 self-directed project teams.[43] Within six years, lack of coordination, confused incentives, and excessive internal politicking caused Oticon to dismantle much of its "spaghetti organization" and reinstitute hierarchical control.[44]

To improve coordination across, between and within organizational capabilities has encouraged companies to align their structures more closely with their internal *processes*. While business process reengineering directs attention to the micro-structure of processes, a focus on organizational capabilities fosters an integrated view of processes that explores how individual processes fit together in sequences and networks of complementary activities. For example, a company's order fulfillment process may span a whole chain of activities from supplying information to potential customers, to customer selection and ordering, to manufacturing, through to distribution. Similarly, the customer relations process embraces the entirety of a company's interactions with its customers through marketing and after-sales services. These macro processes often extend beyond the company: supply-chain management links internal logistics with those of suppliers and suppliers' suppliers. Volvo reorganized ordering, production planning, supply chains, distribution, and dealer relations into an integrated "order fulfillment process" with the goal of a 14-day cycle between customer order and customer receipt of a customized automobile.[45]

Organizing for Adaptability

The need for organizations to coordinate in multiple ways for multiple purposes inevitably means that company structures become more complex. Despite the propensity for CEOs to echo Thoreau in their call to "simplify, simplify," typically the emphasis has been, first, replacing formal systems by informal systems; second, relying less on continuous supervision and more on setting performance goals against which individuals are periodically appraised.

Hands-off Management Complexity theory supports the idea that organizations may be able to do complex things without necessarily resorting to complex structures. Notions of *self organization* and the power of *simple rules* support the idea that human beings are capable of interesting in complex patterns without the need for managers telling them what to do. Loosening the structure may be a critical step towards building the *ambidextrous organization*—one that can combine multiple capabilities and accommodate both gradual change and occasional revolutionary leaps.[46]

The paradox of simplicity is that reducing complexity at the formal level can foster greater variety and sophisticated coordination at the informal level. At GE, Jack Welch's emphasis on "Speed, Simplicity, Self-confidence" resulted in reformulating control systems around just a few performance indicators and using periodic corporate initiatives ("growth," "boundarylessness," and "six-sigma") to drive change. Yet, this paring down of formal systems fostered more complex patterns of coordination and collaboration within GE.[47] In general, the greater the potential for reordering existing resources and capabilities in complex new combinations, the greater the potential for "consensus-based hierarchies" that emphasize horizontal communication over "authority-based hierarchies" that emphasize vertical communication.[48]

Identity Substituting informal structures and systems for formal structures and systems requires focus on organizational context over organizational structure. To manage the organizational context includes influencing social and behavioral norms but these depend on some shared cognition of what the organization is and an emotional attachment towards what the organization represents. These ideas are components of what has been termed *organizational identity*—a collective understanding of what is presumed core, distinctive, and enduring about the character of an organization.[49] A strong consensus around organizational identity provides a powerful basis for coordinated action that permits flexibility and responsiveness to be reconciled with continuity and stability. At some point, organizational identity becomes are impediment to rather than a facilitator of change. (IBM's identity as a vertically integrated supplier of mainframe computers to large organizations hampered adaptation to microcomputing, networking, and web-based computing.) Organizational identity creates an important linkage between a firm's internal self-image and its market positioning. With the increase of symbolic influences on consumer choices, the linkage between product design, brand image, and organizational identity becomes increasingly important. For companies such as Nokia, Apple, Alessi, and Bang & Olufsen, product design is an important vehicle for establishing and interpreting organizational identity.[50]

Breaking Down Corporate Boundaries Even with informal coordination mechanisms, modular structures and sophisticated knowledge management systems there are limits to the range of capabilities that any company can encompass. Indeed, converging technologies and the need for rapid new product development means that outsourcing capabilities is often preferable to developing them internally. The implication is less distinction between what happens within the firm and what happens outside it. Interfirm networks, as we saw in the previous chapter, permit stable yet flexible patterns for integrating the capabilities of different firms while also sharing risks. "Contingent workforces"—comprising people who work for companies but are not covered by long-term employment contracts—similarly permit access to a wide range of skills while avoiding fixed costs.

While localized networks of firms—such as those that characterize Italy's clothing, furniture, and industrial machinery industries—offer potential for building trust and interfirm routines, web-based technologies permit much wider networks of collaboration. The open innovation efforts described in this book—Procter & Gamble's "Connect & Develop" approach to new product development and IBM's "Innovation Jam" (see Chapter 12)—both point to the power of ICT technologies to enable firms to draw upon ideas and expertise across the globe. Increasingly innovation requires the combination of very different technologies: the Nike + iPod Sport Kit involving sensors in Nike running shoes providing real time information that can be read on an Apple iPod is just one example of a phenomenon that is breaking down barriers between industries as well as between companies.[51] Cisco Systems has pioneered the development of web-based business integration with its suppliers, customers, and collaborations. The collaborative potential of the internet is most strongly revealed in open-source communities that build highly complex products such as Linux and Wikipedia through global networks of individual collaborators.[52]

Interfirm networks facilitate the design and production of complex products that require a wide range of technical and commercial capabilities in sectors subject to rapid change. In automobiles, fashion clothing, aerospace, machine tools, and telecom equipment, networks allow each firm to specialize in a few capabilities while providing the close linkages needed to integrate these different capabilities. The flexibility of these linkages offers the potential for the capabilities resident within an interfirm network to be reconfigured in order to adapt quickly to external change.[53]

New Modes of Leadership

Changing external conditions, new strategic priorities, and different types of organization call for new approaches to leadership. The era of restructuring and share-holder focus has been associated with "change-masters"[54]—highly visible, individualistic, often hard-driving management styles of CEOs such as Lee Iacocca at Chrysler, John Browne at BP, Michael Eisner at Disney, and Rupert Murdoch at News International. These leaders have been, first and foremost, strategic decision makers, charting the direction and redirection of their companies, and making key decisions over acquisitions, divestments, new products and cost cutting. The changing circumstances of management I have outlined imply that the "buck-stops-here" peak decision-making role may no longer be feasible, let alone desirable. One simple observation is that most companies are too complex for the CEO to be able to access the information necessary to act as peak decision maker. Recent contributions to the literature on leadership point to business leaders that are capable of creating an organizational environment consistent with the company's strategic needs—including the potential for rapid evolution.

Gary Hamel argues the need to redefine the work of leadership:

> The notion of the leader as a heroic decision maker is untenable. Leaders must be recast as social-systems architects who enable innovation . . .
>
> In Management 2.0, leaders will no longer be seen as grand visionaries, all-wise decision makers, and ironfisted disciplinarians. Instead, they will need to become social architects, constitution writers, and entrepreneurs of meaning. In this new model, the leader's job is to create an environment where every employee has the chance to collaborate, innovate, and excel.[55]

If strategy is founded in organizational identity and common purpose, and if organizational culture is the bedrock of capability, then a key role of top management is to clarify, nurture and communicate the company's purpose, *heritage*, personality, values, and norms. To unify and inspire the efforts of organizational members, leadership requires providing meaning to people's own aspirations. Ultimately this requires attention to the emotional climate of the organization.[56]

If business leadership is less about decision making and more about guiding culture, identity, and vision, then the managers will require different knowledge and skills. Research into the psychological and demographic characteristics of successful leaders has identified few consistent or robust relationships—successful leaders come in all shapes, sizes, and personality types. However, research based upon McClelland's *competency modeling* methodology pointed to the role of a set of personality attributes that have been referred to by Daniel Goleman as *emotional intelligence*.[57] These comprise: *self-awareness*—the ability understand oneself and one's emotions, *self-management*—control, integrity, conscientiousness, and initiative; *social awareness*—particularly the capacity to sense others' emotions (empathy) and *social skills*—communication, collaboration and relationship building.

Jim Collins' concept of "Level 5 Leadership" also emphasizes individual qualities—notably a combination of personal and intense resolve.[58] This combination allows business leaders to avoid the hubris and megalomania associated with outsized egos and to devote themselves to team building and organizational development. Philip Morris's Joseph Cullman, Kimberley-Clark's Darwin Smith, Nucor's Ken Iversen, P&G's L.G. Laffey, and IBM's Sam Palmisano are all transformational leaders who did not succumb to the cult of personality.

Probably the greatest error in Western thinking about leadership in organizations is the heavy emphasis on the role of individuals. Tappin and Cave argue that *team leadership* is best suited to today's troubled times where the top management team members are bound together by close bonds of fellowship. Their model is the Nokia leadership team that comprised Jorma Ollila, Matti Alahuhta, Pekka Ala-Pietilä, Sari Baldauf, and his replacement as president and chief operating officer, Olli-Pekka Kallasvuo. An effective top management team comprises, ideally, just three or four people who share extensively and openly, who have specialized roles but are also able to cover for one another.[59]

However, it is important to acknowledge that, despite the urge to uncover "the secrets of leadership," there is no dominant model of leadership or profile of the successful leader. The main lesson from empirical research is that successful leadership is associated with many different leadership approaches and many different leader characteristics. At the same time, different situations will respond to different leadership approaches. In responding to the present crisis, it is notable that several of the leadership trends that we have identified have gone into sharp reverse for many companies. In order to take fast decisive actions to cut costs, conserve cash and shore up balance sheets, many companies have recentralized management and moved to a much more interventionist and directive top management style.

Summary

In responding to the environments in which their companies find themselves, business leaders experience two major difficulties. First, the outlook for the future is highly uncertain—for many countries, 2009 saw the fastest decline in economic activity since 1930. How the world economy will develop during the second decade of the twenty-first century is unknown. Even in the short-term we do not know how deep the present recession will be, how long it will last, whether governments' monetary and fiscal initiatives will work, or what the political consequences will be. Looking longer term, there is the potential for the recent crisis to lead to fundamental changes in the capitalist system.

Second, the capacity for managerial action has been confounded by a conflict between short term and longer term forces. Over the longer term, several forces for change are influencing our thinking about strategy and management in general. These include increasing competition (arising in particular from internationalization), turbulence, technology and changing social attitudes. In the short term the overwhelming priority is surviving the present downturn.

The central problem is that the two sets of challenges require responses that are often conflicting. While meeting the challenges of increased competition and technological change is likely to require developing new capabilities, survival requires intense focus on cash conservation that is likely to inhibit all forms of investment. Similar observations can be made about styles of leadership. Complex organizations operating at high levels of evolutionary fitness require leaders that foster decentralized adaptation and initiative.

Yet, effective responses to the financial crisis of 2008–9 necessitated radical shifts in strategy that have necessitated, in most companies, a dramatic recentralization of power in order to "circle the wagons."

In many ways this dilemma of reconciling short-term survival with longer term fitness is merely an extreme example of the paradoxes that almost define the challenge of management in the twenty-first century. Several years have passed since Charles Handy identified paradox as the fundamental feature of business—and, indeed society. Yet it is only recently that the challenges of reconciling cost cutting with innovation, global integration with local differentiation, scale with responsiveness, and systematization with improvisation have been acknowledged.

At the same time, emerging concepts and theories—complexity thinking, self-organization, real options, organizational identity, open-source innovation and distributed leadership—offer the potential for us to augment our existing standard tools of strategic management. Even more encouraging is the fact that experimentation and innovation at the coal-face of management practice is offering new approaches to dealing both with old problems and with emerging ones. Radical corporate initiatives such as IBM's "Innovation Jam," Google's emergent approach to business development, and W. L. Gore's self-managed teams tend to be found among companies whose survival is not under serious threat. But even among firms that are primarily focused upon survival, management actions are going beyond conventional approaches to restructuring and cost cutting. These include novel forms of financing which are independent of traditional financial institutions, new approaches to employee relations, scenario-based financial planning, and building strategy around options rather than projects.

One of the challenges for strategic management scholars is to be alert to the initiatives and innovations that are being developed across a vast array of different firms, to identify the critical features of these initiatives and innovations, and to deploy the tools of management and social science theory to draw out their significance and potential for diffusion. A key consequence of this type of activity is that, while strategic management continues to draw heavily on concepts and theories drawn from economics, sociology, psychology, biology, systems theory, and other disciplines, in addressing current issues then is scope for strategic management to take on a leading role in developing new conceptual thinking.

Of course, many of the ideas that have developed over recent years—including the characteristics of the "new economy," the potential for employee stock options to resolve agency problems, and the potential for "decoupling" from the world market have been shown to be empty. This reinforces my belief that our basic tools of strategy analysis—industry analysis and the analysis of resources and capabilities—remain valid and robust. At the same time, there is vast potential for developing new thinking about management—not just in relation to strategy but also in terms of the role of people within organizations, the relationships among companies themselves, and those between companies and government.

Notes

1 U.S. National Intelligence Council, *Global Trends 2025:L A Transformed World* (Washington DC, November, 2008): www.dni.gov/nic/NIC_2025_project.html, accessed July 8, 2009.

2 W. B. Arthur, "Increasing Returns and the New World of Business," *Harvard Business Review* (July–August 1996): 101–8.

3 "The Skype Guys," *Time* (April 30, 2006).

4 A. Y. Lewin, C. B. Weigelt and J. D. Emery, "Adaptation and Selection in Strategy and Change" in M. S. Poole and A. H. van de Ven (eds.), *Handbook of Organizational Change and Innovation* (New York: Oxford University Press, 2004): 108–60.

5 S. Jonsson, H.R. Greve, and T. Fujiwara-Greve, "Undeserved Loss: The Spread of Legitimacy Loss to Innocent Organizations in Response to Reported Corporate Deviance," *Administrative Science Quarterly*, 54 (2009): 195–228.

6 P. F. Drucker, *Managing in the Next Society* (London: St. Martin's Press, 2003), S. Ghoshal, C. A. Bartlett and P. Moran, "A New Manifesto for Management," *Sloan Management Review* (Spring 1999): 9–20; C. Handy, *The Age of Paradox* (Boston: Harvard University Press, 1995).

7 "Sustainable Business," *Financial Times* (October 9, 2006): special section.

8 "Head in, Hands on: Ram Charan on How to Lead Now," *Harvard Management Update*, (Harvard Business School: February 11, 2009).

9 "LG Considers Job Cuts Overseas," *Korean Times* (February 9, 2009): http://www.koreatimes.co.kr/www/news/biz/2009/02/123_39214.html, accessed July 8, 2009.

10 P. Bromiley, P. Navarro and P. Sottile, "Strategic business cycle management and organizational performance: a call to action," *Strategic Organization*. 6 (2008): 207–19.

11 C. Jamison, "What Every Board Director Should Know About Financial Leadership During a Recession," Tatum LLC (2009): www.tatumllc.com.

12 "Managing in the Fog," *Economist* (February 28, 2009): 71–2.

13 P. J. Williamson and M. Zeng, "Value-for-Money Strategies for Recessionary Times," *Harvard Business Review* (March, 2009):

14 R. P. Rumelt, "Strategy in a Structural Break," *McKinsey Quarterly* (December, 2008): 24–31.

15 R. G. McGrath, "A Real Option Logic for Initiating Technology Positioning Investment," *Academy of Management Review* 22 (1997): 974–96.

16 H. T. J. Smit, "Acquisition Strategies as Option Games," *Journal of Applied Corporate Finance* (2001): 79–89.

17 M. J. Leiblein and D. D. Miller, "An Empirical Examination of the Effect of Uncertainty and Firm Strategy on the Vertical Boundaries of the Firm," *Strategic Management Journal* 24 (2003): 839–60.

18 K. M. Eisenhardt and J. A. Martin, "Dynamic Capabilities: What are They?" *Strategic Management Journal* 21 (2000): 1105–21.

19 I. Berlin, *The Hedgehog and the Fox* (New York: Simon & Schuster, 1953).

20 J. Collins, *Good to Great* (New York: HarperCollins, 2001).

21 K. Laursen and N. J. Foss, "New Human Resource Management Practices, Complementarities and the Impact on Innovation Performance," *Cambridge Journal of Economics* 27 (2003): 243–63.

22 R. Whittington, A. Pettigrew, S. Peck, E. Fenton and M. Conyon, "Change and Complementarities in the New Competitive Landscape," *Organization Science* 10 (1999): 583–600.

23 P. Bak, *How Nature Works: The Science of Self-organized Criticality* (New York: Copernicus, 1996).

24 M. J. Wheatley and M. Kellner Rogers, *A Simpler Way* (San Francisco: Berrett-Koehler, 1996).

25 P. Anderson, "Complexity Theory and Organizational Science," *Organization Science* 10 (1999): 216–32.

26 Among the sources I draw upon are: S. L. Brown and K. M. Eisenhardt, *Competing on the Edge: Strategy as Structured Chaos* (Boston: Harvard Business School Press, 1998); W. McKelvey, "Energizing Order-creating Networks of Distributed Intelligence: Improving the Corporate Brain," *International Journal of Innovation Management* 5 (June, 2001): 132–54; D. A. Levinthal, "Adaptation on a Rugged Landscape," *Management Science* 43 (1997): 934–50.

27 S. A. Kaufman, *The Origins of Order: Self Organization and Selection In Evolution* (New York: Oxford University Press, 1993).

28 For discussion of the role of rules in strategy making, see K. M. Eisenhardt and D. Sull, "Strategy as Simple Rules," *Harvard Business Review* (January–February 2001): 107–16.

29 W. McKelvey, "A Simple Rule Approach to CEO Leadership in the 21st Century" (Paper presented at the ISUFI Conference, Ostuni, Italy, September 11–13, 2003).

30 K. M. Eisenhardt and S. L. Brown, "Patching: Restitching Business Portfolios in Dynamic Markets," *Harvard Business Review* (May–June 1999): 72–84.

31 K. M. Eisenhardt and D. C. Galunic, "Coevolving: At Last, a Way to Make Synergies Work," *Harvard Business Review* (January–February 2000): 91–101.

32 W. McKelvey, "A Simple Rule Approach to CEO Leadership," op. cit.

33 H. Mintzberg, *The Rise and Fall of Strategic Planning* (New York: Free Press, 1994); H. Mintzberg, B. Ahlstrand and J. Lampel, *Strategy Safari: A Guided Tour through the Wilds of Strategic Management* (New York: Free Press, 1998).

34 R. M. Grant, "Strategic Planning In a Turbulent Environment: Evidence from the Oil Majors," *Strategic Management Journal* 24 (2003): 491–518.
35 M. E. Porter and N. Siggelkow, "Contextuality Within Activity Systems and Sustainable Competitive Advantage," *Academy of Management Perspectives* 22 (May, 2008): 34–56.
36 J. Strikwerda, "The Emergence of the Multidimensional Organization" (April, 2008). Available at SSRN: http://ssrn.com/abstract=1077363, accessed July 8, 2009.
37 J. G. March, "Exploration and Exploitation in Organizational Learning," *Organization Science* 2 (1991): 71–8.
38 G. Bushe and A. B. Shani, *Parallel Learning Structures* (Reading, MA: Addison-Wesley, 1991).
39 O. M. Bjelland and R. C. Wood, "An Inside View of IBM's 'Innovation Jam,'" *MIT Sloan Management Review* (Fall, 2008): 32–40.
40 J. R. Katzenbach and D. K. Smith, "The Discipline of Teams," *Harvard Business Review* (March–April, 1993): 111–20.
41 G. Hamel and W. Breen, *The Future of Management* (Boston: Harvard Business School Press, 2007): Chapter 6.
42 Ibid: Chapter 5.
43 D. Ravasi and G. Verona, "Organizing the Process of Knowledge Integration: The Benefits of Structural Ambiguity", *Scandinavian Journal of Management* 17 (2001): 41–66.
44 N. J. Foss, "Internal Disaggregation in Oticon: An Organizational Economics Interpretation of the Rise and Decline of the Spaghetti Organization" (Department of Industrial Economics and Strategy, Copenhagen Business School, October, 2000).
45 S. Hertz, J. K. Johansson and F. de Jager, "Customer-focused Cost Cutting: Process Management at Volvo," *Journal of Supply Chain Management* 6, no. 3 (2001): 128–41.
46 C. A. O'Reilly III and M. L. Tushman, "The Ambidextrous Organization," *Harvard Business Review* (April, 2004): 74–81. M. L. Tushman and C. A. O'Reilly III, "The Ambidextrous Organization: Managing Evolutionary and Revolutionary Change," *California Management Review* 38, no. 4 (Summer, 1996): 8–30.
47 "Jack Welch and the General Electric Management System," in R. M. Grant, *Cases to Accompany Contemporary Strategy Analysis,* 6th edn (Oxford: Blackwell, 2008).
48 J. A. Nickerson and T. R. Zenger, "The Knowledge-based Theory of the Firm—A Problem-solving Perspective," *Organization Science* 15 (2004): 617–32.
49 D. A. Gioia, M. Schultz and K. G. Corley, "Organizational Identity, Image and Adaptive Instability," *Academy of Management Review* 25 (2000): 63–81.
50 D. Ravasi and G. Lojacono, "Managing Design and Designers for Strategic Renewal," Long Range Planning, 38, No. 1. (February, 2005): 51–77.
51 "Apple and Nike, Running Mates," *Business Week* (May 24, 2006).
52 A. Wright, "The Next Paradigm Shift: Open Source Everything" *Brighthand.com* (July 9, 2008): http://www.brighthand.com/default.asp?newsID=14348, accessed July 8, 2009.
53 R. Gulati, N. Nohria and A. Zaheer, "Strategic Networks," *Strategic Management Journal* 21 (2000): 203–15.
54 R. M. Kanter, *The Change Masters* (New York: Simon & Schuster, 1983).
55 G. Hamel, "Moon Shots for Management?" *Harvard Business Review* (February 2009): 91-98.
56 J. C. Collins and J. I. Porras, *Built to Last* (New York: Harper Business, 1996).
57 D. Goleman, "What Makes a Leader?" *Harvard Business Review* (November–December 1998): 93–102. See also: J. C. Hayton and G. M. McEvoy,. "Developing and Assessing Professional and Managerial Competence" *Human Resource Management* 45 (2006): 291–4.
58 J. Collins, "Level 5 Leadership: The Triumph of Humility and Fierce Resolve," *Harvard Business Review* (January 2001): 67–76.
59 S. Tappin and A. Cave, *The Secrets of CEOs: 150 Global Chief Executives Lift the Lid on Business, Life and Leadership* (London: Nicholas Brealey Publishing, 2008).

CASES TO ACCOMPANY CONTEMPORARY STRATEGY ANALYSIS

SEVENTH EDITION

profitable than others and for the identification of key success factors in the industry.

From its humble origins in Bentonville, Arkansas, Wal-Mart has grown to be the world's largest retailer and the world's biggest corporation (in revenue). In the intensely competitive world of discount retailing, what is the basis of Wal-Mart's competitive advantage? Understanding the basis of Wal-Mart's success requires careful analysis of the resources and capabilities that Wal-Mart has built over time. What does the future hold for Wal-Mart? Will growing size and success blunt Wal-Mart's drive for cost efficiency? Will Wal-Mart's competitive advantage be undermined either by imitation by competitors or by changing market circumstances?

For nearly two decades, Manchester United has been the most successful English soccer club. The club now faced the prospect of retirement by the primary architect of that success: veteran team manager, Sir Alex Ferguson. What should be the approach of the Manchester United board and CEO in planning the continued development of the club? The case probes the interaction between financial and team performance in professional sport and explores the determinants of team-based capabilities in the intensely-competitive world of European professional soccer. A critical issue for Manchester United—and for any professional sports team—is whether exceptional team-based capabilities are the result of superior resources (players in particular) or of superior coordination and international among the resources.

Eastman Kodak faces the challenge of adjusting to the transformation of technology in the photographic imaging industry. Kodak has staked its future on being a leader in digital imaging. Yet, despite massive investment and a string of acquisitions and strategic alliances, Kodak's ability to establish competitive advantage within the digital imaging sector and to generate satisfactory returns from its investments remains in doubt. The case describes Kodak's digital imaging strategy and explores the challenges faced by CEO Antonio Perez in developing the organizational capabilities required to succeed in the fast-moving digital imaging sector.

[1] This case was written by Robert M. Grant with assistance from Simon I. Peck, Christopher Carr and Timothy Smith.

[2] This case was prepared by Robert M. Grant. It draws upon information contained in three earlier case studies: "P&G Japan: The SK-II Globalization Project," Harvard Business School Case No. 9-303-003, (2003); "Procter & Gamble: Organization 2005," Harvard Business School Case No. 9-707-519 (2007); "Procter & Gamble: Organization 2005 and Beyond," ICFAI Knowledge Center, Case No. 303-102-1 (ECCH, 2003).

[3] Written by Robert M. Grant. The case draws upon a report written by Sara Buchholz, Nadia Fabio, Andrés Ileyassoff, Laurent Mang, and Daniele Visentin, "AirAsia – Tales from a long-haul low cost carrier" Bocconi University (2009) and from an earlier case by Thomas Lawton and Jonathan Doh, "The Ascendance of AirAsia: Building a Successful budget Airline in Asia," Ivey School of Business, Case No. 9B08M054 (2008). © 2009, Robert M. Grant

an innovatory food ingredient, stanol ester, which reduces cholesterol levels in the human body. Its margarine *Benecol*, which includes stanol ester, has become a runaway success in Finland. The question presented by the [A] case is: how should Raisio exploit its innovation on the world market?

The [B] case takes up the story two years later when Raisio's global partnership with Johnson & Johnson is encountering difficulties and Raisio is has competition from Unilever to contend with. What has gone wrong and what can Raisio do to get back on track?

In 2009, the world market for video game consoles has reached an interesting stage. After over a decade of domination by Sony, Nintendo has emerged as the surprising winner in the seventh generation of video consoles. The case provides a history of competition in the industry and requires an analysis of key success factors in this winner-take-all industry. The success of Nintendo's Wii points to a significant change in the dynamics of competition in the industry. The balance of power between hardware and software suppliers has shifted, online game playing has grown, and the industry has lost several of its winner-take-all attributes. The three leading players—Nintendo, Microsoft and Sony—are gearing up for the next generation of video game consoles. To recommend strategies for each of the participants, the case requires an analysis of the potential for network externalities, the implications of changing technology and demographics, and the resource and capability strengths of each firm.

Toshiba's announcement of February 19, 2008 that it was stopping production of its HD-DVD marked the end of the standards war between Sony and Toshiba for leadership in the next generation of high capacity DVDs. This account of the two-year struggle between Toshiba and Sony offers insight into the dynamics of standards war and allows us to consider what Toshiba might have done differently in order to succeed against Sony's Blu-ray.

During 2009, the New York Times Company is struggling against declining revenues, large losses, and difficulties in refinancing its borrowings. These problems reflect both the current recession and the long-term decline in newspaper readership. The group address its financial problems through cost reduction while also seeking a new business model that addresses the shift of news readership and advertising from print media to the internet.

* This case was written by Robert M. Grant, Ellen A. Drost, and Stephen J.J. McGuire. It draws upon an earlier case by Ellen A. Drost, Stephen McGuire, Christina Eaves, Lisa Tousant, Sandy Johnson, Sheridan Mascarenhas and William Drescher.

The author and publisher gratefully acknowledge the permission granted to reproduce the copyright material in this book:

Tables 5.1, 5.5, and the Appendix in Chapter 5. Extracts taken from walmartstores.com. Used with permission of Wal-Mart Corporate Communications.

Tables 9.4 and 9.5. Taken from S. Buchholz, N. Fabio, A. Ileyassoff, L. Mang, and D. Visentin, "AirAsia – Tales from a Long-haul Low Cost Carrier," coursework submitted as part of the MSc international management degree, Bocconi University, May 31, 2009. Used with permission of the authors.

Case 17 draws extensively on M. L. Taylor, G. M. Puia, K. Ramaya, and M. Gengelback, "Outback Steakhouse Goes International," in A. A. Thompson and A. J. Strickland, *Strategic Management: Concepts and Cases*, 11th edn, McGraw-Hill, New York, 1999. Copyright © 1997 by case authors and North American Case Research Association. Used with permission of Marilyn L. Taylor.

Exhibit 19.1. Extract taken from "When Global Strategies Go Wrong," *Wall Street Journal Asia,* April 4, 2002. Used with permission.

Exhibit 22.2. Extract taken from Jordi Canals, "Universal Banks Need Careful Monitoring," *Financial Times,* October 19, 2008. Used with permission of Jordi Canals.

Appendix 22.3. Taken from Shawn Tully, "The Golden Age for Financial Services is Over," *Fortune,* September 29, 2008. Used with permission.

Exhibits 24.1 and 24.2. Extracts taken from www.gore.com. Used with permission of W. L. Gore & Associates.

Every effort has been made to trace copyright holders and to obtain their permission for the use of copyright material. The publisher apologizes for any errors or omissions in the above list and would be grateful if notified of any corrections that should be incorporated in future reprints or editions of this book.

Case 1 Madonna*

Desperately Seeking a Start

In July 1977, shortly before her nineteenth birthday, Madonna Louise Ciccone arrived in New York City with $35 in her pocket. She had left Ann Arbor where she was majoring in dance at the University of Michigan. The third of eight children, she was raised in the suburbs of Detroit; her mother had died when she was six years old. Her prospects in the world of show business looked poor. Apart from her training in dance, she had little musical background and no contacts.

Life in New York was a struggle. "I worked at Dunkin' Donuts, I worked at Burger King, I worked at Amy's. I had a lot of jobs that lasted one day. I always talked back to people and they'd fire me. I was a coat-check girl at the Russian Tea Room. I worked at a health club once a week."[1] She spent a few months training with the Alvin Ailey Dance Theater and had a succession of modeling engagements for photographers and artists. During 1979, Madonna began to explore New York's music and acting scenes. With boyfriend Dan Gilroy, his brother Ed and bassist Angie Smit, "Breakfast Club" was formed—Madonna sharing vocals and drums with Dan. For six months she was dancer and backup singer to French singing star Patrick Hernandez, accompanying him in Europe and North Africa. In August 1979, Madonna was offered the lead role in underground movie director Stephen Lewicki's low-budget film A *Certain Sacrifice*. She was paid $100.

After breaking up with Dan Gilroy, Madonna invited her former Michigan boyfriend, Steve Bray, to New York. They moved into the Music Building—a converted 12-storey building crammed with studios, rehearsal rooms and striving, impoverished young bands. Together they worked on writing songs and developing their sound while Madonna maintained a continuous stream of calls to managers, agents, record companies and club owners. Camille Barbone offered a management contract—but only for Madonna. However, Barbone was unable to deliver success fast enough for Madonna and after 18 months Madonna fired her.

Finding a Sound, Finding a Style

During 1981, Madonna's music and image moved in a new direction. Influenced by the emerging dance scene in New York, Madonna moved increasingly from Pretenders/Pat Benatar rock to the dance music that was sweeping New York clubs. In addition to working with Steve Bray to develop songs and mix demo tapes, she worked on her image—a form of glam-grunge that featured multilayered, multicolored combinations of thrift-store clothing together with scarves and junk jewelry. She adopted "Boy Toy" as her "tag name" and prominently displayed it on her belt buckle. It was a look that she would continue to develop with the help of jewelry designer Maripole. Her trademark look of messy, badly dyed hair, neon rubber bracelets, black lace bras, white lace gloves, and chunky belt buckles would soon be seen on teenage girls throughout the world.

Madonna was quick to recognize the commercial implications of the new musical wave. The dance clubs were crucial and the DJs were the gatekeepers. Armed with her demo tapes, Madonna and her friends frequented the hottest dance clubs where they would make a splash with their flamboyant clothing and provocative dancing. At Danceteria, one of the staff referred to her as a "heat-seeking missile targeting the hottest DJs." DJ Mark Kamins introduced her to Mike Rosenblatt and Seymour Stein of Sire Records, a division of Warner Records. A recording contract and $5000 were soon hers. The first release was a 12-inch single with different versions of *Everybody* on each side. The record was played extensively in dance clubs.

Madonna began working on her first album. Although she had allegedly promised longtime friend and music collaborator Steve Bray and DJ Mark Kamins the job of producer, she dumped both in favor of Warner Records' house producer, Reggie Lucas. Together with Warner Records' national dance promoter, Bobby Shaw, Madonna began a relentless round of courting DJs and pushing her record for play time. Central to the promotion plan was New York's number one DJ, John "Jellybean" Benitez, who Madonna began dating in November 1982.

Her second single, *Burning Up,* released in March 1983 was a dance-club hit, reaching number three in the dance charts. With the attention and resources of Warner Brothers, and a network of DJs, Madonna had most of the pieces she needed in place—but not quite. Early in 1983 she flew to Los Angeles to visit Freddie DeMann, then manager of megastar Michael Jackson. DeMann remembers the meeting vividly: "I was knocked off my feet. I've never met a more physical human being in my life." In a short time DeMann dropped Michael Jackson in favor of managing Madonna.

Breakthrough

The album *Madonna* was released in July 1983. By the end of 1983, the record was climbing the U.S. album charts supported by the success of single release *Holiday*. In April 1984, another single from the album, *Borderline,* reached the top ten. At Madonna's national TV debut on *American Bandstand*, presenter Dick Clark asked her, "What do you really want to do when you grow up?" "Rule the world," she replied.

Within little more than a year Madonna was part way there. The fall of 1984 saw Madonna filming in *Desperately Seeking Susan*. Although initially hired as support for the movie's star, Rosanna Arquette, Madonna progressively hijacked the movie. By the time the shooting was complete, it was essentially a movie about Madonna playing herself, wearing her own style of clothes, and featuring her own music. Its release coincided with a surge of Madonna-mania. Her second album, *Like a Virgin,* had gone triple platinum (over 3 million copies sold) in February 1985, while the singles charts featured a succession of individual tracks from the album. Madonna's first concert tour was a sell out. Her marriage to bad-boy actor Sean Penn on August 16, 1985 further reinforced her celebrity status. When Madonna took up residence in Los Angeles during 1985 she was already a star and seldom far from the popular press headlines.

Fame, Fortune, Notoriety

In the next two decades, little came between Madonna and her quest for fame. She released six albums between 1986 and 1990. The 16 single releases from these albums gave her a near-continuous presence in the charts, including a remarkable seven number-one hits. In the process, Madonna rejected the industry's conventional wisdom of "Find a winning formula and stick to it." Madonna's career was a continuous experimentation with new musical ideas and new images, and a constant quest for new heights of fame and acclaim. Having established herself as the queen of popular music, Madonna did not stop there. By the end of the 1980s she was destined to be "the most famous woman on the planet."

Madonna in Charge

Madonna's struggle for fame revealed a drive, determination and appetite for hard work that would characterize her whole career. "I'm tough, I'm ambitious, and I know exactly what I want—and if that makes me a bitch, that's okay," she told the

London *News of the World* newspaper in 1985. On the set of *Desperately Seeking Susan* she maintained a blistering pace. "During the shoot we'd often get home at 11:00 or 12:00 at night and have to be back at 6:00 or 7:00 the next morning. Half the time the driver would pick up Madonna at her health club. She'd get up at 4:30 in the morning to work out first."[2]

There was never any doubt as to who was in charge of managing and developing Madonna's career. While Madonna relied on some of the best minds and strongest companies in the entertainment business, there was little doubt as to who was calling the shots. Her swift exit from her marriage with Sean Penn further emphasized her unwillingness to allow messy personal relationships to compromise her career goals. For her third album—*True Blue*, released in June 1986—Madonna insisted on being co-producer.

The documentary of her 1990 "Blonde Ambition" tour, *Truth or Dare,*[3] clearly reveals her hands-on management style. The tour itself was a masterpiece of the pop concert as multimedia show embracing music, dance and theater. The tour's planning began in September 1989. Madonna was involved in every aspect of the show's design and planning, including auditioning dancers and musicians, planning, costume design, and choice of themes. For example, Madonna worked closely with Jean-Paul Gaultier on the metallic, cone-breasted costumes that became one of the tour's most vivid images. On the tour itself, the *Truth or Dare* movie revealed Madonna as both creative director and operations supremo. In addition to her obsessive attention to every detail of the show's production, she was the undisputed organizational leader responsible for building team spirit among the diverse group of dancers, musicians, choreographers and technicians; motivating the troupe when times were tough; resolving disputes between her fractious and highly strung male dancers and establishing the highest standards of commitment and effort.

The "Blonde Ambition" tour in the summer of 1990 marked new heights of international obsession with Madonna. The tour coincided with the release of *Dick Tracy*, the Disney movie that was a vehicle for the high-profile lovers, Madonna and Warren Beatty. The film did much to rectify a string of Hollywood flops and scathing reviews of Madonna's own acting capabilities. Madonna's portrayal of Breathless Mahoney exuded her natural talents for style and seductiveness.

Fame and Controversy

As a superstar, Madonna began increasingly to court notoriety, and push up against the boundaries of acceptability. Her overt sexuality together with audacious, expletive-laced talk, and use of crucifixes as items of jewelry raised disquiet within conservative and religious circles. Madonna's explanation only added fuel to the fire: "Crucifixes are sexy because there's a naked man on them." Among her efforts to enthrall and shock the American public, her *Like a Prayer* album, released in March 1989, proved to be a landmark.

Piggy-backing on Madonna-mania, Pepsi-Cola paid Madonna $5 million for a commercial based on the album's title track *Like a Prayer*. What Pepsi had not taken into account was that Madonna was making her own music video of *Like a Prayer* to accompany the launch of the record. The day after the first broadcast of the Pepsi commercial, Madonna's own *Like a Prayer* video appeared on MTV. The video was a stunning mixture of sex and religion that featured Madonna dancing in front of burning crosses, making love on an altar, and revealing stigmata on her hands.

Threatened by boycotts from Christian groups and the American Family Association, Pepsi pulled its Madonna commercial.

The explicit sexuality of the "Blonde Ambition" tour and its mixing of sexual and religious imagery resulted in Madonna achieving new heights of controversy—and public awareness. In Toronto, city authorities threatened to cancel the show. The Vatican condemned the show as "blasphemous." The *Justify My Love* video released in November 1990 set a new record for Madonna—it was banned by MTV for its portrayal of homosexuality, voyeurism, nudity, sado-masochism, and oral sex. Again, Madonna was quick to turn controversy into profit: the *Justify My Love* video was rush-released for retail sale, and the single soon topped the charts.

Sex also provided the basis for Madonna's entry into book publishing. Her photographic "art" book, *Sex,* featured Madonna in an array of sexual poses. Despite its high price ($49.95 for 120 pages) the book sold half a million copies in its first week.

Evita

Madonna has been compared to previous superstars and goddesses of sex and glamour—Greta Garbo, Marilyn Monroe, Mae West, Brigitte Bardot—but she has gone further in creating a persona that transcends her work as an entertainer. Those female superstars were defined by their movie roles. The big names in popular music, from Lena Horne to Janet Jackson, have been famous primarily for their music. Madonna achieved a status that was no longer defined by her work. By the 1990s, Madonna was no longer famous as a rock singer or an actress—she was famous for being Madonna. For the next decade she worked to reinforce this status. Strategically, superstar status has much to commend it. Joining the pantheon of superstars acts as insulation from comparison with lesser mortals. As her web site proclaims, she is "icon, artist, provocateur, diva, and mogul."

In her acting roles the key was to take roles that were primarily vehicles for Madonna to be Madonna. Her successes in *Desperately Seeking Susan* and *Dick Tracy* were the result of roles where Madonna could be herself. However, both these roles were to be eclipsed by Madonna's portrayal of Eva Peron in the movie version of the Andrew Lloyd Webber musical *Evita.* Madonna had coveted the role for years and mounted a vigorous campaign to gain the support of director Alan Parker and Argentine President Carlos Menem. While in previous roles Madonna had been able to use her talents as a singer, a poser, a sharp talker and a seductress; in *Evita* Madonna could present her own life. Like Madonna, Evita had working-class origins, a burning ambition, and had used sex and shrewd judgment to become a legend in her time. The film, released in December 1996, was a huge commercial and critical success. As *Q* magazine's Paul Du Noyer remarked, "If ever there was an ideal vehicle for Madonna's dream of transcendent stardom, this must be it."[4]

Motherhood and More

During most of the filming of *Evita*, Madonna was coping with her pregnancy. On October 14, 1996, she gave birth to Lourdes Maria Ciccone Leon at the Good Samaritan Hospital in Los Angeles. The baby's father was Carlos Leon, Madonna's personal trainer.

In terms of her life, image, and career, motherhood was a major discontinuity for Madonna. The press began reporting a host of lifestyle changes. Madonna abandoned pumping iron in favor of yoga. She began to study Kabbalah (a " mystical interpretation of the Old Testament," she explained). She developed a closer circle of women friends. She spent increasing amounts of time writing music. She became less available to the media. Her interviews were amazingly devoid of sex, expletives and shock value. "I think [motherhood] made me face up to my more feminine side. I had a much more masculine view of the world. What I missed and longed for was that unconditional love that a mother gives you. And so, having my daughter is the same kind of thing. It's like that first, true, pure, unconditional love."[5]

The clearest revelation of these changes was in Madonna's new album, *Ray of Light*, which was unlike any previous Madonna album. Working with William Orbit, the album incorporated a host of new influences: electronic music; traditional Indian music; Madonna's musings on the troubles of the world and the hollowness of fame; reflections on her own emotional development and her unhappy childhood. In performing tracks from the album both on TV and on video, Madonna revealed a series of entirely new looks including Madonna as Goth-girl (black hair, black clothes, black nail polish), Madonna as Shiva (multi-armed with henna tattoos on her hands), Madonna as geisha (straight black hair, kimono and white makeup).

The new persona was the most ambitious and risky reinvention of Madonna's career, insofar as it was the first that was not founded on sexuality and sexual aggression. Yet this transformation was met with no loss of popularity or worldwide acclaim. *Ray of Light* hit number two on the album charts and went triple platinum on the basis of U.S. sales alone. At the MTV Video Music Awards Madonna walked away with a total of six awards followed by three Grammy Awards.

Madonna as Mogul

Madonna's preoccupation with her "art" and her "freedom of artistic expression," has extended to an acute interest in her intellectual property rights. London's *Sunday Times* noted:

> Her early hits, "Holiday," "Like a Virgin" and "Papa Don't Preach," had been written by professional songwriters, who pocketed a quarter of the monies earned. Since 1986, and despite her limited musical ability, Madonna's has always been the first name to appear on her song credits. Her co-writers, meanwhile, have often been talented unknowns, like Pat Leonard, with whom she composed and performed her most successful album, the 24m-seller from 1986, True Blue. As soon as their names have benefited from the connection with her hits—and their asking price has consequently risen—she drops them and hires somebody new, and usually cheaper. [6]

Not only did Madonna maintain control over her own content—she increasingly wanted a cut in distribution. In April 1992 she signed a $60 million deal with Time Warner, Inc. The joint venture, Maverick Records, was a music production company (together with TV, video, and music publishing wings) that was to provide a vehicle for Madonna's creative and promotional talent. Warner Records provided distribution.

Although Madonna remained contracted to Warner Records for her own recordings, Maverick offered an avenue for her to develop and promote other singers and musicians. Among Maverick's early signings included Alanis Morissette, whose *Jagged Little Pill* album sold over 30 million copies, William Orbit, Prodigy, the Deftones, and Michelle Branch. Madonna also assisted in the U.S. launch of British comedian Sacha Baron Cohen (of Ali G and *Borat* fame).

Madonna's interest in new musicians and producing their music was linked to her own widening musical interests. Following *Ray of Light* Madonna became increasingly involved in both in electronic and world music, including collaboration with the French electro-boffin, Mirwais.

The Reinvention Goes On

During the first decade of the twenty-first century, neither Madonna's career nor her command over media attention showed much sign of flagging.

Madonna's family life continued to be a major focus of media interest. The birth of her second child, Rocco, was followed by marriage to Rocco's father, British actor and director Guy Ritchie. As a British resident, "Madge" became a staple feature for the British tabloid press.

Madonna also showed her ability to extend her media appeal beyond the celebrity-obsessed tabloids. Her adoption of a 13-month-old Malawian, David Banda, in October 2006, created a furor that engaged Third World politicians, anti-globalization activists, religious leaders and assorted intellectuals. Madonna became immersed in a global debate over "cash for babies" and "one law for the rich; another for the poor." A second adoption attempt, two years later, was blocked by the courts in Malawi.

On the career front, Madonna was quick to recognize the emerging business model in popular music. In the pre-digital world, live performances were primarily vehicles to publicize new album releases. Seeing the emergence of concert tours as dominant revenue stream, Madonna returned to concert touring in 2001. The "Drowned World" tour was followed by the "Re-invention" tour of 2004 and the "Confessions" tour of 2006.

When music revenues shifted from recordings to concerts, Madonna reorganized her own commercial arrangements. When Maverick began losing money (along with most other record companies), Madonna's exit was credited by industry observers as strategic brilliance. Maverick sued Warner Music for "improper accounting." Afraid of bad publicity and long-running litigation, Warner resolved the matter by buying out Madonna's share of Maverick for $10 million in 2004.

Free of Maverick, Madonna was able to court a new business partner. In 2007, she signed a $120 million, 10-year contract with Live Nation, the world's largest concert promotion company. "The business paradigm has shifted," she said upon signing. "As a creative artist and a businesswoman I have to acknowledge that." There seemed little doubt as who had gained the better part of the deal. Dismayed at the near-impossibility of making a profit from the deal, Live Nation was reported to be considering licensing Madonna's next album back to her old record company, Warner.

Madonna's "Sticky and Sweet" tour, which began in August 2008, set new standards in global scope, longevity, and revenue generation. With 85 concerts spanning every continent of the world except Australia over 14 months, the tour was forecast to gross over $400 million. Madonna's sell-out performances confirmed her ability to recruit a whole new generation of fans, many of whom had not been born when she recorded her debut album.

Outside of music, Madonna's artistic efforts met less success. A London stage performance in the comedy *Up for Grabs* and a movie co-starring with Guy Ritchie, *Swept Away*, were disasters. *The English Roses*, the first in series of children's books achieved modest commercial success.

Following the final concert of her "Sticky and Sweet" tour in September 2009, it seemed likely that Madonna would begin her next metamorphosis. With her divorce from Guy Ritchie finalized early in 2009, her "English gentlewoman" period was over. Part of the divorce settlement included the transfer of her 120-acre Wiltshire country mansion to Ritchie. What her next reincarnation would be was anyone's guess, however, as the London *Telegraph* noted: "What doesn't change, and hopefully never will, is Ms. Ciccone's hypercaffeineated zeal to make the world pay attention."[7]

Notes

1 M. Bego, *Madonna: Blonde Ambition*, Cooper Square, New York, 2000, p. 46.

2 C. Arrington, "Madonna," *People*, March 11, 1985.

3 Released as *In Bed With Madonna* outside North America.

4 "Commanding" (Review of Evita), *Q*, December, 1996, see www.pauldunoyer.com/pages/journalism/journalism_item.asp?journalismID=250, accessed October 29, 2009.

5 M. Murphy, "Madonna Confidential," *TV Guide*, April 11–17, 1998.

6 "Why Madonna's Still a Material Girl," *Sunday Times*, April 5, 2009, http://entertainment.timesonline.co.uk/-tol/arts_and_entertainment/music/article6015124.ece, accessed October 5, 2009.

7 "Madonna, Mistress of Metamorphosis," *Daily Telegraph*, August 10, 2008.

Case 2 Starbucks in 2009: The Coffee Goes Cold

After 20 years of continuous expansion accompanied by rising profits and a soaring stock price, Starbucks' downturn was unexpected and rapid. Starbucks' stock-market valuation was the leading indicator of the problems to come. After reaching a peak of $40 in October 2006, the share price declined by more than 75% over the next two years (see Figure 2.1). During 2007 growth of same-store sales and operating profits slowed. Amidst increasing concern over Starbucks' current strategy and future prospects, chairman and founder, Howard Schultz, returned as CEO at the beginning of 2008. His turnaround strategy comprised a sharp cutback in planned U.S. new store openings, revised operational and human resources practices aimed at improving customer service, "reigniting the connection with customers," and reallocating resources from the U.S. to overseas. In the summer of 2008, Schultz announced the closure of 600 U.S. stores and withdrawal from Australia.

FIGURE 2.1 Starbucks' share price and trading volume, 2000 to February 2009

Source: www.bigcharts.com

Starbucks' financial results for the year ending September 2008 revealed the damage being done by the economic downturn to same-store sales and margins. However, it was the results for the final quarter of 2008 that showed just how badly Starbucks was being hurt: net income was down by almost 70% and the company had experienced its first ever decline in quarterly revenues. Tables 2.1 and 2.2 show annual and quarterly results. The announcement prompted a 33c decline in Starbucks' share price to $9.33. Chairman and CEO Howard Schultz commented:

> In the midst of the weakening global consumer environment, Starbucks is following a well-developed plan to strengthen our business through more efficient operations and by preserving the fundamental strengths and values of our brand. We remain focused on driving the discipline and rigor necessary to create long-term shareholder value, and we are taking aggressive steps to excite customers by providing relevant value and innovation, even during this challenging time.[1]

CFO Troy Alstead, added:

> With a solid balance sheet, strong cash flow and healthy liquidity, Starbucks is well-positioned to weather the challenging global economy. We will continue to take the actions necessary to scale our cost structure to meet current business trends while positioning the company to drive margin expansion when the environment improves.[2]

Further retrenchment measures included: 300 store closures, 6700 job losses (including 700 in corporate and support positions), $500 million in operating cost savings for 2009 and a reduction in new openings of company-owned stores from 270 to 170. Schultz cut his own salary from $1.2 million to $10 000 and put two of Starbucks' three corporate jets up for sale.[3]

While deteriorating sales and profit performance could be blamed primarily on the global economic recession, Starbucks' languishing share price reflected broader concerns about the company's future. Had Starbucks' U.S. expansion resulted in excessive store density in some metropolitan areas? Had the growth of competition—not just from other specialist coffee chains but also from major fast-food chains such as McDonald's

TABLE 2.1 Starbucks Corporation: financial and operating performance 2004–8

Year ended September 30 (in $, millions)	2008 (52 weeks)	2007 (52 weeks)	2006 (52 weeks)	2005 (52 weeks)	2004 (53 weeks)
RESULTS OF OPERATIONS					
Net revenues:					
Company-operated retail	8771.9	7998.3	6583.1	5391.9	4457.4
Specialty:					
Licensing	1171.6	1026.3	860.6	673.0	565.8
Foodservice and other	439.5	386.9	343.2	304.4	271.0
Total specialty	1611.1	1413.2	1203.8	977.4	836.8
Total net revenues	10383.0	9411.5	7786.9	6369.3	5294.2
Cost of sales	4645.3	3999.1	3178.8	n.a.	n.a.
Store operating expenses	3745.1	3215.9	2687.8	n.a.	n.a.
Other operating expenses	330.1	294.2	253.7	n.a.	n.a.
Depreciation and amortization expenses	549.3	467.2	387.2	n.a.	n.a.
General and administrative expenses	456.0	489.2	479.4	n.a.	n.a.
Restructuring charges	266.9	—	—	n.a.	n.a.
Total operating expenses	9992.7	8465.6	6986.9	n.a.	n.a.
Operating income	503.9	1053.9	894.0	780.5	606.5
Net earnings	315.5	672.6	564.3	494.4	388.9
Net cash provided by operations activities	1258.7	1331.2	1131.6	922.9	862.9
Capital expenditures (net)	984.5	1080.3	771.2	643.3	416.9
BALANCE SHEET					
Working capital (deficit)	(441.7)	(459.1)	(405.8)	(17.7)	604.6
Total assets	5672.6	5343.9	4428.9	3513.7	3386.3
Short-term borrowings	713.0	710.3	700.0	277.0	—
Long-term debt	550.3	550.9	2.7	3.6	4.4
Shareholders' equity	2490.9	2284.1	2228.5	2090.3	2469.9
STORE INFORMATION					
Percentage change in same store sales:					
United States (%)	(5)	4	7	9	11
International (%)	2	7	8	6	6
Consolidated (%)	(3)	5	7	8	10
Stores opened during the year (net) of closures):					
United States					
Company-operated stores	445	1065	810	580	521
Licensed stores	438	723	733	596	417
International					
Company-operated stores	236	286	240	177	160
Licensed stores	550	497	416	319	246
Total	1669	2571	2199	1672	1344

TABLE 2.2 Starbucks Corporation: consolidated statement of earnings, final quarter 2008

($ millions) 13 weeks to:	Dec 28, 2008	Dec 30, 2007
Net revenues:		
Company-operated retail	2176.2	2351.5
Specialty:		
Licensing	334.3	304.8
Food service and other	104.7	111.3
Total specialty	439.0	416.1
Total net revenues	2615.2	2767.6
Cost of sales (including occupancy costs)	1196.8	1186.0
Store operating expenses	936.6	927.3
Other operating expenses	72.6	85.7
Depreciation and amortization expenses	134.3	133.2
General and administrative expenses	105.2	125.9
Restructuring charges	75.5	—
Total operating expenses	2521.0	2458.1
Operating income	117.7	333.1
Interest expense	(13.0)	(17.1)
Earnings before income taxes	98.3	326.7
Income taxes	34.0	118.6
Net earnings	64.3	208.1

and Dunkin' Donuts, which had added gourmet coffee to their menus—fundamentally changed the attractiveness of the retail market for brewed coffee? Had Starbucks failed to maintain the uniqueness of the "Starbucks Experience," which had differentiated the company from its competitors? And was this "Starbucks Experience" something that was really recognized and valued by consumers?

The Starbucks Story[4]

The rise of Starbucks from a single coffee store in Seattle's Pike Place market to a Fortune 500 company (number 261 on Fortune's 2009 listing) is now an American business legend.

Howard Schultz lived in New York where he managed the U.S. operations of a Swedish kitchenware company. Intrigued as to why a small Seattle company, Starbucks Coffee, Tea and Spice, was ordering large quantities of an unusual kind of coffee filter—a plastic cone on top of a thermos—he visited the store in 1981. The cup of coffee he was given there, made with freshly ground Sumatra beans, was a revelation. "I realized the coffee I had been drinking was swill." The owner-managers of Starbucks were Gerald Baldwin and Gordon Bowker, former University of San Francisco students who had been running the company for 10 years. Schultz was captivated by the vision of a national chain of coffee stores. Despite their reservations about the threat of Schultz's energy and ambition to the mellow ambiance of their business, Baldwin and Bowker eventually hired Schultz as their head of marketing.

Within a year of joining Starbucks, Schultz's vision of the company shifted radically. On a business trip to Milan he discovered "the romance of the Italian coffee bar" and recognized the opportunity for Starbucks to be a place where people would come to share the experience of drinking great coffee rather than to simply buy coffee beans. "It crystallized in my mind that coffee brought people together . . . and that as far as I could envision, at the time there did not exist in the U.S. a place that brought people together with coffee as the conduit."

Unable to convince his Starbucks bosses of his vision, Schultz left to open his own Italian coffee bar, Il Giornale, in 1986. A year later he bought the Starbucks company and its six stores, merged it with his three Il Giornale bars and adopted the Starbucks name for the enlarged company. By the time Starbucks went public in 1992 it had grown to 165 outlets. With the $27 million raised from the stock offering, Starbucks accelerated its expansion. From its west-coast bases in Seattle and Vancouver, Starbucks expanded nationally in both the U.S. and Canada. Expansion followed a cluster pattern—opening multiple stores in a single metro area. The idea was to increase Starbucks' local brand awareness and facilitate customers' ability to find a Starbucks anywhere within their home town. International expansion included entry into Japan in 1996 and the U.K. in 1998.

Starbucks' organic growth was augmented by selected acquisitions: the U.K.-based Seattle Coffee Company in 1998, Seattle's Best Coffee and Torrefazione Italia in 2003, and Diedrich Coffee in 2006.

Starbucks' Strategy

The Appendix describes Starbucks' business and provides data on its performance.

The Starbucks Experience

Central to Starbucks' strategy is Schultz's concept of the "Starbucks Experience." Starbucks stores—like the original Il Giornata coffee bars—were founded on Schultz's idea of creating a "third place": somewhere other than home and work where people could engage socially amidst the shared experience of drinking good coffee. Despite his original idea of replicating Italian coffee bars where customers mostly stand to drink coffee, Schultz adapted his vision to "the American equivalent of the English pub, the German beer garden and the French café."[5] With the addition of wi-fi, Starbucks stores become a place to work as well as to socialize. The Starbucks Experience combined a number of elements:

- The coffee beans of high, consistent quality. As explained in the Appendix under "Product Supply," Starbucks forms long-term arrangements with coffee growers in order to ensure that Starbucks' requirements are met while ensuring the economic viability of the growers.
- Employee involvement. The counter staff at Starbucks stores—the baristas—played a central role in creating and sustaining the Starbucks Experience. Their role was not only to brew and serve excellent coffee but to engage customers in the unique ambiance of the Starbucks coffee shop. Starbucks' human-resource practices with regard to firing, training and remunerations

were very different from those of other U.S. restaurant chains. "Schultz felt he had to make employees partners in his vision. He had to infuse them with the Starbucks culture, provide them with personal security, and give them a reason to be involved in the success of the business."[6] Starbucks' employee selection was careful and rigorous—placing a heavy emphasis on adaptability, dependability, capacity for teamwork and willingness to further Starbucks' principles and mission. Its training program extended beyond basic operating and customer-service skills to educating employees abut coffee. Unique among catering chains, Starbucks provided health insurance for almost all regular employees.

- Community relations and social purpose. Schultz's approach to human resource management was not simply about the role of Starbucks' employees as key agents in transmitting the Starbucks' Experience, but also part of a broader vision of a common humanity: "I wanted to build the kind of company my father never had the chance to work for, where you would be valued and respected wherever you came from, whatever the color of your skin, whatever your level of education. Offering heathcare was a transforming event in the equity of the Starbucks brand that created unbelievable trust among our people. We wanted to build a company that linked shareholder value to the cultural values that we want to create with our people."[7] Schulz's vision was of a company that would earn good profits but would also do good in the world: "Perhaps we have the opportunity to be a different type of global company. One that makes a profit but at the same time demonstrates a social conscience."
- The layout and design of Starbucks stores were seen as critical elements of the experience. Starbucks has a store design group that is responsible for the design of the furniture, fittings and layout of Starbucks' retail outlets. Like everything else at Starbucks, store design is subject to meticulous analysis and planning—following Schultz's dictum that "retail is detail." While every Starbucks store is adapted to reflect its unique neighborhood, "there is a subliminal unifying theme to all the stores that ties into the company's history and mission—"back to nature" without the laid-back attitude; community-minded without stapled manifestos on the walls. The design of a Starbucks store is intended to provide both unhurried sociability and efficiency on-the-run, an appreciation for the natural goodness of coffee and the artistry that grabs you even before the aroma. This approach is reflected in the designers' generous employment of natural woods and richly layered, earthy colors along with judicious high-tech accessorizing . . . No matter how individual the store, overall store design seems to correspond closely to the company's first and evolving influences: the clean, unadulterated crispness of the Pacific Northwest combined with the urban suavity of an espresso bar in Milan."[8]
- Starbucks' location strategy—its clustering of 20 or more stores in each urban hub—was viewed as enhancing the experience both in creating a local "Starbucks buzz" and in facilitating loyalty by Starbucks' customers. Starbucks' analysis of sales by individual store found little evidence that closely located Starbucks stores cannibalized one another's sales. Recognizing that convenience of location was critical to driving sales, Starbucks began adding drive-though windows to some of its stores and locating stores specifically to capitalize on drive-through customers.

Diversification

Broadening Starbucks' product range was partly about responding to customer demand (for example, requests for iced coffee eventually led to Frappuccino) and partly about building the Starbucks Experience. "The overall strategy is to build Starbucks into a destination," explained Kenneth Lombard, then head of Starbucks Entertainment. This involved adding food, music, books and videos. As a music publisher and retailer of CDs, Starbucks was hugely successful—particularly its "Artists Choice" series where well-known musicians chose their favorite tracks. "I had to get talked into this one," says Schultz. "But then I began to understand that our customers looked to Starbucks as a kind of editor. It was like, 'We trust you. Help us choose.'"

However, Starbucks was also expanding beyond its company-owned stores. As the Appendix illustrates, Starbucks expansion has included:

- Licensed stores. The desire to reach customers in a variety of locations eventually caused Starbucks to abandon its policy of only selling through company-owned outlets. Its first licensing deal was with Host Marriot, which owned a number of food and beverage concessions in U.S. airports. This was followed by licensing arrangements with Safeway and Barnes & Noble for opening Starbucks coffee shops in their stores. Overseas, Starbucks increasingly relied upon licensing arrangements with local companies.
- Distribution of Starbucks retail packs of Starbucks coffee through supermarkets and other retail food stores.
- Licensing of Starbucks brands to PepsiCo and Unilever for the supply of Starbucks bottled drinks (such as Frappuccino and Tazo teas).
- Financial services, notably the Starbucks/Bank One Duetto Visa card, which combined a store card with a Visa credit card.
- *Via* instant coffee. On February 12, 2009, news broke of Starbucks' plan to introduce an innovative instant coffee. The product was the result of long-term R&D project that had been revived by Schultz as part of his drive to reinvigorate innovation at Starbucks. *Via* was based upon a proprietary patented process which allowed the company to "absolutely replicate the taste of Starbucks coffee." It would sell through Starbucks stores at $2.95 for a pack of three. Other commentators were less sanguine. Andrew Hetzel of coffee consultancy Cafemakers, stated: "I have an expectation of what it will be like, and I think it will be harmful for the brand."[9]

Managing Turnaround

Since his return as CEO in January 2008, Schultz's redirection of Starbucks' strategy has involved more than retrenchment. Central to his hyperactive leadership was his belief that the company needed to rediscover and revitalize the "Starbucks Experience" and reestablish its connection with its customers.

During 2008, Starbucks employees from all parts and all levels of the company met to reconsider the company's purpose and principles. The result was a revised mission statement (see the Appendix). Also important to the reaffirmation of Starbucks' core identity was a renewed emphasis on corporate social responsibility.

In October 2008, Starbucks held its annual leadership meeting in New Orleans—the first time the meeting had been held outside Seattle. Starbucks used the convention as an opportunity to field 10 000 volunteers on a variety of community projects ranging from repainting damaged houses to cleaning up neighborhoods. Other initiatives included:

- *Starbucks Shared Planet*— a set of environmental sustainability, community service and ethical targets to be achieved by 2011.
- Increased commitment to small-scale coffee farmers by doubling Starbucks purchases of Fair Trade Certified Coffee in 2009.
- Partnership with Bono and the Global Fund to donate 5 cents from the sale of each serving of certain Starbucks' beverages to support AIDS programs in Africa.

Schultz also reviewed operating practices to examine their consistency with the Starbucks Experience and Starbucks image. One key change was a return to "hand-made" coffee. To speed coffee making Starbucks had replaced its La Marzocco espresso machines, which required baristas to grind coffee for each cup, with automatic Verismo machines, which merely required baristas to press a button. During 2008, Starbucks spent millions installing new coffee machines where cups of coffee were made individually from freshly ground beans. Schultz also insisted on revising Starbucks' food menu—notably withdrawing toasted breakfast sandwiches whose aromas masked those of the coffee: "The breakfast sandwiches drive revenue and profit but they are in conflict with everything we stand for in terms of the coffee and the romance of the coffee."

Most of all, Schultz traveled Starbuck's far-flung empire meeting with employees ("partners") with a view to reinforcing Starbucks' values and reigniting their drive and enthusiasm. Jenny Wiggins of the *Financial Times* describes an October 2008 meeting at London's Barbican Center for 1000 Starbucks store managers from Britain and Ireland. In addition to inspiring tales that exemplified the "humanity of Starbucks" and the role that managers played in creating an experience that "values and respects" customers, Schultz challenged his store managers with the severity of the current situation and the need to return to the values and practices that had made Starbucks a special place.[10]

By re-emphasizing Starbucks' core values, reversing store expansion, eliminating non-core products and returning to the quality of the coffee and customer service, Schultz was doing much to correct the errors of the past. The question is whether the Starbucks concept has the same distinctiveness and appeal in the second decade of the twenty-first century as in the last decade of the twentieth century. According to Don Williams, CEO of brand consultants Pi Global: "Starbucks must seriously and rapidly re-evaluate what the brand stands for, what it sells, and what the consumer experience should be. Far from exuding an air of everyday indulgence, the often slightly dog-eared assembly line that is your average Starbucks store is suffering the double whammy of being both too familiar and overpriced."

Even if Schultz succeeds in reinvigorating Starbucks, it is clear that the market for gourmet coffee, especially in North America, has changed greatly over the past two decades. Despite a widely held view that Starbucks has saturated its market, it is clear that competition is strong, with Starbucks being attacked from below (McDonald's, Dunkin' Donuts) and above (Illy, Lavazza) (see Exhibit 2.1).

EXHIBIT 2.1

Competition in the U.S. Coffee Shop Market

Sales of premium, brewed coffee were estimated to have grown by 157% between 2000 ($3258 million) and 2005 to reach some $8372 million. The total number of coffee shops in the U.S. increased by 70% between 2000 and 2005, bringing the total to a staggering 21400 or one coffee house for every 14000 Americans.

Although Starbucks was the primary driver of this growth and far-and-away the market leader, it was also subject to competition from numerous directions.

- Starbucks' traditional competitors were independent coffee shops and cafes, some of which had grown into local chains.
- Starbucks had also spawned a number of imitators who aspired to grow into national chains. Of these Caribou Coffee, with 495 coffee shops in 15 states, was its nearest competitor.
- Starbucks competed with a range of catering establishments that supplied coffee as part of a broader menu of food and beverages. Increasingly these outlets were seeking to compete more directly with Starbucks by adding premium coffee drinks to their menus. McDonald's had introduced a premium coffee (which *Consumer Reports* rated more highly than Starbucks' coffee) and was adding *McCafes* to many of its burger restaurants. Burger King and Dunkin' Donuts had also moved upmarket in their coffee offerings. McDonald's and Dunkin' Donuts both targeted Starbucks in their advertising. The McDonald's web site, Unsnobbycoffee.com implicitly identified Starbucks as overpriced and "snobbish." Dunkin' Donuts' web site, DunkinbeatStarbucks.com, encourages emailed messages such as: "Friends don't let friends drink at Starbucks."

Outside of the U.S., Starbucks faced different competitive situations country-by-country. In most of them competition was even more intense than in the U.S. Starbucks' withdrawal from Australia was a consequence of a highly sophisticated coffee market developed and educated by immigrants from southern Europe (Italy in particular) and the Middle East.

High standards of coffee preparation and strong local preferences were also a feature of most European markets. Moreover, Starbucks also had to contend with international expansion by the Italian coffee roasters—most notably Illy, which had successfully established itself at the pinnacle of quality. A key challenge that Starbucks faced is that, once it had educated North Americans about the joy of good coffee, these new coffee connoisseurs would go on to seek superior alternatives to Starbucks.

Competition was not only in the form of other coffee-shop chains. Increasingly coffee drinkers were being introduced to the secrets of good coffee at home. A widening range of home espresso makers included sophisticated, easy-to-use coffee systems introduced by Nescafé (Nespresso) and Lavazza (A Modo Mio).

TABLE 2.3 Starbucks, Caribou Coffee and McDonald's: Financial Comparisons, 2005–8

	Starbucks, year ended				Caribou Coffee, year ended				McDonald's, year ended			
	August 2008	*August 2007*	*August 2006*	*August 2005*	*December 2008*	*December 2007*	*December 2006*	*December 2005*	*December 2008*	*December 2007*	*December 2006*	*December 2005*
Sales ($m)	10383	9411	7787	6369	253.9	256.8	236.2	198.0	23522	22787	20895	19117
Depreciation and amortization ($m)	549	467	389	n.a.	24.9	32.2	21.5	16.4	1208	1193	1191	1172
General and admin. expense ($m)	456	489	479	n.a.	29.1	32.3	25.9	22.7	2355	2367	2296	2118
Operating income ($m)	504	1,054	894	781	(15.5)	(30.4)	(9.5)	(4.1)	6443	3879	4433	3984
Net income ($m)	316	673	564	494	(16.3)	(30.7)	(9.1)	(4.9)	4313	2395	3544	2602
Company operated outlets	9217	8536	7185	6135	414	432	440	386	6502	6906	8166	8173
Total outlets	16680	15011	12440	10241	511	484	464	395	31967	31377	31 046	30766
Sales per co. outlet	0.988	1.018	0.988	0.953	0.553	0.551	0.546	0.554	2547	2.204	1.885	1.715
Total assets ($m)	5673	5344	4429	3514	89.6	111.8	136.3	148.0	28462	29392	28 974	29989
Shareholders' equity ($m)	2491	2284	2229	2090	43.9	59.3	88.4	96.9	13382	15280	15 458	15146

Appendix: Extracts from Starbucks Corporation 10-K report for Fiscal Year 2008

Part I

Item 1: Business

General Starbucks Corporation was formed in 1985 and today is the world's leading roaster and retailer of specialty coffee. Starbucks (together with its subsidiaries, "Starbucks" or the "Company") purchases and roasts high-quality whole bean coffees and sells them, along with fresh, rich-brewed coffees, Italian-style espresso beverages, cold blended beverages, a variety of complementary food items, a selection of premium teas, and coffee-related accessories and equipment, primarily through Company-operated retail stores. Starbucks also sells coffee and tea products and licenses its trademark through other channels such as licensed retail stores and, through certain of its equity investees and licensees, Starbucks produces and sells a variety of ready-to-drink beverages. All channels outside the Company-operated retail stores are collectively known as specialty operations.

The Company's objective is to establish Starbucks as one of the most recognized and respected brands in the world. To achieve this goal, the Company plans to continue disciplined expansion of its retail operations, to grow its specialty operations and to selectively pursue other opportunities by introducing new products and developing new channels of distribution.

Revenue Components The following table shows the Company's revenue components as a percentage of total net revenues and related specialty revenues for the fiscal year ended September 28, 2008:

Revenues	Percentage of total net revenues	Percentage of specialty revenues
Company-operated retail	84	
Specialty:		
Licensing:		
Retail stores	8	48 %
Packaged coffee and tea	3	21 %
Branded products	1	4 %
Total licensing	12	73 %
Foodservice and other:		
Foodservice	4	25 %
Other initiatives	<1	2 %
Total foodservice and other	4	27 %
Total specialty	16	100 %
Total net revenues	100	

Company-operated Retail Stores The Company's retail goal is to become the leading retailer and brand of coffee in each of its target markets by selling the finest quality coffee and related products and by providing each customer a unique

Starbucks Experience. The *Starbucks Experience*, or third place beyond home and work, is built upon superior customer service as well as clean and well maintained Company-operated retail stores that reflect the personalities of the communities in which they operate, thereby building a high degree of customer loyalty.

Starbucks' strategy for expanding its retail business is to increase its market share by selectively opening additional stores in existing markets and opening stores in new markets to support its long-term strategic objectives. As described in more detail in Management's Discussion and Analysis in this 10-K, the Company committed in June 2008 to close approximately 600 underperforming Company-operated stores in the U.S. The decision was an integral part of its transformation strategy, first announced in January 2008, and was a result of a rigorous evaluation of the U.S. Company-operated store portfolio. The store closures were initiated in the fourth quarter of fiscal 2008 and are expected to be completed by the end of fiscal 2009.

Starbucks Company-operated retail stores accounted for 84% of total net revenues during fiscal 2008. The following table summarizes total Company-operated retail store data for the periods indicated:

	Net stores opened year ended		Stores open as of	
	Sept. 28, 2008	**Sept. 30, 2007**	**Sept. 28, 2008**	**Sept. 30, 2007**
United States	445	1065	7238	6793
Canada	104	97	731	627
United Kingdom	84	66	664	580
China	37	42	178	141
Germany	27	36	131	104
Thailand	24	18	127	103
Singapore	12	8	57	45
Australia	(64)	4	23	87
Other	12	15	68	56
Total international	236	286	1979	1743
Total Company-operated	681	1351	9217	8536

At the end of fiscal 2008, the Company operated approximately 2800 drive-through locations, compared to approximately 2300 at the end of fiscal 2007, representing approximately 35% and 31%, respectively, of Company-operated stores in the U.S. and Canada combined.

All Starbucks stores offer a choice of regular and decaffeinated coffee beverages, a broad selection of Italian-style espresso beverages, cold blended beverages, iced shaken refreshment beverages, a selection of premium teas and distinctively packaged roasted whole bean coffees. Starbucks stores also offer a variety of fresh food items, including several healthy choice selections. Food items include pastries, prepared breakfast and lunch sandwiches, and salads as well as sodas, juices, and bottled water. Starbucks continues to expand its food warming program in the United States and Canada, with approximately half of these stores as of September 28, 2008 providing warm food items, primarily breakfast sandwiches. A range of coffee-making equipment and accessories are also sold in the stores. Each Starbucks store varies its product mix depending upon the size of the store and its location. Larger stores carry a broad selection of the Company's whole-bean coffees in various sizes and types of packaging, as well as coffee and espresso-making equipment and accessories. Smaller Starbucks stores and kiosks typically sell a full line of coffee beverages, a limited selection of whole-bean coffees and a few accessories such as travel tumblers and logo mugs.

Retail sales mix by product type for Company-operated stores was as follows:

Fiscal year ended	Sept. 28, 2008	Sept. 30, 2007	Oct. 1, 2006
Beverages (%)	76	75	77
Food (%)	17	17	15
Coffee-making equipment and other merchandise (%)	4	5	5
Whole bean coffees (%)	3	3	3
Total (%)	100	100	100

Specialty Operations Specialty operations strive to develop the Company's brands outside the Company-operated retail store environment through a number of channels. Starbucks strategy is to reach customers where they work, travel, shop and dine by establishing relationships with prominent third parties that share the Company's values and commitment to quality. These relationships take various forms, including licensing arrangements, foodservice accounts and other initiatives related to the Company's core businesses. In certain situations, Starbucks has an equity ownership interest in licensee operations. During fiscal 2008, specialty revenues (which include royalties and fees from licensees, as well as product sales derived from specialty operations) accounted for 16% of total net revenues.

Licensing—Retail Stores In its licensed retail store operations, the Company leverages the expertise of its local partners and shares Starbucks operating and store development experience. Licensee partners provide improved and, at times, the only access to desirable retail space. Most licensees are prominent retailers with in-depth market knowledge and access. As part of these arrangements, Starbucks receives license fees and royalties and sells coffee, tea and related products for resale in licensed locations. Employees working in licensed retail locations are required to follow Starbucks detailed store operating procedures and attend training classes similar to those given to employees in Company-operated stores.

During fiscal 2008, 438 Starbucks licensed retail stores were opened in the U.S. and, as of September 28, 2008, the Company's U.S. licensees operated 4329 stores. During fiscal 2008, 550 International licensed stores were opened. At September 28, 2008, the Company's international operating segment had a total of 3134 licensed retail stores. Product sales to and royalty and license fee revenues from U.S. and international licensed retail stores accounted for 48% of specialty revenues in fiscal 2008.

At fiscal year end 2008, Starbucks total licensed retail stores by region and specific location were as follows:

Asia Pacific		Europe/Middle East/Africa		Americas	
Japan	814	Turkey	107	United States	4329
China	269	Spain	76	Mexico	241
South Korea	254	Greece	76	Canada	231
Taiwan	221	United Arab Emirates	69	Other	44
Philippines	150	Saudi Arabia	65		
Malaysia	113	Kuwait	57		
Indonesia	69	France	46		
New Zealand	43	Switzerland	42		
		Other	147		
Total	1933	Total	685	Total	4845

Licensing—Packaged Coffee and Tea Through a licensing relationship with Kraft Foods, Inc. ("Kraft"), the Company sells a selection of Starbucks and Seattle's Best Coffee branded packaged coffees and Tazo® teas in grocery and warehouse club stores throughout the United States. Kraft manages all distribution, marketing, advertising and promotion of these products.

The Company sells packaged coffee and tea internationally both directly to warehouse club customers, such as Costco, and through a licensing relationship with Kraft in Canada and the U.K.

By the end of fiscal 2008, the Company's coffees and teas were available in approximately 37 000 grocery and warehouse club stores, with 33 000 in the U.S. and 4000 in international markets. Revenues from this category comprised 21% of specialty revenues in fiscal 2008.

Licensing—Branded Products The Company licenses the rights to produce and market Starbucks branded products through several partnerships both domestically and internationally. Significant licensing agreements include:

- the North American Coffee Partnership, a joint venture with the Pepsi-Cola Company in which Starbucks is a 50% equity investor, manufactures and markets ready-to-drink beverages, including bottled Frappuccino® beverages and Starbucks DoubleShot® espresso drinks;
- licensing agreements for the manufacturing, marketing and distribution of Starbucks Discoveries®, a ready-to-drink chilled cup coffee beverage, in Japan and South Korea;
- a licensing agreement established in August 2008 with Unilever and Pepsi-Cola Company for the manufacturing, marketing and distribution of Starbucks super-premium Tazo® Tea ready-to-drink beverages in the U.S. and Canada;
- the International Coffee Partnership, another joint venture with the Pepsi-Cola Company, to manufacture, market and distribute ready-to-drink beverages internationally, which currently includes bottled Frappuccino® beverages in China and Mexico.

Collectively, the revenues from these branded products accounted for 4% of specialty revenues in fiscal 2008.

Foodservice The Company sells whole bean and ground coffees, including the Starbucks and Seattle's Best Coffee brands, as well as a selection of premium Tazo® teas and other related products, to institutional foodservice companies that service business and industry, education, healthcare, office coffee distributors, hotels, restaurants, airlines and other retailers. The majority of the Company's direct accounts are through national broadline distribution networks with SYSCO Corporation and U.S. Foodservice. Starbucks foodservice sales, customer service and support resources are aligned with those of SYSCO Corporation and U.S. Foodservice.

The Company's total foodservice operations had over 19 000 accounts, primarily in the U.S., at fiscal year end 2008. Revenues from foodservice accounts comprised 25% of total specialty revenues in fiscal 2008.

Product Supply Starbucks is committed to selling only the finest whole-bean coffees and coffee beverages. To ensure compliance with its rigorous coffee standards, Starbucks controls its coffee purchasing, roasting and packaging, and the distribution of coffee used in its operations. The Company purchases green coffee beans from coffee-producing regions around the world and custom roasts them to its exacting standards for its many blends and single origin coffees.

The supply and price of coffee are subject to significant volatility. Although most coffee trades in the commodity market, high-altitude *arabica* coffee of the quality sought by the Company tends to trade on a negotiated basis at a substantial premium above commodity coffee prices, depending upon the supply and demand at the time of purchase. Supply and price can be affected by multiple factors in the producing countries, including weather, political and economic conditions. In addition, green coffee prices have been affected in the past and may be affected in the future, by the actions of certain organizations and associations that have historically attempted to influence prices of green coffee through agreements establishing export quotas or by restricting coffee supplies.

To help ensure sustainability and future supply of high-quality green coffees in Central America and to reinforce the Company's leadership role in the coffee industry, Starbucks operates the Starbucks Coffee Agronomy Company.

SRL is a wholly owned subsidiary located in Costa Rica. Staffed with agronomists and sustainability experts, this first-of-its-kind Farmer Support Center is designed to respond proactively to changes in coffee-producing countries that impact farmers and the supply of green coffee. During fiscal 2008, the Company expanded this sustainability program to Africa by establishing a Farmer Support Center in Rwanda.

The Company buys coffee using fixed-price and price-to-be-fixed purchase commitments, depending on market conditions, to secure an adequate supply of quality green coffee. Due to volatility in green coffee commodity prices, the Company has historically used fixed-price purchase contracts in order to bring greater certainty to its cost of sales in future periods and promote sustainability by paying an equitable price to coffee producers. When green coffee commodity prices are high for sustained periods of time, the Company is less likely to enter into fixed-price contracts on favorable terms and more likely to increase the use of price-to-be-fixed contracts to meet its demand for coffee. These types of contracts state the quality, quantity and delivery periods and fix the price relative to a green coffee commodity benchmark, but allow the benchmark price to be established after contract signing. An increased use of price-to-be-fixed contracts instead of fixed-price contracts decreases the predictability of coffee costs in future periods until the price of green coffee becomes "fixed" by either Starbucks or the seller.

The Company depends upon its relationships with coffee producers, outside trading companies and exporters for its supply of green coffee. The Company believes, based on relationships established with its suppliers, the risk of non-delivery on such purchase commitments is remote.

Operating Segments Segment information is prepared on the same basis that the Company's management reviews financial information for operational decision-making purposes. Starbucks has three reportable operating segments: U.S., international and CPG . . .

United States The U.S. operating segment sells coffee and other beverages, complementary food, whole bean coffees, and coffee-brewing equipment and merchandise primarily through Company-operated retail stores. Specialty operations within the U.S include licensed retail stores, foodservice accounts and other initiatives related to the Company's core business.

Fiscal year ended	Sept. 2008 ($ millions)	Sept. 2007 ($ millions)	Change (%)	Sept. 2008	Sept. 2007
				(As percentage of U.S. total net revenues)	
Net revenues:					
Company-operated retail	6997.7	6560.9	6.7	88.7	89.3
Specialty:					
Licensing	504.2	439.1	14.8	6.4	6.0
Foodservice and other	385.1	349.0	10.3	4.9	4.7
Total specialty	889.3	788.1	12.8	11.3	10.7
Total net revenues	7887.0	7349.0	7.3	100.0	100.0

Company-operated retail revenues increased primarily due to the opening of 445 new Company-operated retail stores in the last 12 months, partially offset by a 5% decrease in comparable store sales for fiscal 2008. The U.S. Company-operated retail business continued to experience deteriorating trends in transactions during the year, driven by the U.S. economic slowdown.

Licensing revenues increased primarily due to higher product sales and royalty revenues as a result of opening 438 new licensed retail stores in the last 12 months. Foodservice and other revenues increased primarily due to growth in new and existing foodservice accounts.

Fiscal year ended	Sept. 2008 ($ millions)	Sept. 2007 ($ millions)	Change (%)	Sept. 2008	Sept. 2007
				(As percentage of U.S. total net revenues)	
Cost of sales including occupancy costs	3371.7	2956.2	14.1	42.8	40.2
Store operating expenses[a]	3081.0	2684.2	14.8	39.1	36.5
Other operating expenses[b]	219.6	204.8	7.2	2.8	2.8
Depreciation and amortization expenses	401.7	348.2	15.4	5.1	4.7
General and administrative expenses	72.7	85.9	(15.4)	0.9	1.2
Restructuring charges	210.9	—	nm	2.7	—
Total operating expenses	7357.6	6279.3	17.2	93.3	85.4
Income from equity investees	(1.3)	0.8	nm	—	
Operating income	528.1	1070.5	(50.7)%	6.7%	14.6%

[a] As a percentage of related Company-operated retail revenues, store operating expenses were 44.0% and 40.9% for the fiscal years ended September 28, 2008 and September 30, 2007, respectively.

[b] As a percentage of related total specialty revenues, other operating expenses were 24.7% and 26.0% for the fiscal years ended September 28, 2008 and September 30, 2007, respectively.

Operating margin contracted significantly primarily due to restructuring charges incurred and to softer revenues due to weak traffic, as well as higher cost of sales including occupancy costs and higher store-operating expenses as a percentage of revenues. Restructuring charges of $210.9 million had a 270 basis point impact on the operating margin. The increase in cost of sales including occupancy costs was primarily due to higher distribution costs and higher rent expenses as a percentage of revenues. Higher store operating expenses was due to the softer sales, higher payroll-related expenditures and charges from canceling future store sites and asset impairments.

International The international operating segment sells coffee and other beverages, complementary food, whole-bean coffees, and coffee brewing equipment and merchandise through Company-operated retail stores in Canada, the U.K. and nine other markets. Specialty operations primarily include retail store licensing operations in nearly 40 other countries and foodservice accounts, primarily in Canada and Japan. The Company's international store base continues to increase and Starbucks expects to achieve a growing contribution from established areas of the business while investing in emerging markets and channels. Many of the Company's international operations are in early stages of development that require a more extensive support organization, relative to the current levels of revenue and operating income, than in the U.S. This continuing investment is part of the Company's long-term, balanced plan for profitable growth.

Fiscal year ended	Sept. 2008 ($ millions)	Sept. 2007 ($ millions)	Change (%)	Sept. 2008	Sept. 2007
				(As a percentage of international total net revenues)	
Net revenues:					
Company-operated retail	1774.2	1437.4	23.4	84.3	84.7
Specialty:					
Licensing	274.8	220.9	24.4	13.1	13.0
Foodservice and other	54.4	37.9	43.5	2.6	2.2
Total specialty	329.2	258.8	27.2	15.7	15.3
Total net revenues	2103.4	1696.2	24.0	100.0	100.0

Company-operated retail revenues increased due to the opening of 236 new Company-operated retail stores in the last 12 months, favorable foreign currency exchange rates, primarily on the Canadian dollar, and comparable store sales growth of 2% for fiscal 2008. In the fourth quarter of fiscal 2008, Company-operated retail revenues grew at a slower rate year-over-year of 12% and comparable store sales were flat compared to the same quarter in fiscal 2007, both driven by slowdowns in the U.K. and Canada, due to the weakening global economy.

Specialty revenues increased primarily due to higher product sales and royalty revenues from opening 550 new licensed retail stores in the last 12 months.

Fiscal year ended	Sept. 2008 ($ millions)	Sept. 2007 ($ millions)	Change (%)	Sept. 2008	Sept. 2007
				(As a percentage of international total net revenues)	
Cost of sales including occupancy costs	1054.0	824.6	27.8	50.1	48.6
Store operating expenses[a]	664.1	531.7	24.9	31.6	31.3
Other operating expenses[b]	88.5	69.9	26.6	4.2	4.1
Depreciation and amortization expenses	108.8	84.2	29.2	5.2	5.0
General and administrative expenses	113.0	93.8	20.5	5.4	5.5
Restructuring charges	19.2	—	nm	0.9	—
Total operating expenses	2047.6	1604.2	27.6	97.3	94.6
Income from equity investees	54.2	45.7	18.6	2.6	2.7
Operating income	110.0	137.7	(20.1)	5.2	8.1

[a] As a percentage of related Company-operated retail revenues, store operating expenses were 37.4% and 37.0% for the fiscal years ended September 28, 2008 and September 30, 2007, respectively.

[b] As a percentage of related total specialty revenues, other operating expenses were 26.9% and 27.0% for the fiscal years ended September 28, 2008 and September 30, 2007, respectively.

Operating margin decreased primarily due to higher cost of sales including occupancy costs driven by continued expansion of lunch and warming programs in Canada, higher distribution costs and higher building maintenance expense due to store renovation activities. In addition, restructuring charges of $19.2 million recognized in fiscal 2008 had a 90 basis point impact on the operating margin, nearly all due to the closure of 61 Company-operated stores in Australia.

Global Consumer Products Group The Global Consumer Products Group (CPG) operating segment sells a selection of whole bean and ground coffees and premium Tazo® teas through licensing arrangements in the U.S. and international markets. The CPG also produces and sells a variety of ready-to-drink beverages through its joint ventures and marketing and distribution agreements.

Fiscal year ended	Sept. 28, 2008	Sept. 30, 2007	Change (%)	Sept. 28, 2008	Sept. 30, 2007
				As percentage of CPG total net revenues	
Net revenues:					
Licensing	392.6	366.3	7.2	100.0	100.0
Total specialty	**392.6**	**366.3**	**7.2**	**100.0**	**100.0**

Total net revenues increased primarily due to higher royalties and product sales in the international ready-to-drink business and increased sales of U.S. packaged tea and international club packaged coffee.

Fiscal year ended	Sept. 28, 2008 ($ million)	Sept. 30, 2007 ($ million)	Change (%)	Sept. 28, 2008	Sept. 30, 2007
				As a % of CPG total net revenues	
Cost of sales	219.6	218.3	0.6	55.9	59.6
Other operating expenses	22.0	19.5	12.8	5.6	5.3
Depreciation and amortization expenses	—	0.1	—	—	—
General and administrative expenses	6.4	6.3	1.6	1.6	1.7
Total operating expenses	248.0	244.2	1.6	63.2	66.7
Income from equity investees	60.7	61.5	(1.3)	15.5	16.8
Operating income	205.3	183.6	11.8	52.3	50.1

Growth of operating margin was primarily due to lower cost of sales as a percentage of related revenues, partially offset by lower income from equity investees. Lower cost of sales was primarily due to a sales mix shift to more profitable products.

Notes

1 Starbucks Corporation, press release, Starbucks Reports First Quarter Fiscal 2009 Results, January 28, 2009.
2 Starbucks Corporation, press release, Starbucks Reports First Quarter Fiscal 2009 Results, January 28, 2009.
3 Starbucks Corporation, press release, Starbucks Reports First Quarter Fiscal 2009 Results, January 28, 2009.
4 This draws upon information from "Starbuck's Timeline and History," www.starbucks.com/aboutus/timeline.asp, accessed October 6, 2009 and J. Wiggins "When the Coffee Goes Cold," *Financial Times*, December 13, 2008.
5 J. Wiggins "When the Coffee goes Cold," *Financial Times*, December 13, 2008.
6 *Trouble Brews at Starbucks* (Ivey School of Management, University of Western Ontario, Case No. 9B09A, 2009).
7 Quoted in: *Howard Schultz: Building the Starbucks Community* (Harvard Business School Case No. 9-406-127, 2006).
8 "Starbucks: A Visual Cup o' Joe," Contemporary Design Foundation, www.cdf.org/issue_journal/starbucks_a_visual_cup_o_joe.html, accessed May 15, 2009.
9 "Starbucks Instant: Will It Pass The Taste Test?" Fortune, February 13, 2007, http://money.cnn.com/2009/02/13/news/companies/starbucks_instant.fortune/, accessed May 19, 2009.
10 J. Wiggins "When the Coffee goes Cold," *Financial Times*, December 13, 2008.

Case 3 The U.S. Airline Industry in 2009

Here's a list of 129 airlines that in the past 20 years filed for bankruptcy. Continental was smart enough to make that list twice. As of 1992, in fact—though the picture would have improved since then—the money that had been made since the dawn of aviation by all of this country's airline companies was zero. Absolutely zero.

Sizing all this up, I like to think that if I'd been at Kitty Hawk in 1903 when Orville Wright took off, I would have been farsighted enough, and public-spirited enough—I owed this to future capitalists—to shoot him down. I mean, Karl Marx couldn't have done as much damage to capitalists as Orville did.

WARREN BUFFETT, CHAIRMAN, BERKSHIRE HATHAWAY

The year 2009 marked a century of passenger air travel. On November 19, 1909, Deutsche Luftschiffahrt AG had been formed to fly passengers by Zeppelin airships between Berlin, Potsdam and Dusseldorf.[1] The centenary passed without commemoration or celebration in the U.S. airline industry. Most airline executives were too busy struggling to remain solvent in the face of the worst economic downturn since the 1930s.

The financial crash of 2008 was a disaster for the airline industry: passenger traffic declined sharply and profit margins evaporated. All the leading airlines with the exception of Southwest reported large losses for 2008 (see Table 3.1). It was a dramatic end to the mood of optimism that had prevailed during 2006–7 when the industry had experienced a sharp upturn in profitability and was anticipating a rare period of financial stability. But dashed hopes were business-as-usual for the airlines. The previous period during which the industry had experienced a resurgence in profitability was 1999 to mid-2001. September 11, 2001 had brought a decisive end to that interlude of prosperity.

The short-term prospects for the industry looked grim. In March 2009, the International Air Transport Association (IATA) raised its estimate of total 2008 losses for the global industry from $5 billion to $8.5 billion. For 2009, revenues were expected to decline by 12%— steeper than in 2002 following September 11, 2001; net losses were forecast to be $4.7 billion. "The state of the airline industry today is grim. Demand has deteriorated much more rapidly with the economic slowdown than could have been anticipated even a few months ago . . . The industry is in intensive care."[2] The only comparative bright spot was the U.S., where airlines had shrunk capacity in line with demand. As a result IATA was forecasting a small profit for 2009.

First quarter results for U.S. airlines for 2009 confirmed IATA forecasts. While most leading U.S. airlines reported revenue reduction of between 10% and 20% on the year-ago period, all reported smaller losses.

The results of these capacity cuts were visible from satellite pictures of the deserts of California and Arizona where the majority of the world's 2300 surplus airliners were parked. The secondhand market for commercial jet planes also reflected this excess capacity: in March 2009, Air New Zealand was trying to sell one of its Boeing 747-400 jumbos for $5 million—compared to a new price of about $240 million.[3]

Despite fragments of evidence that the U.S. economy might be bottoming out by late 2009, the immediate prospects for any sustained revival in demand looked bleak. The efforts by the Treasury Department and the Federal Reserve Board to support

TABLE 3.1 Revenues, profits, and employment of the seven largest U.S. airlines

	Revenue		Net margin		Return on assets[a]		Employees	
	2007 $ billion	2008 $ billion	2007 (%)	2008 (%)	2007 (%)	2008 (%)	2002	2008
AMR	22.9	23.8	2.3	(9.3)	2.5	(7.9)	109 500	84 100
UAL	19.1	19.3	2.0	(27.1)	2.6	(24.2)	72 000	53 000
Delta	19.2	22.7	8.4	(12.2)	0.3	(10.0)	76 100	83 822
Northwest	12.6	13.8	16.7	(45.6)	9.1	(29.6)	44 300	38 000
Continental	13.1	14.6	5.1	(4.4)	5.8	(5.1)	43 900	40 120
U.S. Airways Group	11.7	12.1	3.6	(17.7)	6.1	(26.4)	46 600	32 671
Southwest	9.9	11.0	6.5	1.6	7.0	3.8	33 700	35 512

[a] Return on assets = net income/total assets.

Source: 10-K Reports of companies.

the financial system and unfreeze credit markets appeared to be successful but the aftermath would be strained balance sheets for government, business and households. It looked as though air travel would be a major casualty of budget cuts by both firms and individuals. In addition, the relief provided by lower fuel prices was drawing to a close: during the first five months of 2009, the price of crude had almost doubled from its December 2008 low.

The primary focus for most CEOs in the industry was short-term survival. Not only were most airlines losing money but these losses were being borne by weak balance sheets. Years of operating losses, restructuring costs and support for underfunded retiree benefits had resulted in an erosion of equity and build-up of debt. However, as prospects for reaching breakeven improved, so the attention of senior executives turned to the longer term prospects for the industry. Was the U.S. airline industry doomed to endure the fierce price competition, low margins and frequent encounters with bankruptcy that had been the norm for most of its history, or was there a prospect that airlines might become a "normal" industry where firms were able to cover their cost of capital most of the time?

Among industry executives and investment analysts, opinions on the prospects for the U.S. airline industry were mixed. Some pointed to a new climate of realism and financial prudence in the industry. As a result of losses and competition from low-cost carriers (LCCs) such as Southwest and Jet Blue, the "legacy carriers" had made major progress in getting cost under control. In particular, they had confronted the labor unions and gained substantial concessions on pay, benefits and working practices. They had gained efficiency benefits from outsourcing, made better use of information technology and retired many of their fuel-inefficient older planes. The speed with which the airlines reduced capacity and the way in which they avoided costly fare wars as demand plummeted in 2008–9 showed that they had learned from harsh experience. Consolidation in the industry was also conducive to profitability, both through exploiting scale economies and reducing the pressure of competition. Following America West's merger with U.S. Airways in 2005 and Delta's merger with Northwest in 2008, many airline executives believed further consolidation was both desirable and inevitable: "We think consolidation is good for the industry, and if it makes sense for us to participate, we will. Consolidation is a natural phase for the evolution of an industry as mature as ours," observed Jack Brace, UAL's CFO, predicting that the domestic airline industry would consolidate around two to four legacy network carriers, with three being the most likely number.

Others were less sanguine. The problems of the airline industry could not be attributed to the specific circumstances of the time: international terrorism, high fuel prices and the credit crunch of 2007–9. For decades the industry had generated poor returns on capital invested in it—not just in the U.S. but in other countries too. Nor could poor industry performance be attributed to inept management. It was notable that, while the legacy carriers (such as AMR, UAL, Delta, U.S. Airlines, and Continental) struggled to remain solvent, few of the LCCs were successful and the low-cost carriers were beginning to struggle. Jet Blue and Air Tran both lost money during 2008 and Southwest only just broke even. The pessimists pointed to two unfortunate features of the industry. First, when times were bad, airlines entered Chapter 11 bankruptcy but seldom liquidated. Second, whenever demand began to revive, airlines would add capacity and new airlines would enter the business, setting up the conditions for the next profit slump. "We've been here before, many times," observed one industry veteran. "Just when the industry seems to be climbing out of the mire, the industry's dire economics reassert themselves."

From Regulation to Competition

The history of the U.S. airline industry falls into two main phases: the period of regulation up until 1978, and the period of deregulation since then.

The Airlines Under Regulation (Pre-1978)

The first scheduled airline services began in the 1920s—primarily for carrying mail rather than passengers. By the early 1930s, transcontinental routes were controlled by three airlines: United Airlines in the north, American Airlines in the south, and TWA through the middle. New entry and growing competition (notably from Delta and Continental) led to the threat of instability in the industry, and in 1938 Congress established the Civil Aeronautics Board (CAB) with authority to administer the structure of the industry and competition within it. The CAB awarded interstate routes to the existing 23 airlines, established safety guidelines and priorities, and strict rules for fares, airmail rates, route entry and exit, mergers and acquisitions and interfirm agreements. Fares were set by CAB on the basis of cost plus a reasonable rate of return. The outcome was an ossification of industry structure—despite more than 80 applications, not a single new carrier was approved between 1938 and 1978.

During the 1970s, a major shift occurred in political opinion as increasing support for economic liberalism resulted in demands for less government regulation and greater reliance on market forces. Political arguments for deregulation were supported by new developments in economics. The case for regulation had been based traditionally on arguments about "natural monopoly"—competitive markets were impossible in industries where scale economies and network effects were important. During the early 1970s, the *theory of contestable markets* was developed. The main argument was that industries did not need to be competitively structured in order to result in competitive outcomes. So long as barriers to entry and exit were low then the potential for "hit-and-run" entry would cause established firms to charge competitive prices and earn competitive rates of return. The outcome was the Airline Deregulation Act, which, in October 1978, abolished the CAB and inaugurated a new era of competition in the airline industry.[4]

The Impact of Deregulation

The abolition of controls over entry, route allocations and fares resulted in a wave of new entrants and an upsurge in price competition. By 1980, 20 new carriers—including People Express, Air Florida, and Midway—had set up.

Deregulation was also accompanied by increased turbulence in the industry: the oil shock of 1979, recession and the air traffic controllers' strike of 1981. During 1979–83, the industry incurred widespread losses that triggered bankruptcies (between 1978 and 1984 over 100 carriers went bust) and a wave of mergers and acquisitions. Despite strong expansion from 1982 onwards, the industry experienced a profit slump in 1990–4. Figure 3.1 shows industry profitability since deregulation. Profitability is acutely sensitive to the balance between demand and capacity—losses result from industry load factors falling below the breakeven level (see Figure 3.2). The role of competition in driving efficiency is evident from the near-continuous decline in real prices over the period (see Table 3.2).

FIGURE 3.1 Profitability of the U.S. airline industry, 1978–2008

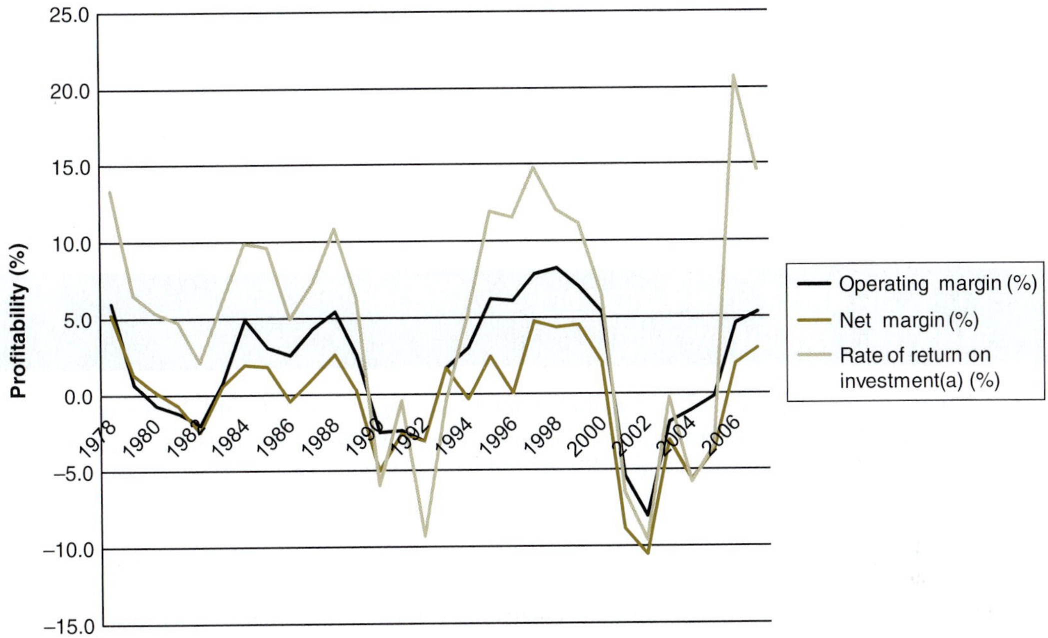

Source: Bureau of Transportation Statistics.

FIGURE 3.2 Load factors in the U.S. airline industry, 1978–2007

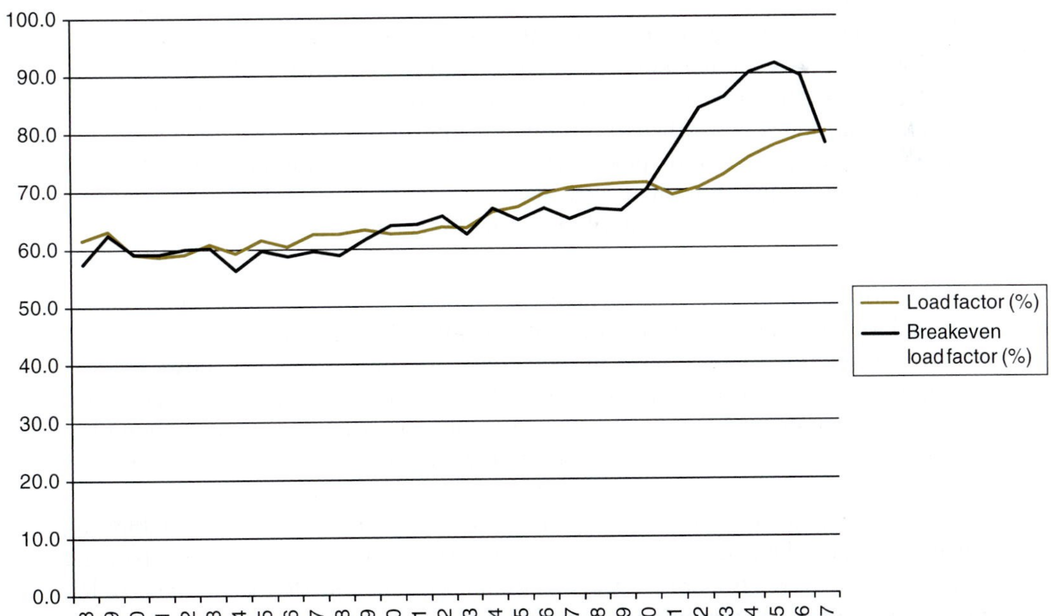

Source: Air Transport Association, Annual Economic Reports (Various Years); Bureau of Transportation Statistics.

TABLE 3.2 The falling price of air travel: revenue per passenger seat mile (cents)

	1960	1965	1970	1975	1980	1985	1990	1995	2000	2008
At nominal prices	6.1	6.1	6.0	7.7	11.5	12.2	13.4	13.5	14.6	12.7
At constant 1984 prices	20.3	19.4	15.4	14.3	14.0	11.3	10.2	8.9	8.5	6.1

Source: Bureau of Transportation Statistics.

Firm Strategy and Industry Evolution after Deregulation

Changes in the structure of the airline industry during the 1980s and 1990s were primarily a result of the strategies of the airlines as they sought to adjust to the new conditions of competition in the industry and gain competitive advantage.

Route Strategies: The Hub-and-Spoke System

During the 1980s the major airlines reorganized their route maps. A system of predominantly point-to-point routes was replaced by one where each airline concentrated its routes on a few major airports linked by frequent services using large aircraft, with smaller, nearby airports connected to these hubs by shorter routes using smaller aircraft. This "hub-and-spoke" system offered two major benefits:

- It allowed greater efficiency through reducing the total number of routes needed to link a finite number of cities within a network and concentrating traveler and maintenance facilities in fewer locations. It permitted the use of larger, more cost-efficient aircraft for interhub travel. The efficiency benefits of the hub-and-spoke system were reinforced by scheduling flights so that incoming short-haul arrivals were concentrated at particular times to allow passengers to be pooled for the longer haul flights on large aircraft.
- It allowed major carriers to establish dominance in major regional markets and on particular routes. In effect, the major airlines became more geographically differentiated in their route offerings. Table 3.3 shows cities where a single airline held a dominant local market share. The hub-and-spoke system also created a barrier to the entry of new carriers who often found it difficult to obtain gates and landing slots at the major hubs.

The hub-and-spoke networks of the major airlines were extended by establishing alliances with local ("commuter") airlines. Thus American Eagle, United Express and Delta Shuttle were franchise systems established by AMR, UAL and Delta, respectively, whereby commuter airlines used the reservation and ticketing systems of the major airlines and coordinated their operations and marketing policies with those of their bigger partners.

TABLE 3.3 Local market share of largest airline for selected U.S. cities (by number of passengers), 2009

City	Airline	Share of passengers (%)
Dallas-Forth Worth	American	73
Miami	American	71
Minneapolis-St. Paul	Northwestern	59
Detroit	Northwestern	54
Houston	Continental	62
Atlanta	Delta	53
Charlotte	U.S. Airways	55
Baltimore	Southwest	53
Newark	Continental	52
San Francisco	United	37
Denver	United	37
Cincinnati	Delta	33

Source: Bureau of Transportation Statistics.

Mergers

New entry during the period of deregulation had reduced seller concentration in the industry (see Table 3.4). However, the desire of the leading companies to build national (and international) route networks encouraged a wave of mergers and acquisitions in the industry—some triggered by the financial troubles that beset several leading airlines. Consolidation would have gone further without government intervention on antitrust grounds; however, Department of Justice approval of the Delta-Northwest merger pointed to a more lenient approach to airline mergers. Figure 3.3 shows some of the main mergers and acquisitions. During 2002–5, concentration declined as a result of capacity reduction by the major bankrupt

TABLE 3.4 Concentration in the U.S. airline industry

Year	CR4 (%)	Year	CR4 (%)
1935	88	1987	64.8
1939	82	1990	61.5
1949	70	1999	66.4
1954	71	2002	71.0
1977	56.2	2005	55.4
1982	54.2	2008	49.1

Note: The four-firm concentration ratio measures the share of the industry's passenger-miles accounted for by the four largest companies. During 1935–54, the four biggest companies were United, American, TWA, and Eastern. During 1982–2005, the four biggest companies were American, United, Delta, and Northwest. The 2008 data relate to American, United, Delta and Southwest.

Source: U.S. Department of Transportation.

FIGURE 3.3 Mergers and acquisitions among major U.S. passenger airlines, 1981–2009

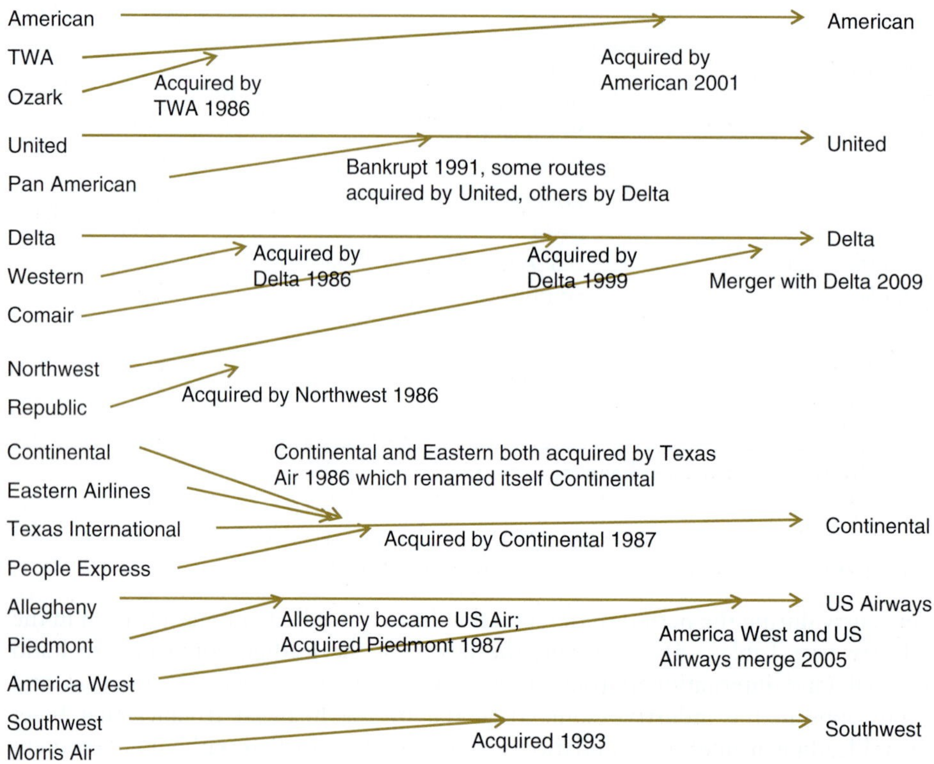

Source: Updated from S. Borenstein, "The Evolution of U.S. Airline Competition," *Journal of Economic Perspectives*, 6(2), 1992, p. 48.

airlines (United, Delta and Northwest) and market share gains by low-cost carriers.

Prices and Costs

Intensification of competition following deregulation was most apparent in the pricing of air tickets. Price cutting was typically led either by established airlines suffering from weak revenues and excess capacity, or by low-cost carriers. The new, low-cost entrants played a critical role in stimulating the price wars that came to characterize competition after deregulation. People Express, Braniff, New York Air and Southwest all sought aggressive expansion through rock-bottom fares made possible by highly efficient cost structures and a bare-bones service (the low-cost carriers economized on in-flight meals, entertainment and baggage handling). Although most of the low-cost newcomers failed during the early years of airline deregulation, they were soon replaced by new entrepreneurs eager to start up their own airlines.

In response to the price initiatives of the low-cost airlines, the major carriers sought to cut prices selectively. Fare structures became increasingly complex as airlines sought to separate price-sensitive leisure customers from price-inelastic business travelers. As a result, fare bands widened: advanced-purchased economy fares with Saturday night stays were as little as one-tenth of the first-class fare for the same journey.

Price cuts were also selective by route. Typically the major airlines offered low prices on those routes where they faced competition from low-cost rivals. Southwest, the biggest and most successful of the economy carriers, complained continually of predatory price cuts by its larger rivals. However, the ability of the major airlines to compete against the budget airlines was limited by the majors' cost structures—in particular, restrictive labor agreements, infrastructure and commitment to extensive route networks. To meet the competition of low-cost newcomers, several of the majors set up new subsidiaries to imitate the strategies and cost structures of the budget airlines. These included: Continental's Continental Lite (1994), UAL's Shuttle by United (1995), Delta's Song (1993) and United's Ted (1994). The closure of United's Ted airline in 2008 marked the end of attempts by the legacy carriers to create their own budget airlines.

During the crisis years of 2001–9, the major airlines made strenuous efforts to cut costs. Union contracts were renegotiated, inefficient working practices terminated, unprofitable routes abandoned and employment numbers reduced. Nevertheless, the budget airlines still maintained a substantial cost advantage over the majors. Higher fuel prices hit the major airlines more heavily than the low-cost carriers. Not only did the low-cost carriers have newer, more fuel-efficient planes but their stronger financial positions allowed them to make forward purchases to protect against escalating fuel prices.

The Quest for Differentiation

Under regulation, the inability to compete on price resulted in airline competition shifting to nonprice dimensions—customer service and in-flight food and entertainment. Deregulation brutally exposed the myth of customer loyalty: most travelers found little discernible difference among the offerings of different major airlines and were becoming more indifferent as to which airline they used on a particular route. As airlines increasingly cut back on customer amenities, efforts at differentiation became primarily focused upon business and first-class travelers. The high margins on first- and business-class tickets provided a strong incentive to attract these customers by means of spacious seats and intensive in-flight pampering. For leisure travelers it was unclear whether their choice of carrier was responsive to anything other than price and the low margins on these tickets limited the willingness of the airlines to increase costs by providing additional services.

The most widespread and successful initiative to build customer loyalty was the introduction of frequent flyer schemes. American's frequent-flyer program was launched in 1981 and was soon followed by all the other major airlines. By offering free tickets and upgrades on the basis of miles flown, and setting threshold levels for rewards, the airlines encouraged customers to concentrate their air travel on a single airline. By the end of 2006, airlines' unredeemed frequent-flyer distance had surged to over 10 trillion miles. By involving other companies as partners—car rental companies, hotel chains, credit card issuers—frequent-flyer programs became an important source of additional revenue for the airlines, being worth over $10 billion annually.

The Industry in 2009

The Airlines

At the beginning of 2009, the U.S. airline industry (including air cargo firms) comprised 151 companies, many of them local operators. Table 3.5 lists those with annual revenue exceeding $100 million. The industry was dominated by seven major passenger airlines—United, American, Delta, Northwestern, Continental, U.S. Airways, and Southwest (see Table 3.6). The importance of the leading group was enhanced by its networks of alliances with smaller airlines. Given the perilous financial state of so many of the leading airlines, most observers expected that the trend towards consolidation in the industry would continue.

Market for Air Travel

At the beginning of the twenty-first century, airlines provided the dominant mode of long-distance travel in the U.S. For shorter journeys, cars provided the major alternative. Alternative forms of public transportation—bus and rail—accounted for a small proportion of journeys in excess of a hundred miles. Only on a few routes (for example, between Washington, New York and Boston) did trains provide a viable alternative to air.

Most forecasts pointed to continued growth in the demand for air travel—but at a much slower rate than in earlier decades. During the 1980s and 1990s, passenger miles flown grew at a rate of 5% per annum, then slowed during the next decade. In March 2009, the FAA predicted a fall in passenger miles flown of 7.8% for 2009, with a long-term trend rate of growth of 2% to 3% through 2025.[5] Several observers thought this overoptimistic: economizing by both firms and consumers would depress demand. Moreover, an upsurge in video conferencing suggested that the long-anticipated shift from face-to-face business meetings to virtual business meetings had finally arrived.

Important changes were occurring within the structure of demand. Of particular concern to the airlines was evidence that the segmentation between business and leisure customers was breaking down. Conventional wisdom dictated that the demand for air tickets among leisure travelers was fairly price elastic; that of business travelers was highly inelastic. Hence, the primary source of airline profit was high-margin business fares. During 2008–9, increasing numbers of companies changed their travel policies to limit or eliminate employee access to premium-class air travel.[6]

Some of the increased pressure on prices could be attributed to changes in the distribution of airline tickets. The advent of the internet had decimated traditional travel agencies—retailers that specialized in the sale of travel tickets, hotel reservations and vacation packages. Meanwhile the companies were developing their direct sales organizations using both telephone and Web-based reservations systems. However, the airlines were slower than e-commerce startups in exploiting the opportunities of the internet. Despite the launch of Orbitz (the airlines' own online reservations service) in June 2001, Expedia and Travelocity lead online air ticket sales. As well as wielding greater bargaining power than traditional travel agencies, they also provided consumers with unparalleled price transparency, permitting the lowest price deals to be quickly spotted.

TABLE 3.5 The U.S. airline companies in 2008

	Employees		Employees
Major carriers			
ABX/Airborne Express	4983	Federal Express	144 237
Airtran	7825	Frontier	4850
Alaska Airlines	10 195	Jet Blue	11 852
American	75 074	Mesa	2940
American Eagle	9976	Northwest	29 137
Atlantic Southeast	4454	Skywest	9889
Comair	5720	Southwest	35 852
Continental	37 720	United	48 571
Delta	48 248	United Parcel	6115
Express Jet	5403	US Airways	33 809
National carriers			
Air Transport Int'l	409	Mesaba	4374
Air Wisconsin	2930	Miami Air	418
Allegiant	1560	Midwest Express	1183
Amerijet	559	North American	840
Arrow	514	Omni Air	1074
Astar	895	Pinnacle	4204
Astar Air Cargo	895	Polar Air Cargo	366
Atlas Air	1249	PSA Airlines	990
Continental Micronesia	1250	Ryan Int'l	576
Evergreen	484	Spirit	2410
Executive	1891	Sun Country	766
Florida West	61	USA 3000	556
Hawaiian	3707	USA Jet	191
Horizon	3751	World	1494
Kalitta Air	962		
Large regional carriers			
Aerodynamics	244	Lynx	375
Aloha Air Cargo	393	Northern Air Cargo	235
Capital Cargo	217	Pace	482
Casino Express	123	Republic Airlines	1432
Centurion Air Cargo	625	Shuttle America	1255
Colgan	1324	Southern Air	544
Compass	761	Tatonduk	291
GoJet	445	Tradewinds	69
Gulf & Caribbean	63	Virgin America	1305
Lynden Air Cargo	160		

Source: Bureau of Transportation Statistics.

TABLE 3.6 The cost structure of the U.S. airline industry by activity, 2002, 2005, and 2007

	Percentage of total operating costs		
Cost item	*2002*	*2005*	*2007*
Flying operations	30.1	36.5	37.9
Aircraft and traffic servicing	15.9	14.1	13.6
Maintenance	12.2	10.3	10.2
Promotion and sales	9.3	5.7	5.2
Transport related	10.0	16.7	16.9
Passenger services	8.3	6.2	5.4
Administrative	7.5	6.0	6.5
Depreciation and amortization	6.7	4.5	4.3
TOTAL	100.0	100.0	100.0

Source: Air Transport Association.

The decline of the traditional travel-agent sector was hastened by the reduction or elimination of commissions paid to travel agents. By 2008, commissions paid by airline companies to resellers fell to less than 1% of operating expenses (see Table 3.6), down from 6.2% in 1991. By 2008, the traditional travel agency industry was dominated by a few global leaders such as American Express and Thomas Cook.

Airline Cost Conditions

A little more than one-third of airline operating costs are accounted for by flying operations whereas servicing and maintenance account for another one-quarter (see Table 3.6). Labor and fuel costs are by far the biggest individual cost items

TABLE 3.7 Operating costs in the U.S. airline industry, 2006 and 2008

		Percentage of total operating expenses	
Cost item	**Increase in cost (%) 2002–8**	**2006**	**2008**
Labor	–6.0	23.8	24.36
Fuel	327.9	25.5	35.94
Professional services	49.9	7.8	8.07
Food and beverage	–11.4	1.5	1,25
Landing fees	31.4	2	1.93
Maintenance material	34.6	1.4	2.29
Aircraft insurance	–52.0	0.1	0.48
Passenger commissions	–27.0	1.3	0.97
Communication	4.3	0.9	1.01
Advertising and promotion	2.2	0.8	0.60
Transport-related expenses	167.4	14.7	19.23
Other operating expenses	93.6	7.6	3.86

Source: Bureau of Transport Statistics.

(see Table 3.7). A key feature of the industry's cost structure is the very high proportion of costs that are fixed. For example, because of union contracts, it was difficult to reduce employment and hours worked during downturns. The majors' need to maintain their route networks added to the inflexibility of costs—the desire to retain the integrity of the entire network made the airlines reluctant to shed unprofitable routes during downturns. An important implication of the industry's cost structure is that, at times of excess capacity, the marginal costs of filling empty seats on scheduled flights are extremely low.

Labor The industry's labor costs are boosted by the high level of employee remuneration—average pay in airlines was $55 950 in 2007; almost 40% higher than the average for all private industries.[7] Labor costs were also boosted by low labor productivity that resulted from rigid working practices agreed with unions. Most airline workers belong to one of a dozen major unions, the Association of Flight Attendants, the Air Line Pilots Association, and the International Association of Machinists and Aerospace Workers being the most important. These unions have a tradition of militancy and have been highly successful in negotiating pay increases far above the rate of inflation.

Between 2002 and 2009, the airlines forced major concessions from their employees. As a result, average compensation (including benefits) declined from $79 356 in 2003 to $74 786 in 2007. Industry employment fell from a peak of 680 000 in 2000 to 532 000 in 2008.[8]

Fuel How much a carrier spends on fuel depends on the age of its aircraft and its average flight length. Newer planes and longer flights lead to higher fuel efficiency. The fuel efficiency of different aircraft varies widely, primarily dependent on the number of engines. Fuel prices represent the most volatile and unpredictable cost item for the airlines due to fluctuations in the price of crude oil. Between January 2002 and June 2008, New York spot crude prices rose from $19 to $140 a barrel before falling to $40 in December 2008. By April 2009, crude prices were back above $50 a barrel.

Equipment Aircraft were the biggest capital expenditure item for the airlines. At prices of up to $250 million each (the A380 sells at around $350 million), the purchase of new planes represented a major source of financial strain for the airlines. While Boeing and Airbus competed fiercely for new business (especially when their order book was low, as in 2002–4), aggressive discounts and generous financing terms for the purchase of new planes disguised the fact that a major source of profits for the aircraft manufacturers was aftermarket sales. Over the past 20 years the number of manufacturers of large jets declined from four to two. Lockheed ceased civilian jet manufacture in 1984; McDonnell Douglas was acquired by Boeing in 1997. The leading suppliers of regional jets were Bombardier of Canada and Embraer of Brazil. During 2005–8, Boeing's return on equity averaged 21.3%.

Airport Facilities Airports play a critical role in the U.S. aviation industry. They are hugely complex, expensive facilities and few in number. Only the largest cities are served by more than one airport. Despite the rapid, sustained growth in air transport since deregulation, Denver is the only major new airport to have been built. Most airports are owned by municipalities; they typically generate substantial revenue flows for the cities. Landing fees are set by contracts between the airport and the airlines and are typically based on aircraft weight. New York's La Guardia airport has the highest landing fees in the U.S., charging over $6000 for a Boeing 747 to land. In 2007, the airlines paid over $2 billion to U.S. airports in landing fees and a further $3.0 billion in passenger facility charges.

Four U.S. airports—JFK and La Guardia in New York, Chicago's O'Hare, and Washington's Reagan National—are officially "congested" and takeoff and landing slots are allocated to individual airlines where the airlines assume *de facto* ownership. The cutback in airline capacity during 2008 and 2009 has temporarily relieved problems of congestion and reversed the escalation in the value of takeoff and landing slots.

Cost Differences between Airlines One of the arguments for deregulation had been that there were few major economies of scale in air transport; hence large and small airlines could coexist. Subsequently, little evidence has emerged of large airlines gaining systematic cost advantages over their smaller rivals. However, there are economies associated with network density—the greater the number of routes within a region, the easier it is for an airline to gain economies of utilization of aircraft, crews, and passenger and maintenance facilities. In practice, cost differences between airlines are due more to managerial, institutional and historical factors rather than the influence of economies of scale, scope, or density. The industry's cost leader, Southwest, built its strategy and management systems around the goal of low costs. By offering services from minor airports, with limited customer service, a single type of airplane, job-sharing among employees and salary levels substantially less than those paid by other major carriers, Southwest together with Jet Blue has one of the industry's lowest operating costs per available seat mile (CASM) despite flying relatively short routes. Conversely, U.S. Airways has the highest operating costs among major airlines—partly because of route concentration in the north-east (short routes, adverse winter weather) but also as a result of low productivity arising from restrictive union agreements. Table 3.8 shows differences in unit costs, unit revenues and capacity utilization among the airlines.

A critical factor determining average costs is capacity utilization. Because most costs, at least in the short run, are fixed, profitable operation depends on achieving breakeven levels of capacity operation. When airlines are operating below breakeven capacity there are big incentives to cut prices in order to attract additional business. The industry's periodic price wars tended to occur during periods of slack demand and on routes where there were several competitors and considerable excess capacity. The industry's ability to reduce losses during the first quarter of 2009 was a result of the airlines reducing capacity in line with falling demand.

Achieving high load factors while avoiding ruinously low prices is a major preoccupation for the airlines. All the major airlines have adopted yield-management systems—highly sophisticated computer models that combine capacity and purchasing data and rigorous financial analysis to provide flexible price determination. The goal is to earn as much revenue on each flight as possible. Achieving this goal has meant a proliferation of pricing categories.

Entry and Exit

Hopes by the deregulators that the U.S. airline business would be a case study of competition in a "contestable market" were thwarted by two factors: significant barriers to both entry and exit and evidence that potential competition was no substitute for actual competition in lowering fares on individual routes.[9] The capital requirements of setting up an airline can be low (a single leased plane will suffice)

TABLE 3.8 Operating data for the larger airlines, 2006 and 2008

	Available seat miles (billions)		Load factor (%)		Operating revenue per available seat mile (cents)		Operating expense per available seat mile (cents)	
	2006	2008	2006	2008	2006	2008	2006	2008
American	175.9	150.4	82.0	82.2	12.48	14.50	12.47	15.73
United	139.8	123.2	82.1	81.3	13.13	14.88	13.08	16.18
Delta	133.5	117.3	77.8	82.3	12.98	16.25	13.57	16.25
Northwest	91.8	72.0	82.7	85.0	14.33	16.63	14.47	17.35
Continental	85.5	91.4	83.1	81.4	13.51	15.15	13.26	15.53
Southwest	85.2	94.9	73.0	71.2	9.52	10.65	8.46	10.25
U.S. Airways	83.9	68.3	77.6	81.8	15.68	16.80	15.20	19.18
Air Tran	15.4	21.9	74.4	78.9	10.10	10.70	9.79	10.98
Jet Blue	23.8	29.7	82.5	80.5	7.55	10.48	7.48	10.18
Alaska	23.2	22.3	76.4	77.3	11.32	13.30	11.52	13.40

Source: Bureau of Transportation Statistics; 10-K reports of companies.

but offering an airline service requires setting up a whole system comprising gates, airline and aircraft certification, takeoff and landing slots, baggage handling services and the marketing and distribution of tickets. At several airports, the dominance of gates and landing slots by a few major carriers made entry into particular routes difficult and forced start-up airlines to use secondary airports. Despite the challenges of entry barriers and the dismal financial performance of the industry there seemed to be no shortage of willing entrepreneurs attracted to the apparent glamour of owning an airline. International airlines were also potential entrants into the U.S. domestic market. However, the depressed state of the industry has prevented a comprehensive E.U.–U.S. open skies agreement that would allow access by European airlines to intra-U.S. routes.

A key factor intensifying competition in the industry has been the barriers to exit that prevent the orderly exit of companies and capacity from the industry. The tendency for loss-making airlines to continue in the industry for long periods of time can be attributed to two key exit barriers: first, contracts (especially with employees) give rise to large closure costs; second, Chapter 11 of the bankruptcy code allows insolvent companies to seek protection from their creditors (and from their existing contracts) and continue operation under supervision of the courts. A critical problem for otherwise financially healthy airlines was meeting competition from bankrupt airlines, which had the benefit of artificially lowered costs.

Looking to the Future

At the end of May 2009, most industry observers were pessimistic about the outlook for the industry. While it looked as though the U.S. economy would avoid an outright depression, the first fruit of the "green shoots" of economic recovery was a rebound in the price of oil.

The mood of pessimism was reflected in stock-market valuation of airline companies and in their credit ratings. The total market capitalization of all quoted U.S. passenger airline companies at the end of May 2009 was $17.4 billion—less than half the value of its largest supplier, Boeing, and a mere 4% of the market value of Exxon Mobil. The market's view of the airlines' debt was similarly bleak. Only Southwest had an investment grade credit rating; all other airline debt was rated "junk" (below BBB−) by S&P. In the second quarter of 2009, Fitch downgraded the debt ratings of both AMR and UAL to CCC.

On the positive side, the legacy airlines had been successful in reducing their cost base through productivity improvements and reductions in compensation and benefits. As a result the cost gap between the LCCs and the legacy airlines had narrowed. However, although this had improved the competitive situation of the legacy airlines relative to the LCCs, it appeared that industry-wide cost reductions—whether from lower fuel prices or greater efficiency—did little to improve the profitability of the airline industry as a whole. The intensity of price competition meant that industry-wide cost reductions tended to be passed on to customers in lower fares.

The key issue was whether industry consolidation and a greater willingness to reduce capacity might lead to firmer pricing on the industry. The speed of capacity adjustment during 2008 and 2009 suggested that the airlines were more willing to adjust capacity to demand—and also more able to do so as a result of more flexible union agreements. The key issue was whether the new discipline would survive the next upturn in the industry. It was possible that the tightening of credit markets might help maintain a more cautious approach to capacity expansion. The long-term failure of the industry to earn a rate of return that came close to covering its cost of capital was likely to imply continuing difficulties for the airlines in financing new planes and other capital equipment. Doug Parker, U.S. Airways CEO, observed: "We have in this business been able to fund long-term losses with outside capital . . . and that is going to be harder to do in the future," citing "fundamental" changes for airlines' financial partners such as banks, aircraft makers, lessors and other suppliers.[10]

The evidence of past revivals in the industry suggested that they came to an end either as a result of external events or by the industry's own propensity to overinvest. In the case of the two previous upturns—1996-99 and 2006-08—external events were the critical factors (the September 11 terrorist attacks and the financial crisis of 2008). But even without adverse external events, the industry had shown a tendency towards over-optimism and lack of financial discipline that has fuelled investment in new capacity both by established airlines and new start-ups. With forecasts that demand for air travel would pick up gradually during the latter part of 2009 and into 2010, the key question was whether the airlines would be able to maintain the disciplined approach to cost control, capacity, and pricing that they had shown since the onset of the financial crisis.

Most encouraging was the success of the airlines in cost cutting. Yet, the efforts of the major airlines in improving operational efficiency also raised some perplexing questions. The widespread assumption had been that, if the major airlines could reduce their costs to the level of Southwest and the other low-cost carriers, they could enjoy profit levels similar to those experienced by Southwest. Despite the efforts of the majors, Southwest, Jet Blue and the other budget airlines still retained a substantial cost advantage over the legacy carriers. Even if the major airlines could continue to reduce costs, who would the beneficiaries be—the long-suffering shareholders of the companies, or travelers as competition to fill seats encouraged the airlines to pass on cost reductions to customers in the form of lower prices?

Notes

1 U.S. Centennial of Flight Commission, "The Early Years of German Commercial Aviation," www.centennialofflight.gov/essay/Commercial_Aviation/germany/Tran19.htm, accessed October 7, 2009.

2 "Airline Industry in Intensive Care," *Financial Times,* March 25, 2009.

3 "Deserts Littered by State of Airline Industry," *Financial Times,* March 5, 2009.

4 Abolition of the CAB meant that the primary responsibility for airline regulation was with the Federal Aviation Administration, which was responsible for airline safety.

5 "FAA: Air Travel will Fall 7.8% in '09," CNN, March 31, 2009, http://money.cnn.com/2009/03/31/news/companies/Airlines/index.htm, accessed October 29, 2009.

6 "Business Travel Blues," *Washington Post,* March 17, 2009, http://www.washingtonpost.com/wp-dyn/content/article/2009/03/17/AR2009031701280.html, accessed October 209, 2009.

7 Air Transport Association, *2008 Economic Report,* ATA, Washington DC.

8 Air Transport Association, *2008 Economic Report,* ATA, Washington DC.

9 On the principles of contestability and its application to the U.S. airline industry see: S. Martin, "The Theory of Contestable Markets," discussion paper, Department of Economics, Purdue University, July 2000.

10 "Airlines: Where Capital Goes to Die," *Business Week,* May 5, 2009.

Case 4 Ford and the World Automobile Industry in 2009

Ford in Crisis

By June 2009, Ford Motor Company was the only remaining member of Detroit's "Big Three" to have escaped bankruptcy. Chrysler had filed for Chapter 11 protection on April 30; General Motors had followed on June 1. For Chief Financial Officer, Lewis Booth, the eight months since his appointment in November 2008 had involved unremitting pressure. The financial crisis that followed the collapse of Lehman Brothers in September 2008 had engulfed the entire U.S. automobile sector. By the time President Obama took office in January 2009, U.S. auto sales were half of those a year previously. This fall in demand was unprecedented in the industry's history. Ford reported a \$14.7 billion loss for 2008; a result of which was the elimination of stockholders' equity.[1]

TABLE 4.1 Ford estimates of U.S. sales and its own financial needs

	Forecast U.S. auto sales (million units)			Ford's estimated additional financing requirement ($ billion)
	2009	2010	2011	
GDP decline of 3%; recession persists throughout 2009	11.0	12.5	14.0	9
More severe slump persisting into 2010	10.5	11.0	12.0	13

Source: Ford Motor Company, Business Plan Submitted to the Senate Banking Committee, December 2, 2008.

Booth's attention had, by June 2009, shifted from short-term survival to the longer term financial outlook for Ford. The evidence that Ford had submitted to the Senate Banking Committee in December 2008 had estimated the company's financing needs on the basis of "current-rates" and "worst-rates" growth scenarios (See Table 4.1). Since then the world economy had stabilized and some forecasters were predicting that the U.S. economy would begin growing again in 2010. For the world auto industry, government incentives for scrapping old cars and purchasing new, fuel-efficient models had done much to stabilize demand—especially in Europe. Ford's results for the first quarter of 2009 showed signs of improvement: despite a continuing fall in sales, its $1.4 billion loss for the quarter was much smaller than the loss in each of the previous two quarters.

As the short-term threat of insolvency receded, Booth turned increasingly to Ford's longer term financial outlook. In December 2008, Booth had forecast that Ford would break even in 2011. Ford's cost-reduction measures had already begun to bear fruit—it had started its restructuring long before GM and Chrysler. During 2009 it would see the benefits of its plant closures, its early switch to smaller, more fuel-efficient cars and the sale of its loss-making Jaguar, Land Rover and Aston Martin subsidiaries.

However, Booth recognized that Ford's return to profitability would depend not only on its own efforts, but also upon the state of the automobile industry in a post-recessionary world. While the short-term outlook of the industry improved over the later part of 2009, the long-term outlook became more alarming.

Booth had taken comfort in the fact that Ford's stronger operational and financial performance would allow it to emerge as one of the survivors of the crisis while weaker competitors failed. A similar view was taken by Daimler Benz's CEO who predicted that 2009 would be a "Darwinian year" for the auto industry. Yet, by June 2009, there was little evidence of competitive selection:

> [I]nstead of natural selection, something else happened: governments around the world, from Canada and Brazil to Russia and South Korea, stepped in with prodigious amounts of cash to keep car plants open and assembly lines running.
>
> All told, automakers have benefited from well in excess of $100 billion of direct bail-out funds or indirect state aid, such as scrappage schemes, since global sales collapsed last October—in nominal terms, the biggest ever short-term intervention in manufacturing.
>
> All this money has preserved jobs in car making, still the linchpin of many industrial economies. But the money has also prevented a necessary shake-out in an industry that has long had too many producers. Consultants at PwC

> estimate the industry has the capacity to build 86 million units this year, almost a record—and 31 million more than the 55 million vehicles that it will sell. "What appeared to be a unique opportunity to address the industry's biggest issue—excess capacity—has been missed," says Michael Tyndall, an analyst with Nomura. In Europe not a single plant has closed permanently, thanks to bail-outs.
>
> "The shape of the industry looks all but the same, except that governments have tipped lots of money in and prevented Darwinian selection," says Max Warburton, analyst at Sanford Bernstein. "It has been a good reminder of what this industry is: a government-supported job creation scheme."
>
> Long-term observers of the industry point out that it has never operated on the pure free-market principles. Governments have always intervened in hard times. The status of many carmakers as national champions is bolstered by dynastic family owners at about half the big producers, who often rank continuity and control above shareholder value. Both they and governments form a big obstacle to consolidation.[2]

The thought of an industry structure that was barely changed from that of the past decade was profoundly depressing to Booth: between 1990 and 2008 the world's five biggest auto makers (GM, Toyota, Ford, Daimler-Chrysler and Volkswagen) had earned on average net margin of 1.1%; their return on invested capital had been far below their cost of capital and together they had destroyed billions in shareholder value. However, even in the absence of consolidation among existing auto makers, it was clear that the structure of the industry was far from remaining static. The shifting of demand from the mature industrial nations to the growing markets of Asia, Eastern Europe and Latin America was accompanied by the emergence of new competitors from these same regions. At a more fundamental level, the combined forces of technology and environmental concerns were redirecting the industry's evolutionary path. Ford planned to introduce all-electric commercial vans in 2010 and all-electric automobiles in 2011.[3]

Development of the World Automobile Market[4]

The Evolution of Market Demand

During the 1880s, the first internal-combustion powered vehicles were produced in Europe—notably by Gottlieb Daimler and Karl Benz in Germany. By the turn of the century hundreds of small companies were producing automobiles both in Europe and in America. The subsequent 120 years saw the industry developing at different rates in different parts of the world. The U.S. market saw its fastest rates of growth during 1910–28 and then after the Second World War. Since the mid-1960s, the combined output of autos and trucks was broadly stable—despite cyclical fluctuations (see Figure 4.1). Western Europe and Japan also experienced maturing of their markets with production peaking in 1989–90. In all the advanced industrial countries, the tendency for cars to last longer created a downward trend in the demand for motor vehicles well before the 2008 recession (see Figure 4.2).

As a result, the automobile producers looked increasingly to the newly industrializing countries for market opportunities. During the 1980s and 1990s,

FIGURE 4.1 U.S. motor vehicle production, 1900–2008

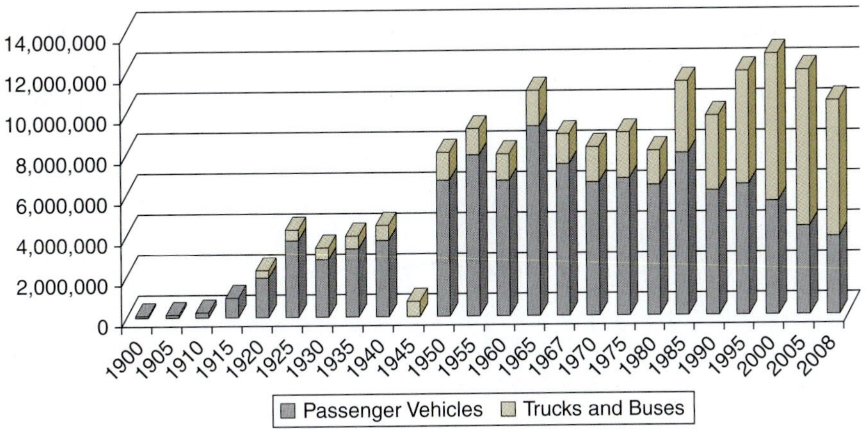

FIGURE 4.2 Median age of passenger cars in the U.S.

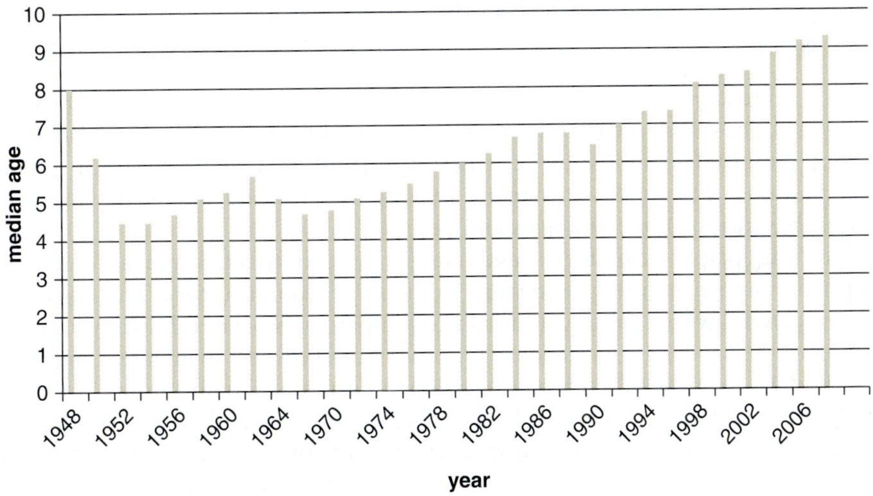

Source: R. L. Polk & Co.

newly industrializing countries such as Korea, Malaysia, Thailand, Turkey, and Argentina offered the best growth prospects. During 2000 to 2009, the BRIC countries (Brazil, Russia, India, and China) were the world's primary growth markets. As a result, the world production of cars and trucks continued to grow (see Figure 4.3).

The Evolution of the Automobile

The early years of the industry were characterized by considerable uncertainty over the design and technology of the motorcar. Early "horseless carriages" were precisely that—they followed design features of existing horse-drawn carriages and buggies.

FIGURE 4.3 World motor vehicle production, 1950–2008

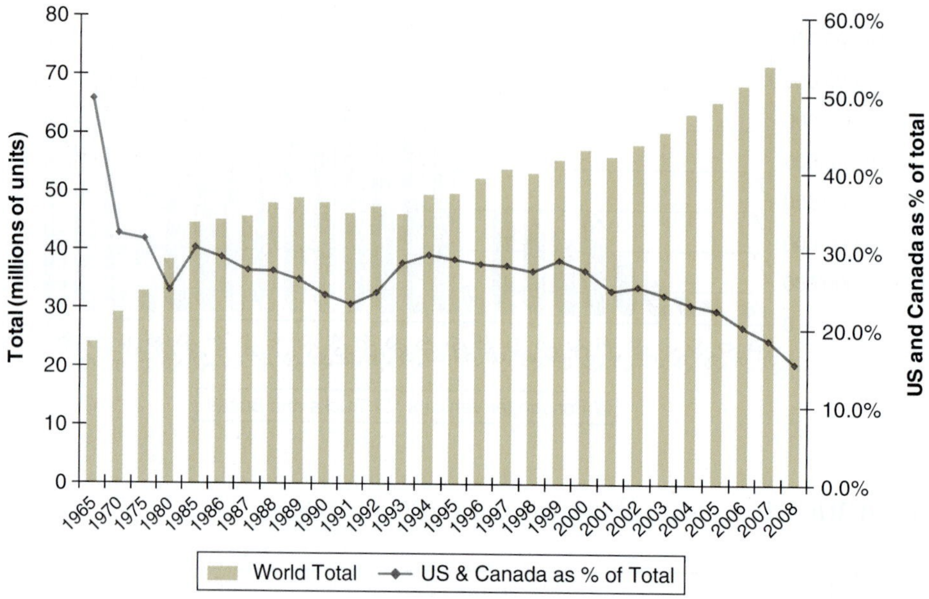

Early motorcars demonstrated a bewildering variety of technologies. During the early years, the internal-combustion engine vied with the steam engine and eclectic motors. Internal combustion engines featured a wide variety of cylinder configurations. Transmission systems, steering systems and brakes all displayed a remarkable variety of technologies and designs.

Over the years, technologies and designs tended to converge as competition relegated many once-promising designs to the scrapheap of history. The Ford Model T represented the first "dominant design" in automobiles—the technology and design features of the Model T set a standard for other manufacturers to imitate. Convergence of technologies and designs continued throughout the twentieth century. During the 1920s, all manufacturers adopted enclosed, all-steel bodies. The final decades of the twentieth century saw the elimination of most distinctively different designs: the VW Beetle with its rear, air-cooled engine, the Citroën 2-CV and its idiosyncratic braking and suspension system, Daf with its "Variomatic" transmission, and the two-stroke engines favored by some Soviet-bloc manufacturers. Engines became more similar: typically four cylinders arranged in line, with V-6 and V-8 configurations for larger cars. Front-wheel drive became standard on smaller cars; suspension, steering, braking systems and body shapes became more similar. Technological progress was incremental: innovations primarily involved new applications of electronics, new materials and new safety features. The main advances were multi-valve cylinders, traction control systems, all-wheel drive, electronic fuel injection, variable suspensions, intercooled turbos, satellite navigation systems, collision-avoidance radar and intelligent monitoring systems.

Despite less differentiation between manufacturers, new product segments have continued to appear. New vehicle types include a number of "crossovers" such as luxury SUVs and "mini-SUVs."

Convergence also occurred across countries. The same market segments tended to emerge in different countries. The major differences between countries were in the *sizes* of the various segments. Thus, in the U.S., the "mid-size" family sedan was the largest segment, with the Honda Accord and Toyota Camry the leading models. In Europe and Asia, small family cars ("subcompacts") formed the largest market segment. Yet for all the emphasis by manufacturers on global models, distinctive national differences persist. For example, during 2000–8 light trucks (pickups and SUVs) outsold passenger cars in the U.S. In Japan, microcars, such as the Suzuki Cervo, have grabbed 35% of the total car market.

This trend toward design convergence and slowing of technological change was interrupted by one major technological development. In 1997 both Toyota and Audi introduced mass-production hybrid cars—almost 100 years after Ferdinand Porsche had developed the first hybrid car in which an internal combustion engine powered an electric motor. By 2009, hybrids accounted for 12% of the Japanese market and 3% of the U.S. market. Several major automobile manufacturers, including GM, Daimler, Mitsubishi, and Subaru, planned to launch all-electric cars in the latter part of 2009 through to 2010, once more revisiting the early years of the auto industry—in 1900, 28% of all automobiles produced in the U.S. were all electric.

The Evolution of Manufacturing Technology

At the beginning of the twentieth century, car manufacture, like carriage-making, was a craft industry. Cars were built to order according to individual customers' preferences and specifications. In Europe and North America there were hundreds of companies producing cars, few with annual production exceeding 1000 vehicles. When Henry Ford began production in 1903, he used a similar approach—even for early versions of his Model T. His vision of an affordable, mass-produced automobile depended on the development of more precise machine tools that would permit interchangeable parts. By 1913, he had overcome the technical challenges of his new system of production. Components were produced either in batches or continuously and were then assembled on moving assembly lines by semi-skilled workers. The productivity gains were enormous. In 1912 it took 23 man-hours to assemble a Model T; just 14 months later it took only four. The resulting fall in the price of cars opened up a new era of popular motoring.

"Fordism" was the first major revolution in process technology; Toyota's "lean production" was the second. The system was developed by Toyota in postwar Japan at a time when shortages of key materials encouraged extreme parsimony and avoidance of inventories and waste. Key elements of the system were statistical process control, just-in-time scheduling, quality circles, teamwork and flexible production (more than one model manufactured on a single production line). Central to the new manufacturing was the transition from static concepts of efficiency optimization towards continuous improvement to which every employee contributed. During the 1980s and 1990s all the world's car manufacturers redesigned their manufacturing processes to incorporate aspects of Toyota's lean production.

New process technologies reduced the extent of scale economies in assembly. Optimal manufacturing efficiency once required giant assembly plants with outputs of at least 400 000 units a year. After 1990, most new assembly plants had capacities of between 150 000 and 300 000 units per annum. Scale economies in components and subassemblies were much more important. The minimum efficient scale for an engine plant was around 1 million units annually.

New Product Development

Scale economies were far more important in new product development: huge development costs needed to be amortized over large numbers of vehicles.

Increasing design complexity, the application of electronics, and new safety and environmental standards caused the cost of developing new models to rise steeply. By the 1990s the cost of creating an entirely new, mass-production passenger car from drawing board to production line was in excess of $1.5 billion. Ford's Mondeo/Contour—its first entirely global model—launched in 1994 cost a total of $6 billion (including tooling costs).

Smaller manufacturers could survive only by avoiding these massive product development costs. One way was to avoid new model changes. Prior to its acquisition by Ford, Jaguar's two models, the XJ6 and XJS, were almost two decades old. The tiny Morgan car company has made the same model since the late 1930s. The alternative was to license designs from larger manufacturers. Thus, Tofas of Turkey built Fiat-designed cars. Proton of Malaysia built Mitsubishi-designed cars. Maruti of India produced Suzuki-designed cars.

The cost of new product development has been the major driver of mergers and acquisitions in the industry. Economies from sharing development costs also encouraged increased collaboration and joint ventures. In 2009, the automobile industry was a global network of collaborative arrangements. These included joint-venture plants, technology alliances, component supply agreements and joint marketing agreements. In emerging market countries, most new auto plants were joint ventures between local and overseas companies. Figure 4.4 shows Ford's alliances with other automobile producers.

During the 1990s, new product development emerged as the critical organizational capability differentiating car manufacturers. Designing, developing and putting into production a completely new automobile was a hugely complex process involving every function of the firm, up to 3000 engineers, collaboration with several hundred suppliers and up to five years from drawing board to market launch. The team-based approach to new product development put in place by Toyota and Honda became models for all the major manufacturers. The result was a significant reduction in product development time.

Attempts to lower product development costs focused around three concepts. First, modular designs: the disaggregation of the vehicle into a number of separate subassemblies. Second, "virtual prototyping": the use of 3D computer graphics to design and test prototypes. Third, the development of shared platforms for multiple models. A "platform" comprised a vehicle's architecture including its floorpan, suspension system and layout of powertrain and major components. From 2000 to 2009 there was an important trend towards building multiple models on a single platform in order to exploit scale economies and to facilitate new product development. For example, Ford's C1 platform is used for the Ford Focus, the Mazda 3, the Ford C-max, and the Volvo S40 and G50. In engines, Ford moved to three engine families: V-8/V-10, V-6 and I-4 (four in-line cylinders). The I-4 engine has over 100 variations; it has an annual volume of 1.5 million and is built at three

FIGURE 4.4 Ford's alliances with other automakers

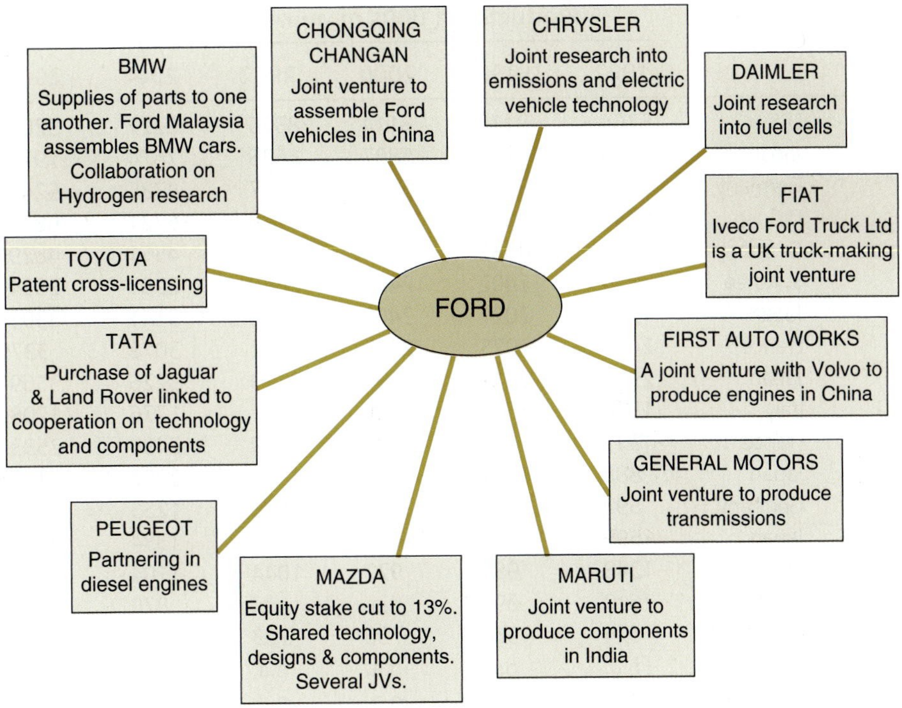

different plants—one in North America, one in Europe and one in Japan. *Automotive News* explained: "The idea is to share systems in areas that customers can't see and feel, and differentiate the brands in areas they can."

The Industry

The Manufacturers

The major automobile manufacturers are shown in Table 4.2. The ranks of the leading producers were dominated by U.S., Japanese, and European companies; outside of these countries only Hyundai of Korea was among the leading manufacturers. All the major manufacturers are multinational: both GM and Ford produce more cars outside the U.S. than within it; Honda produces more Accords in the U.S. than in Japan. As a result some countries—notably Canada, Spain, and the UK—are significant auto-producing countries without having any significant domestic auto companies. Over the past two decades the industry has consolidated through mergers and acquisitions (see Table 4.3). The financial problems of Japanese and Korean auto companies during the late 1990s accelerated this process. As a result, U.S. and European carmakers acquired significant proportions of the Japanese and Korean auto industries. The financial crisis of 2008–9 resulted in little consolidation: Fiat's acquisition of Chrysler was the only major merger. In fact, the

TABLE 4.2 The world's leading auto manufacturers

		Production ('000s of autos and commercial vehicles)						
		1992	1996	2000	2002	2004	2005	2007
GM	U.S.	6764	8176	8114	8326	9221	9200*	9350
Toyota	Japan	4249	4794	5897	6626	7674	7974*	8534
Volkswagen	Germany	3286	3977	5106	5017	4785	5243*	6268
Ford	U.S.	5742	6611	7206	6729	6721	6818*	6248
DaimlerChrysler	Germany	2782	4082	4666	4456	4551	4829*	4635
Hyundai[a]	S. Korea	874	1402	2488	2642	2283	2534*	3987
Honda	Japan	1762	2021	2469	2988	3141	3391*	3912
Peugeot	France	2437	1975	2879	3262	3078	3375	3457
Nissan	Japan	2963	2712	2698	2719	3226	3569*	3431
Fiat	Italy	1800	2545	2639	2191	1776	1708*	2679
Renault[b]	France	1929	1755	2515	2329	2490	2533*	2669
Suzuki	Japan	888	1387	1434	1704	2392	2630	2596
BMW	Germany	598	641	835	1091	1255	1328*	1542
Mitsubishi	Japan	1599	1452	1613	1821	1334	1381	1412
Mazda	Japan	1248	984	972	1044	1104	1149*	1287
Daihatsu	Japan	610	691	n.a.	n.a.	870	909	856
AvtoVAZ	Russia	674	562	756	703	727	732	736
FAW	China	n.a.	n.a.	n.a.	n.a.	n.a.	n.a.	691
Tata	India	n.a.	n.a.	n.a.	n.a.	n.a.	n.a.	588
Fuji (Subaru)	Japan	648	525	581	542	555	571	585
Isuzu	Japan	473	462	572	437	578	642	532

n.a. = not available.

* Sales data.

[a] Including Kia.

[b] Including Dacia and Samsung.

Source: Ward's Automotive Yearbook

main outcome was further fragmentation (e.g. GM's attempts to sell its Saab and Opel subsidiaries). In the meantime, a number of domestically focused manufacturers—especially from China and India—were building a global presence.

Outsourcing and the Role of Suppliers

Henry Ford's system of mass production was supported by heavy backward integration. At Ford's giant River Rouge plant, iron ore entered at one end, Model Ts emerged at the other. Ford even owned rubber plantations in the Amazon basin. The trend of the past 30 years has been towards increasing outsourcing of materials, components, and services in order to achieve lower costs and increased flexibility. At the end of the 1990s GM and Ford both spun off their component manufacturing businesses as separate companies: Delphi and Visteon, respectively. Relationships with suppliers also changed. The Japanese model of close,

TABLE 4.3 Mergers and acquisitions among automobile manufacturers, 1986–2009

Year	Acquirer	Target	Notes
2009	Volkswagen	Suzuki	Acquires 20% stake
2009	Fiat (Italy)	Chrysler	
2009	Volkswagen	Porsche	Merger agreed
2009	Beijing Automotive Industry Corp.	Fujian Motor; Changfeng Motor	
2008	Tata (India)	Jaguar Cars, Land Rover (U.K.)	Acquired from Ford
2008	SAIC Motor Group (China)	Nanjing Automobile	SAIC now owns both MG and Rover brands
2005	Nanjing Automobile (China)	Rover (U.K.)	
2005	Toyota	Fuji Heavy Industries	Acquired 8.7% stake from GM
2002	GM (U.S.)	Daewoo (South Korea)	42% of equity acquired
2000	Renault (France)	Samsung Motors (South Korea)	70% of equity acquired
2000	GM (U.S.)	Fiat (Italy)	20% of equity acquired
2000	DaimlerChrysler (Germany)	Hyundai (South Korea)	10% of equity acquired
2000	DaimlerChrysler (Germany)	Mitsubishi Motors (Japan)	34% of equity acquired
1999	Renault (France)	Nissan (Japan)	38.6% of equity acquired
1999	Ford (U.S.)	Volvo (Sweden)	Acquires car business only
1999	Ford (U.S.)	Land Rover (U.K.)	Acquired from BMW
1998	Daimler Benz (Germany)	Chrysler (U.S.)	Biggest auto merger ever
1998	VW (Germany)	Rolls Royce Motors (U.K.)	Acquired from Vickers plc
1998	Hyundai (South Korea)	Kia (S. Korea)	
1998	Daewoo (South Korea)	Ssangyong Motor (South Korea)	
1998	Daewoo (South Korea)	Samsung Motor (South Korea)	
1997	Proton (Malaysia)	Lotus (U.K.)	
1997	BMW (Germany)	Rover (U.K.)	
1996	Daewoo (South Korea)	FSO (Poland)	
1996	Daewoo (South Korea)	FS Lublin (Poland)	
1995	Fiat (Italy)	FSM (Poland)	
1995	Ford (U.S.)	Mazda (Japan)	
1994	Daewoo (S. Korea)	Oltcit/Rodae (Romania)	
1991	VW (Germany)	Skoda (Czech Republic)	
1990	GM (U.S.)	Saab-Scandia (Sweden)	50% of equity acquired
1990	Ford (U.S.)	Jaguar (U.K.)	
1987	Ford (U.S.)	Aston Martin (U.K.)	
1987	Chrysler (U.S.)	Lamborghini (Italy)	
1986	VW (Germany)	Seat (Spain)	

Source: newspaper reports.

collaborative long-run relationships with their "first-tier" suppliers has displaced the U.S. model of contract-based, arm's-length relationships. United States' and European automakers now have long-term relationships with a far smaller number of suppliers. As the leading component suppliers have gained increasing responsibility for technological development—especially in sophisticated subassemblies such as transmissions, braking systems, and electrical and electronic

TABLE 4.4 Revenues and profitability of the biggest automotive component suppliers

	Revenues ($ billion)			ROA (%)
	1994	2000	2008	2008
Robert Bosch (Germany)	19.6	29.1	58.5	1.7
Denso Corp. (Japan)	11	18.2	40.3	6.7
Johnson Controls (U.S.)	7.1	17.2	35.9	0.6
Aisin Seiki (Japan)	7.3	8.9	27.1	4.4
Magna International (Canada)	–	10.5	23.7	0.1
Delphi Automotive (U.S.)	–	29.1	18.1	n.a.
Eaton (U.S.)	4.4	8.3	15.4	6.6
Lear Corp (U.S.)	3.1	14.1	13.6	(1.0)
Valeo SA (France)	3.8	8.9	11.4	(3.2)
Visteon (U.S.)	–	19.5	9.5	1.2
Dana (U.S.)	5.5	12.7	8.7	n.a.

n.a. = not available.

Source: Company financial statements, Forbes.

equipment—they have also grown in size and global reach. Bosch, Denso, Johnson Controls and Delphi are almost as big as some of the larger automobile companies (see Table 4.4).

The Quest for Cost Reduction

Increasing competition in the industry has intensified the quest for cost reduction among automobile manufacturers. Cost-reduction measures have included:

- *Worldwide outsourcing*. Outsourcing has grown from individual components to major subassemblies (such as engines and steering systems) to complete cars as has been noted above. In addition, auto firms have developed original equipment manufacturer supply arrangements amongst themselves: Chery of China and Hyundai each produce cars for Chrysler, which are sold under the Dodge badge in North America.
- *Just-in-time scheduling*, which has radically reduced levels of inventory and work-in-progress.
- *Shifting manufacturing to lower-cost locations*. VW's North American production is based in Mexico and it moved production from Germany to the Czech Republic, Spain, and Hungary; Japanese companies have moved more and more production to lower cost locations in Southeast Asia; Mercedes and BMW developed greenfield plants in the deep south of the U.S.
- *Collaboration*. Ford's alliances (see Figure 4.4) are typical of the joint technology and product development among automobile companies intended to share costs.

Despite constant efforts at lowering costs, the major automakers were unable to achieve the unit costs of upstart producers in China, India, and other low labor cost countries. Tata Motors' launch of its Nano model in 2009 underlined the challenges faced by the global majors. The Nano was a four-seater, 623cc city car, which achieves almost 70 miles per gallon of gasoline. However, what gained the attention of all the world's automakers was its price: at 115 000 rupees ($2420) it was the world's cheapest new car.

Excess Capacity

The greatest structural problem of the industry was excess capacity. Ever since the early 1980s, the growth of production capacity had outstripped the growth in the demand for cars. Import restrictions had exacerbated the problem. During the 1980s and early 1990s, North American production capacity grew substantially as a result of Japanese companies building greenfield "transplants." The opportunities presented by the growth of private motoring in Eastern Europe, Asia and Latin America during the 1990s resulted in a rush by all the world's leading automakers to build new plants in these countries. Further big additions to world production capacity resulted from the expansion of the Korean car industry during 1992–7. Even where demand was growing fastest—such as China, where sales grew annually by almost 50% between 2002 and 2008—growth of capacity outstripped growth in demand. At the beginning of 2009, CSM Worldwide estimated global excess capacity at 34 million units (see Table 4.5).

Looking ahead, it appeared as though capacity reductions by Ford, GM and a few other companies would be more than offset by the new plants that would begin production during 2007–9. These included three new Toyota plants (one in India, two in China), two new Honda plants in North America, Hyundai plants in the Czech Republic and U.S., PSA in Slovakia, and at least a dozen other new plants in China and India.

Internationalization

Accessing growing markets, exploiting scale economies in purchasing, technology, and new product development were the main drivers of international

TABLE 4.5 Automobile production capacity, January 2009

	Production capacity (millions of units per year)	Production (millions of units per year)	Excess capacity (millions of units per year)
North America	17.3	10.1	7.2
South America	5.5	3.7	1.8
Europe	27.3	17.8	9.5
Middle East and Africa	2.5	1.7	0.8
Japan and Korea	17.3	13.9	3.4
South Asia	8.3	4.7	3.6

Source: CSM Worldwide.

expansion. Although Ford and General Motors began international expansion back in the 1920s, until the 1970s the world auto industry was made up of fairly separate national markets where each national market was dominated by indigenous producers. Each of the larger national markets was supplied primarily by domestic production and manufacturers tended to be market leaders. Internationalization has meant that, while there are now far fewer automakers in the world as a whole, concentration has declined in most national markets. For example, in 1970 the "Big Three" (GM, Ford, and Chrysler) held close to 85% of the U.S. market, VW and Daimler Benz dominated the market in Germany, as did Fiat in Italy, British Leyland (later Rover) in the U.K., Seat in Spain, and Renault, Peugeot, and Citroën in France. Internationalization meant that all the world's leading manufacturers were competing in most of the countries of the world. As a result, the market dominance of local firms was undermined (see Table 4.6).

The rise of new markets and the quest for low production costs has resulted in major shifts in global distribution of production (see Tables 4.7 and 4.8). Between

TABLE 4.6 Automobile market shares in individual countries (%)

	1988	2006		1988	2006
U.S.			**U.K.**		
GM	36.3	23.5	Ford	26.3	18.5
Ford	21.7	16.7	GM (Vauxhall)	13.7	12.7
DaimlerChrysler	11.3	10.8	Peugeot	8.7	10.0
Toyota	6.9	13.9	VW	n.a.	12.9
Honda	6.2	8.8	BMW/Rover	15.0	4.6
France			**Japan**		
Renault	29.1	24.8	Toyota	43.9	40.4
Peugeot	34.2	28.2	Nissan	23.2	14.0
VW	9.2	11.6	Honda	10.8	12.2
Ford	7.1	6.0	Suzuki	n.a.	12.1
Italy			**Korea**		
Fiat	59.9	28.5	Hyundai	55.9	50.0
VW	11.7	10.8	Kia	25.0	23.3
Ford	3.7	7.8	Daewoo	19.1	10.0
Peugeot	n.a.	9.6			
Renault	7.1	6.4			
Germany					
VW/Audi	28.3	27.8			
GM (Opel)	16.1	9.7			
Ford	10.1	8.0			
Mercedes	9.2	11.3			

n.a. = not available.

Sources: Japan Automobile Manufacturers Association; Korean Automobile Manufacturers Association; A. K. Binder (ed.), Ward's Automotive Yearbook, 2009, Wards Communications, Southfield MI, 2009.

TABLE 4.7 World motor vehicle production by countries and regions (percentage of world total)

	1960	1989	1994	2000	2005	2008
U.S.	52.0	23.8	24.5	22.2	20.0	18.6
Western Europe	38.0	31.7	31.2	29.9	28.4	20.7
Central and E. Europe	2.0	4.8	4.3	4.6	5.4	9.5
Japan	1.0	18.2	21.2	17.7	17.0	16.7
Korea	–	1.8	4.6	5.0	5.3	5.5
Other	7.0	19.7	14.4	20.6	24.0	29.0
Total units (millions)	12.8	49.5	50.0	57.4	66.8	69.4

Source: A. K. Binder (ed.), Ward's Automotive Yearbook, 2009, Wards Communications, Southfield MI, 2009.

1990 and 2008, China, Korea, Brazil and India established themselves among the world's leading motor-vehicle producers as a result of rapidly growing domestic markets and low production costs. Nevertheless, the continued leadership of Germany, Japan and the U.S., despite their high costs, pointed to the power of agglomeration effects in maintaining the competitiveness of long-established production centers.

TABLE 4.8 Top-15 automobile-producing countries, 2008 (thousands of cars; excludes trucks)

	1987	1990	1995	2000	2005	2008
Japan	7891	9948	7664	8363	9017	9916
China	n.a.	n.a.	356	620	3118	6341
Germany	4604	4805	4360	5132	5350	5532
U.S.	7099	6077	6338	5542	4321	3777
Brazil	789	663	1312	1348	2009	2561
Korea	793	987	1893	1881	2195	2436
France	3052	3295	3051	2883	3113	2144
Spain	1403	1679	1959	2445	2098	2014
India	n.a.	n.a.	n.a.	541	999	1507
Russia*	1329	1260	834	967	1288	1469
U.K.	1143	1296	1532	1641	1596	1448
Mexico	266	346	710	1130	846	1217
Canada	810	1072	1339	1551	1356	1195
Poland	301	256	260	533	527	840
Italy	1701	1874	1422	1442	726	659

*U.S.S.R. in 1987 and 1990.

Sources: Japan Automobile Manufacturers Association; Korean Automobile Manufacturers Association; A. K. Binder (ed.), Ward's Automotive Yearbook, 2009, Wards Communications, Southfield MI, 2009.

TABLE 4.9 Hourly compensation for motor vehicle workers (U.S.$ per hour, including benefits)

	1975	1984	1994	1998	2002	2004	2006
Germany	7.89	11.92	34.74	34.65	32.20	44.05	45.93
U.S.	9.55	19.02	27.00	27.21	32.35	33.95	35.12
U.K.	4.12	7.44	15.99	20.07	21.11	29.40	29.95
France	5.10	8.20	18.81	18.50	18.73	26.34	29.41
Japan	3.56	7.90	25.91	22.55	24.22	27.38	27.84
Spain	–	5.35	15.37	15.34	15.11	21.55	24.18
Korea	0.45	1.74	7.81	7.31	12.22	15.82	19.04
Italy	5.16	8.00	16.29	16.44	15.67	21.74	18.62
Mexico	2.94	2.55	2.99	2.21	3.68	3.50	3.73

Source: U.S. Department of Labor, Bureau of Labor Statistics.

The Outlook

As he revisited his financial forecasts for the next planning period, Booth realized that Ford's ability to generate profit would depend not just upon the recovery of demand in the world automobile market but also upon how competition would affect the kinds of profit margin that the industry would be earning over the next four years. What would happen in terms of mergers, capacity rationalization, and entry by emerging market manufacturers into world markets would clearly have a major impact on the overall margins that the industry would earn. As of June 2009, there was little evidence that the structural changes anticipated by many industry insiders were materializing. In particular, there was no evidence that recession and scale economies were pushing the industry towards radical consolidation. Despite the widely held belief that the minimum efficient scale for a full-line automobile producer was five million units annually, some of the industry's most successful companies— such as BMW, Suzuki, SAIC, and Tata Motor—had output far below this threshold. Meanwhile, General Motors and Ford with output well in excess of five million units annually were struggling for survival.

Booth also recognized that, despite the appearance of the industry becoming ossified by government support for existing carmakers, there was also the potential for radical change. The combination of environmental concerns and technological change might lead to a number of different scenarios. With global warming accelerating, government regulation and consumer preferences seemed likely to accelerate the shift from large to small cars and hasten the obsolescence of the internal combustion engine. The transition to electric vehicles would offer opportunities for a range of new entrants into the industry—particularly those companies with well-developed capabilities in electrical engineering. Environmental concerns—particularly rising urban congestion—might also result in a dramatic decline in private transportation in favor of public transportation, or possibly private motoring based upon short-term rental rather than car ownership.

Booth was particularly cognizant of the industry's propensity to retain outmoded assumptions concerning the automobile market and its economic drivers—indeed, this was a primary reason why the Detroit "Big Three" were in such a dire predicament. These deeply entrenched assumptions included: the belief that scale economies were the primary drivers of competitiveness, that there was no viable alternative to the internal combustion engine, that efficiency required offering a full range of models, that big cars were more profitable than small cars, and that consumers always preferred more—in terms of size and accessories—to less. Recent events had confounded many of these assumptions. Conventional notions about the attractiveness of different product segments appeared to be breaking down: some of the most popular—and profitable—new product launches had been small cars: the BMW Mini and Fiat Cinquecento in particular. The global success of the Toyota Prius and Honda Insight pointed to environmental awareness among consumers even in the absence of government inducements. New approaches to product development—including virtual prototyping, modular design and collaborative design and development—have the potential to overturn conventional relationships between scale and competitiveness. The efficiency-based logic of mass production is also being challenged by new developments in flexible manufacturing and increased opportunities for customization. Part of the appeal of the BMW Mini and Fiat Cinquecento has been their vast potential for customization.

Appendix

TABLE 4.10 Company sales ($ billion)

	1980–4[a]	1985–9[a]	1990–4[a]	1995–9[a]	2000-4[a]	2005	2006	2007	2008
GM	68	110	128	169	186	193	207	181	149
Ford	42	77	96	149	166	177	160	172	146
Chrysler	13	28	39	58	–	–	n.a.	60	n.a.
Daimler[b]	12	34	59	71	166	177	200	146	135
Toyota	18	42	82	107	125	173	179	203	265
VW	16	28	48	64	96	113	138	160	160
Honda	8	18	35	50	62	80	84	94	121
Fiat	18	27	42	50	59	55	68.4	86.1	83.7
Nissan	16	26	51	57	58	81	89	109	91
Peugeot	13	19	28	35	58	67		89	77
Renault	15	31	31	37	44	47	55	60	53
BMW	5	10	21	34	45	55	65	82	
Mitsubishi	12	14	25	32	27	20	41	43	61
Hyundai Motor	n.a.	n.a.	n.a.	18	38	58	68	74	
Mazda	n.a.	12	21	18	19	25	25	28	35

[a] Annual average.

[b] Daimler Chrysler 2000–6.

n.a. = not available.

Source: Company financial statements; Hoovers.

TABLE 4.11 Company profitability (return on equity, %)

	1980–4[a]	1985–9[a]	1990–4[a]	1995–9[a]	2000–4	2005	2006	2007	2008
GM[b]	11.4	11.8	3.2	27.5	11.7	n.c.	n.c.	n.c.	n.c.
Ford	0.4	21.8	5.9	35.4	(7.7)	18.8	n.c.	(48.2)	n.c.
Chrysler	66.5	20.8	2.0	24.5	–	–	n.a.	n.a.	n.a.
Daimler	24.3	18.3	6.9	22.1	7.7	8.0	9.5	13.1	5.5
Toyota	12.6	10.6	6.1	6.8	10.1	13.6	12.6	12.9	(5.0)
VW	1.6	6.3	(0.4)	11.1	6.8	4.7	7.3	13.0	13.4
Honda	18.1	11.8	5.3	15.1	13.2	11.9	11.3	11.1	1.3
Fiat	10.9	18.7	6.8	7.6	(24.2)	3.5	16.0	28.3	23.3
Nissan	10.3	4.7	3.6	(0.1)	29.3	17.2	13.0	13.7	(8.9)
Peugeot	(15.2)	36.7	12.5	3.0	13.4	n.a.	n.a.	5.8	(3.8)
Renault	(152.4)	51.1	9.1	11.0	14.7	17.6	14.2	12.7	3.2
BMW	14.8	10.4	9.7	(4.0)	15.4	13.2	14.5	11.8	12.7
Mitsubishi	10.0	7.9	4.8	(5.3)	(113.3)	(131.7)	3.7	11.2	(25.7)
Hyundai Motor	n.a.	n.a.	n.a.	4.4	10.6	n.a.	10.7	12.5	11.0
Mazda	n.a.	4.8	5.0	6.3	(34.2)	17.1	4.9	12.0	15.8

[a] Annual average.

[b] GM made a net loss of $2billion in 2006, $39 billion in 2007 and $31 bn. in 2008.

n.a. = not available.

n.c. = not calculable (shareholders' equity negative).

Source: Company financial statements; Hoovers.

Notes

1 Ford's stockholders' equity was negative $17.3 billion at the end of 2008.

2 "U.S. Car Industry: Back on the Road," *Financial Times,* June 17, 2009.

3 Ford Motor Company, Business Plan Submitted to the Senate Banking Committee, December 2, 2008, p. 16.

4 Note that different statistical authorities apply different definitions of "automobile." The basic distinction is between automobiles (or "passenger cars") used to transport people and commercial vehicles ("trucks") used to transport goods. The problem is that, in the U.S., sport-utility vehicles and pick-up trucks used primarily for personal transportation are classed as light trucks. Ideally we would like to define the automobile industry as comprising automobiles and light trucks (vans, pick-up trucks, SUVs, passenger vans), i.e. excluding heavy trucks and large buses. However, most of the statistics we use aggregate automobiles and all commercial vehicles.

Case 5 Wal-Mart Stores Inc., 2009

If you don't want to work weekends, you shouldn't be in retail.

—SAM WALTON (EXPLAINING THE SATURDAY CORPORATE MEETING)

On February 1, 2009, Mike Duke took over from Lee Scott as CEO of Wal-Mart Stores, Inc., the world's biggest retailer. His new office—the same CEO office that had been occupied by founder, Sam Walton—typified the contrast between Wal-Mart's vast size, \$401 billion in sales and over two million employees, and its values of parsimony and simplicity. *Fortune* described the office as "no bigger than a child's bedroom."[1]

Wal-Mart's transformation from a small chain of discount stores in Arkansas, Missouri and Oklahoma in 1970 to the world's second largest company (in terms of revenue) was one of the most remarkable corporate success stories of the twentieth century. Its founder, Sam Walton, had combined folksy charm and homespun business wisdom with cutting-edge information technology and supply-chain management to create the world's most efficient retail organization. Under Lee Scott's leadership, Wal-Mart had embarked on its next stage of development. During his nine years as CEO, Scott had hugely expanded Wal-Mart's operations outside the U.S. and had engineered a transformation in Wal-Mart's external image through embracing social and environmental responsibility and a less aggressively anti-labor union stance. The success of Scott's leadership was apparent in the financial results for the financial year that closed on January 31, 2009: in the face of America's worst economic downturn in 60 years, Wal-Mart reported revenue growth of 7.2% and net income growth of 5.3%.

Despite this transformation, Duke's first report to Wal-Mart's shareholders placed primary emphasis on continuity in the company's leadership:

> My first day in the new job fell on the first Sunday in February. So my wife Susan and I took a few hours to move some boxes and belongings into my new office. But we didn't replace the carpet, furniture, or even Sam Walton's old wood paneling. With the exception of a couple of pictures on the wall, we kept it as the same office in which Sam Walton, David Glass and Lee Scott made the decisions that built our great Company. I could not be more honored or more humbled to sit at their desk now.[2]

The strategy he outlined suggested little deviation from that of his predecessor:

> Our Company is well positioned for today's difficult economy and tomorrow's changing world. We have an exceptionally strong management team, able to execute our strategy, perform every single day, and deliver results . . .
>
> Our team is very focused on working to improve return on investment (ROI). Our capital efficiency process drives expansion decisions. The Company has stepped up investments in technology to maintain leadership in an area that always has been a driver of our success. These efforts will contribute to Wal-Mart's increased efficiency through our use of capital, technology and logistics . . .
>
> Our strategy is working, and we're building more and more momentum. We will maintain our focus on price leadership in every market, whether we're talking to the working mom in São Paulo or the businessman in Tokyo. . .
>
> I'm certain of our strategy, our opportunity and our ability to perform as individuals and as a Company. By executing well and adhering to our values, we plan to distance ourselves even further from the competition and do even more to "save people money so they can live better."[3]

At the same time, Duke wondered whether a "more-of-the-same" strategy would be sufficient to maintain Wal-Mart's remarkable performance record during the new decade. During the decade 2000–9, Wal-Mart had grown sales at an average annual rate of 10% and earned an average return on equity of 21%—remarkable in the mature, intensely competitive business of discount retailing. Yet, maintaining that performance would become increasingly difficult.

As Wal-Mart continually expanded its range of goods and services—into groceries, fashion clothing, music downloads, online prescription drugs, financial services and health clinics—so it was forced to compete on a broader front. While Wal-Mart could seldom be beaten on cost, it faced competitors that were more stylish (T. J. Maxx), more quality-focused (Wholefoods), more service oriented

(Lowe's, Best Buy), and more focused in terms of product range. In its traditional area of discount retailing, Target was proving an increasingly formidable competitor. In March 2009, Target signaled its competitive intent by opening a store in Rogers, Arkansas—the site of the first ever Wal-Mart discount store.[4] Wal-Mart was also facing a "return of the zombies": several retailers that it had crushed earlier—Kmart, Sears and J. C. Penney—had been revitalized by new management. In warehouse clubs, its Sam's Clubs ran a poor second to Costco.

Increasing size boosted Wal-Mart's buying power but it also brought problems. Wal-Mart's success had rested heavily upon its ability to combine huge size with remarkable speed and responsiveness. Critical to this was its short chain of command and close relationship between the top management team and individual store managers. A key component in this linkage had been Wal-Mart's Saturday-morning meeting at its Bentonville HQ. In January 2008, the growing size of the meeting and increasing difficulty of getting all Wal-Mart executives back to Bentonville resulted in the company changing these meetings—which the company had described as "the pulse of our culture"—from weekly to monthly.[5]

Increased size also made Wal-Mart a bigger target for opponents. For years Wal-Mart had been under attack by organized labor seeking to unionize Wal-Mart's two million employees. More recently, "The Beast of Bentonville" has attracted the ire of environmentalists, antiglobalization activists, women's and children's rights advocates, small-business representatives and a growing number of legislators of varying political hues. Under Duke's predecessor, Wal-Mart had become increasingly image conscious and was a late but enthusiastic convert to social and environmental responsibility. The result was a series of senior appointments to new executive positions—a head of global ethics and a new executive vice president of government relations—plus more top management time spent in Washington and with the media.

Wal-Mart's growing geographical scope also raised complex strategic and organizational issues. Unlike other successful global retailers (such as IKEA), Wal-Mart did not have a consistent approach to different national markets. Moreover, its success varied greatly from country to country. Overall, its profitability was significantly lower internationally than in the U.S. What were the implications of the growing importance of its overseas operations for Wal-Mart's identity and culture, both of which were firmly rooted in Wal-Mart's Southern U.S., small-town heartland?

Looking ahead, Mike Duke realized that his first challenge would be to maintain and strengthen the principles and capabilities that had driven Wal-Mart's success for four decades: its unremitting quest for cost efficiency, its leading-edge logistics, its commitment to customers and ability to instill loyalty and commitment within its employees. His second challenge was to prepare Wal-Mart for a future that would inevitably be different from the past, would require meeting new customer requirements and new competitive challenges, and would inevitably require developing new capabilities.

History of Wal-Mart

Between 1945 and 1961, Sam Walton and his brother, Bud, developed a chain of 15 Ben Franklin franchised variety stores across rural Arkansas. Experiencing increasing price competition from newly established discount retailers with large format stores offering a broad range of products, Sam and Bud began developing their own discount store concept. At the time discount stores were located within large towns—it was believed that a minimum population of 100 000 was necessary to support a discount store. Sam Walton believed that, if the prices were right, discount stores could be viable in smaller communities: "Our strategy was to put good-sized stores into little one-horse towns that everyone else was ignoring."[6] The first Wal-Mart opened in 1962; by 1970 there were 30 Wal-Mart stores in small and medium-sized towns in Arkansas, Oklahoma, and Missouri.

Distribution was a problem for Wal-Mart:

> Here we were in the boondocks, so we didn't have distributors falling over themselves to serve us like our competitors in larger towns. Our only alternative was to build our own distribution centers so that we could buy in volume at attractive prices and store the merchandise.[7]

In 1970, Walton built his first distribution center, and in the same year took the company public in order to finance the heavy investment involved. Replicating this structure of large distribution hubs serving up to 100 discount stores formed the basis for Wal-Mart's expansion strategy. By 1980, Wal-Mart had 330 stores across the South and into the Midwest. By 1995, Wal-Mart was in all 50 states. Geographical expansion was incremental. In developing a new area, Wal-Mart built a few stores that were served initially by extending distribution from a nearby cluster. When a critical mass of stores had been established, Wal-Mart would build a new distribution center. As Wal-Mart became a national retail chain, so it entered more developed retailing areas, including larger cities, where it met stronger competition from other discount chains. In its early days, the local Wal-Mart was the only discount store in town—by 1993, 55% of Wal-Mart stores faced direct competition from Kmart and 23% from Target.[8]

Diversification

Wal-Mart experimented continuously with alternative retail formats. Some, like Helen's Arts and Crafts and Dot Deep Discount Drugstores, were unsuccessful. Others—Sam's warehouse clubs and the Supercenters—grew rapidly to become important components of Wal-Mart's business.

Sam's Clubs imitated a distribution concept established by Price Club. The warehouse clubs were not retailers as they were not open to the public. They were clubs where access was through membership. They carried a small number of lines and most items were available in multipacks and catering-size packs. The clubs were literally warehouses with products available on pallets and minimal customer service. The rationale was to maximize economies in purchasing, minimize operating costs and pass the savings on to members through very low prices. Competition among warehouse clubs was ferocious, resulting in rapid consolidation of the sector. Wal-Mart acquired The Wholesale Company in 1991 and Kmart's PACE clubs in 1993, while Costco Wholesale and PriceCo merged in 1993.

Supercenters were Wal-Mart's large-format stores (averaging 187 000 square feet, compared with 102 000 square feet for a Wal-Mart discount store and 129 000 square feet for a Sam's Club). Supercenters were modeled on the European concept of the "hypermarket" that had been pioneered by the French retailer Carrefour.

A Supercenter combined a discount store with a grocery supermarket: in addition, a Supercenter incorporated a number of specialty units such as an eyeglass store, hair salon, dry cleaners, and photo lab. The Supercenters were open for 24 hours a day, seven days a week. The Supercenter stores and Sam's Clubs were supplied through a separate distribution network from the Wal-Mart discount stores. In 1998, Wal-Mart opened the first of its Neighborhood Markets—supermarkets with an average floorspace of 42 000 square feet.

Wal-Mart also built a substantial online business through its web sites walmart.com and samsclub.com. Its online presence was extended through its online pharmacy and music download service.

International Expansion

Fear of saturation at home encouraged expansion abroad. In 1992, Wal-Mart established a joint venture with Mexico's largest retailer, Cifra S.A., and began opening Wal-Mart discount stores and Sam's Clubs in several Mexican cities. In 2000, Wal-Mart acquired 51% of Cifra and took control of the joint venture. By 2003, Wal-Mart Mexico was the country's biggest retailer.

In 1994, Wal-Mart entered the Canadian market by acquiring 120 Woolco stores from Woolworth and converting them to its own discount stores format. Again, Wal-Mart established itself as the country's largest retailer.

In Europe, Wal-Mart has struggled. In the U.K. its Asda subsidiary failed to take sales from market leader Tesco. In Germany, Wal-Mart sold its 85 stores to Metro after eight years of losses.

During the past decade, its international expansion has concentrated upon Latin America and Asia. Asia has been a mixed experience. Wal-Mart withdrew from South Korea in 2006 and at its Seiyu chain in Japan (51% Wal-Mart owned) its low-price strategy met a poor response from Japan's quality-obsessed shoppers.[9] In China, greenfield entry consisted of 138 Wal-Mart Supercenters and three Sam's Clubs. Moreover, through its 30% stake in the Chinese supermarket chain Trust-Mart, Wal-Mart owned 102 Trust Mart stores. Table 5.1 shows Wal-Mart's international development.

Overall, Wal-Mart's performance in overseas markets has been inconsistent. Its strongest performance was in adjacent countries—Mexico and Canada.

Sam Walton

Wal-Mart's strategy and management style was inseparable from the philosophy and values of its founder. Until his death in 1992, Sam Walton was the embodiment of Wal-Mart's unique approach to retailing. After his death, Sam Walton's beliefs and business principles continued to be the beacon that guided Wal-Mart's development. As Harry Cunningham, founder of Kmart Stores, observed: "Sam's establishment of the Walton culture throughout the company was the key to the whole thing."[10]

For Sam Walton, thrift and value for money were a religion. Undercutting competitors' prices was an obsession that drove his unending quest for cost economies. Walton established a culture in which every item of expenditure was questioned. Was it necessary? Could it be done cheaper? He set an example that few of his senior colleagues could match: he walked rather than took taxis, shared

TABLE 5.1 Wal-Mart stores by country, January 2009

Country	Stores	Notes
U.S.	3960	Included 2176 Supercenters, 1100 discount stores, 574 Sam's Clubs, and 110 Neighborhood Markets
Mexico	1197	Entered 1991: JV with Cifra. Chains include Wal-Mart, Bodegas, Suburbia, Vips and Mercamas
Puerto Rico	56	Entered 1992
Canada	318	Entered 1994: acquired Woolco
Argentina	28	Entered 1995: greenfield venture
Brazil	345	Entered 1995: JV with Lojas Americana. Includes Todo Dias, Bompreço, and Sonae stores
China	243	Greenfield entry in 1996; acquired 35% of Trust-Mart and 102 stores in 2006
U.K.	358	Entered 1999 by acquiring Asda. Operates Wal-Mart superstores and Asda supermarkets/discount stores
Japan	386	Entered 2002: acquired 38% of Seiyu. Mainly small stores but some superstores
Costa Rica	164	Acquired 30% of
El Salvador	77	CARHCO, a subsidiary
Guatemala	160	of Royal Ahold in 2005
Honduras	50	Shareholding later
Nicaragua	51	increased to 51%.
Chile	197	Entered January 2009 by acquiring Distribución y Servicio SA
Total	**7590**	

Source: www.walmartstores.com.

rooms at budget motels while on business trips and avoided any corporate trappings or manifestations of opulence or success. For Walton, wealth was a threat and an embarrassment rather than a reward and a privilege. His own lifestyle gave little indication that he was America's richest person (before being eclipsed by Bill Gates). He was equally disdainful of the display of wealth by colleagues: "We've had lots of millionaires in our ranks. And it drives me crazy when they flaunt it. Every now and then somebody will do something especially showy, and I don't hesitate to rant and rave about it at the Saturday morning meeting. I don't think that big mansions and flashy cars is what the Wal-Mart culture is supposed to be about."[11]

His attention to detail was legendary. As chairman and chief executive, he was quite clear that his priorities lay with his employees ("associates"), customers and the operational details through which the former created value for the latter. He shunned offices in favor of spending time in his stores. Most of his life was spent on the road (or in the air piloting his own plane), making impromptu visits to stores and distribution centers. He collected information on which products were selling well in Tuscaloosa; why margins were down in Santa Maria; how a new display system for children's clothing in Carbondale had boosted sales by 15%. His passion for detail extended to competitors' stores as well as his own: as well as visiting their stores, he was known to count cars in their parking lots.

Central to his leadership role at Wal-Mart was his relationship with his employees—the Wal-Mart associates. In an industry known for low pay and hard working conditions, Walton created a unique spirit of motivation and involvement. He believed fervently in giving people responsibility, trusting them, but also continually monitoring their performance.

After his death in 1992, Sam Walton's habits and utterances became hallowed principles guiding the company and its employees. For example, Wal-Mart's "10-foot attitude" pledge is based on Sam Walton's request to a store employee that: "I want you to promise that whenever you come within 10 feet of a customer, you will look him in the eye, greet him and ask if you can help him."[12] The "Sundown Rule"—that every request, no matter how big or small, gets same-day service—has become the basis for Wal-Mart's fast-response management system. Sam Walton's contribution to the management systems and management style of Wal-Mart is reflected in Wal-Mart's web site's description of "The Wal-Mart Culture" (see the Appendix).

Sam Walton's ability to attract the affection and loyalty of both employees and customers owed much to his ability to generate excitement within the otherwise sterile world of discount retailing. He engendered a positive attitude among Wal-Mart employees and he reveled in his role as company cheerleader. Wal-Mart's replacement of its mission slogan, "Everyday Low Prices" by "Save Money, Live Better" was intended to reflect Walton's insistence that Wal-Mart played a vital role in the happiness and well-being of ordinary people.

Wal-Mart in 2009

The Business

Wal-Mart described its business as follows:

> Wal-Mart Stores, Inc. operates retail stores in various formats around the world and is committed to saving people money so they can live better. We earn the trust of our customers every day by providing a broad assortment of quality merchandise and services at everyday low prices ("EDLP") while fostering a culture that rewards and embraces mutual respect, integrity and diversity. EDLP is our pricing philosophy under which we price items at a low price every day so that our customers trust that our prices will not change under frequent promotional activity.
>
> Our operations comprise three business segments: Walmart U.S., International and Sam's Club.
>
> - Our Walmart U.S. segment is the largest segment of our business, accounting for 63.7% of our fiscal 2009 net sales and operates stores in three different formats in the United States, as well as Wal-Mart's online retail operations, walmart.com. Our Walmart U.S. retail formats include:
>   - Discount stores, which average approximately 108 000 square feet in size and offer a wide assortment of general merchandise and a limited variety of food products;

- Supercenters, which average approximately 186 000 square feet in size and offer a wide assortment of general merchandise and a full-line supermarket; and
- Neighborhood Markets, which average approximately 42 000 square feet in size and offer a full-line supermarket and a limited assortment of general merchandise.

- At January 31, 2009, our International segment consisted of retail operations in 14 countries and Puerto Rico. This segment generated 24.6% of our fiscal 2009 net sales. The International segment includes numerous different formats of retail stores and restaurants, including discount stores, supercenters and Sam's Clubs that operate outside the United States.
- Our Sam's Club segment consists of membership warehouse clubs in the United States and the segment's online retail operations, samsclub.com. Sam's Club accounted for 11.7% of our fiscal 2009 net sales. Our Sam's Clubs average approximately 133 000 square feet in size.[13]

Table 5.2 shows sales and profits for these three business segments.

Performance

Table 5.3 summarizes some key financial data for Wal-Mart during the period 1994 to 2006. Table 5.4 shows Wal-Mart's recent performance compared with other discount retailers.

TABLE 5.2 Wal-Mart: performance by segment (year ending January 31)

	2000	2001	2002	2003	2004	2005	2006	2007	2008	2009
Sales ($ billion)										
Wal-Mart Stores	108.7	121.9	139.1	157.1	174.2	191.8	209.9	226.3	239.5	255.7
Sam's Clubs	24.8	26.8	29.4	31.7	34.5	37.1	39.8	41.6	44.4	46.9
International	22.7	32.1	35.5	40.8	47.6	56.3	62.7	77.1	90.6	98.6
Sales increase										
Wal-Mart Stores (%)	14.0	12.1	14.1	12.9	10.9	10.1	9.4	7.8	5.8	6.8
Sam's Clubs (%)	8.4	8.1	9.7	7.8	8.8	7.5	7.3	4.5	6.7	5.6
International (%)	85.6	41.4	10.6	14.9	16.7	18.3	11.4	30.2	17.5	9.1
Operating income ($ billion)										
Wal-Mart Stores	8.70	9.70	10.30	11.80	12.90	14.20	15.30	16.62	17.52	18.76
Sam's Clubs	0.85	0.94	1.03	1.02	1.13	1.30	1.40	1.48	1.62	1.61
International	0.82	1.11	1.46	2.00	2.40	3.00	3.30	4.26	4.77	4.94
Operating income/sales										
Wal-Mart Stores (%)	8.0	8.0	7.4	7.5	7.4	7.4	7.3	7.3	7.3	7.3
Sam's Clubs (%)	3.4	3.5	3.5	3.2	3.3	3.5	3.5	3.6	3.6	3.4
International (%)	3.6	3.5	4.1	4.9	5.0	5.3	5.3	5.5	5.2	5.0

Source: Wal-Mart Stores Inc., 10-K Reports.

TABLE 5.3 Wal-Mart Stores Inc.: financial summary 1998–2009 (year ended January 31)

	1998	1999	2000	2001	2002	2003	2004	2005	2006	2007	2008	2009
Net sales	118.0	137.6	165.0	191.3	217.8	229.6	256.3	285.2	312.4	345.4	374.5	401.2
Net sales increase (%)	12.0	17.0	20.0	16.0	4.0	5.0	12.0	11.3	9.5	11.7	8.6	7.2
U.S. same-store sales increase (%)	6.0	9.0	8.0	5.0	6.0	6.0	4.0	3.3	3.4	2.0	1.6	3.5
Cost of sales	93.4	108.7	129.7	150.3	171.6	178.3	198.7	219.8	240.4	264.2	286.5	306.2
SG&A expenses	19.4	22.4	27.0	31.6	36.2	40.0	44.9	51.2	56.7	64.0	70.3	76.7
Interest expense	0.6	0.5	0.8	1.1	1.1	0.8	0.7	0.9	1.2	1.6	1.8	1.9
Income taxes	2.1	2.7	3.3	3.7	3.9	4.4	5.1	5.6	5.8	6.2	6.9	7.1
Operating income	3.4	4.2	5.4	6.1	6.4	7.8	8.9	10.5	11.4	12.2	12.9	13.3
Net income	3.5	4.4	5.4	6.3	6.7	8.0	9.1	10.3	11.2	11.3	12.7	13.4
Current assets	19.4	21.1	24.4	26.6	28.2	30.7	34.5	38.9	43.8	47.0	47.6	48.8
Inventories	16.8	17.5	20.2	21.6	22.7	24.4	26.6	29.8	32.2	33.7	35.2	34.5
Fixed assets	23.6	26.0	36.0	40.9	45.8	51.4	58.5	68.1	79.3	88.4	97.0	95.7
Total assets	45.4	50.0	70.3	78.1	83.5	94.8	104.9	120.2	138.2	151.6	163.5	163.2
Current liabilities	14.5	16.8	25.8	28.9	27.3	32.5	37.4	43.2	48.8	52.2	58.5	55.3
Long-term debt	7.2	6.9	13.7	12.5	15.7	16.6	17.1	20.1	26.4	27.2	29.8	31.3
Long-term lease obligations	2.5	2.7	3.0	3.2	3.0	3.0	3.0	3.2	3.7	3.5	3.6	3.2
Shareholders' equity	18.5	21.1	25.8	31.3	35.1	39.5	43.6	49.4	53.2	61.6	64.6	65.3
Current ratio	1.3	1.3	0.9	0.9	1	0.9	0.9	0.9	0.9	0.9	0.8	0.9
Return on assets[a] (%)	8.5	9.6	9.5	8.7	8.5	9.0	9.0	9.3	8.9	8.8	8.5	8.4
Return on equity[b] (%)	19.8	22.4	22.9	22.0	20.1	21.0	21.0	22.6	22.5	22.0	21.0	21.2
Other year-end data (number of units)												
U.S. discount stores	1921	1869	1801	1736	1647	1568	1478	1353	1209	1075	971	891
U.S. Supercenters	441	564	721	888	1066	1258	1471	1713	1980	2256	2447	2612
U.S. Sam's Clubs	443	451	463	475	500	525	538	551	567	579	591	602
U.S. Neighborhood Markets	–	4	7	19	31	49	64	85	100	112	132	153
International units	601	715	1004	1071	1170	1272	1355	1587	2285	2757	3121	3615
Employees (000s)	825	910	1140	1244	1383	1400	1400	1600	1800	2100	1900	2100

[a] (Net income before minority interest, equity in unconsolidated subsidiaries and cumulative effect of accounting change)/Average assets.

[b] Net income/Average shareholders' equity.

Source: Wal-Mart Stores Inc., 10-K Reports.

TABLE 5.4 Wal-Mart and its competitors: performance comparisons ($ billions except where noted)

	Wal-Mart		Target		Dollar General		Costco	
	2007	2008	2007	2008	2007	2008[a]	2007	2008
Income								
Sales revenue	348.7	378.8	59.5	63.4	9.2	5.6	56. 5	63.5
Gross profit	84.5	92.3	20.1	21.5	2.4	1.6	8.0	9.0
Gross profit margin (%)	24.2	24.4	33.8	33.9	26.1	28.6	12.3	12.4
Sales, general &	58.5	64.0	13.5	14.5	2.1	1.0	5.8	6.4
administrative expense	5.5	6.3	1.5	1.8	0.28	0.15	0.57	0.66
Depreciation and amortization								
Operating margin (%)	5.9	5.8	8.5	8.3	2.7	6.6	2.5	2.7
Total net income	11.3	12.7	2.8	2.8	−0.008	−0.005	1.08	1.28
Net profit margin (%)	3.2	3.4	4.7	4.5	−0.3	−0.1	1.7	1.8
Financial position								
Cash	7.37	5.57	0.81	2.45	0.12	0.22	3.36	3.28
Inventories	33.69	35.18	6.25	6.78	1.43	1.29	4.88	5.04
Total current assets	46.59	47.59	14.71	18.91	1.74	1.52	9.32	9.46
Total assets	151.19	163.51	37.35	44.56	3.04	8.66	19.61	20.68
Short-term debt	8.28	11.27	1.36	1.96	0.008	0.003	0.11	0.14
Total current liabilities	51.75	58.45	11.12	11.78	0.83	0.86	8.58	8.87
Long-term debt	30.74	33.40	8.68	15.13	0.26	4.28	2.11	2.21
Total liabilities	89.62	98.91	21.72	29.25	1.29	5.95	10.98	11.49
Shareholder's equity	61.57	64.61	15.63	15.31	1.75	2.70	8.62	9.19
Financial ratios								
Total asset turnover	2.31	2.32	1.59	1.42	21.18	8.37	2.88	3.07
Inventory turnover	8.51	7.51	6.70	5.81	6.43	4.34	13.01	11.20
Debt/equity	1.46	1.53	1.39	1.91	0.74	2.20	1.27	1.25
Return on assets (%)	7.46	7.79	7.46	6.39	4.54	−0.15	5.52	6.20
Return on equity (%)	18.33	19.70	17.83	18.61	7.90	−0.47	12.56	13.95

[a] 47 weeks only.

Wal-Mart Stores' Operations and Activities[14]

Purchasing and Vendor Relationships

The size of Wal-Mart's purchases and its negotiating ability means that Wal-Mart is both desired and feared by manufacturers. Being accepted as a Wal-Mart vendor offers access to a huge share of the U.S. retail market. At the same time, Wal-Mart buyers are well aware of their ability to take full advantage of economies of scale available to their suppliers and to squeeze their margins to razor-thin level. Purchasing is centralized. All dealing with U.S. suppliers takes place at Wal-Mart's Bentonville headquarters. Would-be suppliers are escorted to one of 50 cubicles on "Vendor Row." Furnishings comprise just a table and folding chairs—sometimes no chairs. Suppliers regarded the experience of selling to Wal-Mart as intimidating and grueling: "Once you are ushered into one of the spartan little buyers' rooms, expect a steely eye across the table and be prepared to cut your price."[15] Another vendor commented: "All normal mating rituals are verboten. Their highest priority is making sure everybody at all times in all cases knows who's in charge . . . They talk softly, but they have piranha hearts, and if you aren't totally prepared when you go in there, you're in deep trouble."[16] The requirements that Wal-Mart imposes on its suppliers extend well beyond low prices. Increasingly Wal-Mart involves itself in its suppliers' employment policies, including workplace safety, working hours and absence of child labor.

All negotiations are directly between manufacturers and Wal-Mart: Wal-Mart refuses to do business with manufacturers' representatives and agents. To avoid dependence on any one supplier, Wal-Mart limits the total purchases it obtains from any one supplier. The result is an asymmetry of bargaining power. Thus, Wal-Mart's biggest supplier, Procter & Gamble, accounts for about 3% of Wal-Mart's sales—but this represents 18% of P&G's sales.

International expansion has allowed Wal-Mart to increase its purchasing muscle through global procurement. By 2003, Asda was sourcing over 2000 products from Wal-Mart's global network. This network included 23 procurement offices in 23 countries.[17]

Wal-Mart combines ruthless bargaining with close collaboration with its bigger suppliers. Wal-Mart's cooperation with Procter & Gamble provided a model for these relationships. The companies began electronic data interchange (EDI) at the beginning of the 1990s, and by 1993 there were 70 P&G employees working at Bentonville to manage sales and deliveries to Wal-Mart.[18]

By the mid-1990s, Wal-Mart had extended EDI to cover about 70% of its vendors. Through Wal-Mart's "Retail Link" system of supply-chain management, data interchange included point-of-sale data, levels of inventory, Wal-Mart's sales forecasts, vendors' production and delivery schedules, and electronic funds transfer.

Collaboration with Cisco Systems enabled Retail Link to move to the internet during the mid-1990s, allowing suppliers to log on to the Wal-Mart database for real-time store-by-store information on sales and inventory for their products. Suppliers could then collaborate with Wal-Mart buyers forecasting, inventory management, and shipping. The result was faster replenishment, lower inventory, and a product mix tuned to local customer needs. A key benefit to suppliers is in matching production schedules to Wal-Mart's sales.

Warehousing and Distribution

Wal-Mart is regarded as one of the world's leaders in logistics. It distributed a higher proportion of goods to its own stores than any other discount retailer. While most discount retailers relied heavily upon their suppliers to undertake distribution to individual stores, 82% of Wal-Mart's purchases were shipped to Wal-Mart's own distribution centers from where they were distributed in Wal-Mart trucks. The efficiency of the system rested on Wal-Mart's "hub-and-spoke" configuration. Distribution centers ("hubs") spanned over a million square feet, operated 24 hours, and served between 75 and 110 stores within a 200 mile radius. Deliveries into distribution centers were either in suppliers' trucks or Wal-Mart trucks, then deliveries were made to Wal-Mart stores. Grouping of Wal-Mart stores allowed trucks to deliver partial loads to several Wal-Mart stores on a single trip. On backhauls, Wal-Mart trucks would bring returned merchandise from stores and also pick up from local vendors. As a result, trucks were more than 60% full on backhauls. Unlike other retailers (and many manufacturers), which outsourced trucking, Wal-Mart owned over 4000 trucks and some 15 000 trailers.

Wal-Mart was continually seeking ways to make its logistics system cheaper, faster and more reliable. It was an early adopter of "cross-docking"—a system where goods arriving on inbound trucks were unloaded and reloaded on outbound trucks without entering warehouse inventory. In 2005, Wal-Mart introduced its "Remix" system designed to reduce inventories, speed deliveries to stores, and eliminate stock-outs. The new system created a new tier to Wal-Mart's distribution system. Third-party logistic companies were made responsible for making smaller, more frequent pickups from suppliers, establishing "consolidation centers" throughout the U.S., then making frequent deliveries to Wal-Mart's distribution centers. The new system would allow Wal-Mart to order from suppliers on a five-day rather than four-week basis and would lead to lower inventories in both distribution centers and retail stores.

In 2005, Wal-Mart extended its supply chain internationally. Its "direct import" initiative involved, first, purchasing directly from overseas suppliers rather than through importers and, second, taking control of import logistics. Covering 4 million square feet, its import distribution center in Baytown, Texas was America's largest distribution facility devoted to a single company's products. Not only did the new distribution center give Wal-Mart the opportunity to exert greater control over its supplies of imports—it allowed it to avoid the delays and congestion of west-coast ports such as Long Beach.[19]

In 2003 Wal-Mart announced the adoption of radio frequency identification (RDFI) and became the leading pioneer of this technology. However, slow adoption of RDFI by its suppliers has meant that, by 2009, Wal-Mart has been unable to eliminate manual bar code scanning for inventory control purposes.

Wal-Mart continuously seeks incremental improvements to its logistics systems. In the year ended January 2009 it reported higher inventory turnover and lower distribution costs as a result of packing its trucks more tightly.

In-Store Operations

Wal-Mart's management of its retail stores was based upon its objective of creating customer satisfaction by combining low prices, a wide range of quality products carefully tailored to customer needs and a pleasing shopping experience. Wal-Mart's management of its retail stores was distinguished by the following characteristics:

- *Merchandising*. Wal-Mart stores offered a wide range of nationally branded products. Between 2006 and 2009 it had expanded its range of brands—with a quest for more upscale brands in particular. Wal-Mart has become an important distribution partner for Apple, Dell, Sony, Dyson, and Kitchen Aid. Traditionally Wal-Mart placed less emphasis on own-brand products than other mass retailers; however, during 2008–9, Wal-Mart made major investments in its range of *Great Value* private-label products. Under its "Store of the Community" philosophy, Wal-Mart has long sought to tailor its range of merchandise to local market needs on a store-by-store basis. Over time, greater sophistication in analyzing point-of-sale data for individual stores has greatly increased Wal-Mart's responsiveness to local needs (see below).

- *Decentralization of store management.* Individual store managers were given considerable decision-making authority in relation to product range, product positioning within stores, and pricing. This differed from most other discount chains where decisions over pricing and merchandising were made either at head office or at regional offices. Decentralized decision-making power was also apparent within stores, where the managers of individual departments (for example, toys, health and beauty, consumer electronics) were expected to develop and implement their own ideas for increasing sales and reducing costs.
- *Customer service.* Discount stores were open 9 a.m. to 9 p.m. weekdays, with shorter hours on weekends. Supercenters were open continuously. Despite the fanatical emphasis on cost efficiency, Wal-Mart went to great lengths to engage with its customers at a personal level. Stores employed "greeters"—often retired individuals—who would welcome customers and hand out shopping baskets. Within the store, all employees were expected to look customers in the eye, smile at them and offer a verbal greeting. To encourage customer loyalty, Wal-Mart maintained a "Satisfaction Guaranteed" program. This program assured customers that Wal-Mart would accept returned merchandise on a no-questions-asked basis.

Marketing

Wal-Mart had been founded on Sam Walton's belief that: "There is only one boss: the customer." For Wal-Mart, the essence of customer service was low prices. Hence, Wal-Mart's marketing strategy was built upon its slogan "Everyday Low Prices": Wal-Mart's customer appeal was as a price leader across its entire product range, all the time—it did not engage in promotional price cutting.

The centrality of "Everyday Low Prices" to Wal-Mart's relationship with its customers had important implications for its marketing activities. Wal-Mart was able to rely on word-of-mouth communication of its merits and was able to spend comparatively little on advertising and other forms of promotion. Advertising typically involved one home-delivered advertisement circular per month by each store and some television advertising. As a result, Wal-Mart's advertising/sales ratio during the past three financial years was 0.55%—most of its rivals had advertising/sales ratios of between 1.5% and 3.0%. Nevertheless, with an advertising budget of over $2 billion, Wal-Mart was among the world's biggest advertisers.

Beyond its emphasis on serving customers by providing unbeatable value-for-money, the values that Wal-Mart projected were traditional American virtues of hard work, thrift, individualism, opportunity, and community. This identification with core American values was buttressed by a strong emphasis on patriotism and national causes.

However, as Wal-Mart increasingly became a target for politicians and pressure groups, former CEO Lee Scott initiated a major shift in the image that Wal-Mart projected to the world. In 2004, Wal-Mart issued its first annual report on ethical sourcing where it published results of its audit of suppliers' adherence to its code of conduct. In November 2005, Scott committed Wal-Mart to a program of environmental sustainability and set ambitious targets for renewable energy, the elimination of waste and a shift in product mix towards environmentally friendly products.[20] Two years later, Wal-Mart published the first of its annual sustainability reports.

Commitment to social and environmental responsibility can be seen as part of a wider effort by Wal-Mart to broaden its consumer appeal and counter the attempts by activist groups to characterize Wal-Mart as a heartless corporate giant whose success was built upon exploitation and oppression. Wal-Mart broadened its customer base to include more upper income consumers and expanded its geographical base into the more politically liberal parts of the U.S. (for example, the west coast and New England) and beyond U.S. borders, so building an appeal that extended beyond "everyday low prices."

In 2008, Wal-Mart launched a company-wide image makeover that involved a new corporate logo and a redesign of its stores. The new logo replaced upper-case characters by lower-case, eliminated the star-hyphen ("Wal*Mart"), and added a "sunburst" design. According to branding consultant, Marty Neumeier: "The new "sunburst" looks organic. My sense is they are trying to say, 'we're an eco-aware company,'" Tobias Frere-Jones, a professor of typography, observed that lower case letters tend to be interpreted as more casual and approachable.[21] The new logo coincided with a program of store redesign that included wider aisles, improved lighting, and lower shelves.[22]

Information Technology

Wal-Mart was a pioneer in applying information and communications technology to support decision making and promote efficiency and customer responsiveness. During the 1970s, Wal-Mart was among the first retailers to use computers for inventory control, to initiate EDI with its vendors, and to introduce bar code scanning for point-of-sale and inventory control. To link stores and cash register sales with supply chain management and inventory control, Wal-Mart invested $24 million in its own satellite in 1984. By 1990, Wal-Mart's satellite system was the largest two-way, fully integrated private satellite network in the world, providing two-way interactive voice and video capability, data transmission for inventory control, credit card authorization, and enhanced EDI.

During the 1990s Wal-Mart was pioneering the use of data-mining for retail merchandising:

> At Wal-Mart, information technology gives us that knowledge in the most direct way: by collecting and analyzing our own internal information on exactly what any given shopping cart contains. The popular term is "data-mining," and Wal-Mart has been doing it since about 1990. The result, by now, is an enormous database of purchasing information that enables us to place the right item in the right store at the right price. Our computer system receives 8.4 million updates every minute on the items that customers take home—and the relationship between the items in each basket.
>
> Data analysis allows Wal-Mart to forecast, replenish, and merchandise on a product-by-product, store-by-store level. For example, with years of sales data and information on weather, school schedules and other pertinent variables, Wal-Mart can predict daily sales of Gatorade at a specific store and automatically adjust store deliveries accordingly.[23]

Point-of-sale data analysis also assisted in planning store layout:

> There are some obvious purchasing patterns among the register receipts of families with infants and small children. Well-thought-out product placement not only simplifies the shopping trip for these customers—with baby aisles that include infant clothes and children's medicine alongside diapers, baby food and formula—but at the same time places higher-margin products among the staples . . . Customers who buy suitcases are likely to be looking for other items they might need for traveling too—such as travel alarms and irons, which now, logically enough, can be found displayed alongside luggage at many Wal-Mart stores.
>
> The common thread is simple: We are here to serve the customer; and customers tend to buy from us when we make it easy for them. That sounds like a simple idea. But first you must understand the customer's needs. And that's where information comes in.[24]

The role of IT was most important in linking and integrating the whole of Wal-Mart's value chain:

> Wal-Mart's web of information systems extends far beyond the walls of any one store. Starting from the basic information compiled at the checkout stand, at the shelves, and gathered by associates equipped with hand-held computer monitors, Wal-Mart works to manage its supplies and inventories not only in the stores, but all the way back to the original source. Wal-Mart has given suppliers access to some of our systems, which enables them to know exactly what is selling, and to plan their production accordingly. This not only helps us keep inventories under control, but also helps the supplier deliver the lowest-cost product to the customer. With sales and in-stock information transmitted between Wal-Mart and our supplier-partners in seconds over the internet, buyers and suppliers are privy to the same facts and negotiate based on a shared understanding—saving a significant amount of time and energy over more traditional, low-tech systems.
>
> Our buyer benefits from the supplier's product knowledge, while the supplier benefits from Wal-Mart's experience in the market. Combine these information systems with our logistics—our hub-and-spoke system in which distribution centers are placed within a day's truck run of the stores—and all the pieces fall into place for the ability to respond to the needs of our customers, before they are even in the store. In today's retailing world, speed is a crucial competitive advantage. And when it comes to turning information into improved merchandising and service to the customer, Wal-Mart is out in front and gaining speed. In the words of Randy Mott, Senior Vice President and Chief Information Officer, "The surest way to predict the future is to invent it."[25]

Human Resource Management

Wal-Mart's human-resource practices in 2009 were based upon Sam Walton's beliefs about relations between the company and its employees and between employees and customers. All employees—from executive-level personnel to checkout clerks—were known as "associates." Wal-Mart's relations with its associates were to be founded on respect, high expectations, close communication and clear incentives.

Wal-Mart's employees received relatively low pay—the median rates for hourly paid retail workers in 2009 was between $8.46 and $12 an hour. However, these rates were, on average, slightly above those paid in the retail trade generally. Employee benefits included a company health plan that covered 94% of Wal-Mart employees and a retirement scheme, which covered all employees with a year or more of service.

A key feature of Wal-Mart's compensation system was its profit incentives, which extended to hourly employees. A stock purchase plan was also available to employees. Wal-Mart retirees included a large number of millionaires—not all of whom were managers: in 1989, the first millionaire hourly associate retired from the company.

Wal-Mart resisted the unionization of its employees in the belief that union membership created a barrier between the management and the employees in furthering the success of the company and its members. Despite strenuous efforts by unions to recruit Wal-Mart employees, union penetration remained low. Between 2000 and 2008, the United Food and Commercial Workers union together with AFL-CIO fought a concerted campaign to recruit Wal-Mart workers, but to little effect.[26]

Associates enjoyed a high degree of autonomy and received continuous communication about their company's performance and about store operations. Every aspect of company operations and strategy was seen as depending on the close collaboration of managers and shop-floor employees. To control "shrinkage" (theft), the company instituted a system whereby a store's cost savings from reduced shrinkage were shared between the company and the store's employees. Wal-Mart's shrinkage was estimated to be just above 1%, versus an industry average of 2%.

Wal-Mart's approach to employee involvement made heavy use of orchestrated demonstration of enthusiasm and commitment. The central feature of Wal-Mart meetings from corporate to store level was the "Wal-Mart Cheer"—devised by Sam Walton after a visit to Korea. The call and response ritual ("Give me a W!" "Give me an A!" . . .) included the "Wal-Mart squiggly," which involved employees shaking their backsides in unison.

Fortune suggested that the Wal-Mart Cheer's mixture of homespun and corporate themes provided an apt metaphor for what it called "the Wal-Mart paradox":

> The paradox is that Wal-Mart stands for both Main Street values and the efficiencies of the huge corporation, aw-shucks hokeyness and terabytes of minute-by-minute sales data, fried-chicken luncheons at the Waltons' Arkansas home and the demands of Wall Street.
>
> Critics of Wal-Mart call the homespun stuff a fraud, a calculated strategy to put a human face on a relentlessly profit-minded corporation. What is paradoxical and suspect to people outside Wal-Mart, however, is perfectly normal to the people who work there. It reflects a deal that Sam Walton, Wal-Mart's founder, made with the people who worked for him.
>
> The deal was a lot more than just a matter of the occasional visit from Mr. Sam. Wal-Mart demonstrated its concern for workers in many ways that were

> small but specific: time-and-a-half for work on Sundays, an "open-door" policy that let workers bring concerns to managers at any level, the real chance of promotion (about 70% of store managers started as hourly associates).[27]

The paradox of Wal-Mart's human resource practices continues. The enthusiasm it generates among employees supports a level of involvement and empowerment that is unique among large retail organizations. At the same time, the intense pressure for cost reduction and sales growth frequently results in cases of employee abuse. Wal-Mart suffered reversals in class action lawsuits by current and former employees. In a series of adverse court decisions, Wal-Mart was forced to compensate current and former employees for unpaid overtime work, for failure to ensure that workers received legally mandated rest breaks, and for systematically discriminating against women in pay and promotion.

Organization and Management Style

Wal-Mart's management structure and management style had been molded by Sam Walton's principles and values. As Wal-Mart grew in size and geographical scope, Walton was determined that corporate executives should keep closely in touch with customers and store operations. The result was a structure in which communication between individual stores and the Bentonville headquarters was both close and personal. Wal-Mart's regional vice presidents were each responsible for supervising between 10 and 15 district managers (who, in turn, were in charge of eight to 12 stores). The key to Wal-Mart's fast-response management system was linkage between the stores and headquarters. Former CEO, David Glass explained the system:

> The idea is very simple. Nothing very constructive happens in the office. Everybody else had gone to regional offices—Sears, Kmart, everybody—but we decided to send everybody from Bentonville out to the stores Monday though Thursday. And bring them back Thursday night. On Friday morning we'd have our merchandising meetings. But on Saturday morning we'd have our sales for the week. And we'd have the other information from people who'd been out in the field. They're telling us what our competitors are doing, and we get reports from people in the regions who had been traveling though the week. So we decide then what corrective action we want to take. And before noon on Saturday the regional manager was required to be hooked up by phone to all his district managers, giving them direction as to what we were going to do or change. By noon on Saturday we had all our corrections in place. Our competitors, for the most part, got their sales results on Monday for the week prior. Now, they're already ten days behind, and we've already made the corrections.[28]

The Saturday morning meeting was preceded by three other key corporate meetings. The operations meeting was on Thursday afternoon. This was attended by 70 senior executives and logistics, planning, and information managers. The meetings reviewed non-merchandising matters—including inventory management, supply chain efficiencies, and new store development. The meetings were held standing to encourage brevity.

Fridays began with the 7 a.m. management meeting, which involved Wal-Mart's 200 most senior managers. To attend these meetings Wal-Mart's 39 regional vice presidents needed to return on Thursday evening from their territories to the Bentonville "home office." The meetings dealt with strategic and critical operational matters. At lunchtime, in the same auditorium, the merchandising meeting took place. Here, buyers and corporate executives meet. The purpose of the meeting was, first, to give buyers direct insights into what was selling and what was not; second, to give the regional VPs a means to get instant action to solve merchandising problems in their stores; third, to report on what the competition was doing. The meeting dealt with stockouts, excess inventory, new product ideas, and a variety of merchandising errors. By the early afternoon, the regional VPs and merchandisers were emailed a "priority note" of specific actions that they should take action on by the end of the day.

It was the two-and-a-half-hour Saturday morning meetings, however, that were the week's high point and the clearest representation of Wal-Mart's unique management style:

> The meeting is the soul of this behemoth . . . It is the template for other vital gatherings that have evolved throughout the company, ranging from the daily shift-change meetings at the stores to the weekly management, merchandising, and operations meetings at the home office to the five company-wide mega-meetings each year that draw more than 10 000 participants apiece. Not only do these assemblies reinforce and personalize Wal-Mart's almost evangelical culture among its 1.5 million "associates" worldwide, but they are also largely responsible for the retailing giant's amazing agility in the aisles. The meetings enable the company to continue to operate its entire business on a weekly and sometimes a daily basis, just as the founder managed his first five-and-dime, moving quickly to outflank competition and growing almost as a matter of routine.[29]

The Saturday meetings were a mixture of information sharing, educational inputs and motivation recharging. They began with a review of the week's performance data, then involved question-and-answer sessions targeting examples of good and bad performance. They also included presentations that focused on merchandising best practices or new product lines and guest appearances that might include CEOs such as Carlos Ghosn, Steve Jobs, or Jack Welch, or celebrity entertainers or sports stars. The meetings closed with a talk from the CEO. By 2008, it became apparent that Wal-Mart's increasing size was making these meetings increasingly cumbersome—not to mention the fact that Wal-Mart's largest auditorium could no longer accommodate the participants. In January 2008, Wal-Mart announced that its legendary Saturday meeting would occur monthly and would be held at nearby Bentonville High School.

Some managers saw the downgrading of the Saturday morning meeting as a long-overdue recognition that one of the world's biggest corporations could no longer be run with the same personalized, Arkansas-focused management style put in place by Sam Walton. Others interpreted it differently: Wal-Mart was losing the unique spirit and driving force that had been the basis of its success for four decades.

Appendix: The Wal-Mart Culture[30]

As Wal-Mart continues to grow into new areas and new mediums, our success will always be attributed to our culture. Whether you walk into a Wal-Mart store in your home town or one across the country while you're on vacation, you can always be assured you're getting low prices and that genuine customer service you've come to expect from us. You'll feel at home in any department of any store . . . that's our culture.

Sam Walton's Three Basic Beliefs

Sam Walton built Wal-Mart on the revolutionary philosophies of excellence in the workplace, customer service and always having the lowest prices. We have always stayed true to the Three Basic Beliefs Mr. Sam established in 1962:

Respect the Individual

> "Our people make the difference" is not a meaningless slogan—it's a reality at Wal-Mart. We are a group of dedicated, hardworking, ordinary people who have teamed together to accomplish extraordinary things. We have very different backgrounds, different colors and different beliefs, but we do believe that every individual deserves to be treated with respect and dignity. (Don Soderquist, Senior Vice Chairman, Wal-Mart Stores, Inc.)

Service to Our Customers We want our customers to trust in our pricing philosophy and to always be able to find the lowest prices with the best possible service. We're nothing without our customers.

> Wal-Mart's culture has always stressed the importance of Customer Service. Our Associate base across the country is as diverse as the communities in which we have Wal-Mart stores. This allows us to provide the Customer Service expected from each individual customer that walks into our stores. (Tom Coughlin, President and Chief Executive Officer, Wal-Mart Stores division.)

Strive for Excellence New ideas and goals make us reach further than ever before. We try to find new and innovative ways to push our boundaries and constantly improve. "Sam was never satisfied that prices were as low as they needed to be or that our product's quality was as high as they deserved—he believed in the concept of striving for excellence before it became a fashionable concept." (Lee Scott, President and CEO.)

Sam's Rules for Building a Business People often ask, "What is Wal-Mart's secret to success?" In response to this ever-present question, in his 1992 book *Made in America*, Sam Walton compiled a list of ten key factors that unlock the mystery. These factors are known as "Sam's Rules for Building a Business."

Rule 1. Commit to your business. Believe in it more than anybody else. I think I overcame every single one of my personal shortcomings by the sheer passion I brought to my work. I don't know if you're born with this kind of passion, or if you can learn it. But I do know you need it. If you love your work, you'll be out there every day trying to do it the best you possibly can, and pretty soon everybody around will catch the passion from you—like a fever.

Rule 2. Share your profits with all your Associates, and treat them as partners. In turn, they will treat you as a partner, and together you will all perform beyond your wildest expectations. Remain a corporation and retain control if you like, but behave as a servant leader in a partnership. Encourage your Associates to hold a stake in the company. Offer discounted stock, and grant them stock for their retirement. It's the single best thing we ever did.

Rule 3. Motivate your partners. Money and ownership alone aren't enough. Constantly, day-by-day, think of new and more interesting ways to motivate and challenge your partners. Set high goals, encourage competition, and then keep score. Make bets with outrageous payoffs. If things get stale, cross-pollinate; have managers switch jobs with one another to stay challenged. Keep everybody guessing as to what your next trick is going to be. Don't become too predictable.

Rule 4. Communicate everything you possibly can to your partners. The more they know, the more they'll understand. The more they understand, the more they'll care. Once they care, there's no stopping them. If you don't trust your Associates to know what's going on, they'll know you don't really consider them partners. Information is power, and the gain you get from empowering your Associates more than offsets the risk of informing your competitors.

Rule 5. Appreciate everything your Associates do for the business. A paycheck and a stock option will buy one kind of loyalty. But all of us like to be told how much somebody appreciates what we do for them. We like to hear it often and especially when we have done something we're really proud of. Nothing else can quite substitute for a few well-chosen, well-timed, sincere words of praise. They're absolutely free—and worth a fortune.

Rule 6. Celebrate your successes. Find some humor in your failures. Don't take yourself so seriously. Loosen up, and everybody around you will loosen up. Have fun. Show enthusiasm—always. When all else fails, put on a costume and sing a silly song. Then make everybody else sing with you. Don't do a hula on Wall Street. It's been done. Think up your own stunt. All of this is more important, and more fun, than you think, and it really fools the competition. "Why should we take those cornballs at Wal-Mart seriously?"

Rule 7. Listen to everyone in your company. And figure out ways to get them talking. The folks on the front lines—the ones who actually talk to the customer—are the only ones who really know what's going on out there. You'd better find out what they know. This really is what total quality is all about. To push responsibility down in your organization, and to force good ideas to bubble up within it, you must listen to what your Associates are trying to tell you.

Rule 8. Exceed your customers' expectations. If you do, they'll come back over and over. Give them what they want—and a little more. Let them know you appreciate them. Make good on all your mistakes, and don't make excuses—apologize. Stand behind everything you do. The two most important words I ever wrote were on that first Wal-Mart sign, "Satisfaction Guaranteed." They're still up there, and they have made all the difference.

Rule 9. Control your expenses better than your competition. This is where you can always find the competitive advantage. For 25 years running—long before Wal-Mart was known as the nation's largest retailer—we ranked No. 1 in our industry for the lowest ratio of expenses to sales. You can make a lot of different mistakes and still recover if you run an efficient operation. Or you can be brilliant and still go out of business if you're too inefficient.

Rule 10. Swim upstream. Go the other way. Ignore the conventional wisdom. If everybody else is doing it one way, there's a good chance you can find your niche by going in exactly the opposite direction. But be prepared for a lot of folks to wave you down and tell you you're headed the wrong way. I guess in all my years, what I heard more often than anything was: a town of less than 50 000 population cannot support a discount store for very long.

Notes

1 "Changing of the Guard at Wal-Mart," *Fortune,* February 18, 2009.
2 Wal-Mart, Annual Report, 2009, p. 3.
3 Wal-Mart, Annual Report, 2009, pp. 2–3.
4 "Target Thrives in Wal-Mart Country," *Fortune,* June 10, 2009.
5 "Wal-Mart Alters Regular Saturday Meeting," *Morning News,* January 14, 2008, www.nwaonline.net/articles/2008/01/14/business/011508bizsatmeetings.txt, accessed October 16, 2009.
6 S. Walton, *Sam Walton: Made in America,* Bantam Books, New York, 1992.
7 *Forbes,* August 16, 1982, p. 43.
8 *Wal-Mart Stores, Inc.* (Harvard Business School Case No. 9–974–024, 1994).
9 "Why Wal-Mart Can't Find Happiness in Japan," *Fortune,* July 27, 2007.
10 From the Wal-Mart web site: www.walmart.com.
11. S. Walton, *Sam Walton: Made in America,* Bantam Books, New York, 1992.
12 See www.walmart.com/cservice/aw_samsway.gsp, accessed October 16, 2009.
13 Wal-Mart Inc., 2009 10-K Report.
14 This description of Wal-Mart's retailing operations refers primarily to its U.S. discount stores.
15 Bill Saporito, "A Week Aboard the Wal-Mart Express," *Fortune,* August 24, 1992, p. 79.
16 Bill Saporito, "A Week Aboard the Wal-Mart Express," *Fortune,* August 24, 1992, p. 79.
17 "At Wal-Mart, Less is More," *Journal of Commerce,* November 2005. Reprinted in *DSC Logistics and Supply Chain Management,* http://www.dsclogistics.com/newsrelease_05NovJournalofCommerce.php, accessed 29 October 2009.
18 For an insightful account of the development of Wal-Mart's relationship with P&G see: "Lou Pritchett: Negotiating the P&G Relationship with Wal-Mart" (Harvard Business School Case No. 9-907-011, 2007.)
19 "Inside the World's Biggest Store," *Time Europe,* January 20, 2003.
20 "The Green Machine," *Fortune,* July 31, 2006.
21 "Wal-Mart Gets a Facelift," *Business Week,* July 2, 2008, http://www.businessweek.com/innovate/content/jul2008/id2008072_324653.htm, accessed October 29, 2009.
22 "Wal-Mart Moves Upmarket," *Business Week,* June 3, 2009, http://www.businessweek.com/innovate/content/jul2008/id2008072_324653.htm?campaign_id=rss_daily, accessed October 29, 2009.
23 Wal-Mart Stores, Annual Report, 1999, p. 9.
24 Wal-Mart Stores, Annual Report, 1999, p. 9.
25 Wal-Mart Stores, Annual Report, 1999, p. 11.
26 "Unions vs. Wal-Mart: Up against the Wal-Mart," *Fortune,* May 17, 2004.
27 "Sam Walton Made us a Promise," *Fortune,* March 18, 2002.
28 "The Most Underrated CEO ever," *Fortune,* April 5, 2004, pp. 242–8.
29 "Wal-Mart's $288 Billion Meeting," *Fortune,* April 18, 2005.
30 "The Wal-Mart Culture" from www.walmartstores.com; "Sam's Rules for Building a Business," from Sam Walton and John Huey, *Made in America.* (New York: Doubleday, 1992).

Case 6 Manchester United: Preparing for Life without Ferguson*

In July 2009, David Gill, the Chief Executive of Manchester United Football Club Limited (MUFC), was accompanying the Manchester United team on its Asia Tour. The series of matches against local teams in Malaysia, Indonesia, Korea, and China was ostensibly part of the team's pre-season training—in reality its goals were almost wholly commercial.

The tour's itinerary was determined primarily by existing deals: the game in Kuala Lumpur was a reward for Telekom Malaysia's £2 million sponsorship of the tour; the games in South Korea, China and Indonesia reflected deals with Kumho Tyres and Hi Seoul (Korea), Aigo (China) and 3 Indonesia. It was most important to maintain the

---

* This case was written by Robert M. Grant with assistance from Simon I. Peck, Christopher Carr and Timothy Smith.

enthusiasm and commitment of Manchester United's vast army of fans in these countries. In Asia as a whole, Manchester United estimated that it had 80 million supporters. "Our fans in Asia generate money for the club, and the reception United get in Asia is unlike anywhere else on earth," observed David Gill.[1] In South Korea there were 1.2 million Manchester United credit-card holders.

When the Manchester United plane touched down at Kuala Lumpur on July 16, the 73 people on board included a number of Manchester United employees who had no direct involvement in the next day's game against the Malaysia national team. They included a group from Manchester United's commercial office in London led by commercial director Richard Arnold. Their role was to finalize a series of lucrative sponsorship deals, partnerships and territory-specific agreements.

Manchester United's Asian fan base was a key factor for their £80 million four-year sponsorship deal with AON—whose corporate logo would replace that of AIG on Manchester United shirts. According to David Prosperi, AON's VP of Global Public Relations:

> The first year after AIG's sponsorship agreement began, they came from nowhere on the list of the world's top 100 brands to 47th. Manchester United has no equal in sports when it comes to global brand awareness, particularly in Asia. We believe that Asia, particularly India and China, are prime targets for revenue growth and being associated with the Manchester United brand will, we believe, help us to greatly build our brand and grow our business in this region.[2]

For David Gill, the number one issue on his mind was not Manchester United's commercial deals. So long as the team kept winning games and playing exciting football the commercial revenues—from shirt sales, broadcasting and sponsorship—would continue to flow. The biggest cloud on Manchester United's horizon was the imminent retirement of its veteran team manager, Sir Alex Ferguson—the prime architect of the team's success over the past 23 years and winner of more honors for Manchester United than in their entire history prior to his appointment. Although Ferguson had given no indication of his intention to retire, Gill thought it likely that Ferguson would choose to go at the end of the 2009-10 season. Even if Ferguson did decide to stay on beyond the end of next season, Gill could not imagine that it would be for long—at the end of 2009 Ferguson would be 68 years old.

The implications of Ferguson's departure for Manchester United were far reaching. In his 23 years at the club, Ferguson had built an entire infrastructure of scouting, training, team discipline, and team tactics and strategy. In seeking a successor to Ferguson, Gill was forced to look beyond the desirable characteristics for a new team manager and to ponder the fundamental issues of what determined success in English and European soccer.

The Competitive Environment

The English League

The top league in English professional football is the Premier League, comprising the 20 best English teams. Each team plays every other team twice, once at home and once away, with teams receiving three points for a win, one for a tie, and zero for a loss. At the end of every season, the three teams at the bottom of the Premier

TABLE 6.1 The top performing clubs in English football, 1980–2005

	League champion	Second place	Third place	FA Cup winner
2009	Manchester United	Liverpool	Chelsea	Chelsea
2008	Manchester United	Chelsea	Arsenal	Portsmouth
2007	Manchester United	Chelsea	Liverpool	Chelsea
2006	Chelsea	Manchester United	Liverpool	Liverpool
2005	Chelsea	Arsenal	Manchester United	Arsenal
2004	Arsenal	Chelsea	Manchester United	Manchester United
2003	Manchester United	Arsenal	Newcastle United	Arsenal
2002	Arsenal	Liverpool	Manchester United	Arsenal
2001	Manchester United	Arsenal	Liverpool	Liverpool
2000	Manchester United	Arsenal	Leeds United	Chelsea
1999	Manchester United	Arsenal	Chelsea	Manchester United
1998	Arsenal	Manchester United	Liverpool	Arsenal
1997	Manchester United	Newcastle United	Arsenal	Chelsea
1996	Manchester United	Newcastle United	Liverpool	Manchester United
1995	Blackburn Rovers	Manchester United	Nottingham Forest	Everton
1994	Manchester United	Blackburn Rovers	Newcastle United	Manchester United
1993	Manchester United	Aston Villa	Norwich City	Arsenal
1992	Leeds United	Manchester United	Sheffield Wednesday	Liverpool
1991	Arsenal	Liverpool	Crystal Palace	Tottenham Hotspur
1990	Liverpool	Aston Villa	Tottenham Hotspur	Manchester United
1989	Arsenal	Liverpool	Nottingham Forest	Liverpool
1988	Liverpool	Manchester United	Nottingham Forest	Milton Keynes Dons
1987	Everton	Liverpool	Tottenham Hotspur	Coventry City
1986	Liverpool	Everton	West Ham United	Liverpool
1985	Everton	Liverpool	Tottenham Hotspur	Manchester United
1984	Liverpool	Southampton	Nottingham Forest	Everton
1983	Liverpool	Watford	Manchester United	Manchester United
1982	Liverpool	Ipswich Town	Manchester United	Tottenham Hotspur
1981	Aston Villa	Ipswich Town	Arsenal	Tottenham Hotspur
1980	Liverpool	Manchester United	Ipswich Town	West Ham United

Source: www.european-football-statistics.co.uk.

League are replaced by the top three in the league below. The Premier League team that accumulates the most points throughout the season wins the English League Championship.

The governing body for English football is the Football Association (FA). The FA Cup pits teams from all the English leagues in a single elimination tournament—allowing little-known teams from the lower divisions to compete (and sometimes win) against the top clubs. Table 6.1 shows the top performing teams in the English league between 1980 and 2009.

The European League

The Champions League is composed of the 32 top teams in European football. Teams qualify by finishing at or near the top of their respective national leagues.

TABLE 6.2 The top 25 European football clubs 2000–2009

Club	Total points 2000–9	Club	Total points 2000–9
Manchester United (England)	1460	Olympique Lyonnais (France)	1076
Barcelona (Spain)	1411	Olympiakos SF Pireas (Greece)	1001
Real Madrid (Spain)	1314	FK Dynamo Kyiv (Ukraine)	948
Bayern München (Germany)	1314	SV Werder Bremen (Germany)	923
Arsenal (England)	1310	Glasgow Celtic (Scotland)	921
Chelsea (England)	1276	Deportivo de La Coruña (Spain)	919
Liverpool (England)	1199	Juventus (Italy)	917
AC Milan (Italy)	1178	Ajax Amsterdam (Netherlands)	914
Internazionale FC (Italy)	1177	Panathinaikos AO Athina (Greece)	910
FC do Porto (Portugal)	1170	FK Shakhtar Donets'k (Ukraine)	903
Valencia (Spain)	1105	Sporting CP (Portugal)	881
PSV (Netherlands)	1088	Glasgow Rangers (Scotland)	872
AS Roma (Italy)	1083		

Note: Points are based upon club performance in national leagues, national cup competitions and European Champions League and Intertoto cup. National performance is adjusted according to the standard of competition in the national leagues.

Source: www.european-fooball-statistics.co.uk.

In England the top four teams qualify for the Champions League; in Scotland, the top two teams qualify. Qualifying for the Champions League is a critical objective for the aspiring clubs in each of the major national leagues because of the substantial TV and gate revenues that it offers. The latter phase of the Champions League season is a knockout competition that results in one team winning the European Cup. Winning this championship represents the highest accomplishment in European club football, both competitively and financially.

Table 6.2 shows the top teams in Europe based on performance in both national and European competitions.

The inauguration of the European Champions League in 1992 and the revenues and prestige that it conferred had a major impact on English league football. A widening financial gap appeared between the top performing teams—Manchester United, Chelsea, Liverpool, and Arsenal—and the rest as revenues from the European competition fueled the purchases of top-class players, reinforcing the tendency for the leading group of clubs to break away from the pack.

The Players

The critical determinant of team performance in professional soccer is the quality of the players that make up the team. The world's leading players in 2008–9 are shown in Table 6.3.

Competition for superstar players has intensified in recent years as a result of two factors. First, the growing global market for football and football merchandise has greatly increased the value of top-class players in terms of their contribution to team performance and their individual market pull. Second, there has been an influx of new finance into football—especially into the acquisition of English Premier League clubs

TABLE 6.3 FIFA world player rankings, 2008–9

Rank	Player	Nationality	Team
1	Cristiano Ronaldo	Portugal	Manchester United
2	Lionel Messi	Argentina	Barcelona
3	Fernando Torres	Spain	Liverpool
4	Kaká	Brazil	Milan
5	Xavi	Spain	Barcelona
6	Steven Gerrard	England	Liverpool
7	Samuel Eto'o	Cameroon	Barcelona
8	Iker Casillas	Spain	Real Madrid
9	Andrés Iniesta	Spain	Barcelona
9	David Villa	Spain	Valencia
11	Andrei Arshavin	Russia	Zenit St. Petersburg
12	Frank Lampard	England	Chelsea
13	Didier Drogba	Cote d'Ivoire	Chelsea
14	Michael Ballack	Germany	Chelsea
14	Cesc Fàbregas	Spain	Arsenal
16	Zlatan Ibrahimović	Sweden	Internazionale
17	Emmanuel Adebayor	Togo	Arsenal
18	Franck Ribéry	France	Bayern Munich
19	Ruud van Nistelrooy	Netherlands	Real Madrid
20	Sergio Agüero	Argentina	Atlético Madrid
21	John Terry	England	Chelsea
22	Gianluigi Buffon	Italy	Juventus
23	Deco	Portugal	Barcelona and Chelsea

Note: Based on assessment by 157 managers and 145 captains of national teams.

Source: www.fifa.com.

from U.S., Middle East and Russian investors. As a result, despite the global recession, transfer fees hit new highs during the summer of 2009. Table 6.4 shows some of the biggest transfer deals.

Football Finances

If the critical resource determining a team's performance is the quality of its players, then the ability to acquire quality players depends on a club's financial resources. There are two major sources of a club's financial resources: its cash flows from its commercial activities and its financing by investors and lenders.

Revenues

The principal revenue sources for a club are:

- *Matchday revenues.* Revenues from the sale of tickets are determined by the number of home games played, the average attendance and average seat

TABLE 6.4 Biggest player transfers in European football (prior to the end of June 2009)

Rank	Player	From	To	Transfer fee ($ millions)	Year
1	Cristiano Ronaldo	Manchester United	Real Madrid	93.1	2009
2	Zinédine Zidane	Juventus	Real Madrid	76.0	2001
3	Zlatan Ibrahimović	Internazionale	Barcelona	66.0	2009
4	Kaká	Milan	Real Madrid	65.1	2009
5	Luís Figo	Barcelona	Real Madrid	58.5	2000
6	Hernán Crespo	Parma	Lazio	53.6	2000
7	Gianluigi Buffon	Parma	Juventus	49.2	2001
8	Robinho	Real Madrid	Manchester City	49.0	2008
9	Christian Vieri	Lazio	Internazionale	48.3	1999
10	Andriy Shevchenko	Milan	Chelsea	46.5	2006
11	Dimitar Berbatov	Tottenham	Manchester United	46.4	2008
12	Pavel Nedvěd	Lazio	Juventus	46.2	2001
13	Rio Ferdinand	Leeds United	Manchester United	43.9	2002
14	Gaizka Mendieta	Valencia	Lazio	43.8	2001
15	Ronaldo	Internazionale	Real Madrid	43.0	2002
16	Juan Sebastián Verón	Lazio	Manchester United	42.4	2001
17	Karim Benzema	Lyon	Real Madrid	34.9	2009

Source: www.wikipedia.org

price. Among the leading teams in Europe, attendance depends upon stadium capacity. In recent years most of the leading teams have redeveloped their stadiums—others (e.g. Arsenal) built entirely new ones. The great majority of income from tickets was from season tickets. A major source of revenue growth was the sale of corporate boxes and VIP hospitality packages.

- *Broadcasting revenues*. Outside of North America and Japan, football is the world's most popular televised sport. The world's most popular sporting event is the Football World Cup. The 2006 World Cup was televised in 213 countries to a cumulative audience of 26 billion viewers; the final was watched by an audience of 715.1 million. Club-level games are broadcast on national TV and increasingly on overseas TV networks. In England, broadcasting rights are negotiated between the Premier League and the TV networks. In 2006, TV rights to Premier League games were sold to Sky TV, Sentana, the BBC, and overseas TV networks for a total of £2.7 billion—each Premier League club receiving an average of £45 million annually between 2007 and 2010. TV rights for the Champions League are managed by the European governing body for football, UEFA. The international TV audience for Champions League games resulted in a massive revenue boost for those teams that qualified for the league. During 2008/9, Manchester United, Barcelona, Chelsea and Bayern Munich each received more than €30 million from UEFA.
- *Sponsorship and commercial revenues* comprise payments from companies for advertising rights at stadiums and on club web sites, sponsorship agreements

and licensing arrangements—payments to license a club's trademarks for the manufacture of official club merchandise (replica shirts, scarves, games, drinking mugs, toys, and various other products). Most clubs had two leading sponsors: the supplier of team apparel (Nike, Addidas or Puma) and the company whose corporate logo appeared on the team's shirts. Major sponsorship deals included Juventus and Tamoil (€110 million over 5 years), Arsenal and Emirates (£100 million over 15 years), Manchester United and Aon (£80 million over 4 years), and Chelsea and Samsung (£50 million over 5 years). Sponsorship revenues are concentrated on a few leading clubs. In Spain Real Madrid and Barcelona accounted for over 60% of the Primera Liga's sponsorship revenue, while AC Milan, Inter, and Juventus accounted for over 50% of the Serie A's total. The leading European clubs have become increasingly sophisticated in marketing, merchandising and brand management with Real Madrid and Manchester United the leaders in promoting and exploiting their brands globally.

A club's potential sponsorship and commercial revenues depends on both the brand equity of the club and that of its leading players. Real Madrid's signing of superstar players Zidane, Beckham and Cristiano Ronaldo gave massive boosts to the club's licensing and merchandising revenues. Foreign players are especially important in building support in those players' home countries. Manchester United's commercial revenues from South Korea grew substantially after Ji-Sung Park joined the team.

Of the European leagues, England's Premier League is the biggest earner with revenues of €2.4 billion in 2007/08 (up 26% in Sterling terms). Italy's Serie A, Spain's La Liga, and Germany's Bundesliga each had revenues of about €1.4 billion. For the English Premier League during 2007-8, broadcasting contributed £931 million (an increase of 43% on the previous year), commercial revenues £447 million (up 12%), and matchday revenue £554 million (up 3%).[3]

Table 6.5 shows financial data for Europe's leading clubs.

Costs

Wages and salaries—most of which are accounted for by players' salaries—are the biggest cost item for European clubs. During 2007–8, wages as a percentage of revenues were 62% for the Premier League as compared with 68% for Serie A and 63% for La Liga. Among the English clubs Chelsea had the highest wage bill, accounting for 81% of total revenue. Manchester United and Arsenal each paid out about half of their revenues in wages. In 2008/9, the world's highest paid footballers were: David Beckham (Los Angeles Galaxy/AC Milan—$42.7 million), Lionel Messi (FC Barcelona—$37.7 million), Ronaldinho (AC Milan—$25.8 million), and Cristiano Ronaldo (Manchester United—$24.1 million).[4]

Other major cost items for the leading soccer clubs are:

- *Player transfer fees.* Players are transferred between clubs both on terms agreed between the two clubs and with the player concerned. Players are signed to clubs on contracts of up to five years. At the end of their contracts they become free agents. Transfer fees are determined primarily by the acquisitions of a few big-spending clubs. During 2000–2, Real Madrid was the key driver; during 2004–6, Chelsea was main inflationary force; during

TABLE 6.5 Financial data from the leading European football clubs

	Country	Revenue €m.	EBITDA[1] €m.	Club Value £m.	Debt £m.
Real Madrid	Spain	365.8	51.6	850	196
Manchester Utd	England	324.8	101.9	1.140	616
Barcelona	Spain	308.8	68.8	960	41
Bayern Munich	Germany	295.3	37.6	774	0
Chelsea	England	268.9	(8.3)	486	447
Arsenal	England	264.4	51.0	690	896
Liverpool	England	210.9	33.3	704	415
AC Milan	Italy	209.5	36.9	691	0
Roma	Italy	175.4	43.9	266	24
Internazionale	Italy	172.9	17.2	258	199
Juventius	Italy	167.5	29.3	419	21
Lyon	France	155.7	59.9	295	53
Schalke 04	Germany	148.4	26.1	356	135
Tottenham	England	145.0	44.6	310	90
Hamburg	Germany	127.9	28.0	n.a	n.a

[1] Earnings before interest, taxes, depreciation and amortization.

[2] Value of team based on fixed assets and player contracts.

Source: www.forbes.com/lists/2009/34/soccer-values-09_soccer-team-valuations_value.html

2008–9, Manchester City's lavishing of £185million on new players had taken player valuations to yet new heights.

- *Stadiums*. Leading clubs have invested substantially in upgrading and expanding their facilities. In some cases this has involved building completely new stadiums. Arsenal's new stadium opened in 2006, cost a total of £430 million.

Sources of Finance

Only a small minority of European football clubs are publicly listed companies (these include Ajax, AS Roma, Celtic, and Lazio), most are privately owned. Traditionally, football club owners have been rich local businessmen. For example, Juventus is owned by the Agnelli family (Fiat), AC Milan by Silvio Berlusconi, Inter Milan by Massimo Moratti, Olympique Marseille by Robert Louis-Dreyfus. In recent years European football has attracted international sources of equity. Among British clubs owned by foreign-born billionaires include Chelsea (Roman Abramovitch), Manchester City (Sheikh Mansour bin Zayed Al Nahyan), Queen's Park Rangers (Lakshmi Mittal of Alcelor Mittal Steel) and Fulham (Mohammed Al Fayed of Harrods). Manchester United and Liverpool were both owned by U.S. investors (the Glaser family and Tom Hicks, respectively), however, because these investors had financed their purchases primarily through debt, neither club had received the influx of cash that permitted the massive investments in new players that had been made by Chelsea or Manchester City.

TABLE 6.6 Profitability of European football clubs 2000–2006

Club	Return on sales (%)[a]
Arsenal	5.6
Chelsea	(60.4)
Liverpool	(1.2)
Man. United	12.6
Celtic	(4.0)
Rangers	(20.9)
Bayern Munich	4.7
Inter-Milan	(78.4)
Juventus	(17.0)
Real Madrid	0.4

[a] Pre-tax profit over sales revenue.

Profitability

Despite its rapid growth in popularity and revenues, European professional football remains a highly unprofitable business. Deloitte's estimates of operating profitability show that the English and German leagues have earned significant levels of operating profit, but the French and Italian leagues earned substantial (and growing) operating losses. Moreover, these measures of profit are before taking account of interest, tax and depreciation (depreciation of players is a particularly important cost). In terms of net profit, Manchester United, Arsenal, and Bayern Munich were the only leading clubs earning significant profits (see Table 6.6).

Teams and Team Building

Measured by the number and ranking of leading players in Table 6.3, Europe's most star-studded teams were Barcelona and Chelsea. There were two routes to acquiring world-class players: to buy them or to develop them. The extent to which a club is reliant upon buying players is indicated by its expenditure on player transfer fees. Table 6.7 shows that Real Madrid and Chelsea were distinguished by their massive expenditures on star players. Other top-performing teams—notably Bayern Munich, Barcelona, Arsenal, and Valencia had placed the emphasis on developing their own players. A few leading clubs were able to generate revenues from developing and selling players—for Porto, AC Milan, and PSV, revenues from selling players exceeded expenditure on players by a sizable margin.

Coaching, Management and Organization

Running a professional football club involves two distinct areas of management: managing the team for on-the-pitch performance and managing commercial activities to generate revenue and profit. Most English and Scottish clubs are organized to achieve a clear separation between these two. Governance is the responsibility of the board of

TABLE 6.7 Expenditures on player transfers

Club	Performance points 2000-9	Gross transfer fees, 2003-9 (£m)[a]	Net transfer fees, 2003-9 (£m)[a]	Size of squad, July 2009	Average age of squad, July 2009 (years)
Barcelona	200.0	362	249	24	26.8
Manchester United	192.5	322	100	34	25.6
Real Madrid	183.0	626	438	29	26.2
Bayern München	179.5	197	122	25	26.5
AC Milan	169.0	164	(66)	30	28.6
Liverpool	162.5	303	157	33	24.5
Arsenal	162.0	173	22	31	23.3
Valencia	155.5	163	98	30	26.5
Chelsea	144.5	589	430	29	27.4
Internazionale	142.0	294	140	31	27.4
Porto	140.0	132	(173)	31′	25.4
Olympique Lyonnais	139.0	127	18	34	24.4
PSV	124.5	75	(17)	25	26.5
Roma	123.0	140	75	46	25.0
Juventus	115.5	233	68	29	28.1

[a] Covers transfers from the beginning of the 2003–4 season to the end of June 2009.

Source: www.transfermarkt.co.uk.

directors, which would appoint a chief executive officer to take charge of administrative and commercial matters and a team manager who would be responsible for coaching, team selection, and recommending the purchase and sale of players (subject to budgets determined by the board).

For some English clubs this separation of management between the team and commercial matters is less clear. The usual cause of a blurring of boundaries is the owners' desire to involve themselves in managing the team. At Chelsea, for example, the departure of team manager Jose Mourihno was the result of friction with owner Roman Abramovitch over matters of player acquisition, team selection and playing style.

In continental Europe, clubs have different organizational structures. Barcelona and Real Madrid are both owned by their local supporters who elected the club president. These presidents oversee both commercial and team management. Real Madrid's recent presidents, Jose Calderon and Florentino Pérez, have been heavily involved in team selection and player acquisition. As a consequence, the tenure of coaches has been short—Real Madrid hired and fired 10 head coaches between 2003 and July 2009.

A second organizational feature of many Continental European clubs is the division of team management between the coach and a "director of football" (or "sporting director"). The rationale is to enable the coach to focus his efforts on the first team, while the director of football handles the management of reserve and youth teams, scouting for new players, and acts as an interface between the coach and the board. The introduction of directors of football at some English clubs has often resulted in conflict with the coach/manager (for example, at Chelsea and Newcastle).

A critical constituency for every club is its fans. Not only are the fans the primary source of club revenues—they are the custodians of a club's culture and heritage, and their support can play a key role in team performance. The commitment and fanaticism of fans can be a two-edged sword—the fans can lift team performance at critical junctures; it can also be disruptive when they turn against the club's coach or owner. At Barcelona, the fans' adulation for coach Josep "Pep" Guardiola has fueled their support for the team as well as bolstering his authority over his team of superstars.

Despite the different roles of coaches (managers) at different clubs, it is apparent that their role in team success is critical. As the primary architect of the team, the principal motivator and disciplinary force, and the source of team strategy and tactics, the coach is the single person most responsible for its success. Sustained success by a team over a series of seasons is almost always associated with a single coach (see Table 6.8).[5] Yet, what determines a great coach is hard to judge. Coaches succeed with very different leadership styles. Ferguson's tough, aggressive style contrasted sharply with Sven Eriksson's (Lazio, England) calm, controlled demeanor, with Arsene Wenger's (Monaco and Arsenal) intellectual approach, or with Jose Mourinho's (Porto, Chelsea, Inter) obsessive, idiosyncratic style. Certain coaching styles are appropriate to different teams and to different circumstances; coaches that achieve outstanding success with one team are often dismal failures with another.[6]

TABLE 6.8 The world's most highly regarded coaches, 1990–2007

Alex Ferguson	St. Mirren 1974–8; Aberdeen 1978–86; Manchester United 1986–
Arsene Wenger	Nancy 1984–7; Monaco 1987–94; Arsenal 1994–
Arrigo Sacchi	Parma 1985–7; AC Milan 1987–91, 1996–7; Italy 1991–6; Athletico Madrid 1998–9; Real Madrid 2004.
Johan Cruyff	Ajax 1986–8; Barcelona 1988–94
Jose Mourinho	Leiria 2001–2; Porto 2002–4; Chelsea 2004–7; Inter 2008–
Marcello Lippi	Cesena 1989–91; Lucchese 1991–2; Atalanta 1992 –3; Napoli 1993–4; Juventus 1994–9, 2001–4, Inter 1999–2000; Italy 2004–6, 2008–
Luiz Felipe Scolari	Juventude 1986–7; Al Quadisiya 1988–90, 1992; Gremio 1993–6; Palmeiras 1997–2000; Cruzeiro 2000–1; Brazil 2001–2, Portugal 2003–8, Chelsea 2008–9
Vicente Del Bosque	Real Madrid 1999–2003; Besiktas 2004–5.
Fabio Capello	AC Milan 1991–6, 1997–8; Real Madrid 1996–7, 2006–7; Roma 1999–2004; Juventus 2004–6; England 2008–
Franz Beckenbauer	West Germany 1984–90; Olympique Marseille 1990–1; Bayern Munich 1994, 1996
Aime Jacquet	O. Lyonnais 1976–80; Bordeaux 1980–9; Montpellier 1989–90; Nancy 1990–1; France 1993–8
Guus Hiddink	PSV Eindhoven 1987–90, 2002–6; Valencia 1991–4; Netherlands 1995–8; Real Madrid 1998–9; Real Betis 1999–2000; S. Korea 2000–2; Australia 2005–6; Chelsea 2008–9; Russia 2006–
Giovanni Trapattoni	Milan 1974–6; Juventus 1976–88, 1991–4; Inter 1986–91; Bayern Munich 1994–5, 1996–8; Fiorentina 1998–2000; Italy 2000–4; Benfica 2004–5; Salzburg 2006–8; Ireland 2008–
Bobby Robson	Ipswich 1969–82; England 1982–90; PSV Eindhoven 1990–2, 1998–9; Sporting Lisbon 1992–4, Porto 1994–6; Barcelona 1996–7; Newcastle 1999–2004
Carlo Ancelotti	Parma 1996–9; Juventus 1999–2001; AC Milan 2001–9; Chelsea 2009–

Source: "Top 50 Managers of All Time," *Times on Line*, September 12, 2007.

However, some common factors are apparent. An eye for talent appears to be critical. The ability to recognize outstanding football potential before it is fully developed is essential to nurturing that talent within a team context. Second, the ability to mix and balance individual players into effective team combinations is critical to team design and development. Finally, all great coaches are able to motivate their players and inspire respect and loyalty from them.

Among Europe's top teams in 2005, it was possible to observe a variety of strategies at work. Real Madrid's approach was simply to buy the world's best players. Real's president Florentino Perez explained: "It's the only possible economic and sporting model for this club . . . We have the best players and we have an important image in the world. Our strategy is for the best players to come and everyone knows who the best players are." AC Milan relied on mature talent: their team included several players in their 30s. Arsenal's Arsene Wenger ("The Professor") focused on molding a group of talented young players into a flexible, interactive team that played fast-moving, attacking football. Manchester United has emphasized the development of outstanding young talent and blending it with mature, highly experienced players.

Despite over a hundred years of football experience by thousands of professional clubs throughout the world, the determinants of team performance remained a mystery. Why one team outplayed another and why the same team could play brilliantly in one game and abysmally in the next depends on a complex mix of factors that defies analysis. Certainly team performance is not simply a product of the quality of the players in the team. Probably the greatest achievement for any coach is to build a great team out of unknown players with meager financial resources. Thus, Alex Ferguson's achievement at Aberdeen, Jose Mourinho's at Porto, Alf Ramsey's at Ipswich, and Jock Stein's at Glasgow Celtic were triumphs of team building from humble resources. Conversely, Real Madrid and Chelsea's lavishing of vast sums of money to build star-studded teams has yielded teams that have failed to achieve greatness.

Manchester United's History

Manchester United was founded in 1878 and became a professional club in 1885. Old Trafford, Manchester United's stadium, saw its first game in 1910. During the 1950s and 1960s, Manchester United rose to prominence under the leadership of its legendary team manager, Matt Busby. However, in 1958, on a return flight from a European game, a plane crash killed eight of the "Busby Babes." Busby's rebuilding of the team was rewarded in 1968 when Manchester United became the first English team to win the European Cup. After Busby's retirement in 1969, Manchester United went into decline and Liverpool became England's pre-eminent club. During the 18 years before the arrival of Alex Ferguson, Manchester United did not win a single league championship and was runner up just once.

The Ferguson Era

Alex Ferguson was recruited by Manchester United in 1986 as a result of his remarkable success at Aberdeen where he had broken the historical dominance by Rangers and Celtic of Scottish football and had taken Aberdeen all the way to the European Cup.

Ferguson was born into a working-class family in Govan, a tough, shipbuilding community close to Glasgow—a city famous for the passion and loyalty of its football fans. Ferguson's life was built around soccer. After a playing career that included the Scottish clubs St. Johnston, Glasgow Rangers and Aidrie, Ferguson took to coaching. He began with bottom-of-the-league East Stirlingshire, moved to St. Mirren, then to Aberdeen.

During his first six years at Manchester United, Ferguson systematically rebuilt the team. Ferguson culled the existing squad, keeping outstanding talent such as Bryan Robson and jettisoning those whom he judged as lacking the necessary talent or commitment, or who simply didn't fit. Despite a new era of team discipline and the acquisition of several talented new players (including Mark Hughes, Paul Ince, Eric Cantona and Roy Keane), success came slowly. In 1990, Manchester United achieved his first major success: the FA Cup, and next year the European Cup Winners' Cup but it was not until 1993 that Ferguson achieved his primary objective: the English Premier League Championship.

While reconfiguring and augmenting Man United's first team, Ferguson was also developing a stable of talented youth players. In 1990, Manchester United won the English League youth team championship with a team that included Ryan Giggs, David Beckham, Nicky Butt, Gary and Phil Neville, and Paul Scholes. Between 1994 and 2003, these homegrown young players formed the nucleus of a Manchester United team that dominated English football. This golden era culminated in 1999 when Manchester United achieved a triumph unprecedented in English football history: the team won the English league championship, the FA Cup, European Cup, and the Intercontinental Cup when they defeated the South American champions, Palmeiras.

Between 2003 and 2008, Ferguson rebuilt the Manchester United team. Key members of the trophy-winning team of 1999 season were sold, including David Beckham, Roy Keane, Peter Schmeichel, Andy Cole, Teddy Sheringham, and Jaap Stam. Their replacements included a number of highly talented young players: Rio Ferdinand, Cristiano Ronaldo, Wayne Rooney, Louis Saha, Edwin van der Sar, Patrice Evra, Nemanja Vidic, Owen Hargreaves, and Michael Carrick, who would play key roles in Manchester United's winning the European Cup in 2008.

Ownership

Between 1991 and 2003, Manchester United FC was a public company, listed on the London Stock Exchange. In 2005, Manchester United was acquired by the American businessman, Malcolm Glazer, owner of the Tampa Bay Buccaneers—a National Football League franchise. The deal created outrage among Manchester United fans; not only was Glazer "a yank who knows nothing about football" but his purchase was financed mainly by debt. Under Glazer's ownership, the board of Manchester United Ltd comprised Glazer's six children with Joel Glazer as chairman.

Despite transitional difficulties, the new ownership created less friction than expected—and much less than at other foreigner-owned clubs, such as Chelsea and Liverpool. The key was the willingness of the Glazer family to play a back seat role in managing the club. Team manager Alex Ferguson and CEO David Gill were given considerable decision making freedom. Moreover, the primary fear—that Manchester United's heavy indebtedness would limit Ferguson's ability to acquire new players—proved groundless.

Ferguson's Management Style

In a business where the performance expectations of owners and fans were focused on the short term, Ferguson's emphasis was on success over the long term:

> My aim in management has always been to lay foundations that will make a club successful for years, or even decades . . . When I joined United on 6 November 1986, they had gone 19 years without a title. No-one had to tell me that if I did not end that drought I would be a failure. Putting them in a position to challenge consistently would, I knew, be a long haul. I would have to build from the bottom up, rectifying the flaws I had recognized and spreading my influence and self-belief through every layer of the organization. I wanted to form a personal link with everyone around the place—not just the players, the coaches and the backroom staff but the office workers, the cooks and servers in the canteen and the laundry ladies. All had to believe that they were part of the club and that a resurgence was coming.[7]

The starting point was training and team discipline. Ferguson declared war on alcohol—a problem endemic to British professional soccer and an indulgence that Ferguson viewed as incompatible with professional sport. The new, more rigorous training regime included meticulous attention to attendance, punctuality and effort. His training sessions built individual and team skills through continuous repetition: "refining technique to the point where difficult skills become a matter of habit."

In terms of long-term team building, Ferguson focused heavily on identifying and developing new talent: "From the moment I became manager of United, I was committed to the creation of a youth policy that would be the envy of every other club in Britain. The first imperative was to find the raw talent."[8]

One of Ferguson first initiatives at Manchester United was to expand the scouting staff from five to over 20 and instructed them to seek only the most outstanding talent. Manchester United's Youth Academy was built into what Ferguson declared was the finest youth coaching program in the country. Increasingly, Manchester United's scouts would scour the world for new players. In 2008, the club appointed two full-time scouts to seek out new players in Brazil.[9]

To Ferguson, team building was much more than acquiring and developing talented players, developing their skills and building coordination between them:

> The best teams stand out because they are teams, because the individual members have been so truly integrated that the team functions with a single spirit. There is a constant flow of mutual support among the players, enabling them to feed off strengths and compensate for weaknesses. They depend on one another, trust in one another. A manager should engender that sense of unity. He should create a bond among his players and between him and them that raises performance to heights that were unimaginable when they started out as disparate individuals.[10]

Ferguson's approach to motivating his players involved a combination of loyal support and, where he identified unnecessary mistakes or lack of effort, withering criticism. His ability to induce exquisite performances from the brilliant but volatile

Frenchman, Eric Cantona, owed much to Ferguson's unflinching support during Cantona's conflicts with authority. At the same time, Ferguson was renowned for his temper and the ferociousness of his verbal tirades. These were delivered to players at such close range that they became known as "Ferguson's hairdryer." One confrontation resulted in David Beckham requiring stitches above his eye—the result of Ferguson kicking a football boot at him. Ferguson's half-time talks to his team could have a powerful effect in re-energizing their second-half efforts. At the European Cup Final in 1999, Man United was losing 1–0 at the end of the first half. He told his team: "At the end of this game, the European Cup will be only six feet away from you and you'll not even be able to touch it if we lose. And for many of you that will be the closest you will ever get. Don't you dare come back in here without giving your all."

Central to Ferguson's approach to managing players has been his insistence that no player is bigger than the club. The result has been well publicized clashes with some of his leading players—typically resulting in them being dropped from the first team for several games or being sold to other clubs.

In terms of team strategy and match tactics, Ferguson was committed to control over the midfield. This required "controlled, sustained possession that calls for players adept at holding the ball and spreading calculated and accurate passes . . . A high standard of passing in central midfield was the core of United's football."[11] Ferguson had long admired the ability of the top Italian teams to vary the pace of their game—to slow the game with a period of low-energy, possession football, followed by a sudden, lightning attack. Ferguson's team design was characterized as a closely coordinated midfield group built around players such as Keane, Scholes, Beckham, Giggs and Ronaldo supporting creative strikers such as Cantona, van Nistelrooy, Cole and Rooney.

Ferguson has been a pioneering exponent of "squad rotation"—reconfiguring a team to rest players and to adapt tactics in order to exploit opponents' vulnerabilities. During consecutive games, Manchester United's starting team can vary substantially and, in the course of a game, Ferguson made extensive use of substitutes. This team flexibility calls for players to develop broad repertoires of coordination—they must get used to playing in different combinations and adapting their style of play according to the different talents of different team mates.[12]

Although Manchester United was one of Europe's top spending teams on new players, Ferguson's purchases were matched by a willingness to sell players that were valued more by other teams. Major sales have included: David Beckham, Juan Veron, van Nistelrooy and Ronaldo (for a world record transfer fee of £80 million). As a result, Manchester United's net expenditure on player transfers has been relatively modest compared to other leading European clubs.

Manchester United's Commercial and Financial Performance

Manchester United and Real Madrid are regarded as the most commercially focused clubs in European football. In building a global fan base then converting that support into revenues, Manchester United was a model for other European clubs.

"We're not just a sports club, we are an international brand . . . and building that brand is very important," former commercial director Andy Anson observed. In addition to the overall Manchester United brand, the club developed several sub-brands: "Fred the Red" was designed to appeal to children; the "MUFC" brand is targeted at teenagers, while "Red Devil" products are directed mainly towards adults. Other brands are associated with specific licensing deals – notably "Red Cafes" and "Theatre of Dreams" restaurants. A subsidiary, Manchester United International, was created in 1998 for the purpose of developing Man United's business opportunities outside the U.K.—in North America and Asia especially.

In addition to primary sponsors Nike and AIG (to be replaced by Aon in 2010) Manchester United's sponsors have included:

- Budweiser, "the official beer of Manchester United."
- Audi, "the official car supplier to Manchester United."
- Betfred, "the official betting partner of Manchester United."
- Hublot Watches, "official timekeeper of Manchester United."
- Tri Indonesia, "official telecommunications partner of Manchester United for Indonesia."
- Bharti Airtel, "official telecommunications partner of Manchester United in India."
- There were seven other sponsors.

Commercial initiatives have included:

- MU Finance, which offered credit cards, mortgages, and retirement planning products.
- MU Mobile, which offered SMS and video streaming services to Manchester United fans.
- MUTV, which showed Manchester United games on webTV.
- Manchester United Soccer Schools, offered in Manchester and other locations within the U.K. and in the U.S., Canada, Switzerland, Singapore, Malaysia and other countries. There are also Manchester United soccer schools at Disneyland in Paris and Hong Kong.
- The Manchester United Superstore offers a wide range of Manchester United licensed products both through the Old Trafford retail store and online through http://store.manutd.com.
- Manchester United's Old Trafford stadium hosts a wide variety of events. Regular attractions include the Manchester United museum and stadium tour. In addition, suites, bars and a ballroom can be rented for conferences, receptions, parties, weddings and dinners. Expansion of the stadium in 2006 gave a substantial boost to Manchester United's revenues—primarily from the 7500 additional seats.

It was one of the first of the English clubs to go public and the most successful in establishing effective corporate governance. The Glazer acquisition changed the club's financial structure but otherwise had limited impact on Manchester United's financial performance. The club continued to grow its commercial revenues—especially from overseas—however, it was not evident that Manchester United derived any significant benefit from Malcolm Glazer's much lauded promotional expertise.

The Appendix shows financial information for Manchester United plc.

July 2009

As the "Reds" returned from their Asia tour on July 28, 2009, media interest focused upon whether the club would spend the cash from the sale of Cristiano Ronaldo on a bid for Bayern Munich's Franck Ribery. Meanwhile, Sir Alex was setting out his expectations for the forthcoming season: at least 100 goals to be scored of which Rooney was expected to score at least 18 and new signing, Michael Owen 15.

At the same time, anticipation that Sir Alex would retire in the summer of 2010 was attracting a number would-be candidates for his job. Ferguson's former assistant and coach to the Portuguese national team, Carlos Queiroz, had made no secret of his desire to lead Manchester United. Ferguson's former adversary and current coach of Inter Milan, Jose Mourinho, also announced his interest in the post.[13] Another favored candidate was Gordon Strachan, one of Ferguson's former players who had been a highly successful manager of Celtic.

As Manchester United's CEO, David Gill, evaluated the possible successors to Sir Alex, he realized that the club faced a difficult dilemma. After 24 years of Ferguson's leadership, it was important to maintain as much as possible of the system of training, scouting, and team development that Sir Alex had put in place. This would favor appointing Ferguson's former assistants, Queiroz, or one of his current ones, Mike Phelan, Ole Gunnar Solskjær, or Brian McClair. The problem was whether anyone who had been successful as an assistant to Ferguson could have the presence and strength of personality needed to exert leadership and authority over Manchester United's high profile soccer stars. Conversely, if Manchester United was to appoint a manager with proven leadership skills—Jose Mourinho, for example—it was likely that this would involve a revolutionary change in coaching strategy in which much of Ferguson's infrastructure would be taken down and rebuilt.

Appendix: Manchester United: Selected Financial Data, 2000–2008 (£, thousands)

	2008[a]	2007[a]	2006[a]	2005[a]	2004[b]	2003[b]	2002[b]	2001[b]	2000[b]
Turnover	257 118	212 189	167 751	157 171	169 080	173 001	146 062	129 569	116 005
Group operating profit before depreciation and amortization	86 005	79 786	46 254	46 131	58 340	57 269	41 402	38 194	35 125
Depreciation	(7271)	(7630)	(5147)	(6054)	(6591)	(7283)	(6923)	(6514)	(5052)
Amortization of players	(35 481)	(24 252)	(23 427)	(24 159)	(21 839)	(21 018)	(17 647)	(10 173)	(13 092)
Exceptional costs				(7286)	—	(2197)	(1414)	(2073)	(1300)
Group operating profit	42 821	47 797	17 680	8632	29 910	26 771	15 418	19 434	15 681
(Loss)/profit on disposal of players	21 831	11 760	12 462	(556)	(3084)	12 935	17 406	2219	1633
Net interest receivable/ (payable)	462	343	722	2477	1066	(316)	27	727	456
Profit on ordinary activities before taxation	66 416	59 627		10 764	27 907	39 345	32 347	21 778	16 788
Taxation	(19 916)	(17 338)	(9222)	(4224)	(8486)	(9564)	(7308)	(7399)	(4838)
Profit for the period	46 754	42 289	21 603	6540	19 421	29 781	25 039	14 379	11 950
Fixed assets	267 452	283 020	228 989	202 823	204 504	n.a.	n.a.	n.a.	n.a.
Current assets	179 236	115 310	71 765	83 465	24 258	n.a.	n.a.	n.a.	n.a.
Creditors	(81 421)	(82 494)	(31 356)	50 304	53 430	n.a.	n.a.	n.a.	n.a.
Equity Shareholders' funds	294 018	245 304	202 666	180 846	173 354	156 418	137 443	120 457	114 950

Note: The data relate to Manchester United plc for 2000 to 2005 and Manchester United Limited for 2006-2008. Due to accounting changes, the data for 2000–4 are not comparable to those for 2005–8.

[a] 11 months to June 30.

[b] 12 months to July 31.

Source: Annual reports.

Notes

1 "Manchester United's global appeal goes from strength to strength," *Daily Telegraph* (July 16, 2009), www.telegraph.co.uk/sport/football/leagues/premierleague/manutd/, accessed July 25, 2009.

2 "Manchester United's global appeal goes from strength to strength," *Daily Telegraph* (July 16, 2009), www.telegraph.co.uk/sport/football/leagues/premierleague/manutd/, accessed July 25, 2009.

3 Deloitte, *Annual Review of Football Finance, 2009,* highlights, see www.deloitte.com/dtt/cda/doc/content/UK_SBG_ARFF2009_Highlights.pdf, accessed July 29, 2009.

4 "Beckham Again World's Best-paid," *Sports Illustrated,* March 30, 2009.

5 In British football, these included Manchester United under Matt Busby, Liverpool under Bill Shankly and Bob Paisley, Celtic under Jock Stein, Leeds under Don Revie and Nottingham Forest under Brian Clough.

6 Claudio Ranieri was less successful at Chelsea, Athletico Madrid and in his second stint at Valencia than he had been at Fiorentina and his initial term at Valencia; Brian Clough was unable to replicate his remarkable performance at Derby and then Nottingham Forest at either Brighton or Leeds; Bobby Robson's 37-year coaching career included outstanding success at Ipswich, Porto, and Barcelona and poorer team performance at PSV, Sporting Lisbon and Newcastle. "Big Phil" Scolari survived less than one season at Chelsea.

7 Alex Ferguson, *Managing My Life,* Hodder & Stoughton, London, 1999, p. 242.

8 Alex Ferguson, *Managing My Life,* Hodder & Stoughton, London, 1999, p. 274.

9 "Manchester United Invest in Brazilian Talent," *Independent,* October 17, 2008.

10 Alex Ferguson, *Managing My Life,* Hodder & Stoughton, London, 1999, p. 274.

11 Alex Ferguson, *Managing My Life,* Hodder & Stoughton, London, 1999), p. 437.

12 "Sir Alex Ferguson Proves Mastery at Manchester United with Rotation System," *The Times,* May 11, 2009.

13 "Jose Mourinho Wants to Succeed Sir Alex Ferguson at Manchester United," *DailyTelegraph,* July 28, 2009.

Case 7 Eastman Kodak: Meeting the Digital Challenge

On June 1, 2005, Antonio Perez, Eastman Kodak's chief operating officer, took over as CEO from Dan Carp. It was quite clear to him why he had been appointed and what the Kodak board expected from him. He had been recruited from Hewlett-Packard (HP) two years earlier because of his successful leadership of HP's digital imaging initiatives. There he had run HP's inkjet printing business and, subsequently, as CEO of consumer business, he had led HP's efforts to build its business in digital imaging and electronic publishing. As CEO of Eastman Kodak (Kodak) his task was to continue the journey begun by his predecessors, George Fisher and Dan Carp, in transforming Kodak from a photographic company into a world leader in digital imaging.

His first eight months in the job showed progress towards this goal. In 2005, Kodak was U.S. market leader in digital still cameras and ranked third worldwide (see Table 7.1). With its 75 000 retail photo kiosks and the leading online digital

TABLE 7.1 Brand shares of the world market for digital still cameras (by units)

Brand	2005	2004	2003	2002	2001	2000
Sony (%)	15.2	16.7	18	20	25	26
Canon (%)	17.4	17.1	16	14	10	9
Olympus (%)	9.8	7.7	13	16	11	18
Kodak (%)	14.2	11.8	12	10	14	11
Hewlett-Packard (%)	4.4	n.a.	n.a.	3	8	7
Fuji Film (%)	7.8	8.5	10	15	14	12
Total units sold (million)	78	64	48	28	17	n.a.

Source: IDC, The NPD Group/NPD Techworld.

photography service (EasyShare Gallery), Kodak led the retail market for printing digital photographs. In commercial printing, Kodak consolidated its global leadership in high-resolution, color printing systems. In healthcare, Kodak was a leader in digital dental imaging and was expanding its market share in digital X-rays.

However, the financial results told a very different story. Kodak posted an operating loss of $600 million and a net loss of $1362 million for 2005. While Kodak's cash flows from its traditional film business shrank much more quickly than Kodak had anticipated, its digital business—with its intense competition, compressed product cycles and declining product prices—failed to fill the gap. Since hitting a high of $99 in July 1998, Kodak's shares had continued their downward track, closing at $24 at the end of January 2006.

Perez's response was to accelerate Kodak's reallocation of resources from conventional business into digital imaging. In July 2005 he had called for 10 000 job cuts in addition to 15 000 previously announced in order to staunch Kodak's "bleeding year after year." Kodak's manufacturing capacity would be cut by two-thirds. He also called for the phasing out of film: "We need to establish an end point for this transformation and we need to get there soon."[1]

At the Consumer Electronics Show in Las Vegas in January 2006, Perez went further in reorienting perceptions of Kodak: "Soon, I'm not going to be answering questions about film because I won't know. It will be too small for me to get involved." He also played down Kodak's future as a digital imaging hardware company. He described digital cameras as "dinosaurs that cannot evolve as fast as the environment around them." He went on to argue that the future of digital imaging would not be based upon stand-alone cameras but on "technology that allows consumers to search, share and display images on different media such as mobile phones and the internet."[2] Software would play a central role in the industry; it was needed for storing, organizing and sharing digital images:

> Soon you're going to have 10 000 pictures on your computer. It's a complete nightmare . . . If you look at the people we're hiring, you'll be surprised by the number of software people we have. We have human interface experts and people who understand sentiment produced by different colors and shapes. We're becoming a very modern company.[3]

Perez's ambition and optimistic outlook did little to impress the stock market. Chris Whitmore of Deutsche Bank pointed to the difficulty of making money in digital imaging: "They're entering markets that are highly competitive and have low margins and levels of profitability." Commercial printing and medical imaging offered better potential for profitability but it was not clear that Kodak could build a strong competitive advantage in these markets. In commercial printing, Citigroup's Matthew Troy doubted Kodak's ability to integrate its various acquisitions. In medical imaging, he saw Kodak as lacking the critical mass to compete with GE and Siemens: "They're trying to upsell into the field with larger players with much broader expertise . . . They lack the comprehensive scale to compete."[4]

Kodak's History, 1880–1993

George Eastman transformed photography from an activity undertaken by professional photographers working in studios into an everyday consumer hobby. His key innovations were silver halide roll film and the first fully portable camera. In 1901 he established the Eastman Kodak Company in Rochester, New York, to provide the full range of products and services needed to support the amateur photographer. The emphasis was ease of use: "You push the button, we do the rest" was its first advertising slogan. By the time George Eastman died in 1932, Eastman Kodak was one of the world's leading multinational corporations with production, distribution and processing facilities throughout the world with one of the world's most recognizable brand names.

After the Second World War, Kodak entered a new growth period fueled by growing affluence and increased leisure time. Exploiting its polymer technology, its subsidiary, Eastman Chemical, became a major plastics producer. However, by the end of the 1970s, Kodak was facing its first competitive challenges. In cameras, Kodak's leadership was undermined by the rise of the Japanese camera industry, with its sophisticated yet easy-to-use 35 mm cameras. In film, Fuji Photo Film Company embarked on a strategy of aggressive international expansion. Most striking were the new imaging technologies that were emerging. Polaroid pioneered instant photography, Xerox led the new field of electrostatic plain-paper copying, and the personal computer was ushering in an array of new printing technologies.

Early Moves in Electronics, 1980–93

Under Colby Chandler and Kay Whitmore, Kodak launched a series of diversification moves including expansion into healthcare (Eastman Pharmaceutical was established in 1986) and a slew of new imaginative initiatives. These included:

- Eikonix Corp., acquired in 1985, which gave Kodak a leading position in commercial imaging systems that scanned, edited and prepared images for printing.
- Kodak developed the world's first megapixel electronic image sensor with 1.4 million pixels (1986). This was followed by a number of new products for scanning and electronic image capture, including Imagelink for document imaging and Optistar for micrographic digital image capture (1989).
- Kodak became a leader in image storage and retrieval systems. Its KAR4000 Information System provided computer-assisted storage and retrieval of

microfilm images (1983). The Ektaprint Electronic Publishing System and Kodak Image Management System offered integrated systems to edit, store, retrieve, and print text and graphics (1985).

- Kodak became involved in a range of data storage products including floppy disks (Verbatim was acquired in 1985), a 14-inch optical disk capable of storing 6.8 billion bytes of information (1986), and magnetic recording heads for disk drives (through the 1985 acquisition of Garlic Corp.).
- Kodak acquired IBM's copier services business.
- As a result of its collaboration with Philips, Kodak announced its Photo CD system in 1990. Photo CDs allowed digitized photographic images to be stored on a compact disk, which could then be viewed and manipulated on a personal computer.
- In 1991, Kodak introduced its first digital camera, the 1.3 megapixel Kodak DCS-100, which combined a digital back made by Kodak with a camera body produced by Nikon. It was priced at $13 000.

Creating a Digital Strategy: George Fisher and Dan Carp, 1993–2005

By the early 1990s it was clear that Kodak was extended over too many initiatives with too little commitment to any area outside of its traditional imaging business. In 1993, the Kodak board ousted Whitmore and brought in George Fisher, then CEO of Motorola. With a doctorate in applied mathematics and ten years of R&D experience at Bell Labs, Fisher had a scientist's grasp of electronic technology while his experience at Motorola demonstrated an ability to turn new technology into world-beating new products.

From the outset, Fisher's strategic vision for Kodak was as an imaging company: "We are not in the photographic film business or in the electronics business; we are in the picture business."[5] To focus Kodak's efforts on the digital challenge, Fisher's first moves were to spinoff of Eastman Chemical Company and sell most of Kodak's healthcare businesses (other than medical imaging).

Fisher's digital strategy was to create greater coherence among Kodak's many digital imaging projects, in part through creating a single digital projects division headed by newly hired Carl Gustin (previously with Apple Computer and DEC). During his tenure, and continuing through that of his successor, Dan Carp, Kodak developed a digital strategy that comprised the following key themes.

An Incremental Approach

"The future is not some harebrained scheme of the digital information highway or something. It is a step-by-step progression of enhancing photography using digital technology," declared Fisher.[6] This recognition that digital imaging was an evolutionary rather than a revolutionary change would be the key to Kodak's ability to build a strong position in digital technology. If photography was to switch rapidly from the traditional chemical-based technology to a wholly digital technology where customers took digital pictures, downloaded them onto their computers, edited them and transmitted them through the internet to be viewed electronically, then Kodak would face an extremely difficult time. Not only would the new digital value chain make most of Kodak's core competitive advantages redundant (its silver halide technology, its global network of retail outlets and processing facilities)—most of this digital value chain was already in the hands of computer hardware and software companies.

Fortunately for Kodak, during the 1990s digital technology made only selective incursions into traditional photographic imaging. As late as 2000 digital cameras had achieved limited market penetration; the vast majority of photographic images were still captured on traditional film.

Hence, central to Kodak's strategy was a hybrid approach where Kodak introduced those aspects of digital imaging that could offer truly enhanced functionality for users. Thus, in the consumer market, Kodak recognized that image capture would continue to be dominated by traditional film for some time (digital cameras offered inferior resolution compared with conventional photography). However, digital imaging offered immediate potential for image manipulation and transmission.

If consumers continued to use conventional film while seeking the advantages of digitization for editing and emailing their pictures, this offered a valuable opportunity for Kodak's vast retail network. Kodak had installed its first self-service facility for digitizing, editing and printing images from conventional photographs in 1988. In 1994, Kodak launched its Picture Maker, a self-service kiosk located in retail stores where customers could edit and print digital images from a variety of digital inputs, or from digital scans of conventional photo prints. Picture Maker allowed customers to edit their images (zoom, crop, eliminate red-eye and add text) and print them in a variety of formats. George Fisher emphasized the central role of retail kiosks in Kodak's digital strategy:

> Four years ago, when we talked about the possibilities of digital photography, people laughed. Today, the high-tech world is stampeding to get a piece of the action, calling digital imaging perhaps the greatest growth opportunity in the computer world. And it may be. We surely see it as the greatest future enabler for people to truly "Take Pictures. Further."
>
> We start at retail, our distribution stronghold. Here consumers are at the peak moment of satisfaction, when they open their photofinishing envelopes. We believe the widespread photo-retailing infrastructure will continue to be the principal avenue by which people obtain their pictures. Our strategy is to build on and extend this existing market strength which is available to us, and at the same time be prepared to serve the rapidly growing, but relatively small, pure digital market that is developing. Kodak will network its rapidly expanding installed base of Image Magic stations and kiosks, essentially turning these into nodes on a massive, global network. The company will allow retailers to use these workstations to bring digital capability to the average snapshooter, extending the value of these images for the consumers and retailers alike, while creating a lucrative consumable business for Kodak.[7]

Despite the growing ownership of inkjet printers, a very large proportion of consumers continued to use photo-print facilities in retail stores. By the end of 2000, some 30 000 retail locations worldwide offered Picture Maker facilities. By the beginning of 2004, Kodak was the clear leader in self-service digital printing kiosks, with 24 000 installed Kodak Picture Makers in the U.S. and over 55 000 worldwide. The G3 Picture Maker—Kodak's third generation of retail kiosk launched in 2004 could print a picture in as little as five seconds.

Kodak also used digital technology to enhance the services offered by photofinishers. Thus, the Kodak I.Lab system offered a digital infrastructure to photofinishers that digitized every film negative and offered better pictures by fixing common problems in consumer photographs.

Kodak's hybrid approach was also evident in introducing digital enhancement of conventional film. In 1996, Kodak launched its Advantix advanced photo system, which allowed both chemical film images and electronic data to be stored on a single film. The new standard failed to make much impact on the market.

Despite the inferior resolution of digital cameras, Fisher recognized their potential and pushed Kodak to establish itself in this highly competitive market. Kodak's digital cameras addressed both the top end and the bottom end of the market. In January 1994, Kodak launched its DigitalNews Camera, which had been developed in cooperation with Associated Press, was targeted at photojournalists and was priced at $15 000. It also launched the Apple Quicktake computer camera (manufactured by Kodak, marketed by Apple Computer), which, at $75, was the cheapest digital camera available at the time. In March 1995, Kodak introduced the first full-featured digital camera priced at under $1000. During the subsequent six years, Kodak continued to bring out new, more sophisticated digital cameras, including professional cameras developed in conjunction with Canon. By 2000, Kodak offered a wide range of digital cameras. At the top end was its DC4800 camera with 3.1 megapixel resolution; at the other a PalmPix camera that allowed a Palm personal digital assistant to be used as a digital camera.

The Consumer Market: Emphasizing Simplicity and Ease of Use

Fisher advocated different approaches to consumer and commercial markets. While the commercial and professional market offered the test-bed for Kodak's advanced digital technologies, the emphasis in the consumer segment was to maintain Kodak's position as mass-market leader by providing simplicity, quality and value. It was in the consumer market where incremental strategy was most evident; through this it could exploit its brand and distribution strengths. The key was providing an easy pathway for customers from traditional to digital photography.

Kodak continued to be guided by its original vision of "You push the button; we do the rest!" Both Fisher and Carp believed that Kodak's market position in digital imaging should seek to replicate that in traditional imaging: Kodak should be the mass-market leader providing security, reliability and simplicity for customers bewildered by the pace of technological change. This required Kodak to offer a transition path for customers seeking to migrate from traditional to digital imaging. Thus, Kodak would offer an array of services that would allow consumers to digitize conventional photographs, edit digitized images and obtain printed photographs in a variety of formats.

Simplicity and mass-market leadership also implied that Kodak provided the fully integrated set of products and services needed for digital photography. The essential characteristic of the Kodak system would be ease of use. "For Kodak, digital photography is all about ease of use and helping people get prints—in other words, getting the same experience they're used to from their film cameras," Martin Coyne, head of Kodak's Photographic Group, said at the 2002 Kodak Media Forum. He supported his argument with data showing that while 90% of consumers were satisfied with the pictures obtained from traditional photography, for digital photography only between 50% and 70% were satisfied.[8] A systems approach rather than a product approach was based on the recognition that most consumers had neither the time nor the patience to read instructions and to integrate different devices and software. Kodak believed that its integrated system approach would have particular appeal to women who comprised the major part of the consumer market.

The result was Kodak's EasyShare system, launched in 2001. According to Willy Shih, head of digital and applied imaging, EasyShare's intention was to:

> . . . provide consumers with the first easy-to-use digital photography experience . . . Digital photography is more than just about digital cameras. This is just the first step . . . People need to get their pictures to their PCs and then want to share by printing or e-mail. So we developed a system that made the full experience as easy as possible.[9]

The result would be a comprehensive digital system within which consumers could take digital pictures on digital cameras or phone-cameras (or have conventional photographs digitized), could view their images on a variety of devices, and print their digital images at home, at retail kiosks, or through Kodak's online processing service. Figure 7.1 shows Kodak's conceptualization of its EasyShare system.

By 2005, most of the main elements of the EasyShare system were in place:

- Kodak had a broad range of EasyShare digital cameras. Despite a crowded market (by 1998, 45 companies were offering digital cameras) and Japanese dominance in both conventional and digital cameras, Kodak had succeeded in positioning itself among the global big-three. Its EasyShare range resulted in substantial market share gains across the globe.

FIGURE 7.1 Kodak's EasyShare Network: "Your Pictures—Anytime, Anywhere"

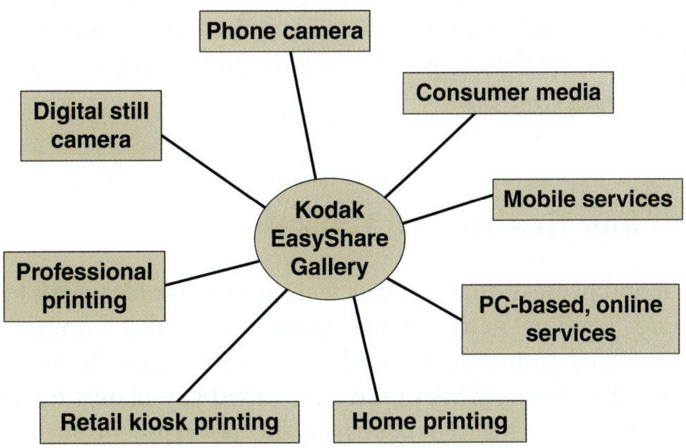

Source: Based upon Bob Brust, "Completing the Kodak Transformation," Presentation, Eastman Kodak Company, September 2005.

- EasyShare software allowed downloading, organization, editing and emailing of images and the ordering of online prints. EasyShare software was bundled with Kodak's cameras as well as being available for downloading for free from Kodak's web site.
- EasyShare camera docks allowed the transfer of digital images from camera to PC at the touch of a button. However, the ability to print photographs without the need for a computer was even more important: EasyShare printer docks enabled photographic prints to be made direct from the camera without the need for downloading to a PC. To provide an integrated offering to consumers, Kodak had begun providing special-purpose printers for producing photographic images. Initially, Kodak sourced inkjet printers from Lexmark. The 2003 EasyShare dock printer represented a major step forward for Kodak: a combined printer and camera dock that offered "one touch simple" thermal-dye printing either with a PC or direct from the camera. In 2002, Kodak acquired Scitex, a leader in continuous-flow inkjet printing, to augment its capabilities in variable data digital printing. Antonio Perez's appointment as COO in 2003 reinforced Kodak's push into printers: "If a company wants to be a leader in digital imaging, it necessarily has to participate in digital output."[10]
- Online digital imaging services. Kodak had been quick to recognize the potential of the internet for allowing consumers to transmit and store their photographs and order prints. According to Willy Shih: "the next killer app . . . is when photography meets the network effect. Or, in other words, when the internet is coupled with digital photography." Kodak's Picture Network was launched in 1997. Consumers could have their conventional photographs digitized by a retail photo store, then uploaded to a personal internet account on Kodak's Picture Network. The following year Kodak launched its online printing service, *PhotoNet,* enabling consumers to upload their digital photo files and order prints of them. Kodak also partnered with AOL to offer *You've Got Pictures,* Kodak providing their printing services and operational support for several of its online photofinishing competitors, including Razorfish. In 2001, Kodak became a leader in online photographic processing when it acquired Ofoto. In addition to online processing, whereby consumers emailed their digital images and received their photographic prints by mail, Ofoto allowed members to build online albums through which family and friends could view and order prints for themselves. In January 2005, Kodak renamed Ofoto "Kodak EasyShare Gallery."

Commercial and Healthcare Markets

The commercial and professional markets were important to Kodak for two reasons. First, they were leading markets for many of Kodak's cutting-edge digital technologies. In digital cameras, the lead users were news photographers and the U.S. Department of Defense, which used unmanned spy-planes for reconnaissance. More generally, the sophisticated needs of the government in satellite imaging, planning military campaigns, weather forecasting, and surveillance activities favored digital technologies for transforming, transmitting, and storing images. In the U.S.

space program, Kodak cameras and imaging equipment accompanied a number of missions, including the Mars probe and the IKONOS Earth-orbiting satellite. In its research activities, Kodak benefitted considerably from Department of Defense and NASA contracts. In both healthcare and in commercial markets, Kodak took a systems approach, seeking to bundle hardware, software and consumables into customer solutions.

In healthcare, medical imaging (especially CT, MRI and ultrasound) required digital technologies for 3D imaging, diagnosis and image storage. In commercial printing, digital imaging provided the basis for a revolution in the publication and printing of newspapers and magazines. Across a wide range of commercial applications ranging from journalism to highway safety to real estate, digital imaging offered huge advantages because of its ability to transmit images (especially through the internet) and link with sophisticated IT management systems for image storage and retrieval. The huge price premium of commercial consumer products (in the case of digital cameras, a professional camera could be up to 100 times that of a basic consumer version; price differentials were similar in color printers) meant that Kodak's R&D was often focused on these leading-edge users in the anticipation of trickle-down to the consumer market.

In commercial printing and publishing (which became the Graphic Communications Group in 2005), Kodak assembled a strong position in commercial scanning, formatting, and printing systems for the publishing, packaging, and data processing industries. This sector comprised NexPress, which supplied a range of high-end color and black-and-white printing machines;[11] Kodak Polychrome Graphics, a leader in graphic communications; Creo Inc., a supplier of pre-press and workflow systems used by commercial printers; Kodak Versamark, a provider of continuous inkjet technology; Encad, a maker of wide-format inkjet printers; and Kodak's Document Products and Services organization, which supplied document scanners, microfilm and support services. Kodak's opportunity was to exploit the transition from traditional offset printing to digital, full-color, variable printing. This opportunity built on two key strengths: first, Kodak's proprietary inkjet technology and, second, its leadership in variable-data printing—printing that required individually customized output (as in personalized sales catalogs or bills).

In the healthcare field, Kodak's market position was similar to that in consumer photography: its strength was in film for X-rays and in related chemicals and accessories. Hence, the encroachment of digital technology offered a major threat. Under Fisher and Carp, Kodak responded by broadening its involvement in medical imaging. Its Ektascan Imagelink system, which enabled medical images to be converted into digital images that could be transmitted via phone between hospitals, was launched in 1995 followed by its Ektascan medical laser printer in 1996. This leadership was extended with the acquisition of Imation's Dry View laser imaging business in 1998. In addition to the printing of medical images, Kodak invested heavily in healthcare information systems, including picture archiving and communications systems (PACS). Kodak also built up a strong, integrated dental imaging business.

In several areas of government service, Kodak used its capabilities in "infoimaging"—the convergence of imaging with information technology to bid on large contracts involving image management and retrieval. Kodak's digital scanning and document management systems were used in national censuses in the U.S., U.K., France, Australia and Brazil. At the German post office, a Kodak team achieved a world record, creating digitized copies of 1.7 million documents in 24 hours.

Hiring, Alliances, and Acquisitions

The traditional Kodak business system was based upon vertical integration and self-sufficiency: at its Rochester base, Kodak developed its own technology, produced its own products and supplied them worldwide through its vast global network. In digital imaging, not only did Kodak lack much of the expertise needed to build a digital imaging business but the pace of technological change was too rapid to rely on in-house development. Hence, as Kodak transformed its capability base from chemical imaging to digital imaging it was forced to look outside for the knowledge it required.

Kodak had traditionally been a lifetime employment company that grew its own senior executives. The arrival of George Fisher from Motorola changed all that. Under Fisher's leadership Kodak launched a major hiring campaign to put in place the executives and technical specialists it needed for its new digital strategy. Key executives who relocated from Silicon Valley to Rochester included Kodak's first head of its digital imaging division, Willy Shih, whose prior experience included Silicon Graphics and IBM. Kodak also brought in senior hires from Xerox, HP, Lexmark, Apple, GE Medical Electronics, Olympus Optical, and Lockheed Martin. Table 7.2 shows the backgrounds of Kodak's top management team.

Fisher's recognition that Kodak's strategy of vertical integration from image capture through to printing photographic images would not work in digital imaging acknowledged that the digital imaging chain already included companies that were well established—sometimes dominant—in particular activities. For example, Adobe Systems dominated image formatting software; HP, Epson, and Canon were leaders in inkjet printers for home use; and Microsoft's control over PC operating systems meant that software for image editing had to be compatible with its Windows system. Willy Shih, head of Kodak's digital imaging products from 1997 to 2003, observed: "We have to pick where we add value and commoditize where we can't."[12] The difficult decision was identifying the activities and product areas where Kodak could add value.

In many cases this meant partnering with companies that were already leaders in digital technologies and hardware and software products. Under Fisher's leadership, Kodak forged a web of joint ventures and strategic alliances. In addition to the already mentioned alliances with Canon, AOL and Heidelberg, Kodak's alliances included:

- Intel Corporation: development and co-marketing of Picture CD; development of digital image storage media and development of an ASP system for archiving and downloading medical images on a pay-per-use basis. Adobe Systems also collaborated with Kodak and Intel in producing software for Picture CD.
- Hewlett-Packard: a primary source of inkjet technology for Kodak, Phogenix Imaging was a joint venture between Kodak and HP to develop high-quality inkjet solutions for micro and mini photo-finishing labs utilizing Kodak's DLS software.[13]
- Microsoft: cooperation to establish standards for Windows-based Picture Transfer Protocols and cooperation in the development of Photo-CDs and development of FlashPix image storage for digital cameras (also with HP).

TABLE 7.2 Eastman Kodak's senior management team, 2005

Name	Position	Joined Kodak	Prior company experience
Corporate officers			
Robert L. Berman	Senior Vice President	1980	Kodak veteran
Charles S. Brown, Jr.	Senior Vice President, Chief Administrative Officer	1973	Kodak veteran
Richard G. Brown, Jr.	Chief Accounting Officer and Controller	2003	Ernst & Young LLP partner,
Robert H. Brust	Chief Financial Officer and Executive Vice President	2000	General Electric, Unisys Corp
Carl E. Gustin, Jr.	Senior Vice President, Chief Marketing Officer	1994	DEC, Apple
Joyce P. Haag	General Counsel and Senior Vice President	1981	Boylan, Brown, Code, Fowler, Vigdor & Wilson LLP
William J. Lloyd	Senior Vice President, Director Inkjet Systems	2003	Inwit, Gemplus, HP
Daniel T. Meek	Senior Vice President, Director Global Manufacturing and Logistics	1973	NYPRO, Verbatim
Antonio M. Perez	Chairman of the Board, Chief Executive Officer	2003	President and CEO of HP
Divisional presidents			
Mary Jane Hellyar	Senior Vice President, President Film and PhotoFinishing Systems Group	1982	Kodak veteran
Philip J. Faraci	Senior Vice President, President Consumer Digital Imaging Group	2004	Phogenix Imaging, Gemplus
James T. Langley	Senior Vice President, President Graphic Communication Group	2003	HP
Kevin J. Hobert	Senior Vice President, President Health Group	2002	General Electric Medical Systems

Sources: Eastman Kodak Annual Report, 2005; www.kodak.com.

- Olympus: sharing digital camera technology; developing common standards for Web-based storage and printing of photographs (each company had over a thousand patents relating to digital cameras and digital photographic systems).
- AOL: Kodak collaborated with AOL to create AOL's *You've Got Pictures* service for uploading, storing and sharing digital photographs.

- Sanyo Electric Co.: joint development of color, active matrix organic electroluminescent (OLED) displays.
- IBM: a manufacturing alliance to produce CMOS image sensors. The first sensors from the alliance were announced in July 2005.

In activities and markets where Kodak believed that a strong proprietary position was essential to its strategy, and in technologies where it needed to complement its own expertise, it used acquisitions. Although Kodak's profits were under pressure for most of the period, its size and balance-sheet strength meant that it was still one of the financially strongest firms in the industry. The bursting of the stock-market bubble in technology stocks in 2000, allowed Kodak to make a number of key acquisitions at for modest outlays. Its major acquisitions over the period are shown in Table 7.3.

TABLE 7.3 Kodak's major acquisitions, 1994–2006

1994	Qualex, Inc.	Provider of photo-finishing services, became key component of Kodak's online photofinishing service
1997	Wang Laboratories	Acquisition of Wang's software unit
1998	PictureVision, Inc.	Provider of PhotoNet online digital imaging services and retail solutions; this service integrated within Kodak's Picture Network business
	Shantou Era Photo Material, Xiamen Fuda Photographic Materials	Kodak strengthens its position in the photographic film market in China
1999	Imation	Kodak acquires Imation's medical imaging business
2000	Lumisys, Inc.	Leading provider of desktop computed radiography systems and x-ray film digitizers
2001	Bell & Howell	Imaging businesses only acquired
	Ofoto, Inc.	Leading online photography service
	Encad, Inc.	Wide-format commercial inkjet printers
2003	Practiceworks	Digital dental imaging and dental practice management software
	Lucky Film Co., Ltd.	Acquires 20% of China's biggest manufacturer of photographic film
	Laser-Pacific Media Corporation	A provider of post-production services for filmmakers
	Algotec Systems Ltd.	Developer of picture archiving systems
	Applied Science Fiction	Digital PIC rapid film processing technology
2004	NexPress	Acquired Heidelberg's 50% of this joint venture, which supplied high-end, on-demand color printing systems and black-and-white variable-data printing systems
	Scitex Digital Printing	A leader in high-speed variable data inkjet printing (renamed Kodak Versamark, Inc.)
	Chinon Industries	Kodak purchases outstanding shares
	National Semiconductor	Kodak acquires National's imaging sensor business
2005	Kodak Polychrome Graphics LLC	Kodak acquires Sun Chemical's 50% stake in the joint venture, which is a leader in graphic communication
	Creo Inc.	Leading supplier of prepress and workflow systems used by commercial printers around the world

Source: Eastman Kodak, 10-K Reports.

Kodak and the Digital Imaging Market in 2006

The digital imaging market—especially the consumer segment—displayed the same features as most other markets that were founded upon digital technologies. Like personal computers, mobile phones, pocket calculators, and DVD players, digital imaging hardware was subject to intense competition, low entry barriers, falling real prices and commoditization. As a result, profit margins on most products were either slim or non-existent.

Digital cameras featured particularly brutal competition. While fierce price competition was restricted to the lower end of the market where Sony, Panasonic, Samsung and other consumer electronics companies were the main players, by 2006 these companies were increasingly moving into the high-price market for digital, single-lens reflex cameras traditionally dominated by Canon and Nikon. Some observers believed that during 2006, the market for digital cameras would begin to decline as more and more consumers relied on their mobile phones for taking digital images.

The situation was similar in printers where about 20 companies—including HP, Canon, Epson, Lexmark, Xerox, Samsung, Brother, Dell, Konica, Fuji, Panasonic, Toshiba, and Apple—supplied inkjet printers. The difference was that, in printers, high margins could be earned on ink cartridges.

For Kodak too, its highest margins were earned on consumables—notably photographic paper. However, in the home market Kodak faced strong competition notably from Xerox, HP, 3M, and Oji, as well as from many minor brands. In supplying photofinishers and commercial printers, Kodak was able to benefit from its leadership in supplying printing hardware. To fight commoditization in printing paper, Kodak pioneered a number of technical advances particularly in inkjet printing paper. Most significant was its Colorlast technology, designed to preserve the fidelity and vibrancy of photographic prints for a hundred years or more. However, across all markets, Kodak was suffering from the growing trend for people to view photographic images and read magazines by electronic display rather than in printed form.

In most other industries based upon digital technology, the primary source of profit was in software rather than hardware. Thus, in PCs, Microsoft earned huge profits from its dominance of operating systems (Windows) and office applications (Microsoft Office). Similarly with Google in internet search. In video games, it was the games developers and publishers rather than the console manufactures who made most money. Software also appeared to be the major source of profit in digital imaging. Thus, in software for creating, manipulating, displaying, and transmitting digital images, Adobe Systems was the major player. During 2005 Adobe earned a return on equity in excess of 30%. In software for editing digital images, programs for basic image manipulation included Microsoft's Picture It, while more comprehensive picture editing and formatting software included Adobe's Photoshop—the leader in this market.

Kodak's software development was primarily focused on the proprietary imaging software included in the systems it supplied to photofinishing lab, retail stores, commercial printers and medical imaging facilities. However, with the launch of its PhotoCD system in 1990 Kodak was heavily involved in developing software for the home market. Kodak's main strengths were in its color management software and its DLS System Management and Enhanced Services Software for managing retail processing and printing operations. In 2003, despite Adobe Systems' domination of the market for image display, formatting, and editing with its Photoshop and Acrobat products, Kodak released its EasyShare software. Adobe quickly followed with Photoshop Album, a $49 derivative of its Photoshop software. Google's introduction of its Picasa free photo-editing software in 2004 was putting additional pressure on prices.

Intense price competition was also a feature of online photosharing and photo-printing services. While Kodak's Easyshare Gallery was the market leader, it competed with a host of other online competitors including: Shutterfly, Snapfish, Walmart Photo Center, FujiFilmNet, Yahoo Photos, and searsphotos.com. As photography increasingly shifted to mobile phones, so Kodak sought to achieve leadership on online photosharing through a mobile phone. In 2003, through collaboration with Nokia and Cingular, Kodak introduced Kodak Mobile Service allowing users to store and organize phone-captured pictures. By 2005, pictures could be uploaded and downloaded by mobile phone to and from Kodak's EasyShare Gallery. Images could also be transmitted by mobile phone to Kodak's retail kiosks for printing.

By the beginning of 2006, it was clear that, under the brand umbrella of EasyShare, Kodak had created a complete digital imaging system for consumers. Kodak was finally a full-system supplier. It was positioned at every stage in the digital imaging chain and, with its EasyShare brand, it was communicating its system capabilities to consumers. Kodak's ability to serve the needs of several types of customer was particularly important. Through its retail network it provided digital scanning, enhancement and storage facilities to consumers who took pictures with conventional film. For consumers with digital cameras it offered editing and printing services both through retail kiosks and online and, with its EasyShare printers, it allowed customers the independence to pursue digital photography without using any of Kodak's retail services.

Kodak's Resources and Capabilities

Digital imaging was a classic "disruptive technology".[14] For traditional photographic companies it was "competence destroying"[15]—the new technological regime meant that many of their resources and capabilities became close to useless. For the camera companies—Nikon, Canon, Olympus and Pentax, for example—digital imaging was not such a threat: digital backs could be added to standard camera architectures; these companies' optical capabilities remained important. In addition, the camera companies had already adopted a good deal of microelectronic technology. For the film companies—Kodak, Fuji Film, Agfa, and Ilford—whose technical capabilities were based on chemical technologies, the threat of digital imaging was much greater. This is why the transition period between traditional and digital imaging was so important for Kodak. So long as the replacement of photographic film was gradual, Kodak could exploit its brand strength and vast distribution system to offer hybrid solutions, while using the time available and its cash flow from film to invest in the resources and capabilities it required for digital imaging. The problem was that many of the companies that Kodak was now competing with in the digital imaging arena had the advantage of well-developed microelectronic expertise: Casio, Ricoh and Hewlett-Packard had entered digital imaging from office electronics and printing,

been leveled at Kodak for its weaknesses in bringing new products to market: Kodak was too slow and its marketers had little understanding of the digital world.

Kodak's product-development process still reflected the company's origins in chemistry. Product development traditionally began with basic research where innovations were exploited through a long and meticulous product-development process before being rolled out onto the world market. One of George Fisher's major initiatives as Kodak chairman and CEO had been to streamline and speed Kodak's cumbersome product development process. In place of Kodak's sequential "phases-and-gates" development process, Fisher transferred approaches that had worked well at Motorola—greater decentralization of new product development and the use of cross-functional development teams to accelerate cycle times. Speed also required collaboration to access the technologies and capabilities of outside companies. Kodak had no problem in establishing collaborative agreements with other companies—its size, brand name and technological strength were sufficient to make it a highly attractive partner for small, technology-intensive firms in digital imaging. The real challenge was for Kodak to overcome a long history of insularity and hierarchical control in order to make its new-found alliances fruitful. Kodak's track record of alliances and joint ventures was mixed. Its Phogenix joint venture with HP to develop digital minilabs for film and image processes was dissolved in May 2003 after three years.[18]

Finances

One of Kodak's key advantages in withstanding the uncertainties and rapid technological changes of the market for digital imaging was its size and financial security. In contrast to the many start-up companies that sought to establish themselves in the sector, Kodak was independent of venture capitalists and the vagaries of the IPO market. In contrast with even some of its large and well established rivals, Kodak had the security of cash flows from its traditional photographic business.

By the beginning of 2004, Eastman Kodak remained a financially strong company but it was no longer the financial powerhouse of yesteryear. Since the late 1990s, debt had risen considerably and retiree healthcare benefits represented a substantial long-term liability. Meanwhile, profitability declined substantially between 2000 and 2003 because of the deterioration of the core photography business and because of the restructuring charges that were becoming a regular feature of Kodak's income statement. As a result, some analysts doubted Kodak's ability to finance its "digital growth strategy," which involved investing some $3 billion in capital expenditures and acquisitions during 2004–6. Tables 7.5 and 7.6 summarize Kodak's recent financial results.

Looking Forward

As he returned to Kodak's headquarters in Rochester, New York, from the Consumer Electronics show in Las Vegas, Antonio Perez reflected on his three years at Kodak—first as COO and then as CEO. For a company that had dominated its traditional market for so long, Kodak's ability to survive the annihilation of its

TABLE 7.5 Eastman Kodak: selected financial data, 2000–5 ($ million)

	2000	2001	2002	2003	2004	2005
From income statement						
Sales	13994	13234	12835	13317	13517	14268
Cost of goods sold	8019	8670	8225	9033	9582	10617
Selling, general, and admin.	2977	2627	2530	2648	2491	2668
R&D costs	784	779	762	781	836	892
Operating earnings	2214	345	793	238	−87	−599
Interest expense	178	219	173	148	168	211
Other income (charges)	96	−18	101	51	161	44
Restructuring and other costs	−44	659	98	484	695	690
Provision for income taxes	725	32	153	−66	−175	689
Net earnings	1407	76	770	265	556	−1362
From balance sheet						
Total current assets	5491	4683	4534	5455	5648	5781
Including:						
Cash and cash equivalents	246	448	569	1250	1255	1665
Receivables	2653	2337	2234	2389	2544	2760
Inventories	1718	1137	1062	1075	1158	1140
Property, plant, and equipment	5919	5659	5420	5094	4512	3778
Other noncurrent assets	1767	2072	3540	4269	3131	3221
Total assets	14212	13362	13494	14818	14737	14921
Total current liabilities	3,275	5,354	5,502	5,307	4,990	5,489
Including:						
Payables	3,403	3,276	3,351	3,707	3,896	4,187
Short-term borrowings	2,058	1,378	1,442	946	469	819
Other liabilities:						
Long-term borrowings	1,166	1,666	1,164	2,302	1,852	2,764
Post-employment liabilities	2,610	2,728	3,412	3,344	3,338	3,476
Other long-term liabilities	671	720	639	601	737	1,225
Total liabilities	10,784	10,468	10,717	11,554	10,917	12,954
Shareholders' equity	3,428	2,894	2,777	3,264	3,820	1,967
Total liabilities (and equity)	14,212	13,362	13,494	14,818	14,737	14,921
From cash flow statement						
Cash flows from operating activities:						
Earnings from continuing operations	1,407	76	770	265	556	−1362
Adjustments for noncash items	−425	1989	1448	1361	590	2542
Net cash provided by operating activities	982	2065	2204	1645	1168	1208
Cash flows from investing activities:						
Additions to properties	−945	−743	−577	−506	−460	−472
Proceeds from sale of businesses/assets	277	0	27	26	24	130
Acquisitions, net of cash acquired	−130	−306	−72	−679	−369	−984
Net cash used in investing activities	−783	−1074	−758	−1267	−120	−1304
Net cash flows from financing activities	−314	−804	−1331	270	−1066	533
Number of employees (thousands)	78	75	70	64	55	51

Source: Eastman Kodak Annual Reports.

TABLE 7.6 Eastman Kodak: results by business segments, 2000–2005 ($ millions)

	2000	2001	2002	2003	2004	2005
Net sales from continuing operations:						
Digital & Film Imaging Systems	10231	9403	9002	9415	9366	8460
Health Group	2220	2262	2274	2431	2686	2655
Graphic Communications Group	1417	1454	1456	967	1343	2990
All other	126	110	103	96	122	163
Consolidated total	13994	13229	12835	12909	13517	14268
Earnings (losses) from continuing operations before interest and taxes						
Digital & Film Imaging Systems	1430	787	771	427	598	362
Health Group	518	323	431	497	452	354
Graphic Communications Group	233	172	192	82	−39	1
All other	−11	−60	−28	−93	−191	−177
Total of segments	2170	1222	1366	913	820	540
Net earnings (losses) from continuing operations:						
Digital & Film Imaging Systems	1034	535	550	370	520	212
Health Group	356	221	313	415	366	196
Graphic Communications Group	90	84	83	35	−8	−9
All other	−2	−38	−23	−95	−163	−98
Total of segments	1478	802	923	725	715	301
Segment total assets:						
Digital & Film Imaging Systems	7100	9225	8798	9129	8458	7070
Health Group	1491	2038	2011	2598	2647	2404
Graphic Communications Group	1045	1438	1405	1011	1638	3543
All other	−92	−16	66	12	98	139
Total of segments	9544	12685	12280	12750	12841	13156

Note: Kodak made several changes in its segment reporting over the period. In 2003, *Photography* became *Digital and Film Imaging Systems*, and *Commercial Imaging* became the *Graphic Communication Group*.

technology was remarkable. For a company to emerge as a leader in a technology that was so radically different from its predecessor was unique. Most of Kodak's competitors in its old photographic business—Agfa, Polaroid, Konica—failed to make the leap; only Fuji Film trumps Kodak in its ability to cross the digital divide—in the period prior to 2005 Fuji grew substantially and was consistently profitable.[19]

From being a near monopolist in silver-halide photographic film, Kodak had emerged as a global leader in digital cameras, online photo storage and processing, light sensors and digital graphic displays. Under his leadership, there was no longer an Old Kodak and New Kodak: the Old Kodak had been buried.

Yet Perez realized that his job was only just beginning. Kodak had successfully crossed over to the other side. It had adopted digital technologies, developed those technologies and introduced a number of highly successful products. But there was no financial return. Kodak continued to bleed cash.

Part of the problem was the restructuring costs that Kodak incurred as it closed plants and shed employees. But this was only part of the story. In the consumer market, Kodak lost money on most hardware products and gave away its software. The commercial and healthcare sectors offered better prospects for margins, but in both of these sectors Kodak was still integrating its multiple acquisitions and building its market presence. Consumables and photofinishing services offered attractive margins, but these too were threatened by the growing tendency for consumers to view their pictures on screens rather than on printed copies.

Kodak's digital strategy had shown considerable awareness of the potential for competitive advantage, most notably in providing customers with integrated solutions, in emphasizing ease of use, and in combining alliances and acquisitions in order to build a presence throughout the digital value chain. The critical issue now was linking these sources of competitive advantage to the generation of profit.

Consumer digital products were unlikely to offer attractive margins—competition was simply too strong. Components offered a better bet: Kodak had strong portfolios of patents protecting its sensor and OLED technologies. However, Perez believed that some of the best opportunities would come from meeting the emerging needs of the consumers of digital images.

Notes

1 "Banishing the Negative: How Kodak is Developing its Blueprint for a Digital Transformation," *Financial Times,* January 26, 2006.
2 "Banishing the Negative: How Kodak is Developing its Blueprint for a Digital Transformation," *Financial Times,* January 26, 2006.
3 "Kodak Zooms in on Software as Industry Focus Shifts to Computers," *Financial Times,* January 9, 2006.
4 "Bill Miller's Kodak Moment," *Fortune,* November 14, 2005.
5 Address to the Academy of Management, Boston, August 1997.
6 "Kodak's New Focus," *Business Week,* January 30, 1995, pp. 62–8.
7 Eastman Kodak Company, "Kodak Leaders Outline Road Ahead to get Kodak 'Back on Track'," press release, November 11, 1997.
8 Eastman Kodak Company, "The Big Picture: Kodak and Digital Photography," www.Kodak.com/US/en/corp/presscenter/presentations/020520mediaforum3.shtml.
9 See www.Kodak.com/US/en/corp/presscenter/presentations/020520mediaforum3.shtml, accessed October 29, 2009.
10 Interview with Antonio Perez, President and COO, Kodak, *PMA Magazine*, February 2004.
11 NexPress was initially a joint venture with Heidelberg; Kodak bought out Heidelberg's share in 2004.
12 "Why Kodak Still Isn't Fixed," *Fortune,* May 11, 1998.
13 Eastman Kodak Company, "Kodak and HP Joint Venture to be Named Phogenix Imaging," press release, August 1, 2000.
14 J. L. Bower and C. M. Christensen, "Disruptive Technologies: Catching the Wave," *Harvard Business Review,* January–February, 1995.
15 M. Tushman, and P. Anderson, "Technological Discontinuities and Organizational Environments," *Administrative Science Quarterly,* 31 (1986): 439–65.
16 Interview with Carl Gustin, Chief Marketing Officer, Kodak, *PMA Magazine* (February 2004).
17 "Kodak's New Focus," *Business Week,* January 30, 1995, pp. 62–8.
18 Jeff Macher and Barak Richman in "Organizational Responses to Discontinuous Innovation: A Case Study Approach," *International Journal of Innovation Management* 8 (2004): 87–114 describe Kodak's joint project with Intel to develop the Picture CD: "Meetings scheduled to discuss the new product suffered from logistical constraints and unsolicited and unnecessary input from neighboring divisions . . . [T]he project's slow start highlighted that the firm's current routines and practices were not capable of developing a new technology for an uncertain, albeit rapidly emerging, market."
19 Fuji Film's operating margin was 2.8% in the year ended March 31, 2006; down from 10.8% four years earlier.

Case 8 Procter & Gamble's Organization 2005 Project*

During the first half of 2000, Procter & Gamble, the world's largest supplier of personal and household products, faced a slumping stock price and a crisis of leadership.

> On March 7, 2000, Procter & Gamble announced it would not meet its projected first quarter earnings, and the stock price abruptly fell from $86 to $60 per share. In total, between January, 2000—when the stock peaked at $116—and March 7th, 2000, P&G stock fell 52 per cent. The biggest crisis at

* This case was prepared by Robert M. Grant. It draws upon information contained in three earlier case studies: *P&G Japan: The SK-II Globalization Project* (Harvard Business School Case No. 9-303-003, 2003); *Procter & Gamble: Organization 2005* (Harvard Business School Case No. 9-707-519, 2007); *Procter & Gamble: Organization 2005 and Beyond* (ICFAI Knowledge Center, Case No. 303-102-1 ECCH, 2003).

P&G was not the loss of $85 billion in market capitalization, however: it was the crisis in confidence—particularly leadership confidence—that permeated the organization. In too many of our businesses, best-in-class competitors were on the attack. P&G business units around the world were blaming headquarters for their problems, while headquarters was blaming the business units.

On the day I was announced as the new CEO, P&G's stock fell another four dollars, and after 15 days on the job, it fell another $3.85—which was not much of a confidence builder.[1]

On June 8, 2000, Procter & Gamble's board of directors fired its CEO, Dirk Jager, and appointed A. G. Lafley as his replacement. Lafley had held a series of senior appointments at P&G, most recently as head of Global Beauty Care.

Lafley immediately embarked upon a series of cost-cutting measures and management changes while beginning work on the more fundamental strategic issues that had been undermining P&G's performance. However, there was one key decision that could not wait. In July 1998, P&G had announced Organization 2005—a plan for a complete redesign of P&G's organization that would involve a shift from a structure based primarily upon geographical regions to one based upon global product divisions. The new structure was implemented in July 1999 but, by the time Lafley took over as CEO, P&G was still in the midst of considerable organizational upheaval.

Given the apparent failure of Organization 2005 to deliver either sales growth or improved margins for P&G and its association with Lafley's predecessor, many P&G senior managers favoured its abandonment and a reversion to P&G's previous regional structure. However, undoing the structure that had been in place for less than a year risked creating even greater upheaval at P&G. Moreover, Lafley acknowledged that Organization 2005 had been a response to widely perceived inadequacies in P&G's ability to coordinate across countries and regions.

The Evolution of P&G's Organizational Structure

P&G began making soap and candles in Cincinnati in 1837. During the twentieth century P&G's diversification across a broad range of branded, packaged consumer goods was a result of three key management innovations. The first was its creation of a central research laboratory (1890), which became the source of a flow of new product introductions. Second was its establishment of a market research department (1924). The third was its invention of brand management—an organizational system where individual products were assigned to entrepreneurial brand managers.

In the U.S., P&G's structure evolved, first, into a divisionalized corporation where each product division had its own manufacturing, marketing and sales functions, then into a matrix organization, where the product divisions formed the primary structure but functional heads within each division had "dotted-line" relationships with corporate-level functional heads. Thus, in the laundry division, the director for manufacturing would report first to the vice president of the laundry division and secondarily to the vice-president of manufacturing at the corporate level.

Overseas expansion had been based around the creation of stand-alone national subsidiaries. The basic principle had been established by the first VP of overseas operations, Walter Lingle: "We must tailor our products to meet consumer demands in each nation. But we must create local country subsidiaries whose structures, policies and practices that are as exact a replica of the U.S. Procter & Gamble organization as it is possible to create." During the 1960s and 1970s, P&G's geographical scope and international sales expanded rapidly. However, duplication of functions at the national level was creating considerable inefficiency. Attempts to consolidate functions around regional headquarters included the creation of a European Technical Center at P&G's European headquarters in Brussels in 1963. It conducted research and process engineering and developed products and processes that country managers could choose to adapt to and launch in their own countries.

Although regional headquarters gained increased authority over the national subsidiaries, there was still limited cross-border integration of product policies, new product introductions, or functional activities. Moreover, while the existing structure allowed P&G to adapt its products and marketing to the needs of existing markets, it did not provide much impetus for expanding into new markets. During the 1980s, Asia—Japan in particular—was offering exciting opportunities for P&G and by the end of the 1980s, the breakup of the Soviet Union and opening of Eastern Europe would lead to a massive expansion in P&G's opportunities for entering unsaturated markets.

The Global Matrix

In 1989, P&G introduced a major change in its organization structure. It created a global product structure where each product category was headed by a president who reported directly to the CEO. The country general managers and their regional bosses retained profit-and-loss responsibilities, HR reporting and career management. However, the new global category executive presidents were given direct control over R&D. For each category a VP of R&D was appointed to manage R&D within the product category worldwide. These VPs of R&D reported directly to their global category presidents. The result was a move towards product-category platform technologies that could be applied globally.

The new structure also strengthened P&G's functional organization. Manufacturing, purchasing, engineering and distribution were integrated into a single supply function headed by a senior vice president. This function was intended to facilitate the end-to-end integration of P&G's global product-supply function. Supply-chain integration was particularly important for integrating the manufacturing and distribution facilities of the acquisitions that P&G was making at this time.

This was followed in 1994 by the reorganization of P&G's sales function into a customer business development (CBD) function. A major goal of this strengthened global sales function was to develop closer relationships with P&G's biggest customers. One of the CBD's first initiatives was to open an office in Wal-Mart's home town of Bentonville.

Figure 8.1 shows a partial picture of P&G's structure in 1990. To show how the geographical structure linked to the products structure, Figure 8.1 shows the detailed products organization for P&G Japan.

The new structure resulted in some improvements in global coordination and allowed cross-border consolidation of some activities and facilities. However, these improvements did little to stimulate growth at P&G. Table 8.1 shows key financial

FIGURE 8.1 Procter & Gamble's organizational structure in 1990

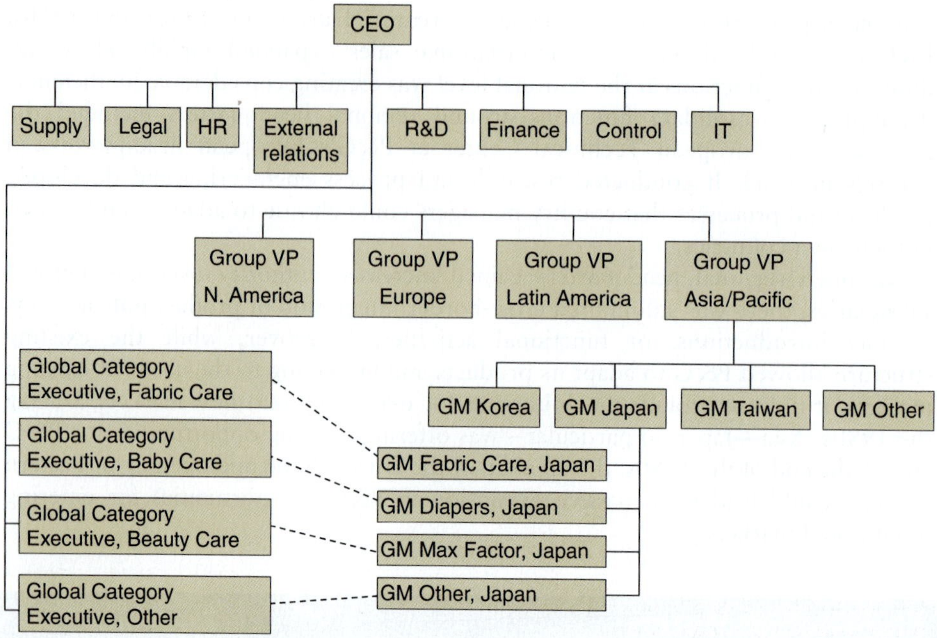

TABLE 8.1 Procter & Gamble: financial data for 1992–2000 (year ended June 30; in $000s except where indicated)

	1992	1993	1994	1995	1996	1997	1998	1999	2000
Net sales	29 362	30 433	30 385	33 482	35 284	35 764	37 154	38 125	39 951
Cost of goods	17 324	17 683	17 338	19 561	20 938	20 510	20 896	21 027	21 018
Gross profit	12 038	12 750	13 047	13 921	14 346	15 254	16 258	17 098	18 933
Total SG&A	9171	9589	9377	9677	9531	9766	10 203	10 845	12 165
Of which: advertising	*2693*	*2973*	*2996*	*3284*	*3254*	*3466*	*3704*	*3639*	*3793*
R&D expense	*861*	*956*	*964*	*1148*	*1399*	*1469*	*1546*	*1726*	*1899*
Operating income	2867	3161	3670	4244	4815	5488	6055	6253	6768
Net income	1872	269	2211	2645	3046	3415	3780	3763	3542
Cash from operation	3025	3338	3649	3568	4158	5882	4885	5544	4675
Cash from investing	(2860)	(1630)	(2008)	(2363)	(2466)	(2068)	(5210)	(2175)	(5345)
Return on equity (%)	23.2	2.9	22.6	25.0	26.0	28.3	30.9	31.2	28.8
Employees ('000)	106	103.5	96.5	99.2	103	106	110	110	110

data for P&G and Table 8.2 shows a breakdown by region. By the time Dirk Jager, P&G's chief operating officer, took over as CEO at the beginning of 1999, the view that P&G was not performing to its full potential had become widespread both within the company and outside. In mid-1999, *The Economist* reported:

> Few companies have suffered as much from price competition as Procter & Gamble. Unwilling to lower its prices and unable to distinguish itself as an

TABLE 8.2 Procter & Gamble: Regional financial performance, 1996–1999 (year ended June 30; in $000s).

		North America	Europe, Middle East, Africa	Asia	Latin America	Corporate and other
Net sales	1999	18 977	11 878	3648	2825	797
	1998	18 456	11 835	3453	2640	770
	1997	17 625	11 587	3573	2306	673
	1996	17 230	11 458	3881	2173	542
Net earnings	1999	2710	1214	279	318	(758)
	1998	2474	1092	174	274	(234)
	1997	2253	956	275	256	(325)
	1996	1953	793	273	219	(192)
Identifiable assets	1999	11 390	6286	2793	1577	10 067
	1998	11 063	5998	2499	1519	9887
	1997	10 280	5433	2726	1389	7716
	1996	10 382	5853	2770	1270	7455

innovator, the firm has failed to increase its volumes in the past three quarters and has lost around 10% of its market share in the past five years . . . P&G's problems reflect its risk-averse culture; its willingness to allow individual country managers a veto over R&D, sales and marketing decisions; and its mish-mash of different manufacturing platforms.[2]

Organization 2005

Jager's primary concern was P&G's low growth of sales during the 1990s. The central problem, in his view, was lack of innovation. P&G's expansion had been based upon innovation: synthetic detergents, fluoride toothpaste, disposable diapers. What had happened to P&G's flow of breakthrough innovations? Jager cited the *Always* range of feminine-hygiene products launched in 1982 as P&G's last major new product innovation. Even when new products were introduced, weak coordination among P&G's complex regional and country organizations resulted in slow global rollout. Pampers disposable diapers were a classic example: launched in the U.S. in 1961, Pampers were introduced into Germany in 1973, France in 1978 and the U.K. in 1981. As a result, in international markets, competitors were often able to launch imitative products before P&G.

Jager's response was an ambitious, six-year program of organizational restructuring that he had been working on while COO. Announcing Organization 2005 in 1999, Jager said:

Success is defined first and foremost in terms of growth. Unless a company grows at an acceptable rate—year in, year out—it can't sustain its organization. Success also means growing profitably. Otherwise, it can't produce the

> resources and capability to invest, to take risks, seizing new opportunities. The program we lay out here today is designed to deliver that growth, at a consistently higher level. Just come back in a couple of years and take a look. I believe that the best way to accelerate growth is to innovate bigger and move faster consistently and across the entire company.[3]

Organization 2005 promised to be one of the biggest upheavals in P&G's history. It involved new processes to boost innovation, plant closures, extensive job losses, and changes in incentives and cultural norms designed to make P&G less risk averse and more responsive. The program had a budget of $1.9 billion.

In his two decades at P&G, Jager had come to regard the organization as bureaucratic, conformist, risk-averse and slow. The goals of greater innovation and responsiveness would require a cultural revolution. By pressuring the organization to increase the rate of new product introductions and speed of rollouts, he hoped to shake up the organization and drive out inertia. Key to a less risk-averse culture was a stronger emphasis on performance. This would be achieved by increasing the importance of performance pay. For senior management, the performance-related variation in annual compensation would change from 20% to 80%. Stock options were extended from the top management team to include middle managers. P&G's complex and tedious budget-setting process was organized into a single integrated business-planning process, built around the agreement of stretch performance targets.

The New Structure

At the heart of Organization 2005 was a fundamental reorientation of P&G's organizational structure. Primary profit responsibility shifted from P&G's four regional organizations to seven global business units (GBUs). The GBUs were given worldwide responsibility for product development, manufacturing and marketing of the products within their categories. The regional organizations were transformed into seven market development organizations whose responsibility was the local implementation of the GBUs' global strategies. Functional services, including accounting, human resources, payroll and IT, were organized into a new global business service unit (GBS). Figure 8.2 shows the new structure.

While the primary strategic mandate of the GBU presidents was developing and rolling out new products, the fact that the GBUs were now responsible for profit and loss meant that they were ultimately responsible for the performance of the whole range of functions within their business. A key objective for the GBU presidents was to increase efficiency through greater cross-border integration. This included standardizing manufacturing processes, simplifying brand portfolios and coordinating marketing activities. For example, the GBU for Baby Care intended to reduce P&G's 12 different diaper-manufacturing processes to one standard production model. By placing emphasis on brands with global potential, P&G identified 300 brands to be closed or sold.

In addition to shifting P&G's primary organizational structure from geographical regions to business divisions, the restructuring also attempted to reduce bureaucracy and enhance accountability by reducing the number of hierarchical levels between the CEO and front line managers. This involved increasing the decision-making authority

FIGURE 8.2 Procter & Gamble's organizational structure in 1999

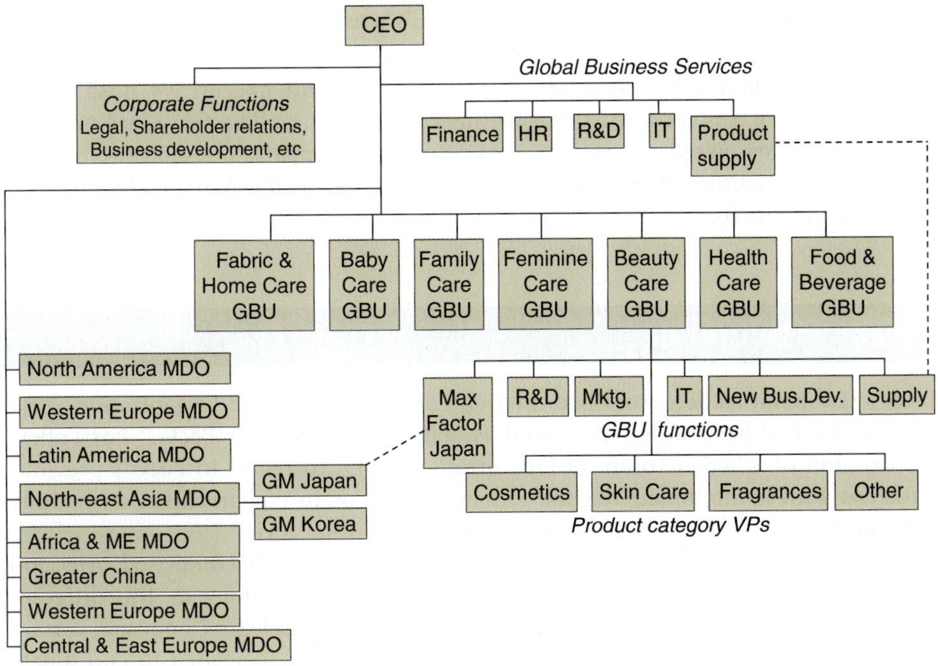

of middle managers. By stripping out much of the hierarchical approval process, it was intended that decision making would become faster and the lag between decisions and their implementation would be reduced.

September 1999 to June 2000

Jager fulfilled his promise to bring far-reaching change to P&G. Where he failed was in delivering the performance improvements that he had targeted. His first year as CEO had gone well—the stock market responded well to his plans for shaking up P&G and even the two quarter-year periods that followed the introduction of Organization 2005—July–December 1999—showed satisfactory sales and profit growth despite the upheaval caused by reorganization. At the end of January 2000, P&G's stock price hit an all-time high. On March 7, 2000, P&G revised its quarterly earnings guidance for the first quarter of 2000: instead of earnings growth of 2%, its earnings would fall by 10% due to higher costs. In fact, earnings for the quarter declined by 18%. The stock market reaction was brutal. On March 7, P&G's stock price fell by 30%; by the end of March it was more than 50% off its peak. On June 8, P&G revised downwards its earnings and sales forecasts for the second quarter of 2000. For a company that had prided itself on the consistency of its performance and achieving its financial targets, this was too much. Jager's credibility in the financial community had been destroyed.

Was Jager's ousting by the board simply a matter of failing in his relations with Wall Street? Two other factors are relevant. First, despite considerable success in increasing P&G's rate of new product introduction, the company's core established brands continued to lose market share. Second, Jager's hard-driving aggressive style generated considerable opposition within P&G's management ranks:

> Jager's resignation also suggests that the 57-year-old executive's push for change may have faced resistance within P&G's culture. The CEO had made clear that his mandate was to shake up the company's risk-averse and bureaucratic culture. And he wasn't afraid to make enemies. Actually, he might have done just that.[4]

Lafley's Decision

Jager's ignominious departure had undoubtedly discredited the Organization 2005 project that had been widely perceived as "Jager's blueprint for P&G." For Lafley, the decision of whether to affirm Organization 2005, to revert to P&G's previous structure with its dominant regional organizations, or to embark upon an entirely new solution would be critical in defining his vision for P&G.

P&G was one of the world's most complex companies. It comprised over 300 brands, thousands of products, and 110 000 employees working in 140 different countries across a broad range of functions. This complexity imposed certain minimal requirements on P&G's organizational structure: it needed to coordinate within each product area, it needed to coordinate within each function and it needed to coordinate within each country. It also needed to coordinate its sales activities in order to meet the needs of multiproduct and multinational customers such as Wal-Mart and Carrefour. While some form of matrix was inevitable, what form should this matrix take? In particular, what should be the responsibilities of each dimension? Until 1999, geographical organization had been paramount. It was responsible for financial control ("profit-and-loss responsibility"), strategic planning and human resource appraisal and control. In 1999 decision-making power had shifted to the business areas. However the case for empowering global product divisions over regional divisions and national subsidiaries was far from clear cut.

The case for global product divisions was based primarily upon the advantages of efficiency and innovation. Global product divisions facilitated cross-border integration and avoiding duplicating functions and facilities by country. Global product divisions allowed pooling research activities around the technologies relevant to different product categories and permitted new products to be rolled out globally in a coordinated way.

Yet, in most of P&G's product markets, national and regional differences between markets remained substantial. Very few of P&G's products were globally standardized (*Pringles* potato chips were among the nearest thing P&G had to a global product). In skin care and cosmetics, household products and most foods, customer preferences were markedly different between countries—and even within countries. Differences in channels of distribution also necessitated nationally differentiated strategies with regard to packaging, product size, marketing, sales, and distribution. In skin care products (see Exhibit 8.1) and in laundry detergents (see Exhibit 8.2) national market differences severely limited the potential for global product strategies.

A key argument in favor of globally standardized products was that the forces of globalization were reducing the national market differences.[5] Yet, as more countries entered the global system of trade and financial transactions—most notably the former communist economies of Russia, China and Eastern Europe—so multinational corporations increasingly sought to develop integrated country-based strategies to develop their businesses within these countries. In the case of P&G, it is notable that the transfer of profit-and-loss responsibility from the regional organizations to the global business units occurred only in the developed countries. For the emerging markets of Eastern Europe, South-east Asia, and Greater China, the regional organizations retained profit-and-loss responsibility. The implication was that, for certain key emerging markets such as China, achieving a coherent country strategy through close cooperation between P&G's different business units took precedence over the need for global coordination within each of these business units.

EXHIBIT 8.1

Organization 2005 in Action: the Case of SK-II

The introduction of Organization 2005 resulted in massive management disruption at P&G. A. G. Lafley, who had only recently been appointed President of the North American regional organization, was appointed President of the new Global Business Unit for Beauty Care. He also retained his North American regional responsibilities as President of the North America Market Development Organization "It was a crazy year," he recalled, "There was so much to build, but beyond the grand design, we were not clear about how it should operate."

Among the large number of initiatives and projects that required his attention, he was attracted towards the case of SK-II, a skin-cleansing product developed by P&G Japan. As part of the management changes ushered in by Organization 2005, Paolo de Cesare, head of P&G's European skin-care business, was promoted to vice president and appointed to head up Max Factor Japan. Under the old structure his primary reporting relationship would have been through P&G Japan to P&G Asia Pacific. Under the new structure he reported to Lafley's Beauty Care GBU and on a dotted-line basis to the head of the MDO for Northeast Asia. At the Beauty Care GBU, de Cesare became a member of the unit's Global Leadership Team whose primary purpose was to develop global brands. The team was chaired by Lafley and comprised business GMs from three key MDOs together with representatives from R&D, consumer research, product supply, human resources, and finance functions. The Japanese Max Factor organization had become increasingly involved in global product development initiatives in beauty care—partly because of Japanese technical leadership in cosmetics and the extremely high-quality demands of Japanese consumers. The development process sponsored by the global category organizations under P&G's former structure involved using consumer research to identify a worldwide unmet consumer need, assigning a lead research center to developing a technical response to the need, then drawing upon marketing expertise from lead markets to build a new product concept on that technology base. In the case of facial cleansing, consumer researchers found that, despite regional differences, there was widespread dissatisfaction among women with existing products and practices. Chris Bartlett describes the next stages:

> *A technology team was assembled at an R&D facility in Cincinnati, drawing on the most qualified technologists from its P&G's labs worldwide. For example, because the average Japanese woman spent 4.5 minutes on her face-cleansing regime compared with 1.7 minutes for the typical American woman, Japanese technologists were sought for their refined expertise in the cleansing processes and their particular understanding of how to develop a product with the rich, creamy lather. Working with a woven substrate technology developed by P&G's paper business, the core technology team found that a 10-micron fiber, when woven into a mesh, was effective in trapping and absorbing dirt and impurities. By impregnating this substrate with a dry-sprayed formula of cleansers and moisturizers activated at different times in the cleansing process, team members felt they could develop a disposable cleansing cloth that would respond to the identified consumer need. After this technology "chassis" had been developed, a technology team in Japan adapted it to allow the cloth to be impregnated with a different cleanser formulation that included the SK-II ingredient, Pitera.*[6]

The result of this global initiative was two very different products for two major national markets. The U.S. marketing team developed an Olay version with a one-step routine that combined the benefits of cleansing, conditioning and toning. The Japanese team developed SK-II version positioned as a "foaming massage cloth" that increased skin circulation through a massage while boosting skin clarity due to the microfibers' ability to clean pores and trap dirt. While the Olay Facial Cloth was priced at $7 in the U.S., SK-II Foaming Massage Cloth was priced at the equivalent of $50 in Japan.

A key goal of Organization 2005 was to speed the global rollout of innovative new products. Yet, as Lafley prepared for his meeting with the Beauty Care Global Leadership Team to discuss the introduction of SK-II in other markets (notably Europe and China), it was clear that there were huge differences between national markets that needed to be taken into account. Not only were women's facial cleansing regimes very different between countries but women also gave different emphasis to the different performance characteristics of cleansing products and their willingness to pay for skin-care products varied in a way that could not be explained simply by disposable income. Moreover, countries varied greatly according to the structure of their distribution channels. SK-II was designed for use in Japanese cosmetics retailing, which made extensive use of beauty consultants who could introduce consumers to the products and demonstrate their use. In the U.S., only upmarket department stores and a few specialized cosmetics stores make use of beauty consultants: the U.S. mass market was made up of drugstores and discount stores, which were totally unsuited to the price point or the customer education requirements of SK-II.

Source: This account draws heavily upon *P&G Japan: The SK-II Globalization Project* (Cambridge, MA: Harvard Business School Case No. 9-303-003, 2003).

EXHIBIT 8.2

Global versus Local Brands

For multinational companies supplying branded goods and services to consumers, deciding whether to replace local brands with global brands is an important and difficult strategic issue. Whether the company has internationalized by acquisition or through setting up wholly-owned overseas subsidiaries, most multinationals find themselves with unwieldy brand portfolios that comprise a few global bands together with a number of local brands, many of which make only minor contributions to overall sales. For example, in 1999, just 25% of Unilever's brands contributed over 90% of its sales. As a result, Unilever launched a program to cull its brand portfolio from 1600 to 400 over a five year period.

Global brands offer two types of advantage over local brands:

- differentiation advantages from the superior status of global bands and their appeal to affluent, globally mobile consumers
- cost efficiencies in advertising resulting from scale economies and spillovers across national borders.

Despite these advantages, many companies retain local brands because of the risks of losing market share when migrating customers from a familiar local brand to a global brand.

Different multinationals have adopted different branding strategies. In retail banking, HSBC and Santander have replaced local bank names with the parent's brand; Unicredit and Royal Bank of Scotland have retained most of their local brands. In household and personal products, Procter & Gamble, Unilever, and Colgate-Palmolive have concentrated upon developing global brands, Henkel has retained national brands where they possessed a strong local identity.

In laundry products, Henkel's different brands exploit national differences in laundry practices. For example, in southern Europe consumers use cooler water than in northern Europe and frequently add bleach to their washes. Packaging practices also vary with northern European consumers preferring compact packages. Henkel markets its leading detergent, Persil, in Germany, France and the Netherlands and uses separate brands for the Spanish and Italian markets. Even with its international brands, Henkel varies product formulation and brand positioning. For example, in France, Persil emphasizes whiteness and stain removal; in the Netherlands Persil is positioned as an environmentally friendly detergent. In Italy, where the preference is for stain-removing ability and blue color, Henkel introduced a brand other than Persil (to allow Persil to fully own the color white in northern Europe). In Spain, the company acquired an existing brand.

Procter & Gamble's moves towards global brands have sometimes encountered local setbacks. In 2000, P&G renamed its popular Fairy laundry detergent in Germany as Dawn. There was no change in the product's formulation, but within a year, P&G's share of the German detergent market had declined drastically.

Source: Draws upon Randall Frost, "Should Global Brands Trash Local Favorites?" BrandHome (March 7, 2005), see http://www.brandchannel.com/features_effect.asp?pf_id=253.

Notes

1 A. G. Lafley, "Getting Procter & Gamble Back on Track," *Rotman Integrative Thinking Seminar*, University of Toronto, April 21, 2003, www.rotman.utoronto.ca/integrativethinking/Lafley.pdf, accessed October 13, 2009.

2 "Procter's Gamble," *The Economist*, June 10, 1999.

3 Quoted in: *Procter & Gamble: Organization 2005 and Beyond* (ICFAI Knowledge Center, Case No. 303-102-1 ECCH, 2003).

4 "What's Driving P&G's Executive Spin Cycle?" *Business Week*, June 8, 2000.

5 This argument was first made by Ted Levitt in "The Globalization of Markets" *Harvard Business Review* (1983): 92–102.

6 C. A. Bartlett, *P&G Japan: The SK-II Globalization Project* (Harvard Business School Case No. 9-303-003, 2003).

Case 9 AirAsia: The World's Lowest Cost Airline*

By 2009, AirAsia had established itself as Asia's most successful low-cost airline. Between January 2002 and March 2009, AirAsia had expanded from two aircraft and 200 000 passenger journeys to 79 aircraft and 11.8 million passengers. Its route network had grown beyond Malaysia to cover 10 South-East Asian countries. In addition to its hub in Kuala Lumpur (KL), Malaysia, it had replicated its system by establishing associated airlines in Thailand and Indonesia.

* Written by Robert M. Grant. The case draws upon a report written by Sara Buchholz, Nadia Fabio, Andrés Ileyassoff, Laurent Mang and Daniele Visentin, *AirAsia—Tales from a Long-haul Low Cost Carrier*, Bocconi University (2009), and from an earlier case by Thomas Lawton and Jonathan Doh, *The Ascendance of AirAsia: Building a Successful Budget Airline in Asia* (Ivey School of Business, Case No. 9B08M054 2008). Used by permission of the authors.

FIGURE 9.1 Costs in U.S. cents per available seat kilometer for different low cost airlines

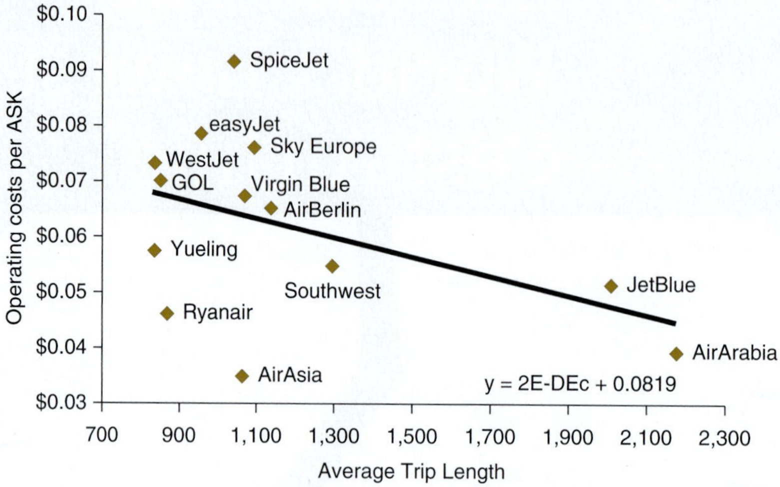

Source: AirAsia Presentation, CLSA Forum, Hong Kong, September 2007

By 2007, UBS research showed that AirAsia was the world's lowest cost airline with costs per available seat kilometer (ASK) significantly below those of Southwest, Jet Blue, Ryanair or Virgin Blue (see Figure 9.1). It was also one of the world's most profitable airlines. In 2008, when very few of the world's airlines made any profit at all, AirAsia earned return on assets of 4%.[1] In 2009 it won the Skytrax Award as "The World's Best Low Cost Airline."

AirAsia had built its business on the low-cost carrier (LCC) model created by Southwest Airlines in the U.S. and replicated throughout the world by a host of imitators. AirAsia had adapted the basic LCC model to the market, geographical and institutional features of South-East Asia while preserving the principal operational features of the strategy. However, in 2007, AirAsia embarked upon a major departure from the LCC model: expansion into long-haul flights by inaugurating routes to Australia and China and then, in 2009, to India and the U.K. The conventional wisdom was that the efficiency of the LCC model was dependent upon short- and medium-distance flights with a single type of aircraft and minimal customer amenities—intercontinental flights required contravening these basic conditions. Very few LCCs had ventured into long-haul; even fewer had made a success of it.

To evaluate AirAsia's potential to expand from being a regional carrier to an international airline would require a careful analysis of the basis of its existing cost advantage and an evaluation of the transferability of these cost advantages to the long-haul market.

The History of AirAsia

The growth of AirAsia is closely associated with the entrepreneurial effort of Tony Fernandes. Son of a Malaysian doctor, Tony was sent to boarding school in Britain with a view to following in his father's footsteps into the medical profession. The son had other ideas and, after an accounting degree at the London School of Economics, went into music publishing, first with Virgin, then Time Warner. He describes his decision to start an airline as follows:

> I was watching the telly in a pub and I saw Stelios [Haji-Ioannou] on air talking about easyJet and running down the national carrier, British Airways. (Sound familiar? Hahaha.) I was intrigued as I didn't know what a low cost carrier was but I always wanted to start an airline that flew long haul with low fares.
>
> So I went to Luton and spent a whole day there. I was amazed how people were flying to Barcelona and Paris for less than 10 pounds. Everything was organized and everyone had a positive attitude. It was then at that point in Luton airport that I decided to start a low cost airline.[2]

He subsequently met with Conor McCarthy, former operations director of Ryanair. The two developed a plan to form a budget airline serving the South-East Asia market.

Seeking the support of the Malaysian government, Prime Minister Mahathir Mohammad encouraged Fernandes to acquire a struggling government-owned airline, AirAsia. With their own capital and support from a group of investors, they acquired AirAsia for 1 Malaysian ringgit (RM)—and assumed debts of RM 40 million (about $11 million). In January 2002, AirAsia was relaunched with just three planes and a business model that McCarthy described as: "a Ryanair operational strategy, a Southwest people strategy, and an easyJet branding strategy."[3]

Fueled by rising prosperity in Malaysia and a large potential market for leisure and business travelers seeking inexpensive domestic transportation, AirAsia's domestic business expanded rapidly. In January 2004, AirAsia began its first international service from KL to Phuket in Thailand; in February 2004 it sought to tap the Singapore market by offering flights from Johor Bahru, just across the border from Singapore, and in 2005 it began flights to Indonesia.

International expansion was fueled by its initial public offering in October 2004, which raised RM 717 million. Airline deregulation across South-East Asia greatly facilitated international expansion. To exploit the market for budget travel in Thailand and Indonesia, AirAsia adopted the novel strategy of establishing joint-venture companies in Thailand (Thai AirAsia) and Indonesia (Indonesia AirAsia) to create new hubs in Bangkok and Jakarta. In both cases, the operations of these companies were contracted out to AirAsia, which received a monthly fee from these associate companies.

From the beginning, Fernandes had set his sights on long-haul travel—guided by the example of his hero, Freddie Laker, the pioneer of low-cost transatlantic air travel. However, this risked his good relations with the Malaysian government because it put AirAsia into direct competition with the national airline, Malaysian Airlines. Hence, Fernandes established a separate company, AirAsia X to develop its long-haul business. AirAsia X is owned 16% by AirAsia (with an option to increase to 30%), 48% by Aero Ventures (co-founded by Tony Fernandes), 16% by Richard Branson's Virgin Group, with the remaining 20% owned by Bahrain-based Manara Consortium and Japan-based Orix Corporation. Operationally, AirAsia and AirAsia X are closely linked.

In 2007, flights began to Australia followed by China. By July 2009, AirAsia X had flights from KL to the Gold Coast, Melbourne and Perth in Australia; Tianjin and Hangzhou in China; and Taipei and London using five Airbus 340s—with three more to be delivered by year end. Planed future routes included Abu Dhabi (October 2009), India (2010) and later Sydney, Seoul and New York. At Abu Dhabi, AirAsia X planned to have a hub that would serve Frankfurt, Cairo, and possibly East Africa too: "You just can't get to East Africa from Asia," observed Fernandes.[4] To support its expansion, AirAsia X ordered 10 Airbus A350s for delivery in 2016.

AirAsia's Strategy and Culture

Strategy

AirAsia described its strategy as follows:

- Safety first: partnering with the world's most renowned maintenance providers and complying with world airline regulations.
- High aircraft utilization: implementing the region's fastest turnaround time at only 25 minutes, assuring lower costs and higher productivity.
- Low fare, no frills: providing guests with the choice of customizing services without compromising on quality and services.
- Streamline operations: making sure that processes are as simple as possible.
- Lean distribution system: offering a wide and innovative range of distribution channels to make booking and traveling easier.
- Point-to-point network: applying the point-to-point network keeps operations simple and costs low.[5]

Prior to its expansion into long haul, AirAsia identified its geographical coverage as encompassing three-and-a-half hours' flying time from its hubs. Fernandes' confidence in his growth strategy rested on the fact that: "This area encompasses a population of about 500 million people. Only a small proportion of this market regularly travels by air. AirAsia believes that certain segments of this market have been under-served historically and that the Group's low fares stimulate travel within these market segments."[6] Its slogan "Now Everyone Can Fly!" encapsulated AirAsia's goal of expanding the market for air travel in Southeast Asia.

To penetrate its target market, AirAsia placed a big emphasis on marketing and brand development. "The brand is positioned to project an image of a safe, reliable low-cost airline that places a high emphasis on customer service while providing an enjoyable flying experience." For an LCC, AirAsia had a comparatively large expenditures on TV, print and internet advertising. AirAsia used its advertising expenditures counter-cyclically: during the SARS outbreak and after the Bali bombings, AirAsia boosted its spending on advertising and marketing. In addition it sought to maximize the amount of press coverage that it received. AirAsia also built its image through co-branding and sponsorship relationships. A sponsorship deal with the AT&T Williams Formula 1 race car team resulted in AirAsia painting one of its A320s in the livery of the a Williams race car. Its sponsorship of Manchester United has resulted in it painting its planes with the portraits of Manchester United players. It also sponsors referees in English Premier League. A cooperative advertising deal with *Time* magazine resulted in an AirAsia plane being painted with the *Time* logo.

Its internet advertising includes banner ads on the Yahoo mobile homepage and a Facebook application for the Citibank-AirAsia credit card with the goal of increasing visibility, encouraging interaction and allowing users to immerse themselves with the AirAsia brand.

This heavy emphasis on brand building has provided AirAsia with a platform for providing services that meet other travelers' needs. AirAsia offers an AA express shuttle bus connecting airports to city centers with seats bookable simultaneously with online booking of plane tickets. Fernandes has also founded Tune Hotels, a chain of no-frills hotels co-branded with Air Asia. Tune Money offers online financial services—again co-branded with AirAsia.

Culture and Management Style

AirAsia's corporate culture and management style reflect Tony Fernandes' own personality:

> Mr. Fernandes says that he came to the industry with no preconceptions but found it rigidly compartmentalized and dysfunctional. He wanted AirAsia to reflect his own unstuffy, open, and cheerful personality. He is rarely seen without his baseball cap, open-neck shirt and jeans, and he is proud that the firm's lack of hierarchy (very unusual in Asia) means anyone can rise to do anyone else's job. AirAsia employs pilots who started out as baggage handlers and stewards; for his part, Mr. Fernandes also practices what he preaches. Every month he spends a day as a baggage handler, every two months as cabin crew, every three months as a check-in clerk. He has even established a "culture department" to "pass the message and hold parties".[7]

The share offer prospectus describes AirAsia's culture as follows:

> The Group prides itself on building a strong, team-orientated corporate culture. The Group's employees understand and subscribe to the Group's core strategy and actively focus on maintaining low costs and high productivity. AirAsia motivates its employees by awarding bonuses based upon each employee's contribution to AirAsia's productivity, and expects to increase loyalty through its ESOS [employee share ownership scheme] which will be available to all employees. The Group's management encourages open communication which creates a dynamic working environment, and meets all its employees on a quarterly basis to review AirAsia's results and generate new ways to lower costs and increase productivity. Employees . . . frequently communicate directly with AirAsia's senior management and offer suggestions on how AirAsia can increase its efficiency or productivity . . .
>
> In addition to the above, AirAsia:
>
> - inculcates enthusiasm and commitment among staff by sponsoring numerous social events and providing a vibrant and friendly working environment
> - strives to be honest and transparent in its relations with third parties . . .

- fosters a non-discriminatory, meritocratic environment where employees are offered opportunities for advancement, regardless of their education, race, gender, religion, nationality or age, and
- emphasizes maintaining a constant quality of service throughout all of AirAsia's operation through bringing together to work on a regular basis employees based in different locations.[8]

AirAsia's Operations

AirAsia's operations strategy comprises the following elements:

- *Aircraft.* In common with other LCCs, AirAsia operates a single type of aircraft, the Airbus A320. (It switched from Boeing 737s in 2005.) A single aircraft type offers economies in purchasing, maintenance, pilot training and aircraft utilization.
- *No-frills flights.* AirAsia offers a single class, which allows more seats per plane. For example, when it was operating its Boeing 737s, these were equipped with 148 seats, compared to 132 for a typical two-class configuration. Customer services are minimal: complimentary meals and drinks are not served on board (but snacks and beverages can be purchased), passengers pay for baggage beyond a low threshold, and there is no baggage transfer between flights—passengers must do this themselves. AirAsia does not use aerobridges for boarding and disembarking passengers—another cost-saving measure. Flights are ticketless and there is no assigned seating. Such simplicity allows quick turnaround of planes, which also permits better utilization of planes and crews.
- *Sales and marketing.* AirAsia engages in direct sales through its web site and call center. As a result, it avoids paying commissions to travel agents.
- *Outsourcing.* AirAsia achieves simplicity and cost economies by outsourcing those activities that can be undertaken more effectively and efficiently by third parties. Thus, most aircraft maintenance is outsourced to third parties, contracts being awarded on the basis of competitive bidding. Most of AirAsia's information technology requirements are also outsourced.
- *Information technology.* AirAsia uses Navitair's *Open Skies* computer reservations system (CRS), which links Web-based sales and inventory system which also links with AirAsia's call center. The CRS is integrated with AirAsia's yield management system (YMS) that prices seats on every flight according to demand. The CRS also allows passengers to print their own boarding passes. In 2006, AirAsia implemented a wireless delivery system which allows customers to book seats, check flight schedules and obtain real time updates on AirAsia's promotions via their mobile phones—an important facility in the Asia-Pacific region because of the high use of mobile phones. While the YMS maximizes revenue by providing trend analysis and optimizing pricing, the APS minimizes operational costs by using the information generated by the YMS to plan and schedule the needed facilities more efficiently. These two IT systems allow Air Asia to reduce costs in

logistics and inbound activities. During 2005, AirAsia adopted an ERP (enterprise resource planning) system to support its processes, facilitate month-end financial closing, and speed up reporting and data retrieval.[9] This was superseded by an advanced planning and scheduling system, which optimizes AirAsia's supply chain management and forecasts future resource requirements.

- *Human resource management.* Human resource management has been a priority for AirAsia since its relaunch under Tony Fernandes. A heavy emphasis is given to selecting applicants on the basis of their aptitudes, then creating an environment and a system with develops employees and retains them. Retention rates are exceptionally high for AirAsia which is important, first, as an indicator of motivation and job satisfaction, but also as a cost saving measure: because employees are multi-skilled, training costs per employee tend to be high for AirAsia. Job flexibility at all levels of the company, including administration, is a major source of productivity for AirAsia.

Air Asia: Cost Information

To offer a comparative view of AirAsia's operational efficiency and cost position, Table 9.1 provides operating and financial information on Malaysia's two leading airlines: Malaysian Airline System (MAS) and AirAsia. Although MAS's route network is very different from that of AirAsia's (MAS has a larger proportion of medium- and long-haul routes), it was subject to similar cost conditions as AirAsia.

For the first time since its relaunch in 2002, AirAsia made a loss in 2008. This was the result of Fernandes' decision to unwind AirAsia's futures contracts for jet fuel purchased. When crude oil prices started to tumble during the latter half of 2008, Fernandes believed that AirAsia would be better off taking a loss on its existing contracts in order to benefit from lower fuel prices.

Going Long-haul

Fernandes was aware that expanding from short-haul flights in South-East Asia into flights of more than four hours to China, Australia, Europe and the Middle East required major changes in operating practices and major new investments—primarily in bigger planes. The creation of AirAsia X was intended to facilitate a measure of operational independence for the long-haul flights while also spreading the risks of this venture among several investors. The investors in AirAsia X also contributed valuable expertise: Virgin Group had experience in establishing and operating four airlines (Virgin Atlantic, Virgin Express, Virgin Blue and Virgin USA), and the chairman of Air Ventures was Robert Milton, the former CEO of Air Canada.

Table 9.2 shows the principal differences in AirAsia and AirAsia X's operations and services.

TABLE 9.1 Comparing operational and financial performance between AirAsia and Malaysian Airline System

	AirAsia	MAS
Operating data		
Passengers carried (millions)	11.81	13.76
Available seat kilometers (millions)	18.72	53.38
Revenue passenger kilometers (millions)	13.49	36.18
Seat load factor (%)	75	67.8
Cost per available seat kilometers (sen)	11.66	22.80
Revenue per available seat kilometers (sen)	14.11	20.60
Number of aircraft in fleet December 31, 2008	78	109
Number of employees	3799	19 094
Aircraft utilization (hours per day)	11.8	11.1
Financial data (RM, millions)		
Revenue	2635	15 035
Other operating income	301.8	466.0
Total operating expense	2966	15 198.3
of which:		
—Staff costs	236.8	2179.9
—Depreciation	347.0	327.9
—Fuel costs	1389.8	6531.6
—Maintenance and overall.	345.1	1146.4
—Loss on unwinding derivatives	830.2	—
—Other operating expenses[a]	139.2	5020.0
Operating profit (loss)	(351.7)	305.5
Finance cost (net)	517.5	60.8
Pre-tax profit (loss)	(869.2)	264.7
After-tax profit	(496.6)	245.6
Total assets	9520.0	10 071.6
of which:		
—Aircraft, property, plant and equipment	6594.3	2464.8
—Inventories	20.7	379.7
—Cash	153.8	3,571.7
—Receivables	694.4	2020.1
Debt	6690.8	433.4
Shareholders' equity	1605.5	4197.0

[a] For AirAsia the main components are aircraft lease expenses and loss on foreign exchange. For MAS the main components were: hire of aircraft, sales commissions, landing fees, and rent of buildings.

Kuala Lumpur to London: Price and Cost Comparisons

A comparison of prices and costs allows a clearer picture of AirAsia's ability to compete in the long-haul market—where AirAsia must position itself against some of the world's major airlines. Between KL and London, AirAsia competes with at least six international airlines, among which the closest competitors are Malaysian Airlines, Emirates and British Airways.

TABLE 9.2 AirAsia and AirAsia X compared

	AirAsia	AirAsia X
Concept	Low cost short haul, no-frills	Low cost long haul, no frills
Flying range	Within four hours flying time from departing city	More than four hours flying time from departing city
Aircraft	Airbus A320 with 180 seats	Airbus A330 with more than 330 seats
Seat type	Single seat	Economy seat and Premium (previously known as XL) seat
Seat option	Free seating with Xpress Boarding option	Assigned seating with advance seat request option
In-flight dining	Wide range of light meals and snacks available for purchase onboard the	Pre-ordered full meals available including Asian, Western, vegetarian and kid's meal; light snacks also available for purchase onboard aircraft

TABLE 9.3 Fare comparisons: AirAsia and its competitors between Kuala Lumpur and London

	AirAsia X[a]	Cheapest other airline[b]	AirAsia price advantage	Cheapest other airlines
KL–London round trip	US$433.96[c]	US$683.68	36.5%	1. Gulf Air, 2. Qatar Air 3. Emirates
London-KL round trip	US$433.96[c]	US$530.35	18.2%	1. Emirates, 2. Etihad, 3. Gulf Air

[a] Average fare between September 1 and October 1, 2009.

[b] Average of lowest airline fare on each day between September 1 and October 1, 2009.

[c] Average outbound fare: U.S.$187.87; average inbound fare: U.S.$209.48; meals and baggage charges: U.S.$36.61.

A comparison of economy, round-trip airfares between the two cities is shown in Table 9.3. As Table 9.4 shows, these fare differentials reflect differences in cost between AirAsia and its long-haul competitors. These cost differences do not take account of differences in load factors, which can make a major effect on the average cost per passenger. AirAsia reports that its KL–London flights have a load factor in excess of 90%. For the airlines as a whole, Table 9.5 shows load factors.

The Outlook for Long-haul

There can be little doubt that AirAsia has been remarkably successful in building a budget airline in South-East Asia. Its cost efficiency, growth rate, brand awareness and awards for customer service, airline management and entrepreneurship all pointed to outstanding achievement, not simply in replicating the LCC business model pioneered by Southwest Airlines but adapting that model and augmenting it with innovation, dynamism and marketing flair that derived from Tony Fernandes' personality and leadership style.

TABLE 9.4 Flight operating cost comparison, Kuala Lumpur to London (in U.S.$)

	AirAsia	British Airways	Malaysia Airlines	Emirates	
Aircraft type [a]	Airbus 340-300	Boeing 747-400	Boeing 747-400	Boeing 777-300	
Route	KUL-STN	KUL-LHR	KUL-LHR	KUL-DXB-LHR	
Maximum passenger capacity	286	337	359	360	
				KUL-DXB	DXB-LHR
Flight fuel cost	79 299	159 522	159 522	77 525	80 822
Leasing costs	5952	0	0	0	0
En route navigation charges	7949	12 294	12 294	1435	6613
Terminal navigation arrival charges	419	645	645	0	645
Landing/parking	1100	2200	2200	2200	2200
Departure handling	6000	12 000	12 000	12 000	12 000
Arrival handling	6000	12 000	12 000	12 000	12 000
Segment totals				105 160	114 280
TOTAL cost per flight [b]	106 719	198 661	198 661	219 440	
Average cost per passenger [b]	373.14	589.50	553.37	609.56	

[a] KUL= Kuala Lumpur, STN = London Stansted, LHR = London Heathrow, DXB = Dubai.

[b] Excluding maintenance, depreciation, meal services and crew salaries.

Source: S. Buchholz, N. Fabio, A. Ileyassoff, L. Mang, and D. Visentin, *AirAsia—Tales from a Long-haul Low Cost Carrier* (Bocconi University, 2009). Data based on NewPacs Aviation Tool Software. Used by permission of the authors.

However, its AirAsia X venture presented a whole set of new challenges. AirAsia had successfully transferred several of its competitive advantages from AirAsia to AirAsia X. The low costs associated with fuel-efficient new planes, secondary airports and human resources practices had allowed AirAsia X to become the low cost operator on most of its routes. The AirAsia brand and reputation provided

TABLE 9.5 Difference between airlines in load factors (%)

	2004	2005	2006	2007	2008
AirAsia	77.0	75.0	78.0	80.0	75.5
Emirates	73.4	74.6	75.9	76.2	79.8
British Airways	67.6	69.7	70.0	70.4	71.2
Malaysia Airlines	69.0	71.5	69.8	71.4	67.8

Source: S. Buchholz, N. Fabio, A. Ileyassoff, L. Mang and D. Visentin, *AirAsia—Tales from a Long-haul Low Cost Carrier* (case report, Bocconi University, 2009). Used by permission of the authors.

AirAsia X with credibility and reputation on each new route it inaugurated. By sharing Web-based and telephone flight booking systems along with administrative and operational services between the two airlines, AirAsia X was able to secure cost efficiencies that would not be possible for an independent start-up.

Nevertheless, doubts remained over AirAsia X's ability to compete against established international airlines. Unlike AirAsia, which was attracting a whole new market for domestic and regional air travel, AirAsia X would have to take business away from the established international airlines whose business models offer some key competitive advantages over that of long-haul LCCs. In particular, its dense domestic and regional route networks offer feeds for their intercontinental flights. These complementarities are supported by through-ticketing, baggage transfer, and frequent flyer schemes. Its sources of profit are very different from the LCCs: most of their profit is earned from first class and business class travelers, which allows it to subsidize its economy class fares.

These challenges pointed towards the advantage of closer integration of AirAsia X with AirAsia. AirAsia X's CEO, Azran Osman-Rani, has argued for the operational and financial rationale of merging AirAsia X into AirAsia: "It would be difficult for AirAsia in the future if it did not have trunk routes as (this) is where the traffic volumes come from, so AirAsia needs growth from AirAsia X and the merger allows it to tap growth opportunities in the long-haul markets." Responding to allegations that the real rationale for the merger was to allow AirAsia to finance AirAsia X's losses, Azran said: "Rubbish, we can clearly dispute that. For the first quarter ended March 31, 2009 our net profit was RM 18 million and we are net cash flow positive. We even had a little cash at RM 3million. We are in a very good position and on a much firmer footing and now is an interesting time to talk about a merger."[10]

Notes

1 Operating profit before depreciation, amortization, and interest as a percentage of average total assets.

2 See www.tonyfernandesblog.com, accessed June 3, 2009.

3 Quoted by T. Lawton and J. Doh, *The Ascendance of AirAsia: Building a Successful Budget Airline in Asia* (Ivey School of Business, Case No. 9B08M054, 2008).

4 "AirAsia X to Hub in Abu Dhabi: AirAsia CEO," *Khaleej Times*, August 5, 2009.

5 "Company Profile," http://www.airasia.com/site/my/en/page.jsp;jsessionid=2FE125E6F301CBFA16C86B62ED064A20?name=Company%20Profile&id=75dbf230-ac1e2082-29962900-ae960618.

6 "AirAsia Berhad," *Offering Circular*, October 29, 2004, p. 3.

7 "Cheap, but Not Nasty," *The Economist*, March 19, 2009.

8 "AirAsia Berhad," *Offering Circular*, October 29, 2004, p. 5.

9 C. Cho, S. Hoffman Arian, C. Tjitrahardja and R. Narayanaswamy, *Air Asia—Strategic IT Initiative* (student report, Faculty of Economics and Commerce, University of Melbourne, 2005).

10 "AirAsia X CEO backs Merger with AirAsia Bhd," *The Star Online*, July 23, 2009, http://biz.thestar.com.my/news/story.asp?file=/2009/7/23/business/4369512&sec=business"

Case 10 Harley-Davidson, Inc., July 2008

You've shown us how to be the best. You've been leaders in new technology. You've stuck by the basic American values of hard work and fair play . . . Most of all, you've worked smarter, you've worked better, and you've worked together . . . as you've shown again, America is someplace special. We're on the road to unprecedented prosperity . . . and we'll get there on a Harley.

PRESIDENT RONALD REAGAN, HARLEY-DAVIDSON PLANT, YORK, PA, MAY 6, 1987

The recovery of this company since the 1980s has been truly remarkable. When you were down in the dumps, people were saying American industry was finished, that we couldn't compete in the global economy, that the next century would belong to other countries and other places. Today, you're not just surviving—you're flourishing, with record sales and earnings; and one of the best-managed companies in America.

PRESIDENT BILL CLINTON, HARLEY-DAVIDSON PLANT, YORK, PA, NOVEMBER 10, 1999

I've been impressed by Harley-Davidsons. It's one of America's finest products. And today I add to my impressions about the product the impressions of the workforce . . . I'm impressed by the esprit de corps, I'm impressed by the fact that these people really enjoy what they're doing, I'm impressed by the fact that they're impressed by the product they make.

PRESIDENT GEORGE W. BUSH, HARLEY-DAVIDSON PLANT, YORK, PA, AUGUST 16, 2006

On May 1, 2009, Keith Wandell took over as CEO of Harley-Davidson, Inc. He faced a dramatically different situation from that which had greeted his predecessors. The financial year 2008 had seen Harley's first decline in revenue since 1984 and a sharp decline in motorcycle shipments (see Figure 10.1). After decades of customer waiting lists and insufficient production capacity, Wandell now had to lay off employees and amalgamate plants in order to cut capacity.

The quarterly financial results released on July 16 showed a further deterioration in demand. During the first half of 2009, motorcycle shipments were down by 12.7% and revenue by 15.1% on the year ago period. The credit crunch was also affecting Harley's balance sheet. A large proportion of Harley's sales were financed by loans from its own financial services subsidiary. Unable to securitize its customer loans, Harley was forced to retain more of these loans on its own balance sheet. With rising default rates on consumer credit, Harley was perceived as much more risky than previously.

Wandell viewed these problems as cyclical. Already the credit markets and macroeconomic forecasts were pointing to the U.S. economy bottoming out and then recovering. Moreover, even with sharply reduced profits, Harley was still the world's most profitable motorcycle company in 2008 with a return on average equity of 29%. Wandell was more concerned with the longer term threats to Harley's business.

Harley's long-term profit growth depended on its ability to keep expanding the sales of its high-priced, heavyweight motorcycles. With the U.S. accounting for 69% of Harley's motorcycle revenues and with the U.S. government and U.S. households facing a painful rebuilding of their balance sheets over the next decade, it seemed likely that the demand for luxury leisure products costing between $8000 and $26 000 would continue to be subdued.

The opportunity for Harley to grow its market share at the expanse of rivals was limited by the fact that Harley already accounted for more than 50% of the U.S.

FIGURE 10.1 Annual shipments of motorcycles by Harley-Davidson

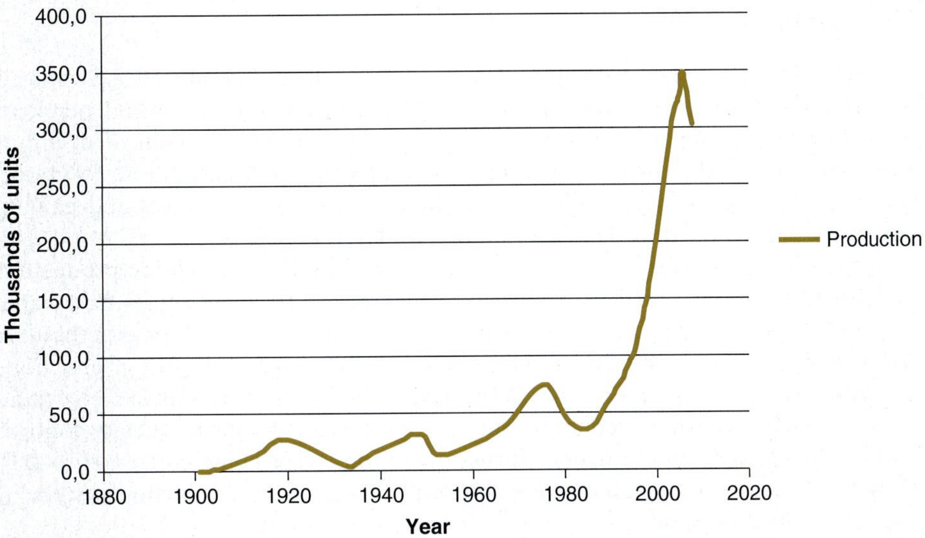

heavyweight motorcycle market. Indeed, Harley's own market might be vulnerable to competition. While no other company could replicate the emotional attachment of riders to the "Harley Experience," there was always the risk that motorcycle riders might seek a different type of experience and become more attracted to the highly engineered sports models produced by European and Japanese manufacturers. Such concerns were fueled by demographic trends. Harley's core market was the baby-boomer generation—and this cohort was moving more towards retirement homes than outdoor sports.

The History of Harley-Davidson

1903–81: From Birth to Maturity

Harley-Davidson, Inc. was founded in 1903 by William Harley and brothers William Davidson, Arthur Davidson, and Walter Davidson. Harley's 1903 model was made in the Davidson family shed and had a three-horsepower engine. In 1909 Harley introduced its first two-cylinder, V-twin engine, featuring the deep, rumbling sound for which Harley motorcycles are renowned. In 1953, the closure of the Indian Motorcycle factory in Springfield, MA, meant that Harley-Davidson was the sole survivor of the 150 U.S. motorcycle producers that had existed in 1910.

The postwar era saw new challenges for Harley-Davidson. Increasing affluence and the rise of youth culture created a growing demand for motorcycles. However, this was satisfied primarily by imports: first the British (by 1959, BSA, Triumph, and Norton took 49% of the U.S. market), then the Japanese. Initially Harley benefitted from the rebirth of motorcycling as a leisure activity, but soon it was facing direct competition: in 1969 Honda introduced its four-cylinder CB750, a huge technical advance on anything produced by Harley or the British. In the same year, Harley-Davidson was acquired by AMF. An expansion of production capacity to 75 000 units a year led to horrendous product quality problems followed by financial losses and a loss of leadership of the U.S. heavyweight motorcycle market.

1981–2008: Rebirth

In 1981, Harley's senior managers, led by Vaughn Beals, organized a leveraged buyout of AMF's Harley-Davidson subsidiary. Harley emerged as an independent, privately owned company, heavily laden with debt. The buyout coincided with a severe recession and soaring interest rates. Harley's sales fell and during 1981 and 1982 it lost a total of $60 million. Only by drastically cutting costs and gaining temporary protection from Japanese import did Harley survive.

At the same time, the management team devoted itself to rebuilding production methods and working practices. Managers visited several Japanese automobile plants and carefully studied Toyota's just-in-time (JIT) system. Less than four months after the buyout, Harley management began a pilot JIT inventory and production-scheduling program called "MAN" (Materials-As-Needed) in its Milwaukee engine plant. The objective was to reduce inventories and costs and improve quality control. Within a year, all Harley's manufacturing operations were being converted to JIT: components and subassemblies were "pulled" through the production system in response to final demand.

With revamped production methods and a new spirit of cooperation between workers and management, Harley increased sales and returned to profitability, allowing it to go public in 1986. With increase investment in new models, plants and its dealership network, Harley's share of the super-heavyweight market (over 850ccs) grew from about 30% in 1986 to over 60% in 1990. The 1990s saw uninterrupted growth in the heavyweight motorcycle market and a continued increase in Harley's market share. The company's biggest challenge was satisfying the surging demand for its products. To overcome this constraint, in 1996, the company announced its Plan 2003 to dramatically increase production capacity during the period preceding Harley's 100th anniversary in 2003. New production plants in Kansas City and York, Pennsylvania, the launching of several new models, and international expansion resulted in sales exceeding 300 000 in 2004 and approaching 342 000 in 2007—a tenfold increase on 1983.

The Heavyweight Motorcycle Market

The heavyweight segment (over 650 cc) was the most rapidly growing part of the world motorcycle market between 1990 and 2007, with the U.S. accounting for a major part of this growth. Sales of heavyweight motorcycles in the major markets of the world almost trebled between 1990 and 2007. North America was the largest market for big bikes, representing 56% of the sales in the major world markets.

In North America, Harley consolidated its market leadership, accounting for almost half of big bike sales. Overseas, however, Harley was unable to replicate this market dominance despite strong sales in a few markets—Harley achieved the remarkable feat of becoming heavyweight market leader in Japan, pushing Honda into second place. In Europe, on the other hand, Harley lagged behind its Japanese competitors and BMW (see Tables 10.1 and 10.2).

TABLE 10.1 Retail sales of heavyweight motorcycles (651+ cc), 2000–8 (in thousands of units)

	2000	2001	2002	2003	2004	2005	2006	2007	2008
North America (total)	365	423	475	495	531	554	579	555	477
Harley-Davidson[a]	163	186	220	238	256	265	282	267	235
Market share (%)	44.6	43.9	46.4	48.1	48.2	47.8	48.6	48.7	49.3
Europe (total)	293	321	332	323	336	351	377	372	384
Harley-Davidson	22	23	24	26	25	30	34	42	45
Market share (%)	7.4	7.1	7.1	8.1	7.3	8.5	9.1	11.3	11.7
Japan/Australia (total)[b]	63	64	64	59	n.a.	n.a.	n.a.	n.a.	n.a.
Harley-Davidson[a,b]	13	14	14	15	10	11	13	23	25
Market share (%)	20.5	21.9	21.2	25.8	n.a.	n.a.	n.a.	n.a.	n.a.

n.a. = not available.

[a] Excludes Buell.

[b] Years 2004–8 include Japan only.

Source: Harley-Davidson 10-K reports.

TABLE 10.2 Market shares in heavyweight motorcycles (651+ cc), 2005–2007 (%)

	North America			Europe		
	2005	2006	2007	2005	2006	2007
Harley-Davidson	47.8	48.6	48.7	8.9	9.1	9.6
Honda	16.6	15.1	14.3	13	14.6	12.3
Kawasaki	6.9	7.1	7.5	12.6	10.7	11.3
Suzuki	12.6	13.1	12.7	13.3	14.8	16.5
Yamaha	9.3	8.8	9.2	15.8	15.5	13.6
BMW	3.3	–	–	17.7	16.5	15.1
Ducati	–	–	–	5.2	5.2	5.9
Triumph	–	–	–	5	5.1	6.5
Other	4.5	7.3	8.3	8.5	8.5	9.2

Source: Harley-Davidson, Annual Reports, 2005, 2007.

The heavyweight motorcycle market comprised three segments:

- *Cruiser motorcycles.* These were "big, noisy, low riding, unapologetically macho cycles,"[1] typically with V-twin, large displacement engines and an upright riding position. Their design reflected the dominance of styling over either comfort or speed. For the urban males (and some females) in congested cities such as Los Angeles, New York, Paris and Tokyo, the cruiser motorcycle was practical transportation but it was primarily a statement of style. The cruiser segment was practically created by Harley and was preeminent in the U.S., representing over half of the heavyweight market. Most of Harley's competitors in this segment had imitated the main features of the traditional Harley design.
- *Touring motorcycles.* These included cruisers specially equipped for longer distance riding and bikes especially designed for comfort over long distances (including the Honda Goldwing and the bigger BMWs). These tourers featured luxuries such as audio systems, two-way intercoms and heaters. While Harley led this segment on the basis of style and image, Honda and BMW had engineered their motorcycles for greater smoothness and comfort over long distances through the use of multi-cylinder, shaft-drive engines, and advanced suspension systems.
- *Performance motorcycles.* These were based on racing bikes, with high-technology, high-revving engines, an emphasis on speed, acceleration and race-track styling; minimal concessions were provided to rider comfort. The segment was the most important in the European and the Asian/Pacific markets, representing 62% and 65% of total heavyweight bike sales, respectively. The segment was dominated by Japanese motorcycle companies, with a significant representation of European specialists such as Ducati and Triumph. Harley entered the performance segment in 1993 through its offshoot, Buell Motorcycles, which it fully acquired in 1998.

Unlike its Japanese competitors, Harley was highly market focused. With the exception of the single-cylinder Buell Blast, Harley's models were not only all heavyweight motorcycles (over 650 ccs engine displacement)—they were concentrated in the narrower super-heavyweight segment (over 850ccs).

Harley-Davidson in 2009

The Brand

Harley's top management team considered the Harley-Davidson image and the loyalty it engendered among its customers to be its greatest assets. Harley-Davidson was an archetype of American style. The famed spread eagle signified not just the brand of one of the world's oldest motorcycle companies, but an entire lifestyle with which it was associated. Harley has been described as "the ultimate biker status symbol . . . a quasi religion, an institution, a way of life."[2] Together with a few other companies—possibly Walt Disney and Levi Strauss—Harley had a unique relationship with American culture. The values that Harley represented—individuality, freedom, and adventure—could be traced back to the cowboy and frontiersman of yesteryear, and before that to the quest that brought people to America in the first place. As the sole surviving American motorcycle company from the pioneering days of the industry, Harley-Davidson represented a tradition of U.S. engineering and manufacturing.

This appeal of the Harley brand was central not just to the company's marketing, but also to its strategy as a whole. The central thrust of the strategy was reinforcing and extending the relationship between the company and its consumers. Harley-Davidson had long recognized that it was not selling motorcycles—it was selling the Harley Experience. Its annual reports made considerable efforts to convey this experience:

> A chill sweeps through your body, created by a spontaneous outburst of pure, unadulterated joy. You are surrounded by people from all walks of life and every corner of the globe. They are complete strangers, but you know them like your own family. They were drawn to this place by the same passion—the same dream. And they came here on the same machine. This is one place you can truly be yourself. Because you don't just fit in. You belong.[3]

If the appeal of the Harley motorcycle was the image it conveyed and the lifestyle it represented, then the company had to ensure that the experience matched the image. To increase Harley's involvement in its consumers' riding experience it formed the Harley Owners' Group (HOG) in 1983. Through HOG, the company became involved in organizing social and charity events. Employees, from the CEO down, were encouraged to take an active role in HOG activities. Each year, senior managers typically attended a total of more than 150 shows, rallies, and rides. The bond between the company and its customers is captured in Willie G. Davidson's phrase: "We ride with you." The HOG provided the organizational link for this sense of community: "the feeling of being out there on a Harley-Davidson motorcycle links us like no other experience can. It's made HOG like no other organization in the world . . . The atmosphere is more family reunion than organized meeting."[4] The loyalty of Harley owners was reflected in their repurchase and upgrading of Harley products. More than half of all sales were to customers who had owned a Harley previously, while about 20% were first-time motorcycle buyers.

Since the 1980s, the demographic and socioeconomic profile of Harley customers had shifted substantially: once blue-collar youngsters, Harley owners were middle-aged and middle class:

> The average U.S. retail purchaser of a new Harley-Davidson motorcycle is a married male in his mid to late forties (nearly two-thirds of U.S. retail purchasers of new Harley-Davidson motorcycles are between the ages of 35 and 54) with a median household income of approximately $87,000. Nearly three-quarters of the U.S. retail sales of new Harley-Davidson motorcycles are to buyers with at least one year of education beyond high school and 32% of the buyers have college/graduate degrees. Approximately 12% of U.S. retail motorcycle sales of new Harley-Davidson motorcycles are to female buyers.[5]

The Products

Broadening Harley's market appeal had major implications for product policy and design. Ever since its disastrous foray into small bikes during the AMF years, Harley had recognized that its competitive advantage lay with super-heavyweight bikes. Here it stuck resolutely to the classic styling that had characterized Harleys since its early years. At the heart of the Harley motorcycle was the air-cooled V-twin engine that had been Harley's distinctive feature since 1909. Harley's frames, handlebars, fuel tanks, and seats also reflected traditional designs.

Harley's commitment to traditional design features may be seen as making a virtue out of necessity. Its smaller corporate size and inability to share R&D across cars and bikes (unlike Honda and BMW) limited its ability to invest in technology and new products. As a result, Harley lagged far behind its competitors in the application of automotive technologies: its motorcycles not only looked old-style, much of the technology was old-style. When Harley introduced its new Twin Cam 88 engine in 1998, *Motorcycle* magazine reported:

> Honda comes out with an average of two new (or reworked) motors every year. The other Japanese manufacturers are good for about one. Count on Ducati and BMW to do something every few years. That leaves only Moto Guzzi and Harley . . . The Twin Cam 88 is Harley's first new engine since the Evolution Sportster motor of 1986, and their first new Big Twin motor since the original Evolution, released in 1984.[6]

Harley's engines were representative of the company's overall technological backwardness. Long after Honda had moved to multiple valves per cylinder, overhead camshafts, liquid cooling, and electronic ignition, Harley continued to rely on air-cooled push-rod engines. In suspension systems, braking systems and transmissions too, Harley lagged far behind Honda, Yamaha, and BMW.

Nevertheless, Harley was engaged in constant upgrading—principally incremental refinements to its engines, frames and gearboxes aimed at improving power delivery and reliability, increasing braking power, and reducing vibration. Harley also accessed automotive technology through alliances with other companies, including Porsche AG, Ford, and Gemini Racing Technologies.

Despite being a technological laggard, Harley was very active in new product development and the launching of new models. By 2009, Harley offered 31 Harley-Davidson models and 10 Buell models. Harley's product development efforts had been assisted by doubling the size of its Product Development Center in 2004 and the creation of a Prototyping Lab. Most of Harley's product development efforts were limited to style changes, new paint designs and engineering improvements. However, between 2000 and 2008, Harley had accelerated technological progress and had introduced more radical new product developments. Its V-Rod model introduced in October 2001 featured innovative styling and an all-new liquid-cooled engine. The Buell range also allowed greater scope for Harley's engineers. The 2002 Buell Firebolt featured a new engine, an all-aluminum frame, and the "naked" styling pioneered by Ducati, while the 2006 Ulysses was Harley-Davidson's first ever "adventure sportbike." In 2006, Harley introduced another new engine, the Twin Cam 96, which featured electronic ignition and was teamed with a new six-speed gearbox.

It is notable that between October 2001 and June 2009, Harley made just 90 patent applications to the U.S. Patent Office. Most of these related to peripheral items: a saddlebag mounting system, footpegs, real light assemblies, an adjustable backrest, an LED fuel gauge. By contrast, over the same period, Suzuki made 247 patent applications, Kawasaki 502, Yamaha 2057, and Honda 3971.

Central to Harley's product strategy was the idea that every Harley rider would own a unique, personalized motorcycle as a result of the company offering a wide range of customization opportunities. New bikes allowed multiple options for seats, bars, pegs, controls, and paint jobs, with the potential for augmentation through a range of 7000 accessories and special services such as "Chrome Consulting."

Reconciling product differentiation with scale economies was a continuing challenge for Harley. The solution was to offer a wide range of customization options while standardizing on key components. For example, among the different Harley-Davidson models there were three engine types (Evolution XL, Twin Cam 88, and Revolution), four basic frames, four styles of gas tank and so on.

The Harley product line also covered a wide price range. The Sportster model was positioned as an entry-level bike beginning at $6999, less than one-third of the price of the Ultra Classic Electra Glide, with "custom coloring" at $22 159. Top of the price range was the three-wheeler Tri-Glide at $31 994 (including non-black paint and a reverse gear).

Buell

Buell offered the opportunity for Harley to broaden its appeal to younger riders and those more interested in speed and maneuverability. Founded by ex-Harley engineer Erik Buell, Buell Motor Company developed bikes that used Harley engines and other components but mounted them on a lighter, stiffer frame. Harley acquired complete ownership of Buell in 1998. The lighter weight and superior handling of Buell models were also seen as appealing to the European customers who put greater emphasis on sporty performance. In the U.S., the age of the typical Buell customer was seven years younger than that of Harley buyers and the price was about $10 000

TABLE 10.3 Harley-Davidson shipments 1997–2006 thousands of units

	1998	1999	2000	2001	2002	2003	2004	2005	2006	2007	2008
H-D motorcycle shipments											
—United States	110.9	135.6	158.9	186.9	212.8	237.7	260.6	266.5	273.2	241.5	206.3
—Export	39.9	41.6	45.8	47.5	50.8	53.5	56.7	62.5	76	89.1	97.2
Motorcycle product mix (%)											
—Sportster	22.5	23.6	22.6	21.7	19.4	19.7	22	21.3	18.5	21.8	20.0
—Custom (a)	51.3	49.6	49.3	50.5	53.7	52	48.6	45.2	46.2	43.7	46.4
—Touring	26.2	26.8	28.1	28	26.8	28.4	29.4	33.5	35.4	34.5	33.6
Buell motorcycle shipments	5.5	6.8	6.9	9.9	10.9	10	9.9	11.2	12.5	11.5	13.1
Company total	156.3	184	211.6	244.3	274.5	301.2	327.2	340.2	361.6	330.6	303.5

compared with an average Harley price of $17 500. The Buell Riders Adventure Group (BRAG) was founded to build the same type of community of riders that HOG had done so successfully. The Buell Blast, with its 490 cc single cylinder engine and a price tag of $4595 was a major departure for Harley: it was Harley's first entry into the middleweight motorcycle market since the 1970s. Yet, despite heavy investments in developing and launching new models, there was little overall growth in Buell's unit sales between 2001 and 2006 (see Table 10.3).

Distribution

Upgrading Harley's distribution network was central to its transformation strategy of the 1980s and 1990s. At the time of the buyout, many of Harley's 620 U.S. dealerships were operated by enthusiasts, with erratic opening hours, a poor stock of bikes and spares and indifferent customer service. If Harley was in the business of selling a lifestyle and an experience, then dealers played a pivotal role in delivering that experience. Moreover, if Harley's target market had shifted towards mature, upper income individuals—Harley needed to provide a retail experience commensurate with the expectations of this group.

Harley's dealer development program increased support for dealers while imposing higher standards of pre- and after-sales service, and requiring better dealer facilities. The dealers were obliged to carry a full line of Harley replacement parts and accessories, and to perform service on Harley bikes. Training programs helped dealers to meet the higher service requirements, and encouraged them to recognize and meet the needs of the professional, middle-class clientele that Harley was now courting. Harley pioneered the introduction of new services to customers. These included test ride facilities, rider instruction classes, motorcycle rental, assistance for owners in customizing their bikes through dealer-based design centers and chrome consultants, and insurance services. Close to 85% of Harley dealerships in the U.S. were exclusive—far more than for any other motorcycle manufacturer.

Given the central role of dealers in the relationship between Harley-Davidson and its customers, dealer relations continued to be a strategic priority for Harley. Its retail environments group liaised closely with dealers with a goal of bringing the same retail experience to customers everywhere in the world. Harley-Davidson University was established to "enhance dealer competencies in every area, from customer satisfaction to inventory management, service proficiency, and front-line sales." Dealer relationships were critical to Harley's goal of growing sales of financial services, parts and accessories and general merchandise. Harley believed that the quality and effectiveness of its dealer network was a key determinant of the strong demand for its products.

Other Products

Sales of parts, accessories, and "general merchandise" (clothing and collectibles) represented 20% of total revenue in 2008—much higher than for any other motorcycle company (see Table 10.4). Clothing sales included not just traditional riding apparel, but a wide range of men's, women's and children's leisure apparel.

Only a small proportion of the clothing, collectibles and other products bearing the Harley-Davidson trademark were sold through the Harley dealership network. Most of the "general merchandising" business represented licensing of the Harley-Davidson name and trademarks to third-party manufacturers of clothing, giftware, jewelry, toys and other products. L'Oréal offered a line of Harley-Davidson cologne. To expand sales of licensed products, Harley opened a number of "secondary retail locations," which sold clothing, accessories and giftware but not motorcycles. Harley-Davidson Financial Services was established to supply credit, insurance, and extended warranties to Harley dealers and customers. Between 2000 and 2007 it was Harley's most rapidly growing source of profit, contributing almost 12% of operating profit in 2007. However, the credit crunch hit the business hard. Unable to securitize its customer loans, Harley was forced to retain these loans on its own books, causing a large increase in its current assets. Some analysts believed that this build up of consumer loans had made Harley more reluctant to extend 100% loans to purchasers which was depressing sales volume.

International Expansion

A key part of Harley-Davidson's growth strategy was expanding sales outside of the U.S. A critical issue was the extent to which Harley needed to adapt its products, image, and customer approach to conditions in overseas markets. Harley's image was rooted in American culture—to what extent was Harley's appeal to European and Asian customers rooted in its status as an American icon? "The U.S. and Harley

TABLE 10.4 Harley-Davidson's non-motorcycle sales, 2000-8 ($, millions)

	2000	2001	2002	2003	2004	2005	2006	2007	2008
Parts and accessories	447.9	509.6	629.2	712.8	781.6	815.7	862.3	868.3	858.7
General merchandise	151.4	163.9	231.5	211.4	223.7	247.9	277.5	305.4	313.8
Financial services	140.1	181.5	211.5	279.5	305.3	331.6	384.9	416.2	377.0

are tied together," observed Hugo Wilson of Britain's *Bike* magazine, "the guy who's into Harleys here is also the guy who owns cowboy boots. You get a Harley and you're buying into the U.S. mystique."[7] At the same time, the composition of demand and the customer profiles were different in overseas markets.

Europe was the focal point of Harley's overseas ambitions, simply because it was the second largest heavyweight motorcycle market in the world. Europe was also a huge challenge for Harley. Unlike in the U.S., Harley had never had a major position in Europe—it needed to fight to take market share from the established leaders in the heavy bike segment: BMW, Honda, Kawasaki, and Yamaha. The European motorcycle market differed significantly from the American market in that 70% of the heavyweight motorcycle market was for performance bikes, while touring and cruiser bikes accounted for just 30%. European buyers were knowledgeable and style conscious but their style preferences were different from those of U.S. riders. European roads and riding styles were also different from the U.S. As a result, Harley modified some of its models for the European market. The U.S. Sportster, for example, had a straight handlebar instead of curled buckhorns and a new suspension system to improve cornering. The name was also changed to the "Custom 53." The Harley Softail also received a new look, becoming the "Night Train." As in the U.S., HOG played a critical role in building brand image and customer loyalty. Harley's centenary celebration in Barcelona on June 2003 attracted some 150 000 people—a large proportion were Harley owners from all over Europe.

Central to Harley's international strategy was building its dealer network. Between 2000 and 2008, Harley expanded its overseas dealership network and built a new European headquarters in Oxford, England. In 2008, Harley had 686 dealers in the U.S., 71 in Canada, 383 in Europe (including the Middle East and Africa), 201 in Asia/Pacific and 32 in Latin America.

Between 2006 and 2008, Harley achieved greater success in penetrating international markets. Non-U.S. sales of motorcycles and related products were $1.75 billion in 2008, representing 31% of net revenue of the motorcycles segment—up from 20% in 2006.

In July 2008, Harley extended its European presence when it announced the acquisition of the Italian motorcycle manufacturer, MV Agusta, for $105 million. According to the Harley press release:

> MV Agusta Group has two families of motorcycles: a line of exclusive, premium, high-performance sport motorcycles sold under the MV Agusta brand; and a line of lightweight motorcycles sold under the Cagiva brand. MV Agusta's F4-R motorcycle, powered by a 1078 cc in-line four-cylinder liquid cooled engine, is rated at 190 hp. The company sells its products through about 500 dealers worldwide, the vast majority of them in Europe. In 2007, MVAG shipped 5,819 motorcycles. During 2008 MVAG has significantly slowed production due to financial difficulties.
>
> "Motorcycles are the heart, soul and passion of Harley-Davidson, Buell and MV Agusta," said Harley-Davidson, Inc. Chief Executive Officer Jim Ziemer. "Both have great products and close connections with incredibly devoted customers. The MV Agusta and Cagiva brands are well-known and highly regarded in Europe. They are synonymous with beautiful, premium, Italian performance motorcycles," Ziemer said.[8]

Operations

As already noted, Harley-Davidson development during the 1980s and 1990s focused heavily on upgrading its manufacturing operations. Investment in plant and equipment included the introduction of advanced process technologies and capacity expansion. Particular emphasis was placed on developing manufacturing capabilities through total quality management, just-in-time scheduling, CAD/CAM, and the devolution of responsibility and decision making to the shop floor. Table 10.5 shows Harley's main manufacturing and development facilities.

Despite constant development of its manufacturing facilities and operational capabilities, Harley's low production volumes relative to Honda and the other Japanese manufacturers imposed significant cost disadvantages. A key cost disadvantage was in the purchasing components. Bought-in, customized components accounted for a large proportion of manufacturing costs and Harley lacked the buying power of Honda or BMW. To compensate for lack of bargaining clout, Harley fostered close relations with its key suppliers and placed purchasing managers at senior levels within its management structure. Its supplier advisory council (SAC) promoted collaboration and best practice sharing within the Harley network.[9] Harley's director of purchasing, Garry Berryman, commented: "Through the SAC, we're able to take some of the entrepreneurial aspects of our smaller, privately held suppliers and inject that enthusiasm, spirit, and energy into those that may be larger, publicly held companies. In this way, the SAC serves not only to improve purchasing efficiency, but also provides a forum to share information, ideas, and strategy."[10]

Harley's capacity for efficiency was also limited by its dispersed manufacturing operations: engine manufacture in Milwaukee, Wisconsin; assembly in York, Pennsylvania and Kansas City, Missouri. To cut costs, Harley initiated a program of plant consolidation. The two Milwaukee-area powertrain plants would be combined

TABLE 10.5 Harley-Davidson's main facilities, 2008

Location	Function	Square Feet
Menomonee Falls, WI	Motorcycle powertrain production	881 600
Milwaukee, WI	Corporate Office	515 000
Wauwatosa, WI	Motorcycle powertrain production	430 000
Wauwatosa, WI	Product Development Center	409 000
Franklin, WI	Distribution Center	255 000
Tomahawk, WI	Fiberglass/plastic parts production and painting	211 000
East Troy, WI	Buell motorcycle assembly	40 000
Kansas City, MI	Motorcycle parts fabrication, painting and Dyna, Sportster	450 000
York, PA	Motorcycle parts fabrication, painting, assembling Softail and touring models	1 321 000
Manaus, Brazil	Assembly of models for Brazilian market	82 000
Varese, Italy	MV Agusta and Cagiva motorcycle assembly	1 378 600
Morazzone, Italy	MV Agusta and Cagiva warehouse	446 500
Adelaide, Australia	Motorcycle wheel production	485 000

Source: Harley-Davidson 10-K Report, 2008.

into a single facility and the separate paint and frame operations at York, Pennsylvania, would be merged into a single plant. The measures announced between January and July 2009 would eliminate about 2400 jobs and reduce costs by about $250 million annually.

People and Management

Central to Harley-Davidson's renaissance was the creation of a new relationship between management and employees. Following the management buyout in 1981, Harley's new management team systematically rethought management-employee relationships, employee responsibilities and organizational structure. The result was a transformation in employee commitment and job satisfaction. Harley's employee relations focused on involvement, self-management, open communication and the provision of generous health and leave benefits. Harley's Kansas City assembly plant, opened in 1998, featured a management structure and working methods designed to promote employee commitment and involvement. The plant manager and other administrators worked in a "bullpen area" on the production floor rather than in separate offices. The entire plant was organized into teams. Production was by eight- to 15-member *natural work groups.* Representatives from these formed four *process operating groups* for fabrication, engine production, assembly and painting. Overall plant management was by a 14-member *plant leadership group* comprising the plant manager, union representatives, elected representatives from the process groups, and six staff members.[11]

Harley's belief in the effectiveness of non-hierarchical, team-based structures in fostering motivation and accelerating innovation and learning was evident throughout the company—including the corporate headquarters. "In our new organization," explained Clyde Fessler, VP for Business Development, "the Harley-Davidson Motor Company has been divided into three broad, functional areas called Circles. They are: the Create Demand Circle (CDC), the Produce Product Circle (PPC), and the Provide Support Circle (PSC). Each Circle is composed of the leaders representing the functions within it."[12] Each Circle operated as a team with leadership moving from person to person, depending on the issue being addressed. Overall coordination was provided by the Strategic Leadership Council (SLC), comprising individuals nominated by each of the three Circles.

Competition

Despite Harley's insistence that it was supplying a unique Harley experience rather than competing with other motorcycle manufacturers, the more it took market share from other manufacturers and expanded its product range and geographical scope, the more it came into direct competition with other producers. The clearest indication of direct competition was imitation: Honda, Suzuki, Yamaha and Kawasaki had long been offering V-twin cruisers styled closely along the lines of the classic Harleys, but at lower prices and with more advanced technologies. In competing against Harley, the Japanese manufacturers' key advantage was the scale advantages deriving from vastly greater volume. However, despite their large price premium, Harley-Davidson motorcycles benefitted from a much smaller rate of depreciation than other brands.

FIGURE 10.2 Cruiser motorcycles, 2009 models

Harley lacked the diversification of its rivals. Honda, BMW, and Suzuki were important producers of automobiles and more than one-third of Yamaha's turnover came from boats and snowmobiles. These companies could benefit from sharing technology, engineering capabilities and marketing and distribution know-how across their different vehicle divisions. In addition, sheer size conferred greater bargaining power with suppliers.

Imitators also included several domestic companies producing retro-styled cruiser bikes. In recent years Excelsior, Polaris (Victory) and a resuscitated Indian had all entered the U.S. super-heavyweight market, mostly selling at prices exceeding those of Harley (the Indian Vintage Chief cost $35 499).

Figure 10.2 shows competitive product offerings while Table 10.6 shows price comparisons. Appendix 2 gives profiles of several leading competitors.

Meeting the Challenges of Tomorrow

In his July 16, 2009 conference call with analysts, CEO Keith Wandell focused upon the short-term problems that Harley was facing in terms of depressed demand and Harley's responses in terms of cost reduction and production cutbacks. Wandell was confident that Harley would emerge from the 2008–9 recession in strong shape. He

TABLE 10.6 Price comparison of V-twin, cruiser motorcycles, 2009

Manufacturer and model	Engine	Recommended retail price ($)
Harley-Davidson		
Sportster 883 Low	V-twin, air-cooled, 883 cc	6999
Fat Boy	V-twin, air-cooled, 1540 cc	15 999
VRSC V-Rod Muscle	V-twin, liquid-cooled, 1131 cc	17 199
Heritage Softail Classic	V-twin, air-cooled, 1450 cc	17 999
Honda		
Shadow Spirit 750	V-twin, liquid-cooled, OHC, 745 cc	7699
VTX1300C	V-twin, liquid-cooled, OHC, 1312 cc	10 299
VTX1800N	V-twin, liquid-cooled, OHC, 1800 cc	13 699
Suzuki		
Boulevard S50	V-twin, liquid-cooled, OHC, 805 cc	7199
Boulevard C90	V-twin, air-cooled, OHC, 1475 cc	11 299
Boulevard M109R	V-twin, liquid-cooled, 1783 cc	13 799
Kawasaki		
Vulcan 900 Classic	V-twin, 8-valve, OHC	7499
Vulcan 1600 Mean Streak	V-twin, air-cooled, 1552 cc	11 099
Yamaha		
V-Star Custom	V-twin, OHC, air-cooled, push-rod, 649 cc	6290
Road Star	V-twin, OHC, air-cooled, push-rod, 1670 cc	12 390
Polaris		
Victory Kingpin	V-twin, 4-valve per cylinder, 1634 cc	16 399

Source: Web sites of different motorcycle manufacturers.

was particularly encouraged by the fact that Harley's 2009 sales were showing greater resilience that those of its main competitors—as a result Harley's share of the U.S. heavyweight market had jumped from 50% to 58%.

The longer term threats were more troubling. A *New York Times* article headed "Harley, You're Not Getting Any Younger," had painted a gloomy picture of Harley's future market position:

> After riding high for two decades, the company that makes the hulky bikes that devoted riders affectionately call Hogs is sputtering. Harley's core customers are graying baby boomers, whose savings, in many cases, have gone up in smoke in the market downturn. Few are in the mood to shell out up to $20 000 or more for something that is basically a big toy, and the company, in turn, has not captured much of the younger market . . .
>
> Its core customers have grayed, and they are buying new bikes less often. The average age of a Harley rider is 49, up from 42 five years ago. But company executives don't seem outwardly worried by the lackluster growth among those 35 and younger, even as it takes steps to turn them into Harley owners.
>
> They say they're confident that the baby-boom generation has 15 more years of riding life. "They're not about to stop riding because they're getting older," Mr. Richer says. "It would be dumb to walk away from our core customer, the most lucrative customer."

As Harley keeps most of its focus on its aging consumers, rivals like BMW, Honda and Yamaha are attracting younger customers who seem less interested in cruising on what their old man rides. United States sales of light sport bikes, intended for the younger crowd, have increased more than 50% in the last five years, and the Japanese makers have popular cruisers of their own. Harley has roughly 30% of the overall United States motorcycle market, but it accounts for half of the heavyweight bikes sold in America . . .

"Harley understands the baby-boomer consumer incredibly well, in a holistic sense," says Gregory Carpenter, a marketing professor at the Kellogg School of Management at Northwestern. "But to grow and thrive, they must create a deep emotional connection with younger consumers."

A decade ago, Harley executives made a decision that now appears to be a major contributor to its current problems. Determined to appease consumers who were stuck on two-year waiting lists, the company ramped up production. Last year, Harley built more than 303,000 bikes, up from 159,000 in 2000 . . .

Now, with so many Hogs in the marketplace, Harley has an issue involving its brand.

"Traditionally, Harley-Davidson had a very loyal consumer," says Anthony Gikas, senior research analyst at Piper Jaffray. "But those riders lost interest in the brand because everyone has a Harley bike. It's not a club anymore."[13]

Reflecting on these challenges, one Milwaukee blogger asked:

So what does Harley do?

One tack would be to stay focused on what it does best: big bikes. While that strategy may make sense on some fronts (focus on what you know, stay loyal to the brand identity, etc.), that approach will mean greatly reduced growth prospects and could doom it if the current consumer spending environment holds out long term. And meanwhile its core audience just gets older.

Or it could do what people have been saying what it should do for years (and what Harley itself has suggested, intermittently, it may do): Make smaller, more affordable bikes. That's easier than it sounds, as it would force Harley to compete against the Japanese manufacturers on their own turf. But if the market is moving away from Harley, does it have a choice?[14]

Appendix 1 Selected Items from Harley-Davidson Financial Statements, 2000–8 ($, millions)

	2000	2001	2002	2003	2004	2005	2006	2007	2008
Income statement									
Net sales	2906	3407	4091	4624	5015	5342	5801	5727	5594
Gross profit	991	1153	1418	1666	1900	2040	2233	2114	1931
R&D	76	130	140	150	171	179	177.7	186	164
Selling, administrative and engineering expense	513	552	639	684	727	762	846	901	985

(Continued)

	2000	2001	2002	2003	2004	2005	2006	2007	2008
Operating income	515	663	883	1149	1361	1470	1603	1426	1029
Of which:									
Financial services	37	61	104	168	189	192	211	212	83
Interest income	18	17	17	23	23	23	27	22	9
Other income/(expense)	16	−7	−13	−6	−5	−5	−5		5
Income before taxes	549	673	886	1166	1379	1488	1624	1448	1034
Provision for income taxes	201	236	306	405	490	528	581	514	379
Net income	348	438	580	761	890	960	1043	934	655
Balance sheet									
Assets									
Cash	419	439	281	329	275	141	238	403	594
Finance receivables held for investment[a]	581	921	1139	1391	1656	1943	2101	1575	1378
Accounts receivable, net	98	119	109	112	121	122	143	181	296
Inventories	192	181	218	208	227	221	288	350	401
Total current assets	1297	1665	2067	2729	3683	3145	3551	3467	5378
Property, plant and equipment, net	754	892	1033	1046	1025	1012	1024	1061	1094
Total assets	2436	3118	3861	4923	5483	5255	5532	5657	7829
Liabilities									
Current portion of long-term debt	89	217	383	324	495	205	832	398	0
Accounts payable	170	195	227	224	244	271	763	300	324
Total current liabilities	498	716	990	956	1173	873	1596	1905	2604
Non-current liabilities									
Long-term debt	355	380	380	670	800	1000	870	980	2176
Other long-term liabilities	97	158	123	86	91	82	109	152	175
Postretirement healthcare benefits	81	90	105	127	150	61	201	193	274
Stockholders' equity	1406	1756	2233	2958	3218	3084	2757	3352	3357
Total liabilities and equity	2436	3118	3861	4923	5483	5255	5532	6796	6786
Cash flows									
Operating activities	565	757	546	597	832	961	762	798	−685
Capital expenditures	−204	−290	−324	−227	−214	−198	−220	−242	−232
Total investing activities	−171	−772	−720	−540	−570	177	−35	391	−393
Financing activities	−158	34	80	81	−316	−1272	−637	−1038	1293
Net increase in cash	236	20	−95	137	−54	−134	97	164	191

[a] In addition Harley-Davidson holds financial receivables (mainly loans to customers) for sale. These amounted to \$2444 million in 2008, up from \$781 million in 2007.

Source: Harley-Davidson 10-K reports (www.harleydavidson.com).

Appendix 2 Comparative Financial Data for Honda, Yamaha, BMW and Harley-Davidson ($, millions, unless otherwise indicated)

	Honda Motor			Yamaha Motor			BMW			Harley-Davidson		
	2006	2007	2008	2006	2007	2008	2006	2007	2008	2006	2007	2008
Revenue	84218	94241	121229	5181	5339	5323	64644	82453	n.a.	5801	5727	5594
Gross profit margin	29.20%	29.10%	28.80%	36.00%	36.00%	37.40%	23.10%	21.80%	n.a.	39.50%	37.90%	33.70%
SGA expense	15015	16988	20080	1631	1652	1671	10215	11737	n.a.	846	901	985
Operating income	7386	7241	9626	234	269	319	5343	6200	n.a.	1603	1426	1029
Net income after tax	4228	4327	5135	273	270	384	3792	4613	n.a.	1043	934	655
Net margin	6.00%	5.30%	5.00%	5.30%	5.10%	7.20%	5.60%	5.90%	n.a.	16.90%	15.20%	11.00%
Op. income/total assets	8.22%	7.08%	7.56%	4.64%	4.95%	6.08%	5.12%	4.73%	n.a.	28.98%	25.20%	13.14%
Total assets	89859	102310	127417	5044	5423	5241	104300	130995	n.a.	5532	5657	7829
Cost of goods sold	59588	66854	86286	n.a	n.a	n.a	49685	64516	n.a.	3742	3817	3958
Inventory turnover	6.76%	6.65%	7.12%	6.80%	6.90%	6.90%	5.54%	5.96%		12.99%	10.91%	9.87%
Inventories	8809	10057	12113	756	798	740	8963	10817	n.a.	288.0	349.7	400.9
Total equity	35069	38102	45897	3109	3410	3327	25238	32005	n.a.	2757	3352	3357
Return on equity	12.06%	11.36%	11.19%	8.78%	7.93%	11.53%	15.02%	14.41%		37.83%	27.86%	19.50%
Operating cash flow	4901	7689	11382	247	385	361	13167	17360	n.a.	762	798	–685
Cash flow from investing activities	–5718	–9611	–17033	–176	–218	407	–18035	–25387	n.a.	–35	391	–393
R&D expenditure	4354	5352	5703	233	235	241	4160	4363	n.a.	178	186	164
Advertising expenditure	3062	2992	2793	250	256	282	5941	6302	n.a.	70	77	89
Motorcycles shipped (thousands of units)	10271	10369	9320	n.a.	n.a.	n.a.	100	102	n.a.	362	331	303
Employees (thousands)	145	167	179	27	26	25	104	104	n.a.	9	9	9

Source: Company financial reports.

Notes

1 G. Strauss, "Born to be Bikers," *USA Today,* November 5, 1997.
2 M. Ballon, "Born to be Wild," *Inc,* November, 1997, p. 42.
3 Harley-Davidson, Inc. *Annual Report,* 2000.
4 See www.harley-davidson.com/experience/family/hog.
5 Harley-Davidson, Inc. 10-K Report for 2008, p. 8.
6 *Motorcycle,* February, 1998.
7 Quoted in: "Motorcycle Maker Caters to the Continent," *USA Today,* April 22, 1998.
8 "Harley-Davidson to Acquire MV Agusta Group Expanding Presence in Europe," press release, Harley-Davidson, Inc., July 11, 2008.
9 K. R. Fitzgerald, "Harley's Supplier Council Helps Deliver Full Value," *Purchasing,* September 5, 1996.
10 A. Millen Porter, "One Focus, One Supply Base," *Purchasing,* June 5, 1997.
11 S. Roth, "Harley's Goal: Unify Union and Management," *Kansas City Business Journal,* May 16, 1997.
12 C. Fessler, "Rotating Leadership at Harley-Davidson: from Hierarchy to Interdependence," *Strategy and Leadership,* July 17, 1997.
13 "Harley, You're Not Getting Any Younger," *New York Times,* March 21, 2009.
14 See http://brewcitybrawler.typepad.com/brew_city_brawler/2009/01/screw-it-lets-ride-is-not-a-strategy.html, accessed July 25, 2009.

Case 11 Raisio Group and the Benecol Launch*

Case A: The Situation in January 1997

During 1996, Raisio Group, a 57-year-old grain-milling company based in Raisio in the south-west of Finland, emerged from obscurity to become the second most valuable public company in Finland (after Nokia) and the focus of worldwide attention. The launch of Benecol, its cholesterol-lowering margarine, at the end of 1995 had attracted the interest of food processors and supermarket groups

---

*This case draws upon an earlier case by Michael H. Moffett and Stacey Wolff Howard, *Benecol: Raisio's Global Nutriceutical* (Thunderbird, The American Graduate School of International Management. Case No. A06-99-0004, 1999). I am grateful to Ayan Bhattacharya for assistance in preparing this case. Copyright © 2008 Robert M. Grant.

throughout the world and fueled a surge of investor interest. Demand for the product had outstripped Raisio's capability to produce the active ingredient in Benecol, stanol ester. On the Helsinki stock market, foreign demand pushed Raisio's share price from FIM61 at the beginning of the year to FIM288 at the end (after touching FIM322 during the summer).[1] CEO Matti Salminen commented:

> 1996 will go down in the Raisio Group's history as the "Benecol year"—such was the role of this new cholesterol-reducing margarine in increasing the Group's visibility and raising its profile in all our sectors of operations. Although we have not been able to meet even the domestic demand for Benecol margarine so far, the product is already known worldwide and great expectations are attached to it. The Benecol phenomenon quintupled the value of our shares, increasing the Group's capitalization by billions of Finnish marks.[2]

It was the international prospects for Benecol margarine (and potentially other food products incorporating stanol ester) that had drawn a bevy of stock analysts and portfolio managers to Raisio's headquarters. Not only was the potential market for Benecol considered huge—the U.S. alone was seen as having a multi-billion market potential—but the profit opportunities also appeared excellent. In Finland, Benecol was selling at about six times the price of regular margarine. In addition to being first to market, Raisio had the ability to sustain its market leadership through its patents relating to the production and use of the active ingredient, stanol ester, and recognition of its Benecol brand name.

However, within Raisio a vigorous debate had broken out as to the best strategy for exploiting the vast commercial potential that Raisio's innovation offered. This debate focused around two issues. The first was whether Raisio's emphasis should be on supplying its Benecol margarine or its active ingredient, stanol ester. Despite the phenomenal success of Benecol margarine in Finland, margarine was only one of a number of potential food and drink products to which stanol ester could be added. Several Raisio managers argued that the company could exploit its innovation more widely if it supplied stanol ester to a number of food and drink companies. A second issue concerned the means by which Raisio would exploit the international potential of its innovation. Although Raisio was a significant margarine manufacturer in Finland, it possessed few facilities and limited experience outside its home market. A number of multinational food companies and leading food retailers had approached Raisio expressing interest in licensing agreements, joint ventures and supply agreements—for Benecol margarine, for stanol ester, or for both. Should Raisio license its intellectual property to other firms, create joint-ventures with foreign companies, or should it keep its technology in-house and use it to build a multinational presence for Raisio?

History

The Raisio Group began life in 1939 as Vehnä Oy, a grain-milling company located in the town of Raisio. In 1950, a vegetable oil factory called Oy Kasviöljy-Växtolje Ab was founded next to the milling plant. The two companies cooperated in introducing rapeseed cultivation to Finland. They eventually merged in 1987 to form Raisio Tehtaat Oy Ab.[3] From cereals and vegetable oil, the company expanded into animal feeds, malt production, potato starch and margarine. In the 1960s, production of starch provided the basis for the supply of a number of chemical products, mainly to the paper industry.

During this period Raisio developed a substantial export business. This began with malt exports to Sweden, followed by exports of margarine, pasta and other food products to the Soviet Union and subsequently to Poland. In the St. Petersburg area of Russia and in Estonia, Raisio's Melia-branded products were market leaders in flour, pasta and muesli. Finland's accession to the European Union in 1995 allowed Raisio to expand its sales in other European countries. By 1996, 39% of Raisio's sales were outside of Finland. Raisio's increased international presence included margarine plants in Sweden and Poland and joint-venture plants supplying starch and other products for the paper industry in Sweden, the U.S., France, Germany and Indonesia.

From its earliest days, Raisio had shown considerable entrepreneurial initiative and technical ingenuity. Its first oil-milling plant was constructed by its own employees using spare parts, scrap metal, and innovative improvisation. Raisio's first margarine plant was built partly to stimulate demand for its own rapeseed oil, which was not widely used in margarine production at that time. Raisio also maintained an active program of R&D. Benecol was the result of Raisio's research into plant sterols. Raisio's annual report tells the story:

> The cholesterol-reducing effects of plant sterols were known as early as the 1950s and ever since that time, scientists all over the world have been studying plant sterols and their properties.
>
> In 1972, a project led by Professor Pekka Puska was launched in North Karelia. The purpose of the project, which enjoyed international prestige, was to reduce the high cardiovascular rates in the region.
>
> In 1988, the Department of Pharmacy at the University of Helsinki started cooperation with the Helsinki and Turku Central Hospitals and the Raisio Group aimed at studying the effect of rapeseed oil on blood cholesterol levels. Professor Tatu Miettinen, who had already done extensive research on fat metabolism, suggested research on plant sterols to the Raisio Group.
>
> The following year, R&D Manager Ingmar Wester (of Raisio's Margarine Sub-division) and his research team found a way of turning plant sterol into fat-soluble stanol ester suitable for food production. A patent application was filed in 1991. This started a period of intense research aimed at producing indisputable evidence of the cholesterol-reducing effect of stanol ester. In 1993, the North Karelia project launched a long-range stanol ester study as part of its other clinical research.
>
> The digestive tract receives cholesterol from two sources, i.e. food and the human body itself. Normally, some 50% of the cholesterol that enters the digestive tract is disposed of and the rest is absorbed by the body. Fat-soluble plant stanol was shown as efficiently preventing the absorption of cholesterol. In a diet containing stanol ester, 80% of the cholesterol entering the digestive tract is disposed of and only 20% is absorbed by the body. The plant stanol itself is not absorbed, but disposed of naturally.
>
> The findings of the North Karelia study were published in the New England Journal of Medicine in November 1995. (The article reported that, after a 14-month trial, a daily intake of 25 grams reduces total cholesterol in the

bloodstream by 10% and the level of more harmful LDL cholesterol by 14%.) At the same time the first patents were issued for the production and use of stanol ester.

The first stanol ester product, Benecol margarine, was introduced on the Finnish market. The interest it aroused soon exceeded all expectations both in Finland and internationally. The registered name, Benecol, has since been confirmed as the common name for all products containing stanol ester.

Production of stanol ester began with experimental equipment, which limited the supply. The availability of plant sterol, the raw material, was another limiting factor. All plants contain small amounts of plant sterol, but it can be recovered economically only from plants processed in very large quantities. Since there had been no demand for plant sterols, no investments had been made in separation facilities.[4]

Exhibit 11.1 describes the cholesterol reducing properties of sterols and stanols. The Appendix gives information on Raisio's main patents relating to stanol ester.

Raisio in 1997

At the beginning of 1997, the Raisio Group had annual sales of $866 million and 2594 employees. The group comprised three divisions:

- Foodstuffs (47% of total sales), including the subdivisions: margarine (39% of sales), Melia Ltd (flour, pasta, breakfast cereal, muesli), oil milling, potato processing (mainly frozen French fries), malting, and Foodie Oy (rye products, pea soup, frozen pastry dough, salad dressings).
- Chemicals (34% of sales).
- Animal feeds (19% of sales).

Outside of Finland, Raisio had subsidiaries in Sweden, Estonia, Latvia, the U.K., France, Spain, Germany, Belgium, Poland, Canada, the U.S. and Indonesia. Raisio also had joint ventures in Mexico (49% ownership) and Chile (50%). Figure 11.1 shows Raisio's share price. Table 11.1 shows Raisio's financial performance.

EXHIBIT 11.1

Sterols and stanols

Sterols play a critical role in maintaining cell membranes in both plants and animals. Plant sterols (phytosterols) can reduce the low-density lipoprotein (LDL) in human blood, therefore reducing the risk of coronary heart disease. In plants, more than 40 sterols have been identified, of which sitosterol, stigmasterol and campesterol are the most abundant.

Plant stanols (phytostanols) are similar to sterols and are also found naturally in plants—though in much smaller quantities than sterols.

The effect of plant sterols in lowering human cholesterol levels has been known since the 1950s. Sitosterol has been used as a supplement and as a drug (Cytellin, marketed by Eli Lilly) to lower serum cholesterol levels. However, the use of plant sterols was limited by problems of poor solubility.

An important breakthrough was made by Finnish chemist Ingvar Wester, who hydrogenated plant sterols (derived from tall oil, a byproduct of pine-wood pulp) to produce stanol, then esterified the stanol to produce stanol ester, which is fat-soluble. Unlike sterol ester, stanol ester is not absorbed by the body. Clinical trials in Finland showed that stanol ester reduced total blood serum cholesterol in humans by up to 15%.

Plant sterols can also be produced as a byproduct of vegetable oil processing. One of the final stages of the processing of vegetable oil is deodorization—high-temperature distillation that removes free fatty acids. Sterols can be recovered from the resulting distillate.

Plant sterols themselves have a waxy consistency and a high melting point, creating solubility issues for the food processor. While they are oil-dispersible to some extent in their raw form, the amount required to produce an efficacious effect in a finished product can cause granulation. The answer to this problem is esterification: to make stanols and sterols fat soluble. During 1996, Unilever was working on the esterification of plant sterols. Meanwhile, Archer Daniels Midland was believed to be developing processes that would allow the introduction of sterols into nonfat systems, thus creating entirely new product lines (for example, adding sterols to beverages).

FIGURE 11.1 Raisio's share price (unrestricted shares, Helsinki Stock Exchange)

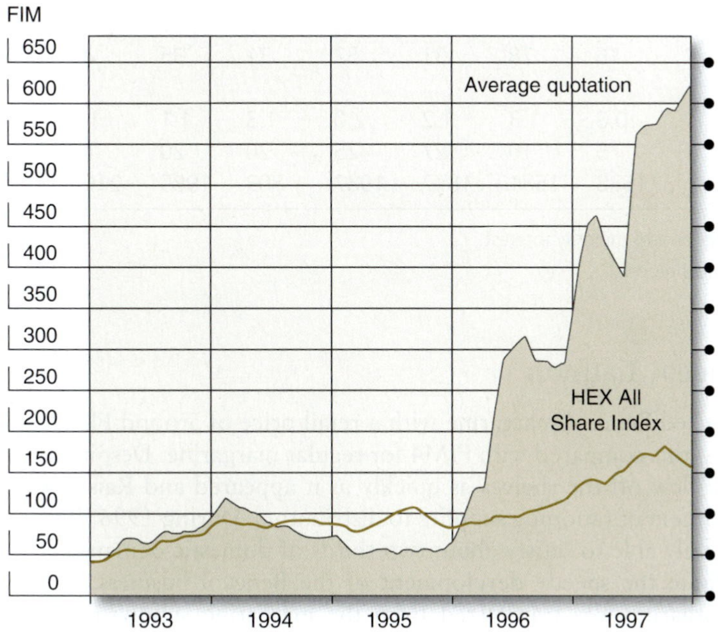

TABLE 11.1 Raisio's financial performance, 1987–1996

	1987	1988	1989	1990	1991	1992	1993	1994	1995	1996
Sales (FIM m)	2011	2184	2487	2557	2315	3070	3549	3518	3224	3928
Change (%)	+9	+9	+14	+3	−9	+33	+16	−1	−8	+22
Exports from Finland (FIM m)	126	106	110	136	172	241	389	358	519	735
International sales (FIM m)	288	16	189	217	279	405	561	568	886	1541
Operating margin (FIM m)	214	247	232	213	316	431	492	428	383	420
Percentage of turnover	10.6	11.3	9.3	8.3	13.6	14.0	13.9	12.2	11.9	10.7
Profit after depreciation (FIM m)	147	167	120	90	185	252	294	230	183	196
Percentage of turnover	7.3	7.6	4.8	3.5	8.0	8.2	8.3	6.5	5.7	5.0
Pre-tax profit[a] (FIM m)	97	98	91	64	63	114	185	35	140	162
Percentage of turnover	4.8	4.5	3.7	2.5	2.7	3.7	5.2	1.0	4.3	4.1
Return on equity (%)	15.5	15.3	5.4	0.1	6.9	10.3	10.3	9.4	6.8	5.8
Return on investment (%)	12.6	13.1	9.0	5.8	10.7	13.7	12.4	10.3	8.5	8.5
Shareholders' equity (FIM m)	670	994	1123	1224	1246	1246	1517	1564	1648	1973
Balance sheet total (FIM m)	1831	2257	2493	2872	2702	3268	3302	3071	3175	3678
Equity ratio (%)	36	44.3	46.0	46.7	47.3	44.3	46.5	51.4	52.1	54.0
Quick ratio	0.8	1.0	0.8	0.8	0.9	0.8	1.0	1.1	0.9	1.1
Current ratio	1.6	1.7	1.6	1.5	1.6	1.5	1.6	1.6	1.6	1.8
Gross investments (FIM m)	101	329	269	462	197	293	174	188	380	387
Percentage of turnover	5.0	15.1	10.8	18.1	8.5	9.5	4.9	5.3	11.8	9.9
R&D expenditure (FIM m)	16	28	31	52	31	35	40	54	54	87
Percentage of turnover	0.8	1.3	1.2	2.0	1.3	1.1	1.1	1.5	1.7	2.2
Direct taxes (FIM m)	5	10	27	25	20	20	47	21	32	64
No. of employees	1538	1581	1877	1987	803	1985	2106	1958	2054	2365

[a] Before appropriations, taxes and minority interest.

Source: Raisio Group annual reports.

The Benecol Launch

Raisio launched Benecol margarine with a retail price of around FIM25 ($4.50) for a 250 g tub—this compared with FIM4 for regular margarine. Despite the high price, the product flew off the shelves as quickly as it appeared and Raisio was forced to institute a system of rationing supplies to distributors. During 1996, Raisio estimated that it was only able to satisfy about two-thirds of domestic demand.

To facilitate the speedy development of the Benecol business, in March 1996 Benecol margarine was transferred from the margarine subdivision to a separate

Benecol unit. The unit was headed by Jukka Kaitaranta, who reported to deputy chief executive and head of the Food Division, Jukka Maki. It was intended that, during 1997, Benecol would become a separate division within Raisio. The Benecol Unit was responsible for developing all aspects of the business. It was responsible for acquiring plant sterol, producing stanol ester, managing international publicity for the project and conducting research.

The key problem was limited supplies of the active ingredient, stanol ester. While plant sterols—the raw material from which stanol ester is produced—are a common byproduct of industries that mass-process vegetable matter, almost no one had the systems in place to collect them. Raisio's primary source of supply of plant stanols was UPM-Kymmene, Europe's biggest pulp and paper company. During 1996, it negotiated increased supplies from UPM-Kymmene and also sought access to sterols from vegetable oil processors. Also in 1996, the Group built its first stanol ester plant, which was located in Raisio, and announced plans for a second plant to bring total stanol ester capacity up to 2000 tonnes a year by January 1998. Mr. Kari Jokinen, chief executive of Raisio's margarine division, estimated that this production of stanol ester would allow the production of 25 million kg of margarine, which could supply a total market of 60 million people.[5] The Benecol Unit also began work on a new 1500 m^2 R&D laboratory at Raisio's main industrial site.

During 1996, Raisio began planning for the international launch of Benecol. Its first overseas market was to be Sweden. The Swedish launch would be facilitated by Raisio's acquisition of a 77.5% stake in Carlshamm Mejeri AB, one of Sweden's main margarine producers, for $44.4 million. However, Raisio's horizons were not limited to Scandinavia—nor even to Europe. Benecol margarine was seen as having a huge international potential. Sales to the U.S. market could be massive, given that Americans spent some $33 billion a year on health foods and slimming products. Some estimates suggested that sales of Benecol margarine could reach $3 billion.

By January 1997, Raisio was being bombarded with requests and proposals from all over the world. Sainsbury's, at the time Britain's leading supermarket chain, requested an own-label version of Benecol margarine.[6] Other food processing companies were interested in purchasing licenses either for Benecol margarine or for Raisio's stanol ester technology, or for both.

Raisio's senior executives recognized that product formulation, marketing strategy and distribution policies would need to be adapted to the requirements of different national markets. Moreover, there were complex national regulations relating to the marketing of food products—especially those that included additives claiming to have health benefits. The Raisio executives were especially interested in an approach from McNeil Consumer Products, a division of the U.S.-based pharmaceutical and consumer products company Johnson & Johnson. McNeil was the world's biggest supplier of over-the-counter medicines and was known by its leading brand-name products such as Tylenol, Imodium, and Motrin. McNeil was headquartered in Fort Washington, Pennsylvania and was able to field a range of relevant resources—not least Johnson & Johnson's worldwide marketing and distribution system.

Competition

In formulating a strategy for the global exploitation of Benecol, Raisio faced a number of uncertainties. One issue that especially concerned Raisio executives was the potential for Benecol to encounter competition. In 1991, Raisio had filed its first patent relating to its process for the production of stanol ester from plant sterols and for its use in reducing cholesterol as an additive to human foods. In 1996, its first U.S. patent relating to stanol ester was issued. In the same year, Raisio filed a broader patent relating to the processing and use of stanol ester (see the Appendix). However, a number of competing products were available for reducing cholesterol. In particular, the cholesterol-reducing properties of naturally available plant sterols were well known. While Raisio believed it owned the only effective means for converting plant sterols into a fat-soluble form, it thought it likely that other processes might offer alternative approaches to the use of plant sterols as a food additive. Tor Bergman, head of chemicals (and soon to be appointed head of the Benecol Division as well) reckoned that Raisio had an 18- to 24-month lead over competitors.

Apart from plant sterols and stanols, a growing array of cholesterol-reducing drugs was available on the market. The major category was statins, which included lovastatin (brand name Mevacor), simvastatin (brand name Zocor), pravastatin (brand name Pravachol), fluvastatin (brand name Lescol) and atorvastatin (brand name Lipitor). Statins worked through slowing down the production of cholesterol by the body and by increasing the liver's ability to remove the LDL-cholesterol already in the blood.

In addition there are a number of natural food products that have the effect of reducing cholesterol within the blood. These include fish oil, garlic, flax seed, dietary fiber, policosanol (fatty alcohols derived from waxes of sugar cane) and guggulipid (an ancient herb from India).

Regulation

Benecol margarine falls into a wide category of products generally referred to as "nutraceuticals" or "functional foods." These are food products or supplements that may have a functional or physiological effect that is beneficial. Nutraceuticals have traditionally included food supplements such as vitamin pills, herbal products and more recently food products with additives that offer particular nutritional benefits—energy-enhancing drinks, vitamin-enriched cereals and the like. Nutraceuticals occupy a middle ground between food and medicines. The regulations relating to them also fall between food regulations and drug regulations. They also vary greatly between countries. Japan was one of the few countries that recognized functional foods as a distinct category and, since 1991, has had a well-developed administrative system for vetting and approving health claims relating to food. Canada, on the other hand, made no distinction between functional foods and drugs in relation to health claims—inevitably, this resulted in a highly restrictive regulatory climate for functional foods. Typically, regulations required that claims regarding the beneficial effects of food products could only be *health* claims (improved health) and not *medicinal* claims (claims relating to the prevention or cure of a disease). The most important markets for Benecol would be the U.S. and European Union. Here the regulations were far from clear cut (see Exhibit 11.2).

The Emerging Strategy

Until the beginning of 1997, Raisio had pursued a largely self-sufficient strategy for the exploitation of its stanol ester technology. It had fabricated stanol ester itself in its own plant using its own technology. Rather than selling the stanol ester to other

EXHIBIT 11.2

Country Regulations Relating to "Functional Foods"

United States

Under the 1990 Nutrition Labeling and Education Act (NLEA), the U.S. Food and Drug Administration allowed health claims in the case of certain well-documented relationships, for example between calcium and osteoporosis and sodium and hypertension.

The 1997 Food and Drug Administration Modernization Act (FDAMA) allowed for two types of health claim:

- Authoritative statement health claims (for example, relating to whole grain foods and risk of heart disease and certain cancers, and potassium and risk of high blood pressure and stroke).
- Qualified claims restricted to dietary supplements—typically in the form of pills, capsules, tablets or liquids, labeled as dietary supplements and not represented or marketed for consumption as a conventional food or sole item of a meal. Such claims could be based on a preponderance of scientific evidence.

In practice this meant three possible paths for gaining approval of a food product offering stated heath benefits:

- As a dietary supplement. This was the simplest path. The applicant had to file notification to the FDA 60 days prior to commercial rollout together with supporting evidence.
- As a food additive. This was a more time-consuming process involving much stronger evidence and a determination by an independent panel of experts assembled by the applicant and reporting to the FDA.
- As a pharmaceutical. Finally, a new food product could be approved as a drug. This process typically required several years.

Canada

The Canadian Food and Drug Act stipulated that all products represented for the cure, treatment, mitigation, prevention, risk reduction, and correction or modification of body structure and function are regulated as a "drug" regardless of the available scientific evidence.

European Union

During the 1990s the EU was in the process of harmonizing legislation among its individual member countries regarding health claims for food products. Regulation No. 258/97 concerning novel foods and novel food ingredients applied to new foods or ingredients that were primary molecular structures, micro-organisms, or were isolated from plants or isolated from animals (but this was not applicable to food additives). Such novel foods were to be assessed by the government of a member state, which would make an initial assessment to determine whether the product met EU standards of safety and accurate labeling and whether an additional assessment was needed.

> *If neither the Commission nor the Member States raise an objection, and if no additional assessment is required, the Member State informs the applicant that he may place the product on the market . . . Any decision or provision concerning a*

novel food or food ingredient which is likely to have an effect on public health must be referred to the Scientific Committee for Food.

Fast-track approval was possible for products that were essentially similar to products already on the market but entirely new products required a full assessment by the Scientific Committee for Food. It would appear that Benecol was a new food product (given its first-time use of stanol ester). However, the fact that it had already been marketed in Finland before the EU's regulation had taken effect might provide it with a loophole to avoid full-assessment approval.

Japan

In 1991, Japan became the first global jurisdiction to implement a regulatory system for functional foods. Under the Japanese system, "foods for specific health use" (FOSHU) had a specific regulatory approval process separate from foods fortified with vitamins and minerals and dietary supplements not carrying FOSHU claims. "Foods for specific health use" are defined as "foods in the case of which specified effects contributing to maintain health can be expected based on the available data concerning the relationship between the foods'/food's contents and health, as well as foods with permitted labeling which indicates the consumer can expect certain health effects upon intake of these particular foods." Approved FOSHU bear a seal of approval from the Japanese Ministry of Health, Labor and Welfare (MHLW) identifying their role in disease prevention and health promotion. To achieve FOSHU status and an approved health claim, companies submit a scientific dossier to MHLW, which includes scientific documentation demonstrating the medical and nutritional basis for the health claim, including the recommended dose of the functional ingredient. The MHLW has established a detailed approval process, which typically takes about one year to complete. Japan was estimated to have the world's second largest functional food market behind the U.S.

Sources: Michael H. Moffett and Stacey Wolff Howard, *Benecol: Raisio's Global Nutraceutical*, (Thunderbird, The American Graduate School of International Management, 1999). Sean A. MacDonald, "A Comparative Analysis of the Regulatory Framework Affecting Functional Food and Functional Food Ingredient Development and Commercialization in Canada, the United States (U.S.), the European Union (E.U.), Japan and Australia/New Zealand," *Agriculture and Agri-Food Canada*, (August, 2004).

food manufacturers for incorporation into their own products, it had followed a strategy of vertical integration. Its stanol ester was used only in its own branded margarine, Benecol, which was produced in its own factories and marketed and distributed through its own sales and distribution system.

If it was to exploit the full potential of its innovation, Raisio would need to draw upon the resources of other companies. Clearly the market for cholesterol-reducing foods was worldwide. Moreover, the potential for using stanol ester in foods was not restricted to margarine. Raisio envisaged its use in a variety of health-food products, including salad dressings, dairy products and snack bars. If Raisio's stanol ester technology was to be exploited effectively throughout the EU, in North America, the Far East, and Australasia, then this would require food-processing facilities, market knowledge, regulatory know-how, and distribution facilities, the provision of which was quite beyond Raisio's ability. Time was a critical issue. Raisio patents related to its own process of producing stanol ester and incorporating it within food products. While Raisio's technology and the patent protection it had received bought it a few years' lead-time, it was likely that other companies would find alternative approaches to the use of plant sterols as a cholesterol-reducing food additive.

In Johnson & Johnson, Raisio had a potential partner that had the capabilities needed to introduce Benecol margarine—and other Benecol products—to the world market. Johnson & Johnson possessed global manufacturing, marketing, and distribution capabilities, together with extensive experience in the food and drug approval procedures of the U.S., Europe and most other countries. It was widely considered to be one of the most effective health product-marketing companies in the world, with an outstanding reputation for quality and social responsibility, a global sales and distribution reach, and vast experience in guiding products through government regulations relating to foods and drugs. It viewed nutraceuticals as an important strand of its growth strategy. Its first nutraceutical was Lactaid for people unable to digest lactose. Lactaid was sold in caplets and as lactose-reduced milk and lactose-free foods. It also supplied sucralose, a low-calorie sweetener that had been approved by the U.S. Food and Drug Administration and was sold in nearly 30 countries.

At the same time, there were voices within Raisio that saw risks in an exclusive relationship with Johnson & Johnson. If stanol ester was a potential additive to a wide range of products, did it make sense for Raisio to become identified with a single product—margarine—and was it desirable for Raisio to link its fortunes with a single partner? An alternative approach for Raisio would be to focus on the supply of its key ingredient, stanol ester. At one meeting of Raisio's executive committee, the case of Monsanto and NutraSweet was discussed. It was noted that following the development of NutraSweet (the branded name for aspartame), Monsanto did not forward integrate into the production of diet foods and beverages, but became a supplier of NutraSweet to a wide range of different beverage suppliers and food processors.

In relation to the production and supply of stanol ester, Raisio also faced some critical strategic choices. The crucial problem in 1996 appeared to be limited capacity for producing stanol ester. Even with a new plant planned for 1997, Raisio would still be unable to supply the potential market for Benecol margarine in Finland and nearby markets. If, as anticipated, the demand for Benecol products was to be worldwide, it would need to produce stanol ester in all regions where Benecol products were manufactured and marketed. Thus, even if Raisio agreed a licensing agreement with Johnson & Johnson to produce and market Benecol products, Raisio would need to specify the terms under which stanol ester would be supplied. All Raisio's sterol requirements were supplied by the pulp and paper group, UPM-Kymmene. Raisio had cooperated closely with UPM-Kymmene in developing the technology for separating plant sterols during wood pulp processing. To ensure access to adequate supplies of plant sterols for its stanol ester production, Raisio would need to collaborate closely with the processors of forest and agricultural products. Raisio was considering forming a joint venture with UPM-Kymmene specifically for the extraction and supply of plant sterols. Irrespective of whether the global licensing deal with J&J for the production and distribution of Benecol products went ahead, Raisio faced critical decisions with regard to the production of stanol ester and the supply of plant sterols. Should it keep its production of stanol ester in-house, or should it license this technology also?

Case B: Developments 1997–2000

The Agreement with Johnson & Johnson

During 1997, negotiations between Raisio Group and Johnson & Johnson's McNeil subsidiary progressed to the point where an agreement was signed between the two companies. Raisio's 1997 annual report outlined the deal:

> In July 1997, the Raisio Group signed a cooperation agreement with the American McNeil Consumer Products Company, which is part of the Johnson & Johnson Group. The contract gives McNeil the sole right to use the Benecol trademark and patents on the U.S., Canadian, and Mexican markets. The Raisio Group retains the right to supply the stanol ester required for the products. McNeil aims to introduce the first products during 1998. Raisio received a lump payment for assignment of these license rights and will receive remunerations related to operative development and royalties for the sales of Benecol products and for deliveries of stanol ester.
>
> Johnson & Johnson is the world's biggest and most versatile producer of health-related products. Its turnover totaled U.S.$21.6 billion in 1996 and it has 170 operative companies in 50 countries.
>
> In November a new letter of intent was signed, which will extend cooperation with Johnson & Johnson to global dimensions. Europe and Japan will take their places by the side of the United States as the chief Benecol markets. The agreement also includes a plan to strengthen the position of the Benecol brand by cooperating with other companies producing strong brands that fit in with the Benecol product family. The letter of intent leads to a final agreement on March 2, 1998.
>
> These agreements confirm the principle that the Raisio Group will keep the entire production of stanol ester in its own hands and will develop Benecol production and marketing in Finland and neighboring areas. Global marketing will be carried out with a strong and skilled cooperation partner.[7]

Expectations for Benecol were high. Raisio's consultants estimated total worldwide sales of nutraceuticals at $35 billion a year, excluding supplements (such as vitamins and minerals). Of these, functional foods comprised about one-third ($10–12 billion) with an annual growth of 25–35%. If consumer reaction to Benecol in other industrialized nations was anything like that in Finland, Benecol promised to be a blockbuster. By the beginning of 1998, Raisio's share price exceeded EUR12—up 1200% over three years.

The agreement would involve close cooperation between Raisio and Johnson & Johnson. Not only would Raisio be supplying J&J with stanol ester—the agreement also provided for the two companies to coordinate medical and clinical research and marketing and cooperate in product development on a project-by-project basis.

Putting together the partnership with J&J was the dominant priority of Raisio's top management during the first half of 1997. As a result, several other initiatives were put on hold. Raisio's 1997 annual report noted that: "The introduction of Benecol products was delayed on the Finnish market because of the extensive license negotiations at group level and the need to adopt a common approach on all markets."[8]

Stanol Ester Production

Given the optimism for worldwide sales of Benecol and Raisio's current inability to meet home demand because of a shortage of stanol ester, the worldwide launch of Benecol margarine depended critically on expanding the production of stanol ester.

The first priority was increasing Raisio's purchases of plant sterol. Raisio's 1997 annual report described the quest:

> The plant sterol needed to produce stanol ester has from the very beginning been supplied by Kaukus Oy, part of the UPM-Kymmene Group. Kaukas separates the sterol during the pulp cooking process and is a pioneer in sterol separation techniques.
>
> In April 1997, Raisio and UPM-Kymmene set up a joint venture called Sterol Technologies Ltd. Raisio's holding is 65%. The company develops sterol separation methods and markets them to the forest industry. In October 1997, Sterol Technologies began to build an experimental sterol recovery unit at the Kaukas mill, which is scheduled for completion in March 1998.
>
> An agreement has been made with the French company Les Derives Raisiniques et Terpeniques to achieve a major increase in its sterol production. The new plant covered by the agreement should go on stream in 1999. The entire additional capacity has been reserved for Raisio Benecol.
>
> In August, a letter of intent was signed with the American Westvaco Corporation on cooperation in studying ways of producing plant sterol in America. The aim is to build a sterol production plant in South Carolina to go on stream in 2000.
>
> In November, an agreement was signed with the Chilean company Harting S.A. on establishing a joint venture called Detsa S.A. in Chile. Raisio's holding is 49%. Detsa will build a sterol plant and Sterol Technologies will be responsible for the technology.
>
> When the Detsa plant is completed in 1999, Raisio Benecol will have close to 400 tonnes of raw sterol a year at its disposal. Refined into stanol ester, this amount will satisfy the daily needs of 4 million people. If the percentage of population accounted for by users of Benecol settles at the same level as in Finland, this amount will be sufficient to supply markets comprising close on 200 million consumers.[9]

Raisio had been operating a prototype stanol ester plant at its headquarters since 1996. It had planned to build an adjoining unit to expand stanol ester production. However, following the J&J deal Raisio decided that the priority was to begin stanol ester production in America. Hence, in June 1997, Raisio began construction of a stanol ester plant at Charleston, South Carolina.

The International Launch

United States

During 1998, J&J planned for the launch of Benecol margarine both in the U.S. and Europe. After considerable analysis and discussion, J&J decided that, for the purposes of meeting the FDA regulations, it would introduce Benecol spreads to the U.S. market as a dietary supplement. As Exhibit 11.2 explains, this would involve the least delay and would allow J&J to promote Benecol's cholesterol-reducing benefits.

However, in October 1998, a letter from the FDA torpedoed the U.S. launch:

> The purpose of this letter is to inform you that marketing the product with the prototype label . . . would be illegal under the Federal Food, Drug and Cosmetic Act . . . The label for the Benecol spread, through the statement that the product replaces butter or margarine, vignettes picturing the product in common butter or margarine uses, statements promoting the texture and flavor of the product, and statements such as ". . . helps you manage your cholesterol naturally through the food you eat," represents this product for use as a conventional food. Therefore, the product is not a dietary supplement.

As a food with an additive that had not been approved as safe, Benecol margarine was subject to FDA regulation and J&J would have to embark on the protracted process of submitting evidence of stanol ester's safety and efficacy.

Johnson & Johnson halted the U.S. launch of Benecol and decided that it would introduce the product as a food product without any explicit health claims. By early 1999 Benecol received "Generally Recognized As Safe" (GRAS) status from a panel of independent experts that allowed Benecol to be launched in May 1999.

Europe

In Europe, J&J avoided the regulatory tussles that had delayed the U.S. launch of Benecol, principally because the 1995 introduction into Finland had predated the new EU regulations. Nevertheless, the European launch still needed to take account of different national regulations and Benecol's formulation also needed to be adapted to different national preferences. In March 1999, Benecol was launched in the U.K., and in Belgium, the Netherlands, and Luxemburg in September. The European launch comprised four products: regular and low-fat Benecol spread (margarine) and a natural and a herb cheese spread. In the fall of 2000, Benecol products were launched in Sweden and Denmark.

Competition

Unilever

The delays to Benecol's international launch eliminated Raisio's first-mover advantage in cholesterol-reducing margarine. Almost simultaneous with Benecol's U.S. debut, Unilever launched its rival product, Take Control, which contained sterol esters derived from vegetable oil. Because Take Control's sterol esters were simpler and less expensive to prepare than Raisio's stanol ester (it did not require a complex hydrogenation process), the Unilever product could be sold at a lower price. Initially, Raisio and J&J were not overly concerned at the price differential, in the belief that stanol ester was more effective than sterol ester in cholesterol reduction. However, some new research suggested that the differential was probably very small.

In September 2000, Raisio and J&J received some rare good news from the FDA. After a careful review of the evidence, the FDA had determined that J&J could issue explicit health claims for the effects of stanol ester within Benecol margarine in reducing coronary heart disease. The only downside was that the ruling gave equal rights to Unilever for its sterol ester ingredient.

Despite overcoming the regulatory hurdles, the market reaction to Benecol was disappointing. Johnson & Johnson spent $49 million on advertising Benecol within the U.S., but U.S. retail sales for Benecol between May and December 1999 reached just $17 million. Another estimate put U.S. sales between May 1999 and August 2000 at $42 million.

Unilever's initial launch met similar results. During 1999 it was estimated that Take Control was supported by $15 million in advertising only to generate $13 million in sales. By January 2000, Take Control had gained 1.6% of the U.S. margarine market, with Benecol holding 1.2%. In response to this poor consumer response, J&J shifted the emphasis of its marketing strategy from consumer advertising to providing information to U.S. doctors on the health benefits of Benecol.

In Europe, J&J was able to enter the market for cholesterol-reducing margarine before Unilever in most countries. Unilever launched its sterol ester margarine as "Pro-activ"—an extension to its existing Flora and Becel ranges of low saturated fat margarines. In the U.K., Unilever's Flora Pro-activ was launched early in 2000—nine months after Benecol. Yet, Unilever's superior sales and distribution for grocery products and its lower price (Benecol retailed at £2.49 per 250 g pack compared with Flora Pro-activ at £1.99) meant that Unilever soon had twice the market share of Benecol. Market observers also noted that Unilever's marketing was more effective than J&J's:

> The brand is backed by the Flora Project, a nutrition marketing effort that educates people about heart disease prevention including diet, smoking cessation, lifestyle habits and exercise. Flora sponsors the London marathon, as well as other sporting events. Before Pro-activ came onto the market, tubs of regular Flora already bore the words, "as part of a healthy diet helps lower cholesterol," a statement scientifically backed by Unilever. Moreover, the Flora name had a massive "share of mind"—from the 1980s until the mid-1990s, the Flora brand accounted for 60% of media spending in the spreads category. Because Flora was associated in consumers' minds for 30 years with heart health—and with good taste—it was logical to leverage the Flora brand assets.
>
> The London Flora marathon seamlessly became the London Flora Pro-activ marathon. There is little company communication about the ingredient—the words "plant sterols" are mentioned only on about page six of the information leaflet. But that is as it should be—Unilever is selling the benefits of Flora, a known and trusted food brand; it is not selling plant sterols, specifically.
>
> In contrast, rival Johnson & Johnson's McNeil Consumer Products group had no pre-existing supermarket brand to extend when it launched the cholesterol-lowering spread, Benecol, in Finland in late 1995 (then owned by Raisio). Benecol, therefore, started out with zero brand equity in the U.K. By the time Pro-activ joined it on the market, Benecol had garnered $30 million in sales—no small achievement for an entirely new brand—and it held a 0.5 per cent volume share and 2.5 per cent value share.
>
> As the brand creator, Benecol had to set the price point, which it did at seven times the price of regular spreads. In response, Unilever added to Pro-activ's competitive advantage by bringing it to market 25 per cent cheaper than Benecol.
>
> Add to these factors the massive brand equity of the Flora name, and it is no surprise that Flora Pro-activ is now outselling Benecol in the U.K. by a factor of almost three-to-one.[10]

Other Competitors

Unilever was not the only company interested in the market for stanol and sterol esters. By 2000, some of Raisio's worst fears were being realized. Several companies had either entered the market for cholesterol-reducing nutraceuticals, or had announced their intention to enter:

- *Forbes Medi-Tech and Novartis*. In April 1999, the Swiss pharmaceutical company Novartis signed a five-year agreement with Canadian biotechnology company Forbes Medi-Tech to license Phytrol—a plant sterol-based ingredient with similar cholesterol-reducing properties to stanol ester. Novartis would become responsible for clinical trials, regulatory submissions, and commercialization of end products. Phytrol (marketed also as Reducol) received FDA "Generally Recognized As Safe" approval in May 2000.[11] In 2000, Novartis announced a joint venture with Quaker Oats to form Altus Foods, which would manufacture healthy foods containing Phytrol. Novartis launched a number of products including breakfast cereals and cereal bars under the Aviva brand name. However, market response was, at best, tepid. In the U.K., the Aviva range was withdrawn six months after the launch.
- *Paulig*. In July 1999, Finland's Paulig (a company known for its coffee and spice operations) announced its own plant sterol ingredient, Teriaka, derived from maize, soy and pine trees. Because its manufacture utilizes normal processing technology and does not require chemical synthesis or high temperatures/pressures, it was believed that it could gain quick approval under the EU's Novel Foods Regulations.
- *Procter & Gamble* introduced a line of cooking oils containing sterol esters under the brand name CookSmart.
- *Archer Daniels Midland* developed a patent-pending sterol ingredient that is dispersible in liquids, allowing sterols to be added to beverages, milk products, and other water-based and non-fat products.
- *Monsanto* in 2000 received a patent on a "phytosterol protein complex" composed of sterols, proteins, and edible oil. The product claimed to enhance the cholesterol-reducing effects of sterols.

Mounting Crisis

During 2000, Raisio was incurring rapidly increasing losses from its Benecol Division. During the first half of 2000, it reported losses of €44.0 million, mostly resulting from a non-recurring charge of €38.0 million. This compared with a profit that totaled €11.2 million during the corresponding period in 1999 (although this resulted entirely from a one-time payment under the agreement with J&J). Between the first half of 1999 and first half of 2000, revenues for the first six months of Raisio's Benecol Division were down from €47 million to €16 million, reflecting the end of payments from J&J and sharply reduced sales of stanol ester to J&J. Tables 11.2 and 11.3 show Raisio's financial performance between 1996 and 2000.

The company's report for the first half of 2000 analyzed the problems:

> The development of the Group's Benecol business derives from a vision dating back to 1996–7 which predicted a rapid and impressive rise in Benecol

TABLE 11.2 Raisio Group financial indicators, 1996–2000

	1996	1997	1998	1999	2000
Sales and operations					
Turnover (€m)	661	858	833	763	800
Change (%)	+22	+30	−3	−8	+5
Exports from Finland (€m)	124	135	178	145	131
Total international turnover (€m)	259	423	421	374	399
Percentage of turnover	39.2	49.3	50.5	49.0	49.9
Gross investments (€m)	65	73	75	61	49
R&D expenditure (€m)	15	17	18	16	18
Percentage of turnover	2.2	1.9	2.1	2.1	2.3
Average personnel	2365	2817	2904	2897	2775
Profitability					
Operating result (€m)	33	41	52	16	−32
% of turnover	5.0	4.8	6.3	2.1	−4.0
Result before extraordinary items (€m)	28	35	42	6	−47
Result before taxes and minority interest (€m)	27	20	39	−2	−47
Percentage of turnover	4.1	2.3	4.7	−0.3	−5.8
Return on equity (ROE) (%)	4.5	7.8	9.2	0.4	−14.9
Return on investment (ROI) (%)	9.2	10.1	11.1	4.0	−4.2
Financial and economical position					
Shareholders' equity (€m)	291	298	317	304	260
Net interest-bearing liabilities (€m)	119	143	174	233	251
Balance sheet total (€m)	619	643	690	744	750
Equity ratio (%)	47.3	46.6	46.0	41.0	34.7
Quick ratio	1.1	0.8	0.7	0.6	0.7
Current ratio	1.8	1.5	1.2	1.2	1.2
Cash flow from business operations	43	60	47	6	16

Source: Raisio Group 2000 Annual Report.

TABLE 11.3 Raisio Group divisional performance, 1997–2000 (millions of euros)

		1997	1998	1999	2000
Benecol	Turnover	16	48	52	23
	Operating profit	n.a.	n.a.	7.5	−45.6
Margarine	Turnover	282	235	200	204
	Operating profit	n.a.	n.a.	79.5	78.0
Grain	Turnover	287	274	235	244
	Operating profit	n.a.	n.a.	0.8	0.7
Chemicals	Turnover	278	277	299	347
	Operating profit	n.a.	n.a.	20.3	11.9

n.a. = not available.

Source: Raisio Group annual reports, 1998–2000.

> products containing stanol ester into global functional foods. This vision was based on Raisio and McNeil's joint assessment and on market and need analyses by leading international consultants.
>
> Raisio then made safeguarding long-term availability of the main raw material in Benecol products—sterol—its strategic goal. Action aimed at large-scale procurement of sterol was therefore taken immediately on both the plant and the wood sterol markets. Plant sterols were acquired under long-term purchasing agreements, as world supply was limited and indeed inadequate for the targets then set for Benecol operations.
>
> The limited nature of plant sterol production thus faced Raisio with a strategic challenge, in view of which several projects were launched aimed at developing more wood sterol separation. The biggest are a tall oil and sterol separation project in Chile (Detsa) and the Westerol project planned for North America. Supplies of wood sterol were also ensured through various contracting and financing arrangements.
>
> Since the launch in Finland in 1995, however, Benecol products have actually reached the market only in the U.S.A., U.K., Ireland and the Benelux countries, and mainly only in the second half of 1999, and in Sweden and Denmark this autumn. Market penetration has thus been slower than expected, partly due to regulatory obstacles. Current experience suggests that the expectations concerning cholesterol-reducing foods on which Raisio's plans were based were overly optimistic. So far, less than 20% of the targets have been achieved.
>
> As a result of its high expectations and targets, Raisio has tied up substantial resources in both wood sterol projects and sterol and stanol stocks. In today's market situation, however, the company has had to review and reassess its sterol strategy and the preconditions for completing ongoing projects, as well as the value of the sterols and stanols already procured.

To stem the losses, Raisio renegotiated several of its long-term sterol purchase agreements, withdrew from its sterol separation joint venture in Chile and suspended its Solexin plant sterol project in New Zealand. Other sterol separation projects were to be reviewed on a case-by-case basis. Inventories of sterol and stanol were revalued at current market prices and several of the fixed assets involved written down.

The central problem, Raisio believed, lay with the agreement with J&J. Johnson & Johnson's worldwide license meant that Raisio was completely dependent on J&J's commitment to Benecol and the success of J&J's marketing strategy. Observing Unilever's ability to push Benecol into second place in the U.S. and Europe, many at Raisio believed that the company had backed the wrong horse. Despite J&J's expertise with FDA regulations and healthcare, and its massive R&D budget, in terms of marketing food products and selling to supermarkets, J&J like other big pharmaceutical companies had limited expertise and channel power in branded, packaged foods.

During 2000, Raisio's share price was in free fall. By October 2000, Raisio's shares had lost 85% of their value compared with the peak in mid-1998 (see Figure 11.2). CEO Tor Bergman, who, as head of Raisio's Chemical Division and head of the Benecol Division, had been the primary architect of the Benecol strategy, was the main casualty of the collapse. He left Raisio in August 2000 and was replaced as CEO by Lasse Kurkilahti. The new CEO's review of 2000 was in

FIGURE 11.2 Raisio Group plc, price of unrestricted shares (Helsinki Stock Exchange).

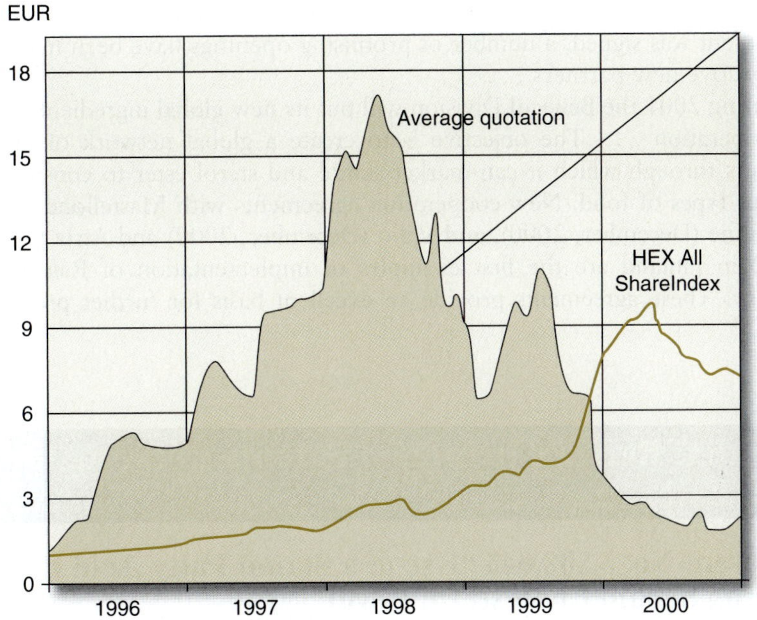

Note: Figures 11.1 and 11.2 are not directly comparable because of a 10:1 share split in June 1998. Figure 11.2 shows Raisio's share price adjusted for the share split.

sharp contrast to the optimistic tone of previous communications to shareholders. After acknowledging 2000 to be "the worst in the past ten years," he went on to outline the challenge of Raisio competing internationally:

> Earlier, Raisio competed with Finnish and Nordic companies; now, its competitors are European or global players . . . The diversified enterprises that formed during the '80s in a closed economy will not survive in today's open economy, where a business's only hope lies in being competitive. The Raisio Group has to focus its resources on the fewer fields.[12]

Benecol would occupy a prominent position among these "fewer fields." However, to succeed, the Division needed a new strategy. The starting point was a new relationship with J&J. By December 2000, a new agreement was reached:

> . . . This gives the Benecol Division the opportunity to implement a global strategy concentrating on functional food ingredients—that is, stanol and sterol ester—in certain clinical areas. The new agreement covers two main aspects of the Benecol stanol ester business. The companies agreed that McNeil would concentrate on markets in North America, the EU (excluding Finland, Sweden and Denmark), Japan and China. Raisio's market area, in turn, comprises Scandinavia, the Baltic region, the former East European countries, the Near East, Latin America, the Far East and Oceania. The two

companies also agreed on a new market-driven delivery agreement for Benecol ingredients. Further, Raisio acquired global rights to sell and market sterol ester. Both companies may agree independently to involve third parties in their market areas in order to expand the product range. Since the agreement was signed, a number of promising openings have been made with prospective new partners . . .

During 2001 the Benecol Division will put its new global ingredient strategy into operation . . . The objective is to create a global network of business partners through which it can market stanol and sterol ester to consumers in various types of food. New cooperation agreements with Mastellone Hnos in Argentine (December, 2000), and Valio (December, 2000) and Atria (January, 2001) in Finland are the first examples of implementation of Raisio's new strategy. These agreements provide an excellent basis for further progress in 2001.[13]

Appendix: Raisio's Principal Patents Relating to Stanol Ester

U.S. Patent No. 5,502,045 "Use of a Stanol Fatty Acid Ester for Reducing Serum Cholesterol Level"

Inventors: Tatu Miettinen, Hannu Vanhanen, Ingmar Wester.

Assignee: Raision Tehtaat Oy AB

Filed: November 22, 1993

Awarded: March 26, 1996

Abstract

The invention relates to a substance which lowers cholesterol levels in serum and which is a .beta.-sitostanol fatty acid ester or fatty acid ester mixture, and to a method for preparing the same. The substance can be used as such or added to a food.

Claims

We claim:

1 The method of reducing the absorption of cholesterol into the bloodstream comprising orally introducing into the body an effective amount of a substance containing a .beta.-sitostanol fatty acid ester prepared by the interesterification of .beta.-sitostanol with a fatty acid ester containing between 2 and 22 carbon atoms in the presence of an interesterification catalyst.

2 The method according to claim 1, wherein the interesterification of .beta.-sitostanol is carried out in a solvent free food grade process.

3 The method according to claim 2, wherein the interesterification occurs at a temperature of approximately 90 degree-120 degree C and a vacuum of approximately 5–15 mmHg.

4 The method according to claim 3, wherein the catalyst is sodium ethylate.

5 The method of claim 1, wherein the fatty acid ester comprises a mixture of fatty acid esters.

6 The method according to claim 1, wherein the .beta.-sitostanol is prepared by hydrogenation of a commercial .beta.-sitosterol mixture.

7 The method according to claim 1, wherein the interesterification is carried out in the presence of a stoichiometric excess of the fatty acid ester.

8 The method according to claim 1, wherein an effective amount of the substance is between about 0.2 and about 20 grams per day.

Extract from "Description" Section

. . . The present invention relates to the use of a sterol of an entirely different type for lowering the cholesterol level in serum. What is involved is fatty acid esters of alpha-saturated sterols, especially sitostanol fatty acid esters (sitostanol = 24-ethyl-5.alpha. -cholestane-3.beta.-ol), which have been observed to lower cholesterol levels in serum with particular efficacy. The said esters can be prepared or used as such, or they can be added to foods, especially to the fatty part of a food. The sitostanol fatty acid ester mixture is prepared by hardening a commercial .beta.-sitosterol mixture (sitosterol = 24-ethyl-5-cholestene-3.beta.-ol). .beta.-sitostanol can be prepared by a prior-known cholesterol hardening technique by hardening .beta.-sitosterol by means of a Pd/C catalyst in an organic solvent . . . This mixture has the approval of the FDA (Cytellin, Eli Lilly). A hardening degree of over 99% is achieved in the reaction. The catalyst used in the hardening is removed by means of a membrane filter, and the obtained sitostanol is crystallized, washed and dried. In accordance with the invention, the .beta.-sitostanol mixture, which contains campestanol approx. 6%, is esterified with different fatty acid ester mixtures by a commonly known chemical interesterification technique . . . A methyl ester mixture of the fatty acids of any vegetable oil can be used in the reaction. One example is a mixture of rapeseed oil and methyl ester, but any fatty acids which contain approx. 2 to 22 carbon atoms are usable. The method according to the invention for the preparation of stanol fatty acid esters deviates advantageously from the previously patented methods in that no substances other than free stanol, a fatty acid ester or a fatty acid ester mixture, and a catalyst are used in the esterification reaction. The catalyst used may be any known interesterification catalyst, such as Na-ethylate.

U.S. Patent No. 5,958,913 "Substance for Lowering High Cholesterol Level in Serum and Methods for Preparing and Using the Same"

Inventors: Tatu Miettinen, Hannu Vanhanen, Ingmar Wester.

Assignee: Raisio Benecol Ltd.

Filed: November 5, 1996

Awarded: September 28, 1999

Abstract

The invention relates to a substance which lowers LDL cholesterol levels in serum and which is fat soluble .beta.-sitostanol fatty acid ester, and to a method for preparing and using the same. The substance can be taken orally as a food additive, food substitute or supplement. A daily consumption of the .beta.-sitostanol ester in an amount between about 0.2 and about 20 grams per day has been shown to reduce the absorption of biliary and endogenic cholesterol.

Claims

What is claimed is:

1 A food composition suitable for reducing blood serum cholesterol levels or reducing absorption of cholesterol from the intestines into the bloodstream, the food composition comprising a nutritional substance and a blood serum cholesterol level reducing or cholesterol absorption reducing effective amount of a sterol component comprising at least one 5.alpha.-saturated sterol fatty acid ester.

2 The food composition as claimed in claim 1, wherein the sterol component comprises .beta.-sitostanol fatty acid ester.

3 The food composition as claimed in claim 1, wherein the fatty acid contains about 2 to 22 carbon atoms.

4 The food composition as claimed in claim 2, wherein the fatty acid contains about 2 to 22 carbon atoms.

5 The food composition as claimed in claim 1, wherein the 5.alpha.-saturated sterol fatty acid ester is produced by esterifying the alpha-saturated sterol and a fatty acid ester in a solvent-free food grade process.

6 The food composition as claimed in claim 2, wherein the .beta.-sitostanol fatty acid ester is produced by esterifying .beta.-sitostanol and a fatty acid ester in a solvent-free food grade process.

7 The food composition as claimed in claim 5, wherein the esterifying step is conducted in the presence of an esterification catalyst.

8 The food composition as claimed in claim 6, wherein the esterifying step is conducted in the presence of an esterification catalyst.

9 The food composition as claimed in claim 7, wherein the esterification catalyst comprises sodium ethylate.

10 The food composition as claimed in claim 8, wherein the esterification catalyst comprises sodium ethylate.

11 The food composition as claimed in claim 5, wherein the esterifying step is conducted at a temperature of about 90–120 degree C under a vacuum of about 5–15 mmHg.

12 The food composition as claimed in claim 6, wherein the esterifying step is conducted at a temperature of about 90–120 degree C under a vacuum of about 5–15 mmHg.

13 The food composition as claimed in claim 5, wherein the esterifying step is conducted without the presence of additional interesterifiable lipids.

14 The food composition as claimed in claim 6, wherein the esterifying step is conducted without the presence of additional interesterifiable lipids.

15 The food composition as claimed in claim 1, wherein the nutritional substance comprises a member selected from the group consisting of

cooking oil, margarine, butter, mayonnaise, salad dressing and shortening.

16 The food composition as claimed in claim 2, wherein the nutritional substance comprises a member selected from the group consisting of cooking oil, margarine, butter, mayonnaise, salad dressing and shortening.

17 A method for reducing the cholesterol level in blood serum of a subject in need thereof, comprising orally administering to the subject the food composition as claimed in claim 1, wherein the sterol component is present in a blood serum cholesterol level reducing effective amount.

18 A method for reducing the cholesterol level in blood serum of a subject in need thereof, comprising orally administering to the subject the food composition as claimed in claim 2, wherein the sterol component is present in a blood serum cholesterol level reducing effective amount.

19 The method as claimed in claim 17, wherein about 0.2 to 20 grams per day of the sterol component are orally administered.

20 The method as claimed in claim 18, wherein about 0.2 to 20 grams per day of the sterol component are orally administered.

21 A method for reducing the absorption of cholesterol from the intestines into the bloodstream of a subject in need thereof, comprising orally administering to the subject the food composition as claimed in claim 1, wherein the sterol component is present in a cholesterol absorption reducing effective amount.

22 A method for reducing the absorption of cholesterol from the intestines into the bloodstream of a subject in need thereof, comprising orally administering to the subject the food composition as claimed in claim 2, wherein the sterol component is present in a cholesterol absorption reducing effective amount.

23 The method as claimed in claim 21, wherein about 0.2 to 20 grams per day of the sterol component are orally administered.

24 The method as claimed in claim 22, wherein about 0.2 to 20 grams per day of the sterol component are orally administered.

Brief Description of the Invention

The present invention relates to a sterol of an entirely different type for lowering the cholesterol levels in blood serum. The substance comprises a fatty acid ester of alpha saturated sterols, especially sitostanol fatty acid esters, which have been observed to lower cholesterol levels in serum with particular efficacy.

The present invention includes a method of reducing the absorption of cholesterol into the bloodstream from the digestive tract by orally introducing into the body an effective amount of a fatty acid ester of a beta-sitostanol. More preferably, the invention further includes orally introducing between about 0.2 and about 20 grams per day of beta-sitostanol fatty acid ester into the body. The ester is introduced either as a food additive, a food substitute or a food supplement. When used as a food additive, the fatty acid ester of the beta-sitostanol may be added to food products such as cooking oils, margarines, butter, mayonnaise, salad dressings, shortenings, and other foods having an essential fat component.

Notes

1 FIM = Finnish marks. The average exchange rate during 1996 was U.S.$1 = FIM4.54.
2 Raisio Group, "Chief Executive's Review," Annual Report, 1996, p. 3.
3 The company was renamed Raisio Group plc in September 1997. Throughout this case we shall refer to the company as "Raisio Group."
4 Raisio Group, Annual Report, 1997, p. 38.
5 "Market Split over 'Miracle' Margarine," *Financial Times,* October 25, 1996, p. 26.
6 "Wonder spread from Finland," *The Grocer,* May 18, 1996, p. 9.
7 Raisio Group, Annual Report, 1997, p. 39.
8 Raisio Group, Annual Report, 1997, p. 39.
9 Raisio Group, Annual Report, 1997, p. 40.
10 J. Mellentin, "Trusted Brands Sell Healthy Hearts," *Functional Foods and Nutraceuticals,* June 2002.
11 See http://resources.bnet.com/topic/cholesterol+and+fda.html, accessed 29 October, 2009.
12 Raisio Group, Annual Report, 2000, p. 5.
13 Raisio Group, Annual Report, 2000, p. 19.

Case 12 Rivalry in Video Games

By summer 2009 the world video games industry had entered a new and unusual stage of its development. Between 1995 and 2006 the industry had been dominated by Sony, whose PlayStation had accounted for well over half of world console sales during the previous two product generations. However, in the new generation of video game consoles—the seventh since the industry's origins at the beginning of the 1970s—an entirely new situation had emerged. What was once believed to be a winner-take-all market was now a three-way battle between Sony, Microsoft and Nintendo with unusually small differences between them in market share.[1]

In terms of unit sales, Nintendo's Wii was the outright winner in all three of the world's major markets (see Table 12.1). However, in revenue terms, market shares were almost equal, reflecting the fact that the PS3 ($399 in the U.S.) was considerably more expensive than either the Xbox 360 ($199 in the U.S.) or the Wii ($149 in the

TABLE 12.1 Cumulative sales of leading models of video game console in major markets to March 31, 2009

Console	Japan	U.S.	Europe
Nintendo Wii (million)	8.1	20	15
Microsoft Xbox 360 (million)	1.0	14	9
Sony PlayStation 3 (million)	3.0	7	9

Sources: Estimates based on information from http://en.wikipedia.org/wiki/Seventh-generation_video_game_console; Forrester Research.

U.S.). The emergence of Nintendo as the new market leader after several years of lagging as a weak third to Sony and Microsoft was a major reversal of fortune. Many observers had written off Nintendo as a serious contender—it seemed to lack the financial or technological muscle to compete against Sony or Microsoft.

As Sony and Microsoft's product development teams prepared for the next generation of competition—both companies were rumored to be planning the launch of new consoles in 2012—the unexpected success of Nintendo's Wii had created considerable confusion for their video game strategies.

The Nintendo Wii had challenged several deeply entrenched assumptions about the video game industry. The evolutionary trajectory of the video game console had been perceived to be towards greater multifunctionality. One of the reasons that Sony and Microsoft had placed so much emphasis on their video game businesses and devoted so many resources to them was because they viewed the video game console as a general-purpose home entertainment device and a mechanism for linking with the internet. As a result, both Sony and Microsoft viewed video game consoles not just as important products in their own right but as critical components of their strategies for building strength within the fast-moving market for home entertainment. For example, Sony had used the PS3 as its standard bearer in its standards battle with Toshiba over technical standards for high-definition video disks. Wii had severely dented this logic—it was a dedicated gaming machine with few of the general entertainment features of PS3 or Xbox 360.

Wii's success also pointed to a major shift in the market for video gaming. The conventional wisdom of the industry had been that the video games market was concentrated among males aged between 11 and 30 and in order to access this demographic group the console makers needed to court "hardcore gamers" when developing and launching new models. The way to attract these sophisticated, intensive consumers was through hardware with immense processing power and brilliant graphics and games that combined cinematic-quality and graphic realism with strong characters and complex storylines. Yet, Wii's main market was among casual gamers. Compared to PS3 and Xbox 360 it was seriously underpowered in terms of both processing speed and graphics. The appeal of its games was the speed with which they could be learned rather than their sophistication.

In developing their video game strategies and their next-generation consoles, a critical issue for Sony and Microsoft was whether Wii was an outlier. If it was, the two companies could continue with the strategic logic that had guided their efforts since the beginning of the twenty-first century. If it was not, then Sony and Microsoft had better imitate the key elements of the Wii strategy. The stakes were high. In recent years the world market for video game hardware and software was about $25 billion. The fact

FIGURE 12.1 Worldwide unit sales of video game consoles by product generation

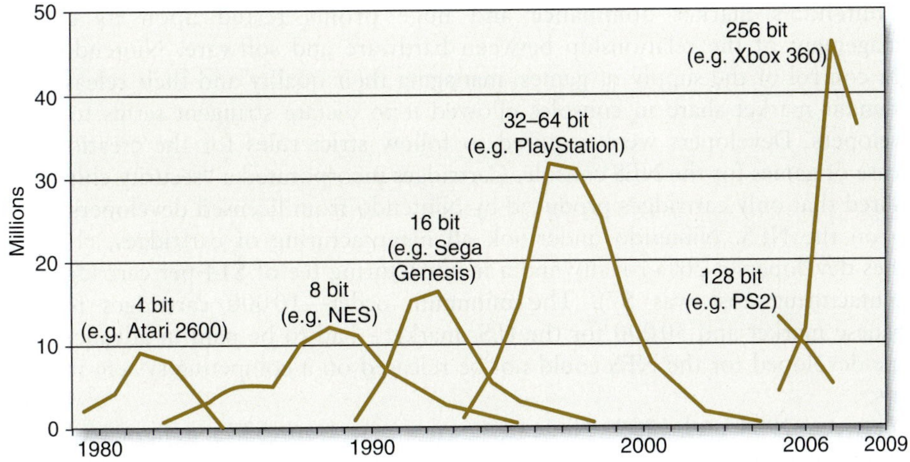

that every new generation of consoles had surpassed the sales of its predecessor (see Figure 12.1), reinforced both firms' interest in capturing market leadership in the future.

History of the Video Game Industry, 1972–2007

Atari and First and Second Generation Consoles: 1972–1985

The home video games market emerged during the late 1970s as an extension of arcade video games. The first generation of home video consoles were dedicated machines that embodied a single game. One of the first of these was *Pong*, created by Nolan Bushnell in 1972. He formed Atari to market this game player. In 1976 Atari was acquired by Warner Communications, Inc.

The second generation of players featured 4-bit processors and interchangeable cartridges. Bushnell designed the Atari 2600 home video game console, which, following the release of *Space Invaders* (1979) and *Pac-Man* (1981), unleashed a craze for video games. By 1982 Atari held almost 80% of the video game market.

Atari was unable to prevent independent software developers from marketing games for the Atari 2600. During 1982, 20 new suppliers of Atari-compatible consoles entered the market and 350 new game titles were released in that year. Declining sales of consoles and oversupply of games caused video game sales to decline from $3 billion in 1982 to $100 million in 1985, resulting in massive losses for Warner.

Nintendo and Third Generation Consoles: 1986–1991

In 1983, Nintendo, the leading Japanese supplier of arcade video games, released its 8-bit Famicom home video system. The U.S. launch of Famicom—renamed the Nintendo Entertainment System (NES)—in fall 1985 was a huge success, selling over a million units during the first year. Nintendo Entertainment System's sales were driven by a series of games created by legendary games developer Sigeru Miyamota: *Donkey Kong*, *Legend of Zelda* and *Super Mario Brothers* (which eventually sold 40 million copies worldwide). By 1988, Nintendo had an 80% market share of the $2.3 billion U.S. video games industry.

Nintendo's market dominance and huge profits rested upon its careful management of the relationship between hardware and software. Nintendo kept tight control of the supply of games, managing their quality and their releases. Its dominant market share in consoles allowed it to dictate stringent terms to game developers. Developers were required to follow strict rules for the creation and release of games for the NES console. Cartridges incorporated a "security chip" that ensured that only cartridges produced by Nintendo from licensed developers could run on the NES. Nintendo undertook all manufacturing of cartridges, charging games developers a 20% royalty and a manufacturing fee of $14 per cartridge (the manufacturing cost was $7). The minimum order—10 000 cartridges for the Japanese market and 50 000 for the U.S. market—had to be paid in advance. Any game developed for the NES could not be released on a competing system for two years.

Between 1984 and 1992, Nintendo's sales rose from $286 million to $4417 million. By 1990, one-third of U.S. and Japanese households owned an NES and in both countries its share of the home video console market exceeded 90%. Nintendo's return on equity over the period was 23.1%, while its stock market value exceeded that of both Sony and Nissan during most of 1990–1.

Sega and Fourth Generation Consoles: 1992–5

Sega's origins, like Atari and Nintendo, were in arcade games machines. Sega launched its 16-bit Genesis home video system in Japan in October 1988 and in the U.S. in September 1989. Despite graphics and sound that were superior to Nintendo's 8-bit system, sales of Genesis were initially sluggish until the introduction of *Sonic the Hedgehog* in June 1991. With strong support from independent games developers, 130 software titles were available for the Genesis by September 1991.

Nintendo launched its 16-bit machine, the Nintendo Super-NES, in September 1991. Its huge installed base, brand awareness, and distribution strength, allowed it to maintain its leadership in Japan. However, in the U.S. and Europe, Sega's bigger library of 16-bit titles (320, compared with 130 for Nintendo by January 1993) allowed it to split the market with Nintendo.

Sony PlayStation and Fifth Generation Consoles: 1995–8

The new generation of 32-bit consoles was initiated by Sega with the launch of its Saturn console in November 1994. A month later Sony introduced its PlayStation console—the result of a six-year development effort led by Sony's video games guru, Ken Kutaragi. Both PlayStation and Saturn used CD-ROMs rather than cartridges. However, PlayStation was launched with an impressive number of new game titles—the result of courting top games developers, financing game development and providing comprehensive software development tools. Sony also entered with a powerful array of resources: a strong brand reputation, global distribution capability and content from its movie division. Its launch of PlayStation was well-orchestrated and supported by a massive advertising budget—prelaunch promotion included a number of cryptic and ambiguous advertisements that created strong interest within the gamer community. Sega ill-coordinated its Saturn system—few game titles, haphazard distribution and a shortage of manufacturing capacity meant that Sony was able to overtake Sega's early lead.

Meanwhile, Nintendo attempted to recapture market leadership by leapfrogging Sony in technology. The N-64 system—launched in Japan in June 1996, in the U.S. in September 1996 and in Europe in the spring of 1997—used a 64-bit processor and came with several highly popular new games, including *Super Mario 64*. Although the N-64 had a big price advantage over PlayStation ($199 compared to $299) it retained cartridge storage of games. The production of cartridges involved higher fixed costs and did not allow the flexibility to quickly produce and distribute additional copies of hit games.

The result was that Sony pursued a different software strategy from Nintendo. While Nintendo concentrated on a smaller number of big-selling games (the average N-64 title sold over 400,000 units in 1997), Sony went for a much bigger library of games (over 300 titles at any point of time) many of which targeted minority preferences (the average PlayStation game sold 69 000 copies). The outcome was leadership for the PlayStation in all the world's major markets.

The Sixth Generation: Sony versus Microsoft, 1999–2005

The 128-bit generation of video game consoles was inaugurated by Sega's launch of its Dreamcast console in November 1998. It most innovative feature was the capacity for internet connectivity which allowed interactive games playing. Despite a successful initial launch—900 000 units were sold in Japan and 1.5 million in the U.S. during its first three months of their respective launches—Dreamcast failed to deliver a knockout blow to Sony's market leadership. The advantages of 128-bit over 64-bit technology were marginal and standard internet connections did not support fast-action interactive play. Sega attracted limited support from independent developers and failed to find a killer app for its Dreamcast.

On March 4, 2000, Sony launched PlayStation 2 (PS2) in Japan. Although 17 months behind Dreamcast, Sony's periodic leakage of information about PS2 had supported intense pre-release interest in PS2 and had continually undermined Sega's efforts to popularize Dreamcast. Kutaragi's brief had been to design a games machine with performance that exceeded any PC and with graphics processing power ten times that of the original PlayStation. With cinematic-style graphics, a DVD player and the potential for internet connectivity, PS2 aspired to be a multifunctional tool for accessing the internet, offering online games, e-commerce, email, and playing music and videos. According to Kazuo Hirai, president of Sony U.S.: "PlayStation 2 is not the future of video games entertainment, it is the future of entertainment, period."

Yet, despite billions of dollars spent on product development, new manufacturing plants and a massive worldwide advertising campaign, PS2's launch was marred by a shortage of key components—notably the graphics synthesizer (made by Sony) and the "Emotion Engine" microprocessor (made by Toshiba)—resulting in a shortage of PS2s for the critical U.S. Christmas shopping period. There was also a lack of software. The power and sophistication of PS2, together with its technical quirks, created complex problems for developers—most PS2 launch titles were revisions of earlier titles.

For all the massive resources that Sony brought to the battleground for the new generation, success was far from assured—in November 2001 the industry's competitive landscape was transformed by the entry of Microsoft. The software giant's entry was seen as symbolizing the potential of video games consoles. Once viewed as children's toys, games consoles were emerging as the primary tool for electronic entertainment, with the ability to offer movies, music and many of the communications functions currently performed by PCs.

The Xbox was a technology breakthrough: "Arguably the most powerful games console ever made, developed after consultation with more than 5000 gamers and games creators, it has a staggering array of features: an internal hard disk with a 733MHz processor, 64MB of memory, a DVD player, Dolby Digital 5.1 Surround Sound and an Ethernet port that makes it the only game console that's internet-ready and broadband-enabled."[2] Yet, with successive generations of consoles, technological capabilities were becoming less and less a distinguishing factor and the critical differentiator—software—was a problem for Microsoft. Xbox was launched with 19 games available, compared with 200 for PS2.

Despite a successful U.S. launch with 1.5 million sold in the six-week Christmas shopping period, Japan proved to be a difficult market for Xbox—not only were launch sales disappointing but Xbox's reputation was damaged by complaints that it caused scratching of CDs and DVDs. Microsoft's ability to establish itself in a strong second place to Sony rested on three factors: Microsoft's formidable reputation in IT, its launch of blockbuster games *Halo* and *Halo2*, and Xbox's online capabilities. In November 2002, Microsoft launched its Xbox Live online gaming service with interactive gaming and direct downloading of new games. A few days after the launch of Xbox, Nintendo joined the fray with its GameCube console.

The major casualties of the intense competition between Sony and Microsoft were Sega and Nintendo. Despite massive price cutting, Dreamcast sales went into sharp decline even before Microsoft's entry. At the end of 2000, Sega announced its withdrawal from video games hardware to focus on software. Meanwhile Nintendo was trailing both Sony and Microsoft in sales. By December 2006, Sony had sold around 111 million PS2s, compared to 24 million Xboxes, 21 million GameCubes and over 10 million Dreamcasts.

The Seventh Generation: Nintendo Bounces Back

The next round of competition in video game consoles—the seventh generation—featured the three survivors from the previous round: Sony, Microsoft and Nintendo. However, both Sony and Microsoft believed that the market was tending towards a duopoly. Nintendo had neither the financial nor the technological resources to match those of Sony and Microsoft. Yet, these new round of competition would feature some major changes in the competitive dynamics of the video game industry and some surprising reversals of fortune.

Microsoft Xbox 360

The first of the seventh generation video game consoles was Microsoft's Xbox 360 released on November 25, 2005. Xbox 360 was the first major console with a near simultaneous global launch as opposed to a phased rollout. The Japanese launch occurred just two weeks after the North American launch. The launch also features a major shift in the market positioning of Xbox. Compared with the original Xbox, which emphasized processing power and focused on hardcore gamers, Xbox 360's positioning eschewed technology in favor of versatility, design and coolness. The Xbox 360 strategy emphasized the hardware's multifunctionality for home entertainment and Microsoft's strong online presence. Through Xbox Live, users could purchase and download video games, in-game extras such as weapons and costumes, and movies and TV shows—including high-definition TV shows.

Sony PS3

Meanwhile, Sony's launch of its PS3 was dogged with multiple delays. Most of the problems related to the technological ambitiousness of the hardware. PS3's revolutionary multicore cell processor, developed jointly with IBM and Toshiba, proved difficult and expensive to manufacture—it was estimated that each cell processor cost Sony $230 per unit. Even more problematic was the delayed Blu-ray DVD drive, the initial production of which was believed to cost about $350 per unit. Merrill Lynch estimated that the total cost of the components for the PS3 could amount to $900 per unit.[3]

The Blu-ray drive was a central element of Sony's strategy. It was engaged in a fierce standards battle with Toshiba over the technical format of the next generation of high definition DVDs. PS3 was to be a key product in gaining market acceptance of Blu-ray.

Software was another problem for PS3. The complexity and power of the hardware extended the potential and the cost of games written for PS3. Software development costs were estimated at four or five times those of PS2. To encourage developers to write for PS3, Sony was obliged to cut its royalties. At its initial launch, Sony had 15 titles available for PS3, although few made full use of PS3's technical capabilities. The most popular of the new games was *Resistance: Fall of Man.*

PS3's launch in Japan on November 11, 2006 and in North America on November 17 was marred by lack of product. Following both launches, PS3s were selling on online auction sites in Japan and the U.S. at a substantial premium to their retail list prices. The European and Australian launches were set for March 23, 2007. One of the results of product shortage was continuing strength of Sony's PS2. During the critical month of December 2006, Americans bought 1.4 million PS2s, outselling PS3 (491 000 units), Xbox 360 (1.1 million units) and Nintendo Wii (604 000 units).

Nintendo Wii

One of the biggest surprises of the new round of competition was the strong initial showing of Nintendo's Wii. Technologically, the Nintendo Wii lacked the advanced features of either the Xbox 360 or PS3; its primary innovative feature was its remote wand-like controller that was sensitive to a range of hand movements. As a result, Nintendo claimed that its Wii was more intuitive than other consoles and could be learned more easily. This linked with a marketing strategy that aimed to recruit new games players and targeted a very broad demographic—including older consumers. Wii was launched in North America on November 19, 2006, on December 2 in Japan and December 8 in Europe. The launch was accompanied by 16 new games for Wii—of which several were new versions of existing franchises (for example, *Legend of Zelda: Twilight Princess).* Nintendo also mounted its biggest ever advertising campaign.

Table 12.2 compares the rival seventh generation consoles. Table 12.3 shows unit sales of leading video game consoles across the different product generations.

TABLE 12.2 Comparison of seventh-generation games consoles

Console	Hardware	Connectivity	DVD	Games	Price (December 2006)
Sony PS3	Cell Broadband Engine 550 MHz RSK GPU HDTV-capable	*20 GB version:* Bluetooth 2.0, an ethernet port and four USB docks. *60 GB version:* Compact flash, SD and memory stick duo, WiFi.	Integrated Blu-Ray player. Backwards compatible with DVD	50 titles available at end of 2006	*20GB version:* $499 *60GB version:* $599
Microsoft Xbox360	IBM Xenon, Power-PC CPU 500MHz ATI custom GPU HDTV-capable	Option to purchase WiFi adapter. *Core version:* Three USB docks, ethernet port *20GB version:* Wireless controllers	DVD player. Additional HD-DVD drive available for $199	130 titles at end of 2006 (of which 65 allow interactive play through Xbox Live). Backwards compatible	*Core version:* $299 *20 GB version:* $399
Nintendo Wii	IBM Broadway Power-PC CPU GPU developed with ATI EDTV video output	Bluetooth, two USB docks, SD slot, internet via IEEE 802.11 or a Wii LAN adaptor	No current DVD playback. Plans to launch integrated DVD version in Japan in 2007	c. 30 titles at time of launch. Backwards compatible with GameCube	$250

TABLE 12.3 Worldwide sales of video game consoles by platform (millions)

	Second generation	Third generation	Fourth generation	Fifth generation	Sixth generation	Seventh generation (to end-March 2009)
Nintendo	–	NES: 60	Super NES: 49	N-64: 32.9	GameCube: 21.2	Wii: 50.4
Sega	–	Master System: 13	MegaDrive/ Genesis: 29	Saturn: 9.3	Dreamcast: 10.6	–
Sony	–	–	–	PlayStation:100	PS2: 140	PS3: 26.7
Microsoft	–	–	–	–	Xbox: 24.0	Xbox 360: 30.2
Others	Atari 2600, Fairfield Channel F, Magnavox Odyssey	Atari 7800: <0.3	NEC TurboGrafx: 11	3DO: 1.2		

Source: Various newspaper articles.

The Video Games Industry in 2009

The Video Games Market

During 2009, the world video games industry was experiencing contraction after consumer expenditures hit a peak in 2007 and 2008. Unit sales for all three leading consoles were down sharply—partly as a result of market saturation and partly as a result of global recession. Sales of games had contracted too—refuting the widely held assumption that video games were recession-proof. In the U.S. the decline in consumer expenditure was especially severe (see Figure 12.2).

However, most observers believed that the recent slump was cyclical rather than an indicator of a longer term decline. As a form of entertainment, video game playing was continuing to grow. In the U.S. over 40% of households owned video game consoles and annual expenditures on consoles and games exceeded cinema box office receipts. Although prices on consoles had been cut during 2008 and 2009, video games consoles had not suffered the same decline in prices that had afflicted computers.

Central to the long-term expansion of the video games market was a broadening of the consumer base. Not only was video game playing expanding from Japan, North America and Western Europe to most of the world—its demographic appeal was broadening. Once the preserve of teenage boys, by 2008, the majority of the age group 18–44 were video games players and even among the 55–64 age group, 24% played video games. Female participation had also increased strongly. While children who grew up playing video games continue to do so as adults, game preferences changed greatly with age. Adolescents were more concerned with what

FIGURE 12.2 Worldwide consumer expenditure on video game hardware and software, 1990–2009

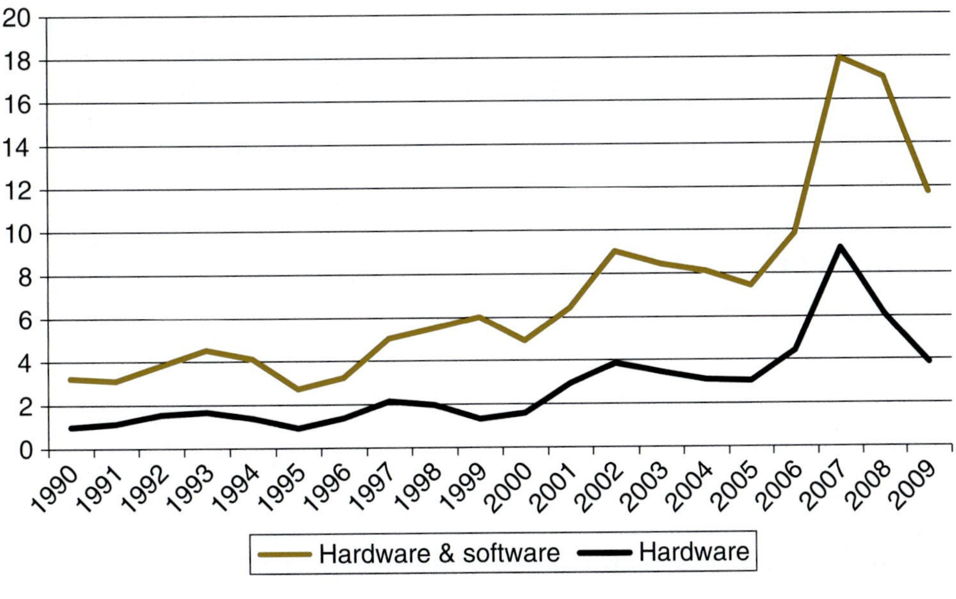

was "in" and "hot." The adult market comprises numerous niches, each with an interest in a different type of game. Adults like titles that fit in with their lifestyle and interests. Sports-based games were very popular among adult males. However, in terms of intensity of game playing, teenage boys remained clear leaders: U.S. males between the ages of 12 and 17 with a video game console in their home devoted an average of 14 hours a week to game playing. Females in the same age bracket played an average of 4 hours a week. The popularity of Nintendo's Wii had contributed substantially to the growth of video gaming among adults and females.

The growth of video games playing had opened up an entirely new source of revenue for video games publishers: advertising. Product placement within video games generated advertising revenues of $56 million in 2005 in the U.S. alone. Both Microsoft and Google acquired advertising agencies specializing in video game advertisement placement.

Software

Each video game console supplier ("platform provider") licensed third-party software companies to develop and distribute games for its system. Two types of company were involved in video games software: video games; publishers, which were responsible for financing, manufacturing, marketing and distributing video games, and video game developers, which developed the software. Video game publishing was increasingly dominated by a few large companies—the most prominent being Electronic Arts (see Table 12.4). Typically, the software publisher submitted a proposal or a prototype to the console maker for evaluation and approval. The licensing agreement between the software company and the hardware provider gave the console maker the right to approve game content and control over release timing, and provided for a royalty payment from the software company. Game developers were paid a royalty, typically between 5% and 15%, based on the publishers' revenues from the game.

Escalating game development costs were a result of the demand for multifeatured, 3-D, cinematic-quality games made possible by increasingly powerful consoles. Atari's *Pac-Man* released in 1982 was created by a single developer and cost about $100 000. *Halo 2* released for the Xbox in 2004 involved 190 developers and cost $40 million. By late 2006, *Halo 2* had sold 8 million copies at $50 each. For the new generation of consoles, most games cost more than $12 million to develop. In terms of both costs and revenue patterns, video games closely resembled movies, with

TABLE 12.4 Share of U.S. video games market by publisher, 2006

Publisher	Market share by value (%)
Electronic Arts	19.8
Konami	9.8
Take-Two Interactive	9.9
Activision	8.8
Others	52.7

Source: From www.researchandmarkets.com/reports/354861/video_game_industry.htm.

TABLE 12.5 Top-selling console games in the U.S., 2008 (by units sold)

Title/platform	Publisher	Release date	Units sold (000s)	Av. retail price ($)
Wii Play (Wii)	Nintendo	Dec. '06	5280	50
Mario Kart Wii (Wii)	Nintendo	Apr. '08	5000	50
Wii Fit (Wii)	Nintendo	May. '08	4530	90
Super Smash Bros. Brawl (Wii)	Nintendo	Mar. '08	4170	50
Grand Theft Auto IV (Xbox 360)	Rockstar Games	Apr. '08	3290	40
Call of Duty: World at War (Xbox 360)	Activision	Nov. '08	2750	60
Gears of War 2 (Xbox 360)	Microsoft	Nov. '08	2310	40
Grand Theft Auto IV (PS3)	Rockstar Games	Apr. '08	1890	40
Madden NFL 09 (XBox 360)	Electronic Arts	Aug. '08	1870	30
Mario Kart DS (DS)	Nintendo	Nov. '05	1650	40

similar success rates—a mere few became money-spinning blockbusters. Table 12.5 shows the top selling titles of 2008. Like movies too, creating a brand franchise through a succession of sequels had become a key competitive strategy. Rising development costs were a key factor causing consolidation among publishers.

As the power of the publishers had grown and the costs of development had risen, so exclusivity ties had disappeared from most licensing contracts—most leading games titles were cross-platform. For example, several titles that were once PS3 exclusives have been released simultaneously on Xbox 360. These include *Grand Theft Auto IV*, *Final Fantasy XIII*, *Virtual Fighter*, and *Devil May Cry*. Wii has several exclusive titles, most of which were developed by Nintendo.

The development of video games required a blend of technology and creative talent. The development process included game development and design, prototyping, programming, art, computer graphic design, animation, sound engineering, technical writing, editorial review and quality assurance. It took 18 to 36 months to complete a new title based on a new platform. To "port" an existing title to a different platform took up to 9 months. Many games were based on characters and themes that were either owned by the game developer or licensed from third parties. The licensing fees paid by software publishers for exclusive rights to the intellectual property of media companies and sports organizations grew substantially between 1998 and 2002. Securing the license to produce a game based on a hit movie (for example, *Harry Potter)* could cost several million dollars. In the sports market, licenses paid to sports leagues (NFL, NHL, MLB, NBA, FIFA) typically involved an upfront payment, plus a royalty of 5% to 15% of the wholesale price for each unit sold.

Not only did software sales exceed hardware sales—software was responsible for virtually all of the industry's profit. The console makers followed a "razors and blades" business model: the consoles were sold at a loss; profits were recouped on software sales—both games developed internally and royalties received from third-party games publishers. The result was strongly cyclical earnings for the platform providers: the launch of a new console would result in massive cash outflows; only with a substantial installed base would the platform provider begin to recoup the investment made.

The Console Suppliers

For the console makers, 2009 was a troubling year. Sony and Microsoft had achieved revenues that were not far behind Nintendo but both were still losing money on their video game businesses. During the first two years of product launch, losses were to be expected—but Xbox 360 had been on the market for almost four years and PS3 for almost three years. Most observers believed that these losses were primarily the result of the costs associated with the technologically advanced specifications of the two consoles. This was particularly the case with PS3. By contrast, as a result of its inexpensive components, Nintendo had been earning a contribution from its Wii from the outset.

Moreover, profits from software were failing to fill the gap. Only 3.8 PS3 games per console were sold in the U.S. by March 2008 and 3.5 Wii games per console. By contrast, each Xbox 360 user bought an average of 7.5 games. This pointed towards the emergence of Xbox as the preferred platform both for serious game players and for games developers.

For Sony, the losses associated with PS3 pointed to the challenges of designing a console that would be a favorite among game players while also establishing the video game console as a general home entertainment device. The decision to incorporate a Blu-ray DVD player in PS3 had little to do its ability to offer a superior video gaming experience—there were few games that exploited its functionality and few consumers had HDTV.

As the three leading console providers looked towards the future, two issues preoccupied them. First, what factors would determine which of them would emerge as a leader in the competitive battle for the next generation of video game consoles? Second, as the games developers and publishers grew in size and strength, had the console makers lost the capacity to dictate industry evolution and with it the capacity to reap profits?

Appendix: Financial Data on the Console Manufacturers

Nintendo (Yen, billions)

	1998	1999	2000	2001	2002	2003	2004	2005	2006	2007	2008
Total sales	534	573	531	463	554	504	514	515	509	966	1672
Operating income	172	156	145	85	119	100	110	113	91	226	487
Net income	84	86	56	97	106	67	33	87	98	174	257
Op. income/Av. total assets (%)	10.6	9.9	6.1	9.7	9.5	8.9	10.5	9.7	7.9	19.5	27.0
Return on av. equity (%)	14.0	12.9	7.7	12.2	12.0	7.4	3.7	9.6	10.4	16.8	11.0

Sony (Yen, billions)

	1998	1999	2000	2001	2002	2003	2004	2005	2006	2007	2008
Sales *of which:*	6761	6804	6687	7315	7578	7474	7496	7160	7475	1016	1284
Games	700	760	631	661	1004	936	754	703	918	974	1219

Sony **(Yen, billions)**

	1998	1999	2000	2001	2002	2003	2004	2005	2006	2007	2008
Operating income *of which:*	526	348	141	225	135	185	99	114	191	71	374
Games	117	137	77	(51)	84	113	68	43	9	(232)	(124)
Net income (loss)	222	179	122	17	15	116	89	164	124	126	369
Op. income/Av. total assets (%)	6.7	5.5	3.7	3.1	1.7	2.2	1.1	1.2	1.9	0.6	2.9
Return on av. equity (%)	13.2	9.8	6.1	0.1	0.1	4.8	3.6	6.3	4.1	3.94	(3.08)

Microsoft **($, millions)**

	2000	2001	2002	2003	2004	2005	2006	2007	2008
Sales *of which:*	22 956	25 296	28 365	32 187	36 835	39 788	44 282	51 122	60 420
Home & entertainment	n.a.	n.a.	2453	2748	2731	3110	4292	6069	8140
Operating income *of which:*	11 006	11 720	11 910	13 217	9034	14 561	16 472	18 524	22 492
Home and entertainment	n.a.	n.a.	(847)	(924)	(1011)	(451)	(1283)	426	(1969)
Net income	9421	7346	7829	9993	8168	12 254	12 599	14 065	17 681
Op. income/Av. total assets (%)	24.4	21.2	18.8	17.9	10.3	17.6	23.6	29.3	30.9
Return on av. equity (%)	26.9	16.6	15.7	17.6	11.7	19.9	28.6	16.45	42.47

n.a. = not available.

Notes

1 Successive generations of video game consoles have conventionally been designated according to processor bit size. In practice, bit size is a poor indicator of processing power. Beyond 32 bits, bit size has little to do with console performance—processor clock speed is much more important.

2 "Out of the Box at Last," *Financial Times* (Creative Business section), November 20, 2001.

3 "Delays likely for Sony's PlayStation 3," *Financial Times,* February 20, 2006.

Case 13 DVD War of 2005–8: Blu-ray versus HD-DVD

On Tuesday February 19, 2008, Toshiba announced that it would stop manufacturing HD-DVD DVD discs and players. The announcement marked the end of the battle between Toshiba and Sony to establish the format standard for the next generation of digital versatile discs (DVDs).[1]

In the history of standards wars, the HDV format war was surprisingly short. The coalescing of technological development of next-generation DVDs around two competing formats can be traced to 2002. However, open warfare did not commence until summer 2005 when attempts to reach agreement on a single standard finally broke down. Products featuring the new technologies did not appear until April 2006 in the case of HD-DVD and June 2006 in the case of Blu-ray. Yet, after a mere 19 months during which products based upon one or other of the two formats competed for market supremacy, it was all over. Over a period of few weeks, Toshiba's position crumbled and Sony emerged victorious.

The Technology

The optical disc was invented in 1958 by David Paul Gregg whose patent was registered in 1961. The first commercial product using the technology was the laserdisc system launched by Philips and MCA in 1978. However, optical discs were superseded by video cassettes.

The breakthrough for optical discs was Philips and Sony Corporation's development of the compact disc in 1983, which became the dominant medium for audio recordings. The CD was followed by the DVD which was introduced into Japan in 1996, the U.S. in 1997, and Europe in 1998. The successful launch of the DVD was the result of an industry-wide forum that forced the proponents of different formats to agree a common technological standard. This industry group became the DVD Forum.

The impetus for developing a high-definition DVD came from the emergence of high-definition television (HDTV) during the 1990s. With HDTV seen as the next wave in consumer electronics there came the need for a storage medium capable of holding high definition images. The distinctive feature of both HD-DVD and Blu-ray formats was the use of short-wavelength blue-laser technology instead of the red lasers used in earlier generations. Blue lasers allowed a vast increase in the amount of data that could be stored on a standard 12 centimeter disc.

The key difference between HD-DVD and Blu-ray was in the thickness of the DVD's protective plastic layer: the HD-DVD retained the 0.6 mm thickness common to conventional DVDs; Blu-ray featured a 0.1 mm coating. The result was that a dual-layer Blu-ray DVD could hold 50GB (gigabytes) of data, compared to 30GB for a dual-layer HD-DVD. This compared to 8.5GB for a conventional DVD.

For content owners—film studios in particular—Blu-ray had an additional advantage. While both formats incorporated the new AACS (Advanced Access Content System) anti-piracy device, Blu-ray included an additional layer of protection. Microsoft was concerned that the additional protection provided by Blu-ray restricted the ability of PC users to integrate video images with other computer functions. In July 2005, Bill Gates argued that the Blu-ray standard had to change to "work more smoothly with personal computers."

Blu-ray's technical refinements came at some cost. HD-DVDs could be manufactured by modifying the production line used for making ordinary DVDs: "It is a simple and low-cost step to go from manufacturing standard DVDs to producing HD-DVDs," said Mark Knox, a Toshiba spokesman. "The changes [for a factory] cost less than $150,000."[2] Blu-ray discs required major changes in manufacturing processes and manufacturing equipment. The implication was that for content owners and consumers, Blu-ray discs would be more costly.

Neither format could be played on existing DVD players. Moreover, HD-DVD players could not play Blu-ray discs and vice-versa. Hence, movie studios and video games publishers faced the prospect of having to stock media in three formats: HD-DVD, Blu-ray and conventional DVDs. Both HD-DVD and Blu-ray players were backward compatible— they could play conventional DVDs.

As far as economizing on the number of formats that content producers needed to manufacture and distributors needed to stock, one of the advantages envisaged by the HD-DVD camp was the ability to produce an HD-DVD disc of a game or movie that also included a standard DVD version of the content. In September 2006, Toshiba announced: "Toshiba, in collaboration with disc manufacturer Memory Tech Japan, has successfully combined a HD-DVD and DVD to a single 3-layer, twin-format disc. The resulting disc conforms to DVD standards so it can be played on DVD players, and also on HD-DVD players."[3]

Moreover, the benefits of Blu-ray's greater storage capacity were not readily apparent at the time. Existing high-definition formats for full-length movies could be easily accommodated on both types of disc. Blu-ray's ability to "to fit an entire season of a television series" on a single disc, and "offer multiple versions of the same film" seemed marginal benefits to most consumers. The case for Blu-ray over HD-DVD seemed to rest primarily on its potential for accommodating future developments in video entertainment: "You open up a whole new spectrum of creative possibilities," says Tim Baxter, senior vice-president of strategic marketing at Sony Corp. of America. "This format is about gearing up for this holiday season and the next 10 years."[4]

Building Bandwagons

In February 2002 the Blu-ray Disc Association was formed with founder members Hitachi, Panasonic, Pioneer, Philips, Samsung, Sharp, Sony, and Thomson. It was soon joined by Dell Computer, Mitsubishi and TDK.[30] The HD-DVD Promotion Group comprised Toshiba, NEC, Sanyo, Microsoft, Kenwood, Intel, Venturer Electronics and Memory-Tech Corporation. Some companies were members of both groups. These included Hewlett Packard (HP), LG, Acer, Asus, Lite-On, Onkyo, Meridian and Alpine.

Blu-ray was the favorite among the leading film studios: Disney, Fox, Lions Gate, MGM, and of course Sony Pictures had aligned with Blu-ray, while Universal was the only major studio that joined the HD-DVD camp. Paramount (including subsidiaries Nickelodeon Movies, MTV Films, DreamWorks Pictures and DreamWorks Animation) and Warner Bros. supported both standards.

Product Roll-out

Even while both camps were developing products incorporating the two incompatible standards, attempts to avoid a costly format war continued. However, on August 22, 2005, the Blu-ray Disc Association and DVD Forum announced that the negotiations to unify their standards had failed. From then on the race was on to bring discs and hardware to market as quickly as possible in order to build market share leadership.

HD-DVD was first to market with the Toshiba HD-A1 launched in the U.S. on April 18, 2006 at a retail price of $499. The Samsung BD-P1000 was the first Blu-ray disc player. It was launched at the end of June 2006 at a retail price of $999.

In April 2006, Universal and Warner Brothers both began releasing HD-DVDs of existing movies at prices of between $29 and $35. Sony Pictures was first to release movies on Blu-ray—with an initial release of 8 movies at $28.95 to coincide with the launch of the Samsung BD-P1000. However, the early Blu-ray movies suffered from major quality problems. Several movies suffered from poor film-to-disc transfers and until October 2006 only single-layer recording was possible on Blu-ray discs which limited their capacity to 25 gigabytes.[5]

The other two major hardware products incorporating the new-generation DVD drives were personal computers and video game consoles. Both Toshiba and Sony were major players in personal computers. Toshiba released an HD-DVD-compatible notebook, the Qosmio G35-AV650.

In May 2006, Sony launched a Vaio notebook with a Blu-ray drive. By the end of 2006, NEC and HP had introduced notebooks with HD-DVDs, while Dell joined Sony in adding Blu-ray to one of its notebook models.

In video game consoles, the market leaders were Sony with its PlayStation and Microsoft with its Xbox. The battle for the next generation of consoles began with Microsoft's launch of its Xbox 360 in November 2005. The Xbox 360 came with a standard DVD drive. In November 2006, Microsoft launched a HD-DVD drive as a separate plug-in unit for its Xbox 360 priced at $200 in the U.S. and £130 in the U.K. Microsoft's unwillingness to include a built-in HD-DVD player was a result of, first, the lack of games developed to exploit HD-DVD capabilities and, second, its belief that online access to games would displace DVD distributed games within a few years.

For Sony, its new PS3 video game console formed a central component of its Blu-ray strategy. Sony's decision to launch its PS3 with a Blu-ray disc player was widely viewed as a strategic blunder. It delayed the launch of the PS3 giving Microsoft lead time of over a year in the new generation of consoles. It also greatly increased the cost. The cost and complexity of developing games that utilized the technical potential of Blu-ray meant that very few new high-definition games were available at launch. Launched at a price of $499 in the U.S., PS3 was seen as something of a desperate gamble by Sony, faced with the market momentum of Xbox 360 and the low-cost challenge of the Nintendo Wii. At $499 it was estimated that Sony would lose over $200 on every unit sold.

Video games developers and publishers were slower than the movie studios to sign up for one or other of the rival formats. However, on January 7, 2007, Sony received a major boost when Electronic Arts (the world's biggest games software company) and Vivendi Universal Games joined the Blu-ray association.

Distributors bore considerable cost burdens because of the standards war. The leading retailers (including Wal-Mart, Target and Best Buy) and movie distributors such as Blockbuster and Netflix felt obliged to carry both formats.

Shifting Alliances

The central battle was for the support of the movie studios. Despite the initial preference of the majority of the major studios for Blu-ray, financial and other incentives resulted in several defections. Early in 2005, Warner Brothers and Paramount had backed HD-DVD, but in October 2005 both announced support for both formats. However, in August 2007, Paramount and DreamWorks Animation SKG dropped Blu-ray and announced that their high-definition movies would be released exclusively on HD-DVD. The studios mentioned cost and technical advantages but most observers believed that the offer from Toshiba of $150 million in cash and promotional guarantees were a bigger factor. Sony's CEO, Sir Howard

Stringer, was particularly active in using his Hollywood connections to build support for Blu-ray among the studios.

Growing frustration with dual formats resulted in several distributors abandoning HD-DVD. In June 2007, Blockbuster, the largest U.S. movie rental company, adopted Blu-ray exclusively after test-marketing both formats and finding that over 70% of high definition rentals were Blu-ray discs. In July 2007, Target Corporation began carrying only Blu-ray standalone players in its stores.

During 2007, sales of Blu-ray decisively overtook sales of HD-DVD in both hardware and software, with PS3 providing a particularly strong boost for Blu-ray. Home Media Research estimated that for 2007 as a whole, Blu-ray outsold HD-DVD players by three to one in the U.S., 10 to one in Europe, and 100 to one in Japan.

A critical event in the battle was Warner Brothers' announcement on January 4, 2008 that it would drop support for HD-DVD from June 2008. The significance of Warner's move was that it was the biggest player in DVD movies. Toshiba responded by cutting the price of its HD-DVD players by up to 50%; however, there was little it could do to prevent the chain reaction that followed the Warner announcement. In January 2008, U.K. retailer Woolworths said it would stock only Blu-ray discs from March 2008. On February 11, 2008, Best Buy began recommending Blu-ray as the customer's digital format choice. Then, on February 15, 2008 Wal-Mart, the largest DVD retailer in the U.S., announced that it would discontinue HD-DVD products from June 2008. Also in February, Netflix, the largest online video rental service, began phasing out its HD-DVD inventory.

On February 19, 2008, Universal Studios—the only studio to have consistently supported HD-DVD from the outset—defected to Blu-ray. On the same day, Toshiba announced it would cease developing, manufacturing and marketing HD-DVD players and recorders. The next day Paramount, the remaining supporter of HD-DVD, announced its move to Blu-Ray.

Even before Toshiba's announcement the fate of HD-DVD was clear. On February 16, 2008, the *New York Times* published its obituary:

> HD-DVD, the beloved format of Toshiba and three Hollywood studios, died Friday after a brief illness. The cause of death was determined to be the decision by Wal-Mart to stock only high-definition DVDs and players using the Blu-ray format.
>
> There are no funeral plans . . .[6]

Costs and Benefits

No reliable data is available concerning the costs and benefits of the DVD war to the main participants. Clearly Toshiba was the chief loser in financial terms. The Nikkei business daily reported that for its financial year ending March 31, 2008, Toshiba was likely to book a 100 billion yen loss ($986 million) relating to the termination of its HD-DVD project.[7] However, most observers believed that the full cost—including R&D expenditures, incentive payments to partners, forced price reductions on hardware and inventory write-offs—would be much greater.

To what extent was Sony a winner? Its costs included not only the massive R&D expenditures on Blu-ray but also the costs of supporting its alliance partners, price cuts in hardware and software and the significant costs of delaying the launch of PS3 until Blu-ray was ready. Moreover, the revenues generated by Sony's Blu-ray technology would be limited, first, by Sony's offer of highly favorable licensing terms in order to attract supporters to the Blu-ray camp and, second, by the likelihood that the commercial life of Blu-ray would be short. Professor Pai-Ling Yin of MIT's Sloan School of Management argues:

> . . . technology markets are characterized by waves of innovation, where the latest and greatest of last year is replaced by the latest and greatest of next year. Joseph Schumpeter described this pattern as "the perennial gale of creative destruction." Blu-ray and HD-DVD are simply the next generation of discs, replacing the standard DVD of the last generation. Thus, there is but a limited amount of time (until the appearance of the next generation technology) for the firms and the technology of this generation to reap the rewards of being the shiny new item on the block.[8]

By failing to agree on a common standard, the time available to exploit the current generation of media storage technology before it is rendered obsolete was greatly reduced: "The reality is that relative to the sales that could have been garnered from faster and higher volumes of DVD players had Sony & Toshiba been able to come to some agreement, both firms have lost."[9]

Notes

1 The correct interpretation of the DVD acronym is a matter of dispute. The two most common are "digital versatile disc" and "digital video disc."

2 "Format Wars: Everyone Could End Up Losing," *Financial Times,* April 3, 2006.

3 See http://news.digitaltrends.com/news-article/11271/three-layer-disc-combines-dvd-hd-dvd, accessed October 17, 2009.

4 "Format Wars: Everyone Could End Up Losing," *Financial Times,* April 3, 2006.

5 "Two years of battle between HD-DVD and Blu-ray: a retrospective," www.engadgethd.com/2008/02/20/two-years-of-battle-between-hd-dvd-and-blu-ray-a-retrospective/, accessed November 12, 2008.

6 "Taps for HD-DVD as Wal-Mart Backs Blu-ray," *New York Times,* February 16, 2008.

7 "The Fall of HD-DVD Will Cost Toshiba $986 Million," March 17, 2008, www.dailytech.com/article.aspx?newsid=11069, accessed October 17, 2009.

8 "What Are the Lessons of the Blu-ray/HD-DVD Battle?" A Freakonomics Quorum, March 4, 2008, http://freakonomics.blogs.nytimes.com/2008/03/04/what-are-the-lessons-of-the-blu-rayhd-dvd-battle-a-freakonomics-quorum/, accessed November 12, 2008.

9 "What Are the Lessons of the Blu-ray/HD-DVD Battle?" A Freakonomics Quorum, March 4, 2008, http://freakonomics.blogs.nytimes.com/2008/03/04/what-are-the-lessons-of-the-blu-rayhd-dvd-battle-a-freakonomics-quorum/, accessed November 12, 2008.

Case 14 *New York Times*

Troubled Times for the "Good Gray Lady"

The early months of 2009 were a difficult period for the New York Times Company (NYT), publisher of the *New York Times* and *Boston Globe* and the owner of a number of regional titles as well as several nonprint media businesses. In common with other U.S. newspaper publishers, the NYT was suffering from the cyclical problem of cutbacks in advertising budgets and the long-term problem of declining readership as newspapers increasingly lost ground to online sources of information.

During January and February, the company was subject to repeated speculation concerning its ability to meet its financial obligations—in particular, the refinancing of a $400 million line of credit due to expire in May. In January the

TABLE 14.1 New York Times Company, Inc.: selected financial data ($000s, except where indicated)

	2008	2007	2006	2005	2004
Revenues	2 948 856	3 195 077	3 289 903	3 231 128	3 159 412
Operating costs	2 791 613	2 928 070	2 996 081	2 911 578	2 696 799
Impairment of assets	197 879	11 000	814 433	–	–
Gain on sale of assets	–	(28 578)	–	122 946	–
Operating (loss)/profit	(40 636)	227 429	(520 611)	442 496	462 613
Interest expense, net	47 790	39 842	50 651	49 168	41 760
Income from continuing operations	(66 139)	108 939	(568 171)	243 313	264 985
Discontinued operations – Broadcast Media Group	8300	99 765	24 728	15 687	22 646
Net income	(57 839)	208 704	(543 443)	253 473	287 631
Property, plant and equipment	1 353 619	1 468 013	1 375 365	1 401 368	1 308 903
Total assets	3 401 680	3 473 092	3 855 928	4 564 078	3 994 555
Total debt	1 059 375	1 034 979	1 445 928	1 396 380	1 058 847
Stockholders' equity	503 963	978 200	819 842	1 450 826	1 354 361
Return on average stockholders' equity (%)	−8	23	−48	18	21
Total debt to total capitalization (%)	68	51	64	49	44
Operating profit/revenues (%)	−1	7	−16	14	15
Current assets to current liabilities	0.60	0.68	0.91	0.95	0.84
Employees (full-time equivalent)	9346	10 231	11 585	11 965	12 300

Source: New York Times Company, Inc., 10-K Report, 2008.

company bought itself breathing space with a $250 million loan at 14% interest from the Mexican billionaire, Carlos Slim. In February it eliminated its dividend for the year.

The annual results for 2008 showed revenues contracting at a faster pace than the company could cut costs. Once impairment charges were taken into account (mainly relating to write-downs of goodwill and the masthead values), NYT made a net loss of almost $58 million (see Table 14.1).

The NYT's share price reflected the general pessimism concerning the company's prospects. In September 2008, its shares had been trading at above $14. On February 20, 2009, they closed at $3.44. At the shareholder's annual meeting on April 29, 2009, Board Chairman Arthur Sulzberger Jr. addressed the company's problems and the board's strategy for dealing with them:

> In our remarks this morning, both Janet Robinson, president and CEO of The New York Times Company, and I will talk about the actions we and our colleagues are taking to steer our organization through the current financial downturn, advertising decline and technological fragmentation—which, collectively, are having a brutal effect on all in the media business.
>
> As you will hear and see this morning, The New York Times Company is no exception. As the Times Company's board of directors and senior management

continue to lead our enterprise through this uncertain era, we are guided by four underlying premises:

- First, quality will remain the distinguishing feature of all that we have to offer;
- Second, business will continue to be difficult, but we are absolutely committed to creating greater shareholder value;
- Third, there is no one single solution that will return us to revenue growth;
- And fourth, we will aggressively go where our new thinking and analysis take us.

Let me expand on these last two thoughts: we recognize that the answers for national and international media outlets such as the *New York Times* and the *International Herald Tribune* will be different than those for our local papers such as the *Sarasota Herald-Tribune* and the *Wilmington Star-News*. And, of course, About.com faces yet a different set of issues and solutions.

Of all our properties, the *Boston Globe* has been most dramatically affected by the secular and cyclical forces that are roiling the entire media industry. We have responded by consolidating printing facilities, raising circulation prices and reducing headcount. But more needs to be done to align the *Globe*'s costs and revenues . . .

We know that there are considerable challenges before us, but past experience teaches us that the outcome will be determined by our ability to adhere to the formula that has successfully driven this Company for so long. That formula can be summed up in this thought: quality journalism attracts a quality audience which, in turn, attracts quality advertisers.

It is this idea, expressed various ways over numerous decades, which has seen The New York Times Company through previous grim economic periods and has enabled *The Times* to emerge as the world's most powerful journalistic voice. Our quality journalism is the fundamental asset our shareholders have. And just three days ago that quality was again recognized as five Pulitzer Prizes were awarded to the men and women of *The New York Times* . . .

Now let me turn to a basic question that I am repeatedly asked: Can quality journalism exist in this new economic environment?

Let me rephrase that question with the one we ask ourselves: How can we enhance our digital revenue sufficiently so that we have the financial foundation necessary to support our news gathering operations, be they at *The New York Times*, the *Boston Globe* or any of our regional news outlets?

At The New York Times Company, we are focusing on three key levers to achieve this essential goal: attracting more users, deepening their engagement and then earning revenue from their usage. To do all this effectively has and will continue to require our making bets on how this new medium will evolve and then making investments in that vision. This is certainly not an easy task, but our insights into human behavior and digital evolution are helping to guide us.

Throughout 2008 and the first months of 2009, we have continued to create a new form of web journalism that is both informative and compelling. Our goal is to respond to our audiences' demand for interactivity, community and multimedia, as well as news and information on an increasingly wide range of topics. We are aggressively responding to our readers' desire to do something with our content. Our readers want to share it, or blog it, or comment on it. They want to use our journalism as raw material for what they make . . .

> Our strategy is rooted in the fundamental premise that we must be OF the internet, not ON it, requiring all of us to move from merely publishing our content on the web to becoming full web publishers.
>
> Presently, we are doing this with an increasing battery of online initiatives, but we are not yet bringing in the revenue we will need in the long-term. We are currently examining a vast array of tactics and options that will enable us to adapt financially to the new realities of our business. As we chart our course toward a sustainable digital future, we have come to recognize with increasing clarity that online success will require substantial re-conceptualization, thoughtful execution, and a great willingness to take full advantage of the web, an amazing laboratory for entrepreneurs, technologists and, of course, journalists.
>
> While we have talked a lot about our Company's online efforts, I am sure that some shareholders wonder whether all this web activity portends the end of print.
>
> Of course not! . . . [A]pproximately 88% of our Company's revenues come from print. There are currently more than 830 000 readers who have subscribed to *The New York Times* for two years or more, what we call loyalists. This is up from 650 000 in the year 2000. Across the Company, circulation revenues made up 38% of our total in the first quarter, significantly higher than others in the industry and a sizeable and stable base. As other newspapers cut back on international and national coverage or, in some sad cases, cease operations, we believe there will be opportunities for *The Times* in print to fill this void, resulting in increased revenue from circulation, news services and other products.[1]

Sulzberger closed his presentation by reminding shareholders of the consistency and steadfastness of the NYT's long-term strategy:

> The path to our digital future is not a new one. Let me repeat something I said to my colleagues a decade ago, at my 1999 annual speech to the staff:
>
> "At the heart of this presentation are plans for ensuring that, a decade from now and a century from now, *The New York Times* will still be the leader in its field of quality journalism, regardless of how it is distributed. These plans entail our moving from a strategy focused on the specific products we produce to one built around our audience—*a quality audience strategy*. Our goal is to know our audience better than anyone else; to meet their informational and transactional needs—by ourselves where we can; in partnership with others when necessary; and to serve them in print and digitally, continuously and on-demand."
>
> Ten years later, we have done this and much more with the tools and platforms that are now at our disposal. We understand this audience and they come to us in what once would have been unimaginable numbers. Now, because of secular and cyclical changes that are transforming our marketplace, we are in the process of fundamentally re-conceptualizing our relationship with that audience.
>
> What does this mean?
>
> Specifically we are in the process of rethinking the value of what we are offering. As you will hear in the months ahead, we will be:
>
> - Engaging in a thoughtful analysis of brand loyalty and circulation revenue.
> - Exploring a new online financial strategy.

- Leveraging the added value we bring to advertisers in terms of brand, technology and thought leadership.
- And thinking about how mobiles, e-readers and social networking can be brought more deeply into the equation.

Fundamentally, we are taking an increasingly deeper look at the role that quality journalism plays in the twenty-first century. We will be determining how best to take what we know, and create a more effective business model. Of course, this search for long-term financial stability is taking place throughout the media industry and each enterprise will have its own answers.

At The New York Times Company, our new relationship with our audience will be guided by our cornerstone belief that world class news, opinion, photography, videography and blogging will grow in value as the interconnection between what happens in the world and the lives of our readers becomes more personal, immediate and direct.

This is why we unequivocally believe in our future.[2]

Sulzberger's faith in the future of the NYT was not widely shared. Skeptics pointed to the decline in newspaper circulation, the sharp decline in newspaper readership among the young, the shift of advertising from print media to online and the failure of the major newspapers to establish a viable business model for their online publishing. There were also concerns regarding the financial acumen of the family-controlled board of directors. In 2006, NYT's board rejected a bid led by former General Electric chairman, Jack Welch, to buy the *Boston Globe* for $600 million. The *Globe* had subsequently become the NYT's biggest cash drain. In 2007, NYT moved into a new $500 million headquarters in midtown Manhattan. Between 1997 and 2004 the company spent $3 billion on stock repurchases at an average price of $37. Some shareholders viewed Chairman Sulzberger, the great-grandson of the newspaper's founder, as part of the problem rather than its solution. However, with NYT's dual-class share structure, the Sulzberger family had been able to dominate the board ever since the NYT had gone public in 1969. Media tycoon, Rupert Murdoch, has referred to the *New York Times* as "his favorite train wreck" and puts the blame firmly on the shoulders of Arnold Sulzberger, who he blamed for loosening *The Times*' links with New York in his urge to make *The Times* a national newspaper.[3]

The New York Times Company in 2009

The Business

The NYT comprises two business segments:

- The News Media Group, which consists of:
  - The New York Times Media Group, which includes *The Times*, NYTimes.com, the *International Herald Tribune* and a New York City radio station, WQXR-FM;
  - The New England Media Group, which includes the *Boston Globe* (the *Globe*), Boston.com, the *Worcester Telegram and Gazette* and related web sites;

- The Regional Media Group, which includes 15 daily newspapers in Alabama, California, Florida, Louisiana and the Carolinas, plus other print publications.
- The About Group, which consists of the web sites of About.com, ConsumerSearch.com, UCompareHealthCare.com and Caloriecount.about.com.

In addition NYT owns equity interests in a Canadian newsprint company, a paper maker in Maine and Metro Boston (a free daily newspaper), 18% of the Boston Red Sox and Fenway Park stadium, 80% of New England Sports Network (the regional cable sports network), and 50% of Roush Fenway Racing, a leading NASCAR team.

The News Media Group comprised by far the largest part of the company's operations. However, shrinking advertising revenues, declining circulation and increasing competition from free newspapers and nonprint sources of news had placed major pressures on margins. Table 14.2 shows results for NYT's two business segments. Table 14.3 shows circulation for NYT's three major newspaper titles, while Table 14.4 shows traffic to NYT's web sites.

Within the News Media Group, *The Times* was the company's jewel. It is the only general daily newspaper to be distributed in all 50 states of the U.S. In terms of journalistic reputation it is unsurpassed. By 2009, its tally of Pulitzer prizes was 101—more than double that of any other newspaper. Its columnists include Nicholas Krista, Thomas Friedman and Nobel Prize-winning economist, Paul Kurgan. The company has attributed its ability to raise the cover price of *The Times* (up from $1 to $2 between July 2007 and May 2009) to the appeal of its quality journalism.

Web revenues were almost wholly generated by advertising while newspaper revenues were primarily dependent upon advertising. Hence, as Table 14.5 shows, the great majority of NYT revenues were provided by advertisers.

TABLE 14.2 New York Times Company: segment results ($000s)

	2008	2007	2006
Revenues			
News Media Group	2 833 561	3 092 394	3 209 704
About Group	115 295	102 683	80 199
Total	2 948 856	3 195 077	3 289 903
Operating profit			
News Media Group	(30 392)	248 567	(497 276)
About Group	39 390	34 703	30 819
Corporate	(49 634)	(55 841)	(54 154)
Total	(40 636)	227 429	(520 611)
Net income/(loss) from joint ventures	17 062	(2618)	19 340
Interest expense, net	47 790	39 842	50 651
(Loss)/income from continuing operations before income taxes and minority interest	(71 364)	184 969	(551 922)

Source: New York Times Company, Inc. 10-K Report, 2008.

TABLE 14.3 Average daily circulation of New York Times Company newspapers (000s of copies)

	2008	2007
New York Times (Monday–Friday)	1033.8	1066.6
New York Times (Sunday)	1451.3	1529.7
International Herald Tribune	240.3	241.6
Boston Globe (Monday–Friday)	323.9	364.6
Boston Globe (Sunday)	500.0	544.1

Source: New York Times Company, Inc., 10-K Report, 2008.

TABLE 14.4 New York Times Company principal web sites, 2008

	Average monthly U.S. visits 2008 (millions)	Content	Revenue source
NYTimes.com	19.5	*New York Times* web sites	Advertising
IHT.com	6.3*	International Herald Tribune web site	Advertising
Boston.com	5.2	*Boston Globe* web site	Advertising
About.com	39.0	Information on over 70 000 topics prepared by 770 advisers	Advertising
ConsumerSearch.com	n.a.	Expert and user-generated consumer product reviews	Advertising
UCompareHealthCare.com	n.a.	Information on the quality of certain healthcare services	Advertising
Caloriecount.about.com	n.a.	Weight management tools, social support and nutritional information	Advertising

*Worldwide visitors

Source: New York Times Company, Inc., 10-K Report, 2008.

Cost Cutting

The principal response by NYT management to shrinking revenues had been to cut costs. In her presentation to shareholders at the 2009 Annual General Meeting, CEO Janet Robinson identified five areas of cost savings:

- Consolidation of operations. The *Times* had consolidated two of its New York printing plants into a single facility, saving $30 million annually. The *Globe* would do the same with its two printing plants, saving about $18 million annually.
- Closure of businesses that did not meet their financial targets. In early 2009, NYT closed City & Suburban, its retail and news-stand distribution business in the New York area. This would improve operating profit by an estimated $27 million annually.

TABLE 14.5 New York Times Company: principal revenue and cost components ($000s)

	2008	2007	2006
Total revenues	2 948 856	3 195 077	3 289 903
of which:			
—Advertising	1 779 699	2 047 468	2 153 936
—Circulation	910 154	889 882	889 722
—Other	259 003	257 727	246 245
Total production costs	1 315 120	1 341 096	1 435 456
of which:			
—Raw materials	250 843	259 977	330 833
—Wages and benefits	622 692	646 824	665 304
—Other	441 585	434 295	439 319
Selling, general and administrative costs	1 332 084	1 397 413	1 398 294
Depreciation and amortization	144 409	189 561	162 331
Total operating costs	2 791 613	2 928 070	2 996 081

Source: New York Times Company, Inc., 10-K Report, 2008.

- Streamlining the organization—principally through outsourcing functions such as advertising service, circulation telemarketing, customer service and financial back-office functions. At some of the smaller newspapers, printing would be outsourced.
- Reducing the resources devoted to marginal areas of circulation.
- Reducing newsprint consumption and production costs by eliminating some newspaper sections (e.g. magazines and TV guides) and reducing the page size of *The Times*.[4]

Asset Sales

The New York Times Company has divested a number of non-core businesses. In 2007 it sold its nine local television stations; in 2008 it sold Alabama-based *Times Daily*. In 2009, it was negotiating to sell its 18% stake in New England Sports Ventures (owner of the Boston Red Sox and Fenway Park) and its 80% holding in New England Sports Network (a cable TV network).

The Quest for a New Business Model

Arnold Sulzberger's notion of the NYT providing "quality journalism, regardless of how it is distributed" was appealing to many who perceived that NYT's core competence was journalism, yet its primary distribution medium—printed newspapers—was in long-term decline. Sulzberger's vision also lacked a well-articulated business model.

Amidst the carnage of the U.S. newspaper industry, profitable titles tend to be those where costs have been slashed by radical outsourcing and those that have been able to establish strong differentiation through strongly focusing upon local needs.

Where all newspapers have experienced difficulty is in establishing a viable business model for their online editions and establishing a synergistic relationship between their web and print editions. In the case of NYTimes.com, fees were initially collected from international users then, in 1997, the online edition became free in an effort to increase the online audience. In 2005, NYTimes.com moved to a mixed model—TimesSelect charged a fee for premium content and access to *The Times'* online archives. By 2007, the desire to build advertising revenues resulted in NYTimes.com providing free access. By 2009, the company was once again evaluating the best approach to charging for content.

Creating a viable online business model for a newspaper represents a challenge that has yet to be met. Rick Wartzman, Director of the Drucker Institute, has proposed an online-only solution: "The web needs to be embraced much more fully than most papers have done. This means no more tentative, halfway initiatives. Dead-tree editions must immediately yield to all-internet operations. The presses need to stop forever, with the delivery trucks shunted off to the scrapyard." As an example, he proposed that if the *Los Angeles Times* went online only it could operate with a staff of 275 and earn a net margin of 10%.[5] The *Huffington Post* has been viewed as a model for an online newspaper.

The central debate over online newspapers has been between advocates of "charging-for-content" and those that see the advertising-only approach as the only viable business model. Eric Schmidt, CEO of Google, comes down firmly on the side of free content and revenues for advertising. Only where content is unique, he argues, will users be willing to pay. For the great majority of news, there is no alternative to providing it free because it is available from so many online sources. The opportunity for online newspapers was to offer targeted advertising—that's where he sees Google as being an essential partner for the newspaper companies. In terms of the design of online newspapers, he suggested that critical features for an online newspaper were, first, it should remember which stories each reader had read so that content could be customized and, second, it should allow the reader to go deeper into topics in which he/she was interested.[6]

However, the discussion of business models for online newspaper content raised the question of what the traditional business model was for print newspapers? The history of the newspaper industry in the U.S. and in other countries of the world, suggested that profit typically took a second place behind political influence and ego projection among most newspaper proprietors. The attraction of newspaper ownership to already rich individuals could mean that a newspaper could be financially viable even if its costs exceeded its revenues. The attraction of *The Times* to the rich and famous was indicated by the presence of a number of potential suitors—in addition to Rupert Murdoch and Carlos Slim, Hollywood and record mogul David Geffen had expressed interest in taking a stake in it.

A key issue was whether the financial problems of the newspapers would stretch the willingness to pay of potential "rich daddies." The *Financial Times* warned that:

> Even wealthy patrons have reason to be wary, however. Sam Zell, the highest profile recent new entrant into the newspaper business, saw his $8.2bn purchase of the Tribune Company end last month in the bankruptcy courts. Having long

> been seen as useful assets for burnishing their proprietors' reputations, newspapers now pose as much risk of tarnishing their owners' names.[7]

A major reason why the financial plight of the newspaper industry has attracted so much attention and concern is that newspapers have been regarded as a valuable public service—the "fourth estate" that can shine the light of public exposure on the wrongdoings of politicians and powerful individuals. If a free press is a central component of a democratic state, then an alternative business model might be that of a charity. Penelope Muse Abernathy of the University of North Carolina, has proposed four options for newspaper funding: establishing an endowment that funds a paper's news department; charitable support for some aspects of the paper's coverage, such as foreign or cultural coverage; purchase of the paper by a university or other educational institution; and sale to an angel investor who would run the paper as a "low-profit limited liability corporation."[8]

Non-profit organizations are also entering the field of journalism. ProPublica, led by Paul Steiger, a former senior editor at the *Wall Street Journal*, funds investigative journalism from charitable endowments. It then makes its stories available to *The Times* and other newspapers. *The Times* also collaborates with Spot.Us, a web site on which journalists can post story ideas they wish to pursue and what it will cost them to do it, raising the money from the public $20 at a time.[9]

Notes

1 The New York Times Company 2009 Annual Meeting of Stockholders, April 23, 2009.
2 The New York Times Company 2009 Annual Meeting of Stockholders, April 23, 2009.
3 "Feeling the Pinch," *The Economist,* December 4, 2008. "All the News that's Free to Print," *The Economist,* July 21, 2009.
4 The New York Times Company 2009 Annual Meeting of Stockholders, April 23, 2009.
5 "Out with the Dead Wood for Newspapers," *Business Week,* March 10, 2009.
6 "View from the Top: Eric Schmidt of Google," *Financial Times,* May 21, 2009.
7 "Playthings for Rich Men could be Unsafe Toys," *Financial Times,* January 21, 2009.
8 Penelope Muse Abernathy, "A Nonprofit Model for The New York Times?" Duke Conference on Nonprofit Media, May 4–5, 2009.
9 "All the News that's Free to Print," *Economist,* July 21, 2009.

Case 15 Eni SpA: Building an International Energy Major

May 2009 marked the beginning of Paolo Scaroni's fifth year as CEO of the Italian energy giant, Eni. Under his leadership, production of hydrocarbons had grown by 11% (most other oil and gas majors had experienced declining output), sales had risen by 86% (in euros) and operating income by 50% (in euros). Eni's market capitalization had declined from €69 billion to €57 billion—nevertheless, Eni had outperformed the market indices on all three of the stock markets where its shares were listed (Milan, London and New York). Moreover, Eni remained Italy's most valuable company with a market capitalization that was almost double that of second-placed ENEL (where Scaroni had been CEO prior to coming to Eni).

The change in leadership had not resulted in any major shifts in strategy for Eni. Scaroni had continued the two main strategic thrusts of his predecessor, Vittorio Mincato:

- A heavy emphasis on upstream investment with the organic growth of Eni's oil and gas reserves supplemented by selective acquisitions.
- A commitment to developing a vertically integrated natural gas business, which was built around linking Eni's gas production in north and west Africa with its downstream gas business in Europe through developing pipelines and liquefied natural gas (LNG), collaborating with Gazprom (the Russian gas giant), extending Eni's downstream gas business into other European countries and developing Eni's power-generation business.

However, in pursuing this strategy, Scaroni was forced to navigate an exceptionally turbulent environment. During his four years at Eni, oil prices had oscillated between $32 and $148 a barrel, European refining margins had widened then shrunk rapidly, and relations with producer governments had become contentious as a result of nationalism, Middle East conflict, and producer countries demanding a bigger share of production and profit from their hydrocarbon resources. In Venezuela and Kazakhstan, Eni had been forced into major concessions by the host governments.

Looking ahead, Eni remained committed to its strategy of growth—both upstream in oil and gas production and downstream in the European gas market. However, a number of uncertainties clouded Eni's future.

Its most immediate problem was the global recession that had reduced the demand for oil, gas and power and had resulted in sharp reductions in energy prices. In its first-quarter results for 2009, Eni had reported a decline in net profit of 43% compared with the first quarter of 2008.

However, the greatest uncertainties related to Eni's future over the long term. Oil and gas reserves were becoming increasingly difficult to find. Exploration in increasingly remote and geologically complex locations was causing finding and lifting costs to rise rapidly. The fragile geopolitical state of the world greatly increased investment risks. Because of its upstream activities in Kazakhstan, Russia, Iran, Libya, Algeria, Nigeria, Congo and Angola, Eni was viewed as especially vulnerable to political instability.

The threats to Eni's vertically integrated natural gas strategy were not all at the upstream level. National gas giants such as Eni and Gaz de France were viewed by the European Commission as critical obstacles to its program of liberalizing Europe's gas market. The Commission was particularly concerned at the monopoly power that resulted from the ownership of the gas-distribution infrastructure. As a result Eni had been required to separate its domestic pipeline and gas-storage assets into a separate company, Snam Rete Gas. The Commission was concerned that Eni's international pipelines represented a barrier for competitors.

The growing problem of global warming was an emerging threat to the oil and gas industry. Although the global recession had shifted attention away from climate issues, there was increasing awareness that the global warming may have reached "tipping point", where the forces driving climate change accelerate and become irreversible.

The History of Eni

Mattei and the Creation of Eni, 1926–62[1]

In 1926, Italian Prime Minister Benito Mussolini established Agip (Azienda Generali Italiana Petroli) as a state-owned oil company.[2] At the end of the Second World War, Enrico Mattei, a former partisan, was appointed head of Agip and instructed to dismantle this relic of fascist economic intervention. Contrary to instructions, Mattei renewed Agip's exploration efforts and, in 1948, discovered a substantial gas field in northern Italy's Po Valley. In 1949, Mattei also took over the management of SNAM, the Italian gas distribution company. With the opportunity to create a national energy system based upon the newly found gas reserves, pipelines were laid at a frantic rate. "Mattei built the pipelines first and negotiated afterwards . . . He simply ignored private and public rights and the law . . . Much of the work was done at night on the theory that by morning the work would be so far along that there would not be very much that anybody could do about it."[3]

On February 10, 1953, the government merged Agip, SNAM and other state-owned energy activities to form Ente Nazionale Idrocarburi (Eni) with the task of "promoting and undertaking initiatives of national interest in the fields of hydrocarbons and natural gases." Mattei was appointed its first chairman and chief executive. Eni's 36 subsidiaries extended well beyond oil and gas to include engineering services, chemicals, soap and real estate.

Under Mattei's leadership, Eni became committed to building an integrated, international oil and gas company that would ensure the independence of Italy's energy supplies and make a substantial contribution to Italy's postwar economic regeneration. Mattei soon established himself as a national hero: "He embodied great visions for postwar Italy—antifascism, the resurrection and rebuilding of the nation, and the emergence of the 'new man' who had made it himself, without the old boy network."[4]

Mattei's daring and resourcefulness was especially evident in Eni's international growth. The international oil majors—which Mattei referred to as the "Seven Sisters" because of their collusive tendencies—had tied up most of the world's known sources of oil in the Middle East and Latin America. The production-sharing agreement that Mattei signed with the Shah of Iran in 1957 marked the beginning of a fundamental shift of power from the oil majors to producer governments and established Eni as the *enfant terrible* of the oil business. The Iranian agreement was revolutionary. It created a jointly owned exploration and production company headed by an Iranian chairman and with the proceeds shared between Eni and the Iranian National Oil Company. The "Mattei formula" was the basis on which Eni extended its upstream interests to Libya, Egypt, Tunisia and Algeria between 1958 and 1960. Mattei also concluded a barter deal for crude oil from the Soviet Union. By 1960, Italy was the Soviet Union's biggest oil customer after China.

All the time Mattei was building political support within Italy. This typically involved Eni in politically motivated investments, especially in acquiring struggling companies. By 1962, Eni was "engaged in industries as various as motels, highways, chemicals, soap, fertilizers, synthetic rubber, machinery, instruments, textiles, electrical generation and distribution, contract research, engineering and construction, publishing, nuclear power, steel pipe, cement, investment banking, and even education, to mention only a few."[5]

Eni under State Control, 1962–92[6]

Mattei died in a plane crash on October 27, 1962 at the age of 56. He left a sprawling corporate empire whose strategy had been Mattei's own vision and whose integrating force had been Mattei's charisma and personal authority. At the time of his death, Mattei was president not just of Eni but also of its main operating companies.[7] Without Mattei's leadership, power shifted to the politicians; increasingly Eni became an instrument of government economic, industrial and employment policies.[8] After 1975, the chairman of Eni lost direct control of its operating companies—their chief executives were appointed by government on the basis of political considerations. Nevertheless, Eni continued to expand its oil and gas interests. Major initiatives included the purchase of natural gas from the Soviet Union (which involved Eni building a pipeline from the Austrian-Czechoslovak border to Italy), the Trans-Med Pipeline from Algeria and Tunisia to Italy, and offshore projects in West Africa, Congo and Angola. But financial performance remained weak—Eni earned significant profits only during 1988–90 (see Table 15.1).

The Bernabè Era: Privatization and Transformation, 1992–8

By 1992 the Italian government was facing pressure from the European Commission and the new European Monetary Union to cut the public-sector deficit and free up industry from state intervention. In June 1992, reformist Prime Minister Giuliano Amato announced the first steps in granting Eni greater autonomy—Eni became a joint-stock company and its relations with government were transferred to the Treasury. At the same time, Franco Bernabè, a 44-year-old economist, was appointed CEO. Although lacking line-management experience, Bernabè possessed a clear vision of Eni's future as a privatized, integrated energy company, shorn of its various diversified businesses.[9]

Bernabè's opportunity for leading a radical transformation of Eni came with the corruption scandal that swept Italy in 1993. During March 1993, Eni's chairman Gabriele Cagliari and several senior Eni board members and executives were arrested on corruption charges.[10] In the following three months Bernabè led a comprehensive restructuring of management. The boards of Eni and its main subsidiaries were forced to resign and some 250 new board members were appointed.[11]

Bernabè's corporate strategy was "to reduce Eni from being a loose conglomerate to concentrate on its core activity of energy."[12] The sale of Nuovo Pigone (a turbine manufacturer) was followed by halving capacity at EniChem—Eni's troubled chemicals business. During 1993, Bernabè's first whole year as chief executive, 73 Eni businesses were closed or sold and employment was cut by 15 000. Cost savings and asset sales resulted in a profit of almost $2 billion in 1994.[13]

Eni's initial public offering of 15% of its total equity on November 21, 1995 raised €3.3 billion for the Italian treasury and on November 28, Eni shares commenced trading in Milan, London, and New York. After more than 40 years of looking to politicians in Rome for guidance, Eni's top management had to adjust to a new set of masters—the investment community in the world's financial capitals.

Commitment to shareholder value provided impetus for further refocusing: "Eni's strategy is to focus on businesses and geographical areas where, through size, technology, or cost structure, it has a leading market position. To this end, Eni intends to implement dynamic management of its portfolio through acquisitions, joint

TABLE 15.1 Eni's sales, profits, employment and production, 1985–2008

	1985	1986	1987	1988	1989	1990	1991	1992	1993	1994	1995	1996
Sales ($m)	24 328	22 557	24 464	25 220	27 105	41 764	34 594	38 659	33 595	30 670	35 335	37 973
Net income ($m)	406	42	544	1006	1176	1697	684	–768	154	1977	2704	2930
Employees (000s)	129	130	119	116	136	131	131	126	109	92	86	83
Oil and gas produced (000s boe/day)	371	384	443	490	538	590	618	860	901	941	982	984

	1997	1998	1999	2000	2001	2002	2003	2004	2005	2006	2007	2008
Sales ($m)	34 323	33 177	31 225	46 000	43 607	51 379	59 322	72 394	91 423	108 492	119 541	158 978
Net income ($m)	2980	2891	3019	5671	7333	4816	6323	9020	10 897	11 613	13 715	14 050
Employees (000s)	80	79	72	70	71	81	77	71	72	73	75	78
Oil and gas produced (000s boe/day)	1021	1038	1064	1187	1369	1472	1562	1624	1737	1770	1736	1797

Source: Eni annual reports for various years.

ventures, and divestments. Eni also intends to outsource non-strategic activities."[14] Capital investment became increasingly concentrated upon upstream activities. In refining and marketing and petrochemicals, costs were reduced and assets sold.

The results were striking. Between 1992 and 1998, Bernabè halved Eni's debt, turned a loss into a substantial profit and reduced employment by 46 000. However, 1998 was to be Bernabè's last year at Eni: his success had made him prime candidate to lead the turnaround of another newly privatized giant—Telecom Italia.

The Mincato Era 1998–2005: From Restructuring to Growth

Vittorio Mincato brought a different background and a different style of management to Eni. Twelve years Bernabè's senior, Mincato had already spent 42 years at Eni—including 15 years as chairman of EniChem where he had pioneered turnaround and restructuring.

If Bernabè's strategy was to focus on Eni's core energy businesses, Mincato's was to grow them. In the 1999 annual report, Mincato outlined the strategy he intended to pursue:

> The four-year plan approved at the end of 1999 derives from a new strategic vision that features, on one side, an aggressive growth option in upstream activities and, on the other, a customer-oriented approach in the energy markets.
>
> For the upstream sector we devised a plan calling for 50% growth in hydrocarbon production by 2003. Such an objective will be made up of two components. The first is represented by ordinary growth . . . the second component of growth is related to mergers and acquisitions . . .
>
> In the natural gas sector, Eni has been active at three levels. First, it followed an internationalization strategy in downstream activities with the aim of selling at least 10 billion cubic meters of natural gas per year by 2003 in foreign growth markets . . . Second, with the creation of EniPower, Eni started to restructure its activities in the electricity sector, an area which represents a necessary step to strengthen its position in the gas chain, in view of the fact that most of the growth in demand for natural gas in Europe will come from the expansion of combined cycle electricity production.
>
> To support the opening up of the natural gas market in Italy, we started to restructure our activities at Snam, separating . . . transport activities from supply and sale.
>
> The scope of the changes affecting our industry will require on our part the achievement of strong efficiency improvements. For this reason, plans to cut costs have been revised, raising to €1 billion (an increase of €250 million) the amount of savings that Eni plans to achieve through cost cutting by 2003 . . . While costs will be cut across all sectors, strong measures will be taken in the Petrochemical sector—whose weight in terms of net capital will decline to 7% by 2003.[15]

By the time he retired in 2005, Mincato had won plaudits from the investment community and from industry insiders both for the clarity of Eni's strategy and the effectiveness of its execution. Upstream, Eni extended its exploration activities in Kazakhstan (where Eni took over operatorship of the huge Kashagan oilfield), West Africa, Iran and the Gulf of Mexico. In addition it acquired British Borneo in

May 2000 for €1.3 billion, LASMO in December 2000 for €4.1 billion and Fortum's Norwegian oil and gas assets in November 2002 for $1.1 billion.

In its natural gas business, Eni embarked on several major projects to link gas production with markets. The biggest and most ambitious was the Blue Stream project, a 50–50 joint venture with the Russian gas giant, Gazprom, to build a gas pipeline under the Black Sea from Russia to Turkey. This was followed by the Greenstream pipeline from the Libya to Italy. Both projects were undertaken by Eni's affiliate, Saipem.

Outside of Italy, Eni acquired several gas distribution companies including major stakes in Spain's Union Fenosa Gas (50%), GVS in Germany (50%) and Galp Energia in Portugal (33%). Eni also entered the downstream gas markets of Hungary, Greece and Croatia. Within Italy, Eni began investing heavily in power generation.

Downstream, Eni pursued rationalization and cost reduction in both refining and distribution. Between 1999 and 2005, refining capacity was cut from 664 000 to 524 000 barrels per day and the number of retail service stations was halved. Eni's chemical business was consolidated into a separate company, Polimeri Europa.

Internally, Mincato sought to make Eni a more integrated corporation. Between 2000 and 2004, Mincato transformed Eni from a holding company into a multidivisional corporation. The main subsidiaries companies, which had operated with their own boards of directors and chief executives, were reorganized into three divisions: exploration and production, gas and power, and refining and marketing. A key aspect of integration was a company-wide human resources strategy that emphasized training, appraisal and career planning over traditional "personnel" activities.

To forge a clearer identity and image for Eni, the slogan "Eni's Way" was adopted as the company's tag line in advertising and corporate communication. The key themes that "Eni's Way" embraced were technological strength, originality, spirit of adventure, and social and environmental responsibility.

Eni's Strategy under Scaroni's Leadership, 2005–9

Prior to his appointment as CEO of Eni, Paolo Scaroni had been CEO of Enel, Italy's largest electricity supplier, and CEO of Pilkington, the British glass company. He was a graduate of Bocconi University and held an MBA from Columbia University. His appointment as CEO of Eni had been greeted initially by dismay from some outside observers:

> Corporate governance [in Italy] continues to suffer big reverses, none bigger than the ousting last week by the government of Vittorio Mincato, the boss of Eni, the world's sixth-largest oil and gas company. Not only was this talented and apolitical manager replaced by somebody who knows nothing of the industry (Paolo Scaroni, boss of Enel, Italy's electrical utility); but also that ignorance is now shared by Eni's entire board.[16]

During the following 12 months, Scaroni allayed these early fears by his effectiveness in communicating with the investment community and in his leadership of Eni's international initiatives—particularly in relation to producer countries. From the outset, Scaroni made it clear that he would not deviate substantially from the strategy put in place by Mincato. In an interview with the *Financial Times* he committed Eni to a ten year strategy of turning Eni into one of world's oil and gas majors: "This is my vision, and it's shared within the company. Eni has moved from a small company to being close to becoming a major. It's closer than it was five years ago. We will use our unique features to build a long-term growth strategy." This growth would be achieved organically: "I do not see a climate for acquisitions today. If there is a target, then everybody would be in a position to get it because everyone has the money for it. In the game of cash, we are not the richest."

Achieving growth would require Eni to draw upon its unique strengths, such as its long experience of politically sensitive, oil-producing states, where it was seen as an even-handed player: "We want to use the dimensions of our company and the dimensions of our country as a positive." Unlike his previous position at Enel, his job at Eni did not require extensive restructuring: "At Eni the strategy is solid and good. If it isn't broken, don't fix it."[17]

Upstream Growth

Annual capital expenditure more than doubled between 2005 and 2008 with more than two-thirds going into exploration and production. Eni's principal upstream initiatives included the following:

- In Kazakhstan, Eni's giant Kashogan oilfield with upward of 15 billion barrels of oil was the world's biggest oil find in 30 years. Eni held an 18.5% stake and was the field's operator. It was Eni's biggest upstream project. However, it was also Scaroni's biggest challenge. As the oil price rose during 2006–8 and development suffered from recurrent cost overruns (the estimate of the total project cost rose from an initial \$57 billion to \$136 billion) and delays (the date for first oil production was pushed back from 2005 to 2013). The relationship with the Kazak government was the number one item on Scaroni's agenda during his first four years at Eni. The Kazak government complained about Eni's mismanagement of the project, while Eni referred to the technical, geological and logistical complexities of the project and the world shortage of engineers, geologists and technicians. A new agreement, signed in October 2008, reduced the share of Eni and its partners in the project and provided for a joint operating company to replace Eni as the developer of the field.
- In Russia, Eni built upon its historical relationship as one of biggest customers for Soviet gas, to broaden its relationship with Gazprom. In April 2007, Eni acquired equity stakes in four Russian oil companies, including 20% of Gazprom's oil business, for €3 billion. However, Gazprom retained an option to repurchase these assets which it exercised in April 2009.[18] In November 2007, it formed a joint venture with Gazprom to build South Stream—a pipeline to ship gas from Central Asia to Southern Europe.
- In Congo, Eni negotiated an agreement with the Republic of Congo that some observers hailed as a model for the future oil company relations with host governments. The May 2008 agreement involved Eni investing \$3 billion in a variety of projects. In addition to onshore and offshore exploration and production (E&P) projects, Eni will build two power plants that will use associated gas from Eni's M'Boundi oil field. The project includes distribution infrastructure and will provide 80% of Congo's electricity needs. In addition, Eni will develop a palm oil plantation to produce biofuels. The Eni Foundation is funding local health clinics and a program of vaccination of children.

- In Libya, Eni built on its status as Libya's longest partner in oil production and biggest buyer of Libyan oil by extending its concession for a further 25 years and agreeing with the Libyan government to sell it a 10% equity stake in Eni.[19]
- Some of Eni's most important new upstream initiatives concerned the development of its LNG business. This was strategically important for Eni. Hitherto, Eni's vertically integrated natural gas business had been built around the use of pipelines to link sources of gas in North Africa and Russia to its large domestic market in Italy. With LNG, Eni could extend geographically both its production and marketing of gas. LNG projects included Egypt, Algeria, Nigeria, Angola, and Indonesia. In Qatar, Eni's agreements to purchase LNG provided the basis for an alliance with Qatar Petroleum to pursue gas and oil exploration projects in Africa and the Mediterranean region.

Table 15.2 shows Eni's geographical distribution of production and reserves.

A key feature of Eni's upstream strategy is a focus on countries that are conventionally viewed as difficult places to do business. According to petro-politics expert, Steve LeVine: "Italy's Eni continues to pioneer a successful path to survival in Big Oil's treacherous new world—get in bed, don't compete with the world's state-owned oil companies . . . It has grown into a hugely successful heir to the Seven Sisters, the most successful of the West's Big Oil companies at finding comfort with the world's autocrats. Where its brethren bicker with Hugo Chavez and Vladimir Putin, Eni has found a comfortable embrace."[20]

Scaroni's response to accusations of being opportunistic and unprincipled was matter-of-fact: "We deal with countries that have gas. If Switzerland had gas, we would deal with Switzerland." At the root of Eni's flexible, innovative approach to

TABLE 15.2 Eni's hydrocarbon production and reserves by geographical region (thousands of barrels of oil equivalent per day)

	Italy	North Sea	North Africa	West Africa	Rest of world	World
Production						
2008	199	237	645	335	381	1797
2007	212	261	594	327	342	1736
2006	238	282	555	372	323	1770
2005	261	283	480	343	370	1737
2004	271	308	380	316	349	1624
2003	300	345	351	260	306	1562
2002	316	308	354	238	256	1472
2001	308	288	317	233	223	1369
2000	333	168	306	225	155	1187
1999	358	154	269	206	77	1064
1998	394	156	236	196	56	1038
1997	404	155	229	180	54	1021
Reserves						
2008	681	510	1922	1146	1983	6242

Source: Eni annual reports for various years.

relationships with producer countries was acceptance of a changed balance of power between producer countries and the Western oil and gas companies: "The fact is, the oil is theirs . . . If you are looked at as a partner, you are allowed to exploit their oil; if not, you are pushed aside."[21]

Eni also continued to increase its oil and gas reserves through selective acquisitions—both of particular assets and of entire companies. In addition to its Russian investments, Eni purchased:

- Maurel and Prom's assets in Congo for $1.4 billion (February 2007);
- a Gulf of Mexico oilfield from Dominion Resources for $4.8 billion (April 2007);
- Burren Energy Plc, whose principal assets were gas fields in Turkmenistan for €2.36 billion (January 2008);
- First Calgary Petroleum Ltd (with upstream assets in Algeria) for €0.7 billion (November 2008).

The strategic plan invented by Scaroni in February 2009 committed Eni to continuing its steady growth in hydrocarbon production (see Appendix 4).

Downstream: Building the European Gas Business

Unlike most other oil and gas majors, the oil refining and the marketing of oil products was a comparatively minor part of Eni's downstream business, accounting for a mere 11% of Eni's total assets. Refining and marketing were heavily focused on Italy, which accounted for 70% of its sales of oil products, representing almost 31% of the Italian market in 2008. Outside of Italy, Eni's main markets for oil products were Austria, Hungary, Slovakia, Switzerland and Germany. Nowhere did it have a maximum market share of more than 12%. Under Scaroni, Eni continued to shrink its refining capacity and reduce its number of retail outlets. It also reduced the geographical scope of its refining and marketing activities—earlier withdrawals from Africa and northern Europe were followed by the sale of its downstream businesses in Spain and Portugal.

In gas, Scaroni continued to pursue expansion of Eni's European gas presence—in part to compensate for the undermining of its dominance of the Italian market by the EU's attempt to promote a competitive European gas market. In France, Eni bought a 27.8% stake in Altergaz in 2007. In Belgium, Eni bought 57% of gas operator Distrigas NV. In Russia Eni contracted to supply gas to a Russian electricity generator, making Eni the first European company to enter the Russian downstream gas market.

Scaroni regarded Eni's vertical integration as its key competitive advantage in the European gas market:

> Eni has a very distinctive way of dealing with the gas in Europe. We are both upstream with our E&P division, and downstream in distribution, transport and sales. Just to give you an idea of how integrated these two divisions are, 35% of our equity gas is sold through our Gas & Power division, so we are already where most of our competitors in the midstream and downstream business of gas would like to be: integrated upstream, and generating our sales from our own equity gas. . . Then of course we have a wide portfolio of sourcing of gas, which goes from Algeria to Libya, Poland, Norway, and of course, Russia.

> To summarize, we combine a strong upstream position in gas, with an extensive and well balanced infrastructure, a strong marketing position in Italy and in Europe. There is no other player that has such a privileged position in the European market—I hope we will demonstrate to you that for each segment of our business— and we have exciting opportunities for growth.

According to Marco Alvera, in charge of gas supplies, Eni's vertical integration in gas offered five main advantages:

> Our gas, be it equity or contracted, comes from ten different countries. This gives us considerable diversity and security of supply. Second, we can leverage on a growing integrated LNG business. Third, we have attractive contractual structures and terms. Fourth, we have access to a very large set of transportation and storage assets across Europe from north to south and east to west. Finally, we have significant commercial flexibility that allows us to vary, on a daily basis, the amounts of gas produced or drawn from each of our contracts. Let's look at these points one by one.[22]

On the fourth of these points, Alvera pointed to the key role of Eni's transportation infrastructure:

> We have direct access to every key gas consuming or producing country around Europe. It gives us an ideal position to support the growth of our non-Italian business. Historically, our transport and significant storage have been developed to bring gas into fixed ebb and flows, where into Italy the model was Italian-centric. They pumped gas into Northern Europe, or Eastern or Western Europe. All we need to do is simply take the gas that's transiting through those regions, on its way to Italy, and stop it exactly where we need it. If we add our ability to complement this with an LNG strategy, and with swap agreements, this effectively means that we can have gas in all our markets in Europe, or all target markets, at no additional costs. This is pretty unique.
>
> This gives us a unique flexibility that we can really sum up in three points. We have strong structural flexibility in our gas contracts, as well as the necessary transport infrastructure to use it. The difference between the maximum quantities we can take from our contracts and the minimum quantities that we must draw from these contracts is 14 billion cubic meters per year. To put this into perspective, this is almost 3% of total European gas demand.
>
> Second, thanks to our presence in most downstream, midstream and upstream markets around Europe, we have a broad and deep understanding of our industry, and finally, of course, we can leverage a unique set of relationships, which in some cases date back 50 years, and our engagements with the broad sets of really strategic partners.
>
> Summing up, I would say that no other operator in the European gas market can claim to have the same scale and asset backed flexibility as Eni's Gas and Power division. Enhancing our optimization capabilities, as we continue our transition from former state monopoly in Italy to a true European leader in the gas market, will further push us even further into a league of our own.

The key obstacle to Eni's vertically integrated gas strategy was the European Union's goal of a competitive European gas market. European directives on competition in natural gas required Eni to limit its share of the Italian downstream gas market to 50% and vest its gas storage and gas transportation assets into separate, regulated companies.

Eni's response was to transfer all its regulated gas businesses to a separate company. In 2001, Snam Rete Gas was created to own and manage Eni's primary (high pressure) gas distribution system. In 2008, Eni sold its gas storage company, Stogit and Italgas, to Snam Rete Gas for a total of €4.8 billion.

Eni's vertical chains for oil and gas are shown in Figure 15.1. It is interesting to note that, despite Eni's commitment to international expansion in both upstream and downstream gas, its sales and assets were still heavily concentrated in Italy (see Figures 15.2 and 15.3).

FIGURE 15.1 Eni's vertical chains in oil and gas

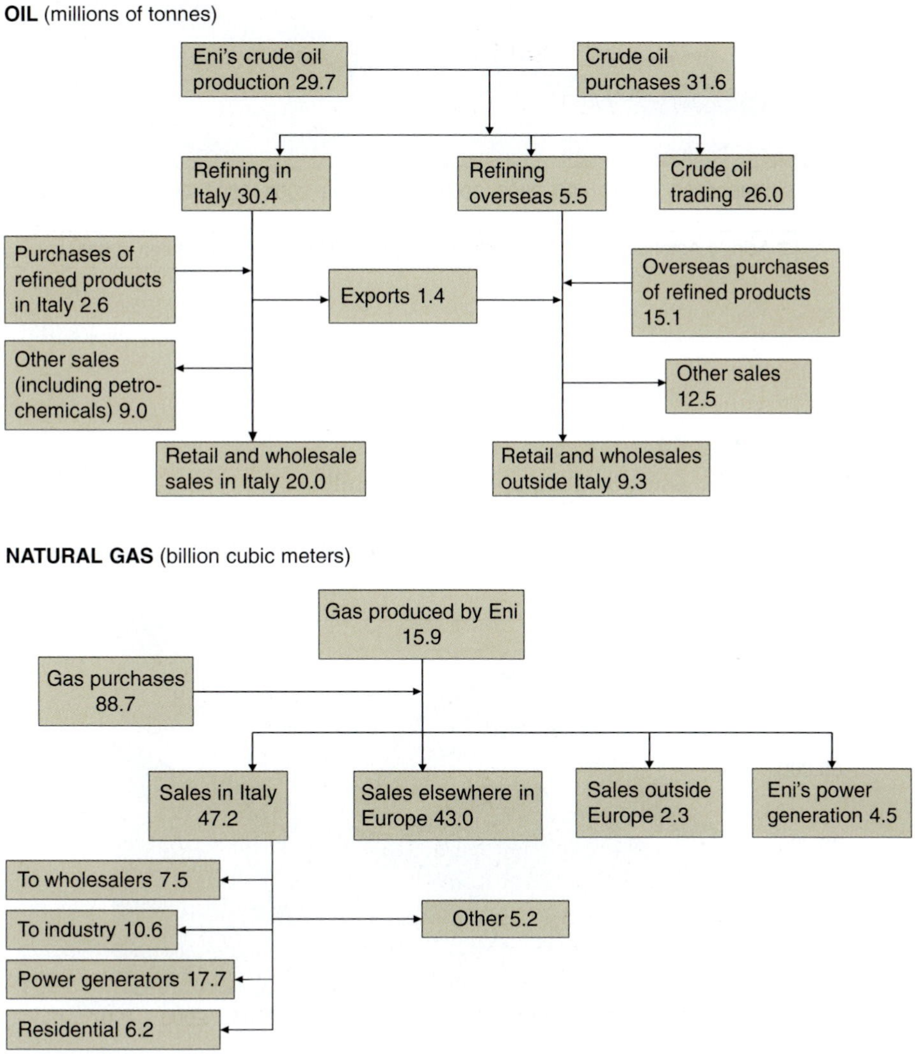

Source: Eni Fact Book 2008, www.eni.it/attachments/publications/reports/reports-2009/fact_book_2008.pdf, accessed October 29, 2009.

FIGURE 15.2 Eni's sales by geographic area ($ millions)

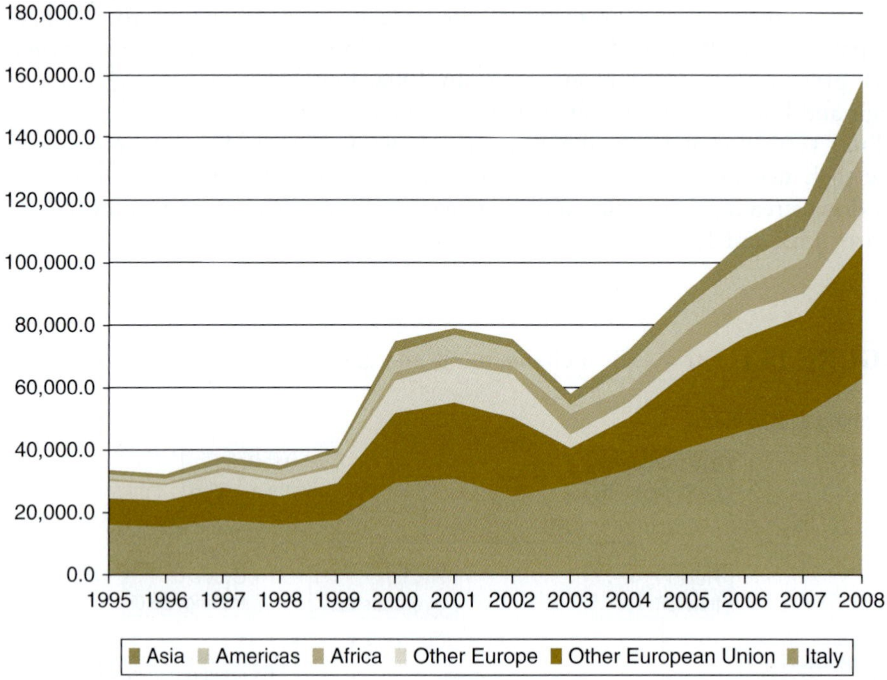

FIGURE 15.3 Eni's assets by geographic area ($ millions)

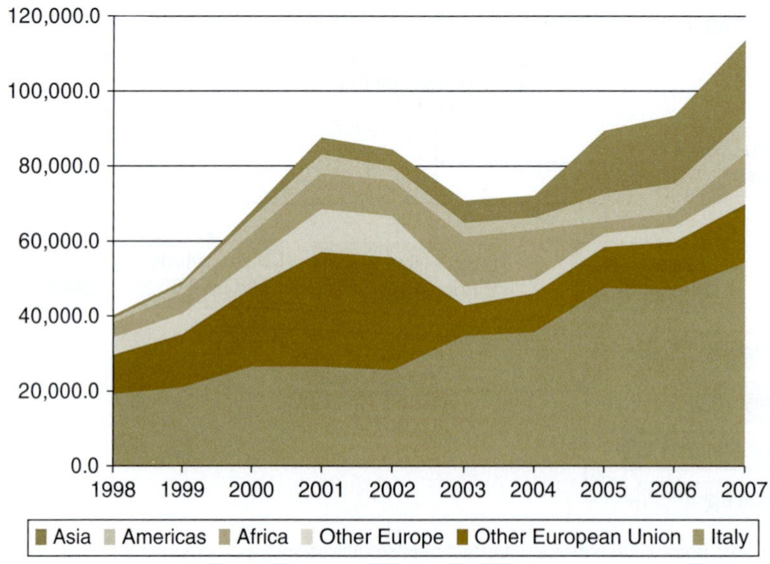

The Petroleum Sector in 2009

The petroleum sector comprises two major segments: *upstream*, comprising exploration and production, and *downstream*. Downstream is further divided into the refining and marketing of oil products and the distribution and marketing of natural gas. Between upstream and downstream are mid-stream activities comprising the transportation of oil and gas (pipeline and marine) and trading.

The Companies

The petroleum sector features three main types of company:

- *The oil and gas majors* are characterized by their age, size, international scope, and vertical integration. They are among the oldest and largest companies in the industry. Between 1998 and 2002 a wave of mergers and acquisitions resulted in the emergence of an elite group of "super majors" comprising Exxon Mobil, BP, Royal Dutch Shell, ChevronTexaco, ConocoPhillips and Total (see Table 15.3). Some of the majors are also major petrochemical producers (for example, Exxon Mobil, Royal Dutch Shell, Total).

TABLE 15.3 Major mergers and acquisitions in the oil and gas industry[a]

Major oil companies in 1995	Revenues in 1995 ($ bn)	Date merged	Major oil companies in 2008	Revenues in 2008 ($ bn)
Exxon	124		**Exxon Mobil Corp.**	425
Mobil	75	1999		
Royal Dutch/Shell Group	110		**Royal Dutch Shell**	458
Enterprise Oil	1	2002		
British Petroleum	56		**BP**	361
Amoco	28	1998		
Arco	16	2000		
Chevron	31	2001	**Chevron**	255
Texaco	36	2001		
Total	28		**Total**	223
PetroFina	n.a.	1999		
Elf Aquitaine	n.a.	2000		
Conoco	15		**ConocoPhillips**	225
Philips Petroleum	13	2002		
Tosco	n.a.	2001		
Eni	36		**Eni**	158
Repsol	21		**Repsol YPF**	68
YPF	5	1999		

[a]Only includes acquisitions of companies with revenues exceeding $1 billion.

Others divested most of their chemical activities (BP, Chevron). The real economic benefits from these mergers and acquisitions remain unclear. There are advantages to spreading risks across a portfolio of major upstream projects. Pursuing multiple projects also offers potential for innovation and learning. However, there was little evidence that scale economies offered significant advantages to "super majors" over mere "majors."

- *The national oil companies (NOCs)* are the state-owned monopolies created by producer governments to manage their countries' petroleum reserves. In terms of production and reserves, the NOCs dominate the ranks of the leading petroleum companies (see Table 15.4). Most were created between the mid 1960s and the early 1980s by nationalizing the oil assets of the majors. During 2000–8, the relationship between the majors and the NOCs shifted substantially. Rising crude prices and growing nationalism among oil producing countries resulted in increasing desire by the NOCs for greater control over the countries' hydrocarbon resources and bigger shares of production and revenues. In Venezuela, Bolivia and Russia, foreign oil companies were forced to transfer upstream assets to the national government or to local companies. Elsewhere higher taxes were imposed and participation agreements renegotiated. Increasingly the NOCs have become direct competitors of the majors. Some, such as Petrobras and CNOOC, have become important international players. Others such as Saudi Aramco, Kuwait Petroleum and PDVSA have established large downstream (and petrochemical) businesses, which have depressed margins in refining and bulk chemicals. With the help of oil service companies such as Halliburton and Schlumberger, the NOCs have access to modern technologies and have become less dependent upon the majors.
- *Independents.* At all vertical levels, specialist companies play an important role. In exploration and production, companies such as Devon Energy, Anadarko, Cairn Resources, and Woodside Petroleum are important players, especially in exploring frontier regions. Their operational and financial success contradicts the arguments of the majors that huge size is an essential requirement in the petroleum industry. In refining, independent refiners such as Valero in the U.S. have grown as the majors have sold off downstream assets. (Appendix 3 lists the world's largest oil and gas companies with publicly traded shares.)

Vertical Integration Strategies

A key feature of the strategies of majors has been vertical integration throughout the value chain from exploration through to retailing gasoline and other refined products. The basis for vertical integration was the need for downstream outlets for a company's upstream production. In the case of oil, the development of a global infrastructure of transportation and storage, competitive markets for both crude and refined products, and the presence of specialist companies at every stage of the value chain has reduced (if not eliminated) the advantages of vertical integration. In response, the majors have dismantled their vertical integrated structures. This has involved dissolving close operational linkages between upstream and downstream and withdrawing from some vertical stages—for example outsourcing oilfield services, marine transportation, IT—and selling off chemical plants. Nevertheless, all the majors maintained their presence in exploration, production, refining, and

TABLE 15.4 *Petroleum Intelligence Weekly's* top 40 petroleum companies

Rank 2005	Rank 2004	PIW Index	Company	Country	State Ownership (%)
1	1	30	Saudi Aramco	Saudi Arabia	100
2	2	36	Exxon Mobil	U.S.	0
3	4	39	NIOC	Iran	100
4	3	44	PDV	Venezuela	100
5	5	48	BP	U.K.	0
6	6	59	Royal Dutch Shell	U.K./Netherlands	0
7	9	68	PetroChina	China	90
8	8	78	Chevron	U.S.	0
8	7	78	Total	France	0
10	9	83	Pemex	Mexico	100
11	11	94	ConocoPhillips	U.S.	0
12	12	96	Sonatrach	Algeria	100
13	13	100	KPC	Kuwait	100
14	14	106	Petrobras	Brazil	32
15	24	108	Gazprom	Russia	50
16	19	130	Lukoil	Russia	0
17	16	132	Adnoc	UAE	100
18	17	134	Eni	Italy	0
19	18	137	Petronas	Malaysia	100
20	21	143	NNPC	Nigeria	100
21	20	152	Repsol YPF	Spain	0
22	25	156	LibyaNOC	Libya	100
23	22	168	INOC	Iraq	100
24	23	183	EGPC	Egypt	100
24	26	183	QP	Qatar	100
26	31	185	Rosneft	Russia	75
26	27	185	Surgutneftegas	Russia	—
28	28	189	Sinopec	China	55
29	30	191	Statoil	Norway	71
30	32	224	ONGC	India	74
31	33	241	Marathon	U.S.	0
32	29	242	Yukos	Russia	—
33	15	253	Pertamina	Indonesia	100
34	37	277	SPC	Syria	100
35	34	283	PDO	Oman	60
36	50	292	OMV	Austria	32
36	36	292	Socar	Azerbaijan	100
38	41	298	TNK-BP	Russia	0
39	40	303	EnCana	Canada	0
40	35	310	Ecopetrol	Colombia	100

Note: The *Petroleum Intelligence Weekly* ranking uses a combination of output and financial measures.

marketing—even if the emphasis was increasingly on the upstream businesses and little attempt was made to ensure close upstream-downstream coordination.

In gas the situation is different. The physical difficulties of transporting and storing gas have meant that monetizing gas reserves requires dedicated investments in transportation, liquefaction, and storage that can link production to consumption. However, unlike oil, most of the majors lack a historical presence in the downstream gas business. Increasingly the majors have forward integrated into the downstream gas sector, either directly or through alliances and long-term contracts with gas marketing companies. In an effort to exploit gas fields that are far from major markets, LNG has been a critical area of investment for most of the majors.

The desire for vertical integration in gas was also a powerful incentive for entering electricity generation. By 2005, Exxon Mobil owned 3700 MW of generating capacity and had invested $2 billion in electricity production.

For all the majors, gas was a key priority during the first decade of the twenty-first century. Once regarded as a worthless impediment that was flared, the world demand for gas was growing at twice the rate as that of oil. By 2008 gas consumption (in terms of oil equivalency) was almost 80% that of oil. If the twentieth century was the "age of oil," the first half of the twenty-first century has been declared the "era of gas" by some observers.

Technology and Knowledge Management

The quest for reserves has taken the petroleum majors to the Arctic and the depths of the ocean. It has encouraged the companies to develop enhanced recovery techniques in order to extend the lives of mature fields. It has resulted in the production of synthetic crudes from sulfur-heavy petroleum, from coal and from tar sands and oilshale. Gas-to-liquids technologies are being deployed to produce gasoline from natural gas.

The result has been increased dependence upon technology. Nevertheless, investments in R&D by the majors have been modest (less than 0.3% of revenues in recent years). Increasingly the majors have outsourced technology-intensive activities to other companies. Upstream, the technological leaders in directional drilling, 4-D seismic modeling, and "intelligent oilfield" management were the oil service companies, Schlumberger in particular.

However, the knowledge requirements of the petroleum business extended beyond technology. The technical, logistical, political and financial complexities of the business meant that a critical driver of competitive advantage was the ability to learn from experience and transfer that learning throughout the company. By the early years of the new century, all the leading oil and gas companies had adopted some form of knowledge management to increase the efficiency of their knowledge capture, storage and utilization. Many of the new knowledge management systems relied heavily on Web-based technology, distributed computing, and digital wireless communication to enhance the speed and quality of decision making.

What Drives Profitability in the Petroleum Sector?

Exploration and Production

The oil price rise of 2002–8 had reinforced the industry's conventional wisdom that upstream provides the primary source of profit for the energy industry. As Table 15.5 shows, upstream was substantially more profitable for the majors than downstream or chemicals. Although upstream activities accounted for only one-fifth

TABLE 15.5 Profitability differences between the majors' business segments, 2006–8 (%)

	Exploration and production		Refining and marketing		Gas and power		Chemicals		Corporate and other	
	ROA 2006–8	Share of total assets 2008	ROA 2006–8	Share of total assets 2008	ROA 2006–8	Share of total assets 2008	ROA 2006–2008	Share of total assets 2008	ROA 2006–2008	Share of assets total 2008
Exxon Mobil	28.45	46.83	13.37	25.60	n.a.	n.a.	19.47	8.84	−0.65	18.73
Royal Dutch Shell	20.40	37.70	7.38	28.51	6.03	17.41	5.32	5.46	4.47	6.86
BP	24.87	59.88	3.53	33.00	n.a.	n.a.	n.a.	n.a.	−6.16	8.36
ChevronTexaco	18.22	58.20	9.26	27.43	n.a.	n.a.	10.90	2.56	−5.55	11.81
Eni	20.99	42.53	4.15	11.22	10.82	32.30	−1.38	2.66	−29.60	0.80
Total	32.96	53.91	14.32	24.87	n.a.	n.a.	6.84	11.89	6.47	9.33
Repsol	19.07	34.27	11.22	34.40	14.97	10.23	10.09	5.68	−3.65	15.41

Note: ROA has been calculated as follows:

For Exxon Mobil: earnings after income taxes/segment assets.

For Royal Dutch Shell: earnings for the period/segment assets.

For BP: profit before interest/segment assets.

For ChevronTexaco: segment earnings/segment assets.

For Eni: adjusted net profit/segment assets.

For Total: net operating income/capital employed.

For Repsol: segment operating profit/segment assets.

Source: Company annual reports.

TABLE 15.6 Oil and gas production and reserves by country, 1991 and 2007

	Oil production (000 barrels/day)		Gas production (bn cubic meters/day)		Oil reserves (bn barrels)	Gas reserves (trillion cu. meters)
	2007	*1991*	*2007*	*1991*	*2007*	*2007*
Saudi Arabia	10413	8820	75.9	35	264.2	7.17
U.S.	6879	9076	545.9	510	29.4	5.98
Russia	9978	9326	607.4	600	79.4	44.65
Iran	4404	3500	111.9	26	138.4	27.80
Mexico	3477	3126	46.2	28	12.2	0.37
Venezuela	2613	2501	28.5	22	87.0	5.15
Norway	2556	1923	89.7	27	8.2	2.96
China	3743	2828	69.3	15	15.5	1.88
Canada	3309	1980	183.7	105	27.7	1.63
U.K.	1636	1919	72.4	51	3.6	0.41
U.A.E.	2915	2639	49.2	24	97.8	6.09
Iraq	2145	279		–	115.0	3.17
Kuwait	2626	185	12.6	1	101.5	1.78
Nigeria	2356	1890	28.4	4	36.2	5.30
Algeria	2000	1351	83.2	53	12.3	4.52

Source: BP Statistical Review of World Energy, 2008.

of revenues for large oil firms, they contributed over two-thirds of overall profits during 2004–8. The reasons why upstream has been so profitable are not altogether clear. The structure of the industry—many producers and a commodity product—does not appear particularly attractive. However, one key structural influence is the role of the Organization of Petroleum Exporting Countries (OPEC), which accounts for over half of world oil production and maintains prices through setting production quotas for its members. When OPEC's discipline over oil production disintegrates, prices drop—sometimes catastrophically (as in 1986 and at the end of 1998). However, the massive rise in oil prices (and upstream profits) during 2002–8 was mainly the result of capacity shortage in the face of rising demand from China and India. As Table 15.6 shows, the problem is not a lack of reserves (except in the U.S. and Europe where reserves are becoming exhausted; the problem is limits on production due to underinvestment (Russia, Iran, Libya), internal unrest (Iraq, Nigeria) and poor management (Venezuela, Mexico).

The high prices of 2006–8, combined with restricted access to existing reserves, caused the companies to move increasingly to deep water exploration and nonconventional oils (tarsands, oil shale). The result has been rapidly increasing finding and lifting costs (see Table 15.7).

The desire to control rising upstream costs has encouraged the oil and gas companies to outsource more and more of their E&P activities. Drilling, seismic surveys, rig design, platform construction and oilfield maintenance are increasingly undertaken by oilfield service companies. As these companies have developed proprietary technologies, deepened their experience and grown through mergers and

TABLE 15.7 U.S. energy companies' finding costs by region, 1993–2007 (2007 dollars/barrel of oil equivalent)

	U.S. onshore	U.S. offshore	Canada	OECD Europe	Africa	Middle East	Other Eastern hemisphere	Other, Western hemisphere	Worldwide
1993–1995	4.53	4.58	6.35	5.25	3.32	3.23	5.51	2.66	4.65
1998–2000	5.21	10.52	7.18	7.85	2.93	5.92	7.88	4.59	6.14
2001–2003	9.16	10.24	12.26	9.86	5.79	6.22	4.05	3.98	7.35
2004–2006	11.54	65.49	19.89	23.41	26.36	5.41	13.03	43.87	17.65
2005–2007	13.38	49.54	17.01	31.58	38.24	4.77	20.56	30.30	18.49

Source: Energy Information Administration, U.S. Department of Energy.

TABLE 15.8 Capital investment by business sector among the majors, 2003–7

	Average annual capital expenditure ($ million)	Exploration and production (%)	Refining and marketing (%)	Chemicals (%)	Gas and power (%)	Corporate and other (%)
Exxon Mobil	16.975	78.2	14.7	4.0	2.6[a]	0.5
Royal Dutch/Shell	16400	68.0	17.8	3.2	9.3	1.7
BP	17900	69.3	17.0	—	3.3	6.0
TotalFinaElf	12193	72.3	17.4[b]	9.9	—	0.4
Chevron Texaco	10800	77.0	17.6	1.6	—	3.8[c]
Conoco Phillips	11425	57.9	16.2	—	—	25.9[d]
Eni	9611	65.7	8.6	1.5	17.6	6.8[e]

Notes:

[a] Coal and Power; downstream gas included in refining and marketing.

[b] Includes downstream gas.

[c] Includes Power.

[d] Major item was investment in Lukoil.

[e] Includes engineering and construction.

Source: Company annual reports.

acquisitions, so sector leaders such as Schlumberger, Baker Hughes, Halliburton and Diamond Offshore Drilling have emerged as powerful players within the petroleum industry.

The attractive rates of return earned in the upstream sector have meant that capital investment by the integrated majors has become increasingly focused upon the upstream sector. Between 2000 and 2008, the leading majors invested between three and four times as much upstream as downstream (see Table 15.8). During previous decades, capital investment was split more evenly between upstream and downstream.

Refining and Marketing In oil, downstream businesses include refining and the wholesale and retail marketing and distribution of refined oil products. The main refined products in order of importance are: gasoline, diesel fuel, aviation fuel, heating oil, liquefied petroleum gas (LPG) and petrochemical feedstocks (e.g. naphtha). Historically, downstream has been less profitable than upstream (see Table 15.9). Both refining and retail distribution have been subject to intense competitive pressure as a result of excess capacity.

During 2004–6, refining margins increased sharply. Mergers between companies and the impact of environmental regulations reduced excess capacity; in the U.S. refinery shutdowns created a temporary squeeze. However, recession, increased fuel efficiency, and new refining capacity in Asia and the Middle East caused profitability to fall during 2007–8. In retailing, profitability was dismal due to excess capacity and new entry by supermarket chains into gasoline distribution (especially in France and the U.K.).

TABLE 15.9 Return on investment by line of business for U.S. petroleum companies, 1980–2007 (%)

	1980–4	1985–9	1990–4	1995–9	2000–3	2004–7
U.S. oil and gas production	15.40	4.00	5.80	10.10	14.40	18.99
U.S. refining and marketing	5.10	8.00	2.70	5.70	7.90	22.33
Foreign oil and gas production	19.30	12.20	9.10	12.40	12.90	21.48
Foreign refining and marketing	10.40	6.80	10.10	7.00	6.20	19.73
Nuclear, nonconventional, and coal	5.50	4.70	2.90	6.10	3.70	16.02

Source: Energy Information Administration, U.S. Department of Energy.

Downstream Gas and Power Among the petroleum majors, Eni was unusual in being established on natural gas rather than oil. For most of the majors, oil had been their dominant interest and, as a result, few had pursued the same strategy of vertical integration that they had in oil. As the result, in most countries the gas chain was more fragmented than the oil chain with exploration and production undertaken by the petroleum companies and distribution traditionally undertaken by state-owned or state-regulated utilities. As demand for natural gas increased during the 1980s and 1990s, the petroleum majors reoriented their upstream activities towards gas. However, gas reserves were valueless unless they could be brought to market. Hence all the majors developed interests in the transportation and downstream distribution of gas. Regulation of downstream gas markets and privatization of publicly owned gas utilities created the opportunities that the petroleum majors needed to increase their presence in gas marketing and distribution. Similar deregulation in electricity generation and market produced further opportunities for the majors. Not only could they enter the electricity business directly—they could also seek to supply natural gas to independent power producers.

Although downstream gas and power offered growth opportunities for the petroleum majors, these activities typically did not offer rates of return comparable with their upstream businesses. The newly liberalized gas and electricity markets attracted entrants from a number of different sectors and were fiercely competitive. Moreover, the oil majors were relative newcomers to these markets compared with the traditional utilities. Fierce competition coupled with overinvestment could decimate profitability. During 2002, wholesale prices for electricity plunged in the U.S. and U.K. forcing a number of power producers into acute financial difficulty.

Chemicals The petrochemical sector displayed many of the same structural features as oil refining: capital-intensive processes producing commodity products, many competitors, and a continual tendency for excess capacity (much of it resulting from new investment by Asian and Middle East producers) to drive down prices and margins. Competitive advantage in chemicals depended upon scale economies, technological advantages (such as patented products and processes) and low costs of feedstock. Among the oil and gas majors there were two distinct views about chemicals. Some, like Eni, saw chemicals as a fundamentally unattractive industry and believed that chemical plants were better run by chemical companies. Others (including Exxon, Shell, and Total) viewed chemicals as part of their core business and believed that integration between refining and petrochemicals offered them a cost advantage.

The Outlook for Eni in 2009

The steady evolution of Eni's strategy under its past three CEOs, Bernabè, Mincato, and Scaroni, had provided stability and a clear sense of identity and direction within the Group. Eni was an international energy major with a strong focus on E&P and a commitment to being Europe's leading supplier of natural gas. Upstream it was focused on the core areas of the Caspian Sea and Africa; downstream upon Italy and nearby European countries. Its technically strong engineering and oil services sector allowed it to link the two. Its emphasis on organic growth, capital discipline and shareholder returns had done much to build its reputation within the industry and the international financial community. Looking ahead, its emphasis upon natural gas and its proven ability to work effectively as a valued partner in politically challenging producer countries positioned it well for the future.

Yet, for all Eni's solid achievement, Scaroni was aware that Eni's outstanding performance had taken place under very favorable external circumstances. The next five years posed uncertainties both for the industry and for Eni. Almost certainly maintaining production growth, increasing profits and creating value for shareholders would be more difficult in the future than in the past. By 2006, Eni had divested most of its noncore businesses and eliminated most of the inefficiencies that it had inherited from its state-owned past. Increasing profits in the future would require pursuing profitable growth opportunities, more effective exploitation of existing competitive advantage and building new sources of competitive advantage.

Upstream, Eni—along with the other majors—faced the risk of growing marginalization as the producer countries sought a bigger share of the value from their oil and gas reserves and their national oil companies extended their ambitions to expand downstream and internationally. Despite being among the world's biggest companies, the oil and gas majors were far from being the biggest players in the industry in terms of oil and gas reserves (see Appendix 3). Moreover, they were high-cost producers compared with many of the national oil companies. So far the increased assertiveness of many producer governments had allowed Eni to position itself as a collaborative partner. However, Eni's difficulties in Kazakhstan pointed to the conflicts between petroleum majors and host governments that characterized the oil business. Ongoing tensions between the EU and Russia provided an awkward context for Eni's closer relationships with Gazprom.

Even without these threats, fulfilling Eni's potential would require developing the responsiveness and coordination that it needed to combine technology, physical assets, expertise, and human ingenuity to exploit the opportunities constantly emerging in the world's fast-changing energy markets. Despite the transformation of Eni from a loose-knit holding company to a more tightly integrated divisional corporation, it still faced internal challenges to the successful execution of its strategy. A key challenge was internationalization. Downstream, Eni was heavily dependent on the Italian market (see Figure 15.1) and, overall, Italy accounted for almost half of Eni's sales and assets

TABLE 15.10 Valuation multiples for petroleum majors (28 April 2009)

	Price/earnings ratio	Price/book ratio	Price/sales ratio	Price/cash flow
Exxon Mobil Corp.	7.38	2.83	0.67	5.36
British Petroleum plc	8.17	1.31	0.63	4.77
ChevronTexaco Corp.	5.44	1.48	0.47	4.32
TotalFinaElf S.A.	5.59	1.76	0.53	5.11
Royal Dutch Petroleum Co.	6.96	1.70	0.32	4.23
Eni SpA	3.77	1.35	0.56	3.56
Repsol YPF, S.A.	3.65	0.87	0.30	n.a.
ConocoPhillips	negative	1.08	0.24	2.62
Industry median	7.50	1.08	0.24	3.30

Source: Hoover's Online (www.hoovers.com); *Financial Times*.

(see Figure 15.2 and 15.3). The strong domestic orientation was reflected in Eni's culture and personnel—there were very few non-Italians among the ranks of senior managers.

The second internal challenge was that of integration. Eni's large downstream gas business offered a market for its upstream gas production, and its internal engineering and construction capabilities provided the means to link the two. Eni's ability to pursue vertical integration in gas represented a significant source of competitive advantage for the company. However, to realize this potential required effective collaboration between Eni's different divisions and subsidiaries. Despite the creation of a divisional corporation, effective coordination in exploiting overseas opportunities increasingly required close, flexible coordination across Eni's traditionally independently-minded businesses.

Finally, the issue of size remained an open question. Eni's commitment to organic growth had been applauded by investment analysts. However, investment projects in the industry were growing steadily in complexity and cost. Did Eni have the necessary size to play with the big boys and the diversity of locations and projects to spread technical and political risks? For all Eni's ability to generate strong shareholder returns, Scaroni continued to be dismayed by the stock market's lack of appreciation for Eni's investment qualities. Eni's valuation ratios remained below those of its peers in the international petroleum industry (see Table 15.10).

Appendix 1: Eni SpA: Selected Financial data, 2002–8

Income statement (U.S.$ millions)	2002	2003	2004	2005	2006	2007	2008
Revenue	51 379	59 322	73 063	92 412	109 479	120 674	160 024
Cost of goods sold	33 440	39 132	47 550	60 223	72 437	79 705	112 320
Gross profit	17 939	20 190	25 513	32 189	37 041	40 968	47 704

(Continued)

Income statement (U.S.$ millions)	2002	2003	2004	2005	2006	2007	2008
Gross profit margin	34.9%	34.0%	34.9%	34.8%	33.8%	33.9%	29.8%
SG&A expense	3253	3584	4024	4155	4599	5206	5886
Depreciation and amortization	5771	5831	6028	7168	8090	9913	14428
Operating income	8915	10774	15375	20865	24352	25849	27402
Operating margin	17.4%	18.2%	21.0%	22.6%	22.2%	21.4%	17.1%
Nonoperating income	45	19	3210	3882	5206	6103	11738
Nonoperating expenses	206	7	3404	4336	5003	6239	12051
Income before taxes	8664	10580	16198	21545	25693	27438	28298
Income taxes	3279	3669	5770	10079	13316	12630	14247
Net income after taxes	4816	6323	9781	11466	12377	14808	14050
Net profit margin	9.4%	10.7%	13.4%	12.4%	11.3%	12.3%	8.8%
ROACE	13.7%	15.6%	16.6%	19.5%	20.0%	20.5%	15.7%
Balance sheet (U.S.$ millions)	**Dec 02**	**Dec 03**	**Dec 04**	**Dec 05**	**Dec 06**	**Dec 07**	**Dec 08**
Cash	3423	4113	1244	1653	5021	2896	2850
Trade and other receivables	14186	17043	17030	22198	23687	28326	32666
Inventories	3355	4031	3530	4418	5988	7534	8941
Other current assets	1868	2244	3135	3018	3131	7569	10121
Total current assets	22832	27431	24939	31288	37826	46325	54578
Net fixed assets	35327	42443	50327	55816	55833	68688	86958
Other noncurrent assets	10840	13024	15072	16870	17614	23987	29851
Total assets	69000	82898	90338	103974	111273	139000	171387
Accounts payable	5806	6975	7238	10131	13265	15196	18507
Short-term debt	8273	9939	5146	5719	4284	10635	10155
Other current liabilities	8560	10285	10696	12029	12374	15602	23304
Total current liabilities	22639	27199	23080	27879	29924	41433	51966
Long-term debt	6868	8251	9433	9490	9335	15522	20476
Other noncurrent liabilities	9766	11734	13755	17976	20103	23317	27636
Total liabilities	39274	43783	46268	55345	59362	80272	100078
Minority interest	2196	2638	3926	2913	2734	3341	5989
Total shareholders' equity	27530	35714	44070	48629	51911	58728	71310
Cash flow statement	**2002**	**2003**	**2004**	**2005**	**2006**	**2007**	**2008**
Net operating cash flow	11091	12257	15500	18521	21421	21258	32047

Appendix 2: Eni's Operating Performance, 1999–2008

Exploration and production	1999	2000	2001	2002	2003	2004	2005	2006	2007	2008
Proved hydrocarbon reserves (mmboe)	5534	6008	6929	7030	7272	7218	6837	6436	6370	6600
Reserve life index (years)	14.0	14.0	13.7	13.2	12.7	12.1	10.8	10.0	10.0	10.0

Exploration and production	1999	2000	2001	2002	2003	2004	2005	2006	2007	2008
Hydrocarbon production (kboe/d)	1064	1187	1369	1472	1562	1624	1737	1770	1736	1797
Gas and power										
Worldwide gas sales (bcm)	63.08	65.50	67.10	68.54	78.33	87.03	94.21	98.10	98.96	104.23
Electricity sold (TWh)	0	4.77	6.55	6.74	8.65	16.95	27.56	31.03	33.19	29.93
Refining and marketing										
Refinery throughput (mm tonnes)	40.65	41.27	39.99	37.73	35.43	37.69	38.79	38.04	37.15	35.84
Refinery capacity (kbbl/d)	664	664	664	504	504	504	524	534	544	544
Sales of refined products (mmtonnes)	51.82	53.46	53.24	52.24	50.43	53.54	51.63	51.13	50.14	50.68
Retail sales (mmtonnes)	14.21	13.92	14.11	13.71	14.01	14.40	13.72	12.48	12.65	12.67
Service stations at year end (units)	12 489	12 085	11 707	10 762	10 647	9140	6282	6294	6441	5956
Average service station throughput (kliters/year)	1543	1555	1621	1674	1771	1970	1926	2470	2486	2502
Engineering and construction										
Orders acquired (€ million)	2600	4726	3716	7852	5876	5784	8395	11 172	11 845	13 860
Order backlog (€ million)	4439	6638	6937	10 065	9405	8521	10 122	13 191	15 390	19 105

Appendix 3: Oil and Gas Companies among the Forbes Global 2000, April 2009 ($ bn)

Rank	Company	Country	Sales ($bn)	Profits ($bn)	Assets ($bn)	Market value ($bn)
2	Royal Dutch Shell	Netherlands	458.36	26.28	278.44	135.10
4	ExxonMobil	U.S.	425.70	45.22	228.05	335.54
5	BP	U.K.	361.14	21.16	228.24	119.70
9	Chevron	U.S.	255.11	23.93	161.17	121.70
11	Total	France	223.15	14.74	164.66	112.90

(Continued)

Rank	Company	Country	Sales ($bn)	Profits ($bn)	Assets ($bn)	Market value ($bn)
13	Gazprom	Russia	97.29	26.78	276.81	74.55
14	PetroChina	China	114.32	19.94	145.14	270.56
18	ENI	Italy	158.32	12.91	139.80	80.68
25	Petrobras	Brazil	92.08	14.12	120.68	110.97
33	Sinopec-China Petroleum	China	154.28	7.43	100.41	93.50
53	StatoilHydro	Norway	93.38	6.20	82.42	53.30
64	Rosneft	Russia	46.99	11.12	77.40	34.07
76	Lukoil	Russia	66.86	9.51	59.14	26.62
101	Repsol-YPF	Spain	68.48[E]	3.95	68.79	18.95
121	Reliance Industries	India	34.03	4.87	43.61	35.95
124	EnCana	Canada	30.06	5.94	47.25	29.69
132	Occidental Petroleum	U.S.	24.48	6.86	41.54	42.03
135	Marathon Oil	U.S.	70.25	3.53	42.69	16.47
145	Schlumberger	Netherlands	27.56	5.43	31.99	45.52
152	Oil & Natural Gas	India	24.04	4.95	35.35	28.91
163	BG Group	U.K.	18.34	4.56	35.83	48.10
168	Surgutneftegas	Russia	24.25	3.61	40.29	19.65
193	Hess	United States	41.09	2.36	28.59	17.84
199	Anadarko Petroleum	U.S.	15.72	3.26	48.92	16.07
207	Indian Oil	India	51.66	1.97	33.64	10.20
211	TNK-BP Holding	Russia	36.25	5.94	27.94	9.45
230	Ecopetrol	Colombia	15.42	5.29	22.16	33.38
231	Transocean	Switzerland	12.67	4.20	35.17	19.11
233	Nippon Oil	Japan	65.46	1.49	45.98	7.05
234	Suncor Energy	Canada	24.37	1.73	26.35	19.51
244	PTT Public Company	Thailand	57.08	1.47	25.21	12.18
246	Cnooc	China	11.97	4.12	24.62	39.17
249	Husky Energy	Canada	20.01	3.04	21.48	18.21
251	Canadian Natural Res	Canada	11.47	4.04	34.55	17.44
271	OMV Group	Austria	35.57	1.91	29.52	7.91
273	Petro-Canada	Canada	22.51	2.54	24.61	10.72
305	Sasol	South Africa	16.62	2.87	17.71	15.98
322	Formosa Petrochemical	Taiwan	21.62	2.15	15.15	15.22
325	XTO Energy	U.S.	7.70	1.91	38.25	18.35
346	National Oilwell Varco	U.S.	13.43	1.95	21.48	11.16
365	Halliburton	U.S.	18.28	1.54	14.39	14.63
366	Inpex	Japan	12.05	1.74	17.96	16.34
372	Apache	U.S.	12.39	0.71	29.19	19.78
380	ConocoPhillips	U.S.	225.42	-17.00	142.87	55.29
394	SK Holdings	South Korea	69.66	1.48	61.16	2.62
395	Cepsa	Spain	25.85	1.02	13.90	12.68
405	Chesapeake Energy	U.S.	11.63	0.72	38.44	9.77
414	Enbridge	Canada	13.07	1.08	20.01	11.20
434	Murphy Oil	U.S.	27.51	1.74	11.15	7.97

Appendix 4: Eni 2009–12 Strategic Plan and Targets

London, 13 February 2009—Paolo Scaroni, CEO of Eni, today presented the company's 2009–12 strategic plan to the financial community.

In spite of the uncertain and volatile energy markets, Eni confirms its strategy of delivering hydrocarbon production and reserve growth, based on a solid portfolio of quality projects. Eni will also strengthen its leadership in the European gas market and maintain a dividend yield amongst the highest in the sector.

Exploration and Production

Eni confirms its strategy of delivering production growth, with an average annual rate of 3.5% for the 2009–12 period. This growth strategy is based on organic development plans carried out with a reserve replacement ratio of 130%. Beyond the four-year plan, Eni expects to maintain robust production growth with an average annual growth rate of 3% up to 2015.

In 2012, hydrocarbon production will exceed 2 million boe/day, based on a $55 per barrel price scenario. In 2009, hydrocarbon production will exceed 1.8 million boe/day, based on a $43 per barrel price scenario.

Production growth will be focused on three main strategic areas: Africa, OECD countries and Central Asia/Russia. More than 90% of production and investments to 2012 will be concentrated in these areas.

Eni will maintain a steady growth, even in lower oil price conditions, thanks to its focus on conventional activities and to the quality of its portfolio, which is located largely in low cost production areas and is based upon giant projects with economy of scale benefits.

In the next four years, more than 0.5 million boe/day of new production will come on stream, 85% of which is related to projects that will be profitable even under an oil price scenario below $45 per barrel.

Gas and Power

Eni will strengthen its leading position in the European gas market, where it holds a unique competitive position, thanks to diversification and the size of its large supply contracts as well as to a vast infrastructure system and customer base.

Despite the lower growth we expect in the European gas markets, Eni will grow its international gas sales by an average 7% a year, thanks also to the contribution of Distrigas. This growth will enable the company to reach total gas sales of 124 billion cubic meters by 2012.

Beyond continuing to grow its market share in core European countries, Eni will increase sales in the U.S., thanks to the monetization of the gas produced in the Gulf of Mexico.

In the four-year plan Eni, thanks to the growth in regulated activities and its expansion in international markets, will achieve in G&P a total pro-forma adjusted EBITDA of €20 billion, 1 billion higher than the target set in the previous plan.

Refining and Marketing

Eni's strategy in the R&M sector focuses on the selective strengthening of its refining system, the improvement of quality standards of its marketing activities and the widespread increase in operating efficiency, targeting an improvement of €400 million in EBIT by 2012 excluding scenario effects.

In refining, Eni plans to increase the complexity and the yield in medium distillates, exploiting proprietary technologies.

In marketing, Eni's target is to consolidate its leadership in the Italian market, increasing its market share to 32% by 2012, through loyalty programs and the broadening of nonoil products sales.

Investment Plan and Efficiency Program

In the 2009–12 plan, Eni will invest €48.8 billion, slightly less than in the 2008–11 plan. Investments in exploration and production are estimated at €34 billion and will sustain the production growth over the next four years and beyond.

With regard to the efficiency, Eni doubled the program launched in 2006, after having achieved almost 1 billion in cost reductions by the end of 2008. The new plan will enable Eni to double costs reduction to about €2 billion by 2012, both in real terms and versus the 2005 baseline.

Source: Eni 2009–12 Strategic Plan and Targets, www.eni.it/en_IT/attachments/media/press-release/2009/02/eni-2009-2012-strategic-plan-and-targets.pdf, accessed October 29, 2009.

Notes

1 We refer throughout the case to "Eni." For most of its history, the company's full name was Ente Nazionale Idrocarburi, but was known by its acronym, ENI. In August 1992, the company's name was changed to Eni SpA.

2 In common with other European governments, Italy recognized the growing strategic importance of oil and wished to avoid dependence upon foreign-owned multinationals for its fuel supplies. The British government had purchased a controlling interest in BP in 1914 and France had established the Compagnie Française des Pétroles (Total) in 1924.

3 D. Votaw, *The Six-Legged Dog: Mattei and ENI—A Study in Power,* University of California Press, Berkeley, CA, 1964, p. 15.

4 Daniel Yergin, *The Prize,* Simon & Shuster, New York, 1992, p. 502.

5 Daniel Yergin, *The Prize,* Simon & Shuster, New York, 1992, p. 23.

6 Section sourced from company report, "L'Eni di Fronte a un Bivio," Eni S.p.A, 2002.

7 D. Votaw, *The Six-Legged Dog: Mattei and ENI—A Study in Power,* University of California Press, Berkeley, CA, 1964, p. 71.

8 "L'Eni di Fronte a un Bivio," Eni S.p.A, 2002, p. 5.

9 *Franco Bernabè at Eni* (Harvard Business School Case 9-498-034, April 7, 1998).

10 Chairman Gabriele Cagliari later committed suicide in prison.

11 "L'Eni di Fronte a un Bivio," Eni S.p.A, 2002, p. 11.

12 "Eni Savors the Taste of Freedom", *Financial Times,* June 9, 1994.

13 ENI SpA, Securities and Exchange Commission, Form 20F, 1996.

14 Securities and Exchange Commission, *ENI S.p.A., 20-F for 1996,* p. 3.

15 "Letter to Shareholders," Eni, Annual Report, 1999, pp. 4–5.

16 "Italy: The Real Sick Man of Europe," *The Economist,* May 19, 2005.

17 "Eni's New Chief Intends to become a Big Player," *Financial Times,* September 22, 2005.

18 Lex column, "Gazprom/Eni," *Financial Times,* April 7, 2009.

19 "Rome's Colonial Past key to Libya's Eni Stake," *Financial Times,* December 9, 2008.

20 See http://oilandglory.com/labels/ENI.html, accessed October 19, 2009.

21 "How Italy's ENI Vastly Boosted Oil Output," *Business Week,* April 20, 2009.

22 Eni S.p.A. Gas seminar conference call, December 1, 2006.

Case 16 American Apparel: Vertically Integrated in Downtown L.A.*

December 2008 marked the end of American Apparel's first year as a public company. On December 19, 2007, its shares had begun trading on the American Stock Exchange under the symbol APP. The year 2008 had been eventful for the Los Angeles-based T-shirt and casual clothing company. Fueled by capital from its public listing, it had embarked upon a new phase of expansion: over 80 new stores were opened—including first-time entry into Spain, Brazil, China and Australia—and sales grew by 62% over 2007. Its status as "one of the hottest brands around" was confirmed by its second place (after Nike) in the *Cassandra Report*'s listing of "Top Trendsetter Brands of 2008"—beating Apple (third place). Chief executive Dov Charney was named "Retailer of the Year" in the 2008 Annual Michael Awards.

This success was achieved despite a strategy that defied the conventional wisdom of the "rag trade." In mass-market fashion apparel, outsourcing production to low-wage countries was viewed as the only viable strategy. Yet American Apparel had built a highly profitable business following a vertically integrated model with production concentrated in Los Angeles. American Apparel believed that the higher costs of manufacturing in the U.S. could be offset by the price premium from superior quality, styling, and image, and by the advantages of speed to market. Critical to these advantages were American Apparel's tight linkage between design, manufacture, marketing, and retailing. It was not just the labor costs of producing in California rather than in China that boosted American Apparel's manufacturing costs. Its cost base was further elevated by paying employees premium wage rates and offering benefits that were unheard of in the dog-eat-dog world of garment manufacture. Employee benefits included health care, retirement pensions and a variety of employee amenities.

The source of American Apparel's distinctiveness was its founder and chief executive, Dov Charney. Charney was a self-proclaimed hustler whose lifestyle and management style generated controversy that most publicly traded companies eschewed. Charney's open and frank attitude about progressive social issues and sex stirred up media feeding frenzies from fashion magazines to nationally syndicated television. While the provocative photos he selected for American Apparel's ad campaigns were praised for their ability to grab people's attention, much of the publicity he garnered was highly critical. In the media and on the Web, he was portrayed as an exhibitionist and sexual predator. Even in taking American Apparel public, Charney succeeded in being nonconformist and innovative. Rather than launch an initial public offering (IPO) underwritten by a leading investment bank, American Apparel chose to be acquired by Endeavor Acquisition Corp—a "special purpose acquisition corporation" (otherwise known as a "blank check company")—a listed company set up specifically to acquire other companies. Observers noted that the deal "allowed Mr. Charney to go public without the scrutiny that attends most stockmarket listings."[1]

Looking ahead, Charney believed that American Apparel faced tremendous future growth potential. He saw American Apparel as operating in an "attractive, underserved market segment with large potential." This potential related both to cities and countries where American Apparel was not yet present and customer segments other than American Apparel's core "metropolitan, young adult segment." The long-term goals he outlined included unit growth of 20% annually, an operating margin of 15% and growth of earnings per share of 20%–25%.[2]

These ambitious growth targets presented new challenges for American Apparel. As it grew in size and its retail stores spanned more of the globe, doubts were raised about the scalability of its business model. Expanding output had already forced American Apparel to acquire new plants in Los Angeles. International expansion meant longer supply chains and increased logistical complexity. The impressive growth in same-store sales had been achieved through expanding its product range—American Apparel had expanded from T-shirts and knitted cotton garments into a wide range of clothing and accessories. The increasing product range added further complexity to purchasing, manufacturing and distribution. Overall, American Apparel's tightly coordinated, vertically integrated business model was being stretched in multiple directions. In addition to the challenges of growing size and scope, Charney also had to come to terms with American Apparel's new status as a public company. This raised questions about his personality and management style. To what extent would increased regulation and financial market scrutiny require a more conventional approach to leadership?

The T-Shirt Business

T-shirts—like denim jeans—are quintessentially American clothing products. About 1.4 billion cotton T-shirts are sold in North America annually with a retail value of about $20 billion. Originally underwear garments, T-shirts are the most common summer outerwear garment for weekend Americans. The designs and words they carry are important statements of personal identity indicating affiliation with a sports team, college, political movement, religion, charity or specific social event. Yet despite the T-shirt's place in American culture, the vast majority are imported—with China, Mexico and Central America the major source. Many imports are by U.S. manufacturing firms such as Gildan Activewear, Hanesbrands and Delta Apparel that have plants in Mexico, Latin America and the Caribbean. A high proportion of imported T-shirts are made from cotton grown in the U.S. and knitted into fabric in China. (The U.S. is the world's largest exporter of cotton fiber.)[3] The average import price of a T-shirt was $1.51 in December 2005.[4] Despite import protection, the U.S. garment industry as a whole had shrunk dramatically. When the quota system known as the Multifiber Agreement was created in 1974, 1.4 million Americans worked in the garment industry. By the time it was abolished in 2006, the total was down to 270 000.

The U.S. T-shirt market features a wide range of suppliers. At the wholesale level, blank T-shirts are sold by major suppliers (such as Gildan Activewear, Hanesbrands, Russell Athletic and Fruit of the Loom) to screen printers that add their own designs or corporate and club logos. At the retail level, many different types of retailer compete—independent specialty stores, department stores, and chains such as Gap, Urban Outfitters, H&M, American Eagle, and Forever 21. The price dispersion is wide: at Sears, a basic T-shirt retails at $6.99, while at Nordstrom, a Versace limited edition T-shirt costs $225. Table 16.1 shows some leading suppliers of casual clothing.

Dov Charney and the Development of American Apparel

Dov Charney's character could be described as brilliant to boisterous, clever to crass, and daring to democratic. The native Canadian had a passion for T-shirts and capitalism. Charney believed that "nationalism is over" and "there was something special about the 'can do' spirit of the U.S.A."[5]

Charney's entrepreneurial interest in the garment business was first demonstrated at age 16, when he purchased American-made T-shirts from K-Mart in the U.S. and then drove them to Canada in a U-Haul truck. He sold them outside the old Montreal Forum at concerts.[6] During his senior year at Tufts University, he dropped out, borrowed $10 000 from his father, moved to South Carolina, and started his T-shirt business: "Heavy, The American Apparel Company." He was successful with a line of form-fitting women's T-shirts before going bust when its main contract manufacturer closed down production.[7]

TABLE 16.1 Sales and profits of leading fashion apparel companies, 2009

	Sales ($ bn)	Net income ($ bn)	Return on assets (%)
Gap (U.S.)	14.53	0.97	12.3
Inditex (Spain)	14.00	1.86	18.0
Hennes & Mauritz (Sweden)	10.91	1.88	30.5
VF (U.S.)	7.64	0.60	9.3
Next (U.K.)	6.62	0.70	21.6
Ross Stores (U.S.)	6.40	0.30	12.1
Esprit Holdings (China)	4.77	0.83	30.3
Hannesbrands (U.S.)	4.25	0.13	2.0
Abercrombie & Fitch (U.S.)	3.54	0.27	5.9
J. Crew (U.S.)	1.43	0.05	7.6
Gilden Activewear (U.S.)	1.25	0.14	7.9
American Apparel (U.S.)	0.55	0.01	4.2

Source: www.hoovers.com and company annual reports.

Charney moved to California where in 1998 he met Sam Lim, an owner of a cutting-and-sewing facility located under a freeway in Los Angeles.[8] Charney went into business with Sam Lim and Sam Kim, both Korean. Together they formed a company named "Two Koreans and a Jew."[9] Eventually Sam Kim sold his stake in the partnership and Charney and Lim went on to develop the business into American Apparel.

Charney established American Apparel as a T-shirt manufacturer that was integrated from knitting, through cutting and sewing, to dyeing and finishing. Initially, the main customers were private-label apparel companies who printed their own logos and retailed the products. Recognizing that this was a cut-throat market, Charney shifted focus to specialty screenprinters: "Your client is always looking to make it cheaper. There's no loyalty . . . And there is so much supply, from all corners of the world that it doesn't make it feasible to focus in that one area. So we de-emphasized private label packages and we're focusing on our brands for the imprintable T-shirt industry that services the specialty industry."[10]

American Apparel's main competitors were the blank T-shirt giants Hanes and Fruit of the Loom. American Apparel differentiated itself by focusing on quality and design. In contrast to the standard loose-fitting, heavy-knit T-shirts, American Apparel offered tightly-fitting women's and men's T-shirts with finer thread and a closer knit. In October 2003, American Apparel opened its first retail store. Charney viewed the Los Angeles store more as an experiment than a new business: "It's supposed to be a place for some of the intellectuals of the company and customers to hang out . . . It's not a money-maker—let's put it that way."[11] The Los Angeles store was quickly followed by others in New York and Montreal. By the end of 2004, American Apparel operated 34 stores in North America and three in the U.K. Charney then committed totally to developing the business. As late as 2005, as CEO of American Apparel, he drew a salary of less than $100 000: long-term development of the company took priority over his personal enrichment. "We need to dig in deeper, to penetrate the market we're in right now . . . We're building our foundation right now. We want to be the best at what we do, and once we are . . . once we're strong, then we can take on the world."[12]

Charney's Controversial Image

Dov Charney's key fashion innovation was in turning T-shirts into garments that enhanced the sexual attractiveness of the wearer. However, sexuality played a wider role in the success of American Apparel. In addition to its sexually provocative advertising, the company had a culture that acknowledged the sexual drives of its customers and its employees and embraced sexual conduct and sexual content as part of openness and creativity. If American Apparel's key product differentiation was the sex appeal of its fashion garments, then sexual openness within the company might enhance its ability to design and market these products.

Charney's own contribution to this culture included his wearing solely his American Apparel underwear while in the office and sexual relationships with his employees. "I'm not saying I want to screw all the girls at work," stated Charney, "but if I fall in love at work it's going to be beautiful and sexual."[13] Between 2005 and 2007, American Apparel faced four sexual harassment lawsuits, three of which were dropped after confidential settlements were reached. The fourth resulted in a wider investigation by the Los Angeles office of the Equal Employment Opportunity Commission into sexual harassment at American Apparel.[14] Charney attributed the lawsuits to disgruntled employees seeking personal gain by exploiting California's litigious culture.[15]

As a result of the lawsuits, American Apparel required employees to sign a document that declared:

> American Apparel is in the business of designing and manufacturing sexually charged T-shirts and intimate apparel, and uses sexually charged visual and oral communications in its marketing and sales activities. Employees working in the design, sales, marketing and other creative areas of the company will come into contact with sexually charged language and visual images. This is a part of the job for employees working in these areas.[16]

American Apparel in 2009

By the beginning of 2009, American Apparel had grown to be one of the leading suppliers of T-shirts to the U.S. market—both blank T-shirts sold to screen printers and final products supplied under its own brand through its own retail stores. Despite a tiny share of the overall U.S. garment industry (about one-half of one percent), it was one of the biggest garment manufacturers in the U.S. This reflected the fact that it was one of the few U.S. garment manufacturers that produced at home: most fashion clothing companies concentrated on design, marketing and distribution, with manufacturing outsourced and offshored. American Apparel's Los Angeles headquarters was the biggest cut-and-sew production facility in the U.S.

The distinctive feature of American Apparel was its high level of vertical integration: not only did it undertake most stages of production at its Los Angeles headquarters, it performed its own design, marketing and advertising, and owned and operated all its retail stores, even its overseas stores. Table 16.2 shows financial information for the company.

TABLE 16.2 Selected financial data, 2005–8 ($ million)

	2008	2007	2006	2005
Selected items from operating statement				
Net sales	545.1	387.0	264.7	188.1
Cost of sales	245.9	171.6	138.4	101.0
Gross profit	299.2	215.5	126.3	87.1
Operating expenses	263.1	184.40	135.1	76.8
of which:				
Selling	168.5	115.6	84.0	45.8
Warehouse and distribution	15.6	10.7	6.7	4.2
General and administrative	78.9	58.1	36.8	26.9
Income from operations	36.1	31.1	9.3	10.2
Interest expense	13.9	17.5	10.8	6.3
Income before income taxes	21.4	15.3	(0.3)	4.0
Income tax provision	7.3	(0.2)	1.3	0.4
Net (loss) income	14.1	15.5	(1.6)	3.6
Selected balance sheet items				
Current assets	187.0	152.8	97.0	85.8
of which:				
Inventories	148.2	106.4	76.5	67.5
Total assets	333.0	233.4	163.1	124.2
Current liabilities	74.3	150.7	59.8	44.9
of which:				
Overdraft and current bank debt	3.8	102.8	6.2	9.3
Accounts payable	26.3	21.9	30.1	18.3
Long-term debt	100.0	0.6	52.7	43.0
Total liabilities	196.6	171.5	136 455	110 280
Stockholders' equity	136.4	171.5	11.7	13.9
Cash flows				
Net cash from operating activities	21.2	(5.4)	7.7	(1,1)
Net cash used in investing activities	(72.2)	(23.8)	(16.9)	(15.9)
Net cash provided by financing activities	41.2	44.5	10.6	17.4

Source: American Apparel, 10-K reports.

Product Development and Design

Recreating the T-shirt as a fashion garment was fundamental to American Apparel's business concept. This involved careful attention to fit, texture, shape-retention and color. "We've fashionized and brought fashion to the commodity setting," Charney explained, arguing that his main achievement was "feminizing the blank T-shirt industry"[17] Previously, T-shirts were "bulky, one-size-fits-all" garments that were not gender specific. The company explained that:

> American Apparel's design vision and aesthetic are intended to appeal to young, metropolitan adults by providing them with a core line of iconic, timeless styles offered year-round in a wide variety of colors at reasonable

> prices. Since its founding, American Apparel has operated with the belief that there is a large potential market among young adults for well-designed, high-quality fashion essentials.[18]

American Apparel employed an in-house team of designers at its Los Angeles headquarters. The team was led by Dov Charney, who personally approved all new garment designs. Charney personally hired each member of the product-development department, searching for designers he felt had the "eye for what's next."[19] The team didn't read fashion magazines and paid little attention to catwalk fashion trends. The team took its inspiration from classic styles of the past, as well as to emerging style trends among young adults living in metropolitan cities such as Los Angeles, London and New York. Its clothing was reminiscent of 1970s urban apparel and represented a retro urban chic style. Designers often went to vintage clothing stores to find inspirations for new designs.

By 2009, the company had expanded its product range well beyond the T-shirt. It offered over 20 000 stock keeping units (SKUs) including fabric shirts, dresses, denim jeans, sweaters, jackets, swimwear, babywear, and a variety of accessories including bags, hats, scarves, sunglasses and other products—even sweaters for dogs. American Apparel intended to continue to introduce new merchandise to complement its existing products and draw new customers.

Manufacturing

American Apparel's headquarters and main manufacturing facility was the former Southern Pacific Railroad depot in downtown Los Angeles comprising 800 000 square feet of floorspace. Dying and finishing were at a separate facility in Hawthorne, California. Despite three-shift working, capacity shortage at its Los Angeles facility resulted in American Apparel expanding production to newly acquired plants in South Gate, California and Garden Grove, California in 2008. It described its production operations as follows:

> American Apparel purchases yarn which is sent to knitters to be knit into "greige" fabric, which is fabric that is not dyed or processed. The Company currently conducts a portion of its knitting operations in-house at its knitting facilities in Los Angeles and Garden Grove, California. The Company operates circular and flat knitting machines, producing jersey, piqué, fleece and ribbing using cotton and cotton/polyester yarns. The Company also utilizes third-party commission knitters. The Company's knitting facilities knit approximately 80% of the total fabric used in American Apparel's garments, and employed a staff of approximately 100 people, as of December 31, 2008.
>
> Knitted greige fabric produced at the Los Angeles and Garden Grove facilities or other commission knitters is batched for bleaching and dyeing and transported to the Company's dyeing and finishing facilities, or other commission dye houses. In some cases, dyed fabric is transferred to subcontractors for fabric laundering. The Company's dyeing and finishing facilities in the Los Angeles metropolitan area dye approximately 80% of the total fabric used in American Apparel's garments, and employed a staff of approximately 900 people, as of December 31, 2008.

> Most fabric is shipped to the Company's primary manufacturing facility in downtown Los Angeles where it is inspected and then cut on manual and automated cutting tables, and subsequently sewn into finished garments. Some fabric is purchased directly from third parties, along with all trims. Garments are sewn by teams of sewing operators typically ranging from five to 15 operators, depending on the complexity of a particular garment. Each sewing operator performs a different sewing operation on a garment before passing it to the next operator. Sewing operators are compensated on a modified piece-rate basis. Quality control personnel inspect finished garments for defects and reject any defective product. American Apparel also manufactures some hosiery in-house at this facility, where it does knitting, inspection, and packing, and uses off-site contractors for washing and boarding. Approximately 3,900 employees were directly involved in the cutting, sewing, and hosiery operations at the downtown Los Angeles facility as of December 31, 2008.
>
> American Apparel purchases yarn, certain fabrics and other raw materials from a variety of vendors over time. American Apparel does not have any major suppliers of raw materials that it relies on exclusively to support its production operations. The inputs that American Apparel uses are produced competitively by a large number of potential suppliers. Since the inputs are commodity in nature, American Apparel believes that it could easily source its inputs from other vendors if its current suppliers were not able to meet its needs.[20]

According to Marty Bailey, Vice President of Operations, "In order for us to be successful, we have to make a good product. . . . [I]f your product is no good, you can count out repeat business. A turd is still a turd no matter how you market or package it."[21] Bailey believed that American Apparel's success was based on four factors: implementing sound quality control, being committed to quick turnaround using lean production, having a specific target market, and careful oversight of manufacturing operations. Bailey continued, "Anytime that you can have your arms around your business, you're in good shape. We are a domestic company and have visibility. We can make commitments to our customers that other people can't."[22]

Workers were organized by the type of garment produced, in modular manufacturing teams. Members rotated positions regularly to alleviate stress and boredom. An average shift included 100 sewing teams. Quality-control supervisors stood across the aisle from the sewing teams and carefully measured and inspected one out of every 24 garments to ensure size and quality consistency.[23] Piece workers spent 11 to 13 seconds per person per piece of garment; the average garment required 140 seconds to manufacture. About 250 000 garments were produced each day and 1.25 million each week. To minimize fatigue and stress, each shift was interrupted by a five-minute stretch or aerobic exercise session accompanied by loud pop music.

An employee's occupation was indicated by attire. Piece workers wore casual clothes of jeans and t-shirts. Supervisors, mechanics, cleaners, and cutters wore t-shirts of a particular color with their position labeled in both English and Spanish on the front. Quality control supervisors wore purple shirts, line supervisors blue shirts, and mechanics red shirts.

Retail and Wholesale Distribution

At the beginning of 2009, American Apparel owned and operated 260 retail stores in 19 countries (see Table 16.3). These were served by distribution centers in Los Angeles, Montreal, and Neuss (Germany). It described its retail operations as follows:

> American Apparel's retail operations principally target young adults aged 20 to 32 through its unique assortment of fashionable clothing and accessories and its compelling in-store experience. American Apparel has established a reputation with its customers, who are culturally sophisticated, creative, and independent-minded. The product offering includes women's and men's basic apparel and accessories, as well as new lines for children and pets. Stores average approximately 2500–3000 square feet of selling space. American Apparel's stores are located in large metropolitan areas, emerging neighborhoods, and select university communities.[24]

American Apparel favored locations away from traditional high streets using nontraditional retail buildings with unique environments. Store selection and design was undertaken by Jordan Parnass of Jordan Parnass Digital Architecture (JPDA), a lifelong friend of Dov Charney. Location scouts searched cities for areas that were populated by artists and musicians and for the hangouts of young adults. Once an ideal location for a store was spotted, designers from JPDA researched the "regional flavor" and developed design concepts that incorporated this regional flavor together with the characteristics of the building's structure.[25] Examples of some unique storefronts included a movie theater marquee that was installed with colored fluorescent triangle lights, and a former auto-garage.[26]

American Apparel's wholesale business sold to about a dozen authorized distributors and over 10 000 screen printers. The latter printed blank products with corporate logos, brands and other images. Wholesale customers were served by a call center at its Los Angeles headquarters. The company prided itself on fast turnaround of orders: orders received before 4:30 pm were shipped the same day.

American Apparel operated online retail sales through its www.americanapparel.com web site. The web site further broadened American Apparel's range of offerings to include shoes, pens, Swiss army knives, audio CDs and even a video described as "the perfect merger of classic pornographic excellence and modern motion."[27]

Tables 16.4 and 16.5 show American Apparel's sales, profits and assets by distribution channel and by geography.

TABLE 16.3 American Apparel's retail outlets

Number of retail stores	Dec. 31, 2008	Dec. 31, 2007	Dec. 31, 2006	Dec. 31, 2005	Dec. 31, 2004
U.S.	148	105	93	66	25
Canada	37	30	26	20	9
International	75	47	30	18	3

Source: American Apparel, 10-K Report for 2008.

TABLE 16.4 American Apparel's financial results by business segment ($ million)

	2008	2007	2006
U.S. wholesale			
Sales	162.7	144.5	127.8
Gross profit	46.9	40.1	31.7
Operating income[a]	21.0	19.7	14.2
Identifiable assets	178.1	125.4	n.a.
Capital expenditure	7.1	5.3	4.3
U.S. retail			
Sales	168.7	115.6	80.2
Gross profit	127.9	88.8	63.0
Operating income[a]	33.5	24.8	11.5
Identifiable assets	98.9	60.0	n.a.
Capital expenditure	30.9	9.3	8.6
Canada			
Sales	67.3	42.4	30.6
Gross profit	40.1	27.1	19.2
Operating income[a]	10.8	1.5	3.5
Identifiable assets	17.1	16.5	n.a.
Capital expenditure	4.7	2.0	1.7
International			
Sales	146.4	84.5	46.4
Gross profit	84.2	59.4	31.7
Operating income[a]	8.0	14.8	4.7
Identifiable assets	38.9	31.5	n.a.
Capital expenditure	18.3	7.1	2.4

[a] Before corporate expense, interest, other income, and foreign currency adjustment

Source: American Apparel, 10-K Report for 2008.

TABLE 16.5 Geographical distribution of sales and fixed assets, 2007 and 2008 ($ million)

	2008	2007
Net sales by location of customer		
United States	331.3	206.1
Canada	67.3	42.4
Europe (excluding U.K.)	74.3	45.1
United Kingdom	35.7	17.6
Japan	14.9	9.8
Korea	10.5	9.2
Other foreign countries	11.1	2.8
Total Consolidated Net Sales	545.1	387.0
Property and equipment, at Dec. 31		
United States	79.3	44.0
Canada	7.3	6.6

	2008	2007
Europe (excluding U.K.)	12.7	7.3
United Kingdom	6.4	4.6
Japan	3.3	1,6
Korea	0.7	0.5
Other foreign countries	2.8	0.2
Total Consolidated	112.4	64.9
Total property and equipment		48 532

Source: American Apparel, 10-K Report for 2008.

Employee Relations: A "Sweat-Shop" Free Environment

American Apparel offered year-round employment and rates of pay where even the lowest paid workers earned around double the minimum wage. Piece-workers started out at $8 an hour and could earn up to $25 an hour based on their productivity. Workers were offered subsidized healthcare for themselves and their families, subsidized lunches (25% paid by American Apparel), free parking, bus passes and low-cost auto insurance. There were five on-site massage therapists who provided regular services for all employees. Yoga classes were also available, along with a health-and-wellness specialist who provided counseling. Workers could take bathroom breaks at any time and use their cell phones for quick personal calls during working hours. Other employee benefits included subsidized public transportation and a bicycle-lending program in which a bicycle, helmet and chain were provided.

Workers received training to improve their job and management skills. American Apparel also offered English and math lessons, classes in human relations and teamwork, and monthly supervisor and management training. The human resources department also assisted employees in gaining the tax benefits available to them and opening bank accounts by inviting a bank to the factory.

Despite a campaign by a garment workers union, American Apparel employees had not elected to form a union. Charney felt that they had no reason to do so. He commented on the failed unionizing campaign:

> The union issue is something that's brought here from a New York-based union. It's a lot of smoke and mirrors. There's not one cut and sew factory in this city that unionized. If the workers wanted a union, they'd have one . . . There's got to be a reason to take on management. There's got to be a reason to say, they're not treating us well enough, we need to rise up and put a gun in management's face.[28]

As noted by *The Economist*:

> The benefits he provides are expensive: subsidizing health insurance costs his firm $4m–5m a year; subsidizing meals costs another $500 000. Even so, Mr. Charney says he has no plans to scale back these benefits. He considers his contented workers the reason for his success. Treating them well means they are less likely to leave, for one thing, which saves money. "American Apparel is not an altruistic company," says Mr. Charney. "I believe in capitalism and self-interest. Self-interest can involve being generous with others."[29]

Marketing and Advertising

American Apparel developed all of its marketing and advertising in-house. The photographs used in advertising and promotion were often taken by Charney and other amateur photographers. Models were all amateurs who posed without makeup or fancy hair-dos. Many were employees, customers, friends, or just women whom Charney wanted to photograph:

> [T]he models in American Apparel's print ads challenge conventional notions of beauty. Before the ballyhooed Dove soap campaign, Charney embraced the notion of "real" advertising, photographing young ethnic and mixed-race men and women with asymmetrical features, imperfect bodies, blemished skin and visible sweat stains on the clothes they are modeling — the kind of artsy, latter-day-bohemian, indie-culture-affiliated young adults who live and shop in the neighborhoods where American Apparel stores are located.
>
> The ads are also highly suggestive and not just because they are showcasing underwear or clingy knits. They depict young men and women in bed or in the shower; if they are casually lounging on a sofa or sitting on the floor, then their legs happen to be spread; frequently they are wearing a single item of clothing but are otherwise undressed; a couple of the young women appear to be in a heightened state of pleasure. These pictures have a flashbulb-lighted, lo-fi sultriness to them; they look less like ads than photos you'd see posted on someone's Myspace page . . . These aren't ads that you'll see on the side of a bus or in famous magazines. American Apparel places advertising in the blogosphere, linking from pop-culture sites like Gawker.com to photo essays and copy on its own web site; on the back pages of alternative newspapers like The Village Voice, L.A. Weekly or The Onion; in slightly obscure art-hipster publications like Purple Fashion and Fantastic Man; and in the profane, anti-P.C. lifestyle magazine Vice, whose louche tastes and attitudes run in close concert with Charney's.[30]

American Apparel's use of internet marketing reached beyond its extensive online catalog and web site. In June 2006, it partnered with Linden Lab to become "the first real life company to open a store in the virtual world of 'Second Life.'"[31] Second Life was an online 3-D virtual world where visitors created alter egos called "avatars." Patrons purchased virtual versions of American Apparel clothing for their avatars for token sums.

Social and Environmental Responsibility

American Apparel took an activist stance on social and political issues and infused social responsibility into its operating practices. The company offered employment to people on the fringes of mainstream society. For example, it hired employees from Homeboy Industries, an organization that assisted at-risk youths and former gang members. An immigrant himself, Charney was active in the Los Angeles immigrant community and was a prominent supporter of free trade and immigrant rights. On May 1, 2006, Charney gave the company's Los Angeles employees a paid day off, a T-shirt with a pro-immigration message, and encouraged them to join a demonstration being held in Los Angeles to protest lack of immigrant rights. American Apparel also supports several international causes, and has used its "Made in USA" and "Sweatshop Free" credentials as part of its advertising messages.

American Apparel also emphasized environmentally friendly manufacturing and clothing. Because most cotton was grown with a very heavy use of insecticides and other pollutants, in 2004 American Apparel introduced its *Sustainable Edition* line made from 100% organic cotton. American Apparel recycled 1 million pounds of fabric scraps annually. Charney remarked: "Actually, the reason we started a panty line was to use all our excessive scraps."[32]

Speed-to-Market

The fundamental performance attribute of American Apparel's business system was its speed and flexibility:

> The Company's vertically integrated business model, with manufacturing and various other elements of the Company's business processes centered in downtown Los Angeles, allows the Company to play a role in originating and defining new and innovative trends in fashion, while enabling the Company to quickly respond to market and customer demand for classic styles and new products. For the Company's wholesale operations, being able to fulfill large orders with quick turn-around allows American Apparel to capture business. The ability to respond to the market quickly means that the Company's retail operations can deliver on-trend apparel in a timely manner, adhere to a policy of not discounting product at retail stores and maximize sales on popular styles by replenishing product that would have otherwise sold out.[33]

From design concept to the American Apparel store rack, a garment took as little as two weeks. Within a day, a designer could come up with an idea, design a garment, create a pattern, cut and have it sewn together. By the evening, the garment could be photographed on a model and emailed for Charney's immediate opinion. If the garment was approved by Charney, then it would be prepared for testing in a few American Apparel retail stores.[34] Customer purchases were tracked and analyzed, and if the product were successful, it would be put into full production for shipping to the rest of American Apparel's retail locations.[35]

Figure 16.1 depicts American Apparel's vertically integrated business system.

The Future

In its presentation to investors in April 2009, American Apparel outlined its long-term goal of becoming "the #1 destination for basic apparel—the first name that consumers think of for T-shirts, sweatpants, underwear, socks, etc." Achieving that goal would require American Apparel to seize the opportunities available for growth and internal development. The opportunities it identified included:

- grow the store base
- expand in underpenetrated urban markets in the U.S., Canada and internationally

FIGURE 16.1 American Apparel's vertically integrated business system

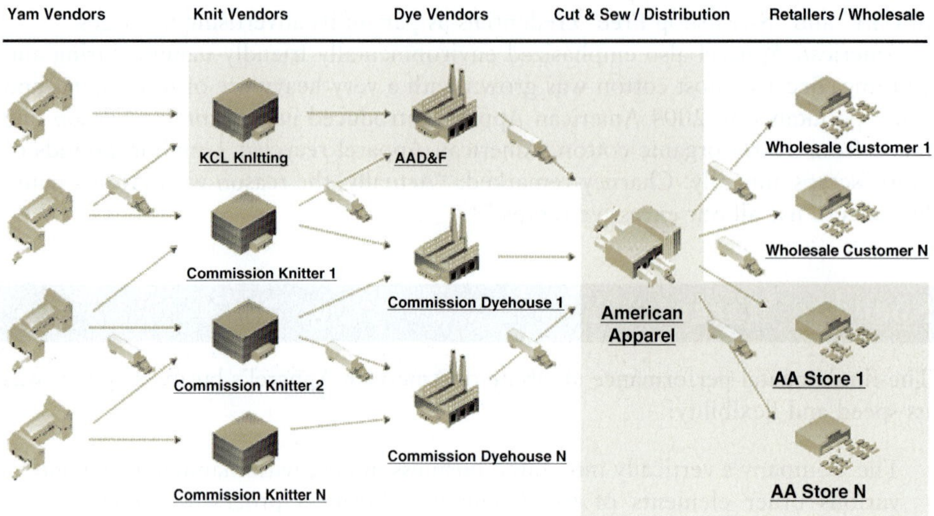

Source: American Apparel, Investors' Presentation (March 2009).

- enter new markets
- improve production efficiency with better supply-chain management and materials resource planning with enterprise resource planning (ERP)
- produce the right SKUs in the right quantities
- improve merchandise allocation in the stores
- improve store productivity by capturing more sales and increasing inventory turns
- add categories to provide customers with a more complete product assortment of basics (jackets, bottoms, wovens, etc.)
- improve store productivity by increasing customer visits, transactions, and average unit revenue
- improve execution through key management hires
- expand brand awareness and reach beyond young metropolitan adults.[36]

During 2009, however, American Apparel's primary emphasis would be efficiency and effectiveness rather than growth. It forecast that only 25 new stores would be opened in 2009 and sales growth would slow to between 5% and 10%. Efforts to improve production efficiency and logistical effectiveness included the implementation of an ERP system and improvements in financial management through implementing the Hyperion Financial Management system and hiring senior finance executives. Improving financial management had become a priority because of "material weaknesses" in American Apparel's financial reporting system identified by its auditors.

American Apparel has shown a remarkable capacity to adapt to change and seize new opportunities. It grew from being a local, wholesale supplier of T-shirts to a multinational corporation vertically integrated from the purchase of cotton yarn to the retailing of garments. Nevertheless, in many respects it is still a medium-sized entrepreneurial company where the founder is engaged in activities that ranges from the approval of new designs, to taking advertising photographs, to selecting sites for new retail stores. Will expansion necessitate a fundamentally different management structure for American Apparel and can its Los Angeles-based production system serve an increasingly global retail network? As American Apparel enhances its profile, will it attract increasing numbers of imitators? Can American Apparel continue to charge the same premium prices for its stylish, socially-responsible, "Made in USA" garments? Dov Charney once described his dream for American Apparel as becoming the "Starbucks of the garment industry." Given Starbucks' forced retrenchment after overexpansion, this is perhaps no longer such an appealing vision.

Notes

1 "American Apparel's Unusual Flotation is Typical of Dov Charney, its Founder," *The Economist,* January 4, 2007.

2 American Apparel, Investor Presentation June 2009, Piper Jaffray Consumer Conference, June 9, 2009, http://investors.americanapparel.net/events.cfm, accessed October 29, 2009.

3 P. Rivoli, *The Travels of a T-Shirt in the Global Economy: An Economist Examines the Markets, Power, and Politics of World Trade*, 2nd edn, John Wiley & Sons, Ltd, Chichester, 2009.

4 "T-shirt Prices are Falling," Trade Fact of the Week, Progressive Policy Institute, February 15, 2006, http://www.ppionline.org/ppi_ci.cfm?contentid=253748&knlgAreaID=108&subsecid=900003, accessed October 29, 2009.

5 D. Charney, interview, "Charlie Rose," KQED9 (TV broadcasting station), July, 2006.

6 D. Charney, interview, "The New Rich," *20/20*, ABC, 2006; M. Mendelssohn, "Sweatshop-Free Zone," *The Gazette,* May 23, 2004.

7 D. Charney, interview, "The New Rich," *20/20*, ABC (2006); M. Silcott, "Dov Charney, 32, Senior Partner, American Apparel," *The Counselor,* April, 2001.

8 J. Elwain, "American Apparel Takes on the T-Shirt," *Bobbin Magazine,* May, 2001.

9 A. A. Nieder, "The Branding of Blank Tees," http://americanapparel.net/presscenter/articles/20000818caapparelnews.html, accessed August 18, 2008.

10 J. Elwain, "American Apparel Takes on the T-Shirt," *Bobbin Magazine,* May, 2001.

11 C. M. Chensvold, "American Apparel Opens Three Retail Stores," *California Apparel News,* October 31, 2003)

12 J. Elwain, "American Apparel Takes on the T-Shirt," *Bobbin Magazine,* May, 2001.

13 J. Mankiewicz "Sexy Marketing or Sexual Harassment?," NBC Dateline, http://www.msnbc.msn.com/id/14082498/, accessed July 28, 2006.

14 American Apparel, 10-K Report for 2008, 2009, p. 31.

15 "Living on the Edge at American Apparel," *Business Week,* July 27, 2007.

16 "And You Thought Abercrombie & Fitch Was Pushing It," *New York Times,* April 23, 2006.

17 D. Charney, Interview, "Worldwide," Chicago Public Radio, November 13, 2003.

18 American Apparel, 10-K Report for 2008, 2009, p. 2.

19 D. Charney, interview, "Charlie Rose," KQED9, July 2006.

20 American Apparel, 10-K Report for 2008, 2009, p. 5.

21 H. Aquirre, "Go Team," *The Manufacturer,* June, 2004.

22 H. Aquirre, "Go Team," *The Manufacturer,* June, 2004.

23 A. Lopez, interview by case authors, April 2007.

24 American Apparel, 10-K Report for 2008, 2009, p. 5.

25 A. DiNardo, "The Anti-Brand," *Visual Store,* December 4, 2006.

26 A. DiNardo, "The Anti-Brand," *Visual Store,* December 4, 2006.

27 See http://store.americanapparel.net/sexctydvd.html, accessed July 2009.

28 "The Apprenticeship of Dov Charney," CBC Radio, March 20, 2005.

29 "American Apparel's Unusual Flotation is Typical of Dov Charney, Its Founder," *The Economist,* January 4, 2007.

30 J. Wolf, "And You Thought Abercrombie & Fitch Was Pushing It?" *New York Times Magazine,* April 23, 2006.

31 "American Apparel's Virtual Clothes," *Business Week,* June 27, 2006.

32 "American Apparel to Recycle over One Million Pounds of Cotton Cutting per Year," *American Apparel Media Advisory,* August 13, 2002.

33 American Apparel, 10-K Report for 2008, 2009, p. 3.

34 A. Lopez, interview by case authors, April 2007.

35 D. Charney, interview, "Charlie Rose", KQED9, July, 2006.

36 American Apparel, Investor Presentation June 2009, Piper Jaffray Consumer Conference, June 9, 2009, http://investors.americanapparel.net/events.cfm, accessed October 29, 2009.

Case 17 Outback Steakhouse: Going International*

By 1995, Outback Steakhouse was one of the fastest growing and most acclaimed restaurant chains in North America. Astute positioning within the intensely competitive U.S. restaurant business, high quality of food and service, and a relaxed ambiance that echoed its Australian theme propelled the chain's spectacular growth (see Table 17.1).

---

*By Marilyn L. Taylor and Robert M. Grant. This case is an abridged version of an earlier case "Outback Steakhouse Goes International" by Marilyn L. Taylor, George M. Puia, Krishnan Ramaya and Madelyn Gengelbach (used by permission of the authors). It has been augmented with material from company reports and from "A Stake in the Business," by Chris T. Sullivan, *Harvard Business Review*, September 2005, pp. 57–64.

TABLE 17.1 Outback Steakhouse, Inc.: growth and profitability, 1990–5

	Revenue ($ m)	Net income ($ m)	Return on average equity (%)	Company-owned restaurants	Franchised and JV restaurants	Total restaurants
1990	34	2.3	41.2	23	0	23
1991	91	6.1	34.4	49	0	49
1992	189	14.8	23.6	81	4	85
1993	310	25.2	22.2	124	24	148
1994	516	43.4	27.4	164	50	214
1995	734	61.3	27.0	262	58	320[a]

[a]Of these, 297 were Outback Steakhouses and 23 were Carrabba's Italian Grills.

Chairman and co-founder Chris Sullivan believed that at the current rate of growth (around 70 new restaurants each year), Outback would be facing market saturation within five years. Outback's growth opportunities were either to diversify into alternative restaurant concepts (it had already started its Carrabba's Italian Grill restaurants) or to expand internationally.

> We can do 500–600 [Outback] restaurants, and possibly more over the next five years . . . [however] the world is becoming one big market, and we want to be in place so we don't miss that opportunity. There are some problems, some challenges with it, but at this point there have been some casual restaurant chains that have gone [outside the U.S.] and their average unit sales are way, way above the sales level they enjoyed in the United States. So the potential is there. Obviously, there are some distribution issues to work out, things like that, but we are real excited about the future internationally. That will give us some potential outside the United States to continue to grow as well.[1]

In late 1994, Hugh Connerty was appointed President of Outback International to lead the company's overseas expansion. Connerty had considerable experience in the restaurant business and had been Outback's most successful franchisee, developing a number of Outback restaurants in northern Florida and southern Georgia. Connerty grasped the opportunity enthusiastically:

> We have had hundreds of franchise requests from all over the world. [So] it took about two seconds for me to make that decision [to become President of Outback International] . . . I've met with and talked to other executives who have international divisions. All of them have the same story. At some point in time a light goes on and they say, "Gee we have a great product. Where do we start?" I have traveled quite a bit on holiday. The world is not as big as you think it is. Most companies who have gone global have not used any set strategy.[2]

Connerty's challenges were to decide in which countries to locate; whether to franchise, directly manage, or joint venture; how the Outback restaurant concept should be adapted to overseas markets and what pace of expansion to target.

Outback's Strategy

Outback was founded by Chris Sullivan, Bob Basham and Tim Gannon. The three had met as management trainees at the Steak and Ale restaurant chain. Although red meat consumption was declining, they believed that this was primarily the result of less meat being consumed at home: steakhouses remained extremely popular. They saw an untapped opportunity for serving quality steaks at an affordable price—filling the gap between high-priced and budget steakhouses. Using an Australian theme associated with the outdoors and adventure, Outback positioned itself as a place providing not only excellent food but also a cheerful, fun and comfortable experience. The company explained its strategy as follows:

> The Company believes that it differentiates its Outback Steakhouse restaurants by:
>
> - emphasizing consistently high-quality ingredients and preparation of a limited number of menu items that appeal to a broad array of tastes;
> - featuring generous portions at moderate prices;
> - attracting a diverse mix of customers through a casual dining atmosphere emphasizing highly attentive service;
> - hiring and retaining experienced restaurant management by providing general managers the opportunity to purchase a 10% interest in the restaurants they manage; and
> - limiting service to dinner (generally from 4:30 p.m. to 11:00 p.m.), which reduces the hours of restaurant management and employees.[3]

Quality of food was central to the chain's differentiation. This began with the raw materials. Outback viewed suppliers as "partners" and was committed to work with them to ensure quality and develop long-term relationships. Outback's food costs were among the highest in the industry—not just in terms of ingredients but also in preparation, with most items prepared from scratch within each restaurant. For example, Outback's croutons were made daily on site with 17 different seasonings and cut into irregular shapes to indicate that they were handmade.

The emphasis on quality extended to service. Among Outback's "principles and beliefs" was "No rules, just right"—employees will do whatever is needed to meet the needs and preferences of customers.

Inevitably, this emphasis on quality and service meant working practices that at other restaurant chains would be regarded as inefficient. Chairman Chris Sullivan explained that Outback had a different management model:

> There are three kinds of turnover in the restaurant business—customer, employee and table. Most restaurant chains worry about the first, resign themselves to the second, and encourage the third. At Outback it's not as straightforward as that; we believe that all three are integrally related. Specifically, our management model and approach reflect the importance we place on fighting employee turnover. One of our catchphrases is "fully staffed, fully trained." You can't be either of those things if a restaurant is a revolving door. Besides, customers like to see a familiar face.
>
> Restaurant work can be stressful. The better the staffers, the more intent they will be on doing things right—and the more frustrated they will become with the facilities and tools they've been given if they get in the way, whether the problem

> is dull knives or not enough burners . . . Bob Basham insisted on making all of our kitchens at least 2500 square feet and keeping lots of cool air flowing through them. The kitchens occupy half of the typical Outback restaurant's floor plan space that other restaurants allocate to revenue-producing tables. But we wanted to offer a bigger menu than the typical casual restaurant did in the 1980s, so we knew we would have to give the cooks and prep people the space to pull it off.
>
> Likewise, we never assign our servers to cover more than three tables; the industry standard is five or six . . . A wide range of customers choose to dine with us on a variety of occasions . . . It has to be the customer who sets the pace for the meal, not the server or the kitchen staff. But for that to happen our servers need time to figure out the mood and expectations of a given table on a given evening, and the kitchen has to be well enough staffed and equipped to turn around orders without delay . . .
>
> We think that employees who are not overstressed stay in their jobs longer than those who are; that employees who stay have time to master their jobs, become familiar with their regular customers' preferences, and learn to operate as teams; that the combination of mastery, memory, and calm is more likely to afford customers themselves a relaxing, enjoyable experience; and that diners who are not hustled through their meals are more likely to come back. In short, low employee turnover leads to well-paced table turnover, which ultimately leads to low customer turnover.[4]

This model linked closely with two other distinctive features of Outback's strategy. First, Outback served only dinner. According to Sullivan, the conventional wisdom that restaurants needed to be open for lunch and dinner in order to make efficient use of capital ignored the hidden costs of longer hours of opening. These included the costs associated with extra hiring and employee turnover, the disruptive effects of shift changes and the fact that employees who worked lunchtime would be tired in the evening—the time when they needed to be at their freshest. Similarly for the food—with preparation of food brought forward to the morning, it would lose its freshness by the evening.

Second, Outback located in residential areas rather than downtown. This reinforced the merits of evening-only opening, kept rents low and encouraged customer and employee loyalty. As Sullivan explained: "The suburbs are our outback."

Outback's management and ownership structure was also unusual. Each of Outback's directly owned restaurants was a separate partnership where Outback Steakhouse, Inc. was the general partner with an ownership of between 71% and 90%. Each restaurant was headed by a "managing partner" while between 10 and 20 restaurants within an area were overseen by a regional manager who is called a "joint venture partner" or "JVP." Sullivan explained the relationship as follows:

> The terms "managing partner" and "joint venture partner" aren't symptoms of title inflation. They straightforwardly describe people's roles and relationships to the organization. All managing partners, most of whom start as hourly employees, must invest $25 000 of their own money—not because Outback needs the capital, but because their financial contributions make them committed investors in the business they'll be running. They must also sign a five-year contract, and they are granted roughly 1000 shares of restricted stock, which vest only at the end of their contracts. In return, managing partners can

> keep 10% of the cash flow their restaurants generate each year. The idea is to ensure that at the end of five years each of them will have stock worth around \$100 000 . . . At the end of five years, successful managers are encouraged to sign up with the same restaurant or to manage a different one . . .
>
> Outback's JVPs, who number around 60, must invest \$50 000, which entitles them to 10% of cash flow of all the restaurants they oversee after the partners have received their 10%. Whereas the managing partners focus on operations and community relations, the Japes focus on monitoring performance, finding and developing new locations, and identifying and developing new managers, managing partners, and Japes like themselves. The Japes are the only management layer between the six operations executives at headquarters and the managing partners at the individual restaurants.[5]

Initially, Outback intended its restaurants all to be directly owned and managed. However, in 1990, requests for franchising led to Outback agreeing to franchise to well-known acquaintances of the founders. Outback was very careful in its choice of franchisees to ensure that all were fully committed to Outback's principles and beliefs.

Management of hourly employees was very different from most other restaurant chains. One executive described Outback's approach as: "Tough on results, but kind with people." Employee selection was rigorous and included aptitude tests, psychological profiles and interviews with at least two managers. The goal was to create an entrepreneurial climate that emphasized learning and personal growth. All employees were eligible for the company's stock ownership plan and health insurance was made available to all employees.

Part of the culture of "no rules" and commitment to quality and service is a constant drive for innovation and improvement:

> Almost all our innovations bubble up from the individual restaurant, often originating with our servers or kitchen staffers. They'll suggest an idea to the restaurant manager who will try it on an experimental basis. If the recommended menu or process change clicks, the managing partner communicates the idea to his or her JVP . . . If the suggested change meets company standards, videos and other materials showing how to implement it are distributed to other JVPs. Each is free to take it or not.[6]

During 1993, Outback formed a joint venture with Houston-based Carrabba's Italian Grill. In January 1995, Outback acquired the rights to develop Carrabba's nationally. Carrabba's Grills were run with almost identical operating and management practices and ownership structure to Outback Steakhouses.

Preparing for International Expansion

Hugh Connerty, Outback's head of International, outlined his approach to international expansion as follows:

> We have built Outback one restaurant at a time . . . There are some principles and beliefs we live by. It almost sounds cultish. We want International to be an opportunity for our suppliers. We feel strongly about the relationships with our

> suppliers. We have never changed suppliers. We have an undying commitment to them and in exchange we want them to have an undying commitment to us. They have to prove they can build plants [abroad].
>
> I think it would be foolish of us to think that we are going to go around the world buying property and understanding the laws in every country, the culture in every single country. So the approach that we are going to take is that we will franchise the international operation with company-owned stores here and franchises there so that will allow us to focus on what I believe is our pure strength, a support operation.[7]

Connerty believed that his experience in developing Outback franchises in the U.S. would provide the guidelines for overseas expansion:

> Every one of the franchisees lives in their areas. I lived in the area I franchised. I had relationships that helped with getting permits. That isn't any different than the rest of the world. The loyalties of individuals that live in their respective areas [will be important]. We will do the franchises one by one. The biggest decision we have to make is how we pick that franchise partner. That is what we will concentrate on. We are going to select a person who has synergy with us, who thinks like us, who believes in the principles and beliefs.
>
> Trust is foremost and sacred. The trust between [Outback] and the individual franchisees is not to be violated. The company grants franchises one at a time. It takes a lot of trust to invest millions of dollars without any assurance that you will be able to build another one.[8]

As for the geographical pattern of expansion, Connerty's initial thoughts were to begin close to home then tackle Latin America and the Far East:

> The first year will be Canada. Then we'll go to Hawaii. Then we'll go to South America and then develop our relationships in the Far East, Korea, Japan . . . the Orient. The second year we'll begin a relationship in Great Britain and from there a natural progression throughout Europe. But we view it as a very long-term project. I have learned that people [in other countries] think very different than Americans.[9]

Overseas Expansion by U.S. Restaurant Chains

The international market offered substantial growth opportunities for U.S. restaurant chains. For fast-food franchise chains—notably McDonald's, Burger King and Kentucky Fried Chicken—international sales accounted for up to one-half of total sales, although for many "international" was limited to Canada and Puerto Rico. Among "casual dining" chains—such as Denny's, Applebee's, T. G. I. Friday's, and Tony Roma's—relatively few had ventured beyond North America. Table 17.2 shows the international presence of leading U.S. restaurant franchise chains.

The attraction of overseas markets was that their restaurants markets were typically less saturated than those of the U.S. and most of the local competition was independent, family owned restaurants rather than large chains. In overseas markets it was anticipated

TABLE 17.2 The ten largest U.S. restaurant franchise chains, 1994

	Total sales ($m)	International sales ($m)	Total outlets	International outlets
McDonald's	25 986	11 046	15 205	5461
Burger King	7500	1400	7684	1357
KFC	7100	3600	9407	4258
Taco Bell	4290	130	5614	162
Wendy's	4277	390	4411	413
Hardee's	3491	63	3516	72
Dairy Queen	3170	300	3516	628
Domino's	2500	415	5079	840
Subway	2500	265	179	8450
Little Caesars	2000	70	4855	155

Source: "Top 50 Franchises," *Restaurant Business,* November 1, 1995, pp. 35–41.

that market trends would follow those of the U.S.: in particular, that greater affluence and a declining role of family life would result in increased eating away from home.

It was notable that, in overseas markets, not only had success been achieved principally by fast food chains but most of the leaders were subsidiaries of large multinationals with many decades of international experience. For example, KFC, Taco Bell and Pizza Hut were subsidiaries of PepsiCo.; Burger King was a subsidiary of British conglomerate Grand Metropolitan.

A key impetus to overseas expansion was maturing of the U.S. market. By 1994 there were over 3000 franchisers in the U.S., operating close to 600 000 franchised outlets. Not only was competition intense, but growth was slowing. Sales per store were growing at 3% during the early 1990s.

However, overseas markets also represented a substantial management challenge. Among the problems that other restaurant chains had encountered were the following:

- *Market demand.* The extent to which market demand existed for a particular type of restaurant depended on levels of disposable income, urbanization, demographics and a host of other social, economic, and lifestyle factors. Most critical to a specific company were national preferences with regard to cuisine and dining conventions. Even McDonald's, whose name had become synonymous with global standardization, adapted substantially to local differences: "Croque McDos" in France, rice burgers in Hong Kong, "McArabia Koftas" in Saudi Arabia, kosher outlets in Israel, no beef or pork products in India.
- *Cultural and social factors* are critical influences on customer preferences with regard to menus, restaurant facilities and overall ambiance; they are also important with regard to employee management practices and entrepreneurial potential.
- *Infrastructure.* Proper means of transportation and communication, basic utilities such as power and water, and locally available supplies were important elements in the decision to introduce a particular restaurant concept. A restaurant must have the ability to get resources to its location. Easy access to

the raw materials for food preparation, equipment for manufacture of food served, and mobility for employees and customers were essential.

- *Raw material supplies.* Overseas restaurant chains needed local supplies of food and drink. The U.S. International Trade Commission noted that: "International franchisers frequently encounter problems finding supplies in sufficient quantity, of consistent quality, and at stable prices. Physical distance also can adversely affect a franchise concept and arrangement. Long distances create communication and transportation problems, which may complicate the process of sourcing supplies, overseeing operations, or providing quality management services to franchisees."[10] While a franchise chain could develop its own supply chain—for example, McDonald's when it entered the Soviet Union—the investment of management time and money could be substantial.
- *Regulations and trade restrictions.* Import restrictions are relatively unimportant in the restaurant business given that most food products are locally sourced. However, some countries have made the import of restaurant equipment difficult and expensive. Restrictions on foreign direct investment are of major significance only in emerging market countries. Far more challenging are national regulations relating to food standards, business licensing, and business contracts. Establishing new businesses in most countries involves far more regulation than within the U.S. Franchise agreements are an especially difficult area because they involve complex contractual agreements between franchisor and franchisee regarding trademark licensing, royalty payments, requirements for quality control and quality monitoring. Despite the provisions of the Uruguay Round's General Agreement on Trade in Services, most countries failed to make public their restrictions on franchising. In some countries some usual terms of franchise agreements have been viewed as restraints on commerce. Employment law was also important—particularly with regard to restrictions on employers' ability to dismiss or lay off employees and requirements for union recognition and national collective bargaining arrangements over wages and work conditions.

Notes

1 M. L. Taylor, G. M. Puia, K. Ramaya and M. Gengelback, "Outback Steakhouse Goes International," in A. A. Thompson and A. J. Strickland, *Strategic Management: Concepts and Cases,* 11th edn, McGraw-Hill, New York, 1999, pp. C296–7.

2 M. L. Taylor, G. M. Puia, K. Ramaya and M. Gengelback, "Outback Steakhouse Goes International," in A. A. Thompson and A. J. Strickland, *Strategic Management: Concepts and Cases,* 11th edn, McGraw-Hill, New York, 1999, p. C291.

3 Outback Steakhouse, Inc., 10K Report, 1996.

4 Chris T. Sullivan, "A Stake in the Business," *Harvard Business Review,* September, 2005, pp. 57–64.

5 Chris T. Sullivan, "A Stake in the Business," *Harvard Business Review,* September, 2005, pp. 59–60.

6 Chris T. Sullivan, "A Stake in the Business," *Harvard Business Review,* September, 2005, p. 58.

7 M. L. Taylor, G. M. Puia, K. Ramaya and M. Gengelback, "Outback Steakhouse Goes International," in A. A. Thompson and A. J. Strickland, *Strategic Management: Concepts and Cases,* 11th edn, McGraw-Hill, New York, 1999, p. C297.

8 M. L. Taylor, G. M. Puia, K. Ramaya and M. Gengelback, "Outback Steakhouse Goes International," in A. A. Thompson and A. J. Strickland, *Strategic Management: Concepts and Cases,* 11th edn, McGraw-Hill, New York, 1999, p. C297.

9 M. L. Taylor, G. M. Puia, K. Ramaya and M. Gengelback, "Outback Steakhouse Goes International," in A. A. Thompson and A. J. Strickland, *Strategic Management: Concepts and Cases,* 11 edn, McGraw-Hill, New York, 1999, p. C299.

10 U.S. International Trade Commission, *Industry and Trade Summary: Franchising,* Washington, DC, 1995, pp. 15–16.

Case 18 Euro Disney: From Dream to Nightmare*

At the press conference announcing Euro Disneyland SCA's financial results for the year ended September 30, 1994, CEO Philippe Bourguignon summed up the year in succinct terms: "The best thing about 1994 is that it's over."

In fact, the results for the year were better than many of Euro Disneyland's long-suffering shareholders had predicted. Although revenues were down 15%—the result of falling visitor numbers caused by widespread expectations that the park would be closed down—costs had been cut by 12%, resulting in a similar operating profit to that of the previous year. The bottom line still showed a substantial loss (net after-tax loss was FF1.8 billion); however, this was a big improvement on the previous year (FF5.33 billion loss). Tables 18.1 and 18.2 show details of the financial performance.

TABLE 18.1 Euro Disneyland SCA: financial performance 1993–4; operating revenue and expenditure (millions of French francs)

	1994	1993
Revenue:		
Theme park	2212	2594
Hotels	1613	1721
Other	322	559
Construction sales	114	851
Total revenue	4261	5725
Direct costs/expenses:		
Park and hotels	(2961)	(3382)
Construction sales	(114)	(846)
Operating income	1186	1497
Depreciation	(291)	(227)
Lease rental expense	(889)	(1712)
Royalties	–	(262)
General and administration	(854)	(1113)
Financial income	538	719
Financial expenses	(972)	(615)
Loss	(1282)	(1713)
Exceptional loss, net	(515)	(3624)
Net loss	(1797)	(5337)
Employees (cast members)		
Number	11 865	10 172
Annual Cost (FF, millions)	2108	1892

Bourguignon was decidedly upbeat regarding the future. Following the FF13 billion restructuring agreed with creditor banks in June, Euro Disney was now on a much firmer financial footing. As a result of the restructuring, Euro Disneyland SCA was left with equity of about FF5.5 billion and total borrowings of FF15.9 billion—down by a quarter from the previous year. With the threat of closure lifted, Euro Disney was now in a much better position to attract visitors and corporate partners.

Efforts to boost attendance figures included a new advertising campaign, a new FF600 million attraction (Space Mountain), which was due to open in June 1996, and changing the park's name from Euro Disneyland to Disneyland Paris.

Moreover, Euro Disney had made a number of operational improvements. Mr. Bourguignon reported that queuing times had been cut by 45% during the year through new attractions and the redesign of existing ones; hotel occupancy rates had risen from 55% in the previous year to 60% and managers were to be given greater incentives. The net result, claimed Bourguignon, was that the company would break even during 1996.

The stock market responded positively to the results. In London, the shares of Euro Disneyland SCA rose 13p to 96p. However, this did not take the shares much above their all-time low. On November 6, 1989, the first day of trading after the Euro Disneyland initial public offering, the shares had traded at 880p. Since then, Euro

TABLE 18.2 Euro Disneyland SCA: financial statements 1992–4 (under U.S. GAAP)

Balance sheet

	1994	1993	1992
Cash and investments	289	211	479
Receivables	227	268	459
Fixed assets, net	3791	3704	4346
Other assets	137	214	873
Total assets	4444	4397	6157
Accounts payable and other liabilities	560	647	797
Borrowings	3051	3683	3,960
Stockholders' equity	833	67	1,400
Total liabilities and stockholders' equity	4444	4397	6157

Statement of operations

	1994	1993	1992
Revenues	751	873	738
Costs and expenses	1198	1114	808
Net interest expense	280	287	95
Loss before income taxes and cumulative effect of accounting change	(727)	(528)	(165)
Income tax benefit	–	–	30
Loss before cumulative effect of accounting change	(727)	(528)	(135)
Cumulative effect of change in accounting for pre-opening costs	–	(578)	–
Net loss	(727)	(1106)	(135)

Source: Walt Disney Company, 10-K Report, 1994.

Disneyland stock had been on a near-continuous downward trend (see Figure 18.1). The *Financial Times*' Lex column was also unenthusiastic:

> Still beset by high costs and low attendances, Euro Disney will find it hard to hit its target of break-even by the end of September 1996. Costs in the year were reduced by FF500m by introducing more flexible labor agreements (more part-timers, increased job sharing and the use of more students in the peak season) as well as outsourcing contracts in the hotel operation. But the company admits that the lion's share of cost reductions has now been realized. Now it hopes attendances are rising . . . Getting people to spend more once they are at the park might be more difficult. Euro Disney is pinning its hopes on economic recovery in Europe. It'll have to start paying interest, management fees and royalties again in five years' time. Management will not say whether it'll be able to cope then.[1]

Returning to his office at the end of the press conference, Bourguignon sighed. Since taking over from the previous chief executive, Robert Fitzpatrick, in 1993, the 46-year-old had been engaged in a continuing battle to ensure the survival of Euro Disney. Now that survival was no longer an issue, Bourguignon now faced his next

FIGURE 18.1 Euro Disneyland's share price in Paris, 1991–4 (in French francs)

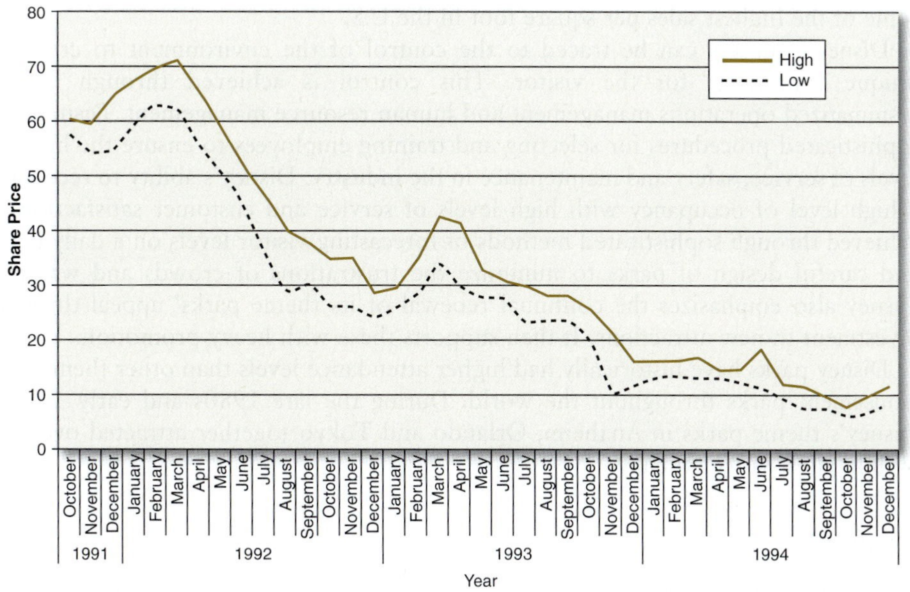

challenge: could Euro Disneyland ever become profitable—especially once Euro Disney had to resume paying licensing and management fees (amounting to some FF500 million a year) to Walt Disney Co. after 1998?

Disney Theme Parks

Walt Disney pioneered the theme park concept. His goal was to create a unique entertainment experience that combined fantasy and history, adventure, and learning in which the guest would be a participant, as well as a spectator. Current Disney-designed theme parks in California, Florida, Japan, and France are divided into distinct lands. All the parks include a number of similar lands with identical attractions. These include Main Street, Frontierland, Tomorrowland, Fantasyland and Adventureland. The objective is to immerse the guest in the atmosphere of the particular land. The theme of each land is reflected in the types of rides and attractions, the costumes of employees, the architectural style of the buildings, and even the food and souvenirs sold within the boundaries of the particular land. Rather than presenting a random collection of roller coasters, carousels and other rides, the Disney parks create an all-embracing experience which envelops the guest in carefully designed, tightly managed fantasy experience such as space flight, a Caribbean pirate attack, a flying ride with Peter Pan, or a race down the Matterhorn in a bob-sleigh.

Disney theme parks benefit from the talent and expertise of the Walt Disney "family" of businesses. Parks are designed by the engineers and architects of a wholly owned subsidiary—WED Enterprises. The themes for the attractions and characters that are featured in them often have their origins in cartoons and live action movies produced by Disney's studios. The parks also benefit from management and merchandising techniques developed over many years at Disney. These techniques have led to tremendous successes. In merchandising, Disney retail stores achieved some of the highest sales per square foot in the U.S.

Disney's success can be traced to the control of the environment to create a unique experience for the visitor. This control is achieved through highly systematized operations management and human resource management. Disney has sophisticated procedures for selecting and training employees to ensure the highest levels of service, safety and maintenance in the industry. Disney's ability to reconcile a high level of occupancy with high levels of service and customer satisfaction is achieved through sophisticated methods of forecasting visitor levels on a daily basis and careful design of parks to minimize the frustrations of crowds and waiting. Disney also emphasizes the continual renewal of its theme parks' appeal through investment in new attractions. It then supports these with heavy promotion.

Disney parks have historically had higher attendance levels than other theme and amusement parks throughout the world. During the late 1980s and early 1990s, Disney's theme parks in Anaheim, Orlando and Tokyo together attracted over 50 million guest visits annually.

Disney's U.S. Parks

The Los Angeles Disneyland theme park was finally opened in July of 1955 on 160 acres of land in Anaheim in California's Orange County. The success of Disneyland created a real estate boom in Anaheim, resulting in Disneyland being surrounded by a ring of hotels, motels, restaurants and other businesses.

For his next theme park project, Walt Disney aimed for undiluted control over the business and its revenue stream. Walt Disney World Resort opened in 1971 on a huge tract of 29 000 acres that Walt acquired outside of Orlando, Florida. Walt Disney World eventually comprised three separate theme parks: the original Magic Kingdom, the Experimental Prototype Community of Tomorrow (EPCOT) Center that opened in 1982 and hosted two themes—*Future World* and *World Showcase*—and Disney-MGM Studios, which opened in 1989.

The experience of creating a theme park as a destination resort represented a major development in Disney's conception of a theme park and was influential in its expansion plans into Europe. The huge site allowed Disney to broaden the scope of its theme park activities to create themed hotels, offer golf courses and other sports, convention facilities, night clubs, a range of retail stores, and even residential housing. The complementary coupling of a theme park with resort facilities that could even host commercial activities (conferences, a technology park) became central to Disney's theme park strategy.

By 1990, Walt Disney World had become the largest center of hotel capacity in the U.S., with approximately 70 000 rooms, of which almost 10% were owned and operated by Disney. Even though the room rates charged by Disney were considerably higher than other hotels in the vicinity, they achieved a remarkable occupancy rate of 94% during the late 1980s.

Tokyo Disneyland

Tokyo Disneyland, which opened in 1983, was a major departure for Walt Disney Company. The Oriental Land Company Limited (OLCL), a Japanese development company, had approached Disney with a proposal to open a Disneyland in Japan. Disney's top management regarded a Disney theme park in another country with a different climate and a different culture as a risky venture. Disney insisted on a deal that would leave OLCL with all the risk: the park would be owned and operated by OLCL while Disney would receive royalties of 10% on the admissions revenues and 5% on receipts from food, beverages and souvenirs. These royalties represented licensing fees for Disney's trademarks and intellectual property, engineering designs for rides and ongoing technical assistance. Despite the challenges of limited space and cold winter weather, Tokyo Disneyland was a huge success. By the late 1980s it was drawing 15 million visitors a year—more than any other Disney park.[2] By 1989, Disney's royalties from Tokyo Disneyland had risen to $573 million—greater than the operating income received from Disney's U.S. theme parks.

Planning and Development

Beginnings of Euro Disneyland

The success of Tokyo Disneyland was clear evidence to Disney's top management of the international potential for Disney's theme parks. Europe was considered the obvious location for the next Disney park. Europe had always been a strong market for Disney movies and there was a strong European demand for toys, books, and comics that featured Disney characters—European consumers generated about one-quarter of revenues from Disney licensed consumer products. The popularity of Disney theme parks with Europeans was evident from the 2 million European visitors to Disneyland and Walt Disney World each year. Moreover, Western Europe possessed a population and affluence capable of supporting a major Disney theme park.

In 1984, Disney management made the decision to commit to development of a European theme park and commenced feasibility planning and site selection. In assessing alternative locations, the following criteria were applied:

- proximity to a high-density population zone with a relatively high level of disposable income;
- ability to draw upon a substantial local tourist population, availability of qualified labor and readily accessible transportation;
- availability of sufficient land to permit expansion of the project to meet increasing demand;
- provision of necessary infrastructure, such as water and electricity.

Two locations quickly emerged as front-runners: Barcelona and Paris. While Barcelona had the advantages of a better year-round climate, Paris offered key economic and infrastructure advantages, together with strong backing from the French government. Disney's interest in a European theme park corresponded with the French government's plans to develop the Marne-la-Vallée area east of Paris. The result was rapid progress of Disney's formal negotiations with the range of local government authorities and public bodies whose cooperation and agreement were essential for a project of this scale. The proposed site's demographic characteristics offered the right set of conditions for a successful theme park. The park rested on a

4500 acre site 32 km east of Paris, providing proximity to a metropolitan area and room for expansion; the high population of the greater Paris area (over 10 million) and Europe (over 330 million) provided a large consumer market and existing and planned transportation equipped the park with access to vital infrastructure. Paris was already a major tourist destination with excellent air, road and rail links with the rest of Europe.

On March 24, 1987, the Walt Disney Company entered into the Agreement on the Creation and the Operation of Euro Disneyland in France (the "Master Agreement") with the Republic of France, the Region of Ile-de-France, the Department of Seine-et-Marne, the Etablissement Public d'Aménagement de la Ville Nouvelle de Marne-la-Vallée, and the Régie Autonome des Transports Parisiens. This was followed by incorporation of Euro Disneyland SCA (the "Company") and the conclusion of an agreement with the SNCF (the French national railway company) to provide TGV (the French high-speed train) service to Euro Disneyland beginning in June 1994. The agreement involved commitments by Disney to establish Euro Disneyland as a French corporation, to develop a major international theme park, and to create 30 000 jobs in the process. The French authorities committed to provide land and infrastructure over the project's 30-year development period ending in 2017. The real estate deal involved Disney acquiring 1700 hectares (approximately 4300 acres)[3] of agricultural land at Marne-la-Vallée. In addition, a further 243 hectares were reserved for public facilities and infrastructure. The purchase price for the land included the raw land price (FF11.1 per square meter or approximately $8360 per acre), direct and indirect secondary infrastructure costs, and certain financing and overhead expenses of the French authorities. The area of the total site was equivalent to one-fifth of the area of the city of Paris. The land for the first phase of the development was purchased outright by Euro Disneyland SCA, with purchase options on the remaining land. Euro Disneyland SCA also had the right to sell land to third parties, as long as the development plans of any purchasers were approved by the French planning authority.

The agreement provided for motorway links to Paris, Strasbourg and the two international airports serving Paris—Charles de Gaulle and Orly, while the planned extension of the RER (the express commuter rail network) would allow visitors to reach the Magic Kingdom from the center of Paris within 40 minutes. Euro Disney[4] would also be linked to France's TGV system, with its own station serving the park. This would also give a rail service from Britain through the Channel Tunnel. In addition to infrastructure, the French government's financial inducements included FF4.8 billion in loans and a favorable tax rate (34%). The total package of incentives added up to roughly FF6.0 billion.[5]

The Market: Demand and Competition

A key factor attracting Disney to Paris was market potential. The greater Paris metropolis has a population of over 10 million. Roughly 16 million people lived within a 160 km radius of the proposed site; within a 320 km radius were 41 million people; and within a 480 km radius were 109 million people. The transportation links of Paris facilitated access to this huge market. As a result, Euro Disneyland would be capable of achieving a high level of capacity utilization, even with much lower market penetration rates than those achieved by Disney's California and

Florida theme parks. European vacation patterns were also seen as conducive to visits—Europeans received substantially more vacation time than U.S. workers and, in addition to their summer vacation, European families frequently took shorter vacations throughout the year. Estimates of numbers of visitors to Euro Disney and their expenditures were made by consultants Arthur D. Little as part of their financial projections for Euro Disneyland SCA (see Appendix 1).

The ability of Euro Disney to achieve its visitor targets would depend not only on the size of the market but also upon the relative attractiveness and number of competing tourist destinations. Although Disney viewed its theme parks as unique in terms of the quality and intensity of the entertainment experience that it offered, the company also recognized that, ultimately, a wide range of family vacation and entertainment experiences compete for household disposable income. Although there were very few large-scale theme parks in Europe to compete directly with Euro Disneyland (most of the world's major theme parks were located in the U.S.) there were a number of family entertainment destinations within Europe that would be potential competitors (see Table 18.3). Moreover, European cities—such as London, Paris, Rome, Prague, Barcelona, and many others—offered a richness and variety of cultural and historical experiences that few U.S. cities could match and represented an alternative to Euro Disney for short family vacations. Furthermore, there was a host of traditional forms of family entertainment in Europe, including fairs, carnivals and festivals, some of which were small and local while others—such as the Munich Bierfest, the Pamplona bull-running festival, the Edinburgh cultural festival, and the Dutch tulip festivals—were major events attracting large numbers of international visitors.

Disney's plans for Euro Disneyland created its own competitors. Within two years of Disney's announcement to build Euro Disney, three French theme parks—Mirapolis, Futuroscope and Zygofolis—had opened in an attempt to pre-empt Disney's entry into the market. By the summer of 1989, two more theme

TABLE 18.3 Attendance at major theme parks

	Estimated attendance in 1988 (millions of guest visits)
Sea World—*Florida*	4.6
Tivoli Gardens—*Denmark*	4.5
Universal Studios Tour—*California*	4.2
Knott's Berry Farm—*California*	4.0
Busch Gardens—*Florida*	3.7
Sea World—*California*	3.4
Six Flags Magic Mountain—*California*	3.1
King's Island—*Ohio*	3.0
Liseberg—*Sweden*	2.8
Alton Towers—*United Kingdom*	2.3
De Efteling—*The Netherlands*	2.3
Phantasialand—*West Germany*	2.2

Source: Euro Disneyland SCA Abridged Offering Circular.

parks—Asterix and Big Bang Schtroumph—opened their gates. However, with aggregate annual losses of about $43 million on a total investment of over $600 million, these parks were considered financial disasters.[6]

The Development Plan

Euro Disney's Development Program provided for a theme park, based closely on the themes and concepts of Disney's U.S. theme parks. It would be the largest theme park and resort development in Europe. The plan established two stages for the project.

Phase 1 Phase 1, the major part of the overall project, was subdivided into two sections. Phase 1A comprised the Magic Kingdom theme park, the Magic Kingdom Hotel (which would serve as the entrance area to the theme park) and a camping ground. These were to be completed at a budgeted cost of FF14.9 billion. Of the 570 acres allocated for Phase 1, Phase 1A would utilize 240 acres. The rest of the land would be developed in Phase 1B to accommodate five additional hotels, an entertainment, restaurant and shopping complex, and sports facilities with an 18-hole championship golf course. Phase 1A also provided for the French government to construct two junctions with the nearby motorway, main access roads to the park, a drinking-water supply and distribution system, storm drainage, sewers, solid waste treatment, and telecommunications networks. The cost of the additional infrastructure, including links with the RER and the TGV, was to be financed by Euro Disneyland SCA.

The Magic Kingdom theme park was to include five themed lands: Main Street USA, the gateway to the park; Frontierland, a reproduction of wooden streets typical of a mid-nineteenth-century frontier town; tropical Adventure Land, the most exotic of the park settings; Fantasyland, with attractions drawn from well-known Disney stories; and Discoveryland, which, through the sophisticated use of technology, illustrates the past and the future. Each offers appropriately themed restaurants and shopping facilities.

To permit year-round operation, Euro Disney included adaptations designed to make attendance less dependent on the weather, with more interconnected covered areas than at other Disney parks. Many modifications to the themes, architecture and dining facilities were made to tailor the park to the European market. For example, while French is the first language of the park, universal signposting is used wherever possible to aid non-French-speaking visitors, and many attractions are identified by visual cues.

Phase 2 Phase 2 of the Long-Term Development Strategy extended to 2011. It envisioned a second theme park (Disney-MGM Studios) on a site adjacent to the Magic Kingdom; 15 additional hotels, which would increase the number of rooms available by 13 000; a water recreation area and second golf course and residential and commercial development. This phase was left flexible to accommodate the policies of the French authorities, economic and market conditions, participant needs, and visitor preferences.

Construction Disney exercised close control over the design and construction of Phase 1A of Euro Disney. Lehrer McGovern Bovis, Inc. (LMB), an independent construction management firm with international experience in the management of large-scale construction projects, was the main contractor. It reported to Euro Disneyland Imagineering SARL (EDLI), a French subsidiary of Disney, which had overall responsibility for designing and constructing Phases 1 and 2 of the theme park. Also reporting to EDLI were separate Disney companies responsible for design (conceptual and otherwise), engineering, and the development and equipping of attractions.

Participants As with other Disney theme parks, at Euro Disneyland "participants" played an important role in financial and in marketing terms. Participants are companies or organizations that enter into long-term marketing agreements with the company. Typically, these relationships represent a ten-year commitment and physically tie the participant to the Magic Kingdom, where it hosts or presents one or more of the theme park's attractions, restaurants, or other facilities. Relationships with participants may also involve marketing activities featuring the association between the participant and the company. Each participant pays an individually negotiated annual fee, which may contribute to the financing of a particular attraction or facility.

Initial participants at Euro Disneyland included Kodak, Banque Nationale de Paris, Renault, and Europcar.

Financial and Management Structure

For Euro Disneyland, Disney chose a unique financial and management structure. Rather than a pure franchise operation similar to Tokyo Disneyland, Disney chose to retain management and operational control of the park while allowing European investors to take majority ownership and European banks to provide most of the debt financing. The relationship between Walt Disney Company and Euro Disneyland is depicted in Figure 18.2.

Euro Disneyland SCA

Euro Disneyland SCA was formed to build and own Euro Disneyland. The company was a *société en commandite par actions*—the French equivalent of a limited partnership. The company was governed by a supervisory board elected by the shareholders and chaired by Jean Taittinger, the Chairman and Chief Executive of Société du Louvre and Banque du Louvre. Disney took a 49% stake in Euro Disneyland SCA; the remaining 51% of equity was floated through an initial public offering underwritten by three investment banks. The shares were listed on the Paris and London stock markets. Although Disney held 49% of Euro Disneyland SCA equity it contributed only 13% of its equity book value (FF273 million net of incentives received). The difference was "granted" to the company, both as a goodwill "gesture" in recognition of Disney's reputation and credibility in the investment community and as compensation for Disney's assumed risk in the undertaking.

The Management Company

Euro Disneyland SCA was managed by a separate management company, Euro Disneyland SA (the "management company"), a wholly owned subsidiary of Disney.

FIGURE 18.2 The financial and management relationship between Walt Disney and Euro Disneyland

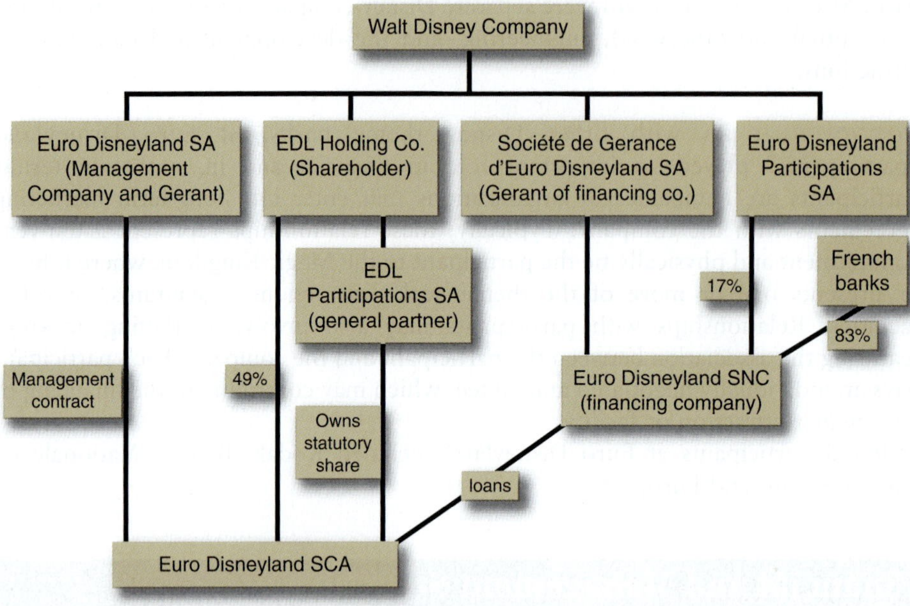

The management company, or *gerant*, was responsible under French law for managing Euro Disneyland SCA and its affairs in the company's best interests. In turn, the management company agreed that the provision of management services to the company would be its exclusive business. Under the Articles of Association, the management company was entitled to annual fees consisting of a base fee and management incentive fees. The base fee in any year was set at 3% of the company's total revenues, and increased to 6% after five years of operation, or after the company had satisfied certain financial targets. On top of the base fee, the management company was entitled to incentive fees based on Euro Disneyland SCA's pretax cash flow. These incentives increased in stages up to a possible maximum of 50% of Euro Disneyland SCA's net profit. The management company also received 35% of pre-tax gains on the sales of hotels. Euro Disneyland SCA was also obligated to reimburse the management company for all its direct and indirect expenses incurred in its management role. The management contract was for five years.

The Shareholding Company and General Partner

Disney's shareholding in Euro Disneyland SCA was held by EDL Holding, a wholly owned subsidiary of Disney. This shareholding company also owned EDL Participations SA, which held the key role of "general partner" in Euro Disneyland SCA—it assumed unlimited liability for the debts and liabilities of Euro Disneyland SCA. As general partner, EDL Participations SA was entitled to a distribution each year equal to 0.5% of Euro Disneyland SCA's net after-tax profits.

The Financing Company

Euro Disneyland SNC was formed to buy the park facilities from Euro Disneyland SCA at book value plus development costs, then lease them back to Euro Disneyland SCA. Euro Disneyland SNC was owned 17% by Disney and 83% by French corporations. The rationale was to allow French corporations to take advantage of the tax benefits of Euro Disneyland's early years of projected losses. Once again, Euro Disneyland SNC was to be managed by a Disney subsidiary and Disney would act as its general partner with full debt default liability.

The License Agreement

Under the License Agreement, Walt Disney Company granted to Euro Disneyland SCA a license to use any present or future Disney intellectual and industrial property rights incorporated in Disney's attractions and facilities and made available to the Company for Euro Disney. These included the Walt Disney name, the Disney characters, and the proprietary technology in theme park attractions. Disney was to receive royalties as follows:

- 10% of gross revenues (net of TVA, the French value-added tax, and similar taxes) from rides, admissions and certain related fees (such as parking, tour guide, and similar services) at all theme parks and other attractions (including the Magic Kingdom and any future theme park);
- 5% of gross revenues (net of TVA and similar taxes) from merchandise, food, and beverage sales in or adjacent to any theme park or other attraction or in any other facility (other than the Magic Kingdom Hotel) whose overall design concept is based predominantly on a Disney theme;
- 10% of all fees due from participants;
- 5% of all gross revenues (net of TVA and similar taxes) from room rates and related charges at Disney-themed accommodations (excluding the Magic Kingdom Hotel).

Cultural Issues

Euro Disneyland presented huge challenges for Disney. Climate was a major problem. The long gray winter of northern France created complex design problems that were absent from Disney's sun-drenched California and Florida parks. However, the challenges posed by adverse weather conditions were mainly technical and amenable to careful analysis. The issues of culture were much less tractable.

While the success of Tokyo Disneyland was a major factor behind the decision to create Euro Disney, the cultural challenges of France were very different from those of Japan. Tokyo Disneyland had been conceived, built, and operated on a wave of popular Japanese acclaim. As a result, Tokyo Disneyland had made very few concessions to Japanese culture. Although, at first, Disney wanted to adapt some of the attractions to the Japanese context (for example, Samurai-Land instead of Frontierland), their Japanese partners strongly resisted efforts to "localize" Disneyland, arguing that the park would attract more Japanese people if it were built as a perfect replica of U.S. Disneyland. They emphasized that Disney's cartoon characters were very familiar to the Japanese people and that visitors would want "the real thing." As a result, only minor changes were made, such as the addition of Cinderella's Castle and the Mickey Mouse Theater.

After the enthusiasm with which the Japanese greeted Disney's entry, the response of the French could not have been more different. France presented a very different situation. French intellectuals had long shown antagonism towards American popular culture and they were supported by widespread nationalistic sentiment that saw the French language and French culture as threatened by the global hegemony of the English language. At the political level too, France had been the most independent of the western European powers in terms of its independent foreign policy and unwillingness to accept U.S. leadership in world affairs. The announcement of the Euro Disneyland project was greeted by howls of outrage from the French media and from the intelligentsia who viewed the park as "a cultural Chernobyl," "a dangerous step towards world homogenization," "a horror made of cardboard, plastic, and appalling colors, a construction of hardened chewing gum and idiotic folklore taken straight out of the comic books written for obese Americans."[7] Euro Disney quickly became a lightning rod for a variety of anti-American issues. For example, shortly after opening, Euro Disney was blockaded by farmers protesting U.S. farm policies.

The design of the park incorporated many adaptations of French and European culture. Disney emphasized the European heritage of many of Disney's characters and storylines (referred to by Chairman Michael Eisner as "European folklore with a Kansas twist"). Some attractions featured European adaptations: Cinderella lived in a French inn and Snow White's home was in a Bavarian village. Other attractions were unique to Euro Disney: Discoveryland (which substituted for Tomorrowland at other Disney parks) was based on themes from Jules Verne and Leonardo da Vinci; "Visionarium" was a 360-degree movie theater showcasing French culture; an Alice-in-Wonderland attraction was surrounded by a 5000 sq. ft. hedge maze. Designing and constructing these European-themed attractions added substantially to the cost of Euro Disneyland.

Some "American" themed attractions were adapted on the basis of market research findings. For example, the finding that European visitors to Disney's U.S. parks responded positively to themes embodying the American West encouraged Disney to redesign several attractions around a Wild West theme—including a mining town setting for one ride, a "Davy Crockett" themed campground, and hotels named the "Cheyenne," "Santa Fe" and "Sequoia Lodge."

Other adaptations were made to cater to European social behavior and culinary tastes. Concern over European aversion to queuing resulted in the provision of video screens, movies and other entertainment for guests waiting in line. Disney's no-alcohol policy was adjusted by allowing wine and beer to be served at Feastival Disney, an entertainment complex just outside the theme park. In the restaurant facilities, greater emphasis was placed on sit-down dining and much less on fast food. At a seminar at UCLA in 1990, Robert Fitzpatrick placed a major emphasis on the Company's determination to provide the highest standards of quality at Euro Disney. This was evident both in the cuisine and in the furnishings and service standards of the hotels. In both areas, Fitzpatrick argued, quality was well in excess of the standards at Disney's U.S. parks.

Human relations management posed further cultural challenges. Central to the Disney theme park experience was the way in which "cast members" interacted with the guests. Disney was famous for its meticulous approach to recruitment, its commitment to employee training and the maintenance of rigorous standards of employee conduct. For example, Disney's employee handbook spelled out a strict code with respect to dress and appearance, including:

- above average height and below average weight;
- pleasant appearance (straight teeth, no facial blemishes);
- conservative grooming standards (facial hair and long hair is banned);
- very modest make-up, very limited jewelry (for example, no more than one ring on each hand);
- employees were required to wear specific types and colors of underwear; only neutral colors of pantyhose were allowed.[8]

Training embraced general principles and specific knowledge and behaviors. For example, employees were instructed that their behavior on the job should be governed by three major rules: "First, we practice a friendly smile. Second, we use only friendly phrases. Third, we are not stuffy."

To what extent could locally recruited employees provide the level, quality and consistency of service at Euro Disney that would match that of other Disney theme parks, and to what extent could Disney simply transplant its U.S. human resource management practices? Euro Disney's selection and training were closely modeled on Disney's U.S. approach. A Euro Disney branch of Disney University was opened and recruitment of 10 000 employees began in September 1991. Selection criteria were "applicant friendliness, warmth, and liking of people." The rules for job applicants were spelled out in a video presentation and in the employee handbook, "The Euro Disney Look." The rules went far beyond weight and height requirements, describing the length of the men's hair, beard and mustache requirements, tattoo coverage requirements and hair color specifications (for example, hair had to be of a natural-looking color, without frosting or streaking). Only moderate use of cosmetics was allowed. Women could wear one earring in each ear with the earrings' diameter not to exceed three-quarters of an inch.[9] The goal was a nationality mix that would match that of Euro Disney's customers, about 45% of whom were French. However, in response to local pressure and the greater availability of local applicants, some 70% of employees were French. At the management level, Disney relied on importing about 200 managers from other Disney parks and training 270 locally recruited managers (this involved training at Disney's other theme parks).

Disney's recruiting practices and employee policies produced a storm of protest. French labor unions started protesting from the moment that Euro Disney started interviewing applicants. Representatives of the General Confederation of Labor handed out leaflets in front of Euro Disney's HQ warning applicants that the Disney hiring practices represented "an attack on individual freedom." Many of Disney's normal U.S. hiring and employment practices contravened French law. Workforce flexibility was limited by the restrictions on terminating employees with more than two years with the company and the high severance payments involved. There were also legal limits over the recruitment and dismissal of seasonal workers. As for Disney's dress and personal grooming codes, French law prohibited an employer from restricting "individual and collective freedoms" unless the restrictions could be justified by the "nature of the objective to be accomplished and were proportional to that end." Since Disney estimated that no more than 700 employees would be involved in "theatrical actions," dress code limitations could only be imposed on those employees, not on those who would only be "back stage."

The First Year

Euro Disney's opening on April 12, 1992 combined both fanfare and protest. An extravagant opening ceremony involved some of the world's leading entertainers and was televised in 22 countries. Michael Eisner proclaimed Euro Disney to be "one of the greatest man-made attractions in the world" while the French Prime Minister described the park as an "incredible achievement which transcends national frontiers . . . We are deeply attached to the links of friendship between our continent and yours. Euro Disney is one of the symbols of this transatlantic friendship." However, the opening was marred by a demonstration of local residents, a train strike affecting lines leading to the park and a terrorist bomb threat. By the end of the first day, park attendance had been way below capacity and only one-half of the anticipated number.

The park ran into early teething problems. Design problems ranged from insufficient breakfast facilities to an absence of toilet facilities for bus drivers and a shortage of employee accommodation. During the first nine weeks of operation, 1000 employees left Euro Disney, about one-half voluntarily. Long hours and hectic work pace were the main reasons given for leaving. Nevertheless, visitor reactions were mainly highly positive. Negative comments related to frustration with long periods of waiting in line and the high cost of admission, food and souvenirs. Some voiced concern over the multinational, multicultural flavor of Euro Disney: "They haven't yet figured out whether it's going to be an American park, a French park, or a European park . . . Differences in waiting line behavior is striking. For instance, Scandinavians appear quite content to wait for rides, whereas some of the southern Europeans seem to have made an Olympic event out of getting to the ticker tape first." Some visitors had difficulty envisaging Disney within a European context: "Disney is very much an American culture. Florida is the true Disney World, the true feeling of Disney, what Disney is trying to project. Americans are part of that, the French aren't."[10]

Start-up difficulties were normal in the theme park business—all major theme parks, including those of Disney, experienced some teething problems during the period of initial operation. Universal Studios in Florida had a disastrous first few months but subsequently rebounded. With 30 000 visitors daily during the summer of 1992, it seemed that Euro Disney might reach its projected target of 11 million visitors annually. However, it was soon clear that, despite good visitor numbers during the summer, Euro Disney's profitability would fall far below expectations. There was a larger number of day visitors and fewer period visits than had been anticipated. As a result, Euro Disney cut hotel rates by up to 25%. Moreover, average visitor expenditure on beverages, food and gifts was 12% less than the $33 per day that had been anticipated. Part of the problem was the economic situation—during 1992, most of Western Europe was mired in one of the worst economic downturns since the Second World War. The depressed state of the French real estate market also prevented Euro Disney from boosting revenues through land sales.

By the end of Euro Disney's first full financial year, the extent of the financial underperformance was becoming clear. Even with exceptional items, the company lost over FF1.7 billion. In terms of U.S. GAAP, Euro Disneyland's pretax loss was over half a billion dollars. Top-line performance was a key problem. Instead of the 11 million visitors forecast, Euro Disney attracted 9.8 million visitors during its first full year. Equally serious was the fact that average visitor spending was below target, and much lower than at Disney's U.S. and Japanese parks. Fewer visitors than projected were staying in Disney theme hotels, deterred by room rates that were much higher than in comparable hotels in Paris. Hotel occupancy rates were below 50% in contrast to the 60% figure projected. On the cost side, Disney's emphasis on quality had boosted both construction and operating costs, while higher than anticipated debt together with rising interest rates caused interest charges to spiral upward. Labor costs amounted to a huge 24% of sales, rather than the forecasted level of 13% of sales. Much of the cost overruns could be attributed to Disney's belief that "Lacoste and Polo loving" Europeans would not tolerate anything unsophisticated or cheap. For example, in the U.S., "The Walt" restaurant had wallpaper but at Euro Disney the walls were covered in Moroccan leather. Yet, when it came to trading off sophistication for lower prices, most Euro Disney customers opted for the latter.

For Walt Disney Company, the financial returns were better than they were for Euro Disneyland's other shareholders. During 1992 and 1993, Disney's 49% share of Euro Disneyland's losses was offset by royalties from its licensing agreement. These amounted to $36.3 million in 1993 and $32.9 million in 1992; however, Disney agreed to defer its management fees for 1992 and 1993.

Restructuring

During the winter of 1993/4, Euro Disney visitor numbers plummeted. Despite the French franc falling against the U.S. dollar, many Europeans found that Disneyland Florida was not only a more attractive destination during the winter months but it was also cheaper. "It's cheaper to go on a two-week holiday in Florida than to come to Euro Disney for five days," remarked one British traveler with a family of four. With low transatlantic fares, European visitors to Walt Disney World in Orlando increased sharply during 1992 and 1993. By early 1994, Euro Disney was in crisis. Faced with mounting losses, rising debt and doubts about the company's capacity to cover its interest payments, rumors were rife that the park would be forced to close.

The financial restructuring package agreed between Euro Disneyland and its creditors in June 1994 involved the following measures:

- A $1.1 billion rights offering of which Disney agreed to take up 41%.
- The provision by Disney of $255 million in lease financing at an interest rate of 1%.
- The cancellation by Disney of $210 million in receivables from Euro Disneyland.
- The agreement by Disney to waive royalties and management fees for five years.

- The agreement that Disney would receive warrants for the purchase of 28 million Euro Disneyland shares and would receive a development fee of $225 million once the second phase of the development project was launched. Euro Disneyland's lenders agreed to underwrite 51% of the Euro Disney rights offering, to forgive certain interest charges until September 2003 and to defer all principal payments for three years. In return, Euro Disneyland issued the lenders ten-year warrants for the purchase of up to 40 million shares of Euro Disneyland stock.

In a separate agreement, Disney agreed to sell 75 million shares, equivalent to 10% of Euro Disneyland's total shareholding, to Prince Alwaleed Bin Talal Bin Abdulaziz Al Saud. The sale reduced Disney's shareholding in Euro Disneyland to 39%.

Looking Ahead

While the restructuring package had staved off disaster for the time being, the traumas of the past year made Bourguignon cautious about the future. Despite heavy advertising, the addition of new attractions and the fine-tuning of Disney's image, customer service, and offering of food, drinks, and souvenirs, Euro Disney had yet to reach the initial forecast of 11 million visitors annually. Significant cost reductions had been achieved; however, the scope for further cost reductions was limited if Euro Disney was to maintain Disney's standards of customer service excellence. While Bourguignon was convinced that the company would be generating operating profits by 1995, such profits would be the result of Disney's agreement to forgo its royalties and management fees. Once these were reinstated, Euro Disney's costs would increase by about FF500 million annually.

Bourguignon believed that many of the problems that had dogged Euro Disney from the beginning had been resolved. In particular, the renaming of the park as Disneyland Paris had helped alleviate ambiguity and conflict over the park's identity. Disneyland Paris was to be a Disney theme park located close to Paris. Dropping the "Euro" prefix released the company from the public's mistrust of all things Euro and helped the park to avoid the debate over what European culture and European identity actually meant. Moreover, the new name firmly associated Euro Disney with the romantic connotations of the city of Paris. In terms of the need to differentiate Euro Disney from Disney's other theme parks, the experience of the past two years suggested that Euro Disney's expensive adaptations to meet European tastes and European culture were not greatly appreciated by customers. For the most part, visitors were delighted by the same rides as existed in Disney's U.S. parks and generally preferred fast food over fine dining.

Over the next six months, Bourguignon recognized that key decisions needed to be taken:

- To what extent should Euro Disney cut admission prices in order to boost attendance? An internal study had estimated that a 20% reduction in admission prices would boost attendance by about 800 000 visitors; however, the net result would still be a reduction in total revenues of about 5%.

- The problems of insufficient demand related primarily to the winter months. In previous winters some senior managers had argued for the closure of the park. However, so long as most of Euro Disney's employees were permanent staff, such a closure would do little to reduce total costs.
- Bourguignon had already deferred Phase 2 of the development plan—construction of a Disney-MGM Studios theme park. The other members of his senior management team were urging him to go ahead with this phase of development. Only with a second theme park, they believed, would Euro Disney's goal of becoming a major destination resort become realized. However, Bourguignon was acutely aware of Euro Disney's still precarious financial situation. With net equity of about FF5.5 billion and total borrowings of FF15.9 billion, Euro Disney was not well placed to begin the large-scale capital expenditures that Phase 2 would involve.

As Bourguignon arranged the papers on his desk at the end of a long day, he reflected on his success at pulling off the rescue plan and the continuing uphill struggle to realize the ambitions that had driven the project in the early days. The wartime words of Winston Churchill summed up the situation well: "This is not the end. It is not the beginning of the end. It is the end of the beginning."

Appendix 1: Euro Disneyland SCA's Financial Model

The company has prepared a financial model, based on the principal assumptions described below, which projects revenues, expenses, profits, cash flows, and dividends of the company for 12-month periods beginning 1 April, 1992 and ending 31 March, 2017 as summarized in Table 18.4. Although the company's accounting year end is 30 September, years beginning 1 April have been used for the projections in order to represent whole operating years from the projected date of opening of the Magic Kingdom. The projections contained in the model do not constitute a forecast of the actual revenues, expenses, profits, cash flows or dividends of the company. The model assumes that the company will complete Phase 1 as described in this document and will develop the remaining elements of Euro Disneyland according to the long-term development strategy. As discussed above, the company retains the flexibility to change the long-term development strategy and the designs for Phase 1B in response to future conditions. Table 18.5 summarizes the principal components of the development plan.

TABLE 18.4 Euro Disneyland SCA: projected revenues and profits (FF millions)

1992–6 12 months commencing April 1	1992	1993	1994	1995	1996
Revenues					
Magic Kingdom	4246	4657	5384	5835	6415
Second theme park	0	0	0	0	3128
Resort and property development	1236	2144	3520	5077	6386
Total revenues	5482	6801	8904	10930	15929
Profit before taxation	351	620	870	1,676	1,941

(Continued)

TABLE 18.4 *(Continued)*

1992–6 12 months commencing April 1	1992	1993	1994	1995	1996
Net profit	204	360	504	972	1121
Dividends payable	275	425	625	900	1100
Tax credit or payment	0	138	213	313	450
Total return	275	563	838	1,213	1550
Per share (FF)	1.6	3.3	4.9	7.1	9.1

Later years: 12 months commencing April 1	2001	2006	2011	2016
Revenues				
Magic Kingdom	9730	13055	18181	24118
Second theme park	4565	6656	9313	12954
Resort and property development	8133	9498	8979	5923
Total revenues	22428	29209	36473	42995
Profit before taxation	3034	4375	6539	9951
Net profit	1760	2538	3793	5771
Dividends payable	1750	2524	3379	5719
Tax credit or payment	536	865	1908	2373
Total return	2286	3389	5287	8092
Per share (FF)	13.4	19.9	31.1	47.6

Source: Euro Disneyland SCA Abridged Offering Circular.

TABLE 18.5 Planned development of Euro Disneyland

	Phase 1A	Phase 1B	Long-term development	Total
Theme parks	1	–	1	2
Hotel capacity (rooms)	500	4700	13000	18200
Camping ground (campsite plots)	595	–	1505	2100
Entertainment center (sq. meters)	–	22000	38000	60000
Offices (sq. meters)	–	30000	670000	700000
Corporate park (sq. meters)	–	50000	700000	750000
Golf courses		1	1	2
Single-family homes	–	570	1930	2500
Retail shopping center (sq. meters)	–	–	95000	95000
Water recreation area	–	–	1	1
Multi-family residence	–	–	3000	3000
Time-share units	–	–	2400	2400

Source: Euro Disneyland SCA Abridged Offering Circular.

The model is based on other assumptions developed by the company in light of Disney's experience with existing theme parks and resorts, after taking into account analyses of local market conditions and an assessment of likely future economic, market, and other factors. The major assumptions have been reviewed by Arthur D. Little International, Inc. ("ADL"), the independent consultancy firm retained by the Company to test and verify their reasonableness. Set out at the end of "The financial model" is a letter from ADL regarding its reports. While the Company believes that the assumptions underlying the model are reasonable, there is no certainty that the projected performance of the company outlined below will be achieved.

Principal Assumptions and Rationale Underlying the Financial Model

Theme Park Attendance

To project the number of visitors expected to visit the Euro Disneyland theme parks, several internal and external studies were commissioned. The most recent of these studies was undertaken by ADL in 1989 to verify and confirm the methods and assumptions used in the previous studies and to make its own estimates of attendance.

The Magic Kingdom The model assumes that the Magic Kingdom will be constructed as described in this document and that it will open and be fully operational by April 1992.

Summary figures for assumed attendance at the Magic Kingdom are shown in the table below. Attendance is measured in terms of the total numbers of daily guest visits per annum. For example, a visitor who enters a theme park on three separate days will count as three daily guest visits.

	1992	1996	2001	2011
Magic Kingdom (in millions of persons)	11.0	13.3	15.2	16.2

The assumed attendance of 11 million for the first full year of operation of the Magic Kingdom is in line with the average attendance achieved in the first year of operation of the Magic Kingdom theme parks in Florida and Japan and is below the range of potential initial attendance estimated to be between 11.7 and 17.8 million in the attendance study conducted by ADL. Depending on its seasonal distribution, the higher end of the range could require acceleration of the attraction investment program. Arthur D. Little concluded that the attendance target of 11 million can be achieved if the development program envisaged for Phase 1A is accomplished and a well-conceived marketing campaign tailored to European patterns is carried out to support the opening of the Magic Kingdom.

Attendance at the Magic Kingdom is assumed to grow over the period covered by the financial model at an average compound rate of 2% per annum. This growth rate compares with an average growth rate of 3.8% per annum for the three Magic Kingdom theme parks in California, Florida and Japan.

The assumed growth rate, which is higher in early years, consists of a basic growth rate, adjusted for the effect of the addition of new attractions every two to three years and for the effect of the opening of a second theme park. The overall assumed growth rate is broken down as follows:

Years	2–5	6–10	11–20	20+
Annual growth (%)	4.9	2.7	0.6	0.0

The method used by ADL involved three steps: first, individual target markets were identified by distance and population: second, penetration rates (the percentage of the total population in a target market which visits the theme park) were estimated for each target market; and third, the average number of annual visits per guest from each target market was estimated.

Arthur D. Little noted that a number of factors, including the following, contribute to the high attendance levels at Disney-designed theme parks:

- The design and scope of a Magic Kingdom theme park are such that a complete visit requires more than one full day. This means that visitors are likely either to extend their stay or to return at a future date.
- The quality and capacity available at Disney hotels allow the demand for longer stays to be satisfied.
- The level of recognition of the Disney name and the quality of the experience make Disney theme parks popular holiday destination resorts.

In the opinion of ADL these factors distinguish Disney-designed theme parks from existing theme parks and amusement parks in Europe, which are much smaller and are basically designed for single-day visits. Accordingly, in determining potential penetration rates and the number of annual visits per guest to derive projected attendance levels at Euro Disneyland, ADL relied largely on the experience at Disney-designed theme parks.

Arthur D. Little concluded that because of the large number of people living within a convenient traveling distance of Euro Disneyland, the assumed attendance figures in the model could be achieved with market penetration rates at or below those experienced at other Disney-designed theme parks.

The company believes that these factors will exist at Euro Disneyland and will support the assumed penetration rates and attendance levels, which are consistent with those experienced at Disney-designed theme parks. The company also believes that the location of the site at the center of an area of high population density with well-developed transport links will enable Euro Disneyland to draw visitors from both local and more distant markets.

Second Theme Park The model assumes that a second theme park will be completed and will open to the public in the spring of 1996. Summary figures for assumed attendance at the second theme park are as follows:

	1992	1996	2001	2011
Second theme park (in millions)	–	8.0	8.8	10.1

Attendance at the second theme park is assumed to grow at an average compound rate of 2% per annum over the first ten years, and 1% per annum for the next ten years until 2016. These assumptions are primarily based on Disney's experience of opening a second theme park at Walt Disney World, where EPCOT Center drew attendance of over 11 million guest visits in its first year of operation.

Per Capita Spending Theme parks derive their revenues principally from admission charges, sales of food and beverages consumed by visitors while at the park and from sales of merchandise available at the park's shopping facilities. Revenues from these sources are measured in terms of *per capita* expenditure, which is the average sum spent per daily guest visit.

The company has assumed *per capita* expenditure figures separately for the two theme parks under the four categories below:

	Magic Kingdom		Second theme park	
	Amount in 1988 FF[a]	*Annual growth rate (%)*	*Amount in 1988 FF*[a]	*Annual growth rate (%)*
Admissions	137.6	6.5	137.6	6.5
Food and beverage	56.7	5.0	53.2	5.0
Merchandise	74.9	5.0	46.5	5.0
Parking and other	5.2	5.0	5.2	5.0

[a]Excluding value-added tax.

The assumed real growth rate of admission prices of 1.5% per annum is less than the average 2.6% experienced at the Disney theme parks since 1972.

The *per capita* spending assumptions are based on experience in theme parks designed by Disney, adjusted for local conditions. A separate report on *per capita* spending was undertaken by ADL. To evaluate the reasonableness of the assumed admission prices, ADL reviewed the admission prices charged in Paris for major attractions which could be considered competitive in terms of entertainment value and also the prices charged by European theme and amusement parks. These reviews showed that the assumed admission prices for Euro Disneyland, although higher than those charged at other European theme and amusement parks, (i) could be considered low when related to prices charged in the Paris region for quality adult-oriented entertainment, and (ii) appeared in line with prices charged for other family-oriented attractions. Arthur D. Little concluded that the company's assumed admission prices were justified, having regard for the destination resort features of Euro Disneyland and the high quality of its entertainment.

To evaluate the reasonableness of the assumed prices for food and beverages at Euro Disneyland, ADL analyzed the prices paid by residents of, and tourists to, Paris in those areas that were particularly attractive to visitors. They also examined food and beverage prices at other European theme and amusement parks and reviewed typical food and beverage expenditure patterns in France as compared with the U.S. They concluded that Euro Disneyland's assumptions concerning food and beverage expenditure were reasonable.

Arthur D. Little determined, in the case of assumed merchandise sales, that there was no comparable experience in the Paris region of small, high-intensity retail shops, exposed to a high volume of visitor traffic, as are found at Disney-designed theme parks. They concluded that it was reasonable to forecast Euro Disneyland's retail sales revenue on the basis of that at other Disney theme parks.

Revenues Total revenues projected in the financial model for the two theme parks are summarized in the table below (in FF millions):

	1992	1996	2001	2011
Magic Kingdom				
Admissions and parking	1909	2981	4664	9314
Food, beverage and merchandise	1759	2692	4065	7401
Participant fees and other	229	303	417	421
Second theme park				
Admissions and parking	–	1788	2697	5794
Food, beverage and merchandise	–	1178	1660	3107
Participant fees and other	–	162	208	412

The first two categories of projected revenues are based on the attendance and *per capita* spending assumptions described above. Projected participant fees are based on the assumption that approximately ten participant contracts will have been signed by the opening of the Magic Kingdom. Four contracts have been signed, each with a term of at least ten years.

Operating expenses The principal operating expense assumptions are based on the following estimates. Labor costs (including related taxes) have been estimated on the basis of experience at Disney parks, adjusted to the conditions of the French labor market. They include a premium on operating labor rates of approximately 10% over the market average, intended to attract high-quality personnel. On this basis, it has been assumed that gross operating labor costs will be FF424 million for the Magic Kingdom and FF232 million for the second theme park (measured in 1988 French francs) in the respective opening years of these parks and that they will increase at the rate of inflation, taking into account increased employment associated with higher attendance levels. Cost of sales has been estimated on the basis of experience at Disney parks, adjusted to reflect factors specific to Euro Disneyland. The assumptions are:

	Cost of sales (% of revenue)
Magic Kingdom	
Merchandise	40–43[a]
Food and beverage	31
Second theme park	
Merchandise	41.5
Food and beverage	31

[a]Declining from 43% in 1992 to 40% in 1996 and thereafter.

Other operating expenses have similarly been based on Disney experience, adjusted to reflect local market conditions. Individually they are assumed to be as follows:

- Maintenance expenses:
  - Magic Kingdom: 6% of revenues;
  - Second theme park: 6.5% of revenues;

- General and administrative expenses (which include marketing, legal, finance and data processing):
  - Magic Kingdom: 14% of revenues;
  - Second theme park: 16% of revenues;
- Property and business taxes, which have been estimated according to the French tax regime:
  - the base management fee.

Operating Income Operating income is the difference between revenues and operating expenses but before royalties, financing costs and interest income, depreciation and amortization, lease expense, management incentive fees, and income taxes. The summary table below shows the operating income projected by the financial model for the two theme parks:

	1992	1996	2001	2011
Magic Kingdom (in FF millions)	1603	2773	4226	8006
Second theme park (in FF millions)	–	1334	1921	4293
Total	1603	4107	6147	12 299

Cost of Construction The cost of construction of the Magic Kingdom is assumed to be FF9.5 billion and the total cost of Phase 1A is assumed to be FF14.9 billion, in accordance with the estimated cost for Phase 1A. The construction cost of the second theme park has been assumed to be FF5.9 billion, with construction and related expenditures being incurred equally in 1994 and 1995. The construction cost of the second theme park has been estimated on the basis of Disney's direct experience of recent theme park construction, notably in completing the Disney-MGM Studios Theme Park within Walt Disney World. The construction cost of that theme park was then adjusted for capacity considerations, inflation, and the construction cost differential between Florida and the Paris region.

Table 18.6 summarizes Walt Disney Company's financial results during 1984–8.

TABLE 18.6 Summary of Walt Disney Company financial results, 1984–8 (U.S.$ millions)

	1984	1985	1986	1987	1988
Revenue					
Theme parks and resorts	1097.4	1257.5	1523.9	1834.2	2042.0
Filmed entertainment	244.5	320.0	511.7	875.6	1149.2
Consumer products	109.7	122.6	130.2	167.0	247.0
Operating income					
Theme parks and resorts	185.7	255.7	403.7	548.9	564.8
Filmed entertainment	2.2	33.7	51.6	130.6	186.3
Consumer products	53.9	56.3	72.4	97.3	133.7
Net income	97.8	173.5	247.3	444.7	522.0

Source: The Walt Disney Company, annual reports.

Appendix 2: Excerpt from Walt Disney 1994 Annual Report

Investment in Euro Disney

1994 vs. 1993 The Company's investment in Euro Disney resulted in a loss of $110.4 million in 1994. The loss consisted of a $52.8 million charge recognized in the third quarter as a result of the Company's participation in the Euro Disney financial restructuring and the Company's equity share of fourth quarter operating results. The prior year's loss reflected the Company's equity share of Euro Disney's operating results and a $350.0 million charge to fully reserve receivables and a funding commitment to Euro Disney, partially offset by royalties and gain amortization related to the investment. The funding commitment was intended to help support Euro Disney for a limited period, while Euro Disney pursued a financial restructuring.

A proposed restructuring plan for Euro Disney was announced in March 1994. During the third quarter of 1994, the Company entered into agreements with Euro Disney and the Euro Disney lenders participating in the restructuring (the "Lenders") to provide certain debt, equity and lease financing to Euro Disney.

Under the restructuring agreements, which specify amounts denominated in French francs, the Company committed to increase its equity investment in Euro Disney by subscribing for 49% of a $1.1 billion rights offering of new shares; to provide long-term lease financing at a 1% interest rate for approximately $255 million of theme park assets; and to subscribe, in part through an offset against fully reserved advances previously made to Euro Disney under the Company's funding commitment, for securities reimbursable in shares with a face value of approximately $180 million and a 1% coupon. In addition, the Company agreed to cancel fully reserved receivables from Euro Disney of approximately $210 million, to waive royalties and base management fees for a period of five years and to reduce such amounts for specified periods thereafter, and to modify the method by which management incentive fees will be calculated. During the fourth quarter of 1994, the financial restructuring was completed and the Company funded its commitments.

In addition to the commitments described above, the Company agreed to arrange for the provision of a ten-year unsecured standby credit facility of approximately $210 million on request, bearing interest at PIBOR. As of September 30, 1994, Euro Disney had not requested that the Company establish this facility.

As part of the restructuring, the Company received ten-year warrants for the purchase of up to 27.8 million shares of Euro Disney at a price of FF40 per share. The terms of the restructuring also provide that, in the event that Euro Disney decides to launch the second phase of the development of its theme park and resort complex, and commitments for the necessary financing have been obtained, the Company will be entitled to a development fee of approximately $225 million. On receipt of the development fee, the Company's entitlement to purchase Euro Disney shares by exercise of the warrants described above will be reduced to 15 million shares.

In connection with the restructuring, Euro Disney Associes SNC ("Disney SNC"), an indirect wholly owned affiliate of the Company, entered into a lease arrangement (the "Lease") with the entity (the "Park Financing Company"), which financed substantially all of the Disneyland Paris theme park assets, and then entered into a sublease agreement (the "Sublease") with Euro Disney. Under the

Lease, which replaced an existing lease between Euro Disney and the Park Financing Company, Disney SNC leased the theme park assets of the Park Financing Company for a noncancelable term of 12 years. Aggregate lease rentals of FF10.5 billion ($2.0 billion) receivable from Euro Disney under the Sublease, which has a 12-year term, will approximate the amounts payable by Disney SNC under the Lease.

At the conclusion of the Sublease term, Euro Disney will have the option to assume Disney SNC's rights and obligations under the Lease. If Euro Disney does not exercise its option, Disney SNC may continue to lease the assets, with an ongoing option to purchase them for an amount approximating the balance of the Park Financing Company's outstanding debt. Alternatively, Disney SNC may terminate the Lease, in which case Disney SNC would pay the Park Financing Company an amount equal to 75% of its then-outstanding debt, estimated to be $1.4 billion; Disney SNC could then sell or lease the assets on behalf of the Park Financing Company to satisfy the remaining debt, with any excess proceeds payable to Disney SNC.

As part of the overall restructuring, the Lenders agreed to underwrite 51% of the Euro Disney rights offering, to forgive certain interest charges for the period from April 1, 1994 to September 30, 2003, having a present value of approximately $300 million, and to defer all principal payments until three years later than originally scheduled. As consideration for their participation in the financial restructuring, Euro Disney issued to the Lenders ten-year warrants for the purchase of up to 40 million shares of Euro Disney stock at a price of FF40 per share.

Euro Disney has reported that it expects to incur a loss in 1995, which will have a negative impact on the Company's results. The impact on the Company's earnings, however, will be reduced as a result of the sale by the Company in October 1994 of approximately 75 million shares, or 20% of its investment in Euro Disney, to Prince Alwaleed Bin Talal Bin Abdulaziz Al Saud. The sale will reduce the Company's ownership interest in Euro Disney to approximately 39%. Beginning in 1995, the Company will record its equity share of Euro Disney's operating results based on its reduced ownership interest. The Company has agreed, so long as any obligations to the Lenders are outstanding, to maintain ownership of at least 34% of the outstanding common stock of Euro Disney until June 1999, at least 25% for the subsequent five years, and at least 16.67% for an additional term thereafter.

1993 vs. 1992 The Company's investment in Euro Disney resulted in a loss of $514.7 million in 1993, including the charge referred to below, after being partially offset by royalties and gain amortization related to the investment. The operating results of Euro Disney were lower than expected, due in part to the European recession, which affected Euro Disney's largest markets.

During 1993, Euro Disney, its principal lenders and the Company began exploring a financial restructuring for Euro Disney. The Company agreed to help fund Euro Disney for a limited period, to afford Euro Disney time to pursue the financial restructuring. The operating results for the fourth quarter and the year, and the need for a financial restructuring, created uncertainty regarding the Company's ability to collect its current receivables and to meet the funding commitment to Euro Disney. Consequently, the Company recorded a charge of $350.0 million in the fourth quarter to fully reserve its current receivables and funding commitment.

In 1992, the Company's investment in Euro Disney contributed income of $11.2 million. Although Euro Disney incurred a loss in 1992, the Company's 49% share of the net loss was offset by royalties and gain amortization related to the investment.

Source: Walt Disney Annual Report, 1994.

Notes

1 "Euro Disney," *Financial Times,* October 30, 1996.

2 "Disney Goes to Tokyo," in D. Ancona, T. Kochan, M. Scully, J. Van Maanen and E. Westney, *Organizational Behavior and Processes,* Southwestern College Publishing, Cincinnati, OH, 1999, pp. M-10, 25.

3 The conversion factors used in the case are: 1 hectare = 2.47 acres, and 1 acre = 4,047 square meters. The U.S. dollar/French franc exchange rates at the beginning of each year were: 1987 6.35, 1988 5.36, 1989 6.03, 1990 5.84, 1991 5.08, 1992 5.22, 1993 5.59, 1994 5.93.

4 "Euro Disney" is used to refer to the Euro Disneyland theme park: "Euro Disneyland SCA" or "the company" refers to the company that owns Euro Disney.

5 J. D. Finnerty, "Case Study: The Euro Disneyland Project" in *Project Financing: Asset-based Financial Engineering,* John Wiley & Sons, Inc., New York, 1995, pp. 338–50.

6 "No magic in these kingdoms," *Los Angeles Times,* December 15, 1989.

7 "Disneyland Goes to Europe," in D. Ancona, T. Kochan, M. Scully, J. Van Maanen and E. Westney, *Organizational Behavior and Processes,* Southwestern College Publishing, Cincinnati, OH, 1999, pp. 38–9.

8 "Disneyland Goes to Europe," in D. Ancona, T. Kochan, M. Scully, J. Van Maanen and E. Westney, *Organizational Behavior and Processes,* Southwestern College Publishing, Cincinnati, OH, 1999, p. 15.

9 From J. Neher, "France Amazed, Amused by Disney Dress Code," *New York Times,* October 5, 1995.

10 *Euro Disney: the First 100 Days* (Harvard Business School Case No. 9-693-013, 1993), p. 14.

Case 19 Vodafone: Rethinking the International Strategy

May 2009

On May 19, 2009, Vittorio Colao, Vodafone's CEO, presented the group's results for the year ended March 31, 2009. Despite Colao's emphasis on Vodafone's increases in revenue, adjusted operating profit and free cash flow (see Table 19.1), the results left analysts unimpressed. The reported gains were wholly the result of foreign exchange movements (the euro had appreciated significantly against the British pound during the year); underlying revenues had contracted by 0.4%. Once "impairment charges" (mainly asset write-downs in Spain) had been taken into account, net profit was down by more than a half. Vodafone's shares closed down almost 4% on the day. For Vodafone's long-suffering shareholders, the results raised further questions about how the world's leading wireless telecommunications operator would generate attractive profits from its extensive global empire.

Colao's appointment in July 2008 marked a new phase in the strategy embarked upon by his predecessor Arun Sarin. Under Sarin's leadership, Vodafone's strategic priority had shifted from growth to consolidation. Under Vittorio Colao, this emphasis shifted even more strongly from top-line growth and bold strategic initiatives to the more mundane tasks of cutting costs and improving efficiency. In November 2008, Colao outlined his strategy for Vodafone. The *Financial Times* reported:

> Vittorio Colao compared himself to a ship's captain as the Vodafone chief executive set a new course for the world's largest mobile phone operator by revenue.
>
> Mr Colao's strategy, unveiled yesterday at his first public presentation since becoming chief executive in July, involved bigger than expected changes to the direction taken by Arun Sarin, his predecessor, in 2006.
>
> But the scale of the changes points to the challenges confronting the Italian-born Mr Colao: a potent mix of economic, competitive and regulatory pressures.
>
> "It's a bit like sailing, you know," said Mr Colao, a former McKinsey partner, when asked how much his strategy had in common with Mr Sarin's legacy. "Every new captain takes the boat from where the boat was, and suddenly the wind changes and the sea changes, and you have three sailors who are sick."

TABLE 19.1 Vodafone Group plc: financial highlights 2005–9 (£ millions, except where indicated)

(Year ended 31 March)	2009	2008	2007	2006	2005
Consolidated income statement data					
Revenue	41017	35478	31104	29350	26678
Operating (loss)/profit	5857	10047	(1564)	(14084)	7878
Adjusted operating profit [a]	11757	10075	9531	9399	8353
(Loss)/profit before taxation	4189	9001	(2383)	(14853)	7285
Net (loss)/profit for the financial year	3080	6756	(5297)	(21821)	6518
Consolidated cash flow data					
Net cash flows from operating activities	12213	10474	10328	10190	9240
Net cash flows from investing activities	(6834)	(8544)	3865	(6654)	(4122)
Free cash flow[b]	4987	5540	6127	6418	6592
Consolidated balance sheet data					
Total assets	152699	127270	109617	126738	147197
Shareholders' equity	86162	78043	67067	85425	113800
Total liabilities	67922	50799	42324	41426	33549
Profit ratios					
Operating profit/total assets (%)	3.8	8.0	(1.4)	(11.1)	5.4
Return on equity[c] (%)	3.6	8.7	(7.8)	(23.6)	5.9

[a] Excludes non-operating income of associates, impairment losses and other income and expense.

[b] Free cash flow measures cash available for reinvestment, shareholder returns or debt reduction. It is calculated by subtracting expenditures on fixed assets from operating cash flow.

[c] After tax (loss)/profit as a percentage of shareholders' equity.

> The most tangible element of his strategy is to focus on improving Vodafone's bottom line performance. He wants to reduce costs by £1bn by 2010–11 and does not rule out going further if the global recession is deep. The promised savings are centered on Vodafone's core European businesses, which are mature operations given that most people own a mobile phone.
>
> But there will be a revenue-boosting element to the strategy, too. This will be led by a push to persuade more consumers to buy mobiles that are capable of connecting to the internet. Mr Colao also wants to intensify Vodafone's efforts to sell telecoms services to companies.
>
> An even sharper focus on making the most of Vodafone's existing businesses in emerging markets is also central to Mr Colao's thinking. Vodafone believes its expansion into developing countries, which began in 2005 and last year involved the $10.9bn (£7.1bn) purchase of a controlling stake in Indian mobile operator Hutchison Essar, may well be close to accomplished.
>
> Mr Colao is reserving the right to do further deals in developing countries, but says there are few large markets that interest him. Across the board, he will take a relatively conservative approach to future deals, in line with a pledge to be more disciplined on capital management.
>
> Vodafone supports consolidation in its existing markets, notably Europe, because of concerns that too many mobile operators are slugging it out. Mr Colao said Vodafone might buy rival operators, although he stressed any significant acquisition would likely be funded through disposals. He declined to specify the nature of any disposals, but signaled there would be no exit from Vodafone's core European businesses in Germany, Italy, Spain and the U.K. Mr Colao also signaled that, like his predecessor, he wants to retain Vodafone's 45% stake in Verizon Wireless, the second-largest U.S. mobile operator.
>
> The capital discipline that Mr Colao talked about yesterday also involves a greater focus on free cash flow—loosely defined as operating cash flow minus capital spending. Vodafone is targeting £5bn–£6bn of annual free cash flow and its future performance guidance is likely to focus on this measure.[1]

In his May 19, 2009 presentation, Colao acknowledged the weakness of user demand—primarily a result of the recession—and continuing pressure on margins as a result of intensifying competition. He announced an acceleration in Vodafone's cost-cutting program.

Most commentators applauded Vodafone's commitment to cost cutting—"After years of acquisition-fuelled growth, a focus on the more mundane matter of efficiency is just what the world's biggest mobile operator needs"[2]—but there was also a concern that cost cutting might not be enough to restore Vodafone's fortunes given growing maturity and commoditization of Vodafone's principal markets. The most distinctive feature of Vodafone's competitive positioning within wireless communication services was its international spread—with 302 million mobile customers and a presence in 52 countries of the world, Vodafone offered a global presence that was unmatched in the industry (see Tables 19.2 and 19.3). A critical issue for Colao was how far Vodafone could better exploit its global presence through closer cross-border integration of its functions and operations and whether Vodafone should regard itself as a portfolio of largely independent national operators sharing a common brand and a common approach to business.

TABLE 19.2 Vodafone's global reach, March 2009

Country	Ownership (%)	customers[a] (000s)	Country	Ownership (%)	customers[a] (000s)
Subsidiaries			Turkey	100.0	15481
Germany	100.0	35471	Egypt	54.9	10405
Italy	76.9	22914	Kenya	40.0	5345
Spain	100.0	16910	South Africa	50.0	30149
U.K.	100.0	18716	Australia	100.0	3970
Albania	99.9	1395	Fiji	49.0	339
Greece	99.9	5899	New Zealand	100.0	2502
Ireland	100.0	2175	***Associates and investments***		
Malta	100.0	201			
Netherlands	100.0	4618	U.S.	45.0	38948[b]
Portugal	100.0	5639	China	3.2	15324
Czech Republic	100.0	2909	France	44.0	8620
Hungary	100.0	2562	India	51.6	46065
Poland	24.4	3555			
Romania	100.0	9588			

Partner agreements[c]

Country	*Operator*	*Country*	*Operator*
Afghanistan	Roshan	Latvia	Bité
Armenia	MTS	Lithuania	Bité
Austria	A1	Luxembourg	Tango
Bahrain	Zain	Macedonia	VIP operator
Belgium	Proximus	Malaysia	Celcom
Bulgaria	Mobiltel	Nor way	TDC
Caribbean	Digicel	Panama	Digicel
Chile	Entel	Russia	MTS
Croatia	VIPnet	Serbia	VIP mobile
Cyprus	Cytamobile-Vodafone	Singapore	M1
Denmark	TDC	Slovenia	Si.mobile-Vodafone
Estonia	Elisa	Sri Lanka	Dialog
Faroe Islands	Vodafone Iceland	Sweden	TDC
Finland	Elisa	Switzerland	Swisscom
Guernsey	Airtel-Vodafone	Thailand	DTAC
Honduras	Digicel	Turkmenistan	MTS
Hong Kong	SmarTone-Vodafone	Ukraine	MTS
Iceland	Vodafone Iceland	United Arab Emirates	Du
Japan	SoftBank	Uzbekistan	MTS
Jersey	Airtel-Vodafone		

[a] Total number of customers of the country subsidiary or associate.

[b] *These amounts are not included in related group totals as Verizon Wireless is an associated undertaking.*

[c] Partnerships in Latin America are through America Móvil.

Source: Vodafone Group plc, Annual Report 2009.

TABLE 19.3 Vodafone's customer base by country, 2005–8 (customers at year end)

	2008 000s	2007 000s	2006 000s	2005 000s	Prepaid customers (%)
Germany	35471	33920	30622	29165	54.4
Italy	22914	22791	20129	18208	92.1
Spain	16910	15810	14464	12923	45.9
U.K.	18716	18447	16939	16325	60.6
Albania	1395	1127	920	749	96.9
Greece	5889	5438	4961	4438	68.5
Ireland	2175	2265	2178	2047	74.0
Malta	201	201	188	177	89.9
Netherlands	4618	4038	3817	3981	46.9
Portugal	5639	5111	4618	4119	79.5
Sweden	–	–	–	1573	
Czech Republic	2909	2658	2413	2142	n.a.
Romania	9588	8808	7717	6132	n.a.
Hungary	2562	2304	2134	2038	n.a.
Turkey	15481	16116	12748	–	n.a.
Poland	3555	2638	2355	1774	n.a.
Egypt	10405	13333	8704	6125	92.7
Kenya	5345	3698	2134	1395	98.3
South Africa	16521	16521	14103	7524	89.3
India	46065	39865	3197	1633	87.2
Australia	3970	3573	3278	3126	73.5
New Zealand	2502	2309	2200	2024	76.4
Fiji	339	186	135	95	95.2
	6811	6068	5613	5245	75.7
Group	**327181**	**221157**	**159954**	**127713**	**74.9**
Associates					
United States	38948	29568	26230	22785	5.4
Other	25194	22784	17714	17780	76.4
Proportionate customers	**391323**	**252301**	**198584**	**164549**	**68.9**

Building the World's Leading Wireless Communications Provider, 1984–2003

Vodafone was originally Racal Telecom Limited, formed in 1984 as a subsidiary of Racal Electronics Plc—a British-based defense and electronics company. It was established to exploit the opportunities made available by the new cellular technology for wireless communication. In 1983, Racal and Cellnet (a subsidiary of British Telecom) won licenses to supply cellular wireless communication in Britain. In 1988, 20% of Vodafone's equity was sold to the public. In 1991, the Vodafone Group was fully demerged from Racal.

Under CEO Gerald Whent, Vodafone steadily expanded its international reach primarily through minority equity stakes in other wireless telecom companies and by establishing joint ventures to bid for licenses and develop new wireless businesses. The appointment of Chris Gent as CEO in 1997 marked a new era in Vodafone's development. With the goal of becoming the world's leading mobile communications companies and fueled by an escalating share price, Vodafone embarked upon a rapid succession of acquisitions. The acquisitions of Airtouch in the U.S., Mannesmann in Germany and Japan Telecom were three huge takeovers that established Vodafone as the world's largest wireless telecom company in terms of number of customers. Table 19.4 lists milestones in Vodafone's expansion.

TABLE 19.4 Vodafone's international acquisitions and divestments, 1989–2009

Year	Company	Country	Subscribers	Notes
1989	Telecel	Malta	n.a.	Joint venture with TeleMalta. Vodafone owns 80%
1990	SFR	France	60 000	4% of equity acquired by Vodafone
1991	AB Nordic Tel	Sweden, Denmark	n.a.	10% of equity acquired by Vodafone
1991	Pacific Link Communication Ltd	Hong Kong	42 000	30% of equity acquired by Vodafone
1993	Vodacom	S. Africa	n.a.	Joint venture established, Vodafone owns 35%
1993	Panafon	Greece	n.a.	Joint venture established, Vodafone owns 45%
1996	Talkland	U.K.	400 000	Vodafone acquired outstanding two-thirds equity of the service provider for £30.6m.
1996	Peoples Phone	U.K.	n.a.	Retailer /reseller with 181 stores acquired for £77 million
1996	Astec Communications	U.K.	n.a.	Service provider with 21 stores acquired for £77 million
1998	Misrfone	Egypt	n.a.	Misrfone consortium (Vodafone owns 30%) wins license to build Egypt's second mobile network
1998	Bell South New Zealand	New Zealand	138 000	Acquired and renamed Vodafone New Zealand
1999	Airtouch Communications, Inc.	U.S.	3.2 million	$62 billion merger to create Vodafone Airtouch. Included 1m. subscribers in Germany, Italy (Omnitel), Poland, Japan, and India
2000	Verizon Wireless	U.S.	n.a.	Joint venture formed from U.S. wireless assets of Vodafone and Bell Atlantic
2000	Mannesmann	Germany	9.5 million	Acquired for £112 billion

TABLE 19.4 *(Continued)*

Year	Company	Country	Subscribers	Notes
2001	Eircell	Ireland	1.2 million	Acquired for €5 million, rebranded Vodafone Ireland
2001	TDC Mobil	Denmark	n.a.	First "Partner Networks" agreement. Vodafone offers co-branded services to Danish market
2001	China Mobile (Hong Kong)	Hong Kong	n.a.	Strategic alliance agreed
2001	Swisscom Mobile	Switzerland	n.a.	25% of equity acquired
2001	Airtel Movil SA	Spain	n.a.	Equity interest increased to 91.6%
2001	Japan Telecom and J-Phone	Japan	11 million	Acquired 69.7% of J-Phone, Japan's third-largest mobile operator and 66.7% of Japan Telecom, its parent
2002	Radiolinja	Finland and Estonia	n.a.	Partner Network Agreements signed
2002	Vizzavi	France/U.K.	n.a.	Vodafone buys out Vivendi's 50% share of the Vizzavi mobile internet portal for €142.7 million
2003	Mobilcom, Bité,	Austria, Lithuania	n.a.	Partner Network Agreements signed
2004	Cyta	Cyprus	n.a.	Partner Network Agreements signed
2004	AT&T Wireless	U.S.	n.a.	$38 billion offer fails; Cingular bids higher
2005	Connex	Romania	n.a.	Equity stake raised to 99%; also buys Czech mobile operator
2005	Oskar	Czech Republic	n.a.	Acquired
2006	Vodafone Sweden	Sweden	n.a.	Sold for €970 million (£660 million)
2006	Vodafone Japan	Japan	n.a.	97.7% stake sold to Softbank £6.9 billion
2006	Belgacom Mobile SA; Swisscom Mobile AG	Belgium & Switzerland	n.a	25% interests in the two companies sold for total of £3.1 billion
2007	Hutchison Essar	India	22.9 million	Acquired 52% of India's 4th biggest wireless operator for $10.9 bn
2007	Bharti Airtel	India	n.a.	Sold Group's 5.60% direct shareholding in Bharti Airtel for $1.6 bn

(*Continued*)

TABLE 19.4 *(Continued)*

Year	Company	Country	Subscribers	Notes
2007	Tele2	Italy and Spain	n.a.	Acquisition of 100% of Tele2 Italia SpA and Tele2 Telecommunications Services SLU for €775 million
2007	The Qatar Foundation	Qatar	n.a	A consortium comprising Vodafone and The Qatar Foundation was named as the successful applicant in the auction to become the second mobile operator in Qatar
2008	Arcor	Arcor	n.a.	Increased its stake in Arcor for €460 million and now owns 100% of Arcor
2008	Ghana Telecommunications	Ghana	n.a.	Acquired 70% of Ghana Telecommunications for £486 million
2008	BroadNet	Czech	n.a.	100% sale of BroadNet Czech a.s. shares to Vodafone Czech Republic
2008	Crazy John's	Australia	n.a.	Control of Crazy John's 83% stake
2009	Verizon Wireless/Alltel	U.S.	n.a.	Verizon Wireless acquires Alltel Corp. for $5.9 billion
2009	Hutchison Telecommunications (Australia)	Australia	n.a.	Joint venture formed between Hutchison Telecommunications (Australia) and Vodafone Australia
2009	Vodacom	South Africa	n.a.	Additional 15% of equity acquired for £1.6 billion
2009	Central Telecom	U.K.	n.a.	Acquired of U.K.-based systems integrator

n.a. = not available or not applicable.

Source: Vodafone annual reports.

International strategy

Under Chris Gent, Vodafone's international expansion had been opportunistic and aggressive but not lacking in strategic rationale. Group strategy director, Alan Harper, explained:

> We have always been mobile focused. In 1995, when I joined Vodafone it was mobile focused . . . It had a turnover of £8 billion, 80% in the U.K. Today we are still mobile focused with a turnover of £100 billion—only 10% in the U.K. . . .

> Our vision has been to leverage scale and scope benefits, reduce response time and ensure effective delivery to customers. This we have achieved by collecting or acquiring national operating companies and giving them a mission of a challenger company . . . For example, Vodafone with SFR is a challenger to France Telecom in France, Vodafone U.K. is a challenger to British Telecom in the U.K., Vodafone Germany is a challenger to Deutsch Telecom in Germany. With this challenger mindset we nurture and instill an entrepreneurial spirit among Vodafone companies and in this respect we do not behave as a traditional telephone company . . . [T]he cultural alignment of people within Vodafone is a key issue in sustaining this challenger and entrepreneurial mindset. To focus on this cultural alignment we give autonomy to the local entity and reiterate that the local entity did not join a global company like IBM or HP. The local entity has to work within a matrix structure and keep alive the "challenger mindset" on fixed line telephony and other incumbents, challenge the status quo every day, and evolve by being local entrepreneurs.[3]

This notion of local autonomy meant that Vodafone did not deploy any standard template in integrating its international acquisitions. It preferred to migrate its subsidiaries to the Vodafone brand; in some cases this was almost immediate, in others (where the existing local brand was strong as in Italy and Germany) it took many years. In some cases Vodafone saw virtue in transferring its operating and marketing practices and its pricing structure—but only where there was adequate compatibility. Apart from promoting Vodafone as a global brand and encouraging challenge and entrepreneurship among its operating companies, Vodafone also encouraged a common competitive strategy across the group. In selecting acquisition targets and in developing its acquisitions, Vodafone sought to be first or second in market share in every country it operated—this was critical to spreading the fixed costs of infrastructure, technology, and marketing. In competing for market share Vodafone eschewed price competition in favor of differentiating itself through a premium offering through value-adding content, network quality and customer care.

Twenty-first Century Challenges

The new century saw the beginning of more difficult times for Vodafone. The company was hit heavily by two developments. First was governments' auctioning of licenses for third generation wireless communication. Between 2000 and 2001, Vodafone paid over $30 billion for the new licenses (including $9.5 billion for a single 3G license in the U.K.). It soon became apparent that, like many of its competitors, Vodafone had greatly overestimated the commercial potential of 3G wireless communication and had grossly overpaid for its licenses. The second factor was the bursting of the "TMT" (technology, media, telecommunications) stock-market boom. In the first quarter of 2001, Vodafone's share price hit an all-time peak. During the next 30 months it would decline by 72%.

The outcome was a massive hit to Vodafone's bottom line. During the four-year period 2001 to 2004, Vodafone's net losses totaled £45 billion—primarily the result of write-offs of goodwill on over-priced acquisitions and amortization of 3G license costs. The impact of these various "impairments" is evident from the difference between operating profit and adjusted operating profit in Table 19.1.

When Arun Sarin replaced Chris Gent as CEO in 2003, Vodafone's management changed in both substance and style. "All that Gent and Sarin have in common," noted one insider, "is a love of cricket." While Gent was a quintessential Englishman, Sarin was a citizen of the world; he was born in India but his career had primarily centered on the U.S. While Gent was a deal maker, Sarin was an operations man with a strong technological background.

The "One Vodafone" Project

During 2004 it became increasingly clear that the greatest challenge facing Vodafone was deriving additional value from its sprawling global empire. Towards the end of 2004, Arun Sarin launched an ambitious program to unify its disparate global network and derive value from its unrivalled global reach. The drivers of this quest for a new international strategy were threefold. First, Vodafone became pressured by investors—especially institutions—for improved bottom-line performance and shareholder returns. Second, the "bigger is better" mantra that accompanied the telecoms M&A binge was increasingly questioned by those who argued that international spread gave few benefits, most of the economies of size in telecoms related to market share within a single country. Finally, the potential offered by 3G offered opportunities for a global rollout of new services—mobile internet access in particular. *The Economist* describes some key features of the initiative:

> Sir Chris [Gent] collected the pieces: Mr. Sarin's mission was to fit them together to achieve economies of scale and so to justify Vodafone's bigger-is-better strategy. For the past 15 months, Mr. Sarin has been doing just that, though mostly behind the scenes. Only now is the curtain finally being raised, with the launch this month of "third-generation" (3G) mobile services in 12 European countries and a relaunch in Japan. The roll-out of 3G, Mr. Sarin agrees, will provide litmus tests of both his own leadership and Vodafone's ability to function as a unified entity.
>
> Redrawing organisation charts, rationalising back-room systems and cutting costs are hardly the sorts of activities that generate headlines, so Vodafone seems a less dynamic firm than it was under Sir Chris. But this dull-but-necessary work is what Mr. Sarin is good at, and what Vodafone needs to bring its sprawling divisions together. His "One Vodafone" project has sorted out the behind-the-scenes spaghetti at Vodafone's national affiliates, so that they are now all using the same technology. This cuts costs by making it possible to develop a new service once, and then introduce it in many markets simultaneously.
>
> Mr. Sarin has also restructured Vodafone's management. The bosses of its large regional operations now report directly to him. The head of marketing at each national operator now reports to the group head of marketing, rather than simply to his local boss, and so on. The aim is to bind the national operators together and give Mr. Sarin more direct control of his firm. Aligning structure with strategy in this way will, he hopes, enable the firm to "execute flawlessly."

> This is not rocket science. Simplifying Vodafone's structure, he believes, is the foundation for making 3G a success, for it enables Vodafone to reap the benefits of its global scale. A single technology platform allows it to test handsets or services in one market and then deploy them everywhere. It ensures seamless international roaming, even for video calling. And it has allowed Vodafone to use its Japanese operation as a test-bed for 3G.
>
> By far the greatest benefit of Vodafone's scale is its resulting clout with handset-makers. It has set strict standards for its 3G handsets, and even the biggest handset-makers have no choice but to comply with them if they want Vodafone's business. Using the same technology in both Japan and Europe means that Vodafone can offer Japanese handset-makers access to European markets and Western firms access to the Japanese market, while playing them off against each other.[4]

The One Vodafone strategy involved reorganizing the corporate structure to facilitate closer linkages between the corporate center and the operating companies and enhanced integration. The new structure introduced at the beginning of 2005 included:

- Six geographically defined businesses that would report directly to the CEO. These included: the U.K., Germany, Italy, Asia-Pacific, other EMEA subsidiaries,[5] and European and non-European affiliates (including the U.S., South Africa, China, France and several other countries).
- Strengthened global functions, each of which would report directly to the CEO. Marketing would include a new multinational corporate unit serving global corporate customers. Marketing would also take care of global handset procurement. Technology would be responsible for standardized network design and IT shared services. Business Development was a new function "responsible for driving Vodafone's product and services portfolio into affiliates and Partner Networks."
- The establishment of two management committees to oversee the execution of the strategy set by the main board. The Executive Committee would focus on strategy, financial structure and organizational development; the Integration and Operations Committee would be responsible for operational and budgetary planning, and product and service development. Both committees were chaired by Arun Sarin.

Alan Harper, head of strategy, explained:

> . . . With acquisitions all over the world, one of our challenges is to integrate seamlessly not only technology (which, by the way, is more or less similar across the world) but also people . . . The challenge of this restructuring program is to balance the need for coordination and synergies with local initiatives . . . We are trying to integrate national operating units . . . and trying to leverage scale and scope while trying to retain the local autonomy and responsiveness of our challenger national units.[6]

The One Vodafone program involved business integration across a wide range of activities including billing (in 2005 Vodafone operated with eight different billing systems), network design, procurement, IT (including billing, back office, ERP/HR, and data center processes), service-center platforms, roaming, customer services and retail operations. According to Harper:

> What One Vodafone tries to achieve is to simplify the integration issues in terms of brand strength and integrating local culture and processes. We centralize all our marketing efforts, branding and product development. Technology is standardized. Network design is coordinated. Best practices are benchmarked by Advance Services. Knowledge is shared . . . We keep and encourage local initiatives such as customer services, and sales . . .[7]

Adjusting the International Strategy

The limits of the One Vodafone program were immediately apparent in three very important markets. Japan and the U.S. used cellular wireless technologies that differed from the GSM European standard used by Vodafone across most of its markets. Verizon Wireless used CDMA wireless technology. Its incompatibility with GSM meant that meant that Vodafone was unable to exploit any significant economies between its U.S. presence and the rest of its international operations. Vodafone's minority equity position in Verizon wireless and the absence of the Vodafone brand further isolated Vodafone's U.S. investment from the rest of Vodafone.

These technological distinctions were reinforced by other distinctive features of these markets. Japan (together with Korea) was regarded as the world's most advanced wireless market, adopting new wireless technologies at least two years earlier than Europe. Vodafone's introduction of its global range of handsets in Japan led to an exodus of Japanese subscribers: the phones were seen as technologically backward. The U.S., on the other hand, lagged both Europe and the Far East in the adoption of new wireless technologies—mainly because of its multiple incompatible wireless standards.

France, too, represented a problem in terms of integrating into Vodafone's global network. As with Verizon Wireless, Vodafone possessed a minority share of SFR (44%) and had not moved SFR to the Vodafone brand. Moreover, SFR supplied mobile, fixed line, and internet communication services, while Vodafone had avoided involvement in fixed line.

During the next 12 months, further changes in Vodafone's international strategy ensued. Strong competitive and regulatory pressures in the mature markets of North America, Western Europe, and Japan encouraged Vodafone to shift its focus to the growing markets of Eastern Europe, Africa, and Asia. Vodafone sold its majority holding in Vodafone Japan in March 2006. This was followed by divestments in Sweden, the Netherlands, Belgium, and Switzerland, and by acquisitions in Egypt, Hungary, Romania, South Africa, and India.

Vodafone also expanded its non-equity modes of internationalization. Initially, Vodafone's partnering arrangements with overseas mobile operators related only to roaming services. However, under Sarin, Vodafone's partner network moved to closer arrangements for supplying Vodafone services and content to partners' own customers. In 2006, Iceland became the first franchise partner to adopt the Vodafone brand.

Vodafone's International Strategy 2008–9

During his first 10 months as Vodafone CEO, Vittorio Colao made several changes to the international aspects of Vodafone's strategy initiated by Sarin. In particular:

- Colao slowed Vodafone's expansion into emerging markets. Under his leadership, the only significant emerging market acquisitions were of Ghana Telecom and an increase in Vodafone's ownership of Vodafone South Africa.
- Increasing Vodafone's presence in the corporate market through expanding Vodafone Global Enterprise, which manages relationships with Vodafone's 270 largest multinational corporate customers: "VGE simplifies the provision of fixed, mobile and broadband services for MNCs who need a single operational and commercial relationship with Vodafone worldwide. It provides a range of managed services such as central ordering, customer self-serve web portals, telecommunications expense management tools and device management coupled with a single contract and guaranteed service level agreements."[8]
- Colao sought to build Vodafone's influence in technology development in the industry—particularly in mobile internet applications. However, for the most part, Vodafone operated with a high degree of national autonomy. This is evident from Vodafone's organizational chart. Thus, each national operating subsidiary is headed by a CEO with profit-and-loss responsibility to headquarters.

Scale Economies in Telecom Services

In evaluating the benefits of international presence and the potential for cross-border linkages, a key issue for Vodafone was the sources and extent of global-level scale economies. There was little doubt that scale economies were very important at the national level: infrastructure, marketing, sales and billing all involved substantial fixed costs, which needed to be spread over a large base of users. However, at the global level these economies were less evident. Table 19.5 offers no clear evidence that profitability is associated with either size or international spread.

The most obvious cost benefit from global scale was in centralized purchasing. In addition to its own equipment and software needs, Vodafone was one of the world's biggest purchasers of handsets (in many countries consumers bought their handset bundled with a service contract). Vodafone's handset requirements gave it massive clout when striking deals with handset makers.

However, these scale advantages from purchasing depended upon all of Vodafone's subsidiaries using the same technology—in second-generation wireless (2G) this was largely true: Vodafone had adopted the European GSM standard. The major exception was the U.S. where its associate company, Verizon Wireless, used CDMA—an incompatible wireless technology.

A global brand also provided economies in advertising and brand development due to spillovers in advertising across national borders and the potential to use media and promotional events that attracted global audiences. Other economies were available from centralizing certain functions. Technology development, Web support, financial reporting and legal services were all centralized.

FIGURE 19.1 Vodafone: organization chart, March 2009

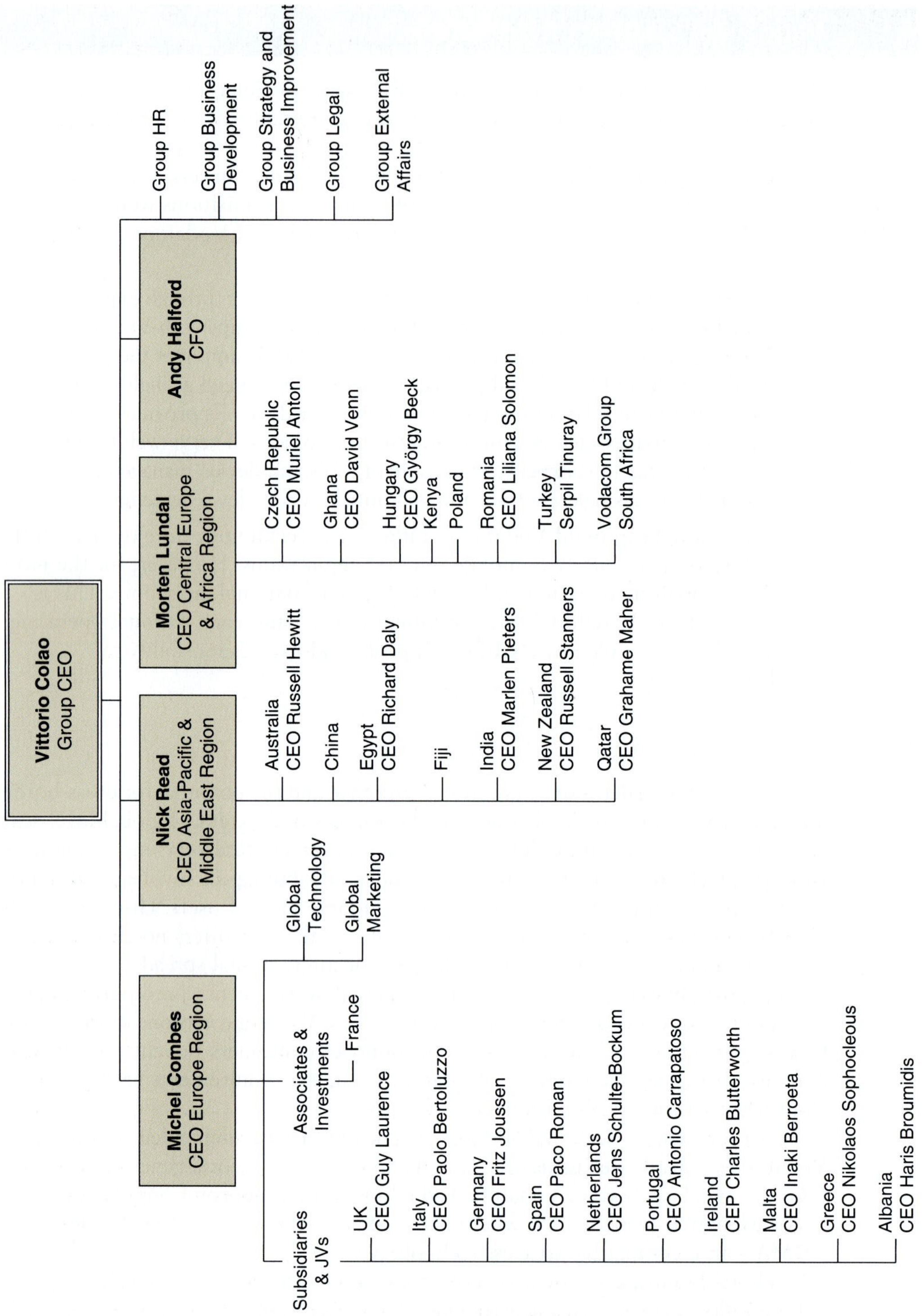

TABLE 19.5 World's largest telecommunication service companies, 2008

	Revenue ($ million)	Net profits ($ million)	Net margin (%)
1 AT&T	124028	12867	10.4
2 Nippon Telegraph and Telephone	103684	5362	5.2
3 Verizon Communications	97354	6428	4.4
4 Deutsche Telekom	90260	2171	2.4
5 Telefónica	84815	11112	13.1
6 France Télécom	78290	5956	7.6
7 Vodafone	69138	5188	7.5
8 China Mobile Communications	65015	11442	17.5
9 Telecom Italia	45118	3241	7.2
10 Vivendi	37166	3810	10.2
11 BT	36626	–140	(0.4)
12 Sprint Nextel	35635	–2796	(7.9)
13 KDDI	34814	2217	6.4
14 Comcast	34256	2547	7.4
15 China Telecommunications	31814	–51	(0.0)
16 América Móvil	31012	5337	17.2
17 Softbank	26608	430	1.6
18 Telstra	22371	3304	14.8
19 China United Telecommunications	21981	2840	12.9
20 Royal KPN	21373	1950	9.1

Source: Fortune Global 500 (2009).

Economies were also available from standardizing administrative and operational practices. A key aspect of the "One Vodafone" project was that it sought opportunities for such standardization. Booz Allen describes its role in this process:

> This program was not just an integration of two functions or two countries, or a merger of two companies, but really an integration program that spanned the 16 countries which had diverse people and diverse markets," says Klaus Hölbling, a principal in Booz Allen's Vienna office. "We couldn't assume we would integrate one operation the way we'd done another because the markets were very different. A customized approach was needed."
>
> Wave 0 of the engagement focused on the business case for integration. Wave 1 established common planning and design standards, elevated management of the supply chain to a global level, and created the architecture for a common service platform. In Wave 2, the work encompassed new operating models, assessing how global and local business would be conducted, and development of a new organization structure and implementation plan . . .
>
> Vodafone is still learning to find the right balance of local versus global—however, the transformation has already resulted in significant cost savings as well as innovative market strategies, more competitive and differentiated pricing, and leading product and service offerings. The new organization facilitates rapid movement of resources and talent, and sharing of best practices and expertise.[9]

It was also questionable whether exploiting the economies from a global brand or standardized global systems necessitated ownership of overseas telecom companies. Vodafone's partner network allowed Vodafone to earn licensing income from providing its brand and particular services to local operators without any need to invest in those countries.

Beyond these cost economies associated with global presence there were also user benefits resulting from international presence. This was certainly the case in serving corporate global accounts. In the case of individual users, international roaming could be offered through access agreements with local service providers. The key roaming benefits of having subsidiaries in different countries was the ability to offer "seamless" roaming services—identical services in each country. It also allowed the flexibility to offer promotional deals. For example, in summer 2009 Vodafone's Passport program offered: "No Roaming Charge in Over 35 Countries This Summer!"

Adapting to Local Market Needs

A key issue for Vodafone was not simply the existence and extent of these potential benefits from global scale but whether the pursuit of these benefits compromised Vodafone's ability to adapt to the local market requirements. Observing the failed international strategies of Swissair and DoCoMo, the Japanese mobile operator, the *Asian Wall Street Journal* drew three lessons for global strategy (see Exhibit 19.1).

EXHIBIT 19.1

Three Lessons for Global Strategy from Swissair and DoCoMo

[T]he first lesson is to start with the microeconomics: Understand what drives superior economic performance in your business and don't take your domestic success for granted. Both the airline and the telecoms businesses are highly regulated, technology driven and capital-intensive industries with high fixed and very low marginal costs (per airline seat or per mobile call minute) . . . In the mobile industry, the significant fixed-cost components of the business (networks, product development, and brand advertising and promotion) provide unit cost advantages to the national market leader compared with its followers . . .

Despite regulatory changes, the economics of the mobile industry remain primarily national in nature. That is, it is clearly better to be a market leader in one country than a follower in two countries. There are obvious trends suggesting that broader geographic scope adds value in mobile. Increased subscriber roaming and higher mobile penetration rates are shifting an increasing portion of cross-border traffic from fixed to mobile networks.

Both trends favor a mobile operator with domestic leadership positions in a number of major city markets within a continental regional market such as Europe or North America. Value has been created by such "regional" consolidators. Vodafone accomplished this in Europe, now owning the No. 1 or No. 2 mobile operator in most major national markets . . .

When both NTT DoCoMo and Swissair convinced themselves they needed to expand beyond domestic boundaries to survive, the race to fulfill their global aspirations seems to have resulted in a set of investments more focused on the number of flags on a boardroom map rather than on these basic economics driving superior profitability in their industries. The risks of these two aggressive expansion strategies were further compounded by not having control over most of their international investments.

That means the third lesson from the two companies' problems is to move to management control if you are serious about capturing acquisition synergies . . . Similarly, in short order DoCoMo accumulated direct or indirect stakes in nine mobile operators—most for cash, at the peak of the telecom bubble. But this acquisition spree resulted in equity stakes in only two market leaders and these were in relatively minor geographic markets—KPN Mobile domestically in the Netherlands and Hutchison in Hong Kong. All the others were lesser players. DoCoMo acquired stakes in the No. 3 U.S. player AT&T Wireless, Taiwan's No. 4 player KG Telecom, U.K. No. 5 player Hutchison U.K., and distant followers KPN Orange in Belgium and E-Plus in Germany. Worse still, all these investments were minority stakes and so would appear to give DoCoMo limited ability to exert control over critical strategic and operational issues at these operators . . .

In contrast, Singapore Telecom appears to be pursuing a more focused strategy. Withdrawing from an early set of unfocused European investments, SingTel has focused more recently on mobile operators in South Asia. It now has stakes in the No. 1 or the strong No. 2 mobile operator in Singapore, Thailand, Indonesia, the Philippines and Australia.

Source: "When Global Strategies go Wrong," *The Asian Wall Street Journal* (April 4, 2002). Reproduced with permission.

Vodafone's experience in Japan underlined some of the risks inherent in a global approach to wireless telephony. Vodafone took control of J-Phone, Japan's third-largest operator, in 2001. Migrating J-Phone to the Vodafone brand, to Vodafone's European 3G technology (UMITS), and to Vodafone's global range of handsets proved disastrous. After losses in market share, Vodafone sold its Japanese subsidiary to Softbank in 2006. According to *The Economist*, the sale of Vodafone Japan signaled a definitive end to Vodafone's famous "big is beautiful" strategy, pointing the way towards a more focused regional strategy. For example, in Europe, Vodafone concentrated upon exploiting its scale advantage within an increasingly unified market.[10]

Compared to its nationally focused competitors, Vodafone was also looking disadvantaged by its mobile-only business focus. A key trend was towards the integration of fixed and mobile networks offering bundled services to customers. A number of operators offered "quadruple play" bundles comprising fixed and mobile telephony, broadband internet access and television services. Vodafone was slow in responding to the trend towards bundling: "Vodafone management has no strategy for convergence," observed one analyst in 2006.[11]

A key theme of Colao's November 2008 strategy review was a push into "total communications services":

> [T]he three target areas are mobile data, enterprise and broadband. Vodafone has already made significant progress on mobile data, with annual revenue of £3 billion, 26% higher on an organic basis than that of a year ago, but the opportunity remains significant as the proportion of the customer base that regularly uses data services is only around 10% in Europe. In the enterprise segment, Vodafone has a strong position in core mobile services, mainly amongst larger corporations. The aim is to build upon this position and expand into the broader communications market, serving small and medium sized businesses with converged fixed and mobile products and services and to continue to increase the Group's penetration of multinational accounts. In fixed broadband, the Group has a presence in all of its European markets and 4.6 million customers globally.[12]

Total communications involved Vodafone in leasing fixed line capacity from other telecom providers. In Britain, Vodafone is acting as a wireless partner to BT, Britain's fixed-line incumbent, which lacks a mobile network. Vodafone has also acquired some of its own fixed line capacity; in 2008 it acquired Tele2's fixed-line and broadband services in Italy and Spain.

Developments in Technology

Adding further complexity to the assessment of benefits and cost of internationalization were the technological changes affecting the industry. Vodafone, along with a number of other new wireless telephony startups such as Orange, Nextel and Wind, were created to exploit the new technology of cellular wireless communication. A quarter of a century later that technology was changing rapidly. Although several potential substitutes for cellular wireless communication had lacked commercial success (for example, paging systems, the Iridium satellite communication system), the pace of technological change appeared to be accelerating. The most visible technological changes were in hardware. Cellular phones were adding new functions and technological convergence was blurring functional distinctions between cellular phones, PDAs, handheld game players (such as Nintendo Gameboys) and portable music players. The remarkable success of Apple's iPhone pointed to the extent to which our conceptions of cell phones were changing.

The implications for wireless telephony providers were complex. At one level, the increasing number of wireless communication devices and the increased demand for mobile internet access greatly increased the total demand for wireless communication. However, an increasing range of alternatives was becoming available. The potential for WiFi to compete with cellular networks was being increased by the creation of city-wide WiFi networks and the advent of WiMax. More direct competition was likely through the opening of new segments of radio frequency for wireless communication. In March 2008, Federal Communications Commision auctioned licenses to the "C-block" spectrum, which conferred the right to operate the 700 MHz frequency band. A surprise bidder was Google. Together with its Android operating platform, Google was signaling a clear intention to become a central player in the development of mobile technology.[13]

While new technology offered opportunities for developing new content and services, the problem for Vodafone and the other cellular service providers was that the new technologies were controlled either by hardware companies (Nokia, Apple, Intel, Qualcomm, for example), or software companies (such as Google, Microsoft). The success of Apple's iPhone was especially alarming for Vodafone. Because of Apple's exclusive deal with O2 (owned by Telefónica), Vodafone was shut out of the widening array of mobile services provided for iPhone users.[14] The iPhone had also positioned Apple as a key gateway into the 3G mobile services through Apple's applications store, which offered support for third-party developers, creating services and content for the iPhone. In response, Vodafone launched its own software applications store—the Joint Innovation Lab—in May 2009. Verizon Wireless, China Mobile and Softbank partnered in the venture whose aim was to produce a single platform for developers to create mobile widgets and applications on multiple operating systems and access the partners' combined 1.1 billion customer base.[15] However, Apple was not the only hardware company seeking to build a strong strategic position from which it could influence the evolution of the wireless technology. Nokia was the world's largest handset supplier and it owned Symbian, the most widely used operating system for mobile phones.

The power battle between hardware suppliers and service provides had important implications for Vodafone's gobal strategy. If Apple, Nokia, Research in Motion, and Google were increasingly their control of wireless technology and content, there was a risk that wireless services would be increasingly commoditized. In this event, the potential for creating value from supplying wireless services across national boundaries would become progressively smaller.

Notes

1 "Captain Colao Takes the Helm and Changes Course in Stormy Seas," *Financial Times,* November 12, 2008.
2 "Vodafone," Lex column, *Financial Times,* May 19, 2009.
3 "Vodafone: Out of Many, One" (ESSEC Business School Case Study, 2005).
4 "Foundation and Empire," *The Economist,* November 25, 2004.
5 Europe, Middle East and Africa.
6 Quoted in "Vodafone: Out of Many, One" (ESSEC Business School Case Study, 2005): 9.
7 Quoted in "Vodafone: Out of Many, One" (ESSEC Business School Case Study, 2005): 9.
8 Vodafone Group Plc, Annual Report, 2009, p. 20.
9 See www.boozallen.com/media/file/06_2005AR_PEA .pdf, accessed April 16, 2008.
10 "Vodafone: Not-so-big is Beautiful," *Economist,* March 9, 2006.
11 "Vodafone: Calling for a Rethink," *Economist,* January 26, 2006.
12 Vodafone Group plc, Annual Report, 2009, p. 9.
13 "An Auction That Google Was Content to Lose," *New York Times,* April 4, 2008. See www.nytimes.com/2008/04/04/technology/04auction.html?_r=1&oref=slogin, accessed October 22, 2009.
14 "Vodafone in Consolidation Call," *Financial Times,* July 24, 2009.
15 See www.jil.org, accessed May 28, 2009.

Case 20 Richard Branson and the Virgin Group of Companies in 2007*

Despite celebrating his 57th birthday, Richard Branson showed no signs of flagging energy or loss of entrepreneurial vigor. During the last two weeks of January 2007, Virgin announced a slew of new initiatives. These included the creation of Virgin Bioverda—a joint venture to develop ethanol plants in the U.S.—a bid for a vacation company (First Choice) and a proposal to take over rail services between London and Edinburgh. At the same time, Branson was negotiating an alliance with Tata Group to establish Virgin Mobile in India and preparing to buy 50 acres of land in Macau to build a $3 billion casino and leisure complex. Meanwhile, Virgin

America—Branson's San Francisco-based low-cost airline—was struggling to get approval from the U.S. Department of Transportation. Some believed that Virgin Galactic—Branson's passenger spaceship service—might be first into the air.

Yet despite being lauded for his entrepreneurship, eccentricity and embodiment of "the friendly face of capitalism," his Virgin group of companies remained a mystery to most outsiders—and to many insiders as well. At the beginning of 2007 there were 215 Virgin companies registered at Britain's Companies House, of which 20 are identified as recently dissolved. However, most operations are conducted through the 36 companies listed on the Virgin web site (see the Appendix). While a number are Virgin companies identified as "holding companies"—they exist only to own and manage other Virgin companies—there is no overall parent company for the group.

The opacity of Virgin's structure and finances encouraged frequent speculation about the overall performance of the group. During the late 1990s, there was consistent evidence that the group as a whole was not performing well. *The Economist* observed that: "Virgin Travel is the only one of Virgin's businesses to make a large profit . . . The rest of Mr. Branson's firms lost money in total."[1] The *Financial Times* pointed to a net cash outflow and a negative economic value added for the group as a whole.[2] During recent years, overall financial performance was strengthened by profit growth at Virgin's wireless telecommunications businesses and the post-2002 recovery in the airline industry. Nevertheless, several Virgin companies continued to generate losses.

As ever, Branson was dismissive of outside criticism, claiming that analysts and financial journalists misunderstood his business empire. Each Virgin company, he argued, was financed on a stand-alone basis; hence attempts to consolidate the income and assets of the companies were irrelevant and misleading. Moreover, Branson had little regard for accounting profits, preferring cash flow and capital value as the critical performance indicators. Thus, most of the Virgin companies were growing businesses that were increasing in their real value and long-term cash-generating potential, even if accounting profits were negative:

> The approach to running a group of private companies is fundamentally different to that of running public companies. Short-term taxable profits with good dividends are a prerequisite of public life. Avoiding short-term taxable profits and seeking long-term capital growth is the best approach to growing private companies.[3]

Apart from questions about financial performance, outside observers also pondered the strategic direction of this motley collection of over 200 separate companies. The Virgin group covered a remarkable range of business, from airlines to bridal stores. In an era of corporate refocusing and the nurturing of core competences, what possible business rationale could explain the structure and composition of the Virgin group? It was not only Virgin's financial resources that risked being stretched. Was there a risk that the Virgin brand would become overextended and that its appeal and integrity would be damaged? With regard to Branson himself, should he attempt to involve himself personally in guiding the various Virgin companies? As the group expanded and Branson became more of a strategic and charismatic leader rather than a hands-on manager, did Virgin need to establish a more systematic approach to control, risk management, and strategy?

The Development of Virgin

Richard Branson's business career began while he was a student at Stowe, a private boarding school. His startup magazine, *Student*, was first published on January 26, 1968. The early success of the magazine encouraged Branson to leave school at 17 years old, before taking his final exams. Agreeing to the boy's request to leave, the headmaster offered the prophetic statement, "Richard, you will end up in prison or as a millionaire." Both predictions were to be fulfilled.[4]

This early publishing venture displayed features that would characterize many of Branson's subsequent entrepreneurial initiatives. The magazine was aimed at baby-boomers between 16 and 25 years old and was designed to appeal to the optimism, irreverence, antiauthoritarianism, and fashion consciousness of the new generation. It would also fill a "gaping hole in the market." *Student* was to be the "voice of youth" and would "put the world to rights." Its eclectic style reflected its founder's ability to commission articles by celebrities and to identify subjects not touched by many well-established magazines. Norman Mailer, Vanessa Redgrave and Jean-Paul Sartre contributed pieces, which appeared among articles on sex, rock music, interviews with terrorists and proposals for educational reform.

Virgin Records

Branson's next venture was mail order records. Beginning with a single advertisement in the last issue of *Student* magazine, Branson found that he was able to establish a thriving business with almost no up-front investment and no working capital, and could easily undercut the established retail chains. The name "Virgin" was suggested by one of his associates who saw the name as proclaiming their commercial innocence, while possessing some novelty and modest shock-value. Virgin Records brought together Branson and his childhood friend Nik Powell, who took a 40% share in the company and complemented Branson's erratic flamboyance with careful operational and financial management. In 1971 Branson opened his first retail store—on London's busy Oxford Street.

Expansion into record publishing was the idea of Simon Draper, one of Virgin's record buyers. Draper introduced Branson to Mike Oldfield, who was soon installed at Branson's Oxfordshire home with a fully equipped recording studio. *Tubular Bells*, launched in 1973, was an instant hit, eventually selling over 5 million copies worldwide. The result was the Virgin record label, which went on to sign up bands whose music or lifestyles did not appeal to the major record companies. Among the most successful signings were the Sex Pistols.

The recession of 1979–82 was a struggle for Virgin. Several business ventures failed and several of Branson's close associates left, including Nik Powell, who sold his share-holding back to Branson for £1 million plus Virgin's cinema and video interests. Despite these setbacks, the 1980s saw rapid growth for Virgin Records, with the signing of Phil Collins, Human League, Simple Minds and Boy George's Culture Club. By 1983, the Virgin group was earning pretax profits of £2 million on total revenues of just under £50 million.

Virgin Atlantic Airways

Virgin Atlantic began with a phone call from Randolph Fields, a Californian lawyer who proposed founding a transatlantic, cut-price airline. To the horror of Branson's executives at Virgin Records, Branson was enthralled with the idea. On June 24, 1984, Branson appeared in a First World War flying outfit to celebrate the inaugural flight of Virgin Atlantic in a second-hand 747 bought from Aerolinas Argentina. With the launch of Virgin Atlantic, Branson had embarked upon a perilous path strewn with the wreckage of earlier entrepreneurs of aviation, including Laker, Braniff and People Express. Unlike Branson's other businesses, not only was the airline business highly capital intensive—it also required a completely new set of business skills, in particular the need to negotiate with governments, regulatory bodies, banks, and aircraft manufacturers.

Private to Public and Back

By 1985, a transatlantic airfares price war and the investment needs of Virgin Atlantic had created a cash squeeze for Virgin. Branson became convinced of the need to expand the equity base of the group. Don Cruikshank, a Scottish accountant with an MBA from Manchester and Branson's group managing director, was assigned the task of organizing an initial public offering for Virgin's music, retail, and vision businesses, which were combined into the Virgin Group plc, a public corporation with 35% of its equity listed on the London and NASDAQ stock markets.

Branson was not happy as chairman of a public corporation. He felt that investment analysts misunderstood his business and that the market undervalued his company. A clear conflict existed between the financial community's expectations of the chairman of a public corporation and Branson's personal style. With the October 1987 stock market crash, Branson took the opportunity to raise £200 million to buy out external shareholders.

As a private company, Virgin continued to expand, using both internal cash flows—mainly from Virgin Atlantic Airways—and external financing. The retailing group moved aggressively into new markets around the world. The Virgin Megastore concept provided the basis for new stores in Japan, the U.S., Australia, the Netherlands and Spain. This growth was facilitated by the formation of a joint venture with Blockbuster Corporation, the U.S. video-store giant. New ventures launched during the early 1990s included Virgin Lightships, an airship advertiser; Vintage Airtours, an operator of restored DC-3 aircraft between Orlando and Key West; Virgin Games producing video games; West One Television, a TV production company and Virgin Euromagnetics, a personal computer company. Meanwhile, Virgin Atlantic Airways expanded its network to 20 cities including Tokyo and Hong Kong. It also won many awards for its customer service.

1990–2006: Continued Expansion, Selective Divestment

Expansion pressured cash flow and the Persian Gulf War of 1990–1 cut airline profits. Branson relied increasingly on joint ventures to finance new business development. The partnering arrangements were primarily in retailing and included one with Marui, a leading Japanese retailer, and another with W. H. Smith, a prominent U.K. retail chain.

Ultimately, the capital needs of Virgin Atlantic forced Branson to take drastic action. In March 1992, Branson sold his most profitable and successful business, Virgin Music, the world's biggest independent record label, to Thorn EMI for £560 million (close to $1 billion). Virgin Music's tangible assets had a balance sheet value of only £3 million. The sale marked a dramatic shift in focus for Virgin away from its core entertainment business towards airlines and travel. It provided the capital to support new business ventures.

In the meantime, Branson's long-standing rivalry with British Airways took a nasty turn. Evidence emerged that British Airways had pursued a "dirty tricks" campaign against Virgin. This included breaking into Virgin's computer system, diverting Virgin customers to BA flights, and spreading rumors about Virgin's financial state. The outcome was a U.K. court case that resulted in BA paying $1.5 million dollars in damages to Branson and Virgin.

The second half of the 1990s saw acceleration in Virgin's business development activities, with a host of new ventures in disparate markets. Virgin's new ventures were a response to three types of opportunity:

- *Privatization and deregulation*. The rolling back of the frontiers of state ownership and regulation in Britain (and elsewhere) created business opportunities that Richard Branson was only too eager to seize. Virgin's most important privatization initiative was its successful bids for two passenger rail franchises: the west coast and cross-country rail services. The resulting business—Virgin Rail—was a joint venture with transportation specialist, Stagecoach. Deregulation in the world's airline sector also created opportunities for Virgin. In 1996, Euro-Belgian Airlines was acquired and re-launched as Virgin Express, and in Australia, Virgin Blue began operations during 2000. Branson's bid to operate the British National Lottery was unsuccessful, but in 2001, Virgin Atlantic was part of the consortium that acquired a stake in the British air traffic control system.
- *Direct selling of goods and services to consumers*. Branson was continually on the lookout for business opportunities offering a "new deal" to consumers. Most of these ventures involved direct sales to consumers and passing on the cost savings from bypassing traditional distribution channels. Virgin Direct, launched in 1995 as a joint venture with Norwich Union, offered telephone-based financial services to consumers. In subsequent years, Virgin Direct expanded the range of financial products it offered and moved to the internet. Virgin Car and Virgin Bike challenged the existing dealership system of the automobile and motorcycle manufacturers by offering direct sales of cars and motorbikes at discounted prices. Virgin Wine was also launched.
- *TMT*. The "TMT" (Technology, Media, Telecom) boom of 1998–2000 created a tremendous buzz within Virgin. Virgin's origins lay in media, while the internet offered a new channel for Virgin to reach consumers. In 1997 Virgin Net, an internet service provider and portal, was launched as a joint venture between Virgin and cable operator NTL. The next year Virgin Mobile, a joint venture with Deutsche Telecom's One-to-One wireless telephone service began business in Britain. The success of Virgin Mobile in Britain—half a million subscribers were signed up within the first year and four million by 2004—encouraged Virgin to expand into the U.S., Australia, South Africa and South East Asia. Virgin's increasing online presence was seen as offering important e-commerce opportunities to the Virgin group as a whole. The Train Line Company (www.thetrainline.com) was set up as an online reservation service for train passengers. Virgin Direct offered music downloads. The Virgin.com portal became a shopfront for all of Virgin's consumer offerings.

Other new ventures appeared to be largely the result of Branson's whims and opportunism and defied any kind of categorization. These included a chain of health clubs (Virgin Active), space flight (Virgin Galactic), and biofuels (Virgin Fuels, Virgin Bioverda).

To fund so many new ventures, Branson sought to release equity from some of his established and growing businesses. Major divestments included:

- Virgin Atlantic: 49% was sold to Singapore Airlines for £600 million in 1999;
- Virgin Megastores, France was sold to Legardere Media in 2001 for £100 million;
- Virgin One: Virgin's home loan business was sold to Royal Bank of Scotland in 2001 for £100 million;
- Virgin Blue: 50% was sold to Patrick Corporation for £250 million in 2001; a further 25% of Virgin Blue was sold in that company's 2003 IPO, raising a similar amount;
- Virgin Mobile (U.K.) was acquired by cable operator NTL for £962 million in 2006.

Moreover, Virgin Express—Virgin's loss-making, Brussels-based airline—merged in 2005 with SN Brussels Airlines to form SN Airholdings, in which Virgin held a 30% stake. The appendix shows a timeline of Virgin's development.

The Virgin Group of Companies in 2007

Among the 200-plus companies forming the Virgin Group, the major businesses in terms of revenues and market presence are shown in Table 20.1. The principal commonalities between this diverse range of enterprises are, first, their use of the Virgin brand name and, second, the role of Richard Branson as their instigator and, in most cases, their major investor.

The Virgin Brand

The Virgin brand was the group's greatest single asset. There are few brands that encompass so wide a range of products as Virgin. Can a brand that extends from train travel and financial services to night clubs and music downloads have any meaningful identity? The Virgin web site explains the Virgin brand as follows:

> All the markets in which Virgin operates tend to have features in common: they are typically markets where the customer has been ripped off or underserved, where there is confusion and/or where the competition is complacent. In these markets, Virgin is able to break into the market and shake it up. Our role is to be the consumer champion, and we do this by delivering to our brand values, which are:

- *Value for Money:* Simple, honest and transparent pricing—not necessarily the cheapest on the market.
- *Good Quality:* High standards, attention to detail, being honest and delivering on promises.

- *Brilliant Customer Service:* Friendly, human and relaxed; professional but not corporate.
- *Innovative:* Challenging convention with big and little product/service ideas; innovative, modern and stylish design.
- *Competitively Challenging:* Sticking two fingers up to the establishment and fighting the big boys—usually with a bit of humor.
- *Fun:* Every company in the world takes itself seriously so we think it's important that we provide the public and our customers with a bit of entertainment—as well as making Virgin a nice place for our people to work.[5]

These attributes were communicated to customers in a variety of ways. Virgin Atlantic pioneered a range of innovative customer services (principally for its business class passengers). These included inflight massages, hair stylists, aromatherapists and limousine and motorcycle home pickup services. In 1998 it offered speedboat rides along the Thames from Heathrow to the City of London, allowing executives and bankers to dodge London traffic jams. British Airways—huge, stodgy and bureaucratic—provided the ideal adversary against which Virgin Atlantic could position itself. When British Airways was experiencing problems erecting its giant Ferris wheel, the London Eye, Virgin positioned a blimp above the site bearing the message "BA Can't Get It Up!"

TABLE 20.1 Main businesses within the Virgin Group, 2006

Virgin Active	Chain of health and leisure clubs in the U.K. and South Africa
Virgin Atlantic	London-based airline serving 20 destinations in the U.S., Caribbean, South Africa and Asia
Virgin Atlantic Cargo	Air freight using Virgin Atlantic's network
Virgin Balloon Flights	Passenger balloon flights in the U.K., Holland and Belgium
Virgin Blue	Low-fare airline flying in Australia
Virgin Books	Publishes books on music, sport, TV, movies, and comedy
Virgin Brides	Chain of bridal retail stores
Virgin Comics	Collaboration with writer Deepak Chopra, filmmaker Shekhar Kapur and Sir Richard Branson
Virgin Cosmetics	Direct sales of specially formulated cosmetics
Virgin Credit Card	Credit card issued by Virgin Money
Virgin Digital	Online digital music collection
Virgin Drinks	Distributes Virgin-branded soft drinks
Virgin Experience Days	Offers innovative leisure experiences, from bungee jumping to Ferrari driving
Virgin Express	Brussels-based airline offering scheduled flights to U.K. and other European destinations
Virgin Galactic	Offers opportunities for space travel
Virgin Games	Online gaming
Virgin Holidays	U.K.-based tour operator specializing in long-haul holidays to America, the Far East, Australia, and South Africa, using Virgin Atlantic flights

TABLE 20.1 *(Continued)*

Virgin Jewellery	Offers a range of silver and fashion jewelry
Virgin Limited Edition	Offers vacation packages at exclusive hotels worldwide
Virgin Limobike	Motorcycle taxi service in London
Virgin Limousines	Limos serving northern California
Virgin Megastores	Eighty megastores in Europe, Japan, and North America sell music, movies, computer games and books
Virgin Mobile	Wireless telephone resellers offering easy-tariff service with no line rental or fixed-term contract
Virgin Money	Online financial services offering loans, mutual funds, and stock trading
Virgin.net	U.K.-based internet service provider
Virgin Play	Distributor, marketer, and promoter of computer and interactive games in Spain
Virgin Radio	U.K. digital radio broadcaster
Virgin Spa	Spa services in South Africa
Virgin Trains	Major U.K. operator of passenger train services and facilities and allows booking of Virgin Train tickets online
Virgin Unite	Charitable, volunteer organization supporting grassroots charities
Virgin Vacations	Vacation packages
Virgin Ware	Retail and online vendor of underwear
Virgin Wines	Direct seller of wines
V2 Music	Independent record label (artists include the Stereophonics, Tom Jones, Moby and Underworld)
Pacific Blue	Airline operating daily services between Australia and New Zealand

Source: www.virgin.com.

Some of Branson's ventures seemed to be inspired more by a sense of fun and eagerness to "stick it to the big boys" than by commercial logic. Virgin Cola was introduced in 1994 packaged in a "Pammy" bottle modeled on the body of *Baywatch* star Pamela Anderson. The goal, according to Branson, was to "drive Coke out of the States."[6] By 1997, Virgin Cola was losing £5 million on revenues of £30 million.

Virgin's ability to extend its brand so widely pointed to the broad appeal of Virgin's values and business principles. Much of this appeal was linked with Richard Branson's persona and style. The values and characteristics that the Virgin brand communicated are inseparable from Richard Branson as entrepreneur, joker, fair-playing Brit and giant killer. The Virgin brand was identified too with the innovation and unconventional strategies and marketing that characterized most Virgin startups. Branson went to great lengths to differentiate his new enterprises from established market leaders. Thus, the difference between Virgin Atlantic and BA, between Virgin Cola and Coke, and between Virgin Money and the leading banks was not primarily about products; it was more about the nature of the companies and how they related to their customers. As Virgin internationalized, a critical issue was whether Branson and the Virgin brand could achieve the same rapport with consumers in other countries as they did in Britain. Although Branson was well known in Europe and

North America, in many respects he was a quintessentially British character who was a product of time and place.

A continual issue for Virgin was the risk that the brand might become overextended. The head of brand identity at consultant Landor Associates commented: "He's still way too unfocused. He should get out of businesses that don't fit the Virgin/Branson personality, such as beverages, cosmetics, certainly financial services, or come up with another brand name for them."[7] Widespread public dissatisfaction with rail services in Britain suggested that Virgin's vision of new standards of service for rail travelers might be unattainable given the structural problems of Britain's congested rail infrastructure.

Despite his renown, Branson, too, might be waning in market appeal. Was there a risk that, having seen Branson as flight attendant, Branson in a wedding dress, Branson with successive prime ministers, and Branson attempting to fly around the world in a hot-air balloon, the public might tire of his exploits?

During the late 1990s, Virgin had moved to consolidate around a number of core businesses, notably travel, entertainment, and retailing. However, this trend was short lived: the telecom and internet revolution offered Branson a host of new entrepreneurial opportunities that were irresistible.

Branson as Entrepreneur

Almost all of the Virgin businesses were new startups. From the founding of *Student* magazine through to the formation of Virgin Galactic, Branson's primary strength as a businessman was in conceiving and implementing new business ideas—not that Branson was the source of all of Virgin's new business ideas. Branson acted as a magnet for would-be entrepreneurs and Virgin actively encouraged the submission of new business ideas to its corporate development offices in London, Sydney and New York. Virgin employees, too, were encouraged to develop proposals for new businesses. The idea for Virgin Bride had originated with a Virgin Atlantic employee dismayed by the products and services offered by existing U.K. bridal stores. Nelson Mandela once offered a business idea to Branson, suggesting that Branson acquire a South African health club chain that had gone bankrupt putting thousands of jobs at risk. Virgin Active South Africa is now the country's biggest chain of health clubs.

Yet Branson's leadership of the Virgin Group extended beyond his role as a source of entrepreneurial ideas. As the creator of Virgin and its unique corporate culture, and the primary promoter of its image and entrepreneurial spirit, Richard Branson was synonymous with Virgin. To many of his generation he embodied the spirit of "New Britain." In a country where business leaders were members of "the establishment" and identified with the existing social structure, Branson was seen as a revolutionary. Despite a privileged family background (his father was a lawyer and Richard attended a private boarding school), Branson had the ability to transcend the social classes that traditionally divided British society and segmented consumer markets. As such, he was part of a movement in British culture and society that has sought to escape the Old Britain of fading empire, class antagonism, Victorian values, and stiff-upper-lip hypocrisy. Richard Branson symbolized the transition from "Rule Britannia" to "Cool Britannia."

Informality and disrespect for convention were central to Branson's way of business. Branson's woolly sweaters, beard, windswept hair and toothy grin were practically a trademark of the Virgin companies. His dislike of office buildings and the usual symbols of corporate success was reflected in the absence of a corporate head office and his willingness to do business from his family homes, whether a houseboat in Maida Vale or Necker Island Caribbean retreat. This lack of separation between work, family, and leisure—indicated by the involvement of cousins, aunts, childhood friends and dinner-party acquaintances in business relationships—reflected a view of business as part of life which, like life, should involve excitement, creativity and fun.

An earlier case study on Virgin explains Branson's approach to new business startups:

> Much of the operating style was established not so much by design but by the exigencies of the time when Virgin was getting started. It has proved to be a successful model that Branson can replicate. His philosophy is to immerse himself in a new venture until he understands the ins and outs of the business, and then hand it over to a good managing director and financial controller, who are given a stake in it, and are then expected to make the company take off. He knows that expansion through the creation of additional discrete legal entities not only protects the Virgin Group, but also gives people a sense of involvement and loyalty, particularly if he trusts them with full authority and offers minority share holdings to the managers of subsidiaries. He is proud of the fact that Virgin has produced a considerable number of millionaires. He has said that he does not want his best people to leave the company to start a venture outside. He prefers to make millionaires within.[8]

His use of joint ventures was an extension of this model reinforced by his dealings with the Japanese. Branson was impressed by the Japanese approach to business, admiring their commitment to long-term development and focus on organic growth. His only major acquisition was the parts of British Rail that formed Virgin Rail. Prior to that, Branson had made only two significant acquisitions: Rushes Video for £6 million and the airline that became Virgin Express. He saw similarities between Virgin and the Japanese *keiretsu* system (multiple companies interlocking through managerial and equity linkages in a collaborative network). Virgin's network of small companies combined "small is beautiful" with "strength through unity." He explained this and other business maxims that he believed to be necessary for success in a speech to the Institute of Directors in 1993. "Staff first, then customers and shareholders" should be the chairman's priority if the goal is better performance. "Shape the business around the people," "Build don't buy," "Be best, not biggest," "Pioneer, don't follow the leader," "Capture every fleeting idea," and "Drive for change" were other guiding principles in the Branson philosophy.

Branson's values of innocence, innovation and irreverence for authority were apparent in his choice of new ventures. He drew heavily on the ideas of others within his organization and was prepared to invest in new startups even in markets that were dominated by long-established incumbents. His business ventures, just like his sporting exploits, reflected a "just live life" attitude and a "bigger the challenge, greater the fun" belief. In identifying opportunity he was particularly keen to identify markets where the conservatism and lack of imagination of incumbent firms meant that they were failing to create value for customers. Branson entered markets with a "new" and "anti-establishment attitude" that sought to offer customers a better alternative. An example of this was Virgin's entry into financial services. Into a business that was long regarded as conservative and stuffy, Branson hoped to bring "a breath of fresh air."

At the same time, the affection of the British public for Branson reflected the fact that Branson's values and his sense of fair play were consistent with many traditional values that defined the British character. His competitive battles against huge corporations like British Airways and Coca-Cola linked well with the heroes of yesteryear who battled against tyranny and evil: King Arthur, Robin Hood, and St. George. Resisting British Airways' "dirty tricks" campaign and his other battles with corporate giants resonated well with the British sense of decency. Even his willingness to appear in outlandish attire reflected a British propensity for ludicrous dressing-up, whether for fancy-dress parties, morris dancing, or the House of Lords.

Virgin's Management Structure

Of Virgin's 200-plus companies, the majority are operating companies that own assets, employ people, and offer goods and services. These operating companies are owned and controlled by some 20 holding companies; most of these own several operating companies within the same line of business. For example, Virgin Travel (Holdings) Limited owns Virgin Group's investments in Virgin Atlantic, Virgin Blue, Virgin America and SN Airholdings. Overall ownership of most of the Virgin Group lies in the hands of Virgin Group Investments Limited—a private company registered in the British Virgin Islands. Virgin Group Investments Limited is owned by Richard Branson and a series of trusts, the beneficiaries of which are Branson and his family members.

The most striking feature of the Virgin Group is its legal complexity. For example, Virgin's passenger train companies are Virgin West Coast Mainline and Virgin Cross Country. These are owned by Virgin Rail Group Holdings Ltd, 51% of which is owned by Ivanco (No. 1) Ltd, which is owned by Virgin Group Investments Ltd.

This financial and legal structure reflects Branson's unconventional ideas about business and his wariness of the financial community. The intricate structure involving offshore private companies cloaks the Virgin empire in a thick veil of secrecy. This is reinforced by the use of "bearer shares" by several of the Virgin holding companies through which minority shareholders (venture capitalists and other investors) cannot be identified. However, Branson also views the loose-knit structure of the group as consistent with his vision of people-oriented capitalism:

> We're structured as if we are 150 small companies. Each has to stand on its own two feet, as if they are their own companies. Employees have a stake in their success. They feel—and are—crucial to their company because they are one-in-fifty or one-in-a-hundred instead of one-in-tens-of-thousands. They indeed are all under the Virgin umbrella, but they are generally not subsidiaries. I'm over them to see if one company can't help another, but otherwise they are independent. Some people like the idea of growing fiefdoms—companies that brag about sales of over $5 billion a year—but there is no logical reason to think that there is anything good about huge companies. History in fact shows the opposite. Those huge corporations with tentacles and divisions and departments become unwieldy, slow growing, stagnant. Some chairmen want them like that so that one division's loss can make up for

another's profit, but we'd rather have a lot of exciting companies that are all making profits—as are all of ours.[9]

The Virgin Group has been likened both to a brand franchising operation and to Japanese *keiretsu*, where member companies have financial and management links and share a common sense of identity. The reality, according to *Management Today*,[10] is somewhere between the two. Will Whitehorn, Branson's long-time strategist and business developer, describes Virgin as "a branded venture capital organization."

The formal linkages between the companies include:

- *Ownership*. Most of Branson's equity interests are owned by Virgin Group Investments Ltd.
- *The brand*. Virgin's trademarks—including the Virgin name and logos—are owned by Virgin Enterprises Ltd. Neil Hobbs, intellectual property lawyer for Virgin Enterprises, explains: "Our role is both to optimize and enhance the value of the brand and to protect that by ensuring that that value is not diminished through infringement by third parties. VEL licenses companies both within and outside the Virgin Group to use the Virgin brand."[11] One third-party licensee is EMI Records, which owns Virgin Records and is licensed to use the Virgin name.
- *Management*. Virgin Management Ltd is the management arm of the Virgin Group. It manages the appointment of board members and senior executives to the different Virgin companies, assists in coordination between the companies, and is responsible for the development of new business enterprises. In 2005, Virgin Management Ltd had 87 employees at Virgin's London headquarters.

However, the key to the management of the Virgin Group is the informal relations between Branson and a small core of long-term associates who form the senior management team of the Virgin Group and occupy key executive positions within individual operating companies. Among Branson's inner circle are:

- Will Whitehorn, originally Branson's press spokesman, who has been Virgin's director of brand development and corporate affairs for the past decade and is currently CEO of Virgin Galactic. He is widely viewed as Branson's second-in-command and key strategic thinker.[12]
- Gordon McCallum, who joined Virgin in 1997 as group strategy director from McKinsey & Company. He has pioneered Virgin's entry into mobile telecommunications and since September 2005 has been CEO of Virgin Management Ltd.
- Patrick McCall, who was formerly an investment banker at UBS Warburg. At Virgin he is a director of Virgin Management and has been a board member of a number of Virgin companies, including Virgin Rail and Virgin Blue.
- Stephen Murphy, who joined Virgin from Quaker Oats. He was Virgin Group's finance director from 1994 to 2000, and since 2001 has been a board member of Virgin Management as executive director.

FIGURE 20.1 The Virgin Group of companies

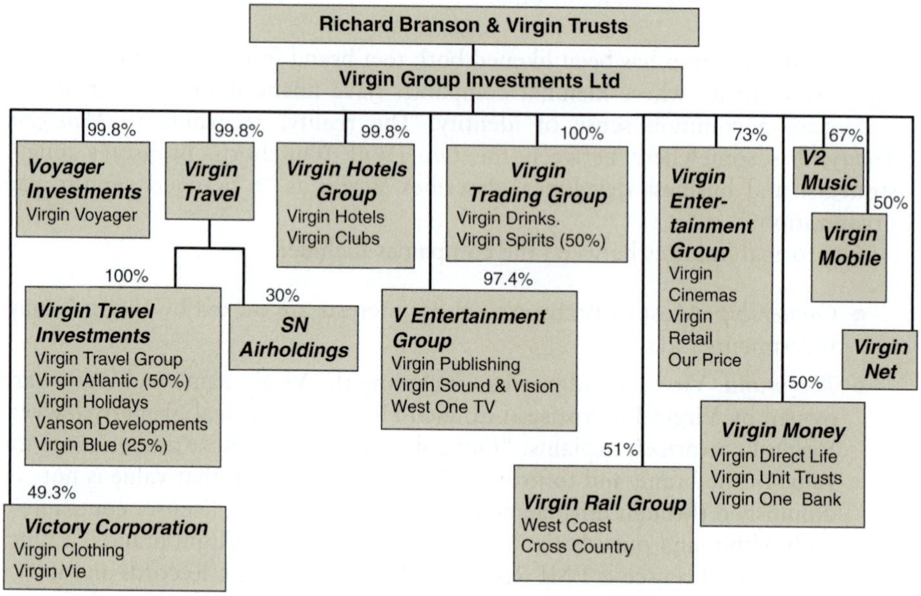

Source: Financial Times, August 13, 1998, p.25, updated from www.virgin.com.

Note: This figure is intended to provide a general view of the structure of the Virgin Group, but it includes only some of Virgin's 2001 companies.

- Rowan Gormley, who joined the Virgin Group as corporate development director after working as an accountant with Arthur Andersen & Co. He led Virgin's move into financial services in 1995 as chief executive of Virgin Direct. In January 2000, he became CEO of Virgin Wine.
- Frances Farrow, who joined Virgin Atlantic as commercial services director from the law firm Binder Hamlyn. She became CEO of Virgin USA, Inc.

Figure 20.1 shows the structure of the Virgin Group of companies, including some major operating companies and the holding companies that own them.

Virgin's Organizational Culture

The ability of the Virgin Group to operate effectively with so little formal structure or management systems owes much to the group's unique organizational culture. This is defined almost entirely by Branson's own values and management style. It reflects his eccentricity, sense of fun, disrespect for hierarchy and formal authority, commitment to employees and consumers and belief in hard work and individual responsibility. The group provides an environment in which talented, ambitious people are motivated to do their best and strive for a higher level of performance. While the working environment is informal, anticorporate and defined by the popular culture of its era, expectations are high. Branson expects a high level of commitment, the acceptance of personal responsibility and long hours of work when needed. Financial rewards for most employees are typically modest but nonpecuniary benefits include social activities, company-sponsored weekend getaways and impromptu parties.

The apparent chaos of the Virgin Group, with its casual style and absence of formal structure and control systems belies its sharp business acumen and forceful determination. It is easy for more traditional business enterprises to underestimate Virgin—a key error of British Airways. Virgin possesses considerable financial and managerial talent, and what it lacks in formal structure is made up for by commitment and close personal ties. The Virgin organizational structure involves very little hierarchy, offering short lines of communication and flexible response capability. Employees are given a great deal of responsibility and freedom in order to stimulate idea generation, initiative, commitment, and fun. The lack of formal controls is conducive to teamwork and entrepreneurial spirit.

Virgin's Financial Performance

Financial reporting by the Virgin companies was fragmented, hard to locate and difficult to interpret. No consolidated accounts existed for the group as a whole. Not only were there multiple operating companies but ownership of these companies lay with a number of holding companies, some of which consolidated subsidiary accounts while others did not. Tracking financial results over time was difficult because investments in Virgin operating companies were frequently transferred within the group. Individual Virgin companies (at least those registered in the U.K.) submitted audited financial statements to Companies House (a government agency). Table 20.2 shows results for some of the Virgin's operating and holding companies.

The financial structure of the Virgin Group has changed substantially over the years. In particular, Virgin's near collapse during the 1990–2 recession has resulted in a more conservative approach to financing. During the past 15 years, Branson has relied increasingly on equity partners to finance his new business ventures. Typically, joint venture partners have taken 49% or 50% of the equity of the new venture despite supplying the majority of the equity capital. The power of the Virgin brand and Branson's celebrity status and promotional capabilities has meant that Branson has acquired equity stakes in new ventures that were disproportionate to the size of his financial investment—which was typically small. For example, Branson put up only £2000 initially for minority stakes in Virgin Clothing and Virgin Vie; at Virgin Blue, Branson's initial investment was a mere A$12 million. Virgin's joint ventures include:

- Virgin Atlantic, which was 49% owned by Singapore Airlines.
- Virgin Rail, which was 49% owned by Stagecoach.
- Virgin Retail had different partners and investors. These included Blockbuster and Marui.
- Virgin Trading drinks ventures had been launched with investments from William Grant and Cotts.
- Victory Corporation, the fashion and toiletries company, was pioneered by entrepreneur and investor Rory McCarthy. In addition, outside investors owned 25% of the equity. McCarthy also held one-third of V2 Music.
- Virgin Express was a subsidiary of SN Airholdings in which Virgin held a 30% equity stake.
- Virgin Blue was a publicly traded company where Virgin held 25%.
- In addition, private investors (including major equity and venture capital funds) held equity stakes in some Virgin businesses.

TABLE 20.2 Financial results for selected Virgin companies

Company	Revenue (£ m)	Net profit (£ m)	Total assets (£ m)	Employees (incl. directors)	Financial year ending	Comments
Virgin Group Ltd	0.2	(151.4)	69.9	4	March 31, 2005	Investment holding company. Owns Voyager Group Ltd and Virgin USA, Inc. Exceptional loss of £151 m in 2005
Virgin Enterprises Ltd	13.3	3.3	129.3	4	March 31, 2006	Owns and licenses Virgin brand
Virgin Management Ltd	5.7	(13.3)	548.7	97	March 31, 2006	Management of other Virgin companies. Owns Virgin Bride Ltd, Virgin Mobile (Singapore), Vanson Group Ltd, and Virgin Life Care Investments Ltd
Virgin Travel Group Ltd	0	0.7	250.1	10	February 28, 2006	Holding company. Owns Virgin Atlantic Airlines Ltd and Virgin Holidays Ltd
Virgin Atlantic Ltd	1912.3	60.3	1196.7	8939	February 28, 2006	Airline
Virgin Leisure Ltd	0	36.9	216.2	n.a.	March 31, 2006	Investment holding company that owns Virgin Active Group Ltd
Virgin Mobile Holdings (U.K.) Ltd	563.1	44.9	106.3	1488	March 31, 2006	Telecommunications. Acquired by NTL on July 4, 2006
Virgin Mobile Group (U.K.) Ltd	80.0	65.8	374.8	3	March 31, 2006	Holding company. Owns Virgin Mobile Telecoms Ltd

Virgin Money Ltd	51.1	12.8	20.0	4	December 31, 2005	Online financial services, primarily credit cards
Virgin Money Holdings (U.K.) Ltd	258.2	8.5	40.3	376	December 31, 2005	Online financial services, primarily personal investment products
Virgin Rail Group Holdings Ltd	717.1	(1.2)	372.6	4456	March 4, 2006	Owns West Coast Trains Ltd and CrossCountry Trains Ltd
Virgin Retail Group Ltd	0	(82.6)	39.2	4	March 31, 2004	Holding company. Owns Virgin Retail Ltd and Vspace Ltd (internet cafés).
Virgin Retail Ltd	376.3	(74.7)	203.7	3240	March 27, 2004	Holding company. Owns Virgin Atlantic Airways Ltd and Virgin Holidays Ltd
Virgin Trading Group Ltd	0	(7.0)	7.6	4	March 31, 2005	Investment holding company. Owns Virgin Drinks Group Ltd

n.a. = not available.

Source: Company annual reports submitted to Companies House.

Looking Ahead

During early 2007, Virgin Group appeared to be relatively free of the cash-flow and debt-service problems that had plagued it in the past. While a number of Virgin businesses were making losses and others (for example, Virgin Atlantic) were only marginally profitable, recent divestments had replenished the group's coffers. Longer term, however, there were fundamental strategic questions about the future shape and rationale for the Virgin Group. What kind of enterprise was Virgin? Was it a brand management and franchising company, an incubator of startup businesses, a vehicle for Richard Branson's personal ambitions, or a novel form of conglomerate? Was Virgin a unified, if diversified, business or a loose confederation of many independent businesses?

Whatever the identity and rationale of the Virgin Group, it was not apparent that the existing structure or organization fitted with any of these categories:

- If Virgin was a brand franchising organization, then the critical role for the Virgin Group was to develop and protect the brand and maximize the licensing revenues from its use by other companies. Clearly Branson would need to play a role in promoting the brand but it was not necessary that he should have any strategic, operating, or ownership role in the companies using the brand.
- If Virgin was to be an incubator of new startups then there needed to be a more systematic approach to evaluating new business opportunities and monitoring their progress and development.
- If Virgin was a conglomerate, then did this imply a stronger corporate role? What kind of strategic planning and financial controls were needed to ensure that value was not being dissipated? And could Virgin really perform across so wide a range of businesses?

Whichever path Virgin followed, it appeared that organizational changes would be needed in order to manage intercompany linkages. Although Branson liked to maintain that the different companies were independent and "stood on their own two feet," the reality was somewhat different. Some companies had been strong cash generators; others were heavy loss makers. Relationships between the companies were largely *ad hoc* and Branson was proud of the fact that no consolidated financial statements were prepared, even for internal management purposes. Moreover, changes to Britain's capital gains tax laws threatened to eliminate the advantages of multiple, offshore holding companies. Indeed, to obtain the tax benefits from Virgin's loss-making businesses, there were clear advantages in consolidation. Key questions also surrounded the management of the Virgin brand. To the extent that the brand was a common resource, how could it be best protected? The experiences of Virgin Rail suggested that adverse publicity from one company could negatively affect the overall status of the Virgin brand.

As always, the future of the Virgin Group could not be considered without taking account of Branson himself. What kind of role did he anticipate now that he had celebrated his 57th birthday? If Branson was to become less active as chief entrepreneur, public relations director and strategic architect for the Virgin companies, who or what would take his place?

Appendix

The history of Virgin

1968—First issue of *Student* magazine, January 26.
1970—Start of Virgin mail order operation.
1971—First Virgin record shop opens in Oxford Street, London.
1972—Virgin recording studio opens at The Manor near Oxford, England.
1977—Virgin record label launched with Mike Oldfield's *Tubular Bells*.
—Virgin Records signs the Sex Pistols.
1978—Virgin opens The Venue night club in London.
1980–2—Virgin Records expands overseas. Signs Phil Collins and Boy George/Culture Club.
1983—Virgin Vision (forerunner of Virgin Communications) formed to enter broadcasting and produce and distribute films and videos.
—Vanson Developments formed as real-estate development company.
—Virgin Games (computer games software publisher) launched.
—Virgin Group earns pre-tax profit of £2.0 million on sales of £50 million.
1984—Virgin Atlantic Airways and Virgin Cargo launched.
—First hotel investment (Deya, Mallorca).
—Virgin Vision launches The Music Channel, a 24-hour satellite-delivered music station and releases its first feature film, *1984*, with Richard Burton and John Hurt.
1985—Virgin wins Business Enterprise Award for company of the year.
—Virgin Vision extends film and video distribution internationally.
—Virgin Holidays formed.
1986—Virgin Group, comprising the Music, Retail & Property, and Communications divisions, floated on London Stock Exchange. Placement of 35% of equity raises $56 million.
—Airline, clubs, holidays, and aviation services remain part of the privately owned Voyager Group.
1987—Virgin Records forms subsidiaries in the U.S. and Japan.
—British Satellite Broadcasting (Virgin a minority partner) awarded satellite broadcasting license. (Virgin sells its shareholding in 1988.)
—Virgin acquires Mastertronics Group, distributor of Sega video games in Europe.
—Virgin Airship & Balloon Company launched to provide aerial marketing services.
1988—Recording studios opened in Barnes, London.
—New international record label, Virgin, launched.
—Virgin Broadcasting formed to further develop Virgin's radio and TV interests.
—Virgin Hotels formed.
—Virgin Megastores opened in Sydney, Paris, and Glasgow.
—Branson takes Virgin private with £248 million bid for outstanding shares.
1989—Virgin Music Group sells 25% stake to Fujisankei Communications for $150 million.
—Virgin Vision (video distribution) sold to MCEG of Los Angeles for $83 million.
1990—Virgin Retail Group and Marui form joint venture company to operate Megastores in Japan.
—Virgin Lightships formed to develop helium airships for advertising.

1991—W. H. Allen plc acquired. Merged with Virgin Books to form Virgin Publishing.
—Sale of Virgin Mastertronic to Sega. Remaining part of the business becomes Virgin Games.
—Virgin Retail Group forms 50:50 joint venture with W. H. Smith to develop U.K. retail business.
1992—Sale of Virgin Music Group to Thorn EMI plc.
—Joint venture with Blockbuster to develop Megastores in Europe, Australia, and U.S.
—Virgin Communications gains license for Britain's first national commercial rock station (Virgin 1215AM goes on the air in April 1993).
—Virgin acquires Euro-Magnetic Products, distributor of personal computer consumables.
—Vintage Airtours established to fly Orlando-Florida Keys in vintage DC-3s.
1993—Virgin Games floated as Virgin Interactive Entertainment plc with Hasbro and Blockbuster taking minority equity stakes.
—Virgin Euromagnetics launches a range of personal computers.
1994—Virgin Cola Company formed as joint venture with Cott Corp.
—Agreement with W. Grant to launch Virgin Vodka.
—Virgin acquires W. H. Smith's 75% stake in Our Price retail music stores.
—Virgin Retail Group forms joint ventures to develop Megastores in Hong Kong and South Korea.
—Virgin City Jet service launched between Dublin and London City Airport.
1995—Virgin Direct Personal Financial Service is launched as a joint venture with Norwich Union (whose stake is later acquired by Australian Mutual Provident).
—Acquisition of MGM Cinemas, U.K.'s biggest movie theater chain, to create Virgin Cinemas.
1996—Virgin Travel Group acquires Euro-Belgian Airlines to form Virgin Express.
—V2 record label and music publishing company launched.
—London & Continental Railways (in which Virgin a major shareholder) wins £3 bn contract to build the Channel Tunnel Rail Link and operate Eurostar rail services.
1997—Virgin Rail awarded franchise to operate the West Coast train services.
—Virgin Net, an internet service provider, formed with NTL.
—Branson acquires a 15% stake in the London Broncos rugby league team.
—Victory Corporation, a joint venture with Rory McCarthy, launches the Virgin Clothing and Virgin Vie toiletry products.
—Majority share in Virgin Radio sold to Chris Evans's Ginger Media Group.
—Virgin Bride retail chain formed.
—Virgin One telephone bank account and "one-stop integrated financial service" launched in collaboration with Royal Bank of Scotland.
1998—Virgin Entertainment acquires W. H. Smith's 75% stake in Virgin/Our Price.
—Virgin Cola launches in the U.S.
1999—Virgin sells its U.K. cinema chain to UGC for £215 million.
—Virgin launches mobile phone service in joint venture with Deutsche Telecom's One-to-One (November).
—49% of Virgin Atlantic sold to Singapore Airlines for £600 million.
—Restructuring and relaunch of loss-making Our Price record stores.
2000—Virgin Mobile launches U.S. wireless phone service in joint venture with Sprint. Virgin Mobile Australia (a joint venture with Cable & Wireless) launched.
—Virgin Net, Virgin's portal and ISP venture, closes its content division.

—Virgin announces the closing of its clothing company (February).
—Virgin Cars, online sales of new cars, launched.
—Virgin and Bear Stearns form Lynx New Media, a $130 million venture capital fund.
—Inaugural flight of Virgin Blue, Virgin's low-cost Australian airline.
—Branson knighted by the Queen: becomes Sir Richard Branson.
—Virgin fails to win franchise to run Britain's government-owned National Lottery.

2001—50% of Virgin Blue sold to Patrick Corporation for A$138 million.
—Virgin expands into Singapore and SE Asia with joint ventures with local companies in radio stations, cosmetic retailing, and wireless phone services.
—Virgin.net merges its ISP and portal businesses.
—16 French Virgin Megastores sold to Lagardere Media for €150 million.

2002—Virgin Bikes (U.K.) begins direct sale of new motorcycles at discount prices.
—Virgin Mobile offers wireless telecom services in the U.S.

2003—Virgin Blue initial public offering; Virgin retains 25% of equity.

2004—50% stake of Virgin Money repurchased from AMP for £90 million.
—Virgin Digital launched. Offers online music store and digital music download capabilities.
—Virgin Cars and Virgin Bikes sold to MotorSolutions Ltd of the U.K. for an undisclosed amount.

2005—Virgin Mobile launched in Canada.
—Virgin Atlantic increases services to Shanghai and begins flights to Beijing.
—Virgin Atlantic introduces self-service check-in for all passengers.

2006—Launch of Virgin Atlantic credit card.
—NTL acquires Virgin Mobile.
—Virgin Mobile and Virgin Money launched in South Africa.

Source: www.virgin.com.

Notes

1 "Behind Branson," *The Economist,* February 21, 1998, pp. 63–6.
2 "The Future for Virgin," *Financial Times,* August 13, 1998, pp. 24–5.
3 Richard Branson, letter to *The Economist,* March 7, 1998, p. 6.
4 Branson is one of Britain's richest individuals, with a net worth exceeding $2 billion. Branson also spent a night in Dover police cells when arrested for tax offenses after he sold through his Virgin store a batch of Virgin records intended for export. The case was settled out of court.
5 "The Virgin Brand," www.virgin.com/aboutvirgin/howitallworks/, accessed October 23, 2009.
6 P. Robison, "Briton Hopes Beverage will Conquer Coke's Monopoly," *Bloomberg News,* December 14, 1997.
7 M. Wells, "Red Baron," *Fortune,* July 3, 2000.
8 R. Dick, *The House that Branson Built: Virgin's Entry into the New Millennium,* INSEAD Fontainebleau, France, 2000.
9 R. Dick, *The House that Branson Built: Virgin's Entry into the New Millennium,* INSEAD, Fontainebleau, France, 2000.
10 C. Blackhurst, "At the Court of King Richard," *Management Today,* May 1998, pp. 40–5.
11 "Consolidating and Protecting the Licensed Virgin Brand," www.cscorporatedomains.com/ downloads/IPScan_issue1 0_virgin.pdf, accessed March 3, 2007.
12 "Will Whitehorn: Galactico of the Airways," *Independent,* November 27, 2006.

Case 21 Google Inc.: Running Amuck?

July 2009

Google's announcement on July 7, 2009 that it would be adding a computer operating system to its Chrome internet browser set off shock waves through the IT community. The much-heralded battle between Google and Microsoft for dominance of cyberspace had taken a major step closer. This emerging "Battle of the Titans" was a gift for news editors. Stock analysts were less impressed; they were awaiting the announcement of Google's second quarter financial results on July 15. Their key concern was that Google's many ambitious new initiatives were adding cost and distracting management at a time when advertising revenues were being squeezed by the economic downturn. Chris O'Brien of the San Jose Mercury summed up the feelings of many in a blog entitled "Google's growing identity crisis":

> There are a handful of reasons people generally cite for Google's success. The power of its search engine algorithm. The elegance of a business model that matches text ads to searches. A restless, innovative culture continually striving to improve and evolve its products.
>
> Here's what always struck me about Google: its simplicity. At the start, Google did one thing phenomenally well. Its search engine was so superior that the company's name became synonymous with search itself. And its home page was, and remains, a visual model of simplicity: a sea of white space, the Google logo, a search box, a couple of links—and no ads.
>
> The homepage aside, though, Google increasingly feels like a company running in a thousand directions at once. Over the past year, it has released a steady stream of high-profile products that seem to have little or no relation to the core identity expressed on its corporate homepage: "Google's mission is to organize the world's information and make it universally accessible and useful." The problem is that in expanding into so many different areas—productivity applications, mobile operating system, a Web browser—that the identity of Google itself has become muddled. No doubt, this all follows some clear logic from inside the Googleplex. But from the outside, it's getting harder every day to articulate what Google is. Is it a Web company? A software company? Something else entirely?[1]

For Sergey Brin, one of Google's co-founders, the growing breadth of Google's empire was a source of pride:

> Every minute, 15 hours worth of video are uploaded to YouTube . . . Today we are able to search the full text of almost 10 million books. While digitizing all the world's books is an ambitious goal, digitizing the world is even more challenging. Beginning with our acquisition of Keyhole (the basis of Google Earth) in October 2004, it has been our goal to provide high-quality information for geographical needs . . . Last year, AdSense (our publisher-facing program) generated more than $5 billion dollars of revenue for our many publishing partners . . . In addition to Gmail and Google Docs, the Google Apps suite of products now includes Spreadsheets, Calendar, Sites, and more . . . Google Translate supports automatic machine translation between 1640 language pairs . . .[2]

The concern of many stock analysts was that most of Google's diversifying initiatives did nothing to boost revenue, let alone generate profit. The *Financial Times*' Lex column dubbed Google a "one-trick pony": "Google has what amounts to a license to print money. By inserting itself between the shops and shoppers of the world, the search provider takes a small commission every time it connects the two." Beyond its core search business, Google's activities only added cost:

> [J]ust look at YouTube, the video-sharing website Google bought for $1.8bn—paid mostly in stock—in 2006. The site supplies about 40 per cent of all videos watched online worldwide for free. That generosity comes at tremendous cost, as very few of its videos carry advertising. Credit Suisse estimates YouTube's running costs will be between $500m and $1bn this year, while revenues will only be in the region of $240m. Even with the addition of more professionally created content, the economics appear unsustainable.[3]

TABLE 21.1 Google Inc.: Key financial data

	2004	2005	2006	2007	2008
Income data:					
Revenues	3189	6139	10605	16594	21796
Costs and expenses:					
Cost of revenues	1469	2577	4225	6649	8622
Research and development	395	600	1229	2120	2793
Sales and marketing	296	468	850	1461	1946
General and administrative	188	387	752	1279	1803
Total costs and expenses	2549	4121	7055	11510	15164
Income from operations	640	2017	3550	5084	6632
Interest income and other, net	10	124	461	590	316
Income before income taxes	650	2142	4011	5674	5854
Net income	399	1465	3077	4204	4227
Balance sheet data:					
Cash and marketable securities	2132	8034	11243	14218	15845
Long-term liabilities	43	107	128,	610	1226
Total stockholders' equity	2929	9418	17039	22689	28238

Source: Google, 10-K Report, 2008.

With Google's revenue growth hit by the 2008 recession while its costs continued to rise rapidly, some investors believed that it was time to rein in Google's chaotic expansion and develop a more focused strategy founded upon a clear recognition that the basis of Google's business model was the advertising revenues that flowed through which its dominance of internet word searches. Table 21.1 shows financial data for Google.

Google's Founding

Google was created by Larry Page and Sergey Brin, PhD students at Stanford University. In January 1996, Page's search for a dissertation topic led him to examine the linkage structure of the World Wide Web. Page and Brin developed a page-ranking algorithm that used backlink data (references by a Web page to other Web pages) to measure the importance of any Web page. Although several rudimentary Web search engines were in existence, most selected Web pages on the basis of the frequency with which a particular search word appeared. They called their search engine "Google" and on September 15, 1997 registered the domain name google.com. They incorporated Google Inc., on September 7, 1998 in Menlo Park, California. Google's "PageRank" algorithm was granted a patent on September 4, 2001.

Google met an essential need of the rapidly growing number of people who were turning to the World Wide Web for information and commercial transactions. As the number of web sites grew exponentially, locating relevant web content became a critical need. Page and Brin were not alone in recognizing the potential for a search engine. Among the early crawler-based Web search engines were WebCrawler, Lycos, Excite, Infoseek, Inktomi, Northern Light, and AltaVista. Several of these search engines became popular "portal sites"—web sites that offered users their first port of entry to the Web. Given that the primary purpose of a portal was to guide users to the information and commercial services offered by the web, other portal sites soon recognized the need to offer a search facility. Yahoo! licensed AltaVista's search engine, then in 1998 replaced AltaVista with Inktomi.

The Google search engine attracted a rapidly growing following because of its superior page ranking and its simple design—it did not compromise its search functionality by attempting to become a portal. In 2000, Google began selling advertisements—paid web links associated with search keywords. These "sponsored links" were brief, plain text ads with a click-on URL, which appeared alongside with Web search results for specific keywords. Advertisers bid for keywords; it was these "cost-per-click" bids weighted by an ad's click-through rate (CTR) that determined the order in which a sponsored links would appear. In offering a Web-based advertising system linking third-party advertisers to a search engine of informational web site, Google's system copied many of the features of the then market leader, Overture. After 2000, Google experienced explosive growth and was boosted in May 2002 by AOL's decision to adopt Google's search engine and its paid listings service.

Page and Brin's initial funding was a $100 000 contribution from Andy Bechtolsheim, co-founder of Sun Microsystems. In June 1999, larger funding was obtained from venture capital firms Kleiner Perkins Caufield & Byers and Sequoia Capital. On August 19, 2004 an initial public offering of about 7% of Google's shares raised $1.67 billion, giving Google a market capitalization of $23 billion.

Google's Expansion, 2004–9

The financial boost provided by Google's IPO fueled even more rapid development of its business. In its core Web search business, Google was continually seeking to improve users' search experiences while finding ways to better monetize its dominance of web search through advertising. However, the most striking feature of Google's development was its determination to grow beyond its core web search business. This expansionist urge reflected the company's *raison d'être*: it had never seen itself just as a supplier of an internet search engine, its declared mission was ". . . to organize the world's information and make it universally accessible and useful." Google's IPO prospectus had elaborated this intent:

> We serve our users by developing products that enable people to more quickly and easily find, create and organize information. We place a premium on products that matter to many people and have the potential to improve their lives, especially in areas in which our expertise enables us to excel.
>
> Search is one such area. People use search frequently and the results are often of great importance to them. For example, people search for information on medical conditions, purchase decisions, technical questions, long-lost friends and other topics about which they care a great deal. Delivering quality search results requires significant computing power, advanced software and complex processes—areas in which we have expertise and a high level of focus.[4]

Google's quest to meet the information needs of society caused it to continually seek opportunities for accessing new information and provide it through additional media channels. As Exhibit 21.1 shows, Google's quest to provide accessibility to the

EXHIBIT 21.2

Google Timeline

January 1996. Larry Page and Sergey Brin begin collaborating on a search engine called BackRub.

September 1998. Google Inc. establishes operations in a friend's garage in Menlo Park, California and hires its first employee.

June 1999. Google obtains $25 million in venture capital funding. Google moves to its new Googleplex headquarters in Mountain View, California.

September 1999. Google.com officially launched.

2000. Continued enhancements to Google including the Google Directory, the ability to search via wireless devices and the first 10 non-English language versions Google officially becomes the world's largest search engine. Google introduces AdWords, a self-service ad program that could be activated online. Introduction of the Google Toolbar allowing users to perform a Google search without visiting the Google homepage.

February 2001. Acquires the assets of Deja.com and begins organizing its huge Usenet archive into a searchable format.

August 2001. Dr Eric Schmidt, former CEO of Novell and CTO of Sun Microsystems, becomes CEO of Google.

September 2001. Google becomes profitable.

December 2001. Launch of Google Image Search and Google Catalog Search (allowed more than 1100 mail order catalogs to be searched). Year-end Google Zeitgeist summarizes search patterns, trends, and top search terms of 2001.

February 2002. Introduction of the Google Search Appliance allowing search to be extended beyond firewalls to company intranets, e-commerce sites, and university networks. Google Compute allows available processing on users' computers to help solve computation-intensive scientific problems.

May 2002. AOL selects Google to provide search and advertising to its 34 million members.

September 2002. Google News launched: access to 4500 leading news sources worldwide.

December 2002. Froogle, a product search service launched.

April 2003. Acquisition of Applied Semantics; launch of Google AdSense: generates revenue through placement of highly targeted ads adjacent to their content.

January 2004. Local Search allows geographically focused web search and personalized search on Google Labs, enabling users to specify their interests and customize their search results.

April 2004. Launch of Gmail, a web-based mail service. Gmail designed to deliver relevant ads adjacent to mail messages.

July 2004. Acquires Picasa, Inc., a digital photo management company that helps users to organize, manage and share their digital photos.

August 2004. Initial public offering of GOOG on NASDAQ through a Dutch auction process.

October 2004. Release of Google Desktop Search. Also Google SMS launched: instant, accurate answers to queries through text messaging, using a cell phone or handheld device. Acquisition of Keyhole Corp., a digital and satellite image mapping company.

November 2004. Google index of Web pages numbers 8 billion.

December 2004. Launch of Google Groups: allows users to create and manage their own email groups and discussion lists. Google Book Search begins scanning of books from many of the world's leading libraries.

January 2005. Launch of Google Mini, search tool for small and medium-sized businesses. Launch of Google Maps providing map views and satellite views.

June 2005. Google Labs offers Personalized Homepages. Launch of Google Earth.

August 2005. Launch of Google Talk: free internet telephony.

September 2005. Release of Google Blog Search.

October 2005. Launch of Google Reader combines blog, Web page and news sources onto a single screen.

November 2005, Launch of Google Base to upload content in a structured format that searchers can then find. Google Analytics replaces "Urchin" as an online advertising management tool.

January 2006. Google Video Store offers range of content using a new Google Video Player. Google domain in China announced.

February 2006. Google Chat: integrates email and instant messaging within a Web browser. Updated version of Google Desktop released. Google Page Creator facilitates simple design and creation of Web pages.

March 2006. Debut of Google Finance: financial and business information.

April 2006. Release of Google Calendar for easy accessing and sharing of personal calendars.

June 2006. AdWords launches click-to-play Video Ads. Launch too of Google Checkout to provide a faster, safer and more convenient online shopping. Google Maps available to businesses for embedding in their own web sites.

August 2006. Agreement with Fox to access their newly acquired MySpace. SketchUp acquired. Partners with EarthLink in a proposal for free WiFi for the city of San Francisco.

November 2006. Google Apps for Education expands offer of Google services to teachers and students. Google for Educators, a new outreach program offers elementary teachers Google Certification through the Google Teacher Academy,

October 2006. Acquisition of YouTube. Release Web-based applications Docs and Spreadsheets. Acquisition of Jobspot, a collaborative wiki platform, which later becomes Google Sites.

December 2006. Release of Patent Search indexing more than 7 million U.S. patents.

January 2007. Partnership with China Mobile announced.

February 2007. Acquisition of Adscape, producer of in-game advertising producer.

April 2007. Acquisition of DoubleClick. Froogle changed to Google Product Search. Acquisition of Zenter, software to create and share online presentations. Acquisition of TiSP, a home broadband service.

May 2007. First steps towards universal search—integrated search of video, news, books, images and local results.

June 2007. Acquisition of Feedburner, provides tools for sitefeed management and analysis.

September 2007. AdSense for Mobile introduced. Presently, a new application for making slide presentations, added to Google Docs.

November 2007. Android, the first open platform for mobile devices, and a collaboration with other companies in the Open Handset Alliance, announced. Google.org announces REC for supporting low cost electricity from renewable sources.

January 2008. Google bids in the 700MHz spectrum auction.

February 2008. Launch of Google Sites (based upon the acquisition JotSpot), allows creation of collaborative web sites with embedded videos, documents, and calendars.

March 2008. Completion of acquisition of DoubleClick.

May 2008. Release of Google Health—allows secure online collection, storage and management of individuals' medical records and health information.

June 2008. Google Finance offers real-time stock quotes. Launch of Google Site Search—site owners can enable Google-powered searches on their own web sites.

September 2008. Announcement of Chrome, new open source web browser. T-Mobile announces the G1, the first phone built on the Android operating system.

February 2009. Google Latitude mobile devices allows sharing your location.

March 2009. Launch of Google Ventures, a venture capital fund to support innovation and new technology.

May 2009. Launch of Sky Map for Android: allows identification of stars and planets via Android phone.

world's information had taken it into new communication media (notably wireless telephony, but also radio, TV and video games) and sources of information beyond third-party web sites.[5] These new sources of information included images (Google Image Search), maps (Google Maps), academic articles (Google Scholar), books (Google Book Search), satellite imagery (Google Earth), news (Google News), patents (Google Patent Search), video (Google Video; YouTube), finance (Google Finance), and Web logs (Google Blog Search).

However, Google's entrepreneurial and technological dynamism also resulted in initiatives that extended beyond the accessing and organizing of information. Since the introduction of Gmail in 2004, Google offered a widening array of software and services for communicating, creating and manipulating 2D and 3D images, producing documents, creating Web pages, managing time and social networking. For example: Google Docs is a suite of software for creating, storing and sharing text documents, spreadsheets, and presentations; Blogger is software that allows individuals to create their own Web logs; Google Groups allows individuals to establish and support communication within a group formed around a particular interest or identity; Orkut is a social networking service; Picasa is downloadable software for organizing, editing and sharing photographs. The Appendix describes Google's products and services.

Most of these additional products and services offered no new revenue opportunities for Google. However, Google was also expanding its advertising-based revenue model. Google's primary source of advertising revenue is AdWords launched in 2000. Advertisers specify the words that should trigger their ads and the maximum amount they are willing to pay per click. When a user searches google.com, short text

TABLE 21.2 Google's revenues ($ millions)

	2006	2007	2008
Advertising Revenues			
Google web sites	6332.8	10624.7	14413.8
Google Network web sites	4159.8	5787.9	6714.7
Total advertising revenues	10492.6	16412.6	21128.5
Licensing and other revenues	112.3	181.4	667.1
Total revenues	10604.9	16594.0	21795.6

Source: Google Inc., 10-K Report 2008.

advertisements appear as "sponsored links" on the right side of the screen. AdWords also places advertisement on third party web sites through the Google Partner Network.

AdSense uses an advertisement placement technology developed by Applied Semantics which Google acquired in 2003. It allows Google to place ads on third party web sites. In 2008, 32% of Google's advertising revenue was derived from partners' web sites, and 68% from its own web sites.

The Appendix explains AdWords and AdSense in greater detail. Table 21.2 shows Google's revenues from advertising.

In 2007 and 2008, Google's diversification efforts took a dramatic new turn with Google's entry into mobile telephony and Web browsers.

Android and Mobile Telephony

In November 2007, Google, in collaboration with its partners in the Open Handset Alliance, announced its Android wireless communication software platform. *PC Advisor* commented:

> Google's announcement of the Android mobile development platform . . . is yet another example of the lengths the company will go to keep its advertising business growing at a jaw-dropping rate. It is also another awe-inspiring—or terrifying, depending on one's perspective—display of the engineering and business resources Google can unleash and of the power it has to influence, disrupt and rearrange markets . . .
>
> "What we have here is Google trying to move the whole mobile internet forward through this alliance," said industry analyst Greg Sterling of Sterling Market Intelligence.
>
> In a nutshell, Google announced a free, open-source application development platform called Android for mobile devices with the intention of eclipsing existing operating systems from Microsoft, Symbian, Palm and others . . .
>
> Android will have a complete set of components, including a Linux-based operating system, middleware stack, customizable user interface and applications.
>
> Google envisions that with Android, developers will flood the mobile market with new applications and online services that can be written once and deployed in many phones, something that, as Google sees it, the current mobile technical fragmentation prevents.
>
> The goal: to radically improve the creation, delivery and provision of mobile online services and applications, in the hope that as people find the experience more satisfying, their mobile web and internet usage will balloon, along with online ad revenue . . .
>
> Ultimately, what is propelling Google in this effort is its core advertising business, which the company recognizes it must extend to the mobile market. A small market today, mobile advertising is expected to attain a significant size in coming years. According to Opus Research, mobile advertising spending in North America and Western Europe will reach a combined $5.08bn by 2012, up from an estimated $106.8m at the end of this year. This represents a compound annual growth rate of 116%. Opus Research, which released the forecast last week, said that improving the mobile user experience will prompt more people to spend more time using the internet via their mobile phones. This in turn will fuel ad revenue growth.

> In the end, independently of what ends up happening, Google's entry into the mobile market is a welcome development, Dulaney said. "We need powerful players from the 'wired' internet market to get into the mobile space to break up the tight control carriers have had on content," Dulaney said. "So far, carriers have controlled all the content and they've been bad at it. Innovation has been stifled."[6]

A few weeks later Google announced its intention of bidding in the Federal Communication Commission's upcoming auction of 700MHz wireless spectrum. The interesting feature of Google's bid was that it had no desire to win the auction. Its intention was to force the major telecom service providers into the auction so that a new section of the wireless spectrum would be developed for the wireless internet service. Google lobbying had already ensured that whoever developed this portion of spectrum would be required to allow users to download any software application they wanted on their mobile device and to use any mobile devices they liked on that wireless network. In January 2008, the FCC announced that AT&T and Verizon had won the auction bidding a total of $16 billion. Many observers believed that the real winner was Google: while AT&T and Verizon would bear the costs of developing the 700MHz waveband, Google would be able to offer its Android system and mobile internet services without any of the upfront costs.[7]

Chrome

Google's announcement of its Chrome Web browser on September 2, 2008, generated huge publicity, but little surprise. It was widely known that founders Brin and Page had wanted to launch a Web browser since Google's early days. For several years Google had been the main source of technical and financial support for Mozilla's Firefox browser. According to the Google's head of product development, Sundar Pichai: "Google's entire business is people using a browser to access us and the web." Google's explanation of its decision to launch its own browser emphasized the improved functionality for users: "Google Chrome is a browser that combines a minimal design with sophisticated technology to make the web faster, safer, and easier," claimed Google's web site. Microsoft's internet Explorer by contrast was limited by the legacy of its 15 year history, which meant that it was optimized for JavaScript or Web 2.0.

However, most observers believed that Google's strategic intent was not simply a superior user experience. An additional motive imputed to Google was its desire to protect the threat posed by the new version of Microsoft's internet Explorer (IE). Version 8 of IE launched in beta mode in August 2008 allowed an "InPrivate" protection mode that would delete cookies and make it more difficult to track users' browsing habits. The result would be to limit Google's ability to use such information for targeted advertising.

Others believed that Google's primary intention was not so much to protect itself against Microsoft as to launch a direct attack upon Microsoft's dominance of personal computing and to speed the transition of computing to a new online environment:

> [Google Chrome] is an explicit attempt to accelerate the movement of computing off the desktop and into the cloud—where Google holds advantage.

And it's an aggressive move destined to put the company even more squarely in the crosshairs of its rival Microsoft.[8]

The announcement 10 months later that Google would add an operating system to its Chrome browser was seen as confirmation that the primary motivation of Chrome was to strike against the core of Microsoft's market strength.

Google's Management and Capabilities

Google's phenomenal growth and capacity for innovation rested upon a management system that was unique, even by the unorthodox standards of Silicon Valley. In his book, *The Future of Management*, Gary Hamel identified several key features of the management system built by founders Larry Page (President of Products) and Sergey Brin (President of Technology), and their "adult supervisor" Eric Schmidt (Chairman and CEO):

1. *Hiring policy*. Google only employs people who it believes to be exceptionally talented: "Google's leaders believe that one exceptional technologist is many times more valuable than one average engineer; hence they insist on hiring only the brightest of the bright—folks out on the right-hand end of the bell-shaped curve. They also believe that if you let one 'bozo' in, more will surely follow. Their logic is simple: A-level people want to work with A-level people—fellow savants who will spark their thinking and accelerate their learning. Trouble is, B-level people are threatened by A-class talent, so once they get in the door, they tend to hire colleagues who are as unremarkable as they are."

2. *A "dramatically flat, radically decentralized" organization:* "In many ways, Google is organized like the internet itself: it's highly democratic, tightly connected, and flat. Like so much of Google's culture, the source of the company's radical decentralization can be traced back to Brin and Page, both of whom attended Montessori schools and credit much of their intellectual independence to that experience. Says Mayer: 'They don't like authority and they don't like being told what to do.' Brin and Page understand that breakthroughs come from questioning assumptions and smashing paradigms."

3. *Small, self-managing teams:* "Roughly half of Google's 10 000 employees—all those involved in product development—work in small teams, with an average of three engineers per team. Even a large project such as Gmail, which might occupy 30 people, is broken into teams of three or four, each of which works on a specific service enhancement, such as building spam filters or improving the forwarding feature. Each team has an 'über-tech leader,' a responsibility that rotates among team members depending on shifting project requirements. Most engineers work on more than one team, and no one needs the HR department's permission to switch teams."

4. *Rapid, low-cost experimentation.* "Evolutionary adaptation isn't the product of a grand plan, but of relentless experimentation . . . Google's 'just-try-it' philosophy is applied to even the company's most daunting projects, like digitizing the world's libraries. Like every new initiative, Google Book Search

began with a makeshift experiment aimed at answering a critical question; in this case: how long does it take to digitize a book? To find out, Page and Mayer rigged up a piece of plywood with a couple of clamps and proceeded to photograph each page of a 300-page book, using a metronome to keep pace. With Mayer flipping pages, and one half of Google's founding team taking digital snapshots, it took 40 minutes to turn the ink into pixels. An optical character recognition program soon turned the digital photos into digital text, and within five days the pair had ginned up a piece of software that could search the book. That kind of step-wise, learn-as-you-go approach has repeatedly helped Google to test critical assumptions and avoid making bet-the-farm mistakes."[9]

The result was a constant impetus towards creativity, innovation, and entrepreneurial initiative. Indeed, given the caliber and characteristics of Google's employees, it was difficult to see how Google could not be a hotbed for innovation:

> Our employees, who have named themselves Googlers, are everything. Google is organized around the ability to attract and leverage the talent of exceptional technologists and business people. We have been lucky to recruit many creative, principled and hard working stars. We hope to recruit many more in the future. We will reward and treat them well . . . Because of our employee talent, Google is doing exciting work in nearly every area of computer science . . . Talented people are attracted to Google because we empower them to change the world; Google has large computational resources and distribution that enables individuals to make a difference. Our main benefit is a workplace with important projects, where employees can contribute and grow . . . [10]

The culture of creativity and innovation was institutionalized through Google's "70-20-10" rule which stipulated that Google would devote 70% of its engineering resources to developing the core business, 20% to extend that core into related areas, with 10% allocated to fringe ideas.

Underlying Google's capacity for innovation and the effective implementation of new initiatives was a set of resources that few other technology-based companies could match. With an operating cash flow of $7.9 billion in 2008 and a cash pile of $15.8 billion, Google was a financial powerhouse matched only by Microsoft, IBM, HP, and Apple. This financial strength allowed Google to buy its way through acquisition into almost any market or area of technology. Most of the time Google did not need buy its way into new market: like Apple, its brand (valued by Interbrand in 2008 at $25 billion—the world's tenth most valuable) offered it instant credibility. Most important was a user base unmatched by any other IT company. With 776 million unique visitors to its web site every day, it reached an estimated 77% of the world's internet audience daily.

Future Challenges

For all Google's vitality and its manifest destiny to lead the next generation of information technology, there were those—both within Googleplex and outside—who perceived danger in Google's trajectory. Despite a slowing during 2008, Google was expanding rapidly. Between 2003 and 2007 its revenues had grown from $1.5 billion to $21.8 billion and employees from 1628 to 20 222.[11] Coordination was a growing problem; while the majority of Google's employees were concentrated at its Mountain View, California, headquarters, Google had additional research and development and sales and support offices in 18 other cities throughout the U.S., as well as facilities in Argentina, Austria, Australia, Belgium, Brazil, Canada, China, Czech Republic, Denmark, Egypt, England, Finland, France, Germany, Hungary, India, Ireland, Israel, Italy, Japan, Korea, Mexico, New Zealand, Norway, Poland, Russia, Singapore, Spain, Sweden, Switzerland, Taiwan, Turkey and United Arab Emirates.[12]

Growing size and complexity were recognized by Google as significant sources of risk:

> We have experienced rapid growth in our headcount and operations, which has placed, and will continue to place, significant demands on our management, operational and financial infrastructure. If we do not effectively manage our growth, the quality of our products and services could suffer, which could negatively affect our brand and operating results. Our expansion and growth in international markets heightens these risks as a result of the particular challenges of supporting a rapidly growing business in an environment of multiple languages, cultures, customs, legal systems, alternative dispute systems, regulatory systems and commercial infrastructures. To effectively manage this growth, we will need to continue to improve our operational, financial and management controls and our reporting systems and procedures.[13]

As Google increasingly displaced Microsoft as the world's pre-eminent IT company, it would be a target for criticism and regulatory pressures. Under the headline "Is Google Too Powerful?," the potential for Google to dominate the Web and media advertising was noted by *Business Week* early in 2007:

> . . . Google has come to represent all our hopes, dreams, and fears about the disruptive promise and dangers of the internet. As this clash plays out over the next couple of years, the outcome could determine the way we'll entertain ourselves, shop, socialize, and do business on the internet. The overriding question: Will the vast commercial landscape of the Net, like so many other tech markets in the past, condense to one dominant force for the foreseeable future? Will we just Google everything?[14]

By 2009, the dominant concern was less about market power in a traditional sense and more about the sheer mass of personal data that Google had access to. Google's cookies allow it to track every Google user's web browsing. Its online map service, "Street View," allows views inside individuals' home properties and the observation of visitors to those homes. Gmail allows Google an intimate view of personal communications of Gmail's 30 million account holders.

These growing concerns about privacy and market power would impose additional pressures on Google's top management team. Had the time come for Google's leading trio—Brin, Page, and Schmidt—to scale back Google's ambitions and draw boundaries around Google's corporate strategy?

Appendix: Description of Google's business and products (extracts from Google, 10-K Report for 2008)

Overview

Google is a global technology leader focused on improving the ways people connect with information. Our innovations in web search and advertising have made our web site a top internet property and our brand one of the most recognized in the world. We maintain a large index of web sites and other online content, which we make freely available via our search engine to anyone with an internet connection. Our automated search technology helps people obtain nearly instant access to relevant information from our vast online index.

We generate revenue primarily by delivering relevant, cost-effective online advertising. Businesses use our AdWords program to promote their products and services with targeted advertising. In addition, the thousands of third-party web sites that comprise the Google Network use our AdSense program to deliver relevant ads that generate revenue and enhance the user experience . . .

Our Mission

Our mission is to organize the world's information and make it universally accessible and useful. We believe that the most effective, and ultimately the most profitable, way to accomplish our mission is to put the needs of our users first. We have found that offering a high-quality user experience leads to increased traffic and strong word-of-mouth promotion. Our dedication to putting users first is reflected in three key commitments:

- We will do our best to provide the most relevant and useful search results possible, independent of financial incentives. Our search results will be objective and we do not accept payment for search result ranking or inclusion.
- We will do our best to provide the most relevant and useful advertising. Advertisements should not be an annoying interruption. If any element on a search result page is influenced by payment to us, we will make it clear to our users.
- We will never stop working to improve our user experience, our search technology and other important areas of information organization.

We believe that our user focus is the foundation of our success to date. We also believe that this focus is critical for the creation of long-term value. We do not intend to compromise our user focus for short-term economic gain.

How We Provide Value to Our Users

We serve our users by developing products that quickly and easily find, create, organize and share information. We place a premium on products that matter to many people and have the potential to improve their lives.

Some of the key benefits we offer include:

Comprehensiveness and Relevance Our search technologies sort through a vast and growing amount of information to deliver relevant and useful search results in response to user queries. This is an area of continual development for us. When we started the company in 1998, our Web index contained approximately 30 million documents. We now index billions of Web pages and strive to provide the most comprehensive search experience possible . . .

Objectivity We believe it is very important that the results users get from Google are produced with only their interests in mind. We do not accept payment for search result ranking or inclusion. We do accept fees for advertising, but the advertising is clearly marked and separated and does not influence how we generate our search results. This is similar to a newspaper, where the articles are independent of the advertising . . .

Global Access We strive to provide our services to everyone in the world and the Google interface is available in 120 languages . . .

Ease of Use We have always believed that the most useful and powerful search technology hides its complexity from users and gives them a simple, intuitive way to get the information they want. We have devoted significant efforts to create a streamlined and easy-to-use interface based on a clean search box set prominently on a page free of commercial clutter . . .

Pertinent, Useful Commercial Information The search for information often involves an interest in commercial information—researching a purchase, comparing products and services or actively shopping. We help people find commercial information through our search services and advertising products . . .

Multiple Access Platforms The mobile phone is the primary way that many people around the world access the internet. We have continued to invest in improving mobile search and have introduced applications that allow users to access search, email, maps, directions and satellite imagery through their mobile devices.

Improving the Web We want to make the Web experience as good as possible for users around the world. This includes providing platforms for developers to build, deploy and run increasingly rich applications. For users, we are investing in areas to improve their experience in using web-based applications, including making browsers more stable and powerful.

Products and Services for our Users

Our product development philosophy involves rapid and continuous innovation, with frequent releases of early-stage products that we then iterate and improve. We often make products available early in their development stages by posting them on Google Labs, at test locations online or directly on Google.com. If our users find a product useful, we promote it to "beta" status for additional testing. Once we are satisfied that a product is of high quality and utility, we remove the beta label and make it a core Google product. Our main products and services are described below:

Google.com—Search and Personalization We are focused on building products and services on our web sites that benefit our users and let them find relevant information quickly and easily. These products and services include:

Google Web Search In addition to providing easy access to billions of Web pages, we have integrated special features into Google Web Search to help people find exactly what they are looking for on the Web.

Google Image Search Google Image Search is our searchable index of images found across the web. To extend the usefulness of Google Image Search we offer advanced features, such as searching by image size, format and coloration and restricting searches to specific web sites or domains.

Google Book Search Google Book Search lets users search the full text of a library-sized collection of books to discover books of interest and to learn where to buy or borrow them . . .

Google Scholar Google Scholar provides a simple way to do a broad search for relevant scholarly literature including peer-reviewed papers, theses, books, abstracts and articles . . .

Google Finance Google Finance provides a simple user interface to navigate complex financial information in an intuitive manner . . .

Google News Google News gathers information from thousands of news sources worldwide and presents news stories in a searchable format within minutes of their publication on the Web . . .

Google Video Google Video lets users upload, find, view and share video content worldwide.

Google Blog Search Google Blog Search enables users to search the blogging universe more effectively and find out users' opinions on a wide variety of subjects. The Google Blog Search index includes every blog that publishes a site feed.

iGoogle and Personalized Search iGoogle connects users to the information that is most useful and important to them in an easy-to-use and customizable format . . .

Google Product Search Google Product Search helps users find and compare products from online stores across the web and directs users to where they can buy these products . . .

Google Custom Search Google Custom Search allows communities of users familiar with particular topics to build customized search engines . . .

Google Base Google Base lets content owners submit content that they want to share on Google web sites . . .

Google Webmaster Tools Google Webmaster Tools provides information to webmasters to help them enhance their understanding of how their web sites interact with the Google search engine . . .

Applications

Information created by a single user becomes much more valuable when shared and combined with information from other people or places. Therefore our strategy for products we develop in this space is simple: develop tools for our users to create, share and communicate any information generated by the user, thus making the information more useful and manageable. Examples of products we have developed with this strategy in mind include:

Google Docs

Google Docs allows our users to create, view and edit documents, spreadsheets, and presentations from anywhere using a browser . . .

Google Calendar

Google Calendar is a free online shareable calendar service that allows our users to keep track of the important events, appointments and special occasions in their lives and share this information with anyone they choose . . .

Gmail

Gmail is Google's free webmail service that comes with built-in Google search technology . . . We serve small text ads that are relevant to the messages in Gmail.

Google Groups

Google Groups is a free service that helps groups of people to connect to information and people that have interest in them. Users can discuss topics by posting messages to a group, where other people can then read and respond . . .

Google Reader

Google Reader is a free service that lets users subscribe to feeds and receive updates from multiple web sites in a single interface . . .

Orkut

Orkut enables users to search and connect to other users through networks of trusted friends. Users can create a profile, personal mailboxes, post photos and join or manage online communities.

Blogger

Blogger is a Web-based publishing tool that lets people publish to the Web instantly using weblogs, or "blogs."

Google Sites

Google Sites allows users to easily create, update and publish content online . . .

YouTube

YouTube is an online community that lets users worldwide upload, share, watch, rate, and comment on videos, from user generated, niche professional, to premium videos . . . YouTube offers a range of video and interactive formats for advertisers to reach their intended audience.

Client

Google Toolbar

Google Toolbar is a free application that adds a Google search box to web browsers (internet Explorer and Firefox) . . .

Google Chrome

Google Chrome is an open-source browser that combines a minimal design with technologies to make the web faster, safer, and easier to navigate.

Google Pack

Google Pack is a free collection of safe, useful software programs from Google and other companies that improve the user experience online and on the desktop . . .

Picasa

Picasa is a free service that allows users to view, manage and share their photos . . .

Google Desktop

Google Desktop lets people perform a full-text search on the contents of their own computer, including email, files, instant messenger chats and web browser history . . .

Google GEO—Maps, Earth and Local

Google Earth

Google Earth lets users see and explore the world and beyond from their desktop. Users can fly virtually to a specific location and learn about that area through detailed satellite and aerial images . . .

Google Maps

Google Maps helps people navigate map information . . .

Google Sketchup and Sketchup Pro

Google Sketchup is a free tool that enables users to model buildings in 3D . . . The Pro version of this tool is sold to professional designers and includes additional features.

Google Mobile and Android

Google Mobile

Google Mobile lets people search and view both the "mobile Web," consisting of pages created specifically for wireless devices, and the entire Google index. Users can also access online information using Google SMS by typing a query to the Google shortcode and checking their email using Gmail Mobile. Google Mobile is available through many wireless and mobile phone services worldwide.

Google Maps for Mobile

Google Maps for Mobile is a free Java client application that lets users view maps and satellite imagery, find local businesses and get driving directions on mobile devices.

Blogger for Mobile

With Blogger for mobile devices, users can take pictures with their camera phones and then post their pictures and text comments to their blog using MMS or email.

Google Gmail, News and Personalized Home for Mobile

Several of our services, such as Gmail, News and Personalized Home are also available as mobile applications.

GOOG-411

GOOG-411 is a free, speech-enabled application allowing users to call 1-800-GOOG-411 to search for businesses by name or category.

Android

Android is a free, open-source mobile software platform which allows developers to create applications for mobile devices and for handset manufacturers to install . . .

Search by Voice

Search by Voice lets users do a Google Web search just by saying what they are looking for . . .

Google Checkout

Google Checkout is a service for our users, advertisers and participating merchants that is intended to make online shopping faster, more convenient and more secure . . .

Google Labs

Google Labs is our test bed for our engineers and adventurous Google users . . .

The Technology Behind Search and Our User Products and Services

Our Web search technology uses a combination of techniques to determine the importance of a Web page independent of a particular search query and to determine the relevance of that page to a particular search query.

Ranking Technology

. . . PageRank is a query-independent technique for determining the importance of web pages by looking at the link structure of the Web.

Text-Matching Techniques

Our technology employs text-matching techniques that compare search queries with the content of web pages to help determine relevance . . . By combining query independent measures such as PageRank with our text-matching techniques, we are able to deliver search results that are relevant to what people are trying to find.

Infrastructure

We provide our products and services using our homegrown software and hardware infrastructure, which provides substantial computing resources at low cost. We currently use a combination of off-the-shelf and custom software running on clusters of commodity computers . . .

How We Provide Value to Our Advertisers and Content Owners

Google AdWords

For advertisers seeking to market their products and services to consumers and business users over the internet, we offer Google AdWords, an auction-based advertising program that lets advertisers deliver relevant ads targeted to search queries or Web content across Google sites and through the web sites of our Google network, which is the network of online and offline third parties that use our advertising programs to deliver relevant ads with their search results and content . . . AdWords is accessible to advertisers in 41 different interface languages.

Advertisers in our AdWords program create text-based or display ads, bid on the keywords that will trigger the display of their ads and set daily spending budgets. AdWords features an automated online signup process that lets advertisers quickly implement ad campaigns on Google properties and the web sites of our Google Network members. Ads are ranked for display in AdWords based on a combination of the maximum cost-per-click pricing set by the advertiser and click-through rates and other factors used to determine the relevance of the ads. This favors the ads that are most relevant to users, improving the experience both for the person looking for information and for the advertiser who is generating relevant ads . . .

Google AdSense We are enthusiastic about helping content owners monetize their content, which facilitates the creation of better content to search . . . Our Google AdSense program enables web sites that are part of the Google Network to deliver AdWords ads that are relevant to the search results or content on their pages. It also allows offline media companies, such as television and radio stations, to deliver ads and audio ads to the content they provide. We share most of the revenue generated from ads shown by a Google Network member with that member. The key benefits we offer to Google Network members include:

Access to Advertisers Many small web-site companies and content producers do not have the time or resources to develop effective programs for generating revenue from online advertising. Even larger sites, with dedicated sales teams, may find it difficult to generate revenue from pages with specialized content. Google AdSense promotes effective revenue generation by providing Google

Network members access to Google's base of advertisers and their broad collection of ads . . .

Improved User Satisfaction Many web sites are cluttered with intrusive or untargeted advertising that may distract or confuse users and may undermine users' ability to find the information they want . . . Our AdSense program extends our commitment to improving the overall Web experience by enabling web sites to display AdWords ads in a fashion that we believe people find useful rather than disruptive.

Better Storage, Management, Access and Visibility We have developed new storage, management and access technologies to allow content owners and producers to distribute and, if they wish, monetize more types of online and offline content . . .

Syndicated Search We provide our search technology to partners of all sizes, allowing Google search service to be offered through these partners' properties. For commercial partners, we provide an extensive range of customization options.

Display Advertising

Display advertising is internet advertising that typically includes static or animated images as well as interactive audio or video media, such as the banner ads you see on the tops or sides of many popular web sites. Our goal is to make it easy for anyone to use display advertising. We want advertisers to realize a better return on their display advertising campaigns and publishers to maximize the value of the content on their web sites by providing tools, platforms and channels for ad management and delivery.

We completed our acquisition of DoubleClick in March 2008 and are in the process of integrating DoubleClick's online ad serving and management services into Google's advertising solutions. DoubleClick provides Google with a platform for delivering display advertising. DoubleClick also provides services related to the delivery of display advertising, including media planning, buying, implementation and measurement tools for advertisers and agencies and forecasting and reporting tools for publishers. Through these tools we also provide publishers with access to agencies and advertisers to help them sell their advertising inventory and ways to streamline the ad sales process.

We also offer advertising solutions on YouTube in a range of video, static or animated images, and interactive formats.

The Technology Behind Google's Advertising Programs

Our AdWords and AdSense programs serve millions of relevant, targeted ads each day based on search terms people enter or content that they view on the Web. The key elements of our advertising technology include:

Google AdWords Auction System

The Google AdWords auction system lets advertisers automatically deliver relevant, targeted advertising. Every search query we process involves the automated execution of an auction, resulting in our advertising system often processing hundreds of millions of auctions per day. To determine whether an ad is relevant to a particular query, this system weighs an advertiser's willingness to pay for prominence in the ad listings (the cost-per-click or cost-per-impression bid) and interest from users in the ad as measured by the click-through rate and other factors . . . The AdWords auction system also incorporates the AdWords Discounter, which automatically lowers the amount advertisers actually pay to the minimum needed to maintain their ad position . . .

AdSense Contextual Advertising Technology

Our AdSense technology employs techniques that consider factors such as keyword analysis, word frequency and the overall link structure of the web to analyze the content of individual web pages and to match ads to them almost instantaneously . . . Our display advertising programs provide advertisers and publishers services related to the delivery of branded display advertising. The key elements of our display advertising technology include:

DoubleClick Advertiser Platform

The DoubleClick Advertiser Platform provides tools for media planning, buying, selling, ad delivery, measurement, and optimization . . .

YouTube

YouTube offers video ads solutions to advertisers that provide advertisers with a way to promote their content to the YouTube community as well as to associate themselves with content being watched by their target audience . . .

Google Enterprise

Schools and businesses are increasingly moving towards Web-based applications and away from licensed software. Since Web-based applications require minimal up-front investment, businesses can pay as they use them and download updates.

Google Apps

Google Apps provides hosted communication and collaboration tools for organizations such as businesses, schools and groups. Google Apps includes communication features such as Gmail, Google Calendar, Google Video, Google Sites, and Google Talk and collaboration features such as Google Docs. It is available on an organization's own domain . . .

Google Mini

The Google Mini is targeted at small-and medium-sized businesses who want to let employees and customers search designated documents, intranets and web sites.

Google Search Appliance

The Google Search Appliance is similar to the Google Mini except that it can handle more documents and offers more advanced features. Some advanced features of the Google Search Appliance include integration with advanced corporate security protocols, integration with other enterprise applications, such as content management systems, portals and other systems and real-time search of business applications . . .

Notes

1 "Google's Growing Identity Crisis": Chris O'Brien's blog, July19, 2009, www.mercurynews.com/ci_12853656?IADID, accessed July 20, 2009.
2 Quoted in D. Rowan, "Inside Google: The Man with All the Answers," *Wired,* August 2009, p. 77.
3 "Lex: Google the One-trick Pony," *Financial Times,* April 17, 2009.
4 Google Inc. SEC form 424B3, filed November 23, 2004.
5 At the March 2008 Federal Communications Commission's auctioning of licenses to "C-block" spectrum, Google was one of the bidders. Google was delighted to lose out to winning bids to AT&T and Verizon that together amounted to over $18 billion because the FCC had decreed that the new spectrum owners would be required to open their networks to third-party providers. Hence, Google would be free to offer its wireless service without the need to invest in infrastructure. See: "An Auction that Google was Content to Lose," *New York Times,* April 4, 2008, www.nytimes.com/2008/04/04/technology/04auction.html?_r=1&oref=slogin, accessed October 23, 2009.
6 "Analysis: Google's Android Mobile Strategy Explained," *PCAdvisor,* November 6, 2007, www.pcadvisor.co.uk/news/index.cfm?newsid=11248, accessed July 21, 2009.
7 "Wireless Auction: Google Likely Out, and Happy," *Forbes,* February 6, 2008.
8 "Inside Chrome: The Secret Project to Crush IE and Remake the Web," *Wired Magazine,* October 16, 2008.
9 G. Hamel, *The Future of Management,* Harvard Business School Press, Boston MA, 2007.
10 Letter from the Founders, "An Owner's Manual" for Google's Shareholders, http://investor.google.com/ipo_letter.html, accessed 30 March, 2008.
11 These consisted of 7254 in R&D, 8002 in sales and marketing, 3109 in general and administrative and 1857 in operations.
12 Google Inc., 10-K Report to the SEC for 2007, p. 33.
13 Google Inc., 10-K Report to the SEC for 2008, p. 20.
14 "Is Google Too Powerful?" *Business Week,* April 9, 2007.

Case 22 Bank of America's Acquisition of Merrill Lynch

December 2008

On the afternoon of Monday December 22, 2008, Ken Lewis, Chairman and CEO of Bank of America Corporation, was preparing for a special meeting of Bank of America's board of directors, which would be held by telephone at 4 p.m.

The meeting was critical to the future of Bank of America and to the future careers of Lewis and his top management team. The meeting offered the board its final opportunity to pull the plug on its acquisition of Merrill Lynch & Company, which was to be consummated in ten days' time (January 1, 2009).

The acquisition, announced on September 15, 2008 (see Exhibit 22.1 for the press release), would create America's biggest financial services company in terms of total assets. It was the culmination of a quarter of a century of almost continuous acquisition by the Charlotte, North Carolina, banking corporation. Under Hugh McColl, its CEO from 1983 to 2001, North Carolina National Bank first became NationsBank, then, after its 1998 acquisition of San Francisco-based BancAmerica, it changed its name to Bank of America Corporation. Table 22.1 shows Bank of America's principal acquisitions.

Despite the size of the acquisition, it was not the result of careful strategic planning. The merger announcement came the same day that Lehman Brothers filed for Chapter 11 bankruptcy protection amidst growing fears that the global financial system was going into meltdown. Anticipating that Merrill Lynch might be the next major financial institution to fail, the acquisition was hastily brokered by Federal Reserve Board chairman Ben Bernanke and U.S. Treasury Secretary, Hank Paulson. Announcing the merger, Bank of America's Chairman and CEO, Ken Lewis, stated: "The fact that we

EXHIBIT 22.1

Press Release: Bank of America Buys Merrill Lynch Creating Unique Financial Services Firm

CHARLOTTE (September 15, 2008)—Bank of America Corporation today announced it has agreed to acquire Merrill Lynch & Co., Inc. in a $50 billion all-stock transaction that creates a company unrivalled in its breadth of financial services and global reach. "Acquiring one of the premier wealth management, capital markets, and advisory companies is a great opportunity for our shareholders," Bank of America Chairman and Chief Executive Officer Ken Lewis said. "Together, our companies are more valuable because of the synergies in our businesses." "Merrill Lynch is a great global franchise and I look forward to working with Ken Lewis and our senior management teams to create what will be the leading financial institution in the world with the combination of these two firms," said John Thain, chairman and CEO of Merrill Lynch.

Under the terms of the transaction, Bank of America would exchange 0.8595 shares of Bank of America common stock for each Merrill Lynch common share. The price is 1.8 times the stated tangible book value. Bank of America expects to achieve $7 billion in pretax expense savings, fully realized by 2012. The acquisition is expected to be accretive to earnings by 2010. The transaction is expected to close in the first quarter of 2009. It has been approved by directors of both companies and is subject to shareholder votes at both companies and standard regulatory approvals. Under the agreement, three directors of Merrill Lynch will join the Bank of America Board of Directors.

The combined company would have leadership positions in retail brokerage and wealth management. By adding Merrill Lynch's more than 16 000 financial advisers, Bank of America would have the largest brokerage in the world with more than 20 000 advisers and $2.5 trillion in client assets. The combination brings global scale in investment management, including an approximately 50% ownership in BlackRock, which has $1.4 trillion in assets under management. Bank of America has $589 billion in assets under management. Adding Merrill Lynch both enhances current strengths at Bank of America and creates new ones, particularly outside of the United States. Merrill Lynch adds strengths in global debt underwriting, global equities and global merger and acquisition advice. After the acquisition, Bank of America would be the number one underwriter of global high yield debt, the third largest underwriter of global equity and the ninth largest adviser on global mergers and acquisitions based on *pro forma* first half of 2008 results.

Source: http://newsroom.bankofamerica.com/index.php?s=43&item=8255, accessed August 13, 2009.

could put this transaction together in less than 48 hours is a great statement on the strength of both our teams, but also on the great strategic fit which, from the instant that we talked about it, became clear that this transaction would make a lot of sense."

Others were less convinced that the transaction made sense. The biggest concern was that Bank of America was overpaying. The *Financial Times*' Lex column commented:

> Even if Merrill is being taken out at a third of its 52-week high, it is, in the circumstances, hardly a steal at 1.8 times tangible book value and 12 times 2009 earnings. Mr. Thain's willingness to accept market realities has enabled Merrill shareholders to escape a total wipe-out. As Jamie Dimon noted after acquiring Bear Stearns, there is a difference between buying a house and buying a house that's on fire. While flames are licking at Merrill's outhouses, Mr. Thain has persuaded BofA's Ken Lewis there is still plenty of time to douse them. But until Mr. Lewis can prove that Merrill has suffered only cosmetic damage, he will struggle to get investors excited about promised savings worth $7bn or 10% of the cost base. BofA's shares fell 15%, destroying $23bn of value.

TABLE 22.1 Bank of America's growth by acquisition

Year	Company acquired	Notes
1960	Security National Back of Greensboro merges American Commercial Bank of Charlotte	Merged bank names North Caroline National Bank (NCNB)
1982	First National Bank of Lake City (Florida)	First out-of-state acquisition by NCNB
1991	C&S/Sovren of Atlanta	NCNB changes its name to NationsBank
1993	MNC Financial of Maryland	
1998	BancAmerica Corporation of San Francisco	NationsBank renames as Bank of America
2004	Fleet Boston Financial Corporation	Expands into Northeast
2006	MBNA	Bank of America becomes largest U.S. credit-card issuer
2007	U.S. Trust	Bank of America establishes leading position in private banking for wealthy individuals
2007	ABN AMBRO North America	Principal subsidiary is La Salle Bank Corporation
2008	Countrywide Financial	Bank of America becomes largest mortgage lender in U.S.
2008	Merrill Lynch & Company, Inc.	September 15 bid to take effect January 1, 2009

> If the deal proceeds to plan, BofA would secure the Merrill brand and the largest retail broker network in the U.S., with a 17 000-strong herd of financial advisers as well as a leading investment bank and wealth management franchise. There are, though, two big dangers. First, much of the risk Merrill has "offloaded" in its vendor-financed sale of toxic securities could come back to haunt its new owner. Second, a culture war between two workforces remunerated according to different pay systems seems unavoidable.[1]

During the final quarter of 2008, pessimism about the merger continued to grow—Bank of America's share price declined from $29.55 on September 16, 2008 to $13.53 on December 22. The critical concern was Merrill's balance sheet. On October 16, Merrill reported a third-quarter loss of $5.1 billion resulting mostly from a writedown in the value of its CDOs (collateralized debt securities and real-estate related assets).

By mid-December it was becoming clear that Merrill's fourth-quarter results would be even worse that the dreadful third-quarter figures. On December 14, 2008, Bank of America's Chief Financial Officer, Joe Price, advised Ken Lewis, Bank of America's CEO, that Merrill Lynch's financial condition was deteriorating. During the previous week Merrill Lynch's projected fourth-quarter losses had risen from $9 billion to $12 billion.

These revelations about the full horrors of Merrill's financial position removed any lingering doubts over whether Bank of America had overpaid for Merrill: current losses and future write downs probably meant that Merrill Lynch was worth absolutely nothing. The issue for Lewis and the board was whether to invoke the "MAC clause" in the merger agreement, which allowed the merger to be called off in the event of a "materially adverse event" occurring.

There followed a flurry of communications between Lewis, Federal Reserve Chairman Bernanke and Secretary Paulson and officials of the U.S. Treasury. After informing them of Bank of America's desire to exit the merger, Lewis became a target of sustained pressure from the Department of the Treasury in particular.

Secretary Paulson reminded Lewis of the risks to the entire U.S. financial system that would result from Bank of America's rescinding the merger agreement—risks that would inevitably have a major impact upon Bank of America itself. Paulson also indicated that, should Bank of America invoke the MAC clause, the U.S. government would seek the removal of Bank of America's board and top management team. However, if Bank of America went ahead with the merger, the Treasury and Federal Reserve System would provide whatever assistance was needed by Bank of America to restore its capital and to protect it against the adverse impact of "toxic" Merrill Lynch assets.[2]

As Lewis got ready to speak to his fellow board members, he realized that he was faced with the most difficult decision of his entire career. If Bank of America went ahead with the merger, Merrill's appalling financial situation would be a major drag on Bank of America's performance, would depress its share price and would undoubtedly anger shareholders. However, beyond the short term—probably the next two to three years—he believed that shareholders would reap considerable long-run benefit from the strategic advantages of the new global colossus. Rescinding the deal would free Bank of America from Merrill Lynch's acute financial problems—but the implications were troubling. It would postpone—possibly forever—Lewis's desire to create the world's pre-eminent universal bank. Even more serious, it might be the trigger for the financial calamity that President Bush had forewarned in his recognition that: "This sucker might go down!" The implications for Bank of America, especially if Paulson made good on his threat to remove Bank of America's board, were hardly appealing.

The potential conflict between Lewis's moral obligations to his shareholders and to his country was further complicated by his legal duties. As chairman and CEO, Lewis was required to inform shareholders of company matters relevant to their interests. Although shareholders had on December 5 approved the acquisition of Merrill Lynch, this was without the new projections of Merrill's fourth-quarter losses. When Lewis had raised issues of disclosure with Bernanke and Paulson he had been given the opinion that such disclosure would not be conducive to the stability of the U.S. financial system.[3]

The Strategic Issues Arising from the Merger

The strategic arguments in favor of the merger were outlined in a joint press conference by the two CEOs—Ken Lewis and John Thain—made on September 15, 2008. Lewis saw Merrill Lynch as adding critical strengths to Bank of America in relation to both individual financial services and corporate financial services. Figure 22.1 shows two slides from their presentation.

In terms of individual financial services, Merrill Lynch's U.S.-wide network of local offices and its army of financial advisers would represent a massive extension of Bank of America's existing brokerage and wealth-management services. In addition, Bank of America anticipated that the combination of the largest U.S. wealth-management organization with one of America's biggest retail banks with presence in 31 states would offer considerable opportunity for offering a wider range of financial services to the clients of each.

Merrill Lynch's much bigger presence outside of the U.S. would also offer Bank of America the opportunity to build a truly international wealth-management business.

In terms of Bank of America's corporate and investment banking, the merger would transform Bank of America from a provider of corporate banking services with comparatively small-scale investment banking activities into one of the world's leading investment banks. Not only was Merrill strongly positioned in all the world's major financial centers—it had also established a strong position in the emerging markets of Asia, Eastern Europe, Latin America, Africa and the Middle East—most notably in the BRIC countries. Appendices 22.1 and 22.2 provide information on the businesses and performance of the two companies.

Some of the contentious aspects of the merger extended beyond the specifics of the Merrill Lynch acquisition to the overall strategy of Bank of America. Bank of America was one of a small number of U.S. banks—the others were Citigroup and J.P. Morgan Chase—that had taken advantage of the repeal of the Glass-Stegall Act to combine commercial and investment banking. This so-called "universal banking model" was common in Europe where UBS, Deutsch Bank, Credit Suisse, BNP-Paribas, Barclays, Royal Bank of Scotland and Unicredit long combined conventional banking services with capital market activities, corporate advisory services, market making and proprietary trading.

The financial crisis of 2008–9 had confirmed the robustness of the universal banking model. Among the major U.S. investment banks, only Goldman Sachs and Morgan Stanley had survived. The universal banks were able to pick up the pieces: in addition to Bank of America's acquisition of Merrill Lynch, J.P. Morgan Chase had acquired Bear Stearns. The universal banks had demonstrated the advantages of risk spreading as a result of diversification, plus the stability advantages of financing through retail bank deposits rather than relying on wholesale money markets. In addition there were

FIGURE 22.1 Extract from Merger Presentation by Ken Lewis and John Thain

Creating the Premier Financial Services Company in the World

Ken Lewis
Bank of America
Chairman and CEO

John Thain
Merrill Lynch
Chairman and CEO

Strategic Rationale

- ***Diversify business mix***
- ***Significant enhancement to our investment banking capabilities***
  - ***Creates leading positions in***
    - ***Global Debt Underwriting***
    - ***Global Equities***
    - ***Global M&A Advisory***
- ***Leadership position in retail brokerage and wealth management***
  - ***20,000 financial advisors (16,690 Merrill Lynch advisors)***
  - ***$2.5 trillion in client assets***
- ***Brings global scale in investment management***
  - ***50% ownership stake in BlackRock with $1.4 trillion in AUMs***
  - ***Columbia funds have $425 billion in AUMs (total BAC AUMs $589 billion)***

(AUM = Assets Under Management)

A Bank of America and Merrill combination yields a diverse business mix

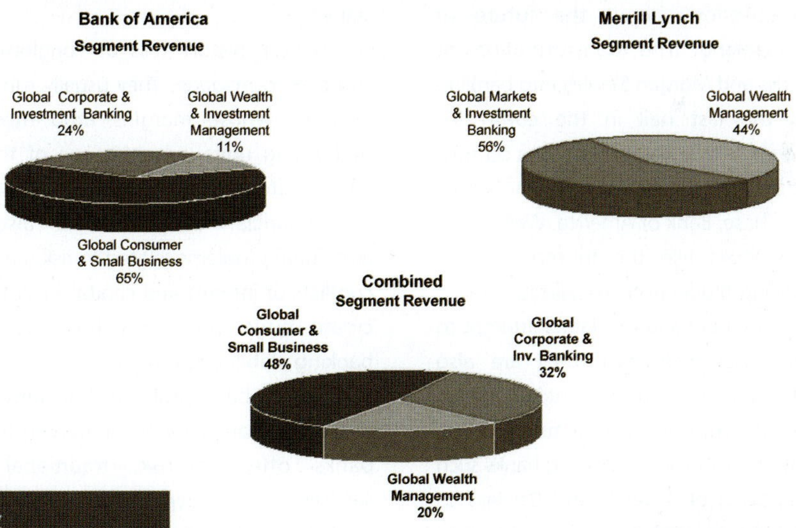

Merrill Lynch

Bank of America

the strategic advantages that had traditionally been argued for the universal banks. First, the "one-stop-shopping" benefits in relation to both individual and corporate/institutional customers of offering a comprehensive range of products and services. Second, the vertical integration benefits of having a retail distribution network to support investment banking activities such as underwriting and securitization.

There were others who believed that the benefits of combining investment and commercial banking were small, while the costs were potentially great. These critics pointed to the fact that few financial institutions had been able to make "cross-selling" financial products work well, while the organizational and management difficulties of administering diversified, multinational financial service companies were huge. Citigroup was often quoted as an example of a financial service company whose size and complexity had made it unmanageable. Part of the problem was in designing management systems that exploit the synergies between commercial and investment banking while avoiding the inherent conflict of interests that multiple relationships with the same client posed (see Exhibit 22.2).

EXHIBIT 22.2

Universal Banks Need Careful Monitoring

The recent failure of Bear Stearns, Lehman Brothers and Merrill Lynch as independent banks has raised questions about the future of investment banking. The transformation of Goldman Sachs and Morgan Stanley into banking holdings is the last nail in the coffin for investment banks as we knew them for a century. At the same time, the growth of new giants such as JPMorgan Chase, Bank of America, Wells Fargo and Barclays looks like the triumph of the universal banking model over specialized banks.

As the U.S. Treasury and regulators attempt to stop the financial meltdown, they are also redefining the banking model in unintended ways that may sow the seeds of financial turbulence in the future. By encouraging or allowing banks such as JPMorgan, Bank of America and Barclays to rescue weaker banks, useful as it is in the short term, they are also nurturing bigger universal banks. Their sheer size will not only strengthen the unwritten TBTF principle ("too big to fail"). The emerging banking model, based on financial conglomerates with a high degree of diversification, also creates problems for banking stability.

Financial history tells us conglomerates are complex to manage. They usually run profitable business whose margins fund other under-performing units, which is one of the reasons why investors put a discount on their share price. But financial conglomerates also involve additional problems related to risk management, conflicts of interest and capital allocation, which create huge challenges for regulators and banking stability as a whole.

The first basic problem that universal banks face is risk management. On the one hand, these banks offer low-risk, traditional banking services—such as deposit-taking and commercial lending—with guaranteed deposits and an insurance mechanism set up by governments. Yet they also run trading units, lend money for mergers and acquisition, manage individuals' portfolios, invest their savings in exotic products and design complex structured loans. These banks look more stable because they are more diversified, but in this diversification lies the problem.

There are a few universal banks in the U.S., such as Bank of America and JPMorgan, which have weathered the storm so far reasonably well. It is also true that European banks such as Santander or BBVA have been successful with a universal model, although they are strong retail banks and not as diversified as their U.S. competitors. If one leaves these exceptions aside, managing the traditional banking business together with risky financial operations not only makes the basic banking function riskier, but also puts pressure on the whole bank. This is one of the reasons for the huge problems at the heart of the financial woes of Merrill Lynch, UBS, Fortis and Wachovia.

In universal banks, conflicts of interest are ubiquitous. This is an old story that often comes back. It happened during the internet bubble, when some banks played different roles for different parties: advising on M&A, lending to fund some acquisitions, leading initial public offerings or managing portfolios. Chinese walls were torn down and some bankers unethically exploited those conflicts of interest. Public uproar and some regulatory changes calmed the storm but did not eradicate the intrinsic problem.

Disclosure and shareholders' protection is another important issue. By definition, capital allocation in conglomerates is complex to make and complex to discern. Unless banks make a huge effort to explain it in a clear way, neither investors nor regulators really understand where their risk lies, as the recent crisis has shown.

The conflicts of interest inherent in universal banks are not enough to forbid their existence or to go back to the U.S. Glass–Steagall Act.

But regulators should monitor them more closely and ask them to separate legally and operationally the basic banking intermediary function from other financial services. Banks should fully disclose their capital allocation and risk in a clearer way, both for shareholders and investors.

Auditors can also help here. Just have a look at the annual reports of some of the failed banks over the past three years and one gets the feeling, most of the time, that they were almost immune to risk.

A dynamic economy needs well functioning banks. But the universal model needs a clear separation of regulated and unregulated activities and better transparency and disclosure. Unless we address this challenge, we may end up not only with larger banks but with a weaker financial system in the future.

Source: J. Canals, Universal banks need careful monitoring, *Financial Times*, October 19, 2008. Reproduced by permission of Prof. Jordi Canals, IESE Business School, University of Navara.

Appendix 1: Bank of America Corporation: The Business and Performance

General

Bank of America Corporation ("Bank of America" or the "Corporation") is a Delaware corporation, a bank holding company and a financial holding company under the Gramm-Leach-Bliley Act. Our principal executive offices are located in the Bank of America Corporate Center, Charlotte, North Carolina 28255.

Through our banking subsidiaries (the "Banks") and various nonbanking subsidiaries throughout the U.S. and in selected international markets, we provide a diversified range of banking and nonbanking financial services and products through three business segments: *Global Consumer and Small Business Banking, Global Corporate and Investment Banking* and *Global Wealth and Investment Management*. We currently operate in 32 states, the District of Columbia and more than 30 foreign countries. The Bank of America footprint covers more than 82% of the U.S. population and 44% of the country's wealthy households. In the U.S. we serve approximately 59 million consumer and small business relationships with more than 6100 retail banking offices, more than 18 500 ATMs and approximately 24 million active online users. We have banking centers in 13 of the 15 fastest growing states and hold the top market share in six of those states...

As of December 31, 2007, there were approximately 210 000 full-time equivalent employees within Bank of America and our subsidiaries. Of these employees, 116 000 were employed within *Global Consumer and Small Business Banking*, 21 000 were employed within *Global Corporate and Investment Banking* and 14 000 were employed within *Global Wealth and Investment Management* . . .

($ millions, except where indicated)	2007	2006	2005	2004	2003
Income statement					
Net interest income	34 433	34 591	30 737	27 960	20 505
Noninterest income	31 886	37 989	26 438	22 729	18 270
Total revenue, net of interest expense	66 319	72 580	57 175	50 689	38 775
Provision for credit losses	8385	5010	4014	2769	2839
Noninterest expense, before merger and restructuring charges	36 600	34 792	28 269	26 394	20 155
Merger and restructuring charges	410	805	412	618	–
Income before income taxes	20 924	31 973	24 480	20 908	15 781
Income tax expense	5942	10 840	8015	6961	5019
Net income	14 982	21 133	16 465	13 947	10 762
Performance ratios					
Return on average assets (%)	0.94	1.44	1.30	1.34	1.44
Return on average common shareholders' equity (%)	11.08	16.27	16.51	16.47	21.50
Return on average tangible shareholders' equity (%)	22.25	32.80	30.19	28.93	27.84
Total ending equity to total ending assets (%)	8.56	9.27	7.86	9.03	6.76
Total average equity to total average assets (%)	8.53	8.90	7.86	8.12	6.69
Dividend payout (%)	72.26	45.66	46.61	46.31	39.76

($ millions, except where indicated)	2007	2006	2005	2004	2003
Market price per share of common stock					
Closing ($)	41.26	53.39	46.15	46.99	40.22
High closing ($)	54.05	54.90	47.08	47.44	41.77
Low closing ($)	41.10	43.09	41.57	38.96	32.82
Market capitalization	183 107	238 021	184 586	190 147	115 926
Average balance sheet					
Total loans and leases	776 154	652 417	537 218	472 617	356 220
Total assets	1 602 073	1 466 681	1 269 892	1 044 631	749 104
Total deposits	717 182	672 995	632 432	551 559	406 233
Long-term debt	169 855	130 124	97 709	92 303	67 077
Total shareholders' equity	136 662	130 463	99 861	84 815	50 091
Asset quality					
Allowance for credit losses	12 106	9 413	8 440	9 028	6 579
Nonperforming assets measured at historical cost	5 948	1 856	1 603	2 455	3 021
Allowance for loan and lease losses as % of total loans and leases outstanding (%)	1.33	1.28	1.40	1.65	1.66
Allowance for loan and lease losses as % of total non performing loans and leases (%)	207	505	532	390	215
Net charge-offs	6 480	4 539	4 562	3 113	3 106
Net charge-offs as % of average loans and leases outstanding	0.84	0.70	0.85	0.66	0.87
Nonperforming loans and leases as a percentage of total loans and leases (%) outstanding measured at historical cost	0.64	0.25	0.26	0.42	0.77
Nonperforming assets as % of total loans, leases and foreclosed properties (%)	0.68	0.26	0.28	0.47	0.81
Ratio of the allowance for loan and lease losses at December 31 to net charge-offs	1.79	1.99	1.76	2.77	1.98
Capital ratios (period end)					
Risk-based capital:					
Tier 1	6.87	8.64	8.25	8.20	8.02
Total	11.02	11.88	11.08	11.73	12.05
Tier 1 Leverage	5.04	6.36	5.91	5.89	5.86

Global Consumer and Small Business Banking

2007 ($ millions)	Total	Deposits	Card services	Consumer real estate	ALM other
Net interest income	28809	9423	16562	2281	543
Noninterest income:					
Card income	10189	2155	8028	6	–
Service charges	6008	6003	–	5	–
Mortgage banking income	1333	–	–	1333	–
All other income	1343	(4)	943	54	350
Total noninterest income	18873	8154	8971	1398	350
Total revenue, net of interest expense	47682	17577	25533	3679	893
Provision for credit losses	12929	256	11317	1041	315
Noninterest expense	20060	9106	8294	2033	627
Income (loss) before income taxes	14693	8215	5922	605	(49)
Income tax expense (benefit)	5263	2988	2210	234	(169)
Net income	9430	5227	3712	371	120
Net interest yield* (%)	8.15	2.97	7.87	2.04	n/m
Return on average equity	14.94	33.61	8.43	9.00	n/m
Efficiency ratio*	42.07	51.81	32.49	55.24	n/m
Period end—total assets	442987	358626	257000	133324	n/m

* The *efficiency ratio* measures the costs expended to generate a dollar of revenue; *net interest yield* evaluates how many basis points we are earning over the cost of funds.

The strategy for *GCSBB* is to attract, retain and deepen customer relationships. We achieve this strategy through our ability to offer a wide range of products and services through a franchise that stretches coast to coast through 32 states and the District of Columbia. We also provide credit-card products to customers in Canada, Ireland, Spain and the United Kingdom. In the U.S. we serve approximately 59 million consumer and small-business relationships utilizing our network of 6149 banking centers, 18 753 domestic branded ATMs, and telephone and internet channels. Within *GCSBB* there are three primary businesses:

- *Deposits* provides a comprehensive range of products to consumers and small businesses. Our products include traditional savings accounts, money market savings accounts, CDs and IRAs, and noninterest and interest-bearing checking accounts. Debit card results are also included in *Deposits*.
- *Card Services,* which excludes the results of debit cards (included in *Deposits*), provides a broad offering of products, including U.S. Consumer and Business Card, Unsecured Lending, and International Card. We offer a variety of cobranded and affinity credit-card products and have become the leading issuer of credit cards through endorsed marketing in the U.S. and Europe. During 2007, Merchant Services was transferred to *Treasury Services* within *GCIB*.
- *Consumer Real Estate* generates revenue by providing an extensive line of consumer real estate products and services to customers nationwide.

Consumer Real Estate products are available to our customers through a retail network of personal bankers located in 6149 banking centers, mortgage loan officers in nearly 200 locations and through a sales force offering our customers direct telephone and online access to our products. *Consumer Real Estate* products include fixed and adjustable rate loans for home purchase and refinancing needs, reverse mortgages, lines of credit and home equity loans. Mortgage products are either sold into the secondary mortgage market to investors while retaining the Bank of America customer relationships or are held on our balance sheet for ALM purposes. *Consumer Real Estate* is not impacted by the Corporation's mortgage production retention decisions as *Consumer Real Estate* is compensated for the decision on a management accounting basis with a corresponding offset recorded in *All Other.*

- The *Consumer Real Estate* business includes the origination, fulfillment, sale and servicing of first mortgage loan products, reverse mortgage products and home equity products. Servicing activities primarily include collecting cash for principal, interest and escrow payments from borrowers, disbursing customer draws for lines of credit and accounting for and remitting principal and interest payments to investors and escrow payments to third parties. Servicing income includes ancillary income derived in connection with these activities such as late fees.

Global Corporate and Investment Banking

2007 ($ millions)	Total	Business lending	Capital Market and advisory	Treasury Services
Net interest income	11 217	5020	2786	3814
Noninterest income:				
Service charges	2769	507	134	2128
Investment and brokerage services	910	1	867	42
Investment banking income	2537	–	2537	–
Trading account profits (losses)	(5164)	(180)	(5050)	63
All other income	1148	824	(971)	1092
Total noninterest income	2200	1152	(2483)	3325
Total revenue, net of interest expense	13417	6172	303	7139
Provision for credit losses	652	647	–	5
Noninterest expense	11925	2158	5642	3856
Income (loss) before income taxes	840	3367	(5339)	3278
Income tax expense (benefit)	302	1246	(1977)	1213
Net income (loss)	538	2121	(3362)	2065
Net interest yield	1.66	2.00	n/m	2.79
Return on average equity	1.19	13.12	(25.41)	26.31
Efficiency ratio	88.88	34.98	n/m	54.02
Period end—total assets	776107	305548	413115	180369

Global Corporate and Investment Banking provides a wide range of financial services both to our issuer and investor clients, who range from business banking clients to large international corporate and institutional investor clients, using a strategy to deliver value-added financial products and advisory solutions. Global Corporate and Investment Banking's products and services are delivered from three primary businesses: *Business Lending, CMAS* and *Treasury Services* are provided to our clients through a global team of client relationship managers and product partners. In addition, *ALM/Other* includes the results of ALM activities and other *GCIB* activities (such as commercial insurance business, which was sold in the fourth quarter of 2007). Our clients are supported through offices in 22 countries, which are divided into four distinct geographic regions: U.S. and Canada; Asia; Europe, Middle East and Africa; and Latin America.

- *Business Lending* provides a wide range of lending-related products and services to our clients through client relationship teams along with various product partners. Products include commercial and corporate bank loans and commitment facilities, which cover our business banking clients, middle market commercial clients and our large multinational corporate clients. Real-estate lending products are issued primarily to public and private developers, homebuilders and commercial real-estate firms. Leasing and asset-based lending products offer our clients innovative financing solutions. Products also include indirect consumer loans, which allow us to offer financing through automotive, marine, motorcycle and recreational vehicle dealerships across the U.S. *Business Lending* also contains the results for the economic hedging of our risk to certain credit counterparties utilizing various risk mitigation tools.
- *Capital Markets and Advisory Services* provides financial products, advisory services and financing globally to our institutional investor clients in support of their investing and trading activities. We also work with our commercial and corporate issuer clients to provide debt and equity underwriting and distribution capabilities, merger-related advisory services and risk management solutions using interest rate, equity, credit, currency and commodity derivatives, foreign exchange, fixed income and mortgage-related products. The business may take positions in these products and participate in market-making activities dealing in government securities, equity and equity-linked securities, high-grade and high-yield corporate debt securities, commercial paper, mortgage-backed securities and ABS. Underwriting debt and equity, securities research and certain market-based activities are executed through *Banc of America Securities, LLC,* which is a primary dealer in the U.S.
- *Treasury Services* provides integrated working capital management and treasury solutions to clients worldwide through our network of proprietary offices and special clearing arrangements. Our clients include multinationals, middle-market companies, correspondent banks, commercial real estate firms and governments. Our products and services include treasury management, trade finance, foreign exchange, short-term credit facilities and short-term investing options. Net interest income is derived from interest-bearing and noninterest-bearing deposits, sweep investments, and other liability management products. Deposit products provide a relatively stable source of funding and liquidity. We earn net interest spread revenues from investing this liquidity in earning assets through client-facing lending activity and our ALM activities.

Global Wealth and Investment Management

2007 ($ millions)	Total	U.S. Trust	Columbia Management	Premier Banking and Investments
Net interest income	3857	1036	15	2655
Noninterest income:				
Investment and brokerage services	4210	1226	1857	950
All other income	(144)	57	(366)	146
Total noninterest income	4066	1283	1491	1096
Total revenue, net of interest expense	7923	2319	1506	3751
Provision for credit losses	14	14	–	27
Noninterest expense	4635	1592	1196	1700
Income before income taxes	3274	741	310	2024
Income tax expense	1179	274	114	749
Net income	2095	467	196	1275
Net interest yield	3.06	2.69	n/m	2.70
Return on average equity	18.87	17.25	11.29	72.44
Efficiency ratio	58.50	68.67	79.39	45.31
Period end—total assets	157157	51044	2617	113329

Global Wealth and Investment Management provides a wide offering of customized banking, investment and brokerage services tailored to meet the changing wealth management goals of our individual and institutional customer base. Our clients have access to a range of services offered through three primary businesses: *U.S. Trust, Bank of America Private Wealth Management (U.S. Trust); Columbia Management (Columbia)* and *Premier Banking and Investments (PB&I)*.

U.S. Trust, Bank of America Private Wealth Management In July 2007, we completed the acquisition of U.S. Trust Corporation for $3.3 billion in cash combining it with *The Private Bank* and its ultra-wealthy extension, *Family Wealth Advisors*, to form *U.S. Trust*. The results of the combined business were reported for periods beginning on July 1, 2007. Prior to July 1, 2007, the results solely reflect that of the former *Private Bank. U.S. Trust* provides comprehensive wealth management solutions to wealthy and ultra-wealthy clients with investable assets of more than $3 million. In addition, *U.S. Trust* provides resources and customized solutions to meet clients' wealth structuring, investment management, trust and banking services as well as specialty asset management services (oil and gas, real estate, farm and ranch, timberland, private businesses and tax advisory). Clients also benefit from access to resources available through the Corporation including capital markets products, large and complex financing solutions and its extensive banking platform.

Columbia Management *Columbia* is an asset-management business serving the needs of institutional clients and individual customers. *Columbia* provides asset management products and services, including mutual funds and separate accounts. *Columbia* mutual fund offerings provide a broad array of investment strategies and products including equity, fixed income (taxable and nontaxable) and money market (taxable and nontaxable) funds. *Columbia* distributes its products and services directly to institutional clients and distributes to individuals through *U.S. Trust, PB&I* and nonproprietary channels including other brokerage firms.

Premier Banking and Investments Premier Banking and Investments includes *Banc of America Investments*, our full-service retail brokerage business and our *Premier Banking* channel. Premier Banking and Investments brings personalized banking and investment expertise through priority service with client-dedicated teams. It provides a high-touch client experience through a network of approximately 5600 client-facing associates to our affluent customers with a personal wealth profile that includes investable assets plus a mortgage that exceeds $500 000 or at least $100 000 of investable assets.

Appendix 2: Merrill Lynch & Co., Inc.: The Business and Performance (extracts from 10-K report for 2007)

The Business

Merrill Lynch was formed in 1914 and became a publicly traded company on June 23, 1971. In 1973, we created the holding company, ML & Co., a Delaware corporation that, through its subsidiaries, is one of the world's leading capital markets, advisory and wealth management companies with offices in 40 countries and territories. In our Global Wealth Management ("GWM") business, we had total client assets in GWM accounts of approximately $1.2 trillion at December 26, 2008. As an investment bank, we are a leading global trader and underwriter of securities and derivatives across a broad range of asset classes and we serve as a strategic advisor to corporations, governments, institutions and individuals worldwide. In addition, as of December 26, 2008, we owned approximately half of the economic interest of BlackRock, Inc. ("BlackRock"), one of the world's largest publicly traded investment management companies with approximately $1.3 trillion in assets under management at the end of 2008 . . .

Our activities are conducted through two business segments: Global Markets and Investment Banking ("GMI") and GWM. In addition, we provide a variety of research services on a global basis.

Global Markets and Investment Banking

The Global Markets division consists of the Fixed Income, Currencies and Commodities ("FICC") and Equity Markets sales and trading activities for investor clients and on a proprietary basis, while the Investment Banking division provides a wide range of origination and strategic advisory services for issuer clients. Global Markets makes a market in securities, derivatives, currencies, and other financial instruments to satisfy client demands. In addition, Global Markets engages in certain proprietary trading activities. Global Markets is a leader in the global distribution of fixed income, currency and energy commodity products and derivatives. Global Markets also has one of the largest equity-trading operations in the world and is a leader in the origination and distribution of equity and equity-related products.

Further, Global Markets provides clients with financing, securities clearing, settlement and custody services and also engages in principal investing in a variety of asset classes and private equity investing. The Investment Banking division raises capital for its clients through underwritings and private placements of equity, debt and related securities and loan syndications. Investment Banking also offers advisory services to clients on strategic issues, valuation, mergers, acquisitions and restructurings.

Global Wealth Management

Global Wealth Management, our full-service retail wealth management segment, provides brokerage, investment advisory and financial planning services, offering a broad range of both proprietary and third-party wealth management products and services globally to individuals, small- to mid-size businesses and employee benefit plans. Global Wealth Management comprises Global Private Client ("GPC") and Global Investment Management ("GIM").

Global Private Client provides a full range of wealth management products and services to assist clients in managing all aspects of their financial profile through the Total Merrill℠ platform. Total Merrill℠ is the platform for GPC's core strategy offering investment choices, brokerage, advice, planning and/or performance analysis to its clients. Global Private Client's offerings include commission and fee-based investment accounts, banking, cash management and credit services, including consumer and small business lending and Visa® cards; trust and generational planning; retirement services and insurance products.

Global Private Client services individuals and small- and middle-market corporations and institutions through approximately 16 090 financial advisors as of December 26, 2008.

Global Investment Management includes our interests in creating and managing wealth management products, including alternative investment products for clients. GIM also includes our share of net earnings from our ownership positions in other investment management companies, including BlackRock.

	GMI	GWM
Clients	Corporations, financial institutions, institutional investors, and governments	Individuals, small- to mid-size businesses, and employee benefit plans
Products and businesses	***Global Markets*** *(comprising Fixed Income, Currencies and Commodities ("FICC") and Equity Markets)* Facilitates client transactions and makes markets in securities, derivatives, currencies, commodities and other financial instruments to satisfy client demands Provides clients with financing, securities clearing, settlement, and custody services Engages in principal and private equity investing, including managing investment funds, and certain proprietary trading activities	***Global Private Client ("GPC")*** Delivers products and services primarily through our Financial Advisors ("FAs") Commission fee-based investment accounts Banking, cash management, and credit services, including consumer and small business lending and Visa(r) cards Trust and generational planning Retirement services Insurance products

(continued)

GMI	GWM
Investment Banking	***Global Investment Management ("GIM")***
Provides a wide range of securities origination services for issuer clients, including underwriting and placement of public and private equity, debt and related securities, as well as lending and other financing activities for clients globally Advises clients on strategic issues, valuation, mergers, acquisitions and restructurings	Creates and manages hedge funds and other alternative investment products for GPC clients Includes net earnings from our ownership positions in other investment management companies, including our investment in BlackRock

Results by geographical area, 2008

($ millions)	2008	2007	2006
Net revenues			
Europe, Middle East and Africa	(2390)	5973	6896
Pacific Rim	69	5065	3703
Latin America	1237	1401	1009
Canada	161	430	386
Total non-U.S.	–923	12869	11994
United States	–11670	–1619	21787
Total net revenues	(12593)	11250	33781
Pretax earnings from continuing operations			
Europe, Middle East, and Africa	(6735)	1211	2091
Pacific Rim	–2559	2403	1204
Latin America	340	632	357
Canada	5	235	181
Total non-U.S.	–8949	4481	3833
United States	–32882	–17312	5977
Total pretax earnings from continuing operations	(41831)	(12831)	9810

Results by business segment, 2008

($ millions)	GMI	GWM	MLIM	Corporate	Total
Noninterest revenues	(25416)	10464	–	(1675)	(16627
Net revenues	(26460)	12778	–	1089	(12593
Noninterest expenses	15084	10432	–	3722	29238
Pretax (loss)/earnings from continuing operations	(41544)	2346	–	(2633)	(41831
Year-end total assets	568868	97849	–	826	66754

(continued

Results by business segment, 2008

($ millions)	GMI	GWM	MLIM	Corporate	Total
2007					
Non-interest revenues	(4950)	11 719	–	(1068)	5701
Net revenues	(2668)	14 021	–	(103)	11 250
Non-interest expenses	13 677	10 391	–	13	24 081
Pre-tax (loss)/earnings from continuing operations	(16 345)	3630	–	(116)	(12 831)
Year-end total assets	920 388	99 196	–	466	1 020 050

Appendix 3: "The Golden Age for Financial Services is Over" By Shawn Tully

The New Most Powerful Man in Finance, Bank of America CEO Ken Lewis, Talks about the Future of Wall Street and the Economy

To reach the new power center of Wall Street, hop into a cab to La Guardia, board a flight for Charlotte, stride into a beige granite tower, go past the allegorical murals of the common man at work, then take the elevator to the 58th floor. You're at the headquarters of Bank of America, and you're about to enter the glass-framed suite of CEO Ken Lewis.

A world away from Manhattan money and its ethos—which, by the way, he detests—Lewis presides over a company that represents the future of finance. BofA's deal to buy Merrill Lynch for $50 billion sets the template. Sure, rival institutions—notably J. P. Morgan Chase and Citigroup—combine investment and consumer banking. But the Bank of America/Merrill union creates a colossus of unprecedented size and scope.

It isn't clear whether the deal will enrich shareholders or how the market chaos will play out. But it's certain that Lewis is realizing the epic vision he has long dreamed of. "I approached [former Merrill CEO] Stan O'Neal a few years ago, but he showed no interest," says Lewis. Now the crisis brings the missing piece within his grasp: "We've fulfilled the strategic picture we sketched on blank sheets of paper."

The Merrill merger will make BofA just what Lewis wants it to be, the dominant player almost across the board in financial services. By capturing Merrill's "thundering herd" of 16 700 financial advisors, BofA becomes the world's biggest brokerage, with $2.5 trillion in client assets. If both firms keep their current market shares, BofA will rise from the second tier in investment banking to first place in global debt and equity underwriting. After years of acquisitions that created the first true nationwide banking brand, BofA already ranks first in credit cards, retail banking (with 6000-plus branches) and mortgages via its recent acquisition of Countrywide. BofA is now a full-blown financial supermarket, a business model that is succeeding at J.P. Morgan under CEO Jamie Dimon but failing at Citigroup.

Lewis, who's 61, clearly thinks he has an advantage over those two because he's bigger—in more businesses, in more places. Seated in his sun-splashed office adorned with American Impressionist and Hudson River school paintings, he's describing the future of finance in terms perhaps best characterized as cautious exultation. He predicts an end to profligate pay and a witheringly tough market ahead that will leave a few giant champions and a field of casualties. That's not all bad news as far as Lewis is concerned. After all, he hates Wall Street's inflated pay; the market crisis brought him Merrill Lynch; and any decline in the rest of the investment banks out there is good for him. "We'll take a lot of their business," he says.

Lewis is under no illusion that the next few years will be easy. "The Golden Age for financial services is over," he tells Fortune. "It will never be the same, not in my career. Revenues will be far harder to get in the future." For Lewis the biggest problem is the plight of the consumer. He sees the credit pie shrinking as Americans, stretched by high mortgage payments and gas prices, their jobs frequently in jeopardy, recognize that they can't afford the debt they already have, let alone add more. "The consumer is deleveraging, just like many of the banks," says Lewis.

The banks, in his view, are just as weak as the consumer. As a result, they'll be hard-pressed even to satisfy the demand for mortgage, car and credit card loans. "We'll see big write-downs all the way through next year that won't abate until 2010," says Lewis. "Over that period a number of big banks won't have enough capital to make a lot of loans." Lewis sees a rare opportunity to grab market share by extending credit while his competitors languish on the sidelines.

Lewis says his edge isn't just a plentiful pool of capital. He also claims that he'll soon enjoy a big advantage over the best soon-to-be-ex-investment banks in the business, as well as the only ones that remain independent, Goldman Sachs (GS, Fortune 500) and Morgan Stanley (MS, Fortune 500). Both firms are turning into bank holding companies. That will allow them to fund their loans and investments with stable deposits rather than short-term debt that can evaporate in a financial crisis. But it will also force them to radically shrink their balance sheets.

But Lewis believes that transformation will make them far less formidable forces in capital markets. Why? It's complicated, but here goes: since Goldman and Morgan must shrink their balance sheets by reducing their towering leverage, they won't be able to offer the same financing options their corporate customers increasingly demand—that's because corporations that give Goldman and Morgan their underwriting business will expect the banks to extend revolving credit facilities and bridge loans as part of the package. Says Lewis: "As bank holding companies, Morgan Stanley and Goldman will be forced to shrink their balance sheets when expanding your balance sheet is a key to getting corporate business. That will make them less competitive." How does Lewis feel about facing the two storied firms in battling for credit card customers and branch deposits? "We have something of a headstart," he says with a sly smile. "I'm not losing any sleep."

Even as the world moves Lewis's way, he still faces some obstacles. One is the issue of BofA's capital. With the bank's acquisitions of Countrywide and Merrill, even BofA's war chest has become a bit crimped. Unless the bank bolsters its equity, its regulatory capital-to-assets ratio will fall to around 7.4% after the Merrill deal, below Lewis's target of 8% to 8.5%. Lewis is pondering a radical solution: cutting BofA's almost \$3 billion quarterly dividend, which amounts to \$11.8 billion annually. "For the first time, the dividend is on the table," says Lewis. "The Merrill deal is a factor, along with everything that's happening in the economy. The need to build capital is more apparent and intense."

Shrinking the dividend, however, will disappoint investors who flocked to BofA stock because of its reliable, ever-rising payout. It also represents a retreat for Lewis, who until recently told investors that a cut was unlikely. "A lot of investors will be upset, and the stock price may go down if he makes the cut," says Meredith Whitney of Oppenheimer & Co.

The other big issue for BofA is whether it overpaid for Merrill. Lewis calls the deal "the strategic opportunity of a lifetime." But was it really such a bargain? BofA is paying an extremely high price in a market where assets are going for a song, although the deal could prove profitable in the long run. Until Friday, September 12, Lewis was weighing the acquisition of Lehman Brothers, then on the verge of bankruptcy. Lehman had $85 billion in toxic real estate loans. "We figured that the $85 billion in troubled loans was at least $10 billion underwater," says Lewis. He calculated that the value of Lehman's good assets—its investment bank and asset-management arm—wasn't nearly enough to compensate for the potential $10 billion-plus loss on the mortgage assets. He wanted the government to take $65 billion to $70 billion of the most dangerous securities on its books. Over the phone on Friday evening, Lewis told Treasury Secretary Hank Paulson he couldn't buy Lehman without government assistance. When Paulson said he couldn't help, Lewis walked.

On Saturday morning, September 13, Merrill CEO John Thain phoned Lewis in Charlotte to propose a merger, and the two made the giant deal in 36 hours. The huge question is why Lewis paid $50 billion, or $29 a share, a 70% premium over Merrill's closing price on Friday. Over that weekend, with markets heading for a meltdown on Monday, Lehman's looming bankruptcy threatened to bring down Merrill as well. Indeed, Lehman failed on Monday morning; the following week Barclays got a sweet deal buying its North American investment bank and headquarters for $1.7 billion.

So why didn't Lewis wait until Monday, when Merrill might have faced bankruptcy or, even if it survived, been forced to settle for a fire-sale price? Lewis explains that if Merrill went bankrupt, BofA would have had a harder time buying the business it most coveted, Merrill's brokerage franchise. "In a bankruptcy we'd have to bid against other potential buyers, and that asset would have been worth a lot on its own," says Lewis. And if Merrill avoided bankruptcy, Lewis feared that Thain would make another deal. "Both Goldman Sachs and Morgan Stanley were in the mix," says Lewis. So Lewis eliminated his chance of losing Merrill by acting in a flash. He won't talk much about the negotiations with Thain. "He started at a higher price, and I started at a lower price," he says simply.

It may be true that Lewis would have lost Merrill had he waited. But he has no regrets about the price. "Merrill is worth significantly more than $50 billion," he says. He is promising shareholders that he'll cut costs by a staggering $7 billion before taxes. Unattainable? Not if you consider the extraordinary cost savings Lewis wrung from the Countrywide merger, and the Fleet acquisition in 2004. Lewis is especially anxious to attack Merrill's pay scales. "Merrill was paying typical Wall Street pay," he says. "Their staff people were making a lot more than our staff people. That won't last. We intend to pay market instead."

And if his new employees aren't happy about the pay—or any of Lewis's grand transformations, for that matter—they probably shouldn't waste their time griping to the CEO. Lewis isn't known for his tolerance of complaint. A few years ago one of his top lieutenants wrote the boss a long memo complaining that he'd been undermined by another executive. A few days later he found the memo on his desk. At the top, Lewis had scribbled three words: "Get over it."

Source: S. Tully, The Golden Age for financial services is over,' *Fortune*, September 29, 2008, http://money.cnn.com/2008/09/28/news/companies/tully_levis.fortune/index.htm. Reproduced with permisson.

Notes

1 "BofA/Merrill Lynch," *Financial Times,* September 16, 2008.

2 See: A.M. Cuomo, "Bank of America—Merrill Lynch Merger Investigation," State of New York Office of the Attorney General (April 29, 2009), http://online.wsj.com/public/resources/documents/BofAmergLetter-Cuomo4232009.pdf, accessed July 3, 2009.

3 The facts regarding conversations between Lewis and U.S. government officials are unclear on this point. See: A.M. Cuomo, "Bank of America—Merrill Lynch Merger Investigation," State of New York Office of the Attorney General (April 29, 2009), http://online.wsj.com/public/resources/documents/BofAmergLetter-Cuomo4232009.pdf, accessed July 3, 2009.

Case 23 Jeff Immelt and the Reinventing of General Electric, 2009

April 2009

On April 22, 2009, Jeff Immelt, chairman and CEO of the General Electric Company, was in Orlando, Florida, preparing for the annual shareholders' meeting—his eighth since becoming CEO. The meeting would lack the upbeat, celebratory atmosphere that had been the norm under his predecessor Jack Welch. General Electric's stock was trading a little below $12 that day—up from the low of $6 it reached six weeks earlier but well down on the $53 that GE's shares were trading at when Immelt's appointment had been announced late in 2000. Shareholders' anger was further fuelled by GE's decision to slash its dividend—the first dividend cut since 1938.

Since taking up the leadership of GE, Immelt had become familiar with adversity. If taking over from Jack Welch—"living legend" and "best manager of the past half-century"—was daunting enough, external events soon revealed just how tough his job would be.

Four days after Immelt took over the chairman's suite, two hijacked airliners ploughed into New York's World Trade Center, setting off a train of events that would profoundly affect GE's business environment. A month later, Enron's collapse precipitated a crisis of confidence over corporate governance, executive morality and financial reporting. The scandal at Tyco International—a company that had explicitly modeled itself on GE—and its decision to break up into three separate companies reinforced suspicion of the conglomerate business model. Controversy over financial statement manipulation and executive compensation soon engulfed GE. After being lauded by analysts for its smooth earnings growth it became apparent that GE systematically massaged its quarterly earnings through the use of reserves and end-of-quarter asset sales. More serious criticism was directed at GE's alleged disguising of the true risks of its businesses by consolidating the financial statements of its industrial businesses and its financial services business, GE Capital. In March 2002, Bill Gross, of the IPCO fund management group, argued that GE was primarily a financial services company but, with the support of GE's industrial businesses, GE Capital had been able to operate on a narrow capital base while maintaining a triple-A credit rating. Further problems for Immelt emerged when in September 2002 the details of Welch's startlingly generous retirement package from GE were leaked to the press.

By 2006, it seemed that Immelt was successfully exorcizing the ghost of Jack Welch and winning the war against external adversity. Between 2003 and 2006, Immelt's new growth strategy was achieving its targets for both revenue and profit. Better communication with the investment community and more detailed financial reporting were helping to restore investor confidence in GE. From 2003 to early 2007, GE's stock price experienced a sustained recovery. GE's rehabilitation was confirmed by its reclaiming the title of Fortune's "Most Admired Company" in 2005 and 2006.

Then came the financial crisis of 2008–9. The problems of sub-prime, mortgage-backed securities ballooned into a global credit crunch and forced the demise or government bailout of many of America's biggest financial institutions: Bear Stearns, Lehman Brothers, AIG, Fannie Mae and Citigroup. It profoundly affected GE. GE Capital, GE's financial services arm, was one of America's biggest financial services businesses. For two decades GE Capital had been GE's primary growth engine. It was now seen as "ticking time bomb" of bad debts and asset writedowns.

Two weeks before the end of the first quarter of 2008, Immelt confirmed that GE would meet its quarterly earnings expectations of \$0.50 to \$0.53 per share. The news, six weeks later, that GE had earned only \$0.44 per share was a massive disappointment—GE had a long record of reliable earnings guidance and invariably meeting or exceeding its financial targets. Former CEO Jack Welch was outraged: "I'd get a gun out and shoot him if he doesn't make what he promised now. Here's the screw-up: you made a promise that you'd deliver this, and you missed three weeks later. Jeff has a credibility issue."

As the financial crisis deepened, Immelt was forced to take radical action to shore up GE's balance sheet. On September 25, he suspended GE's stock buyback program but reaffirmed that GE had no need for outside capital. Yet, one week later, Immelt made an agreement with Warren Buffett for a \$3 billion equity injection with a guaranteed annual dividend of 10%. Investor confidence waned further: the fear for shareholders was that GE Capital, which had provided 42% of GE's profits in 2007, might bring down the whole of GE. As James Quinn observed in seekingalpha.com:

> Most people know GE as an industrial conglomerate that makes light bulbs, appliances, and jet engines. The truth is that . . . GE is a bank disguised as an industrial conglomerate . . . Being a bank during the boom years of 2004 to 2007 did wonders for GE's bottom line. Being a bank now is a rocky path to destruction.[1]

Central to the "earnings magic of GE Capital" was GE's AAA credit rating, which allowed GE Capital to finance itself at a lower cost of capital and with a weaker balance sheet than other financial institutions. On March 12, Standard & Poor's (S&P) downgraded GE from AAA to AA+, further damaging the reputation of the company and its CEO.

The address by Immelt and CFO Keith Sherrin to the shareholders' meeting on April 22, 2009, focused on two key strategic issues. Sherrin addressed how GE was shoring up its financial strength in order to weather the current downturn. Immelt concentrated upon GE's longer term strategy. For the most part, he reiterated the principal elements of the strategy that he had been developing since he took over as CEO seven-and-a-half years earlier. In particular, Immelt emphasized GE's commitment to organic growth; exploiting technological innovation and globalization; creating new business opportunities through matching GE's existing capabilities to emerging opportunities in environmental conservation, infrastructure, and healthcare; and developing the leadership needed for GE to prosper in the coming era. At the same time, Immelt emphasized how the current financial and economic crisis represented a once-in-a-generation "reset." Key changes were likely to include a reduced role for financial services in the future, an increased role of government, lower levels of wealth, and a growing emphasis on reputation and trust.

Immelt identified five themes for how GE would "get through the cycle and then . . . build the franchise over the long term":

- "Build strong businesses." GE's four major businesses—energy infrastructure, technology infrastructure, GE Capital and NBC Universal—would be the foundation for GE's growth and cash generation into the future. GE had already divested its least attractive businesses (such as insurance and reinsurance, and plastics and silicones) and had entered several high-potential industries: renewable energy, oil and gas, water, healthcare information technology, avionics and cable. The principal change in the GE portfolio would be a shrinking of GE Capital through exiting some of the product lines and focusing increasingly on building links between GE Capital and GE's other businesses (as in leasing aircraft).
- "Invest in innovation, services, and globalization." During the current decade, GE had invested about $50 billion in research and development. Key innovations included GE's investment in Smart Grid, which would allow massive savings in energy. General Electric's new sodium battery offered vast improvements in power storage with potentially valuable applications to power generation and transportation (locomotives in particular). In media GE had developed Hulu, the world's largest video content site after YouTube. In brain imaging and clean power generation from coal GE was also a world leader. In all its industrial businesses, services in the form of customer and technical support and maintenance would be an important source of growth and a major contributor to the bottom line.

- "Position in essential themes." Essential themes are key areas of emerging opportunity for GE. The most important of these was "ecoimagination"—business innovation and development in environmentally responsible activities such as green energy. For the immediate future, GE had identified infrastructure as a tremendous opportunity. GE's quest for opportunities would also be focused on countries where the biggest increases in public expenditure on infrastructure, healthcare and energy were likely to be, these included the U.S., Canada, China, Brazil, U.K., France, Germany, and the Middle East.
- "Drive competitiveness." As always, ambitious performance targets were fundamental to GE's strategy. After a dominant focus on using top line growth as the primary driver of profitability, in 2009, Immelt shifted GE's priorities to cost cutting, setting a target of reducing costs by $5 billion annually.
- "Commitment to people." Immelt reiterated GE's commitment to developing people including investment in training, emphasis on retention, and nurturing of loyalty.[2]

Despite the greater financial stability and a recovery of GE's share price during March and April 2009, unease over GE's future prospects and the strategy being developed by its chairman and CEO continued. Most concerns related to the central role of GE Capital within the company. Despite Immelt's intention of shrinking GE Capital, it would continue to represent a major part of GE's assets for the foreseeable future. As such, it would be a continuing source of risk for GE. With the loss of GE's triple-A credit rating, the financial synergies between the industrial and financial parts of GE were less apparent.

A further concern was whether Immelt's strategy of organic growth based upon innovation and exploiting "essential themes" could deliver the long-term profit growth that investors had come to expect of GE. As Harvard's Clay Christensen observed:

> The major growth engine at GE has been GE Capital . . . But the fact that it's been a great growth engine in the past means it likely won't be in the future. That's my biggest worry for GE. I don't see a new engine of growth that's comparable to what they had in the past. One challenge is that the bigger a business gets, the less and less interest it has in small opportunities. And all the big growth markets of tomorrow are small today.[3]

GE has shown a capacity for internal growth. However, most of GE's growth has been the result of acquiring major new businesses then expanding them through internationalization and the application of GE's strong management systems.

Moreover, the major growth opportunities that GE was pursuing involved the development and sales of whole systems of products and services. In healthcare, GE was pursuing deals that involved supplying not just medical imaging equipment, but generators, technical support, training and finance. In infrastructure, GE is engaged in multi-faced deals that involve hardware systems, support services, finance and training. Developing these types of business opportunities required high levels of coordination across multiple organizational units—inevitably creating increased organizational complexity and making GE's systems for linking individual incentives to individual and organizational performance even more difficult to implement.

Ultimately, Immelt had to face the question of whether General Electric made sense any more. For close to 20 years conglomerates had been deeply unfashionable both with investors and management theorists. Most had either reorganized themselves as more focused businesses (for example, Textron, General Mills, TRW, BTR) or had broken up completely (ITT, Hanson, Vivendi-Universal, Tyco). While the break up of GE had been suggested many times in recent years, the idea had attracted little serious support: GE was the exception; its quality of management was such that it had avoided the problems that had beset other large, highly diversified corporations. That reasoning held less credence in April 2009. GE's broad diversification had done little to offer it stability throughout the economic cycle—the dividend cut was a clear indication of this. Even more serious, GE's managers had lost much of their hero status. Immelt's retractions of the assurances he had given on earnings, funding needs and the dividend and the inability to foresee the vulnerability of GE Capital's dependence upon the wholesale credit markets for financing its business had seriously undermined the credibility of Immelt and the belief that GE's management was wiser than the market.

For most of GE's 120-year history it had been a pioneer of modern management providing many of the principles and methods that form the basis upon which large companies are managed today. The critical question posed by Immelt's notions of a fundamental "reset" of the business environment following the 2008–10 recession was whether this new business environment would offer GE the opportunity for a new era in its corporate development or whether it would expose the frailties of a corporate giant whose business model rested on the management logic of a previous century.

Table 23.1 summarizes GE's financial performance during 2002–8.

TABLE 23.1 General Electric: selected financial data, 2002–8

($ millions)	2008	2007	2006	2005	2004	2003	2002
General Electric Consolidated							
Revenues	182 515	172 488	151 568	136 262	123 814	113 421	111 967
Net earnings	17 410	22 208	20 742	16 720	17 222	15 561	12 998
Cash from operating activities	48 601	43 322	31 455	37 691	36 493	29 229	28 766
Cash used for investing activities	(40 901)	(69 504)	(52 647)	(35 099)	(38 423)	(21 843)	(61 227)
Return on average shareowners' equity	15.9%	20.4%	19.8%	18.1%	18.8%	20.0%	25.2%
Stock price range ($)	38.52–12.58	42.15–33.90	38.49–32.06	37.34–32.67	37.75–28.88	32.42–21.30	41.84–21.40
Year-end closing stock price ($)	16.20	37.07	37.21	35.05	36.50	30.98	24.35
Total assets	797 769	795 683	697 273	673 210	750 252	647 834	575 018

(continued)

TABLE 23.1 *(Continued)*

($ millions)	2008	2007	2006	2005	2004	2003	2002
Long-term borrowings	330067	319013	260749	212167	207784	170309	138570
Total employees	323000	327000	319000	316000	307000	305000	315000
U.S.	152000	155000	155000	161000	165000	155000	161000
Other countries	171000	172000	164000	155000	142000	150000	154000
GE data (industrial businesses)							
Short-term borrowings	2375	4106	2076	972	3252	2555	8786
Long-term borrowings	9827	11656	9043	8986	7561	8388	970
Shareowners' equity	104665	115559	111509	108633	110181	79666	63979
Total capital invested	123545	137824	128172	123899	128230	91684	74763
Return on average total capital invested	14.8%	18.9%	18.5%	16.7%	16.9%	18.1%	24.0%
Borrowings as a percentage of total capital invested	9.9%	11.4%	8.7%	8.0%	9.0%	11.9%	13.0%
Working capital	3904	6433	7527	7853	7788	5282	3821
GECS data (financial services businesses)							
Revenues	71287	71936	61351	54889	50320	43513	38456
Net earnings	7055	10301	10658	7577	8728	7974	2491
Shareowner's equity	53279	57676	54097	50812	54379	45790	37202
Total borrowings	514601	500922	426262	362042	355463	316593	267014
Ratio of debt to equity at GE Capital	8.76:1	8.10:1	7.52:1	7.09:1	6.45:1	6.62:1	6.48:1
Total assets	660902	646485	565258	540584	618614	554877	489602

Source: General Electric, 10-K reports 2006 and 2008.

The General Electric Company

The GE that Jeffrey Immelt inherited in 2001 was the world's most valuable company and was widely regarded as the world's most successful. It is the only company to have remained a member of the Dow Jones industrial index since the index was created in 1896. The key to its success had been to combine massive size with constant adaptation. Over the decades GE had adapted both its business portfolio and its management systems to the demands and opportunities of a changing world.

It was founded in 1892 from the merger of Thomas Edison's Electric Light Company with the Thomas Houston Company. Its business was based upon exploiting Edison's patents relating to electricity generation and distribution, light bulbs, and electric motors. Throughout the twentieth century GE was not only one of the world's biggest industrial corporations, it was also "a model of management—a laboratory studied by business schools and raided by other companies seeking skilled executives."[4] Under the leadership of Charles Coffin, between 1892 and 1922, GE successfully married Edison's industrial R&D laboratory to a business system capable of turning scientific discovery into marketable products. After the Second World War, Chairman Ralph Cordiner, assisted by Peter Drucker, pioneered new approaches to the systematization of corporate management. Under Fred Borch (CEO 1963–72), GE established a system of strategic management based on strategic business units and portfolio analysis that became a model for most diversified corporations. Reg Jones, GE's chairman from 1973 to 1981, further developed GE's system of corporate management linking techniques of strategic planning to systems of financial management.

During his two decades at GE's helm, Jack Welch had led one of the most comprehensive strategic and organizational upheavals in GE's long history. General Electric's business portfolio had been reformulated through a massive exit from extractive and manufacturing businesses where GE lacked the potential for global leadership, together with a major shift into services—financial services in particular. By the time he retired, GE Capital was responsible for close to half of GE's revenues and the majority of its assets. At the heart of Welch's remaking of GE was the creation of a performance culture supported by comprehensive systems for setting and monitoring performance targets and providing powerful incentives for their achievement.

> Changing the culture—opening it up to the quantum change—means constantly asking not how fast am I going, how well am I doing versus how well I did a year or two before, but rather, how fast and how well am I doing versus the world outside. Are we moving faster, are we doing better against that external standard?
>
> Stretch means using dreams to set business targets—with no real idea of how to get there . . . We certainly didn't have a clue how we were going to get to 10 inventory turns [a year] when we set that target. But we're getting there, and as soon as we become sure we can do it—it's time for another stretch.[5]

Welch declared war on GE's elaborate bureaucracy and stripped out layers of hierarchy. His management style was based upon direct human contact—often confrontational—in which managers committed to ambitious performance targets, then pressured themselves and their own subordinates to deliver. Every aspect of GE's management systems was redesigned from the ground up, from strategic planning to human resource management. In addition to remaking the GE culture and infrastructure, every few years Welch would introduce a major new corporate initiative that would shift GE's strategic direction. These included: "Be #1 or #2 in your global industry"; "Work-out," a process for company meetings that allowed grassroots ideas about organizational change to be implemented; "Six Sigma," a program of company wide initiatives to improve quality and reliability; and "Destroy your business dot.com," an initiative to encourage exploitation of internet technologies.

The outcome was two decades of outstanding corporate performance. Between 1981 and 2001, revenues had grown from $30 billion to $126 billion, net income from under $2 billion to $14 billion, and stock market capitalization from $14 billion to $510 billion—an average annual return to stockholders of 24%.

Jeff Immelt

Jeffrey R. Immelt was appointed CEO of GE at the age of 44. He had previously been head of GE's Plastics business and, most recently, head of Medical Systems. He had an economics and applied math degree from Dartmouth and an MBA from Harvard. He claimed that his own experience of GE extended beyond his two decades with the firm—his father spent his entire career at GE. On being recruited from Harvard by GE in 1982, Immelt was identified as a "young high potential" whose progress was tracked by senior executives at GE. In 1987, Immelt was invited to attend the executive development course at Crotonville, GE's management development center. This course was considered the gateway to the executive ranks of GE. At GE Appliances, GE Plastics and GE Medical Systems, Immelt acquired a reputation for turning around troubled units, driving customer service and exploiting new technologies. He also demonstrated the ability to motivate others—an aptitude that he had revealed as an offensive tackler for Dartmouth's football team in the 1970s.[6]

In December 1994, the GE board began to consider possible candidates to replace Jack Welch. Immelt was one among a list of some 20 GE executives submitted by Welch for board consideration. After five years of careful monitoring and assessment the list had shrunk to three: Jim McNerney, Bob Nardelli and Immelt.

Immelt's emergence as front runner owed much to his outstanding success at GE Medical Systems, which he was appointed to lead in 1997. In addition to rigorous cost cutting and exceeding his budget forecasts, Immelt showed the ability to pick good managers, motivate them, pioneer new technologies, and expand the business. His strength was in energizing and motivating others: "He brought the life and energy that drives major growth," commented GE's head of HR.

Immelt had developed a personality and leadership style that contrasted sharply with those of Welch. Yet, they seemed to be similarly effective in driving business performance. *Business Week* observed: "Where Welch ruled through intimidation and thrived as something of a cult figure, Immelt opts for the friendlier, regular-guy approach. He prefers to tease where Welch would taunt. Immelt likes to cheer people on rather than chew them out. That style has given him a very different aura within

GE. He may not be a demigod, but it's his man-of-the-people nature that draws praise from the top ranks to the factory floor."[7] Immelt knew that his different style of leadership would have important implications for his role as CEO and the ways in which he would influence GE's strategy, structure, and systems. However, Immelt believed that the principal changes that he would initiate at GE would be a result of the changing environment and the shifting priorities that GE faced.

GE's Business Environment, 2001–9

The remarkable growth in profits and stock market valuation that Welch had achieved was against a backdrop of an economy effused by optimism, confidence and growth. The new century presented a whole new set of challenges. In his first letter to shareholders, Immelt observed: "The exuberance of the late 1990s and the inevitable downturn have created difficult times. Entire industries have collapsed, poor business models have been exposed, large companies have filed for bankruptcy and corporate credibility has been called into question."[8]

In a world of geopolitical and economic turbulence, Immelt believed that GE's diversified portfolio of businesses would provide GE the stability to weather business cycles: "The GE portfolio was put together for a purpose—to deliver earnings growth through every economic cycle. We're constantly managing these cycles in a business where the sum exceeds the parts."[9]

However, 2008–9 revealed the limits to this "stability through diversity" thesis. General Electric escaped the dire consequences of the credit crunch that engulfed many financial service firms, the problems of GE Capital posed a major threat to the whole corporation that required urgent remedial attention—including the equity injections from Warren Buffet.

A further key change in the business environment was the discrediting of the 1990s' obsession with shareholder value maximization. From the outset, Immelt was anxious to disassociate himself from cruder versions of shareholder value maximization. In all his communications to shareholders, Immelt was emphatic that the job of the CEO was not to manage the stock price but to manage the company for the long-term earnings growth that would drive the stock price: "We all want the stock to go up. But to do that we have to manage the company. In fact, the only way you can run GE is to believe that performance will ultimately drive the stock."[10] Apart from providing the underlying earnings growth, the only other influence that management could play was to offer transparency to investors through detailed financial reporting. If the annual report had to be "the size of the New York City phone book, that's life," commented Immelt. Nevertheless, despite the "new transparency" many of the fears that depressed GE's stock price during the first quarter of 2009 were exacerbated by uncertainty over GE Capital's financial obligations.

However, the most crucial issue for GE, Immelt believed, was to identify the likely sources of profit in the future. Under Welch, the potential for value creation through cost reduction and the elimination of underperforming assets had probably been fully realized. Immelt would need to look to new areas. Top-line growth would have to be the driver of bottom-line returns. Yet, opportunities for value creation were likely to be meager: "I looked at the world post-9/11 and realized that over the next 10 or 20 years, there was not going to be much tailwind." The primary driver of such growth, figured Immelt, was organic growth—given the level of M&A activity and the huge volume of funds flowing into private equity funds, acquisitions could easily destroy shareholder value. With a generally poor outlook for growth in the world economy, the central challenge was to identify where the most promising opportunities for profitable growth would lie.

In identifying opportunities for profitable organic growth, Immelt sought to identify key global trends that would offer business opportunities for GE. Between 2001 and 2009, there were several revisions in Immelt's view of what these trends would be. For example early in 2007, Immelt identified the key growth trends that GE could exploit as: infrastructure, emerging markets, environmental solutions, digital connections, global liquidity and demographics.[11] Two years later, the "big themes" were infrastructure, emerging market growth, clean energy, and sustainable healthcare.[12] Across the 2001–9 period as a whole, four key external trends were paramount:

- *Demography*. The aging of the world's population would create opportunities for goods and services required by older people—healthcare services in particular. Population growth in the developing world would also offer expanding demand for many other of GE's businesses—including entertainment.
- *Infrastructure*. GE predicted massive investments in infrastructure by 2015. GE's positioning in infrastructure products, services and financing offered it opportunities in energy, aviation, rail transportation, water, and oil and gas production.
- *Emerging markets*. China, India, Eastern Europe, Russia, Middle East, Africa, Latin America and South East Asia would offer rates of GDP growth around three times that of the world as a whole. These countries would be key centers of business opportunity for GE.
- *Environment*. The challenges of global warming, water scarcity and conservation would become increasingly pressing creating the need for technologies and innovatory responses to alleviate these problems.

GE's Growth Strategy

Growth—organic growth in particular—became the central theme of Immelt's strategy for GE. In 2002, he committed GE to an organic growth rate of 8% per annum (under Welch organic growth had averaged 5% a year) and to "double digit" earnings growth. This 8% revenue growth was based upon the idea that GE should be able to grow at between two and three times that of world GDP. Profits would grow faster than revenues, explained Immelt, because of reductions in general and administrative expense as a percentage of sales and higher margins resulting from new products and services. Between 2002 and 2007, GE comfortably met these targets: revenues grew at 13% each year, operating earnings at 14%. However, during 2008, revenue growth was only 6% and earnings declined by 19%.

Immelt's growth strategy comprised several elements.

Reshaping the Business Portfolio

To position GE for stronger growth, the company would need to exit slow-growth businesses, reallocate resources to businesses where growth prospects were strong, and enter new businesses. Despite Immelt's focus on organic growth, repositioning would require acquisition. Immelt stressed that GE's acquisitions would be selective and focused: "We don't acquire companies just because we can. We don't go for unrelated fields. We acquire companies that give us new growth platforms where GE capability can improve financial performance and build shareholder value."[13]

Immelt's first five years were a period of intense acquisition activity for GE. Between September 2001 and March 2009, GE's major acquisitions were in five major areas:

- *Broadcasting and entertainment.* The acquisitions of Telemundo and Bravo TV networks, Vivendi Universal's entertainment business, and Oxygen Media represented a massive expansion of GE's presence in movies and TV.
- *Healthcare.* Key acquisitions included: Amersham (U.K. diagnostics and medical equipment company), HPSC (financial services for medical and dental practices), and Abbott Diagnostics (the world's leading provider of *in vitro* diagnostics).
- *Energy.* Major growth areas were in alternative energy sources (e.g. acquisitions of Enron's wind energy business, BHA Group Holdings—emission reduction equipment, ChevronTexaco's coal gasification business, AstroPower—solar energy products; and Vetco Gray and Hydril Pressure Control (petroleum drilling equipment).
- *Technology infrastructure.* Key acquisitions were in security systems (InVision Technologies explosive detection systems; Edwards Systems Technology, fire detection; Interlogix, security systems); water treatment (Ionics and BetzDearborn); and aerospace (Smiths Aerospace, avionics and aircraft components).
- *Finance.* GE Capital continued to make acquisitions in the area of equipment leasing, commercial finance, credit cards and consumer finance.

Table 23.2 shows GE's main acquisitions and divestments during 2001–9. Table 23.3 shows basic financial data for GE's business segments, while Table 23.4 gives detailed information for GE Capital.

TABLE 23.2 General Electric's principal acquisitions and disposals, 2001–8

2001	NBC acquires Telemundo, a leading Spanish language television networks.
2003	GE Healthcare acquires Instrumentarium.
2003	GE Capital acquires Transamerica Finance from AEGON, who retained the rest of Transamerica Corporation.
2004	NBC acquires the entertainment assets of Vivendi Universal, excluding Universal Music. This forms NBC Universal, of which General Electric owns 80%.
2004	GE Healthcare acquires Amersham plc.
2004	GE Capital acquires Dillard's credit card unit for U.S.$1.25 billion.
2004	GE sells 60% stake in GE Capital International Services (GECIS) to private equity companies, Oak Hill Capital Partners and General Atlantic, for $500 million.

(continued)

TABLE 23.2 *(Continued)*

2004	GE's life and mortgage insurance businesses spun off as Genworth Financial.
2004	GE Security acquires InVision Technologies, a leading manufacturer of airport security equipment.
2005	GE Commercial Finance acquires the financial assets of Bombardier, a Canadian aircraft manufacturer for U.S.$1.4 billion.
2006	GE Healthcare acquires IDX Systems, a medical software firm, for U.S.$1.2 billion.
2006	GE Advanced Materials division is sold to Apollo Management for U.S.$3.8 billion.
2006	GE Water & Process Technologies acquires Zenon Environmental Systems for $758 million.
2006	Sale of GE Insurance Solutions and GE Life to Swiss Re.
2007	GE-Aviation acquires Smiths Aerospace for $4.6 billion.
2007	GE Oil and Gas acquires Vetco Gray for $1.4 billion.
2007	GE Plastics is sold to Saudi Arabia Basic Industries Corp. for $11.7 billion.
2007	GE NBC-Universal acquires Oxygen Media (cable TV channel).
2008	GE Co. acquires Vital Signs Inc. for $860 million.
2008	GE Energy Infrastructure acquires Hydril Pressure Control (oilfield equipment).
2008	GE Capital finance acquires Merrill Lynch Capital, CitiCapital and Bank BPH.

TABLE 23.3 General Electric: segment performance, 2004–8 ($ millions)

	2008	2007	2006	2005	2004
Revenues					
Energy Infrastructure	38571	30698	25221	21921	19841
of which:					
Energy	29309	22456	19406	–	–
Oil and Gas	7417	6849	4340	–	–
Technology Infrastructure	46316	42801	37687	33873	30142
of which:					
Aviation	19239	16819	13017	–	–
Enterprise Solutions	4710	4462	3951	–	–
Healthcare	17392	16997	16560	–	–
Transportation	5016	4523	4159	–	–
NBC Universal	16969	15416	16188	14689	12886
Capital Finance	67008	66301	56378	49071	43750
Consumer and Industrial	11737	12663	13202	13040	12408
Profit					
Energy Infrastructure	6080	4817	3518	3222	3100
of which:					
Energy	4880	3835	2918	–	–
Oil and Gas	1127	860	548	–	–
Technology Infrastructure	8152	7883	7308	6188	5412
of which:					
Aviation	3684	3222	2802	–	–
Enterprise Solutions	691	697	620	–	–
Healthcare	2851	3056	3142	–	–
Transportation	962	936	774	–	–

(continued)

TABLE 23.3 *(Continued)*

	2008	2007	2006	2005	2004
NBC Universal	3131	3107	2919	3092	2558
Capital Finance	8632	12 243	10 397	8414	6593
Consumer and Industrial	365	1034	970	732	601
Assets					
Energy Infrastructure	33 836	31 466	24 456	–	–
Technology Infrastructure	58 967	57 670	49 641	–	–
NBC Universal	33 781	33 089	31 425	–	–
Capital Finance	572 903	583 965	491 000	–	–
Consumer and Industrial	5065	5351	5740	–	–
Investment (Property, plant and equipment additions)					
Energy Infrastructure	1226	1054	867	–	–
Technology Infrastructure	1395	1954	1389	–	–
NBC Universal	131	306	352	–	–
Capital Finance	15 313	17 832	14 489	–	–
Consumer & Industrial	284	363	373	–	–

Source: General Electric, 10-K Report, 2008.

TABLE 23.4 GE Capital Finance: financial data by business segment (in $ millions)

	2008	2007	2006
Revenues			
Commercial Lending and Leasing	**26 742**	27 267	25 833
GE Money	**25 012**	24 769	19 508
Real Estate	**6646**	7021	5020
Energy Financial Services	**3707**	2405	1664
GE Commercial Aviation Services	**4901**	4839	4353
Profit			
Commercial Lending and Leasing	**1805**	3801	3503
GE Money	**3664**	4269	3231
Real Estate	**1144**	2285	1841
Energy Financial Services	**825**	677	648
GE Commercial Aviation Services	**1194**	1211	1174
Total assets			
Commercial Lending and Leasing	**232 486**	229 608	
GE Money	**183 617**	209 178	
Real Estate	**85 266**	79 285	
Energy Financial Services	**22 079**	18 705	
GE Commercial Aviation Services	**49 455**	47 189	

Source: General Electric, 10-K Report, 2008.

A key theme in Immelt's reshaping of GE's business portfolio towards higher growth was the creation of new "growth platforms." Growth platforms could be extensions of existing businesses or they could be entirely new areas of business. For example, GE's expansion into Spanish language broadcasting (spearheaded by the acquisition of Telemundo) was an example of one of GE's businesses (NBC) expanding into a new, fast-growing market segment. Other growth platforms could be entirely new businesses that drew upon some of GE's existing strengths. For example, renewable energy and security services were entirely new areas of business for GE.

Identifying new growth platforms was established as a central strategic challenge for GE's businesses. The approach involved the analysis and segmentation of markets to identify high-growth segments that offered the potential for attractive returns, then to use a small acquisition as a basis for deploying GE's financial, technical and managerial resources to build a leading position. Immelt explained the role of his acquisitions as follows:

> We did a lot of heavy lifting in our portfolio because we didn't have enough juice. We saw where we needed to go and we found that we wouldn't get there with our existing businesses. So, we bought homeland security, biotech, water—businesses that would give us a stronger foundation for innovation.[14]

General Electric also exited from a number of low-growth, low-margin businesses including insurance and plastics, and consumer financial services in Japan. It was widely believed that appliances and lighting would also be candidates for divestment. Despite, Immelt's assurance that "We'll stay in those businesses. They both return their cost of capital,"[15] General Electric's Consumer and Industrial segment was conspicuously absent from Immelt's references to GE's efforts to "build strong businesses." The Appendix describes GE's main businesses at the end of 2008.

Technology

Immelt remarked on the fact that he represented a different generation from Jack Welch and that his generation had a much closer affinity for technology. He identified technology as a major driver of GE's future growth and emphasized the need to speed the diffusion of new technologies within GE and turn the corporate R&D center into an intellectual hothouse. His commitment to technology was signaled by expanding GE's R&D budgets. This began with a $100 million upgrade to GE's corporate R&D center in Niskayuna, New York and was followed by the construction of new Global Research Centers in Shanghai and Munich, Germany. By the end of 2008, GE Global Research had over 2500 researchers working in GE Global Research Centers in New York, Bangalore, Shanghai, and Munich.

Immelt's emphasis on technology reflected his belief that the primary driver of sales was great products: "You can be six sigma, you can do great delivery, you can be great in China, you can do everything else well—but if you don't have a good product, you're not going to sell much".[16] Increasing product quality and product innovation became a critical performance indicator for all of GE's businesses.

Under Welch, the emphasis of R&D had been short-term product development. Under Immelt, the time horizon lengthened and focused upon fewer, bigger projects: the number or projects was cut from over 1000 to just 100. Looking beyond the lifespan of individual projects, five broad areas of technology were given particular emphasis including nanotechnology, advanced propulsion and biotechnology.

Among new projects, Immelt was particularly interested in identifying and supporting projects that offered large-scale market potential. "Imagination Breakthroughs" were promising projects with the potential to create $100 million in sales over a three-year period. By mid-2006, some 100 Imagination Breakthroughs had been identified and individually approved by Immelt. Major Imagination Breakthroughs included

- *Evolution* hybrid locomotive: an energy-saving locomotive that would use energy lost in braking to be stored in batteries.
- *Smart Grid*: a marriage of IT with electrical infrastructure to support twenty-first century energy needs.
- *Sodium batteries*: a novel, patented battery technology for large-scale electricity storage.

Customer Focus and Integrated Solutions

A key feature of Immelt's career at GE was the extent of his customer orientation and the amount of time he spent with customers, building relationships with them and working on their problems. Looking ahead, Immelt saw GE using IT and redesigned processes to become increasingly customer focused. Soon after taking over as CEO, Immelt emphasized the primacy of customer focus: "We're dramatically changing our resource base from providing support to creating value. Every business has functions that add high value by driving growth. These are the functions that deal with the customer, create new products, sell, manufacture, manage the money and drive controllership. Call that the front room. Every business has backroom support functions that sometimes are so large and bureaucratic they create a drain on the system and keep us from meeting our customers' needs and keep us from growing. So we're going to take more of the back-room resources and put them in the front room—more sales people, more engineers, more product designers. We're changing the shape of this company and we're doing it during a recession."[17] The increased customer focus involved increased investment in GE's marketing function—including hiring talented marketing executives and developing processes for identifying new product and service offerings and unmet customer needs. Some of these are discussed below in relation to "Changing the GE Management Model."

An important outcome of GE's enhanced customer focus would be the ability better to meet customer needs through bundling products with support services and combining product and service offerings from different businesses. Every business was encouraged to create customer value through bundling products with a variety of customer service offerings, including technical services, financial services, training, and the like. Across businesses, enterprise selling was given greater prominence. For example, in the case of a new hospital development, there might be opportunities not just for medical equipment but also for lighting, turbines and other GE businesses as well. To exploit new opportunities that cut across GE's existing divisional structure, GE began to create cross-business, high-visibility marketing campaigns.

"Ecomagination" emerged from GE's 2004 strategic planning process as a way for GE to better capitalize on greater environmental awareness through combining initiatives in emissions reduction, energy efficiency, water supply, and scarcity management. The ecomagination proposal then went to the Commercial Council, which planned an initiative involving 17 products.[18]

Increasing GE's capacity to serve customers better with integrated solutions was a key consideration in Immelt's reorganization of GE's structure in which divisions were consolidated into a few broad-based business sectors—the aim being to facilitate closer integration of related businesses. (The changes in GE's organizational structure will be considered in greater detail in the next section.)

Immelt believed that some of the biggest payoffs from greater customer orientation would come from GE's increased success in international markets. This would involve more local product development and an increased emphasis on truly aligning products and services to meet local market needs rather than simply adapting product features. In terms of exploiting opportunities in major growth markets such as India and China, Immelt saw the need to go from a "defeaturing" mindset (providing a stripped-down American product) to a "customer-optimization" mindset.

Exploiting global opportunities also involved globalizing GE's own talent base. Under Immelt's leadership, GE sought to internationalize its workforce—including core corporate functions. By 2006, of 400 younger members of GE's audit staff, about 60 were Indian.

GE's Competitive Advantage

In GE's annual report for 2008, Immelt outlined the basis on which GE would build "solid competitive advantage over the long term":

> OUR STRATEGY
> Our strategy borrows our key strengths from the past and makes them relevant to a new era of global business:
>
> *Be Global.* Our non-U.S. revenues have averaged 13% annual growth this decade. We expect our global growth to outpace the U.S. in 2009. This is a source of competitive advantage for GE. We are perfecting an approach called "connected and scalable localization" whereby we accelerate growth by expanding our local product lines, serving new customers, and creating strong partnerships with local champions. GE has 25 countries each with more than $1 billion in revenues, so empowering our local teams is critical to driving growth. Global diversity is important in this cycle because it diversifies revenues and risk. We expect Healthcare's diagnostic imaging business to suffer in the U.S. as our customers grapple with budget cuts. However, we have a $9 billion global healthcare business that we expect to experience strong demographic growth, offsetting weakness in the U.S.
>
> *Drive Innovation.* We will invest $10 billion in technology and content in 2009, the same level as 2008. Since 2000, we have invested approximately $50 billion in product technology. We'll launch economical "value products" in

2009 such as the 2.6-megawatt wind turbine, which has high efficiency, more capacity, and lower cost. We'll continue to build our innovation pipeline. We launched a venture in digital pathology, which we think will be a $2 billion market over time. We launched hulu,™ a joint venture between NBC Universal and News Corp., which is an innovative digital content platform competing with YouTube.™ We have invested $150 million in battery technology that will power our hybrid locomotives. We will continue to fund innovation through the downturn.

Build Relationships. GE has many ventures and partnerships that help us grow and diversify risk on a global basis. Our multi-business structure makes us a particularly desirable partner for governments and other large investors. A great example is our spectacular success with the Beijing 2008 Olympic Games. This event produced $2 billion of revenues across multiple GE platforms, while building our relationships in China. In 2008, we announced a multifaceted partnership with Mubadala, the commercial investing arm of Abu Dhabi, which includes a commercial finance joint venture, projects in renewable energy, and a training center in Abu Dhabi. Mubadala will also become a "Top 10" GE investor.

Leverage Strengths. We have core processes centered on organic growth, operating excellence, and leadership development. The aim of these processes is to spread best practices across the Company. We compare our progress on common metrics in industrial organic revenue growth, margins, return on total capital, and productivity as measured by revenue per employee with a composite of world-class peers. We continue to perform. In addition, we continue to invest $1 billion annually in our people and leadership development. We value our team. We remain committed to developing broad and "battle-tested" global leaders.[19]

Changing the GE Management Model

The management system that Immelt inherited had been reformulated by his predecessor and mentor, Jack Welch, but as also a product of 120 years of continuous development. Immelt respected GE's management systems and process, and recognized that many of them were so deeply embedded within GE's culture that they were integral to GE's identity and the way it viewed the world. At the core of GE's management system was its management development—its so-called "talent machine"—and its system of performance management.

General Electric is unique among leading corporations for its reliance upon internally developed leadership: all of its CEOs were promoted from within the company. General Electric's meritocratic system of development and promotion was put in place by Charles Coffin, the CEO who succeeded Edison in 1892. Since then GE has been a "CEO factory" that has produced top management talent not only for GE, but for many other corporations. During the 1950s, GE worked on the two key pillars of its management development system: its corporate university at Crotonville, NY, and its "Session C" system of tracking, evaluating, and planning managers' careers and formulating succession plans for every management position at GE from department head upwards. Jack Welch greatly increased senior executives' emphasis on the management development and career planning process emphasis. The Session C reviews became all-day events at each of GE's businesses involving Welch and the business CEO reviewing the performance, values, and potential of each manager.

General Electric's management appraisal and management development processes formed one dimension of a management system devoted to driving high performance. The company's financial planning, strategic planning, and HR appraisal and development were all based upon sophisticated processes for measuring performance and identifying the determinants of superior performance. Under Jack Welch the GE's system of performance management became increasingly based upon quantitative targets that allowed focus and accountability. "Nothing happens in this company without an output metric," observed Immelt. All of Immelt's strategic initiatives—from the 8% organic growth target to productivity improvements, reductions in overhead costs and six sigma—were linked to precise quantitative targets. In 2005 GE standardized its customer satisfaction metrics, focusing on "net promoter scores" (the percentage of customers who would recommend GE to a friend, minus the percentage who wouldn't).

GE's commitment to management development and metrics-based performance management would continue to be the foundation for GE's management system under Immelt's leadership; at the same time, the redirecting of GE's strategy towards a greater emphasis technology, customer focus and increased integration across GE's different businesses also required significant changes to GE's structure and systems. As *Harvard Business Review* editor, Tom Stewart observed:

> Immelt put two of GE's traditional strengths—process orientation and the ability to develop, test, and deploy new management ideas in the service of a different goal. That meant designing a process that could reliably draw new revenue streams form existing businesses.[20]

Changing Organizational Structure

The most visible of the management changes introduced by Immelt concerned the overall structure of the organization. Between 2002 and 2008, Immelt reversed several of the major structural changes that Welch had introduced during the 1980s. As part of "delayering" and his effort to create a more responsive company, Welch had broken up GE's major industrial sectors into smaller divisions. In order to facilitate greater cross-business integration, the bundling of products and services into "systems", and the creation of new "growth platforms", Immelt progressively reorganized GE's divisions into a smaller number of broad-based sectors. Following an initial reorganization in 2002, a further reorganization was initiated in 2005: "In 2005, we restructured the Company into six businesses focused on the broad markets we serve: Infrastructure, Commercial Finance, Consumer Finance, Healthcare, NBC Universal, and Industrial. Each business has scale, market leadership, and superior customer offerings."[21] In 2008, these six businesses were reduced to five. Figures 23.1 and 23.2 show GE's organizational structure in 2001 and in March 2009.

FIGURE 23.1 General Electric's organization structure, 2001

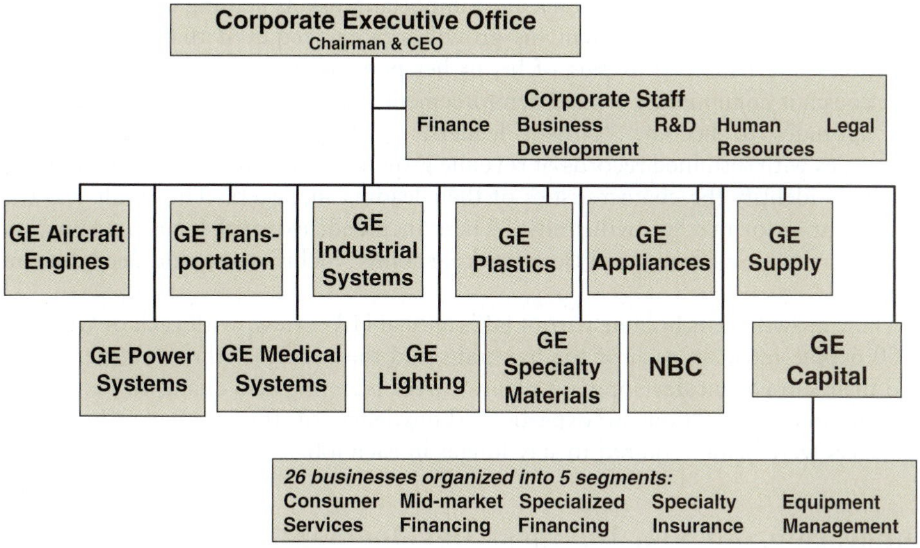

FIGURE 23.2 General Electric's organization structure: segments and businesses, January, 2009

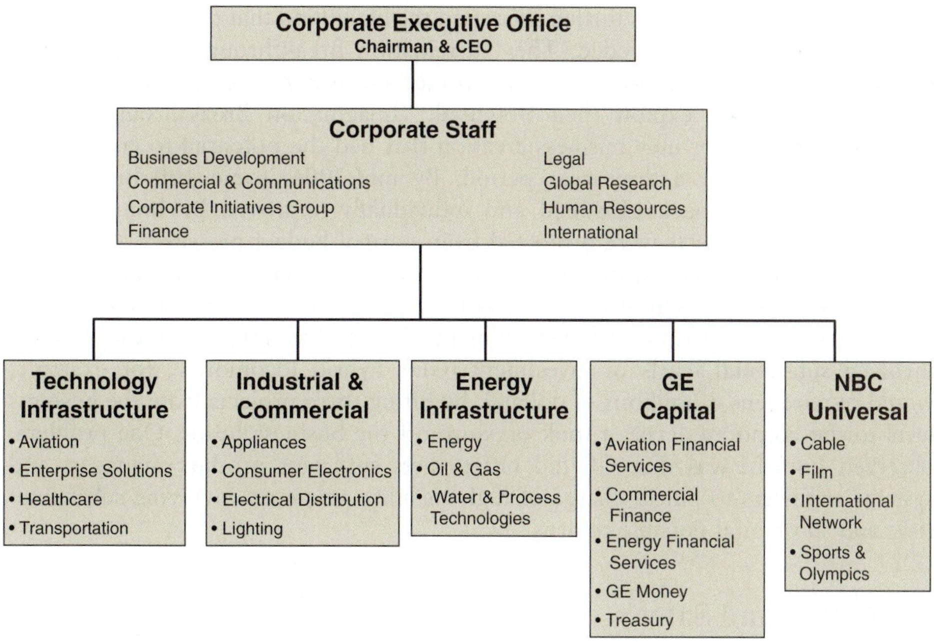

Leadership Development

As with Jack Welch, Immelt saw his most important task as helping to develop GE's managerial talent. To implement his growth strategy required that each of GE's employees internalized it as part of his or her personal mission. This required not only constant communication and reinforcement from the CEO but also the skills and aptitudes to become "growth leaders." A benchmarking exercise on 15 companies with sustained records of revenue growth (for example, Toyota and Dell) sought to identify the characteristics of their leading managers. The result was the categorization of five "growth traits." These included: external focus, imagination and creativity, decisiveness and clear thinking ability, inclusiveness and deep domain expertise.

These growth traits became part of GE's annual HR review, with each of GE's top 5000 people rated on each of the five traits and the results of the assessment built into their subsequent development plans. Career planning also changed: because of the importance of "domain expertise" (knowledge of the particular business), managers were being required to stay longer in each job.

Innovation and New Business Development

A key challenge was to reconcile GE's famous obsession with profitability and cost control with nurturing the innovation that would drive growth. Innovation, especially when it included big, long-term projects, involved substantial risk. The danger was that GE's obsession with performance metrics might discourage business unit heads from making big bets on promising new opportunities. Furthermore, given the fact that many of the biggest opportunities were likely to require cooperation across divisions further increased the likelihood that that they would fail to get the support they needed. The "Imagination Breakthroughs" initiative was designed to ensure that major, innovatory projects would receive the investment and attention needed to exploit their potential. "Imagination Breakthroughs" were promising projects for new business creation that had the potential to create $100 million in sales over a three-year period. By mid-2006, some 100 Imagination Breakthroughs had been identified and individually approved by Immelt. Once approved, these projects were protected from normal budget pressures. About half involved new products and the other half involved changing commercial structure. Immelt saw these Innovation Breakthroughs as a means of focusing attention on the goal of business creation and development. Given that some of these projects involved substantial levels of investment (GE's hybrid locomotive, for example, would require tens of millions of dollars), by lifting these projects from the business level to the corporate level, it took pressure off the business heads. One problem, observed Immelt, was that GE did not possess sufficient product managers and systems engineers to put in charge of high-visibility programs involving substantial risks and substantial possible returns.

Marketing and Sales

A key aspect of Immelt's creation of a customer-driven company was a revitalization of GE's marketing function. "Marketing was the place where washed-up salespeople went."[22] Upgrading GE's marketing was achieved through creating the new senior corporate position of Chief Marketing Officer, the recreation of GE's Advanced Marketing Seminar, developing an Experienced Commercial Leadership Program, and requiring that every business appoint a VP-level head of marketing. Most important was the creation of GE's Commercial Council, which brought together GE's leading sales and marketing leaders to develop new business ideas, to transfer best practices and instill a commercial culture within GE. A key initiative was "At the Customer, For the Customer," a program that deployed six sigma in marketing, sales, and customer relations activities, applied GE's six sigma methodologies to customers' own businesses, and used new metrics to track customer satisfaction and customer attitudes.

As with all aspects of GE's approach to management, marketing was subject to the same systematized, metrics-driven analysis as all other functions within the firm, often with some startling revelations:

> We're getting the sales force better trained and equipped with better tools and metrics. A good example is what we're doing to create discipline around pricing. Not long ago, a guy here named Dave McCalpin did an analysis of our pricing in appliances and found out that about \$5 billion of it is discretionary. Given all the decisions that sales reps can make on their own, that's how much is in play. It was the most astounding number I'd ever heard—and that's just in appliances. Extrapolating across our businesses, there may be \$50 billion that few people are tracking or accountable for. We would never allow something like that on the cost side. When it comes to the prices we pay, we study them, we map them, we work them. But with the prices we charge, we're too sloppy.[23]

The GE Growth Process

By early 2006, GE's various management initiatives with regard to changing GE's performance metrics, revising its management development process, fostering innovation and developing a stronger marketing function were integrated into what Immelt referred to the GE Growth Process. As Immelt explained:

> If you run a big multibusiness company like GE and you're trying to lead transformative change, that objective has to be linked to hitting levers across all of the businesses—and it must keep that up over time. So you've got to have a process. That's true from an internal standpoint, but it's also the only way you get paid in the marketplace. Investors have to see that it's repeatable.
>
> I knew if I could define a process and set the right metrics, this company could go 100 miles an hour in the right direction. It took time, though, to understand growth as a process. If I had worked out that wheel-shaped diagram in 2001, I would have started with it. But in reality, you get these things by wallowing in them awhile. We had a few steps worked out in 2003, but it took another two years to fill in the process.[24]

During 2006, Immelt's view of GE's growth engine as an integrated, six-part process was disseminated throughout the organization and became a key part of Immelt's communication to GE's external constituencies (see Figure 23.3).

FIGURE 23.3 General Electric's six-part growth process

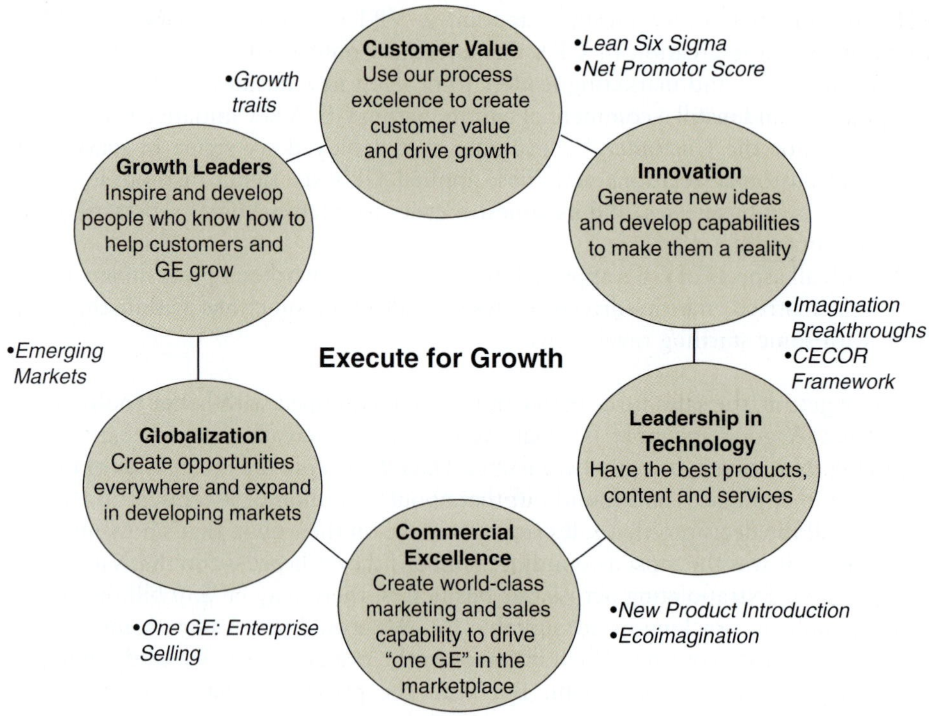

The Challenge of Integration and Complexity

Common to most of the organizational changes initiated by Immelt was the desire to create value through the many parts of GE working together more closely and more effectively. "Working at GE is the art of thinking and playing big; our managers have to work cross-function, cross-region, cross-company. And we have to be about big purposes," observed Immelt.[25]

However, greater integration across GE's different businesses created complex coordination problems. GE has gone beyond cross-selling and product bundling to embrace the concept of "enterprise selling":

> We've always done enterprise selling on an ad hoc basis, but we want to go beyond the convenient cross-selling opportunities and think more systematically about the kinds of customers that can benefit from our broad portfolio. If somebody's building a hospital, that might represent a total package of $1 billion, of which the GE market potential might be $100 million. We're probably already talking to the C-suite because we sell the medical equipment. What we need to do is set things up so that the medical rep can bring in the lighting rep, the turbine rep, and so on.[26]

This concept of enterprise selling has also been applied to whole countries:

> In Qatar, the emir wants to know everybody doing business in his country. In a dinner set up to talk about oil and gas bids, he might say, "Jeff, I'm going to

EXHIBIT 23.1

GE Medical Systems Customer Solutions Initiative

One of the earliest initiatives to exploit opportunities for bundling products and services was to combine the sale of medical imaging equipment with consulting services. In 2001, GE Medical Systems (soon to become GE Healthcare) created a new unit, Performance Solutions, to provide an integrated approach to hospital diagnostic imaging departments by combining equipment with technical support and patient-management systems. A lead customer was Stanford University Medical Center which transitioned to all-digital imaging for its hospital and outpatient unit.

After a promising start, by 2005, Performance Solutions was in trouble. The medical equipment sales people had limited understanding of the consulting services being offered by the Performance Solutions unit and provided few sales leads for the new integrated offering. They were also reluctant to share their customers with sales personnel from Performance Solutions. Meanwhile, the sales personnel from Performance Solutions considered themselves as "solution providers" and felt constrained by having to limit their solutions exclusively to GE offerings.

Source: Based upon Ranjay Gulati "Silo Busting How to Execute on the Promise of Customer Focus," *Harvard Business Review* (May, 2007).

put $10 billion into a hospital," or he might mention that they're going to buy GE engines for Qatar Airways.[27]

Exploiting customer requirements across a range of products and services is highly appealing for a diversified company like GE, but it has complex organizational ramifications. Sales and marketing staff becoming less focused upon their particular business and more oriented towards the opportunities provided from across the company as a whole. In practice, this creates complex problems of organization, expertise, and incentives. Exhibit 23.1 describes the difficulties encountered in the apparently simple bundling of medical diagnostic equipment with consulting services.

As Immelt recognized, organizing to meet customer needs implied a different type of organizational structure from organizing for operational efficiency. Similar challenges existed in relation to GE's efforts to develop large-scale innovations that cut across its existing business-based structure. Reconciling these different coordination needs posed organizational challenges that even GE had not fully resolved:

> I've found that few companies are actually structured to deliver products and services in a synchronized way that's attractive from a customer's perspective. Individual units are historically focused on perfecting their products and processes, and give little thought to how their offerings might be even more valuable to the end user when paired with those of another unit. It's not just

> that the status quo doesn't reward collaborative behavior—although the right incentives are also critical. It's that the connections literally aren't in place.
>
> One way to forge those connections is to do away with traditional silos altogether and create new ones organized by customer segments or needs. Many companies, however, are understandably reluctant to let go of the economies of scale and depth of knowledge and expertise associated with non-customer-focused silos. A company organized around geographies can customize offerings to suit local preferences, for instance, while a technology-centric firm can be quick to market with technical innovations. In many cases, functional and geographic silos were created precisely to help companies coordinate such activities as designing innovative products or gaining geographic focus. A customer focus requires them to emphasize a different set of activities and coordinate them in a different way.
>
> In their initial attempts to offer customer solutions, companies are likely to create structures and processes that transcend rather than obliterate silos. Such boundary-spanning efforts may be highly informal—even as simple as hoping for or encouraging serendipity and impromptu conversations that lead to unplanned cross-unit solutions. But the casual exchange of information and ideas is generally most effective among senior executives, who have a better understanding than their subordinates of corporate goals and easier access to other leaders in the organization.[28]

Extensive collaboration across divisional boundaries also mitigated against some aspects of GE's performance-management systems. Part of the paradox of GE was its reconciliation of cooperation and a one-enterprise culture with strong internal competition—not just competition for resources but also competition between people for recognition and reward. As Immelt pushed cross-business initiatives in innovation, new business development, and marketing and sales, it seemed likely that the intense internal pressures for meeting divisional performance targets would be compromised.

A key feature of the performance driven organization that Welch had created was a clear division between the role of the business division and that of the corporate headquarters. The business divisions with their individual CEOs were responsible for running their own businesses both operationally and strategically. The role of the corporate headquarters was both to support the businesses through various centralized services and to drive business performance by putting divisional top management under intense pressure to deliver.

As headquarters became increasingly involved in promoting and developing developmental initiatives such as GE's "Imagination Breakthroughs" and enterprise selling, increasingly the corporate headquarters became a partner with the business divisions rather than an overseer of divisional performance and interrogator of business strategies.

As a result, much of the simplicity and directness associated with Welch's management style was being supplanted by an emphasis on managing integration which inevitably involved more sophisticated approaches to strategy execution. Developing new products, businesses, and customer solutions required new and more complex cross-business and cross-functional coordination within GE. The new performance requirements were being built on top of GE's existing commitments to efficiency, quality and financial performance. Could this added complexity be borne by a company that was steadily growing larger and encompassing a widening portfolio of businesses and products? Management research pointed to the fact that most companies pursuing the combination of innovation and efficiency in fast-moving business environments were forced to become less diverse in order to maintain outstanding performance. Among the other top-20 companies on *Fortune's* "most admired" list in 2006, Procter & Gamble, Johnson & Johnson, Berkshire Hathaway, and 3M were widely diversified—the other 15 were much more specialized, with most being single-business companies (FedEx, Southwest Airlines, Dell, Toyota, Wal-Mart, UPS, Home Depot, Costco). As Immelt made clear to his top managers, GE was entering uncharted waters: "The business book that can help you hasn't been written yet." While Immelt was extolling the benefits of GE's diversity as a source of strength and opportunity, other companies were moving in the opposite direction, divesting businesses in order to achieve a narrower core-business focus. As Chris Zook, head of global strategy at Bain, commented: "The conglomerates are dead. With some rare exceptions, the conglomerates' business model belongs to the past and is unlikely to reappear."[29]

Appendix: General Electric's businesses (extract from 10-K Report, 2008)

Energy Infrastructure

Energy Infrastructure (21.1%, 17.8% and 16.6% of consolidated revenues in 2008, 2007 and 2006, respectively) is a leader in the field of development, implementation and improvement of products and technologies that harness resources such as wind, oil, gas and water . . .

Energy

Energy serves power-generation, industrial, government and other customers worldwide with products and services related to energy production, distribution and management. We offer wind turbines as part of our renewable energy portfolio, which also includes solar technology. We also sell aircraft engine derivatives for use as industrial power sources. Gas turbines and generators are used principally in power plants for generation of electricity and for industrial cogeneration and mechanical drive applications. We are a leading provider of Integrated Gasification Combined Cycle (IGCC) technology design and development. Integrated Gasification Combined Cycle systems convert coal and other hydrocarbons into synthetic gas that, after cleanup, is used as the primary fuel for gas turbines in combined-cycle systems . . . Nuclear reactors, fuel and support services for both new and installed boiling water reactors are offered through joint ventures with Hitachi and Toshiba . . .

Oil and Gas

Our technology helps oil and gas companies make more efficient and sustainable use of the world's energy resources.

Oil and Gas supplies mission critical equipment for the global oil and gas industry, used in applications spanning the entire value chain from drilling and completion through production, transportation and pipeline inspection and including downstream processing in refineries and petrochemical plants. The business designs and manufactures surface and subsea drilling and production systems, equipment for floating production platforms, compressors, turbines, turboexpanders, high-pressure reactors, industrial power generation and a broad portfolio of ancillary equipment. [O]ur service business has over 40 service centers and workshops in all of the world's main oil and gas extraction and production regions . . .

Water and Process Technologies

Water and Process Technologies offers water treatment solutions for industrial and municipal water systems, including the supply and related services of specialty chemicals, water purification systems, pumps, valves, filters and fluid handling equipment for improving the performance of water, wastewater and process systems, including mobile treatment systems and desalination processes . . .

Technology Infrastructure

Technology Infrastructure (25.4%, 24.8% and 24.9% of consolidated revenues in 2008, 2007 and 2006, respectively) is one of the world's leading providers of essential technologies to developed, developing and emerging countries. Around the world, we are helping build healthcare, transportation and technology infrastructure.

Aviation

Aviation produces, sells and services jet engines, turboprop and turbo shaft engines and related replacement parts for use in military and commercial aircraft. Our military engines are used in a wide variety of aircraft including fighters, bombers, tankers, helicopters and surveillance aircraft, as well as marine applications, and our commercial engines power aircraft in all categories of range: short/medium, intermediate and long-range, as well as executive and regional aircraft. We also produce and market engines through CFM International, a company jointly owned by GE and Snecma, a subsidiary of SAFRAN of France, and Engine Alliance, LLC, a company jointly owned by GE and the Pratt & Whitney division of United Technologies Corporation. New engines are also being designed and marketed in joint ventures with Rolls-Royce Group plc and Honda Aero, Inc., a division of Honda Motor Co., Ltd.

Enterprise Solutions

Enterprise Solutions delivers integrated solutions that improve customers' productivity and profitability. We offer integrated solutions using sensors and non-destructive testing, security and life safety technologies, power system protection and control and plant automation and embedded computing systems. From home to industry to national security, our technology covers the full spectrum of security solutions, including card access systems, high-tech video monitoring, intrusion and fire detection, real estate and property control, and explosives and narcotics detection. We design and manufacture equipment and systems that enable customers to monitor, protect, control and ensure the safety of their critical applications . . .

Healthcare

Healthcare has expertise in medical imaging and information technologies, medical diagnostics, patient monitoring systems, disease research, drug discovery and biopharmaceutical manufacturing technologies. We are dedicated to predicting and detecting disease earlier, monitoring its progress and informing physicians, helping them to tailor treatment for individual patients. Healthcare manufactures, sells and services a wide range of medical equipment that helps provide a fast, non-invasive way for doctors to see broken bones, diagnose trauma cases in the ER, view the heart and its function, and identify early stages of cancers or brain disorders. With X-ray, digital mammography, computed tomography (CT), magnetic resonance (MR) and molecular imaging technologies, Healthcare creates industry-leading products that allow clinicians to see inside the human body more clearly than ever. In addition, Healthcare manufactured technologies include patient monitoring, diagnostic cardiology, ultrasound, bone densitometry, anesthesiology and oxygen therapy, and neonatal and critical care devices . . .

Transportation

Transportation provides technology solutions for customers in a variety of industries including railroad, transit, mining, oil and gas, power generation and marine. We serve customers in more than 100 countries.

Transportation manufactures high-horsepower diesel-electric locomotives . . . We also offer leading drive technology solutions to the mining, transit, marine and stationary and drilling industries. Our motors operate in thousands of applications, from electrical drive systems for large haulage trucks used in the mining industry to transit cars and drilling rigs, and our engines are used for marine power . . .

Transportation also provides a portfolio of service offerings designed to improve fleet efficiency and reduce operating expenses . . .

NBC Universal

NBC Universal (9.3%, 8.9% and 10.7% of consolidated revenues in 2008, 2007 and 2006, respectively) is a diversified media and entertainment company focused on the development, production and marketing of entertainment, news and information to a global audience. NBC Universal, which is 80% owned by General Electric and 20% owned by Vivendi S.A., is engaged in the production and distribution of film and television programming; the operation of leading cable/satellite television networks around the world; the broadcast of network television through owned and affiliated television stations within the United States; and investment and programming activities in digital media and the internet. Our premier film company, Universal Pictures, is engaged in the production and worldwide distribution of theatrical, home entertainment and television programming. We own the world-renowned theme park Universal Studios Hollywood, operate and hold an ownership interest in the Universal Studios Florida theme parks and brand, design and develop international theme parks under exclusive licenses. Our cable/satellite television networks provide produced and acquired entertainment, news and information programming to households worldwide. Our cable/satellite television networks include the USA Network, Bravo, CNBC, the SciFi Channel, MSNBC, Oxygen, UniHD, Chiller, Sleuth, mun2, and branded channels across Europe, Asia and Latin America. The NBC television network is one of four major U.S. commercial broadcast television networks. Together, the NBC television network and Telemundo, our U.S. Spanish-language broadcast television network, serve 210 affiliated stations within the U.S. At December 31, 2008, we owned and operated 26 television stations each subject to U.S. Federal Communications Commission regulation. We have exclusive U.S. television rights to the 2010 and 2012 Olympic Games, National Football League Sunday Night Football and the Super Bowl in 2012 . . .

Capital Finance

Capital Finance (36.7%, 38.4% and 37.2% of consolidated revenues in 2008, 2007 and 2006, respectively) offers a broad range of financial products and services worldwide. Services include commercial loans, operating leases, fleet management, financial programs, home loans, credit cards, personal loans and other financial services . . .

Commercial Lending and Leasing (CLL)

Commercial Lending and Leasing offers a broad range of financial services worldwide. We have particular mid-market expertise and offer loans, leases and other financial services to customers, including manufacturers, distributors and end users for a variety of equipment and major capital assets. These assets include industrial-related facilities and equipment; vehicles; corporate aircraft; and equipment used in many industries, including the construction, manufacturing, transportation, telecommunications and healthcare industries . . .

GE Money

GE Money, through consolidated entities and associated companies, is a leading provider of financial services to consumers and retailers in over 50 countries around the world. We offer a full range of innovative financial products to suit customers' needs. These products include, on a global basis, private-label credit cards; personal loans; bank cards; auto loans and leases; mortgages; debt consolidation; home equity loans; deposit and other savings products; and small and medium enterprise lending . . .

Real Estate

Real Estate offers a comprehensive range of capital and investment solutions, including equity capital for acquisition or development, as well as fixed and floating rate mortgages for new acquisitions or recapitalizations of commercial real estate worldwide. Our business finances, with both equity and loan structures, the acquisition, refinancing and renovation of office buildings, apartment buildings, retail facilities, hotels, parking facilities and industrial properties. Our typical real estate loans are intermediate term, senior, fixed or floating-rate, and are secured by existing income-producing commercial properties. We invest in, and provide restructuring financing for, portfolios of mortgage loans, limited partnerships and tax-exempt bonds.

Energy Financial Services

Energy Financial Services offers structured equity, debt, leasing, partnership financing, project finance and broad-based commercial finance to the global energy and water industries and invests in operating assets in these industries. Energy Financial Services also owns a controlling interest in Regency Energy Partners LP, a midstream master limited partnership engaged in the gathering, processing, transporting and marketing of natural gas and gas liquids . . .

GE Commercial Aviation Services (GECAS)

GECAS is a global leader in commercial aircraft leasing and finance, delivering fleet and financing solutions for commercial aircraft. Our airport financing unit makes debt and equity investments primarily in mid-sized regional airports.

Consumer and Industrial

Consumer and Industrial (6.4%, 7.3% and 8.7% of consolidated revenues in 2008, 2007 and 2006, respectively) sells products that share several characteristics—competitive design, efficient manufacturing and effective distribution and service. Strong global competition rarely permits premium pricing, so cost control, including productivity, is key. We sell and service major home appliances including refrigerators, freezers, electric and gas ranges, cooktops, dishwashers, clothes washers and dryers, microwave ovens, room air conditioners, and residential water systems . . . Consumer and Industrial also provides integrated electrical equipment and systems used to distribute, protect and control energy and equipment. We manufacture and distribute electrical distribution and control products, lighting and power panels, switchgear and circuit breakers . . .

Notes

1 James Quinn "General Electric: Genuine Risk of Collapse?" *Seeking Alfa,* November 17, 2008) http://seekingalpha.com/article/106445-general-electric-genuine-risk-of-collapse, accessed October 24, 2009.
2 Transcript of Presentation to General Electric Annual Shareowners Meeting, April 22, 2009.
3 "The GE Mystique," *Fortune,* March 6, 2006, p. 100. "Less than the Sum of the Parts? Decline Sets in at the Conglomerate," *Financial Times,* February 5, 2007, p. 9.
4 "What Makes GE Great?" *Fortune,* March 6, 2006, pp. 90–6.
5 General Electric, Annual Report, 1993, p. 5.
6 "Running the House that Jack Built," *Business Week,* October 2, 2000.
7 "The Days of Welch and Roses," *Business Week,* April 29, 2002.
8 General Electric, Annual Report, 2002.
9 General Electric, Annual Report, 2002.
10 Address to shareholders, Annual Share Owners' Meeting, Philadelphia, April 26, 2006.
11 General Electric, Annual Report 2006, pp. 4–5.
12 General Electric, Annual Report 2008, pp. 4.
13 General Electric, Annual Report, 2002.
14 "Growth as a Process: An Interview with Jeff Immelt," *Harvard Business Review,* June, 2006.
15 General Electric, Annual Report, 2002.
16 "Growth as a Process: An Interview with Jeff Immelt," *Harvard Business Review,* June, 2006.
17 "Growth as a Process: An Interview with Jeff Immelt," *Harvard Business Review,* June, 2006.
18 "Growth as a Process: An Interview with Jeff Immelt," *Harvard Business Review,* June, 2006.
19 General Electric, Annual Report 2008, pp. 6–7.
20 "Growth as a Process: An Interview with Jeff Immelt," *Harvard Business Review,* June, 2006.
21 "Letter to Shareholders," General Electric, 2005 Annual Report.
22 "Growth as a Process: An Interview with Jeff Immelt," *Harvard Business Review,* June, 2006.
23 "Growth as a Process: An Interview with Jeff Immelt," *Harvard Business Review,* June, 2006.
24 "Growth as a Process: An Interview with Jeff Immelt," *Harvard Business Review,* June, 2006.
25 "Growth as a Process: An Interview with Jeff Immelt," *Harvard Business Review,* June, 2006.
26 "Growth as a Process: An Interview with Jeff Immelt," *Harvard Business Review,* June, 2006.
27 "Growth as a Process: An Interview with Jeff Immelt," *Harvard Business Review,* June, 2006.
28 "Growth as a Process: An Interview with Jeff Immelt," *Harvard Business Review,* June, 2006.
29 "Less than the Sum of the Parts? Decline Sets in at the Conglomerate," *Financial Times,* February 5, 2007, p. 9.

Case 24 W. L. Gore & Associates: Who's In Charge Here?*

"If a man could flow with the stream, grow with the way of nature, he'd accomplish more and he'd be happier doing it than bucking the flow of the water."

W. L. Gore

Malcolm Gladwell (author of *The Tipping Point* and *Outliers*) described his visit to W. L. Gore & Associates:

> When I visited a Gore associate named Bob Hen, at one of the company's plants in Delaware, I tried, unsuccessfully, to get him to tell me what his position was. I suspected, from the fact that he had been recommended to me, that he was one

*This case was prepared by Robert M. Grant. ©2010 Robert M. Grant.

of the top executives. But his office wasn't any bigger than anyone else's. His card just called him an "associate." He didn't seem to have a secretary, one that I could see anyway. He wasn't dressed any differently from anyone else, and when I kept asking the question again and again, all he finally said, with a big grin, was, "I'm a meddler."[1]

The absence of job titles and the lack of the normal symbols of hierarchy are not the only things that are different about W.L. Gore & Associates, Inc. ("Gore"). Since its founding in 1958, Gore deliberately adopted a system of management that contrasted sharply with that of other established corporations. While the styles of management of all start-up companies reflect the personality and values of their founders, the remarkable thing about Gore is that, as a $2.5 billion company with 8500 employees ("associates") in facilities located in 24 countries of the world, Gore's organizational structure and management systems continued to defy the principles under which corporations of similar size and complexity are managed.

The Founding of W. L. Gore & Associates

Wilbert L. (Bill) Gore left DuPont in 1958 after 17 years as a research scientist. At DuPont, Gore had been working on new synthetic material called polytetrafluoroethylene (PTFE) which it had branded "Teflon." Gore was convinced that DuPont's commitment to a business model based on large industrial markets for basic chemical products had caused it to overlook a whole range of innovative applications for PTFE. In forming a business together with his wife, Vieve, Gore was also motivated by the desire to create the energy and passion that he had experienced when working in small research teams at DuPont on those occasions when they were given the freedom to pursue innovation.

Working out of their own home in Newark, Delaware, and with the help of son, Bob, the Gore's first product was Teflon-insulated cable (which was used for the Apollo space program among other applications).

The company's biggest breakthrough was the result of Bob Gore's discovery of the potential of Teflon to be stretched and laced with microscopic holes. The resulting fabric had several desirable properties; in particular, it shed water droplets but was also breathable. Gore-Tex received a U.S. patent in 1976. Not only did it have a wide range of applications for outdoor clothing, the fact that Gore-Tex was chemically inert and resistant to infection made it an excellent material for medical applications such as artificial arteries and intravenous bags. The potential to vary the size of the microscopic holes in Gore-Tex made it ideal for a wide range of filtration applications.

Origins of the Gore Management Philosophy

FundingUniverse.com describes the development of Bill Gore's management ideas as follows:

From their basement office, the Gores expanded into a separate production facility in their hometown of Newark, Delaware. Sales were brisk after initial product introductions. By 1965, just seven years after the business had started, Gore & Associates was employing about 200 people. It was about that time that Gore began to develop and implement the unique management system and philosophy for which his company would become recognized. Gore noticed that as his company had grown, efficiency and productivity had started to decline. He needed a new management structure, but he feared that the popular pyramid management structure that was in vogue at the time suppressed the creativity and innovation that he valued so greatly. Instead of adopting the pyramid structure, Gore decided to create his own system.

During World War II, while on a task force at DuPont, Gore had learned of another type of organizational structure called the lattice system, which was developed to enhance the ingenuity and overall performance of a group working toward a goal. It emphasized communication and cooperation rather than hierarchy of authority. Under the system that Gore developed, any person was allowed to make a decision as long as it was fair, encouraged others, and made a commitment to the company. Consultation was required only for decisions that could potentially cause serious damage to the enterprise. Furthermore, new associates joined the company on the same effective authority level as all the other workers, including Bill and Vieve. There were no titles or bosses, with only a few exceptions, and commands were replaced by personal commitments.

New employees started out working in an area best suited to their talents, under the guidance of a sponsor. As the employee progressed there came more responsibility, and workers were paid according to their individual contribution. "Team members know who is producing," Bill explained in a February 1986 issue of the Phoenix Business Journal. "They won't put up with poor performance. There is tremendous peer pressure. You promote yourself by gaining knowledge and working hard, everyday. There is no competition, except with yourself." The effect of the system was to encourage workers to be creative, take risks, and perform at their highest level.[2]

Bill Gore's ideas about management were influenced by Douglas McGregor's *The Human Side of Enterprise*, which was published as Gore's own company was in its start-up phase. McGregor identified two models of management: the conventional model of management, rooted in Taylor's scientific management; and Weber's principles of bureaucracy which he termed "Theory X." At its root was the assumption that work was unpleasant, that employees were motivated only by money, and that management's principal role was to prevent shirking. "Theory Y" was rooted in the work of the human relations school of management, which assumed that individuals were self-motivated, anxious to solve problems, and capable of working harmoniously on joint tasks.

A key element in Bill Gore's management thinking related to the limits of organizational size. He believed that the need for interpersonal trust would result in organizations declining in effectiveness once they reached about 200 members. Hence, in 1967, Bill and Vieve decided to build a second manufacturing facility in Flagstaff, Arizona. From then on, Gore built a new facility each time an existing unit reached 200 associates.

According to Malcolm Gladwell, Gore's insistence upon small organizational units is an application of a principle developed by anthropologist, Robin Dunbar.

According to Dunbar, social groups are limited by individuals' capacity to manage complex social relationships. Among primates, the size of the typical social group for a species is correlated with the size of the neocortex of that species' brain. For humans, Dunbar estimates that 148 is the maximum number of individuals that a person can comfortably have social relations with. Across a range of different societies, Dunbar found that 150 was the typical maximum size of tribes, religious groups and army units.[3]

Organization Structure and Management Principles

The Gore organization does include elements of hierarchy. For example, as a corporation, it is legally required to have a board of directors—this is chaired by Bob Gore. There is also a CEO, Chuck Carroll. The company is organized into four divisions (fabrics, medical, industrial and electronic products) each with a recognized "leader." Within these divisions there are specific business units, each based upon a group of products. There are also specialized, company-wide functions such as human resources and information technology.

What is lacking is a codified set of ranks and positions. Gore associates are expected to adapt their roles to match their skills and aptitudes. The basic organizational units are small, self-managing teams.

Relationships within teams and between teams are based upon the concept of a lattice rather than a conventional hierarchy. The idea of a lattice is that every organizational member is connected to every other organizational member within the particular facility. In the lattice communication is peer-to-peer, not superior to subordinate. For Bill Gore, this was a more natural way to organize. He observed that in most formal organizations, it was through informal connections that things actually got done: "Most of us delight in going around the formal procedures and doing things the straightforward and easy way."[4]

Leadership is important at Gore, but the basic principle is that of natural leadership: "If you call a meeting and people show up—you're a leader."[5] Teams can appoint team leaders, they can also replace their team leaders—as a result every team leader's accountability is to the team. "Someone who is accustomed to snapping their fingers and having people respond will be frustrated," says John McMillan, a Gore associate. "I snap my fingers and nobody will do anything. My job is to acquire followership, articulate a goal and get there . . . and hope the rest of the people think that makes sense."[6]

New associates are assigned to a "sponsor" whose job is to introduce the new hire to the company and guide him or her through the lattice. The new hire is likely to spend time with several teams during the first few months of employment. It is up to the new associate and a team to find a good match. An associate is free to find a new sponsor if desired. Typically, each associate works on two or three different project teams.

Annual reviews are peer based. Information is collected from at least 20 other associates. Each associate is then ranked against every other associate within the unit in terms of overall contribution. This ranking determines compensation.

The company's beliefs, management principles and work culture are articulated on its web site (see Exhibit 24.1).

EXHIBIT 24.1

W. L. Gore & Associates: Beliefs, Principles and Culture

What We Believe

Founder Bill Gore built the company on a set of beliefs and principles that guide us in the decisions we make, in the work we do, and in our behavior toward others. What we believe is the basis for our strong culture, which connects Gore associates worldwide in a common bond.

Fundamental Beliefs

- *Belief in the individual:* if you trust individuals and believe in them, they will be motivated to do what's right for the company.
- *Power of small teams:* our lattice organization harnesses the fast decision-making, diverse perspectives, and collaboration of small teams.
- *All in the same boat:* all Gore associates are part owners of the company through the associate stock plan. Not only does this allow us to share in the risks and rewards of the company; it gives us an added incentive to stay committed to its long-term success. As a result, we feel we are all in this effort together, and believe we should always consider what's best for the company as a whole when making decisions.
- *Long-term view:* our investment decisions are based on long-term payoff and our fundamental beliefs are not sacrificed for short-term gain.

Guiding Principles

- *Freedom:* the company was designed to be an organization in which associates can achieve their own goals best by directing their efforts toward the success of the corporation; action is prized; ideas are encouraged; and making mistakes is viewed as part of the creative process. We define freedom as being empowered to encourage each other to grow in knowledge, skill, scope of responsibility, and range of activities. We believe that associates will exceed expectations when given the freedom to do so.
- *Fairness:* everyone at Gore sincerely tries to be fair with each other, our suppliers, our customers and anyone else with whom we do business.
- *Commitment:* we are not assigned tasks; rather, we each make our own commitments and keep them.
- *Waterline:* everyone at Gore consults with other associates before taking actions that might be "below the waterline"—causing serious damage to the company.

Working in Our Unique Culture

Our founder Bill Gore once said, "The objective of the Enterprise is to make money and have fun doing so." And we still believe that, more than 50 years later.

Because we are all part owners of the company through the associate stock plan, Gore associates expect a lot from each other. Innovation and creativity; high ethics and integrity; making commitments and standing behind them. We work hard at living up to these expectations as we strive for business success. But we also trust and respect each other and believe it's important to celebrate success.

Gore is much less formal than most workplaces. Our relationships with other associates are open and informal and we strive to treat everyone respectfully and fairly. This type of environment naturally promotes social interaction and many associates have made lifelong friends with those they met working at Gore.

Do Something You're Passionate About

At Gore, we believe it's important to have passion for what you do. If you're passionate about your work, you are naturally going to be highly self-motivated and focused. If you feel pride and ownership, you will want to do whatever it takes to be successful and have an impact. So when you apply for an opportunity at Gore, be sure you're going to be passionate about the work you'll be doing.

The Lattice Structure and Individual Accountability

Gore's unique "lattice" management structure, which illustrates a nonhierarchical system based on interconnection among associates, is free from traditional bosses and managers. There is no assigned authority, and we become leaders based on our ability to gain the respect of our peers and to attract followers.

You will be responsible for managing your own workload and will be accountable to others on your team. More importantly, only you can make a commitment to do something (for example, a task, a project, or a new role)—but once you make a commitment, you will be expected to meet it. A "core commitment" is your primary area of concentration. You may take on additional commitments depending on your interests, the company's needs, and your availability.

Relationships and Direct Communication

Relationships are everything at Gore—relationships with each other, with customers, with vendors and suppliers and with our surrounding communities. We encourage people to build and maintain long-term relationships by communicating directly. Of course we all use e-mail, but we find that face-to-face meetings and phone calls work best when collaborating with others.

Sponsors

Everyone at Gore has a sponsor, who is committed to helping you succeed. Sponsors are responsible for supporting your growth, for providing good feedback on your strengths and areas that offer opportunities for development and for helping you connect with others in the organization.

Source: www.gore.com/en_xx/careers/whoweare/about-gore.html. Reproduced by permission of W.L. Gore & Associates.

Innovation

The success of Gore's unusual management system is its capacity for innovation. Between 1976 and July 2009, Gore received 918 patents. Even more remarkable has been its ability to extend its existing technological breakthroughs to a wide variety of new applications. Central to Gore's ability to innovate is its willingness to allow individuals the freedom to pursue their own projects: each associate is allowed a half day each week of "dabble time". The company's web site gives examples of the results of these initiatives (see Exhibit 24.2).

EXHIBIT 24.2

Examples of innovation at W.L. Gore & Associates

Change Music

How did the creators of GORE-TEX® products—worn by outdoor enthusiasts and people with active lifestyles all over the world—invent a new kind of guitar string?

Although manufacturers have coated their guitar strings for many years to make them last longer by protecting them from perspiration, oil, and dirt the coating severely compromised the quality of the sound.

Gore had no presence in the music industry until one associate envisioned a completely new type of guitar string that would prevent string contamination, last longer, and be more comfortable for musicians to play. Relying on the company's unique culture and mentoring system to support his efforts, he formed a cross-functional team—including Michael and John—to make it happen.

Each member of the Gore team had the knowledge and know-how needed to develop this exciting new product. With the entrepreneurial spirit characteristic of Gore, they took this innovative concept to the marketplace in less than two years.

But the team's commitment to integrity didn't stop in the lab. They asked 15000 musicians to test the new strings for sound quality before the product was introduced. Since then, revolutionary ELIXIR® Strings have inspired a generation of musicians all over the world to pick up their guitars and play. And their ELIXIR® Strings experience and the challenges they overcame have changed their lives too.

Change Lives

How did the creators of GORE-TEX® products—worn by outdoor enthusiasts and people with active lifestyles all over the world—invent material to patch human hearts?

For people with a serious heart problem known as an atrial septal defect, or "hole in the heart," open heart surgery was once the only treatment. The surgeon makes an incision in the chest to expose the heart; a heart-lung bypass machine pumps blood while the heart is stopped and the defect is patched. Many patients with this condition are infants and small children, for whom this surgery poses an even greater risk.

A dedicated team of Gore associates—including Hannah, Nitin, and Sarah—developed a minimally invasive device that physicians implant through a cardiac catheter to permanently close the hole without major surgery. Driven by Gore's core values of integrity, innovation, and quality, the team spent years perfecting the device before taking it to market. Patients treated this way experience much less pain, recover much more easily and quickly, and have less scarring.

Since then, the GORE HELEX septal occluder has changed the way doctors treat patients with this heart defect and has helped thousands of patients throughout the world—more than half of them infants and children—lead normal, healthy lives. And the team's experience with the septal occluder product changed their lives, too.

Change Industries

How did the creators of GORE-TEX® products—worn by outdoor enthusiasts and people with active lifestyles all over the world—invent material that protects firefighters from heat, flames, and hazardous chemicals?

Gore makes a line of protective fabrics based on its patented membrane technologies. These fabrics are used by Gore's customers—garment manufacturers—as one layer of protective clothing for military and law enforcement uniforms, medical protective wear, workwear, and turnout gear for fire and safety personnel.

Firefighters rely on protective gear—including boots, pants, jackets, gloves, and headgear—to keep them safe. While already incorporating waterproof and breathable GORE-TEX® fabric to improve the comfort and quality of their gear, the firefighting industry identified a need for barrier fabrics that also protected firefighters against bloodborne pathogens and common fire ground chemicals. Dave, Henri, and Ron were part of a cross-functional team that set out to engineer high-performance CROSSTECH® protective barrier fabric to meet this need.

By building relationships with firefighters, suppliers, and industry experts, the global Gore team came to understand the extreme conditions that firefighters are exposed to. Harnessing deep knowledge of Gore's membrane technologies and their passion for making a difference, they developed Gore protective barrier fabrics that change the way firefighters respond to emergencies. And their fire service experience and the challenges they overcame have changed their lives, too.

Source: www.gore.com/en_xx/careers/associatestories/12347 22965408.html. Reproduced by permission of W.L. Gore & Associates

Gary Hamel closes his discussion of W.L. Gore and Associates with the following challenge:

> Bill Gore was a 40-something chemical engineer when he laid the foundations for his innovation democracy. I don't know about you, but a middle-aged polytetrafluoroethylene-loving chemist isn't my mental image of a wild-eyed management innovator. Yet think about how radical Gore's vision must have seemed back in 1958. Fifty years later, postmodern management hipsters throw around terms like complex adaptive systems and self-organizing teams. Well, they're only a half century behind the curve. So ask yourself, am I dreaming big enough yet? Would my management innovation agenda make Bill Gore proud ?[7]

Notes

1 M. Gladwell, *The Tipping Point,* Little, Brown & Co., London, 2000.

2 See www.fundinguniverse.com/company-histories/WL-Gore-amp;-Associates-Inc-Company-History.html, accessed October 25, 2009.

3 M. Gladwell, *The Tipping Point,* Little, Brown & Co., London, 2000, pp. 177–81.

4 Quoted by G. Hamel with B. Breen, *The Future of Management,* Harvard Business School Press, Boston MA, 2007, p. 87.

5 Quoted by G. Hamel with B. Breen, *The Future of Management,* Harvard Business School Press, Boston MA, 2007, p. 88.

6 W. L. Gore & Associates, Inc.: Quality's Different Drummer, IMPO, www.impomag.com/scripts/ShowPR.asp?RID=3923&CommonCount=0, accessed October 25, 2009.

7 Gary Hamel with Bill Breen, *The Future of Management,* Harvard Business School Press, Boston MA, 2007, p. 100.

Note: page numbers in *italic* refer to illustrations and tables.